THE BUILDINGS OF SCOTLAND

FOUNDING EDITORS:
NIKOLAUS PEVSNER & COLIN McWILLIAM

DUNDEE AND ANGUS

JOHN GIFFORD

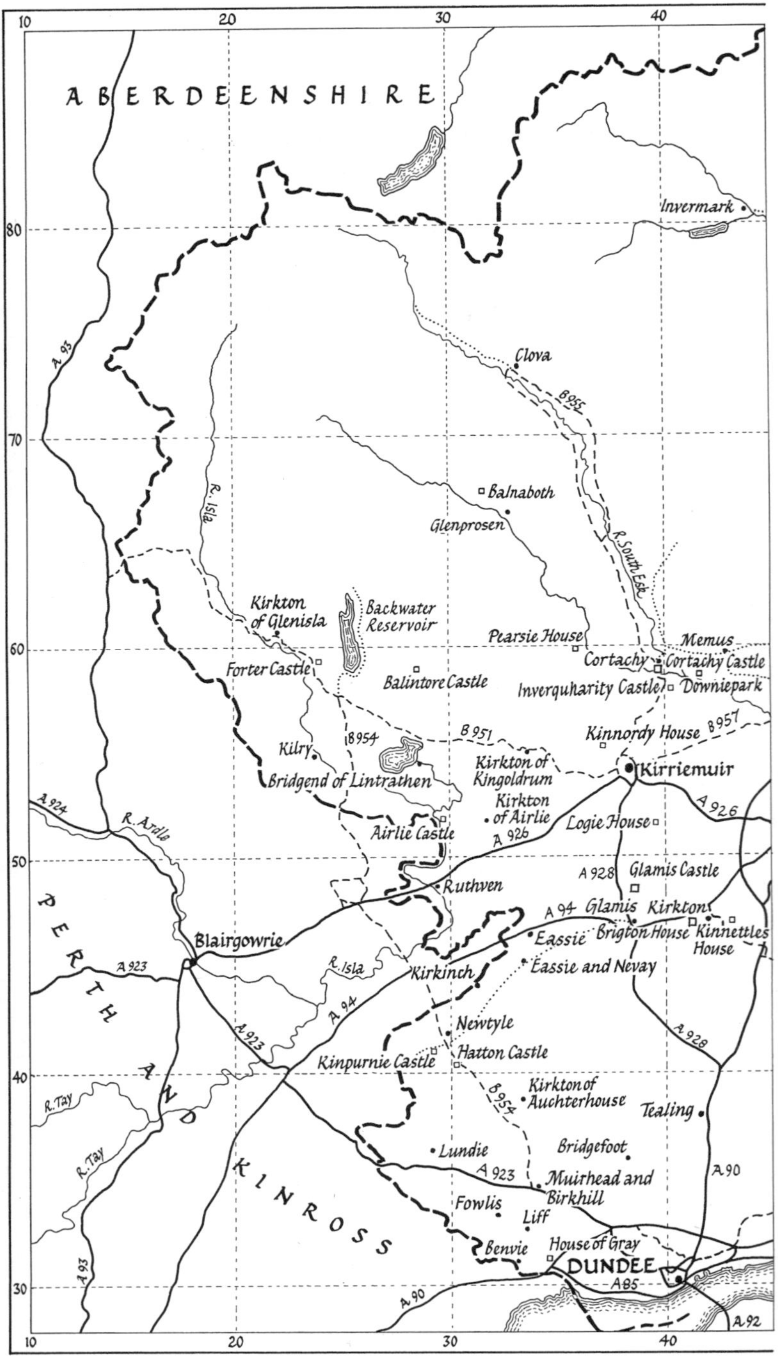

ABERDEENSHIRE
PERTH AND KINROSS
Invermark
Clova
B 955
R. Isla
Balnaboth
Glenprosen
R. South Esk
Kirkton of Glenisla
Backwater Reservoir
Pearsie House
Memus
Cortachy
Cortachy Castle
Forter Castle
Balintore Castle
Inverquharity Castle
Downiepark
B 954
B 951
Kinnordy House
B 957
Kilry
Kirkton of Kingoldrum
Kirriemuir
Bridgend of Lintrathen
A 924
R. Ardle
Kirkton of Airlie
A 926
Logie House
Airlie Castle
A 926
A 928
Glamis Castle
Ruthven
A 94
Glamis
Kirkton
Eassie
Brigton House
Kinnettles House
Blairgowrie
A 923
R. Isla
Kirkinch
Eassie and Nevay
A 94
Newtyle
A 923
A 928
Kinpurnie Castle
Hatton Castle
R. Tay
B 954
Kirkton of Auchterhouse
Tealing
R. Tay
Lundie
Bridgefoot
A 923
A 90
Muirhead and Birkhill
Fowlis
Liff
Benvie
House of Gray
DUNDEE
A 85
A 93
A 93
A 90
A 92

DUNDEE and ANGUS
ABERDEENSHIRE
North
Sea
Tarfside
R. North Esk
B 966
A 90
Edzell Castle
Edzell
Lethnot
Lundie Castle
Stracathro House
Gallery House
A 937
A 92
Menmuir
Newtonmill House
Stracathro
Pert
Balnamoon
Keithock
Logie Pert
Logie
Fern
Langley Park
Hillside
Vayne Castle
Careston
Brechin
Dun
House of Dun
Noranside
Careston Castle
A 935
Tannadice
Kintrockat House
R. South Esk
Montrose
Oathlaw
Aberlemno
Kinnaird Castle
Maryton
Ferryden
Finavon Castle
Craig
Carse Gray
B 9134
Melgund Castle
A 934
Farnell
Usan House
Pitscandly House
Dunninald Castle
Rescobie
B 9113
Lunanhead
Balgavies House
Braikie Castle
Lunan
Restenneth Priory
Kinnell
Red Castle
A 932
Guthrie
Forfar
Inverkeilor
Balmadies House
Friockheim
B 965
Dunnichen
Letham
House of Pitmuies
Gardyne Castle
Middleton
Kinblethmont
Lour House
B 9128
B 961
West Newton House
A 933
Letham Grange
Colliston
Ethie Castle
Inverarity
Auchmithie
Carmyllie
B 9127
St Vigeans
Seaton House
The Guynd
Arbirlot
Affleck Castle & House
Arbroath
Kelly Castle
Gagie House
Monikie
Panmure
B 978
Newbigging
Panbride
Murroes
Barry
B 961
A 930
Carnoustie
Monifieth
Broughty Ferry
'A' roads
'B' roads
Minor roads
Boundary of Dundee and Angus
0 1 2 3 4 5 6 7 8 9 10 miles
0 5 10 15 km
50
60
70
80
40
30

PEVSNER ARCHITECTURAL GUIDES

The Buildings of Scotland was founded by Sir Nikolaus Pevsner (1902–83) and Colin McWilliam (1928–89) as a companion series to *The Buildings of England*. Between 1978 and 2001 it was published by Penguin Books.

For a considerable period the National Trust for Scotland carried the financial responsibility for management and finance of the research programme needed to sustain the first editions of guides in the Buildings of Scotland series. Between 1991 and 2012 that role was taken over by the Buildings of Scotland Trust, sponsored by Historic Scotland (on behalf of Scottish Ministers), The National Trust for Scotland and the Royal Commission on the Ancient and Historical Monuments of Scotland. During its lifetime the Trust received the support of many individuals, charitable trusts and foundations, companies and local authorities. Without that support it would not have been possible to look forward to the completion of the series. From 2012 funding will be administered through the Paul Mellon Centre for Studies in British Art.

Special thanks are due to the following donors:

H.M. The Queen and H.R.H. The Prince of Wales

Binks Trust, Sir James Cayzer, Dulverton Trust
Esmée Fairbairn Charitable Trust
Marc Fitch Fund, Gordon Fraser Charitable Trust
Gargunnock Estate Trust, Jennie Gordon Foundation
A. S. and Miss M. I. Henderson Trust, Historic Scotland
Imlay Foundation Inc., Leng Charitable Trust
Sir Peter and Lady Leslie, Leverhulme Trust, Lindsay Trust
Macrobert Trusts, Colin McWilliam Memorial Fund
Nancie Massey Charitable Trust, Merchants House of Glasgow
National Trust for Scotland, Pilgrim Trust
Radcliffe Trust, Joseph Rank Benevolent Trust
Royal Bank of Scotland plc, Russell Trust
Walter Scott, VisitScotland, James Wood Bequest Fund

and

ABERBROTHOCK CHARITABLE TRUST
TURTLETON TRUST

for their grants towards this volume

and

The Paul Mellon Centre for Studies in British Art
for a grant towards the cost of illustrations

Dundee and Angus

BY

JOHN GIFFORD

THE BUILDINGS OF SCOTLAND

YALE UNIVERSITY PRESS
NEW HAVEN AND LONDON

YALE UNIVERSITY PRESS
NEW HAVEN AND LONDON
302 Temple Street, New Haven CT 06511
47 Bedford Square, London WC1B 3DP
www.pevsner.co.uk
www.yalebooks.co.uk
www.yalebooks.com

Published by Yale University Press 2012
2 4 6 8 10 9 7 5 3 1

ISBN 978 0 300 14171 9

Printed in China
through World Print
Set in Monotype Plantin

TO THE MEMORY OF MY MOTHER

A LYELL OF KINNORDY

ACCESS TO BUILDINGS

Many of the buildings described in this book are public places, and in some obvious cases their interiors (at least the public sections of them) can be seen without formality. But it must be emphasized that the mention of buildings or lands does not imply any rights of public access to them, or the existence of any arrangements for visiting them.

Some churches are open within regular hours, and it is usually possible to see the interiors of others by arrangement with the minister or church officer. Particulars of admission to Ancient Monuments and other buildings in the care of Scottish Ministers (free to the Friends of Historic Scotland) are available from Historic Scotland, Longmore House, Salisbury Place, Edinburgh EH9 1SH or its website, www.historic-scotland.gov.uk. Details of access to properties of the National Trust for Scotland are available from the Trust's head office at Hermiston Quay, 5 Cultins Road, Edinburgh, EH11 4DF or via its website, www.nts.org.uk. Admission is free to members, on whose subscriptions and donation's the Trust's work depends.

Scotland's Gardens Scheme, 42a Castle Street, Edinburgh EH2 3BN, provides a list of gardens open to visitors, also available on the National Gardens Scheme website, www.gardensofscotland.org. Scotland's Churches Scheme, Dunedin, Holehouse Road, Eaglesham, Glasgow G76 0JF, has a searchable database (www.sacredscotland.org.uk) of churches in Scotland including details of opening arrangements and publishes a series of regional guides. *Hudson's Historic Houses, Castles and Gardens Open to the Public*, published annually, includes many private houses open to visitors.

Local Tourist Offices can advise the visitor on what properties in each area are open to the public and will usually give helpful directions as to how to get to them.

CONTENTS

LIST OF TEXT FIGURES AND MAPS

MAPS

MAP REFERENCES

The numbers printed in italic type in the margin against the place names in the gazetteer indicate the position of the place in question on the area map (pages ii–iii), which are divided into sections by the 10-kilometre reference lines of the National Grid. The reference given here omits the two initial letters (formerly numbers), which in a full grid reference refer to the 100-kilometre squares into which the county is divided. The first two numbers indicate the western boundary, and the last two the southern boundary, of the 10-kilometre square in which the place is situated. For example, Auchmithie reference 6040 will be found in the 10-kilometre square bounded by grid lines 60 (on the *west*) and 70, and 40 (on the *south*) and 50; Montrose, reference 7050 in the square bounded by grid lines 70 (on the *west*) and 80, and 50 (on the *south*) and 60.

ACKNOWLEDGEMENTS FOR ILLUSTRATIONS

Royal
Commission on the
Ancient and
Historical
Monuments of
Scotland

We are deeply indebted to Heather Stoddart of the Royal Commission on the Ancient and Historical Monuments of Scotland (RCAHMS) who redrew measured plans for this volume.

Photographs are copyright of the RCAHMS with the exception of the following:

© Niall Benvie / Corbis: 1
© Jan Holm / fotolibra: 2
© Crown Copyright reproduced courtesy of Historic Scotland: 8, 37
Paul Reid / Angus Pictures: 9, 111
Iain McIntosh, St Stephen's & West Church, Broughty Ferry: 26–8
© JFS Architects LLP: 33, 108
Courtesy of Glamis Castle: 43, 44
Courtesy of Dalhousie Estates: 49
Images reproduced with kind permission of the National Trust for Scotland: 51, 52, 67
Nicoll Russell Studios: 77, 105, 106, 109
Courtesy of the University of Dundee: 98
Arcaid / Keith Hunter: 101
Courtesy of Page & Park, photograph by Iain Lindsay: 102
Courtesy of Austin-Smith: Lord / Graeme Duncan Photography: 103
Ian Lindsay, W. H. Brown Construction: 104
Courtesy of Richard Murphy Architects: 107

The plates are included in the indexes of names and places, and references to them are given by numbers in the margin of the text.

FOREWORD

Not long before publication of the last of the first editions of *The Buildings of England*, Sir Nikolaus Pevsner entrusted the oversight of a similar series for Scotland to Colin McWilliam. Colin himself wrote *Lothian*, the first Scottish volume, published in 1978, was co-author of *Edinburgh* and, at the time of his death in 1989, had begun visiting buildings in Dumfries and Galloway. Volumes by other authors published or written before 1989 owed much to his courteous but careful scrutiny and his influence has been strong even on books whose writing had not been begun before he died.

From the start Colin McWilliam was insistent that the writing of the books must be supported by thorough research. I myself as one of the first workers on the project trawled for Scottish references through the C19 and C20 building and architectural journals (*The Builder*, *The Building News*, *The Architect*, etc.) which added greatly to the information available in the frequently terse Government Lists of Buildings of Special Architectural or Historic Interest. For medieval and early modern houses and churches the magisterial works of Charles MacGibbon and Thomas Ross (*The Castellated and Domestic Architecture of Scotland*, 5 vols, 1887–92, and *The Ecclesiastical Architecture of Scotland*, 3 vols, 1896–7) have been consistently useful sources, as has, for C18 and C19 buildings, the late Sir Howard Colvin's *A Biographical Dictionary of British Architects* (4th edn, 2008) and, for Victorian and C20 buildings, David M. Walker's online *Dictionary of Scottish Architects* (www.scottisharchitects.org.uk).

For Dundee and Angus the task of arranging notes and searching through a myriad of histories and descriptions of towns, villages, parishes and individual buildings, the single most important source for the area being Alexander J. Warden, *Angus or Forfarshire* (5 vols, 1880–5), was undertaken by me and Siobhan Marples. We also spent many months looking at ecclesiastical and official records and estate papers held in the National Archives of Scotland, the Dundee City Archive, the Angus Archives and the University of Dundee Archives, whose staff have proved unfailingly helpful and patient, as have many librarians, notably those of the National Library of Scotland, the Scottish and Fine Arts Departments of the Edinburgh Central Public Library, Edinburgh University Library, the Dundee Central Library and of the several libraries in Angus, all of whom have made me welcome. Most long-suffering of all has been the staff of the National Monuments Record of Scotland where the research notes for *Dundee and Angus* will be deposited, as have those of other published volumes in the series.

Information on individual buildings has been given by owners, clergy and members of their congregations. Many historians and architects have contributed much, either by answering specific queries or by discussing the buildings and architecture of the area and of Scotland more generally. Thanks are especially due to the late Sir Howard Colvin, Kitty Cruft, Christopher Dingwall, John Dunbar, Richard Fawcett, Miles Glendinning, Ian Gow, Bob Heath, Yvonne Hillyard, Jeff Hopewell, Tom Davidson Kelly, Andrew Kerr, Aonghus MacKechnie, Allan Maclean, Debbie Mays, Helen Smailes, John Stansfeld, David Walker, Mark Watson, Diane Watters and Charles Wemyss. An exceptionally large expression of thanks is due to Alex Banks of the Dundee City Council who provided a great amount of information on Dundee buildings of the C20 and C21. Gratitude of a rather different sort is owed to David Bassett who has had to suffer my mood swings from depression to despair and, very occasionally, elation, whilst writing this book.

The book's editor at Yale University Press, Charles O'Brien, read the whole text and made many suggestions for its improvement, some of which I have adopted. Bernard Dod has acted as copy editor and Charlotte Chapman as proofreader. Among the Yale team co-ordination of the text has been undertaken by Catherine Bankhurst and illustrations were commissioned and co-ordinated by Sophie Sheldrake and Phoebe Lowndes. I prepared the Index of Artists and Judith Wardman the Index of Places. The map of Angus has been drawn by Reg Piggott. The town maps are by Martin Brown.

As with some previous volumes, the Royal Commission on the Ancient and Historical Monuments of Scotland has given immense help with the illustrations. Heather Stoddart prepared the plans of buildings with customary determination to ensure their accuracy and good humour. Many of the photographs were taken specially by the Commission's photographers, principally Angus Lamb and Steve Wallace. Responsibility for ordering and transmitting photographs held by the Commission was undertaken by Kristina Watson. All this was co-ordinated by Clare Sorensen and Diane Watters.

INTRODUCTION

TOPOGRAPHY, GEOLOGY AND BUILDING MATERIALS

The geology and topography of Angus are formed in bands running from SW to NE. The NW of these, roughly from Bridgend of Lintrathen to Edzell, is a highland area of moorland cut across by the partly wooded gorges of Glen Isla, Glen Prosen, Glen Clova and Glen Esk. The hills, of generally rounded form, rise to 928 m. and 947 m. at the adjacent summits of Mayar and Driesh W of Clova and over 1000 m. at Fafernie and Cairn Bannoch to the NW on the border with Aberdeenshire. The underlying rocks are Dalradian originally formed from sandstone or mudstone sediments laid down in an ocean over 550 million years ago. These, during the Caledonian orogeny (mountain-building period) of about 470 million years ago, were then compressed, folded and metamorphosed to high mountains composed largely of quartzite and slate which, still bare of vegetation, were quickly eroded by the action of rivers. This belt now contains narrow strips of fertile land beside the rivers but, on the steep slopes of the hillsides above, pasture of coarse grass quickly gives way to heather moorland and scree composed of fragments of ice-shattered rocks, the habitat of grouse, mountain hares, deer and sheep of the hardier breeds.

The highland belt of the Angus glens is bounded on the SE by the Highland Boundary Fault, a low-lying narrow but quite fertile strip, its underlying geology largely of coarse-grained conglomerate rocks formed from boulders, cobbles and gravels washed down from the mountains behind. SE of this is the broad belt of Strathmore underlain by Old Red Sandstone rocks formed about 400 million years ago from the finer particles of sand carried down from the mountains and now covered largely by sandy or clayey soil. The landscape is varied, a plain from which rise hills, e.g. Hill of Kirriemuir (148 m. high), Finavon Hill (202 m.) or Turin Hill (262 m.), covered with grass, gorse or broom. The sand or clay soil of the lower-lying land forms rich red earth which when drained, as it has been since the C18, is among the most fertile in Scotland, well suited to the growing of arable crops, fruit and potatoes as well as to pasture for livestock.

Roughly contemporary with the Old Red Sandstone of Strathmore are the Sidlaw Hills to the S which stand in a gentle curve extending from the Perth and Kinross border near Lundie to W of

Carmyllie where they dip down to the coastal plain. These are volcanic in origin, their rocks, formed from molten lava, mingled with the sandstone through which they erupted. On their lower slopes now grow arable crops, the higher are given over to pasture.

The area's SE belt, between the Sidlaw Hills and the sea, is a coastal plain whose N end merges with Strathmore and which is also underlain by Old Red Sandstone, the rock formations dramatically exposed at the steep cliffs which form much of its E edge. As in Strathmore the soil here is admirably suited to arable, fruit and potato crops but the landscape is flatter, the monotony of the plain relieved by the eruptions of the volcanic vents of Downie Hill, near Monikie, and Dundee's Dundee Law and Balgay Hill.

BUILDING STONE in the area, the product of a large number of local quarries, was predominantly of sandstone. Before the C18 it was used mostly for the construction of churches and lairds' houses, the dwellings of the peasantry being built of boulders from the fields intermixed with turf. However, by the end of the C18 the use of quarried stone became more general. The sandstone's colour varies greatly. Much of Victorian and early C20 Dundee is built of stone from the Kingoodie Quarry near Invergowrie (Perth and Kinross), which weathers to a dull brownish-grey, almost khaki colour. Elsewhere, however, is stone of a steelier grey colour and texture better able to refract light. Much of the Angus sandstone is red in colour and at Kirriemuir an almost purple crimson. By the later C19 stone was transported by the railways from elsewhere in Scotland, most notably from the extensive quarries near Dumfries whose durable and red-coloured sandstone was used for the walling of St Mary's Church at Kirriemuir in 1904–5.

A mixture of CLAY and small stones was sometimes used for the walls of houses in the late C18 and early C19, especially in areas where good building stone was not readily available. Covered with harling and sheltered by a projecting roof this was surprisingly durable. Clay was also used for the manufacture of bricks and a sizeable brickworks at Anniston near Inverkeilor was in operation in the C19 and early C20. Bricks and concrete blockwork, almost all imported to Angus and usually covered with harling or render, became the area's common building materials in the mid C20.

TIMBER for buildings was, by the C17, generally imported from the Baltic and Angus has not since grown wood for use in construction. Steel, also from outside the area, has now largely replaced timber as a major structural component of buildings.

Until the end of the C18 the most common ROOFING MATERIALS for all rural buildings except churches and lairds' houses were varieties of thatch, often of turf but sometimes of the more durable straw or heather. By the late C18 sandstone was quarried not only for walls but also as slabs for the paving of floors and, as 'grey slates', for the covering of roofs. The use of 'grey slates' was extensive in late C18 and early C19 Angus but their weight required the use of a disproportionate amount of timber to support them. The development of the railways by the mid C19 led to the replacement of these sandstone slabs by much lighter true slates ('blue slates') from the West Highland quarries of Easdale and Ballachulish. Welsh slates, concrete tiles and metal have, in turn, replaced these as the common covering for roofs in the later C20 and C21.

PREHISTORIC AND ROMAN ANGUS

The earliest inhabitants of Scotland arrived in tiny numbers probably by the beginning of the seventh millennium B.C. after the end of the last Ice Age. These MESOLITHIC (Early Stone Age) hunter-gatherers lived by killing or trapping wild animals and birds, by fishing, and by harvesting shellfish, nuts and berries. They worked stones or flints to form tools such as scrapers, blades, awls and corers. Their presence in Angus has been established by the C19 discovery of a couple of their middens or rubbish dumps containing shells and flints at Broughty Ferry and Stannersgate, Dundee, and more recently of microliths (miniature worked flints) at inland sites, e.g. at Kirkbuddo near Inverarity, Monikie and the Brown Caterthun near Menmuir.

From the beginning of the fifth millennium B.C. new techniques were introduced to Scotland, probably by immigrants from Continental Europe, who may have co-existed with groups of hunter-gatherers for several centuries. This NEOLITHIC (New Stone Age) culture was characterized by settlements, usually on light and easily worked soils, occupied by communities of farmers who grew primitive types of wheat and barley and kept flocks and herds of domesticated sheep and cattle. Tools, still of stone or flint, were worked to more sophisticated patterns and clay was used to make pottery.

Burials, presumably of personages of some importance, were marked by CAIRNS. Some were ring cairns, each consisting of a ring of cairn material (turf and stones), its inner and outer edges defined by kerbs of slabs or boulders, surrounding a roofless central space which contained the burial itself. At Mearns Hill near Kirriemuir stands a ring cairn *c.* 10 m. in overall diameter and with a central space of 5 m. diameter, parts of the ring's kerbs still traceable. The outer kerb of an exceptionally small cairn (only 6 m. in diameter) on Strone Hill overlooking the Loch of Lintrathen has been composed, at least in part, of large slabs. Cairns probably played a part in religious ritual. So probably did the large (65 m. by 19 m.) two-compartment enclosure bounded by posts which was exposed by excavation in the late 1970s and early 1980s at Douglasmuir near Friockheim and for which radiocarbon testing has provided a date of *c.* 2900 B.C. Almost certainly of religious significance and connected with observations of the summer and winter solstices are STONE CIRCLES. The most boldly sited in the area is the now fragmentary circle at Colmeallie near Edzell, standing on a hillside above the valley of the North Esk and composed originally of perhaps twelve stones.

Probably also of Neolithic date are the ROCK CARVINGS pecked with stone axes found on some boulders. These consist of cup marks (shallow circular scoops) or cup-and-ring marks (cup marks set in circles). The surface of a flat boulder on Tullos Hill near Menmuir is indented with more than thirty shallow cup marks. Probably such carved boulders served as territorial markers or, perhaps, ritual monuments or combined both functions.

A further wave of new ideas and skills, probably brought by immigrants, came to Scotland about the middle of the third millennium B.C. at the beginning of the BRONZE AGE. These introduced the art of metalworking to produce bronze implements and weapons. FUNERARY CUSTOMS changed, first with interments of individual bodies in stone-slabbed cists or boxes. Over the most important graves, often located on the tops of hills or ridges, were constructed large round cairns, two of the largest in Angus standing at Dickmontlaw near Arbroath and at Cotelhill near Kirkton of Lintrathen, the second no less than than 30 m. in diameter and, despite later disturbance, still up to 3 m. high. From *c.* 1500 B.C. bodies of the dead were often cremated, the residue of ashes and bone fragments buried, if not directly in the ground, in small cists. Round cairns also marked these interments but they were of much smaller dimensions than earlier ones, suggesting they may have been only of local significance.

Standing stones continued to be erected as ritual monuments. At Balkemback near Tealing there is a 'four-poster', a quadrangular setting of four upright stones (two now fallen). A massive standing stone on the Hill of Kirriemuir seems to be the survivor of a pair.

By 750 B.C. the climate was deteriorating. Consequently, some upland settlements were abandoned, the displaced population having to compete with existing settlers for the more fertile low-lying land. At about the same time yet another influx of ideas and probably immigrants reached Scotland, introducing the technology for the smelting and working of iron. The population seems now to have formed tribes, each based on the labours of peasant farmers but with a martial aristocracy equipped with iron weapons. The major contribution of the IRON AGE to the buildings of Angus was the construction of FORTS. Some were formed on promontories. Castle Rock at Auchmithie and Maiden Castle (*see* Auchmithie) both jut into the sea, high cliffs providing natural defence on these sides. The easier landward approach to each has been fortified, Maiden Castle with a single but massive rampart and ditch, Castle Rock with three ramparts and accompanying ditches. A few promontory forts occupied inland sites, e.g. Hurly Hawkin near Liff which was defended by a rampart and two ditches. Much more prominently sited are the forts erected on hilltops, clearly visible from a considerable surrounding area. Typically each consisted of a roughly oval enclosure, its size varying from *c.* 1.5 ha. to over 6 ha., defended by a rampart and ditch and sometimes, as at Denoon Law near Eassie and Nevay, with further ramparts as supplementary defences on their hills'

gentler slopes. Several, most notably the large fort on the Brown Caterthun near Menmuir, have several roughly concentric ram- 3
parts but these seem to be of different dates corresponding to periods when the size of the forts expanded or contracted. The final phase of development of the Brown Caterthun entailed the construction of a palisaded enclosure of *c.* 100 m. by 60 m., perhaps indicating a shift in the organization of society at the beginning of the first millennium A.D., a period which saw the erection of a number of small forts or DUNS, e.g. on Dumbarrow Hill near Letham or on the lower slope of Pitscandly Hill just E of Lunanhead. One dun, on Turin Hill near Aberlemno, partly overlays the earlier defences of an earlier hilltop fort. At about the same time BROCHS were constructed within and sometimes on top of the ramparts of hill-forts, as at Craighill near Murroes or Hurly Hawkin near Liff. These, rare in Angus although common in NW Scotland and the Northern Isles, are circular enclosures, of 10.6 m. internal diameter at Craighill and 12 m. at Hurly Hawkin, each containing a central hearth and ringed by a thick wall which may have supported a superstructure containing mural chambers and whose inner face probably served as the back wall of single-storey lean-to buildings.

The generality of Iron Age HOUSES of the first millennium B.C. and the first millennium A.D. were circular, between 5 m. and 20 m. in diameter, each built round a central hearth, the inner part of the high-pitched conical roof often supported on a ring of posts, the outer part on a low wall of stone, earth or timber-framed wattle and daub. Often these houses were accompanied by SOUTERRAINS or underground passage-like stores. These were generally curved, often in a banana-shape, *c.* 2 m.–3 m. broad, 1.5 m.–2 m. high and 20 m.–40 m. long. They were formed by the digging of 3 m. deep trenches which were then faced and roofed with stone slabs or timber, the roofs covered with soil up to the level of the surrounding ground. Excavated and now roofless examples can be seen near Newbigging and at Tealing. Still slab-roofed is the souterrain at Kirkton of Airlie, the soffit of one of its lintel stones (presumably reused) bearing Bronze Age cup marks, as does also a stone in the Tealing souterrain.

The ROMANS established a presence in Britain from 43 A.D. In 82 and 83 the governor Gnaeus Julius Agricola undertook campaigns in Scotland N of the Tay. Before his recall to Rome in 83 he had probably planned lines of forts, although their construction seems to have been the work of his successor during the next couple of years. The principal line, together with a road for at least part of its length, crossed the Tay at Bertha just N of Perth and from there ran through Strathmore by way of a fortlet at Cargill (Perth and Kinross) to large forts at Cardean near Ruthven and Stracathro, perhaps with an undiscovered fortlet between them. A second line, whose forts seem intended to control the mouths of the glens to the N or, perhaps, to serve as bases for incursions up them, ran a little to the NW with a fortress at Inchtuthil near Spittalfield (Perth and Kinross) and a fortlet at Inverquharity beside the South Esk. Both the fort at Stracathro and the fortlet at Inverquharity were accompanied by camps, perhaps occupied by soldiers engaged in their construction. These camps are conventional oblongs but with the entrances defended by external projections of the surrounding rampart, one curved, the other straight, together forming a claw-like funnel. The C1 forts and fortlets themselves were also oblongs with rounded corners and defended by ramparts and ditches, the internal enclosure regularly laid out with an array of administration and barracks blocks, their walls constructed of timber-framing infilled with wattle and daub. Hardly had they been completed than they were abandoned, the N frontier of Roman occupation retreating first to the Forth–Clyde isthmus and, by 100, further back to the Tyne–Solway line.

In 208–*c.* 212 the Emperor Septimius Severus and his sons, Geta and Caracalla, responded to raids by the Caledonii, the Celtic tribes of Scotland N of the Tay, by undertaking military campaigns in Perthshire, Angus and the North-East. Physical evidence of these is provided in Angus by the remains, some only discernible from the air, of the army's MARCHING CAMPS at Cardean, Battledykes near Oathlaw of *c.* 50.6 ha. and at Kirkbuddo near Inverarity of *c.* 25.5 ha., all of approximately rectangular shape. Each was defended by a rampart and ditch and contained leather tents in which the soldiers slept during their brief occupation of the camps – up to three days after which local food supplies would be exhausted and the water supply contaminated. These early C3 campaigns led to no permanent occupation and the Roman army again withdrew to the line of Hadrian's Wall between the Tyne and Solway.

PICTISH AND EARLY CHRISTIAN MONUMENTS

The tribes encountered by the Romans in Scotland N of the Forth–Clyde isthmus during their incursions of the C1 and C3 A.D. were named by them as the Caledonii or Dicalydones and by Bede, writing in the C8, as the northern Picts. Pictish kingdoms, latterly under the overlordship of the kings of Fortiu centred on Forteviot, survived until the mid C9 when they fell under the supremacy of the kings of Alba or Scots, successors to rulers of kingdoms founded by Irish immigrants who had settled in Argyll by the C5. The Gaelic language, originally confined to western Scotland, was gradually to supplant that of the Picts in most of the country N of the Forth and Clyde.

The clearest evidence of a specifically Pictish culture is provided by SCULPTURED STONE SLABS erected between the C6 and C9. The purpose of these is uncertain and perhaps various. Some marked graves, others may have identified ownership of a particular tract of land or denoted a meeting place. Common to all is their inclusion of symbols grouped, usually vertically, in twos or threes. Some symbols are realistic depiction of creatures, e.g.
4 a snake on a slab at Aberlemno and another snake, accompanied

by a salmon, on a slab at Glamis or an eagle on a slab now in St Vigeans Museum. Others represent fantastic animals, e.g. the 'Pictish beasts' on the fragments of slabs at Kinblethmont and Balluderon (Martin's Stone) near Kirkton of Auchterhouse. Yet more are stylized representations of objects, their subject matter identified with varying degrees of certainty by historians and now with a generally accepted nomenclature (e.g. 'mirror and comb' or 'double disc'). Often, the stylized symbols are combined with a 'V-rod' or 'Z-rod', apparently representing respectively a broken arrow and a broken spear or, possibly, sceptre. Between twenty and thirty Pictish symbols have been identified, most with a wide geographical distribution throughout Scotland. Their meaning is unknown but the most probable explanation is that they represented names, the pairs of symbols standing for X son of Y and with the triple groups including also the name of a grandfather.

The earliest of the Pictish sculptured slabs display only symbols, e.g. the fragment at Kinblethmont or a couple of slabs at Aberlemno, and date probably from the c6 or c7. After the conversion of the Picts to Christianity in the late c7 one face of each slab was generally carved with a cross, usually decorated with interlacing, a decorative motif perhaps derived from contemporary metalwork. On some slabs the cross, although the dominant motif, is the only specifically Christian subject, the other carvings expressions of secular concerns and pastimes. The cross on the 6
large c8 slab in the graveyard beside Aberlemno Parish Church is flanked by depictions of intertwined beasts. Flanking the cross on the c8 or c9 St Orland's Stone at Cossans near Glamis are intertwined fish monsters. On a slab in the St Vigeans Museum the head of the cross is set between a pair of birds, the shaft between interlaced patterns. On either side of the cross on the slab at Glamis are a lion, a centaur, a cauldron and two warriors 5
engaged in hand-to-hand combat. On other slabs the cross is placed between a mixture of Christian and non-Christian figures. On one slab in St Vigeans Museum the cross is flanked by human figures, two representing St Paul the Hermit and St Anthony of Egypt (emblematic respectively of the eremitical and monastic life) and others probably more saints, but also the depiction of a cow and crouching man. Also in St Vigeans Museum, the 'Drosten Stone's' cross is set between fantastic beasts but has an angel perched on its l. arm. The slab on Hunter's Hill near Glamis is carved with a cross between symbols, animals and a bird-headed man but also an angel. Flanking the shaft of the cross on the slab in Eassie Parish Church are figures of an armed warrior, a deer and a hound but on either side of the cross-head are carved angels. Similarly, one slab at Aberlemno has a cross whose shaft is flanked by beasts but also by angels. The cross on one slab, probably c9, in St Vigeans Museum is notable for its accompaniment of exclusively Christian figurative representations, being flanked by a pair of ecclesiastics, presumably saints. The figures on the back of this slab are also apparently of saints, two of them perhaps of St Paul the Hermit and St Anthony of Egypt. The reverse faces of other slabs bear depictions of purely secular

pursuits. A slab at Aberlemno shows a battle, the warriors of one side bare-headed and long-haired, the others wearing helmets, possibly the commemoration of a battle between Picts and invading Northumbrian Angles. Slabs at Cossans near Glamis, Eassie and Aberlemno display hunting scenes, the pursuit of deer probably the preserve of kings and aristocrats here represented as enjoying the privilege of their status. Unusual is the juxtaposition on a slab at Aberlemno of a hunting scene with smaller panels, one carved with a centaur but the other with the biblical scene of the shepherd boy David (the future King of Israel) killing a lion.

By the C10, as can be seen from the Camus' Cross near Monikie, some monuments at least were without Pictish symbols and displayed almost wholly Christian imagery. Carved from a single slab, this is free-standing and cross-shaped. Each of the two faces of the cross is divided into three panels, the top showing the Crucified Christ on the W and Christ in Glory on the E, the W lower panels with reliefs of a *sagittarius* and scrolls of foliage, the E carved with saints, perhaps the Four Evangelists. Also C10 and without Pictish symbols but also devoid of Christian iconography is the stone unearthed at Bullion near Liff and now in the National Museum of Scotland (a plaster cast in Liff Church) which bears the relief of an aged horse plodding uphill, the equally elderly rider quaffing from a drinking horn.

RECUMBENT GRAVE-SLABS, probably C9 or C10, are now in St Vigeans Museum, one bearing the relief of a mounted warrior, another of a hunting scene overlooked by a scornful manticore, the man-eating beast of Aristotelian 'zoology', a third a depiction of Daniel in the Lions' Den. A fourth whose top's central panel is carved with a cross is the most overtly Christian.

MEDIEVAL CHURCHES

Christianity was adopted by the Picts of Angus *c.* 700. During the next four centuries there seems to have developed an ecclesiastical organization in which clergy were grouped in monastic or quasi-monastic communities, each serving the religious needs of an extensive local area. The churchyard of St Vigeans has produced an abundant display of fragments of cross-slabs dating from the C8 onwards (*see* Pictish and Early Christian Monuments, above), clearly suggesting that this was an ecclesiastical centre of some importance. There is good evidence of the presence of houses of *Céli Dé* ('vassals of God'), inspired by Irish monastic reforms of the C8 and C9, at Brechin (by *c.* 972) and Restenneth (by the later C11). At Restenneth the C11 church consisted of a short nave (only 3 m. long internally) and chancel. Of the early church at Brechin, apparently of greater importance,
7 there survives the originally detached Round Tower which was probably constructed *c.* 1100. Probably of Irish inspiration, this tower, *c.* 33 m. high and, tapering from a diameter of *c.* 4.65 m. at the base to 3.3 m. at the top, is one of only two such circular

Early Christian towers in Scotland, the other of about the same date at Abernethy (Perth and Kinross), where it also stood as a landmark to announce the presence of a community of *Céli Dé*.

From the end of the C11 the Scottish Church underwent sweeping changes, the process greatly encouraged by Malcolm III, his queen St Margaret (both †1093), and their sons, successive Kings of Scots, Edgar (†1107), Alexander I (†1124) and David I (†1153). Principal among these reforms were the foundation of monasteries belonging to international religious orders, the revival of territorially defined dioceses (all of Scotland's previously established bishoprics having been left vacant during the C11) and the creation of parishes, each covering a limited area and usually served by a single resident priest. In Angus a diocese of Brechin was established at about the same time as the Round Tower was built and, soon after, the associated community of *Céli Dé* was transformed into a cathedral chapter of canons. Also in the early or mid C12 the community of *Céli Dé* became a priory of Augustinian canons (a pendicle of Jedburgh Abbey). In 1178 William I ('the Lion') founded the most lavishly endowed and largest of Angus's religious establishments, the Tironensian (reformed Benedictine) abbey of Arbroath. These monastic and diocesan innovations were accompanied by the erection of new buildings. The church at Restenneth was largely rebuilt in the C13 to serve the needs of the new priory. A new choir was erected, 8
capable of accommodating the monks during the performance of their regular monastic offices. At the same time was constructed a longer and broader nave which served as the setting for services for the surrounding parish. The earlier nave survived but as the base of a tower awkwardly placed at the junction of the new nave and choir and with a passage on its N side running between these two parts of the church. Almost twice the size was the church of Arbroath Abbey built in the late C12 and early C13, 10
its length of *c.* 70 m. greater than that of any other monastic church in Scotland except St Andrews Cathedral (the church of an Augustinian priory) and about the same as that of Glasgow Cathedral. The impact of size was magnified by the height and seeming solidity of its three towers.

At both Restenneth Priory and Arbroath Abbey the length of the nave was largely determined by the functional need for it to be long enough to form one side of a quadrangular cloister. This, containing the living quarters of the monks, was by the C12 of standardized form with a covered ground-floor walkway on all sides. The N walk abutted directly the side of the abbey or priory church. On the other sides of the cloister the walks projected from the inner faces of two-storey ranges. The E contained the monks' first-floor dormitory from which a stair descended into the S transept of the church to allow direct access for the night-time services; projecting E from this range was the ground-floor chapter house. In the S range was the refectory and the W contained a guesthouse. Similar provision of a conventual church with a cloister to one side was found at friaries, such as the Franciscan house, a C13 foundation, on the edge of Dundee. The

C12 provision of a bishop for the diocese of Brechin and the transformation of that town's community of *Céli Dé* into a cathedral chapter was followed from the beginning of the C13 by the construction of a new cathedral church of marked but modest pretension, *c.* 42.7 m. long but with a fully aisled nave, transepts
7 and choir, the great NW tower (perhaps an afterthought of the mid C13) an overpowering counterweight to the earlier Round Tower but a fitting affirmation of the building's status.

A later and more grandiose proclamation of status was the
13 50 m.-high W tower added in the C15 to Dundee's 53 m.-long burgh church (forerunner of the present City Churches). This gave visible expression of the place of Dundee among the principal royal burghs of Scotland. Less swaggering assertions of burgh status were given by the towers of the medieval churches of the less important royal burghs of Montrose and Forfar.

The medieval rural PARISH CHURCHES were much more modest and only a handful in Angus have survived. As first built, generally in the C12 or early C13, each seems to have comprised an unaisled nave and chancel, in some cases structurally distinct as at Lundie, in others, as at St Vigeans, originally with the chancel marked off only by a wooden rood screen or beam. St
9 Vigeans Parish Church is also notable both as a medieval survival and as a church which was enlarged in various stages in the C15, first by the broadening of the nave and creation of a N aisle, then by the addition of a W tower and, lastly, by the erection of a S aisle. The addition of these aisles may have been, at least in part, the result of the late medieval need to erect side altars to be used for votive masses, often for the souls of the deceased of a family or trade. In Dundee, the burgh church housed at least twenty-seven such altars by the beginning of the C16. Provision for further altars in a parish church could also be met by the addition of a chapel, usually to serve also as the burial place of a local landed family. Such transeptal chapels or 'aisles' were added to Guthrie Church *c.* 1470, Glamis Parish Church about ten years later and the former Edzell Parish Church in 1549, all with round-headed arches opening into the church itself. The Guthrie Aisle was covered with a tunnel-vaulted oak ceiling painted with depictions of the Crucifixion and Last Judgment, the Strathmore Aisle at Glamis by stone vaulting embellished with heraldry. Erection of the Guthrie Aisle seems to have been part of a scheme by Sir David Guthrie of Guthrie to enlarge the parish church to house a collegiate church whose provost and three (later seven) prebendaries held daily quasi-monastic services there and prayed for the souls of dead members of the founder's family. Another combined parish and collegiate church was St Marnock's Church at Fowlis founded by Andrew, Lord Gray, in 1453, the nave used for parochial services, the chancel for those of the college which consisted of a provost and seven prebendaries. The exterior of this long rectangular building is simple but with a show-off entrance, its ogee-arched hoodmould bearing a heraldic display in celebration of the Gray family.

The FURNISHINGS of any medieval church comprised, at the least, an altar, rood screen or beam to mark off the chancel and for liturgical use in the Holy Week and Easter ceremonies, and font. Hardly any of these survive in Angus. At St Marnock's Church at Fowlis, however, are remarkable examples of parts of the C15 furnishings of a late medieval church of some pretension. The altars themselves no longer exist but a large fragment of the High Altar's reredos, now hung on the N wall, is painted with portraits of Our Lord and saints. The rood screen's gates, ornamented with linenfold panelling, tracery and crocketed pinnacles, now form part of the C19 screen dividing the vestibule from the body of the church. The top of the rood screen, a large panel painted with a depiction of the Crucifixion including characterful 11
depiction of the bystanders, now adorns the N wall and more fragments of this scene are hung on the S wall. Also in St Marnock's Church is the C15 octagonal stone font, its bowl with mutilated scenes from the Life of Our Lord, the base bearing the coats of arms of Lord Gray, founder of the collegiate church, and his wife. The roll-call of late medieval furnishings here is completed by the E gable's stone sacrament house (a stone aumbry 12
in which a consecrated host was reserved for communion of the dying), its ogee-arched door surmounted by a representation of Our Lord flanked by angels. The head of another probable sacrament house of the C15 or early C16 and also with a carved depiction of Our Lord and angels is found in Angus at Cortachy Church. Airlie Church (Kirkton of Airlie) contains a contemporary sacrament house whose arch-head is set between a ringed cross and a carving of the *Arma Christi*. Now without overtly Christian subject matter is the decoration of the sacrament house of *c.* 1480 in the Strathmore Aisle of Glamis Church, the spandrels of its ogee arch bearing heraldic shields.

Burial inside churches was reserved for personages of some standing. The most important might be commemorated by EFFIGIES. One, now headless C14 figure of a robed man was discovered at the E end of Arbroath Abbey's church, its position, although not its likely date unless it was a replacement, suggesting it may have marked the grave of William I ('the Lion'), the abbey's founder. Another effigy at Arbroath Abbey which portrays a bishop may have marked a grave but was perhaps a statue of St Thomas Becket, patron saint of the abbey. Humbler are the grave-slabs of a couple of less highly placed churchmen, the late C14 slab to Ingram of Kethenys, Archdeacon of Dunkeld, in Tealing Parish Church, unusually for the date with an inscription in English, and the slab of 1535 at Arbroath Abbey carved in low relief with the figure of a monk.

POST-REFORMATION CHURCHES

In August, 1560, the Scottish Parliament forbade celebration of the Mass according to Catholic usage, proscribed the recognition of papal authority and adopted a Calvinist Confession of Faith.

In Angus, following the Reformation, the church of Arbroath Abbey and most of its conventual buildings were abandoned and subsequently used as a quarry for building materials. The monastic buildings of Restenneth Priory were also abandoned and largely demolished, although the priory church itself continued to be used as a parish church until 1591 when supplanted by the erection of a new church at Forfar, and part of it was fitted up as a short-lived Episcopalian chapel at the end of the C17. At Brechin the cathedral church's nave was used, as before, as the parish church of the burgh but the choir was abandoned.

Burgh and rural PARISH CHURCHES continued in use but adapted for reformed worship. This placed, in theory, almost equal emphasis on prayer, preaching and the sacrament of the Lord's Supper or Holy Communion, although the reluctance of the laity to communicate weekly led to this being celebrated only occasionally. That the congregation should be able to hear and see the minister was accorded importance and, at least partly in consequence, by 1609 the great burgh church of Dundee was divided to hold three congregations, one in the choir and the others in the transepts. Stone altars were removed, the wooden tables which replaced them often erected only for communion services, and pride of place generally given to a pulpit placed at one end of a church or often in the centre of one of the sides. One early C17 pulpit which has survived, probably because of its
15 exceptional quality, is in Dun Church. Dated 1615, it displays the coat of arms of the then parish minister; its canopy's front is treated as a pelmet and surmounted by an urn finial. Chancels, now functionally redundant, were not infrequently taken over by a local landed family to serve as burial places as at St Marnock's Church (Fowlis), sometimes with a laird's pew or loft above. The chancel of Inverkeilor Church, taken over by the Carnegies of Ethie (later Earls of Northesk), was rebuilt in the 1630s to contain their burial vault and laird's loft, the outside face of its S wall adorned with panels displaying the family's coat of arms together with reliefs of a skeleton and a trumpeting angel trampling emblems of death. Inside, the front of the laird's loft displays heraldry and an enjoyably ignorant parade of classicism. Another medieval chancel rebuilt in the earlier C17 to contain a family pew and burial vault was that of Auchterhouse (Kirkton of Auchterhouse), its S elevation symmetrical, the rectangular door flanked by Gothic survival windows.

A few churches were rebuilt at the end of the C16 and during the C17 and early and mid C18. Generally they were of simple oblong form, the windows often rectangular, a birdcage bellcote the chief embellishment, as at the parish churches of Eassie of *c.* 1600, Carmyllie of *c.* 1609 or Inverarity of 1754–5. More ambi-
14 tious was the rebuilding in 1630 of the nave of Auchterhouse Church with a W tower and an entrance door whose design appears a deliberate evocation of medieval precedent, the segmental-arched head springing from bell-capitalled shafts. When Careston Church was rebuilt in 1636 it was on a T-plan, the N jamb housing the family pew and burial vault of Sir Alexander

Carnegie of Careston. This opens into the church by a round-headed arch in the same way as might have done a late medieval transeptal chapel, but here it is filled by the Artisan Mannerist front of the pew whose C17 occupants faced the pulpit standing at the centre of the church's S side.

Most parish churches rebuilt in the late C18 or beginning of the C19 were hardly more ambitious than the earlier post-Reformation churches. Straightforward oblongs, birdcage bellcotes on their W gables, were put up, for example, at Kirkton of Airlie in 1781–3, Maryton in 1791–2, Stracathro in 1799, Tealing in 1806 and Rescobie in 1820, Maryton's bellcote with an unusually elegant urn finial. Further display was usually restricted to the shape of windows, round-headed at Kirkton of Airlie, but often Gothic as at Maryton, Dunnichen (1801–2) or Monikie (by *David Neave*, 1811–12). Some of these box-like churches were dignified by a W tower. Those of Oathlaw Parish Church of 1815 and Edzell Lethnot Church of 1818 were battlemented but the tower of St Rule's Church, Monifieth, of 1812–13 finished with a plain parapet.

Some NEW CHURCHES of the late C18 and beginning of the C19 were more ambitious. Several were in burghs whose civic pride might demand urban adornments. The medieval churches of Montrose and Dundee were rebuilt but retained their existing towers. The new church at Montrose (by *David Logan*, 1791) was large but unpretentious. At Dundee, the new church occupied 13
the site of the former nave which had been left unrepaired after its destruction by an English army in 1548. Designed by *Samuel Bell* in 1787, this was suavely detailed with Y-traceried Gothic windows and a quatrefoil-studded frieze under the wall-head cornice. Also by Samuel Bell and designed a year later was the new parish church at Forfar (now Forfar East and Old Parish Church), the body a Gothic-windowed box but the tower of the tall steeple with an entrance set in a Roman Doric aedicule, pedimented clock faces and an octagonal top stage serving as a base for the stone spire. Another church designed by Bell (in 1772) was St Andrew's Parish Church in Dundee, originally a 16
chapel of ease but far from utilitarian, the Trades (craft guilds) of the town having met half the cost. In the centre of the S front is a pair of swag-surmounted Venetian windows. On the steeple are more carved swags but above Diocletian windows and, as at Forfar, the tower's top stage is octagonal and serves as a base for the spire. For the smaller burgh of Kirriemuir *James Playfair* provided a simple but dignified church in 1786–8, its pedimented W gable surmounted by a steeple. Unexpectedly smart are a few rural churches, each apparently resulting from the determination of the sole or chief heritor (landowner) of the parish, legally responsible for all or most of the building costs of a parish church, to place architectural quality before financial considerations. Light-hearted Gothick was chosen by William Ramsay Maule, sole heritor of the parish, for Lochlee (now Glenlee) Church in the early C19 and by Sir David Carnegie of Pitarrow, sole heritor of Farnell, for that parish's church designed by *James*

Playfair in 1788–9. Largest and grandest of these rural churches is Craig Parish Church of 1796–9, its architect, *Richard Crichton*, employed at the same time by Hercules Ross, the parish's dominant heritor, on the erection of Rossie Castle. Gothic again but a touch more serious, the battlemented nave flanked by aisles and with an inventively detailed tall tower, its great entrance surmounted by the inscription 'Enter His Gates with Praise'.

The INTERIORS of these late C18 and early C19 churches often contained galleries, either at the ends or, more frequently, also along one side, e.g. the semi-octagonal galleries at St Andrew's, Dundee, of 1772–4. As in the first post-Reformation churches the pulpit held pride of place. At Dunnichen Church (1802) it was bow-fronted, at Glenisla Parish Church (1821) covered with a canopy.

For most of the C18 Roman Catholics were forbidden by law to hold public services and in 1763 their number was said to be only fifty-nine in the whole of the counties of Angus and Fife. Passing of the Catholic Relief Act (Scotland) in 1793 made attendance at Mass lawful but it was not until the 1830s, with the immigration of Irish workers to find employment in the rapidly growing textile industries, that their numbers in Dundee and Angus increased substantially and that purpose-built chapels were erected for Catholic worship. The penal laws of the C18 had applied also to Scottish Episcopalians until 1792. However, a handful of Episcopalian meeting houses seem to have been tolerated before then. Moreover Anglican priests, in orders of the Church of England or Church of Ireland and prepared, unlike the Scottish Episcopalians before the 1790s, to swear allegiance to the Hanoverian monarchy, could function freely. A chapel for the congregation of one such 'qualified' clergyman was built at Montrose in 1724. A very grand one and looking like a town house or the meeting place of a trades incorporation was erected at Dundee in 1783–4. Soon after the repeal of the penal laws an Episcopalian chapel was put up at Kirriemuir (1797) and another (St Paul's) in the newly laid out Castle Street, Dundee, in 1810–12. The Dundee chapel occupied a site intended for a tenement and observed the three-storey height and street line expected of buildings here, the double-height chapel occupying the upper floors and with tall pointed windows and a Tudor Gothic entrance to announce its presence.

More than twenty parish churches in Angus were rebuilt between 1820 and 1850, their architectural ambition generally proportionate to the poverty or wealth of the parish. Some were simple oblong boxes with only bellcotes and pointed, round-headed or segmental-arched windows to distinguish them from domestic buildings, although the churches of Eassie and Nevay of 1833 and Lunan of 1844 also boast quatrefoil windows or dummies. Much more stylishly attired is *David Paterson*'s Cortachy Church (1828–9) where battlements and pinnacled buttresses combine with Perpendicular Gothic windows at the body, and the contemporary Airlie Mausoleum projects like a chancel from one end. Here the Late Gothic manner is continued inside,

its focus the crown-spired canopy of the pulpit. More heavily 18
detailed is the Tudor Gothic canopy of 1848 over the pulpit in Murroes Church. Quite exceptional among these churches of the earlier C19 is the design by *Burn & Bryce* for the rebuilding after a fire of the medieval chancel, transepts and E bays of the nave of the City Churches in Dundee. The new external elevations are in a serious Late Gothic manner. The interior of the former St Paul's (South) Church was covered with plaster groin-vaulting, of Dundee Parish Church (St Mary's) with a wooden hammer-beam roof, and its nave arcades formed of round-headed arches carried on bundle-shafted columns.

At a few churches of the earlier C19 the standard bellcote was replaced by a tower, e.g. St Aidan's Parish Church, Broughty Ferry (by *James Black*, 1824–6) or Dun Church (by *Robert Dalgarno*, 1832–4), both in a Gothic style. Also Gothic but of a Tudor character and more expensively detailed is Liff Church (by *W. M. Mackenzie*, 1838–9), its W tower topped by a stone spire. Far more ambitious and replacing medieval predecessors are the 47 m.-high steeple added to Arbroath's Old Parish Church by *John Henderson* in 1830–1 and the 61 m.-high steeple at the Old Parish
Church in Montrose by *James Gillespie Graham*, 1832–4, the 19
design derived from the Perpendicular steeple of Louth Parish Church (Lincolnshire).

Relief from the rather uninspired generally Gothic design of most new parish churches erected in 1820–50 was provided by a few Church of Scotland chapels of ease built to supplement the parish churches in places whose population was burgeoning. Between 1827 and 1830 chapels of ease, paid for by public subscription, were put up at Dundee, Arbroath and Montrose. All these were Neoclassical and temple-fronted, the Lochee Chapel of Ease at Dundee designed by *David Neave*, Arbroath's Inverbrothock Chapel of Ease by *Archibald Simpson* and St John's
Church at Montrose by *William Smith*. However, another chapel 20
of ease in Dundee, the Wallacetown (now Trinity Parish) Church (by *George Mathewson*, 1839–40), was a large 'Saxon' box with an end tower. Two Secessionist churches in Dundee, the Bell Street United Associate Church of 1840 and the Wishart United Secession Church of 1841, have the character of well-finished Late Georgian tenements, the Bell Street church indeed occupying an end pavilion of what was intended as a palace-fronted terrace. Other denominations were eclectic in their choice of style, the Dundee Congregational Church designed by *James Brewster* in 1832 in a carpenter's Gothic manner, Dundee's Roman Catholic
chapel (now St Andrew's Cathedral) in Nethergate in 1835 in a 21
more earthbound Perpendicular style, its firescreen front a misleading advertisement for the unaisled nave behind. This was by *George Mathewson* who adopted unarchaeological Romanesque and 'Saxon' in his designs for St Thomas of Canterbury at Arbroath in 1846 and St Mary Our Lady of Victories, Dundee, in 1850, both with aisled naves, but the arcades at Arbroath are carried on slender cast-iron columns, those at Dundee on fat stone pillars.

Churches after 1850

The four decades after 1850 saw a huge number of new churches built in Dundee and Angus, as in the rest of Scotland. To a large extent this resulted from splits and unions within the Presbyterian denominations. In 1843 took place the DISRUPTION of the Church of Scotland in which about two-fifths of ministers, generally of Evangelical persuasion, and a larger proportion of the laity, left the established church to found the Free Church of Scotland. From the start the Free Church aimed to set up an ecclesiastical organization in parallel to that of the Church of Scotland, each parish to be provided with a (Free) church, manse and school. In large part this aim was accomplished, many churches being built within a few years. These hurriedly constructed early Free churches were, understandably, cheap and architecturally unadventurous, a bellcote and round-headed or pointed windows often the only embellishments, e.g. the Liff Free Church (Muirhead) of 1843, Mains and Strathmartine Free (now Parish) Church of 1844 or Dunnichen Free (now Letham) Church of 1845. The Tudor Gothic garb of Forfar Free Church of 1843–4 is exceptionally smart for its date.

Four years after the Disruption the two main denominations into which the various C18 Secessionist groupings had coalesced, the United Secession Church and the Relief Church, came together to form the United Presbyterian Church. Already equipped with places of worship there was no immediate United Presbyterian building programme such as had been undertaken by the Free Church. Nevertheless, fairly soon after the union of 1847, some United Presbyterian churches were rebuilt or erected from scratch. In 1851 *James Maclaren* designed Erskine United Presbyterian Church at Arbroath, its Gothic still Georgian in spirit. Also Gothic and of the same date but a more serious presence was the tall Mill Street United Presbyterian (now Knox's Montrose United Free) Church in Montrose.

During the 1850s and 1860s some of the early Free churches were rebuilt and others put up to serve newly populous areas. A few, e.g. Forfar East Free Church of 1851–2, were hardly more adventurous than churches of the years immediately after the Disruption. Others, like *David Bryce*'s Maryton Free Church of 1857 or St Paul's Free (now Melville South Parish) Church at Montrose of 1859–60 were simple but dignified by towers, the use of a pyramid-roofed tower at Maryton recurring also in *J., W. H. & J. M. Hay*'s Early Christian (stripped Romanesque) design for the contemporary Lochlee Free (now Maule Memorial) Church at Tarfside. A tower, although a low one, was used to announce the presence of Panbride Free Church at Carnoustie in 1854–5 and another and much taller that of St Paul's Free (now Meadowside St Paul's) Church in Dundee (by *Charles Wilson*, 1850–2), both these buildings Gothic in style. Also Gothic but more powerful is the East Free Church, by *J., W. H. & J. M. Hay*, 1859–60, at Brechin or, of a muscular rogue variety
29 encrusted with carving, the McCheyne Memorial Free Church

in Dundee designed by *Pilkington & Bell* in 1869. By contrast, Dundee's Albert Square Free Church (by *David Mackenzie II*, 1868–9) is Renaissance in manner, with a hall under the galleried church which occupies the upper floors of a building of secular appearance and quite happy in its present use as offices.

From the 1860s until *c.* 1890 many PRESBYTERIAN CHURCHES in the area, especially in the towns, were built or rebuilt, often to serve burgeoning populations. Worship of all the principal denominations (Church of Scotland, Free Church and United Presbyterian Church) was focused, as it had been since soon after the Reformation, on the pulpit placed at one end or in the centre of one side of the church but, after *c.* 1870, often with an organ occupying a recess behind it. Galleries were common, their access stairs often housed in towers or turrets flanking the entrance vestibule.

Some of these new churches continued the Georgian formula of an oblong building with a bellcote on one end, although generally considerably taller, often with buttresses and Gothic detail copied accurately from medieval sources. Such are the Church of Scotland churches at Hillside (by *Alexander Grieve*, 1869–70) and Kilry (1876–7), the United Presbyterian churches at Newbigging (by *James Maclaren*, 1864) and Carnoustie (by *Robert Baldie*, 1872–3), the Congregational Church at Broughty Ferry (by *James Maclaren*, 1864) or the Montrose Methodist Church (1873–4). The Georgian variant formula of substituting an end tower for a bellcote appears at Fern Parish Church (by *Carver & Symon*, 1883). Another oblong church with a tower but here placed at one side of the front gable is Oathlaw Tannadice Parish Church at Tannadice (by *John Carver*, 1866). The Georgian T-plan kirk appears in tall and determinedly Gothic form at Newtyle Church of 1870, also designed by Carver and with a helm-roofed tower in the inner angle of the jamb and main block.

Many churches, more determined in their attempts to evoke medieval buildings, had side aisles flanking the nave, as at *William Leiper*'s French Gothic Bank Street United Presbyterian (now St Ninian's R.C.) Church at Brechin of 1873–5, *Maclaren & Aitken*'s Queen Street United Presbyterian Church at Broughty Ferry of 1875 or *McKenzie & McMillan*'s Forfar First Free (now St Margaret's Parish) Church. At the Broughty Ferry and Forfar examples, as at *Pilkington & Bell*'s rogue Gothic St Mark's (now Gate) Church of 1867–9 in Dundee, the aisle roofs run at right angles to the naves', the roofs of St Mark's Church of hammer-beam construction. Aisles which served either as passages or, more frequently, to house seating, often at both ground and gallery levels, were commonly separated from the nave, not by the stone arcades which the churches' predominantly Gothic exteriors might suggest but by slender cast-iron columns which hardly interrupted the view of the preacher in the pulpit.

Some churches moved closer to a Gothic Revival ideal by being provided not only with aisled naves but also with transepts. At Broughty Ferry Free (now East) Church (by *Andrew Heiton Jun.*, 1864–5) and Barry Free (now Parish) Church (by *James Maclaren*,

1888), they project from the liturgical E end of the nave, but at *William Aitkenhead*'s East Free Church in Arbroath from the W. These were only tentative steps towards a full embrace of Gothic Revival planning. The earliest Presbyterian churches in the area to display the full panoply of aisled nave, (liturgical) E transepts and chancel were St Stephen's and West Church at Broughty Ferry of 1871 and Arbroath West Kirk of 1879, both designed by *Edward & Robertson* and with the Gothic Revival manner continued inside where the pointed arches to the nave arcades, transepts and chancel were all of stone. Very similar in both planning and its use of medieval detail internally as well as externally was another church in Broughty Ferry, St Luke's Free (now St Luke's and Queen Street) by *Hippolyte J. Blanc*, 1884–5, the nave arcades carried on granite-shafted columns. Less orthodox is Dundee West (originally St John's Free) Church by *James Hutton*, 1882–4, its nave arcades with tall bundle-shafted cast-iron columns.

The almost invariable accompaniment to a Presbyterian church of the later C19 with any pretensions was a tower or steeple. The dissensions within contemporary Presbyterianism sometimes led to churches of rival denominations standing almost cheek by jowl, each with a tower to assert that particular denomination's claim to be the true representative of the Scottish Protestant tradition. In the centre of Dundee, the tall steeple of St Paul's Free (now Meadowside St Paul's) Church challenges the great W tower of the City Churches. In Nethergate a little to the W, St John's Free (now Dundee West), St Mark's (now Gate) and Ryehill United Presbyterian Churches form a multi-denominational procession with the McCheyne Memorial Free Church a short distance away as if about to join the queue.

Gothic, often of C13 type, was the usual dress for High Victorian Presbyterian churches but a few were in different styles. In Dundee, Victoria Street United Presbyterian Church (by *Edward & Robertson*, 1874–5) is Italianate, the square tower at one corner a gratuitous self-advertisement. The Maisondieu United Presbyterian Church at Brechin (by *George Washington Browne*, 1890–2) is free Neoclassical, its corner tower topped by a dome, Ryehill United Presbyterian Church, Dundee (by *Maclaren & Aitken*, 1878–80), Lombardic Romanesque. Also Romanesque are two churches, Auchmithie Parish (now St Peter's Episcopal) of 1884 and St James' Broughty Ferry, of 1890, both designed by *T. S. Robertson*.

In May 1848 the clergy of the Brechin diocese of the Scottish Episcopal Church elected the thirty-year-old Alexander Penrose Forbes their new bishop. Energetic and imbued with the Catholic spirituality of the Oxford Movement, Forbes set about the revitalization of his diocese by the erection of new churches, each with an associated school. The earliest and largest of these was
25 St Paul's Church (now Cathedral) in Dundee. Built in 1852–5 to a design by *G. Gilbert Scott*, it occupies the site of the medieval castle S of the High Street. Simple in conception with an aisled nave, short choir and semi-octagonal sanctuary, it is dominated by the great (liturgical) W tower, its appearance derived from the

medieval tower of the City Churches. The tower serves not only to affirm the church's presence to the passer-by but to stand as a landmark seen from the Firth of Tay. Completion of St Paul's was followed immediately by the construction of St Mary Magdalene's Church, also in Dundee but in an area of working-class housing interspersed with textile mills. Geometrical Gothic in style and raised above a basement occupied by the accompanying school, a gabled bellcote serves as the principal external ornament. It was designed by *Coe & Goodwin*, the partnership formed by two of Scott's former assistants. Also in Dundee and externally an even more austere mission church was the third of Forbes's foundations, St Salvador's Church, sited in the Hilltown, another district of workers' housing and mills. Again the architect, *G. F. Bodley*, was a former pupil and assistant of Scott. In all three churches the focus of attention was undoubtedly the High Altar in the chancel. At St Paul the altar was given a marble-columned and mosaic-decorated reredos in the 1870s. The reredos in St Mary Magdalene, designed by *William Butterfield* and erected in 1865, was also embellished with mosaic. Far more
lavish was the decoration provided at St Salvador's in the 1870s, 24
the walls covered with stencilled patterns, a light but painted and gilt cast-iron screen erected at the entrance to the chancel and, behind the High Altar, a reredos which extends the full height and width of the E wall and is painted with a depiction of the Crucifixion flanked by panels portraying the Twelve Apostles. Contemporary with St Salvador's was another Episcopalian church whose erection owed much to Bishop Forbes but which served as a place of worship for a rapidly growing small town rather than a mission to the working classes. This was St Mary's at Broughty Ferry of 1858, designed, like St Paul's, Dundee, by *Scott*. It is sizeable but austere, lancet windows and a W bellcote the principal features.

Two other Episcopalian churches of the 1850s in Angus were less directly the products of Forbes's energies. Both were designed by *John Henderson*. Decorated Gothic in style and less severe than the churches in Dundee and Broughty Ferry, St Mary's at Arbroath, built in 1852–4, comprised a nave with an aisle and chancel, together with a steeple for vertical emphasis and to announce its presence. Another steeple adorns St Peter's (now St Mary and St Peter) of 1858 at Montrose. This sits on the Links where it appears as a pavilion in a public park, allowing full appreciation of its cruciform shape. St Peter's was built for a Church of England congregation not in communion with the Episcopal Church whose own but humbler place of worship at Montrose had also been designed by Henderson fourteen years earlier.

A new wave of church building in the 1870s and 1880s gave the Episcopal Church further edifices. Least prominent is St Andrew's at Brechin, on the site of a chapel built in 1809. In style it is thrifty Gothic but comprises an aisled nave, transepts and chancel. This was designed by *Ross & Macbeth* in 1888, eight years after *Alexander Ross* had been architect for the church of

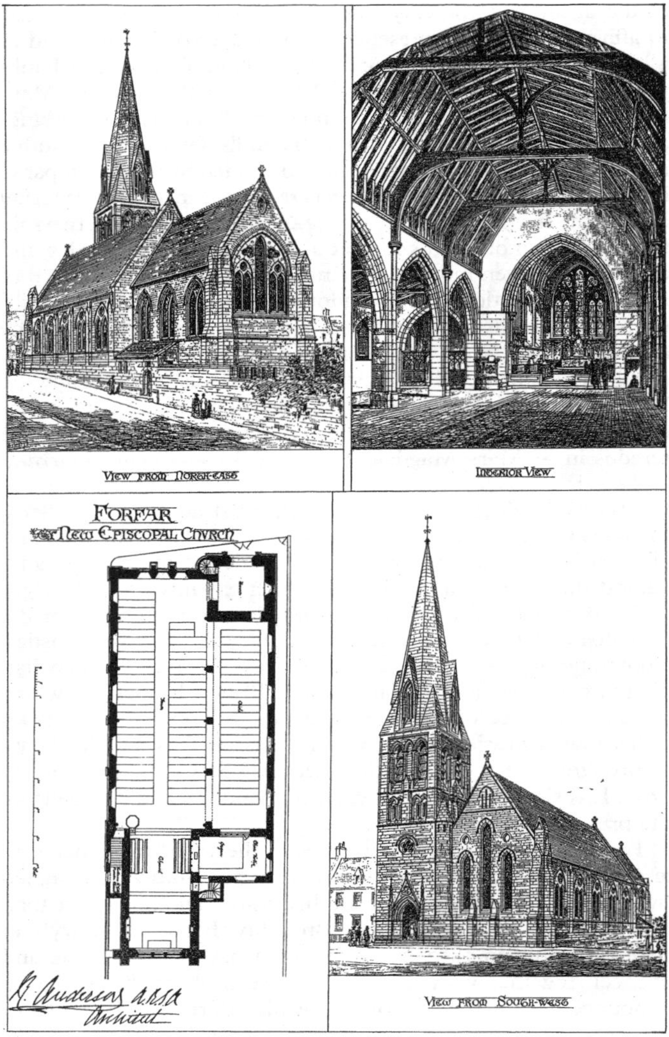

Forfar, St John's Episcopal Church.
R. Rowand Anderson's design of 1879

the Holy Rood at Carnoustie, its conical-roofed tower strongly evocative of the early medieval Round Tower of Brechin Cathedral. Even more assertive would have been the 50 m.-high steeple intended by *R. Rowand Anderson* for the new St John's Church built at Forfar, in 1879–81. Had it been executed the steeple would have dominated the town's High Street, easily asserting superiority over the town's Parish Church. Contemporary but less strident and deliberately evocative of an English village church is St Drostan's at Tarfside (by *Matthews & Mackenzie*), its bellcote idiosyncratically placed below the head of the W gable and covered with a semi-dome. Also of village inspiration were two Episcopalian churches in Dundee designed by the *Rev. Edward Sugden* and built in the later 1880s, St John the Baptist in Albert Street and St Margaret's at Lochee, both now containing surprisingly lavish furnishings introduced a few years later.

The Roman Catholics built only one church of note between 1850 and 1890 but that is the most accomplished work of Pugin-influenced Gothic in the area. Designed by *J. A. Hansom* in 1864, St Mary's provided the Dundee suburb of Lochee with an edifice 22
which served both as mission church for workers in the neighbouring mills and also as a Cathedral-like proclamation of the place of Catholicism in the area. More relaxed Gothic but of comparable size is Dundee's Catholic Apostolic (now St Mary 23
Magdalene's Episcopal) Church by *Edward & Robertson*, 1867.

Churches c. 1890–1914

From the 1890s until the outbreak of the First World War some churches belonging to the main denominations were rebuilt or remodelled. Almost all were Gothic but the style was used in a more relaxed and sometimes less historicist manner than had been the case in the preceding decades and with inspiration found in late medieval architecture. One major influence, especially on the design of Presbyterian churches, was the Aberdeen (later Scottish) Ecclesiological Society founded in 1886. Another was the publication in 1896–7 of David MacGibbon and Thomas Ross's three-volume *The Ecclesiastical Architecture of Scotland*, whose Introduction claimed that the country's late medieval churches formed 'a specially Scottish branch of Gothic architecture'. A meeting of the Ecclesiological Society in 1888 heard a paper read on Brechin Cathedral. Its author spoke of the local 'sense of pride in the ancient church, and a growing sense of no less pleasing dissatisfaction with its present woful [*sic*] state, which may ere long bear fruit in a worthy restoration'.* However, it was not until 1900 that *John Honeyman*'s reconstruction began. This was an attempt both to restore the cathedral as much as possible to its medieval appearance, notably by rebuilding the ruined choir and demolished transepts, and to fit it up as a dignified setting for worship of a Protestant character but in conformity with 'ecclesiological' precepts. These advocated the placing of the communion table in a chancel, whose entrance was to be flanked by the lectern and pulpit, giving visible expression to the early Reformers' vision of worship as a balanced combination of prayer, scriptural reading, preaching and sacrament. At Brechin, as in many churches built or remodelled on 'ecclesiological' lines, these furnishings were augmented by choir stalls in the chancel. Similar in spirit was the remodelling by *D. Wishart Galloway*, 1905, of the very much smaller C17 Careston Church as an

* *Transactions of the Aberdeen Ecclesiological Society*, 1889, 2.

'example of what a small parish church ought to be . . . simple and chaste in the interior; fitted to aid the minister in discharging his duties, and the congregation in rising into the spirit of reverent worship'.* Externally, the remodelling gave this kirk a discreet Gothic flavour, the division of the oblong body into nave and chancel marked by different treatment of the windows. Internally, the E end was fitted up as a chancel to house a communion table and choir stalls, the steps at its entry flanked by a lectern and pulpit. Galloway justified his formation of an E chancel rather than having a pulpit in the centre of the S wall as the main focus of worship, the church's original arrangement, as 'not only more in keeping with the general principles of ecclesiastical architecture, but also as better fitted to express the ideas which underlie the worship of the Christian Church'.† Also part of Galloway's work at Careston was the removal of a wall erected in 1809 which had blocked off the laird's aisle in the jamb from the body of the church and restoration of the C17 front of the laird's pew.

Some NEW CHURCHES followed the precepts of the 'ecclesiologists' but seemingly without enthusiasm, as if repeating a lesson learnt by rote. One such is *John J. Burnet*'s Old Parish Church in Arbroath of 1894–6, its First Pointed style incorporating references to early medieval work at Arbroath Abbey and Dunblane Cathedral, the interior dutifully respectful of 'ecclesiological' teaching. A similarly careful observance of this new orthodoxy, although with only an apse rather than a full-blown chancel to house the communion table, is shown at *Johnston & Baxter*'s Balgay Parish Church, Dundee, of 1900–2. Accomplished but also curiously mechanical in feeling is the large Romanesque Logie and St John's (Cross) Church in Dundee designed by *H. & F. Thomson* in 1911. It adheres fully to 'ecclesiological' planning by providing an aisled nave, transepts, choir and sanctuary. Similar but more appealing, despite the poor quality of its external masonry, is *P. Macgregor Chalmers*'s Carnoustie Parish Church of 1900–2, the style very simple Early Christian, the furnishings enriched with Romanesque and Neo-Celtic motifs. One of the most satisfying of these 'ecclesiological' churches is the Gardner Memorial Church erected at Brechin in 1896–8, the most elaborate of a number in Scotland designed by *John J. Burnet* which were characterized by low churches and halls dominated by a tower. An unselfconscious mixture of motifs including Romanesque, Late Gothic and Neo-Celtic, all with a Scots inflexion, combine here to provide what could be something of the illusion of the centre of a picturesque village to this urban site.

Two further churches come nearest to a full realization of 'ecclesiological' ideals. One is Barnhill St Margaret's at Broughty Ferry. Designed by *Duncan Carmichael* in 1894, its general appearance was modelled on one of the last pre-Reformation churches in Scotland, the 1540s collegiate church of Biggar

* D. Wishart Galloway, 'The Restoration of Careston Church', *Transactions of the Scottish Ecclesiological Society* 2, pt 1, 1906–7, 142.
† *Ibid.* 2, pt 1, 138.

(Lanarkshire), but with details culled from other late medieval
Scottish buildings. It was intended to be cruciform with a cross-
ing tower and a choir and sanctuary occupying the E limb. Even
though the tower was not built and the E limb executed only in
rudimentary form, it stands as a calm and prosperous presence
in its suburban surroundings. Also suburban is the site at Forfar
of the Lowson Memorial Church built in 1912–14 as a memorial
to John Lowson Jun., a Forfar mill-owner and former Provost of
the burgh. Designed by *A. Marshall Mackenzie & Son*, it is cru-
ciform, the nave with low and narrow aisles, the chancel contain-
ing elders' stalls along the side walls and the communion table
at the E end. The W gallery housed the organ and choir. The
design quotes from a variety of Scottish sources from the C13 to
the C15 including Dunblane Cathedral, Sweetheart Abbey, St
Monans Parish Church and King's College Chapel and St Mach-
ar's Cathedral in Aberdeen. A contemporary description in the
Transactions of the Scottish Ecclesiological Society gave its approval:
'The style of architecture is the later Scottish Gothic – the most
distinctly national of all our styles, and one whose character, at
once rich and sturdy, seemed well suited to supply a memorial
to an eminently sturdy and kindly Scot.'*

If the Lowson Memorial Church was the fullest Presbyterian
realization in Angus of the ideals of Scottish ecclesiologists, one
Episcopalian church, St Mary's at Kirriemuir (1904–5), may be 30
seen as the supreme example in Scotland of the wider ecclesio-
logical movement. Its architect, *J. Ninian Comper*, was a native of
Aberdeen and the son of a priest who was one of the leaders of
the High Church wing of the Scottish Episcopal Church. Ninian
Comper had joined the Aberdeen Ecclesiological Society in 1889
or 1890 and, as seen at Kirriemuir and a few years before at St
Margaret's, Braemar (Aberdeenshire), had adopted 'ecclesiologi-
cal' ideals of church planning, albeit with a Catholic Episcopalian
flavour. His choice of Late Gothic for his design of St Mary's
was far more than a stylistic predilection. For him it was a fulfil-
ment of the aim that the building 'should visibly express the claim
which the Episcopal Church makes to be historical and national'.†
Consequently he took features of late C15 or C16 Scottish archi-
tecture (e.g. the porch of St Michael's, Linlithgow, and the tower
of Iona Cathedral) as the starting point. But these were not part
of an exercise in careful historicism but of an attempt to create
the ideal Scottish parish church as it would have developed but
for the Reformation. The ensuing church comprises a nave, N
aisle and chancel. The W bay of the nave forms the base of a
massive tower and houses the baptistery, the E bay of the aisle
serves as the Lady Chapel, the two-bay chancel contains choir
stalls and, at the E end, the High Altar, all lit from large windows,
their heads with inventive Late Gothic tracery and now filled with
stained glass. A much humbler Episcopalian church but with

* James Cooper, 'The Lowson Memorial Church, Forfar', *Transactions of the Scottish Ecclesiological Society* 5, pt 1, 1915–16, 95.

† *The Scottish Chronicle* 1, 1905, 325.

harled walls and crowstepped gables to assert its Scottishness was designed by *Freeman & Ogilvy* in 1901 for the Dundee suburb of Downfield, its intended tower never completed.

Neither 'ecclesiological' in plan nor overtly Scottish in style was a group of idiosyncratic churches designed by *T. Martin Cappon*. The earliest (1894–5) was Dundee's Central Baptist Church, hall-like with Tudor Gothic detail. A few years later he produced a memorably inventive free Perpendicular Gothic design for the Wishart Memorial United Free Church, also in Dundee. For the Roman Catholics Cappon designed St Patrick's in Dundee, its Late Gothic freely treated and with a powerful corner tower. The unaisled interior is dominated by the High Altar contained in a recess whose elliptical arch is covered by a crocketed ogee-arched hoodmould. The altar's reredos, adorned with a huge painted depiction of St Patrick flanked by small statues of St Columba and St Bridget, is an unashamed assertion of the Irish origins of Dundee's Late Victorian Roman Catholic population. At Our Lady of Good Counsel, Broughty Ferry, of 1904 Cappon designed a straightforward Gothic church with a tower, the walling thriftily clad in glazed red brick but the windows' hoodmoulds of red sandstone. Far more dramatic although seen only obliquely, is the front which Cappon added
31 in 1900–2 to the church of St Mary Our Lady of Victories in the Hilltown of Dundee. His design was based on an unexecuted one by C. Harrison Townsend for the Whitechapel Art Gallery in London, with cupola-topped towers flanking the gable and linked across its base by a narthex. Only the narthex's statue of the Virgin Mary and the gable's great window (an insertion by Cappon) are clearly suggestive of an ecclesiastical function.

Churches since 1914

The area's few INTERWAR CHURCHES are almost all in Dundee where they were built to serve new housing developments. The Church of Scotland put up two substantial churches, St David's (by *Thoms & Wilkie*, 1929–30) for the Lawton housing area and Craigiebank Church (by *Frank Thomson*, 1937–8) for the Craigie housing area. Both are in an Early Christian manner and dignified by towers. St David's comprises a nave and chancel, the larger Craigiebank Church is cruciform, the chancel short and low. The interiors were planned on 'ecclesiological' lines. For the Roman Catholics *Reginald Fairlie* designed the sizeable church of St Peter and St Paul at the N end of Hilltown, its simple Romanesque style, red brick walling and pantiled roofs all economical but the interior given dignity by the quasi-Doric octagonal pillars of the nave arcades. The Episcopalians built only St Ninian's at Fintry, a small harled oblong but its saddleback-roofed W tower asserting its presence in the area.

Most of the LATE TWENTIETH-CENTURY CHURCHES in Dundee and Angus were built to serve further housing developments. Many are hall-like and utilitarian. A couple in Dundee were designed by *Thoms & Wilkie* and built in 1959–62. Each has a nave with one narrow side aisle and a tower, that of Camperdown Parish Church a campanile, Menzieshill Parish Church's saddleback-roofed. The same architects' Whitfield Parish Church, Dundee, of 1970–1 comprises an L-plan arrangement of church and hall with a campanile in the inner angle. Also economical is St Columba's (R.C.) Church, Dundee, of 1956, but its walling of glazed red brick, Early Christian detail and octagonal tower give it presence. Also of red brick and not without presence, although far weaker than would have been the huge edifice designed for the site in 1933, is St Francis's (R.C.) Church, Dundee, by *Reginald Fairlie & Partners*, 1957–9, its porch surmounted by *Hew Lorimer*'s stone relief of a scene in the life of St Francis, and with a low tower at one end.

A few churches of the 1970s were more adventurous and show some appreciation of the Modern Movement. In Dundee St Leonard's and St Fergus's (R.C.) Church of 1975 is an ingenious assembly of boxy elements and St Martin's (Episcopal) by *James Parr & Partners*, 1971–2, has a two-storey pavilion-roofed oblong as its main block but with a cantilevered first-floor sanctuary projecting at one end and a low tower at the other. Also by *James Parr & Partners* and in Dundee was St Matthew's (R.C.) Church (now demolished), its long monopitch roof swept down over white-rendered walls. A little later (1985–7) is *James F. Stephen*'s 33
St Anthony's (R.C.) Church in Kirriemuir, economical but accomplished, the interior an exemplar of how to adopt the liturgical reforms which followed the Second Vatican Council.

Stained glass

Stained glass was introduced to churches in the area from the mid C19. Probably the first windows, dating from the 1840s, are in Dundee Parish Church (St Mary's) and display emblems of two of the town's trade incorporations rather than religious themes. The first coherent scheme of specifically religious stained glass was erected in St Paul's (Episcopal) Church (now Cathedral) in Dundee on its completion in 1855. Here the sanctuary lights were filled with glass showing related scenes from the Old and New Testaments. These were the work of *John Hardman* whose firm was also responsible for much of the later C19 stained glass in that church. When the first chapel of what was to develop into St Salvador's (Episcopal) Church, Dundee, was opened in 1859, its W rose window contained stained-glass figures of saints by *Clayton & Bell*. The contemporary W window of St Mary's (Episcopal) Church at Broughty Ferry contained Biblical scenes.

The earliest religious stained glass in a Presbyterian church in Dundee and Angus came in 1867 when a window by *David Small* showing Scenes in the Life of Our Lord was erected in Dundee Parish Church (St Mary's). The first Presbyterian attempt at a scheme of stained glass, considered both as to siting and subjects, was provided by the chancel windows erected in the medieval St Vigeans Parish Church after its restoration in 1871–2. These depict the principal events in the Life of Our Lord from the

Nativity to the Ascension. Also forming a considered scheme but not restricted to scriptural subjects is the stained glass put into St Salvador's (Episcopal) Church, Dundee, between 1870 and 1890. The windows are the work of *Burlison & Grylls*, the firm of decorators and glass-stainers also entrusted with the other decoration of that church. The chancel windows at St Salvador's show biblical saints, the prophet Isaiah and the Virgin and Child but also the Fathers of the Eastern and Western Churches. By contrast, the two large windows erected by *James Ballantine & Son* in Lochlee Free (now Maule Memorial) Church at Tarfside in 1881 as memorials to the Earl of Dalhousie and the divine, Dr Thomas Guthrie, are respectively heraldic and floral, not scriptural but unlikely to lead to idolatry.

From 1880 stained glass became common in churches of all the main denominations. Presbyterians until the end of the C20 favoured the depiction of biblical subjects including heroes and saints of the Old and New Testaments; Episcopalians were happy to contemplate more recent saints, especially those connected with Scotland. One of the most comprehensive of Episcopalian schemes of stained glass is found in St Mary's, Kirriemuir, all of whose windows except one were filled between 1905 and 1948 with glass designed by *J. Ninian Comper*. The array of saints chosen for depiction includes Ninian, Columba, George, Patrick, Martin, Denis, Quintin, Margaret of Scotland, Stephen of Hungary, Elizabeth of Hungary and David, King of Scots. Comper designed almost exclusively for Anglican or Episcopalian churches but many designers can be found working across denominational boundaries. *Mayer & Co.* produced windows both for Dundee's St Andrew's Parish Church *c.* 1880 and for the Episcopalian Church of St Mary the Virgin at Arbroath in 1884–92, *Clayton & Bell* for the Episcopalian St John the Baptist's Church, Dundee, in 1887 and the same city's St Paul's Free (now Meadowside St Paul's) Church in 1898. The most popular firm of glass-stainers in Dundee and Angus during the last years of the C19 and the beginning of the C20 was *Morris & Co.*, usually executing designs by *Edward Burne-Jones*. At St Luke's Free (now St Luke's and Queen Street) Church at Broughty Ferry they provided the apse windows of 1884, depictions of heroic figures of the Bible. In 1895 they filled the great E window of Arbroath Old Parish Church with three tiers of portraits of Old and New Testament characters and two years later the corresponding window of Dundee Parish Church (St Mary's) with depictions of the Twelve Apostles. The most extensive work of Morris & Co.
26–28 in the area and, indeed, in Scotland is at Broughty Ferry's St Stephen's and West Church where, between 1894 and 1915, they filled every window, the result almost too lush.

Of C20 artists *Douglas Strachan* produced characteristically crowded although relatively ordered windows at the Lowson Memorial Church, Forfar, in 1914 and Brechin Cathedral in 1949. Typical examples of the swirling compositions and strong colouring of *William Wilson*'s work of the 1950s are to be found in Brechin Cathedral and Kirriemuir Old Parish Church. More disciplined and notable for clarity of draughtsmanship are the windows of the 1920s and 1930s by *C.E. Kempe & Co. Ltd* at St Mary the Virgin (Episcopal) Church, Arbroath, and Fern Parish Church. Also worth searching out are the portraits of saints made in the 1930s by *Herbert Hendrie* at Brechin Cathedral and Barnhill St Margaret's and Glamis Parish Churches. A wide-ranging collection of stained glass of the mid and later C20 and the beginning of the C21 is on display at St Andrew's Parish Church, Dundee, allowing the visitor to compare windows by *Walter Pritchard*, *Mary Wood* and *Gordon Webster* with more recent work by *John K. Clark*, *Liz Rowley*, *Douglas Hogg* and *Alexander J. Galloway*.

GRAVEYARDS, MONUMENTS, MAUSOLEA, CREMATORIA AND STATUES

In Angus, as elsewhere in Scotland, most GRAVEYARDS are associated with parish churches. By the C18 they were almost all enclosed by stone walls but these were primarily utilitarian, designed to prevent unwanted incursions of animals rather than for architectural display which was generally limited to simply corniced gatepiers at the entrance. However, a few showed greater ambition. The gateway to the parish churchyard of Guthrie is a gabled structure of 1639, its ends and apex topped by stumpy obelisks, the entrance a segmental arch surmounted by the coat of arms of the Guthrie family. At Kinnaird Castle the family burial ground of the Earls of Southesk was formed *c.* 1695, its entrance gatepiers of channelled ashlar faced with banded pilasters and topped by finials carved as flaming urns.

Inside a churchyard, usually built against a wall, might be a hearse house designed, as the name suggests, to accommodate the parish hearse. One such, of 1795, survives at Monikie, a simple rubble-walled oblong roofed with stone slabs.

All the towns in Angus contain one or more graveyards besides those adjoining parish churches. The earliest of these was formed at Dundee in 1564 when the garden of the former Franciscan friary on what was then the N edge of the burgh was laid out as the town's new burial ground (The Howff) replacing the graveyard of the medieval St Clement's Parish Church. The Howff of Dundee was itself supplemented from the C18 by further graveyards. From the mid C19 large cemeteries were laid out in the Angus towns. The first was Rosehill Cemetery at Montrose laid out in 1839–40, followed by the Western Cemetery at Dundee in 1845. By 1870 further cemeteries had been formed at Dundee, Arbroath, Brechin, Forfar and Kirriemuir and, in 1893–4, a second cemetery at Montrose. All are spaciously laid out with broad paths and shrubbery, the 1890s Sleepyhillock Cemetery at Montrose with an arboretum containing plenty of yew trees. The entrance to Dundee's Western Cemetery was designed by *James Findlater* in 1845, a Tudor Gothic screen topped by the statue of an angelic mourner, Brechin Cemetery's approach by *George*

Henderson in 1856–7, with a bridge across the Den Burn leading to a gateway of rusticated ashlar, the keystone of its round-headed arch carved as a death mask and topped by a phoenix. A battlemented Gothic gateway by *William Scott*, 1863, adorned with carving illustrative of the Ages of Man and statues of mourning ladies, forms the entrance of Dundee's Eastern Cemetery, a large classical gateway of *c.* 1870 that of the Western Cemetery at Arbroath.

The Church of Scotland's proscription in 1581 of burial inside churches was circumvented by the more important landed families taking over the sites of medieval chancels or transeptal chapels for burial places, usually in conjunction with the erection of a laird's pew or gallery looking into the body of the church. However, the ban was obeyed by the vast majority. Most burials took place in parish graveyards, usually in unmarked graves which served only as temporary resting places until the body had decomposed and the bones, clean of flesh, could be reinterred somewhere where they took up less space. The prosperous members of the population, such as merchants, craftsmen or, by the late C18, farmers, might wish for permanent grave plots marked by MEMORIALS and be prepared to pay for the privilege, usually by contribution to a parish fund for poor relief. Memorials were not, however, always directly associated with graves. In The Howff at Dundee one wall is embellished with a line of proto-classical recesses, each containing a vestigial sarcophagus. These were erected at the beginning of the C17 as monuments to a few of those buried in the graveyard but did not mark actual graves. Most memorials, however, did mark burial plots, each containing the bodies of several members of a family, all commemorated by a single monument or stone slab. The area's largest and most varied collection of memorials dating from the C17 is in The Howff at Dundee. Some take the form of miniature houses, e.g. the monument of *c.* 1620 to Dr David Kinloch and Grizel Hay, others are sarcophagi, such as the memorial erected in 1673 to commemorate Robert Forrester. More common are table stones. One, of *c.* 1610 to John Baxter, is carved with a relief of Baxter embracing his wife, a skull and bone on their shoulders serving as reminders of mortality. Others, dating from a few years later, bear emblematic figures of Father Time and Christian Virtues copied from Francis Quarles's *Emblems* published in 1635. In Murroes Churchyard the table stone of Alexander Edward †1655 and his grandchildren †1660 is carved with the relief of a trumpeting angel floating above the naked bodies of four human figures. More economical memorials than table stones were grave-slabs. Several in The Howff bear reminders of the trade of the deceased, e.g. the gloves, shears and buckle on the grave-slab of Matthew Watson, skinner (i.e. leather worker), †1603 or the mason's tools on the slab to John Jack †1608, this last commemorating also his wife and son, the final earthly destiny of all three shown by a row of skulls and bones at the top. A pair of waulker's shears are carved on the slab of 1607 to William Greig in Glamis Parish Churchyard. This is one of an exceptional number of C17 slabs here, most decorated with reminders of death and angels' heads (symbols of the soul). One of the largest and best-preserved grave-slabs in the area, possibly originally the top of a table stone, dates from 1742 and is now housed in Liff Church. It commemorates the weaver, James Cock. Flanking the mantled and helmet-topped inscription panel are dowsed torches; at the top of the slab, an angel's head under a crown is set between weavers' shuttles and angel trumpeters, and the bottom is carved with an emblematic figure of Justice and reminders of death.

In the C18 HEADSTONES constituted the most common category of graveyard memorials. Most display angels' heads and symbols of death, sometimes accompanied by trade emblems or coats of arms. A few are more idiosyncratic. In Tealing Parish Churchyard the headstone of 1765 commemorating Margaret Fairweather bears full-length figures of a woman and two children. The headstone of 1759 to Donald Ritchie's children in Lundie Churchyard is carved with scriptural scenes, Adam and Eve and the Serpent in the Garden of Eden on one side, Abraham Preparing to Sacrifice Isaac on the other. Headstones have continued to be erected until the present day but are now seldom adorned with cheerful reminders of death and resurrection or emblems of the trade of the deceased. From the C19 free-standing monuments have become relatively common, especially in urban cemeteries. One of the earliest and more inventive is the monument to James Spence †1813 in Auchterhouse Churchyard, a truncated pyramid whose urn finial is decorated with swags hanging from human faces. However, most are routine productions of firms of monumental masons, often in the form of urns, truncated pillars or androgynous angels.

COMMEMORATIVE MONUMENTS were erected in churches as well as graveyards. An unusually early example, possibly connected with an interment despite the 1581 ban on burial in churches, is in Tealing Parish Church. It commemorates the parish minister, John Ramsay †1618, and is formed by an aedicular frame which encloses a panel carved with a relief of Ramsay kneeling in front of a lectern. Most church monuments of the C18, C19 and C20 are well mannered but dull. Of more than average interest is the white marble monument by *Peter Rouw Yr.* to John Henderson †1836 in St Vigeans Parish Church, its chief feature a kneeling angel shown in the act of writing the inscription. Of restrained grandeur is the Gothic monument erected in 1878 to commemorate Bishop Alexander Penrose Forbes in the Cathedral Church of St Paul at Dundee. Designed, like the cathedral, by *G. Gilbert Scott* and executed by *Farmer & Brindley*, it consists of a marble recess enclosing a sarcophagus on which lies a coped and mitred effigy of the bishop. Worth seeing also are a couple of First World War memorials of *c.* 1920. In the Steeple Church, Dundee, a bronze tablet bears the relief of a sinuous angel framing the inscription. More elaborate is the memorial designed by *Thoms & Wilkie* in Dundee Parish Church (St Mary's), an elaborate Late Gothic tabernacle decorated with heraldry and enclosing a figure of Victory.

Many churchyards contain BURIAL ENCLOSURES. Most consist only of walls or railings marking off the piece of land belonging to a particular family. Some, however, are more consciously architectural. In Airlie Churchyard are a couple of C17 enclosures with roll-and-hollow-moulded surrounds to their entrances, that of one (dated 1609) set between stones incised with skulls and bones and themselves flanked by other stones carved with gloomy but improving texts. One side of Liff Churchyard's burial enclosure of the Watts and Websters of Balruddery is formed by the monument designed in 1809 by *David Neave* to Katherine Webster, the inscription panel set behind a Roman Doric 'portico'. In Inverkeilor Churchyard the back wall of the early C19 burial enclosure of the Raits of Anniston is constructed of V-jointed ashlar masonry and surmounted by a block pediment. On this wall is placed the monument commemorating Elizabeth Guthrie †1814 and her husband, John Rait †1823. This is carved by *M. W. Johnson* with the relief of a lady seated on a chaise longue and clasping her dying husband.

MAUSOLEA were erected in the area in the C18 and C19. Two of these were formed by remodelling medieval former parish churches. The old Dun Church, just S of the walled garden of the House of Dun, was reconstructed, *c.* 1835, in a battlemented Tudor Gothic manner as a mausoleum of the Erskines of Dun. Logie Church was curtailed and recast in 1857 as the mausoleum of the Macpherson Grants of Craigo, the new W gable unabashedly Victorian Gothic. At Lundie, the parish church's medieval chancel was rebuilt in 1787–9 as a saucer-domed classical mausoleum designed by *Robert Mylne* to house monuments to Sir William Duncan, younger brother of the laird of Lundie, and his wife. When Cortachy Church was rebuilt in 1828–9 it was provided with a 'chancel' serving as the mausoleum of the Earls of Airlie. Like the church itself this is Gothic and designed by *David Paterson* but the walling is of polished grey sandstone ashlar in contrast to the stugged red sandstone masonry of the church.

Surprisingly grand is the mausoleum near Kirriemuir built *c.* 1800 for the Kinlochs of Kilrie and Logie, a family of not especially well-off lairds. Not part of a graveyard and standing on a hillside, its isolation emphasized by a surrounding moat, this is a domed octagon of polished red sandstone ashlar, its faces panelled with round-headed arches. Weirdest of funerary buildings in the area is the sculpture-encrusted Gothic Memorial
32 Chapel at the centre of the Arbroath Western Cemetery. Built in 1875–84 at the expense and design of the artist, architectural amateur and local laird, *Patrick Allan-Fraser*, this is a combination of (non-denominational) chapel for funeral services and mausoleum containing the tombs of Allan-Fraser, his wife and her parents. The chapel itself is an oblong but with narrow aisles enclosing first-floor passages which lead to narrow galleries overlooking the nave's W end, the site of the stone bier on which to lay a coffin. Towers, all of different design, stand at the corners, the two E housing stairs, the two W the sarcophagus tombs of the Frasers and Allan-Frasers of Hospitalfield. Perhaps

unsurprisingly, no other local family attempted subsequently to emulate this edifice.

A major C20 change in funerary practice was the introduction and widespread adoption of cremation as a means to dispose of corpses. Two CREMATORIA have been built in Dundee and Angus. The first, the Dundee Crematorium, was erected in 1935–6. Designed by *T. Lindsay Gray*, the red brick chapel is purposeful Romanesque in style and very like an Episcopalian church in arrangement, the E chancel containing an altar with space for a coffin to stand in front of it. Above the chancel rises a sturdy tower which houses the crematorium's chimney. More like a hall and so not unlike a typical late C20 church is the Parkgrove Crematorium (by *Inglis & Carr*, 1993) in a woodland setting near Friockheim.

MONUMENTS unrelated to burial sites top some hills in the area. Near Newtyle the summits of both Keillor Hill and Kinpurney Hill are surmounted by rubble-built towers erected in 1774 by James Stuart-Mackenzie and visible from the grounds of his seat of Belmont Castle (Perth and Kinross) to the N. Privy's Prap on Keillor Hill is a solid 6 m.-high column intended for use in conjunction with a mark on the lawn of Belmont Castle to plot the meridian passage of the sun, Kinpurney Tower a 12 m.-high crudely battlemented oblong. Of greater public import is the 32 m.-high Panmure Testimonial designed by *John Henderson* and erected in 1839 on Downie Hill near Monikie by a grateful tenantry in honour of William Ramsay Maule, Lord Panmure, its urn-finialled column rising within a ring of flying buttresses and standing on an octagonal base containing rooms for visitors. In 1900–1 Tulloch Hill, near Cortachy, was crowned by *T. Martin Cappon*'s Airlie Memorial Tower, a Scottish Baronial tower with corner caphouse, built in memory of the eleventh Earl of Airlie who had been killed in the South African War.

FIRST WORLD WAR MEMORIALS were erected in all the area's towns and many of its villages. Most are routine, often in the form of crosses. Largest and most prominently sited, on the top of Dundee Law, is Dundee's designed by *Thomas Braddock*, a square mausoleum-like structure of polished granite, the round top stage covered with a dome, the resultant appearance disappointingly dumpy. More impressive is the slab of a cenotaph by 96
George Washington Browne at the W entry to Arbroath. *Charles G. Soutar* provided Monifieth with a granite pillar, its top with a recess containing the figure of a knight. Kirriemuir's memorial was designed by *John Kinross*, the tall pedestal bearing the statue of a soldier. Surmounting the memorial at Montrose is a bronze Victory sculpted by *H. S. Gamley*. Memorials to the dead of the First World War were adapted, usually by the addition of another inscription panel, to commemorate also those of the Second World War. However, one striking new memorial to the fallen of that conflict was erected on a hillside just outside Dundee in 1959. This is the Black Watch Memorial, its bronze figure of a soldier sculpted by *Scott Sutherland*.

From the mid C19 STATUES were erected in some Angus towns
to honour the virtues of certain public figures. In the 1850s the
memory of two politicians, the former Prime Minister Sir Robert
Peel and the long-serving Member of Parliament Joseph Hume,
was perpetuated by a brace of stone statues (by *A. Handyside
Ritchie* and *Calder Marshall*) in the centre of the High Street of
Montrose. Later in the C19 a statue, also stone, of the poet Robert
Burns was commissioned from *W. Birnie Rhind* for the same town
although not set up until 1912. In Dundee in the 1870s a
semicircle of statues was placed in front of two sides of the newly
built Albert Institute (now The McManus), composed of bronze
figures of Robert Burns (by *John Steell*), the politician George
Kinloch (also by Steell) and James Carmichael, inventor of the
fan-blast (by *John Hutchison*), representatives of the Arts, Public
Service and Industry. In 1899 they were joined by the squat pres-
94 ence of Queen Victoria seated on a throne (by *Harry Bates*).
Further commemorative statues have been put up in the area
during the last years of the C20 and the opening of the C21. The
centre of Montrose acquired a statue (by *Michael Snowden*, 2005)
of the C17 Royalist hero, the first Marquess of Montrose, a native
of the burgh, and that town's harbour a bronze figure (by *Alan
Beattie Heriot*, 2006) of the dog Bamse, a St Bernard who served
on a minesweeper based at Montrose during the Second World
War. In Dundee in 1997 was placed a statue by *Janet Scrymgeour
Wedderburn* of the sailor and local laird, Admiral Adam Duncan,
to commemorate the bicentenary of his naval victory at the Battle
of Camperdown. The approach to Arbroath from the SW is
marked in flamboyant fashion by *David Annand*'s huge bronze of
2001 celebrating the signing of the Declaration of Arbroath with
statues of King Robert Bruce and Abbot Bernard Linton bran-
dishing the parchment on which was written Scotland's claim to
independence.

CASTLES AND TOWER HOUSES

Much of early medieval Angus formed part of the demesne lands of the Crown and in the C12 William I ('the Lion') granted fiefs in Angus, generally to members of families of Norman or Flemish descent recently imported from England, to be held in return for military service. Between 1165 and 1207 he granted fiefs of the lands of Inverkeilor to Walter de Berkeley, the royal chamberlain, of Fowlis to Roger de Mortimer, of Panmure to William de Valognes, of Tealing to William Gifford and of Guthrie to Walter de la Carneille, each for the service of one knight. Further fiefs, such as Ogilvy to a son of the Earl of Angus, were granted to men of native ancestry, also in return for military service. On each of these fiefs there seems to have been constructed a fortified dwelling. Some occupied artificial sites like the motte, an artificial mound topped by a wooden keep, constructed about this time at Edzell. Others stood on naturally defensible sites, the stronghold of Berkeley's fief of Inverkeilor a coastal promontory (now the site of Red Castle), that of Fowlis a hilltop, that of Guthrie beside the Lunan Water and Panmure a promontory in a bend of the Monikie Burn. The first buildings on these sites seem to have been mostly or wholly of wooden construction and with ditches or earth ramparts supplementing the natural defences. A little later, however, some of the first defences were apparently replaced by stone walls. The most substantial although fragmentary survivor of such C13 CASTLES OF ENCLOSURE in the area is represented by the 32 m.-long W wall of Red Castle. Also probably C13 and stone-walled were the royal castles at the burghs of Montrose, Forfar and Dundee, positioned to command the principal routes of the shire along the E coastal plain and the naturally well-drained land on the W edge of Strathmore. All occupied defensible sites, Montrose's castle on a hillside overlooking the Montrose Basin, Forfar's the conical Castle Hill and Dundee's the volcanic mound at the N end of Castle Street (site of the present Cathedral Church of St Paul). These royal castles were all destroyed during the late C13 and early C14 Wars of Independence and not subsequently rebuilt.

After the Wars of Independence the lands of the Umphraville Earls of Angus, who had been adherents of the pro-English party, were forfeited. New families, notably the Lindsays, Maules, Ogilvys, Lyons and Carnegies, came to wealth and prominence in the C14 and C15. In the earlier and mid C15 two strongholds were built by the Ogilvys, both positioned on the dividing line between the fertile vale of Strathmore and the Highland glens of Angus to the N. One was Airlie Castle for whose construction James I granted a licence in 1432 to Walter Ogilvy of Carcary and Lintrathen, High Treasurer of Scotland. The site is one of great natural strength, a promontory at the confluence of the Melgam
Water and River Isla with almost sheer drops to both rivers. The 38
landward (W) approach is cut off by a ditch backed by a 9 m.-high rubble-built wall with a gatehouse tower over the entrance to the enclosure in which stood the domestic and service buildings of the castle. Almost contemporary is Inverquharity Castle for whose erection Alexander Ogilvy, nephew of Walter Ogilvy the builder of Airlie Castle, obtained a royal licence in 1444. The site beside the River South Esk is not of the same natural strength as that of Airlie Castle but nevertheless easily defensible. On it was
presumably erected an enclosure, the walls now missing, with a 34
large tower house in one corner. This house is austere, an ashlar-walled and battlemented L of four storeys, the third double-height. In common with a few other mid-C15 Scottish TOWER HOUSES, e.g. the nearby Glamis Castle, Cessford Castle (Borders) or Cawdor Castle (Highland and Islands), the main block is constructed of two superimposed vaults, the lower divided by an entresol floor and containing a Lower Hall above stores, the
upper the double-height Great Hall. The stairs were set in the 36
massively thick walling of the main block, and the jamb contained further rooms, the ground floor's with a well and the second floor's possibly a kitchen serving the Great Hall. Of about the same date or a little later but with walls more economically

constructed of harled rubble rather than ashlar are the first phase of the Great Tower of Glamis Castle, begun by Patrick Lyon (later first Lord Glamis) in 1435, and Guthrie Castle, built *c.* 1470 for David Guthrie of Kincaldrum. Like Inverquharity Castle both were L-plan, architecturally austere and with their main blocks constructed with superimposed double-height vaults. At each the lower vault was divided by an entresol floor, the upper occupied by the house's Great Hall. At Glamis, as at Inverquharity, the jamb contained rooms, at Guthrie the house's stair. Probably slightly later and constructionally less ambitious is Affleck Castle, also a rubble-walled L but the main block containing only one double-height vault, the floors above being of wood. Nevertheless, the interior is smartly finished, with stone window seats at both the first-floor Lower Hall and second-floor Upper Hall. There are window seats also at the exceptionally well-appointed Chamber on the third floor with bundle-shafted and foliaged columns to the fireplace. Off the Chamber is a chapel on the top floor of the jamb. The mid-C15 Kelly Castle is T-plan, the jamb containing the stair. It is also the most showy of Angus's C15 tower houses, its S corners adorned with turrets, one round and conical-roofed, the other of two storeys, square and crowstep-gabled and with a tourelle in the inner angle. Architecturally disappointing by contrast, although in a commanding position overlooking the harbour of Broughty Ferry, is Broughty Castle, a four-storey and rubble oblong, the royal licence for its construction granted to Andrew, Lord Gray, in 1490.

Almost certainly each of these C15 tower houses stood in one corner of a courtyard. Along the courtyard's sides stood other buildings. These, often built of wood, included a brew house, kitchen and a hall of a more public character than the hall in the tower house of the laird.* One such hall of public character occupied the upper floor of an originally detached two-storey building just SE of the Great Tower of Glamis Castle.

The idea that a tower house was one element, although usually the most important, in a complex of buildings of varied uses continued throughout the C16. The fullest realization of this is
35 now found at the large complex of Edzell Castle constructed from *c.* 1530 as a proud affirmation of the baronial status of the Lindsays, lords of Glenesk and Edzell since the mid C14. Built round a courtyard, the group's earliest structure, at the SW corner, is a rubble-walled four-storey and attic L-plan tower house, the walls pierced by gunloops and surmounted by a corbelled battlement. N of the tower house is the main two-storey W range, the walling also with gunloops. At the centre of this range is the round-headed entrance to the courtyard, originally surmounted by heraldic panels. The three-storey N range contained a huge first-floor hall, presumably intended as a much more public space than the hall of the tower house. It is placed above a kitchen which supplemented the castle's slightly earlier kitchen in the W range. Further accommodation was provided in the E

* But the main block of Kelly Castle contained a ground-floor kitchen.

and S ranges. Comparable in scale and pretension to Edzell Castle was The Craig, a complex of buildings round two courtyards, which was built in the early C16 for David Wood, the confidant of James V. The entrance to the outer and larger courtyard, probably intended for the humbler buildings of the complex such as stabling, is through a gateway flanked by towers whose prominently positioned gunloops provide a forbidding welcome. Off one side of the outer courtyard is an inner court, whose two-storey S range, which perhaps originally contained the public hall, has been demolished except for its outer (S) wall which stretches between three-storey and attic towers built flush with the wall and so of limited defensive value but perhaps intended to impress from a distance. The other two ranges, now cheerful muddles of different dates, contained domestic quarters, including a C16 kitchen. A third C16 courtyard residence, Mains Castle, now in 39
Dundee's Caird Park, makes a determined attempt to proclaim the status of its owners, the Grahams of Fintry, who had acquired the estate *c.* 1455 but only received a Crown charter and the lands' consequent erection into a barony in 1530. Thereafter they seem to have abandoned Dundee as their principal place of residence in favour of a new house at Mains. The outer face of the courtyard's W range is pierced by gunloops and surmounted by a battlement which contains shot-holes and breaks forward into a round at one corner and a half-round over the entrance. The principal C16 accommodation was in the three-storey N range which is unexceptional except for the stupefying height of its five-storey stair-tower, the top floor remodelled in 1630. The house's W range, built in the late C16 and remodelled in the late C17, would also be unexceptional were it not for the elaborate C16 aedicular frame for a now missing heraldic panel over its doorway, providing another flourish of nouveau riche ostentation. The buildings in the enclosures surrounding most C16 and early C17 lairds' houses have been removed together with the barmkin walls themselves, leaving tower houses, if not engulfed in later additions, to stand as over-emphatic vertical emphases in garden settings.

Most of the tower houses of Angus, as elsewhere in Scotland, were built during the C16 and the first years of the C17. Some, such as Logie House, erected for the Wisharts *c.* 1540, or Gardyne Castle, put up by the Gardynes of that Ilk in the 1560s, were on estates long held by the families of their owners. Others were on estates carved out from larger landholdings and settled on younger sons. One such is Cortachy Castle, constructed early 40
in the C16 on an estate which had been granted to a younger son of Sir John Ogilvy of Inverquharity in 1473. Another was Careston Castle, begun *c.* 1590 for Sir Henry Lindsay of Kinfauns, a younger brother of the Earl of Crawford. Others again were the secondary residences of lairds whose principal houses were elsewhere. Hatton Castle was built in 1575 by the fourth Lord Oliphant as a residence on his estate of Newtyle which was a considerable distance from his chief property and residence of Dupplin Castle (Perth and Kinross). A couple of secondary

residences may have been intended as assertions of the authority of major lairds over outlying estates in the highland glens of Angus whose inhabitants were noted for their disregard of the law. Such may well have been the motive for the eighth Earl of Crawford's erection of Invermark Castle in Glen Esk in the early C16 and the construction of Forter Castle in Glen Isla by John, Lord Ogilvy, in 1608.

A number of houses were built for lairds whose estates had been recently acquired by them or their families. A growth in the number of landowning families in the C15 and early C16 was, at least in part, the result of a new fashion among some owners of great estates to dispose of their lands in feu ferme, i.e. granting possession in perpetuity in return for payment of a lump sum and an annual money rent whose value was quickly eroded by the contemporary depreciation of coinage. The lands on which Mains Castle was to be built had been first granted to the Grahams in feu ferme in 1455. Other lands held in feu included the estate of The Craig granted by the Archbishop of St Andrews in 1535 and the estate of Colliston feued by Arbroath Abbey to John Guthrie ten years later. Another part of the lands of Arbroath Abbey was used *c.* 1530 by its Abbot David Beaton (later also a Cardinal and Archbishop of St Andrews) as the site on which to build Ethie Castle as a rural retreat. Beaton was also to use the wealth obtained from his various ecclesiastical and secular positions to acquire in 1542 the lands of Melgund which he settled on his mistress Marion Ogilvy and their son a year later when construction of a house there was under way.

All the tower houses built in Angus in the C16 and early C17 were built with walls of rubble masonry, generally originally covered with harling and with crowstepped gables. They varied greatly in size, the main block of the diminutive Ballinshoe Castle only *c.* 8.2 m. by 6.7 m., the main block of Forter Castle *c.* 11.9 m. by 7.9 m., but that of Hatton Castle *c.* 20.4 m. by 7.3 m. and of Careston Castle *c.* 23.2 m. by 8.8 m. Most were of three storeys, sometimes with an attic, but a few, e.g. the early C16 Cortachy Castle or Careston Castle of *c.* 1590, were a storey higher. Invermark Castle, as first built in the early C16, was a simple battlemented oblong. Almost all other tower houses were either L-plan, the jamb usually containing the principal stair to the first floor, or, less commonly, Z-plan with jambs at diagonally opposite corners. Cortachy Castle, as first constructed, was unusual in being an irregular T with a long NW jamb and a short SW jamb in the form of a bow-fronted tower.

L-plan tower houses at their simplest, e.g. Ethie Castle or Braikie Castle, were straightforward, the jamb projecting from one end of the side of the main block and with its outer face flush with the walling of the main block's gable. At other tower houses, e.g. Careston Castle or Forter Castle, the jamb was so placed as to project from both the side and one gable of the main block, allowing its gunloops to provide raking fire across two elevations of the main block in the event of attack. The jambs of several L-plan houses, e.g. Ballinshoe Castle, Gardyne Castle or

Logie House, took the form of round towers, also able to provide raking fire in defence of two elevations of the main block. At Z-plan houses, gunloops in the jambs, whether round or rectangular, could provide raking fire across all elevations of the main block.

Elsewhere in Scotland it was not uncommon for there to be a stair-tower in the inner angle of a jamb and the main block of an L- or Z-plan house. In Angus such an arrangement exists at Vayne Castle and Claypotts Castle and probably existed also at Cortachy Castle before the construction of its present principal stair in the early c19. At the Z-plan Claypotts Castle a second turret in the inner angle of its other jamb and the main block also contained a tighter stair, apparently to provide access from the wine cellar to the dais end of the first-floor hall. At a number of houses, e.g. Colliston Castle, Hatton Castle, Braikie Castle and Careston Castle, the principal stair occupied a jamb but rose only to the first floor, access to the floors above being by a turnpike housed in a turret corbelled out in the inner angle of the jamb and main block. At Gardyne Castle the main stair in the jamb rose to the second floor, from which level a tight stair in a corbelled-out turret led to the attic.

An idiosyncrasy of the design of several c16 Angus tower houses is their having jambs which are circular or bow-fronted at their lower stages but surmounted by crowstep-gabled rectangular top floors. At Gardyne Castle the top stage is placed sensibly at right angles to the main block but the top stages of towers at Cortachy Castle and Colliston Castle are set at a diagonal. So too are the top floors of both the round towers of Claypotts 37 Castle. Some of these top stages appear unsure of themselves, timidly corbelled-out as if they had been afterthoughts forced upon a mason unsure as to the structural feasibility or safety of such a feature. However, the top stage of one tower at Claypotts Castle, perhaps because it was built nineteen years after the cautiously detailed top of the other tower, is far more confident and projects boldly.

Despite the title of 'castle' generally enjoyed by these c16 and c17 tower houses, they hardly bristle with serious FORTIFICATIONS. The wall-head of Invermark Castle, as first built at the beginning of the c16, was surmounted by a corbelled battlement extending all round the house. Also battlemented are both the tower and the hall block of Melgund Castle but wall-head battlements are rare in Angus. At Claypotts Castle there were balconies under the gable-heads of the main block but these were probably provided to allow the inhabitants to enjoy the view rather than to defend themselves against attack. The corners of some otherwise unbattlemented tower houses are dressed up with turrets. The closets which they contain were welcome additions to the accommodation of the houses but their exteriors, even when equipped with gunloops and shot-holes, seem intended as displays of taste and status. Both Forter Castle and, probably, Gardyne Castle as originally built had round turrets at their main blocks' three corners not covered by their jambs. These turrets have conical roofs, those of Forter conjectural reconstructions of 1990. Gardyne's, either original or, perhaps more probably, dating from C17 alterations, are tall, rise from within decorative battlements and are studded with pedimented windows and topped by finials. Braikie Castle, Ballinshoe Castle, Old Finavon Castle and Invermark Castle all boast single round turrets, those of the L-plan first three at diagonally opposed corners to the jamb, several with shot-holes in their continuous corbelling.

SHOT-HOLES and GUNLOOPS decorate the walls of many tower houses. A few seem to have been provided for defence rather than show, e.g. the crudely formed gunloops which constitute the only openings to the ground floor of Invermark Castle. Forter Castle eschews gunloops but has shot-holes below all the principal windows, probably a sensible precaution for a symbol of the authority of the laird in a highland glen. Possibly also intended as working defences are the shot-holes and gunloops of the sides of Melgund Castle which were outside the barmkin wall. But other houses display such a plethora of shot-holes and gunloops as to suggest either excessive fearfulness on the part of their owners or a desire to display these as affirmations of baronial status. Such an affirmation seems to have been the motive behind the displays of oval gunloops, sometimes accompanied by circular shot-holes at, for example, Colliston, Claypotts, Finavon, Gardyne and Hatton Castles. More likely a sign of sophisticated taste rather than military purpose is the double-apertured 'pince nez' gunloop on the turret of *c.* 1600 at Invermark Castle.

Displays of HERALDRY are surprisingly rare on the C16 and early C17 houses of Angus. There have been panels, presumably carved with coats of arms, over the gateway to the enclosure of Edzell Castle and above the entrance doors of Claypotts Castle and Hatton Castle. Perhaps originally over the house's entrance but now placed on a side wall is a heraldic panel of 1568 at Gardyne Castle. Also perhaps not *in situ* but apparently erected as part of C17 alterations to the house is Colliston Castle's stone of 1621 bearing the arms of James VI and the initials of Henry Guthrie of Colliston and his wife. Small and looking almost as if designed for a private reassurance of their ownership rather than for public display are the coats of arms of Marion Ogilvy and her son David Beaton carved on window lintels at Melgund Castle and the coat of arms and initials of John Strachan on a skeputt of Claypotts Castle. These understated pieces of heraldry are quite eclipsed by
42 the great display erected at Glamis Castle in the early C17 by the first and second Earls of Kinghorne as part of their scheme of remodelling the house with the addition of two further storeys to the C15 Great Tower and the construction in its inner angle of an ashlar-clad full-height stair-tower. On completion of the work, the roof-line presented a fantastic array of turrets, the (originally coloured) heraldic panels placed across the fronts of the Great Tower and the new stair-tower a colourful affirmation of the lineage of the owners.

The INTERIORS of C16 and early C17 tower houses of whatever size contained standard features. Their ground-floor rooms are almost invariably covered by stone tunnel-vaults.* However, these rooms varied in number from just one cellar at Invermark Castle or Gardyne Castle to three cellars and a kitchen at Careston Castle. The tower of Old Finavon Castle is unusual in containing a tunnel-vaulted store on the ground floor and, on the first floor, a kitchen, also covered with a tunnel vault. Stairs were usually turnpikes, the early C17 stair of Glamis Castle exceptionally broad, but at Hatton Castle there was also a narrow straight stair contained in the thickness of a side wall which rose from a cellar, probably the wine cellar, to the hall. At some houses the principal stair from the ground to the first floor is scale-and-platt, e.g. at Old Finavon Castle or at Hatton or Careston Castles whose flights are covered by tunnel vaults. The first or principal floor contained a hall. The hall of Powrie Castle was double-height and vaulted but generally C16 or early C17 halls in Angus were of single height and with beamed wooden ceilings. They usually occupied the whole first floor of the main block but at the large houses of Hatton Castle and Careston Castle there were inner chambers at the end of the hall. At some houses, e.g. Cortachy Castle and Claypotts Castle, an inner chamber occupied a jamb. The second floor of the main block often contained a couple of rooms and there might be further accommodation in jambs or turrets at this level. Of internal decoration of the C16 and first years of the C17 little now survives beyond fairly simple moulded stone chimneypieces, but there has been an extensive scheme of painted decoration on both the walls and beamed ceilings of Braikie Castle. Such decoration was probably popular in other houses also.

MANSIONS AND COUNTRY HOUSES

Substantial houses of peaceful character had been built on country estates in Angus since at least the C15 when Farnell Castle, a crowstep-gabled oblong with a first-floor external wooden gallery at one end, was constructed as a residence for the Bishops of Brechin. Some houses, such as the two-storey Murroes House as first completed in the mid C16, are too modest in scale to be classified as tower houses although Murroes is L-plan and boasts a round corner tower and plentiful supply of gunloops. However, the larger Gagie House, also two-storey and oblong, of *c.* 1615, makes no such martial bluster, its S gable's tall turrets appearing only as picturesque embellishments, one turret's single shot-hole no more menacing than a C21 burglar alarm. Just as domestic is the two-storey N range of Powrie Castle built along one side of a courtyard in 1604, the ground floor containing a kitchen and bakehouse, the upper floor two self-contained lodgings. Here, display but of an architectural rather than martial character is confined to the S porch's first-floor windows whose proto-classical surrounds hint at worldly sophistication. Even less

* But the ground floor of Ballinshoe Castle was unvaulted.

demonstrative externally is now the early C17 Old Mansion House of Auchterhouse although, perhaps, originally it boasted heraldic dormerheads. However, inside, it contains a ground-floor room, originally the Lower Hall or dining room, whose plaster ceiling and overmantel of 1630 are boldly modelled, the ceiling with pendants and geometrical compartments, the overmantel with a classical surround enclosing strapwork enrichment and reliefs of vases and heraldry including the coats of arms and initials of the house's owners, the Earl and Countess of Buchan.

Similar decoration but on a grandiose scale was introduced in 43 1621 by the second Earl of Kinghorne to the Great Hall of Glamis Castle. He kept the C15 double-height space but covered its semicircular tunnel-vault with compartmented plasterwork and a central row of pendants. In the compartments were set floral, foliaged and heraldic motifs, together with portraits of some of the Worthies of biblical and classical Antiquity (David, Joshua, Hector and Alexander). Above the Hall's fireplace he erected an overmantel, also of plasterwork, bearing the achievement of the Royal Arms set in a border of thistles. This mixture of heraldry and classical allusions in the principal room of the remodelled and heightened Great Tower of Glamis marks a shift in the architecture of the residences of the Scottish aristocracy from an assertion that they held their positions through military strength to one where their learning, allied to lineage, could also be celebrated. A similarly mixed appreciation of contemporary Renaissance art and architecture joined to a pride in family descent is found in the remarkable collection of chimneypieces and overmantels erected in Careston Castle by two successive owners, Henry, Lord Spynie, and Sir Alexander Carnegy of Balnamoon, in the 1620s and 1630s. Derived, at least in part, from engravings published by Jacques Androuet du Cerceau in 1561, their designs are French Renaissance decorated variously with statuary of sphinxes, nudes, satyrs and angels, together with heraldry in celebration of the house's owners.

Despite or perhaps because of the civil wars of the mid C17, houses built after the restoration of the monarchy in 1660 were peaceful in appearance. The change which had taken place since the beginning of the century can be seen at Pitscandly House, built in the late C17 for a minor lairdly family, the Lindsays of Pitscandly. About 1600 they would have put up a tower house. Now they erected a piend-roofed two-storey box, the main embellishments provided by the pedimented centrepieces of both the front and rear elevations, and the steep pediment over the entrance. The house's service ranges are contained in a couple of rear wings which, with the main block, enclose three sides of a neat and regular courtyard. The erection of houses without any hint of the castle about them was adopted by the aristocratic families of Angus as well as by minor lairds. In 1666 the Master Mason to the Crown, *John Mylne Jun.*, contracted to build Panmure House for the second Earl of Panmure. The new house, a replacement for the medieval Panmure Castle, was a gawkily detailed but regular design, the symmetry classical in intent if

Panmure House.
Late seventeenth-century front elevation

not in language. The double-pile main block was of two storeys and an attic above a half-exposed basement, the front's centre advanced and gabled, the end bays also finished with gables which were half covered by taller square and ogee-roofed towers projecting at the corners. The intermediate bays between the front's centrepiece and its ends were lower (the attic storey omitted over the front half of the house's double pile), flat-roofed and fronted by balustrades. Inside Panmure contained, in slightly muddled fashion, elements which were to become common in the planning of most major and many minor nobles' and lairds' houses during the next eighty years – a principal or state stair from the ground floor to the first-floor *piano nobile* where a saloon, at Panmure occupying the full depth of the house's centre, formed the first of a sequence of rooms constituting a state apartment, theoretically for occupation by the King or his deputy, and consisting of an antechamber, state drawing room, state bedchamber and closet.

Similar to Panmure House in their symmetry were other Angus houses built or remodelled in the late C17 and beginning of the C18. In 1677 the Edinburgh mason, *Thomas Wilkie*, began construction of the smaller but not dissimilar Gallery House for Sir John Falconer of Balmakelly, Master of the Mint and a local laird. Like Panmure House Gallery has towers at the front corners but they have pavilion roofs and the main block is a simple oblong, the only decoration the corniced surround to the central entrance and its surmounting heraldic panel. Inside, a long gallery extends the full length of the main block. Over the High Dining Room, the principal room of the house, is a richly modelled plaster ceiling with a vine-leaf border to the central oval and reliefs of eagles in the surrounding panels. Also in the 1670s Charles Maitland, Lord Hatton, brother of the Duke of Lauderdale, remod- 41
elled his newly acquired Dudhope Castle. He made the front approximately symmetrical by rebuilding its N part to balance the existing S, both parts with towers at the outer corners, leaving the towered gatehouse of *c.* 1600 as the central feature of the front. A similar desire to provide an approximately symmetrical entrance front was shown *c.* 1700 at Careston Castle where a second jamb was added to make the existing L-plan elevation into a U, its first- and second-floor windows given rusticated

surrounds in keeping with the up-to-date mansion house appearance.

From 1669 until the end of the century Patrick, third Earl of Kinghorne (Earl of Strathmore and Kinghorne after 1677), carried out major works at Glamis Castle, respecting its character as a huge tower house but extending it so as to make the internal plan that of a post-Restoration mansion. His most important alterations to the exterior were the remodelling of the existing three-storey SE wing and the addition of a new NW wing, both in a rather old-fashioned manner. Inside, the new NW wing's first floor was entered from a passage formed through the C15 Lower Hall (The Crypt) of the Great Tower and contained a suite of rooms for occupation by the Earl and Countess, consisting of a dining room, drawing room, bedchamber and closet. On the floor above was a second and very similarly laid-out suite introduced by the Great Hall. This second suite formed the state apartment, containing also a dining room, drawing room, bedchamber and closets. At the same time as providing these processional sets of rooms the Earl added a discreetly positioned three-storey NE wing at the back of the house. Also entered from the Great Tower, this wing's first floor contained a library and its top floor a chapel
44 whose wood-panelled walls and ceiling were covered with Scenes from the Life of Our Lord, portraits of the Apostles and Christian symbols.

Just before completion of the third Earl of Strathmore and Kinghorne's work at Glamis two other Angus noblemen commissioned designs for the remodelling or rebuilding of their houses. In 1698 the fourth Earl of Southesk procured alternative schemes from *John Slezer* and *Sir William Bruce* and *Alexander Edward* for recasting Kinnaird Castle which then stood as the untidy product of piecemeal development from the C15 to the early C17. Both schemes would have produced a large and dignified although not very exciting classical mansion. Slezer's design had a pedimented five-bay centrepiece to the thirteen-bay main front. Bruce's and Edward's was more economical, their ten-bay main block having a pediment over the central three bays and pavilion-roofed towers at the outer corners from which would have extended low office wings enclosing a forecourt. The execution of any work at Kinnaird was prevented by the Earl of Southesk's death the next year. However, 1698 was also the year in which the fourth Earl of Panmure began a thoroughgoing reconstruction of Brechin
49 Castle to designs by Alexander Edward. When work here was completed in 1711 the result was beautifully restrained, the only external mark of ostentation at the three-storey ashlar-faced main block being a great heraldic achievement carved in the central pediment. Conical-roofed round towers stood at the corners of the main front just as had the square towers at the Panmure House and Gallery House and as had been proposed by Bruce and Edward for Kinnaird Castle. The principal rooms of Brechin Castle formed a state apartment containing a Great Dining Room, Drawing Room, Bedchamber, Dressing Room and Closet, and there was a second suite of rooms for the Earl and Countess.

Completion of Brechin Castle was followed in 1714 by the construction of the last of this group of post-Restoration mansions, the House of Gray built for John, ninth Lord Gray, the design almost identical to that of the slightly earlier Strathleven House (Stirling and Central Scotland). Here also is a piend-roofed main block, its centre advanced under a pediment which contains a heraldic achievement flanked by a pair of oculi and below which is the entrance in a segmental-pedimented surround. Standing at the ends of the front but slightly set back are ogee-roofed towers and, beyond them, lower pavilions which are advanced to flank a shallow forecourt. Here too was a state apartment of dining room, drawing room, bedchamber and closets which filled the ground floor of the main block.

Lairds' houses of the EARLIER EIGHTEENTH CENTURY continued the post-Restoration adoption of the restrained classical box as the model but without the corner towers so characteristic of these exemplars. The main blocks of the early C18 Tealing House, of Kintrockat House built in 1721 and of the House of 50
Pitmuies of *c.* 1730 are all straightforward oblongs with advanced and pedimented centres. Much more idiosyncratic is the tower-like show front of classical inspiration added to the W gable of the C16 Logie House in 1722. Grander than any of these and one of the most striking Scottish houses built in the first half of the C18 is House of Dun designed by *William Adam* and built for a 51
judge and local laird, David Erskine, Lord Dun, in 1730–42. Basically this is an oblong of two storeys above a basement, the centrepieces of the two main elevations both slightly advanced. However, the entrance is placed in a triumphal arch, the idea suggested a few years earlier by *John Erskine, sixth and eleventh Earl of Mar*. Inside, the centre of the ground floor was filled by the entrance hall and great Saloon which were flanked by two suites of rooms, one a state apartment, the other a set of rooms for the family. The decorative plasterwork by *Joseph Enzer* must 52
count among the most ebullient of its date in Scotland, the overmantels of the saloon's chimneypieces displaying huge figures of Mars and Neptune, trophies of arms on the frieze above and reliefs in the cove of the ceiling, one of Minerva seated among battle standards and cannon and with shackled captives at her feet, the other of a sportive dolphin and, surrounding this, the further relief of a hunting scene.

House of Dun was the last house built in Angus to contain a state apartment. Externally, however, the appearance of new lairds' houses built in the area during the LATER EIGHTEENTH CENTURY AND EARLY NINETEENTH CENTURY showed only minor deviations from the formula of the piend-roofed box, its front dignified by a pedimented centre, which had been established by 1700. Examples of this type are Ardovie House, its urn finials memorably oversized, of 1759, Craigo (now demolished) of 1767, Langley Park and Auchenreoch also of the later C18. Simpler still is Reswallie House of 1794 with a chimney-topped gablet in place of a pediment, or the contemporary house built in the N courtyard range of Airlie Castle which has neither

pediment nor gablet but marked the centre with a smartly detailed
Venetian door. Stolider is Lunan House of 1825, a piend-roofed
box, the centre of the front emphasized only by a Tuscan-
columned portico under a three-light window.

Rather more sophisticated were several houses in the form of
VILLAS, some built for lairds of established families, others for
newcomers with recently acquired fortunes, built between 1785
and *c.* 1820. Anniston (demolished), the seat of the Raits, a family
of lairds, was designed in 1785 by *James Playfair*, the severity of
the three-storey and basement main block relieved only by a
pedimented entrance, but this block was set between piend-
roofed lower pavilions, their gable-ends containing large tripartite
windows under overall Diocletian fanlights, from which extended
colonnaded service ranges. Similarly smartly austere is The
59 Guynd, built in 1817 for John Ochterlony whose family had
owned the estate for two centuries, the two-storey and basement
main block with a Roman Doric portico and flanked by bow-
ended pavilions. Also early C19, its main block of *c.* 1800, its
pavilions perhaps added a few years later, is West Newton House,
the exterior plain but the entrance hall in a stylish Adamish
manner, albeit on a small scale.

More show-off externally are some villa-country houses whose
construction was financed by recently acquired wealth. Money
made in the West Indies financed George Keith's construction of
Usan House in 1820, the ends and central pediment of its Ionic-
porticoed front all with urn finials. Pearsie House was built in
1805 by Charles Wedderburn with money accumulated during a
seventeen-year sojourn in India, the elevations of the three-storey
main block tied together by sill and band courses, their red
sandstone ashlar a contrast to the white harl of the main walling,
the columned entrance set in a full-height bow flanked at the first
floor by Venetian windows contained in round-headed over-
arches. The contemporary Downiepark was built for Lieutenant-
Colonel William Rattray, another veteran of India, its main
block's tall central section containing the principal entrance at
57 the N and bulging out as a bow to the S where in 1819 was added
a portico which shelters the basement entrance and whose flat
roof serves as a balcony to the ground floor drawing room. Short
low links join the main blocks to pedimented pavilions. Inside
the house, a stair rises round three sides of the entrance hall to
a first-floor bedroom passage set behind a columned screen.

Another villa-country house whose stair-hall, here containing
a grand imperial stair to the bedrooms, forms the principal
feature of the interior is the simply detailed Balmadies House
built by the agriculturalist Henry Stephens in 1821. Of local
origin was the wealth of Peter Arkley who bought the estate of
Dunninald in 1811 and in 1823–4 built here a house designed by
58 *James Gillespie Graham* in studiously asymmetrical Tudor-Gothic
style with slim square towers at three corners of the main block
and a fat round tower at the fourth, the interior continuing
the Gothic manner into the central stair-hall, dining room and
60 'cloister' passage to the drawing room and circular library.

A few of the largest houses built in Angus in the late C18 and early C19 broke with the Anglo-Dutch classical formula and its derivations. In the 1770s and again in the 1790s a genteel CASTLE STYLE was adopted for alterations and additions to Glamis Castle. Rather heavier in manner and symmetrical in composition was the front block added to Aldbar Castle (now demolished) *c.* 1800. Remodelling of the C16 and C17 tower house of Cortachy Castle to give it a more appropriately castellated 40
appearance, although of light-hearted character, was carried out by *Richard Hogg* in 1787–90 and by *R. & R. Dickson* in 1820–1. Much more thoroughgoing, serious-minded and of vastly greater ambition was *James Playfair*'s re-creation of Kinnaird Castle in 1788–98, transforming it from an untidy agglomeration of parts constructed at various dates into a huge symmetrically ordered castle-style mansion. The works at Glamis, Cortachy and Kinnaird were all commissioned by the heads of aristocratic families but Angus's two other great castle-style Late Georgian mansions (both demolished) were built for nouveaux riches, Rossie Castle (by *Richard Crichton*, *c.* 1795–1800) for Hercules Ross who had acquired a fortune as a naval paymaster, and Lindertis House (by *Archibald Elliot*, 1815–16) for Gilbert Laing Meason who had recently purchased the estate. Both had symmetrical towered main blocks, Rossie Castle's windows round-headed, Lindertis House's Gothic.

Stylistically quite different from these castellated mansions, although sharing the later ones' adherence to symmetry of design,

Kinnaird Castle.
W-front elevation by James Playfair, 1789

are the GREEK REVIVAL houses of Angus. The earliest of these
54 is Camperdown House built in 1820–6 for Robert, second Vis-
count Duncan, son of the victorious British admiral at the Battle
of Camperdown. *William Burn* produced the design, closely
derived from William Wilkins's for The Grange (Hampshire) of
1809 but with an Ionic instead of a Doric portico. Construction
of two further Greek Revival houses, both designed by *Archibald
Simpson*, was begun in 1827. One, Letham Grange, was on an
estate which had been assembled a few years before from lands
in different ownerships by Alexander Hay, merchant and manu-
facturer of Arbroath, and inherited by his sportsman son John,
Simpson's client. The house here has something of the quality of
a villa, the three-bay centrepiece of the main block's entrance
front articulated by giant Roman Doric columns carrying a
shallow pediment, the centrepiece of the garden front a domed
bow fronted by more columns. The other and more starkly Neo-
53 Grec mansion designed by Simpson is Stracathro House, built
for Alexander Cruikshank who had made a fortune in Jamaica.
Blockier and more powerfully detailed than Letham Grange, the
main block has severe book-end end bays between which is
stretched a giant Ionic colonnade which breaks forward as a
pedimented portico at the centre. At the heart of the interior is
55 a domed double-height Inner Hall, its walls clad with scagliola,
its E and W ends divided off by Corinthian-columned screens.
The surrounding principal rooms contain a wealth of colourful
painted and plasterwork decoration.

In the MID AND LATE NINETEENTH CENTURY several Angus houses were built, recast or extended, some on a massive scale. One of these was Letham Grange, remodelled by *John Robertson* and *John Rhind* in 1881–5 in opulent French Second Empire manner for James Fletcher of Rosehaugh, the newly plutocratic pioneer of the import of alpaca wool to Britain. The equally expensive interior is in a grand hotel Neo-Jacobean style. Jacobean Renaissance was also adopted for work at two seats of the Angus aristocracy. Panmure House (demolished), the principal residence of Lord Panmure, was transformed from the gawky building of 1666 into the semblance of an early C17 prodigy house in 1852–5 by *David Bryce* who twenty years later designed a huge extension to Cortachy Castle in the same manner (this extension also demolished) for the Earl of Airlie.

However, SCOTTISH BARONIAL was the generally chosen
style. It was introduced to the area in 1843 at Aldbar Castle
(demolished) by *Alexander Roos* in an attempt to enliven the
house's symmetrical castellated front addition of *c.* 1800, and in
1848 David Bryce added turrets, bay windows and crowsteps to
a plain C18 wing of Guthrie Castle. These, however, were tenta-
tive essays in comparison to the work at Kinnaird Castle. Here,
James Playfair's late C18 castellated mansion was re-created by
Bryce in 1854–60 as a Franco-Scottish Baronial fantasy, the
61 chateau which might have been built as a royal palace had Mary,
Queen of Scots' first marriage produced a son to rule a united
kingdom of Scotland and France. More single-mindedly Scottish

is Balintore Castle designed in 1859 by *William Burn* for David
Lyon, an English Member of Parliament, its towered and turreted
presence dramatically sited on a hillside high above the Loch of
Lintrathen. Also on a hillside and built for a merchant is Kinnet-
tles House of 1865 by *Peddie & Kinnear*, using much the same
language but more relaxed in manner. More relaxed still and
without the hint of aggression shown by the earlier Baronial
houses is *Wardrop & Reid*'s Kinnordy House designed in 1879 63
for a local laird who had just inherited further estates and a
considerable sum of money. The language is decidedly Scottish
but the 'Baronial' elements are reduced to unthreatening conical-
roofed and slender towers while large bay windows dominate the
principal garden front. A restrained display of wealth is reserved
for the interior, English Jacobean Renaissance the dominant sty- 65
listic influence, and with a double-height library serving as the
principal room. More emphatically Baronial is the tower added
in 1891–2 by *R. Rowand Anderson* to the jamb of the early C16
house standing at one corner of the low-key complex into which
Ethie Castle had developed.

Most idiosyncratic of the area's Scottish Baronial houses but
quite at ease with itself is Hospitalfield designed by the artist and 62
amateur of architecture, *Patrick Allan-Fraser*, as the principal
residence on his wife's estate near Arbroath. This is a sprawling
Z-plan given a welcome vertical tautness by towers and turrets,
the elevations enlivened by inventive touches and ample carving.
The interior is the work of a connoisseur, also with a wealth of
carved work, the walls covered with stamped leather and panel-
ling, the chimneypieces of elaborate Jacobean character, the prin-
cipal room a richly decorated Gallery, the setting for much of the 64
Allan-Fraser collection of pictures, statuary and artifacts. More
'correctly' antiquarian is the decoration in some other houses in
Angus. The drawing room (originally laird's hall) of Cortachy
Castle was remodelled in 1873 by *David Bryce* who gave it a
plaster ceiling closely following the design of an early C17 ceiling
in the Old Mansion House at Auchterhouse. Inspired by English
work are interiors introduced to Brechin Castle in 1903–4. The
drawing room formed at this time was designed to house tapes-
tries of *c.* 1700 from Dalhousie Castle (Lothian) but the remain-
der of the walling was panelled, chimneypieces and overmantels
erected and a ceiling installed, all copied from the 'State Room'
of 1606 of the 'Old Palace' at Bromley-le-Bow (London) which
had recently been removed to the Victoria and Albert Museum.
Also taken from an English early C17 source was the design of
the Gallery's ceiling, copied from a ceiling of 1637 in the Rein-
deer Inn at Banbury (Oxfordshire).

A backward look at Scottish lairds' houses of the early C17
characterized several Angus country houses remodelled or built
at the BEGINNING OF THE TWENTIETH CENTURY. Most
accomplished of these are *Robert S. Lorimer*'s reconstruction and
extension of Pitkerro House in 1902–4. Studiously and self-
consciously Scottish without originality are Edwardian houses
designed by *Thoms & Wilkie*. The bay-windowed and crowstep-

gabled Dunlappie of 1901 is gentle Scots Jacobean with shaped dormerheads the principal embellishment. Very much larger is Kinpurnie Castle, a huge villa built for the ship-owner Sir Charles Cayzer in 1907–10, its low harled bulk stretched out along the side of Newtyle Hill. The manner is wholly domestic except for a tower rising flush with the walling on one side and the gentlest of martial hints provided at the turreted entrance gable. Also by Thoms & Wilkie but in an English Arts and Crafts manner is Grayburn of 1905, the style adopted also by *T. Martin Cappon* for the contemporary Kingennie House.

Parks, gardens and estate buildings

Houses of the C16 and early C17 were sometimes accompanied by ORNAMENTAL GARDENS adjoining the barmkin enclosures. A surviving and very stylish example is the garden of Edzell
46 Castle formed in the first years of the C17. Three of the garden's four walls are divided by Doric pilasters into bays which contain alternately heraldry proclaiming the lineage of the Lindsays of Edzell and panels carved with reliefs of the Cardinal Virtues, the
47–48 Seven Liberal Arts and the Planetary Deities, perhaps in part to celebrate the learning and virtues of the garden's owners. A garden like that at Edzell was essentially private and can be seen as a forerunner of later gardens visible only by those allowed to pass through the house to which they are attached. At the outer corners of Edzell Castle's garden were two C17 pavilions, one perhaps a bath house, the other a two-storey summerhouse. At Ethie Castle is a garden house of 1674 and also of two storeys. Almost a century younger is the summerhouse of 1762 in the garden of Gagie House, its ashlar front embellished with Roman Doric pilasters supporting an entablature. SUNDIALS might stand at the centre of C17 gardens. A late C17 multi-faceted
45 example, now isolated on a lawn, stood in the Dial Garden, one of the garden compartments which formerly fronted Glamis Castle. At Kinnaird Castle is a sundial of 1675, its stem a bulbous baluster.

In the late C17 the APPROACHES to some houses passed through a series of enclosures and courts, an external version of contemporary internal planning in which the status of visitors could be measured by how they progressed along the processional suite of rooms making up a laird's or state apartment. The approach to Glamis Castle led through two gateways built in 1680–1 before reaching a third which opened onto a forecourt flanked by garden plots. The first of the gateways was the Satyr Gate (re-erected in 1775 on the edge of the parkland), its tall piers originally with eagle finials. Flanking the central archway itself are panels carved with reliefs of satyrs. The gateway beyond was the Gladiator Gate (also moved in 1775), the ball-finialled corniced piers originally flanked by narrow pedestals on which stood figures of naked gladiators. At each corner of the forecourt stood a brass-coloured lead statue of one of the C17 Stuart kings of Scotland. In the centre of one of the flanking garden plots was a fountain, in the other a sundial. Leading to the outer gateway was a great avenue laid out in the late C17 together with other avenues which radiated from the castle. Similar radial layouts of avenues, together with 'wilderness' areas of denser planting, were made about the same time at Brechin Castle, Panmure House and Kinnaird Castle. In the late C18 and early C19 these formal parkland layouts were replaced by 'naturalistic' planting, with lawns and trees brought right up to the walls of the mansion house, forecourts other than gravel sweeps being done away with.

LATE GEORGIAN PARKLANDS, many still surviving, were settings for buildings. Often incorporated in the landscapes are DOOCOTS, their construction usually predating the formation of the parkland. Built to house pigeons reared to be eaten by the laird's household, a doocot was a symbol of landowning status. One of the earliest in Angus, probably of the mid C16, stands near Edzell Castle. Originally it boasted angle-rounds at diagonally opposite corners. A doocot of more peaceful appearance at Tealing is a simple rubble-walled and crowstep-gabled rectangular structure, one skewputt carved with the date 1595, the other with the coat of arms of the laird, David Maxwell of Tealing. Several C17 doocots are of lectern type with monopitch roofs, e.g. the doocots of *c.* 1600 at Letham Grange and of 1672 at Careston Castle or the large double doocot beside the main approach to Glamis Castle. Something of a rarity is the pyramid-roofed square doocot, probably of the C18, at Newtonmill House.

The parkland of country houses almost always contained WALLED GARDENS in which were grown fruit, vegetables and flowers and which often also served as nurseries for saplings to be later planted on the estate farms or parks. Many walled gardens were formed in the late C18 or early C19. The walls are usually of rubble but sometimes faced with brick as at Dunninald Castle or wholly of brick construction as built at Kinnaird Castle in 1790 or at the late examples of walled gardens at Cortachy Castle in 1857 and Glamis Castle in the 1860s. Less common is a facing of ashlar masonry but such is found at Brechin Castle's walled garden constructed in 1802. That garden is also unusual in being not rectangular but formed as a quatrefoil (later extended to a cinquefoil). Here, a gardener's house, also of 1802, rises above and behind a vine house which is built against one stretch of the garden wall. At Stracathro House's walled garden of *c.* 1830 a pavilion-roofed tower stands behind the greenhouse backing onto the curved N side. For the most part garden walls were unadorned but at Cortachy Castle they are surmounted by stone urns and acorns and at Glamis Castle by heraldic lions. In 1906–7 the walled garden of Dunninald Castle was given enjoyably decorative wrought-iron gates embellished with depictions of birds and flowers.

STABLES AND COACHHOUSES, necessary appendages of C18 and C19 country houses, were usually placed at a short distance from them. Several are coeval with the houses and of the same

architectural character, as at Downiepark where the stables built in 1805 and facing the entrance front of the house occupy a pair of classical blocks. At Stracathro House the stables stand beside
68 the drive as a classical prelude but an octagonal tower gives an idiosyncratic twist to the style. Even when of a different date to the main house, stables sited on the approach can serve as a fitting introduction. At Brechin Castle the stables of 1806 overlook the drive, the three pavilions of the front range all with Diocletian windows; at Airlie Castle the stables designed by *David A. Whyte* in 1813 give a battlemented Gothic foretaste of the high medieval wall and gatehouse fronting the castle itself.

Enjoyment of the parkland of a few country houses required the construction of BRIDGES. Smartest of these has been the Image Bridge at Brechin Castle designed by *James Burn* in 1807, its piers with niches containing statues and originally supporting wooden arches with trellis-work balustrades. Enjoyably lightweight Gothic is a cast-iron footbridge of *c.* 1830 at Stracathro House.

Ornamental in character although also commemorative of events connected with the owners of estates are MONUMENTS in the parks of Panmure House and Glamis Castle. At Panmure James, fourth Earl of Panmure, erected a square ashlar pillar to commemorate his marriage to Margaret Hamilton in 1694, its bearing pilasters panelled with faceted masonry blocks and crossed by bands of pulvinated stonework. About thirty years later his wife erected Margaret's Mount, an urn-topped pedestal celebrating the Earl's escape to France after the failure of the Jacobite rising of 1715–16. Much more recently an urn inside a Postmodern classical aedicule was erected in 2006 as a monument to Princess Margaret at her birthplace of Glamis Castle.

Dome-roofed circular classical TEMPLES standing beside rivers were erected at Kinnaird Castle *c.* 1790 and The Guynd in 1853, the first's columns Roman Doric, the second's Ionic. These were put up to add interest to parkland. So too were FOLLIES such as the Gothic late C18 Artificial Ruin at Panmure House and the battlemented Doulie Tower built in 1796 in the grounds of The Burn (Aberdeen and South Aberdeenshire) near Edzell. Enjoying the view from woodland at Kinnaird Castle is Montrose's View of *c.* 1800, an octagonal Gothic summerhouse constructed with tree-trunk uprights and patterned wattle walling. Also decorative but more functional in purpose is the conical-roofed round Dairy at Balnaboth designed by *David A. Whyte* in 1823–4. Another building which combines the qualities of a folly with functionality is the Museum and Observatory built, probably in the late C18, in the walled garden of Kinnordy House.

At the entrances to the parkland of country houses stand LODGES AND GATEWAYS, built both to guard against undesirable intruders and to announce the nearby presence of the residence of a noble or laird. At Panmure House *Sir William Bruce* designed the West Gate at the W entry in 1672, the banded and corniced ashlar piers surmounted by coroneted ball finials. Very tall gatepiers constructed of channelled ashlar masonry and topped by urns were erected at Dunninald Castle *c.* 1700. Ashlar gatepiers of similar although often simpler corniced design continued to be put up through the C18 and into the C19. The accompanying lodges built from the beginning of the C19 have often survived. The earlier of these were usually single-storey and restrained although far from inelegant in architectural effect. One of the simplest is at Balnaboth. Designed by *David A. Whyte* in 1823, it is picturesquely broad-eaved and with a semi-octagonal projection at the centre of the front. The lodge of *c.* 1820 at Usan House boasts a primitivist pedimented Tuscan portico. In the pedimented front gable of Careston Castle's North Lodge of *c.* 1800 is a Venetian dummy window. Venetian dummy windows also look out from the fronts of the pair of lodges at the entrance to the drive of West Newton House. Perhaps to indicate the owner's aristocratic status a battlemented wall-head was provided at Brechin Castle's Old Lodge of *c.* 1800 whose round-headed windows are set in overarches. Almost playful is the square and pyramid-roofed early C19 lodge of Kintrockat House, its front window containing Gothic lights and flanked by crosslet dummy arrowslits. Much more serious is the Grey Lodge of *c.* 1820 at Cortachy Castle comprising a pair of Tudor pavilions with octagonal turret-buttresses at the corners. These flank the drive's entrance archway set between more turret-buttresses. Larger and more forceful an assertion of the status of the mansion beyond is the West Gateway built at Guthrie Castle in 1838 and serving both as a gate to the parkland and a viaduct for the railway line from Arbroath to Forfar. This is a Tudor arch set in a huge battlemented and turreted surround, the heraldic achievement of the Guthries of Guthrie prominently displayed. Larger still are the East Gates erected by Lord Panmure at Panmure House in 1852. They were designed by *David Bryce* as an introduction to the opulence of the mansion as remodelled by him at the same time. The gateway itself is a swaggering essay in the late C17 classical manner, the lodges an evocation of Scottish architecture of fifty years earlier, a combination of styles used half a century later by *Robert S. Lorimer* for the gates and lodge of Pitkerro House. At the same time as Bryce designed the Panmure gates *Brown & Wardrop* designed the West Lodge of Brechin Castle, another seat of Lord Panmure, the Tudor archway flanked by conical-roofed round towers of different sizes. Similar towers were provided for Bryce's North Lodge of 1861 at Kinnaird Castle but these flank not an archway but coronet-finialled gatepiers. More martial still are the 1890s West Gateway of Letham Grange and the North Lodge of Dunninald Castle, but they offer only feeble competition to the defensive strength of Cortachy Castle's Airlie Lodge of 1889, a battlemented gatehouse equipped with a (dummy) portcullis which straddles the principal approach to the mansion house. At the head of the principal approach to Glamis Castle stand the Queen Mother's Gates erected in 2008. Designed in a late C17 manner by *James F. Stephen*, the gatepiers display the coats of arms of the Angus burghs and are topped by lions, heraldic devices of the Earls of Strathmore. The gateway provides an appropriate introduction to the house which constitutes Angus's most ostentatious display of familial self-celebration.

ROADS, RAILWAYS, HARBOURS AND LIGHTHOUSES

Angus must have had roads or tracks along which livestock could be driven and humans could walk or ride from a very early age, the more important of these probably near rivers. However, few if any would have been suitable for wheeled traffic, large or heavy consignments of goods being carried on boats along the rivers or, for relatively short distances, on sledges. Of MEDIEVAL BRIDGES over the larger rivers there is little written or structural evidence although the existence of Brechin Bridge is recorded in the earlier C13 and the obtusely pointed S arch of the present bridge could be of this date.

In 1617 the Scottish Parliament enacted that ROADS between market towns were to be at least 20 feet (*c.* 6 m.) wide and that they were to be maintained by the inhabitants of each parish they passed through. Further legal provision for roads was given in 1669 when an Act for Repairing Highways and Bridges was passed. This required the tenants in each parish to give their labour for free for a few days each year to repair roads and bridges. It also allowed Commissioners of Supply for each county, themselves drawn from local landowners, to levy taxes on their fellow landowners for the maintenance of roads. Perhaps unsurprisingly the system was of only limited effect.

Those bridges which did exist before the late C18 were, like their medieval predecessors, narrow, like the C16 North Water Bridge over the North Esk which did not have space for carts to pass each other. The bridge over the Water of Mark was too steeply hump-backed for a cart to cross. However, in the 1770s and 1780s public subscriptions or private individuals paid for the erection of new bridges such as a bridge of three arches over the Kerbet Water. Smartest of these was the Bridge of Dun
70 designed by *Alexander Stevens Sen.* in 1785 to carry the road from Forfar to Montrose over the South Esk, its architecture a light-hearted mixture of classical, Gothic and castellated elements.

In 1790 an Act of Parliament was passed for the county of Angus. This provided for the replacement of the use of statute labour for the upkeep of roads and bridges by a financial levy, the money raised to be spent under the direction of county trustees drawn from the local landowners. The act also empowered the trustees to borrow money for the construction or upkeep of major roads, the money to be repaid from the proceeds of tolls levied on those using the roads. As a result, £5,000 or £6,000 was raised each year to be spent on roads and bridges. Within twenty years Angus had been provided with an efficient road system, the main routes leading from Coupar Angus and Meigle (Perth and Kinross) through Strathmore to Forfar, Brechin and from there to the North Water Bridge over the North Esk, from Coupar Angus to Dundee with a spur to Newtyle, from Dundee along the coast to Arbroath and Montrose, from Dundee inland to Forfar with another road from Dundee to Carmyllie, Friockheim and Brechin, from Arbroath to Friockheim and Forfar, and from Brechin to Montrose. Few major new bridges were required but in the 1790s one of three arches was built over the South Esk at Finavon and a wooden bridge (designed by *Alexander Stevens Jun.*) constructed to replace a ferry over that river's mouth at Montrose. In 1828–9 this last bridge was replaced in turn by a 132 m.-long suspension bridge designed by *Captain Samuel Brown.*

After 1879 roads in Scotland became the responsibility of County Road Trustees and, from 1889, the newly created county councils. Two early C20 bridges are memorable if not beautiful. At Justinhaugh near Tannadice, *Crouch & Hogg* were engineers in 1907–8 of a steel bowstring bridge over the South Esk. In 1929–30 *E. Owen Williams* replaced the century-old suspension bridge with a bridge (now replaced) of reinforced concrete cantilever construction, in appearance a horribly heavy-handed evocation of its iron predecessor. Since 1936 trunk roads have been the responsibility of central government. In the late C20 the A90 from Dundee to Aberdeen has been widened to a dual carriageway, now by-passing the towns of Forfar and Brechin. Most of the new bridges are well-mannered but unexciting concrete structures. One stands out because of its 2.2 km. length. This is the forty-two-span Tay Road Bridge joining Dundee to Fife, designed by *William Fairhurst* and opened in 1966.

The construction of an efficient road system from the end of the C18 contributed to the prosperity of the inland towns of Angus. More significant for their C19 industrial development was the construction of RAILWAYS enabling the easy transport of raw materials and finished goods. The earliest in the area was the Dundee & Newtyle Railway opened in 1831, its trains initially pulled along different stretches of the line by horses and by tow-lines from stationary engines. Construction of this line owed much to the enthusiasm of two lairds, the Earl of Airlie and Lord Wharncliffe, who owned much of the land along the route. The railway was soon after extended to Coupar Angus and Glamis but steep inclines along the original route made it far from satisfactory until the 1860s when deviation lines were constructed, including one passing by the great jute factory of the Camperdown Works at Lochee. More important were the railways opened in 1838–9 from Dundee to Arbroath and from Arbroath to Forfar, these forming an L-shape linking two of the major towns in Angus to the recently extended harbour of Dundee. In 1847 was opened the Dundee & Perth Railway through the Carse of Gowrie and the next year Dundee gained railway access via Perth to Glasgow and Edinburgh. An alternative and more direct route to Edinburgh by the line through Fife from Tayport to Burntisland was given attraction in 1851 by the provision of ferries able to carry loaded railway trains across the Tay from Broughty Ferry just E of Dundee to Tayport and across the Forth from Burntisland to

Grantown near Edinburgh. The Scottish Midland Junction Railway from Perth through Strathmore to Glamis and Forfar was opened in 1848. That year saw also the completion of a branch line which left the Arbroath & Forfar Railway at Friockheim and ran via Brechin and Bridge of Dun to Montrose from where a line to Aberdeen was opened in 1850. A branch line from the Scottish Midland Junction Railway to Kirriemuir, opened in 1861, meant that from then all the Angus towns were served by railways. In 1875 was completed a railway bridge over the Tay. Although it collapsed during a storm two years later, a new bridge was then built and opened in 1887. Extensions of the railway system continued during the late C19, notably the construction of a coastal route from Arbroath to Montrose in 1881 and a line from Forfar to Brechin in 1895. Serving the needs of Late Victorian holidaymakers in the Angus glens was the line to Edzell which opened in 1896 simultaneously with the building of a couple of sizeable hotels in that village. All the area's railway lines except the coast line from Perth and the Tay Bridge via Dundee and Arbroath to Montrose and from there to Aberdeen were closed and dismantled in the later C20. The Caledonian Railway between Brechin and Bridge of Dun was reopened for both steam and diesel locomotives by a group of volunteer enthusiasts in 1993.

Fairly few RAILWAY STATIONS survive. The earliest, at Newtyle, is of 1831–2, a tall goods shed with a brick-fronted lower passenger station at one end. Stations at Brechin and Montrose both date from 1848, Brechin's Italianate in style, that at Montrose cottagey, as is the railway station of 1849 at Broughty Ferry. Small but prominently sited and an assertive presence is Lochee's railway station designed by *James Gowans* for the Dundee & Newtyle Railway in 1861, its walls of multi-coloured rubble, the windows in shouldered arches, the eaves of the roof supported on moulded stone brackets. Staider and in a Tudor manner is the railway station built at Arbroath in 1911. Unsurprisingly, the grandest of the area's Victorian stations were in Dundee. Here, rival stations stood beside one another at the foot of what was then Union Street, the Caledonian Railway's Scottish Baronial West Station (now demolished) of 1888–90 with a 26 m.-high clock tower, the contemporary Tay Bridge (now Dundee) Station of the North British Railway much less ambitious architecturally but with the platform awnings supported by four-way brackets and the waiting rooms contained in a two-storey brick building whose upper floor is reached from Riverside Drive by bridges over the track. This station's front block was rebuilt in 1959 as a modernistic box lacking both dignity and the promise of adventure.

The lines of the Angus railways managed generally to avoid the need for large BRIDGES AND VIADUCTS. One far from utilitarian bridge is the Tudor-arched West Gateway to Guthrie Castle built in 1838 by the Arbroath & Forfar Railway, one example of how much a landowner could obtain from the railway companies as the price for allowing a railway to intrude in his parkland. Two massive viaducts were constructed at the S approach to Montrose by the coastal line from Arbroath. One, of *c.* 1880, is brick-built, its seventeen arches carrying the railway across the road along the side of Montrose Basin and the South Esk; the other (by *W. R. Galbraith*, 1882–3, replacing a slightly earlier bridge whose design was deemed unsafe) is sixteen-span, the elliptically arched lattice girder trusses carried on paired iron columns. More workmanlike but of no fewer than seventy-four spans and, at 3.2 km., the longest railway bridge in Britain is *W. H. & C. Barlow*'s Tay Railway Bridge of 1881–7.

The Angus coast is inhospitable with few natural inlets or havens. Fishing HARBOURS before the C19 were no more than sloping beaches sheltered by rocks, as at Broughty Ferry and Auchmithie before the construction of harbours in the mid and late C19. The three principal harbours used for cargo rather than fishing boats were at Montrose, Dundee and Arbroath. All were of medieval origin, the first two of some significance for foreign trade, but these harbours consisted principally of wharfs along the shore and tidal basins which gave shelter to ships but dried out at low tide. From the early C19 these towns began to construct new harbours incorporating wet docks, entered through lock gates which controlled the volume of water inside so that ships could float there at all states of the tide. At Arbroath the medieval wooden pier had been replaced in 1725 by a tidal basin (the Old Harbour). In the 1840s a second basin, also tidal but 2
making use of deeper water, was constructed and in the 1870s the Old Harbour converted to a wet dock. At Montrose quays and wharfs had been built from the Middle Ages until the C19 along the shore at the mouth of the River South Esk. A wet dock was constructed in 1839–43. The medieval harbour of Dundee had comprised a stone pier and wharfs. By the end of the C18 there was a tidal basin bisected by a pier. Major development came in the C19 with the construction of four wet docks between 1815 and 1875 followed in the C20 by the formation of a huge area of wharfs to the E. Elsewhere in Angus a couple of harbours were built in the mid and late C19. At Broughty Ferry a harbour to serve a ferry bearing railway trains across the Tay was constructed in 1847–51 and at Auchmithie a (tidal) basin providing shelter for fishing boats in 1889.

Beside the harbours were erected buildings for goods. The best surviving collection of Victorian structures is at Dundee where railway sheds for goods in transit were built beside the Victoria Dock in the 1860s and 1870s together with a six-storey granary dignified by a clock tower at one end. Also beside Dundee Harbour is the grandly classical 1840s Customs House, the pediment of its front's aedicular centrepiece containing the royal coat of arms in high relief.

The entry to some harbours, especially those placed at the mouths of rivers, was marked in the C19 by BEACONS. Two of these, conical-shaped towers of 1819, still stand on the S bank of the South Esk at Ferryden opposite Montrose. More prominent markers of dangerous rocks as well as of harbour entrances could

be provided by LIGHTHOUSES. Just E of the Ferryden beacons is the Scurdie Ness Lighthouse designed by *D. & T. Stevenson* in 1868, a round tower with light keepers' houses at its foot. It is of minor importance, however, in comparison with the Bell Rock Lighthouse built to *Robert Stevenson*'s design in 1807–11. This rises from a rock in the North Sea 17.7 km. SE of Arbroath, a 30 m.-high round tower faced with painted granite and surmounted by an octagonal lantern. A shore-based adjunct to this
69 lighthouse is the Signal Tower erected in 1813 at Arbroath, a much lower and battlemented and decoratively detailed circular tower standing at the centre of one range of a courtyard of stores and light keepers' family housing.

BURGHS AND VILLAGES

Angus contains one city (Dundee), a few burghs of moderate size, a handful of large villages and a sprinkling of small villages and hamlets. Although the population now lives mostly in towns and, increasingly, in new housing developments on their fringes, the aspect of the area remains predominantly rural.

Burghs and villages before the later eighteenth century

Until the later C18 farming was the chief occupation of the Angus population, mostly living in ferm touns, settlements housing groups of peasants, each engaged in the collective working of a farm. A minority, however, lived in burghs. The most important of these were the royal burghs which held their property and privileges directly of the Crown and whose merchants enjoyed a monopoly of foreign trade over a large surrounding area. In Angus three royal burghs (Dundee, Forfar and Montrose) were founded in the C12. Two other burghs (Brechin and Arbroath) also dated from the C12 but originally were dependencies of the Bishop of Brechin and the Abbey of Arbroath. Both, however, had come by the C16 to be regarded as royal burghs, entitled to the same trading privileges and representation in the Convention of Royal Burghs and Parliament. In the C15 three other burghs (Kirriemuir, Glamis and Auchterhouse) were founded in Angus, all burghs of barony, dependencies of local lairds who appointed their municipal officials, and with their privileges restricted to the right to hold markets for domestic trade and to house craftsmen. Further burghs of barony were founded in the C16 and C17 (East Haven in 1541, Hilltown in 1671 and Newtyle in 1682) although none developing to any size until the C19.

All royal burghs were surrounded by walls or fences, precautions against smuggling rather than military attack, with gates at the road entries. Dundee had a stone wall of which one gateway, the Wishart Arch, its present form dating perhaps from *c.* 1500, survives. Despite possessing such a defence, the town was captured and recaptured several times by pro-English and patriot armies in the early C14, again fell to English armies in 1385 and the 1540s and, during the civil wars of the mid C17, successively to the Marquess of Montrose and General Monk. Dundee's walls were finally removed c. 1760.

By the C16 and probably earlier burghs boasted MARKET CROSSES. The shaft of the market cross of Dundee made by *John Mylne* in 1586 still stands although on a Victorian substructure and not on the original site. Also standing but not on its original site is the substructure of Forfar's market cross of 1683–4, a 6 m.-high battlemented octagonal tower which displays the burgh coat of arms, the King's monogram and the thistle emblem of Scotland. Other marks of burgh status were the trons, beams for weighing goods offered for sale, utilitarian structures no longer in evidence in Angus. As importantly, burghs possessed TOLBOOTHS or TOWN HOUSES built to house the money collected as market dues, lock-up cells for suspected criminals and meetings of the burgh councils or courts. In 1325 Robert I granted Dundee a site for a tolbooth in Seagate and probably by the late C14 this had been replaced by a new tolbooth in High Street. Both these buildings were apparently of wooden construction but in 1562 a new stone-walled tolbooth was erected. A stone tolbooth was put up at Kirriemuir in 1604. Far grander than these was Dundee's replacement in 1732 for the C16 tolbooth, the new Town House designed by *William Adam* in a Palladian manner, with a steeple derived from James Gibbs's St Martin-in-the-Fields in London, a ground-floor loggia and double-height rooms (the Court House and Guild Room for meetings of the merchants' guild) on the upper floor.

SCHOOLS were provided in each parish by the beginning of the C18, fulfilling one aim of the C16 ecclesiastical Reformers. Most of those built before the C19 seem to have been very humble, providing a bare sufficiency of accommodation for the pupils and schoolmaster. The new parish school built at Craig in 1722 was c. 11 m. by 3.7 m. and 1.8 m. high, the walls of stone and the roof slated. In 1747 the school at Maryton was thatched and consisted of two rooms, one a classroom, the other a dwelling for the schoolmaster.

DOMESTIC BUILDINGS before the late C18 survive in Angus only in tiny numbers. Each of the medieval burghs was generally laid out with a broad main street, partly intended as a market place, from which narrow strips of land (burgage tofts) ran back at right angles. Each toft was intended as the site of a combined dwelling and workplace of a burgess and also as ground for a vegetable garden and perhaps orchard. In time the tofts were often subdivided, usually with a second dwelling house built about halfway back and reached by a close or alley along the side of the toft. Late medieval division of tofts has apparently dictated the layout of parts of the main street of Montrose although the buildings are C18 or C19. Set back from the High Street of Dundee is Gardyne's Land, a tall merchant's house of the late C16. Off the same city's Nethergate is a small tenement (now St David's Rooms) of late C16 or early C17 origin, one panelled jamb of a ground-floor archway still in place. The last vestiges of

Dundee's great medieval town house of the Earls of Crawford,
also in Nethergate but with a garden extending to the bank of
the River Tay, were removed in the late C18.

The later eighteenth century to the 1830s

The later C18 in Angus, as elsewhere in Scotland, was a time of
growing prosperity, agricultural improvement getting underway
and industry, especially the weaving of linens, being established.
At the beginning of the C19, during the Napoleonic Wars, further
encouragement to economic development was given by the
blockade on trade which removed foreign competition. Prosper-
ity and optimism were shown by other burghs following the early
C18 example of Dundee and erecting new town houses to accom-
modate their officials and meetings of their councils. All were
dignified examples of Neo-Palladian restrained classicism. The
73 Town House at Montrose was built in 1763–4 and remodelled
and heightened in 1819, the Town and County Hall at Forfar in
72 1786–8, Brechin's Town House in 1789 and Arbroath's in 1803–8.
These were followed by the erection of halls for the burghs'
incorporations of tradesmen and craftsmen. In Dundee the vista
along High Street was closed in 1778 by the smartly detailed
Trades Hall (designed by *Samuel Bell*) and Trinity House for the
Sailors' Incorporation built beside the Harbour in 1790. Less
ostentatious Trades Halls were built at Arbroath and Montrose
in 1814 and 1816.

Other expressions of local or civic pride were SCHOOLS AND
EDUCATIONAL ESTABLISHMENTS. Parish schools, their con-
struction and upkeep still the legal responsibility of the heritors
(landowners of each parish), were becoming more commodious
for both pupils and teachers than had been their C18 predeces-
sors. The school put up at Glamis in 1839, for example, is Jaco-
bean, the schoolmaster's house not luxurious but of decent size.
Hugely more impressive were the large new schools of a proudly
public nature constructed in the early C19 in the burghs of the
area, several bringing previously separate educational establish-
ments under one roof. The Academies of Forfar and Montrose
74 were built in 1815–16 to Greek Revival designs by *David Logan*,
the centrepiece of one having columns of a Doric order, the other
with Ionic columns. Sizeable but simpler was the Arbroath
Academy of 1821 but the High School of Dundee, designed by
George Angus, is again Greek Revival with a boldly projecting
pedimented Doric portico. Rather later and departing stylistically
from the classical idiom were the Neo-Jacobean Webster's Semi-
nary at Kirriemuir (by *James Brewster*, 1837–8) and, at Brechin,
78 the Mechanics' Institute (by *John Henderson*, 1838–42), a Tudor
Collegiate edifice which, as well as containing a public lecture
hall, library and reading room, housed the grammar, parish and
burgh schools of the town. Contemporary with the Mechanics'
Institute and also designed by Henderson but in Greek Revival
79 manner is the Montrose Museum, not a school but of scholarly
purpose. At the same time was erected the Watt Institute in

Dundee which contained a museum, library and lecture hall, George Angus's classical design of Roman rather than Greek inspiration.

SHERIFF COURT HOUSES were the responsibility of the county Commissioners of Supply, committees of local landowners, who provided Angus with one in the earlier C19. This, at Forfar, designed by *David Neave* in 1823, is restrained classical, the centrepieces of the two main elevations with Ionic columns and pilasters. A second and more pompously Roman court house was designed for Dundee by *George Angus* in 1833 but its construction postponed for another thirty years although the side and rear parts of the intended complex (police offices, prison governor's house and prison) were built at this time.

A few HOSPITALS were built in the area in the late C18 and early C19. *John Paterson* was architect of the Dundee Infirmary of 1794–8, a three-storey-and-basement block, the pedimented centre with a Roman Doric portico, looking like the house of a well-to-do laird. More decidedly a public building is the Montrose Royal Infirmary by *James Collie*, 1837–9. These two burghs also contained Angus's first lunatic asylums, the Montrose Asylum, built in 1781 and the first in Scotland, and the Dundee Asylum designed by *William Stark* in 1812.

ASSEMBLY ROOMS AND HOTELS appeared in the early C19. In 1828–30 Dundee acquired the Exchange Coffee Room, its Greek 84 Revival design by *George Smith* giving it the appearance of a public building, its principal rooms (a library and assembly room) also of public character. Less assertive but of quiet pretension is the Crown Hotel built *c.* 1815 at Montrose to serve as a local meeting place as well as to house visitors, its front's pedimented centre and end corners with vase finials. Similar in size and function is Arbroath's White Hart Inn of 1821, the front's centrepiece and the pedimented gable both containing Diocletian windows.

During the late C18 and early C19 a considerable number of the Angus towns' DOMESTIC AND COMMERCIAL BUILDINGS were rebuilt, generally in a plain but seemly manner. Among these were new town houses to accommodate local lairds, merchants, lawyers and bankers. Some of these, like Straton House, The Retreat and Coutts House at Montrose, replaced earlier houses which had occupied the backlands of medieval burgage tofts. Others, together with tenements, occupied hitherto undeveloped sites beside existing roads leading out of the burghs. One road which acquired a short stretch of ribbon development was the W continuation of Dundee's medieval Nethergate carrying the main road from that town to Perth. Here was built from *c.* 1790 a mixture of tenements, among them Morgan Tower, its 83 Venetian-windowed five-storey tower endearingly idiosyncratic, and villas of marked but modest pretension. A terrace of up-market housing was constructed in King Street at Dundee's E end in 1815–19. Villas of similar quality were built at the same time in other Angus towns, e.g. Castlestead in Castle Place, Montrose, or houses at The Shore of Arbroath. New streets were

also formed in Dundee. In the late C18 Crichton Street and Castle Street were both pushed through the medieval toft pattern to provide direct access for wheeled traffic from the Harbour to High Street, the sides of these streets lined with tenements and, in Castle Street, the Theatre Royal which observes the building line but with a pedimented centrepiece to give it presence. In the early C19 expansion of Dundee Tay Street and the lands to the N were laid out for development, and in 1818 *David Neave* designed a palace-fronted terrace for one side of South Tay Street. An Act of Parliament of 1825 provided for the formation of further new streets to be laid out through the medieval fabric of Dundee, the principal one, Reform Street, intended for terraces of uniform design leading to new developments N of the medieval burgh. Also in the early C19 a street (Roseangle and Magdalen
85 Yard Road) SW of the town was developed with villas, The Vine exceptionally smart. Here also was built, *c.* 1835, a two-storey Greek Revival terrace (Windsor Place). Greek Revival was also
87 the style adopted for the houses of the Springfield development N of Perth Road begun in 1830. Mostly Jacobean, by contrast, is the picturesquely laid out double crescent of villas built from 1833 in Laurel Bank and the neighbouring streets on a steep hillside N of the city centre.

Some PLANNED VILLAGES, intended to attract populations of craftsmen or weavers, were laid out for housing in the late C18 and early C19, Letham in 1788, Broughty Ferry *c.* 1790, Carnoustie *c.* 1810, Friockheim in 1811, Newtyle (a C17 burgh of barony which had failed to develop into a village) in 1832, and Edzell *c.* 1840. All were on gridiron plans, Letham's central square giving it a touch of urbanity. The housing was generally of one or two storeys and very plain. At Kirkton, however, is a row of single-storey double houses, the windows in segmental-headed overarches and the paired doors under single long hoodmoulds, the house blocks linked by screen walls.

Victorian and Edwardian burghs and villages

The population of all the Angus burghs increased in the mid and late C19, hugely so at Arbroath and Dundee where textile mills proliferated. Except at Dundee the effect on the towns' commercial centres was limited, although these continued to be redeveloped, their new buildings generally of three storeys and containing flats above shops, the architecture of no great excitement. The construction of new village housing, of one or two storeys, continued.

In the centre of Dundee after 1871 the medieval streets of Nethergate, Murraygate and Seagate and the newer Bell Street and Commercial Street were all widened and new streets (Whitehall Street and Whitehall Crescent) formed between High Street and the Harbour and Railway Station. General control was maintained over the design of the tall new buildings erected in these thoroughfares, a free French Renaissance manner being adopted as the style. Outside the centre of Dundee new settlements appeared, with mixed commercial and domestic buildings along the main traffic routes providing linear centres to the Hilltown and Dens neighbourhoods, and Lochee acquiring the character of a small town.

Plentiful new housing, largely composed of cheaply constructed TENEMENTS to house mill workers, was put up in the late C19. Similar suburban developments but on a much smaller scale were built in other Angus burghs. Some tenements show more architectural ambition, e.g. in Dundee the classically detailed blocks of Gowrie Place designed by *James Maclaren* in 1868 at the W end of Hawkhill or the red sandstone block of 1896 at Nos. 101–103 Magdalen Yard Road which displays Jacobean detail and a corner dome. TERRACED HOUSING was built for the more prosperous inhabitants, sometimes of markedly superior quality as at Montrose's palace-fronted Georgian survival Panmure Terrace or its Neo-Jacobean Melville Gardens, 86
both overlooking the Links, or Dundee's precipitously sloping Windsor Street of 1851–73. Well-heeled inhabitants of the suburbs could enjoy VILLAS, some of routine Georgian survival or mildly Italianate character as in Dudhope Terrace, Dundee, others of more forceful aspect, e.g. *William Aitkenhead*'s Scottish Baronial Caenlochan House at Arbroath, its battlemented tower with a caphouse, or the rogue Romanesque No. 8 Panmure Terrace in Dundee (by *F. T. Pilkington*, 1872). Much larger but unshowy was the decidedly expensive group of villas (most now demolished) built by members of the Cox family of textile manufacturers just N of Lochee, the 1850s Jacobean Clement Park by *James Maclaren* still standing. Other mill-owners were housed in unashamedly opulent displays of plutocratic wealth such as Castleroy designed in 1867 by *Andrew Heiton Jun.* for George Gilroy, owner of the Tay Works, or Carbet Castle by *T. S. Robertson*, 1866, for Joseph Grimond of the Bowbridge Works, both now demolished. Far more architecturally restrained abodes for the wealthy were designed in the early C20, notably in the string of English Arts and Crafts villas along Perth Road on the W edge of Dundee.

Expansion of towns, changes in local government after 1833 and the huge growth of industry in the area were accompanied by the erection of NEW BUILDINGS, many of them of new types. The existing Town Houses of the burghs, sometimes supplemented by rented offices, continued as the formal headquarters of councils, usually without significant alteration although the Kirriemuir Townhouse was remodelled and given a tower in the 1860s and, in 1894–5, Brechin acquired new Municipal Buildings designed by *D. & J. R. McMillan* in a free Scots Renaissance manner. A similar style was adopted for the Municipal Buildings erected at Carnoustie in 1897, a few years after the village acquired burgh status. At the end of the C19 small but decidedly public offices were erected for newly constituted parish councils, the Parish Council Chambers at Brechin of 1897 in Jacobean Renaissance style, those at Dundee of 1899–1901 Italianate and Montrose's of 1915–16 English Baroque.

In 1860 the Government undertook to provide proper funding for new Sheriff Courthouses. As a result construction of the
77 Sheriff Courthouse at Dundee designed in 1833 was finally begun in 1861. Seven years later was started the building of a new Forfar Sheriff Courthouse designed by *Brown & Wardrop* in a Tudor-
76 Baronial manner and standing next to the forbiddingly castellated prison which had been erected in the same town in 1842–3.

Government buildings of a friendlier type were POST OFFICES. Until the end of the C19 those in Angus were housed in buildings rented or bought for that purpose, Dundee's occupying part of the Town House in the later C19. However, between 1895 and 1910, a purpose-built Post Office was erected in every Angus town. Except for the Georgian survival office of 1896 designed by *David Waterston* for Kirriemuir and the Renaissance-style office of 1897–8 by *George Morham* at Forfar, these were the responsibility of architects of *H. M. Office of Works* at Edinburgh.
89 A monster in size and of boldly modelled Franco-Italian Renaissance appearance is the General Post Office built at Dundee in 1895–8. English Baroque was the style favoured for the Edwardian Post Offices at Montrose, Broughty Ferry and Brechin.

A few new HOSPITALS were put up in the area in the mid and later C19. The first was the Arbroath Infirmary opened in 1845. Much larger was the new Dundee Royal Infirmary designed by *Coe & Goodwin* and built in 1852–5. Originally with accommodation for 220 patients, it is Tudor Collegiate in style, the cupola-topped centrepiece containing an elaborate Gothic doorway approached by a double stair. Smaller and plainer were the Forfar Infirmary of 1860–2 and Brechin Infirmary of 1868–9. All these were extended at the end of the C19 or beginning of the C20, most memorably by the Dundee Royal Infirmary's Caird Building of 1902–6, an assemblage of towered pavilions faced with red engineering brick. A new Arbroath Infirmary was built in 1913–16. Generally much smaller are the hospitals built *c.* 1900 at Montrose, Dundee, Brechin, Forfar and Arbroath composed of an administration block surrounded by isolation wards to house patients suffering from different infectious diseases (smallpox, diphtheria, typhoid, scarlet fever, measles, etc.). Of similar character was the Sidlaw Sanatorium for tubercular patients built at Auchterhouse in 1901. Two sizeable LUNATIC ASYLUMS were built in the area, both replacements for earlier establishments. The late C18 Montrose Asylum was replaced in 1857 by the large main block of the Sunnyside Royal Hospital at Hillside, designed by *W. L. Moffat* in an economical Tudor manner. In 1891 *Sydney Mitchell & Wilson* were the architects of a more cheerful free Jacobean Hospital or infirmary block, and in 1895–9 *William Kelly* of the large but villa-like Carnegie Lodge for private patients. A similar course of development occurred at the Dundee Royal Asylum (later Royal Dundee Liff Hospital) at Liff whose thrifty Baronial main block for 400 patients was built in 1877–82 and a large villa (Gowrie House) for private patients in 1898–1901.

In the area was built the first institution in Scotland to provide a home for those with learning difficulties. This was the Baldovan Institution (later Strathmartine Hospital) originally designed by *Coe & Goodwin* in 1853 in the style of a Tudor country house but much extended by *James Maclaren & Sons* in 1900.

The Poor Law Act of 1845 made rather more effective the existing parochial system to aid the destitute and disabled. In the mid C19 several parishes combined to build POORHOUSES to accommodate their paupers. Two were erected at Dundee (in 1854 and 1862) and others at Forfar (1859–60) and Arbroath (1864), all of utilitarian design.

SCHOOLS generally continued to be the responsibility of parish heritors until 1872. However one major educational establishment appeared in 1868 with the opening of the Morgan Hospital (later Academy) on the edge of Dundee. Founded in terms of the will of John Morgan, a native of Dundee and merchant in India, this was originally a boarding school for 100 pupils, all natives of Dundee or other Angus burghs. Sited on what was the edge of Dundee and designed by *Peddie & Kinnear*, it is a huge Franco-Flemish building with a massive tower at the centre of the front.

The Education Act of 1872 made schooling between the ages of five and thirteen compulsory for all children and removed the responsibility for providing and maintaining schools from heritors to elected local school boards. At the same time was set up the Scotch Education Department which laid down national standards for education, including ones for school buildings. Generally these were to consist of a single-storey block containing separate classrooms for infants and older pupils and a school house or dwelling for the schoolmaster, often attached to the classroom block, usually of two storeys and containing a kitchen, parlour and three bedrooms. Many existing parish schools, especially if of recent erection, met these standards or could be made to do so, as at Arbirlot, where a new school house was added in the 1870s to the former parish school of 1855, or at Farnell where the school, also dating from 1855, was enlarged in 1875. Elsewhere, schools were built afresh, e.g. the former Eastern School at Broughty Ferry or Friockheim Public School, both of 1875.

From *c.* 1890 there emerged a second generation of BOARD SCHOOLS. Some of these were straightforward replacements but clad in newly fashionable architectural styles such as the free Jacobean Renaissance used for schools of 1901–2 and 1911 at Edzell and Letham. Others were of two or three storeys, usually planned round a central hall (a requirement of the Scotch Education Department for schools of over 500 pupils after 1906) and, in the burghs, sometimes providing secondary education. In Dundee a remarkable collection of large new schools was put up between 1890 and 1914, all designed by the Dundee School Board architect *James H. Langlands*, Blackness Primary (originally Hawkhill) School of 1892–4 classical in style, the others all Free Jacobean, the most inventive Clepington Primary (originally Stobswell Public) School with touches of Art Nouveau inspiration.

Also large but outside the control of the School Board and of French Renaissance character (by *Alexander McCulloch* and *J. Graham Fairley*) was Dundee's High School for Girls of 1886–90, a sister establishment to the earlier (boys') High School. Larger still and Jacobean but purposefully serious is Dundee's Girls' Industrial School, a reformatory housing 'the waifs and strays of city life', designed by *James Maclaren & Sons* in 1893.

Dundee's two universities can both trace their origins to the 1880s and the philanthropy of a brother and sister in founding COLLEGES for adult education. In 1881 Miss Mary Anne Baxter gave £130,000 to endow a university college at Dundee. It was duly opened two years later, occupying four villas linked by a newly constructed corridor, with chemical and engineering laboratories built behind and with a former church serving as the college hall. In 1887 the trustees of the will of Miss Baxter's brother, the textile manufacturing magnate Sir David Baxter, began construction of a quite separate Technical Institute with money left by Sir David 'for the education of boys and young men in those branches of learning necessary or useful for working mechanics or other craftsmen'. On the walls of the building, designed by *J. Murray Robertson* in an American-influenced free Renaissance style, are reliefs illustrative of the engineering, construction, metallurgical and textile industries. Between 1902 and 1913 the university college developed, with the erection of a large Scoto-Flemish Renaissance School of Medicine and English Renaissance physics, engineering and electrical engineering
98 laboratories (the Geddes Quadrangle), and with the purchase of the Technical Institute after its trustees had built a new and even larger Dundee Technical College and School of Art on a site nearer the city centre in 1907–11. A third institution of further education was built at Dundee in 1912–15, a teachers' training college housed in a Baroque edifice with an adjoining practice school, both designed by *T. Martin Cappon*.

LIBRARIES also provided a means of education or self-improvement. Although after 1854 burghs were able to finance public libraries from the rates it was only from the last years of the C19 when the philanthropy of the Scottish-born Pittsburgh steel magnate, Andrew Carnegie, made charitable funds available for their erection that libraries were properly established in the area. One, designed in a Frenchy free style by *J. McLellan Fairley*, was built at Brechin in 1891–3. The Meffan Institute at Forfar, containing a public library, was put up in 1898, the same year in which was completed the conversion of the 1820s Arbroath Academy to a library. Montrose Library, an accomplished essay in Scots Jacobean by *J. Lindsay Grant*, opened in 1905 as did Dundee's similarly styled Arthurstone Library by *William Alexander*. Soon after, other parts of Dundee acquired libraries, all unequivocally public buildings and designed by the City Architect, *James Thomson*, in assured Baroque and Beaux-Arts classical styles – Blackness and Coldside, both opened in 1908, St Roque's
80 in 1910 and the Central Reading Rooms in 1911. Earlier, the suburb of Lochee had benefited from the generosity of the Cox

family, owners of the Camperdown Works, who, in 1894, had put up a red sandstone Neo-Jacobean building designed by *J. Murray Robertson* containing a library and swimming pool.

BATHS at Dundee had been erected by a private company in 1848 but it was in the 1890s and the first years of the C20 that an adequate number of public baths and washhouses for the cleaning of the populace and its garments was built in the Angus towns. Less utilitarian than these washhouses were the Jacobean-fronted Swimming Pool erected at Forfar in 1909–10 and the solidly worthy Arbroath Public Baths of 1913–15, also containing a swimming pool. Another building intended to contribute to bodily well-being was Dundee's Ward Road Gymnasium constructed in 1890–1 in a Frenchy manner, the pediment over its entrance carved with a relief of Mother Dundee surrounded by healthy children 'illustrating the power of gymnastics'.

HALLS for private or charitable organizations were constructed at the beginning of the C20, Dundee's Foresters' Halls of 1900–2 in a free Tudor manner influenced by designs for Whitechapel Art Gallery, London, Montrose's YMCA Free Jacobean of 1908. Although designed as the hall of a private body, the Dundee Chamber of Commerce, Dundee's Royal Exchange of 1853–6 is 82
very much a public building and its hall intended for public use, *David Bryce*'s design intended to evoke a Flemish cloth hall. Large public halls for meetings, concerts and lectures were built in several Angus burghs, Arbroath's Corn Exchange (a hall as well as a sales place) in 1852–3, Brechin City Hall in 1883 and Kirriemuir Town Hall in 1885. Larger and architecturally distinguished is the Reid Hall at Forfar, designed by *Brown & Wardrop* in 1869 in a stylish Flemish-Baronial manner. Smaller and of Scots Renaissance character is the Inglis Memorial Hall at Edzell, by *C. & L. Ower*, 1896–8. Grandest and most prominently sited of Angus's Victorian halls is the Albert Institute (now The 81
McManus) in Dundee, by *G. Gilbert Scott* in his own version of medieval Flemish style with a Scottish inflexion, its double-height Great Hall filling the first floor of the front block. Most redolent of civic self-importance is Dundee's Caird Hall designed by *James Thomson*, in 1914, a classical edifice filling one side of City Square.

Victorian and Edwardian THEATRES are few in Angus. The Webster Theatre in Arbroath was built in 1865–7 to a Renaissance-style design by *James Maclaren*. More drily classical is the former King's Theatre in Dundee, by *H. & F. Thomson*, 1908–9.

Many HOTELS of the later C19, like their Georgian predecessors, fitted discreetly into the streetscape of Angus towns. The entries to the village of Edzell, however, are dominated by rival hotels, the large and villa-like Glenesk Hotel (by *David Fraser*, 1896) at the S and the half-timbered Panmure Arms (by *T. Martin Cappon*, 1895–7) at the N. In Montrose the Central Hotel (by *John Sim*, 1892) is a Frenchy presence in High Street, one corner with an octagonal tunnel. Also free French Renaissance in manner is the Dundee Sailors' Home (by *Ireland & Maclaren*, 1879–81) which provided cheap lodging for mariners. Again in Dundee are two prominent former temperance hotels, the punchily detailed Jacobean Lamb's Temperance Hotel in Reform Street (by *James Maclaren*, 1867) and the huge free French Renaissance Mathers' Commercial Hotel in Whitehall Crescent (by *Robert Hunter*, 1897–9). Another large Dundee hotel, designed in an inventive mixture of French Renaissance and Gothic styles, is the Queen's Hotel in Nethergate (by *Young & Meldrum*, 1875–8).

Victorian and Edwardian BANKS, despite the commercial nature of their activities, have the character of public buildings. With a certain arrogance they broke the uniformity of design laid down for the elevations of some new C19 streets, as in Dundee's Reform Street and Commercial Street where the Bank of Scotland of 1842, the National Bank of 1854–7 and the Commercial Bank of 1878–80 all seem to assert their exemption from strict obedience to the regulations which must be observed by others. Their number can be astonishing. The small burgh of Kirriemuir had three banks, each in its own purpose-built premises, by the late C19. In 1900 eight banks served Montrose's population of *c.* 13,000. Although the 1860s National Banks at Forfar and Montrose were appropriately clothed in Scottish dress, most Victorian banks occupied palazzi, the ground floor of each containing the banking hall, the upper floors accommodation for the bank's agent, often a local lawyer. Large and architecturally accomplished examples of these are the former Royal and North of Scotland Banks at Montrose of the 1860s (by *Peddie & Kinnear* and *James Matthews*) and the 1890s Royal Bank in Dundee's
92 High Street by *George Washington Browne*. Grandest of the palazzi
91 is the free-standing former Clydesdale Bank (by *William Spence*,
1875–8) closing the vista at the E end of Dundee's High Street.
Brasher but welcome nonetheless are *Johnston & Baxter*'s Edward-
93 ian Baroque designs for the Dundee Savings Banks in Princes
Street and at Lochee. Other financial institutions of apparent probity were the INSURANCE COMPANIES. At Dundee their Late Victorian offices stand in proximity along Meadowside, engaged in stylistic as well as commercial competition, a palazzo (by *Alexander Johnston*, 1897–8) housing the Scottish Provident Institution, a narrow-fronted Flemish-Jacobean block (by *C. & L. Ower*, 1896–8) the Pearl Life Assurance Co., a building in English C17 style (by *J. Murray Robertson*, 1886) the Caledonian Insurance Co., and a red-brick Jacobean edifice (by *A. Waterhouse & Son*, 1895–7) the Prudential Assurance Co. Quite at home in this company is the huge American-style free classical NEWSPAPER OFFICE of the *Dundee Courier* (by *Niven & Wigglesworth*, 1904).

The earlier twentieth century to the present day

HOUSING has been the dominant building type in Dundee and Angus since 1920. Dundee's overcrowded Victorian tenements, containing only rudimentary sanitation and mostly without bathrooms, were supplemented or replaced by massive new housing schemes, until the end of the C20 mostly undertaken by the City Council. In the 1920s and 1930s these were generously laid out, notably at the Logie and Craigie developments, but lacked public or commercial centres. Usually the buildings consisted of two-storey piend-roofed flatted blocks, each often containing four dwellings. A few developments belie the general impression of unimaginative drabness. In Dundee, a group of harled houses with gently assertive gables at their fronts was built in Clive Road and the neighbouring streets N of Kingsway in 1922–4 for the Dundee Garden City Association Ltd, showing how a touch of imagination could make the most of a tight budget. At Montrose, a V-plan block of flats in Ferry Street by *W. M. Patrick & Co.*, 1937–8, gives a touch of cheerful modernity, its cream-harled walls (originally) enlivened by horizontal bands of red brickwork.

Further large-scale housing developments, also mostly for local authorities, was undertaken from the 1950s. This included the layout of huge new estates to the N of Dundee, cut off physically and psychologically from the rest of the city by the arterial traffic route of Kingsway. One of these northern developments, Ardler, was provided in the 1960s and 1970s with a small civic centre at Turnberry Avenue where curved low-rise blocks of flats above shops face a complex which contained a library, halls, theatre and clinic and a pair of primary schools. For most of Dundee's developments, however, individuality of a sort has been provided by randomly sited tower blocks, the most pleasantly sited, among the mature trees of a Victorian garden, the fifteen-storey towers (by *Crudens Ltd*, 1962–4) of Pitalpin Court and Lansdowne Court at Lochee, the most impressive, if only because of their twenty-three- and twenty-four-storey height, the 1960s towers beside Strathmartine Road (by *James Parr & Associates*) and, now demolished, Alexander Street (by *Ian Burke, Martin & Partners*) at Hilltown. In the early C21 well-mannered large blocks of flats have been built along the Waterside of Dundee, well provided with balconies to enjoy views over the Firth of Tay, and more are now (2011) under construction. More joyous is the nine-storey 104
Wishart Place (by *James F. Stephen*, 1996–2000), a nine-storey Postmodern block, colourful with walls of red brick and reconstituted stone and roofs of ribbed blue metal.

The interwar years saw one significant piece of PUBLIC AND COMMERCIAL REDEVELOPMENT in the centre of Dundee, the formation of City Square, a large space stretching back from High Street to the newly completed Caird Hall. Its N side was opened to the street by the removal of the 1732 Town House, the E and W sides developed in 1929–34 in an uninspired classical manner with a mixture of commercial premises, the new City Chambers and municipal offices. Elsewhere, small-scale redevelopment took place, e.g. the erection in Commerce Street, Arbroath, of a single-storey classical savings bank by *Hugh Gavin*, 1924. Polite infill continued into the 1950s, notably with the erection of Royal Exchange Buildings in Meadowside at Dundee in 1956–7, *Gauldie, Hardie, Wright & Needham*'s design carefully detailed in a Modern-traditional manner. Much less polite are Dundee's two main city centre commercial developments of the

1960s and 1970, both removing large parts of the urban fabric. The Overgate Centre was formed in 1961–71 and redeveloped in smarter form in 1998–2000, the Wellgate Centre in 1974–8. More welcome have been office blocks on the northern edge of Dundee; the flat-roofed brown brick Timex Building by *Beard & Bennett*, 1946, a gentle introduction to the Modern Movement, the effectively mannered Olivetti (now Balgray) Building of 1971, and the commanding presence of *James F. Stephen*'s Discovery Centre of 1999–2001.

Most SCHOOLS after 1920 were built to serve new housing areas. One in Dundee, however, the Harris Academy designed by *Thoms & Wilkie* in a Modern-traditional manner in 1928 was built to offer secondary education to pupils of academic ability from a wider geographical area. The Harris Academy is ashlar-faced but usually Dundee schools of the interwar years are brick-walled, of two storeys and designed in a Neo-Georgian manner, e.g. St Joseph's Primary School by *Thoms & Wilkie*, 1931–2 or Rockwell School of 1930–2 and St Mary's Primary School of 1936, both by *Allan & Friskin*, one with Neo-Egyptian detail, the other with hints of awareness of the Modern Movement. Many new schools in the area date from the 1950s and 1960s. Some, like Webster's High School at Kirriemuir of 1954, its walls faced with brick and render, its roofs of shallow pitch, or the curtain-walled Forfar Academy by *J. B. Yates*, 1965, are replacements on new sites for C19 schools. Many more, especially in Dundee, were in new housing developments. Those of the 1950s are generally in a lightweight Festival of Britain manner with shallow-pitch roofs (e.g. schools by the Dundee City Architect, *Robert Dron*, at Charleston, Ardler and Fintry), those of the 1960s usually curtain-walled and flat-roofed. Sizeable new schools, again generally in Dundee but also elsewhere (e.g. at Newtyle), have been built in the early C21, colourful Postmodern the favoured idiom.

One very large HOSPITAL in Dundee was built in 1963–74.
100 This is Ninewells Hospital designed by *Robert Matthew, Johnson-Marshall & Partners*, a huge horizontally proportioned complex on a butterfly plan, faced with pale grey aggregate panels, a ribbed concrete tower providing the needed vertical accent. In
101 the grounds is Maggie's Centre, a day centre for those with cancer, a cheerfully quirky pavilion by *Frank Gehry*, 2001–3. Much smaller and more obviously welcoming than the institutional bulk of Ninewells Hospital is the Whitehills Health and Community Care Centre at Forfar by *MRT Architects*, 2003–5.

Few COLLEGE AND UNIVERSITY BUILDINGS were put up in the interwar years, the only one of significance *Robert Gibson*'s competently classical Dundee School of Economics and Commerce in 1928–31. The 1950s began with Duncan of Jordanstone College's timidly modernistic Crawford Building by *James Wallace*, 1953–65. However, in 1957 *Robert Matthew & Johnson-Marshall*
99 designed the University of Dundee's eleven-storey Tower Building in Scandinavian-inflected Modern Movement style. In 1971–4 *James Parr & Partners* produced the University's Students

Association Building, its front wall of reflective dark glass, and *Baxter, Clark & Paul* Duncan of Jordanstone's self-indulgently Brutalist Matthew Building. Also at the University of Dundee is *Austin-Smith:Lord*'s stylish metal and glass extension of 2005–7 103
to the 1980s Main Library. The University of Abertay Dundee, successor to Dundee's Late Victorian Technical Institute, achieved university status in 1994. Two years later it began construction of the Library to a design by *The Parr Partnership*, the main reading rooms in a glazed four-storey semicircle which projects from the side of a slender block housing the services, and with lecture spaces contained in a massive drum tower. The same architects were responsible for the Student Centre of 2003–5, a wilful although effective mass of glass, cast stone and wood cladding.

FIRE STATIONS were sited in or near housing developments. In 1931 a fire station designed by the City Architect, *David E. Maclay*, was built at Strathmore Avenue, Dundee, and consists of a piend-roofed Neo-Georgian block, the engines garaged on the tall ground floor. The Tayside Headquarters of the fire service at Dundee occupy a straightforward three-storey building and accompanying garage, by *James Parr & Partners*, 1967–70. Smaller but punchier is the same firm's fire station in Macalpine Road, Dundee, the front of its roof's broad eaves supported on red-painted metal piers.

Also governmental in character are the LABOUR EXCHANGES built since the early C20. Dundee acquired one in 1913–15, an authoritarian classical block by *W. T. Oldrieve* of *H.M. Office of Works*, a huge relief of the royal coat of arms on its corner. Another was built in Forfar in 1937, also designed by the architects of *H.M. Office of Works* in bureaucratic Neo-Georgian style. Less redolent of officialdom but hardly welcoming is the area's largest C20 POLICE STATION, the Tayside Police Headquarters in Dundee, by *Gauldie, Hardie, Wright & Needham*, 1974–6, a large three-storey block with narrow vertical windows and jazzy facing panels.

CINEMAS were ubiquitous in Angus towns in the 1920s and 1930s. Very few of these interwar picture houses have survived and none is now in use for its original purpose. Montrose's La Scala Cinema (now a bar), by *W. M. Patrick & Co.*, 1932, still stands, its rendered front with pediments over the front's end bays and exaggeratedly broad eaves at its centrepiece. A fairly faithful replica of the Art Deco tower which rose above the façade of Green's Playhouse in Nethergate, Dundee, designed by *John Fairweather* in 1935–6, was erected in 1996–7. Large and joyless boxes now house the screens of recently built cinemas, Dundee's Cineworld Cinemas of *c.* 2000 a representative example. Other centres of entertainment give more pleasure to the observer. The Art Deco W part of the present Carnoustie Leisure Centre was designed as a concert hall by *Allan & Friskin* in 1934. The Dundee Rep Theatre, by the *Nicoll Russell Studios*, 1979–82, is a strongly modelled assemblage of blockwork and glass hinting at hidden delights within.

VISITOR AND ARTS CENTRES are recent and not unwelcome invaders. Pictavia at Brechin (by *Oliver & Robb*, 1999) efficiently combines two pavilions, one round and containing the exhibition space, the other an octagon housing shops and a restaurant. At
108 Arbroath, the Harbour Visitor Centre by *Baxter, Clark & Paul*, 2006–7, is also a collection of pavilions, here under high aluminium roofs appropriately suggestive of ships' prows. It houses another restaurant, shops and a tourist office. Just missing elegance is Dundee's Discovery Point, by the *Michael Laird Partnership*, 1992–3, a two-storey octagonal visitor centre standing beside the old Ferry Harbour. More focused on the aesthetically or scientifically inquisitive visitor are Dundee's more recent contri-
107 butions. *Richard Murphy*'s Dundee Contemporary Arts of 1997–9, housing cinemas, exhibition and workshop space and a café, is a stylish combination of patinated copper and glass. The Sensation Science Centre, Dundee, by *Merrylees & Robertson*, 1999–2000, is also not without presence, a large monopitch-roofed shed housing the exhibition space and fronted by a narrow metal and glass box containing the circulation areas and café. Potentially the most adventurous of C21 buildings is the planned V&A in Dundee.

RURAL MANSES, FARMHOUSES AND STEADINGS

In Angus, as elsewhere in Scotland, AGRICULTURE BEFORE THE LATER EIGHTEENTH CENTURY was essentially medieval. Land was divided into farms, each worked by about ten to twenty-five families living together in a ferm toun. The arable land, used predominantly for the growing of barley and oats, consisted of a continuously cultivated 'infield' on which was spread all available manure, and an 'outfield' which received no manure but where was practised a rudimentary form of crop rotation including one-third being left fallow each year. Beyond the arable land was rougher pasture ground grazed during the summer by livestock, chiefly consisting of cattle of which many were sold or slaughtered at the onset of winter, the remainder housed in the ferm toun, often under the same roofs as its human inhabitants.

FARM BUILDINGS were generally cruck-framed, the structural supports consisting of pairs of birch crucks pinned together and with each pair joined to the next by thin longitudinal strips of wood. This framework was covered with walling, in Angus usually composed of alternating layers of stone and turf, and roofed with turfs or straw thatch. The humbler houses were without windows. The only opening in the walls of such was the door, sometimes serving as the entrance for both the human occupants and the cattle housed at one end. A further modicum of light and ventilation was provided by a hole in the roof serving as the outlet for smoke from the fire on a central hearth. More prosperous dwellings might have one or two windows and contain a couple of rooms, one the kitchen in which landless servants slept, the other the family's room, perhaps equipped with a hanging chimney.

MANSES were usually the most substantial buildings in the countryside after lairds' houses. In 1663 the Scottish Parliament laid down that the heritors (landowners) of each parish were bound to provide a manse and offices, usually a barn, stable and byre, costing between £400 and £1,000 Scots (*c.* £27–£85 sterling) in accordance with the wealth of the parish. Some late C17 and early C18 manses showed little pretension. In 1721 the upland parish of Lochlee acquired a manse which comprised a slate-roofed main block of *c.* 8.2 m. by 4 m. internally, of two storeys but with walls only 3.6 m. high, containing two rooms on each floor, one of these a kitchen. The offices (a stable and byre) were contained in a 6 m.-long turf-roofed low range. Considerably more substantial was the new manse for the more prosperous parish of Aberlemno whose construction was ordered in 1717 by the Presbytery of Forfar which specified that the two-storey slate-roofed main block was to be 13.4 m. by 6 m. externally and 5.6 m. high.

Following a decision of the Court of Session in 1760 that the upper limit on the cost of a new manse did not apply to the rebuilding of an existing one, more substantial new manses were put up in the late C18 and beginning of the C19. At Lintrathen the old manse ('a wretched hovel, covered with thatch') was replaced in 1795–9 by a new two-storey house containing six rooms, a kitchen, dairy and cellar. Of the same date was Cortachy Manse, its two-storey main block and lower kitchen wing both covered with slated roofs, the roofs over the barn and cartshed of 'grey' slates (sandstone slabs). The main blocks of the manses at Fern and Lethnot, both built in 1808–11, were each of two storeys and measured 12.2 m. by 6.1 m. internally. In 1813 it was reported* that new manses in Angus generally contained two public rooms and four or five bedrooms and that manse offices consisted of a barn, stable, byre, cart house and washing house. A couple of early C19 manses display modest architectural ambition. Craig Parish Manse (now Kirkton House) of 1805 has turret-buttresses at the corners and a parapet decorated with blind arcading. Arbirlot Parish Manse (now The Glebe House) of 1834–5 is L-plan, the inner angle containing a porch whose entrance is placed between Roman Doric columns *in antis*.

Between the 1740s and 1800 corn prices in Scotland rose by over 160 per cent. In 1770 Parliament passed an act 'to encourage the improvement of Lands . . . in that Part of Great Britain called Scotland' which allowed owners of entailed estates to borrow money against the security of their estates on condition that it was spent on such improvements as the enclosure and draining of land, tree-planting and the erection of farmhouses and steadings. Very patchy AGRICULTURAL IMPROVEMENTS, such as the growing of turnips as winter food for livestock, had been in progress for some time but it was in the late C18 that these became general. Between 1771 and 1776 the ninth Earl of

* By James Headrick, *General View of the Agriculture of the County of Angus* (Edinburgh, 1813), 151–2.

Strathmore invested £22,283 in improvements to his Angus estates, and other landowners, such as George Dempster of Dunnichen or Sir David Carnegie of Pittarrow, owner of the Southesk estates, were investing at the same time. The major change to agriculture was the establishment of sizeable farms, each held by an individual tenant on a reasonably long lease (nineteen years was standard by *c.* 1800), laid out in regular fields, with crop rotation practised on arable lands, and with winter shelter and food provided for livestock. A further fillip to improvement was the boom in agricultural prices during the Napoleonic Wars when economic blockade cut off imports from Continental Europe.

Accompanying these changes was the widespread building of NEW FARMHOUSES AND STEADINGS, constructed generally at the expense either of the tenant who was allowed remission of two or three years' rent in compensation or of the landlord who was consequently able to charge a higher rent. Except in the predominantly pastoral upland areas the new farmhouses resembled contemporary manses, being of two storeys, the walls of lime-mortared masonry, the roofs covered with slates or sandstone flags. Often the farmhouse occupied one side of a courtyard whose other ranges were occupied by farm offices. Some steadings were aspirational expressions of status. One block of 1761 in the steading at Ballindarg, near Kirriemuir, boasts a prosperous-looking birdcage bellcote. The entrance built in 1771 to the steading of Old Montrose, near Maryton, was surmounted by an octagonal tower topped by a domed cupola. The steading built at Balmadies by the agricultural theorist, Henry Stephens, in the 1820s extended round three courtyards. These buildings have been largely lost but an exceptionally grand castellated courtyard steading of *c.* 1800 survives at Langley Park, a battlemented tower rising in the centre of one range. One feature common to most steadings of the late C18 and early C19 was a threshing mill, often powered by a horse trudging round the interior of a conical-roofed circular shed, although horse-power was increasingly replaced in the C19 by steam power. New COTTAGES for farm servants by the early C19 were generally built of clay-mortared rubble masonry and thatch-roofed, although the walls of superior examples were lime-mortared and their roofs of sandstone flags. By the mid century they were routinely constructed with lime mortar and often slated.

Both manses and farmhouses later in the C19 often acquired bay windows and an appearance close to that of contemporary middle-class suburban villas. The suburban products of speculative house-builders have too often been the seeming inspiration for new farmhouses and other rural dwellings of the late C20 and early C21.

Agricultural improvement continued for much of the C19, further land being brought into cultivation after it had been reclaimed by drainage, with the introduction of better breeds of cattle, notably the Aberdeen-Angus, and with much of the upland area given over to sheep farming, the bleakest parts serving also as grouse moors and deer forests. Although large-scale grain imports from North America led to a slump in the prices of arable produce from 1870 until the Second World War, except for a prosperous brief interlude during the First World War, livestock prices remained more buoyant. The late C19 and early C20 saw some redevelopment of steadings, often designed to house more cattle.

Major agricultural development in the lowland areas of Angus has taken place since 1950. The policies and subsidies of successive British and Scottish governments and the European Union have ensured that much of the land is intensively farmed with barley, oil-seed rape, vegetables, fruit and potatoes predominant. Mechanization has strengthened the shift to agriculture of a quasi-industrial character accompanied by buildings of similar nature, often constructed of asbestos-cement, fibre cement and pre-cast concrete, the surviving earlier stone-walled former steadings converted to commuter or retirement housing.

INDUSTRIAL BUILDINGS

From medieval times until the end of the C18 tenants of farms were legally bound to bring their grain crops to their laird's mill for threshing, and GRAIN MILLS were among the most prominent buildings in any parish. Usually water-powered although a few were windmills, most stood near a river from which a lade or artificial channel controlled the flow of water to the wheel driving the machinery. After the act of 1799 which allowed for commutation of this servitude for the payment of a sum of money, most of the larger new farm steadings were equipped with their own threshing mills and many of the former lairds' mills were demolished or converted to other uses. However, grain mills did continue in use although in smaller numbers, and several were built or rebuilt in the mid and later C19. Their design is usually straightforward and unpretentious although a distinctive picturesque quality can be given by pagoda-roofed kilns in which grain was dried.

The agricultural improvements of the late C18 and early C19 were served by some industrial processes. One was the crushing of bones to provide phosphate fertilizer, and a steam-powered BONE MILL was built at Dundee in the 1820s and another, also serving as a flax mill, at Newtyle in the 1830s. Another and widespread component of agricultural improvement was the use of lime to increase the fertility of fields as well as for mortar for building. Early LIMEWORKS had been inefficient horizontal or clamp kilns, often of a temporary nature, but from the mid C18 permanent vertical stone-built kilns were constructed in which the lime was burnt over coal-fired furnace pots, the resultant liquid quicklime discharging through draw-holes. Among the earliest in Angus were the kilns built at Boddin near Craig by the landowner, Robert Scott of Dunninald, an early proponent of new agricultural methods. Another component of improvement was the tile drainage of fields and an extensive BRICK

AND TILE WORKS was put up at Anniston near Inverkeilor in the mid C19.

Wheat and barley were used to make beer and whisky, both produced from the early C19 in commercial quantities to serve urban markets. BREWERIES operated at Dundee, Brechin and Montrose in the C19. A couple of DISTILLERIES were founded at Brechin in the early C19 and others were built at Montrose and Arbroath in the 1880s and 1890s. These have been demolished but in Seagate, Dundee, still stand three huge Late Victorian former BONDED STORES, Robertson's Bond in Lombardic Romanesque style with a gable at the centre of the front and a tower at one corner.

Other agricultural products served more specialized industries. Hemp was used in the manufacture of ropes and a large ROPE-WORKS was built at Montrose in the early C19. Arbroath was noted for LEATHERWORKS, the Leadburn Tanworks reputedly the largest in Scotland in the mid C19 although it closed soon after. Also at Arbroath an extensive shoemaking factory was constructed in 1882.

Far and away the major industry in Dundee and Angus from the late C18 until the mid C20 was the spinning and weaving of linen and, later, jute. Originally this was a cottage industry, the raw material being brought to the homes of workers who spun it into thread which they or others could then weave into cloth, but by the end of the C18 TEXTILE MILLS were being built. One of the earliest, of *c.* 1790 and now incorporated into the Claverhouse Bleachworks complex on the edge of Dundee, was a cotton mill but this was exceptional in the area whose mills were overwhelmingly devoted to the spinning and weaving of flax for linens. By *c.* 1795 flax mills had been built in the parishes of Auchterhouse, Glamis, Kinnettles, Lintrathen and Menmuir, the mill at Douglastown (near Kirkton) employing about thirty women and seventy children aged between seven and ten, and further mills were put up in the early C19. The earlier linen mills were water-powered but steam engines were quickly introduced. The flax mill built at Glamis in 1806 was originally powered by water from the Glamis Burn but by then a steam-powered mill had already been constructed at Arbroath, and in 1820 a 10-horsepower steam engine was added to the Glamis mill. By 1835 steam engines were in use at the rural flax mills along the Lunan Water, their sites evidence of the earlier reliance on water power. However, it was not until the mid C19 that steam power became general for both spinning and weaving and that hand looms were replaced by power looms. The first significant part of the Camperdown Works at Lochee was the Lower Factory which, when constructed in 1850, housed both types of loom. Fifteen years later the Camperdown Works acquired a massive boiler house surmounted by Cox's Stack, an 86.5 m.-high chimney dressed up as an Italian campanile. By 1875 all thirty-four of Arbroath's linen works were powered by steam.

In the second half of the C19 the flax mills in villages and the countryside were closed and mostly demolished. By contrast, a

plethora of new mills, some of gigantic size, were built in the Angus towns, all now linked by the railway network to Scotland's major cities and to the harbour of Dundee. Through this harbour, from the late C19, passed great quantities of jute for processing in specially constructed mills or linen mills converted to that purpose. Some of the C19 mills impressed primarily by their size The Chapel Works at Montrose fills one side of Dean's Green at the S end of the Links, the town's public park. The approach to Brechin from the S and E is dominated by the Italianate mass of the Den Burn Works, its presence emphasized by a corner tower. 111
Just W of Dundee's city centre is a stupefying concentration of mills, the Verdant Works almost domestic in comparison with the great E range of the South Mill developed between 1851 and 1875 as a three-storey and attic block of thirty-three bays articulated by pedimented sections. This can be viewed only obliquely. However, the late C20 widening of West Marketgait to a dual carriageway has allowed a full-frontal view of the front of the immense Tay Works, its N block of 1851–4 four storeys and an attic in height and thirty-five bays long, the architecture restrained classical but the central pediment displaying the coat of arms of Dundee and formerly topped by a statue of Minerva, goddess of spinning and weaving. Beside it, the lower S block of 1865 con- 112
tinues in the same manner but in more richly detailed form. Designed to be seen from a distance as well as from the adjacent street is the Seafield Works of 1859–61, its Italianate tower rising from a steep hillside above Dundee's Magdalen Green. Also set back on a hillside from where it stands sentinel above the Harbour of Dundee is the Upper Dens Works built in stages from 1834 to 1850, the main block's centrepiece with large engine-house windows and formerly surmounted by a statue of James Watt, inventor of the modern steam engine, the block's E corner with a tall tower topped by a domed cupola. On the hillside's lower slope stands the same firm's 1860s Lower Dens Works whose asymmetrically designed twin towers proclaim the factory's superiority over the humbler buildings at its foot. Aloof from Dundee and surrounded by what developed as its own company town is Lochee's Camperdown Works, its High Mill spread out 113
along a hillside, its chimney (Cox's Stack) standing on the axis 114
of the great railway bridge over the Firth of Tay.

Other buildings were linked directly or indirectly to the textile industry. CALENDERS, housing machines for the glazing and pressing of finished cloth, were often attached to mills, as at the Camperdown Works. However, they might occupy separate premises. In Dundee the East Port Calender of 1913 was built behind a polite splayed façade of thirty-three bays. Much more assertive is the same city's turreted Flemish-Baronial Victoria 110
Road Calender of 1874–5. Also constructed for the finishing of linens were the area's BLEACH WORKS. The bleaching process required the cloth to be steeped in a hot alkaline solution, from the late C18 usually chlorine-based, and then to have acid, generally vitriol (sulphuric acid) applied. By the late C19 there were works for the manufacture of these CHEMICALS at Carnoustie,

Arbroath and Montrose as well as Dundee. Not surprisingly factories for the manufacture of MACHINERY for mills, as well as for agricultural uses, were also built in the towns of the area.

The growth of towns in the C19 was accompanied by some attempts to provide utilities. GASWORKS, whose redistillation of coal tar produced the fuel for lighting streets and houses, were constructed from early in the C19, the first gas company in Dundee being founded in 1825 and one at Montrose two years later. Initially private companies, from the later C19 they came under the control of burgh councils who sometimes undertook large-scale expansion of capacity; one gasholder at Dundee, when erected in 1881, was the second largest in Scotland.

C19 urban WATERWORKS, replacing or supplementing the supply from earlier wells, were also at first constructed by private companies but then taken into municipal ownership and, by the late C19, reservoirs were formed at considerable distances from towns, Dundee being served by reservoirs at Monikie and, after 1875, from the Loch of Lintrathen. The most prominent buildings associated with these works are WATER TOWERS, one on the
71 N entry to Montrose a tall octagonal Tudor structure of 1841, another, constructed at Arbroath in the 1880s, appearing as a Baronial fortification. Also Baronial and of martial aspect was the sluice chamber built in 1873 at Clepington Road, Dundee, and the Edwardian walls and towers which give Dundee's Stobsmuir Reservoir something of the appearance of a prison. Much smaller and looking like a doocot is the water tower provided at the same city in 1921 to serve a new housing scheme in Stirling Avenue.

GAZETTEER

DUNDEE 4030

INTRODUCTION

The most incoherent of Scotland's cities, Dundee, with a population of over 130,000*, occupies a series of terraces rising from the shore of the River Tay with the volcanic vents of Balgay Hill and Dundee Law serving as dramatic vertical accents.

The city has developed from a royal burgh founded beside a castle in the C12. The castle was destroyed during the Wars of Independence but by the mid C14 Dundee was recognized, together with Edinburgh, Aberdeen and Perth, as one of the four great towns of Scotland. Probably by that date it was surrounded

* Excluding Broughty Ferry, Barnhill, West Ferry and the rural areas now within the City of Dundee boundary.

by a wall, except on the S where the Tay formed the boundary, which ran along the lines of the present West Marketgait, Bank Street and East Whale Lane just E of East Marketgait. Apparently also of medieval origin was the suburb of Hilltown climbing the steep hill to the N and bordering the road to the inland burghs of Angus, this suburb granted the status and privileges of a burgh of barony in 1672.

The late C18 and early C19 was a time of prosperity and growth for Dundee when extensive improvements were made to its harbour, and a flax-spinning and linen-weaving industry grew up in the town and its immediate neighbourhood. The population, which had risen from *c.* 8,000 in the mid C17 to *c.* 12,000 in 1755, soared to over 19,000 by 1788, almost 27,000 by 1801 and over 45,000 by 1831. This was accompanied by a major expansion of the town whose surrounding wall had been removed *c.* 1760. The area N of Bank Street was laid out as a formally planned 'New Town', other regularly formed genteel housing developments constructed on the line and in the vicinity of Nethergate to the W, more randomly sited industrial buildings, some of great size and civic grandeur, erected to the NW and E of the medieval burgh and villas placed beside the Tay to the SW and on the high ground to the N. At the same time was begun a redevelopment of the rural settlement of Lochee as the company town of the massive new Camperdown Works.

Expansion of Dundee and its industry continued through the mid and later C19, this growth accompanied by the development of railway links to other towns and cities from the 1830s and by improvements to the harbour. The population rose to over 90,000 in 1861, over 140,000 in 1881 and more than 160,000 at the end of the C19. The town centre was largely redeveloped with new commercial buildings of a size and dignity worthy of a major city and with broad new streets pushed through the old layout of closes and lanes. Suburban expansion continued with the construction of further factories and mills for the production of linens and later jute, tenements to house the blue- and white-collar workforce of the various enterprises and villas for mill-owners and members of the managerial and professional classes, access to the more distant parts of the conurbation provided from the 1870s by an extensive tramway network. In 1889 Dundee was granted city status.

The interwar years were a period of relative stability for Dundee, its population fairly constant at about 165,000. The major changes were the building, predominantly by the City Council, of a huge amount of new housing and the construction in 1920–34 of a bypass (Kingsway) which runs in an arc round the N side of the urban conurbation and which served as the outer boundary of new developments.

After the Second World War radical changes were made to Dundee. In 1965–80 a dual-carriageway inner ring road (Marketgait) was formed round the rough oblong of the city's commercial centre, cutting it off physically and psychologically from the harbour to the S and housing on the other sides, the physical barrier made the more daunting by the volume of traffic brought to this road by the opening of the Tay Road Bridge in 1966. The city centre itself acquired two new shopping and office complexes, the Overgate Centre and the Wellgate Centre. At the same time the textile industry, the dominant employer of Victorian and early C20 Dundee, suffered terminal decline. All but one of the mills had closed by 2000, several subsequently demolished, others converted to commercial uses or housing. Widespread slum clearance removed many late C19 tenements and Dundee became notable for its 1950s and 1960s tower blocks, many of them now in turn demolished or under threat, as well as extensive lower-rise housing. New factories were constructed along Kingsway, now partly replaced by large shopping complexes. The farmland to the N became the site of huge new housing developments accompanied by only a handful of small shops. Much of this was replaced at the beginning of the C21 by speculatively built private housing, the quality of architecture and generosity of layout hardly noticeable improvements on the municipal estates they have succeeded.

The first years of the C21 have witnessed a massive attempt by Dundee to affirm its civic pride in the 'City of Discovery'. Physically, efforts have been concentrated in the Waterfront area containing the C18 and C19 Harbour left disused by the shift in port activities to the E. New blocks of flats allowing executives to enjoy the views over the Tay to Fife, join with exhibition buildings (most strikingly the yet unbuilt V&A at Dundee), to provide what is intended as the vibrant and culturally dynamic quarter of the city.

CITY CENTRE

The area within the dual-carriageway box of Marketgait, the city's inner ring road. It contains most of the medieval burgh of Dundee and the 'New Town' laid out to its N at the beginning of the C19.

The medieval burgh consisted of a tight-knit layout of closes and alleys running N–S off the broad spine of High Street and Nethergate. In the late C18 and C19 this was cut through by new streets and most of the few surviving early buildings S of High Street were demolished in the early C20 when City Square was formed. In the late C20 large areas N of High Street were replaced by the shopping and office developments of Overgate and Wellgate. At the beginning of the C21 the area still has a vitality which is to be valued.

CHURCHES

ALBERT SQUARE (or GAELIC) FREE CHURCH, corner of Meadowside and Chapel Street. Secularized. More like an office block than a church, Italian Renaissance, by *David Mackenzie II*, 1868–9. Six-bay front of three tall storeys (the ground

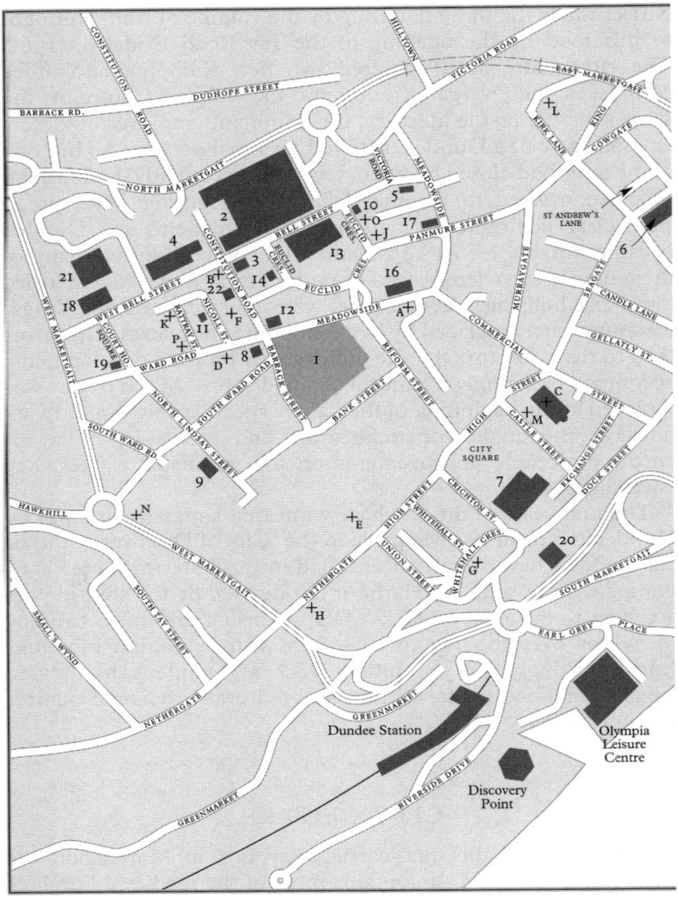

A Albert Square Free Church
B Bell Street United Associate Church
C Cathedral Church of St Paul
D Central Baptist Church
E City Churches
F Dundee Congregational Church
G Gilfillan Memorial Church
H Meadowside St Paul
J Panmure Street Congregational Church
K Rattray Street Baptist Church
L St Andrew's Parish Church
M St Paul's (Episcopal)
N Salvation Army Citadel
O United Original Secession Church
P Ward Road Wesleyan Methodist Church

1 The Howff
2 The University of Abertay Dundee, Old College

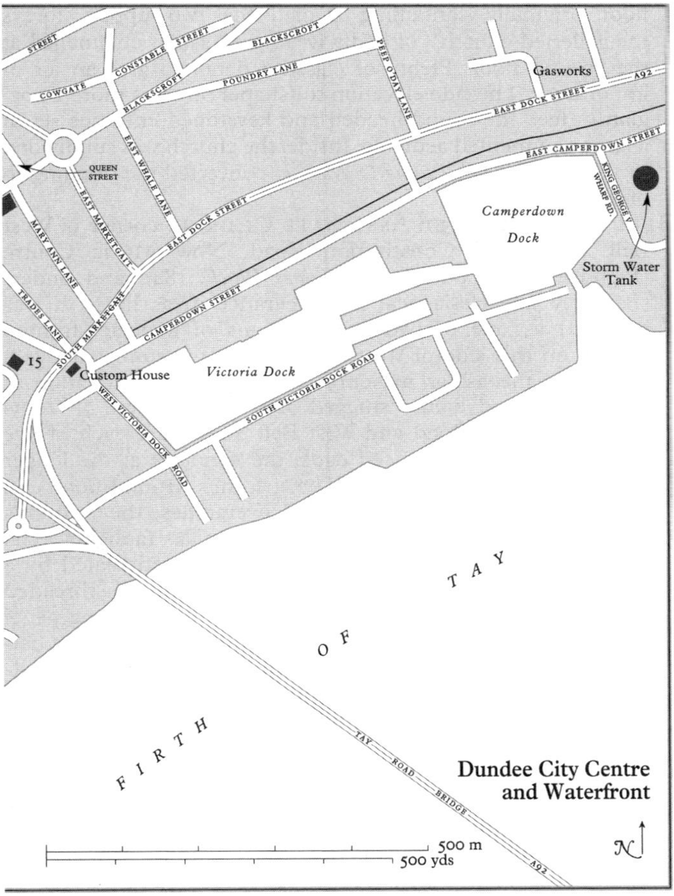

3 The University of Abertay, Student Centre
4 University of Abertay, Library
5 Bonar House
6 Bus Station
7 Caird Hall, City Chamber and Council Offices
8 Central Reading Rooms
9 Dundee House
10 Euclid Crescent School
11 Foresters' Halls
12 General Post Office
13 High School of Dundee
14 Margaret Harris Building
15 Jobcentre Plus
16 The McManus Dundee Art Gallery and Museum
17 Royal Exchange
18 Sheriff Court
19 Strathmore Lodge
20 Tayside House
21 Tayside Police Headquarters
22 Watt Institution

floor originally containing a hall, the two upper storeys the galleried church), of badly weathered ashlar channelled at the ground floor. Plenty of classical detail to give an air of importance. The side elevation to Chapel Street is more Georgian in feel, the round-headed and keystoned entrance set in a large pedimented aedicule. Inside, the church was subdivided in 1959 when *Dick Peddie & McKay* converted the building to offices.

BELL STREET UNITED ASSOCIATE CHURCH, corner of West Bell Street and Constitution Road. Now Music Centre (Dundee City Council). By *James Black*, 1840 and understandably unecclesiastical in appearance if, as likely, it was intended as one of two end pavilions of a palace-fronted terrace on this side of West Bell Street. Two storeys above a basement, the ashlar masonry with V-jointed rustication at the ground and lightly stugged above. The E and N fronts (to Constitution Road and West Bell Street) are each of five bays with slightly advanced ends, the windows at the longer E front more widely spaced. The E front's ground-floor end windows are set in round-headed overarches, the N front's end doorways surmounted by semicircular fanlights. The slightly recessed walling of the first floor is articulated by a procession of Roman Doric pilasters with a sill course threaded through them. Below the sill course, a moulded oblong panel under each window. Above the wall-head entablature are balustrades over the end bays, parapets decorated with round-headed arcading over the intermediate bays and a panelled and shallowly pedimented pedestal over the centre of each front.

CATHEDRAL CHURCH OF ST PAUL (Episcopal), High Street. By *G. Gilbert Scott*, 1852–5. Large urban church (given the status of a cathedral in 1905) intended as the central place of worship for Episcopalians in Dundee. The client was Alexander Penrose Forbes, Bishop of Brechin and Rector of Dundee, who had been strongly influenced by Tractarian ideas and had worked directly with Pusey. The style is Dec, the masonry of coursed snecked and squared rubble, all in line with the precepts of Pugin and, by extension, of 'Catholic' Anglicans.

The body of the church, so hemmed in by other buildings as to be hardly visible, is straightforward, a four-bay nave with tall aisles, their windows rising into gablets, transepts, a one-bay choir flanked by lean-to aisles (one now an organ chamber, the other originally a sacristy but now a chapel), and a semi-octagonal sanctuary. All is solidly buttressed. Well-mannered unassertive detail, e.g. the small gargoyles at the bases of the gablets surmounting the clasping buttresses at the N (liturgical W) corners of the nave, or the foliaged label stops of the windows' hoodmoulds.

What is clearly visible, and visible from a considerable distance, is the N steeple, its dominance the more striking for its being approached by a flight of steps up to the platform on which the church is raised. The general appearance of the steeple's tower is clearly derived from the medieval tower of Dundee Parish Church (St Mary's), as was noted by *The Ecclesiologist* in 1856.* Like the Parish Church tower, that of St Paul's is of two principal stages, each topped by a parapet walk or balcony, the dumpiness of this tiered arrangement offset by the vertical accent provided by the slender stair-turret rising at one corner, its 'perpendicular' quality praised by R.W. Billings in *The Baronial and Ecclesiastical Antiquities of Scotland* to whose publication in 1845–52 Scott had subscribed. However, Scott further emphasized the verticality of the stair-turret by placing it at one corner of the front of the St Paul's tower, not in the inner angle with the nave as at the Parish Church. More importantly, he gave his tower a spire, its height of 71.6 m. from the road below the church to the weathercock making the steeple the tallest then built in Scotland. Most of the detail of the Parish Church tower was eschewed in favour of restrained Dec.

At the base of the tower's N (liturgical W) front, a large pointed and gableted entrance, the bell capitals of the shafts austerely simple. Flanking the entrance, boldly projecting buttresses rising with two offsets, to the level of a string course above which the buttresses are surmounted by small square steeples composed of polished granite shafts with foliaged capitals carrying stone spires rising from between gablets, all decorated with crocketing. Projecting diagonally from the bottom corners of the spires, downward-pointing dragon gargoyles. The NE stair-turret is broached at this level from square to an octagon. Above the tower's entrance, a large two-light window. High up in this second stage of the tower, a pair of small pointed lights under the lower of the tower's two parapet walks or balconies. This walk is projected on simple moulded corbels and fronted by stone parapets decorated with circled quatrefoils (as at the balcony of Dundee Parish Church), the decoration continued as a broad band round the stair-turret; at the corners, large and muscular dragon gargoyles. The upper tier of the tower is slightly set back. In its N face, a twin-arched shafted and hoodmoulded recess containing two tiers of apertures, the lower small pointed single lights, the upper two-light belfry openings. In the tower's E face, a single-light version of this. At the top of the tower, a second parapet walk or balcony identical to the one below except that it is also carried as a projecting walk round the turret which is finished with a small spired caphouse. Within the parapet, a low square pedestal from which rises the octagonal stone spire, studded with five tiers of lucarnes and surmounted by a leafy finial and gilded weathercock. At the corners of the pedestal, solid versions of the steeples over the buttresses flanking the entrance.

* 'Imitated from the ancient tower, still existing, of the great church at Dundee, it surpasses it in elegance, while it has the addition of a spire, which in the other has long since perished.'

25 The abiding impression of the INTERIOR is of height (the apex of the nave roof 20.4 m. above the floor) and of light bouncing off the plaster of the nave walls and the pale ashlar masonry of the choir and sanctuary. Tall nave arcades (no triforium or clearstorey), their quatrefoil-shaped piers with simply moulded capitals. Hoodmoulds over the pointed arches, their label stops carved as angels except at the longer crossing bay where they depict human heads. A pointed arch at the end of each aisle into the transept. Open timber roof carried continuously along the nave and crossing. Over the nave aisles, lean-to roofs interrupted by the jerky lateral intrusion of the windows' gablets. Boarded roofs over the tall transepts. High pointed chancel arch, its clustered shafts carrying leafy capitals. Pointed arch either side of the choir into the organ chamber and Lady Chapel, each entered also through a low arch from the transept. Over the choir and sanctuary, stone rib-vaults. At the N (liturgical W) end of the nave, an arch into a gallery contained in the tower, its stone front pierced with quatrefoils.

REREDOS over the High Altar, designed by *Scott* and made in 1870. At its ends, coloured marble columns with white marble capitals and tall pinnacles. The columns support a gablet decorated with tilework and semi-precious stones. Halfway up each of its crocketed sides, an angel; finial carved as a pelican in piety. In the gablet's tympanum, a high-relief *Agnus Dei*. All this frames a mosaic (executed by the *Venice & Murano Glass & Mosaic Co.* from a design by *Clayton & Bell*, 1875) depicting Our Lord in Glory adored by an angelic choir, orchestra and thurifers. – Immediately to the W (liturgical S) of the high altar, a marble AUMBRY AND PISCINA, fairly routine Gothic from a design by *G. Gilbert Scott* but executed posthumously (by *Farmer & Brindley*) in 1888. – N of that, Gothic SEDILIA of *c.* 1855, made of varicoloured marbles, leafily decorated with carved angels at the bottom corners of the three gablets. In the gablets' tympana, high-relief heads of three men. At the back of each recess, a metal panel painted with stylized foliage and, at the centre panel, birds. – Oak CHOIR STALLS by the *Lord Roberts Memorial Workshops* from designs by *Mills & Shepherd*, 1949–63, of unexciting sub-Lorimer type. – ORGAN by *Hill & Co.*, *c.* 1860, enlarged by *D. & T. Hamilton*, 1869, and rebuilt by *Hill, Norman & Beard*, 1975. – Big double-sided brass LECTERN by *John Hardman*, 1855. – Octagonal stone PULPIT by *Farmer*, 1855, with polished granite shafts at the corners. On each of the four main faces to the church, the high-relief head of an aggressive Evangelist. Suspended over the pulpit, a mid-C20 wooden tester with angels at the corners.

FONT of 1855 in the N (liturgical W) bay of the nave. Its pedestal with squat attached columns at the corners, three of the faces carved with blind arcading, the fourth with foliage, was formerly in the garden of the Parish Manse at Newburgh (Fife); it may be C14. – Simple PEWS of 1855, designed by *Scott* and made by *William Cooper*.

In the W (liturgical S) aisle of the choir, the LADY CHAPEL formed from a sacristy in 1896, its walls partly lined with green-veined white marble in 1922. – The chapel's ALTARPIECE of *c.* 1920 depicts the Annunciation. – The E (liturgical N) transept was fitted up as a CHAPEL in the C20, its altarpiece with statues of the Crucifixion. Contemporary wooden sacrament house.

MONUMENT in the E (liturgical N) wall of the chancel to Bishop Alexander Penrose Forbes †1875, designed by *G. Gilbert Scott* and executed by *Farmer & Brindley*, 1878, a Gothic tomb-recess of veined beige marble with darker marble used for the columns' shafts. On the sepulchre within the recess, a recumbent effigy of the coped and mitred bishop, his pastoral staff lying beside him. On the back of the recess, the impaled arms of the bishop and the diocese of Brechin. – In the floor of the choir, a BRASS of 1877 again commemorating Bishop Forbes, with a full-length portrait; in the upper corners of the slab, the arms of the diocese and of Forbes.

STAINED GLASS. The sanctuary's five two-light windows are filled with glass of 1855 (parallel scenes from the Old and New Testaments – the Expulsion from Eden, and the Annunciation; Isaac carrying the wood to Mount Moriah, and Our Lord Bearing the Cross; the Brazen Serpent, and the Crucifixion; Jonah, and the Resurrection; the Translation of Elijah, and the Ascension). It is by *John Hardman*, with characteristic bright clear colours and barely three-dimensional figures, a decorative complement to the architecture. – Also by Hardman (1856) are the two windows placed above the choir's side arches (on the W, Moses feeding the Israelites with manna, and the Paschal Lamb; on the E, Elijah and the Widow's Cruse, and Melchisedek). – In the small and high-set S windows of the transepts, depictions of the four Evangelists, by *Hardman*, 1856. – In the E (liturgical N) transept's four-light E window, glass (saints) by *John Hardman & Co.*, 1887, more self-consciously 'artistic' and less subordinate to the architecture than the 1850s windows. – The W (liturgical S) transept's W window (Scenes from the life of St Paul) is by *John Hardman & Co.*, 1875, the work midway in feeling between the firm's 1850s and 1880s work. – In the E (liturgical N) aisle, a three-light window of 1910, the glass almost impossible to see because of the building behind. – Also in the aisle's side wall, a window (Scenes in the Life of Our Lord, and emblems of the Evangelists) by *Gibbs*, 1855, strongly coloured and archaic, and (the Transfiguration) by *Hardman & Co.*, 1894. – The aisle's N window (Our Lord as the Light of the World and the Bread of Life) is by *John Scott*, 1864–5. – In the E aisle's side wall, S window (scenes from the early life of Our Lord) by *John Hardman & Co.*, 1875. – Then a window of *c.* 1880 (the Baptism, Fasting and Temptation of Our Lord). – The two windows to its N (miracles, and scenes from the life of Our Lord) are by *Hardman & Co.*, 1881. – The aisle's end window (Our Lord as the Good Shepherd and the Sower) is by *John*

Scott, 1856. – In the Lady Chapel, S window (the Nativity of Our Lord) by *Hardman*, 1864, and two-light W window (the Adoration of the Magi, the Flight into Egypt) also by Hardman, 1865.

CENTRAL BAPTIST CHURCH, Ward Road. Late Gothic, by *T. Martin Cappon*, 1894–5. Red sandstone N front. Large advanced central gable with a ringed cross finial. At the gable's base, a low and broad mullioned and hoodmoulded window (part converted to an entrance in 2001) lighting a hall inside. Above, the shallowly projecting and huge canted oriel window of the church itself. Tudor Gothic detail, each of the three faces with a crocketed and foliaged finial. The gable is flanked by slightly recessed and lower transepts (containing stairs to the church's gallery), each with a three-light first-floor window, the r. above a door set in a hoodmoulded overarch pierced by a trefoil opening, the l.'s inner angle with the main gable containing a battlemented single-storey porch, its entrance also hoodmoulded.

Simple two-storey HALL to the E, by *Oliver Chapman Architect & LJR + H Architects*, 2008–9.

The church's front entrance of 2001 opens into the ground floor's large vestibule (originally church hall). On its walls, early C20 MURALS depicting Landscapes of the Holy Land. The church proper occupies the building's first floor. Gallery round three sides, the supporting full-height two-stage cast-iron columns marking off narrow side aisles. The collars of the roof over the central vessel are pierced with quatrefoils and trefoils. The original pews were replaced by chairs in 2001. Panelled and apsed S sanctuary, the focus of attention originally provided by the pulpit and organ (now removed). – STAINED GLASS. In the sanctuary, a two-light First World War memorial window (a Christian Knight being Received into Paradise by an Angel) of *c.* 1920.

CITY CHURCHES (DUNDEE PARISH CHURCH (ST MARY'S), MARY SLESSOR CENTRE AND THE STEEPLE CHURCH), Nethergate. Complex of Georgian and Early Victorian churches on the site of the medieval burgh church of St Mary. That church, originally founded by David, Earl of Huntingdon, at the end of the C12, had by the beginning of the C16 developed into a vast cruciform building with a great W tower. In 1548 the Duke of Somerset's English army wrecked the church except for the tower. Subsequently the choir and transepts were repaired and fitted up after the Reformation to house several different congregations and in 1788–9 the nave, a roofless ruin since the C16, was rebuilt to house another congregation (now The Steeple Church). In 1841 a fire destroyed the choir and transepts. In 1842–4 the choir was rebuilt to house Dundee Parish Church (St Mary's), followed in 1846–7 by the construction of a new church (St Paul's (South), now the Mary Slessor Centre) on the site of the transepts, both these designed by *Burn & Bryce*.

13 The W TOWER is the only surviving part of the medieval church but a most important one, both for its design and its

City Churches, Tower.
Engraving by R. W. Billings, *c.* 1850

size, *c.* 12.2 m. square and 50.3 m. high, i.e. twice as high as the W tower of the Church of the Holy Rude at Stirling, the near-contemporary church of a burgh of comparable size and importance. Like the tower of the Church of the Holy Rude, the City Churches' tower seems to evidence two distinct phases of construction and design, both probably of the mid or later C15, the lower part finished with a parapet within which rise the two intaken top stages. Walling all of red sandstone ashlar, the base marked off by a string course. This string course, like the ones higher up, is also carried round the splay-sided NW stair-turret which clasps the tower's NE corner.

The two lower stages of the tower's W front are framed by angle buttresses which rise, with two offsets, to gabled and foliage-finialled tops, each tied into the main walling by a flying buttress. Just above the base of each buttress, an image niche, its corbel base carved as a man's head, the canopy decorated with stylized foliage, all this apparently much restored in 1871–3 by *G. Gilbert Scott* who carried out extensive repairs. Between the buttresses, at the bottom of the W front, a low bipartite entrance, the twin round-headed entrances contained in a single segmental overarch enriched with rosettes, the overarch in turn set in a rectangular frame which is provided by the jumping up of one of the tower's string courses. The doorway's jambs and trumeau are multiple-shafted. At the l. jamb, the shafts' capitals are carved with oak twigs and acorns issuing from the mouth of a boar and the frieze with rosettes; at the r., capitals carved with vine branches, a fox at one end and a crude human head at the other, the frieze with stylized foliage. The trumeau's capitals are decorated with thistles and the coat of arms of Dundee. In the tympanum above, inept 1960s carving of the arms of the city (replacing a depiction of the Virgin and Child) above a shield now bearing a star but which formerly displayed the arms of the diocese of Brechin. Over the doorway, a huge pointed window, its six lights divided 3:3 by a central mullion from which springs Y-tracery, the head filled with a pair of daggers. In the head of each half of the window (the l. restored in the 1870s), a spiral of cusped loops. Above the window, a hoodmould with headstops.

At the tower's third stage a large round-headed window, its hoodmould with pendant label stops. The tracery consists of a circle filled with quatrefoils, the reticulated design reminiscent of the W belfry opening in the late C15 crossing tower of Iona Abbey (Argyll and Bute). Above, a small window of two pointed and cusped lights, its hoodmould also with pendant label stops. The walling of the N face of the tower's lower part is unbroken by openings. High up on the S face, the small figure of a saint standing on a leafy corbel and framed by rectangular hoodmoulding. Above, a two-light window like that at the top stage of this lower part of the W front. In the E face, at the tower's third stage, a small image niche containing the figure of a saint. At the fourth stage, a rectangular opening set between four corbels, possibly intended to support more figures but there is no evidence of canopies. Finishing this lower part of the tower is a parapet supported on continuous corbelling and pierced by quatrefoils arranged in groups of three separated from each other by pinnacles, the front of the central W pinnacle with a niche containing a statue of the Virgin and Child, the corner pinnacles placed diagonally.

The tower's two-stage upper part is recessed. At the lower stage of the W, S and E faces, a trio of closely spaced cusped-arched belfry openings, their hoodmoulds with headstops; at the N face, its W end covered by the stair-turret, just two openings. A string course marks off the top stage. In its W, S and E faces, a pair of cusped-arched openings, also with headstops to their hoodmoulds; a single opening at the N face. On each side of the tower the gilded skeletal dial of a clock erected in 1882 to replace an earlier clock which had been removed in the 1870s. This stage is finished with a parapet pierced, like the lower parapet, by quatrefoils but here arranged in groups of five set between piers. These are the stubs of flying buttresses which, if completed would have formed a crown spire. Within this parapet, the tower's saddleback roof looking as if meant to be replaced by a grander termination. The stair-turret rises the full height of the tower, its walling broken only by a tier of small rectangular windows in the NW face and one small opening in the N. At the top, a continuation of the tower's top parapet within which rises a conical-spired roof.

The tower's INTERIOR is entered through an elliptical-arched porch in the thickness of the W wall. Its main space high and ashlar-faced; stone benches along its N and S sides and W end. The splayed E corners are finished with broad moulded capitals from which springs the head of the pointed arch (largely built-up) into the nave (now The Steeple Church). Placed against these splays and in the rectangular W corners are tall columns rising to bell capitals. At this level, along the side walls, are rounded corbels, presumably to support wooden galleries or a floor but, if a floor, presumably stopped short of the arch into the church. Above the bell capitals of the shafts, a second tier delicately detailed but much shorter bundle-shafted and foliage-capitalled columns from which spring the ribs of the tower's groin-vault, its centre pierced by a large hole to enable bells to be hoisted to the belfry above. From the capitals of the W end's upper tier of columns a string course extends W to join to the capitals of slender nook-shafts framing the W window.

THE STEEPLE CHURCH occupying the W two-thirds of the 'nave' is by *Samuel Bell*, 1787–9, and Georgian Gothic, a broad unaisled oblong built of polished red sandstone ashlar. At both the N and S fronts, sill courses link the two-light Y-traceried windows. At each side's wall-head, a quatrefoil-decorated frieze under a cornice projected on simply moulded corbels, the W corners surmounted by plain pinnacles. However, the S elevation is of four bays and its window surrounds have roll-and-hollow mouldings, the N elevation of five bays, the windows more economically set in chamfered surrounds. Here the central window is curtailed to allow space for a pointed door. Battlemented small SW porch built against the face of the medieval tower. 13

This church's INTERIOR originally contained a gallery along the E, W and N sides, with the pulpit standing at the centre of the S wall. This was recast in an architecturally cheerless institutional manner in 1964 when the E and N galleries were removed, a sanctuary formed at the E end and a boarded suspended ceiling introduced. The (altered) W gallery survives, its front's panels enriched with Gothick arcading which springs from drapery pendants. – Routine Gothic bench PEWS of the later C19. – Lorimerian COMMUNION TABLE of 1927. – Behind, a long bow-fronted late C20 PULPIT. – On the N wall, WAR MEMORIALS, the most accomplished of these a bronze tablet of *c.* 1920, the inscription surrounded on three sides by the flowing figure of a drapery-clad angel watched by a child from the bottom l. corner. A rather cruder oak version of this is of *c.* 1950.

ST PAUL'S (SOUTH) CHURCH (now MARY SLESSOR CENTRE) by *Burn & Bryce*, 1846–7, is T-shaped, filling the 'transepts' and the two E bays of the 'nave'. It is also of polished ashlar but its Gothic more serious and stodgier. The buttressed 'nave' bays continue the height of the Steeple Church but the wall-head lacks a frieze and is finished with a simple moulded cornice under a parapet. In each of the sides' W 'nave' bays, a basket-arched door set in a rectangular surround, its spandrels ornamented with cusped panels. The 'nave' windows are each of four lights grouped 2:2 either side of a broad central mullion finished with Y-tracery containing a pair of daggers. The main openings are cusped segmental-headed arches under pointed heads pierced by circles filled by quatrefoils. Windows of the same designs in the sides of the transepts, the W curtailed by doors detailed like those of the 'nave'. The transepts' N and S windows are huge, each of six cusped and pointed lights grouped 2:2:2, with spiralling cusped loops in their heads; cusped loops also in the Y-tracery above. The detail of the S side facing Nethergate, the town's principal street when the church was built, is more elaborate than that on the N, originally fronting the relatively narrow Overgate. At the S windows, bell-capitalled nook-shafts and hoodmoulds with pendant corbels; at the S, no nook-shafts and only the transept's principal N window is hoodmoulded.

The church INTERIOR was converted to halls, offices, etc. (the Mary Slessor Centre) after 1978. Much of the 1840s church survives as the Sports Hall. This is a high space under a groin-vaulted plaster ceiling whose ribs spring from corbels. Simple Late Gothic panelled front to the W gallery. – STAINED GLASS. Huge six-light N window (Our Lord, Old Testament figures, Saints and Christian symbols) by *The Abbey Studio*, 1950, brightly coloured and with small-scale designs, rather in the manner of Douglas Strachan.

The five-bay aisled 'choir' (DUNDEE PARISH CHURCH (ST MARY'S)) of 1842–4 is also by *Burn & Bryce* and of the same general character as St Paul's (South) Church. Aisles finished with plain parapets, their windows with Late Gothic tracery. In the W bay of each side, a door similar to those of St Paul's (South) Church. Near the N side's E end a link to the plain Gothic HALL added by *William Alexander* in 1896–7. Again the treatment of the S elevation is richer, having sturdy gabled buttresses, their front faces with image niches under tall Gothic panels. At the E end of both aisles, clasping buttresses with foliage-finialled pinnacles.

Along the sides of the choir itself, quatrefoil-pierced parapets. These stand on a wall-head cornice through which rise the clearstorey windows, each containing two cusped lights with Y-traceried heads, their ogee-arched tops prettily decorated with carved foliage. In the E gable of each aisle, a two-light window with bell-capitalled nook-shafts. Taller buttresses, also panelled and pinnacled, divide the aisles from the choir's E gable. This is treated like the W end of a medieval church and contains the principal entrance. It is a low depressed-arched door, the bell-capitalled nook-shafts carrying a simple moulding; rectangular surround like that of the aisle doors. Above, a great window of six lights divided 2:2:2 by bell-capitalled shafts, the pointed main openings set below spiralling cusped loops; loops of less exuberant character in the intersecting tracery of the heads.

INTERIOR divided into a clearstoreyed nave and aisles by five-bay arcades, the moulded round-headed arches springing from bundle-shafted pillars with rosettes on their foliate capitals. Over the nave a wooden hammerbeam roof with Neo-Jacobean pendants. Trabeated flat ceilings over the aisles, each compartment with a saltire design. U-plan GALLERY in the aisles and across the W end, its panelled front also Neo-Jacobean. Under the gallery, at the W end, oak PANELLING by the *Lord Roberts Workshops*, 1990. – Plain oak PEWS of 1939–40 by *Leslie Grahame Thomson & Connell*. – At the E end, the oak COMMUNION TABLE of 1884, extended at each end in the same Late Gothic manner in 1976. – Flanking the communion table, a FONT and LECTERN, both by *Ian G. Lindsay & Partners*, 1957–8, their style of late C17 inspiration. Behind the communion table, the PULPIT, also Late Gothic and of 1900. It is backed by a Lorimerian wooden SCREEN designed by Ian G. Lindsay & Partners, 1957. – S of the screen, a LECTERN made in the mid C19 from fragments of woodwork taken from the C17 pulpit of the former Dundee Parish Church. These include enjoyably Artisan Mannerist pilasters with tall foliate capitals. – ORGAN in the W gallery built by *Forster & Andrews*, 1865–6, improved by *John R. Miller*, 1908, and rebuilt in 1939 and again in 1969. Mid-C20 ORGAN CASE.

WAR MEMORIALS. At the E end of the N wall, a bronze tablet of *c.* 1920 bearing the relief of a soldier with rifle reversed. It commemorates the 205th (1st Dundee) Field Company Royal Engineers. – On the E wall, N of the pulpit, the Black Watch First World War memorial by *Thoms & Wilkie*, *c.* 1920. Elaborately carved Late Gothic tabernacle bearing the arms of England, Scotland and Ireland; in the centre, at the top, the badge of the Black Watch supported by angels. Inside the tabernacle, a bronze figure of Victory. The base of the memorial opens to reveal steel tablets engraved with the names of the fallen.

STAINED GLASS. Great E window (the Apostles among stylized lush foliage) by *Morris & Co.*, 1897, the figures from 1870s designs by *Edward Burne-Jones* except for those of St Matthew and St Paul which are of the 1890s and St Bartholomew which is from a design of 1865 by *William Morris*. – This window is flanked, at area level, by a brightly coloured and realistic l. window (St Columba and St Cecilia) by *T. S. Halliday*, 1968. Corresponding pictorial window (the Nativity of Our Lord; the Flight into Egypt) on the r., by *David Small*, 1867. At gallery level, above this window, two lights (the emblems of the smiths' and tailors' incorporations) probably of the 1840s. – In the N wall below the gallery, the E window (St Ninian, the Blessed Virgin Mary and David, Earl of Huntingdon (St David, King of Scots), the reputed founder of St Mary's Parish Church in Dundee), an example of Modernist realism, by *Alexander L. Russell*, 1958. – On its l., a window (Faith, Hope and Charity) of 1882 and also by Morris & Co. using designs of 1870–1 by Burne-Jones. – Next, a lushly coloured window (the Resurrection) by *Cottier & Co.*, *c.* 1890. – In the S wall, under the gallery, the light and clearly drawn E window (the Baptism of Our Lord) is by *Henry Holiday* (executed by *James Powell & Sons*), 1889. – Adjoining, a strongly coloured narrative window (the Good Samaritan) by the *Newcastle Stained Glass Co.*, *c.* 1885. – The next window (the Transfiguration) is darkly realistic and by Cottier & Co., *c.* 1880. – Beside it, a late C19 window (the Agony in the Garden) by *James Ballantine & Son*. – At the W end, under the gallery, the S window (a depiction of David, Earl of Huntingdon, being saved from shipwreck after asking the intercession of the Blessed Virgin Mary, together with eucharistic symbols and views of Dundee buildings) is by *Lorraine Lamond*, 1991. – Corresponding N window (peach and olive trees (symbols of Truth and Wisdom) and motifs from the coat of arms of the High School of Dundee) also by Lamond, 1989–91. – Most of the gallery windows serve as top lights to those below but one window on the N side (the Blessed Virgin Mary, the Dove and a man standing on an orb and looking at the sun) is by *T. S. Halliday*, 1966. – One (N) clearstorey window contains stained glass (Enoch and Abraham), by *Morris & Co.*, 1893, from designs of 1872 by Burne-Jones.

DUNDEE CONGREGATIONAL CHURCH, Constitution Road. Originally Ward Chapel. By *James Brewster*, 1832–3. Simple oblong but dressed up with a carpenter's Gothic front, the outer corners diagonally buttressed. The nave is marked off from the aisles by pairs of crocketed-pinnacled slender buttresses, the narrow wall strips between the buttresses rising into gablets and containing skinny recesses under foliage-carved ogee-arched hoodmoulds. In the front of each aisle, a hoodmoulded Tudorish door under a pair of lancet lights. In the nave's gable, a large four-light Dec window, its hoodmould with carved headstops; on the gable's apex, a chunky foliaged finial. At the W end, facing Nicoll Street, a lower chancel and schoolroom, plain Gothic by *Ireland & Maclaren*, 1880.

Spacious interior, the aisles separated from the nave by four-bay arcades, their depressed arches carried on wooden cluster-shafted columns. Flat ceilings over the aisles; over the nave a ceiling with minimally pointed transverse ribs springing from pendant corbels; the ceiling's lower panels were filled with small panes of obscured glass in diaper-patterned borders in 1901. Over the nave's E bay, a plaster vault of Late Gothic character. In the apse of 1880, a ceiling with heavy beams and stained-glass panels of 1901 depicting flowers. In the aisles and E end of the nave, a U-plan gallery, its oak-panelled front formed into a Gothick aedicule containing a clock at the bowed E end. Under this end, a glazed SCREEN by *Inglis & Carr*, 2003. In pride of place at the W end, the PULPIT (by *John Burnet*, 1850) backed by panelling below the apse's organ gallery. – ORGAN by *Holt & Son*, 1864–5, with stencilled pipes. It was rebuilt in 1880 and again by *John R. Miller*, 1902. – Simple PEWS of 1876–7. – The aisle windows contain decoratively patterned small panes of obscured glass in foliage-patterned STAINED GLASS borders, by *Donald & Smith*, 1902. – E window of 1901, its patterned glazing with stained-glass borders of stylized foliage at the main lights and coloured floral Art Nouveau patterns in the tracery.

DUNDEE PARISH CHURCH. *See* CITY CHURCHES.

GILFILLAN MEMORIAL CHURCH, Whitehall Crescent. By *Malcolm Stark Jun.*, 1887–8, and looking like a major public hall. English Baroque N front of polished ashlar, channelled at the ground floor of the slightly advanced centrepiece. This contains a huge cavetto-moulded round-headed arch, its massive consoled keystone carved with foliage. The arch surrounds the aedicular entrance, the fronts of whose corbelled pilasters are decorated with bowls of fruit and upright cornucopia, the Ionic capitals' upside-down volutes with putti in the centre; steep pediment, its tympanum bearing an inscription cartouche placed among foliage and flaming torches. The centrepiece's ground-floor cornice continues across the outer bays, each containing a shopfront under a three-light mezzanine window; channelled pilasters at the corners. The church itself occupies the tall first floor. Here the centrepiece is treated as a grandiloquent Ionic-pilastered and swan-neck-pedimented aedicule framing a three-light window with Corinthian column-mullions and a radially keystoned semicircular fanlight. In the aedicule's pediment, a relief of floating cherubs either side of an obelisk-finialled pedestal. Behind the pediment the wall-head served as a base for urns and a cupola, all now removed. In each outer bay of the upper floor, a window in a Gibbs surround and, above, a circular opening under a round-headed and drapery-carved hoodmould. Giant Ionic pilasters at the outer corners, their upper third fluted. They support obelisk finials at the ends of the wall-head's balustrades.

GLASITE MEETING HOUSE. *See* ST ANDREW'S PARISH CHURCH, below.

MEADOWSIDE ST PAUL, corner of Nethergate and West Marketgait. Originally St Paul's Free Church. Tall and Gothic with hoodmoulded lancet windows, by *Charles Wilson*, 1850–2. Cruciform, with an unaisled nave, full-height transepts and a minimally projecting S chancel, all built of stugged rough ashlar. Projecting boldly from the pinnacled front gable and set between lean-to porches is the dominant steeple. In the front of its buttressed tower, the steeply gableted entrance. Pairs of very tall openings at the belfry stage. Between these further gableted openings rise through the arcading-corbelled eaves. Octagonal stone spire.

Flanking the porches either side of the steeple are flat-roofed single-storey PAVILIONS designed in 1936 by *W. M. Patrick & Co.* as printers' offices. At the back of the church, an extensive but architecturally undistinguished HALLS complex by *Reid & Greig*, 1988–90.

Inside the church, roofs with spindly collar-braces, hammerbeams and pendants; the flat centre of the nave's boarded wagon roof is pierced by large traceried ventilator openings introduced by *James Maclaren* in 1882. – U-plan GALLERY on cast-iron columns, its front decorated with blind arcading under trefoil ornament. – Sanctuary at the S end, its back wall filled by the massive oak combined PULPIT AND ORGAN CASE designed by *Thoms & Wilkie* in 1902, the organ pipes placed under the three hoodmoulded lancet lights of the S window, the ends rising as towers supported on angels' heads; the ORGAN itself was built in 1901–2 by *E. F. Walcker & Co.* and rebuilt by *Rushworth & Dreaper*, 1971. – In front, a simple oak COMMUNION TABLE by the *Lord Roberts Workshops*, 1982. – FONT of 1902, a stone shaft supporting an octagonal marble bowl, its corners carved with the heads of angels.

STAINED GLASS. In the main S window, crowded and strongly coloured depictions of Faith, Hope and Charity by *Clayton & Bell*, 1898. – These are flanked by lushly realistic gallery windows (Moses; Isaiah) of 1910 in the S walls of the E and W transepts. – Flanking these in turn, two lights (St Andrew; St Columba) by *Alexander L. Russell*, 1949. – In the S wall of the E transept, under the gallery, one light (Purity) of 1910. – In the S wall of the W transept, under the gallery, a corresponding light (Fortitude) also of 1910. – In the E transept's gable, a three-light gallery window (Our Lord Leaving the Judgment Hall and, below, a smaller-scale Last Supper) of *c.* 1910. – The gallery window of the W transept (the Adoration of the Magi, the Baptism and Ascension of Our Lord and, below, smaller depictions of Our Lord Among the Doctors in the Temple, Our Lord Carrying the Cross and the Marriage at Cana) is also of *c.* 1910, a memorial to the parents and sisters of George Duncan and Jane S. Scrymgeour. – In the E transept's gable, under the gallery, two lights (Eunice and Dorcas), accomplished examples of realism of 1910. They flank the lusher depiction of the Good Shepherd of 1906. – In the W transept gable, under the gallery, two lights (St Peter; St John the Evangelist) of *c.* 1910 and like the corresponding windows in the E transept. Between them and much cruder, a light (St Paul of 1905). – The side windows of the nave under the gallery contain Christian symbols (the Dove, *Agnus Dei*, A and Ω, etc) all of 1910. – Under the gallery at the N end, a window (the Sermon on the Mount) of 1912.

PANMURE STREET CONGREGATIONAL CHURCH, corner of Panmure Street and Euclid Crescent. Secularized and now the Trinity Meadowside Building of the High School of Dundee. Decorated Gothic, by *David Bryce*,* 1854–5. Oblong and unpretentious except that the centre of each gable projects to suggest a nave and aisles behind. In the inner angles of the S end, octagonal stair-towers under slated and bellcast-eaved spire roofs with wooden lucarnes and wrought-iron finials. Crocketed and foliage-finialled pinnacles on the gable's diagonal buttresses. Nook-shafted door under a large rose window, the hoodmoulds of both with headstops. Three-light windows in the side elevations, the W side with flattish buttresses.

The interior is now subdivided by the insertion of a floor at gallery level to provide a ground-floor library and first-floor hall. The church's hammerbeam roof survives at the upper level.

RATTRAY STREET BAPTIST CHURCH, Rattray Street. Disused. Quite ambitious but lumpy Lombardic Gothic, by *McCulloch & Fairley*, 1878, the W gable front falsely suggestive of a nave and aisles behind.

ST ANDREW'S PARISH CHURCH, King Street. Originally the Cowgate Kirk. Set well back from the street behind an upward-sloping graveyard garden, an urbanely detailed Late Georgian kirk built as a chapel of ease in 1772–4 to a design by *Samuel Bell*. The work was financed by a public subscription initiated by the Incorporated Trades of Dundee who paid half the cost of construction.

The church is a large two-storey-height rubble-walled oblong 16
with a steeple at the W end. Principal S front of four bays. In each end bay, a door under a window, all round-headed and with projecting imposts and keystones. Between these a pair of large Ionic-pilastered Venetian windows, each surmounted by a carved stone swag; between the swags, an oval panel whose Latin inscription records the foundation of the building by the ministers of the Presbytery and the tradesmen and people of Dundee in 1772. Mutuled wall-head cornice with urns at the ends. Another urn on the E gable where a pair of round-headed ground-floor windows flank a small piend-roofed porch, a tactful addition. Above, a large semicircular window, its stone Y-tracery inserted by *Edward & Robertson* in 1874. Dummy oculus in the head of the gable. The N elevation is straightforward with a double tier of round-headed windows but the centre overlaid by the link to the halls (*see* below). In the W

* *William Scott* was executant architect.

gable each side of the steeple, double tier of round-headed windows under an octagonal attic opening.

The steeple (restored after being struck by lightning in 1970) is square, its tower's lowest stage of the same height as the church's wall-head and containing the familiar round-headed door and window openings. Slightly recessed second stage, with urn-finialled strip quoins at the corners. In each exposed face a Diocletian window under a stone swag; above the swags, oval panels, the S with an inscription recording the church's restoration in 1939. The corniced clock stage is cubical but with cut-out corners; in each side a round clock face (the present CLOCK a replacement of 1867 by *Alexander Keith*). Further recessed is the octagonal belfry, its upper part of polished ashlar and with Ionic columns at the corners; a rather small round-headed opening in each face. Truncated flattened spire roof on which sits the panelled and corniced octagonal base of the stone spire, its faces bearing oval panels; cast-iron weathervane in the form of a wyvern.

INTERIOR. Plaster ceiling with a mutule cornice and a small central rose in a foliaged border. Semi-octagonal panel-fronted GALLERY on Roman Doric columns along the ends and N side. Boxy PEWS of 1874. In the centre of the S side, a Neo-Jacobean PULPIT and surrounding railing, also of 1874 and designed by *Edward & Robertson*. – In front, the COMMUNION TABLE continuing the Neo-Jacobean manner but of 1921 and made by *Francis East & Co. Ltd.* – On its r., an octagonal domed brass FONT with reliefs of St Andrew on four faces, by *Charles Henshaw & Sons*, 1963. – Hung on the end walls under the gallery are Late Georgian BANNERS embroidered with coats of arms of the Trades Incorporations of Dundee. They were placed here in 1981.

STAINED GLASS. Varied and almost complete display of glass-stainers' work from the late C19 to the early C21. The two large S windows flanking the pulpit were filled in 1892 by the Nine Incorporated Trades and the Three United Trades with pictorial glass (Ruth; Our Lord in the Carpenter's Shop), both designed by *Gordon & Watt* and executed by *Lindsay & Scott*. – At this wall's E end, under the gallery, one light (the Good Shepherd) of *c.* 1880 by *Mayer & Co.* and typically painterly. – The corresponding window at the W end (Our Lord and Children) is also late C19. – Under the gallery in the E and W walls, a pair of windows (the Adoration of the Magi; Madonna and Child) by *James Ballantine II*, 1929. – In the N wall under the gallery, the W window (Celebration of the Weaver Craft) by *Alexander J. Galloway*, 2004, depicting a cross set among jute plants and emblems of the jute-making industry, all placed in a border which metamorphoses from the representation of a jute rope to that of a river (the Tay), purple and gold the dominant colours. – Beside it, a window (the Baptism of Our Lord) of 1975, a typical example of the work of *Gordon Webster* with small-scale draughtsmanship and strong colours. – Then, a similar window (the Good Shepherd) by *Walter Pritchard*,

1931. – This wall's semi-abstract and dark-hued E window (Life as Spiritual Phenomenon) is by *Douglas Hogg*, 1991.

At gallery level, the S wall's E window (the Crucifixion) is of 1971 and also by *Gordon Webster*. – Adjoining window (St Andrew) by *Mary Wood*, *c.* 1930, its realism slightly stylized. – At the wall's W end a realist light (St John) of *c.* 1885, a memorial to David Neave, and a colourful window (the Calling of St Peter and St Andrew) by *William Wilson*, 1957. – In the wall of the E gallery, S window (Adoration of the Magi) of 1971 and again by Webster. – The large centre window (depictions of The Howff, St Andrew's Parish Church and the (demolished) C18 Trades Hall, with emblems of the Trades and the Christian Life) is by *John K. Clark*, 1987. – At the S end of the W gallery, a window (Our Lord set among small Scenes of the Acts of Mercy) by *Gordon Webster*, 1967. – In the N gallery, the W window (the Risen Lord Appearing to St Mary Magdalene) was designed by *Neil Hutchison* and executed by *Gordon Webster*, 1973. – Further E, a semi-abstract light (the *Agnus Dei*) by *Douglas Hogg*, 1986. – E window of this wall, ('O Lord Protect us from Our Wisdom', with depictions of the life of the parish) by *Liz Rowley*, 2002.

ORGAN in the N gallery by *William Hill & Son and Norman & Beard*, 1921; rebuilt by *A. F. Edmonstone*, 1994. Simple Neo-Jacobean ORGAN CASE of 1921, by *Francis East & Co. Ltd.*

Bronze South African War MEMORIAL to the Tay Division Royal Engineers (Volunteer) Submarine Miners, on the S wall E of the pulpit, erected in 1910.

HALLS to the E, joined to the church by a dog-leg link from the centre of the rear wall, by *T. H. Thoms* of *Thoms & Wilkie*, 1973–5. Harled and flat-roofed. At the S end, the GLASITE HALL, originally GLASITE MEETING HOUSE, built in 1777 as a place of worship for members of a small Presbyterian denomination, converted to a hall for St Andrew's Parish Church in 1927 and remodelled internally in 1973–5. Two-storey harled octagon under a slated prismatic roof. Double tier of round-headed windows with projecting imposts and keystones. These are centred in the walls but the (blocked) doors, also round-headed, of the SW and NE faces are off-centre. Plain rectangular door in the S wall, presumably an insertion of the earlier C19 when a pedimented porch (now removed) was added here. – On the ground immediately W of the halls, three BELLS, all cast by *Park & Chapman* of London, 1777. Originally in the church steeple, they were removed after it was struck by lightning in 1970.

GRAVEYARD fronted by railing-topped dwarf walls S of the church, containing a few late C18 and C19 HEADSTONES. – GATEPIERS of 1821. Channelled ashlar with a pilaster strip up the centre of each face. They carry stone urns carved with foliage.

ST PAUL (Episcopal), Castle Street. Secularized. Built in 1810–12 on a site intended for a tenement and its height and rough ashlar flat front keeping the expected norm for the street, a two-storey-height chapel above ground-floor shops. The central entrance from the street to the staircase up to the chapel is ecclesiastical, a Tudor-arched door framed by bundle-shafted cast-iron columns and an entablature, the centre of its frieze enriched with a quatrefoil. Fronting the chapel above are three pointed windows, originally with transoms and Y-tracery but their heads now blocked and the glazing pattern below badly altered. Rising through the wall-head's cornice and parapet are corbelled shafts, their pinnacles now lost.

SALVATION ARMY CITADEL, West Marketgait. By *W. M. Patrick & Partners*, 1968. Restless, in brown brick, slate and concrete. Main hall at the S end, its vertical windows set between fins.

THE STEEPLE CHURCH. *See* CITY CHURCHES.

UNITED ORIGINAL SECESSION CHURCH, Euclid Crescent. Now part of the Trinity Meadowside Building of the High School of Dundee. Routine Gothic by *James H. Langlands*, 1891. Two blocks, the S of two storeys and an attic. W front of two bays, with hoodmoulds forming 'gablets' over the first-floor windows; on the wall-head, a pair of unequal-sized stone dormer windows. The two-storey N block presents a slightly advanced gable to the street. Cusped-arched entrance under a crocketed and foliage-finialled hoodmould. At the tall upper floor, a huge hoodmoulded two-light window, a roundel in the head.

WARD ROAD WESLEYAN METHODIST CHURCH, corner of Ward Road and Rattray Street. Secularized and now garishly painted. By *David Mackenzie II*, 1866–7. Spiky Gothic, the S gable front divided by gableted and pinnacled buttresses into a nave and aisles. Headstops to the hoodmoulds over the entrance and the five-light Geometric window above, the entrance's portraying women, the window's men. Procession of sturdy stepped buttresses along the E side. Projecting at the SW corner, a two-storey Tudor Gothic vestry of the late C19.

The church's INTERIOR is divided into a nave and aisles by arcades of pointed arches on cast-iron columns.

THE HOWFF

Meadowside

On the site of a Franciscan friary, the burgh burial ground from 1564 to 1857. The S and E sides are enclosed by the backs of buildings along Bank Street and Reform Street. On the N side, RAILINGS erected by *David Neave* in 1828. On the W, a BOUNDARY WALL, its outer face's S end bearing C17 moulded frames, presumably intended for heraldic panels. In this wall, a classical GATEWAY by *James Black*, 1833, the elliptical-arched entrance set between urn-topped pilasters, the cornice surmounted by the heraldic achievement of the City of Dundee.

The crowded graveyard contains a wondrous array of monuments dating from the late C16 to the mid C19, only a few mentioned here. The earlier are often grave-slabs, sarcophagi or in the form of miniature houses, some bearing reliefs of emblematic figures. By the C18 headstones are usual, frequently displaying the tools of the trade of the deceased together with a parade of grisly reminders of death.

The W WALL'S INNER FACE serves as backing for MONUMENTS. At its N end, a large and badly worn aedicule of 1718 commemorating Alexander Duncan of Lundie. – On top of the wall to the S, a monument erected in 1602 by James Mudie to mark the burial place of his family. Three long horizontal pilastered panels bearing coats of arms and the inscription. – S of this, three steeply pedimented rectangular recesses, probably of the early C17, each containing two compartments framed by paired fluted pilasters and divided by a moulded corbel. – Then a procession of twenty recesses of 1601 interrupted by the gateway of 1833. Each has a round-headed roll-and-hollow-moulded arch springing from attached columns, their bases scalloped, the capitals carved with stylized foliage. In the recesses, narrow stone benches to represent tomb-chests, their fronts decorated with skulls. – S of these, three more recesses, again of the early C17 but they are straight-lintelled aedicules, the steep pediments carried on paired attached columns, the lintels of the inscription panels' moulded surrounds supported on central corbels. In each, a narrow tomb-chest, the front carved with reminders of death. – Placed between the two N of these recesses is the narrow monument to James Guthrie †1710. End pilasters stand on a bracketed sill, each topped by its own steep pediment. The cornice between is surmounted by an oval heraldic panel topped by a grotesque head. – Two more round-headed recesses near the S end of the wall. – At the S end, the BLACKNESS AISLE, a mausoleum erected by Captain Lyell of Blackness in 1615. It is a tall ashlar shed, the large elliptical-arched E entrance flanked by shaft-ringed attached columns. On the back wall of the mausoleum, a big horizontally proportioned monument, presumably also of 1615. Tomb-chest decorated with reminders of death. Above are paired slim columns of a quasi-Ionic order supporting the basket-arched outer frame. Behind the columns are pilasters carrying the outer ends of a pair of basket arches, their inner ends supported on a corbel from which projects a console under the centre of the outer frame. The ground of the cemetery is laid out on a rough gridiron pattern, paths dividing it into compartments.

W BORDER. N COMPARTMENT. At its N end, the Neo-Jacobean sarcophagus monument of 1844 to John Bell. – To the S, the monument to Dr David Kinloch and his wife, Grizel Hay, †1617, like a miniature house, the Latin inscription carved on the pitched roof. – Some way further S, the table tomb of John Baxter, baker burgess of Dundee, †1609. At the top, two panels, each containing a coat of arms. Below these, a relief of Baxter embracing his wife, a skull and a bone perched above their shoulders. – Beside this, three mid-C17 coped table tombs (one to James Wat, flesher, †1641, another to David Vat, skinner burgess, †1646), each with a coat of arms at one end and emblems of death at the other. Two bear figures of Father Time and a man holding an hourglass at the ends of one side and, on the other, the Angel of the Resurrection and a figure emblematic of one of the Christian Virtues (on one it is of Justice), the figures copied from illustrations in Francis Quarles, *Emblems* (1635). – To the SW, another coped grave-slab, dated 1646 and with the initials IL and MC. At one end are carved tools arranged in a wheel, at the other a coat of arms. Strap-work-bordered inscription panels on the sides; at their ends, emblematic figures including one of Justice. – To the W, the broader and more shallowly coped grave-slab of James Goldman, merchant burgess, †1632, a coat of arms at one end, a skull and crossbones at the other; an angel's head peers over the inscription.

W BORDER. S COMPARTMENT. Near the N end, a coped gravestone to William Gibb †1645. At one end, a shield under an angel's head; at the other, an hourglass, skull and cross-bones. Inscription panels on the long sides. One is flanked by figures of Father Time and a boy holding an hourglass, the other by figures emblematic of Christian Virtues. – Exception-ally well preserved version of this stone to its W, now with an inscription to Thomas Scott †1783 but probably originally erected to commemorate Robert Muresone †1637. Has it been re-cut? – W of this, the grave-slab of Johne Kynnair and Eupham Gray †1627. Upper panel containing a coat of impaled arms and pairs of skulls and bones. In the larger lower panel, a relief of a man and woman holding hands, an hourglass in one corner. – S of that, a large broken slab, now with an inscription to Jean Knight but probably originally erected *c.* 1579 to com-memorate Thomas Simson. It is carved with a coat of arms supported by angels. – E of this, the coped slabbed table tomb of Thomas Bevoc, merchant, †1642, a shield at one end, emblems of death at the other. On the sides, inscription panels, one flanked by figures of Father Time and a boy with an hour-glass, the other by figures of Charity and Justice. – At the S end of this compartment, a tomb, probably of the early C18, to members of the Geekie and Steill families. Baluster-pilastered sides, the panels carved in relief, the two scenes still visible depicting St George and the Dragon and a skeleton and trees.

NW COMPARTMENT. In the compartment's NW corner, the monument to John Scrymgeour, Provost of Dundee, †1657, originally set against the N wall but moved when that wall was replaced by railings in 1828. It is an Ionic-columned aedicule, a pair of high-relief cherubs carved in the pediment. The sides of the frame of the missing inscription panel are decorated with fruiting foliage, its top with drapery surmounted by an hour-glass. – To the S, the headstone of Robert Bruce, merchant in Dundee, †1748. The W face is a joyful celebration of the Resur-rection, its top carved with a crown flanked by a pair of floating boys. Below, a helm-crested and mantled shield bearing a merchant's mark (like the figure 4) and flanked by torches surmounted by angels' heads. – E of this, three grave-slabs. One, perhaps of the C16, is carved with crude reliefs of a pair of skulls above a coat of arms. Another, for Cathrine *sic.* Clerk †1616, is incised with no fewer than four sets of skulls and bones. On the third, to James Flescher, merchant, †1584, low reliefs of a skull, shield and the *Agnus Dei.* – To the SW, the C17 coped stone to I.C., wife of Thomas Vichtane, notary burgess of Dundee. Inscription panels on the sloping sides, the S flanked by figures of a seated woman and a man and woman in C17 dress drawing a curtain, the N by a boy carrying a staff and Father Time. At the foot, a winged skull, crossbones and a bell.

In the NW CENTRE COMPARTMENT, a coped C17 gravestone bearing reliefs of Father Time, a boy holding an hourglass, and emblems of death.

Near the NE corner of the SW CENTRE COMPARTMENT, the headstone erected in 1759 by David Miller, maltman, to his sons, with a pair of grinning angels floating above a helm-crested shield. – Further S, an C18 headstone to RM and HB, the E face with a sorrowful angel's head, the W carved in very shallow relief with endearingly inept representations of a skull, bone, hourglass, etc. – Nearby, a very well preserved coped gravestone of 1683 to IM and IK. Narrow top panel carved with reliefs of a handshake and a sexton's tools. On the S side, a strapworked panel flanked by Father Time and a boy with a flail. Similar panel on the N held by trumpeting angels. The head of the stone is carved with a man in a boat, the foot with skulls and crossbones. – To the W, a worn grave-slab, probably C18, with a strapwork border and reliefs of a skull and crossbones. – NW of this, the coped gravestone of James Gourlay, maltman burgess, †1648, the top decorated with panels containing initials and a face, a barley sheaf, and the implements of a maltster. At the head, a coat of arms; a skull, crossbones and hourglass at the foot.

UNIVERSITY OF ABERTAY DUNDEE

Bell Street and West Bell Street

The university began with a bequest by Sir David Baxter †1872, principal partner in the textile firm of Baxter Brothers, who left £20,000 to establish a mechanics' institute in Dundee 'for the education of boys and young men in those branches of learning necessary or useful for working mechanics or other craftsmen'. As a result the Technical Institute (now the property of the University of Dundee, *see* below, p. 159) was built in Small's Wynd in 1887–8. Within twenty years this had become inadequate for the size of the student body and it was decided to relocate to Bell Street where a huge new building was erected. On its completion in 1911, the Technical Institute was rechristened the Dundee Technical College and School of Art, becoming the Dundee

Institute of Art and Technology in 1933.* By 1951 the Institute offered courses leading to external degrees of the University of London. In 1975 it was again renamed the Dundee College of Technology and in 1988 the Dundee Institute of Technology. In 1994 it was granted university status as the University of Abertay Dundee.

OLD COLLEGE (DUNDEE BUSINESS SCHOOL), overpowering the N side of Bell Street and rising above the High School of Dundee on the axis of Reform Street, was built in 1907–11, the massing and layout designed by *Robert Gibson*, the façade by *James H. Langlands*. This is squared-up Baroque on a massive scale, more of a bureaucratic bully than a swaggering Cavalier in character. Three storeys, the windows diminishing in size at each floor, all faced with purplish-coloured polished ashlar. Huge pedimented aedicules at the centre and ends and four-bay intermediate sections. Over the entrance a consoled pediment, the tympanum carved with swags of fruit and a central cartouche under a head of Minerva.

Abutting the W end of Old College's front, a lower 1970s block, its dark brown brickwork relieved only by the name and coat of arms of the University. This serves as a link to the KYDD BUILDING by *T. H. Thoms* of *Thoms & Wilkie*, 1967–75, the S front clad with concrete aggregate panels containing traditionally proportioned windows. Metal and glass entrance added by *The Parr Partnership*, 1995. Narrow addition by *Archial Architects*, 2011, at the W gable, the reconstituted red stone and copper cladding like that of the Student Centre opposite. Also by Archial Architects, 2010–11, the extensive remodelling of the large 1970s rear block.

STUDENT CENTRE on the SE corner of Bell Street and Constitution Road, by *Parr Architects*, 2003–5. Wilful but not without panache. Four storeys, its E end a cubist assemblage of glass and red cast stone and wood cladding. The main block's cast stone front, the roof curved up over its bowed W end, is set at a slight angle to the line of Bell Street, the triangular space in front filled by a narrow full-height second block, its E quarter parallel to the main building, the rest re-establishing the streetline. Above the ground floor, open except for the supporting metal piers of the structure, this front block is faced with copper cladding as far W as its almost fully glazed corner to Constitution Road. The internal layout provides little reason for the building's external division into two parts except for the siting of an agreeable roof terrace over the front block's NW corner.

LIBRARY on the N corner of West Bell Street and Constitution Road. By *The Parr Partnership*, 1996–8. Prominently placed

* The building in Bell Street also housed a school of art founded in terms of a bequest by James Duncan of Jordanstone †1909, and the technical college and school of art shared a single governing body. The Duncan of Jordanstone College of Art in Perth Road opened in 1955 and became a separate institution in 1975. Since 1996 it has formed part of the University of Dundee.

and stylishly designed invitation to students to discover the delights of books and computers. The building is composed of three elements, each with a clear function. At the back, a slim five-storey oblong housing back-up and service areas, clad in red reconstituted stone, the openings relatively few and small. On its S side, a four-storey fully-glazed almost complete semicircle which contains the reading rooms. Clearly visible metal structure; at the top, a boldly projecting canopy formed of metal strips. The semicircle's sweep is broken at the SE by the third element, a sloping-topped drum tower in which are placed lecture spaces. This breaks forward as a mass of red reconstituted stone pierced only by very small windows but with a bold glass band cut out around the ground floor's E segment. The line of the reading rooms' canopy continues N beyond the drum to cover the squared-off fully glazed end wall containing the entrance.

PUBLIC BUILDINGS

BONAR HOUSE, Bell Street. Originally the Dundee School of Economics and Commerce, it is now part of the High School of Dundee. By *Robert Gibson*, 1928–31. Routine classical of three storeys faced with polished red sandstone.

BUS STATION, Seagate. By *Kelvin Construction Co. Ltd*, 1957–8 Two-storey curtain-walled box set between granite-faced wings. The SW wing joins to a glass-sided hexagonal entrance hall (by *Dundee City Council*, 1997, replacing a circular waiting room) whose roof rises in prow-like form over the NE and SE corners.

CAIRD HALL, CITY CHAMBERS AND COUNCIL OFFICES, City Square. Stripped classical U-plan complex with public halls (the Caird Hall) in the S range and the City Chambers and Council Offices in the NW and NE wings.

The concept of a civic square, its S side filled by a new civic hall, had been accepted in 1914 by the Town Council and the jute manufacturer, Sir James K. Caird, who had agreed to give £100,000 towards its cost. At that time it was envisaged that the square's E and W sides would be occupied by new commercial premises, the space under the square by a covered market entered from Crichton Street and Castle Street, and that *William Adam*'s Town House of 1732–4 would continue to stand on the N facing High Street. The civic hall (named, on its completion, the Caird Hall) was built in 1914–21 to a design by the City Architect, *James Thomson*. Designs for the proposed commercial ranges along the square's E and W sides were prepared by Thomson in 1924 and submitted for approval to *John J. Burnet* who also recommended removal of the C18 Town House. Only the men's outfitters, Montague Burton Ltd, showed interest in occupying premises here and the N half of the E range was built for them in 1929–31. This range's S half was then constructed to a different design, by the Deputy City Architect, *J. McLellan Brown*, in 1931–2 as Council Offices, and at the same time was begun the W range, also to a design of McLellan Brown, as the City Chambers, formally opened in 1933 as a replacement for the old Town House which had been demolished the previous year.

The CAIRD HALL is fronted by a long block containing the vestibule, its N façade's polished honey-coloured ashlar walling pierced by only a few high-set windows, a trio of doors in channelled surrounds at the centre and identically detailed single doors at either end. Stretching almost the full length above a stepped base is a Doric portico, the columns set between panelled end piers; mutuled cornice under a high parapet. The taller hall block behind is barely visible from the front but its pedimented W end is fully exposed to Crichton Street as is its rear to Shore Terrace. This elevation is composed of a block of two storeys above an unsunk basement behind which the main part of the hall rises a further storey. Channelled masonry at the basement and ground floor of the lower block; at the first floor, corniced windows. Openings framed by broad anta-pilasters at the end bays of the hall itself.

The three doors in the centre of the colonnade open into a broad but short top-lit and beam-ceilinged entrance hall. Console-corniced surrounds to the doors' inner faces. At the entrance hall's long N and S sides, extravagantly capitalled Corinthian columns. At the short E and W ends, discreetly expensive wooden box offices. Off the corridor on the N is the Caird Hall itself, its decoration in a far from thrifty but not overcrowded Baroque manner. W gallery. At the E end, a shallow recess, its sides with emblematic classical reliefs, its back filed by a huge ORGAN (by *Harrison & Harrison*, 1922–3). Smaller Marryat Hall to the W with a single aisle on the W side. Pâtisserie rococo plasterwork on the coved beams and flats of the compartmented ceiling, the aisle pillars and walls' pilasters. Huge mirrors (now hidden by curtains) covering much of the N and S ends. The basement floor below originally contained meeting rooms and offices for the City Council, the principal of these at the W end later converted to council committee rooms. In Committee Room No. 1 (the former Council Chamber), lavish plasterwork of Louis XV inspiration. More of the same and also an Adamish chimneypiece in Committee Room No. 3 (the former Lord Provost's Room) to the S. Plain but pompous furnishings to the windowless Committee Room No. 4 (former Town Clerk's Office) just to the E, its S end divided off by a pillared screen and presumably originally containing a public counter.

CITY CHAMBERS on the W side of City Square, of four storeys under a mansard roof, the walling also of polished ashlar. Front of seven bays, the centre five advanced and with a granite-faced ground-floor loggia, its arches round-headed. Above the loggia, tall windows rising the height of two storeys and set in channelled surrounds above aprons which are carved in relief with emblems of the industries of Dundee. The central window's depth is curtailed by a door opening onto a granite balcony, intended for ceremonial civic appearances, its front carved with the City's coat of arms. Corbelled out above this *piano nobile*, a continuous 'balcony' in front of small windows. The front's outer sections are stodgy Neo-Georgian with three-light windows at the inner bays. At each end of the ground floor a large shopfront of faintly Art Deco character. The S corner is joined to the Caird Hall by a set-back and lower link faced with a convex shopfront. W elevation to Crichton Street plain Neo-Georgian except for a vertical Art Deco centrepiece and granite-clad basement.

Inside, a central entrance hall opens onto an Art Deco marble-clad grand staircase. Above its half-landing, a large W window filled with STAINED GLASS of 1933 by *Alexander L. Russell*, displaying Celtic symbols and small panels with views of the War Memorial on Dundee Law, the City Churches' steeple and the former Town House. At the first floor, the full frontage of the main block is occupied by the double-height Council Chamber. Plastered ceiling beams decorated with Art Deco motifs. At the S end, a recess containing a small public gallery, its front bearing the coat of arms of Dundee; above its door, a pair of carved wooden griffins which served as the heads of newel posts on the stair of the former Town House of 1732–4. Radiator grilles with emblems of events in the history of the city (e.g. a galley representing the supposed Norse settlement here, the ship in which David, Earl of Huntingdon was saved from wreck on his vowing to build a church at Dundee). Five large E windows, the centre cut into by the door to the balcony overlooking City Square. In all these, STAINED GLASS by Russell, 1933, the central light with the coat of arms of Dundee. In other windows, coats of arms relating to colourful scenes of events in the history of Dundee (Sir William Wallace and Alexander Scrymgeour at the siege of the Castle in 1297, Robert Bruce granting a charter to the burgh of Dundee in 1297, Mary, Queen of Scots' visit to Dundee in 1561 or 1562, James Graham of Claverhouse, Viscount of Dundee, leaving Dudhope Castle before his death at the Battle of Killiecrankie in 1689).

COUNCIL OFFICES on the E side of City Square of the same length as the City Chambers opposite and also with a five-bay principal section but this is placed well S of centre. Most of the detail of the City Chambers reappears but, instead of a loggia, the five-bay section has a large shop window flanked by doors, each surmounted by a panel carved with a relief of fish and flanked by smaller panels which bear the heads of seahorses. Above, a double tier of windows but these openings share tall vertical surrounds to correspond with the openings of the Council Chambers' centrepiece. No ceremonial balcony but the central second-floor window is flanked by large panels, each with the relief of a cow in a galley, emblematic of Dundee's origin as a Norse settlement. Most of the ground floor of this range's N end is occupied by shops. Another concave link and convex shopfront join the S end to the Caird Hall.

CENTRAL READING ROOMS, corner of Barrack Street, Ward Road and South Ward Road. Now McManus Collections Unit.
80 By the Dundee City Architect, *James Thomson*, 1909–11. Baroque, of one very tall storey and an attic above an exposed basement. Walling of polished ashlar, the channelling of the basement's masonry carried up as broad cartouche-topped pilaster-strips framing the bowed corners and the centrepiece of the E front. This façade is of three bays, the main walling of the outer bays' principal floor slightly recessed between tall Ionic half-pilasters and broken by pedimented windows. The centrepiece forms a huge aedicule, its open segmental pediment carried on paired Ionic columns. Within the aedicule a cavetto-moulded low entrance rising a little above the basement level and surmounted by an open pediment carved with large cherubs flanking a cartouche. Over the entrance and also in a cavetto surround, a great round-headed window of three lights, the glazing of the outer openings continued as a semicircular border round the head; consoled keystone carved as a lion's head. Above the façade's mutuled cornice, a tall parapet pierced at the outer bays by Diocletian attic windows in Gibbs surrounds. Another window of the same design in the E face of the large pedestal set back behind the top of the centrepiece; banded masonry along this pedestal's sides and at the corners of its front. The pedestal is the base for a cupola, its design inspired by Wren and Hawksmoor. At the cupola's open first stage, a screen of Ionic columns *in antis* at each face. Above, a low stage whose pinnacled corner pedestals are linked by concave walls pierced by rectangular openings flanking broader elliptical arches. Octagonal third stage, the openings of the four main faces round-headed and keystoned, the others smaller and rectangular but surmounted by panels. Roman Doric columns at the corners; ball-finialled ogee-profile dome.

Inside, a short stone staircase leads to an oval vestibule. Behind, the principal reading room. This is oblong but the ceiling has a large bay-leaf-bordered central oval opening rising through a gallery balustrade at the floor above to the large domed cupola which provides the room's top lighting.

DUNDEE HOUSE, corner of North Lindsay Street and South Ward Road. Administrative headquarters of Dundee City Council, by *Reiach & Hall*, 2009–11, a not very satisfactory combination of respect for Dundee's industrial past and affirmation of its present day civic pride. The front block is the former hackle-making works of Halley Brothers Ltd, designed by *H. & F. Thomson*, 1909–11, in an austere classically derived manner. Four storeys of squared and stugged masonry. E façade divided into five three-bay sections, the windows all tripartite, those of the ground floor now made into doorways to Reiach & Hall's loggia behind. In the centre of each section the ground and first windows combine to form single openings under round-arched and keystoned heads. Joining the outer windows of each section are sill courses which rise as hoodmoulds over the centre windows. Straight sill course at the third floor.

The Edwardian front block is attached to Reiach & Hall's main building behind whose E elevation rises above it as a set-back storey faced with yellow-coloured curtain walling and containing committee rooms. Further set-back is glass-fronted three-storey-height office accommodation. N side elevation to South Ward Road of glass and thin vertical metal strips. The rear is a splayed arrangement of three blocks, their ends with tall piers of pale brickwork forming the verticals of a grid whose horizontals are thin concrete slabs; behind this grid, tall windows in brick-faced walling.

EUCLID CRESCENT SCHOOL, Euclid Crescent. Now the Baxter Hall of the High School of Dundee. Humble collegiate Tudor, by *Alexander MacGregor*, 1868.

FORESTERS' HALLS, Nicoll Street. By *Johnston & Baxter*, 1900–2. Free Tudor, apparently influenced by C. Harrison Townsend's designs for the Whitechapel Art Gallery, London.* Three and four storeys, of red sandstone, the taller ends of the three-bay E façade appearing as towers flanking the centre's recessed upper floors, their wall-heads finished with strapwork parapets between small octagonal corner turrets. The end bays' slated spire roofs, together with the pyramidal roof over the centre, were replaced by flat roofs after a fire in 1963. The centre of the ground floor, its walling on the same plane as that of the ends, forms a porch, its front pierced by an elliptical-headed arch, its back wall by the halls' round-headed principal entrance flanked by rectangular sidelights. Over the porch, a parapet carved with the halls' name set in foliage and flanked by shields bearing emblems of the Ancient Order of Foresters. The parapet now carries a flat-roofed low addition built in 1939 to house a corridor at internal gallery level, its three-light window a squat version of the original first-floor opening. Set well back above this, the top of the first floor's original walling and the second floor which is lit by three closely spaced round-headed and transomed windows. Straightforward rectangular windows at the end towers, those of the second and third floor triplets and small. Over the l. tower's ground-floor entrance, a consoled pediment carved with foliage and a cartouche bearing the initials and motto (UNITAS BENEVOLENTIA ET CONCORDIA) of the Ancient Order of Foresters. At the foot of the r. tower a door inserted in 1939, its round-arched and keystoned head the surviving top of an original oculus in this position.

GENERAL POST OFFICE, corner of Meadowside and Constitution Road. Now in other use. Huge freely detailed Franco-Italian Renaissance, by *W. W. Robertson* of *H.M. Office of Works*, 1895–8, its desire to impress welcomed only tepidly by *The Builder* which noted '. . . the multiplication of detail, its columns and pilasters, strings and cornices, square windows and circular-headed windows, dormers, domes, turrets and vases, carving and sculpture, and many other contents of the 89

* Published in *Academy Architecture* (1896 and 1899).

architectural larder poured into the pot and flavoured with just enough Italian Renaissance sauce to satisfy the public palate'.* Three storeys and an attic, all faced with pale polished ashlar, banded at the very tall ground floor which housed the public office. Wall-head balustrade except at the centre where a panelled parapet is surmounted by a Roman Doric aedicule, the pediment with shell enrichment, forming a recess which contains the Royal Arms. On the roof, a domed cupola, a pedimented aedicule at each of its faces. The S front's main part is of five bays, the urn-topped corners of the slightly advanced broad centre and ends with paired pilasters at the ground floor, their pedimented tops with cartouches under human and animal heads, Ionic pilasters at the first floor and Corinthian columns above. Two-light windows at the ends, the ground floor's large, round-headed and transomed, the first-floor openings rectangular, the second floor's round-headed and baluster-aproned. Similar treatment at the broader centrepiece but its upper windows are of three lights. At its ground floor, a huge doorway (now window), the keystone surmounted by a crown set among foliage. Above the centrepiece's corner pilasters are statues of angelic figures, one holding a post-horn and a letter, the other a thunderbolt (the emblem of electricity), symbolizing the postal and telegraph departments. This front's E bay is also of 1895–8 and treated in similar fashion but the ground floor contains a rectangular vehicle entrance surmounted by panels, the first floor's stonework is channelled and the windows three-light.

At the W corners, identically treated half-round quadrants, their wall-head parapets ringed by upside-down consoles topped by finials carved as fruit; above the parapets, acorn-finialled lead domes. In the central segment of each corner, a dignified but not especially grand Roman Doric aediculed entrance, the pediment carved with shell enrichment. Aedicular stone dormers on the wall-head.

The N elevation to Euclid Street, originally of only one bay, was extended E by *H.M. Office of Works*, 1921–2, the red sandstone addition presenting a stripped classical appearance.

HIGH SCHOOL OF DUNDEE, Euclid Crescent. The cynosure of the vista up Reform Street, a Greek Revival temple of learning built (as The Seminaries) to house the burgh's formerly separate English School, Grammar School and Academy.
75 It is by *George Angus*, 1829–35. Main building faced with polished ashlar. At the long single-storey S front, a pedimented Doric hexastyle portico with antefixae along its sides and containing the corniced entrance. From this centrepiece recessed and lower parapeted six-bay links, a sill course under their architraved windows, to square end pavilions of the same height as the centre. At the front of each pavilion, a framework of coupled Doric pilasters supporting an unadorned entablature and parapet which rises higher at each

* *The Builder*, lxxv, 143.

end; within this frame, a single large window in a lugged architrave surround.

The pavilions' side elevations repeat the front treatment but have only single pilasters at the corners. N pavilions, their sides matching those of the S and joined to them by recessed links of two storeys but lower, their upper windows small, their sidelit and pilastered central entrances contained in elliptical-headed overarches. Both rear wings have been extended N in the manner of the original architecture, the W by five bays (by *William Scott*, 1853–4), the E by three (1857–9 and also by Scott). Facing Bell Street, a stone-faced corniced and parapeted TECHNICAL AND GYMNASIUM BLOCK of two storeys, by *Alexander McCulloch*, 1886, the two bays at each end marked off by giant pilasters. On the gymnasium's E side, a utilitarian two-storey and basement harled block by *Allan & Friskin*, 1936. On the W side and even less welcome, a brick-built block by *Thoms & Wilkie*, 1969–71.

The interior was extensively remodelled in 1957–64 by *Thoms & Wilkie* who divided the early and mid-C19 tall single-storey classrooms by the insertion of an upper floor. Behind the front portico, the entrance hall of 1957–64, its N side opening onto a stair of modernistic character. On the N wall of the E part of the hall, a MONUMENT to the Rev. Richard Low †1879, the Jacobean Renaissance stone surround framing a white marble high-relief portrait bust. On the E wall, the school's bronze SECOND WORLD WAR MEMORIAL by *T. S. Halliday*, the centrepiece a small statue of a High School pupil in front of a scene of ruin and destruction.

Detached LODGE just E of the school, by *James Findlay*, 1928, in a simplified version of Angus's manner.

MARGARET HARRIS BUILDING to the W, on the corner of Euclid Crescent and Euclid Street, by *Alexander McCulloch* and *J. Graham Fairley*, 1886–90. This was built (as the High School for Girls) to accommodate female pupils when first admitted to the High School, although kept segregated from the boys. Large L-plan edifice in best French Renaissance style. Two tall storeys of polished ashlar under high mansard roofs. Very similar fronts to both E and S, their ground-floor masonry banded above a tall base which is pierced by windows to the S. The minimally advanced end bays are marked off by superimposed Roman Doric and swagged Ionic pilasters carrying wall-head pediments. Behind the pediments rise square truncated pyramid roofs topped by antefixae and pierced by circular windows. In each end bay, a Roman Doric-pilastered three-light ground-floor window and, above, a baluster-aproned Venetian window, its Ionic columns and pilasters swagged, the spandrels with corniced panels carved with rosettes. The intermediate bays' ground-floor windows are also of three lights, with banded mullions and flanking pedimented panels bearing flowering and fruiting foliage. First-floor windows also tripartite and with swagged Ionic columns and pilasters but their openings are round-headed and console-keystoned.

The E front's centrepiece is assertive. Like the ends, it is minimally advanced and with superimposed corner pilasters. Here they carry a swan-neck pediment broken by the swagged base of a Corinthian-aediculed two-light attic window, its triangular pediment broken by an urn, which fronts a truncated domical roof. The ground-floor entrance is contained in a segmental-pedimented aedicule with Roman Doric columns *in antis*, the metopes of the frieze carved with rosettes. Inside this aedicule, the pilastered and round-headed door, its keystone carved as a head of Minerva (patron goddess of institutions of learning and the arts), the spandrels with ribbons and flowers; pilastered and keystoned sidelights under segmental-pedimented double-lugged panels carved with swags. Above the entrance, a tripartite window, the central compartment two-light, the Ionic pilasters and central column-mullion all swagged; above the outer lights, lugged-architraved and curvaceously pedimented dummy windows, their blind openings carved with urns in high relief.

The S elevation to Euclid Street is, except for its centrepiece and the windows in its base, a repeat of the E. At the centrepiece, pairs of two-light windows, those of the ground floor repeating the detail of the end bays, the first-floor openings the detail of the intermediate bays. Superimposed corner pilasters like those of the E front but they carry a triangular pediment carved with a relief of foliage spiralling round an oculus and surmounted by a seated stone figure of Study. This, together with the emblematic reliefs of Music, Literature, Science and the Arts in the pediments over the end bays, was designed by *J. Eadie Reid* and, like all the sculptured decoration, carved by *James Bremner*.

Inside, a small vestibule, its side walls with circular niches intended to house busts. The vestibule's E side is formed by a Neo-Jacobean Artisan Mannerist screen, its Ionic columns with shafts of polished granite and swagged capitals carved with sportive putti. Stair-hall behind, the stair itself also Neo-Jacobean. On its back wall, three STAINED GLASS windows by *W. B. Simpson & Sons*, 1890, with emblematic figures of Art, Literature and Science. More stained glass, also with emblematic figures and by Simpson & Sons, 1890, on the secondary stair to the S. In the centre of the S range, a first-floor Assembly Hall, the walls embellished with Artisan Mannerist Ionic pilasters, the upper part of their shafts fluted, their capitals swagged. In many of the classrooms, simple compartmented Neo-Jacobean plaster ceilings. Also Neo-Jacobean and of unexpected refinement the woodwork of dadoes and doors.

JOBCENTRE PLUS, corner of Dock Street and Gellatly Street. Originally Labour Exchange and redolent of authoritarian bureaucracy, by *W. T. Oldrieve* of *H.M. Office of Works*, 1913–15, its two storeys and attic faced with polished ashlar. Giant pilasters at the lower floors. On the corner, the attic storey is filled by a huge carving of the royal coat of arms. Along

Gellatly Street, a single-storey rear wing faced with concrete blockwork, by *H.M. Office of Works*, 1935.

THE MCMANUS DUNDEE'S ART GALLERY AND MUSEUM, Albert Square. Originally the Albert Institute. The most impressive architecturally and best-sited of Dundee's public buildings although constructed and extended in several stages from 1865 to 1889.

After the death of the Prince Consort in 1861 a group of Dundee citizens formed the Albert Institute Co. Ltd to honour his memory by the erection of a building to house a free library, museum and picture gallery, public hall and other rooms. *G. Gilbert Scott* was appointed architect for the work in 1864 and the first phase of the building constructed in 1865–8. This was T-plan, the front (W) block containing library accommodation on the ground floor and a public hall above. Only the N side of the tail was built and contained a passage-hall leading from the principal entrance at its E end to a grand staircase. In 1871 *David Mackenzie II* enlarged Scott's tail to the originally intended thickness, this S addition protruding well beyond the E end of the tail's N part, and added a wing across the addition's E end, making the building a rough H on plan, the new work containing museum and picture gallery rooms. The Albert Institute was sold to the Burgh of Dundee in 1879 and in 1887–7 was further extended by the Town's Architect, *William Alexander*, in celebration of Queen Victoria's Golden Jubilee. Extensive refurbishment was carried out by *Page & Park* in 2006–9 and the building now houses an up-to-date art gallery and museum, the exhibits accompanied by informative study aids, a café and shop providing for the material needs of visitors.

The style of Scott's 1860s work is Gothic of C13 or C14 81
Flemish derivation but with C16 Scottish touches, a combination for whose devising Scott claimed credit, the stonework of stugged and coursed masonry. Main (W) block of two storeys and an attic with an arcaded wall-head balustrade, gableted crowsteps of ecclesiastical appearance and, at the corners, angle buttresses topped by slit-windowed round turrets with tall witches' hat roofs. On the centre of the roof, a tall octagonal spire-roofed flèche. Scott originally intended a tower at the centre of the five-bay front but in the event a full-height and boldly advanced porch was substituted, its upper floor's entrance (to the Albert Hall) given a magnificent swirl of an approach by a horseshoe-shaped external stair. This is Baroque in feel although wholly Gothic in detail, the supporting pointed arches carried alternately on corniced ashlar piers and granite-shafted columns, the balustrades arcaded. At the first floor, a large rectangular doorway contained in a Gothic arch, its head carried on bell-capitalled and granite-shafted columns from which rise two orders, the inner enriched with stylized foliage, the outer with ballflower ornament. Over the doorway, a cusp-arched tympanum carved in relief with foliage surrounding a shield on which is displayed the coat of arms of the Prince Consort. This is contained within a rectangular overarch, its

spandrels with roundels bearing high-relief heads of Queen Victoria and Prince Albert executed, like all the 1860s carving, by *Farmer & Brindley*. In each of the front's outer bays, a ground-floor window of two lights, their bell-capitalled nook-shafts of sandstone (a cheaper substitute for the originally intended polished granite) but the central column-mullion's shaft of granite. Much taller first-floor windows, each of three lights under a round opening in the diapered head. Over the windows are hoodmoulds with small headstops and, under the windows, aprons carved with rosetted roundels placed among foliage.

Each gable of the front block is divided by a central buttress into two broad bays. At the S gable, windows like those of the W front except that the outer roundels of the first-floor aprons are carved with animal heads (a goat, sheep, lion and bull). In the head of this gable, a wheel window flanked and surmounted by roundels carved with rosettes. At the N gable, windows of four lights grouped 2:2 under quatrefoil openings and with plate-traceried sexfoils in the heads. Above, a circular window containing six roundels surrounding a central roundel, all with quatrefoiled plate tracery. At the top of the gable, a round panel carved with a rosette.

Set back to the E of the front block's N gable is the short tail of the 1860s T-plan building. This is of three bays. At the W of these, a fat octagonal stair-tower, each of its two exposed faces containing, at first-floor level, a single tall cusped and pointed light, one with foliaged label stops to its hoodmould, the other's hoodmould with headstops. Near the top of the tower, a corbelled balustrade of Gothic arcading behind which is set a low circular stage pierced by shouldered-arched openings and topped by a conical slated roof with a weathervane finial. The two bays to the E form a two-storey piend-roofed block, originally giving decided presence to this end of the building. In the l. bay, a doorway set in a nook-shafted pointed arch, its head carved with a pair of dragons among foliage and, in the centre, a roundel displaying the heraldic achievement of the Burgh of Dundee.

Mackenzie's additions of 1872–4 are respectful of Scott's work and continue his use of C13 or C14 Gothic. The block on the S side of Scott's tail is designed, as Scott had intended, to form two parts, the W's attic with a trio of crowstep-gabled dormers, the E with a lower roof of shallower pitch on which sits a long glass-roofed rectangular lantern, its side filled with a procession of Gothic lights. In the inner angle with Scott's front block and Mackenzie's new E block are porches, the W of two storeys, the E of one, both topped by Gothic balustrades. In Page & Park's alterations of 2006–9 one ground-floor window was converted to a door by dropping its sill and removing the central column-mullion although leaving its capital in place to disconcerting effect.

The 1870s E extension across the tail's E end is shorter than the corresponding 1860s front block but with its S gable in line with that of the W block, giving symmetry to the building's S elevation. The treatment is generally similar to that of the W block and also with a crocket-spired lead flèche on the roof although without the swagger of its external stair. Alexander's 1880s two-bay N extension of the E block repeated Mackenzie's detail. Similar treatment of the contemporary wing across the N end of this block, its E gable like that of the 1870s E block's S gable but in the head of the W gable, a wheel window and no balcony. Also built to Alexander's design in the 1880s are the simple and unassertive Gothic blocks which fill the inner angle of the NE wing and the tail of Mackenzie's additions.

INTERIOR. The present principal entrance is on the S side of the building's cross-bar. It opens into a shop-cum-café created by Page & Park from rooms of the 1870s, a trabeated plaster ceiling as in the other ground-floor rooms of the 1870s and 1880s the main feature. One window is filled with STAINED GLASS (Scenes from the Life of Mary Slessor, the Dundee mill girl who became a missionary to the Calabar coast of Nigeria) by *William Aikman*, 1923. N of this room, Scott's encaustic-tiled ENTRANCE HALL, the arch-head of its door from the outside carved with the coat of arms of the Burgh of Dundee. This hall's E end is twin-aisled and groin-vaulted, the stone ceiling ribs springing from a granite-shafted central pillar and wall corbels, all with capitals carved with stiff-leaf foliage. W of the hall, a short passage, also encaustic-tiled and groin-vaulted, which opens to the C19 stair-hall through a Gothic screen, the pointed arches carried on columns, also with shafts of polished granite and stiff-leaf capitals. The STAIR-HALL is circular, its domed ceiling patterned with radiating wooden ribs, the stair itself a comfortable turnpike. In the windows, STAINED GLASS by *Clayton & Bell*, 1917, with roundels containing portraits of figures (Sir Walter Scott, Robert Burns, James Watt and Sir Henry Raeburn) representing Scottish Literature, Science and Art. The ground floor of the W block, originally the Lending and Reference Libraries, is now a single twin-aisled exhibition room, the beams of the ceiling supported on a line of cast-iron columns with four-way brackets, their spandrels pierced by roundels. N of the E end of the building's cross-bar is a stair-hall formed in the early C21, the cantilevered steps of the stair spiralling round a vesica-shaped concrete-panelled central lift, tall metal railings forming a cage round the perimeter.

On the first floor, the 1860s stair-hall opens through a large nook-shafted Gothic arch to the LONG GALLERY on the N side of the building's cross-bar. At the Gallery's W end and filling the whole of the W block is Scott's double-height Albert or Great Hall. Entrance through a nook-shafted doorway. The HALL is covered with a panelled and ribbed wooden tunnel vault. The vault's ribs spring alternately from wall-shafts standing on large corbels, the columns' capitals and the corbels both with stiff-leaf ornament, and from higher-set and smaller simply foliaged corbels, these latter ribs carved with small hammerbeams. STAINED GLASS by *Clayton & Bell*, 1913. In the heads of the main windows, depictions of flowers emblematic of Virtues. Above these, in the N gable, are coats of arms of famous people connected with Dundee (David, Earl of Huntingdon; Alexander Scrymgeour, appointed Constable of Dundee in 1298; James Halyburton, the Protestant champion and Provost of Dundee from 1555 to 1588; and Sir William Ogilvy Dalgleish, Chairman for twelve years of the jute and linen manufacturers, Baxter Bros & Co. and the principal donor of electric lighting for the galleries). In the roundel above, the coats of arms of Queen Victoria and the Prince Consort and, in the large circular window in the head of the gable, the arms of the City of Dundee surrounded by floral decoration. More flowers in the wheel window of the S gable. N of the doorway, a fragment of the Hall's original stencilled floral wall decoration.

The first-floor E gallery in the cross-bar is of the 1870s and covered by an elaborate open timber roof with Neo-Jacobean pendants. Above the main roof, an almost wholly glazed rectangular lantern. In the 1880s NE wing, the VICTORIA GALLERY, top-lit from its glass-panelled and ribbed segmental tunnel vault. Dogtooth ornament on the ribs and also, together with stiff-leaf enrichment, on the cornice. At the tops of the end walls, panels which display the Royal Arms of Scotland and the coat of arms of the Burgh of Dundee.

In Albert Square, in front of two sides of the Gallery, are STATUES. On the W, a 3.66 m. bronze seated figure of Robert Burns, by *John Steell*, erected in 1879–80. Corniced pedestal of polished Peterhead red granite. – N of this and also by Steell but only 2.44 m. high, the standing bronze figure of the Radical politician and Member of Parliament for Dundee, George Kinloch of Kinloch, erected in 1872. Kinloch is depicted wrapped in a cloak and holding the text of a speech in one hand. The corniced pedestal is of grey granite. – Framed by the centre of the N elevation, the majestic bronze statue of a throned and crowned Queen Victoria holding an orb and laurel
94 spray, by *Harry Bates*, 1898–9. Dull-polished red Peterhead granite pedestal made by *Bower & Florence* under the architectural direction of *Hadden A. Bower*. On this, bronze panels (also by Bates) depicting scenes in the life of the Queen including the visit by her and the Prince Consort to Dundee in 1844; at the front corners, small statues emblematic of Legislation and the Colonies. – In front of the Gallery's NE corner, the bronze seated figure of James Carmichael, ironfounder and inventor of the fan blast, by *John Hutchison*, 1873–6. Carmichael is shown holding a drawing and foot-rule, one arm resting on a steam cylinder, the other on a model of the fan blast. Polished pink granite pedestal.

ROYAL EXCHANGE, corner of Meadowside and Panmure Street.
82 Built by a consortium to house the Dundee Chamber of Commerce in 1853–6, it was designed by *David Bryce* in best C15 Flemish style and built of pale grey polished ashlar. The ground floor serves as a solid-looking base, its long S side with

mullioned-and-transomed shouldered-arched windows and an elliptical-headed door under an ogee-arched and crocketed hoodmould. The principal floor is high, its very tall and narrow windows, also mullioned-and-transomed, flanked by slender columns; immediately above each window, a tall crocketed-gabled and foliage-finialled stone dormer rising from the wall-head. Plainer Gothic W gable, an octagonal spire-roofed stair-tower at its N corner.

Boldly projecting SE corner tower. In its low first stage, a hoodmoulded S doorway like that of the main block; round-headed and hoodmoulded window in the E face. In each exposed face of the second stage, a two-light Gothic window, a quatrefoil in the head, under a crocketed and finialled hood-mould. Each face of the top stage is pierced by a round-headed opening containing a pair of low Gothic lights under a huge roundel; again, a crocketed and foliage-finialled hoodmould. The corners of this stage's upper half form clasping buttresses which rise from corbels carved as half-length grotesque figures; between these corners, blind cusped arch-heads under the wall-head cornice and pierced Gothic parapet from which dragon gargoyles project near the ends of each face. The tower was intended to carry a two-stage octagonal and crown-spired lantern, sadly unexecuted because of foundation problems. Projecting from the join of the tower's NE corner and the E gable of the main block, a low octagonal stair-tower.

The E gable is crowstepped and narrow, the first-floor window of three tall rectangular lights, the second-floor window with pointed lights. The attic is slightly recessed behind a stone balcony, its front pierced by swirling mouchettes; more mouchettes in the head of the hoodmoulded window. At the r. of the gable, a slender spired turret, its base square, its upper stages octagonal. Inside, the whole of the main block's first floor is filled by a double-height Great Hall, now divided horizontally by a suspended ceiling under an inserted upper floor. Over this, an open wooden roof with two tiers of hammer-beams, the upper tier (deprived of pendants) still visible at the present top floor level. At the W end of this floor, a two-light STAINED GLASS window of 1856 depicting Neptune and Penelope, symbols of Commerce and Spinning. At the present lower level, glass of *c.* 1885 by *John Hardman & Co.*, with figures emblematic of the Arts, Science, Commerce and Agriculture.

SHERIFF COURT, West Bell Street. Heavy-handed Roman classical, by the Town's Architect of Dundee, *William Scott*, 1861–3. The façade is taken from a design of 1833 by *George Angus*. Angus's scheme, for a court house flanked by police offices and the governor's house of a prison occupying the ground behind, had been only partly carried out in 1835–7, the court house left unbuilt on grounds of cost.

The court house's main block is of two storeys above a windowless basement. Front of honey-coloured polished ashlar. Nine bays, the rectangular ground-floor windows with lugged architraves and panelled keystones and linked by a 77 moulded sill course; string course, also moulded, under the panelled aprons of the pilastered and console-keystoned first-floor openings. Giant pilasters between the outer bays. Fronting the three centre bays a pedimented Roman Doric portico, the columns standing on pedestals fronting a channelled base, the pediment carved (by *P. B. Smith*) with the royal coat of arms set among roses, shamrocks and thistles. At the rear of this block, the centre is carried back as a rubble-walled two-storey wing, with round-headed and keystoned first-floor windows and a louvred ventilator-cupola.

Originally at each end there were recessed five-bay single-storey screen walls of 1835–7 with high-set round-headed and keystoned dummy windows set in rectangular overarches at the outer bays, and a large gateway, also round-headed and with a consoled keystone in the centre. The screen walls (the E's r. three bays rebuilt in paler stone) ended with two-storey pavilions, again of the 1830s, the surviving E pavilion also of greyish ashlar. The pavilions' three-bay fronts with giant pilasters, sill courses and wall-head entablatures were of generally similar detail to the outer sections of the main block but less tall and with smaller windows, the ground-floor openings without moulded architraves.

The W screen wall's l. three bays (rebuilt, 1933–4) and W pavilion were demolished *c.* 1974. In 1994–6 the *Nicoll Russell Studios* added a courtroom behind the surviving 1830s two bays of this screen wall, the courtroom's W and N elevations a courteous homage to the 1830s work, its glazed attic storey set behind the cornice. At the E end of the complex, an ashlar-clad flat-roofed low box housing the District Court was built behind the façade of the pavilion by *Gauldie, Wright & Partners*, 1979–81. The larger but discreet addition behind this end's screen wall is of 1994–6 and by the Nicoll Russell Studios who, at the same time, opened up the 1830s dummy windows.

Inside, the double-height Court No. 1 retains much of its Victorian character. On three sides, round-headed windows above a plaster band studded with roundels containing emblems of Justice, Scotland and Dundee. S gallery on slender fluted cast-iron columns. Broad consoled canopy over the judicial bench at the N. Compartmented ceiling, the beams decorated with expensive but appropriately sober plasterwork.

WAR MEMORIAL of 1922 to members of the Dundee City Police to the SE, a granite Celtic cross of routine design.

STRATHMORE LODGE, corner of Courthouse Square and Ward Road. Originally Industrial Schools and converted to a Salvation Army hostel in 1900. By *Charles Edward*, 1855–6. Two-storey rubble-built and institutional-looking. U-plan E front, the gables of the wings and the centre bay of the main range all with quatrefoil openings in their heads. Set back at the S end and containing the entrance, a low tower with a slated spire roof.

TAYSIDE HOUSE, Dock Street. Dominating the entry to the city from the Tay Road Bridge, a sixteen-storey T-shaped and flat-roofed tower built to house the offices of Tayside Regional

Council (established in 1975 and abolished in 1996), by *James Parr & Partners* (partner-in-charge: *Joe Wynne*), 1972–6. Concrete frame behind which the two bottom floors are slightly set back. Above these, a grid of glazed horizontal panels set in simply moulded concrete surrounds. Tall concrete fascia at the top. Taller off-centre service jamb of ribbed concrete. All quite sensible and without frills or pomp but the siting of this monument to local government bureaucracy has understandably made it few friends. Scheduled for demolition (2011).

TAYSIDE POLICE HEADQUARTERS, West Marketgait. By *Gauldie, Hardie, Wright & Needham*, 1974–6. Three-storey oblong round a central courtyard, the vertically proportioned narrow windows set between slender sloping-topped concrete-aggregate buttresses. Under the first- and second-floor windows jazzy yellow panels; individual lead fascias over the windows of the top floor. Part of the rear rises a further two storeys. – HEADQUARTERS ANNEXE to the N, on the corner of West Marketgait and North Marketgait, a flat-roofed late C20 six-storey block, its curtain walling formed of bands of glass and concrete-aggregate.

WATT INSTITUTION, Constitution Road. Now offices. Designed by *George Angus** and built in 1838–9 as the museum, library and lecture hall of a literary and scientific society which had been formed in 1824 to commemorate the engineer and inventor, James Watt. Originally of two storeys above a basement. Five-bay front of polished ashlar, channelled at the ground floor. Heavy Roman Doric-pilastered doorpiece in the centre, its cornice with anthemion finials. Very tall windows to the first floor whose three-bay centrepiece is slightly recessed, its openings round-headed. Tall attic in a French Renaissance manner added by *Alexander Johnston* in 1874 after the building had become the Young Men's Christian Association Rooms. Pedimented wall-head dormers fronting truncated square spires at the ends; a large domical roofed dormer over the centre.

DESCRIPTION

WEST MARKETGAIT is a boundary and entry to the centre. Beside the West Port Roundabout its S end begins with the Salvation Army Citadel (*see* Churches, above). The utilitarian multi-storey WEST MARKETGAIT CAR PARK of 1966 is a surviving original part of the OVERGATE CENTRE of 1961–70. This shopping, hotel and office complex designed by *Ian Burke, Martin & Partners* was mostly redeveloped in 1998–2000, with *Benoy* as the conceptual and *Keppie Design* the executive architects. Bland ashlar-clad department store frontage to West Marketgait with low drum-topped corner towers and large display windows under panels bearing abstract bronze sculptures (Images of Dundee's Past) by *David Wilson*, 2000. Bold entrance canopy at the SW corner. From this stretches to the E the Centre's principal frontage along the NW side of

* *James* and *William Paterson* were executant architects.

NETHERGATE and HIGH STREET. Straight-sided end blocks much like the West Marketgait elevation, the SW with curved corners, the NE a structure of the 1960s but refaced in 1998–2000 when it acquired a curving projection in its inner angle with the 1960s continuation of the block on the corner of High Street and Reform Street. More sculpture by Wilson on these corner blocks. Set behind the NE block, a 1960s office tower faced with cheerless concrete aggregate panels. Between the end blocks and forming a backdrop to the City Churches (*see* Churches, above), a glass-fronted crescent of two storeys under an oversailing ribbed metal roof. The crescent contains a one-sided mall looking out over the churches, its NW back containing the entrances to the shops, those of the upper level fronted by a gallery reached by generously proportioned stairs and escalators and which, at intervals, bulges out over the lower walkway's SE side and extends to balconies outside the glass frontage. Over the circulation space, a 'gull wing' soffit roof. In the SW corner of the open space enclosed by this crescent stands the MARKET CROSS, its octagonal shaft made by *John Mylne* in 1586, a small relief panel bearing the coat of arms of Dundee on its SW face. Originally sited in High Street, it was removed as an obstruction to traffic in 1777 and its substructure destroyed. The shaft and finial were restored and partly renewed in 1874 when was provided an octagonal drum, a miniature version of the original much larger substructure, with foliage-capitalled columns at the corners and blank shields on the faces. Stepped base of 1874. On the shaft's Corinthian capital (a badly weathered replacement of 1874) stands a late C20 replica of its C16 finial, a unicorn bearing a shield carved with the Royal Arms of Scotland.

NETHERGATE'S SE side begins with Meadowside St Paul's Church (*see* Churches, above). To its E is MECCA BINGO, by *Cooper Cromar Associates*, 1996–7. Front of small scale and bland except for a tall metal-clad Art Deco tower, a near replica of the principal external feature of Green's Playhouse (by *John Fairweather*, 1935–6) which formerly occupied the site. Next in Nethergate a small curtain-walled building (Nos. 98–100) before the four-storey mid-C19 Georgian survival Nos. 92–96 with corniced windows to the first floor. Very similar pair of tenements at Nos. 80–90, dated 1850 on the hopper of their shared downpipe. In front, one of the city centre's BUS SHELTERS, their standard design produced by the *Nicoll Russell Studios*, *c.* 2000, having a curved fully glazed wall to the street and a long flower box on the curvaceous canopy. In the close behind No. 86, the three-storey rubble-built ST DAVID'S ROOMS, a small tenement of late C16 or early C17 origin. Three-storey three-bay front, now generally Georgian in appearance. At the W end of the ground floor (now below close level) a broad elliptical arch of *c.* 1600, its W jamb a panelled pilaster. This is dwarfed by the adjacent NETHERGATE BUSINESS CENTRE by *Hugh Wilson & Lewis Womersley*, 1975–7. Four-storey front block (No. 66 Nethergate) of grey-coloured blockwork, an unsuccessful evocation of Georgian regularity but mercifully without tricks. The development's more extensive rear block (WHITEHALL HOUSE) facing Yeaman Shore is crushingly dull, its seven-storey central tower providing additional office space rather than a vertical feature of real interest. On Nethergate the low No. 60 (by *I. B. Murray & Son*, 1962) is followed by the corner block with Union Street.

UNION STREET, its line fixed by *William Burn* in 1825, was formed in 1827–8 as a carriageway between Nethergate and Dock Street, the elevations of its buildings (developed from 1828) designed by *David Neave*. These are dignified four-storey terraces containing flats above shops, cornices over the first-floor windows and moulded architraves at the second floor the principal embellishments. At the top, the W side begins with Nos. 1–7, the broached ashlar now painted. This building (converted to the Royal Hotel in the late C19) was dressed up in 1892 by *James Maclaren & Sons* who added the panelled parapet and pedimented dormer windows. Over the quadrant corner they placed an octagonal turret, a swagged frieze over its round-headed windows, the slated truncated spire roof surmounted by a cupola. The adjoining Nos. 11–19 Union Street, although designed by Neave, broke with his standard design for the street. Built as the THISTLE HALL in 1828–9 it was originally of only three storeys, the presence of the hall itself marked by the height and flashy classical detail of the first floor. This is of five bays articulated by Ionic pilasters, coupled at the centre whose window is of three lights with Corinthian column-mullions *in antis* and a segmental-arched fanlight. Over the windows of the outer bays, triangular pediments with anthemion finials on the outer corners. As part of their 1892–4 remodelling of the Royal Hotel of which this had become part, *James Maclaren & Sons* removed the 1820s second floor and added two new top floors and an attic, this work detailed in a coarse commercial manner. The final block on this side of the street (Nos. 33–47 Union Street and No. 25 Yeaman Shore) is mid-C19, its scale and general appearance following Neave's design but without cornices at the first-floor windows and with large wall-head chimneys.

Union Street's E side is generally to Neave's elevation but the NE block (by *George Matthewson*, 1839–40) has quadrants at both the NE and NW corners. In the centre of the N front to Nethergate, a three-light window, its block cornice carried on heavy consoles, and a stone balcony; another balcony but off-centre at the W front. The ground floor's polished granite pub-front is early C20 but the triglyph frieze above appears original. To the S, blocks of straightforward Neave design (the S without cornices over the first-floor windows) but the stonework badly weathered. At the S corner block's front to Whitehall Crescent crowded detail with the first- and second-floor windows all corniced, a large off-centre wall-head chimney and a fireclay balustrade on the wall-head cornice.

In Nethergate, on the E side of Couttie's Wynd, Nos. 36–38 on the E of *c.* 1920, tall and narrow classical front of American inspiration. Also of four storeys and an attic but much lower the plain Late Georgian No. 32 Nethergate next door.

WHITEHALL STREET, the next thoroughfare from Nethergate towards the harbour, was laid out in 1881–2 as a result of the 1871 Act for the Improvement of the Burgh of Dundee. Control over the elevations of the buildings was maintained by the Dundee Burgh Surveyor, *William Mackison*, but they were not constructed until 1884–91 and with variations, some dictated by the size of individual sites. The style is commercial French Renaissance, the four-storey and attic façades clad in polished ashlar. Corinthian pilasters framing the first-floor windows, pedimented windows at the second floor and double-lugged architraves to the third-floor openings; round-headed and keystoned dormers behind the wall-head balustrades. At the N blocks (of 1885–7, the NW by *Hutcheson & Henderson*), dome-topped semi-octagonal corner towers. Tall oval windows at the centre and S blocks (of 1884–91, presumably all by *Robert Keith* who designed Nos. 5–7, 13–15 and 26–36), the S corners (of 1890–1) topped by pediments.

WHITEHALL CRESCENT was laid out at the same time as Whitehall Street. On the concave N side, W of Couttie's Wynd, a narrow four-storey block (Nos. 17–21) of *c.* 1890, its canted corner rising as a five-storey tower. To its W, the corner block with Union Street (*see* above). In this side's E segment, Nos. 7–9 by *Malcolm Stark & Rowntree*, 1891, continuing the general character of Whitehall Street but the detail more Georgian survival than French Renaissance. This side ends with No. 5 (by *James Parr & Partners*, 1972) on the corner of Castle Street (*see* below).

Dominating Whitehall Crescent's convex S side and the view down Whitehall Street is the Gilfillan Memorial Church (*see* Churches, above). On its E, Nos. 10–22 Whitehall Crescent, dated 1899. Five storeys and an attic, of polished ashlar, channelled at the first floor in which are set round-headed windows. The three storeys above are divided into two three-bay sections, each flanked by three-storey oriel windows. Restrained Victorian classical detail. To the E, with a tightly bowed corner to Castle Street and a return elevation to Dock Street, another block (Nos. 2–8 Whitehall Crescent and Nos. 14–15 Dock Street) of 1898–9 but Georgian survival. The whole of Whitehall Crescent W of the Gilfillan Memorial Church is occupied by the five-storey-and-attic Nos. 26–42 built as Mathers' Commercial Hotel in 1897–9. The design by *Robert Hunter* uses motifs from Whitehall Street but on a larger scale and more thinly spread. Not unimpressive is the W end containing the hotel entrance. Flanked by paired Composite pilasters, this is a broad elliptical arch, its massive console-keystone carved with the portrait of a moustachioed man. Supported on this and on pairs of fluted consoles either side is a balcony. Above, a two-storey oriel window. Surmounting the corner, a Frenchy lead-roofed and iron-crested tower.

HIGH STREET continues Nethergate to the NE. On its corner with CRICHTON STREET, a thoroughfare to the harbour opened in 1783, a late C18 four-storey-and-attic tenement (Nos. 26–28 High Street) built of painted rubble and rather altered. Also of four storeys and an attic the contemporary Nos. 3–9 Crichton Street to the SE, quite plain except for the model of the former Dundee Town House (designed by *William Adam* in 1732 and demolished two hundred years later) erected in 1932 over the entrance to The Pillars bar (its name that of the Town House's nickname). The scale is maintained at Nos. 11–13 but this building is of 1892 by *W. J. Anderson* and enjoyable Flemish in style, faced with glazed red brickwork. Also of four storeys and an attic is the adjoining Late Georgian Nos. 15–19, its front of cherry-cock-pointed rough ashlar. The Late Georgian norm and height continue at No. 21 but its stugged ashlar has been painted and a mansard roof added *c.* 1900. Front of only two bays, perhaps curtailed in the late C19 for the construction of Nos. 23–29 by *Alexander McCulloch*, 1892. This aspires to gentility, its polished ashlar façade with two-light windows in the centre and end bays and timid Renaissance detail. At the junction with Whitehall Crescent, the splay-cornered No. 5 Whitehall Crescent, an insurance company's offices by *James Parr & Partners*, 1971, keeps the scale and streetlines of its neighbours but its dark brown curtain walling is jarring.

The whole of Crichton Street's NE side as far as Shore Terrace is taken up by the side elevation of City Square (*see* Public Buildings: Caird Hall, City Chambers and Council Offices, above). Between Shore Terrace and Dock Street is THE PODIUM, a concrete-framed and glass-walled three-storey 1970s box, containing offices and access to a pedestrian bridge across Dock Street to the tower of Tayside House (*see* Public Buildings, above).

REFORM STREET, running NW from High Street, was laid out as a result of the 1825 Act for Opening Certain Streets in the Burgh of Dundee, the contemporary High School of Dundee as its focus, the University of Abertay Dundee's Old College behind an unintended and less welcome part of the view. Unified elevations for the street frontages were provided in 1832 by *George Angus*. On each side, four-storey central and end blocks linked by three-storey sections, all on the same plane. Dividing the W centre block in two equal halves is Bank Street. Presumably Angus's intention was that the end blocks should be all of the same length but, as built, the N ends are shorter than the S and the N intermediate sections correspondingly longer. Façades all of polished ashlar, mostly now painted. Continuous dentilated cornices and balustrades (much restored in the late C20) above the ground floors in which are set shopfronts (some now altered, others restored) separated by regularly spaced Ionic-columned entrances to the stairs serving the upper floors. Moulded architraves to the first-floor windows. Second-floor sill courses and, above, dentilated cornices under the top floors of the four-storey blocks and along the wall-heads of the three-storey sections. Bowed quadrant corners to High Street, the W with pediments (two triangular, the centre segmental) over the first-floor windows.

The unity of design is broken by buildings on the S corner of Bank Street and at Reform Street's N corners with Meadowside. The first of these is the former BANK OF SCOTLAND (No. 34 Reform Street) designed by *William Burn* in 1842 and remodelled by *G. S. Aitken* in 1879–80. Burn deviated from Angus's design for the site by omitting the Ionic columns at the entrance which he flanked with office windows instead of shopfronts; to the first-floor windows' architraves he added pediments at the front elevation and cornices at the side to Bank Street. Aitken reclothed this genteel intruder in pompous dress, refacing the ground floor with channelled and banded rustication, in which he set a richly carved new entrance, and replacing the continuous balustrade above with Neo-Jacobean balconies, the boldly projecting centre balcony carried on massive consoles finished with high reliefs of female heads, its corners surmounted by lions séjants holding shields carved with saltires. At the rear Aitken added a banking hall, its single tall storey rising the height of two, the wall-head balustraded. The one window to Bank Street is Venetian, the centre light stilted, the surround carved with Greek key ornament, the keystone with the head of a bearded man. On Reform Street's NW corner with Meadowside, MEADOW HOUSE (No. 64) designed as Lamb's Temperance Hotel by *James Maclaren*, 1867, its general appearance following Angus's design but the detail Neo-Jacobean. On Reform Street's opposite corner, the former NATIONAL BANK OF SCOTLAND (Nos. 65–71) by *William Scott*, 1854–7. Generally respectful of Angus's design for the street but with panelled aprons under the ground-floor windows, open pediments on foliaged consoles over the first-floor openings and the second floor's cornice mutuled.

BANK STREET, like Reform Street, was laid out under the 1825 Act for Opening Certain Streets in the Burgh of Dundee.

On the street's N side, No. 5, a palazzo-like four-storey office building by *James Maclaren*, 1868. This is a prelude to the huge block, also ashlar-fronted and with a dignified modicum of classical detail, at Nos. 7–25, built in stages to house the newspaper offices of the *Dundee Advertiser* and *People's Journal*. It was begun by *Charles Edward* in 1859 as a two-storey seven-bay block, the ends slightly advanced. In 1864 the building was extended in mirror-image fashion six bays to the E by *Charles Ower* who heightened the whole block by an additional storey in 1870. Four years later *C. & L. Ower* again extended the building, this time to the W by a further six bays. Then, in 1882–3, a further W extension, also by C. & L. Ower, was built. This was of four storeys, its five E bays very similar in appearance to No. 5 Bank Street, the sixth (W) bay a broader version of the E bay of the newspaper offices. Finally, in 1890, C. & L. Ower raised the whole building to a uniform four-storey-and-attic height, a third floor and attic added to the nineteen E bays, an attic to the six bays at the W end. Projecting from the first floor are elegantly curved and scrolled Victorian iron lamps. On the corner of Barrack Street, Nos. 27–31 Bank Street of 1868, mixing Italian and Jacobean Renaissance detail. Originally of three storeys and an attic, an extra floor was added to the W part later in the C19.

HIGH STREET'S N side W of Reform Street is the setting for a pair of bronze SCULPTURES of Desperate Dan and Minnie the Minx, cartoon figures loved or loathed by readers of the Dundee-published comics, the *Dandy* and *Beano*. These caricatures of caricatures are by *Tony* and *Susie Morrow*, 2001. Behind them, the four-storey Nos. 66–67 of *c.* 1800. Rendered and painted five-bay front, the windows grouped 3:2. Set at a slight splay, the contemporary Nos. 68–69, a mirror image but for the long and horizontal first-floor window inserted *c.* 1930. Also four-storey and rendered but probably of the early C18 Nos. 70–73. Symmetrical front of six bays, the windows grouped 3:3 and with a chimney-topped gablet over the two centre bays. Projecting from the centre of the first floor, a large clock of 1932 surmounted by a model of the former Dundee Town House demolished in 1932. Inside, a third floor room retains early C18 panelling and a round-headed china recess. Off-centre entrance to Gray's Close. In the close, GARDYNE'S LAND occupying the E side is a late C16 merchant's house repaired and converted to a backpackers' hostel by *Simpson & Brown*, 2005–8. The front is composed of two main parts. The slightly set-back l. is of four storeys and an attic with jettying under the second floor and again under the third. Regular two-bay elevation, the attic's single window placed above the r. openings of the floors below, the windows above the ground floor, where original, as also in the r. part, with roll-moulded surrounds. The house's higher and broader r. part rises to a gable whose head is formed by one short and one long slope. All is straightforward enough, although irregularly windowed, above the jettied second floor. The two bottom floors are treated more wilfully. At the l., a bowed tower-like projection containing a moulded door (restored in 2005–8). Above, the walling is jettied out, the continuous corbelling's lowest course containing a stone carved with stars and, in the centre, a panel containing initials of which AS are decipherable; horizontal window like a fanlight above. At first-floor level, a shallowly bowed turret. At the r. of this elevation, a squinch arch over the ground and first floors' recessed walling. The next building fronting High Street is the three-storey Nos. 75–76 of the earlier C19, the upper floors' windows framed by pilasters, the first-floor end windows set in Ionic aedicules. Then, the start of the massive block on the corner of Murraygate (*see* below).

On High Street's S side, opposite the end of Reform Street but disappointingly off-axis, is the frigid civic space of CITY SQUARE (*see* Public Buildings: Caird Hall, City Chambers and
92 Council Offices, above). Immediately E, THE ROYAL BANK OF SCOTLAND (Nos. 3–4 High Street) by *George Washington Browne*, 1897–9, a tall four-storey palazzo faced with polished ashlar, a display of rich but restrained classical detail. The third floor's low, horizontal and apse-ended windows are placed between putti frolicking beside urns. Inside, a square double-height banking hall, the walls covered with round-arched panels between giant Corinthian pilasters. Domed ceiling, a ring of anthemion enrichment at the base, the ribs decorated with bowls of flowers; central glazed cupola.

On the opposite corner of Castle Street, Nos. 1A–2 High Street, a four-storey-and-attic late C18 tenement, the windows of its ten-bay front not quite regularly spaced, their gentle Renaissance detail and the wall-head's urn-topped balustrade embellishments of the mid or later C19 when this was the Royal Hotel. Set at a slight splay to the E gable, the four-storey No. 1 High Street of the later C19, a crowstepped gable to the front, a large first-floor oriel window at the exposed E end. This side of High Street finishes with the flight of steps rising to the Cathedral Church of St Paul (Episcopal), for which *see* Churches, above. In front, a bronze STATUE of Admiral Adam Duncan, victor of the Battle of Camperdown and an Angus landowner, the tail of his frock coat billowing behind, a telescope in his hands. It is by *Janet Scrymgeour Wedderburn*, 1997.

CASTLE STREET was opened in 1795 as a thoroughfare from the city centre to the harbour. On the W side, S of The Royal Bank of Scotland on the corner of High Street (*see* above), the former THEATRE ROYAL (Nos. 7–21, now offices) by *Samuel Bell*, 1808–10, a tall three-storey ashlar-clad block. Front of seven bays, the centre three slightly advanced under an urn-finialled pediment whose dummy oculus contains a small bust of Shakespeare. Originally, the ground floor was a parade of round-headed and keystoned shopfronts (now replaced by late C20 shopfronts). Baluster-aproned and corniced first-floor windows, the centre opening dignified with a pediment. At each end of the wall-head's cornice, a pedestal for a vase (now missing). Beside it, the four-storey-and-attic Nos. 23–25, plain Late Georgian, with a late C20 box dormer. Then, Nos. 27–29 (Castle Court) of *c.* 1800. Three storeys, the very tall second floor formerly containing the Caledonian Hall, its round-headed windows with projecting imposts and keystones. On the wall-head, a chimney-topped gablet containing a dummy oculus. The lower floors were recast in the late C20 with a jolly Victorian-style two-storey shopfront; rectangular pend arch at the l., with mild-steel gates. Three-storey-and-attic early C20 block at Nos. 31–33, the first- and second-floor windows contained in giant round-headed overarches; circular panels in the spandrels. The SE corner of the Caird Hall (*see* Public Buildings, above) fills this end of the street.

On Castle Street's E side, below the corner block with High Street (q.v.), two very plain mid-C19 four-storey rubble-built blocks. More pleasurable the former St Paul's (Episcopal) Chapel (*see* Churches, above). No. 26 is an early C19 three-storey town house of modest pretension with aproned and corniced first-floor windows. Taller but plainer adjoining block (Nos. 28–38) of the earlier C19. The gap between it and the block to the S was filled in 1919 by *Frank Thomson* with the grandiose entrance to the next-door offices of the distillers, Alexander Stewart & Son. The appearance is very like that of a contemporary war memorial. Only one bay wide and one immensely tall storey in height, faced with polished light-grey Persley (Aberdeenshire) granite. The front is filled by a round-headed arch flanked by panelled pilasters from which hang bronze wreaths (made by *H. H. Martyn & Co. Ltd*). The arch's keystone rises to the entablature under the wall-head, the frieze carved with Greek key ornament. Filling the lowest third of the arch, elaborately modelled bronze doors under a transom inscribed STEWART. In the arch's upper two-thirds, small-panes of cathedral glass in a narrow border; in the head, a large roundel, its top covered with bronze drapery. The adjacent block which it serves (Nos. 42–48 Castle Street and Nos. 2–8 Exchange Street) is by *David Mackenzie*, 1832. Four storeys, of stugged ashlar. Pilastered shopfronts and, at the quadrant corner to Exchange Street, an entrance set between fluted Doric columns.

At Castle Street's S end, filling the space between Exchange Street and Dock Street, the Greek Revival former EXCHANGE COFFEE ROOM designed by *George Smith* and built in 1828–30 84
as the meeting place, assembly rooms and library of Dundee's mercantile élite. Two-storey front of polished ashlar, the upper floor very tall, and of five bays. At the ground floor the ends are boldly advanced and contain doors set between Doric piers. At each intermediate bay, a window framed by unfluted Doric columns *in antis*; columns, also Doric, in front of the central entrance. Entablature over the ground floor. All this is a base for the upper floor, the slightly advanced walling of its ends fronted by fluted Ionic columns (the order derived from the Erechtheion at Athens), the bays between framed in Ionic pilasters, coupled at the centre, their anthemion and palmette necking also taken from the Erechtheion. Windows all architraved and console-corniced. Entablature and parapet carried across the front, their upper part returning along the sides. Elevation of eight bays to Dock Street, the three W slightly advanced and two-storey, their lower floors with pilastered shopfronts under an entablature, the tall upper storey with windows like those of the front flanking a central opening of three lights framed by Corinthian (Tower of the Winds order) column-mullions *in antis*. The E bays are the same height but of three storeys and plainer, their shopfronts unadorned, the first-floor windows' cornices without consoles and the wall-head parapet replaced by a balustrade. Plainer still the N side

facing Exchange Street and not viewed on the approaches from Castle Street or the harbour. All of three storeys, the W end's upper windows dummies. Inside, a windowless basement occupied by tunnel-vaulted cellars. On the ground floor the central W door opens into the entrance hall. Empire garlands on the frieze of its compartmented plaster ceiling; rosettes at the intersections of the broad beams. Some of the original richly coloured wall decoration has been exposed. Neoclassical panels with stylized floral designs in the borders and between the panels. At the hall's E end, Greek Doric columns frame the entrance to the imperial stair, its cast-iron balustrades with anthemion decoration. Large console-corniced window at the half-landing. At the first floor, a broad doorpiece, also console-corniced, at the entrance to the former assembly room/library which occupies the full frontage of the building. This is over 9 m. high, its coved ceiling's three panels with Greek key borders and containing laurel garlands. At the room's N end, proscenium arch to a recess for a small orchestra.

In DOCK STREET to the E, a couple of Georgian survival buildings (Nos. 20–22 and Nos. 32–34) of the early or mid C19 flank a block of flats (Nos. 24–26) by *The Wilson Partnership*, 1996–8 in tactful Georgian-survival-revival manner. Four-storey and attic block of 1898–1900 (Nos. 37–40 Dock Street) on the corner of Commercial Street. Commercial French Renaissance, its only exuberance the slated steep dome topped by iron cresting over the corner.

Dock Street between Commercial Street and Gellatly Street is filled by THE HOLIDAY INN EXPRESS, by *Young & Gault*, 2008. Large five-storey block, the main part composed of a frame of dark glass around grey-tiled walling, the W two-thirds of the tiling's base cut through a band of dark glass under a copper fascia. The frame's broad W side is recessed and from it extends a curved copper-clad stair-tower.

On Dock Street's E corner with Gellatly Street, Jobcentre Plus (Nos. 54–55 Dock Street and Nos. 1–3 Gellatly Street), for which *see* Public Buildings, above. E of this, Nos. 56–59 Dock Street, designed as the GREAT EASTERN public house by *J. Murray Robertson*, 1880. English picturesque of a near-symmetrical three bays, built of buff-coloured masonry relieved by bands of red sandstone. Tall canted oriel windows, the outer two gabled, the centre one with a slated low spire, rise from the first floor to the attic, their top storey enjoying applied half-timbering. Beside this, a narrow-fronted three-storey-and-attic building (No. 60) designed by *C. & L. Ower* in 1880 to house a chandler's shop with dwelling house above. Weird Gothic detail and, projecting from the attic's shaped gable, a triangular oriel window. Its bravado is unavailing competition for the adjacent huge five-storey former SAILORS' HOME by *Ireland & Maclaren*, 1879–81. This is free French Renaissance, built of stugged ashlar, channelled at the ground floor. Composite-pilastered ground floor, the shopfronts with cast-iron column-mullions in their shouldered-arched windows.

Round-headed main entrance, its keystone carved as a head of Neptune. Above the entrance an oriel window with stilted elliptical-arched heads to the lights. Under the wall-head cornice and parapet, a frieze carved with the names of illustrious British sailors. In the centre of the parapet a segmental pediment, its tympanum carved with the relief of two sailors studying a globe. Over the canted SE corner, a round tower, its steep lead dome topped by a columned and domed cupola. The plainer side elevation along CANDLE LANE ends with the gable front of the contemporary CHAPEL which formed an adjunct to the Home. This is two-storey, the entrance under a semicircular dummy fanlight and flanked by dummy windows, each containing a pair of round-headed lights. Above, a large round-headed window, its main glazing set within a narrow border formed by mullions and crossed by radial stone spokes above the transom.

HIGH STREET'S E end is dominated by the former CLYDESDALE BANK (Nos. 94–96) standing on the triangular site 91 bounded by High Street, Murraygate and Commercial Street. Italian Renaissance, by *William Spence*, 1875–8, faced with polished ashlar, the lower courses channelled. The building is of two parts and functions. At the front, the two-storey bank itself, a triangle but with its W tip squared off, and, facing Commercial Street, an oblong rear block of the same height but three-storey and designed to contain shops and offices. This is much simpler except for Corinthian aedicules at the first-floor windows.

The bank's narrow W front proclaims civic and financial status. This forms a T, the first-floor level marked by a band of rosetted guilloche enrichment. Giant Corinthian pilasters at the ends and at the corners of the bow-sided and aedicular-fronted central projection where they carry an open segmental pediment surmounted by a statue of Britannia accompanied by an anxious lion (carved, like all the sculpture, by *James Young*). In each side of the projection, a baluster-aproned and Corinthian-aediculed ground-floor window, its segmental pediment carved with shell enrichment; above, a window whose cornice is carried on consoles carved with lions' heads. In the front of the projection a console-corniced first-floor window. Below this, a single-storey porch, its Corinthian corner pilasters standing on panelled bases and carrying a cornice studded with lions' heads and surmounted by a balustrade. This porch contains the bank's entrance, its surround with acanthus-leaf decoration; in the porch's side walls, round-headed windows, their keystones carved as heads of Commerce and Justice. In the W front's windowless end bays, shell-headed ground-floor niches containing figures also of Commerce and Justice. The upper floor's panels, carved with the coats of arms of the cities of Glasgow (home of the Clydesdale Bank) and Dundee, were removed in the early C20. The bank's N and S sides are treated identically, with giant Corinthian pilasters between the windows which are larger versions of the side openings of the W front's projection. Bold wall-head cornice under a parapet panelled with a procession of dummy round-headed slits interrupted by stumpy Ionic pilasters. From the front porch one enters the apsed W end of the banking hall, its doorway's inner side with a segmental pediment containing the coat of arms of the Clydesdale Bank. In the windows of both the porch and the banking hall's apse is STAINED GLASS by *W. & J. J. Kier* depicting putti engaged in banking and commercial activities. The banking hall's walls are finished with a rinceau frieze under a rosetted modillion cornice. In the centre of the coved and panelled ceiling, an anthemion-finialled modillion cornice from which rises the domed cupola, its glass painted (by W. & J. J. Kier) with ovals bearing the coats of arms of the principal Scottish and English towns and cities which contained branches of the Clydesdale Bank, together with emblems of Plenty, Agriculture, Commerce, Manufactures, Justice, Navigation and Peace.

COMMERCIAL STREET cuts through the city's medieval layout. Its SE part, from High Street to Dock Street, was laid out by *James Black* in 1828 but widened in 1874 when the street's upper part extending to Meadowside was formed, the new buildings' elevations based on designs produced by the Burgh Surveyor, *William Mackison*, in conjunction with *John Lessels*, architect to the Edinburgh Improvement Trust. Set back from the lower part's W corner with High Street is the Cathedral Church of St Paul (*see* Churches, above). Beside it and with a front garden to High Street is CASTLE HILL HOUSE, an C18 three-storey town house, the painted rubble front half-hidden by a single-storey link to the Cathedral and a two-storey addition of the earlier C19. Facing Commercial Street to the S, a three-storey block by *Alexander McCulloch*, 1889, originally containing a school (now the Cathedral's hall and offices) above ground-floor shops. Institutional Gothic but not unfriendly, its central cupola with a crocketed lead spire. Then, CALCUTTA BUILDINGS (Nos. 18–32 Commercial Street), a large and asymmetrical free French Renaissance three-storey block of offices above shops by *James Maclaren*, 1877, the canted corners topped by fish-scale-slated and bulbous truncated spires finished with lead-capped cupolas. On the S corner of Exchange Street, No. 6 Commercial Street, *c.* 2000, with a curved frontage and glazed tower but hardly stylish.

EXCHANGE STREET runs E. On the N side, Nos. 22–26, a four-storey-and-attic ship's biscuit factory and warehouse of 1868, a gablet containing the hoist door. Front of cherry-cocked masonry, now with cement dressings and, in front of most of the windows, 'balcony' features added on the building's conversion to flats in 1999. There follows a pair of mirror-image four-storey blocks of flats (Nos. 18–20) by *The Wilson Partnership*, 1999. Postmodern vernacular, the inner corners curved, faced with blockwork and metal cladding. On the S side the three-storey and attic Nos. 13–15 of the earlier C19. Central pend under paired first- and second-floor windows; pedimented gablet between wall-head chimneys.

At the bottom of COMMERCIAL STREET'S E side, plain late C19 tenements. The scale and architectural quality rise at the five-storey and attic polished ashlar front of Nos. 29–35 of 1900. Franco-Jacobean-accented Renaissance, two-storey oriel windows at the ends. Similar but slightly more elaborate block on the corner of SEAGATE (Nos. 37–45) by *John Bruce & Son*, 1887, its Frenchy tower's truncated dome topped by iron cresting.

COMMERCIAL STREET'S SW side N of High Street begins with the commercial rear block of the former Clydesdale Bank (*see* above). Opposite, between Seagate and Murraygate, Nos. 51–85 Commercial Street, a large four-storey and attic block by *Alexander Johnston*, 1877. Expensive commercial Renaissance of Second Empire character faced with polished ashlar. Bowed N corners, the E with a Frenchy fish-scale-slated dome finished with a low octagonal cupola, the W with a segmental-pedimented dormer window. Very tall shopfronts with cast-iron Composite columns. The keystones of the entrances to the upper floors of Nos. 55 and 65 are carved with the heads of bearded gentlemen.

Large block on Commercial Street's corner with High Street and Murraygate. Its W two bays (No. 77 High Street) are of *c.* 1880, the first-floor windows segmental-pedimented, the second floor's round-headed. The next three bays, marked off by giant pilasters, are by *Ireland & Maclaren*, 1876, their tall shops originally with cast-iron Composite columns. The upper storeys' polished ashlar is channelled at the first floor whose outer windows are pedimented as is the central opening of the three-light middle window. Round-headed and nook-shafted windows to the modillion-corniced second floor. Dutch-gabled stone dormerheads front a Frenchy truncated spire, its iron cresting now lost. The channelled first-floor stonework and second-floor cornice continue along the rest of the block, also of 1876 but by *Robert Keith*. A few of the shops' original cast-iron columns survive but their fronts are now mostly early C20 Art Deco black marble. Above, giant pilasters divide the façade into sections, the centre bays of some with two-light first-floor windows under stone balconies. Alternating triangular and segmental pediments over the first-floor windows; round-headed and nook-shafted openings at the second floor. Over the corner of Commercial Street and Murraygate, a slated truncated dome, its elaborate iron cresting intact. This development continues along Commercial Street's SW side to Meadowside. On the N corner, another slated truncated spire, its lid-like top surmounted by a tall cresting of scrolled ironwork.

Commercial Street's NE side between Murraygate and 90
Meadowside (the section at Nos. 89–95 designed by *William Alexander*, 1892–3, and Nos. 97–99 by *Alexander Johnston* in 1878) is also Late Victorian. Similar to the SW side but calmer,

the tall ground-floor shopfronts' cast-iron columns surviving at the SE end. Bowed quadrant corners, each covered with a slated Frenchy truncated dome topped by scrolled iron cresting. Three-light windows to the corners' upper floors; a richly carved stone surround at the door of the N corner. A variant to the prevailing architectural norm and the masonry without channelling is provided by the two lower floors of the former COMMERCIAL BANK OF SCOTLAND (Nos. 85–87) by *David Rhind*, 1878–80. At the ground floor, tall windows set in architraves and a pilastered entrance; over this floor, a triglyph frieze. Baluster-aproned and Corinthian-pilastered first-floor windows under a symmetrical disposition of triangular and segmental pediments, the segmental pediment over the tripartite centre window's principal light larger than the others. The tall banking hall at the rear of the main block is entered through a Doric screen; on the other sides, Doric pilasters and lunette windows. Above the walls' entablature a panelled cove, its beams decorated with roses, rises to a flat band round an upper tier of coving with the glazed oblong roof in its centre.

SEAGATE continues High Street as a curve to the NE. After the block of 1877 on the corner of Commercial Street (*see* above) the E side begins with the former CAPITOL CINEMA (now bars) by *William M. Wilson*, 1955–6. Rendered front of two storeys, the very tall first-floor windows exaggeratedly vertical. Huge windows in the red brick N elevation to GELLATLY STREET. Further down that street, the GELLATLY STREET CAR PARK by *Kerr Duncan McAllister*, 1998, a Postmodern attempt to escape functionalism. On Gellatly Street's NE corner with Seagate, a four-storey Renaissance tenement (Nos. 65–67 Seagate) by *J. & F. Salmond*, 1880, the stonework badly eroded. Also of four storeys and an attic but much lower the mid-C19 Nos. 69–77, its ground-floor masonry and the lower parts of the corners' pilaster-strips channelled. Alternating triangular and segmental pediments over the first-floor windows, lugged architraves at the second floor's. E of this, The Bond (*see* Industrial Buildings, below).

On Seagate's W side, after the corner with Commercial Street, Robertson's Bond (*see* Industrial Buildings, below). Abutting its N end, the low and bland late C20 back of No. 45 Murraygate (*see* below). Between Horse Wynd and Peter Lane, Nos. 62–64 Seagate, a narrow-fronted four-storey block of *c.* 1860. Georgian survival and with a quadrant corner. This is answered on the far side of Peter Lane by the canted corner of VIRGINIA BUILDINGS (No. 74 Seagate) by *Charles Ower & Co.*, 1903–14 (altered in 1914 by *George Jamieson*) decorated with stylized strapwork carving. Under the shopfront's cornice are pendant corbels. A cornice and corbels of the same design continue across the front of the single-storey enjoyably Edwardian commercial No. 78, also by *Charles Ower & Co.*, 1903–14. These carry an arcaded parapet with, at its centre, a gablet surmounted by a dragon-finialled segmental pediment, the tympanum carved with shell-head enrichment. The original glazing design survives in the large plate-glass windows, the horizontal upper lights with Neo-Jacobean patterned panes. Then, a tenement (Nos. 110–116) by *Edward & Robertson*, 1894, a two-storey oriel window splayed across the corner with St Andrew's Street.

On Seagate's E side N of Candle Lane, Watson's Bond (*see* Industrial Buildings, below). Behind and extending E of Allan Lane, a traditionally detailed four-storey housing development by *George Johnston*, 1995. Between the two wings of Watson's Bond, Nos. 95–97 Seagate, the former hall of the Loyal Order of Ancient Shepherds by *Johnston & Baxter*, 1907. Two storeys, of red brick with stone dressings. Asymmetrical English late C17 style, the windows mullioned and transomed. On the N corner of Trades Lane, the Bus Station (*see* Public Buildings, above).

A little way down TRADES LANE, on the N side, DISCOVERY WHARF by *ARKTX*, 2007. Four-storey pitched-roofed blocks of flats, the walls faced with red brick and render. Metal balconies and semicircular stair-towers clad in glass bricks give the needed touches of interest. At the foot of Trades Lane and facing SOUTH MARKETGAIT is the three-storey-and-attic MARITIME BUILDINGS by *James Maclaren & Sons*, built for the ship-owners R. A. Mudie & Sons in 1881 and the head office of the Dundee, Perth & London Shipping Co. since 1915. Pompous free Renaissance five-bay façade of polished ashlar, channelled at the ground floor. Across the front, superimposed pilasters, channelled and swan-neck-pedimented at the ground floor where they carry a cornice, decorated with panels carved with lions' heads at the first floor, and, at the second, Ionic and surmounted by the wall-head's balustraded entablature. Central entrance in a pilastered surround of polished red granite.

In ST ANDREW'S LANE, the SEA CAPTAIN'S HOUSE (No. 48 St Andrew's Lane), a harled two-storey three-bay house of the early C19. On the E side of Sugarhouse Wynd, the surviving buildings of the Dundee Calender (*see* Industrial Buildings, below). On Seagate's E corner with QUEEN STREET, MAGNUM HOUSE (Nos. 138–140 Seagate) designed in 1934 by *Cornelius Armour* as a Scottish Co-operative Society grocery warehouse. Large and lumpy Art Deco, the relief of a galley's prow in allusion to Dundee's supposed Norse origin over the entrance. Set-back top storey added by *Pask & Pask* on the building's conversion to flats in 1992.

MURRAYGATE leading N from the E end of High Street was one of Dundee's medieval thoroughfares but widened in the 1870s. At its start, outside the former Clydesdale Bank (*see* High Street, above), a bronze SCULPTURE ('The Dragon') executed by *Tony Morrow* in 1994 from a maquette by *Alistair Smart*. On the W side, after Commercial Street (*see* above), the slightly projecting Nos. 12–14, originally late C18 and of three storeys and an attic but heightened and remodelled in an English Jacobean manner by *Gauldie & Hardie*, 1911. The adjoining four-storey harled block (Nos. 16–20) was rebuilt in 1987–8 when the *Comprehensive Design Group* produced a not especially faithful replica of the C18 building on the site. Then, a pair of two-storey blocks by *Hugh Martin & Partners*, 1984 in a sort of traditional manner. No. 32 is by *H. Wilson*, 1922, of three storeys, the stripped classical façade clad in white tiles; garlanded metal panels between the first- and second-floor window openings. Small and nondescript infill of 1984 at Nos. 42–44. The three-storey No. 46 was built in 1877, its first-floor masonry channelled; carved rosettes between the second-floor windows which rise into gabled dormerheads. Also three-storey Nos. 48–60, of 1924, built as the Dundee store of *F. W. Woolworth & Co. Ltd* to a design by their own architects' department, the Art Deco cinema-like front set back from the building line. This line but not the scale is re-established at Nos. 62–64, by *McLaren, Murdoch & Hamilton*, 1987–9, an insubstantial-looking clock tower on one corner. No. 66 at the entrance to Pullar's Close is of *c.* 1900, the tall shopfront (now altered) under a broad pedimented two-storey oriel window. Some rubble walling, perhaps of the early C19, at the upper storey of Nos. 68–70, followed by Nos. 72–78 Murraygate and Nos. 27–29 Panmure Street. This is by the *Douglas McConville Partnership*, 1998, of two and three storeys, faced with red sandstone ashlar. Modern-traditional but with a flashy glazed round tower on the corner with Panmure Street.

On Murraygate's E side N of the corner with Commercial Street, Nos. 7–15 by *William Alexander*, 1896. Commercial Renaissance of three storeys and an attic in polished ashlar, the first-floor windows of one and two lights with Corinthian column-mullions and pilastered jambs. A drop in scale at Nos. 17–23 of the later C19. Only of two storeys and an attic and three bays, the first-floor windows set in Neo-Jacobean moulded architraves, the outer openings of three lights. The dignified Late Georgian No. 31 was built *c.* 1830 as the BRITISH LINEN CO.'S BANK. Polished ashlar three-storey front of seven bays, the first-floor windows corniced. In 1870 the ground floor was converted to shops (their fronts replaced in the C20). At the l. end, a basket-arched and Gothic-detailed doorway of 1870. Also of polished ashlar and three storeys but taller, this bank's successor (Nos. 35–39) designed by *David*
88 *Cousin* in 1868. Five-bay façade, a dentilated cornice over the ground floor. Anthemion-finialled Corinthian portico containing the central entrance; in the outer bays, console-corniced windows and a door to the agent's house above. First-floor windows also with consoled cornices but with the addition of pediments, the centre window in a Corinthian-columned and pedimented aedicule. The smaller second-floor openings are set back from the wall-plane and shouldered-arched. Above, a rosetted frieze under the wall-head's modillion cornice. Inside, a square double-height banking hall, each wall divided by Corinthian pilasters into three bays crossed by a deep band enriched with anthemion and palmette between Greek key decoration. Set just inside the walls is a second square formed

by Corinthian columns supporting a dome pierced by glazed panels.

Across Horse Wynd, the tame Art Deco rendered frontage of No. 45 by *James M. Monro & Son*, 1936. Murraygate's ensuing traditionally detailed harled infill of the later C20 is followed by three attempts to break with such unexciting tact. The first (Nos. 53–63 Murraygate) is by *Carl Fisher, Sibbald & Partners*, 1987–8. Tall three storeys in an Edwardian-revival stripped classical manner. Next, Nos. 65–69, originally by *Bronek Katz & R. Vaughan*, 1960, with shopfronts below a two-storey rectangular frame enclosing walling broken only by ventilation panels. In 1987–8 this upper part was remodelled, again by *Carl Fisher, Sibbald & Partners*, and given windows set between tapering fins, the resultant appearance better suited to a seaside ice cream parlour than the building's use as a city centre bank. The third (Nos. 71–73) is by *Carl Fisher, Sibbald & Partners*, 1990–1, in red brick with concrete trimmings, a weird and joyless collision of 'Greek' Thomson and Art Deco influences.

COWGATE leads E from the top of Murraygate. On the corner DISCOVERY HOUSE (Nos. 5–9 Cowgate and Nos. 75–79 Murraygate), a joyless five-storey block of polished red sandstone ashlar, by *James Sibbald*, 1910. A few touches of Jacobean Renaissance detail; cupola skied above the corner. On its E and also of polished red sandstone ashlar but only three-storey, CAXTON HOUSE (Nos. 11–19 Cowgate), a former printing works by *Maclaren, Sons & Soutar*, 1908. Quiet Queen Anne with a central wall-head pediment. The polished red sandstone ashlar and three-storey height continue at the former KING'S THEATRE (now a nightclub) by *H. & F. Thomson*, 1908–9. Spare classical with hints of Art Deco. Recessed Doric columns under the canopy at the main entrance; tall windows to the second floor. Splayed corner to St Andrew's Street where the theatre's S end rises an additional two storeys above a very tall channelled masonry base.

KING STREET shares a V-shaped corner with Cowgate. On this, THE TOWN HOUSE, a substantial four-storey and basement house of *c.* 1815. The bowed front (W) gable was remodelled by *Edward & Robertson* in 1876 when the building was used as offices by the jute-making firm of J. & A. D. Grimond. In this remodelling the ground floor was refaced with channelled ashlar which is carried up as pilasters at the corners of the first floor. Also of 1876 the round-headed entrance, the architraves to the upper floors' windows, the consoled cornice over the first floor's centre window and the pediment over the window above. The rubble-built splayed sides along Cowgate and King Street, both with wall-head gablets and the King Street elevation with a couple of corniced first-floor windows, were left alone.

King Street continues with a superior two-storey and basement flat-fronted terrace (Nos. 5–19) of 1815–19. Twenty-four-bay ashlar front, now painted. Along the whole terrace, band courses under the ground and first floors, also with sill courses linking their windows (the first-floor sill course now broken by the deepening of the windows at No. 11). Wall-head cornice and blocking course, set slightly higher over the six bays at each end. At these bays, V-jointed rustication to the ground floor and paired centre doors; symmetrically positioned entrances in the intermediate bays. All the doors have sidelights and segmental-arched fanlights and are contained in broad pilastered and corniced surrounds. Some of the rubble-built rear elevations along Cowgate, a couple with full-height bows, follow the line of that street, possibly incorporating earlier work or later extended over small back gardens. On the terrace's blank E end (now faced in late C20 blockwork), a large sculptured metal ROUNDEL by *Keith Donnelly*, 1996, each radial panel displaying the relief of a hand holding a locket on which is displayed the emblem of one of the Nine Trades of Dundee. Opposite this terrace, St Andrew's Parish Church and the former Glasite Chapel (*see* Churches, above).

THE WELLGATE CENTRE, occupying the whole N side of Cowgate, stretches back up a steeply sloping site to Victoria Road. Designed by *James Parr & Partners* in 1974 and opened in 1978, it comprised three-storey shopping frontages under two floors of offices at the S end but is only of one and two storeys above a basement at the N. The NE corner was designed to contain the Steps Theatre and Central Library (*see* below) with a multi-storey car park in the centre of the E side; a second multi-storey car park on the W side. The basic concept has survived the various alterations since the 1970s. Of these the most significant are at the Cowgate front. Originally, the curtain-walled top floors, supported on pilotis, provided a boldly oversailing top to the set-back shopfronts, only parts of which broke forward like pods. However, in 2004 the shops were extended to the same line as the offices and given a bland and curiously blank façade. From the main S entrance a straight shopping mall extends the full depth of the development, intermittently open as atria to the glazed roof, the upper shopping levels reached by centrally positioned escalators. At the N end, the mall emerges under a glazed awning (added *c.* 2000) into an irregularly octagonal open-air space from which formidable flights of steps lead to the much higher level of Victoria Road. At the top of the N flight, a large Victorian cast-iron BAILIE'S LAMP made by the *Sun Foundry*, a tall fluted column with Neo-Egyptian decoration. The blockwork sculptural forms of the Centre's N end extend E to house the curve-walled Steps Theatre and Central Library, their shared entrance under a bold glass canopy and set behind a forecourt formed in 1996 by *Dundee City Council*. On the Library's upper floor, generously sized S windows overlooking St Andrew's Parish Church (*see* Churches, above) and the curved glass covering constructed over a roof terrace, also by *Dundee City Council*, in 2002–3 to form the Wighton Heritage Centre. Inside the Library entrance, a bronze PLAQUE with a relief portrait of Nelson Mandela, by *Tony* and *Susie Morrow*, 1998.

The Wellgate Centre's NW inner angle is filled by earlier developments fronting VICTORIA ROAD. Abutting the end of the Library, the two-storey-and-attic curved block of VICTORIA HOUSE (Nos. 5–15), 1938, with horizontally proportioned first-floor windows. Vertical windows at KANDAHAR HOUSE (Nos 71–83 Meadowside) on the corner of Meadowside. This is by *Allan & Friskin*, 1930, and built as lettable offices for the Lord Roberts Memorial Workshops, a stone balcony carved with a lion's head over the W entrance.

PANMURE STREET, continuing the line of Cowgate W of The Wellgate Centre, is an introduction to the city centre's educational and office area which grew up on land laid out for development in 1836. On the S, after the corner building with Murraygate (*see* above), the mid-C19 four-storey Nos. 21–25. The adjoining block (Nos. 11–15), designed by *Alexander Johnston* in 1872, is a swaggering Mannerist expression of commercial and industrial might. The three lower floors are of polished grey ashlar. Ten bays but reading as two identical five-bay sections. At each a pair of shops flanks the entrance to offices above. At the ends and centre, paired pilaster-strips crossed by vermiculated bands and rising into triplet consoles carved with grapes. The office entrance is round-headed, the keystone carved as the head of a bearded man; foliaged consoles on the frieze. At the two principal floors above, giant attached Corinthian columns at the ends forming the sides of an open-pedimented narrow aedicule in the centre. Entablature over the second floor, its frieze carved with rosettes and lions' heads. The third floor is low and plain, faced with yellower stonework, and appears as a cheaply constructed afterthought although of the same date as the rest. Canted dormer windows along the roof. W of this as far as Meadowside, a single-storey range of shops of *c.* 1900.

Panmure Street's N side W of The Wellgate Centre begins with a large but routine Italianate-classical four-storey block (No. 10) of *c.* 1865. This block's height, polished ashlar and cornices continue at the mid-C19 No. 8, staider Georgian survival, the first-floor windows all corniced. On the corner of Meadowside, the former UNION BANK OF SCOTLAND (Nos. 2–6 Panmure Street) by *Alexander Johnston*, 1872. Low-key Renaissance palazzo of polished ashlar, rusticated at the ground floor and with channelled pilaster-strips at the corners. Slightly advanced two-bay 'centrepiece' containing round-headed doors (one now a window), their keystones carved as hirsute mens' heads; in front a screen of Doric piers, the cornice surmounted by a Jacobean Renaissance parapet. Above the centrepiece the wall-head balustrade is broken by an urn-finialled segmental-pedimented panel bearing the coat of arms of the Union Bank of Scotland. Narrow quadrant SW corner where the wall-head balustrade is broken by a segmental-headed panel carved with a monogram of the Union Bank's initials.

MEADOWSIDE was laid out under the 1825 Act for Opening Certain Streets in the Burgh of Dundee as a curve from Panmure Street SW to Barrack Street and extended N *c.* 1888. In this N stretch, after the Union Bank, the former SCOTTISH PROVIDENT INSTITUTION building (No. 49) by *Alexander Johnston*, 1897–8, a five-storey palazzo, the upper storeys of polished grey sandstone ashlar, the pilastered ground floor of grey granite. Also four-storey the mid-C19 Georgian survival Nos. 51–53 to the N.

On Meadowside's W corner with Panmure Street, the Royal Exchange (*see* Public Buildings, above). To its W, ROYAL EXCHANGE BUILDINGS designed by *Gauldie, Hardie, Wright & Needham* and built in 1956–7 as the head office of the Royal Exchange Assurance Co. Bland Modern-traditional front faced with Blaxter sandstone ashlar. Beside it, on the corner of Euclid Crescent, the former Panmure Street Congregational Church (*see* Churches, above). These form the N side of ALBERT SQUARE, the semi-formal setting for The McManus and accompanying public sculpture (*see* Public Buildings, above).

On Meadowside's W side, N of the Royal Exchange, are the former PEARL LIFE ASSURANCE offices by *C. & L. Ower*, 1896–8. Vertical and narrow front of polished red sandstone ashlar in an extravagant Flemish-Jacobean manner ('very ornate and rather fantastic', said *The Builder**). Lavishly carved gableted attic windows and a spire-roofed tower at the NE corner of Royal Exchange Lane. Across the lane and on the corner of Bell Street, MEADOWSIDE HALLS, an insubstantial-looking block of flats for students at the University of Abertay Dundee, by *Ian Burke Associates*, 1994–6. It lacks the presence required by its site and function. In BELL STREET, opposite Bonar House (*see* Public Buildings, above), MEADOW PLACE BUILDINGS designed by *James Maclaren & Sons* and built as the public office of the jute manufacturers, Cox Brothers, in 1883–6. Large Second Empire Renaissance but without panache, a dumpy low spire on the canted SE corner. N continuation to Victoria Road in plain but pompous Georgian survival manner, by *Robert Gibson*, *c.* 1920. The block was converted to housing in 1980. On the E corner of VICTORIA ROAD and Bell Street, INDIA BUILDINGS (No. 86 Bell Street) by *J. Murray Robertson*, 1874–6. Three storeys of polished ashlar, with Ægypto-Greek detail and incised ornament in the manner of 'Greek' Thomson but without his originality. To the W, CHAPELSHADE HOUSE (Nos. 78–84 Bell Street), two-storey 1930s *moderne*. Very plain late C19 tenements at Nos. 58–76 (Nos. 72–76 by *Alexander Johnston*, 1869). Also Late Victorian but more ambitious MERCANTILE BUILDINGS (Nos. 48–54) by *James Maclaren & Sons*, 1893. Thinly detailed Jacobean Renaissance, the first-floor windows an almost continuous glazed band across the red sandstone front. The rest

* *The Builder*, lxxv, 1898, 143.

of Bell Street's N side is filled by the University of Abertay Dundee's buildings and, on the S, its Student Centre W of the former Euclid Crescent School and the backside of the High School of Dundee.

MEADOWSIDE S of Panmure Street has buildings only on the E. These begin with the late C20 two-storey brown brick rump of Nos. 48–60 Murraygate. Much better suited are the former CALEDONIAN INSURANCE CO. offices (No. 33 Meadowside) by *J. Murray Robertson*, 1886. Symmetrical English C17 manner with a Dutch gable and two-storey oriel windows enriched with bands of crisply carved thistles; carved decoration also but more weathered on the wall-head parapet. Beside it, another but taller insurance company office, that of the PRUDENTIAL ASSURANCE CO. (No. 31) by *A. Waterhouse & Son*, 1895–7. Jacobean Renaissance and symmetrical but the walling is of red brick with dressings of polished red sandstone. Too small for the site and too timid is the two-storey-and-attic No. 27 by *Baxter, Clark & Paul*, 1975–7, the triple-gabled front faced with dark brown brick. More assertive and of polished ashlar the late C19 No. 21, *c.* 1896, a small-scale display of free Mannerist bluster, followed by the corner blocks to Commercial Street (*see* above).

Meadowside now turns W to form the S side of Albert Square, its centre occupied by The McManus (*see* Public Buildings, above). After the Commercial Street corner, the former Albert Square (Gaelic) Free Church (*see* Churches, above). The ground floor of the adjacent No. 3 Meadowside (the former head office of the DUNDEE SAVINGS BANK) by *T. Lindsay Gray*, 1968, makes deferential reference to the former church whose height it continues.

NW of Albert Square and on the axis of Reform Street, the High School of Dundee's main building in the central segment of EUCLID CRESCENT and, to its W, the Margaret Harris Building (*see* Public Buildings, above), the buildings of the University of Abertay Dundee (q.v.) rising up behind.

On Meadowside's NW corner with Euclid Crescent, its E end facing directly across Albert Square to The McManus, is COURIER PLACE (No. 2 Albert Square) by *Niven & Wigglesworth*, 1904–6. Built as the head office of the *Dundee Courier* and its sister publications, this huge American-influenced free classical edifice is closer in spirit to a dignified financial institution than a purveyor of journalistic sensationalism. Five storeys, all of polished red Closeburn (Dumfriesshire) sandstone ashlar, channelled at the ground and quasi-mezzanine first floors, the channelling carried up as strip quoins at the narrow quadrant E corners. In the ground floor, large doors and windows, all round-headed; over the principal entrance in the S front, a crowned globe flanked by half-length figures of Liberty and Justice by *Albert Hodge*. Small windows, also round-headed and with heavily corbelled sills, light the first-floor mezzanine whose cornice serves as a plinth for the giant panelled pilasters which frame each bay of the three floors above. In all these, three-light windows which form two-storey canted oriels at the centre of the E end and the three central bays of the S front. Mutuled cornice at the wall-head. The W bay of the building's N side is gently curved out of respect for the streetline of Euclid Crescent. Ill-considered attic addition over part of the roof. Lower and plainer NW block, also of 1904–6. At the building's SW corner, a massive and tall tower by *T. Lindsay Gray*, 1960–1. The two lowest storeys are inaccurate quotations from the Edwardian main block. Above, seven storeys in a stripped classical style, rather in the manner of A. E. Richardson; fully glazed NE corner housing a stair. In Meadowside immediately to the W, a concrete-framed four-storey block (POST OFFICE) of *c.* 1950, unworthy of its position between Dundee's most prominent commercial edifice and its former General Post Office (*see* Public Buildings, above). Opposite, The Howff (*see* above).

BARRACK STREET'S NW corner is filled by the former Central Reading Rooms (*see* Public Buildings, above). S of South Ward Road, FRIARFIELD HOUSE, the sizeable office block of the adjacent but now demolished Ward Mills. This is by *Maclaren & Aitken*, 1873–5. Restrained French Renaissance, the ashlar masonry channelled at the ground floor and stugged above. Rounded NE corner containing the entrance set in a Roman Doric piered and balcony-topped surround; pedimented first-floor windows. Over the corner, a slate-roofed truncated round spire finished with iron cresting. On Barrack Street's SW corner with Willison Street, WILLISON HOUSE by *Findlay & Stewart*, 1934. Faience-clad four storeys in a very restrained Art Deco manner.

CONSTITUTION ROAD continues the line of Barrack Street N of Ward Road. Its W side starts with a splay-cornered three-storey commercial and office block (Nos. 1–2 Constitution Road and Nos. 1–7 Ward Road) by *Edward & Robertson*, 1869, the first- and second-floor windows set in giant overarches. Immediately N, Dundee Congregational Church followed by the former Watt Institution (*see* Churches and Public Buildings, above).

On Constitution Road's E side after the former General Post Office (*see* Public Buildings, above) and on the corner of EUCLID STREET, the former DUNDEE SAVINGS BANK (No. 2 Euclid Street). This is Tudor by *James Maclaren*, 1865–7. Two tall storeys of stugged ashlar. Basket-arched door and windows to the ground floor. Tracery-panelled aprons under the first-floor openings, all these linked by a continuous hoodmoulding-string course which rises between the S front's first-floor windows to form 'gablets' containing shields carved alternately with the coat of arms of Dundee and the monogrammed initials of the bank. Stiff-leaf-capitalled attached columns rise from corbels at the string-course level to the foliage-enriched wall-head cornice where they support gableted buttresses in front of the stepped merlons of the parapet. In the centre of the W elevation a three-light window, its column-mullions with granite shafts and stiff-leaf capitals, and, above, the heraldic achievement of the burgh of Dundee under a gablet formed by the string course. N of the bank, a pair of very plain late C19 tenements (Nos. 3–5 Constitution Road).

WEST BELL STREET was laid out by the Dundee Town's Architect, *James Black*, in 1839. It starts off, at its S corner with Constitution Road, with the former Bell Street United Associate Church (*see* Churches, above), its design (by Black) suggesting that it was intended to be one of two identical end pavilions of a palace-fronted terrace. The adjoining three-storey, basement and attic house (No. 1) of *c.* 1840 continues the putative terrace, its badly weathered ashlar stonework V-jointed at the ground floor, like that of the former church. Also of three storeys with a basement and attic and faced with eroded polished ashlar but much taller and free Italian in style is the former CURR NIGHT SHELTER by *David Maclaren* of *Ireland & Maclaren*, built to provide food and beds for outcasts and vagrants in 1880–2. Channelled masonry to the ground floor, its windows' semicircular blind heads decorated with rosettes. In the head of the entrance, also semicircular, the relief of a Lady Bountiful (Charity) welcoming the homeless and inscribed I WAS A STRANGER AND YE TOOK ME IN; framing the entrance, a pedimented aedicule, its stumpy Corinthian columns' shafts of polished granite. The former PARISH COUNCIL CHAMBERS (No. 9) by the Dundee City Architect, *William Alexander*, 1899–1901, continues the height and general appearance but in more classical form. Opposite, the University of Abertay Dundee Library (*see* University of Abertay Dundee, above).

West Bell Street's S side ends with the WEDDERBURN BUILDING (No. 15) by *Ian Burke Associates*, 1972, a large but graceless office block faced in concrete-aggregate, the red cast stone of the attic failing to give cheer. On the N, the Sheriff Court and behind, its principal front to West Marketgait, the Tayside Police Headquarters (for these, *see* Public Buildings, above).

WARD ROAD is a W continuation of Meadowside. On the S, after the former Central Reading Rooms, the Central Baptist Church (*see* Churches and Public Buildings, above). Then the two-storey No. 12 built in 1897 as the Dundee Water Commission's offices. It was designed by *Alexander Johnston* in a Scots C17 town house manner, the front of stugged grey ashlar enlivened by dressings of polished red sandstone. Three oriel windows project from crowstepped gablets; off-centre elliptical-arched vehicle entrance. On its W and also of two storeys but taller, the WARD ROAD GYMNASIUM (No. 14) by *Alexander McCulloch*, 1890–1, but reconstructed in 1926–7 after a fire. Five-bay front of polished pale ashlar, the ends and broad centre slightly advanced. Two- and three-light windows, the first-floor openings round-headed, those of the ends with fleur-de-lis finials to their keystones. The centrepiece, originally tall, was lowered in height and its first floor remodelled, and both it and the end bays lost their high French roofs in 1926–7. The round-headed and console-keystoned entrance of 1890–1 survives. It is set in an Ionic-pilastered aedicule, the segmental pediment containing the relief of 'Mother Dundee reclining, surrounded by a group of hearty, healthy children, illustrating the power of gymnastics'.* On the corner of North Lindsay Street, LINDSAY HOUSE (No. 30 Ward Road) by *Rip Fleming*, 1975, a five-storey office block faced with horizontal bands of glass and splay-topped concrete-aggregate panels.

NICOLL STREET leads off the N side of Ward Road. On its W, the former Foresters' Halls (*see* Public Buildings, above). In Ward Road W of Nicoll Street, Nos. 9–13, a sizeable tenement of faintly Jacobean inspiration, by *David Mackenzie II*, 1864. This forms the SE corner with RATTRAY STREET. For the Rattray Street Baptist Church and the former Ward Road Wesleyan Methodist Church on the W corner of Rattray Street and Ward Road, *see* Churches, above. After the intrusion of a S wing of the Wedderburn Building (*see* West Bell Street, above), on Ward Road's corner with COURTHOUSE SQUARE, the five-storey former CENTRAL HOTEL (No. 1 Courthouse Square) built in 1927–8 to a design by its first proprietor, *J. Hall Nicol*. Of red sandstone ashlar but plain except for a few simplified and idiosyncratic details to give a hint of Jazz-Modern; canted SW corner. On the other side of Courthouse Square the former Industrial School, now Strathmore Lodge (*see* Public Buildings, above). On Ward Road's SW corner with North Lindsay Street and entered from JOHNSTON STREET, a five- and seven-storey block of student flats (COURTHOUSE APARTMENTS) by *Mackie Ramsay Taylor*, 2003. Elevations angled to the various streetlines and rather restless in red cast stone, harling and metal cladding but with a certain panache and far from drab.

NORTH LINDSAY STREET properly begins with the Lindsay Street Mill (*see* Industrial Buildings, below). S of the Lindsay Street Mill and stretching to South Ward Road, the three-storey former BUS STATION (Nos. 64–72) by *Gordon & Scrymgeour*, 1933–5, long and horizontally proportioned in a timid *moderne* manner. More vertical and with more style is the two-storey block (Nos. 43–45) opposite, also by *Gordon & Scrymgeour*, 1932; metal panels enriched with reeding and stylized foliage between the ground- and first-floor windows. At its S end, a building (No. 41) by *Mackie, Ramsay & Taylor*, 1978, its piended roof and drydash and glass walling hesitating between modernity and tradition. To its E, on South Ward Road's N side, a former engineering works (*see* Industrial Buildings, below). The W side of North Lindsay Street's final stretch S of South Ward Road begins with the huge Dundee House (*see* Public Buildings, above) followed by a pair of tenements (Nos. 32–36 North Lindsay Street) by *William Alexander*, 1871, both faced with polished ashlar and with consoled cornices over the first-floor windows. The ground floor of the

* *The Dundee Year Book . . . for 1891*, 1892, 142.

l. tenement contained shops, the r. the offices of the *Dundee Courier and Argus* set behind round-headed arcading.

INDUSTRIAL BUILDINGS

THE BOND, No. 81 Seagate. Three-storey bonded warehouse by *Robert Blackadder*, 1867–8. In the channelled ashlar ground floor broad basket-arched and keystoned cart entrances and round-headed windows with panelled aprons; elliptical-arched windows to the upper floors. Lotus-flower vases on the E end of the wall-head's parapet.

DUNDEE CALENDER, Sugarhouse Wynd. Surviving fragments of an extensive calender complex begun 1822. On the W side of Sugarhouse Wynd, a two-storey rubble-walled and piend-roofed block, its W front of six bays at the upper floor, the S bay a hoist opening. To the S, three gables of a late C19 rubble warehouse building.

ENGINEERING WORKS, South Ward Road. Now in other use. Late C19. Tall single-storey and rubble-built, with a quartet of piended gables to the street.

LINDSAY STREET MILL, North Lindsay Street, Johnston Street and South Ward Road. Large rubble-built jute mill, now in other use. On the corner of North Lindsay Street and Johnston Street, a three-storey-and-attic block by *Maclaren & Aitken*, 1874–5. Simplified Lombardic Romanesque large gable; at the S corner, a tower under a slated French pavilion roof. The building extends W along Johnston Street in plain fashion. Rusticated quoins mark the W end of the 1870s work. The building was extended to the corner of South Ward Road in 1881 by *G. S. Aitken* who also added a SW wing. All quite plain except for the splayed W corner which is dressed up with rusticated quoins and a battlement.

ROBERTSON'S BOND, No. 38 Seagate. By *Johnston & Baxter*, 1897–8, the huge former bonded warehouse of the whisky distillers, John Robertson & Son. Four-storey and attic red sandstone Jacobean. Symmetrical and without fussy detail. Transomed windows, some also mullioned. Domed semi-octagonal turrets flank the pedimented gables which contain the two principal entrances. Above the heavily corbelled wall-head cornice, battlements which rise into crowstepped gablets over the end sections; over the centre, scooped-out parapets and a gablet.

WATSON'S BOND, Nos. 93–99 Seagate. Now housing. Huge office and bonded warehouses designed by *Johnston & Baxter* and built for the whisky blenders, James Watson & Co., in 1906–8. External walling all of glazed red brick with some polished ashlar dressings, the main structure within of reinforced concrete. Irregular U-shaped W frontage, the cavity filled by Nos. 95–97 Seagate (*see* Description, above). Five-storey-and-attic S wing, its three-bay W façade pierced by three-light windows, those of the four lower floors contained in giant round-headed overarches. Moulded corbels under the wall-head's tall battlements whose centre rises into a stepped gablet pierced by a round-headed window. Stepped gable at the W end of the S elevation to Candle Lane, all the openings contained in a giant overarch; the remainder of this lane frontage quite plain. The five-storey N wing's W façade is of seven bays. Banded and obelisk-finialled pilaster-strips at the corners and to mark off the centre whose open pediment breaks the line of the outer bays' wall-head parapets. Round-headed windows and a corniced central pend opening at the ground floor; elliptical-arched windows above. The building's cut-out NW corner to Trades Lane is now filled by a nondescript 1930s two-storey block. E of this, the back of the wing of the main building advances to the street, its N façade a large but similarly detailed version of the Seagate frontage. The warehouse was rebuilt as flats behind the façades in 1995 when *George Johnston* provided more genteel versions of the original faced in paler brick.

WATERFRONT

Long, skinny coastal strip containing the dockland and former dockland of Dundee and reclaimed land on the N bank of the Tay. It is cut off from the rest of the city by the railway line opened in the 1830s and the dual carriageway roads constructed in the late C20. Since the 1990s efforts have been made to develop the W of the area as a fashionable residential and entertainment quarter.

HARBOUR

Originally the harbour of Dundee seems to have consisted only of the N bank of the Tay between the present Discovery Wharf and Caledon West Wharf. Here a concave-shaped sloping beach, well behind the present line of docks and wharves, was sheltered except from the S wind. In 1447 James II granted Dundee Town Council the right to levy shore dues on goods shipped from the port and thereafter harbour works seem to have been carried out. By the C16 and perhaps for some time before it comprised, beside wharves on the river bank, a stone pier protected by a breakwater each side, the resultant pair of tidal basins stretching forward from Dock Street between the present Union Street and Castle Street. Frequent repairs were made in the C17 and C18, perhaps most notably after a storm in 1668 and by *John Smeaton* in 1770. By the beginning of the C19 the harbour consisted of a tidal basin of *c.* 1.82 ha. bisected by a pier and protected by a pair of diagonally placed island breakwaters but with neither wet dock nor dry dock.

In 1815 Parliament passed the Dundee Harbour Act which transferred responsibility for the harbour from the Town Council to Harbour Commissioners. They adopted proposals by *Thomas Telford* for construction, on the E side of the existing harbour, of a 2.63 ha. wet dock and associated small graving or dry dock in its SE corner. They also provided for the reconstruction of the existing harbour with an angled SW breakwater and an answering breakwater extending from the SE corner of the new wet dock to give a shared entrance harbour serving both the tidal harbour and the new wet dock. Telford's design was carried out in 1815–25, with *David Logan* as the resident engineer, the new wet dock being later named King William IV's Dock. During the course of the work a second Dundee Harbour Act was passed in 1819 as a result of which a tidal ferry harbour with a long sloping pier was formed on the W side of the main tidal harbour. Following Parliament's passing a third Dundee Harbour Act in 1830 by which the Harbour Commissioners were replaced by the Dundee Harbour Trust, the old tidal harbour was developed in 1832–4 as a second wet dock (the Earl Grey Dock) of *c.* 2.12 ha., also designed by Telford but in conjunction with *James Jardine* and *John Gibb* and with *James Leslie* acting as Superintending Engineer.

In 1835, immediately after completion of the Earl Grey Dock, James Leslie produced plans for a third wet dock. This was to be on the E side of King William IV's Dock and entered from a new tidal harbour to its E. Construction was begun but halted in 1837 by a financial crisis. Twenty years later work resumed, now with *Charles Ower* as engineer, at the E end of the project but, instead of forming a tidal harbour, another wet dock (the Camperdown Dock) was constructed. In 1871–5 Leslie's unfinished wet dock (the Victoria Dock) was completed to a revised plan and with a dry dock at one corner, all designed by *David Cunningham*, Ower's successor as Harbour Engineer.

From the late C19 the provision of docks to shelter vessels has been accompanied and largely superseded by the formation of riverside wharfs to the E of the harbour. Land reclamation of parts of the foreshore E of the Camperdown Dock was carried out in 1872–4 in anticipation of building work although the first actual construction work of new wharfage was the lengthening in 1885–6 of the existing Western Wharf (further lengthened in 1891) on the S side of the Victoria and Camperdown Docks. Development some way to the E of the existing harbour began in 1890–1 with construction of the Eastern Wharf and, immediately to its E, a cattle depot with accompanying wharf and sheds. The Fish Dock, built beside the cattle depot to house the Dundee trawler fleet, was opened in 1900 and the Eastern Wharf, originally of timber, was reconstructed in reinforced concrete and widened, 1903–9.

The major work of the earlier C20 was the construction, in three stages between 1913 and 1930, of the King George V Wharf between the E entrance to the Camperdown Dock and the Eastern Wharf. Loss of docks and further provision of wharfs took place in the mid and late C20. The Western Wharf, still of timber construction, was partly rebuilt in reinforced concrete in 1952–5 and renamed the Queen Elizabeth Wharf. Soon after, in 1962–3, the William IV and Earl Grey Docks, at the N end of the new Tay Road Bridge, were infilled. After the opening of that bridge in 1966 the Ferry Harbour, now redundant, was reconstructed and lost its long pier. Also in 1966 was completed a reconstruction of the Fish Dock and its renaming as the Tidal Harbour. The W end of the Eastern Wharf was rebuilt in the later C20 to form the Caledon West Wharf and the Princess Alexandra Wharf, the latter extended in 1974. E of the Tidal Harbour, the Caledon East Wharf was also constructed in the later C20 and the Prince Charles Wharf in 1977–9 and extended in 2003.

The harbour is now partly, at the W end, a historically evocative but functionally redundant setting for hotel, leisure and commercial buildings, together with large amounts of housing (for all these, *see* Description, below), and partly, for its E stretch, a grimly purposeful expanse of wharfs covered by a utilitarian C20 development of industrial sheds, oil depots and refineries (for the Storm Water Tank, *see* Public Buildings, below).

At the W end, the former FERRY HARBOUR of *c.* 1820, its walls faced with ashlar. The long sloping pier which projected from the W side was removed on the harbour's reconstruction as a wet dock in the 1980s to house the RRS *Discovery*, a ship constructed by the *Dundee Shipbuilding Co.* in 1901 for Captain Robert F. Scott's National Antarctic Expedition. Beside it was the EARL GREY DOCK of 1832–4, now infilled but its outer wall survives. This is of bull-nosed ashlar. Slipway, the stone ramp partly covered with concrete, at the W end; at the E, a pair of rounded bastion-like projections, each accompanied by a stone staircase down to the river. Beyond the site of the King William IV Dock, now the footing of the N end of the Tay Road Bridge and its accompanying access roads, the VICTORIA DOCK. This is roughly rectangular, of *c.* 4.3 ha. in extent, faced with stugged masonry, the large blocks of rough ashlar slightly bigger at the N and W walls built in 1869–75 than at the E and S which date from 1835–7. At the SE corner, a small DRY DOCK of 1869–75. Moored on the S side of the Victoria Dock are two ships. The NORTH CARR LIGHTSHIP was built in 1933 and placed here in 1997. To its E, the frigate HMS *Unicorn* constructed in 1824 and which served as a drill ship for the Dundee section of the Royal Naval Reserve after 1873. At the Victoria Dock's entrance from the Camperdown Dock to the E, a segmental-arched cast-iron SWING BRIDGE, the sides pierced by round holes which diminish in size towards the centre; coat of arms of the Dundee Harbour Trust as the fulcrum. The CAMPERDOWN DOCK of 1857–65 is a rough rectangle covering *c.* 3.4 ha., the sides mostly built of rough ashlar but part of the S side is constructed of cast iron set behind a concrete frame.

PUBLIC BUILDINGS

CUSTOM HOUSE AND HARBOUR CHAMBERS, Dock Street. A work of sober classical dignity built in 1840–3. The design was by *James Leslie*, Resident Engineer of the Dundee Harbour Works, in collaboration with *John Taylor*, Surveyor of Buildings to H.M. Customs, who was chiefly responsible for the façade. Three storeys, the front and sides of polished ashlar, channelled at the ground floor which is finished with a cornice. N front of thirteen bays, with five-bay outer sections and a three-bay centrepiece. The centre of each outer section is slightly advanced at the ground floor and contains a round-headed and console-keystoned entrance (the W to the Dundee Harbour Trust offices, the E to the Custom House) under a stone-balustraded balcony. This fronts the first-floor window which is set between scrolls and topped by a consoled pediment. Sill course linking the architraved and corniced outer windows of the first floor. Moulded architraves also at the smaller second-floor openings. Wall-head entablature and set-back parapet. The centrepiece's ground floor projects as a loggia with round-headed and console-keystoned arches standing in front of the windows; carved wreaths in the spandrels. The loggia is surmounted by a balustrade punctuated by the pedestals of the giant Ionic columns of the upper floors' 'portico'. In the 'portico's' pediment, a high-relief carving (renewed by *Graciella Ainsworth* in 1992) of the Royal Arms of Scotland. Behind the 'portico', windows like those of the outer bays, the first floor's centre opening pedimented.

The W end elevation is of three bays, treated like the centre bay of one of the outer sections of the front. Slightly set back at the S end, a single-storey cartshed, its segmental-arched entrance under a balustrade. The E elevation was extended from three to five bays by *C. & L. Ower*, 1881–4, and a further single-storey extension, a canted bay window at its S end, was added by *Maclaren, Soutar & Salmond* in 1936. Harled addition of *c.* 1920 on the rubble-walled rear elevation.

DISCOVERY POINT, Discovery Quay. Visitor centre, by the *Michael Laird Partnership*, 1992–3, and almost stylish. Two-storey octagon, the walls of horizontally droved blockwork and glass; roof of coated ribbed aluminium rising with one step to a glass-sided domed cupola. Fully glazed E side overlooking the Ferry Harbour and the RRS *Discovery*.

DUNDEE ORPHAN INSTITUTION, Carolina Port. Now housing. By *William Chalmers*, 1869–70. Two-storey-and-attic rubble-built U in a cheap mixture of Jacobean and French Renaissance. The main front is to the S where two-storey canted bay windows under shaped gablets flank the aediculed doorpiece. Ball-finialled ends with minimally projecting rectangular bay windows.

DUNDEE STATION, South Union Street. Originally the Tay Bridge Railway Station. Built in 1887–9. Booking hall and entrance contained in a modernistic boxy building of 1959, faced in metal cladding and glass but without style. The rest is mainly of the 1880s. Stair down to the gently curved island platform which is placed in a cutting below the level of the adjacent streets. Over the platform, ridge-and-furrow awnings carried on squat cast-iron columns, their necks decorated with rosettes. From them spring large four-way brackets, their spandrels pierced by circular openings. At the platform's E end, a central two-storey building, of red brick with buff stone dressings and pedimented gables. On the S side, this building's upper floor is reached from Riverside Drive by bridges over the track, their superstructures formed by frameworks of cast-iron piers infilled with glazing and surmounted by double-pitch roofs with obelisk finials on the gables.

EAST WHALE LANE CAR PARK, corner of East Marketgait and East Dock Street. By *Dundee City Council*, 2011. Five-storey oblong, a tower at the centre of the S end.

NEW OLYMPIA CENTRE, corner of East Marketgait and Seagate. Swimming pool and ancillary facilities, by *Dundee City Council*, 2011. Large and shaped like a ship's prow, the W end narrowing and rising gently under a long sloping roof.

OLYMPIA LEISURE CENTRE, Earl Grey Place. By *David Bell*, of *James Parr & Partners*, 1970–4. Lump of painted blockwork barely relieved by the tiling of the W elevation. Tall roofless 'portico' with a ribbed concrete fascia along the N (entrance) side. Snakework of colourful ducts on the back.

ROODYARDS CEMETERY, Broughty Ferry Road. A rubble-walled enclosure first opened as a graveyard in 1561 when Plague victims were buried here, the present headstones mostly of the earlier and mid C19. – In the centre, the late C18 GUTHRIE MAUSOLEUM. It is a domed square of polished ashlar with coupled Ionic pilasters at the corners; at each face, a keystoned round-headed panel.

106 STORM WATER TANK, Camperdown Dock. By the *Nicoll Russell Studios*, 2002. Large and low rotunda, not unlike a Martello tower, of buff-coloured GRP cladding under a silvery dish roof oversailing the open top floor.

TAY RAILWAY BRIDGE. At 3.26 km. the longest railway bridge in Britain but unexciting. It was built in 1881–7 to replace the earlier bridge of 1871–8 (designed by *Thomas Bouch*) which had been destroyed in a storm in December 1879. *W.H. & C. Barlow* were the engineers and they placed the new structure *c.* 18.3 m. upstream of its predecessor, the bases of whose piers are still visible and many of whose girders were reused. Sloping very gently from N to S, it is of eighty-four spans, seventy-four of these crossing the river itself in a straight line except at the N end where it curves to the E. The piers are each constructed with an underwater part consisting of brickwork columns, *c.* 9.7 m. apart, enclosing concrete cores and enclosed in wrought-iron cylinders. Above the water they are formed of pairs of octagonal hollow legs of wrought iron joined by a round-headed arch, the piers rising higher at the thirteen navigation spans over the centre of the river. At the outer spans the piers support lattice girders on which are laid the twin railway tracks. At the navigation spans they support hogback-shaped lattice girders through which the tracks are threaded.

TAY ROAD BRIDGE. The 2.22 km.-long but disappointingly utilitarian crossing of the Firth of Tay, by *William Fairhurst*, 1962–6. A shorter route to the E was ruled out because of the cost of long spans necessary to allow passage for large ships into Dundee harbour, a route to the W clear of the city centre because here the river bed was 'littered with expensive Post Office cables'.

Forty-two spans, increasing in length from 24.4 m. at the ends to 54.9 m. at the centre, so counteracting the optical illusion occurring with a bridge of equal-length spans when viewed from the shore that the end spans appear longer than the centre. The spans are constructed of steel box girders (made by the *Caledon Shipbuilding and Engineering Co. Ltd* in conjunction with *Sir William Arrol & Co. Ltd*) resting on boat-shaped piers, tapering towards the bottom, of shuttered concrete. On the box girders, a concrete roadway of four vehicular lanes and a central walkway. On the outer sides, inward-leaning concrete balustrades; metal balustrades and paired lamp standards along the centre.

V&A AT DUNDEE, Earl Grey Place. Proposed large gallery beside the River Tay, the 'iconic' building of Dundee's Waterfront. *Kengo Kuma & Associates* were appointed the architects in 2010 after a competition for the design of the building to house exhibitions mounted by Dundee City Council in partnership with the Victoria and Albert Museum, London. Construction is scheduled to begin in 2012 and be completed in 2014. The general appearance is that of a pair of conjoined ships' hulls but rising from the river embankment rather than the water itself and constructed of horizontal bands of concrete clad in reconstituted stone.

DESCRIPTION

RIVERSIDE DRIVE is the approach road from the W, passing under the Tay Railway Bridge (*see* Public Buildings, above) which forms a gateway to the area. Then a roundabout followed, on the S, by a small PUMPING STATION of *c.* 2005. Oval of pale brown brick under an angular and boldly oversailing monopitch roof of ribbed copper. On the other side of the road, the long and low shopping shed of TESCO of 1989–90, the yellowish concrete blockwork enlivened by red coloured bands under green copper ribbed roofs. A couple of gablets and low towers on the S side, the SE tower pagoda-like. At the W end, a mirrored screen between the store's car park and the road. The screen extends E to the veranda fronting the store itself. Opposite Tesco's E end, a SCULPTURE by *Jeremy Cunningham* and *Paul Grimes*, 2004. Rectangular archway of diagonally droved stone, the inner faces of the jambs and lintel of white painted metal. In it is suspended the framework of a boat containing nautical appendages (e.g. a buoy and foghorn). To the E, a pair of three-storey office blocks, QUADRANT HOUSE and COMPASS HOUSE, by the *Holmes Partnership*, 2001–2 and 2005–6, joined by a glazed link. Quadrant House's N and S elevations are divided vertically into three sections by broad strips of yellowish ashlar which also forms a fascia under the broad-eaved roof; in each section, green and blue vertical panels. Projecting from the N side of the E section, a large but low round tower faced with granite and glass. At each of Compass House's main elevations, a rectangular frame containing horizontal bands delineating the floors and vertically proportioned windows divided by grey-blue and yellow mullions. At the W end of the N front, a rectangular tower, its sides metal-clad, its front glazed. At both buildings, long slatted visors over the S windows. E of Compass House, the two-storey PREMIER INN of 1994, its would-be traditional manner failing to evoke either dockland purpose or seaside frivolity. On its E, beside the river wall, the ALEXANDRA FOUNTAIN presented to the community by Lord Provost William Longair, *c.* 1905. Classical square shelter with granite-shafted Roman Doric columns, a swagged frieze and a crown-finialled dome. Inside, the figure of a putto holding a dolphin. It was formerly at the foot of South Union Street. It stands beside the visitor centre of Discovery Point which looks N over the road to Dundee Station and E over Craig Harbour to the Olympia Leisure Centre (for all these, *see* Harbour and Public Buildings, above). Further E, in EARL GREY PLACE, the five-storey box of the HILTON HOTEL of 1988, and extended in 1996–7. Surprisingly mean-windowed except for the fully glazed S wall of a single-storey S projection overlooking the Tay. Large but low brick-walled and metal-roofed GALA CASINO of *c.* 2000 to the N. Then the Tay Road Bridge (*see* Public Buildings, above) crosses over the footpaths and road. Just W of the bridge, a large concrete 'STANDING STONE' bearing bronze plaques by *Charles Henshaw* recording the bridge's opening in 1966.

E of the Tay Bridge, WEST VICTORIA DOCK ROAD leads S from the Custom House on Dock Street (*see* Public Buildings, above) to the Tay. On its W side, overlooking the end of the Victoria Dock (*see* Harbour, above), the seven-storey APEX CITY QUAY HOTEL by *Ian Springford Architects*, 2001–3. Straightforward grid frontage of wood (now painted) and glass above a horizontal band of brick and glass at the two lower floors. Further S, a pair of sleek and soulless five- and six-storey office blocks (RUSHTON COURT and RIVER COURT) by *Comprehensive Design Architects*, 2008–9. On the N side of Victoria Dock, the CITY QUAY SHOPPING CENTRE formed in 2000–1, incorporating much of the structure of the RAILWAY GOODS SHEDS designed in 1875 by the Dundee Harbour Engineer, *David Cunningham*, with *C. & L. Ower* as consultants. Long single-storey range, the N elevation all Victorian. It is built of brick with stone used for rusticated quoins at the large former shed openings and stone frieze under the eaves.

Originally the W gable was entirely of wood but a sizeable expanse of glazing was introduced in 2000–1. The S side's wall (formerly composed entirely of wooden sliding doors) has been rebuilt in wood and glass but the tie-beam metal structure of the roof survives. It projects as an awning supported on cast-iron beams carried on columns (by *John Stewart & Son* of Irvine), their integral rainwater hoppers modelled as bearded human heads. On the far side of the railway track S of this range (relocated from its working position to the N of the sheds), a second but shorter range, all of 2000–1 and standing on a narrow stretch of infill of the dock. U-plan and timber-clad, with large windows and a ribbed metal roof. Two-storey centrepiece, its roof a bold display of double pitches and broad eaves; large bowed balcony to the S. Fronting this range, a wooden walkway cantilevered out over the Victoria Dock. At the E end of the N of these two ranges, the CLOCK TOWER, a six-storey former granary by *David Cunningham*, 1877, converted to housing by *Archial Architects*, 2008. Broad stugged ashlar oblong; projecting from the pedimental W gable, a clock tower with ball finials on the corners of the crowning balustrade. The main block's openings form alternating tiers of windows, the top floor's round-headed, and former hoist openings contained in giant round-headed overarches. At the E gable, a tier of balconies in a bowed projection was added in 2008. E of the Clock Tower, a RAILWAY GOODS SHED by the Dundee Harbour Engineer, *Charles Ower*, 1865. Single-storey and broad, brick-built with rusticated stone quoins at the corners and the large goods doorways. Big round-headed windows above the doors in the gables. Attached to the E side, an addition of *c.* 1885 overlooking Camperdown Dock. Cast-iron structural framework in which are set wooden sliding doors. On the E side of Camperdown Dock, the Storm Water Tank (*see* Public Buildings, above).

SOUTH VICTORIA DOCK ROAD bounds the S side of Victoria Dock. Extensive development of the early C21 to its S. On the E side of West Victoria Dock Road, a pair of almost identical monopitch-roofed six-storey and attic blocks of flats, PANMURE COURT and UNICORN COURT by *Ritchie, Dagen & Allan*, *c.* 2005, their walls faced with red brick and render and with wood cladding to the top floors, the S block with S balconies overlooking the Tay. These form the W side of a courtyard. On its short S side, a plain rubble-walled range of the later C19 heightened by two storeys *c.* 2000. On the N side of the courtyard, a three-storey and attic sawtooth-roofed range of *c.* 2010. On the courtyard's E side, a two-storey and attic rubble-built range of WORKSHOPS (converted to housing by *Ritchie, Dagen & Allan*, 2006–8) designed for the Panmure Shipyard by *James Leslie*, 1837, and extended N by six bays *c.* 1850. The W elevation is quite straightforward except for segmental-arched cart openings and a pend gateway. On the E side, a tall and square tapering chimney of brick above a masonry base. In the courtyard, remains of a mid-C19 PATENT

SLIP (now infilled). It forms a long bow-ended ramp with segmental-arched openings in the stugged rough ashlar walling. On the E side of CHANDLERS LANE, a two-storey and attic range of shipyard WORKSHOPS of the later C19, the windows originally all elliptical-headed. Further E, two more courtyards between THORTER LOAN and THORTER ROW with three-storey ranges of terraced housing to E and W and six-storey blocks of flats facing South Victoria Dock Road to the N and MARINE PARADE WALK beside the Tay on the S, all faced with brick, render and dark-coloured metal cladding. Yet another courtyard bounded by blocks of flats E of Thorter Row but lower, only the corner blocks rising to five and six storeys and an attic, and with wood cladding much in evidence. Similar but taller courtyard on the E extending to THORTER NEUK. E of this, yet more blocks of flats built in 2011 around a courtyard but dourer. At Victoria Dock's E end, on the N side of South Victoria Dock Road, a single-storey PUMP HOUSE by *David Cunningham*, 1875. Ashlar-faced with ball finials on the gable and a couple of metal ventilators on the roof.

NETHERGATE, MAGDALEN YARD AND PERTH ROAD

A long wedge extending W from the City Centre to which its E extremity belonged until the formation of the dual carriageway of West Marketgait in the 1960s. Land N of this was laid out for the 'New Town' of South Tay Street at the beginning of the C19. At the same time villas began to appear along Perth Road and in Roseangle and Magdalen Yard Road to its S. The mid and later C19 and early C20 brought more concentrated development, a juxtaposition of tenements, terraced housing and detached villas sprinkled with a complement of churches and public buildings. The mid and late C20 and the opening years of the C21 have been notable for the University of Dundee's occupation and development of much of the area between Nethergate and Perth Road on the S and Hawkhill on the N.

CHURCHES

DUNDEE METHODIST CHURCH, West Marketgait. By *Reid & Greig*, 1965. Small two-storey box, the front's upper floor of ribbed concrete, the ground floor glazed.

DUNDEE WEST CHURCH, corner of Perth Road and Roseangle. Originally St John's Free Church. Spikily detailed Decorated Gothic, by *James Hutton*, 1882–4. Basically the shape is cruciform but with 'chapels' to the S (liturgical E) of the transepts and a transeptal vestibule across the N (liturgical W) end. Steeple in front of the E aisle and, in front of the W, a tall gabled outshot with a baptistery-like projection to its W. At the front of the vestibule, a four-light window under a trio of gablets.

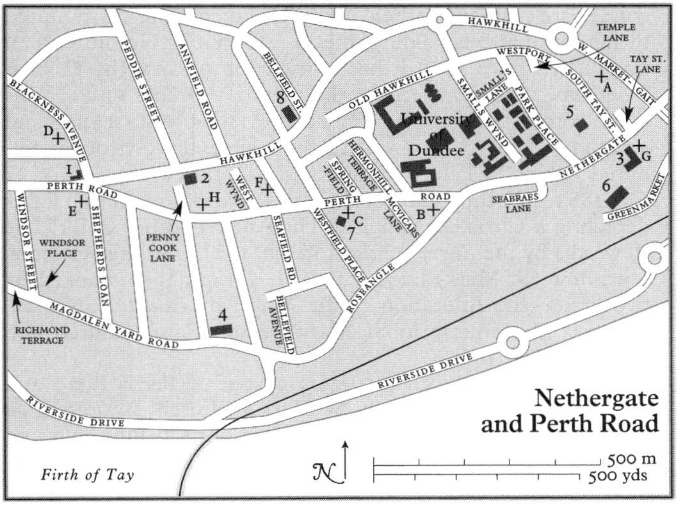

A	Dundee Methodist Church	1	Blackness Library
B	Dundee West Church	2	Blackness Primary School
C	Gate Church International	3	Dundee Contemporary Arts Centre
D	Logie and St John's (Cross) Parish Church	4	Dundee Institution for the Blind
E	McCheyne Memorial Free Church	5	Dundee Rep Theatre
F	Ryehill United Presbyterian Church	6	Sensation Science Centre
G	St Andrew's (R.C.) Cathedral	7	White Top Centre
H	St Peter's Free Church	8	Whitehall Theatre

Behind and above rises the nave gable finished with a pierced parapet. It contains a four-light window, the head filled with a rose carved by *James Bremner* with reliefs of flowers and the heads of the Protestant heroes, Martin Luther, John Knox and Thomas Chalmers, first Moderator of the Free Church of Scotland. To the r., pinnacled buttresses frame the gabled projection fronting the W aisle. In this, a door, its gablet's tympanum with a cusped roundel decorated with carved foliage. Similar door at the base of the steeple. Its tower's two lowest stages are square but with chamfered corners. Broaching under the tall and slender belfry from whose corners project carved beasts. Rising between the belfry's gableted openings, the elegant stone spire. The other elevations are simpler, Late Gothic tracery in the windows and an abundance of carved work. To the W, a plain harled HALL by *Joseph Johnston*, 1937–8.

The church INTERIOR is high and spacious, divided into a nave and aisles by very tall and slender foliage-capitalled and bundle-shafted cast-iron columns. Under the ends of the roof trusses are pendant corbels, those at the crossing surmounted by figures of angels holding shields. – Elaborate Gothic NORTH GALLERY. Since 1969 it has housed the ORGAN (by *C. & F. Hamilton*, 1896) formerly at the S end. – Gothic PEWS, their backs comfortably raked. – Late C20 COMMUNION TABLE and PULPIT. – STAINED GLASS. In the S apse, three strongly coloured lights (St Peter, St John and St Andrew) by *F. Holt & Co.*, 1883. – At the S ends of the aisles, two war memorial lights depicting a Christian Knight ('The Answer to the Call'; 'The Reward') by the *Stephen Adam Studio*, 1921. – In the vestibule, a window (St Mark) by *Alexander L. Russell*, 1952, flanked by two lights (the Adoration of the Magi) by *Douglas Strachan*, *c.* 1927, all formerly in St Mark's (now Gate) Church and moved here *c.* 1968.

GATE CHURCH INTERNATIONAL, corner of Perth Road and Greenfield Place. Originally St Mark's Church. By *Pilkington & Bell*, 1867–9. Rogue Gothic, the masonry of buff-coloured snecked ashlar with polished dressings, the tall steeple prominent in the streetscape. The principal front faces N. Main gable with a stepped roof to suggest a nave and aisles behind, the 'aisles' with round-headed arcading under the eaves. In front of each 'aisle', a lower gabled outshot containing a window of two acutely pointed lights, the central mullion's capital carved with stiff-leaf; rose window above. At the lower stage of the 'nave', a porch containing a bipartite door, the openings' arched heads sharing a foliage-capitalled column; over the openings, more carved foliage pierced by a sexfoil. All this is contained in a single broad arch springing from foliage-capitalled squat columns. The porch's parapet is also decorated with carved foliage and a central roundel containing a cross; above this, the parapet rises to form a fleur-de-lis-finialled gablet. Behind and above the porch the 'nave' gable contains a pair of two-light windows, their columns with tall foliaged capitals, the arch-heads carved with foliage and pierced by a quatrefoil. Framing both windows, a single giant pointed over-arch, its head also decorated with foliage and pierced by a sexfoil. To the r. of the 'nave' gable, a low stair-tower under a tall Frenchy spired roof; from it projects a single-storey outshot, its front with a two-light window, its parapet carved with rosettes. To the l. of the 'nave' gable is another outshot, of one tall storey, the window of its gable front with a broad central mullion carved with stiff-leaf; above, a sexfoil opening. Rising behind is the steeple. Its tower is sturdy, the two lower stages gripped by clasping buttresses; gabled porch at the E face. Tall octagonal belfry, each of its main faces pierced by an opening of two louvred lights under a sexfoil set in a circle; empty image niches on the narrow intermediate faces. Above the belfry, a tall stone spire.

Behind the façade the church is two-storeyed, originally with an oblong apse projecting from the splayed S end; single-storey bowed outshots on the E and W sides. In 1879–80 *Ireland & Maclaren* extended the building S by one further bay, reducing the apse to a barely projecting organ chamber. Also of 1879–80 and by Ireland & Maclaren are the Gothic hall, classroom and vestry attached to the S end. The hall further S was added by *Wilson & Wilson* in 1934–6.

INTERIOR divided into a nave and aisles by columns, their lower shafts of stone, their upper of cast iron. Hammerbeam roofs; over the aisles, they run transversely. Galleries, their fronts articulated by attached barley-sugar columns, at the N end and E and W sides, the side galleries extended S in 1879. The focus is on the exceptionally roomy PULPIT of 1879–80 fronting the contemporary ORGAN CASE (now empty). – Victorian PEWS, those of the area arranged in semicircular disposition. – STAINED GLASS. Under the W gallery, a four-light window (David and Jonathan, a memorial to George Jarvis Bell-Belmont and his friend, William Kidd) by *Stephen Adam & Son*, 1898. – Under the E gallery, another four-light window (the Virtuous Woman, a memorial to James Muirhead) by *Stephen Adam*, 1904.

LOGIE AND ST JOHN'S (CROSS) PARISH CHURCH, Blackness Avenue. Originally St John's Parish Church. By *H. & F. Thomson*, 1911–14. Impressively large-scale Romanesque, built of hammer-dressed masonry. Clearstoreyed nave rising from between low aisles, tall transepts and W chancel. In the SE inner angle of nave and S aisle, the base of an uncompleted tower. NE corridor link to a contemporary hall designed as a miniature version of the church. At the hall's NE end an assertive brown-brick addition by *Robbie & Wellwood*, 1970–1, a slate-hung low tower at its NE corner.

The principal E entrance opens into a vestibule covered by a boarded elliptical-arched tunnel vault; above it, the end gallery. The red-tiled floor of the nave and passage aisles slopes down towards the W end. Over the nave, another boarded tunnel vault, also elliptical-arched. Nave arcades of round-headed arches with scalloped cushion capitals. Tall two-bay arcades to the transepts. On the S side, a third and equally tall arch from the one-bay choir, entered through a tall chancel arch and raised three steps above the nave, into the organ chamber. On the choir's N side, blind arcading as if to frame sedilia, the W arch containing the entrance to the hall passage under a small window. The sanctuary is raised a further four steps. On its W (end) wall, blind arcading. FURNISHINGS (including the pulpit on the S of the chancel arch, the font (circular and of stone) on the N, choir stalls and, in the sanctuary, elders' pews and communion table) of 1914. All, except the font, of oak with Romanesque detail intermingled with Neo-Celtic touches. – ORGAN by *Allan Watson*, 1925.

STAINED GLASS. Three-light W window (the Risen Lord with St John and St James) by *J. & W. Guthrie & Andrew Wells Ltd*, 1922, an accomplished design with brightly coloured figures set against a background of obscured glass. – In the N wall of the choir, a window (female saint) by the *St Enoch Glass Co.*, 1931. – In the W wall of the N transept, a depiction of St

Cecilia by *Alexander L. Russell*, 1951. – The aisle windows are filled with brightly coloured and realistic Scenes from the Life of Our Lord of *c.* 1950–65, mostly designed and executed by *Alexander L. Russell.*

McCheyne Memorial Free Church, Perth Road. Disused. By *Pilkington & Bell*, 1869–70. Characteristically Rogue Gothic exhibiting a proliferation of carved detail, the tall steeple a local landmark.

29 N façade, its walling of stugged ashlar with dressings of polished stone, composed of the nave gable flanked on the l. by the steeple and on the r. by the slightly lower double-pitch-roofed W aisle's gable with a lower vestry beyond. The base of the nave gable is pierced by a long and low window, its five squat and stilted square-headed lights separated by foliage-capped broad mullions. Above, a large Decorated Gothic window, the five lights grouped 2:1:2, the outer pairs surmounted by quatrefoils, the central opening by a rose. In the gable of the W aisle, a plain pointed door under an outsize rose window filled with trefoils surrounded by small quatrefoils. The lower and parapeted vestry outshot to its r. is of two storeys. Ground-floor window of two stilted square-headed lights; at the first-floor, a large quatrefoil opening.

The steeple dominates. Square low tower, its two bottom stages battered, the lowest's N face filled by a Gothic aedicular inscription panel commemorating the Rev. Robert McCheyne †1843, the Evangelical minister of St Peter's Church, in whose honour this church was named, the E face containing the entrance whose squat columns' exaggeratedly tall foliaged capitals support a cusped and pointed blind arch, the tympanum carved with stylized foliage. Between the first and second stages of the tower, a band decorated with rosettes. At each face of the second stage, a cusp-arched narrow window. Above this stage, a bully-boy show of broaching to a tall octagonal belfry, the faces all rising into etiolated gables pierced by circular dummy openings. At each of the cardinal points, an opening of two narrow cusped and louvred lights, their column-mullions granite-shafted and foliage-capitalled. Under the gables of the intermediate faces, rosetted square panels between trefoil-decorated bands. From within the belfry's gables rises the tall and slender octagonal stone spire.

The church is built on ground which slopes steeply to the S, so the E and W sides stand above a basement which becomes a full ground floor at the end. Aisle roofs at right angles to the nave. In each side, a trio of transeptal gables, the outer with three-light ground-floor windows, their openings, as elsewhere, stilted and square-headed and set between broad mullions, the taller gallery windows Decorated Gothic. Projecting from each centre bay is a single-storey-and-basement bow, its main window of five lights; in the gable above, a large rose window. In 1898–9 *Sydney Mitchell & Wilson* extended the church S by one bay, the bowed sides of their addition pierced by plain Gothic lights; flèche over the junction of the old and new work.

At the S end the nave was continued as an oblong apse, the S gable containing a high-set rose window, its tracery consisting of three large trefoils set among quatrefoils probably reused from the original S window. In the SE inner angle, a conical-roofed turret. Attached to the S end of the church, a plain two-storey house, also of 1898–9.

The INTERIOR'S three N bays of 1869–70 form an oblong consisting of a nave with its aisles occupying the transeptal outshots at the sides. Gallery across the N end and in the aisles, its Neo-Jacobean wooden fronts supported on foliage-capitalled cast-iron columns; above, a superimposed tier of columns supports the vaulting ribs of the nave roof and the beams under the aisle roofs. Collar-braced roof decorated with rosetted hammerbeams. Bench pews arranged in elliptical curves in the area of the church. The roomy PULPIT of 1870 and the ORGAN of 1899 at the S end form the focus of the building. – STAINED GLASS by *Henry Holiday*, 1919–20, and *Alexander L. Russell*, *c.* 1950.

RUSSELL INDEPENDENT CHAPEL, corner of Hawkhill and Ure Street. Now part of The Whitehall Theatre (*see* Public Buildings, below). Cheap Gothic in stugged masonry, by *James Maclaren*, 1868–9. The pinnacled S gable provides the principal front, a plate-traceried three-light window over the entrance.

RYEHILL UNITED PRESBYTERIAN CHURCH, Perth Road. Now housing. By *Maclaren & Aitken*, 1878–80. Lombardic Romanesque, a tall tower at the SE corner. The large windows were partly blocked and partly altered with smaller openings on the church's conversion to flats in 1984–5.

ST ANDREW'S (R.C.) CATHEDRAL, Nethergate. Large Perp Gothic box of a church (given cathedral status in 1923) by *George Mathewson*, 1835–6. Facing the street, a fire-screen N front clad in polished ashlar. It is divided by buttresses, topped by tall panelled and crocketed pinnacles, to suggest a nave and aisles behind. Straightforward angle buttresses at the outer corners. Projecting from the central pair of buttresses are lower ones, each topped by an octagonal pinnacle rising into a crocketed finial. Over each 'aisle', a sloping battlement with deep and narrow crenelles; the 'aisle' fronts are pierced by tall two-light windows, their hoodmoulds' label stops carved as bearded men's heads. Under each window, a canopied image niche in which is placed a pedestal, presumably intended for a statue. The walling of the 'nave's front is carried up higher, ignoring the line of the roof behind, and finished with a plain parapet. The full width of the 'nave' below this parapet is filled by a trio of windows, all with slender bundled shafts, the outer opening of two lights and simple, the much taller centre window of three lights under a double tier of tracery and surmounted by a hoodmould, its label stops carved as women's heads. Below these windows, a shallow battlemented porch. In its centre, a pointed entrance, its orders with elided capitals. Above, a crocketed ogee hoodmould with male headstops, the 21 finial topped by a cross. At the S (liturgical E) end, an apse added by *Charles J. Menart* in 1920–1. It cuts into the CLERGY HOUSE of 1835. This was originally of three storeys but raised to four and given a flat-roofed bowed extension jettied out at the upper floors in 1920–1.

INTERIOR. The unaisled nave is covered by a Tudor-arched plaster ceiling, the main transverse ribs springing from heavy corbels, their soffits modelled as foliaged pendants. Also springing from these corbels are the depressed arches of plaster panels along the E and W walls. In these side walls, tall two-light traceried windows, their depressed arches carried on tall shafts, their capitals elided. In the N (liturgical W) bay of the nave, a gallery which extends back over the vestibule and is carried on four depressed arches which flank the narrower and more steeply pointed arch over the central passage. At the nave's S (liturgical E) end, a depressed arch springing from corbels carved as angels. It opens into the wedge-shaped and marble-clad choir and sanctuary added by Menart in 1920–1. Nine steps up to the choir and then, under an elliptical arch, a dizzying further seven to the sanctuary. – Curved behind the high altar, a REREDOS, presumably of 1921, the tabernacle surmounted by a large Gothic panel behind the crucifix, surmounted by crocket-finialled tabernacle work. Each side of this, three Gothic panels, each painted with an angel. – On the nave walls, four tall PAINTINGS of SS Catherine, Andrew, Margaret and George. They look early C20. – STAINED GLASS. In the sanctuary, central (S) window (the Martyrdom of St Andrew) flanked by two windows depicting saints, all probably of the 1920s. – The other chancel windows contain insipid heraldic glass of the later C20. – In the nave, the two N windows each side (on the E, St John at the Last Supper and Our Lord's Commission to St Peter; on the W, St Teresa, the Conversion of St Paul) are of 1928, the others (Saints, and the Mysteries of the Rosary) probably a little earlier. – In the baptistery at the church's NE corner, a two-light window (the Baptism of Our Lord; Our Lord with Little Children), probably early C20.

ST PETER'S FREE CHURCH, St Peter Street. Originally a chapel of ease and set behind a small graveyard. Prosperous if not architecturally advanced Late Georgian in appearance, the steepled church was designed and constructed in 1836 by the Dundee builder-architects, *David Hean & Sons*. The body is formed by a broad box faced with rough ashlar. On the roof, a couple of Victorian ventilators. Two-storey elevations, the side windows elliptical-arched below and round-headed above where they light the galleries. A pair of tall round-headed windows under a dummy oculus in the W gable. At the pedimented E end, a pair of round-headed gallery windows flank the boldly projecting steeple. This is of five stages, the lower three, rising as high as the body of the church and crossed by string courses, faced with the same masonry. In each exposed face of the bottom two stages, round-headed openings, the second stage's smaller than the first's. Smaller again and also round-headed the louvred belfry openings in the N and S sides of the third stage but the E opening is square. This stage is finished with an entablature of polished ashlar, the facing material of the top stages. In each front of the slightly intaken fourth stage, a pilastered and keystoned round-headed panel framed by coupled anta-pilasters supporting an entablature. Above this the tower's top stage is further intaken and with cut-out corners. It is taller, each front formed as a pilastered and pedimented aedicule now containing the face of a clock by *Alexander Keir*, 1872. Octagonal spire, its polished ashlar pierced by oculi. Extending from the N face of the tower, a single-storey C20 link to a two-storey HALL, built in the mid C19 as a school and extended *c.* 1870. N of this, a CHURCH OFFICER'S HOUSE, also of two storeys but pyramidal-roofed and pierced by a pend.

Inside the church, a U-plan gallery on slender cast-iron columns with foliate capitals. – At the W end, a pair of STAINED GLASS windows (Our Lord and Children: the Good Shepherd) of 1919.

WESTERN CEMETERY
Perth Road

Laid out in 1845 by *James R. Findlater* who also designed the entrance GATEWAY. This is a Tudor Gothic screen of polished ashlar above a base of pebble rustication. In the centre, panelled octagonal turrets with fish-scale-slated domical tops (the E now missing) clasp the sides of the tall and broad battlemented hearse and carriage entrance, the central merlon surmounted by the figure of a mourning angel. Extending from either side, walls bearing Gothic inscription panels and pierced by buttress-flanked pedestrian entrances under draped urns. At each end of this screen, a tall pier finished with a crown spire. The line of the gateway is carried E and W by dwarf walls, also with pebble-rusticated bases but now bereft of railings. At the E end, a single-storey Gothic LODGE of 1845, its buttressed elevation to Perth Road with round-headed dormer windows.

Inside the cemetery, in the place of honour on the axis of the gateway, the MONUMENT to Ann Spark Wood †1850, a pedestal topped by the figure of a girl mourning beside an urn. It typifies the other Victorian memorials which display the repertoire of obelisks, urns, columns (some shattered) and angels; the wall monuments are generally Gothic aedicules. About two-thirds of the way back, the cemetery's original NE and NW corners are occupied by Gothic MAUSOLEA (the E belonging to the Colville Carruthers family). Each has a buttressed front wall; lions' heads at the ends of the cornice and wreaths on the stepped parapet above. The cemetery was extended N in 1868 following plans drawn by *Patrick Findlater*.

UNIVERSITY OF DUNDEE

The genesis of the University came in 1881 with the gift of £130,000 from Miss Mary Ann Baxter, sister and heir of the textile magnate Sir David Baxter, supplemented by a further £10,000 from her cousin, Dr John Boyd Baxter, a former Procurator Fiscal of Forfar. The money was used to provide premises and an endowment for a university college for 'promoting the education of persons of both sexes and for the study of science, literature and the fine arts'. University College, Dundee, was opened officially in 1883, the new institution occupying four villas fronting Nethergate together with new chemical and engineering laboratories and the former St John's Free Church of 1844, which was converted to a college hall (now demolished). The academic staff consisted of a Principal and five Professors.

In 1890 University College was affiliated to the University of St Andrews, a union not fully effective until 1900 by which date a medical school had been founded at Dundee, its premises built a few years later on the site of the former college hall. Further buildings, notably science and engineering laboratories, were put up before the First World War. The interwar years were a period of stagnation for University College, its students in 1939 numbering only 250, mostly reading medicine or scientific subjects.

In 1953 University College was renamed Queen's College and soon after added faculties of Law and Social Science. By the mid 1960s student numbers had increased to over 2,000 and in 1967 a divorce from St Andrews was finalized and Queen's College became the independent University of Dundee. Since then it has continued to develop and strengthen its existing faculties and also acquired new ones for arts subjects. In 1997 the Duncan of Jordanstone College of Art joined the University. The last years of the C20 and the opening years of the C21 have seen major building work.

Descriptions of the University buildings between Nethergate and Hawkhill are here grouped by streets beginning at the E end of the area and, in each street, from S to N.

BONAR HALL, Park Place. Student hall of residence, by *Gillespie, Kidd & Coia*, 1974–7. Facing Nethergate, a stepped arrangement of blocks, their yellow brick walling almost unbroken. To Park Place, large windows set in horizontal boarding.

SCRYMGEOUR HALL AND COMPUTING CENTRE, Park Place. Originally Dundee's Training College (a teachers' training college) and the associated Practice School, now housing the University's Faculty of Laws and Computing Centre. By *T. Martin Cappon*, 1912–15. The former training college is squared-up static Baroque, faced with red Dumfriesshire sandstone ashlar, channelled at the basement above which rise the three principal storeys. Front of seventeen bays, the corners of the advanced ends clasped by superimposed pilasters, the giant lower order channelled and rising to the top of the first-floor, the upper order stumpy and panelled. In the front face of each of these end bays, a trio of round-headed and keystoned basement windows. At each of the ground and first floors, a corniced three-light window; at the second floor, a Diocletian window, its keystone hanging from a swagged rectangular panel flanked by a pair of circular panels, also swagged. This window sits above a cornice which is carried over the top of the corners' lower pilasters and continues across the main block to its centrepiece.

In the main block's outer bays, round-headed and keystoned windows, corniced at the ground floor. The centrepiece is of three bays, the outer bays' walling channelled at the three lower floors, the first-floor openings set between swagged square blocks and corniced dummy openings flanking the second-floor windows. Double stair, its front decorated with Empire garlands, to the central entrance. This is a massive Roman Doric aedicule with banded columns, the tympanum of its open segmental pediment carved with acanthus-leaf ornament above armorial shields. A cupola used to stand behind on the ridge of the roof.

The former Practice School to the N, also clad in polished red sandstone, appears like a younger brother to the Training College but with Roman Doric porticoes in the inner angles of the U-plan front.

DUNDEE DENTAL HOSPITAL AND SCHOOL, Park Place. The part at the S end is of 1949–52 by *Findlay, Stewart & Robbie* who joined together a pair of detached two-storey and basement houses of the earlier C19, each faced with stugged ashlar and with an anta-pilastered doorpiece. The linking section is Neo-Georgian, of polished ashlar. Swagged cartouche above the corniced entrance, keystoned and round-headed first-floor window. In 1963–7 *Robbie & Wellwood* added an eleven-storey tower faced with panels of concrete aggregate and, behind the earlier part to the S, a three-storey 'Fyfestone'-walled block. To the N, a timidly Modernist ashlar-clad block by *Findlay, Stewart & Robbie*, 1952.

TOWER BUILDING, corner of Nethergate and Small's Wynd. 99
Built to house the University's library, administration and some teaching departments, by *Robert Matthew & Johnson-Marshall*, 1957–61. Scandinavian-influenced Modern Movement, an eleven-storey oblong tower, faced with rubble, vertically boarded timber cladding and glass. Part of the fourth floor is cantilevered out at the SW corner; near the N end of the W side, a top-floor balcony. Low horizontally proportioned blocks extend to E and W, the E of 1957–61, the W intended from the start but not built until 1966–8.

OLD TECHNICAL INSTITUTE, Small's Wynd. Originally The Technical Institute and independent of University College, it now houses the University's Geology Department. American-influenced Free Renaissance, by *J. Murray Robertson*, 1886–8. Greenish-buff walling of stugged thin ashlars. Two storeys above a high basement and with a roof-lit attic. Front of three very broad bays, the centre minimally advanced under a foliage-decorated pediment. At each floor of the end bays, a four-light window, the first floor's mullions with Neo-Egyptian tops, too blocky to be categorized as capitals. The entrance is placed at an intermediate level between the centrepiece's basement and ground floor, the pediment of the wooden surround rising at the latter into the central opening of a broad window of three lights, the outer two round-headed, the centre segmental-arched; mullions in the form of stumpy pilasters with rosetted necks. Under the five-light first-floor window are panels carved with reliefs depicting activities of engineering and of the construction, textile and metallurgical industries. Behind, the contemporary COLLEGE HALL (originally an engineering laboratory), its mansard roof supported on lattice trusses.

OLD MEDICAL SCHOOL AND CARNELLEY BUILDING, Small's Wynd and College Green. Now the University's School of Life Sciences. The former School of Medicine at the W is of 1902–4 by *James Findlay* adapting sketch designs produced by *J. Murray Robertson* before his death in 1901. Scoto-Flemish Renaissance; four storeys and an attic, built of stugged ashlar. Main (S) front of eleven bays with two-storey domed turrets projected on continuous corbelling at the outer corners. Slightly advanced and Dutch-gabled centrepiece containing the entrance under a round-headed 'fanlight' (first-floor window) and battlement within which rises a two-storey oriel window. The roof's cupola is now missing.

ENTRANCE FOYER link to the adjoining Carnelley Building by the *Nicoll Russell Studios*, 2002–3. Glass front wall; fixed to its centre, a large ashlar panel.

The CARNELLEY BUILDING, originally Chemistry Department, was built in stages. All are Neo-Georgian and without panache. The first, by *Ireland & Maclaren*, 1886, was of a single storey and basement. Principal (S) façade of polished ashlar, channelled at the ground floor of the main block. Three-light windows at the centre of the SE jamb. In 1888–9 *J. Murray Robertson* made the front a U by the addition of a SW jamb to balance and replicate the SE. A rear extension came in 1905. Then in 1950 an upper floor in the same manner was added by *T. Lindsay Gray* who, in 1958, gave the building an attic contained in a dormer-studded mansard roof.

EWING BUILDING, S corner of Small's Wynd and Small's Lane. Built to house the Engineering Department, it is by *Reginald Fairlie & Partners*, 1950–4. Originally of two tall storeys above a basement. Long E front in an authoritarian manner, articulated by giant anta-piers; metal glazing in the windows. Low attic addition of the later C20.

FULTON BUILDING, N corner of Small's Wynd and Small's Lane. The Civil and Mechanical Engineering Department, by *Walter Underwood & Partners*, 1960–7. Four-storey main block, the ground floor faced with crazy-paved rubble. The upper floors, partly projected on pilotis, form a bland expanse of polished ashlar broken by traditionally proportioned windows. Lower but equally bland N part now joined by a rendered and blue-painted link to the CIVIL ENGINEERING RESEARCH LABORATORIES of 2000, a two-storey box of grey brickwork.

FLEMING BUILDING, Small's Wynd. Originally The Fleming Gymnasium gifted to University College, Dundee, by the financier, Robert Fleming, a native of the city. Neo-Georgian of a sort by *Mills & Shepherd*, 1904–5. Seven-bay S façade of one tall storey, built of stugged ashlar with polished dressings. At the ends, corniced doors under inscription panels; between them, round-headed and keystoned windows set in rectangular overarches. At the W a less assertive but contemporary block containing fives courts.

GEDDES QUADRANGLE, off Small's Wynd. The closest the University comes to having a collegiate-looking centre, a not very grand semi-formal space reached by lanes squeezed between the ends of buildings. Its S range is provided by the rear of the Fleming Building (*see* above), the other ranges front the quadrangle. In its centre, a SUNDIAL commemorating the meeting of the British Association for the Advancement of Science at Dundee in 1912. Stone pillar with a faceted head supporting a metal hemisphere. The quadrangle's W side is formed by the CARNEGIE BUILDING, originally Carnegie Laboratory of 98 Physics, by *Rowand Anderson & Paul*, 1908–9. English Renaissance, of two storeys and an attic, the ground floor faced with grey sandstone ashlar, the first-floor with red sandstone enlivened by dressings of grey stone and with rusticated corner quoins; piended roof covered with small tile-like slates and with steeply pedimented dormers. The E front simultaneously suggests and belies symmetry. It is of eleven bays but the advanced 'centrepiece' is N of centre. Surmounting the 'centrepiece', a segmental pediment carved with the swagged coat of arms of the University of St Andrews. At the ground floor, in the 'centrepiece's' l. bay, a door set in a lugged architrave under a curvaceous pediment carved with a book flanked by foliage. On the roof behind the 'centrepiece', a cupola of late C17 inspiration. The 'centrepiece's first floor is occupied by a large Venetian window. In the outer bays of the ground floor, segmental-arched windows except at the S end where the two l. windows are circular. Corniced first-floor windows placed above apron-like projecting panels; the two l. bays are windowless but contain an inscription panel.

Cliff-like S gable rising above a basement fully exposed in the fall of the ground. The centre is advanced under a pediment, its tympanum bearing the heraldic achievement of the City of Dundee. First-floor Venetian window with an exceptionally tall central light; corniced sidelights which are topped by corniced rectangular panels pierced by bullseye windows.

The Geddes Quadrangle's N side is filled by the HARRIS BUILDING, originally New Engineering Laboratory, of 1910–13 and also designed by *Rowand Anderson & Paul* in an English Renaissance manner with a ground-floor of grey sandstone and upper floor of red stone with grey dressings and rusticated quoins. The main block's front is of eight bays. As at the Carnegie Building, the ground-floor windows are segmental-arched. At the E end the penultimate bay is windowless and the final bay contains the entrance, the door set in a moulded architrave under a panel bearing a coat of arms flanked by putti. First-floor windows with moulded architraves, cornices and deep aprons but the penultimate window at the E end has a consoled pediment and balustered apron and the window over the entrance is without an apron. Mutuled wall-head cornice and a piended roof, covered, like that of the Carnegie Building, with small tile-like slates. The N elevation is faced more economically with hammer-dressed red sandstone masonry. Rising at its centre, a square tower of five stages, the top two visible from the Geddes Quadrangle and clad in polished red sandstone ashlar with grey stone dressings. Oculi at the fourth stage and segmental-pedimented small windows at the top. Ogee-profiled lead roof with a wrought-iron finial. The Harris Building's SE wing bounds the E side of the Quadrangle. It displays the same contrast of red and grey sandstone as at the main block and the Carnegie Building. Lighting the ground floor is a trio of three-light windows.

Immediately W of the Harris Building and just outside the Geddes Quadrangle, the PETERS BUILDING, originally the Peters Electrical Engineering Laboratory. Also English Renaissance and of two storeys, the lower floor faced with grey sandstone, the end bays of the upper with red stone and grey dressings, it is of 1908–10 and designed by *Mills & Shepherd*. S front of three bays. The outer windows are segmental-arched at the ground floor and of three lights at the first. The centre is all of grey stone and slightly advanced under an open segmental pediment containing a cartouche and the date 1909. Corniced door under an inscription panel at the ground floor; above, a wooden-mullioned tripartite window.

MAIN LIBRARY, corner of Small's Wynd and Cross Row. Built in two stages. The earlier, by *Faulkner Brown 'Hendy' Watkinson & Stonor*, 1985–6, is at the W. Three storeys of aggregate concrete cladding above a glazed base. Much more stylish and
103 larger is the library's second stage, fronting Small's Wynd, by *Austin-Smith:Lord*, 2005–7. S elevation of metal and glass with slatted canopies to the windows and an oversailing roof. Fully glazed E elevation fronting the main reading rooms. The ground floor is recessed except at the rendered S corner. Cut-out NE corner. The N elevation is a horizontally boarded gentle curve joining to the earlier part.

CHAPLAINCY CENTRE, Cross Row. By *James Parr & Partners* (partner-in-charge: *Gordon Farquharson*), 1973–4. Drydashed, a two-storey block of offices and meeting rooms at the S. To the N, a bow-ended block of the same height but of only one storey which contains the chapel. At the join of the two, a glazed entrance to the foyer which divides and connects the two parts. The chapel's interior is orientated to the NE. Top-lit, the light filtered round the edges of a suspended wooden ceiling. At the NE end, a stylized realist SCULPTURE (the Crucifixion) carved from Darney stone by *Hew Lorimer*, 1985–6. – On the W wall, ceramic STATIONS OF THE CROSS, also in a stylized realistic manner, by *Frank Partridge*, 1978. – CHAMBER ORGAN by *Peter Collins*, 1978.

DALHOUSIE BUILDING, W corner of Old Hawkhill and Hunter Street. Teaching block, by *Campbell & Arnott*, 2006–7. L-plan main building of three storeys (four in the fall of the ground to the E), rendered above a black-tiled base. Cut-out SE corner and a curved E elevation. Horizontal windows, those of the SW wing and NE corner set behind a balcony-like mesh-filled metal framework. Bowed stair-towers faced with glass bricks project on the W side of the NE wing and at the W end of the SW. Filling the inner angle, a large red-painted rotunda.

STUDENTS ASSOCIATION, Airlie Place and Balfour Street. By *James Parr & Partners* (partner-in-charge: *Gordon Farquharson*), 1971–4. The main façade looks S down Airlie Place. Elegantly unexpressive wall of reflective dark glass above a blockwork base. This fronts a large drydashed box. NW extension by *James F. Stephen*, 2003–4, the ground floor of dark brickwork, the oversailing upper floor faced with horizontal-boarded timber cladding and glass.

QUEEN MOTHER BUILDING, Balfour Street. Housing part of the University's School of Computing. By *Page & Park*, 2003–6. 102
Of three storeys, covered in white render. Long core, the S side gently curved, from which project segments of circular pods housing laboratories on the W, a lecture theatre at the N end, and seminar room, research theatre and cyber café on the E. At the S end, the pod containing the set-back entrance; second-floor balcony.

BELMONT TOWER AND FLATS, Balfour Street, Old Hawkhill and Mount Pleasant. BELMONT TOWER, built as a University hall of residence, is by *Gauldie, Hardie, Wright & Needham*, 1962–6. Two flat-roofed blocks. The SE is horizontal, of three storeys, the ground floor a piazza of transverse elliptical tunnel vaults, the upper floors with traditionally proportioned windows. At the N end, an eleven-storey tower, the E and W ends of ribbed concrete, the sides composed of aggregate panels; taller W jamb just recessed from the N end and projecting beyond the S. Windows also of traditional proportions. Contemporary buildings to the W were replaced in 2004 by the four- and six-storey blocks of BELMONT FLATS. Restrained and lacking any hint of panache, by *Boswell, Mitchell & Johnston*.

HEATHFIELD FLATS, W corner of Old Hawkhill and Heathfield Place. Student flats by *Smith Scott Mullan Associates*, 2006. Large but unexciting. Four and five storeys, clad in render and red and black brickwork, with a sparing use of reconstituted stone.

INSTITUTE OF SPORT AND EXERCISE, corner of Old Hawkhill and Kincardine Street. The earliest part is at the N and W, a two-storey L-plan building of 1978–9, the cladding provided by metal panels above a blockwork base. On the S side, a much larger three-storey blockwork and render extension of 1995–6. At its E end, a tall rotunda clad in horizontal strips of dark- and light-coloured aluminium, by the *Nicoll Russell Studios*, 2005.

DUNCAN OF JORDANSTONE COLLEGE OF ART AND DESIGN, CRAWFORD BUILDING, E corner of Perth Road and Hawkhill Place. Timidly modernistic, by *James Wallace*, 1953–65, the building bearing only a family resemblance to Wallace's competition-winning design of 1938 in which the entrance formed the dominant central feature of the façade. Four-storey and attic complex round a courtyard. The main front looks S over Perth Road, a curtain wall of glass and metal contained in a smooth-finished concrete frame, the end bays faced with buff brickwork and containing the entrances. Two-storey brick outshot at the E end; at the W, a glazed stair-tower.

DUNCAN OF JORDANSTONE COLLEGE OF ART AND DESIGN, MATTHEW BUILDING, Hawkhill Place, Perth Road and Hermonhill Terrace. By *Baxter, Clark & Paul*, 1971–4. Constructed of blockwork and concrete panels, its self-indulgent Brutalist bluster sets a bad example to the students. The name commemorates Chessor L. Matthew, Principal of Duncan of Jordanstone College from 1964 to 1978.

BIOLOGICAL SCIENCES INSTITUTE, Dow Street. A smaller version of the Medical Sciences Institute (*see* below). It was built in 1969–72 and also designed by *Mackie, Ramsay & Taylor*.

MEDICAL SCIENCES INSTITUTE, Dow Street. By *Mackie, Ramsay & Taylor*, 1967–70. Brutalist array of grey concrete panels.

SIR JAMES BLACK CENTRE, WELLCOME TRUST BUILDING AND COLLEGE OF LIFE SCIENCES, Well Road, Old Hawkhill and Miller's Wynd. Built in stages between 1995 and 2005, all designed by *Boswell, Mitchell & Johnston*. Large spread of five storeys plus an attic containing the services, faced with white panelled cladding. It is sensible and unexciting, disappointingly prominent on the approach to Dundee over the Tay.

PUBLIC BUILDINGS

BLACKNESS LIBRARY, corner of Perth Road and Blackness Avenue. By the Dundee City Architect, *James Thomson*, 1907–8. On a triangular site, a Beaux Arts classical edifice faced in polished red sandstone ashlar, channelled at the blunt SE corner whose paired Ionic columns support an entablature. These form a surround to the entrance, a Roman Doric-columned aedicule, its open pediment containing a cartouche and with emblematic ladies (sculpted by *Albert Hodge*) seated on the sloping sides. Above, a relatively small square window. Identical S and E fronts with advanced ends serving as broad piers between which are stretched screens of attached Ionic columns.

Inside, an oval vestibule ringed by Roman Doric columns. A pair of bronze PLAQUES bearing reliefs of John Robertson, donor of the site, and Andrew Carnegie, who paid for the construction, are signed by *W. Richardson & Co.* of London.

BLACKNESS PRIMARY SCHOOL, Hawkhill. Originally Hawkhill School. Classical, by *James H. Langlands*, 1892–4. Two-storey N façade of polished ashlar, channelled at the ground floor. Front of nine bays, the centre three recessed. At the corners of each three-bay outer section, superimposed pilasters, the lower order with swan-neck pediments, the upper with Ionic capitals. In the centre of each outer section, a first-floor window in a segmental-pedimented aedicule; cornices over the other windows. Broader centrepiece, the pediment of the centre first-floor window's aedicular surround carved with shell enrichment. Cut-out NE and SW corners containing the originally separate boys' and girls' entrances.

BOTANIC GARDEN, Riverside Drive. The University of Dundee's Botanic Garden was opened in 1977. VISITOR CENTRE by the *Arkos Design Partnership*, 1982. Harled V, the slated monopitch roof rising dramatically to the SW point.

DUNDEE AIRPORT, Riverside Drive. Laid out on land reclaimed from the River Tay. A grass airstrip suitable for light aircraft was opened in 1963, tarmaced in the early 1970s and extended to a length of *c.* 1,400 m. in the 1990s. Flat-roofed TERMINAL BUILDING and CONTROL TOWER by Yorkon Ltd, 1996–7. – To their E, the metal-clad and curvaceously roofed HANGAR by *Dundee City Council*, 1999. – On the N side of Riverside Drive, a 20 m.-long stainless steel SCULPTURE ('On the Wing') by *Diane Maclean*, 1995. It is made up of two rows of tapered poles topped by arrow-shaped forms.

DUNDEE CONTEMPORARY ARTS, Nethergate. Cinema, exhibition, workshop and café complex, by *Richard Murphy*, 1997–9. 107
Built on a precipitously sloping site, it is L-plan, the SW wing incorporating at its lower floors a utilitarian brick-walled garage of *c.* 1930. Murphy gave this a patinated copper and glass top, the use of these materials continued along the new NE wing which thrusts forward to the building line of Nethergate. This wing is double-pile, the E part's monopitch roof sloped down to the W where it forms a glass strip, the shorter and narrower W part's fully glazed roof sloped down to the E. Rounded and fully glazed end to the E section. Inside, the NE wing serves as an introduction to the complex containing a small shop and gallery and generous stair down to the two-storey café at the hinge of the L. This opens E to a cinema and W towards the Print Room. Outside the café, in the L's inner angle, a terrace gives a sheltered outdoor space for the enjoyment of refreshments and nicotine.

DUNDEE INSTITUTION FOR THE BLIND, Magdalen Yard Road. Now housing ('SERVITE'). By *Alexander Johnston*, 1883–5. Two storeys of symmetrically composed collegiate Gothic faced with weathered stugged ashlar, a tall slated flèche rising from the centre of the roof. Set back at the W end, a one-bay addition of 1889–91 in the same style.

DUNDEE REP THEATRE, Tay Square. By the *Nicoll Russell Studios*, 1979–82. Economical assemblage of blockily detailed elements achieving an undeniable presence and not without elegance. The main element is the auditorium, expressed externally as a windowless rectangular mass of blockwork. This is carried on two storeys, also of blockwork, the upper floor surmounted on the S side by a horizontal strip of glazing. Most of the E front is cut out and glazed. In this, a splayed section which contains the entrance placed under the first-floor landing of the stair whose flight of steps supports a great glazed screen. Inside, two levels of circulation space and bars are wrapped round the E and W side of the auditorium. On the roof, a tactful addition, the SCOTTISH DANCE THEATRE by the *Nicoll Russell Studios*, 2004.

SW extension by the *City of Dundee District Council*, 1990.

HARRIS ACADEMY, Perth Road. By *Thoms & Wilkie*, 1928–31. Huge but self-effacing educational edifice in Modern-traditional dress, the street (N) frontages clad in polished ashlar, the other elevations economically rendered. The site slopes steeply to the S, the building being of two storeys at the front and three at the back. Hexagonal shape with a short N block containing the entrance from which splay back the NW and NE wings, their ends joined by relatively short E and W ranges to the long S block. Bisecting the hexagon, a hall block running N–S. Only the top floor of the principal (N) façade stands above the level of Perth Road from which a bridge over the area gives access to the central block. Timidly detailed squared-up English Renaissance canopy over the entrance, a Wrenaissance cupola rising behind. Late C20 extension at the W end.

SENSATION SCIENCE CENTRE, Seabraes. By *Merrylees & Robertson*, 1999–2000. A building of two parts. The main part, containing the exhibition spaces, is at the N, a blue metal shed under a shallow monopitch roof which rises to the S from a long and windowless side wall; large rectangular windows pierce the E end. In front, housing the foyer, café, etc., a narrow metal and glass block with a steeply sloped roof.

THE WHITE TOP CENTRE, Perth Road. A day-care centre for the severely physically handicapped, by the *Nicoll Russell Studios*, 1993–4. Splayed front faced with stone, brick and glass. Prominent roof of ribbed metal rising to a pagoda-like central cupola (the 'white top').

THE WHITEHALL THEATRE, Bellfield Street. Originally the Alhambra Cinema. By *Frank Thomson*, 1928–9. Brick-built shed behind a rendered front block containing the foyer. Low café extension of *c.* 2005 along the S side.

DESCRIPTION

Greenmarket, South Tay Street and Hawkhill

GREENMARKET, the name borrowed from a former street removed for the formation of City Square, was laid out on the site of former railway yards from *c.* 1990. At its W end, the four-storey SEABRAES COURT, student housing by *James Paul Associates*, 1995 and extended in 2004, sensible but cheerless. Beside it, VISION @ SEABRAES, *Keppie Design*'s Postmodern conversion and extension of the C19 Seabraes Mill to exhibition and office space in 2004–5. Also offices but more straightforward is SEABRAES HOUSE, a four-storey L of metal, glass and terracotta curtain walling with a glazed stair-tower at the back, by *James Barr Architecture*, 2006–7. To the E, the Sensation Science Centre, its car park overlooked by the utilitarian backside of the Dundee Contemporary Arts Centre (for these, *see* Public Buildings, above).

On Greenmarket's S side, the GREENMARKET CAR PARK by *Dundee City Council*, 2005, of yellow brick and green coloured metal in a Postmodern manner. To the E, CALEDONIAN HOUSE, by *The Holmes Partnership*, 1990–2, also Postmodern but lumpy, clad in yellow and red brickwork crossed by black bands. Much suaver the pair of identical office blocks (Nos. 1–3 Greenmarket) by the *Holmes Partnership*, 2005, the dark windows of the two lower floors set in tall frames of buff-coloured reconstituted stone. Horizontal strips of glazing under the broad eaves; set-back attic. At the ends of the fronts, glazed sections containing the entrances and stairs. Slatted canopies over the S windows shielding them from the view of the railway station.

On Greenmarket's corner with WEST MARKETGAIT, a gapsite stretching to the SW corner of Nethergate. On the NW corner of Nethergate and West Marketgait, the red sandstone BANK OF SCOTLAND by *Davis Duncan Harrold*, 1994–6, a lumpy late C20 version of Neo-Georgian but with a very tall window in the centre of the full-height shallow bow on the E elevation and a fully glazed bow at the centre of the S, this front set back from the line of Nethergate in a refusal to recognize the importance of the corner. The S bow contains STAINED GLASS by *Liz Rowley*, 1996, a spiral shape bearing the names of ancient and modern trades and professions of Dundee. In West Marketgait to the N, the ALLIANCE TRUST HEADQUARTERS (No. 8 West Marketgait) by *RMJM Scotland Ltd*, 2008, its black presence created by dark glass and antiqued copper cladding but relieved by bright blue strips of cold cathode tubes. For the adjoining Dundee Methodist Church, *see* Churches, above.

NETHERGATE, together with its continuation, Perth Road, is the principal route leading W through the area. The S side starts with an Italianate palazzo, No. 132, by *Young & Meldrum*, 1873. The brick-built No. 134 is of only a low two-storey height and narrow but fun. It was designed by *James Hutton* in 1893 as a studio for the photographers, A. & G. Taylor. Gabled front with a canted first-floor oriel window on moulded brackets; above, a relief of foliage. At the splayed W corner, a corniced small window, its boldly projecting sill supported on a moulded corbel. There follows a three-storey-and-basement rubble-built tenement (Nos. 136–148) of *c.* 1790. Not very formal palace front, the outer corners with rusticated quoins. Five-bay end sections, their openings grouped 3:2, joined by slightly recessed one-bay links to a seven-bay centrepiece, its openings grouped 3:1:3. Symmetrical disposition of doors in Gibbsian surrounds. At the rear the basement is fully exposed in the fall of the ground and placed above a sub-basement. Symmetrical elevation again, with a pair of projecting bows. Beside this, St Andrew's (R.C.) Cathedral followed by the set-back Dundee Contemporary Arts (*see* Churches and Public Buildings, above). Immediately E of these, NETHERGATE HOUSE (No. 158) built in 1790 for Alexander Riddoch, merchant and Provost of Dundee. The villa's main block, built of cherry-cock-pointed rough ashlar with rusticated quoins, is of two storeys above a basement. Front of three bays, the doorpiece with attached Ionic columns supporting a mutuled cornice. The sashes of the first-floor windows are gently bowed. Slightly recessed at each end, a single-storey-and-basement lateral wing of one bay, also with rusticated quoins but the pointing not cherry-cocked.

On Nethergate's N side, W of the Bank of Scotland, the street line is established by No. 81, a parapeted single-storey block, its E elevation incorporating a blind arcade of four pointed arches, the splayed SE corner a foliaged capital and the S front the lower part of a Gothic door. It is by *Edward & Robertson*, 1872–4, the survivor of two shops which flanked the forecourt to the contemporary St Enoch's Church which stood on the site of the Bank of Scotland. The scale rises at Nos. 89–97, a four-storey-and-attic red sandstone tenement with ground-floor shops, by *J. Murray Robertson*, 1890, freely mixing Flemish and Jacobean Renaissance motifs. To the W, Nos. 99–103, a Georgian survival block by *James Foggie*, 1890.

After Tay Street Lane, Nethergate continues at Nos. 105–113 with the ten-bay side elevation of a building fronting South Tay Street which leads into a long diversion along the W and N sides of the area. In the side facing Nethergate, ground-floor shopfronts, architraved and corniced windows to the first floor, a second-floor sill course and a pair of broad chimneys on the wall-head. At the front to the uphill-sloping SOUTH TAY STREET, the ground-floor acquires the status of a basement and the building is revealed as the S end of a thirty-bay palace-fronted block (Nos. 1–27 South Tay Street) which was designed by *David Neave* in 1818–19. Façade of stugged ashlar. At the centre of each of the six-bay end sections and centrepiece, paired and corniced doors are flanked by architraved and corniced windows (the architraves now missing at the centre section and at No. 27); first-floor sill course. The doorpieces of the end sections have Ionic pilasters, those of the centrepiece columns. The first-floor windows of the N section (Nos. 25–27) were deepened, *c.* 1830, and given cast-iron balconies, their fronts with anthemion and palmette decoration. Slightly recessed intermediate sections, also six-bay, their centres' paired doors console-pedimented and flanked by console-corniced windows; sill course at the first-floor. The entrance halls of Nos. 15–17 have sunburst enrichment in the centre of their panelled plaster ceilings and open to the stairs behind through screens of Ionic columns *in antis*.

The street continues as a three-storey terrace, also early C19 but slightly advanced from the earlier building line. PALAIS HOUSE (No. 31) is of four bays and with rougher masonry. Blocky consoles under the window sills; consoles of the same type support the cornices of the ground-floor windows. It was given a wide and pedimented new doorway by *James Sibbald* in 1905 when this became the premises of the auctioneers, James A. MacLean & Sons. The door-jambs are Neo-Jacobean, their pedestals carved with lions' heads from whose mouths issue swags of fruiting foliage; above the pedestals, half-length female figures. No. 33 was reconstructed by *C. & L. Ower* in 1888 to house the Young Women's Christian Association. Originally it seems to have boasted little more than moulded architraves to the ground- and first-floor windows, the ground-floor windows also corniced. The Owers added foliage-capitalled columns, their shafts of polished granite, to the central entrance, a balcony, its front pierced by round-headed arcading, to the window above, and, over the wall-head cornice, a pair of shell-headed dormer windows. Less altered are Nos. 37–39, their rough ashlar masonry cherry-cock-pointed. Architraved windows, the sills supported on blocky consoles, at the ground and first floors. Door squeezed into the centre, its cornice supported on leafy consoles. The masonry of Nos. 41–47 is also cherry-cock-pointed. Pilastered and corniced doorpiece with a triglyph frieze. The two r. windows of the first and second floors are of three lights. Pilastered and corniced doorpiece at No. 49 on the corner of Palais Court. South Tay Street's W side is bittier. At the S end, after the block on the corner of Nethergate (*see* below), the early C19 Nos. 6–10, its front of cherry-cock-pointed rough ashlar with rusticated quoins and a pilastered and corniced doorpiece. To TAY SQUARE to the N it presents a single-storey piend-roofed wing of *c*. 2000. At the S end of the square's W side, the NETHERGATE MEDICAL CENTRE (No. 3), a harled traditionally detailed block of four storeys, by *Blaikie Johnston Withers*, 1992–3. The rest of this side is filled by the Dundee Rep Theatre (*see* Public Buildings, above). On Tay Square's N side, a rubble-walled double house (Nos. 9–11) of the early C19, its doors with dentilated cornices carried on consoles, those of No. 11 decorated with foliage.

In South Tay Street N of Tay Square, the three-storey and attic No. 20 of *c*. 1840. Rendered front of two bays, the ground-floor window corniced and the doorway with a block pediment. Also rendered is the adjoining mid-C19 double house (Nos. 24–26), its paired doors with consoled cornices. The ground-floor band course and wall-head cornice continue along the contemporary Nos. 28–32. Fifteen-bay façade, originally with symmetrically placed console-corniced doors but an additional and plain entrance has been formed from a window at No. 30 and a window inserted above. The block at Nos. 34–36 was designed as premises for the motor engineers, Rossleigh, by *William Gauldie*, 1908. Harled and low-key English Renaissance with superimposed pilasters along the two-storey front, the central first-floor window contained in a segmental-pedimented aedicule. In ARTILLERY LANE behind, the broad-eaved and rubble-built single-storey mission buildings designed by *William Scott* in 1861 for the now demolished Tay Square United Presbyterian Church. On North Tay Street's N corner with CROSS LANE, late C20 flats dressed up with Neo-vernacular touches. They are followed by No. 50 South Tay Street, a very plain late C19 block.

WEST PORT leads W from the end of South Tay Street. On the corner, a four-storey tenement (Nos. 52–56 South Tay Street and Nos. 2–18 West Port) by the Dundee City Architect, *David B. McLay*, 1933, the splayed NE corner finished with a steep gablet. On West Port's E corner with TEMPLE LANE, a four-storey block of brick-faced flats by *Baxter, Clark & Paul*, 1994–6, in a tricksy Scots Neo-vernacular manner. On the opposite corner, Nos. 30–34, a tenement of the later C19 with a splayed quadrant corner and sparing use of minimally Italianate detail. On West Port's N side, on the corner of JOHNSTON'S LANE, THE GLOBE BAR, Georgian survival dated 1864. On the centre of the wall-head, a pilastered square cupola, a clock face in the E front and round-headed belfry openings in the sides. On Johnston's Lane's W side, Nos. 3–13 OLD HAWKHILL (CRAIGOWL PLACE), a late C19 rubble-built tenement, its E corner splayed. To the W, an unassertive English Renaissance block (Nos. 21–25 Old Hawkhill) by *James Findlay*, 1930. From here Old Hawkhill as far W as its junction with Hawkhill is lined with late C20 and early C21 University buildings (*see* University of Dundee, above).

HAWKHILL'S W stretch is the chief traffic route along the N of the area's E part, its junction with Old Hawkhill marked by The Whitehall Theatre (*see* Public Buildings, above) on the W side of BELLFIELD STREET. N of the theatre is a multi-gabled LAUNDRY of *c.* 1890. Red brick, of three storeys and ten bays. In 1983 the elliptical-headed windows were filled with grey ceramic PANELS by *Keith Donnelly*. W of the theatre, on the corner of Hawkhill and URE STREET, the former Russell Independent Chapel (*see* Churches, above).

On the W side of ANNFIELD ROAD the former Baltic Works (*see* Industrial Buildings, below). The ball-finialled S gable of one of its buildings has been incorporated in the HAWKHILL MEDICAL CENTRE by *McLaren, Murdoch & Hamilton*, 1992–3. In ANNFIELD STREET to the N, ANNFIELD HOUSE, a piend-roofed villa of 1793. Rubble-built and with cherry-cock pointing. S front of five bays, the centre three contained in a broad shallow bow, its first floor's anthemion-decorated cast-iron balcony an addition of the earlier C19.

Hawkhill's final stretch begins on the S with Blackness Primary School (*see* Public Buildings, above). On the N, a pair of late C19 tenements (Nos. 273–283). More impressive are the tenements of GOWRIE PLACE (Nos. 289–297 Hawkhill) by *James Maclaren*, 1868. Three storeys and a mansard-roofed attic, faced with coursed and squared rubble. The front is divided by giant urn-finialled pilasters into sections, each containing windows grouped 2:2 either side of a central door, its cornice carried on blocky brackets, the walling above carried up to a broad chimney. The windows in the outer bays of each section are two-light and surmounted at the ground floor by stylized scrolls and shields. Pilastered and corniced first-floor windows, aprons under the second-floor openings. The development continues as VIEWFORTH PLACE at No. 299 Hawkhill and, round the corner, at Nos. 1–3 BLACKNESS AVENUE, also apparently designed by *Maclaren*. W front divided by urn-finialled pilasters of the same design as those at Gowrie Place into three-bay sections, each surmounted by a broad wall-head chimney and containing three-storey canted bay windows, their centre lights at the ground and first floors adorned with consoled cornices and floriated friezes; at the first floor, aprons decorated with interlaced circles. In the centre of each section is the entrance closely flanked by windows, all under a single bracketed cornice and with foliaged friezes. No. 5 Blackness Avenue, on the corner of Gowrie Street, is in the same manner but it is of five bays, with more restrained detail and topped by a pair of chimneys. N of Gowrie Street, No. 7 Blackness Avenue is another late C19 four-storey tenement with full-height canted bay windows but the channelled and polished ashlar masonry of the ground floor and the wall-head's balustrade are Georgian survival. Also with bay windows and a ground floor of channelled ashlar are the late C19 tenements at Nos. 9, 11–15 and 17–21 Blackness Avenue, those at Nos. 11–15 and 17–19 with pediments consoled out above the doors. Similar treatment to the N at the tenement (Nos. 23–25 Blackness Avenue and No. 2 Lytton Street) by *James Sibbald*, 1904. On Blackness Avenue's W side, Logie and St John's (Cross) Church (*see* Churches, above) and, on the corner of Perth Road, the Blackness Library (*see* Public Buildings, above) marks the end of this N diversion.

West end of Nethergate and start of Perth Road

On NETHERGATE's W corner with South Tay Street, an early C19 three-storey-and-attic rubble-built block (Nos. 115–121 Nethergate and Nos. 2–4 South Tay Street). Its height is continued W by the contemporary Nos. 123–131 Nethergate. Also of *c.* 1800 but faced with rough ashlar is the one-bay No. 133 topped by a wall-head chimney. It abuts MORGAN TOWER 83
(Nos. 135–139), a rubble-walled tenement built by a sea captain, Daniel Morgan of Westfield, *c.* 1795. The eponymous tower occupying the r. bay is of five storeys. Shopfront at the

ground-floor. At each of the upper floors, a Venetian window, the top floor's much smaller than the others and with dummy sidelights and flanked by a pair of rectangular openings. The tower is finished with an ogee-profiled dome surmounted by a crescent moon finial. Rear elevation built of much redder sandstone rubble; splay-cornered stair-tower. Behind, No. 145 Nethergate, the former VESTRY of Tay Square United Secession Church (demolished, 1991). Originally by *David Mackenzie*, 1833–4, and of one storey, the gently curved front of stugged and coursed masonry with an anta-pilastered doorpiece towards the E end. In 1843–4 it was given an upper floor to house a day school. Adjoining Morgan Tower, Nos. 141–143 Nethergate of *c.* 1800, also rubble-walled and originally of four storeys but in the later C19 the two bottom floors were combined as one. The building's r. bay is aligned with the main block of Morgan Tower, the bays to the l. set slightly forward, establishing a new building line to the street.

The QUEEN'S HOTEL on Nethergate's S side, by *Young & Meldrum*, 1875–8, is a large Gothic prelude to the street's final stretch. Near-symmetrical but the NE corner is bowed, the NW right-angled. The ends are finished with tall French roofs which rise within quatrefoil-pierced parapets, the recessed centre with a granite-shafted and foliage-capitalled portico projecting from its broad gable. Inside, some Jacobean detail at the staircase and the plaster ceilings of the rooms in the NE corner, the first floor's with coats of arms in some of the compartments. The hotel is followed by three closely spaced villas, the first two uncomfortably so. All are of two storeys above a basement. No. 162, faced with roughish ashlar, was built for a merchant, Robert Jobson, *c.* 1790. Front of five bays, the centre advanced under a pediment pierced by an oculus; overall semicircular fanlight above the door and sidelights. A slate-hung bridge now connects the house to No. 164. This was put up by James Jobson, *c.* 1785, the three-bay front's masonry cherry-cock-pointed and with rusticated quoins. Venetian doorpiece but the central opening is relatively narrow and its round-headed top stilted. No. 166, the most relaxed and smartest of the three, was designed by *David Neave* in 1817. Built of stugged ashlar, it is of three bays, the centre slightly advanced and finished with a fluted and panelled parapet. Side-lit entrance under a segmental fanlight, its heavy surround a replacement of *c.* 1930 for the original Ionic-columned doorpiece. The ground-floor windows of the outer bays boast aprons and consoled cornices. Set further apart are the next villas. The late C18 No. 170 (CAIRD COTTAGE), built of rough squared masonry with rusticated quoins, is of three bays, the door framed by a moulded architrave. The house is now joined by a short two-storey link to No. 172 (CAIRD HOUSE), a sizeable two-storey villa of *c.* 1840. U-plan front of stugged ashlar. At its ends are canted projections; in the faces, ground-floor windows with lugged architraves and cornices and, at the first-floor, with moulded architraves and aprons. Similarly treated windows at the three-bay centre, its porch entered through a screen of Ionic columns *in antis*. S elevation with a tall console-corniced central stair window of three lights and a full-height bow at the E end.

PERTH ROAD continues the line of Nethergate. On the N, after Small's Wynd and set behind a garden, are a pair of early C19 two-storey-and-basement villas, ELLENBANK and UNION MOUNT (Nos. 1–3 Perth Road), joined by a link added in 1928–9 by *Mills & Shepherd*. Ellenbank is faced with weathered stugged ashlar crossed by a first-floor string course. Front of three bays, the pedimented centre containing a balustraded porch, its console-corniced entrance framed by Ionic columns *in antis*. The ground floor's outer windows are corniced and aproned. Union Mount was designed by *David Neave* for John Alison, the polished ashlar of its façade now badly worn. Five bays, the centre advanced under a pediment; from it projects an Ionic portico flanked by corniced and aproned windows. At the W end, two additions, one of two storeys with two-light windows and of *c.* 1900; fronting this, a single-storey extension of the earlier C19, its windows copying the original openings.

AIRLIE PLACE leads uphill to the N, its end filled by the Students Association building (*see* University of Dundee, above), its sides formed by two terraces of mid-C19 housing, all faced with polished ashlar. The E terrace (Nos. 1–15) was built from 1851, a would-be palace front but stepped up the slope. The design was apparently by *Charles Edward* but based on one by *John Dick Peddie*.* Three-storey-and-basement end pavilions, each of three bays with a channelled ground floor and cornices over the first-floor windows. At the S pavilion (No. 1), a long first-floor balcony and a tall attic with large and pedimented dormer windows added by *C. & L. Ower* in 1881. The N pavilion (No. 15) has a two-storey-and-basement canted bay window, a band of guilloche ornament between the ground and first floors. Two-storey and basement intermediate sections join the pavilions to the centrepiece, each of six bays, the ground-floor openings round-headed and keystoned. At the S section (Nos. 3–5) cast-iron balconies have been added to some of the first-floor windows in the mid or later C19 and a balustrade and pedimented dormer windows erected on the wall-head in the late C19. At the N section (Nos. 11–13) an attic has been added over the S three bays. The terrace's centrepiece (Nos. 7–9) is of three storeys above a basement, the ground floor's masonry channelled. In its centre, a pair of corniced doors (now windows). At the first floor, architraved, corniced and aproned windows.

* In 1849–50 *John Dick Peddie* produced various plans and elevations for development of the street but these were not carried out. By 1851 *Charles Edward* had prepared the adopted feuing plan but it was stipulated that houses at the street's SW corner 'should be in keeping with the houses then being erected on the east portion of the property of Airlie Lodge of which John Dick Peddie Architect in Edinburgh is declared thereby to be the sole judge'.

Airlie Place's two-storey and basement W terrace (Nos. 2–14) was also begun in 1851 and completed *c.* 1860, the design probably by *Charles Edward* adapting one by *John Dick Peddie*. Its S house (No. 2) is of three bays with a piered portico flanked by corniced and aproned ground-floor windows. At the centre of the wall-head's balustrade a pedestal on which stands a pair of scroll-sided chimneystacks linked by balustrading. Bowed quadrant SE corner. Stepping uphill to the N, Nos. 4–14 Airlie Place formed of three six-bay sections, each containing a pair of plain houses with balustraded wall-heads. The four-storey and basement Nos. 16–18 to the N survive from a tenement development designed by *James Maclaren* in 1872. Three-bay front with full-height canted bay windows at its ends and a wall-head chimney at the centre. More of the same at the NE wing which contains three-light windows, corniced at the first and second floors. W of Airlie Place, the mid-C19 villa of No. 11 Perth Road, its polished ashlar front now painted, the heavy piered portico flanked by corniced ground-floor two-light windows. Beyond lies the Crawford Building of Duncan of Jordanstone College of Art (*see* University of Dundee, above).

PERTH ROAD'S S side starts with a plain pair of three-storey tenements (Nos. 2–8) by *James Black*, 1828, their wall-head gablets swept up to exceptionally broad chimneystacks. Nos. 10–16 are mid-C19 and of four storeys, with pilastered shopfronts at the ground floor. The block at Nos. 18–28, also of four storeys, its front of stugged ashlar, is of two periods of construction. The first, *c.* 1865, produced the four-bay E section with corniced shopfronts at the ground floor. In 1873 a second almost identical block was built to the W. At the same time the space between the two blocks was filled with a one-bay 'centrepiece' marked off by channelled pilaster-strips and surmounted by a pediment, its tympanum carved with a heraldic achievement. The stugged ashlar walling and four-storey height continue, with the addition of an attic, at Nos. 30–36, a three-bay block by *Hutcheson & Henderson*, 1883, the outer bays with shallowly projecting three-storey oriel windows. At No. 40, a slightly set-back tenement of *c.* 1840, the ground floor pilastered. It is followed by a public garden overlooking the Tay which extends to the corner of Roseangle.

Roseangle and Magdalen Green

ROSEANGLE is the beginning of a crescent-shaped diversion round the S part of the area. At the top of its steep slope, on the E corner of Perth Road, No. 2, designed by *David Neave* for David Martin, a merchant, *c.* 1815. It is of two storeys above a high basement. At the street front, faced with stugged ashlar, corniced and aproned ground-floor windows flank a pedimented mid-C19 porch which projects from the Greek Doric columns of the original doorpiece. At the rear, an advanced and pedimented centre. A slated cupola, lighting the stair inside, was added to the roof in 1880 by *Leslie Ower* who also added an oriel window at the rear. Downhill, to the S, Nos. 4–6 Roseangle, a double house, also of *c.* 1815 and faced with stugged ashlar but plain. Contemporary but smarter the two-storey-and-basement three-bay villa at No. 8 erected for the shipbuilder, John Calman, the front's centre slightly advanced with a three-light first-floor under a blocking course. The ground-floor windows are set in rectangular overarches and flank a porch added in the mid C19 to the original Ionic-columned doorpiece. Roseangle continues with a mixture of Late Georgian villas and plain tenements of the late C19 and of *c.* 2000. Among these, on the W side, No. 15 of *c.* 1810 but its door's pilastered and corniced surround added by *David Neave* in 1819. Then, No. 17, also faced with stugged ashlar and with a Roman Doric portico. It was built in 1820 for William Wyllie, master of the Academy or English School of Dundee. Almost opposite on the E, No. 22 of *c.* 1815. U-plan, the main block built of cherry-cock-pointed reddish-coloured rough ashlar. Three-bay front, its Roman Doric portico's roof serving as a balcony to the pedimented attic window which rises through the eaves. The wings project boldly at either end. No. 26's stugged ashlar masonry and rusticated quoins are also of a reddish colour but the villa was built *c.* 1860 and is stolid. No. 28 of *c.* 1830 is single-storey with a basement and attic. At the centre of the front, a doorpiece with coupled anta-pilasters and a large pedimented dormer window. No. 23 opposite is Georgian survival of *c.* 1860. To the W, ROSEANGLE HOUSE (No. 27), also mid-C19 and of two storeys. The entrance at the pedimented centrepiece is set behind a screen of Greek Doric columns *in antis*. Set well back is the early C19 BISHOP'S HOUSE (No. 29), of two storeys and an attic, the three-bay front vertically proportioned; anthemion- and palmette-decorated cast-iron balcony at the first-floor. At the house's W end, a small CHAPEL added in the early C20 after this had become the residence of the Roman Catholic Bishop of Dunkeld. On the street's S side, No. 36 of the earlier C19, its porch decorated with upside-down empire garlands. Mid-C19 symmetrical Jacobean double house at Nos. 38–40. In SEAFIELD ROAD Nos. 72–82, by *James Hutton*, *c.* 1895, at the E side's S end, a parade of two-storey bay windows and dormer windows with decoratively pierced pediments.

MAGDALEN YARD ROAD continues the line and numbering of Roseangle along the N side of Magdalen Green. At the street's E end THE VINE (No. 43), an exceptionally smart Greek Revival villa built in 1836 for George Duncan, a merchant and 85
M.P. for Dundee. It is a single-storey rectangle of three by five bays faced with polished ashlar. The principal elevations front E and S, each with an advanced centre containing an entrance, the E set between recessed Greek Doric columns. Lugged architraves with exaggerated entasis to the large window and door openings. Piers, incised with ornament, clasp the corners and rise through the wall-head's entablature and parapet to

pedestals; smaller round-headed pedestals over the walling between the S front's windows. Empire garlands on the main frieze; more garlands on the round-headed pedestals of the S front. Anthemion finials on the parapets above the doorways. Rising from the centre of the roof, a domed cupola surmounted by an urn finial. On Magdalen Yard Road's corner with BELLEFIELD AVENUE, tenements of 1894, No. 1 Bellefield Avenue in buff-coloured sandstone and with an octagonal corner tower, No. 2 Bellefield Avenue in red sandstone with a bowed corner.

The villas of Magdalen Yard Road resume on the E corner of Thomson Street with the mid-C19 No. 53 Magdalen Yard Road, the corniced ground-floor windows flanking a badly weathered Roman Doric portico. On the piended roof, agreeably pompous pedimented dormers and a domed cupola of the later C19. On Thomson Street's W corner, BRIDGE VIEW HOUSE (No. 55) of *c.* 1840, also of two storeys and three bays but the door is set behind a screen of Greek Doric columns *in antis*. To the r., a three-light window; at the advanced l. bay, a canted bay window. No. 57 originated *c.* 1830 as a two-storey villa, its three-bay S front of polished ashlar with an anta-pilastered doorpiece and an anthemion finial over the centre of the parapet. Recessed E extension of *c.* 1860. In 1873 *C. & L. Ower* provided the broad canted bay windows either side of the entrance. A full-height canted bay window of *c.* 1890 was the house's final addition. On the W side of Paton's Lane, at No. 59 Magdalen Yard Road, the former Dundee Institution for the Blind (*see* Public Buildings, above).

Villas continue to the W. No. 61 Magdalen Yard Road of *c.* 1820 is enjoyable. Two piend-roofed storeys of stugged ashlar but the broad centrepiece rises above the wall-head to a battlement formed by a pair of chimneystacks. Attached Roman Doric columns at the entrance. Nos. 65–67 were originally two identical two-storey houses designed by *David Neave c.* 1817, each with a three-bay front, the slightly advanced and pedimented centre containing an Ionic-columned doorpiece. At the outer bays, corniced and aproned ground-floor windows. About 1860, No. 65 acquired bay windows, one rectangular, the other canted, and cast-iron balustrading on the top of the doorpiece. Mid-C19 Jacobean on a small scale at No. 69. Then, tenements on the corners of Taylor's Lane, the E brick-faced, by *Baxter, Clark & Paul, c.* 2000, the W by *George A. Harris*, 1896–8, its splayed corner carried up as a tower. This development continues along Magdalen Yard Road with full-height bay windows at Nos. 87–89. There follows a mid-C19 two-storey piend-roofed villa, SEAFIELD LODGE (Nos. 91–93). Polished ashlar façade of three bays, the ground-floor's two r. windows of two lights and corniced. The W bay is advanced and pedimented; projecting from it, a canted bay window. This house looks over to Magdalen Green's BANDSTAND, a product of *Walter Macfarlane & Co.*'s *Saracen Foundry*, 1889. Open-sided octagon with scrolled cast-iron railings at the bottom of the sides. At each corner, a slender Corinthianish column rising from a foliaged fat base from which spring elaborately decorated cast-iron arches under an ogee-profiled and gilt-finialled dome, its eaves studded with acroteria. Magdalen Yard Road continues to Shepherd's Loan with a lumpily detailed short late C19 terrace of two-storey-and-attic houses (Nos. 95–99). The E side of SHEPHERD'S LOAN is filled with the former Seafield Works (*see* Industrial Buildings, below).

On the W corner of Shepherd's Loan and Magdalen Yard Road, an accomplished tenement (Nos. 101–103 Magdalen Yard Road), 1896, the crisp stonework of red sandstone ashlar and with gentle Jacobean detail, a dome over the rounded SE corner. Double house (OSBORNE VILLA AND RAEWOOD VILLA) on the corner of Osborne Place. It is dated 1872. Light-hearted seaside architecture with carved bargeboards. At the ground floor, bay windows and a Corinthian-columned entrance to the S porch; windows of stilted and round-headed lights at the upper floor. On Osborne Place's W corner, No. 2, a villa of the later C19. Georgian survival but with a full-height canted bay window at the W end. Also Georgian survival of the mid or later C19 but with a pair of bay windows is ASHBANK (No. 107 Magdalen Yard Road).

WINDSOR PLACE was laid out *c.* 1835 on land acquired by Patrick Hunter Thoms, merchant and banker. It forms a two-storey palace-fronted terrace of *c.* 1835, faced with polished ashlar and with a wall-head parapet and balustrade. At the ends, three-bay houses with Greek Doric colonnaded ground-floors. Intermediate two-bay sections, each with a two-light window in the outer bay and a Greek Doric portico in the inner, join to the slightly advanced four-bay centrepiece. Here are paired Greek Doric porticoes flanked by two-light windows. The house at the W end (No. 6) presents a three-bay W front to the steeply rising WINDSOR STREET where it serves as a slightly advanced end pavilion to the E side. This side of the street is filled by a stepped terrace of two-storey housing, the N houses built above basements, all constructed between 1851 and 1873 and originally with wall-head balustrades (some now missing) and masonry of polished ashlar (much now painted or rendered). It begins at the S with four pairs of six-bay double houses (Nos. 1–8 Windsor Street) built in 1851–7, the second and third pair slightly advanced. In the centre of each double house, a pair of architraved and corniced doors; aprons under the first-floor windows. Then, five more double houses (Nos. 9–18), a development of *c.* 1870 by the builder, *William Brownlee*. They also have paired doors but with consoled pediments. Lugged architraves to the ground-floor windows; at the first-floor, windows with keystoned elliptical-arched heads, the outer openings set in lugged architraves, the centre lights in pilastered surrounds. Some round-headed dormers, all of identical design, have been added, those at Nos. 15–16 in 1876 and the work of *Ireland & Maclaren* who were probably responsible for the design of all. At Nos. 19–20, a pair of four-bay houses, also probably of the 1870s, similarly treated except that the centre first-floor windows are not pilastered. Nos. 21–26, all designed and built by *William Brownlee* in the 1870s, are simpler versions of the houses to the S. Finally, before the tenement on the corner of Perth Road (*see* below), a double house (Nos. 27–28) built by *Robert Lickley* in 1871, the detail also simplified but the doors paired at the centre and with consoled pediments.

RICHMOND TERRACE continues the line of Magdalen Yard Road. It is formed by two two-storey-and-attic terraces of late C19 housing with full-height bay windows and consoled cornices over the doors. The first terrace's end at Minto Place is marked by a Frenchy truncated spire over the splayed corner. Bowed corner at the beginning of the second terrace.

Perth Road West of Roseangle

PERTH ROAD W of Roseangle resumes with the spiky Gothic presence of Dundee West Church (*see* Churches, above). Beyond, No. 140 Perth Road, a villa of *c.* 1830, the parapeted porch flanked by corniced windows. The ensuing four-storey block at Nos. 142–148 is late C19 cheap Renaissance. Another villa but of *c.* 1790 at No. 150, the front now covered with cement render lined out as ashlar. Round-headed door under a squat Venetian window; a three-light window to the second-floor. On the W corner of MCVICAR'S LANE, a tall and busily detailed block of flats (Nos. 2–24 McVicar's Lane) by *KDM Architects*, 2006. There follows a pair of two-storey ashlar-fronted houses (Nos. 152–154) of the earlier C19, each of three bays with a consoled cornice over the entrance door (the r. house's converted to a window in 1880). They are joined by a pompous Artisan Mannerist link containing a console-pedimented door. It was designed by *Ireland & Maclaren* in 1880 when the houses had been taken over as offices by James Valentine & Sons, the printers. Adjoining, another villa, GREENFIELD HOUSE (No. 156) of the earlier C19 but slightly taller. Then, the Gate Church International (*see* Churches, above). Perth Road's N side starts with the Crawford and Matthew Buildings of Duncan of Jordanstone School of Art (*see* University of Dundee, above). There follows a pair of three-storey-and-attic bay-windowed tenements (Nos. 23–25) by *John Bruce & Son*, 1889, dressed up with a few free Flemish touches. Behind, HERMONHILL TERRACE containing a pair of houses. The E (HERMONHILL HOUSE) is an early C19 villa; at its E gable, a single-storey porch, its round-headed door in a Roman Doric-columned surround. The W house is of *c.* 1890. Canted bay windows at the ends of the S front; central door-piece with Roman Doric columns *in antis*.

The SPRINGFIELD development fronting Perth Road and forming a street to the N now begins. This was laid out in 1830 'according to a much approved plan by an eminent architect

in Edinburgh', probably *George Angus*,* and completed by 1851. It begins on Perth Road with No. 32 Springfield, a two-storey house of two bays with a Greek Doric portico, full-height bay window and a wall-head balustrade. The height and the balustrade continue at Nos. 30–31, a double house with paired porticoes, also Greek Doric as throughout the development. Facing the steeply rising street of Springfield itself, a stepped pair of mirror-image houses (Nos. 28–29 Springfield), each of three bays with a portico at the outer bay, windows set in lugged architraves and corniced at the ground floor. No. 29's mansard roof is a late C19 addition. Uphill, the same detail but here are double houses with paired porticoes. At the N end of the E terrace, a single house (No. 17), also with a portico. Across the N end of the street, a double house (Nos. 15–16), a colonnade across the ground floor. On the W side of Springfield, paired houses (Nos. 5–14) of the same design as those 87
on the E but the S house (No. 4) is single and with the portico at the centre of the front. The development returns to the W along Perth Road with Nos. 1–3 Springfield, Nos. 2 and 3 forming a double house with paired porticoes, No. 1 with a porch at its W gable.

On Perth Road's S side after the Gate Church International, a tall late C19 Renaissance tenement (Nos. 166–172) on the E of Westfield Avenue. Behind, the White Top Centre (*see* Public Buildings, above). On Westfield Avenue's W corner, Nos. 172A–182 Perth Road, a two-storey-and-basement Late Georgian terrace, the paired doors with consoled cornices. Roughly contemporary and of the same height but rubble-built, plainer and now altered is No. 184. In WESTFIELD PLACE, the single-storey harled WESTFIELD COTTAGE (No. 11) by *David Logan*, 1818, its piended roof with broad eaves. Boldly projecting SW wing with a canted bay window.

The N side of Perth Road W of Miller's Wynd is composed largely of late C19 tenements and some slightly earlier and humbler vernacular buildings. Among these, the former Ryehill United Presbyterian Church (*see* Churches, above), on the corner of Mid Wynd. On WEST WYND's E corner, a rubble-built three-storey tenement (Nos. 93–95 Perth Road) of the earlier C19, quite plain except for the figures of a pair of otters standing on the skewputts. In ST PETER STREET, St Peter's Free Church (*see* Churches, above) and, on the E side, a Late Victorian tenement whose N gable has been painted by the *Edinburgh Artists Collective*, 1982, with a mural depicting the C19 industries of Dundee (whaling, jute-spinning, paper-making, engineering) and vignettes of prominent streets in the city. Just W of St Peter Street, on Perth Road's S side, plain early C19 housing (Nos. 228–240) of two storeys above a basement.

* According to the Register of Sasines, the feuing plan was made out by *William Paterson*, architect in Dundee. William Paterson and his brother, James, acted as executant architects for buildings in Dundee designed by the Edinburgh-based Angus in the 1830s.

On the N side, at the E corner of PENNYCOOK LANE, PENNYCOOK COURT by *Page & Park*, 1987–90, sheltered housing faced with pink and grey blockwork. Display of Postmodern tricks including an extensive use of metal balconies. Just W of Pennycook Lane, SALISBURY HOUSE (No. 155 Perth Road) of the mid C19 with a pilastered and pedimented doorpiece. W of this Perth Road takes on something of the atmosphere of a small town's commercial centre with a jumble of mid- and late C19 tenements, shops occupying their ground floors. This N side meets the junction with Hawkhill with a three-storey block (Nos. 189–205) of the mid C19, the W gable rebuilt with a canted bay window to a design by *Ron Weir*, 1987, when the terrace's end gave place to a slip road. On the side of Perth Road, the McCheyne Memorial Free Church (*see* Churches, above).

Beyond the church and set back, an energetically crowstepped Scots Jacobean villa (No. 334) of the mid C19. Contemporary but plain a single-storey cottage (No. 336) and two-storey-and-basement flatted housing (Nos. 338–341) on the E corner of Strawberrybank. W of Strawberrybank, larger but plain tenements of the later C19 up to the corner of Windsor Street, Nos. 344–354 Perth Road with elliptical-arched ground-floor windows. W of Windsor Street, an even plainer block (Nos. 358–390), consoled cornices over the doors the only embellishments. MAGDALEN VIEW is a set-back terrace of town houses by *Peter Inglis*, 2004, horizontal timber cladding the main feature. Even further recessed the timidly modernistic office block Nos. 400–410 by *G. P. K. Young & Son*, 1965–6. The street line is re-established by Nos. 412–418, single-storey-and-basement flatted housing of *c.* 1830. Behind this, THE BINNS (No. 412), a contemporary harled cottage, also of one storey above a basement, the S front, facing away from the street, with a pair of gables flanking the recessed entrance bay; slightly later wing set back at the W end. Horizontal-paned glazing in the windows. Another single-storey-and-basement terrace of *c.* 1830 at Nos. 426–428.

On Perth Road's N side, after the Blackness Library (*see* Public Buildings, above), BLACKNESS CRESCENT (Nos. 227–229 Perth Road), a pair of four-storey-and-attic tenements of 1877, faced with polished ashlar, channelled at the ground floor. At each, full-height canted bay windows at the ends; between them, two-light windows at the upper floors, their column-mullions with lotus-leaf capitals, and a ground-floor pedimented doorpiece decorated with incised Ægypto-Greek ornament. Adjoining, a two-storey double house (Nos. 231–233) by *William Burn*, 1827. Six-bay front, its doors paired, the first-floor windows with aprons. Blackness Crescent now ends with a pair of late C20 houses faced with 'Fyfestone'. There follows WINDSOR TERRACE (Nos. 239–257 Perth Road), a development laid out in 1870 by the builder, *William Brownlee*, who may have been responsible for the design, and completed by 1874. It consists of a procession of two-bay houses, each composed of a full-height canted bay window and a straight section, most of the houses forming mirror-image pairs. The W house's bay window is broader than the others and its entrance placed at the gable. Across a lane, SEYMOUR LODGE (No. 259 Perth Road) of *c.* 1880, a large two-storey-and-attic villa built for a grocer, Henry McGrady. It is designed in a very free Jacobean manner with carved bargeboards, dormer windows rising into jerkin-head gablets, mullioned-and-transomed windows and a band of Gothic decoration between the ground and first floors. Next door, the mid-C19 No. 261 Perth Road, plainer but also bargeboarded, followed by the contemporary No. 263, restrained small-scale Jacobean. More mid-C19 Jacobean at No. 267 and at No. 269 on the corner of Hyndford Street. On HYNDFORD STREET's E side, No. 1, an asymmetrical bay-windowed and bargeboarded villa of *c.* 1870. The bay-windowed gable at the r. end of the front was added by *Ireland & Maclaren* in 1880. On the W side of Hyndford Street, Nos. 2–6, a triple house by *C. & L. Ower* 1883, embellished with energetic Free Jacobean Renaissance detail, decorative ironwork, carved bargeboards and a turret.

W of Hyndford Street, Perth Road's N side continues with the two-storey-and-attic CLARENDON TERRACE (Nos. 271–297 Perth Road) developed by the builder, *William Brownlee*, *c.* 1875, the façade of polished ashlar (now mostly painted). The houses at Nos. 271–287 are each of two bays, the r. containing a Corinthianesque portico, the l. a two-storey canted bay window. The W houses (Nos. 289–297) are each of three bays and also with bay windows and porticoes (now missing from No. 297). In ROCKFIELD STREET Nos. 3–7 of 1885 virtually repeat the design of Nos. 2–6 Hyndford Street (*see* above) and are also presumably by *C. & L. Ower*. W of Rockfield Street, Perth Road's N side continues with villas of the mid and later C19, none of much originality. There follows GROSVENOR TERRACE (Nos. 307–311 Perth Road and No. 1 Grosvenor Road) designed by *Ireland & Maclaren* in 1882 and completed by 1886. Two-storey-and-attic symmetrical façade of polished ashlar with two-storey canted bay windows and balcony-topped Neo-Jacobean doors. Over the W end, the roof rises into a French pavilion roof providing a vertical stop before the Western Cemetery (*see* above).

On Perth Road's S side, facing Grosvenor Terrace, the rubble-built two-storey GREYWALLS (No. 452), designed by *Patrick Thoms* of *Thoms & Wilkie*, 1929, for himself in a fidgety Cotswold Arts and Crafts manner, a conical-roofed low round tower beside the N entrance, a small loggia and two-storey bow window to the S. The broad-eaved single-storey L-plan No. 454A Perth Road is by *Ireland & Maclaren*, 1880, a flat-roofed porch in the inner angle, stone canopies over the gables' windows. This was the lodge to BINROCK (No. 456 Perth Road), a late C18 villa originally of one storey but raised to two and remodelled *c.* 1820 by *David Neave*. At the l. end of the S front, a full-height bow. The main block's W elevation is of three bays, the central door and segmental-arched fanlight introduced by *Mills & Shepherd* in 1924 when they moved the entrance to this side. Undistinguished mid-C19 additions at the N. THE RIDGES (No. 458), a harled and Rosemary-tiled English Arts and Crafts villa, is by *Thoms & Wilkie*, *c.* 1928. Then, the Harris Academy (*see* Public Buildings, above). Opposite, the WEST PARK CONFERENCE CENTRE, a complex developed round a sizeable but unexciting Italianate villa of *c.* 1860 extended in the late C20 and set well back from the road. At the entrance to the drive, a late C19 piend-roofed LODGE with a pedimented doorway. E of the house, the four-storey blocks of WEST PARK FLATS, student housing by *Smith Scott Mullan*, 2006–7, clad in render brick and timber. At the W of the group, the SIDLAW SUITE by *James F. Stephen*, 1990–2, faced with brick and glass; monopitch roof and a bowed SE gable. W of West Park Road, large but generally routine late C19 villas. The two-storey piend-roofed FERNBRAE (No. 329 Perth Road) is Georgian survival of *c.* 1860 with a portico of Ionic columns *in antis* and corniced ground-floor windows. On the W side of WESTGROVE AVENUE beyond, THE BOREEN (No. 6 Westgrove Avenue) by *Thoms & Wilkie*, 1911. Rubble-walled English Arts and Crafts under a prominent roof. On the S side of Perth Road, TAYPARK (No. 484) of *c.* 1865, Jacobean with a pedimented Corinthian portico and a corner turret. Contemporary crowstep-gabled LODGE beside the main road. Beyond and set well back, CIDHMORE (No. 488) dated 1868. Very large but uninspired Italianate. Contemporary LODGE in the same manner at the entrance to the drive. No. 494 to the W is Scottish Baronial of 1888, built of hammer-dressed masonry; a wood and glass porch of *c.* 2000 on the NE corner. Opposite, on the corner of FARINGTON STREET, FARINGTON HOUSE (No. 1 Farington Street) by *T. Martin Cappon*, 1906, relaxed Queen Anne in red sandstone ashlar. A little further out, on the S side of Perth Road, WESTDENE (No. 506) by *Watson & Salmond* of Glasgow, 1903. English Arts and Crafts but appearing curiously tense. Also unrelaxed but in a Queen Anne style is *T. Martin Cappon*'s No. 512 of 1907. More Arts and Crafts but with a Scottish Renaissance twist at NYOORA (No. 514) by *Thoms & Wilkie*, 1905. The masonry is of hammer-dressed red sandstone; touches of crowstepping and, over the door, a turret topped by an elongated dome. More self-consciously but routinely Scottish S front but with the garden entrance in a recess fronted by a round-headed arch. Similar treatment of the garden entrance at the next-door ARDVRECK (No. 516) by *Mills & Shepherd*, 1907–9, a large and asymmetrically composed villa, its appearance surprisingly plain.

GLAMIS ROAD leads N from Perth Road. On its E side the large DUNCRAIG HOUSE (No. 3) by *C. & L. Ower*, 1890. Scottish Baronial horror as if designed to house the Addams family. RIVERSIDE DRIVE exits Perth Road to the S. On its E side, the University of Dundee Botanic Garden (*see* Public Buildings, above), followed by VERNONHOLME, a large Italianate villa by *Johnston & Baxter*, 1910. It was converted to flats and given accompanying housing by *Architectus*, 1999.

INDUSTRIAL BUILDINGS

BALTIC WORKS, Annfield Road and Peddie Street. Little more than the octagonal chimney of 1864 survives of Mitchell & Graham's textile mill. That is impressive enough, tall and tapering, built of patterned red and white brickwork; the top cornice was removed in 1987. To the W, some single-storey weaving sheds, by *Pearce Bros*, 1872.

SEAFIELD WORKS, Shepherd's Loan. Substantial remains of the large Victorian textile works (now housing) of D. & J. Thomson & Co. The main building is the HIGH MILL, designed by *Robertson & Orchar* in 1861. It is of four tall storeys and an attic, faced with stugged ashlar. N elevation of twenty-one bays, the centre three slightly advanced. At the first floor of this centrepiece, only two windows but these are tripartite and lit the engine house; elliptical-headed window above. Projecting from the W bay of this front, an Italianate square tower of five stages, the lower pierced by round-headed windows, the top with tall two-light belfry openings. The mill's S elevation is straightforward, all the windows rectangular; small off-centre wall-head gablet carved with the construction date. This side formerly rose above the five parallel single-storey weaving sheds of the POWERLOOM FACTORY built in 1859. Their W gables survive, forming a ten-bay wall along Shepherd's Loan, the two bays at each end slightly advanced, their large windows with projecting keystones and imposts and placed above aprons; in the intermediate bays, openings with lugged architraves and bracketed sills. NE of the High Mill, single-storey sheds and, returning to the W from the N of these, the cast-iron skeleton of a boiler house, its braced kingpost roof carried on columns.

SUBURBS SOUTH OF KINGSWAY

CHARLESTON, MENZIESHILL AND NINEWELLS

Large semicircular area of housing, predominantly of the later C20, sprawling round the land rising from the River Tay at the W end of Dundee, the mass of Ninewells Hospital a huge presence on the approach to the city (see map on p. 186).

CHURCHES

CAMPERDOWN PARISH CHURCH, Brownhill Road. By *T. H. Thoms* of *Thoms & Wilkie*, 1959–61. Harled oblong with a W campanile and shallowly double-pitched felted roof. In the N side, tall and angular pointed windows. On the S, a narrow aisle, its windows domestic in appearance, and a clearstorey.

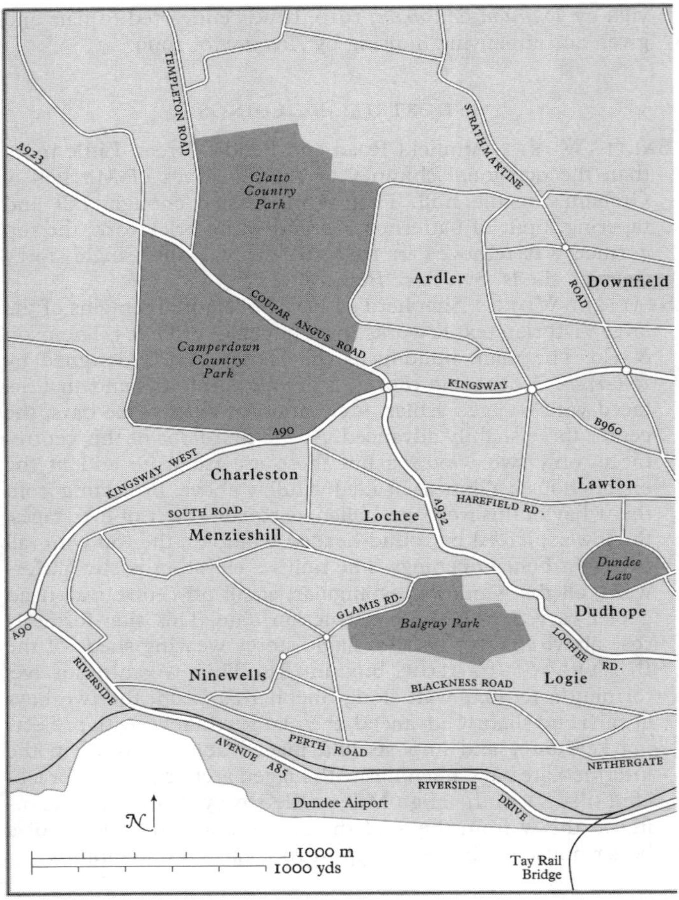

MENZIESHILL PARISH CHURCH, Charleston Drive. T-plan complex of church and halls, by *T.H. Thoms* of *Thoms & Wilkie*, 1961–2, mostly drydashed. The W part of the cross-bar is formed by the church itself, its steeply sloped double-pitch roof covered with concrete tiles. Tall S windows; on the N side, a square-windowed narrow aisle. Saddleback-roofed SE tower. At the centre of the cross-bar and faced with crazy-paved masonry, a flat-roofed porch serving the church and halls. Very shallowly pitched roof over the small hall to the E. The T's tail is formed by the large hall, its double-pitch roof more prominent. Flat-roofed contemporary MANSE making a SW wing.

ST CLEMENT (R.C.), Craigowan Road. By *Allan & Friskin*, 1962. Hall-like, the drydashed walls with cement dressings;

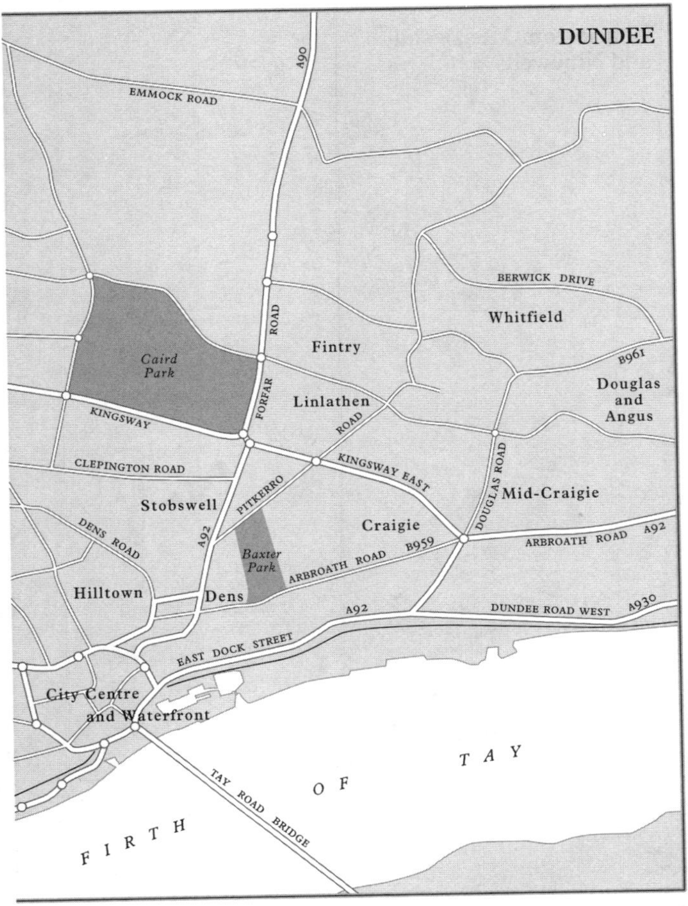

shallowly pitched broad-eaved roof except at the S (liturgical E) end where a monopitch roof covers the sanctuary. Gently scalloped walls pierced by tall rectangular windows.

Inside, a flat ceiling over the nave, a sloping ceiling over the sanctuary which is lit by a clearstorey window at its junction with the nave. – FURNISHINGS of the 1960s. On the S wall, behind the altar, a large MOSAIC of Our Lord Reigning from the Cross flanked by figures of St Peter and St Clement. – In the NE baptistery, a diagonally fluted goblet-shaped stone FONT.

ST NINIAN (R.C.), Dickson Avenue. Small and drydashed by *Peter Whiston*, 1969, with tall rectangular windows along the sides. M-roofed SW tower and porch. Single-storey CLERGY HOUSE to the W.

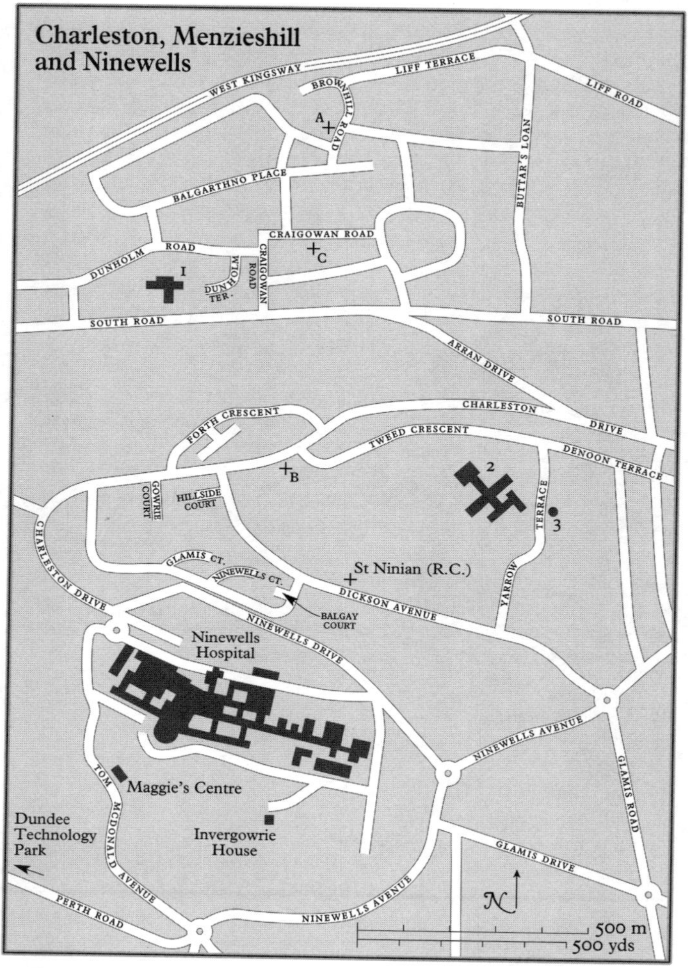

A Camperdown Parish Church
B Menzieshill Parish Church
C St Clement (R.C.)

1 Charleston Primary School
2 Menzieshill High School
3 Menzieshill Service Reservoir

PUBLIC BUILDINGS

CHARLESTON PRIMARY SCHOOL, Dunholm Terrace. By the Dundee City Architect, *Robert Dron*, 1957–60. In the Festival of Britain manner, with shallow-pitched roofs. *See also* St Clement's Primary, Balgartho Place, of the same period.

MENZIESHILL HIGH SCHOOL, Yarrow Terrace. 1969–72, by the Dundee City Architect, *John W. Kidd*, and almost identical to his contemporary Craigie High School (Dens, Craigie and Stobswell). Low and boxy Modern Movement but without flair, faced with brownish red brick, aggregate and glass.

MENZIESHILL SERVICE RESERVOIR, Yarrow Terrace. Hilltop water tower built in 1961. Tall round tank on a pedestal ringed by tapering narrow stilts, all rendered.

NINEWELLS HOSPITAL, Ninewells Drive. Huge complex, by *Robert Matthew, Johnson-Marshall & Partners* (partner-in-charge *Tom Spaven*), 1963–74, boldly strung out on a hillside overlooking the Carse of Gowrie and the W approach to
Dundee. The principal building is butterfly-plan consisting 100
of a flat-roofed block housing the concourse from which extend two unequal-sized ranges of interlinked blocks containing wards, treatment and teaching rooms and offices which surround courtyards (some infilled before the hospital was opened). Generally of four storeys but only two at the N, the walls all clad with pale grey aggregate panels which form continuous horizontal bands between the floors and narrow vertical strips between the three-light windows. A much needed and powerful vertical accent is provided at the centre (i.e. immediately E of the concourse block) by the massive tall tower of ribbed concrete, composed of rounded elements of different heights. In 1995–9 *Keppie Architects* extended the concourse block, originally set back from the S fronts of the ward blocks, to the S. The extension is of the same height as the ward blocks but thrusts forward between them, its S end faceted in unconvincing imitation of a bow and the three upper floors faced with glaring white panels, an unhappy intrusion into the decorous subfusc of the original design. – Earlier additions and ancillary buildings, mostly to the E and SE and in the same manner and materials as the main building.

MAGGIE'S CENTRE, off Tom McDonald Avenue, to the SW. 101
A day-centre for cancer sufferers, it is by *Frank Gehry* (with *James F. Stephen* as executant architects), 2001–3. Small and irregularly shaped, with harled walls under a pitched roof of pleated stainless steel. Rising from near the W end, a sturdy tapering rounded tower, admirably sculptural with a curved roof and a sloping canopy over the S windows. Beautifully finished interior, the E end containing a kitchen and dining area, the tower a library whose curved stair rises to a gallery; largely glazed area to the W.

DESCRIPTION

CHARLESTON, its main thoroughfare provided by South Road, consists mostly of traditional housing of the 1950s and 1960s, with walls of exposed concrete blockwork or drydashed, the roofs covered with concrete tiles. Some Victorian and Edwardian housing E of Buttar's Loan.

MENZIESHILL'S E end, bordering on Lochee Park and Balgay Hill and encircled by Charleston Drive and Glamis Road, contains bungalows of the late 1930s. The area W of this, bordering Charleston Drive, was developed in the later C20 with unexciting houses and low-rise blocks of flats, the walls drydashed or of exposed brickwork, the house roofs covered with concrete tiles, the flats' with metal sheeting. Uphill to the S, an informal layout of monopitch-roofed blocks, of *c.* 1965, the drydash relieved by some weatherboarding, many enjoying open views to the N or S. W of Dickson Avenue, five identical fifteen-storey cruciform tower blocks (GOWRIE COURT, HILLSIDE COURT, GLAMIS COURT, NINEWELLS COURT and BALGAY COURT), by *G. Bowie*, Chief Architect to *Crudens Ltd*, in association with the Dundee City Architect, *John W. Kidd*, 1960–5. Cheerless but very prominent landmarks on the approach to Dundee from the W.

NINEWELLS to the S is dominated by Ninewells Hospital (*see* Public Buildings, above), with the Dundee Technology Park (*see* below) sitting at the foot of the hillside. E and S of Ninewells Avenue, small-scale suburban housing of the mid and later C20, bungaloid in character and often in actuality. At the E end of GLAMIS DRIVE, several architecturally accomplished and substantial harled villas of the 1920s.

DUNDEE TECHNOLOGY PARK

Explorer Road, Gemini Crescent and Mariner Drive

Extensive collection of two- and three-storey late C20 and early C21 office buildings and warehouses, neatly packaged with walls generally of brick, glass and blockwork under shallow-pitched and piended metal or slate roofs. – PROSPECT BUSINESS CENTRE, Gemini Crescent, a large but thriftily detailed two-storey villa (originally The Gows) by *Peddie & Kinnear*, 1864. Much gabled and gableted, with bracketed broad eaves. – GRIANAN BUILDING, Gemini Crescent, by the *Nicoll Russell Studios*, 1988. Two-storey L, the outer sides elegant with glazed walls, dark at the ground floor and clear above where they tilt outwards under the broad eaves of the shallow monopitch roofs carried on internal columns topped by three-way brackets. Rubble-faced inner angle containing the entrance. – HILL-
105 CREST HOUSING H.Q., Explorer Road. By the *Nicoll Russell Studios*, 2009–10. Three-storey offices, glass-walled above a 'caged'-walled ground floor. 'Caged' walling also at the broch-like curved projection at the r. end of the front.

INVERGOWRIE HOUSE

off George Pirie Way

Beleaguered by the buildings of Ninewells Hospital, a laird's house of *c.* 1600 much enlarged and remodelled by *William Burn*, 1937, in Scots manorial manner.

The lands of Invergowrie, formerly held by Scone Abbey, were acquired by Sir Patrick Gray, a younger brother of the fourth Lord Gray, in the later C16 and he seems to have been responsible for the erection of the house's W block. This is a crowstep-gabled three-storey rubble-walled oblong with conical-roofed turrets (apparently restored in 1837) on continuous corbelling at the W corners, the S turret serving the two upper floors, the N only the top. Front of five bays but lengthened to the N by a further bay, perhaps in the late C17 or C18. Probably of the late C18 is the bowed stair-tower at the rear. In his remodelling of the house for Alexander Clayhills, whose family had bought the estate in 1641, Burn enlarged the existing first- and second-floor windows, built up the central one at the first floor, replaced the two to its l. by a large rectangular oriel, added a stone balcony in front of the two to the r., and provided the second floor openings with gabled stone dormerheads; to the S gable, he added a canted first floor oriel.

Fully as far-reaching in their effect on the mansion house as the remodelling of the W block were Burn's extensions to it. He added a three-storey SE wing in the same manner as the remodelled W block but of only three bays and without oriel windows. At the SW corner, a conical-roofed round tower rising from the ground and, at the SE corner, a turret like that on the SW corner of the main block. The NE wing is similar in manner and also of three storeys but the ground floor, half-hidden by the rise of the ground on this side, serves as a basement. Conical-roofed NW corner turret. In the gabled porch have been placed a couple of dormerheads, probably originally on the W block. One bears the date 1601 and the initials and impaled coats of arms of (Sir) Patrick Gray of Invergowrie and Agnes Napier, his wife, the other a weathered coat of arms and the motto TRVST.IN.GOD.

The main block and wings form three sides of a service court at the back of the house, its fourth enclosed by a bowed office range of 1837 but perhaps incorporating work of 1786.

DENS, CRAIGIE AND STOBSWELL

Large and disparate area of SE Dundee cut off from Hilltown (q.v.) by the gorge of the Dens Burn (now the site of Dens Road) and by Kingsway East from Mid Craigie. Rural until the mid C19 except for an industrial pocket between Cowgate and King Street, some villas and the Dundee Lunatic Asylum. Victorian development of mills and tenements along Albert Street to the N and Arbroath Road to the E then took place, with the Morgan Academy and Baxter Park and the Eastern Cemetery serving as psychological and physical barriers to the further spread of industry. By about 1900 the whole area between Baxter Park and Dens Road was filled with a medley of factories and tenements, the land around Forfar Road N of the Morgan Academy and between Baxter Park and the Eastern Cemetery reserved for

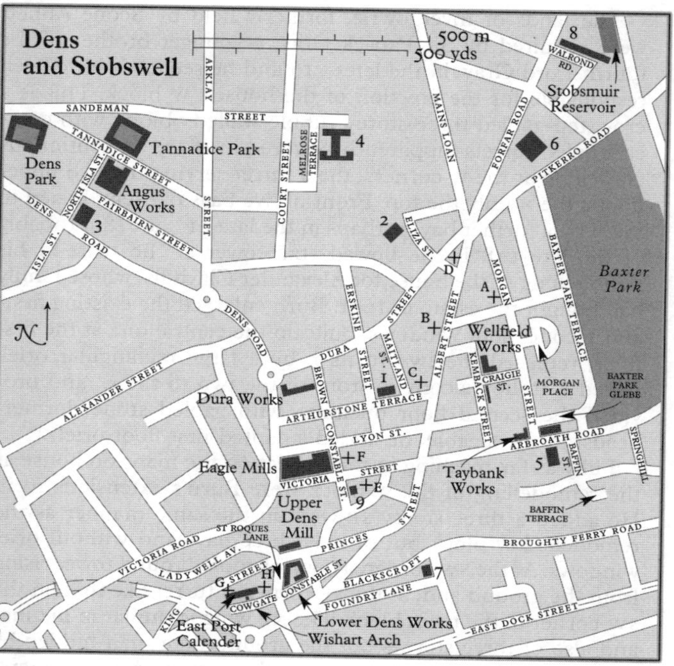

A	Park United Presbyterian Church	I	Arthurstone Neighbourhood Library
B	St John the Baptist (Episcopal)	2	Clepington Primary School
C	St Patrick (R.C.)	3	Dens Road Primary School
D	Stobswell Parish Church	4	Dundee College Melrose Campus
E	Trinity Parish Church	5	Glebelands Primary School
F	Victoria Street United Presbyterian Church	6	Morgan Academy
G	Wishart Memorial United Free Church	7	St Roque's Library
H	Wishart United Secession Church	8	Tramway Depot
		9	Wallacetown Nursery School

villas. After the First World War Craigie, SE of the Eastern Cemetery, was laid out along garden suburb lines as a curiously isolated housing development, and housing of similar character but less cut off from urban life was put up around the city's two major football stadia in the area's NW corner. The closure of most of the mills in the later C20 has been followed by the conversion of some to flats and the redevelopment of the sites of others and of Victorian tenements for new housing.

CHURCHES

CRAIGIEBANK CHURCH, corner of Craigie Avenue and Greendykes Road. Prominently sited in the centre of the Craigie housing development, a cruciform church, by *Frank Thomson*, 1937–8, in a simple Early Christian manner, the harled walls with buff reconstituted stone dressings, the roofs covered with red Rosemary tiles. Sloping-topped buttresses between the tall side windows of the nave. In the transept gables, triplets of windows under small single lights; unassertive windows placed quite high in the sides of the transepts and the S gable of the nave. Short and low N chancel. The dominant feature is the S tower. Ashlar-faced bottom stage containing the entrance, its elliptical-arched door in a round-headed billet-moulded surround, with cushion-capitalled nook-shafts and a tympanum carved with a Maltese cross in shallow relief, perhaps intended to suggest a consecration cross. The tower's two upper stages are harled but with rusticated quoins and narrow openings of diminishing size. Inside, round-headed arches to the transepts and chancel. – ORGAN by *Frederick Rothwell & Sons*. – HALL across the N end, like a miniature version of the church but without a tower. It is of 1931–2 and also by Frank Thomson.

DUNDEE UNITED FREE CHURCH, Marryat Street. Harled and pitch-roofed oblong, by *Allan & Friskin*, 1931–2. Small buttresses along the sides; rectangular windows. Full-height but narrow W porch, the round-headed entrance, its arched head blind, in a moulded and corniced classical surround. Harled HALL of 1933, also by Allan & Friskin, across the E end.

PARK UNITED PRESBYTERIAN CHURCH, corner of Park Avenue and Morgan Street. Now a medical centre and housing. By *Leslie Ower* of *C. & L. Ower*, 1888–9. Austere Gothic, built of stugged grey ashlar. Cruciform, the SW inner angle containing a two-storey porch to the W hall added in 1890–1. Placed diagonally across the SE inner angle, a tall tower containing the church's gabled entrance. The tower is plain except at the slightly recessed belfry, each of its faces pierced by a three-light opening whose triangular mullions rise as angular mouldings on the merlons of the surmounting battlement. Within the battlement, a small slated and wrought-iron-finialled spire. In the inner angles of the tower and the church's S and E limbs, bowed projections, the taller on the NE containing the gallery stair. Identically treated E and S gables, each with gableted corner buttresses and a sloping-topped central buttress. In each half of the gable, a four-light mullioned window (those of the S gable now converted to doors) under a Y-traceried window of two lights.

ST JOHN THE BAPTIST (Episcopal), Albert Street. Small and villagey rubble-built Late Gothic, by the *Rev. Edward Sugden*, 1886–7, exactly orientated so rather awkwardly placed to the street. Nave with lean-to aisles, a lower semi-octagonal chancel and NE vestry; the NW porch was added in 1896. Rectangular windows containing pointed lights to the aisles and chancel; continuous band of round-headed lights in the clearstorey. Enjoyably flowery wrought-iron finial on the chancel; a tall bellcote with a French pavilion-style truncated spire on the nave's W end. – To the S, a single-storey-and-attic HALL of 1893 and also by Sugden. Hoodmoulded door and windows in the gable fronting the street.

Inside, a hammerbeam roof over the nave whose arcades are composed of elliptical-headed arches carried on wooden pillars. Green painted aisle walls stencilled with gold fleurs-de-lis. Pointed stone chancel arch. Projecting from its S side, a PULPIT of 1914. On its stone base an oak superstructure, the faces carved in relief with Scenes from the Life of Our Lord. Also of 1914 the stone rail at the chancel entrance. Simple roof over the choir; in the apsed sanctuary the collars meet at a central pendant. On the walls of the choir, elaborate PANELLING of Late Gothic character designed by *Thoms & Wilkie*, 1908, with crocketed pinnacles and thistle finials; on the panels, religious emblems. Contemporary oak CHOIR STALLS with griffon arm-rests at the ends. – Also of 1908 and in the same manner the ORGAN CASE on the N side of the choir. The ORGAN itself is by *George Sixsmith*, *c*. 1985. In the apse, its walls stencilled with green-coloured foliage patterns, the REREDOS of 1914 with figures of kneeling angels; the centrepiece is a triptych painted by *William Hole* of the Adoration of the Magi flanked by depictions of St John the Baptist and St John the Evangelist. – Stone FONT of 1914 at the W end of the nave, its steepled cover of oak. – Painted STATIONS OF THE CROSS, also of 1914.

STAINED GLASS. In the apse, four lights of 1887 (St Ambrose, the Blessed Virgin Mary, St Andrew and St Gregory the Great) by *Clayton & Bell*, 1887. – Also of 1887 and by Clayton & Bell the choir's N window (St Augustine of Hippo). – The corresponding modernistic S window (Millennium Window) is of *c*. 2004. – At the W end of the nave, a pair of lights (the Blessed Virgin Mary and the Infant Jesus with St John the Baptist, Elizabeth and Zacharias; Our Lord Blessing Children) under a roundel (the Baptism of Our Lord), all by the *Newcastle Glass Co.*, 1904.

ST PATRICK (R.C.), Arthurstone Terrace. Freely treated Late Gothic, by *T. Martin Cappon*, 1897–8. Big buttressed box, built of hammer-dressed Berrymuirhead (Forfar) red stone, the polished dressings also of red sandstone but from Ayrshire. Powerfully buttressed and curvaceously parapeted outshots containing confessionals along the sides. Gabled flush transepts at the N (liturgical E) end. Cusped-loop and quatrefoil tracery in the heads of the side windows. Art Nouveau cupola on the nave roof. The main interest is at the S front. In the gable, a crocketed gableted and foliage-finialled entrance containing an elegant Gothic wrought-iron gate flanked by similarly treated small windows. Above, a hoodmoulded window of six lights, its traceried head filled with cusped loops spiraling round a central quatrefoil. In the gable-head, a stepped arrangement of three small louvred openings. The gable is divided by buttresses into a 'nave' and 'aisles', the W 'aisle's front carried up as the face of a square corner tower and containing a niche in which stands a figure of St Patrick. The tower's slightly recessed low top stage is the belfry, each face's large round-headed opening containing a pair of squat louvred lights under a quatrefoil-filled head, the mullions and tracery of wood. Stone griffons project from the tower's upper corners. Surmounting the tower, an octagonal wooden cupola, its slated low spire rising to an iron weathervane.

Unaisled INTERIOR covered with a roof whose collars rise from dwarf marble columns standing on pendant stone corbels. At the N (liturgical E) end, altars of the Immaculate Conception and Sacred Heart, both in round-headed niches under leafily crocketed ogee-arched hoodmoulds. These flank the elliptical-arched recess, also with a crocketed and ogee-arched hood-mould, containing the High Altar. On the E sides of this arch, remains of foliage-stencilled decoration of 1898. Over the High Altar, a REREDOS painted with a huge figure of St Patrick; in tabernacled niches either side, small statues of St Columba and St Bridget. – In front, a free-standing ALTAR of 1898, its front painted with a depiction of the dead Christ; formerly it stood in the Mortuary Chapel. – At the church's S end, a GALLERY over the vestibule which is flanked by the baptistery on the E and Mortuary Chapel on the W. – In the gallery, an ORGAN by *Andrew Watt & Son* in a divided case. – In the groin-vaulted BAPTISTERY, the disappointingly routine Gothic FONT designed by *Cappon*, 1898, its wooden cover a crocketed crown spire.

CLERGY HOUSE of 1899 and also by Cappon to the N. Vertically proportioned three storeys with mullioned-and-transomed windows, the lower floors' with curvaceously moulded lintels. – To the NE, the detached ST PATRICK'S WAR MEMORIAL HALL, by *Reginald Fairlie*, 1926–7, plain except for the round-headed and splay-moulded entrance in the W gable, this end stone-faced, the other walls drydashed.

ST TERESA OF AVILA (R.C.), Graham Street. Disused. Designed by *Allan & Friskin* in 1938 but not completed until 1955. Built of gently variegated brown and red brick. Simple Early Christian detail. Stepped and scooped bottom corners to the W gable from which projects a shallow porch. Blind arched heads to the side windows which rise into gablets. Flat-roofed NW baptistery.

STOBSWELL PARISH CHURCH, Albert Street, Dura Street and Eliza Street. Originally Ogilvie Free Church. On a triangular site, a mission hall of 1874 and church of 1875–6, both by *Edward & Robertson* and of roughly stugged masonry in a thriftily detailed Gothic manner.

The hall at the N is lancet-windowed. From its semi-octagonal N end extends a lower chancel-like projection whose original gablets were replaced in 1978 by a crushingly heavy 'mansard' roof.

The church itself is basically L-plan, with a nave (orientated N–S) and, at its S end, a twin-gabled long E transept from whose SE corner extends a semi-octagonal vestry, but there is also a minimally projecting W transept, again twin-gabled. Triangular steeple in the inner angle of the nave and E transept.

In the nave's S gable and the end of the W transept, pairs of tall two-light windows with quatrefoil heads, the nave's surmounted by a rose window under a vesica opening. Two-storey arrangement of windows in the end of the E transept, the upper windows two-light with quatrefoil heads, the lower windows and those in the transept's sides single lancets. In the W side of the nave, another two-storey treatment, the upper windows rising into gablets. Rose window in the N gable.

The steeple gives presence to the church. Chamfered corners at the tower. Over its entrance, an ogee-arched hoodmould with a stiff-leaf finial; above, a diagonally stepped string course and lancets disclose the rise of the gallery stair inside. Pairs of tall belfry openings with bell-capitalled nook-shafts. Parapet decorated with blind arcading; splay-foot slated spire.

Inside, between the hammerbeam-roofed nave and transeptal two-bay E aisle, depressed-arch arcade carried on stone columns, their capitals carved with stiffleaf. Gallery, its front with Late Gothic panels, on slender cast-iron columns in the aisle and across the nave's N end and with a splay across the inner angle. Sanctuary formed in 1997 in the SW corner of the nave.

STAINED GLASS. At the nave's S end, a pair of large windows (Scenes from the Life of Our Lord), colourful but disciplined, by *William Wilson*, 1953, and formerly in Park United Presbyterian Church. – In the W wall at gallery level, a narrative window (Our Lord with Martha and Mary) of *c.* 1950. – At the S end of the E aisle, a pair of lights. One (St Luke) is of *c.* 1980, the other and more accomplished (St John the Evangelist) signed by *W.C. Cameron*, 1965. – In the aisle's E side, a window (the Risen Lord Appearing to St Mary Magdalene) of *c.* 1950 and, in the flanking lights, a pair of reused mid-C20 panels (the Ascension; the Dove at the Ending of the Flood) from the head of a window.

TRINITY PARISH CHURCH, Crescent Street. Originally Wallacetown Church. By *George Mathewson*, 1839–40, and built as a chapel of ease. Large 'Saxon' box, the walling of stugged ashlar, now badly weathered, the nave's tall round-headed windows of two lights. Projecting from the front (E) gable, a tower originally of two principal stages, the lower containing the hoodmoulded entrance under a window of three tall stepped lights and finished with a cornice carried on round-arched corbelling. The upper stage was the belfry with, at each exposed face, a single opening whose head rises into blind arcading under the heavy moulded corbels supporting the cornice. The Romanesque top stage was added in 1877 by *C. & L. Ower*. Two-light belfry openings under boldly projecting chevron-carved hoodmoulds, the clock faces (by *George Rattray*) provided in 1891. Wall-head parapet pierced by round-headed arcading; at the corners, panelled and conical-spired drums. Extending from the nave's W end, a full-height short chancel, the gable window of three stepped lights under a circular opening.

INTERIOR. On the vestibule's W wall, in the position of a doorway of 1840, a WAR MEMORIAL of *c.* 1920, a round-headed recess of Early Christian inspiration but the carving unusually elaborate. The church itself is divided into a nave and aisles by giant bundle-shafted and bell-capitalled cast-iron columns. From these spring round-headed arches over the nave's low clearstorey windows (originally lit from roof-lights over the aisles) and transverse Tudor-arched trusses, their spandrels with cusped arcading, under the roof of the central vessel. The focus of attention was originally on the E end but the plans of the seating and gallery were reversed in 1877 when C. & L. Ower moved the pulpit from the E to the W end of the church. – Gothic bench PEWS, probably of 1877, in the aisles; the central pews were replaced by chairs *c.* 2005. – At the W end, an early C20 COMMUNION TABLE standing in front of the octagonal stone PULPIT. This is of 1840, with stumpy columns at the corners. – Behind the pulpit, a splay-sided apse entered through a Tudorish arch. This is of 1840 but in 1892 *C. & L. Ower* erected a Gothic-panelled wooden SCREEN across the arch's lower part and formed an organ gallery above, the present ORGAN, in a divided case, built by *Rushworth & Dreaper* in 1955. – STAINED GLASS. Narrative three-light window ('Come Unto Me All Ye That Labour and Are Heavy Laden . . .') of 1892 in the W wall of the apse.

Low HALL in a very simple Romanesque manner to the N. It was built as a school in the later C19 and converted to a hall by C. & L. Ower in 1888.

VICTORIA STREET UNITED PRESBYTERIAN CHURCH, corner of Victoria Street and Brown Constable Street. Secularized. Italianate, by *Edward & Robertson*, 1874–5. Broad piend-roofed two-storey box faced with badly weathered stugged ashlar, the windows round-headed. At the S front, a four-bay centrepiece under a pediment, its tympanum containing a dummy oculus. Console-keystoned entrance at the W end. Within the parapet above rises a square belfry, each face panelled with a giant overarch springing from corner pilasters and containing a two-light opening under a dummy oculus. The belfry's wall-head is finished with a bracketed cornice and circle-pierced parapet, its corners topped by obelisks. In the W elevation to Brown Constable Street, paired round-headed windows in giant shouldered overarches. Contemporary HALL, also Italianate but lower, to the SE.

WISHART MEMORIAL UNITED FREE CHURCH, King Street. Secularized. By *T. Martin Cappon*, 1899–1901. Free Perpendicular, built of hammer-dressed grey Burghmuirhead stone with a liberal admixture of red Dumfriesshire sandstone dressings. In the front (N) gable, a huge window divided by a transom into two stages, the tracery elaborate but disciplined; ogee-arched hoodmould. NE tower, its N face with an entrance like that of the gable but the surround's head is carved with a relief portrait of the C16 Protestant reformer and martyr, George Wishart, in a multi-foil panel set among thistles, and the entrance's hoodmould is segmental-arched and with crocketed pinnacles at the ends. Immediately above the entrance, a tripartite low window. The tower's lower two-thirds are finished with a cornice, griffons projecting at the corners. Above the cornice, a tall belfry, its corner pilasters with foliaged capitals; in each face, a hoodmoulded tall two-light opening. Overall battlements, also with griffons under the tall panelled and crocket-finialled corners.

The exposed rubble-walled W side of the nave rises into a trio of gables, the S containing a tall three-light window, a simplified version of the main window in the front gable. W transept at the S end. On the nave roof, an Art Nouveau cupola, its lead roof rising from extravagantly bellcast eaves to a slender spirelet.

WISHART UNITED SECESSION CHURCH, Cowgate. Secularized. Built in 1841, an urbane ashlar-fronted oblong, the stonework now badly weathered, containing a hall-like church above shops, the ground floor, pierced by a pend, much altered in the C20. The church itself was of one very tall storey, its height allowing for a gallery, but, after its secularization in 1901, a floor was inserted which cuts across the S windows whose round-arched heads were infilled at the same time. S façade of seven bays, the outer two at each end slightly advanced under a parapet and containing pairs of closely set windows. Broader windows at the three centre bays which are finished with a very shallow block pediment. Two tall windows, also round-headed, in the E gable. In the N elevation, two tiers of windows to the church, the lower rectangular, the upper round-headed and still with the original glazing pattern.

PARK AND CEMETERY

BAXTER PARK, Arbroath Road, Baxter Park Terrace, Pitkerro Road and Bingham Terrace. The park covering *c.* 15 ha. was given to Dundee by the textile-manufacturing magnate, Sir David Baxter, and two of his sisters in 1863. The landscaping was designed by *Joseph Paxton* and its execution superintended by *Frank Richmond*. Flat at the S end from which the ground rises to the well-planted slope at the N, the park's two halves are divided by a terrace along which runs a gravel walk. Behind the centre of the terrace and fronted by a broad flight of steps up to it, the MAIN PAVILION built in 1863 and designed by Paxton's nephew and partner, *G. H. Stokes*. This is Jacobean Renaissance, of one tall storey faced with polished Bannockburn ashlar. Front composed of a five-bay loggia between slightly taller square pavilions (the W originally a ladies' room, now café, the E a refreshment room, now entrance hall), all with balustraded wall-heads, the pavilions' balustrades surmounting panelled parapets and with corner pedestals topped by obelisk finials on scrolled bases. At the pavilions' corners, coupled Ionic pilasters standing on tall plinths. In the S face of each pavilion, a large Palladian window, its keystone formed by a cartouche, the l. bearing the initials S/M, the r. H/I/N. The central loggia's round-headed arches, glazed in 2005–6, are carried on coupled Roman Doric columns and with keystones also formed as cartouches, the central cartouche carved with the Baxter coat of arms. Inside the loggia (now a function and exhibition space), the end and back walls are panelled with giant round-headed arches. In the centre of the N wall, a niche containing a marble STATUE by *John Steell*, 1863, of the frock-coated Sir David Baxter, a cloak over one shoulder, holding a scroll on which is depicted the plan of the park.

PARK CENTRE to the NW, by *Dundee City Council*, 2003–4. Postmodern, a glazed box under a ribbed metal roof whose broad eaves are supported on fat metal columns. – NORTH LODGE, Pitkerro Road. Single-storey Scots Jacobean of 1863. – Contemporary GATEWAY at the park's SW corner. Jacobean Renaissance, the gatepiers of channelled ashlar with touches of strapwork on the friezes and surmounted by double-handled urns.

EASTERN CEMETERY, Arbroath Road. Laid out by *William Scott*, the Town's Architect and Surveyor, in 1862. GATEWAY of 1863 and also by Scott. Aggressive battlemented Gothic, the large archway for carriages and hearses flanked by lower archways for pedestrian mourners, their hoodmoulds carved with rosetted and floriated panels, the headstops with portraits of variously aged men, women and children. The inner order of each arch is decorated with foliage and springs from bell-capitalled nook-shafts. Flanking the archways are offset and gableted buttresses finished with crocketed finials, the two central buttresses with cusped niches containing small figures of mourning ladies. On the centre battlement, the coat of arms of the Burgh of Dundee. From the ends of the gateway dwarf walls curve out under high quatrefoil-pierced parapets to join the straight walls, sadly bereft of their railings, which line the road. – Plain Jacobean LODGE, also of 1863 and by Scott, at the cemetery's N corner.

MONUMENTS. Just inside the S gateway, a large Gothic sarcophagus memorial to George Kirkland, dated 1870, its base and the shafts of the leafily capitalled columns of the arches under the canopy all of polished red and black granite. – To the NW, beside the uphill-curving path, a version of the Choragic Monument of Lysicrates, erected as a memorial to James Smieton †1866. – Fair number of Celtic crosses. One, on top of the central hillock, commemorates Alexander Gilroy †1879. Of polished granite, the faces of the arms carved with interlace work, the front of the shaft with reliefs of the Dove Descending (the Holy Spirit) and the Good Shepherd. It is signed by *Davidson*, probably *Andrew Davidson* of Inverness.

PUBLIC BUILDINGS

ARTHURSTONE NEIGHBOURHOOD LIBRARY, corner of Arthurstone Terrace and Maitland Street. By the Dundee City

Architect, *William Alexander*, 1902–5.* Scots Jacobean Renaissance in polished red sandstone ashlar, the gables and gablets with formidable crowsteps and segmental or triangular pediment finials. More pediments over the Composite-pilastered entrance and several of the mullioned-and-transomed windows. Between the five-light ground- and first-floor windows of the E wing's S gable, a strapwork-balustraded stone balcony carried on massive foliaged corbels, their faces carved with human heads, whose mouths are stuffed with leaves. On the roof, a Wrennish octagonal cupola.

Inside, stair-hall with a dado of honey-coloured tiles decorated with sunburst and foliage designs. On the first floor, the E range is occupied by the principal reading room (now an office), its arch-braced and queen-strut roof largely glazed.

CLEPINGTON PRIMARY SCHOOL, Eliza Street. Originally Stobswell Public School and containing a secondary department which included the sciences, both natural and domestic, among its subjects. By *James H. Langlands*, 1906–8. Large and tall, built of hammer-dressed rubble, it is triple-pile, the central block of three storeys and an attic, the outer ranges a storey lower, all above a basement which is fully exposed in the fall of the ground to the SW. The principal front, in a confident Free Jacobean manner with Art Nouveau touches, is composed of the NE ends of the three blocks. The centre's gable is of two bays with four-light mullioned-and-transomed windows to the principal floors, their aprons carved with Art Nouveau foliage, the second-floor windows round-headed and their mullions and transoms of wood rather than stone; simply shaped top enclosing a large panel. Slightly set back from this gable, low towers containing the principal entrances for boys and girls, each approached by a flight of steps and covered by a massively canopied semicircular stone hood; above, small two-light stair windows and a circular window to the top landing. On top of the towers, low octagonal attic cupolas under flattened lead domes, their windowless faces panelled, their corners tied by stone scrolls to the corners of the towers' wall-heads. Set back from these towers are the crowstepped gables of the outer blocks, their low four-light windows serving cloakrooms; in the inner angles with the main block's towers, low bowed projections which housed janitors' rooms. The long side elevations are much plainer but, at each end, a curvaceously parapeted double gable, the outer half containing cloakroom windows like those to the front and the inner pierced by stair windows, the top landing enjoying a round-headed and mullioned four-light window. Over the tall classroom windows of the intermediate bays are pedimented dormers. Roofs with bracketed broad eaves and surmounted by an array of Art Nouveau cupolas, their domes' wrought-iron finials in the form of pierced hearts.

* The building was completed, after Alexander's death in 1904, by his successor as City Architect, *James Thomson*.

CRAIGIE HIGH SCHOOL, Garnet Terrace. 1968–70, by the Dundee City Architect, *John W. Kidd*, and almost identical to his contemporary Menzieshill High School (*see* Charleston, Menzieshill and Ninewells). Loosely composed and horizontally proportioned low blocks clad in brown brick and drydash relieved by wooden fascias.

DENS PARK, Tannadice Road. Dundee Football Club's ground since 1899. Long and minimally angled late C20 V-plan NORTH STAND, with a double-pitch roof. Also with a double-pitched roof the short SOUTH STAND by *Hiddleston, Hynd & Feist*, 1992. The EAST and WEST STANDS are by *James Paul Associates*, 1998–9, their monopitch roofs forming canopies over the spectators. All the back and side walls are of ribbed metal sheeting.

DENS ROAD PRIMARY SCHOOL, corner of Fairbairn Street and North Isla Street. By *James H. Langlands*, 1908–11. Free Style, built of hammer-dressed masonry. Three main two-storey sections, the central section composed of two back-to-back piend-roofed blocks, each with an Art Nouveau cupola. Cupolas also on the end sections. Their NE elevations are piend-roofed and plain. More exciting the SW overlooking Dens Road. Here the outer bay of each end section is carried up as a simply detailed Jacobean gable. Protruding from the inner end of each is a curvaceously parapeted tower, of the same height as the rest but containing five storeys of small windows, the top floor's forming a continuous mullioned band. Below, at each half of the front, bands of windows but set at different levels, those of the half next the centre block lighting cloakrooms and placed higher than the outer half's windows which light the stair whose third-floor landing enjoys a huge round-headed and mullioned opening. At the ground floor of each of these towers, an entrance under a semicircular hood carried on heavy consoles. At the first floor of the end elevations, tall Diocletian windows.

To the SW, a contemporary single-storey round structure designed to house the air intake of the school's heating system. Rubble-built under an open clearstorey, the lead roof rising into a spirelet.

DUNDEE COLLEGE GRAHAM STREET CAMPUS, Graham Street. Originally St Michael's School. By the Dundee City Architect, *David B. McLay*, 1937. Large red brick and drydash U, the centre block of two storeys, the wings of three. Utilitarian except for the most sparing of Neo-Georgian touches. – To the SE, a single-storey-and-attic red brick JANITOR'S HOUSE with a steeply pitched roof and prominent chimneystacks at the ends.

DUNDEE COLLEGE MELROSE CAMPUS, Melrose Terrace. Originally Stobswell Boys School. By the Dundee City Architect, *David B. McLay*, 1938. Two- and three-storey H, of red brick and harling. Generally Neo-Georgian without frills but horizontally proportioned first-floor windows at the centre block.

Morgan Academy.
View from south-east

GLEBELANDS PRIMARY SCHOOL, Baffin Street. By *James H. Langlands*, 1913–15. Three tall storeys and bleak except for some thrifty Jacobean touches, only the small cloakroom windows and the cupola reminders of the Art Nouveau influence evident at Dundee Board Schools of a few years earlier.

MORGAN ACADEMY, corner of Forfar Road and Pitkerro Road. Franco-Flemish edifice by *Peddie & Kinnear*, 1862–8. Originally on an almost rural site and, although now bordered by villadom, still aloof from the city's industry, commerce and blocks of flats, this is Dundee's most conspicuous advertisement of Victorian philanthropy.

John Morgan (†1850), a native of Dundee who had acquired considerable wealth as a merchant in India, left instructions in his will that a sum be taken from his estate sufficient to build and endow a 'Hospital' (i.e. a school providing free board, lodging and education) to accommodate 100 boys chosen from the children of natives of Dundee and three other Angus burghs. Built at a cost of *c.* £18,000, the Morgan Hospital served its original purpose for only twenty-one years before it was acquired by the Dundee School Board who changed its name from 'Hospital' to 'Academy' and its function from a charity boarding school to a selective secondary day school (comprehensive since the later C20). Gutted by fire in 2001, the buildings were reconstructed by *Dundee City Council* in association with *Simpson & Brown*, 2001–4.

As built in the 1860s the school was an oblong of four two-storey ranges enclosing a courtyard (roofed over as a gymnasium in 1914–15). The principal front faces S. The ends are formed by the crowstepped and advanced gables of the E and W ranges, their corners with angle buttresses at the ground floor and nook-shafts above, the face of each bisected by a very tall chimney corbelled out from first-floor level. At the first floor, a pair of foliage-finialled single windows from whose cusp-topped transoms spring quatrefoil-headed arches. Under the windows, a sill course which is carried all round the building. These ends are joined to the front's centrepiece by mirror-image four-bay sections. At each the three outer bays contain mullioned-and-transomed windows of two basket-arched lights, the upper windows breaking through the eaves into gablets in front of the wall-head's pierced parapet. At each gablet, a quatrefoil-decorated round panel and foliage-finialled pinnacles. The taller inner bay of each linking section, marked off by a stepped buttress, rises into a crowstepped gable. At the upper floor a rectangular oriel window covered by a mono-pitch roof.

The front's centre tower, a proud assertion of the munificence of the institution's founder, is of three principal stages. The lowest is angle-buttressed and contains the elliptical-arched main entrance under an ogee-arched and crocketed hoodmould. Very tall second stage, its cut-out corners filled with nook-shafts. Hoodmoulded and mullioned three-light window, its upper tier of openings with Gothic traceried heads. Projecting from this, a bracketed stone balcony, the front pierced by Gothic arcading. Fish-scale-slated tourelles at the corners of the third stage. In each side, a round clock face under a hoodmoulded low window. Finishing this stage is a quatrefoil-pierced parapet carried on multi-moulded corbels. Set back within the parapet, a gableted Flemish Gothic attic under a tall iron-crested French pavilion roof, its two steeply pitched and slated tiers interrupted by a vertical wooden belfry containing Gothic openings.

Side elevations in the same manner and with tall lead-spired octagonal cupolas on the iron-crested roofs of the back wings.

ST ROQUE'S LIBRARY, Blackscroft. Disused. French-flavoured Edwardian Baroque, by the Dundee City Architect, *James Thomson*, 1909–10. Tall single-storey, the principal three-bay N and W façades faced with polished ashlar. These are almost identical, each with lugged architraved and aproned windows set in frameworks of channelled stonework at the outer bays and with an advanced centrepiece, its walling wholly channelled. In each centrepiece, a round-headed and keystoned recess containing an entrance. The E doorway (for juveniles) is corniced, the W (to adults' reading rooms) framed in an Ionic-columned aedicule, the pediment broken by a shield. Above the continuously corniced wall-head, balustrades over the outer bays and, over the N and W centrepieces, heavy stepped parapets, each carved with the head of a thoughtful cherub above a swag-surmounted cornucopia. – At the W end of the small front garden's railings, a contemporary cast-iron GATE under an overthrow, the design of late C17 inspiration.

STOBSMUIR RESERVOIR, Clepington Road. By the Dundee Water Engineer, *George Baxter*, 1908. The reservoir itself, first constructed after the formation of the Dundee Water Company in 1845, is a utilitarian concrete-roofed oblong. Surrounding walls of bull-nosed masonry built in 1908, their battlements with unusually long merlons. At the W end, a substantial square tower (the Chart Room) and, near the centre of this side, a second but smaller tower (the Valve House), both also battlemented. Much smaller towers to the E and, at the enclosure's NE corner, an L-plan arrangement of small towers linked by concave walling. Further small towers along the E and W sides of the enclosure.

TANNADICE PARK, Tannadice Road. The stadium of Dundee United Football Club, its NORTH, EAST and WEST STANDS all by *James Paul Associates*, 1991–5. Ribbed metal outer walling and boldly oversailing upswept monopitch roofs over the two tiers of seating. SOUTH STAND of 1961, also with ribbed metal walls but the roof of two uneven pitches.

TRAMWAY DEPOT, corner of Forfar Road and Walrond Road. Now in other use. Built in 1901, a tall single storey of red brick. A pair of shaped gables to the W. The long S elevation to Walrond Road is divided into panels, their sawtooth heads of black brick, enclosing black brickwork diamond patterns.

WALLACETOWN NURSERY SCHOOL, Brown Constable Street. Early C21, of concrete blockwork and glass with a low-pitched pavilion roof. – The W GATEPIERS were erected for a school built here in 1858 by the textile manufacturers, Baxter Bros, to provide part-time education for their child workers. Bell-capitalled cast-iron round piers surmounted by elegant vases, also of cast iron, bearing Neoclassical reliefs emblematic of the Arts and Learning, a smart reminder of Dundee mill-owners' adherence to liberal social as well as economic principles.

WISHART ARCH, Cowgate. Rubble-built relic of Dundee's town walls (demolished in the C18), preserved because of the story that the Protestant reformer and martyr, George Wishart, preached from its battlement during the plague of 1544. The gateway may be of *c.* 1500. Round-headed arch, a double-keyhole gunloop to its N; in the stub of walling to the S, a rectangular doorway for pedestrians crudely inserted, perhaps *c.* 1800.

DESCRIPTION

Cowgate to Arbroath Road

COWGATE E of East Marketgait was a principal thoroughfare from the medieval burgh of Dundee towards Broughty Ferry. No longer a thoroughfare, it now forms the N boundary of an extensive car park. The buildings on the S side have been demolished. On the N corner with East Marketgait and stretching uphill N to King Street, WISHART PLACE, a block of flats
104 by *James F. Stephen*, 1996–2000. Rising to a height of nine storeys, it is determinedly cheerful Postmodern of Scots vernacular inspiration in red brick and reconstituted stone, with

painted metal trimmings and blue-coloured ribbed roofs. To the E and much more restrained, the long former East Port Calender (*see* Industrial Buildings, below). In front of this, the rubbly Wishart Arch (*see* Public Buildings, above), a reminder of pre-industrial Dundee. Next to the East Port Calender and still clinging to gentility, the former Wishart United Secession Church (*see* Churches, above) on the corner of ST ROQUE'S LANE. Filling the whole of the next block, its S entrance from CONSTABLE STREET (Cowgate's E continuation) and bounded by DENS STREET on the E and Princes Street on the N, the Lower Dens Works, one of the city's most swaggering assertions of industrial enterprise, and, across Dens Street, its former flax warehouse (for these, *see* Industrial Buildings, below). S of the car park, on the far side of BLACKSCROFT, the civic swagger of the former St Roque's Library (*see* Public Buildings, above).

KING STREET, behind and parallel to Cowgate, starts at the W with Wishart Place (*see* above) on the S and, on the N, the lower part of the LADYWELL AVENUE housing development by the *City of Dundee District Council*, 1975–7, the low-rise blocks of flats grouped in a zigzag arrangement on the steep slope, their layout, drydashed walls and concrete-pantiled roofs valiant attempts to evoke the spirit of Scottish East Coast small burghs and fishing villages. After Wishart Place, the former Wishart Memorial United Free Church (*see* Churches, above), its architectural references also Scottish but culled from different sources. Immediately to its E, at Nos. 63–67 King Street, the former head office of the jute-manufacturing firm of Low & Bonar formed *c.* 1913 by *Robert Gibson* who reconstructed and refronted a former flax-spinning mill of *c.* 1835 for the purpose. Two-storey-and-attic nine-bay front of roughish ashlar. At each end was a Jacobean Renaissance door under a Diocletian fanlight (the l. entrance and fanlight now combined as a single round-headed opening) and, at the first floor, a three-light window, the sill supported on rounded corbels. Wall-head parapet, its taller ends pierced as simplified balustrades, its centre rising to a curvaceous gable containing a Diocletian window. There follow plain late C19 tenements (Nos. 75–89). In PRINCES STREET E of St Roque's Lane, the Lower Dens Works (*see* Industrial Buildings, below) and, E of Dens Street, fairly humble tenements (Nos. 11–25) of the earlier or mid C19, two with central gablets. On Princes Street's N side, between Dens Brae and Weaver's Yard, the massive façade of the Upper Dens Works (*see* Industrial Buildings, below).

At it E end Princes Street bends to run NE. Off the l. side, FERGUSON STREET, its W end closed by Trinity Parish Church (*see* Churches, above). On Princes Street's corner with VICTORIA STREET, the former DUNDEE SAVINGS BANK EASTERN BRANCH by *Johnston & Baxter*, 1914–15. Baroque, 93
a tall tower at the join of the acutely angled E and N elevations. These are identical, each of one very high storey and of five bays, the walls faced with polished ashlar above a

hammer-dressed base. The narrow end bays are treated as panelled antae containing pedimented Gibbsian small windows and, high up, panels under rectangular swags. Between the ends, attached Ionic column screens framing large windows, also in Gibbsian surrounds, under circular openings whose surrounds are decorated with ribbon enrichment. Above the mutule-corniced entablature, a balustrade between scroll-topped pedestals, their faces carved with cornucopia. The tower is wedged uncomfortably between the inner ends of the main fronts, its rounded corners forming strips of channelled masonry. At the NE face, a portico, its Composite columns with granite shafts, the pediment displaying the Royal Arms of Scotland; behind the pediment, a parapet with urn-finialled corners. The doorway itself is cavetto-moulded and keystoned. Above, the tower rises sheer except for a ribbon-moulded window opening in each side and, at the front, the bank's coat of arms in a corniced surround. Mutuled wall-head cornice carrying segmental-pedimented large pedestals fronted by clock faces and joined by short balustrades to urn-topped small pedestals on the corners. Within these, a ball-and-spike-finialled stone dome. On the opposite corner, Nos. 1–42 Victoria Street, a block of flats of 2005. Splayed SE corner, its large windows fronted by metal balconies which follow the building lines of the streets.

ARBROATH ROAD continues the line of Victoria Street E of Princes Street. On the NW corner with Kemback Street, Nos. 34–38 by *Nicoll Russell Studios*, 1996, a pitched-roofed four-storey block of flats, the pale-coloured blockwork walls enlivened by a few Postmodern touches. In KEMBACK STREET and extending along the N side of CRAIGIE STREET, the former Wellfield Works. Most of Arbroath Road's N side between Kemback Street and MORGAN STREET is occupied by the frontage of the former Taybank Works Jute-Spinning Mill (for these, *see* Industrial Buildings, below). Off Morgan Street, N of Craigie Street, MORGAN PLACE, a square of three-storey blocks of flats by the Dundee City Architect, *David B. McLay*, 1935–9. Walls faced with hammer-dressed masonry, the chief inspiration C17 Scots domestic architecture but with a hint of Art Deco. Off Arbroath Road's S side, just E of Morgan Street, Glebelands Primary School (*see* Public Buildings, above). On the N of Arbroath Road E of Morgan Street, the former Taybank Works Jute-Spinning Mill and Power Loom Factory (*see* Industrial Buildings, below). Then the bottom of BAXTER PARK TERRACE jinks off to the l., a fussy Postmodern block of flats, by *Architectus*, 1997, at the start. The terrace's late C19 and early C20 tenements to the N, all overlooking Baxter Park (*see* Park and Cemetery, above), are more satisfactory. Four-storey and plain except for Georgian survival doorpieces and a sparing provision of canted bay windows. Nos. 17–18 of *c.* 1890 are by *James Maclaren & Son* who may have designed others. At the N end, Nos. 1–3, by *Alexander McCulloch*, 1885–6, the doorpieces of Jacobean Renaissance derivation, a spired octagonal tower on the corner with Pitkerro Road.

In Arbroath Road S of Baxter Park, late C19 Renaissance tenements (Nos. 85–93) on the E side of Baffin Street. Another pair of late C19 tenements (Nos. 95–97 and No. 99) flank the entrance to Eden Street, their canted corners topped by pilastered and ogee-roofed cupolas. In SPRINGHILL, No. 15 (SPRINGBANK), a two-storey Late Georgian villa overlooking the Tay. Three-bay S front with a central bow; the ground- and first-floor windows of the r. bay were enlarged to tripartites in the late C19.

East of Baxter Park to Craigie

E of Baxter Park, on Arbroath Road's N side, Nos. 94–96, a late C19 bargeboarded two-storey double house. At the centre of the front, a pair of jerkin-head gables with canted bay windows at their ground floor and cushion-mullioned three-light openings above; wooden end porches on which sit ogee-domed semi-octagonal window projections. To the N a predominantly bungaloid area developed in the 1920s and 1930s. However, in BINGHAM TERRACE, prosperous-looking villas, mostly Late Victorian or Edwardian. On the S, No. 7 designed for himself by the artist *F. M. Henderson*, 1960. Flat-roofed *moderne* in drydash with brick trim. Large S windows and a bowed corner to the SW jamb. On the N, No. 6 (TILLYDRINE) by *James Foggie & Son*, 1907, two-storey, asymmetrical and broad-eaved. Jerkin-head gable to the front, the lights of its top-floor window set between broad wooden mullions. Over the entrance, a domed small tower with a canted oriel and a curvilinear parapet. The ashlar-faced No. 8 (THE ANCHORAGE) by *C. & L. Ower*, 1895, was built for a ship-owner, Captain William Ovenstone. Two storeys and an attic, with full-height canted bay windows at the ends of the front and, at its centre, a short veranda-porch and elliptical-headed dormer window. On the roof, wrought-iron cresting and a fish-scale-slated domed cupola. The single-storey-and-attic Nos. 14–16 form a white-harled double villa by *James Foggie & Son*, *c.* 1910. At the front's M-roof gabled centrepiece, a pair of broad canted bay windows; recessed broad porches at the ends. Art Nouveauish dormer windows and chimneys. Unfortunately, the original glazing pattern has been lost at No. 16. At Bingham Terrace's E end, a group of harled two-storey double houses (Nos. 38–56) by *Hutton & Tough*, 1909, all set behind steeply sloping front gardens. At the centre of each, an M-roofed double gable, bargeboarded and partly half-timbered, containing three-light windows. Linking the centrepiece to spire-roofed octagonal end towers are two-storey verandas surmounted by balconies sheltered under the projecting eaves. In the sides of the houses, large stair windows containing some Glasgow-style stained glass. At the E end of Bingham Terrace, the Eastern Cemetery (*see*

Park and Cemetery, above), its main entrance from Arbroath Road.

DALGLEISH ROAD leading downhill from Arbroath Road is mostly C20 bungaloid. In BROUGHTY FERRY ROAD, between its S end and Greendyke Road, a group of Late Victorian villas, almost but not quite enjoyable. More suggestive of seaside fun is a group in EAST HADDON ROAD to the N, the houses all on the N side of that street's SE stretch and standing high up to enjoy formerly uninterrupted views over the Tay. Here, Nos. 5–7 and Nos. 11–17 make up three bargeboarded and broad-eaved two-storey double houses of *c.* 1900, each with a central M-roofed double gable, its head half-timbered, from which projects a pair of bay windows covered by concave-sloped roofs. Also of *c.* 1900 and bargeboarded but a single house and of only one storey is No. 9. Centre door under a canopy which extends over the canted bay windows at the gabled ends of the front. Contemporary pair of single-storey-and-attic double houses at Nos. 19–25, the roofs carried down over the bay windows and Art Nouveauish veranda; at each, piend-roofed dormer windows flank a large dormer window in a half-timbered gablet. Jerkin-heads to the end gables. Further up the street, on the E, Nos. 45–51, a couple of Arts and Crafts double houses by *Freeman & Ogilvy*, *c.* 1911, with gabled porches and piended dormer windows. Elsewhere in East Haddon Road, double houses with M-roofed twin-gabled fronts and canted bay windows, by the Dundee City Architect, *James Thomson*, 1921–4.

Craigie

The CRAIGIE housing development E of East Haddon Road was laid out by *James Thomson* in 1919. Bounded to the N and S by Arbroath Road and Broughty Ferry Road, its principal streets form a circus (CARLOCHIE PLACE) surrounded by an oval (NORAM AVENUE and BALGAVIES AVENUE), both intersected by the saltire formed by the tree-lined dual carriageways of GREENDYKES ROAD and CRAIGIE AVENUE, the central reservation of Craigie Avenue originally carrying tramlines. The inner angles of the saltire were intended for a church, school, institute and block of shops, the necessary appurtenances of a garden city suburb. Of these, only Craigiebank Church (*see* Churches, above) was built, the sites of the others now partly occupied by discreet but unexciting mid-C20 four-storey blocks of flats. The original housing, designed by a number of local architects' practices (*Allan & Friskin*; *J. R. Gordon*; *J. Lowe & Co*; *F. Thomson*) and built in 1922–8, is contained in two-storey blocks, piend-roofed and with bracketed cornices or canopies over the doors, looking like semi-detached dwellings but containing two flats on each floor.

In BROUGHTY FERRY ROAD between Greendyke Road and Craigie Avenue, some Victorian villas and a couple of less welcome late C20 houses. Among them, Nos. 306–308 of *c.* 1890. Broad-eaved, bargeboarded and bay-windowed but with some Italianate detail. M-roofed double gable at the centre of the front; bracketed and gabled canopies over the side entrances. No. 310 (INGLESIDE) is an early C19 two-storey villa. Polished ashlar front of three bays, the ground-floor windows with lugged architraves, the entrance set in a screen of Roman Doric columns *in antis* at the slightly recessed centre, now with a wrought-iron porch added in the late C20. Opposite and placed below road level, No. 137 (THE MOUNT) of *c.* 1840 and also of two storeys and three bays, the masonry rendered, the piended roof with tall diagonally placed chimneys. Bracketed cornice over the N entrance. At the S front overlooking the Tay, a canted bay window at the advanced and gabled centre.

Albert Street, Forfar Road and streets off

ALBERT STREET continues the line of Princes Street from the W end of Arbroath Road. Late C19 tenements of the plainest description dominate but, on the S corner of Raglan Street, Nos. 21–29 boast a domed three-storey turret. In LYON STREET to the W, a former brewery (*see* Industrial Buildings, below). On Albert Street's S corner with ARTHURSTONE TERRACE, a bow-angled tenement (Nos. 48–52 Albert Street and Nos. 2–6 Arthurstone Terrace) by *Alexander Johnston*, 1895–1900. Conical-roofed three-storey oriel windows and a central crowstepped gable flanked by tourelles. Just to the W, on Arthurstone Terrace's N side, St Patrick's (R.C.) Church and the Arthurstone Neighbourhood Library. To the NW, off the N end of Brown Constable Street, on the N side of COWAN STREET and stretching to DENS ROAD, the former Dura Works (*see* Industrial Buildings, below).

ALBERT STREET, N of Arthurstone Terrace, is, for the most part, grimly tenemental but on the W side St John's (Episcopal) Church. In PARK AVENUE to the E, among respectable but still plain four-storey late C19 housing, the former Park Church. At the top of Albert Street and turning its NE corner with PITKERRO ROAD, a gentle convex curve of Georgian survival four-storey tenements of 1885 (Nos. 165–223 Albert Street) gives a welcome sense of occasion. Opposite, on the acutely angled corner of Albert Street and DURA STREET, Stobswell Parish Church and, presiding over a car park to the NW, Clepington Primary School (*see* Churches and Public Buildings, above).

FORFAR ROAD continues Albert Street to the N, its start dominated by the Morgan Academy (*see* Public Buildings, above). N of the Academy, a pair of single-storey-and-attic bay-windowed late C19 double houses (Nos. 1–7 Forfar Road) with carved bargeboards and Gothic porches and windows. More carved bargeboards at Nos. 7–11 MADEIRA STREET of 1870, a triple house, also of one storey and an attic, the asymmetrically composed front with three platformed and one double-pitch gable. On Madeira Street's NW corner another single-storey-and-attic double house (Nos. 9–11 Forfar Road) of 1870 but with bow windows, their mullions leafily capitalled. Gabled and columned surrounds, also with foliaged capitals, to the doors, the tympanum of No. 9 carved with the relief of a man's head, that of No. 11 with flowering foliage. At Nos. 13–19 Forfar Road, a four-house terrace by *William Bruce*, 1871–2, canopies over the three-light column-mullioned windows and, supported on idiosyncratically modelled heavy stone brackets, above the paired doors. To the N, as far as Clepington Road, bay-windowed two-storey or two-storey-and-attic late C19 terraced housing redolent of respectability. On Forfar Road's N corner with WALROND ROAD, the former Tramway Depot (*see* Public Buildings, above), its brickwork an industrial jolt to the genteel stone facing of the suburban houses around. S of CLEPINGTON ROAD's E end, the martial wall protecting the Stobsmuir Reservoir (*see* Public Buildings, above).

Along FORFAR ROAD's N stretch between Clepington Road and Kingsway, Late Victorian and Edwardian villas. The double house at Nos. 53–55 (E side) designed in 1905 by *James H. Langlands* for his unmarried sisters stands out, stylistically a free mixture of American summer resort and Art Nouveau. Piend-roofed single-storey main block, the walling of bull-nosed red sandstone ashlar; tapering chimneys finished with lid-like cornices. At the corners of the front, squat ogee-roofed and Art Nouveau-finialled pavilions, their outer faces fully glazed above the base courses. Advanced centrepiece composed of a pair of open-pedimented gables, their tympana harled, the front below fully glazed above the stone base; in the centrepiece's inner angles, curvaceously battlemented low towers with Art Nouveau finials. The entrance doorways between these towers and the corner pavilions are recessed under the bracketed broad eaves of the main roof. In the upper panes of the windows of the centrepiece and the pavilions, stylized STAINED GLASS designs in a Glasgow School manner. Art Nouveau gatepiers. Next, (HILLSIDE) is by *Hutton & Tough*, *c.* 1905. Two storeys, the ground floor of bull-nosed ashlar, the upper floor harled. Over the door, a steeply pitched canopy which extends to form roofs over the broad canted bay windows either side. These narrow at the upper floor where they flank the fully glazed centre fronted by a wooden balcony. Piended roof, its small central platform designed to carry a large chimneystack, now sadly missing.

In CLEPINGTON ROAD W of Forfar Road, quite prosperous but modestly sized villas of the late C19 and early C20. On the N, Nos. 65–67 form a double house of *c.* 1890, the broad-eaved roofs of the front's bowed ends rising as conical spires. The adjoining contemporary double house (Nos. 69–71) is piend-roofed. In the centre of the front, a pair of full-height bay windows, canted at the ground floor and rectangular above, with half-timbering under their four-light openings; the l. window finished with a half-timbered gable, the r. with an ogee-profiled piended roof. To the W, in GRAHAM STREET off Clepington Road's N side, St Teresa of Avila (R.C.) Church and Dundee College Graham Street Campus (*see* Churches and Public Buildings, above).

S of Clepington Road, FLEMING GARDENS, an oval-shaped model housing scheme built for the Fleming Trust (a charitable foundation to provide housing, set up in 1928, the endowment of £130,000 provided by the Dundee-born merchant banker, Robert Fleming, the trustees consisting of the Lord Provost, magistrates and councillors of the City of Dundee). Two-storey blocks of flats by the Dundee City Engineer, *George Baxter*, 1929–30, the drydashed walls trimmed with brick and artificial stone, the roofs variously gabled or piended. Dourer local authority housing of two and three storeys, also of 1929–30 and by *George Baxter*, in the streets bordering CAIRD AVENUE just to the W. Among this, in MARRYAT STREET, the Dundee United Free Church. Leading E along the S boundary of the Fleming Gardens scheme is SANDEMAN STREET. Off its far end, Dundee College (Melrose Campus) and, on its S side and bordering TANNADICE STREET, the stadia of Dundee's two best-known sporting institutions, Dundee Football Club's Dens Park and Dundee United Football Club's Tannadice Park (*see* Public Buildings, above). In FAIRBAIRN STREET, just S of Tannadice Park, the Angus Works (*see* Industrial Buildings, below) facing Dens Road Primary School set aloof from a remorseless line of Late Victorian tenements bordering the gorge of DENS ROAD.

INDUSTRIAL BUILDINGS

ANGUS WORKS, Fairbairn Street. Now in other use. Jute-spinning mill built for William Ritchie & Co. in 1879. Two tall storeys, of squared masonry. At the three-bay 'centrepiece', an oculus in the gable and a segmental-arched and keystoned entrance; another entrance to the same design just to the r. Single-storey weaving sheds behind.

BREWERY, Lyon Street. Now housing. Built in 1876 for Joseph Brown, the design by *T. M. Black*. Rubble-built, of three storeys with a piended roof. The N front is of six bays with evenly spaced windows but the stonework provides evidence of further first-floor openings (now blocked) and there was originally a kiln at the W end.

DURA WORKS, corner of Dura Street and Cowan Street. Now housing. Rubble-built L-plan textile mill (originally for flax spinning) constructed for J. & H. Walker between 1834 and 1855. The earliest part, built in 1834–6, is the three-storey NW range fronting Dura Street. Twelve-bay façade, the position of the engine house near the N end disclosed by three-light windows at the lower floors; hoist door in the S gable. The E two-thirds of the two-storey-and-attic SE range along Cowan Street is of *c.* 1840. Rubble-walled and plain except for a cornice placed below the wall-head and a small oculus in the E gable; the metal-fronted attic storey is a 1990s replacement. The six bays linking this to the original mill were added *c.* 1855.

Stair-towers of harling and glass were added at the back on the building's conversion to housing in the 1990s.

EAGLE MILLS, Dens Road, Victoria Street and Brown Constable Street. The only jute-spinning mill erected in Dundee between the First and Second World Wars, it is by *Robert Gibson*, 1929–30, incorporating the 1864 pattern shop of Baxter Brothers & Co.'s foundry. The former pattern shop, of two storeys and a mansard-roofed attic, has a plain fifteen-bay S front to Victoria Street. Gibson extended this E by a further nine bays of the same height and in the same manner and added a two-storey two-bay block of faintly Art Deco character on the W. Also of 1929–30 is the single-storey block W of that with a splayed corner to Dens Road. Saw-toothed weaving sheds of 1929–30 behind, their gable-ends of rubble.

EAST PORT CALENDER WORKS, Cowgate. The façade by *Robert Gibson*, 1913–14, was retained in 1997–2000 when flats were built behind and the present attic added. The early C20 work is of two tall storeys, faced with stugged and coursed squared rubble masonry. Gently splayed thirty-three-bay frontage. Round-headed cart entrances, two of them (one now a window) paired as part of the off-centre 'centrepiece' where they are flanked by round-headed windows; six round-headed windows above. The tall ground floor has been divided horizontally by a mezzanine floor, its openings and those of the original first floor now with metal balconies added in 1997–2000.

LOWER DENS WORKS, Princes Street, Dens Street, Constable Street and St Roque's Lane. On a steeply sloping site, a massive roughly quadrangular textile mill complex (now in other uses), mostly erected in the 1860s for Baxter Brothers & Co., the world's largest late C19 firm of linen manufacturers. The tallest range, prominent in views of Dundee from the approach up the Firth of Tay, is the BELL MILL on the E side of St Roque's Lane. Designed by *Peter Carmichael* in 1866, it is of iron-framed construction faced with stugged ashlar. Five storeys and a mansard attic, the main cornice placed in characteristic mill fashion below the wall-head. Pedimented N gable with a cast-iron vase finial on the apex; pedestals for missing finials on the ends. Near the long S end of the mill's long W side, a round-headed entrance in a surround of channelled ashlar and flanked by round-headed doors (partly blocked). The S end is the works' showpiece. Pedimental gable like the N but its corners are gripped by towers, the oblong E one (containing a hoist) flush with the gable's face, the square W one (a stair-tower) minimally projecting from it, both towers projecting from the sides of the mill. In the exposed faces of each tower, a single round-headed window at each floor below the top stage. This is marked off by a band course, contains a tall two-light window and is finished with a cornice carried on moulded corbels, the E tower's cornice topped by a balustrade with slender Neo-Jacobean finials on the corners. Surmounting the W tower, a tall cast-iron cupola, its segmental-pedimented faces formed of paired round-headed arches springing from Roman Doric columns *in antis* and carrying a domed drum. Tall addition in the N inner angle of the E tower. A large rectangular brick chimney was placed in the NE inner angle of the Bell Mill and the North Mill (*see* below) in the C20.

In front of the Bell Mill, a S LODGE of 1889, originally single-storey but partly heightened and much altered in the C20. It stands on the W side of the courtyard's entrance. On the entrance's E side, the seven-bay front of ST ROQUE'S MILL, a rubble-built textile mill erected originally for the firm W. R. Morison, *c.* 1835. Three storeys above a basement which is partly exposed in the fall of the ground to the W. Roof-lit mansard-roofed attic added in 1889 after this mill had been acquired by Baxter Brothers & Co. as an extension to the Lower Dens Works. The pedimental treatment of the gables and their cast-iron vase finials are also of 1889. Corniced doorpiece, probably of the earlier C19 in the W gable. Extending N up Dens Street is the DENS STREET MILL by *Peter Carmichael*, 1865. Twelve-bay E elevation, faced in rough ashlar masonry, of four storeys and a roof-lit mansard-roofed attic, the pedimental N gable with an oculus and the usual cast-iron vase finials. Linking the N ends of the Dens Street Mill and the Bell Mill is the NORTH MILL, by *George Pyott*, 1935. The Princes Street (N) elevation, faced with narrow-stoned ashlar, is of two storeys and a roof-lit attic. Four-storey elevation, taking advantage of the drop in the ground, to the courtyard behind, the lower three floors of glass in an exposed concrete frame, the top floor of brick.

On the E corner of Dens Street and Constable Street, the Works' flax warehouse, built for William Baxter & Son in 1828. Three-storey, rubble-walled and piend-roofed. S front of six bays, the openings grouped 3:3; hoist doors in the second and fifth bays of the upper floors. Widely spaced openings in the broad E and W gables. Twin-gabled rear elevation.

TAYBANK WORKS JUTE-SPINNING MILL, W corner of Arbroath Road and Morgan Street. Only the outer walls of the mill built in 1947–9 remain (the area behind redeveloped for housing in 2007–8). These are by *Kenneth F. Masson*, Chief Architect of the *Scottish Co-operative Welfare Society* in a *moderne* manner, not without style. S front to Arbroath Road, a long red brick rectangular framework, the l. jamb pierced by portholes above a door. This frame encloses a façade clad in large glazed tiles. At the ground floor, three clusters of openings, each of six almost square windows grouped 3:3, with broad entrance doors between them; at the first floor, a continuous band of glazing broken only by broad mullions of polished grey granite. The mill's SE corner is treated as a low tower, its splayed centre containing the Art Deco entrance under a huge window set in a deeply recessed and tiled surround. Simpler version of the S front along the steep slope up Morgan Street, part of this elevation demolished for access to the houses behind.

TAYBANK WORKS JUTE-SPINNING MILL AND POWER LOOM FACTORY, E corner of Arbroath Road and Morgan Street. Mill (now housing) built for Storrier, Brough & Co. in 1873–4. Two storeys and a mansard-roofed attic. Rubble-walled S front of eight bays although the designs show that a further seven were originally intended. Of the Power Loom Factory to the W, only the S façade survives as a screen wall. This is of nine bays, the windows (two dummies) set in large square recessed panels, their lintels carried on rounded corbels.

UPPER DENS WORKS, Princes Street. Now housing. Huge linen mill faced with roughish ashlar. It was built in two stages for the firm of Baxter Brothers & Co. The first, designed by the engineers and millwrights, *John Kerr & Umpherston* of Dundee, in 1833, produced a three-storey-and-attic block with an engine house at the W end and a stair-tower projecting from the SE corner. In 1850 *Peter Carmichael* in collaboration with the Glasgow engineers and millwrights, *Randolph, Elliott & Co.*, heightened the existing building and doubled the main block's length, providing at the addition's E end a second engine house abutting the first. The building was converted to housing by *Baxter, Clark & Paul* in 1984–7.

The S front to Princes Street is symmetrical, of four storeys with a mansard-roofed attic and, exposed in the fall of the ground to the W, a basement whose windows are now built up. Quite plain ten-bay sections either side of the very slightly advanced centrepiece on which formerly stood a statue of James Watt, the inventor of the modern steam engine. This contained the two engine houses, its windows lining through with those of the outer sections only at the top floor. At each of the two main floors, a pair of three-light windows with pilaster-mullions and segmental-arched fanlights, the l. first-floor window in a giant overarch formed when the doorway below was inserted in the 1980s. Between these two floors, a rosetted band course and, above them, a moulded cornice-like string course. Along the whole frontage, a wall-head cornice and parapet which return across the gables (the W splayed) with pedimental effect and round the NE tower and along the N elevation's wall-head. The gable-heads are pierced by oculi and adorned with cast-iron vase finials. The stair-tower projects N of the E gable. Lower stages quite plain except for windows (some dummies) in the E and N faces which line through with those of the main block; on the N face, a cast-iron roundel bearing the date 1841 which was brought here in the 1980s from the Dens Works' demolished office and stable block. In the stage above the level of the main block's wall-head cornice, a round-headed E window. In each face of the top stage, a moulded round panel, perhaps intended for a clock face. Surmounting the tower is a circular cupola composed of round-headed arches placed between Roman Doric columns which support an entablature, all these of cast iron. Above, a slated dome from which rises a slender fish-scale-slated spire.

The N elevation of the main block is nearly symmetrical, the engine house centrepiece marked off by narrow stone soil chutes projected on cast-iron brackets from above the ground floor. In the centrepiece, two large ground-floor entrances, the l. rectangular, the r. sidelit and with a fanlight filling the head of the round-arched opening.

The mill's other buildings were replaced in 1984–7 by blocks of flats along the E and W boundaries of the steeply sloping site and houses along the N side, all designed by *Baxter, Clark & Paul*, straightforward but without excitement. Extensive terracing and landscaping of the central space was designed by the *Building Design Partnership*, including the erection of a GAZEBO which mimics the cupola on the mill's stair-tower, a needlessly gratuitous act of homage.

WELLFIELD WORKS, corner of Kemback Street and Craigie Street. Jute mill built for Ireland & Boase in 1865–6. The principal building faces Craigie Street. Rubble-built main block of two tall storeys and an attic. In the head of the W gable, a triangular arrangement of two oval openings under an oculus. Thirteen-bay S front. Projecting at its E end, the open-pedimented tall gable of the mill's original engine house, with a huge three-light window and a dummy oculus in the pediment. On the E side of this engine house, a second engine house added in 1907, its S end containing a trio of very tall round-headed and keystoned windows, the outer openings of decidedly skinny proportions. N of this mill building, fronting Kemback Street and slotted between the gables of a couple of single-storey piend-roofed blocks of the 1860s, the works' entrance and office. Large segmental-arched entrance (dated 1865) in a pilastered and corniced surround topped by a ball-finialled curvilinear gablet. To the l. of the entrance, the two-storey office, also of 1865, with two-light windows and a chimney rising from the wall-head's parapet. The office was extended N in 1913. This addition's pilastered and corniced main section contains a broad canted oriel window set in a segmental-headed and keystoned overarch. Buttressing the wall-head's cornice are scrolls, the l. placed on top of the addition's narrow and lower E bay, the r. on the parapet of the 1860s office.

DUDHOPE AND LAWTON

Largely composed of C19 and C20 housing circling Dundee Law but hard pressed by the tighter-knit tenemental and industrial Hilltown (q.v.) to the E. Land of the Dudhope estate round Dudhope Castle on the Law's S slope was laid out and developed mostly as sizeable villas for the more prosperous citizens of Dundee from the 1830s. Smaller villas to the N were put up in the late C19 and local authority housing N of these in the earlier C20.

CHURCHES

ST DAVID'S HIGH KIRK (THE HIGH KIRK), Kinghorne Road. Originally High Free Church. Decorated Gothic, by *Ireland &*

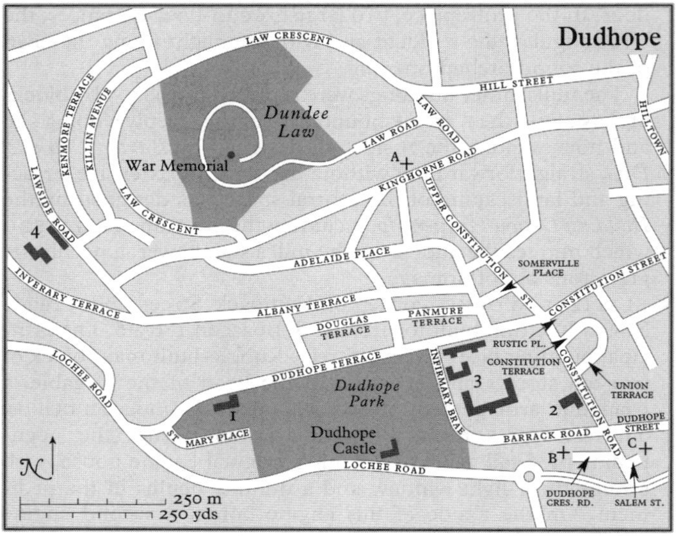

A St David's High Kirk (The High Kirk)
B St Mary Magdalene (Episcopal)
C United Reformed Church (Salem Chapel)

1 Dudhope Arts Centre
2 Dundee College (Constitution Campus)
3 Dundee Royal Infirmary
4 Lawside Convent

Maclaren, 1877–8, built of stugged and squared buff-coloured stone (badly eroded at the S front). Nave and E and W transepts, these added in 1886. In the SW inner angle, a parapeted porch and pyramidal-roofed low tower; tall tower in the SE inner angle. Two-storey elevations, the small and cusped lower windows under continuous hoodmoulding, the nave's upper windows with column-mullions, their shafts of red sandstone, their capitals carved with foliage; more foliage on their hoodmoulds' label stops. Plate-traceried heads in the large three-light windows of the transept gables and the five-light S window.

The SE tower dominates. Tall lower stage with nook-shafted corners. At the S face, under a hoodmoulded round window, the church's principal entrance contained in a Gothic aedicule, its columns' shafts of polished red granite. Cusped underside to the aedicule's gable; carved flying angels at the outer corners, a ringed cross on the apex. The tower's angle-buttressed upper stage is set back. In each face, a two-light plate-traceried window below a pair of keystoned circular openings. Wall-head cornice under a parapet pierced by quatrefoils and with pinnacled octagonal piers at the corners.

Plain two-storey HALL by *Joseph Johnston*, 1936–7, at the rear.

INTERIOR. In the tower's vestibule, a glass and wood SCREEN by *Douglas Gray*, *c.* 1980, at the entrance to the church. In the church itself, a GALLERY round three sides, the S corners splayed. Of gentle Neo-Jacobean character with pendants under the front and supported on Corinthian-capitalled cast-iron columns, it was erected at the S end by Ireland & Maclaren in 1881 and extended along the E and W sides in 1928. – At the church's N end, an early C20 COMMUNION TABLE of simple Gothic character on which stands a TABLE LECTERN by *Douglas Gray*, 1972, the front with silver and enamel panels. – Behind, the PULPIT which is integral with the ORGAN CASE (ORGAN itself by *Wadsworth & Co.*), both of 1904. – STAINED GLASS. Two S windows (Job; St Paul and Saints) by *W. C. Cameron*, 1970.

ST DAVID'S HIGH KIRK (ST DAVID'S), corner of Wetherby Place and Strathmore Avenue. Originally St David's North Parish Church. Early Christian with a tower, by *Thoms & Wilkie*, 1929–30, the walling of ashlar, the roofs red-tiled. Nave, narrower S chancel, slightly lower E and W transepts and a W porch, all gabled and with clasping buttresses at the corners. Sloping buttresses along the sides. Tall windows in the gables. Slightly smaller windows in the sides of the transepts and the E side of the nave. Smaller still at the porch and the nave's W side where they are arranged as triplets contained in giant overarches. Italianate square cupola near the N end of the nave roof. In the S inner angle of the nave and W transept, the pyramid-roofed tower. Above its low base the main walling is set back from the corners and broken only by the paired belfry openings. Vestry on the tower's S side.

Studiously simple INTERIOR, the walls plastered above half-height ashlar cladding, the nave's cladding panelled with round-headed blind arcading; a tunnel vault over each limb. Stone chancel arch, its semicircular head ornamented with dentilated blocks, the supporting pilasters with Celtic foliaged capitals. On the E side of the chancel arch, a simple Early Christian octagonal PULPIT, its stone base carrying an oak body, each of its faces panelled with a pair of round-headed arches which spring from pilasters only at the corners. – FONT and COMMUNION TABLE of similar character originally in Roseburn Free (later Wester Coates) Church, Edinburgh. – ORGAN by *J. J. Binns*, 1899, also originally in Roseburn Free (later Wester Coates) Church, Edinburgh, and rebuilt here by *Ronald L. Smith*, 1975. – STAINED GLASS. Three lights in the chancel (the Good Shepherd, flanked by the *Agnus Dei* and Dove) of 1977.

ST MARY MAGDALENE (Episcopal), Dudhope Crescent Road.
Originally Catholic Apostolic Church. By *Edward & Robertson*, 23
1867. Long and tall, its simply detailed Early Gothic not without style, the walling of squared and stugged buff-coloured masonry. Nave and chancel under a continuous roof finished with iron cresting; the tall zigzag patterned lead flèche towards the E end, also by Edward & Robertson, was added in 1882.

Lean-to aisles the full length of the nave, the S aisle's W bay carried up as a gabled two-storey porch, its roof also iron-crested; piend-roofed transeptal organ chamber at the E end of the N aisle, a vestry at the W. The chancel projects as a buttressed full-height semi-octagon from the nave's E end, its gableted 7.3 m.-high windows with cusped lights under quatrefoil heads. The side walls of the aisles and clearstorey are articulated by simple buttresses and pierced by paired lancets. Hoodmoulded S entrance with stiff-leaf capitals to the nook-shafts; above, a window of two lights under a quatrefoil. Hoodmoulded windows in the ends of the aisles, two-light to the E and single-light to the W. In the W gable, three lancet lights under a large circular opening. – HALL to the NE, by *George A. Harris*, 1901–3, also Gothic and with a conical-roofed squat tower containing the entrance.

INTERIOR. Gothic stone arcades, the pillars with stiff-leaf capitals, some with animals among the foliage. Scissor-truss roof over the 20 m.-high nave. The W bay of the N aisle is the baptistery, its side wall stencilled with the Ten Commandments in a Gothic surround. Wooden parclose screens divide off the aisles' E bays, the N containing the organ, the S a chapel. Between these the nave's E end is raised by three steps as a choir open to the apsidal sanctuary whose floor is covered with encaustic tiles, its walls with a Gothic panelled dado surmounted by stencilled foliage (restored by *Allan Blow*, 1979–81) on the walls and ceiling. – Bench PEWS in the nave, rather more elaborate STALLS in the choir, all of 1867. – Octagonal stone FONT in the baptistery, also of 1867, its idiosyncratic Gothic almost Spanish. – On the N side of the entrance to the choir, PULPIT by the *Lord Roberts Workshops*, 1946–7, brought here from the former St Mary Magdalene's Episcopal Church in Blinshall Street (Logie, Blackness and Balgay) in 1952. – On the S side of the choir entrance, a Victorian Gothic brass double-desk LECTERN. – ORGAN by *Peter Conacher*, 1867, rebuilt in 1937 (by *Frederick Rothwell*) and again in 1986 (by *Nicholson & Co.*). Stencilled pipes in a Gothic case.

STAINED GLASS. Extensive scheme, many of the windows imported in the late C20. In the sanctuary, five colourful and accomplished windows of 1867 (Our Lord the Good Shepherd, flanked by Prophets and Saints). – Circular W window, a modernistic sunburst, by *John Baird*, 1979. – The S aisle's E window (the Risen Lord Appearing to St Mary Magdalen) is of 1911. – In this aisle's E side window, two brightly coloured and gently stylized lights (St Andrew and St George) by *Alexander L. Russell*, *c.* 1920, and formerly in St Mary Magdalene's Episcopal Church, Blinshall Street. – Fragments of a window (the Crucifixion) of *c.* 1900. – Then, four windows (Scenes from the Life of St Peter) of *c.* 1900 formerly in St Peter's, Oxford and one (the Empty Tomb) by *Heaton, Butler & Bayne*, 1875, formerly in St John's Church, Highbury (London). – The E window of the N aisle is late C19, abstract and colourful. – In this aisle's side windows, one (the Prodigal Son) is of the later

C19 and three (the Good Samaritan) came from a church in Wales. – This aisle's W window (Acts of Mercy) was formerly in H.M. Borstal, Feltham (Middlesex). – In the porch, two lights (Acts of Mercy), also brought here from H.M. Borstal, Feltham.

UNITED REFORMED CHURCH SALEM CHAPEL, Salem Street. Small Gothic oblong, by *William Alexander*, 1872. Front (W) gable divided by pinnacled buttresses into a 'nave' (fronted by a porch) and 'aisles'. The 'nave's' W window is of three lights under a roundel, all cusped; hoodmould with little heads peering out from the carved foliage of its label stops. Hood-moulded and cusped single lights at the ends of the 'aisles'. Plain lancets in the side elevations.

PUBLIC BUILDINGS

DUDHOPE ARTS CENTRE, St Mary Place. Originally Dudhope School. Two blocks. The W, by *David Maclaren*, of *Ireland & Maclaren*, 1874–5, is of one tall storey, built of squared masonry. Six-bay S front, the ends slightly advanced and gabled with windows of three elliptical lights under round-headed dummy openings. NW porch. Asymmetrical two-storey E block by *James H. Langlands*, 1893–4. Plain except for elliptical-arched windows at the first floor.

DUNDEE COLLEGE (CONSTITUTION CAMPUS), Constitution Road. Originally Dundee College of Commerce. By *Ian Burke, Martin & Partners*, 1966–70. L-plan arrangement of a pair of flat-roofed blocks, one of seven, the other of five storeys, joined by low links. Exposed concrete frames with panel infill.

DUNDEE ROYAL INFIRMARY, Infirmary Brae. Partly demolished, 2000, and the surviving buildings converted to housing by *Kerr Duncan McAllister*, 2000–7. The principal building (REGENTS HOUSE) at the S is by *Coe & Goodwin*, 1852–5. Collegiate Tudor, built of brown rubble, and originally intended to accommodate 220 patients. Symmetrical S front, the outer sections of three storeys, with segmental-arched lights in the mullioned-and-transomed openings and canted bay windows at the advanced and gabled ends. Boldly advanced four-storey centrepiece, like a gatehouse with octagonal corner towers and surmounted by a domed octagonal cupola. Double stair to the elaborately treated Gothic first-floor entrance; above, a battlemented and broad oriel window. The centrepiece is finished with a battlement which rises in the centre as a surround for a shield. At the corner towers, cusped segmental-headed windows and, high up, carved shields. Wall-head cornice with animal gargoyles projecting at the corners and surmounted by a battlement. Towards the S end of the building's side elevations, four-storey octagonal towers, also battlemented.

DALGLEISH HOUSE to the NW, by *Alexander Johnston*, 1896–7, was built as a nurses' home. Three-storey-and-attic, plain Jacobean with battlemented bay windows and a wall-head parapet. – To the N, THE CAIRD BUILDING, by *James*

Findlay, 1902–6. Large and unabashedly red-coloured, the walls of engineering brick, the roofs covered with Rosemary tiles. Administration block flanked by wards, all treated as pavilion-roofed towers; lower towers in the NE and NW inner angles. Bridge-like open-sided corridors link the three main blocks. Lower additions, also of red brick, by *Johnston & Baxter*, 1930 to the SE.

FIRE STATION, Strathmore Avenue. By the Dundee City Architect, *David B. McLay*, 1931. Piend-roofed Neo-Georgian, of three storeys. Red brick ground floor containing the garaging, the centre minimally advanced under a balcony. White-harled upper floors of five bays with advanced ends.

KING'S CROSS HOSPITAL, Clepington Road. Originally the Dundee Infectious Diseases Hospital. By the Dundee Burgh Engineer, *William Mackison*, 1888–9. The ashlar-faced two-storey main building was the administration block. Routine Jacobean, the N front with gabled end bays and an iron-crested French pavilion-roofed tower above the entrance. Detached ward blocks of the 1880s, 1894, 1898, 1902 and early C20 (by *James Thomson*). Utilitarian except for a domed wooden clock tower and some iron cresting. Along the boundary with Clepington Road, anthemion-finialled wrought-iron RAILINGS by *Walter MacFarlane & Co.* of the *Saracen Foundry*, 1889.

LAWSIDE CONVENT AND DIOCESAN CENTRE, Inverary Terrace. Large-scale and confident but simply detailed institutional Gothic, begun by *Archibald Macpherson*, 1892–4, extended by *T. Martin Cappon* in 1897–8 and with a chapel added by *Reginald Fairlie* in 1921, all built of hammer-dressed masonry.

The earliest part is the three-storey and attic S range, some of its windows mullioned-and-transomed and containing shouldered-arched lights; broad-eaved roof with flat-topped dormer windows C20 additions. Massively crowstepped and double-chimneyed gables at the W end and, off-centre, at the front, both with elegantly detailed Late Gothic overarches. Projecting from the front gable, a canted bay window finished with a parapet; in the top of the gable, a niche containing a large statue of the Virgin and Child. Over the entrance at the front's E end, a stone relief of the Annunciation. Cappon's addition (a House of Mercy for training girls for domestic service) forms a SE wing of the same height. Two-light mullioned windows in the front gable; cusped blind heads to the second-floor openings which are surmounted by multifoil attic openings. Full-height bay window at the N end of the wing's E side. The wing at the NE is Fairlie's chapel, the exterior in a simplified Romanesque manner. The chapel interior is cruciform. Very short E limb consisting of a splay-sided apse, its walls clad in green and grey marble, housing the marble-faced ALTAR of 1925, also to Fairlie's design. Round-headed arches from the crossing to the transepts, the N containing a panel-fronted wooden gallery for visitors, the S intended for the girls in the House of Mercy. Wagon-roofed nave (originally serving as the conventual choir), its walls with high oak-panelled Neo-Georgian dadoes incorporating seating for the nuns. Dividing off the nave from the passage-like W bay is an oak screen, also Neo-Georgian. Against the W wall, the ORGAN by *Andrew Watt & Sons*, its case of sober early C18 character. – STAINED GLASS. In the side windows of the apse, two lights (Angel Musicians) and in the W wall, three lights (the Crucifixion with St Mary Magdalene at the Foot of the Cross, flanked by the Virgin Mary and St John), all strongly coloured work of the 1920s.

ROCKWELL SCHOOL, corner of Lawton Road and Strathmore Avenue. By *Allan & Friskin*, 1930–2. Two tall storeys of mixed red and dark brown brickwork with cement dressings, the piended roofs slated. Gentle Neo-Egyptian detail.

ST JOHN'S R.C. HIGH SCHOOL, Harefield Road. The three-storey SE block is by *T. H. Thoms* of *Thoms & Wilkie*, 1958–61. Curtain-walled with blue panels, the pitched roof's ribbed metal sheeting of 2004–6. Two-storey brown brick W block. It links to a large extension by *Dundee City Council*, 2004–6. This is large and sensible, of four and five storeys, the walls clad in render broken by large expanses of glass; shallow-pitched metal roofs. At the SW corner, a single-storey brick-walled pavilion and, to the N, a long low wing (swimming pool), these also of 2004–6.

WAR MEMORIAL, Law Road. Just S of the summit of Dundee Law (the summit itself occupied by a television mast of 1964) and visible from much of what then constituted the built-up area of the city, Dundee's tribute to its dead of the First World War is by *Thomas Braddock*, 1922–5. Tall mausoleum of polished grey granite standing on a circular pedestal. Battered and stepped square base; in its W side, a bronze door bearing the City's coat of arms. The main part above, unbroken by openings, is also battered and with chamfered corners. Open-sided circular top stage under a truncated dome surmounted by a bronze funerary urn.

DESCRIPTION

Dudhope

NORTH MARKETGAIT at the area's SE corner begins with OPAL 1, a gently concave cliff of student flats by the *Hurd Rolland Partnership*, 2009–10. Variegated cladding of horizontally ribbed grey metal, red and orange blockwork and copper panels. In DUDHOPE CRESCENT ROAD, set back from the dual carriageway of North Marketgait, the Gothic presence of St Mary Magdalene's Episcopal Church (*see* Churches, above) a stylish introduction. CONSTITUTION ROAD ascends from its E end. On that street's SE corner, CONSTITUTION HOUSE (originally PUBLIC HEALTH INSTITUTE), bureaucratic Neo-Georgian by the City Engineer and Architect, *George Baxter*, 1925–8. Behind, off Constitution Road at the E end of SALEM STREET, the United Reformed Church Salem Chapel. Further up

Constitution Road, on its SW corner with Barrack Road, GARLAND PLACE (Nos. 20–24 Constitution Road and Nos. 2–4 Barrack Road), a bow-cornered tenement of 1867 with hoodmoulded Gothic windows and doors. Probably it is by *William Alexander* who, in 1871, designed the W continuation (Nos. 6–10 Barrack Road), also bay-windowed but without the Gothic detail. At the W end of Barrack Road, an entrance to Dudhope Park surrounding Dudhope Castle (*see* below).

DUDHOPE STREET continues the line of Barrack Road E of Constitution Road. On its SW corner, a tenement of 1870–5 (RUSTIC PLACE, Nos. 63–69 Constitution Road and Nos. 1–5 Dudhope Street), Free Renaissance with consoled pediments to the doors and a Frenchy roof (now deprived of cresting) on the bowed corner. On Dudhope Street's N side, villas of the early and mid C19. No. 4 is a two-storey *cottage orné* with carved bargeboards. Then, Georgian survival, the single-storey No. 6 with a pedimented porch, the taller No. 8 with a Doric-columned doorpiece. More architecturally adventurous No. 10. Jacobean Renaissance pediments over the first-floor windows of the advanced and crowstep-gabled end bays, fluted Doric columns at the central door.

Set back from Constitution Road's W side is Dundee College (Constitution Campus) (*see* Public Buildings, above). Much more pleasurable are the two crescents (LAUREL BANK and PROSPECT PLACE; UNION TERRACE and CONSTITUTION TERRACE) laid out for villas by *David Mackenzie* in 1833 and mostly developed within the next thirty years although not finally completed until the 1890s. At Nos. 6–8 Laurel Bank, a two-storey double house, the polished ashlar front's advanced end bays with lugged architraves to the ground-floor windows and block pediments on the wall-head cornice. Multi-gableted Jacobean No. 11. Another ashlar-fronted double house at Nos. 4–6 Prospect Place of *c.* 1850, its windows three-light with segmental pediments over the central openings of the ground floor's. At the entrance to the N crescent, TERRACE HOUSE (No. 2 Union Terrace) with a balustraded portico fronted by Ionic columns *in antis*. At the E end of Constitution Terrace, the Jacobean No. 16 of *c.* 1860. Shaped gables, a canted and battlemented bay window and a battlemented porch with a turret-buttress at one corner. Also Jacobean, with shaped gablets and a strapworked door, the triple house of Nos. 6–10 Constitution Terrace, dated 1851. Ogee-domed cast-iron gatepiers to the front gardens. Gatepiers of the same design at Nos. 2–4, Jacobean again, a domed turret-buttress at a corner of the porch.

SOMERVILLE PLACE runs W from the top of Constitution Road. On the N side, two harled double houses by *James Black*, 1830, both with canted bay windows and cast-iron latticed verandas, Nos. 1–2 single-storey, Nos. 3–4 two-storey and with an off-centre gabled cupola-attic room and a bowed E gable.

DUDHOPE TERRACE, W of Somerville Place, is prosperous, the C19 houses standing on the N side and looking over Dudhope Park and the city below to the hills of Fife. It starts with Nos.

1–3, three two-storey houses built to a unified design by *George Angus*, 1840. Each has a three-bay front with two-light ground-floor windows flanking the entrance's screen of Greek Doric columns *in antis* but the block-pedimented centres of Nos. 1 and 3 are recessed, that of No. 2 slightly advanced. Opposite and entered from INFIRMARY BRAE, the buildings of the former Dundee Royal Infirmary (*see* Public Buildings, above). In Dudhope Terrace W of Law Street, No. 9 of the earlier C19 with an anta-pilastered and pedimented doorpiece. There follow pleasant mid-C19 villas, Georgian survival or with Italianate touches, most with bay windows. No. 12 has an Ionic-columned portico but segmental-arched Italianate windows at the first floor. Bracketed pediment over the entrance to No. 13. W of Inverlaw Place, set back in a miniature park, is DUDHOPE HOUSE, a large Scots Jacobean villa by *Charles Wilson*, 1849–53, with touches of strapwork and a double row of corbels under the wall-head parapet. Mansard-roofed single-storey-and-attic red brick W extension added by *Johnston & Baxter*, *c.* 1930 when the house was converted to a nurses' home. In the grounds, to the W, a broad-eaved pavilion (CENTRE FOR CHILD HEALTH) of *c.* 2000, the walls of glass and buff brick. S of Dudhope Terrace, in ST MARY PLACE at the area's SW corner, DUDHOPE COURT, a fifteen-storey flat-roofed tower block by *James Parr & Partners*, 1962–5. T-plan, the arms slightly splayed and meeting at a recessed hub whose angled sections suggest a concave curve; S tail. Recessed and balconied centres to the ends of the limbs. Beside the W entrance to Dudhope Park, Dudhope Arts Centre (*see* Public Buildings, above).

PANMURE TERRACE, on the higher ground behind Dudhope Terrace's E end, is one-sided, the houses all on the N. Beginning at the E, a pair of single-storey villas (Nos. 1–2) of the earlier C19, joined by a slightly set-back four-bay link, its ends formed by the fronts of piend-roofed outshots, its centre a screen wall. The corniced main block of each house was originally identical, with a pedimented Doric portico flanked by tall two-light windows, but No. 1's masonry is now rendered and No. 2 has lost its portico although it boasts an additional slightly recessed pavilion and garden gateway at the W end. No. 3, by *Edward Tough*, 1909, is two-storey and more assertive. Stugged ashlar walling and tile-crested roofs. Full-height canted bay windows at the ends of the front whose broad centre is filled with a segmental arch containing the fanlit and doubly sidelit entrance; five-light first-floor window above. Art Nouveau influence is manifest but the symmetry is static. Asymmetrical Rogue Romanesque appears at the two-storey No. 8, designed by *F. T. Pilkington* in 1872. Stugged ashlar front of three bays. Panels boldly carved with foliage over the r. ground-floor window and central door. First-floor r. window of two lights whose stilted round-headed arches spring from foliage-capitalled column-mullions; gablet above decorated with a quatrefoil niche containing the relief of a ball. At the front's l. end, a full-height and gabled canted bay window, its lower stage's sides extravagantly battered, the walling above scooped in under the tall and column-mullioned upper window. DOUGLAS TERRACE to the W continues the prosperous villa character. At the broad-eaved No. 3 of *c.* 1883, an Italianate tower. In ALBANY TERRACE to the N, respectable but smaller late C19 houses, mostly semi-detached and bay-windowed, some with bargeboarded gables, No. 7 by *Alexander Johnston*, 1871. The tall and broad-eaved double house at Nos. 10–11 is by *Young & Meldrum*, 1877, its bay windows canted at the ground floor and brought to the square above. Italianate tower set back at the E end.

LAWSIDE ROAD's SE end begins with late C19 houses. Further up the road and in KENMORE TERRACE and KILLIN AVENUE to the E, two-storey traditional blocks of flats by the Dundee City Architect, *David B. McLay*, 1931, their walls' drydash covering relieved by brick bases and door surrounds. LAW CRESCENT and KINGHORNE ROAD circle the volcanic peak of Dundee Law surmounted by the city's war memorial and television mast (*see* Public Buildings, above). In Kinghorne Road, St David's High Kirk (The High Kirk) (*see* Churches, above). Just to the NE, on an island site at the foot of LAW ROAD, the driveway to the Law's summit, a former WATER TOWER of 1921, by the Dundee City Engineer and Architect, *George Baxter*, constructed as part of a district heating system for the contemporary housing in Stirling Avenue to the S. Looking like a square pyramidal-roofed doocot, built of hammer-dressed masonry. Tall batter-sided ground floor, the upper storey low and slightly set-back.

Lawton

LAWTON, between the N slope of Dundee Law and Strathmore Avenue, was developed for local authority housing from *c.* 1925. In BYRON CRESCENT and the nearby streets, two-storey white-harled blocks with pantiled piended roofs, each looking like a double house but containing four flats. Rockwell School (*see* Public Buildings, above) and plain rubble-walled and piend-roofed three-storey blocks of flats to the E. All these are by the Dundee City Architect, *David B. McLay*. To the N, set back from HAREFIELD ROAD's E end, St John's R.C. High School (*see* Public Buildings, above). On the N side of STRATHMORE AVENUE and the E of JOHNSTON AVENUE, an L of two-storey semi-detached houses, of 1925–6. Harled, with red-tiled or slated roofs; paired gables to the fronts and jerkin-head end gables. Inside the L, contemporary but plainer piend-roofed houses. To the N, in CLEPINGTON ROAD W of Strathmartine Road, bungaloid development of *c.* 1930 on the S side, unexciting late C19 small villas on the N. Among these is No. 373, an aggressively ashlar-clad Baronial SLUICE CHAMBER designed for the Dundee Waterworks by *J. & A. Leslie* in 1873. Single-storey and battlemented, a round tower at the W end. Further E, King's Cross Hospital (*see* Public Buildings, above).

DUDHOPE CASTLE

Dudhope Park, off Barrack Road

On the lower S slope of Dundee Law, overlooking the city, a long-limbed harled L, its appearance an unresolved mixture of mansion house, mill and barracks.

A third of the lands of Dudhope were granted in feu to Sir John Scrymgeour, fifth hereditary Constable of Dundee and Standard Bearer of Scotland, in 1461, and his son, James, was entitled lord of Dudhope by 1481. At about this time and almost certainly by 1527 when there is mention in a charter of the 'tower and fortalice' (*turre, fortalicio*) of Dudhope there was constructed here a tower house, standing in the NE corner of a roughly oblong enclosure. About 1600 James Scrymgeour, tenth Constable of Dundee, added a tall gatehouse on the S side of the tower house, a three-storey-and-attic block which occupied the remainder of the enclosure's E side, with a round tower at its SE corner, and a long but lower range along the enclosure's S side. In 1668 the Dudhope estate was acquired by Charles Maitland, Lord Hatton (later, third Earl of Lauderdale). Hatton carried out an extensive refurbishment of Dudhope Castle in 1672–5. Probably he was also responsible, shortly after, for replacing the original tower house with a new block and NE tower to give the E front an approximately symmetrical appearance, and for adding a tower at the S range's W end.* Ownership of the house passed in 1684 to the local laird and professional soldier, John Graham of Claverhouse (created Viscount of Dundee in 1688), and, after his death at the Battle of Killiecrankie in 1689, to the Douglas family who lived there only occasionally in the C18 although the estate factor occupied the S range. In 1792 the house was leased to the British Woollen Co. for use as a textile mill and, after that firm's bankruptcy the next year, to the Government which converted it to barracks. Disused after 1880, Dudhope Castle was acquired by the City of Dundee in 1893, primarily to maintain its surrounding parkland as open space. The house itself was used only as storage and clubrooms until 1985–8 when the *City of Dundee District Council* (project architect *A. B. Anderson*) carried out major repairs and further remodelling. It is now used by the University of Abertay Dundee.

The E front, at first glance, appears unified, a three-storey range 41
with conical-roofed round corner towers and a centrepiece marked off by semicircular drum towers, also conical roofed, and surmounted by a birdcage bellcote. The centrepiece, containing an elliptical-arched pend entrance (now glazed) under a low horizontally proportioned window, is of *c.* 1600 but its height was reduced *c.* 1795 when at least one storey was removed. The present wall-head is finished with a corbelled-out ashlar gablet containing a clock and surmounted by a tall

* If the work was carried out for Hatton it was presumably executed before his loss of office and accompanying income in 1680. Less probably it was done for John Graham of Claverhouse after his acquisition of Dudhope in 1684.

birdcage bellcote but, although the bellcote's design could well be of *c.* 1795, the gablet looks more like work of *c.* 1840. The drum towers are also of *c.* 1600, each with a projecting high base finished with a splayed offset and with an inward-facing moulded surround for a heraldic panel, but their conical roofs are conjectural restorations of 1985–8.* The E range S of the centrepiece is again of *c.* 1600, its projecting splay-topped base lower than that of the adjacent drum tower. The base is now cut through by very tall ground-floor windows, the l. window much broader than the r. They may have been formed in the late C17, possibly in the place of gunloops, usual appurtenances of late C16 and early C17 lairds' and nobles' houses but of which none survive here. If so, they were probably heightened after 1792. Two windows at the first floor. They were formerly surmounted by panels, probably from dormerheads erected when this storey was added. They bore the initials of James Scrymgeour of Dudhope and his second wife, Magdalene Livingstone, providing a date of *c.* 1600.† Large wall-head chimney at the S end.

The E front N of the centrepiece was built in the late C17, replacing the tower house of *c.* 1500 in this position. Originally it was of the same height as the part to the S but contained three storeys and an attic. No projecting base and regularly spaced windows. As at the S part, the wall-head was raised above the attic's window heads after 1792. In 1985–8 the internal floor levels were altered so as to make it of three rather than four storeys, the present tall first-floor openings formed by partly blocking and partly amalgamating the previous first- and second-floor windows. Also of the 1980s is the wall-head chimney at the N end, balancing the chimney of the S part of the front.

Both E corner towers are round and conical-roofed but otherwise dissimilar. The S, of *c.* 1600, is larger and taller than the late C17 N tower and with a projecting base pierced by windows, their chamfered surrounds restored in the 1980s. This tower's top-floor windows are skied, suggesting that it may have been heightened in the late C17. The N tower is regularly fenestrated, the very tall ground-floor windows formed in the 1980s by amalgamating two tiers of earlier openings. At the NW segment, a large wall-head chimney.

In the E range's S gable, the windows are generally aligned above each other but the basement window has been enlarged and the attic window (reopened in the 1980s when a window to its r. was built up) is asymmetrically placed.

The house's S front is also a mixture of work of different periods. As built *c.* 1600 it was of two storeys and an attic with

* Such roofs are shown in John Slezer's late C17 engraved view of Dundee but they were removed soon after 1792 and the towers given parapets (removed in the 1980s).

† James Scrymgeour (†1612) had married Magdalene Livingstone in 1581. A datestone of 1600 was formerly visible above a window on the W side of the centrepiece.

a basement exposed in the fall of the ground. Large basement window at the W end, a slightly smaller one to its r., and then three small windows, all with chamfered surrounds and probably original. The ground- and first-floor windows are grouped 3:3 but not quite regularly spaced. Between two of the ground-floor openings, the jamb of a blocked window showing that the fenestration has been altered, perhaps in the late C17. Further evidence of alteration is provided by a small central rectangular window at a level between the present first- and second-floor (originally attic) openings. In the alterations after 1792, the wall-head was first raised above the lintels of the attic windows and then by a further full storey. Roll-and-hollow mouldings survive at the three E windows of the present second floor.

The SW corner tower is smaller than the SE, although probably also of *c.* 1600. Corbelled out in its SE inner angle but from above the present first-floor level of the S range is a tight stair-turret. The unmoulded door in the tower's NE inner angle is probably a Late Georgian insertion.

In the S range's W gable are roll-and-hollow-moulded windows, the r. of the two at the ground floor tall and perhaps enlarged. At the first floor, a decently sized opening on the r. and a small blocked opening, perhaps originally lighting a garderobe, to its l. Another decently sized window in the centre of the gable at the second floor (originally attic), its lintel with a roll-and-hollow moulding, the remainder of the surround renewed. At the NW corner, a skewputt marking the original height of the wall-head; it bears the initials M^{D}L (for Dame Magdalene Livingstone) round a shield which bore the quartered coats of arms of Scrymgeour and Livingstone.

The principal feature of the S range's courtyard elevation is a bowed and conical-roofed stair-turret rising from above basement level. Except for its base of continuous corbelling this is a restoration of the 1980s, the existence of a turret in this position shown both by the corbelling and blocked doors above but its size conjectural. At the basement's E two-thirds, five small windows with chamfered surrounds, all perhaps original. Towards the W end, a door also with a chamfered surround and perhaps of *c.* 1600. The blocked door to its r. and the horizontally proportioned W window, both with roll-and-hollow moulded surrounds, look late C17. Tall ground-floor windows, all with roll-and-hollow mouldings; one has holes for an iron grating in its sill but none in the jambs, another has holes in both sill and jambs. At the ground floor's E end, a decently sized window set just below the level of the others and slightly smaller, its plain surround suggesting it may be a Late Georgian insertion. So too may be the two first-floor windows and three of the five second-floor (originally attic) openings but the two flanking the turret are broader and with roll-and-hollow mouldings, perhaps of the late C17.

The courtyard elevation of the E range is clearly of two dates, the S part including the gatehouse slightly recessed from the

N. In the S part, the pend entrance at the l. and, at the r., a basement door, its roll-and-hollow moulding probably late C17, which opened onto the principal stair behind. N of the stair landing's window above, a small horizontally proportioned opening. At the upper floors, stair windows and, at different levels, windows to rooms in the main section of the gatehouse. Fairly regularly spaced windows in the late C17 N part of this range. All seem to be post-1792 work except for one which has a chamfered surround and is set at an intermediate level between the ground and first floors and a blocked first-floor opening to its r., not aligned with the other first-floor windows and with a roll-and-hollow moulded lintel. The W third of the N gable, finished with a half-gable, projects from the rest. In this projection, a door inserted in the 1980s.

In front of the house's S range, the former OVERGATE WELL of 1743, a corniced ashlar cube under a dome-surmounted bellcast-eaved and stone-slabbed roof. It was moved from the Overgate to the corner of Tally Street and Mid Kirkstyle in 1828 and to Dudhope Castle in 1897.

The castle's grounds were opened as DUDHOPE PARK in 1893. – L-plan EAST LODGE of *c.* 1895. Single-storey, with bracketed broad eaves. Veranda-like porch in the NE inner angle; a bracketed stone canopy over the NW jamb's two-light gable window.

HILLTOWN

A suburb of Dundee by the C17, Hilltown, variously known also as Rottenrow and Bonnethill, climbs the ascent N from the town between Dundee Law and the gorge of the Dens Burn, now occupied by Dens Road. The settlement became a burgh of barony under the superiority of Charles Maitland, Lord Hatton, the owner of the Dudhope estate in 1672. Twelve years later it was described, with some exaggeration, by John Ochterlony as 'a large towne' and seems to have been a small local centre for the manufacture of woollen goods and ironware. Incorporated into the burgh of Dundee in 1728, by the beginning of the C19 Hilltown was still a linear development of artisan housing along Bonnethill (now Hilltown) with a scattering of isolated villas to the E and W. From the mid C19, however, the lands each side of the thoroughfare were developed for textile mills and associated workers' tenements. By the later C20 the mills had closed and much of the Victorian housing cleared for redevelopment, a not entirely happy mixture of tower blocks and Postmodern evocations of vernacular architecture.

CHURCHES

BUTTERBURN UNITED PRESBYTERIAN CHURCH, corner of Hilltown and Hill Street. Disused. Lancet Gothic, by *R. G. B.*

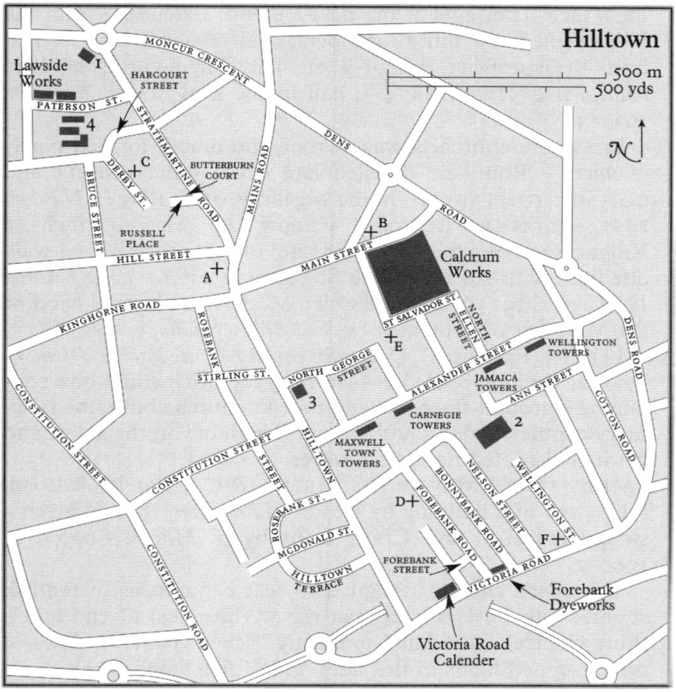

A Butterburn United Presbyterian Church
B Coldside Parish Church
C St Martin (Episcopal)
D St Mary Our Lady of Victories
E St Salvador (Episcopal)
F Wesleyan Methodist Chapel

1 Coldside Branch Library
2 Our Lady's Primary School
3 Police Station
4 St Peter and Paul Primary School

Hay, 1865, the ashlar walling badly weathered. The E gable front is treated as a slightly advanced 'nave' and 'aisles'; pinnacles on the outer corners, a gabled bellcote over the centre. Hoodmoulded door and windows, all with pendant label stops; quatrefoil-traceried round window in the gable-head. In the W end, a pair of tall lancets under a small louvred lancet opening.

COLDSIDE PARISH CHURCH, corner of Main Street and Isla Road. Originally Clepington Church. Lancet Gothic in squared rubble, by *Alexander Johnston*, 1880–1. Aisled and buttressed nave, the aisles stopped short of the W gable. In the gable, vestibule windows under a hoodmoulded three-light gallery window. Battlemented porch in the NW inner angle. In the SW inner angle, a tower, its openings also hoodmoulded, rising to a crowstep-gabled saddleback roof; bowed stair projection at the S face. Transepts at the nave's E end. Extending from the N transept, a low link to the octagonal session house formed from the surviving end of a mission chapel-cum-school by *Maclaren & Aitken*, 1874–5; hall to the E by *Joseph Johnston*, 1932–3.

Inside the church, a wagon roof, the braces formed partly of wire. – Routinely detailed late C19 Gothic PULPIT and COMMUNION TABLE. – In the W gallery, ORGAN by *H. Hilsdon*, 1957. – STAINED GLASS. E window (a Christian Knight; a Knight Receiving the Crown of Life) of *c.* 1920. – In the S wall, one light (Christ's Charge to St Peter) by *Arthur L. & Charles E. Moore*, *c.* 1925. – In the N wall a Modern-traditional window (St Margaret of Scotland) by *The Abbey Studio*, *c.* 1960.

ST MARTIN (Episcopal), Derby Street. By *James Parr & Partners*, 1971–2. Pavilion-roofed two-storey grey brick small box containing a ground-floor hall and roof-lit church above, the sanctuary cantilevered out at the N end. Vestibule on the S; low and pyramidal-roofed harled SW tower.

ST MARY OUR LADY OF VICTORIES (R.C.), Forebank Road. Large box of a building by *George Mathewson*, 1850–1, given a swaggering Arts and Crafts front by *T. Martin Cappon* in 1900–2.

The 1850s church, designed to seat *c.* 3,000, is of reddish rubble, with flush transepts at the W (liturgical E) end and a short chancel. The detail is mostly 'Saxon' with windows of three stepped lights in the sides and of five lights at the chancel's W end. In the gable-heads of the chancel and transepts, Geometric-traceried rose windows; below, a blocked three-light window to the chancel. Very simple low chapels flanking the chancel, the N joined to a still lower vestry fronting the transept, were added by *Reginald Fairlie* in 1926.

31 Cappon's E front, seen only obliquely from the narrow and steeply sloping street, is an unashamed crib from C. Harrison Townsend's first and unexecuted design of 1896 for Whitechapel Art Gallery, London.* Battered towers with rounded corners and surmounted by cupolas joined by a narthex stretched across the gable, all of greyish ashlar masonry, polished at the narthex and base and top of the towers, of stugged smaller stones at the towers' intermediate stages. The towers' bases and narthex form an integrated bottom storey with five close-set small round-headed windows in the front of each tower and a hoodmoulded broad door, also round-headed, in the narthex; on the narthex, a curvaceous parapet containing a niche for a statue of Our Lady. Inside the narthex doorway, wrought-iron gates, the lower uprights with fleur-de-lis finials, the top rail decorated with panels of foliage and surmounted by spire finials and a floriated central cross. Projecting from the outer side of the N tower, a rounded and half-domed low baptistery. Above this ground-floor level the towers rise as severe slabs,

* Exhibited at the Royal Academy in 1896 and illustrated in *Academy Architecture* vol. ix (1896).

the stonework pierced only by two widely separated tiers of bipartite rectangular windows, to belfries (only the N containing bells). Here the rounded corners are carried up as domed circular buttresses which frame a large round-headed opening in each face. Inside the scooped parapet of each tower is a cupola, also with rounded corners and round-headed openings, its concave-sloped pyramidal roof rising from broad eaves to a gilded metal spire finialled with a tall cross. The centre of the 1850s gable between the towers was refaced by Cappon in ashlar and a huge window inserted, of five round-headed low lights under a great circle whose tracery forms a cross with circles between the arms.

INTERIOR. The general appearance is 1850s 'Saxon'. The church contains a seven-bay nave and aisles, the arcades formed by round-headed arches carried on fat columns of bundled shafts with elided capitals, their tall bases intended to be hidden by pews. Over the nave, a plaster semicircular tunnel vault, each bay marked off by a transverse rib with a traceried central boss. At the W (liturgical E) bay, the ceiling over the sanctuary is richly panelled. Each bay of the flat-roofed aisles is delineated by a round-headed arch springing from hefty corbels. Under each of the aisle windows was placed in 1867 a carved marble scene of one of the STATIONS OF THE CROSS resting on a foliaged corbel. Between the windows, fluted corbels surmounted by life-size figures of the Apostles, also of 1867. In the E (liturgical W) gallery, the ORGAN by *Booth & Son*, 1862, rebuilt by *E. H. Lawton*, 1914, and again by *R.C. Goldsmith* in 1980. – Gothic bench PEWS of 1900–2 and lower than the original seats. – On the N side of the sanctuary, a brass eagle LECTERN of 1894, imported here *c.* 2000. – On the sanctuary's S side, an octagonal PULPIT of 1889 remodelled in 1900–2 when were introduced the present round-headed panels carved by *James Bremner* with alternating reliefs of foliage and flowers and heads of the Blessed Virgin Mary, Our Lord and St Joseph. – Mid-C19 brass CANDELABRA of Puginesque design flank the entrance to the sanctuary whose MOSAIC TILING was introduced in 1902. – HIGH ALTAR of 1902, the front divided into round-headed panels containing gilded reliefs of sacred symbols (the Pelican in Piety, vines, the IHS monogram and the *Agnus Dei*). It is surmounted by a domed marble tabernacle and gabled reredos topped by statues of angels and the Virgin and Child, all of 1862. – Free-standing ALTAR in front designed by *Joseph Dagen*, 2001, and made up of the two side chapel altars of 1902, both of marble embellished with gilded metal reliefs. – STAINED GLASS. Stylized foliage designs of 1851 in the W (liturgical E) rose window. – In the E (liturgical W) window, abstract patterns evoking the Mysteries of the Rosary in blue and yellow round a rose-coloured cross, by *Anthony Naylor*, *c.* 2000.

Former SCHOOL at the SE. Its two-storey N part is of *c.* 1860, the front (E) gable with round-headed windows and a squat but heavy 'bellcote' feature. A single-storey S extension in similar manner was added by *Ireland & Maclaren*, 1875. S of this, a two-storey block by *Robert Keith*, 1882–3, its front gable quite ambitious Romanesque. The single-storey link of 1875 was heightened by another floor by *T. Martin Cappon*, 1902.

ST PETER AND ST PAUL (R.C.), corner of Byron Street and Milton Street. By *Reginald Fairlie*, 1927–8. Blocky and very simple Romanesque, the walls of red brick with stone dressings, the roofs pantiled. Broad nave, its front (S) gable containing the entrance flanked by overarched small windows; in the gable-head, a low three-light window under an empty image niche. Flanking the gable are low flat-roofed 'towers' with pierced parapets. These front narrow aisles, also flat-roofed and with windows set high in their sides. At the N (liturgical E) end, a low chancel with clearstorey lights in the sides above the flanking low chapels.

Inside, brick-faced walls. Tall quasi-Doric octagonal pillars divide the nave from the passage aisles and support the beams of the panelled flat wooden ceiling. Broad round-headed arch to the chancel and narrow ones from the aisles to the chapels. In the sides of the chancel, paired arches to the chapels under the small clearstorey windows; elliptical-arched tunnel-vaulted and panelled ceiling.

CLERGY HOUSE of 1927–8, also by *Fairlie* and of red brick to the E. Piend-roofed Neo-Georgian, an off-centre entrance in the six-bay front. Single-storey link to the church's E chapel.

ST SALVADOR (Episcopal), corner of Church Street and St Salvador Street. School and mission church, its economical rubble-walled Gothic exterior containing coloured decoration unequalled in Scotland, all by *G. F. Bodley* and built in stages between 1858 and 1874.

An Episcopalian mission from St Paul's Church (now Cathedral) to the Hilltown area was established by Bishop A. P. Forbes in 1855 and the mission's first building erected in 1858–9. This (now the MAXWELLTOWN INFORMATION CENTRE) is of two storeys, its lower floor containing a classroom, the upper floor designed as a temporary church to accommodate 300. Rubble-built and plain except for the W gable's first-floor window of four lights under a rose and flat-roofed birdcage bellcote, and the short NW wing's jerkin-head gable. Over the entrance in the wing, the coat of arms of the diocese of Brechin.

The church itself to the N was designed in 1865 and built in two stages, the nave in 1867–8, the chancel and Lady Chapel in 1874. Aisled nave, its W gable finished with a ringed cross and fronted by a lean-to porch. The tall clearstorey is articulated by stepped buttresses, their flying bases concealed inside the aisles. Lower and narrower chancel, the Lady Chapel on its S side. Simple Geometric detail in the nave's two-light side windows and four-light W window and in the tall three-light N windows of the chancel.

24 INTERIOR of architectural simplicity but spectacular richness of decoration, quite devoid of tackiness. Over the tall nave,

a kingpost-truss roof with curved struts; diamond-shaped stone flooring slabs. Low pointed arcades into the passage aisles, their sloping roofs supported on transverse half-arches (i.e. the fliers supporting the external buttresses of the clearstorey). Tall pointed chancel arch. Pointed and panelled tunnel-vaulted ceiling over the chancel, its choir raised one step above the nave, the sanctuary raised a further step and with a marble-slabbed floor. On the chancel's S side, three arches, the W containing the organ, the two to the E opening into the Lady Chapel. Over the chapel, a scissor-truss roof.

The walls and ceiling were covered with STENCIL DECORATION designed by Bodley and probably intended from the start but not perhaps executed until the later 1870s or early 1880s. The scheme is still almost complete although the original paintwork, executed in watercolour and tempera, was replaced in oils (by *Mackay & Son* under *C. G. Soutar*'s direction) in 1936 and restored (by *J. & T. Harvey* under *Colin McWilliam*'s direction) in 1972. The stencilling of the high dadoes on the aisles' side walls has been lost but their top band of foliaged decoration survives. In the nave, the spandrels of the arcades are painted in dark bluish-green on a lighter bluish-green ground with a diaper pattern closely derived from the carved work on the mid-C15 tomb of Bishop Thomas Beckynton in Wells Cathedral; under the clearstorey windows, a band inscribed with part of the hymn 'Jerusalem my happy home' ('There Mary sings Magnificat to tunes surpassing sweet . . .'). Above, on a cream-coloured ground, motifs of stylized roses and the letter S (for Salvador) surrounded by crowns. On the nave roof, stencilled gold stars, also on a cream ground. The same diaper pattern as at the nave arcades recurs on the E walls of the aisles and the chancel arch but in red on a black ground. At the springing of the chancel arch, a band inscribed 'Praise ye the Lord ye Lords name be praised'. Above this band the arch-head is surrounded by a pattern of blossoming branches, the design taken by Bodley from the depiction of an angel's cloth of gold cope in a C15 Westphalian painting in Munich, executed in pale green on a gold ground. On the side walls of the chancel, a red and black stencilled low dado. Above and carried up to the springing of the windows' arches, the same diaper pattern and also in bluish-greens as at the nave arcades. From the springing of the arches to the wall-head, the blossoming branch design of the head of the chancel arch but here in red on a cream ground. The choir's ceiling panels are stencilled with roses on a green ground, the panels above the sanctuary adorned with gold stars and sacred monograms on a red ground. In the Lady Chapel, the same stencilled dado pattern as in the chancel; above, the blossoming branch design in green on a cream ground.

CHANCEL SCREEN of 1875 designed by Bodley, the ironwork executed by *Braun & Downing* of Birmingham, the painting and gilding by *A. W. Fairweather* of Dundee (much regilding carried out by the *Rev. Paul Harvie* in the 1990s). It is divided by slender stanchions, partly twisted and gilded, into seventeen vertical compartments crossed by transoms. At the lowest stage, a lattice grille. Above, six of the stanchions bear gilded shields painted in black with the sacred IHS monogram, this second stage finished with an embossed and crenellated transom. At the third stage, cusped arcading springing from the stanchions, the arches containing small shields also painted with the sacred monogram but in gold on black. Above the top rail, large gilded fleur-de-lis finials to the stanchions. Rising in the centre, above a large shield with the gold IHS monogram on a red ground, a tall black and gold cross, elaborately but delicately decorated with foliage sprouting on the stem, the upper arms ending in gilded fleurs-de-lis. An iron chain ties the top of the cross to the head of the chancel arch. – Contemporary PARCLOSE SCREENS in the two arches from the chancel to the Lady Chapel, both with gilded fleur-de-lis finials. – In the arch to the W, the ORGAN by *Wordsworth & Maskell*, 1882 (rebuilt by *Harrison & Harrison*, 1997), its contemporary canopy-topped carved, painted and gilded case designed by *Canon Frederick H. Sutton*; linenfold-panelled front to the organ loft. – On the sanctuary's N wall, a battlemented semi-octagonal SACRAMENT HOUSE in a late medieval manner, coloured red and gold.

REREDOS occupying the full width and height above the altar of the chancel's E wall, designed by Bodley and executed by *Burlison & Grylls*, *c.* 1875 (the painted decoration restored by *Rab Snowden* of the *Department of the Environment* under *Colin McWilliam*'s direction, 1972). Retable painted with octofoils enclosing the IHS monogram. Above, a huge and very flatly modelled painted depiction of the Crucifixion with figures of Our Lady and St John in cusped arches at the foot of the Cross. In the square panels between the upper arms of the Cross, painted open-traceried octofoils containing modelled and gilded lead stars, those at the centre with the IHS monogram. Above, a row of four panels depicting the Archangels. Flanking the reredos's centrepiece, three tiers of copper panels painted with figures of the Twelve Apostles. In the tympanum, a fresco of the Annunciation with some decoration in high relief; triangular corner panels painted with the kneeling figures of Isaiah and Jeremiah. – In the Lady Chapel, an ALTARPIECE, presumably of *c.* 1875, decorated with carved and gilded vines.

Simple bench PEWS of 1868 in the nave and, in the choir, slightly more elaborate Gothic oak STALLS designed by Bodley and executed by *Kidd & Son* in 1875. On the S side of the chancel, wooden SEDILIA, probably also of 1875, the canopy with rosetted bosses, carved and gilded. – N of the chancel arch, a simple box-like wooden PULPIT, perhaps of 1868. – At the W end of the N aisle, a late C19 octagonal FONT, of stone with polished granite shafts. – MONUMENT in the chancel floor to the Rev. James Nicholson †1890, a marble slab inlaid with a bronze border enclosing a floriated cross flanked by a Bible and chalice.

STAINED GLASS. On the chancel's N side, three clearly drawn windows by *Burlison & Grylls*. The E (SS Andrew, Patrick and George, flanked by Fathers of the Eastern Church) is of 1890, the centre window (Isaiah, St John the Baptist and the Virgin and Child, flanked by Fathers of the Western Church) of 1888, and the W (Scottish Saints) of 1876. – Probably also by Burlison & Grylls and of *c.* 1890 are the E clearstorey windows (Archangels) either side of the nave. – Nave W window (St Andrew, St Michael, St Joan of Arc and St George), colourful and less disciplined, by *Clayton & Bell*, 1922. – In the Lady Chapel's S wall, a pair of two-light windows (Scenes from the Life of Our Lady) by *Burlison & Grylls*, 1902. – The chapel's colourful W rose window (half-figures of Saints) is by *Clayton & Bell*, 1859. Formerly in the W window of the school building's upper-floor temporary church, it was moved here in 1874.

VICTORIA CHAPEL, Clepington Road. Disused. Cheap Gothic, by *Johnston & Baxter*, 1898–9. Nave and shorter W aisle, the intended transepts and N apse not built. In the diagonal-buttressed S gable five cusped vestibule windows and three taller and hoodmoulded lancets above. Wooden porch on the W side, stone porch on the E. The HALL at the N was added by *Joseph Johnston* in 1937–8.

INTERIOR. Over the nave, an open wooden roof, the collar-braces decoratively pierced and springing from stone corbels. Three-bay arcade to the W aisle, the pointed arches carried on round pillars at the centre and hefty corbels at the ends. – STAINED GLASS. In the E wall, two lights (Justice and Mercy) of *c.* 1930. – In the W aisle, two Modernist-realist lights (a woman kneeling beside a warrior; the Virgin and Child) by *Douglas Hamilton* and erected as a Second World War memorial in 1951. The windows are intended (2011) to be re-erected in Coldside Parish Church (*see* above).

WESLEYAN METHODIST CHAPEL, corner of Victoria Road and Wellington Street. Now Tayside Islamic Cultural Education Centre (Jamia Masjid Tajdar-e-Madina). By *Alexander Johnston*, 1869. Awkwardly detailed Gothic buttressed box, the masonry now painted. Large rose window above the steeply gabled front porch.

PUBLIC BUILDINGS

COLDSIDE BRANCH LIBRARY, corner of Strathmartine Road and Strathmore Avenue. Edwardian Baroque, by the Dundee City Architect, *James Thomson*, 1907–8. Long segmental-shaped NE front between narrow ends which stand on the building lines of the two streets. Each end is fronted with a giant screen of Ionic columns *in antis*, the piers channelled, the entablature surmounted by a high parapet formed of three stepped pedestals. Framed by the screen, the Roman Doric-columned and open-pedimented aedicular surround to a large and prominently keystoned window; above the window, at upper-floor level, the relief of an open book surrounded by swagged foliage, the carving, as elsewhere on the building, by *Albert Hodge*. The concave frontage between the ends is of nine bays, the ground-floor windows set in a Doric-columned screen supporting an entablature. Aedicular central entrance with coupled columns and an open pediment, its tympanum bearing a cartouche flanked by putti. The upper floor is an unbroken sweep of red brick. Aedicular-faced and domed square cupola on the roof.

Inside, a circular entrance hall, the walls with attached columns in a Roman version of the Ionic order. Plain ground-floor rooms. The first floor's two reading rooms are top-lit from segmental-arched tunnel vaults.

OUR LADY'S PRIMARY SCHOOL, Nelson Street. By *Tayside Regional Council*, 1982. Long and low, of painted brick and glass, curved roof-lights the principal feature.

POLICE STATION, corner of Hilltown and North George Street. By *Dundee City Council*, 1997. Single-storey with a bowed corner, in a 1930s modernistic manner but the walls of blockwork.

ST PETER AND PAUL PRIMARY SCHOOL, Byron Street. By *Allan & Friskin*, 1930, of red brick with dressings of pale buff-coloured cement. Main block of two tall storeys, the appearance generally Neo-Georgian but with horizontally proportioned large windows in the centre of the S front. Projecting at the E end, a short but more powerful block of two and three storeys, Dudok Modern in character but with simplified Romanesque detail.

TAYSIDE ISLAMIC CULTURAL EDUCATION CENTRE (JAMIA MASJID TAJDAR-E-MADINA). *See* WESLEYAN METHODIST CHAPEL, above.

DESCRIPTION

VICTORIA ROAD, laid out in 1871 as a broad thoroughfare on the line of the medieval Bucklemaker Wynd, forms the S boundary of the industrial and post-industrial Hilltown. Part of the city's inner ring road, the road's S side now belongs to the City Centre (*see* above), the N to Hilltown. At the W end, the four-storey VICTORIA CHAMBERS (Nos. 10–14), by *William Alexander*, 1874. Renaissance, the shallowly concave twenty-one-bay façade designed as three identical palazzi. The curve of the terrace is continued at the taller Nos. 16–20, originally the Victoria Brewery. As built in 1875 to a design by the engineering firm of *B. Thomson & Son*, this consisted of a five-storey three-bay main block on the r., its first-floor window surrounds pilastered and corniced. The ground floor, originally dignified with a large segmental-arched entrance, is now covered by a C20 pub front. Also altered is the ground floor of the section to the l. Originally this was of only two storeys, each with a pair of widely spaced and narrow round-headed dummy windows (the first floor's now opened up), but was raised to the same height as the rest *c.* 1914. The scale continues at the corner block with Hilltown. By *Pilkington & Bell*, 1872, this is an idiosyncratic version of an Italianate palazzo but the eccentricity laboured and the very tall ground-floor shop fronts replaced in routine manner and with a mezzanine floor inserted, *c.* 1950.

Victoria Road's E corner building with Hilltown was replaced in the late C20 by a concave wall broken by the fearsome ascent of a stair to the flats of Barclays Square behind (for this and Hilltown N of Victoria Road, *see* below). The street line is re-established by the formidable presence of the Victoria Road Calender (*see* Industrial Buildings, below). Across an alley, No. 76 Victoria Road, a six-storey block of flats by the *Nicoll Russell Studios*, *c.* 2000. Walls faced with ashlar and render, metal balconies and an oversailing roof. Then, a four-storey Baronial tenement (Nos. 78–86 Victoria Road and Nos. 2–4 Forebank Street) by *McCulloch & Fairley*, 1876–7, a slate-spired octagonal tower at the SE corner. Further up FOREBANK STREET, St Mary Our Lady of Victories (R.C.) Church. Another assertion of industrial might, although not ostentatious, in Victoria Road at the former Forebank Dyeworks, now Bonnybank Apartments (*see* Industrial Buildings, below). E of Bonnybank Road, ERROL TERRACE (Nos. 90–94 Victoria Road), four-storey tenements by *McCulloch & Jamieson*, 1895–6, with full-height bay windows, pedimented entrances and Frenchy-domed octagonal corner towers. The tenements continue round the corner in NELSON STREET as ERROL BANK (Nos. 2–8 Nelson Street), also by McCulloch & Jamieson, 1895–7. To the N, No. 8A Nelson Street, a piend-roofed early C19 two-storey villa, its S entrance corniced, the centre bay at the rear carried up as a twin-chimneyed and parapeted attic. A full-height canted bay was added to the S front's E end *c.* 1900. On Nelson Street's E side and overlooking Victoria Road, the GURU NANAK GURDWARA SIKH TEMPLE, originally a piend-roofed house of the earlier C19, a segmental-arched entrance in its stugged ashlar front. W addition of the earlier C20, Georgian in manner but with two-light windows. In Victoria Road W of Wellington Street, the former Wesleyan Methodist Chapel (*see* Churches, above), now the Tayside Islamic Cultural Education Centre (Jamia Masjid Tajdar-e-Madina). Plain late C19 and C20 housing follows. At Nos. 126–140 Victoria Road, on the corner of COTTON ROAD, a four-storey tenement by *Edward & Robertson*, 1877. First- and second-floor windows with cornices, the first floor's carried on consoles at the bowed corner.

HILLTOWN N of its junction with Victoria Road climbs steeply uphill. On the E, No. 25 Hilltown by *Baxter, Clark & Paul*, 1994, four-storey flats, their pseudo-traditional design mixing references to Scottish fishertown vernacular and the Costa del Sol. There follows a four-storey late C19 tenement (Nos. 27–33 Hilltown), Georgian survival with corniced windows but of two lights. Blockwork frontage to the late C20 Nos. 37–39, mostly of traditional appearance but with touches of jettying and some cut-out corners. Then plain tenements (Nos. 57–69 and Nos. 71–75) by the Dundee City Architect, *David B. McLay*, 1936, followed by more late C20 modernistic Scots vernacular but dour.

HILLTOWN TERRACE leads W. On the S side, four fifteen-storey tower blocks (HILLTOWN COURT, BONNETHILL COURT, TULLOCH COURT and DALLFIELD COURT) by the *Scottish Construction Co. Ltd*, 1964–6, harled and flat-roofed, with recessed balconies in the long sides. On Hilltown Terrace's N side, piend-roofed 1930s Neo-Georgian blocks of flats.

On HILLTOWN's W side, N of McDonald Street, No. 114, the former office of the Hillside Works, by *Maclaren, Sons & Soutar*, 1910. Three-storey Neo-Georgian of a sort, the ground floor of red brick, the upper floors rendered and with two-storey oriel windows at the end bays. Broad-eaved roof forming an open pediment over the centre bay whose upper floors are set in a frame of giant pilasters with bases but no capitals. Plain four-storey tenements (MOUNT PROSPECT) of 1894 at Nos. 116–122. Hilltown's stretch between Rosebank Street and Constitution Street contains plain Late Victorian tenements, a few late C20 traditionally detailed buildings and, at Nos. 182–184, a late C19 Georgian survival three-storey block with a pedimented and chimney-topped central gablet.

ANN STREET runs E from Hilltown. On the S side, Our Lady's Primary School (*see* Public Buildings, above). On the E corner of NORTH ELLEN STREET, a four-storey tenement (Nos. 128–130 Alexander Street) of *c.* 1871 and probably designed by *John Bruce* who produced an unexecuted design for the site in that year. Basket-arched windows except at the bowed corner where the upper floors' openings are each of three round-headed lights. Immediately N, at No. 13 NORTH ELLEN STREET, a tenement of *c.* 1875, with carved heads at the window surrounds. To the N, ST SALVADOR STREET, its N side filled with the Caldrum Works (*see* Industrial Buildings, below), its SW corner with St Salvador's Episcopal Church (*see* Churches, above). NORTH GEORGE STREET leads from the church's W end to Hilltown. At its SW corner, the Police Station (*see* Public Buildings, above). On the NW corner, the four-storey CO-OPERATIVE BUILDINGS (Nos. 235–237 Hilltown), dated 1905. Two-bay front in a Queen Anne manner with open pediments over the bipartite first-floor windows, a Dutch gablet crowning the wall-head.

HILLTOWN N of Constitution Street begins on the W with a large corner development (HILLBANK HEALTH CENTRE by *Bell & Farquharson*, 1991 and Nos. 216–222 Hilltown by *Peter Inglis Architects*, 1994), an over-determined display of Postmodern tricks. Patterned brick elevation to Constitution Street. Cut-out SE corner containing a blockwork tower, its glazed top stage under a splay-foot slated spire. To Hilltown, a blockwork front of four storeys, with taller rectangular bay windows jettied out above the ground floor. Beyond, on the S corner of STIRLING

STREET, a Jacobean tenement (Nos. 236–238 Hilltown) of 1885, with a conical-roofed corner turret. Across Stirling Street, the former DUNDEE SAVINGS BANK (No. 1 Stirling Street) by *Johnston & Baxter*, 1903–5. Jacobean Renaissance in red sandstone ashlar, with mullioned-and-transomed windows and a strapwork parapet over the S front. Conical-roofed low round tower containing the open-pedimented entrance. It faces across Hilltown to a mosaic-clad wall erected in 2006 containing large square openings onto a garden behind. The N stretch of Hilltown ends with plain buildings of the late C19 and early C20 and, on the W, the brown brick flats of the late C20 STIRLING COURT, the development ignoring the street line as if to disown the existence of Hilltown. Road junction marked by the HILLTOWN CLOCK designed by the Dundee Burgh Engineer, *William Mackison*, and erected in 1901. Tall cast-iron column carrying the circular clock (by *G. D. Rattray*), each face topped by the Dundee coat of arms. KINGHORNE ROAD goes off to the W. On its S corner with Hilltown, a two-storey flat-roofed and splay-cornered *moderne* block (Nos. 288–290 Hilltown and No. 2 Kinghorne Road) by *W. M. Patrick & Co.*, 1934, the ground floor clad in polished black granite, the E front's windows horizontally proportioned, the N elevation's in surrounds of triangular projection. On Kinghorne Road's N side, a dour rubble-faced three-storey Neo-Georgian block of flats (Nos. 31–35) by the Dundee City Architect, *David B. McLay*, 1934. To the W, on the S, KINGHORNE COURT, by *James Parr & Partners*, *c.* 1980, cliff-like but its brown brick more inviting.

In MAIN STREET, E of Hilltown, a ragbag of late C19 and C20 buildings, two of the more recent at Nos. 12–28 with Postmodern touches. On the corner of Isla Road, Coldside Parish Church, for which *see* Churches, above.

STRATHMARTINE ROAD continues Hilltown to the N. On the W, at the Kinghorne Road corner, LAW HOUSE (No. 2), a brown brick block of flats by *James Parr & Partners*, 1975. At the S corner of Hill Street, the former Butterburn United Presbyterian Church (*see* Churches, above). On Strathmartine Road's E side, a late C19 four-storey tenement (Nos. 7–13), the first-floor windows with simplified Jacobean Renaissance cornices, one with a pediment. Also late C19 and of four storeys with Jacobean Renaissance touches, the tenements at Nos. 17–21 and No. 29, identically detailed but No. 29's upper windows are vertically linked by aprons and its corner to Mid Road is splayed and pedimented. Opposite, on the W side of Strathmartine Road, the late C20 BUTTERBURN SQUARE and RUSSELL PLACE, a not very formal square of five-storey blocks of flats clad in ribbed metal sheeting and with long balconies of grey brick behind the red brick piers which support the eaves. Then, plain Victorian and a few late C20 tenements, only the mid-C19 two-storey-and-attic Nos. 49–53, with an elliptical-headed pend arch and a chimneyed central gablet, hinting that the area once housed a pre-industrial workforce. It faces housing of quite different scale and purpose, two twenty-three-storey tower blocks (BUTTERBURN COURT and BUCKLEMAKER COURT) by *James Parr & Associates*, 1966–70, their present red brick cladding no disguise for their intention to house as many people as possible on the site. Set back between them and entered from DERBY STREET, St Martin's Episcopal Church. To the W, interwar housing and, on the N side of BYRON STREET, St Peter and St Paul (R.C.) Church and Primary School. In PATERSON STREET and MILLTON STREET to the N, the former Lawside Works (*see* Industrial Buildings, below). At the N end of this stretch of Strathmartine Road, on the corner of Strathmartine Avenue, the Coldside Branch Library.

INDUSTRIAL BUILDINGS

CALDRUM WORKS, St Salvador Street. A jute mill by *Robertson & Orchar*, 1872–3, and much extended later although remaining generally utilitarian. The 1870s part is at the W. Rubble-built piend-roofed weaving sheds stretching behind a parapeted wall along Glamis Street. At their S end and facing St Salvador Street, a single-storey calender with, on its E, a two-storey office block with two-light windows. Beside it, a tripartite gateway erected in 1887, the gatepiers with mutule cornices. These support keystoned elliptical arches added in 1912 to carry the front wall of the boardroom above, its façade with a three-light window flanked by bipartites. E of the gateway, the plain two-storey bag factory built in 1887–90. The works' factory and weaving sheds were extended N to Main Street in 1882–90.

FOREBANK DYEWORKS, Victoria Road. Now housing (BONNYBANK APARTMENTS). By *Alexander Johnston*, 1875. Rubble-built and austere in the Late Georgian textile mill tradition, the S front of twelve bays, the corners rounded at the ground floor and corbelled to the square above. Originally the building was two-storey-and-attic but in 1895 it was heightened by a further floor, the large rectangular second-floor windows repeating those below, the attic's round-headed gable openings replicas of those of the earlier attic. Cornice placed below the wall-head, the small windows over the cornice inserted on the works' conversion to flats in 1984–5.

LAWSIDE WORKS, Paterson Street. Converted to housing, 2007. Rubble-built L-plan jute mill of *c.* 1835. At the two-storey S range's W end, the engine house, its ground- and first-floor windows contained in round-headed and keystoned overarches. This is a rebuilding of 1865–6 when this range was remodelled and extended. In Scott Court behind, a detached mechanics' shop built in 1871, its Italianate clock tower with a pyramidal roof topped by a weathervane.

VICTORIA ROAD CALENDER, Victoria Road. Now housing. Vast rubble-walled and crowstep-gabled Flemish-Baronial edifice of 1874–5, by *Robertson & Orchar* with detail designed by *J. F.*

Anderson. Originally of three tall storeys with an attic lit only from windows in the gables. Front of fourteen bays, the l. three minimally advanced and with tall and slender conical-roofed corner turrets at the gable; another turret on the E gable's S corner. The ground- and second-floor windows are elliptically arched, the first-floor openings rectangular. Over all these, continuous hoodmouldings which rise above the centres of the ground-floor openings to frame oblong panels and step up as semicircles over the first-floor windows. At the eleven-bay r. section, under a curtailed window, a broad entrance in a shouldered elliptical arch. Another entrance at this section's W end was formed as part of *James Lowe*'s alterations of 1911–14 when two ground-floor windows were replaced by a broad rectangular door, its lugged architrave with a heavy consoled keystone, and, above, a huge mullioned-and-transomed fanlight (lighting a boardroom behind). Over this section, a parapet carried on tall multi-moulded corbels. At the three-bay l. section, curtailed ground-floor windows, each containing two depressed-arched lights. Below them, a trio of doorways, the outer two like that towards the E end of the r. section, the centre door (now a window) lower and narrower, all under a continuous rope moulding. Two-light windows to the first floor. At the second floor the hoodmould, its outer ends coiled, steps up over the centre window (of two round-headed lights) to enclose a pair of circular panels. Formerly there was a single tall attic window contained within the stepped jettying of the gable's head but this opening has been curtailed and small additional windows inserted below it. A pair of 1870s rear wings were heightened and united as a single block in 1911–14. The calendering and bag-sewing workshops which abutted the N side have been demolished and the back wall was harled and given over-elaborate forestairs to the flats inside in 1997. 110

LOCHEE

Long a part of Dundee but still with its own identity, the area in and around Lochee was, by the beginning of the C19, occupied by settlements of handloom weavers, chiefly employed in linen manufacture, and by a few small mills. From the 1850s, the construction and expansion of Cox Brothers' Camperdown Works (by the late C19 the largest jute mill in the world) was accompanied by the development of Lochee into a small industrial town, its High Street of urban if not especially urbane character, with a complement of churches, public library and baths, banks, shops and tenements, and its own suburban villas to the N and S. Closure of the Camperdown Works and the mid- and late C20 construction of extensive housing estates, now serving as dormitories for the city centre, have deprived Lochee of self-confidence.

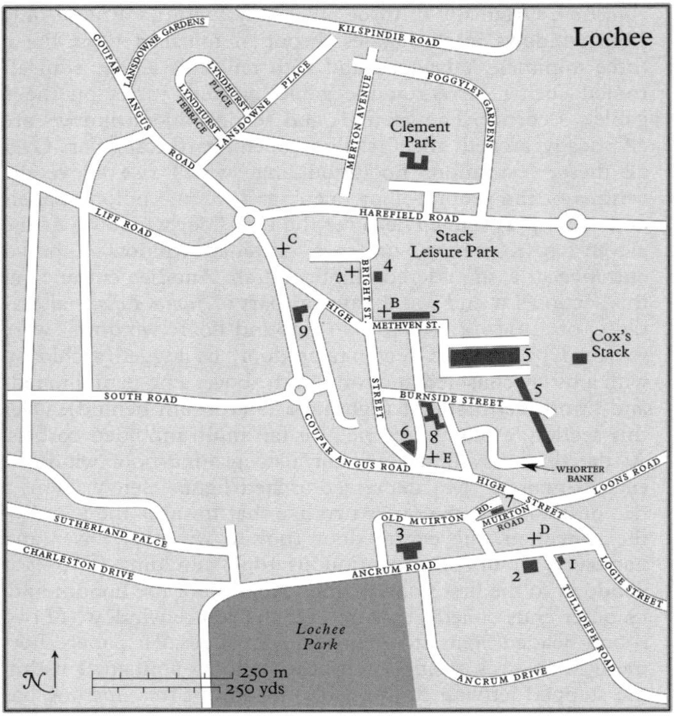

A Central Baptist Church Lochee Centre
B Lochee Chapel of Ease
C Lochee Parish Church
D St Margaret (Episcopal)
E St Mary (R.C.)

1 Albert Halls
2 Ancrum Outdoor Education Centre
3 Ancrum Road Primary School
4 The Boy's Brigade Hall
5 Camperdown Works
6 Lochee Neighbourhood Library and Swimming and Leisure Centre
7 Lochee Railway Station
8 St Mary's Primary School
9 West District Housing Office

CHURCHES

CENTRAL BAPTIST CHURCH LOCHEE CENTRE, Bright Street. Originally Lochee Baptist Church. Built in 1866 but extended and remodelled by *Thomas Keir* in 1884. Rectangle of stugged and squared masonry, the side windows round-headed. A gabled porch and a large circular window at the front gable whose eaves are carried on arcaded cornicing.

LOCHEE CHAPEL OF EASE, corner of Methven Street and Bright Street. Disused. By *David Neave*, 1829–30. Classical two-storey three-bay temple front, with giant anta-pilasters carrying the overall pediment pierced by an oculus. This is surmounted by a corniced and pilastered square belfry which serves as a pedestal to the spire-topped octagonal upper stage pierced by circular openings. Pilastered entrance at the centre of the front. Plain side elevations.

HALL to the NW. Free Renaissance, by *Alexander Johnston*, 1884.

LOCHEE PARISH CHURCH, corner of High Street and Coupar Angus Road. Originally Lochee United Presbyterian Church. By *James Maclaren*, 1869–71. Broad and high Gothic box presiding over Lochee's High Street, the architectural interest concentrated at the S end. Here the broad front gable with a pierced parapet rises above the ridge of the roof and hides its iron cresting. Stretched between the gable's corner buttresses is a battlemented porch, its centrepiece a pinnacled-buttressed pointed doorway with marble nook-shafts and dogtooth ornament on the moulded surround; foliaged label stops to the hoodmould. Five-light window above. On the gable's E side, an apsidal projection containing a gallery stair. On the W, a shorter but taller link to the SW steeple. The steeple's tower is high and finished with a tall octagonal belfry within whose pierced parapet rises the lucarned stone spire.

Economical side elevations. In each, single-light openings alternate with slightly advanced and gabled bays which contain taller mullioned-and-transomed windows, their upper lights with shouldered arches under cusped and pointed heads. At the church's N end, an apsidal-ended chancel of 1890.

The INTERIOR is divided into a broad nave and narrow aisles by tall and slender foliate-capitalled columns which carry pointed arches, their spandrels with quatrefoiled circlets. Wagon ceiling, the central flat with traceried ventilator roses. Gallery along the aisles and across the S end, its corners splayed; Gothic blind arcading on the front. Simple Gothic bench PEWS of 1872. Also Gothic and of 1872, the pine PULPIT in pride of place at the N end. Behind the pulpit, the stone arch to the apse which was added in 1890 to house the contemporary ORGAN by *Hill & Son*. – Late C19 brass eagle LECTERN formerly in Lochee Chapel of Ease. – STAINED GLASS. In the apse, brightly coloured Late Victorian abstract glass in the rose window and two sidelights. – Similar glass in the five-light S window.

HALL to the SE, by *James Maclaren*, 1882–3, with a gambrel roof and sparing Gothic detail.

ST MARGARET (Episcopal), Ancrum Road. English village Gothic by the *Rev. Edward Sugden*, 1888, but not completed until 1948–9 and then to a curtailed and different design by *Thoms & Wilkie*. The N chancel, transepts and one bay of the nave are all of 1888, built of hammer-dressed masonry and drydash. Very similar chancel and transepts, each apsidal-ended, the roof sloped at two different pitches interrupted by a vertical band of clearstorey glazing. In the side walls of the E transept, windows, each of two elliptical-arched lights; shouldered-arched S door to the W transept. The nave roof is also of two pitches with a clearstorey but at the rectangular gable provided in 1949 it is finished with a boldly oversailing jerkin-head. At the nave's SW corner, a low pyramid-roofed tower of 1949. Also of 1948–9 and by Thoms & Wilkie is the piend-roofed and drydashed HALL to the S, almost hiding the church from the street.

The church's INTERIOR contains a magnificent display of woodwork, with arcades carried round the limbs to support the clearstoreys and, under the chancel and transept roofs, collar-braces meeting at bosses. – Wrought-iron CHANCEL SCREEN finished with gilded fleur-de-lis finials. It was designed by *J. Murray Robertson* and executed by *Schryver* of Brussels in 1890. – At the screen's W (liturgical N) end, a brass eagle LECTERN of *c.* 1890. – At the E end of the screen, the PULPIT, perhaps of C16 North German workmanship, the round bowl carved in high relief with crude figures of Our Lord and the Four Evangelists. – Marble FONT of 1904 in the W transept, an Italian copy of Thorwaldsen's Kneeling Angel font at Copenhagen. – In the chancel, canopied wooden CLERGY STALLS, probably contemporary with the REREDOS (designed by Sugden) of 1889 whose canopy rises to a crocketed ogee dome at the centre. It formerly framed a PAINTING by *S. Reid* of Christ the Light of the World hung here in 1892. – Gothic HIGH ALTAR of marble, made in Italy and dedicated in 1907, the central panel of the front carved with the Crucifixion, the end panels with the eucharistic symbols of corn and vines. – On the chancel's W side, serving as the BISHOP'S THRONE, a chair whose back is carved with a relief of Moses Bringing the Tablets from Mount Sion and, below, figures of two saints and a panel inscribed 16xI.DEnSx72, the late C17 date plausible enough. – Also in the chancel, an ORGAN by *John R. Miller*, 1866, from the former St Mary's (Episcopal) Chapel in Adelaide Place (demolished) and rebuilt here by *Wood, Wordsworth & Co. Ltd* in 1978–9.

ST MARY (R.C.), corner of High Street and St Mary's Lane. Decorated Gothic, by *J. A. Hansom*, 1864–6. Despite the hole-in-the-wall site, one of Dundee's most arresting edifices, mixing the ethos of a mission church with that of a cathedral.

Immensely long nave and lean-to aisles, with a transeptal baptistery and porch at the N (liturgical W) end and short transepts at the S from which thrusts forward towards High
22 Street the much taller octagonal chancel, its appearance that of a tower-like chapter house. At the corners of the chancel are massive offset buttresses, their bases pierced by pointed arches. In each face, a tall two-light window, the head filled with three roundels containing trefoils. Spire roof with bands of fish-scale slating. Another but tiny spire on top of the bowed roof of the W transept's S chapel whose walling is broken by a band of cusped lights. In this transept's heavily buttressed gable, a window of two lights under a quatrefoil head. Identical window in the unbuttressed gable of the E transept but the place of a S chapel is taken by a link to the adjoining clergy house. The

nave's side elevations are straightforward, both of twelve bays marked off by buttresses against the aisle and clearstorey walls and containing paired windows, each of two stumpy lights under a circled head; three-light windows with cusping at the clearstorey. Gabled E porch. The W baptistery is a spire-roofed octagon, the high-set hoodmoulded windows each containing three roundels. At the N gable, a central buttress containing a small figure of Our Lady in an image niche. The buttress was originally flanked by trios of cusped arches which are now cut across by doors inserted in the late C20. Higher up, a pair of single-light windows, each with cusping and a trefoil head, the hoodmoulds' label stops left in block. Higher still, a pair of quatrefoiled round panels. The gable is finished with a louvred and gableted wooden bellcote.

INTERIOR. Six-bay arcades between the nave and aisles, the broad pointed arches carried on bell-capitalled columns of banded red and grey stone, the arch-heads of red and grey brick, the spandrels pierced by circlets containing quatrefoils. Corbelled out above the centre of each pillar of the arcade, a bell-capitalled vaulting shaft rising to a string course over the clearstorey and supporting a scissor truss under the steeply pitched roof. Fronting the clearstorey windows are pointed arches carried on columns, also with bell capitals. On each of the ashlar-clad aisle walls, a double tier of pointed arch-heads which spring from rosetted bosses. Interrupting this arcading are gableted stone panels bearing carved and painted STATIONS OF THE CROSS. At the (liturgical) E end of the S aisle, an apsed Lady Chapel. At the ends of the nave, tall and narrow acutely pointed arches of red and grey brick, the (liturgical) W opening to an organ loft over the vestibule, the front of the loft and vestibule screen late C20, the ORGAN by *Forster & Andrews*, 1884. The (liturgical) E arch opens into the semi-octagonal apsed sanctuary under the tower, its walls faced with brickwork (now painted) up to the level of the high-set windows. – The apse's marble HIGH ALTAR was erected in 1897, its front with foliate-capitalled columns at the ends, a roundel displaying a painted relief of the Pelican in Piety at the centre. On the altar, a contemporary elaborate Gothic REREDOS of three compartments. In the ogee-arched outer compartments, figures of thurible-swinging angels. The centre is steepled and contains the tabernacle, its green and gold-coloured metal doors in a frame of veined brown alabaster. – In the nave, low bench PEWS of the 1860s.

STAINED GLASS. Stylized floral designs, probably of 1866, in the aisle windows. In the S wall of the Lady Chapel, a late C19 three-light window (the *Mater Dolorosa* and St Mary Magdalen) by *Mayer & Co.* – In the apse, six lights, also late C19, the centre two depicting the Nativity of Our Lord, the others containing figures of SS Francis of Assisi, Peter, Patrick and Bridget.

SW of the church, the contemporary CLERGY HOUSE, also by *Hansom*. Two-storey, on an obtusely angled L-plan; Gothic detail but domestic in appearance.

LOCHEE PARK

Ancrum Road

The 9 ha. site was gifted to the City of Dundee by Cox Brothers, owners of the Camperdown Works, in 1890 and opened two years later. – At the N entrance, a heavily detailed Gothic LODGE AND GATEWAY, of 1891 by *Johnston & Baxter*, a fish-scale slate-roofed octagonal tower at the lodge's NE corner.

PUBLIC BUILDINGS

ALBERT HALL, corner of Ancrum Road and Tullideph Road. Masonic hall, by *James Lowe & Co.*, 1930. Single-storey squared-up brute classical in polished ashlar.

ANCRUM OUTDOOR EDUCATION CENTRE, Ancrum Road. Originally St Margaret's (Episcopal) School. By the *Rev. Edward Sugden*, 1895–6. One tall storey, the five-bay N front's advanced and gabled centre containing a hoodmoulded window of three stepped lights. Small two-light windows in the intermediate bays; at the end bays, taller windows, also two-light, which rise into bargeboarded gabled dormerheads. Slate-spired square cupola-ventilator on the roof. Rear addition by *James H. Langlands*, *c.* 1905, the canopied boys' and girls' entrances like those of his near-contemporary Ancrum Road Primary School (*see* below).

97 ANCRUM ROAD PRIMARY SCHOOL, Ancrum Road. Two-storey Board School of 1905–7 designed to accommodate 1,400 pupils. It is by *James H. Langlands* who incorporated but completely remodelled some of the structure of its single-storey predecessor (for 529 pupils) of 1874–5 (by *David Maclaren* of *Ireland & Maclaren*). That school's six-bay frontage with three-light windows in the slightly advanced and gabled end bays was retained but heightened by a floor, refaced in stugged and squared purplish masonry and given redesigned windows. These ground-floor openings are now all rectangular and corniced. Corniced windows also to the new upper floor and with aprons of stylized drapery; over the three-light windows of the end bays, segmental pediments, their tympana carved with thistle-surrounded blank shields. These bays are finished with shaped gables containing blind panels above swagged aprons. On each side of the front block, a curvaceously corniced lower projection but of four storeys with mezzanine floors containing cloakrooms. At the ground floor, the boys' and girls' entrances, their doors surmounted by heavily consoled semicircular canopies; mullioned small windows, those lighting the stair placed on the diagonal. On the centre of the piended roof, an Art Nouveauish lead-domed cupola. Cupola of the same design on the large but plain parallel block at the rear. Inside, a central hall on each floor, the upper with a collar-beam roof.

THE BOYS' BRIGADE HALL, Bright Street. By *James Maclaren & Sons*, 1884–5, and built as a school for 'half-time' pupils aged between eight and thirteen working part-time in the

Camperdown Works and for younger children of employees at the works. Scots Jacobean detail.

LOCHEE NEIGHBOURHOOD LIBRARY AND SWIMMING AND LEISURE CENTRE, corner of High Street and St Mary's Lane. By *J. Murray Robertson*, 1894, and extended in 1913. Lochee's only red sandstone building and its principal public edifice, this was a gift to the community by Cox Brothers, owners of the Camperdown Works. Relaxed Jacobean Renaissance, the front's main walling of stugged, the dressings of polished ashlar. The low single-storey-and-attic E end contains the BATHS, entered from St Mary's Lane. At the S front to High Street, a windowless ground floor; squared-up gables containing the attic openings. The W part, of two storeys in the fall of the ground, is the LIBRARY. Front composed of twinned shaped gables, the r. with a very tall mullioned-and-transomed window of three lights surmounted by segmental-arched panels decorated with stylized scrollwork. In the l. gable, a trio of two-light mullioned-and-transomed ground-floor windows; two-light windows, also mullioned and transomed, at the first-floor where they flank a panel carved with a shield bearing the coat of arms of the Cox family. At the SW corner, a domed round tower, the entrance's pediment enriched with egg-and-dart.

LOCHEE RAILWAY STATION, Old Muirton Road. Now Burns Club. By *James Gowans* for the Dundee & Newtyle Railway, 1861. The general shape, a double-pitch-roofed rectangle, is simple enough but the detail is characteristically and engagingly idiosyncratic. Walling of multi-coloured rubble (pink, red, orange and black, with a sprinkling of quartz) crossed, at Gowans's standard 2-foot (0.61 m.) intervals, by hammer-dressed string courses. Above a high and blind basement, tall windows with moulded brackets in their upper corners forming shouldered arches. Extravagantly moulded stone brackets under the eaves of the roof. Flat-roofed late C20 N extension for the building's present use.

ST MARY'S PRIMARY SCHOOL, corner of St Mary's Lane and Burnside Street. Originally two separate schools (for boys and girls) abutting each other. Flat-roofed Neo-Georgian with intimations of the Modern Movement, by *Allan & Friskin*, 1936, faced in red brick with white concrete dressings.

WEST DISTRICT HOUSING OFFICE, Aimer Square. By *Dundee City Council*, 2006–7. Stylish, in white harl above a brick base and with blue-painted trimmings. Butterfly-plan E front, the hinge provided by the semi-octagonal khaki-coloured centrepiece containing the entrance. The wings' large windows are shaded by metal canopies over the ground-floor openings and by the roof's upswept broad eaves at the upper floor, the canopies and eaves joined by metal wires.

DESCRIPTION

ANCRUM ROAD is the SW approach, the arrival of Lochee heralded by Lochee Park (*see* above) on the S and Ancrum Road

Primary School on the N. Then, small-scale late C19 villas and semi-detached houses, No. 35's bargeboarded front gable carved with a vase spouting foliage. Further E, the Ancrum Outdoor Centre and Albert Hall (*see* Public Buildings, above) facing St Margaret's Episcopal Church.

LOGIE STREET, running NW from Ancrum Street's E end towards High Street, contains plain Late Victorian tenements above shops. They are followed by the surviving hammer-dressed W abutment of a demolished RAILWAY BRIDGE of *c.* 1860. The line served the former Lochee Railway Station (*see* Public Buildings, above) standing high above the S side of OLD MUIRTON ROAD. On this road's N side, two single-storey-and-attic bay-windowed double houses, the roofs' broad eaves forming canopies over their centres. Foliaged finials on the bargeboarded gables; broad wooden gablets over the attic windows.

HIGH STREET, although unpretentious, is Lochee's public and commercial centre. Its SE start is overlooked from a distance by WHORTERBANK's two fifteen-storey blocks of flats (BURNSIDE COURT and ANCRUM COURT), by *Crudens Ltd*, 1960–2, each formed of three linked crosses, the long E and W sides rendered, the ends clad in brick. Their cut-out end corners, formerly occupied by balconies, have been infilled. Stylish they are not. High Street now asserts itself, the N side displaying the clergy house and prow-like chancel of St Mary's (R.C.) Church followed by the red sandstone Lochee Neighbourhood Library and Swimming and Leisure Centre.

W of the Library, on the corner where the road bends to the N, is the English Baroque Lloyds TSB Scotland, originally the DUNDEE SAVINGS BANK, by *Johnston & Baxter*, 1905, its ends bowed to turn the corner. At the straight centrepiece, faced like the rest with polished Camperdown ashlar, a broken- and open-pedimented aedicule, the heads of whiskered gentlemen carved in the centres of the Composite columns' upside-down volutes. This frames a three-light ground-floor window with Ionic column-mullions; the first-floor window's consoled pediment encloses a decorative inscription panel. At each bowed corner, a round-headed and keystoned first-floor window. Over the E corner's ground-floor window, a consoled pediment with a shield displaying the Royal Arms of Scotland. More assertive is the NW corner's Ionic aedicule, its pediment's shield bearing the coat of arms of the Dundee Savings Bank, which frames the lugged architrave surround to the bank's cavetto-moulded and round-headed entrance, the keystone carved with the head of a bearded man.

In High Street's stretch N of the Lloyds TSB Bank, a shopping centre of the 1970s on the W. It is of two and three storeys, some of the upper floors occupied by flats. Opposite, plain and small-scale Victorian and Edwardian tenements with ground-floor shops. The height rises to three storeys and an attic at No. 95 which was designed as the NORTH OF SCOTLAND BANK by *C. & L. Ower* in 1875. Ruskinian Gothic of a sort, with heavily moulded corbels under the first-floor balconies and wall-head's parapet. A bowed first-floor oriel window, carried on continuous corbelling, projects from the splayed corner to BURNSIDE STREET, down which is a glimpse of St Mary's Primary School. High Street continues N with the 1970s shopping development on the W facing plain late C19 buildings interrupted by late C20 intrusions. At the point where High Street jinks to the NW, METHVEN STREET exits E past Lochee Chapel of Ease and St Luke's Church to the entrance to the Camperdown Works (*see* below) and BRIGHT STREET runs N with the Central Baptist Church Lochee Centre and The Boys' Brigade Hall facing each other across the road. On the NE corner with Bright Street, the ogee-domed octagonal tower of a late C19 four-storey block (Nos. 139–145 High Street and No. 2 Bright Street). Both sides of High Street's final stretch to the NW are predominantly Late Victorian but the two-storey Nos. 168–174's front, by *Robbie & Wellwood*, 1971, is clad in white tiles, the upper floor projected on convex jettying. Aloof from the street's end, at its junction with Coupar Angus Road, stands the steepled Gothic mass of Lochee Parish Church.

COUPAR ANGUS ROAD'S S end serves as a bypass to High Street. On its E side, the rear of the West District Housing Office (*see* Public Buildings, above). W of a roundabout at the S end, a pair of sixteen-storey tower blocks (ELDERS COURT and ADAMSON'S COURT), by the *Scottish Construction Co. Ltd*, 1967. Each is H-plan, the brick-faced ends gripping the slightly recessed cross-bars, their lower storeys harled, the top five floors clad in ribbed metal sheeting. Surrounding four-storey housing by the Dundee City Architect, *Alan Preston*, 1970.

N of Coupar Angus Road's junction with High Street, HAREFIELD ROAD goes off to the E, with the vehicular access to the former Camperdown Works (*see* below) on the S and Clement Park (*see* below) set back on the N. W of Clement Park and entered off Coupar Angus Road, LANSDOWNE PLACE, LYNDHURST PLACE and LYNDHURST TERRACE were developed in the 1930s with single-storey small villas of traditional design with bellcast-eaved roofs and occasional touches of half-timbering. At the NE end of Lansdowne Place and extending E to MERTON AVENUE, drydashed local authority housing by the Dundee City Architect, *J. McLellan Brown*, 1946–51, still traditional in design with red-tiled piended roofs and jerkinhead front gables. Further E, in FOGGYLEY GARDENS beside Clement Park, four ten-storey cruciform blocks of flats, by the *Scottish Special Housing Association*, 1958–61, each with a small lift tower at the centre of the oversailing flat roof and balconies at the face of each arm. Further W, off Coupar Angus Road, in LANSDOWNE GARDENS, mature specimen trees planted as a setting for The Cottage (demolished). At the street's W end, monopitch-roofed low-rise late C20 housing. This preludes two fifteen-storey tower blocks (PITALPIN COURT and LANSDOWNE COURT) by *Crudens Ltd*, 1962–4, and identical to the contemporary Burnside Court and Ancrum Court (*see* above). More Victorian planting including a large monkey-puzzle in DRYBURGH GARDENS immediately N where the grounds of the demolished Dryburgh House were developed in 1958–9 with four ten-storey blocks of flats by the *Scottish Special Housing Association* to the same design as their blocks in Foggyley Gardens (*see* above).

CLEMENT PARK
Clement Park Place

Jacobean mansion designed by *James Maclaren* for James Cox, senior partner in Cox Brothers, owners of the Camperdown Works, who named the house in honour of his wife, Clementina Carmichael.

It was built apparently in two stages between 1854 and *c.* 1860. The first stage comprised the W part, a vertically proportioned asymmetrical L-plan house, the principal elevations finished with pierced and ball-finialled parapets. These face S over the Camperdown Works to Balgay Hill and W towards the arboreal parkland of Camperdown House. From the S (entrance) front's slightly advanced and gabled W end projects a battlemented two-storey canted bay window. At the front's E end where the parapet rises into a gablet, a single-storey rectangular bay window. The detail of its pierced parapet is repeated but with the addition of a heraldic lion at the entrance portico which extends to the E. Behind the portico, a tall and square tower, its surmounting parapet also pierced, the top-floor windows each of three round-headed lights. Rising above the tower's NE corner, a battlemented turret.

The E range, which extended the original L of the house to a U, seems to belong to a second stage of construction. This range's broad S gable is shaped and finialled, with gargoyles sitting on the cusps. Three-light first-floor window under a stepped hoodmould. At the ground floor, a canted bay window with round-headed lights. Round-headed lights also at the first-floor window in the recessed link to the 1854 tower. In front of this link, a single-storey Gothic conservatory filling the space between the portico and the E range. The side elevations are treated in similar but less assertive manner, wall-head chimneys prominent. At the W range's NE corner, a second tower, with an iron-crested French pavilion roof. The N end of the principal ranges' U is closed by a low service range. NW wing added as a maternity block by *Allan & Friskin*, 1934, when the house was used as a Salvation Army hostel.

CAMPERDOWN WORKS
METHVEN STREET

In the late C19 the largest jute works in the world. There survives a handful of huge buildings, including the great chimney (Cox's

Stack) which, until the advent of tower blocks in the later C20, was Dundee's most prominent architectural landmark on the approaches to the city from the Carse of Gowrie and the Tay Rail Bridge. These stand to the S and SW of an expanse of a car park which serves the leisure and retail centre now built on the other sides of the factory site.

The partnership of Cox Brothers was established in 1840 by four scions of a local family long engaged in the manufacture, bleaching and merchandise of linen. The nucleus of the Camperdown Works, a 3.24 ha. field beside the Lochee Burn was acquired for a water-powered linen works in 1850 and construction of its first major building (the Lower Factory) housing both power looms and handlooms begun in the same year. There quickly followed major expansion of the works and their diversification into the manufacture of jute (its raw material imported from Bangladesh), the Crimean War of 1854–6 having both increased the demand for materials for military equipment and cut off Russian supplies of hemp and flax. The Lower Factory was extended and building of the High Mill to its S begun in 1857. Expansion, with demand for jute further increased by the American Civil War of 1861–5, continued through the 1860s. A branch railway serving the works was opened in 1861, and Dundee Harbour's Camperdown Dock for the direct importation of jute to Dundee in 1865. Also in 1865 was begun the erection of Cox's Stack, the 86.5 m.-high chimney which asserted the works' aspiration to be seen as the most prominent of all the Dundee textile mills. By the end of the C19 the Camperdown Works, with a labour force of 5,000, covered over 11 ha. After the First World War the Scottish jute industry was hit by competition from Indian factories and the economic depression of the 1920s and 1930s, and from the 1950s with introduction of polymer-based manufactures, the demand for jute products decreased sharply. Camperdown Works finally closed in 1981 and all the unlisted buildings on the site were demolished soon after. In the 1990s the Calender was converted to commercial use, the High Mill and some warehouses to housing and Cox's Stack preserved as a landmark.

Methven Street was the approach to the works. On its N side, the former CALENDER designed by *George A. Cox*, the youngest of the Cox brothers and an engineer. Its first stage, built in 1862–5, comprised six parallel ranges covered with piended slated roofs. The long ashlar-faced side fronting the street was of twenty bays, the twelve E bays (originally inside the works' entrance) of one tall storey, the eight to the W with a basement in the fall of the ground. Quite plain except for a wall-head cornice and parapet. The other elevations, except for the E front's S end, were of rubble. Interior divided into longitudinal aisles by cast-iron columns supporting the kingpost-truss roofs. At the NE corner, a parapeted two-storey tower which housed a beam engine. The calender was extended W in the same manner in 1882–3. On its conversion to shopping use by *James*

F. Stephen, 1990–1, the S front's two E bays were unified to contain a huge segmental-arched entrance and all the ranges except the S covered by a single metal-sheet roof; at the E end, a porch dressed up with a pair of cupola-topped pavilion roofs. Much of the C19 internal structure survives in the S range.

The GATEWAY into the works, also by *George A. Cox* and of 1862, extends S from the calender across Methven Street, its present position a little W of the original. Broad central cart entrance, the square ashlar piers with fluted bases and finished with cornices from which rise stepped pedestals surmounted by scrolled and foliaged gaslight holders, their mantles decorated with anthemion ornament. Each side, a mutule-corniced pedestrian gateway.

COUNTING HOUSE of a tall single storey, by *George A. Cox*, 1862, on the S side of Methven Street but only the creeper-clad N and E walls survive to enclose a garden in front of MULLIGAN COURT, a block of flats designed by *James F. Stephen* and built on the site in 1991–3. The dignified but unostentatious frontages are of stugged ashlar (now badly eroded), finished with a wall-head cornice and parapet. At the N front's W end, a round-headed door flanked by round-headed windows (the r. a dummy). Symmetrical ten-bay E elevation facing into the works. Canted bay windows at the last-but-one bays. Centrepiece formed by a pair of three-light windows flanked by keystoned round-headed doors set between piers which carry wall-head projections.

113 The HIGH MILL, a jute-spinning mill and the largest of the works' buildings, occupies most of the S side of the present leisure and shopping centre's huge car park. Designed by *George A. Cox* with assistance from *Peter Carmichael*, it was built in three stages between 1857 and 1868 and converted to housing by *James F. Stephen* in 1993–5. Huge edifice, the main (N) block of three storeys and an attic above a partly exposed basement. 131 m.-long front of forty bays, the procession of regularly spaced large rectangular windows broken by two asymmetrically placed advanced and pedimented sections. Stugged rough ashlar walling composed of narrow blocks, relieved by polished dressings. Cornice placed a little below the wall-head, the masonry above appearing as a parapet. Slated mansard roof, the lower pitch's original continuous band of glazing replaced in the 1990s by a metal strip broken by skylights; dormer windows added at the same time to the upper pitch. The main cornice is carried across the two advanced sections but, above, each is crossed by a pair of band courses, the lower forming the sill of an attic window, the upper the base of a pediment with ball finials at the ends and an elongated urn on the apex; in the tympanum, a large round-headed architraved and keystoned window flanked by stumpy pilasters on scrolled bases. Projecting N from the front's E corner is a tall square clock tower, its lowest stage of channelled and polished ashlar. At the NE corner, a curvaceous wrought-iron lamp bracket of *c.* 1868. Channelled strip quoins at the corners of the two

stages above, their windows in minimally lugged architraves and with simple moulded corbels under the sill ends; cornice just above the cornice of the main range. Taller fourth stage, its strip quoins unchannelled and pilaster-like, the panelled walling of each face containing a large round-headed window. This stage is corniced and balustraded, the N and S balustrades broken by pediments. Slightly set-back and still taller fifth stage, also with pilaster-like strip quoins. In the panelled fronts, two-light windows under round clock faces; modillion cornice. Above, a low octagonal pedestal on which stands a Roman Doric-columned cupola, also octagonal. Delicately foliaged ironwork in the open sides, a ball finial on the ogee-domed roof.

The end elevations of the High Mill are each of four bays. The W of 1857–60 is plain, the change in the roof pitches marked by steps in the gable. At the two centre bays of the basement, a corniced rectangular projection. The E end of *c.* 1865–8 is more elaborate. Round-headed openings to the ground floor. The head of the gable is crossed by band courses whose outer ends are linked vertically by scrolls and pilaster-like strip quoins which hide the lower pitches of the mansard roof. The round-arched and keystoned heads of a pair of windows break though the upper band course which serves as the base of the gable's pedimented head. Oculus in the pediment; elongated urn finial. Regularly windowed but plain S elevation. At its E corner, a lamp bracket like the one on the NE tower.

Projecting S of the High Mill's main range is a full-length and deep block, its E two-thirds built *c.* 1857–62, the W third erected at the same date as a lower boiler house but rebuilt or reconstructed *c.* 1865–8 when it was brought to the same height as the rest. The whole of this block is now a uniform one storey and basement, the basement fully exposed in the fall of the ground to the rear. Quite plain except for a cornice and parapet.

The INTERIOR was all of fire-proof construction, the floors formed on shallow brick tunnel vaults supported by cast-iron columns and beams. The roofs were carried on cast-iron trusses pierced by light-hearted Gothic tracery. At the lower S block whose serrated roof's S pitches were longer than the N, the trusses' off-centre arch-heads are filled with quatrefoils, the spandrels with cusped forms. Each floor of the N block was divided into three longitudinal aisles and the upper floor and E two-thirds of the basement in the S range into five aisles. However, in the W third of this basement the vaults run transversely. The S range's basement (now garaging) retains its C19 form. Also intact is the roof structure of the two N aisles of the S block's upper floor, their covering removed in the 1990s when an internal courtyard was formed here. Four bays of this block's roof structure and supporting columns have also been re-erected in a garden immediately E of the High Mill. At the E end of the N block, its original ground-floor construction is still visible, with the elliptical brick vaults running E–W and carried on sturdier columns than those in the basement of the S block. In the W of the N block's N projections, the beams under the ground-floor vaulting are pierced by ovals.

E of the High Mill and at the same level as its basement is the surviving S wall of the BOILERS, the boiler house to serve the whole works built in 1865–6. It was designed by *George A. Cox* together with Cox's Stack to which it was linked by underground flues. The front is of the usual stugged ashlar, broken by an array of twenty-four round-headed arches, the six at the W end lower than the others.

114 COX'S STACK, on higher ground immediately to the NE, is the works' most prominent feature and the best-known symbol of Dundee as a Victorian industrial city. Cox was engineer for this single 86.5 m.-high chimney which replaced the three separate and utilitarian chimneys which had previously served the different parts of the complex. *James Maclaren* designed its fancy-dress Italian campanile appearance. Rising from a battered base of hammer-dressed ashlar is the square chimney, its red brickwork joyously decorated with bands and ornamentation of white brick. High pedestal with decoratively panelled corner strips and a frieze ornamented with diamonds; in the centre of each face, a double-lugged rectangular panel set among small diamonds. The immensely tall main stage is slightly set back. At each face, banded corner strips form a round-headed overarch. At the bottom, a diamond-shaped panel, its sides extruded to form small diamonds at the corners; above, a nine-stage tier of tiny round-headed dummy windows under a small round light, also a dummy, in the head of the overarch. Closely spaced bands of white brick mark off the next stage which is pierced by pairs of tall dummy windows and finished with a band of Greek key ornament below the rosetted frieze under the cornice, its balustrade and corner finials now lost. The Stack's top stage is a high octagonal 'belfry' decorated with banding; in each face, a round-headed dummy opening. The belfry's moulded cornice has been removed.

All the other buildings of Camperdown Works N of the High Mill have been demolished. On their site, the STACK LEISURE PARK, an expanse of parking fringed by large pavilions with boldly oversailing ribbed metal roofs, by *James F. Stephen*, 1990–3. Walls of red brick, the decorative motifs derived from Cox's Stack in misplaced homage to a great industrial monument.

S of the High Mill's E end, a three-storey range of rubble-built warehouses of 1861–2, presumably designed by *George A. Cox*, which stood on the W side of the branch railway to the works. Small horizontally proportioned windows and ball-and-spike finials on the gables; in the splayed gable to Burnside Street, a round-headed and keystoned attic window. They were converted to housing (CALEDONIAN COURT) by *James F. Stephen* in 1991–3. S of Burnside Street, a second range, of 1872 and extended S in 1882, the splayed N corner with another but dummy attic window of the same design. Over Burnside

Street's E end, a RAILWAY BRIDGE of 1861 which carried the branch line. Splayed elliptical arch of rough ashlar with channelled soffit and hammer-dressed voussoirs; rubble parapets.

LOGIE, BLACKNESS AND BALGAY

Spilling out W from the city centre and now cut off from it by a dual carriageway, Logie developed from the early C19 as an irregularly planned and tight-knit agglomeration of mills and other industrial buildings with some Late Victorian housing laid out to the N and NW between Lochee Road and City Road. In 1919 the generously planned Logie housing scheme was laid out between the C19 industrial area and Balgay Hill whose S slope has acquired a C20 and early C21 fringe of villas and private housing.

CHURCHES AND PLACES OF WORSHIP

BALGAY PARISH CHURCH, corner of Lochee Road and Tullideph Road. Originally St Thomas' Church. By *Johnston & Baxter*, 1900–2. Lancet Gothic, built of stugged and squared buff-coloured masonry. Nave with lean-to aisles, N transepts, a low N apse and a SW porch; SE tower in the inner angle of

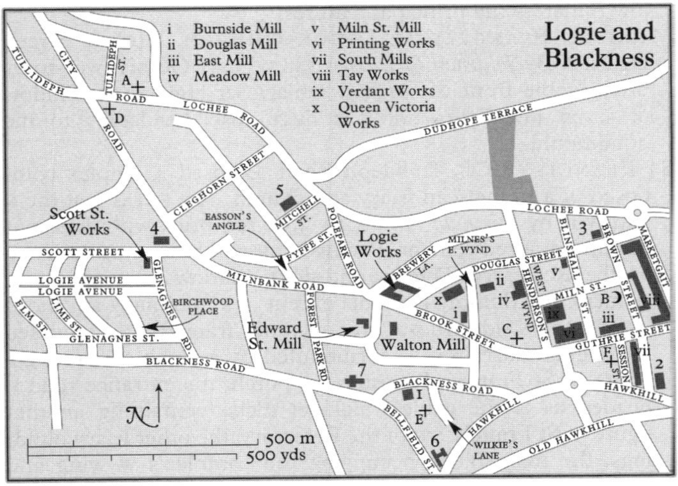

- A Balgay Parish Church
- B Jamia Mosque
- C Morison Evangelical Union Church
- D St Francis (R.C.)
- E St Joseph (R.C.)
- F St Mary Magdalene (Episcopal)
- 1 Al-Maktoum Institute
- 2 Brown Street School
- 3 Drill Hall
- 4 Logie Church Hall
- 5 Mitchell Street Centre
- 6 St Joseph's Primary School
- 7 Tayside Fire and Rescue

the nave and E aisle. The tower is of three stages, with a diagonal buttress extending from the SE corner and a slab-spired octagonal turret at the SW. At the bottom stage, an E door and S window, their hoodmoulds' label stops carved with foliage, small cusped windows at the second stage and hoodmoulded belfry openings at the third. Wall-head finished with a band of ballflower decoration, griffons at the corners and a stepped parapet.

The INTERIOR is divided into a nave and aisles by arcades, the octagonal piers carrying pointed arches. Open wooden roof, its collars pierced by quatrefoils and circlets. S gallery, the space below screened off in 2002 to form a vestibule. N apse entered through a pointed stone arch. – Bench PEWS of 1902. – Simple Gothic PULPIT, also of 1902, on the l. of the chancel arch. – In the apse, a late C20 COMMUNION TABLE by the *Lord Roberts Workshops*. – STAINED GLASS. In the apse, three clearly drawn and brightly coloured lights (the Church Family) by *Susan Bradbury* of the *Stained Glass Design Partnership*, 1995. – In the vestibule, three lights (the Church Built on a Rock Withstanding the Floods), also by Bradbury and of 1997.

HALL to the W, by *Joseph Johnston*, begun in 1939 but not completed until ten years later. Faintly ecclesiastical, with a louvred square cupola. N extension of 1978.

JAMIA MOSQUE (DUNDEE MOSQUE), Miln Street. By *Lucas Dow Design Studios*, 1997–2000. Small and not very ambitious Postmodern version of traditional Islamic architecture with low minarets the principal features.

MORISON EVANGELICAL UNION CHURCH, Guthrie Street. Disused. By *Johnston & Baxter*, 1887. Fussy Gothic two-storey broad gable front of stugged ashlar. Set high up, a window of seven low lights under a huge rose; headstops to the hoodmould.

ST FRANCIS (R.C.), Tullideph Road. Disused. Complex composed of a Franciscan friary and church. The FRIARY at the N and W is by *Reginald Fairlie*, 1933, of red brick with dressings of buff-coloured cement. The two-storey N block was designed as the Refectory. The ground-floor windows are set under semicircular dummy fanlights except at a minimally advanced bay on the S side whose large window, framed by a moulded rectangular surround, is surmounted by a niche containing a figure of St Francis. Two-storey E porch, the entrance round-headed as is the gable's high-set niche containing another figure of St Francis. SW of the Refectory, the other friary buildings, the main block occupying the complex's W wing and fronted by a passage whose external wall's round-headed arcading, blind except for small window openings, suggests a cloister.

The CHURCH itself, occupying most of the E side of the complex, is by *A. R. Conlon* of *Reginald Fairlie & Partners*, 1957–9, and much less dominant than the previously intended edifice. Hall-like, with a large stone CALVARY in a corniced surround on the S gable. Tall round-headed windows in the E side and rectangular clearstorey lights in the W. Stumpy SE tower. Across the S gable, a porch under a stone RELIEF by *Hew Lorimer* of St Francis's Return to Assisi at the End of his Life.

Inside, the vestibule's SE corner under the tower is partitioned off by a wrought-iron screen to form a baptistery (no longer used as such). Boarded wagon roof over the nave. At the N end of its E side, a short aisle containing confessionals. Short and narrower sidelit N chancel. – In the former baptistery, a colourful STAINED GLASS window of *c.* 1960 (the Holy Spirit as a Dove Descending on Dundee).

ST JOSEPH (R.C.), Wilkie's Lane. Partly hidden behind its accompanying clergy house and school (now the Al-Maktoum Institute for Arabic and Islamic Studies, *see* Public Buildings, below), a crowstep-gabled and lancet-windowed cruciform, by *Ellis & Wilson*, 1872–4. Gableted bellcote on the S (liturgical W) gable. Hoodmoulded principal entrance at the E side's slightly advanced and gabled S bay, the two doors divided by a granite-shafted column. Above the entrance, a three-light window, the central opening a dummy which serves as a niche for a figure of St Joseph Holding the Holy Child. Diagonally set porch in the inner angle of the E transept and nave.

Bare INTERIOR, the starker since the walls of the chancel and the (liturgical) E sides of the transepts were stripped of plaster to leave the rubble masonry exposed. – Over the High Altar an elaborate REREDOS designed by *P. P. Pugin* in 1900, its boldly projecting canopy covering the altar's tabernacle. Woodwork and carving by *Boulton & Sons*, painted depictions of angels by *John Hardman & Co.* – Painted STATIONS OF THE CROSS by *Édouard Cabane*, 1875. – ORGAN of the 1870s in the (liturgical) W gallery.

STAINED GLASS. In the chancel's apse, four lights (Evangelists) by *David Small*, 1878. – In the (liturgical) N transept's Chapel of the Sacred Heart, a three-light window (the Sacred Heart with SS Augustine, Francis, Catherine of Siena and Margaret) and, in the flanking lights, St Bridget and St Margaret of Scotland, all by *Barnett & Son*, *c.* 1890. – In the (liturgical) S transept's Chapel of the Immaculate Conception, another three-light window (the Immaculate Conception with SS Joseph, John the Evangelist, Anne and Dominic) flanked by a pair of single lights (St Andrew and St Patrick), all of 1887 and by *Barnett & Son*. – In the (liturgical) N wall of the nave, a three-light window (the Risen Lord Appearing to St Thomas) of *c.* 1905. – In the nave's (liturgical) S wall, another three-light window (the Presentation of Our Lord in the Temple) of 1899. – In the vestibule, one brightly coloured and rather crude light (St John the Baptist) of *c.* 1900.

Ecclesiastical Gothic CLERGY HOUSE, of 1876 and also by *Ellis & Wilson*, on the E side of the chancel.

ST MARY MAGDALENE (Episcopal), Blinshall Street. Now a rock-climbing centre (AVERTICAL WORLD). Geometrical Gothic, by *Coe & Goodwin*, 1853–4. Nave with a N aisle and a lower short chancel; small spire-roofed octagonal stair-tower at the SW corner. At the front (W) gable, a hoodmoulded door under a four-light window and a crowning twin-arched and gableted bellcote. Basement, originally containing a school and vestry, hidden from the street but exposed behind, with mullioned rectangular windows.

Inside, scissor-truss nave roof. Octagonal stone piers carry the pointed arches of the N arcade. Narrow chancel, its entrance arch springing from pendant corbels and flanked by depressed arches (now blocked) to the flanking chapel and organ chamber. The E wall under its three-light window was covered with a mosaic REREDOS designed by *William Butterfield* in 1865.

BALGAY CEMETERY, BALGAY PARK AND VICTORIA PARK

off Balgay Road and Glamis Road

Balgay Cemetery and Balgay Park were laid out by *Alexander Tower* and the Dundee Burgh Superintendent of Cemeteries, *W. R. Mackelvie*, in 1870–1 and extended in 1903. Victoria Park to the SE was opened in 1906.

BALGAY CEMETERY, abundantly planted with evergreens and shrubs, rises to a ridge on whose top stand the principal Late Victorian and early C20 MONUMENTS. Among them is the burial enclosure formed in the early C20 for the bishops and clergy of the Roman Catholic diocese of Dunkeld. At the centre of its segmental screen wall, a gabled and segmental-headed niche containing the coat of arms of the diocese above the small effigy of a bishop. From the cemetery's NE corner a cast-iron FOOTBRIDGE of 1877 designed by the Dundee Burgh Engineer, *William Mackison*, crosses a gorge to the side of Balgay Hill. One broad elliptical span with latticed spandrels and a very short straight-lintelled side span at each end; balustrade of Gothic arches intersecting at top and bottom.

In BALGAY PARK, a (roofless) PAVILION of 1877, the structure rebuilt in 1997 after a fire, on the S side of Balgay Hill. Brick wall fronted by a cast-iron veranda, its centre breaking forward as a half-octagon. Acanthus-capitalled columns carry the pointed arches, their spandrels decorated with scrolls and flowery circles. – In front of the pavilion, a semicircular-topped WELL-HEAD probably of the earlier C19, its round-headed niche with a lion's-head keystone.

THE MILLS OBSERVATORY on the summit of Balgay Hill, built in terms of the will of John Mills, a Dundee linen manufacturer, in 1932–3, was designed by the Dundee City Architect, *David B. McLay*. Latin cross, the ashlar masonry hammer-dressed but polished at the entrance's surround and the parapets, the E, W and S arms single-storey, the N (containing the stair) higher and with canted corners and tall windows. Two-stage centre composed of superimposed octagons, the smaller upper storey surmounted by a rotating papier maché dome which opens to allow the telescope to poke out. On each floor of the main block, a circular room. In its centre, a tapered pier rising from the bedrock to support the cast-iron stand of the TELESCOPE by *Thomas Cooke & Sons*, 1871, formerly at the University of St Andrews and erected here in 1952. Surrounding the central pier, a circular bench, the upper floor's seat pierced with decorative patterns and its back with Gothic arcading.

PUBLIC BUILDINGS

AL-MAKTOUM INSTITUTE FOR ARABIC AND ISLAMIC STUDIES, corner of Blackness Road and Wilkie's Lane. Formerly St Joseph's School. The original (W) part is Free Style, by *James H. Langlands*, 1905–6, built of hammer-dressed squared masonry. Principal block of two storeys, with large round-headed mullioned-and-transomed windows and an Art Nouveauish lead cupola. Taller and curvaceously parapeted tower-like front block containing the entrance hall, stair and cloakrooms. Semicircular canopy on heavy corbels over the doorway. Small windows, the stair's placed diagonally, the cloakrooms' in mullioned horizontal strips. Ashlar-fronted E addition by *Allan & Friskin*, 1933, in a vertical *moderne* manner with narrow canted and tapering buttresses between the windows.

BROWN STREET SCHOOL, corner of Brown Street and Hawkhill. Now a bar. Built *c*. 1855 as a two-storey Neo-Jacobean rectangle. In 1874–5 *David Maclaren* of *Ireland & Maclaren* enlarged it by the addition of a large jamb, also Jacobean in manner, extending from the centre of the W side.

DRILL HALL, Brown Street. Now in other use. By *Leslie Ower*, 1909. Single-storey with a prominent round-headed entrance in the S gable. On the E side, a two-storey office wing of blocky Jacobean Renaissance character but with tapering wall-head chimneys to give a hint of Art Nouveau.

GIRLS' INDUSTRIAL SCHOOL, Blackness Road, W of Balgay Road. Now in other use. By *James Maclaren & Sons*, 1893–6, and built as a reformatory to house 'the waifs and strays of city life'. Jacobean Renaissance, with shaped gables, pedimented dormerheads to the windows of the upper floor, and some strapwork decoration. Conical-roofed corner towers grip the S front's taller centrepiece which boasts a Roman Doric-columned entrance, a canted oriel window and iron-crested French pavilion roof.

LOGIE CHURCH HALL, Scott Street. Now in other use. By *Robert Keith*, 1888. Built of badly weathered stugged masonry, a piend-roofed lancet-windowed box. Hoodmoulded elliptical-arched doors to the S porches; gableted large window in the W gable. Fleur-de-lis finials to the roof's gableted ventilators. Inside, a wagon roof with a herringbone-pattern boarded ceiling above the hammerbeam trusses.

THE MILLS OBSERVATORY. *See* BALGAY CEMETERY, BALGAY PARK AND VICTORIA PARK (above).

MITCHELL STREET CENTRE, Mitchell Street. Originally Mitchell Street School. As first built to *David Maclaren*'s design in 1883–4, this was single-storey. Seven-bay S front, with windows of three steeped lights at the advanced ends and two lights at the centre, all linked by a sill course minimally projected on rounded corbels under the end and central openings. In 1893–5 *James H. Langlands* added an upper storey and French pavilion-roofed low towers on the E and W sides. Piended roof with bracketed eaves. The bowed porch in the E tower's S inner angle was provided, *c.* 2000.

ROYAL VICTORIA HOSPITAL, Elliot Road. Georgian mansion house converted to a hospital for incurables by *J. Murray Robertson*, 1898–9.

BALGAY HOUSE, the principal building of *c.* 1790, built for Captain David Anderson on his return from service in India. Originally of two storeys. Ashlar-faced S front of eleven bays, the centre three minimally advanced under a pediment, its tympanum pierced by an oculus; more boldly advanced two-bay ends. A pair of band courses between the ground and first floors. Robertson placed a dormer-windowed mansard roof over the seven central bays and heightened the ends as low towers with flattened ogee roofs. Also Robertson's is the entrance's Roman Doric aedicular doorpiece. At the W end, a late C20 link to a villa-like two-storey ward block (originally for cancer patients) by *James Findlay*, 1904–6, a verandaed bow, also of two storeys, at the front's l. end. Low-key harled additions of the later C20 at the main building's E end.

ST JOSEPH'S PRIMARY SCHOOL, corner of Hawkhill and Bellfield Street. Neo-Georgian, by *Thoms & Wilkie*, 1931–2. Two-storeyed U of brown brick with white-painted cement dressings and a few tiled decorative panels, the main range piend-roofed. Large but traditionally proportioned windows.

TAYSIDE FIRE AND RESCUE HEADQUARTERS, Blackness Road. By *James Parr & Partners* 1967–70. Three-storey flat-roofed box of aggregate panels and glass. Single-storey brick garage for fire engines at the E end.

DESCRIPTION

WEST MARKETGAIT'S dual carriageway cuts off the tight-knit predominantly industrial quarter of Blackness at the SE corner of the area from the City Centre. At its S end, on the corner with Hawkhill, WESTPORT AND GROSVENOR CASINO, by *James F. Stephen*, 2008–9, a complex also containing flats. Straightforward blocks faced with brown brick, render and glass to the S and W; big bowed corner feature sheathed in green and black cladding. To the N, the long expanse of the former Tay Works (*see* Industrial Buildings, below), the weaving sheds (refronted by *Urquhart Lindsay & Co.*, 1872) of the demolished Dudhope Works forming a small N appendage. Behind, on the SE corner of BROWN STREET and West Port, the former Brown Street Public School (*see* Public Buildings, above). On Brown Street's W side, between West Port and Guthrie Street, the former South Mills (*see* Industrial Buildings, below). N of Guthrie Street, the back of the former Tay Works' N part (Old Mill Complex) faced, on the W, by the car park of the Jamia Mosque (*see* Churches and Places of Worship, above). At the top of Brown Street, on its NW corner with DOUGLAS STREET, a former Drill Hall (*see* Public Buildings, above). On the SW corner of Douglas Street and BLINSHALL STREET, the surviving warehouses of the Miln Street Mill (*see* Industrial Buildings, below). At Blinshall Street's S end, the former St Mary Magdalene Episcopal Church (*see* Churches and Places of Worship, above). It is cut off from WEST PORT by THE HUB, a large five- and six-storey housing development by *James F. Stephen*, 2007, wall-like but cheerful in render, wood and brick. At The Hub's E end, the former South Mills (*see* Industrial Buildings, below) in SESSION STREET and stretching back to Guthrie Street.

GUTHRIE STREET'S N side between Session Street and Blinshall Street is filled by the former East Mill and the next block W by D. C. Thomson's (originally John Leng & Co. Ltd's) printing works with a return along West Henderson Wynd. On the S side of Guthrie Street, between Blinshall Street and Horsewater Wynd, former flax warehouses (for all these, *see* Industrial Buildings, below).

WEST HENDERSON WYND runs N. On the E side and with a wing extending along MILN STREET is the Verdant Works. On West Henderson Wynd's SW corner with Douglas Street, the former Meadow Mill and, to its W, the former Douglas Mill (for these, *see* Industrial Buildings, below).

In GUTHRIE STREET W of West Henderson Wynd, the former Morison Evangelical Union Church (*see* Churches and Places of Worship, above). At the beginning of BROOK STREET, the W continuation of Guthrie Street, on the corner of Milne's East Wynd, a STONE carved in the late C20 with reliefs of mythical animals. In MILNE'S EAST WYND, the former Burnside Mill and, to its N, on the SW corner of Douglas Street, the former Queen Victoria Works and, on the N side of Douglas Street, the Park Mill (for these, *see* Industrial Buildings, below).

In BROOK COURT, S of Brook Street, the former Walton Mill. Very much larger and filling the coffin-shaped space between BROOK STREET, LOWER PLEASANCE and BREWERY LANE is the great edifice of the former Logie Works. EDWARD STREET runs S from Brook Street's W end past the former Edward Street Mill (for these, *see* Industrial Buildings, below).

MILNBANK ROAD exiting W from Brook Street marks the transition from industrial to residential. On its gusset corner with POLEPARK ROAD, a four-storey tenement (Nos. 1–9 Milnbank Road and Nos. 2–12 Polepark Road) by *Young & Meldrum*, 1871. Projecting from the corner, a bow corbelled to the square at the third floor and finished with a steep and narrow crowstepped gable. Elliptical-arched windows to the first floor and huge double-keyhole dummy gunloops. On Milnbank Road's S side, No. 10, a single-storey-and-basement house of *c.* 1840. Three-bay front of badly weathered stugged ashlar, the ground-floor openings corniced, the windows with aprons, the doorpiece pilastered; parapet on the wall-head cornice. Beside it, at No. 12, a warehouse (*see* Industrial Buildings, below). Further W, two Late Georgian piend-roofed villas (No. 24 and No. 32) which flank the entrance to Forrest Park Road. No. 24 is by *David Neave*, *c.* 1815, with corniced ground-floor windows flanking the Ionic-pilastered and pedimented doorpiece. The similar but lower No. 32 is of *c.* 1825. At the S end of Forrest Park Road and fronting BLACKNESS ROAD, the unassertive Tayside Fire and Rescue Headquarters and, to its E, on the corner of WILKIE'S LANE, the Al-Maktoum Institute for Arabic and Islamic Studies, a much more forceful design despite its relatively unimportant position (for these, *see* Public Buildings, above). Behind this former school, St Joseph's (R.C.) Church and, to its S, facing HAWKHILL, St Joseph's Primary School.

In EASSON ANGLE, N of Milnbank Road, a piend-roofed two-storey double house of the earlier C19 (Nos. 3–5), the ashlar front over-cleaned, the paired doors with consoled cornices. The street leads to FLEUCHAR STREET where Nos. 12–18 are four mid-C19 Georgian survival houses, alternately of one and two storeys above a basement, all with heavy corniced doorpieces. In FYFFE STREET to the E, Nos. 1–7, a three-storey block of flats by *J. Morrison*, 1935–6. Basically U-plan but with a notch taken out of the long S side. Squared-up Neo-Georgian in stugged ashlar. In MITCHELL STREET to the N, the Mitchell Street Centre (*see* Public Buildings, above). At the street's E end, LOCHEE ROAD. Its SE stretch leading downhill towards West Marketgait is post-industrial wasteland but, on the corner of Park Street, a solitary Late Georgian survival. Three-storey-and-attic tenement (No. 112), the five-bay front of stugged ashlar and with a chimney-topped central gablet. At the building's E end, a pair of single-storey contemporary cottages. In Lochee Road NW of Mitchell Street late C19 tenements lead towards Balgay Parish Church and St Francis' (R.C.) Church (*see* Churches and Places of Worship, above). A little W of Balgay Parish Church, pyramid-topped panelled ashlar gatepiers of 1837 at the entrance to the former LOGIE GRAVEYARD, its C19 monuments routine.

CITY ROAD descends back to the SE where, off its E side in PITFOUR STREET, etc., are late C19 'colonies' type developments, i.e. two-storey buildings containing flats, the upper and lower entered from different sides, each with a garden. On City Road's W side, late C19 tenements. From its S end, SCOTT STREET exits W. On the N side, the former Logie Church Hall (*see* Public Buildings, above) and on the corner with Glenagnes Road the former Scott Street Works (*see* Industrial Buildings, below). The LOGIE HOUSING DEVELOPMENT to the SW was built in 1919–20 under the general superintendence of the

Dundee City Architect, *James Thomson*, but with individual sections designed by an array of local private architects, *Maclaren, Sons & Soutar, Bruce, Son & Morton, H. Thomson, W. B. D. Keith* and *Thoms & Wilkie*. Short curved streets (SYCAMORE PLACE, ELM STREET, LIME STREET, ASHBANK ROAD, BIRCHWOOD PLACE and GLENAGNES ROAD) extending from the central spine of LOGIE AVENUE and containing piend-roofed two-storey blocks of flats appearing externally as double houses; sparing brick embellishment on the pebble-dashed walls. Unusually for the date, warmth was provided by a communal heating system. At the W end, a viewing platform looking over the Firth of Tay to Fife.

BALGAY beyond is leafy, the Balgay Cemetery, Balgay Park and Victoria Park (*see* above) forming a horseshoe round Balgay Hill, its summit the site of The Mills Observatory, its lower S slope of the former Girls' Industrial School and Royal Victoria Hospital.

INDUSTRIAL BUILDINGS

BURNSIDE MILL, Milne's East Wynd. Surviving mill (converted to housing, 2004) of a jute works. It is a rubble-walled three-storey-and-attic block of *c.* 1865. Seven-bay E elevation, the windows (now with cement margins) generously sized except at the attic where they are low and horizontal under the eaves and at the S end where four floors are contained in the height of the building. Late C20 painted brick addition at the N end.

COFFIN MILL. *See* LOGIE WORKS.

DOUGLAS MILL, corner of Douglas Street and Milne's East Wynd. Rubble-walled mill (now in other use) of a jute works, built *c.* 1835. Two-storey-and-attic, the SE corner rising as a low square tower which served as the base of a brick chimney (removed). Two bays W of the chimney is a full-height engine-house window. Single-storey preparing shed of *c.* 1850 behind.

EAST MILL, corner of Guthrie Street and Blinshall Street. A tannery of *c.* 1792 converted to a flax-spinning mill in 1799 and much extended in the mid C19, this was the first successful steam-powered flax mill in Scotland. All rubble-built (now partly rendered) and unassuming. The original part, at the W, is of two storeys and an attic with a basement partly exposed in the fall of the ground to the E. Ten bays, the ground-floor windows much enlarged in the C20. E extension of 1846–51, also of ten bays and with altered ground-floor windows. The first-floor W window lighting the engine house is taller than the others. Hoist doors in the centre of the E gable.

EDWARD STREET MILL, Edward Street. Converted to housing, 2006. Power-loom mill for the weaving of linen damasks built in 1851. Three-storey-and-attic main block of hammer-dressed ashlar. N front of nineteen bays, the three at each end minimally advanced. Rectangular and oval windows in the E gable.

At the rear the walling of the upper floors is carried on cast-iron columns, the ground floor originally opening into a single-storey block of weaving sheds behind, its eight-bay E front with three-light end windows and a wall-head parapet.

LOGIE WORKS, Brook Street, Lower Pleasance and Brewery Lane. Sprawling flax mill (converted to housing, 1997) of modest architectural pretension. It developed from 1828 on a not very regular U-plan. The earliest part is the four-storey rubble-walled S range built in 1828–33. Regularly windowed twenty-three bay S front, the ground-floor openings now built-up. Each end bay is of the same height but contained an engine house of three tall storeys and with three-light windows, the ground- and first-floor openings with segmental-arched dummy fanlights. The E end was surmounted by a bellcote, its base still extant. Splayed five-bay boiler house to the E, its upper floors added *c.* 1835 to raise it to the same height as the rest of the range. Similar N elevation to the courtyard behind but the ground-floor windows unblocked although some have been enlarged and now serve as garage entrances. At the E end, round-headed doorways (now windows) to the boiler house. Under the second-floor window of the E engine house and the two windows flanking it are large rounded stone corbels which formerly carried a cast-iron balcony which gave access from the mill to the boiler house, the two parts cut off internally by the engine house. At the S range's NW corner, a square stair-tower, its lower two-thirds of the same height as the main mill and contemporary with it, the top three floors and pyramidal roof added *c.* 1835. Also of *c.* 1835 are the three-storey W and N ranges, their top floors' painted metal balconies added in 1997. The walling of the W range's upper floors to the court-yard is carried on cast-iron columns, the ground floor originally opening into a preparing shed (demolished).

MEADOW MILL, corner of West Henderson's Wynd and Douglas Street. The mill building (now in commercial use) of a jute works survives. By *Urquhart, Lindsay & Co.*, 1874, it is iron-framed and rubble-walled, of five storeys, with rusticated quoins and a piended roof. Full-height short NE wing. In the main block's thirteen-bay S side, a very tall blocked opening at the W end. In its W gable, a symmetrical disposition of openings, all now blocked, with five windows to the ground floor, two at the first and one each at the second and third. Regular eight-bay arrangement at the main block's E gable and the E side of the wing. In the wing's three-bay N gable, segmental-arched ground-floor doors.

MILN STREET MILL, corner of Blinshall Street and Douglas Street. One surviving warehouse of the flax mill begun in 1833. It is of three bays by three, triple-pile, the piended roofs running N–S. At the N elevation, broad elliptical-arched door-ways; two more doorways at the E front but a window between them.

PARK MILL, Douglas Street. Rubble-walled two-storey-and-attic former jute mill, built *c.* 1850 and doubled in length to fourteen bays *c.* 1865. Triangular arrangement of first-floor and attic windows in the S gable whose ground floor was refaced with a cement imitation of ashlar and given an off-centre broad Neo-Georgian door in the early or mid C20.

PRINTING WORKS, Guthrie Street, Blinshall Street and West Henderson's Wynd. By *T. Lindsay Gray*, and built for John Leng & Co. Ltd, 1959. Two and three storeys. S and W elevations of mixed red and brown brick, the W with a procession of shallow-pitched gables. E block rendered above a brick ground floor. Faint intimations of the Modern Movement (e.g. the large and horizontally proportioned metal-framed windows) but hardly more than utilitarian.

QUEEN VICTORIA WORKS, corner of Douglas Street and Milne's East Wynd. Disused. Three late C19 rubble-built blocks survive of a jute works, all two-storey-and-attic but the E block lower than the other two and piend-roofed. Double-pitch-roofed weaving sheds to the W.

SCOTT STREET WORKS, corner of Glenagnes Road and Scott Street. The piend-roofed two-storey office block (now housing) of a jute-spinning mill survives. It is by *Thoms & Wilkie*, *c.* 1920, and more like a public library than an industrial building. Wrenaissance. At the main (E) front the l. two-thirds are symmetrical, with three-light windows to the ground floor and rusticated surrounds to the windows of the first floor. In the front's r. part, the dignified entrance, its bracketed cornice supported on channelled antae framing Roman Doric columns.

SOUTH MILL, Brown Street. Converted to housing by *Baxter, Clark & Paul*, 1999–2001. Long three-storey-and-attic mansard-roofed flax mill built in stages between 1851 and 1875 for J. & W. Brown (later Brown & Miller, and O. G. Miller & Co.), all rubble-walled and with a cornice below the wall-head. E front of thirty-three bays, the nine S built in the 1850s, the pedimented three-bay section to their r. and the ten bays beyond in 1864. A further three-bay pedimented section N of this and eight more bays to its r. were added in 1874–5. Each pedimented section is minimally advanced, with segmental-arched windows and a moulded cornice-like string course under the second-floor openings. The l. section's first-floor centre window (formerly lighting the engine house) is larger than the others. In this section, a gaping vehicle entrance inserted *c.* 1930. At the rear elevation the walling of the upper floors of the ten bays added in 1864 is carried on cast-iron Roman Doric columns, the ground floor of the mill originally opening directly into a preparing shed (demolished) behind. – To the W and fronting Session Street, the South Mill's OLD MILL, built *c.* 1825 but rather altered since. Two storeys, of rubble, the W front of fourteen bays.

TAY WORKS, West Marketgait. The huge flax and jute works of Gilroy Bros & Co. (later, Gilroy, Sons & Co.) developed in the mid and late C19 on the site of earlier mills along what was then North Tay Street. The principal buildings, facing West *p. 264*

Dundee, Tay Works.
View from east, 1891

Marketgait, are all in a Georgian manner suggestive of barracks architecture.

The MILL itself (converted to student housing and other uses in 1986 and named OLD MILL COMPLEX) was contained in the range N of Guthrie Street. Four-storey-and-attic thirty-five-bay-long N block, the façade of stugged ashlar, austerely detailed with rectangular windows and a wall-head cornice and parapet. It is, at first glance, all of a piece but was built in two stages. The earlier, comprising the S fourteen bays, is of 1851, by *Gilroy Bros & Co.'s Engineering Department*, the two bays at each end minimally advanced and with rusticated quoins; at the ball-finialled S gable, a large attic window flanked by oculi. The twenty-one bays to the N were added, also by *Gilroy Bros & Co.'s Engineering Department*, in 1863–4, their r. fourteen bays repeating the detail of the earlier part, the l. seven bays forming a taller centrepiece with segmental-arched windows and the attic rising as a stone-faced storey above the line of the wall-head cornice which here becomes a panelled band course. Framing the attic windows are pilasters, finialled alternately with anthemion and urns at the outer bays. Pediment over the attic's three centre bays, its tympanum carved with the coat of arms of the burgh of Dundee, its pedestal finial formerly the base for a statue of Minerva, goddess of spinning and weaving. Almost identical rear (W) elevation but it is rubble-built and with a dummy oculus instead of a coat of arms in the centrepiece's pediment.

112 The lower but flashier block S of Guthrie Street (also converted to housing and other uses in 1986) is by *Joseph Lindsay* of *Gilroy Bros & Co.'s Engineering Department*, 1865, almost doubling the length of the mill. Front also of stugged ashlar but

the cornice is placed below the wall-head to suggest a parapet above. It is of three storeys and an attic, the façade of twenty-three bays, the l. two slightly advanced. The twenty-one bays to their r. form a symmetrical composition except that the presence of an engine house at the N end is marked by a consoled pediment over its (blocked) ground-floor door and the large window above, its round-arched head now built-up. Architectural display is concentrated at the advanced and pedimented five-bay centrepiece. Rusticated quoins above its channelled ground floor whose round-headed windows flank a segmental-arched and keystoned pend entrance. Architraved first-floor windows with panelled aprons and alternating triangular and segmental pediments. The second-floor windows' architraves rise to frame shell niches above the openings. Anthemion finials to the centrepiece's overall pediment, its tympanum carved in high relief with a shield bearing the inscription 'R^{G}A/G^{I}LR^{O}Y [for Robert, George and Alexander Gilroy (i.e. Gilroy Bros)]/1865' set in a surround of thistles and roses above a ribbon inscribed TAY WORKS. At this block's ball-finialled S gable, a large round-headed door (blocked) and an attic window flanked by oculi. Similar treatment of the W gable-head of the SW wing facing Guthrie Street which was added *c.* 1870.

Behind the mill's N block, a surviving part of the former DYEWORKS constructed in the 1920s, a detached two-storey-and-attic brick building. Twin-gabled W front to Brown Street, each gable almost wholly glazed below the attic. Pedimented treatment of the gable-heads, with recessed panels set in mutuled brick surrounds and pierced by keystoned oculi. At the dyeworks' NE corner, the ENGINE HOUSE AND CHIMNEY survive from the weaving factory built to *Gilroy Bros & Co.'s Engineering Department*'s design in 1851 (and demolished, 1983–4) on the ground to the N. The two-storey engine house is square and rubble-walled, a pair of large round-headed windows (partly blocked) in the E face. Rising from its NE corner, the tall and tapering square brick chimney. S of the engine house, the long two-storey WEST MILL erected *c.* 1851, also to *Gilroy Bros & Co.'s Engineering Department*'s design, for batching, preparing and winding the flax. E front of stugged ashlar, its segmental-arched cartshed openings formerly covered by a glazed canopy whose cast-iron brackets are still in place. Brick-built S extension, probably of the earlier C2C. To the SW and fronting Brown Street, the OLD MILL, also originally a flax mill, built for William Boyack in 1834–6. Three-storey-and-attic iron-framed and rubble-walled L. N range of ten bays. At the E end of its S elevation the attic is carried up as a pediment, its tympanum pierced by an oculus; formerly it was finished with a bellcote. Seven-bay SW wing.

CALENDER S of Guthrie Street (now in hotel and commercial use) by *Gilroy, Sons & Co.'s Engineering Department*, 1881. Three-storey-and-attic, the masonry of squared rubble. E front of twenty-one bays, the centre three slightly advanced under a pediment, its tympanum pierced by a low three-light window.

Full-height W wings. All the gables are ball-finialled and display the Tay Works' hallmark of a large attic window flanked by oculi. Behind, a late C19 rubble-built parallel range of one tall storey and an attic, the gables ball-finialled and with oculi-flanked attic windows.

VERDANT WORKS, corner of West Henderson's Wynd and Miln Street. Complete group of buildings (converted to a museum, 1993–6) developed from 1833 as a flax (later jute and tow) spinning mill. The mill building of 1833 itself forms the N range facing Miln Street. Rubble-walled, of two storeys and an attic, with a cornice below the wall-head; mansard roof with a continuous skylight. In the seventeen-bay N front, tall round-headed ground-floor openings at the third and fourth bays from the W. These lit the engine house whose chimney rises at the mill's NW corner, its lower part tower-like and of stone, the tapering upper part (the top 6.1 m. removed) of brick. The S elevation of the mill range faces a courtyard. At the W end, three round-headed ground-floor openings to the boiler house. Most of the remaining length of this elevation is overlaid by the single-storey preparing room added *c.* 1850, its partly glazed roof supported internally on pierced cast-iron trusses.

N of the preparing room, a block containing the batching rooms. Its single-storey E wing is of *c.* 1835. To this was added *c.* 1850 a two-storey block facing the courtyard, its roof piended at the N gable which is joined by a cast-iron bridge running in front of the preparing room to the mill. Cast-iron forestair to the W front's first-floor door. S of the batching rooms, a two-storey-and-attic rubble-walled warehouse of *c.* 1855, a large hoist door in the W gable. SE block of *c.* 1860.

On the W side of the courtyard and abutting the warehouse, a small two-storey office block of the 1830s. To its N the contemporary entrance from West Henderson's Wynd to the courtyard, the heavily corniced gatepiers of stugged ashlar, the N joined by a short screen wall to the mill. Inside the entrance, a cast-iron weighbridge, late C19, by *A. & W. Smith & Co. Ltd.*

WALTON MILL, Brook Court. Now housing. Four-storey L-plan and piend-roofed former jute mill built in 1891, the main block extended S by a further three bays soon after. Large windows to the first and second floors. String course under the third floor whose few and small windows are late C20 insertions. At the rear (W) elevation, the walling of the upper floors is carried on paired cast-iron columns, the ground-floor opening originally onto batching sheds (now removed).

WAREHOUSE, No. 12 Milnbank Road. Built for the Logie Works, *c.* 1865, probably for the storage and finishing of damasks. Two-storey-and-attic ashlar front of eight bays, its two-bay E end slightly advanced, the cornice below the wall-head; some alterations to the openings. The gables and rear are of rubble. Oval dummy windows in the gables. At the rear, a fully exposed basement and a central gabled hoist at the attic.

WAREHOUSES, Guthrie Street and Blinshall Street. Group of rubble-walled flax warehouses built *c.* 1830. Fronting Guthrie

Street, a long two-storey block, the ground-floor doors mostly built-up; small horizontally proportioned windows at the upper floor. Along Blinshall Street to the E, a second block, the two large cart entrances in the centre of its E front flanked by windows; six-bay upper floor, the two central openings taller than the others. W of the Guthrie Street warehouse and at right angles to it, a three-storey piend-roofed block with hoist doors in its N gable. Separated from it by a narrow alley is an L-plan warehouse of *c.* 1860, also piend-roofed.

SUBURBS NORTH OF KINGSWAY

ARDLER AND DOWNFIELD

The area bounded by Camperdown Country Park on the W, Caird Park on the E, Kingsway West on the S and countryside to the N. It contains the mansion houses of Camperdown and Mains Castle as well as outer Dundee housing estates of the later C20, partly redeveloped and extended at the beginning of the C21, each with a complement of churches and schools but, except at the Ardler Complex in Turnberry Avenue, no defined neighbourhood centre. Strathmartine Road, running N through the middle, provides a thoroughfare of earlier date but its Late Victorian development is linear and without a village focus.

CHURCHES

CHALMERS ARDLER CHURCH, Turnberry Avenue. Built in 1968–9. Hall-like, a monopitch ribbed metal roof swept down from the rubble-faced S gable. A few pale brick panels enliven the drydash of the other walls. Double-pitch roofed NE wing containing the hall. In front of this, a rubble-faced square bell-tower.

DOWNFIELD SOUTH CHURCH, Haldane Terrace. Originally Downfield United Presbyterian Church. Gothic with a Late Georgian feel, by *C. & L. Ower*, 1889, the front gable of stugged ashlar, the sides of hammer-dressed rubble. Clearstorey-windowed slate-hung nave and lean-to aisles. W steeple, the tower's front flush with the ends of the aisles but marked off by buttresses which rise to tall panelled pinnacles. At the tower's second stage, a two-light traceried window, its central column-mullion and responds with bell capitals. At the third stage, a trio of narrow openings. Slate-hung belfry with cusped openings under a steep pyramidal spire, also slated.

INTERIOR. The church is divided into a nave and aisles by tall bell-capitalled cast-iron columns supporting the clearstorey. Over the aisles, sloping boarded roofs; flat roof to the nave. Panel-fronted deep W gallery which was extended E in 1896 and 1913. – Simple Gothic PEWS. – At the E end, a combined PULPIT AND ORGAN CASE of 1911, the faintly Neo-Georgian organ case's centrepiece forming a curved canopy over the simple Gothic pulpit. The ORGAN itself is of 1911 and

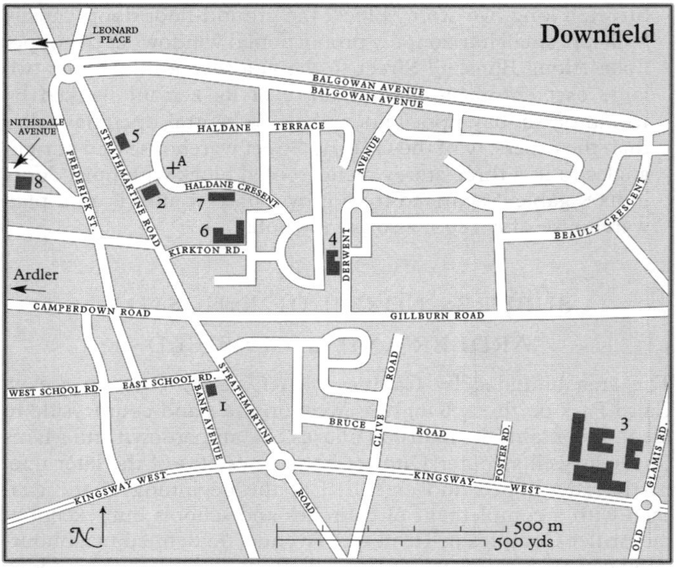

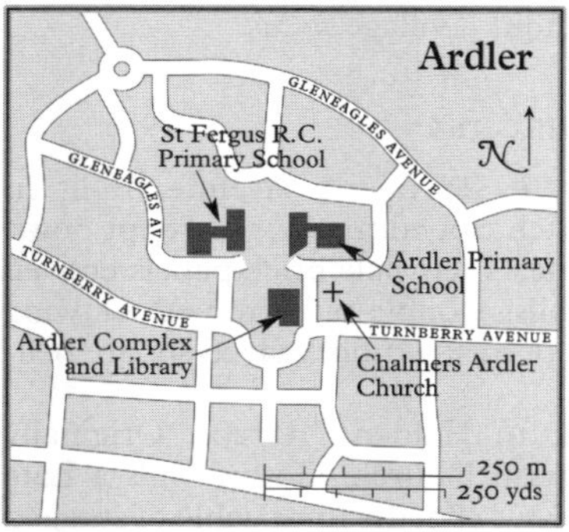

A Downfield South Church

1 Downfield House
2 Downfield Primary School
3 Dundee College Kingsway Campus
4 Kirkton Neighbourhood Centre
5 Scout Hall
6 St Columba's Primary School
7 St Columba's (R.C.) High School
8 St Margarets's (R.C.) Primary School

by *John R. Miller*. – Abstract patterned STAINED GLASS of 1899 in the windows.

MAINS AND STRATHMARTINE PARISH CHURCH, corner of Old Glamis Road and Claverhouse Road. Converted to housing. Rubble-walled box of 1800, the N side now harled. Tall round-headed S windows, the others all rectangular. Two-storey arrangement at the gables. Diocletian window in the pediment of the W gable which is surmounted by a corbelled-out birdcage bellcote. Low rubble-built additions by *Alexander Johnston*, 1895, at the ends, the semi-octagonal E porch finished with a parapet.

ST COLUMBA (R.C.), Derwent Avenue. By *Allan & Friskin*, 1956. Tall and powerfully stark box of glazed red brickwork with an octagonal SE tower, the detail Early Christian. – Neo-Georgian CLERGY HOUSE to the N.

ST LEONARD AND ST FERGUS (R.C.), corner of St Leonard Place and Macalpine Road. By *Burns, Veal & Co.*, 1973–5. Boxy assemblage, the NE part flat-roofed, the taller NW and SE parts with monopitch roofs. The church's W end is joined by a single-storey-and-attic CLERGY HOUSE to the HALL, these both of *c.* 1960.

ST LUKE (Episcopal), St Luke's Road. Harled evocation of a village kirk, by *Freeman & Ogilvy*, 1901–3. Crowstep-gabled rectangle, the sanctuary marked off from the nave by a gable over the chancel arch and crocket-pinnacled and thistle-finialled buttresses. On the sanctuary's S side, the base of an intended tower; on the N, a vestry. Hoodmoulds over the round-headed doors to the N side and S porch. In the sides, slit and diamond-shaped ventilation openings below the large windows. These are rectangular, each filled with a pair of round-headed and cusped lights. Small moulded corbels under the gutter. Hoodmoulded and pointed window in the W gable; in the E, a Late Gothic window of four lights, the head filled with cusped looped tracery. – To the N, a small early C20 HALL with a pedimented porch.

STRATHMARTINE PARISH CHURCH, Strathmartine Road. Originally Mains and Strathmartine Free Church, it was built to a design by *William Paterson* in 1844 (the date of 1843 on the S side refers to the formation of the congregation) but heightened, completely remodelled and given a new W front by *Alexander Johnston*, following a sketch design by the church's minister, the *Rev. Robert Lorimer*, in 1892.

The general conception, a broad box faced with buff-coloured stugged ashlar masonry, is of the 1840s but the detail all of 1892. This is chaste Romanesque. In the front (W) gable, a large wheel window, the outer moulding of its surround studded with reliefs of tiny capitals and human heads. Below, a minimally advanced gabled surround to the entrance, the door's arch enriched with chevron ornament; in the tympanum, carved panels bearing the Chi-Rho and A and Ω emblems. The gable is surmounted by a bellcote, panelled with intersecting round-headed arches and finished with a stone-slabbed pyramidal roof. Projecting from the church's SE corner, a low bow-ended session house of 1844, enlarged in Romanesque manner as a bow-ended hall by *Johnston & Baxter*, 1896. Further large E extension in brick and drydash, by *McCabe & MacDonald*, 1993.

The INTERIOR is a big and bare single space. – WEST GALLERY of 1955. – Bench PEWS. At the E end of the N wall, the ORGAN CHAMBER formed in 1892, its round-headed arch constructed of red and yellow brickwork. In it, the ORGAN, its pipes stencilled, built by *John R. Miller*; rebuilt by *Ronald L. Smith*, 1987. – In the E sanctuary, an octagonal PULPIT of 1892, constructed of ebonized cypress wood on a short stone pillar, the faces with intersecting Romanesque arcading under small rectangular panels. Behind is a recess whose back's round-headed panel bears the IHS monogram. – In front, a small COMMUNION TABLE, also of 1892 and of ebonized cypress wood, the legs provided by cushion-capitalled columns. It is copied from an altar in Ratisbon Cathedral. – The MINISTER'S AND ELDERS' CHAIRS are in the same style but probably early C20; round-headed panels on their backs. – On the S side of the sanctuary, an early C20 LECTERN, also of ebonized wood and with a gilded cross on the front. – On the sanctuary's N side, the FONT made in 1892, its stone pedestal carved with the relief of a dove. The bowl is formed from a capital, its front bearing the Royal Arms of Scotland, believed to have come from the (demolished) 1582 Tolbooth of Dundee.

CAIRD PARK

between Kingsway and Claverhouse Road

Open space of *c.* 109 ha. comprising the Den of Mains and adjoining land acquired by the City of Dundee in 1913 with money given for the purpose by Sir James K. Caird, owner of the Ashton Works and Craigie Mill, and opened to the public in 1920. Most of the land W of Mains Loan, which provides a road through the park, is now laid out as a golf course. E of Mains Loan, an athletics stadium and, close by the road, the old Mains Parish Churchyard and Mains Castle (*see* below) facing each other across the gorge of the Gelly Burn. Beside the entrance to Mains Loan, the road running N through the park, the CAIRD FOUNTAIN originally erected at the W end of High Street in 1879 and moved here in the C20. Classical, a cast-iron rotunda on a circular base of polished red granite.

MAINS PARISH CHURCHYARD. The site of a medieval church demolished after the construction in 1800 of Mains and Strathmartine Parish Church (*see* Churches, above) to serve the two recently united parishes. Of the CHURCH itself, which stood roughly in the graveyard's centre, only fragments of the rubble walling of a transeptal S chapel survive. Now featureless, the gable contained a window of three lancet lights.* In the graveyard's S part, a number of C17 GRAVE-SLABS decorated in shallow relief with emblems of death. – At the SE corner, an C18 HEADSTONE erected by David and Rhoderick Ormond to their father, Alexander, a bleacher. On the swan-neck pedimented E face, a pair of angels' heads (souls) which flank a panel bearing a crossed pair of hooked poles. – Beside it, a HEADSTONE of 1765 to the children of David Smith, vigorously carved with a skull, crossbones and hourglass.

PUBLIC BUILDINGS

ARDLER COMPLEX AND ARDLER CLINIC, Turnberry Avenue. The Complex was designed by the Dundee City Architect,

* As recorded by David MacGibbon and Thomas Ross, *The Ecclesiastical Architecture of Scotland*, iii (1897), 455–6.

Alan M. Preston, 1973–5, to contain a public library, halls and theatre but lacks civic presence. Flat-roofed, of one and two storeys, the walls of reddish-brown brick, with fins projecting between the side windows. At the centre of the S front, a fully glazed canted bay window under a deep fascia. Serving as a single-storey SW pavilion but with walls of paler brick is the Ardler Clinic, by *James Parr & Partners*, 1967–9.

ARDLER PRIMARY SCHOOL, East Scotscraig Lane. By *Leonard & Partners*, 1965–8. Flat-roofed boxes, the walls finished with drydash and dark brick.

BALDRAGON ACADEMY, Burn Street. Originally Kirkton High School. By the Dundee City Architect, *Robert Dron* (architect-in-charge: *Gordon W. H. Mechan*), 1957–60. Three- and five-storey main blocks, curtain-walled above brick bases, joined by a curvaceously roofed hall block. Lower buildings to the N.

CRAIGOWL PRIMARY SCHOOL, St Columba Gardens. By *SMC Parr Architects*, 2007. Large building of two storeys covered by shallowly pitched roofs.

DOWNFIELD HOUSE, corner of East School Road and Bank Avenue. Originally Downfield School. By *Peter Cunningham*, 1909–11. Large and solid-looking asymmetrical Georgian survival, built of squared and stugged masonry. Two tall storeys; piended roof. At the NW corner is incorporated a more picturesque predecessor by *J. & F. Salmond*, 1878. This is single-storey and bargeboarded. Three-light windows to the W and N, the W hoodmoulded.

DOWNFIELD PRIMARY SCHOOL, Strathmartine Road and Haldane Crescent. By the *Holmes Partnership*, 2009–10. Rendered walls, their predominantly dazzling white colour relieved by splashes of red and blue paintwork. It is curiously reminiscent of a factory.

DUNDEE COLLEGE KINGSWAY CAMPUS, Old Glamis Road. The first development, by the *Scottish Education Department*, 1962–4, provided single-storey brick-built workshops and, at the SE corner, a straightforwardly boring seven-storey block, its concrete frame filled with aggregate panels and glass. Similar three-storey block to the N. Unexpectedly adventurous is THE SPACE to the W. Designed by the *Nicoll Russell Studios*, it was 109
built in 2000–2 for the Scottish School of Contemporary Dance. Tall ovoid-plan auditorium, reminiscent of a steelworks' cooling tower but stylishly clad in dark cladding and with the concentric walls of its circulation spaces wrapped round the base. Projecting from the N end, the upswept roof over the entrance and foyer. On the W side, a range containing semi-basement offices surmounted by studios, the studios lit by a band of continuous glazing separated by a deep band from a glazed clearstorey under the sinuous roof. Inside, a circulation 'artery' leads from the foyer past the auditorium to the double-height and top-lit 'buzz' area intended for student interaction between classes and for spontaneous events. The studios' view over dreary playing fields rather than a wild landscape is a disappointment.

DUNDEE CREMATORIUM, Macalpine Road. The CHAPEL is the main building. Wholly ecclesiastical-looking, by *T. Lindsay Gray*, 1935–6. Powerfully detailed and buttressed sturdy Romanesque, the walls of red brick. Nave and parapeted aisles which extend one further bay W (containing rooms) and return across the W end as a porch from which a *porte cochère* extends to the W and N. Three-light W window. Single lights in the nave's clearstorey, three-light windows at the sides of the aisles. One high-set window in the nave's E end above which rises a slim tower (tactfully heightened, *c.* 1985) which contains the chimney flues of the oven. Low flat-roofed semi-octagonal chancel-like outshot E of the tower. Transeptal outshots at the E ends of the aisles.

Inside, the ashlar-clad W vestibule's round-headed N and S doors open into rooms whose oak panelling bears commemorative inscriptions to those whose ashes are stored behind, the E door into the crematorium chapel. The chapel has round-headed nave arcades; ashlar-panelled dadoes in the aisles. The E bay of the nave forms a narrower chancel, its end wall clad with marble, the floor intended to carry a bier standing in front of the altar. On the chancel's S side, the ORGAN (replacing an instrument of 1936) by *Henry Willis & Sons*, 1954. – STAINED GLASS. E window (the Almighty) by *Alexander L. Russell*, *c.* 1940. – In the S clearstorey, a modernistic light of *c.* 1965. – In the side wall of the S aisle, the E window's centre light (Naomi) is by *T. S. Halliday*, *c.* 1965. The centre light of the central window (Boaz) is also by Halliday, *c.* 1960. Two lights of this aisle's W window are filled with a stylized depiction of James and Jemima Boyd in the local hills, *c.* 1995 and 1999. – In the N aisle, the E window's centre light is of *c.* 1975 and also by Halliday. – Two lights of the central window contain modernistic glass (Walking the Hills) by *Ian Cargill*, 1983.

NW of the chapel, a U-plan CLOISTER begun *c.* 1950 and extended later, the back walls and piers of brick, the piended roofs covered with green tiles. – At the E entrance to the drive, a single-storey-and-attic brick-walled LODGE of 1935–6 and by Gray, the tall piended roof enlivened with fish-scale slating; bow on the W side.

FIRE STATION, Macalpine Road. By *James Parr & Partners*, 1971–2. Tall yellow brick garage, the front's broad eaves supported on red-painted metal piers; shallow-pitched and piended ribbed metal roof.

KINGSPARK SCHOOL, Gillburn Road. By *Tayside Regional Council*, *c.* 1985. Single-storey, informally composed and sculptural, of dark brown brickwork, drydash and glass, with rooflights projecting at the top.

KIRKTON NEIGHBOURHOOD CENTRE AND LIBRARY, Derwent Avenue. By *Gauldie, Hardie, Wright & Needham*, 1969–72. L-plan of drydash and ribbed metal walling, the glazed entrance canted across the SE inner angle added in 1998.

LAWSIDE R.C. ACADEMY, Rannoch Road. By the Dundee City Architect, *John W. Kidd*, 1964–6. Long and lightweight-looking, of one and two storeys.

ST COLUMBA'S PRIMARY SCHOOL, Kirkton Road. By the Dundee City Architect, *Robert Dron*, 1955–8. Three-storey main block, concrete-framed and with infill panels of ribbed metal and glass. Modernistic brick boiler house tower at the NE.

ST FERGUS PRIMARY SCHOOL, Scotscraig Lane. A mirror image of the contemporary Ardler Primary School (*see* above).

SCOUT HALL, Strathmartine Road. Originally Public Hall. Late C19 and ecclesiastical Gothic in character. Slender NW tower finished with a lead-spired belfry.

TECHNOTOTS NURSERY, Brunel Road. By *Rod Davidson*, 2001. Appropriately small and fun. Of two storeys, the walls painted blue, grey and white. Monopitch roof projecting W over brightly painted metal posts to form a veranda. Some porthole windows.

DESCRIPTION

ARDLER's housing of the 1950s and 1960s S of Birkdale Place was largely replaced at the beginning of the C21, the garden-fronted dwellings predominantly two-storey faced with brick or render and laid out in short streets. Should the newly planted trees survive, the area may in time be pleasantly arboreal. At the estate's SE corner, drydashed two- and three-storey blocks of flats by *Johnston & Baxter*, 1962, their roof pitches meeting at windowless 'clearstoreys'. TURNBERRY AVENUE contains the estate's D-plan centre, the curved S side formed by blocks of flats by *James Parr & Partners*, 1970–3, straightforward and humanely scaled, their E and W wings containing ground-floor shops and with green slate panels to enliven the reddish-brown brickwork. On the straight N side, the Ardler Complex and Ardler Clinic with the playground separating the Ardler Primary School and St Fergus Primary School behind and Ardler Chalmers Church to the E.

DOWNFIELD is more varied. SE of Strathmartine Road is the small development (Nos. 301–343 KINGSWAY, CLIVE ROAD, FOSTER ROAD and BRUCE ROAD) designed by three architectural practices (*Ogilvy & Stewart*, *Maclaren, Soutar & Salmond* and *Donald Ross*) for the Dundee Garden City Association Ltd, and built in 1922–4, the harled houses with gabled fronts, some with boarded heads. The scheme was extended W of Clive Road by *W. Curtis Green & Partners* and *Maclaren, Soutar & Salmond* in 1934–5.

STRATHMARTINE ROAD running N from Kingsway to the edge of the city is the principal street, composed mostly of small and unexciting Late Victorian and C20 villas. Only near the junction with Haldane Street, whose E end is closed by Downfield South Church (*see* Churches, above), does a sense of urban scale appear with a couple of dour three-storey tenement blocks (Nos. 397–399 Strathmartine Road of 1895 and Nos. 490–492 Strathmartine Road of 1900). Just to their N but set back on the E side is the late C19 Scout Hall (*see* Public Buildings, above) followed by a U-plan double villa (Nos. 423–425 Strathmartine Road) of the later C19, with bargeboarded gables at the advanced end bays; in each inner angle, a fleur-de-lis-finialled porch sporting a pair of carved human heads. At Strathmartine Road's N end is the former Mains and Strathmartine Parish Church.

INDUSTRIAL AND OFFICE BUILDINGS

BALGRAY BUILDING, corner of Harrison Road and Faraday Street. Originally designed as offices for Olivetti, by *Edward Cullinan, Michael Chassay, Julian Bicknell, Giles Oliver*, 1971. Mannered two-storey block, the upper storey projected on pilotis at the W and S sides where the first-floor walls slope outwards to meet the edges of the pitched copper roof, its eaves serrated by the backward-sloped triangular tops of the windows. Parkland warmed by Mediterranean sun would be a more appropriate setting than a Dundee industrial estate.

CLAVERHOUSE BLEACHWORKS, Barns of Claverhouse Road and Heron Rise. Sizeable remains of a bleachfield whose first building was erected as a cotton mill, *c.* 1790. A long rubble-built range (much altered and now housing) at the W of the complex probably survives from that mill. Originally single-storey but with two-storey additions of 1834–5. Beside Barns of Claverhouse Road is a yarn store (also now housing) of 1835, the walling of red rubble. The E elevation to the road is simple single-storey with a slightly advanced and chimney-gabled 'centrepiece'. The W elevation, taking advantage of the steep fall in the ground, is of two storeys. Advanced centre containing the elliptical-arched entrance under a segmental-headed window and surmounted by a birdcage bellcote projected on heavy moulded corbels. Across the range's S end is a two-storey house (perhaps originally a school for the works' child labourers), the upper windows with gablet dormerheads. – To the N, a mid-C19 tall and tapering square chimney, brick-built above a masonry base. Behind, two bays of weaving sheds.

DISCOVERY CENTRE, Fulton Road. By *James F. Stephen*, 1999–2001. Huge mass of yellowish orange brick cut into and across by dark glass and covered with ribbed blue metal roofs. Symmetrical frontages, the N with an advanced centre, the S, overlooking Kingsway West, with a fully glazed centrepiece between bowed towers which support the oversailing eaves.

NCR BUILDING, off Myrekirk Road. Originally the Timex Building. Well-mannered but unexciting, by *Beard & Bennett*, 1946. Flat-roofed two storeys of pale brown brick, the ground-floor windows horizontal, those of the first floor vertical.

CAMPERDOWN HOUSE

off Angus Road

Greek Revival mansion built in 1820–6 for Robert, second Viscount Duncan (later, first Earl of Camperdown), who named it in honour of his father's victory over the Dutch fleet at the Battle of Camperdown in 1797. *William Burn*'s design is a (presumably unashamed) crib of William Wilkins's for Grange Park (Hampshire) of eleven years earlier but using an Ionic rather than a Doric order for the great portico. 54

The house is of two tall storeys, with an underground basement and an attic hidden by the parapet. Walling of polished white Cullalo (Fife) sandstone. Entrance (E) front of seven bays, the advanced ends framed by giant pilasters which form antae for the screen of two widely spaced Ionic columns across the centre. Fronting this screen, a hexastyle Ionic-columned and pedimented portico, its soffit coffered. Simple detail, the ground-floor openings at the end and centre bays architraved and corniced; aprons under the windows flanking the door. Narrower windows at the second and sixth bays; smaller windows at the upper (bedroom) floor. The main block is joined by a recessed screen wall to a NE pavilion containing the house's kitchen. This is cruciform, the E limb's corniced front, clearly visible on the approach, with coupled corner pilasters framing an architraved and corniced window.

The S front, except for the recessed r. bay, is of nine bays, the ground-floor windows all architraved and corniced. Slightly advanced three-bay centrepiece, the design derived from the Temple of Thrasyllus in Athens, the ends of the parapet surmounted by podia; low flight of steps in front. Similar treatment at the W elevation but it is of only five bays (the basement partly exposed at the N two) with a one-bay advanced centrepiece. The centrepiece contains the garden entrance, a sidelit French window with pilaster-mullions and an overall segmental fanlight. Set back from the main block's N end is a single-storey-and-basement piend-roofed wing ending with a corner pavilion. Between this wing and the E screen wall and NE pavilion is a service court, its N side bounded by a low range, its ground floor pierced by a segmental-arched cart entrance, the upper floor with piended dormerheads over the windows. On the courtyard side of the NE pavilion, a gabled canopy sheltering a bell.

Inside, ENTRANCE HALL with a coffered ceiling and brute classical marble chimneypiece. To the N, the T-shaped BILLIARD ROOM, its tail projecting to the E. At the W wall and the tail's S side, grey marble chimneypieces with reeded jambs and lintels, their ends with rosettes. Entered through double doors at the W end of the entrance hall and occupying the middle of the main block is the SALOON. Its square double-height central 56
compartment opens through screens of scagliola columns *in antis* (the lower Ionic, the upper Corinthian of slender

proportions and with foliaged cast-iron balustrades) at E and W onto ground floor lobbies and first floor passages; at the N and S sides, console-corniced large first-floor openings to passages behind. Over the central compartment, a dome on pendentives, the panels of its coffered ceiling containing clear glass in patterned borders of the same liverish colour as the columns of the E and W screens and the chimneypiece, also of brute classical design. Corniced doorcases on all sides, the double doors at the E opening onto the STAIR HALL. Imperial stair with simply detailed cast-iron balusters and oak handrails and newel posts of Jacobean rather than Greek inspiration. Coffered ceiling with a glazed oblong lantern rising at the centre.

The interconnected principal rooms (DINING ROOM, LIBRARY and DRAWING ROOM) extend along the S front of the main block, all with identical coffered ceiling, their large panels bordered by expensive but restrained plasterwork executed, as elsewhere in the house, by *James Annan*. Corniced doorcases and, in the dining room and library, window pelmets with anthemion and palmette decorated friezes, and black marble chimneypieces, yet again of brute classical character. The drawing room chimneypiece is of alabaster carved in high relief with flowers, foliage and cherubs' heads. Double doors between these three rooms but the N wall of the library is set slightly S of the line of the N walls of the dining room and drawing room so here these doors are disconcertingly off-centre. In the library, built-in bookcases, their fronts of copper latticing with rosettes at the intersections. The windows in the drawing room's W end have been blocked by the erection of a thin wall just inside them, this wall, like the others in the room, with large plasterwork panels, rosettes at the corners of the borders. On the house's W side N of the drawing room were the family's private rooms, all now unremarkable except for a circular small sitting room.

In the basement of the main block, a windowless central HALL, its ends marked off by primitivist Tuscan columns.

SAWMILL of the earlier C19 WNW of the mansion house. Single-storey rubble-built U, quite unassuming except for a lunette in the W range's N gable and some elliptical-arched cartshed openings to the courtyard. – To its NNE, the single-storey DAIRY COTTAGE, also of the earlier C19. Piended roof with broad eaves. Three-bay S front originally with hoodmoulded two-light windows (one now much enlarged). Door, also hoodmoulded, at the slightly advanced centre, its gable topped by a stone obelisk finial. – S of the house, the WALLED GARDEN, by *John Hay*, 1807. At its E end, the WILDLIFE CENTRE, by *Dundee City Council*, 2011. Walls of wood and glass under a prominent double-pitched metal roof with jerkin-head gables. – Lavishly treed PARKLAND laid out by *David Taylor* in the early C19, the surrounding WALL built by *Adam Will* in 1867–8.

GREYSTANE (THE LANDMARK HOTEL)

off Kingsway West

Scottish Baronial villa-mansion designed by *Campbell Douglas* and built in 1870 for David Matthew Watson, owner of the Bullionfield Paper Mill at Invergowrie, and his wife, Hannah Parker, their initials scattered liberally around the house. In the later C20 this became a hotel for which large additions have been constructed. On the house's E side these form an L, enclosing two sides of an entrance court open to the S, their design inoffensive enough in a pseudo-vernacular manner but their bright white harling something of an affront to the main block's sober stonework.

The Victorian house is only of two principal storeys above a fully exposed basement but vertical in appearance, the walling of bull-nosed squared masonry. The projecting NE corner is treated as a tower, the N gable's crowstepped head set back behind a parapet, the E face with a Neo-Jacobean stone dormerhead above its attic window, In the E front of the main block and reached by a flight of steps is the principal entrance. Above it, a window in an aediculed surround, the slender banded columns with foliate capitals and flanked by strapwork, the apron beneath inscribed PAX.INTRANTIBVS/ SALVS.EXEVNTIBVS, the steep pediment broken by a thistle finial, its tympanum with the Scottish royal motto NEMO ME IMPUNE LACESSIT.

Near-symmetrical S front, badly compromised by late C20 additions. At the N elevation, a large oriel window. Below its continuous corbelling are hefty individual moulded corbels inscribed GIF.VE.DEID AS.VE.SOUVLD.VE.MYGHT.HAIF.AS. VE.VALD. To the r. of the oriel window, a panel with the impaled coats of arms of Watson and Parker, the border's inscription recording the construction of the house in 1870 by David Matthew Watson and Hannah Parker; below, a further inscription GOD.GIVE.THE.BLISING.TO.THE.PAPER.CRAFT.IN THE. GOOD.REALM.OF.SCOTLAND.

Inside the front door, a vestibule, its plaster ceiling with a central pendant, and a flight of steps up to the principal floor's stair-hall. Here, a Jacobean wooden stair and boarded ceiling. Stone chimneypiece, the frieze inscribed with the initials of David Watson and Helen Parker and the words VAH.INCALVI. VIDI.IGNEM. Strapwork embellishments at the overmantel which bears a coat of arms. Off the stair-hall's W side, the former dining room, the heavy elliptical arch of its sideboard recess carved with birds, beasts and grapes. Some stencilled decoration depicting birds survives on the wall above.

MAINS CASTLE

Mains Loan

Perched on the edge of a ravine cut by the Gelly Burn but with rising ground behind leaving it vulnerable to artillery attack, the 39

C16 and C17 house of the Grahams of Fintry combines a proud affirmation of baronial status with the domesticity of a villa.

About 1455 George, fourth Earl of Angus, granted the lands of Mains of Earls Strathdichty to Robert Graham of Fintry in feu ferme, and in 1530 Robert Graham's great-grandson, William Graham, received a Crown charter of the lands which were erected into a barony. The Grahams' principal residence seems to have been in Dundee until the mid C16 when they began the expansion of a very modest house at Mains into a sizeable courtyard complex. Work was presumably well advanced by 1562 or 1566 when a stone bearing the date and the initials of Sir David Graham, fifth of Fintry, and his wife Dame Margaret Ogilvy was erected over the entrance to the courtyard.* Further work was carried out in 1582 and again in the C17. The house was abandoned as a laird's residence in the mid C18. In 1913 the buildings, by then partly roofless, were acquired by the City of Dundee. The E range was inhabited until 1959 but no attempt was made to restore the rest of the complex until 1976. In that year repair of the surviving buildings and restoration of the roofless N range were begun by the *City of Dundee District Council*. Work was completed in 1985.

The complex is all rubble-walled, built round a courtyard which was formed in the mid C16. The WEST WALL was formerly backed by buildings. At its N end, the wall incorporates the S two-thirds of the broad gable of an earlier two-storey house, its N end demolished when the present courtyard house was constructed. This earlier house, probably built in the later C15 as a grange or occasional residence, was remodelled in the C16 as an appendage to the new N range. It is now roofless but in the surviving part of its W gable are a pair of ground-floor windows (now blocked), one a slit, the other square, and one first-floor opening, also blocked. The house's E gable, now the lower part of the main N range's W wall, contains at the ground floor a slit window and a slightly larger opening and at the first floor a square window (all now blocked).

From the N corner to a little past its mid-point the W wall is finished with an ivy-clad battlement pierced by shot-holes. At this battlement's N end, remains of an angle-round carried on continuous corbelling and, at its S end, a half-round on individual double corbels with shot-holes between them. Under the half-round, the courtyard's entrance, a round-headed doorway with a roll-and-hollow moulding. S of the entrance the W wall has been altered to serve as the outer wall of a block built probably in the early C17 but now demolished except for this side. It has been of at least two storeys. In the W wall, a ground-floor window with chamfered jambs. At the

* The date, no longer visible but said to have been carved on the keystone, is given as 1562 by A. H. Millar, *The Historic Castles and Mansions of Scotland: Perthshire and Forfarshire* (Paisley and London, 1890), 396, and as 1566 by Alexander J. Warden, *Angus or Forfarshire*, iv (Dundee, 1884), 292.

first floor, three windows, the N with fluted half-columns banded with a rope moulding, the other two (the S fragmentary) with roll-and-hollow-moulded jambs.

The NORTH RANGE is, except for its W end (*see* above), also of the 1560s. Main block of three storeys, its ends gabled crowsteps restored in 1976–85. At the external (N) elevation's ground floor, slit windows (blocked) and a large door (also built-up) which has been inserted, perhaps in the late C17. More blocked openings to the first floor, two of them large; the smaller opening at a lower level lit the screens passage at the hall's W end. Two second-floor windows with chamfered jambs, their lower parts C16, their upper rising into gabled stone dormerheads, conjectural restorations of the late C20. Also of the late C20 is the lean-to outshot built against the E gable and filling its inner angle with the E range. The main front of the N range is to the courtyard. Slit windows (blocked) to the ground floor and, at its W end, a door in a weathered chamfered surround, probably inserted in the C17. The first-floor openings, all with roll-and-hollow surrounds, consist of two large windows and a third whose size has been reduced, probably in the C17. Second-floor windows with chamfered surrounds and pedimented dormerheads, all restored in the late C20 but the lower part of the l. window original. Over the W end of this range, a crowstepped half-gable. This abuts the boldly advanced stair-tower, the house's dominant feature. It rises over 21 m. high for a dizzying five storeys, the lower four broken only by smallish windows and the roll-and-hollow-moulded entrance. The top floor, projected on individual corbels and with a chimney-topped gable at each face, was rebuilt in 1630 by David Graham, seventh of Fintry (the date and his initials on one skewputt). In the E inner angle with the main block, a bowed stair-turret finished with a catslide roof is carried on continuous corbelling above the first floor.

Inside the N range, an unvaulted ground floor. Plaster has been stripped from the remainder of the interior which is now uncomfortably rubbly. Two rooms (hall and chamber) at each of the first and second floors reached by a comfortable turnpike stair in the tower. At the first-floor hall, tall elliptical-headed window embrasures. The high-set small window in the W wall may be an insertion. This wall's other (blocked) window is placed low down and opened from the now roofless C15 house on the W. Plain E chimneypiece with a roll-and-hollow moulding. The chamber to the E has, unusually, a fireplace at each end, both apparently contemporary and simply moulded, although it seems always to have been a single room. Cupboards in the N and S walls, the S in the place of a former door to the E range. The wall thickness of the NE corner has contained a private turnpike stair (removed) to the floor above. On the second floor, simply moulded stone chimneypieces. The upper floors of the tower above the principal turnpike stair are reached from a tighter turnpike contained in the stair-turret, its external continuous corbelling continued inside above a pendant carved with a human face. At each floor, one room with a fireplace.

The two-storey EAST RANGE is of two periods. The E bay, presumably originally projecting into the courtyard and containing a straight stone stair to the upper floor, is of 1582.* Here is the main entrance, a door with a roll-and-hollow moulding surmounted by a badly weathered horizontal panel. Above this, the surround for a heraldic panel, the framework of double-tier balusters standing on moulded bases and supporting a cornice. The four bays to the N, built of much larger blocks of rubble, date from a late C17 remodelling in which this block was thickened to the W, the new roof piended at the S end. Plain ground-floor openings, the doors now converted to windows.

Of the SOUTH RANGE only some of the N wall survives. It seems to be late C16. Doorway at the E end; another towards the W end seems a later insertion. A couple of relieving arches disclose the presence of blocked openings. At the first floor one jamb of a former window or door.

FINTRY, WHITFIELD, LINLATHEN, MID CRAIGIE, AND DOUGLAS AND ANGUS

Sprawling housing estates at the NE corner of Dundee, N of Kingsway East and Arbroath Road, developed from the 1930s.

CHURCHES

MID CRAIGIE PARISH CHURCH, Longtown Terrace. Harled hall church, by *Joseph Johnston*, 1938, a pyramid-roofed cupola-bellcote on the red-tiled roof; semi-octagonal NE porch. – Flat-roofed HALL.

OUR LADY OF SORROWS (R.C.), Finlarig Terrace. Hall-like, by *W. W. Friskin* of *Allan & Friskin*, 1967, the walls harled above a brick base. At the N end, a parapeted and buttressed stone porch; above, an overarched window of three round-headed lights, the overarch's head a brick panel.

ST NINIAN (Episcopal), Longtown Road. By *William Gauldie* of *Gauldie, Hardie & Sharpe*, 1938. Harled and slate-roofed oblong, with sloping buttresses along the sides and semi-octagonal heads to the windows. Low saddleback-roofed W bell-tower. – To the E, the contemporary single-storey-and-attic RECTORY, the upper floor jettied at the S front.

ST PIUS X (R.C.), Balerno Street. By *W. W. Friskin* of *Allan & Friskin*, 1961. Drydashed box, the long E and W sides buttressed. Above the entrance in the N gable front, a large window, its round-arched head blind. – A contemporary two-storey NW wing of Neo-Georgian inspiration contains the CLERGY HOUSE, a N bow its principal feature.

* The date formerly visible on the panel above the entrance.

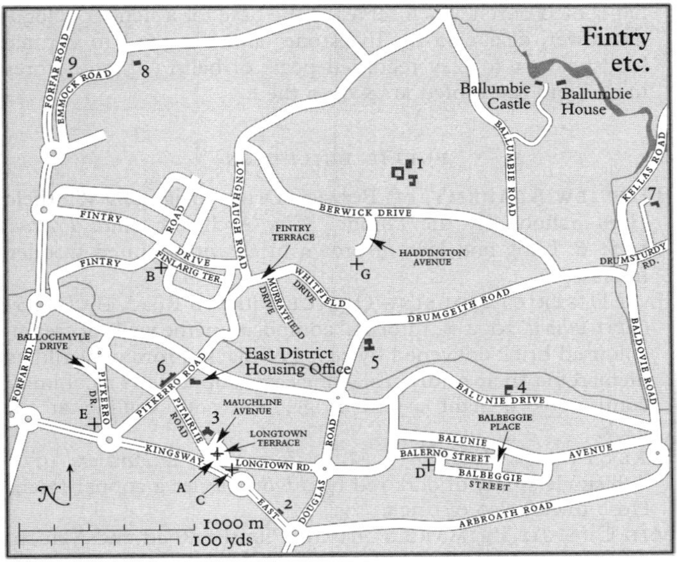

A Mid Craigie Parish Church
B Our Lady of Sorrows (R.C.)
C St Ninian (Episcopal)
D St Pius X (R.C.)
E St Vincent de Paul (R.C.)
G Whitfield Parish Church

1 Braeview Academy
2 Fire Station
3 Mid Craigie Primary School
4 Police Station
5 St Saviour's High School
6 St Vincent's Primary School
7 Pitkerro House
8 Powrie Castle
9 Black Watch Memorial

ST VINCENT DE PAUL (R.C.), Pitkerro Drive. By *W. W. Friskin* of *Allan & Friskin*, 1950–3. Big but barely detailed rectangle, flat-roofed except at the E end where a double-pitch roof rises into a low tower. Above the E porch, its image niche containing a statue of St Vincent de Paul, five closely set round-arched lights. – To the W, SERVITE PRIORY, also by *Allan & Friskin*, 1950–3, the two-storey piend-roofed front block with an off-centre gabled porch. Round-headed panels above the ground-floor windows; cushion-capitalled column-mullions at the two-light upper windows.

WHITFIELD PARISH CHURCH, Haddington Avenue. White-harled L of church and hall, by *T. H. Thoms* of *Thoms & Wilkie*, 1970–1. Over the church, a monopitch roof sloping down from the 'Fyfestone'-clad W gable. Lower N and S aisles, also mono-pitch-roofed, their W ends splayed; rectangular side windows. Double-pitch roof over the NE hall. In the inner angle, a flat-roofed porch which serves as the base for a slender octagonal tower, also clad in 'Fyfestone' and designed to contain loudspeakers to play recorded peals of bells. – Single-storey harled and tile-roofed MANSE to the E.

PUBLIC BUILDINGS

BRAEVIEW ACADEMY, off Berwick Drive. Originally Whitfield High School. By the Dundee City Architect, *Alan Preston*, 1974–6. Long and low, of brown brick with painted wooden fascias.

EAST DISTRICT HOUSING OFFICE, Pitkerro Road. By *Dundee City Council*, 2004–5. Informal composition, the walls of cream-coloured brick enlivened by strips of black. Prominent ribbed metal roofs, their boldly projecting eaves supported on columns; continuous skylight at the ridge. Sawtooth walling at the back.

FIRE STATION, Kingsway East. By *James Parr & Partners*, 1972. Tall single storey of dark red brickwork under a copper fascia. Hose tower, also of brick.

MID CRAIGIE PRIMARY SCHOOL, Pitairlie Road and Mauchline Avenue. Timidly Modern, by the Dundee City Architect, *David B. McLay*, 1935. Harled and flat-roofed, of two storeys, the metal-framed windows linked by sill and lintel courses. Butterfly-plan S front. At each end, a projecting bay containing an entrance under a tall stair window; blocky shallow porch at the centre.

POLICE STATION, Balunie Drive. By *Gauldie, Hardie, Wright & Needham*, designed in 1975 but not built until 1980–1. Efficient-looking assemblage of brown-brick blocks.

ST SAVIOUR'S HIGH SCHOOL, Drumgeith Road. By the Dundee City Architect, *Alan Preston*, 1970–4. Boxy, of one, two and three storeys, the drydashed walls with coloured panels and generously sized windows.

ST VINCENT'S PRIMARY SCHOOL, Pitkerro Road. By the Dundee City Architect, *J. McLellan Brown*, 1950–1. Flat-roofed and drydashed, of three storeys. The long E front is articulated by piers between the vertical windows; continuous shallow canopy over the first-floor openings. Two-storey lateral end wings.

DESCRIPTION

The LINLATHEN development in the SW corner of the area is by the Dundee City Architect, *David B. McLay*, 1936, mostly composed of two-storey double houses with red-tiled piended roofs. Timber-clad walls, the boards horizontal at the ground floor and vertical above.

In MID CRAIGIE the SE corner, along the N side of LONGTOWN ROAD and in MAUCHLINE AVENUE, was built in 1935–7, to designs by *David B. McLay*. Two-storey blocks, the walls drydashed but with brick embellishments, full-height canted bay windows and red-tiled roofs. For the rest, housing of the later C20 and early C21.

FINTRY is largely a development of the 1940s and 1950s by the *Scottish Special Housing Association*. To the N, on a hillside beside EMMOCK ROAD, the BLACK WATCH MEMORIAL, an over-life-size bronze figure of a soldier, by *T. Scott Sutherland*, 1959, looking across Dundee to Fife. E of Emmock Road is Powrie Castle (*see* below).

WHITFIELD had a tentative beginning *c.* 1940 when the S side of FINTRY TERRACE (Nos. 1–27) was built at its W end. Harled two-storey housing, the upper-floor windows rising into gabled dormerheads. The front garden of No. 5 boasts a monkey-puzzle tree. Much of the rest of the area was covered with housing in 1967–75 but further development and redevelopment took place at the end of the C20 and the beginning of the C21, the recent buildings mostly of two storeys and harled, some monopitch-roofed. Off MURRAYFIELD DRIVE, in the area's SW corner, four-storey blocks of flats of *c.* 1970, the boarding under the windows and red-tiled roofs half-hearted attempts to relieve the monotony.

In DOUGLAS AND ANGUS, traditionally designed 1950s housing, the walls of drydash or concrete blockwork, the roofs covered with concrete tiles.

PITKERRO MILL, Nos. 13–14 Kellas Road. Now housing. Rubble-walled and piend-roofed grain mill of 1812. The overshot wheel survives.

BALLUMBIE CASTLE AND HOUSE

Elm Rise

BALLUMBIE CASTLE is the substantial rubble-built and ivy-clad ruin of the residence of the Lovells who held the lands of Ballumbie from, probably, the C13 until 1576. This is a curtain-walled stronghold occupying a mound in a bend of the Fithie Burn, its general appearance of a rectangle with corner towers suggestive of a C13 or C14 date but its details, notably wide-mouthed oval gunloops, indicating the early or mid C16 as the probable period of its erection or reconstruction. Bowed towers at the E corners, the SE with a stair turret on continuous corbelling in its N inner angle, both towers with high-set gunloops. Another gunloop in the E wall in which is also placed a large panel carved with the coat of arms of the McGavin family, owners of the estate for much of the C19. The castle's W side has been rebuilt as a Late Georgian stable block, its U-plan front with a segmental-arched carriage opening in the shallowly recessed centre. At the ends, rectangular carriage entrances under three-light first floor windows.

BALLUMBIE HOUSE to the E (now converted to flats after many years of dereliction) began as a three-storey laird's house built in 1810 for David Miller, then the owner of the Ballumbie estate. However, in 1906 *James Findlay* recast and enlarged it for Alexander Gilroy of the textile firm of Gilroy, Bros & Co., owners of the Tay Works. The appearance is almost all of 1906, a large harled villa, the details of uninspired and unexciting Scots C17 character.

PITKERRO HOUSE
off Drumsturdy Road

White-harled L-plan laird's house of some size but modest pretension, the SE wing largely C16 and C17, the NW range and other additions built in 1902–4 for Lieutenant-Colonel A. C. Douglas Dick designed by *Robert S. Lorimer*.

The lands of Pitkerro were acquired by John Durham, a merchant and burgess of Dundee, in 1534 and either he or his son James probably built the earliest part of the present house. This forms the S two-thirds of the SE wing. Simple three-storey oblong, *c.* 13 m. by 6.7 m. Projecting from the centre of its E side, a taller D-plan stair-tower containing the original entrance and topped by a crowstep-gabled rectangular caphouse; in the stair-tower's S inner angle, a round turret containing a stair from the main block's second floor to the study in the caphouse. At the SW corner of the main block, a round turret on continuous corbelling. Probably in the earlier C17 this wing was extended N and with a second turret on the addition's NW corner, perhaps C16 work reused. All this was remodelled in the C18 or early C19 with regularly spaced and comfortably sized windows and the wall-head raised to the top of the second-floor windows. Lorimer restored the wall-head and roof to their likely C16 and C17 appearance, placed crowsteps on the gables, dormerheads over the second-floor windows (all boat-shaped except for the pedimental head to the centre window on the W side) and gave the turrets low ogee-profile roofs. Lorimer also remodelled a sizeable two-storey addition, perhaps of the early C19, which had been built against the N half of the wing's E side, adding crowsteps to its E gable whose attic window he dressed up with a curvaceously pedimental surround. He also gave an extra floor to a single-storey corridor link from this addition to the stair-tower.

Lorimer's NW range is considerably larger than the earlier house. Of the same height, it contains only two (taller) storeys. The manner is resolutely Scottish domestic of early C17 inspiration. At the E end of the N elevation, a broad chimneyless crowstepped gable. Adjoining, the recessed main entrance under a panel set in a Neo-Jacobean aedicular surround. To the r., a crowstepped and chimney-topped gable and, r. of that and on the same plane, a straightforward three-bay end section containing a tall stair window, a pedimented first-floor opening and a single-storey canted bay projection, the windows in its sides (originally lighting a chapel) with cusped heads. Another canted bay but of two storeys at the range's W gable, the ground-floor windows in its sides also with cusped lights, a tall first-floor window in the W face. The main features of the S front overlooking the garden are pedimental dormerheads to the l. first-floor windows and a broad chimneyless M-roofed double gable projecting at the r. In the gable's W inner angle, a conical-roofed low tower, its first-floor door opening onto a forestair.

Harled single-storey-and-attic LODGE, also by Lorimer, 1902–4, and doggedly Scotstyle with a steep bellcast roof, bowed jamb at the S side and pedimental dormer window to the S. – Beside it, contemporary ashlar GATEPIERS in a late C17 manner, the stonework with faceted blocks, topped by the sloping ends of a pediment whose centre is replaced by the floral-ornamented and armorial cast-iron overthrow to the gates themselves.

POWRIE CASTLE

off Emmock Road

Part of one range and the whole of another of the C16 and early C17 courtyard house of the Fothringhams of Powrie.

The earlier part is at the E end of the SOUTH RANGE, its other buildings demolished, together with those of the E and W ranges. This is a rubble-walled tower house, probably of the early or mid C16. It has been Z-plan, the main block *c.* 13 m. by 9 m., the SW jamb now missing but probably circular and of about the same size as the round NE jamb which is *c.* 8.5 m. in diameter. Bowed stair-turret in the NE jamb's inner angle with the main block. The house now stands to a height of two storeys but originally must have been of three or, more probably, four. Entrance at the E end of the main block's N side, the chamfered elliptical-arched doorway under a hoodmould with headstops. Wide-mouthed oval gunloops at the ground floor on all sides of the main block and round the NE jamb; window in a chamfered surround in the jamb's S segment. Windows of reasonable size, also with chamfered margins, at the first floor where the masonry of most of the W gable and part of the S wall has been removed.

Inside, the entrance opens onto a vaulted lobby in the thickness of the N wall. On its S side are paired doors to two vaulted stores. A passage through the N wall's E end leads to a kitchen in the NE jamb. This is rectangular and also tunnel-vaulted. Segmental-arched fireplace, its surround chamfered, in the N wall, its W ingo containing the opening to a round oven. Slop drain in the S wall. Off the N side of the passage to the kitchen, a stone turnpike stair to the first floor. Here the main block has been filled by a double-height hall covered with an ashlar semicircular tunnel vault which springs from continuous corbelling. Broad chimneypiece, the cornice of its moulded rectangular surround rising at the centre as if to contain a panel; salt-box in the E ingo. The embrasure of the adjoining window has contained stone seats. In the NE jamb, a rectangular chamber, also tunnel-vaulted. Fireplace in the E wall. Garderobe in the NW corner; stone seats in the embrasure of the S window.

The NORTH RANGE was built in 1604 (the date on the lintel of one of the first-floor windows), perhaps partly as a jointure or dowry house. It is also rubble-walled. Long main block of *c.* 23.3 m. by 6.1 m. and a round NW jamb *c.* 4.5 m. in diameter, both of two storeys; two-storey S porch. In 1977 the jamb's conical roof was renewed, the C19 catslide dormerheads over the main block's first-floor windows replaced by gablets, and the porch's catslide roof replaced by a piended one. Two large chimneystacks rise from the wall-head on the N side. Windows only at the first floor of the jamb. In the main block's W gable, a built-up pedimented first-floor window. Most of the door and window openings along the S front are simply moulded and some altered. Modest and now rather weathered display is reserved for the first floor of the porch, its W face jettied on two tiers of continuous corbelling. In the W face, a window whose jambs have fluted pilasters rising from bulbous bases to capitals carved with stylized foliage, the lintel a frieze decorated with ovals. In the porch's S face, the first-floor window is framed by superimposed attached slender columns with bulbous bases and capitals.

The range seems to have contained ground-floor rooms intended to serve the complex as a whole and, on the first floor, two separate dwellings, one entered from a door (blocked) in the porch's E side, the other by a door at the E end of the main block's S front, both presumably reached by wooden forestairs. The present internal stair is a later introduction, perhaps of the C18. The ground floor's E room (now dining room) was an early C17 kitchen, its E end filled by an elliptical-arched fireplace. At the W end of the ground floor, a large tunnel-vaulted store (now kitchen) off whose NE corner is the entrance to a huge bread oven on the ground floor of the jamb. On the first floor of the main block are three rooms, the present stair now intruding into the W end of the centre room. Originally, the E and centre rooms may have formed one dwelling and the W room together with the room in the jamb a second. The main block's E and W rooms were given boarded tunnel-vaulted ceilings in 1977.

ANGUS

ABERLEMNO 5050

Just the church, manse and one farm, with a handful of 1950s local authority housing and a remarkable group of Pictish cross-slabs at Crosston 0.4 km. to the N.

PARISH CHURCH. Late Georgian kirk altered in the mid C19. The church designed by *Samuel Bell* and built in 1799 was of rubble (now sneck-harled). Its T-shape survives, as does the W gable's birdcage bellcote, its stepped roof topped by a pinnacle. It was extensively remodelled in 1856 by *James Maclaren* who heightened the walls and inserted Gothic windows, those of the S front with inelegantly traceried heads. The vestry in the NE inner angle and partly covering the gable of the N jamb is also probably of 1856 as is the addition containing a stair to the gallery built in the NW inner angle.

Inside, the semi-octagonal GALLERY is carried on cast-iron columns; it seems to be of 1799. – The PEWS and PULPIT (stripped of varnish *c.* 1962) are of 1856. – Round stone FONT BOWL of the C12 or C13 formerly at Aldbar Chapel. It is panelled with round-headed arches above a rope moulding. – HERALDIC STONE from Melgund Castle (q.v.) which bears the Beaton coat of arms, the initials JB and EM (for James Beaton and Elizabeth Menzies, his wife) and the date 1604.

MONUMENTS. On the S wall, a small bronze First World War memorial tablet of *c.* 1920; relief of kneeling male and female angels holding scrolls. – On the W wall, a stone monument of 1803 to George Jarron of Balbinnie. Urn at the top; inscription panel bordered by a rope moulding and with the relief head of a determined angel above the lettering. – On the N wall, an early C18 monument to Thomas and Agnes Mitchell. It is aedicular with fluted Ionic columns and a semicircular pediment whose tympanum displays a mantled shield flanked by open books. The monument is flanked by two others (to Jean Craw †1809 and Elizabeth Sedgwick †1821), each with Roman Doric pilasters and a cornice surmounted by a semicircular panel carved with the relief of a flower.

GRAVEYARD. Immediately W of the church, a large C8 CROSS-SLAB. The W face is carved with a ringed cross decorated with interlacing. In the background panels flanking the shaft are reliefs of intertwined beasts, the bottom r. pair serpentine-tailed horses; at the top, a pair of hippocamps. The E side has two Pictish symbols (a 'notched rectangle and Z-rod' and 'triple disc') below which is a battle scene. – To the S and E of the church, a sizeable number of C18 HEADSTONES, several pilastered, carved with some or all of the area's funerary repertoire of mantled shields, angels' heads and reminders of death. – Against the E wall, C18 GRAVE-SLABS displaying the same motifs as the headstones. Also some C17 slabs bearing shields and crudely carved skulls.

MANSE to the E. Plain harled double-pile built in 1782 to a design by *David Jamie* but much enlarged sixty years later.

KIRKTON to the W of the Parish Church. Harled farmhouse of *c.* 1840, the cornice of the doorpiece supported on heavy consoles. The house forms the N range of a three-sided court open to the E. On this court's S side, a cottage range. On the W side, the E range of a courtyard steading, its roof still partly covered with stone slabs. All these buildings look early C19.

PICTISH SLABS, Crosston. Three Pictish carved slabs, probably of the C7 and C8, all on the SE side of the B9134. The first, probably of the C8, is just NE of the School. Its front is carved with an interlaced background from which stands out a Celtic
6 cross, the shaft flanked by sorrowful angels with drooping heads and wings, holding books in their hands. At the bottom, the shaft is flanked by beasts. On the back, the 'crescent and V-rod' and 'double-disc and Z-rod' symbols above a large hunting scene. At the foot, two panels, one carved with a centaur, the other with the figure of David, when a shepherd boy, killing the lion. – To the NE, a smaller slab of much redder sandstone. Its incised carvings are now almost completely defaced but there are traces of a crescent and a curved line. This may be C7 work. – To the NE again, a slab of pale pinky
4 grey stone, the front carved, probably in the C7, with a serpent, 'double-disc and Z-rod', and 'mirror and comb' symbols. At the bottom of the stone are incised cup marks, probably dating from the second millennium B.C., so the slab seems to have been reused.

SCHOOL, Crosston, 0.4 km. N. Plain Tudor school and school house of 1864–5.

FLEMINGTON, 0.5 km. E. Superior ashlar-walled and piend-roofed two-storey FARMHOUSE, dated 1823 at the minimally advanced and parapeted centre, its doorpiece's cornice carried on block consoles; band course under the first floor. Extensive buildings to the rear, the single-storey N range's E gable containing a window with dummy sidelights and topped by an overall fanlight, also a dummy.

FLEMINGTON CASTLE to the S was built *c.* 1600 for the Mortimers of Flemington. Now semi-derelict, it is a largely ivy-covered rubble-walled L of two storeys and an attic, the jamb projecting to both N and E. In each inner angle, a turret carried on continuous corbelling, the S splayed and rising only from the first floor to an entresol, the taller S turret bowed. At the ground floor of the jamb, a large round shot-hole to the N and an oval shot-hole to the S; in the E face, a double shot-hole like a pair of pince-nez. Doorway with a roll-and-hollow moulding in the S face of the jamb; to its l., a slit window with a chamfered margin. Most of the windows of the main block seem to have been enlarged *c.* 1700.

Inside, the main block's ground floor contains two tunnel-vaulted rooms. The S was the kitchen, its fireplace with a round-headed arch. The principal stair (now missing) in the jamb led to a first-floor hall, later subdivided.

FORT, Hill of Finavon, 1.6 km. W. Remains of a fort constructed *c.* 700 B.C. The site is the summit of a hill with fairly gentle slopes on three sides but a much steeper ascent from the S. Surprisingly, the fort is set back from the edge of the S slope leaving a flat space unfortified either naturally or artificially in front of the rampart on this side. The fort is a rough oblong, *c.* 150 m. by 40 m., enclosing an area of *c.* 0.7 ha., defended by a massive stone rampart *c.* 6 m. wide and standing up to 5 m. in height. In places the rampart's masonry shows evidence of vitrifaction, so it has been laced with wood which has later caught fire either accidentally or as the result of an attack. At the E end is a bone-shaped outer defence. There was a well or cistern (no longer visible) in a depression at the enclosure's W end. Near the E end, an (infilled) shaft cut through the rock, probably a cistern.

MELGUND CASTLE. *See* p. 604.

AFFLECK CASTLE AND HOUSE

4030

2.4 km. W of Monikie

Late C15 tower house of the Auchinlecks of that Ilk sitting beside Affleck House, its successor as the residence of the owners of the estate since the late C18.

The tower house (AFFLECK CASTLE), built of local red sandstone rubble, is of four storeys and an attic, L-plan with a main block of *c.* 11.6 m. by 8.2 m., the jamb of *c.* 3.7 m. by 1.8 m. projecting from the S end of the main block's E side. At the ground floor, an inverted keyhole gunloop in each of the main block's N, S and W walls and in the E face of the jamb. At the first, second and third floors of the main block, a window in each of the S, E and W walls, the second-floor openings larger than the others. Slit stair windows up to the second-floor level of the jamb and rather larger openings above. At the main block's upper floors are small S windows lighting wall chambers and, at its SW corner, slit stair windows above the second floor. At the wall-head, an ashlar parapet, perhaps a Late Georgian replacement for a battlement but the supporting individual corbels are C15. It breaks forward into round turrets carried on continuous corbelling at all corners except the SW

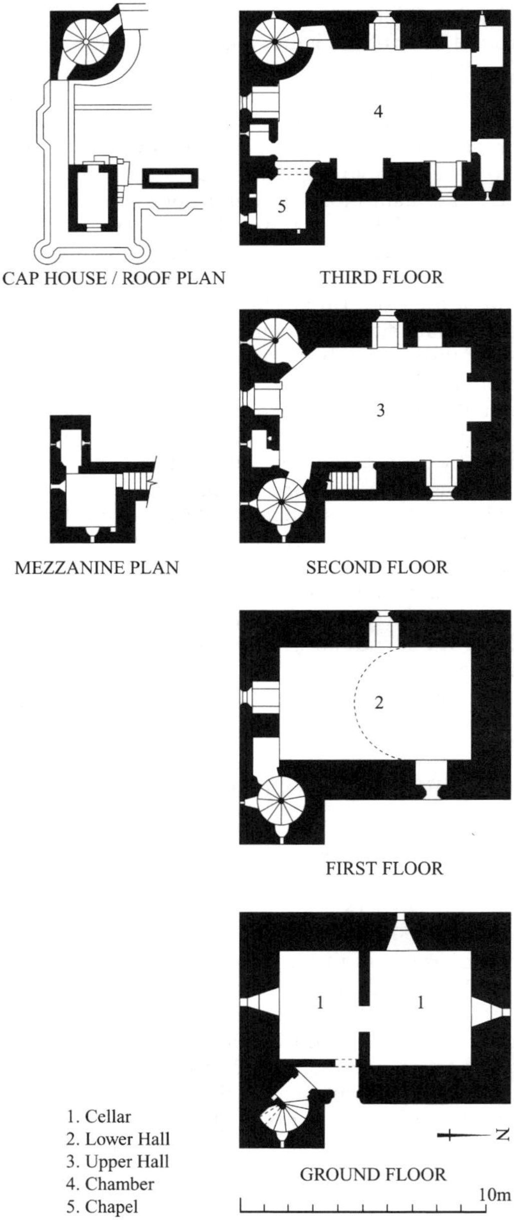

Affleck Castle.
Plans

and into machicolated bartizans at the centre of the S side and, in front of a wall-head chimney, over the house's E entrance. The main walling of the SW corner rises above the parapet as a caphouse with its own parapet; another caphouse, also parapeted, over the jamb but set back behind the main wall-head parapet. Also set back within the wall-head parapet is the main block's crowstep-gabled attic, a chimney on its N end. Segmental-arched entrance, formerly containing an iron yett behind the door, at the main block's S end immediately beside the projection of the jamb. Directly above but set quite high, a couple of recesses. The lower is square and may have contained an armorial panel; the upper rises into a cusped ogee arch.

(Inside, the ground and first floors of the main block are covered by a single round-headed tunnel vault divided horizontally by an entresol floor. On the ground floor, a few steps below the entrance level, a pair of intercommunicating cellars lit only from gunloops. The turnpike stair in the jamb rises to the second floor. On the first or entresol floor is the Lower Hall, its elliptical-headed window embrasures' stone seats giving a suggestion of comfort belied by the absence of a fireplace. The second floor's wooden-ceilinged Upper Hall is much better appointed. Its rather larger windows, their embrasures segmental-arched, are also equipped with seats. At the room's N end, a large fireplace. In the N end of the W wall, a big cupboard and, in the wall thickness of the SE corner, a garderobe with a small window to the S. A door in the Hall's E side opens onto a straight stair leading up through the wall thickness to a small room above the SE jamb's stairhead, a lamp recess in its E wall, a small window in the S; garderobe with a peephole into the Hall off its W side. In the splayed SW corner of the Upper Hall, a door to the house's second turnpike stair. Of the same size as the stair from the ground to the second floors, this rises to the wall-walk. Off it is the Chamber which occupies the third floor of the main block. This is quite low and covered by a wooden ceiling but exceptionally well finished. Stone seats in the round-headed window embrasures. At each end of the N wall, a mural chamber provided with a small window. Garderobe, also with a window, at the E end of the S wall. Just S of the centre of the room's E side is the fireplace, the capitals of its jambs' bundle-shafted columns formed as stylized foliage, the high lintel finished with a cornice. Immediately r. of the fireplace is the entrance to a Chapel in the jamb. The round-headed entrance is very like a chancel arch, the chamfered jambs with curve-splayed bases and moulded capitals, the arch-head with a concave-moulded chamfer. In the inner faces of the jambs are slots for a wooden screen. Corbelled out from the S jamb's E face is a heptagonal stoup, three of its faces bearing shields, one displaying three lozenges. Above the chapel, an ashlar semicircular tunnel vault. Flanking the site of the altar at the E end are a pair of horizontally moulded corbels, probably intended as stands for statues. Light on the altar came from a window at the E end of the S wall. Beside this window, a combined piscina and credence niche. The piscina is a horizontally moulded semi-hexagon tapering downwards to a small corbel carved with a human face. Above is the credence niche, a pointed arch whose head is flanked and surmounted by three consecration crosses.)

AFFLECK HOUSE immediately S is an unexciting harled laird's house built *c.* 1760 for James Yeaman, a bailie of Dundee, or his son and enlarged by *Alexander MacGregor*, *c.* 1850.

AIRLIE *see* KIRKTON OF AIRLIE

2050
AIRLIE CASTLE

1.9 km. NW of Kirkton of Airlie

House of two personalities, disparate but complementary, a high C15 castle wall fronting a courtyard whose N side is occupied by a wholly pacific Georgian house.

In the early C15 Sir Walter Ogilvy of Carcary and Lintrathen, High Treasurer of Scotland and progenitor of the Earls of Airlie, acquired lands in the barony of Lintrathen. In 1432 he obtained a licence from James I to construct his tower of Airlie in the form of a castle and the castle of Airlie is on record in 1459. In 1640 Airlie Castle, a Royalist stronghold, was destroyed by the Marquess of Argyll's Covenanting force. Subsequently, Cortachy Castle (q.v.) became the principal seat of the Earls of Airlie and Airlie Castle was abandoned as a residence until the 1790s when David, titular Earl of Airlie, built a house on the site of part of the former N range. Originally 'intended merely as an occasional summer resort', this house was soon after extended W. About the same time or a little later, low service buildings and a cottage completed the range. The buildings were repaired by *Ian G. Lindsay & Partners* in 1956–7 and, *c.* 1960, were remodelled by *Stewart Tod* as the principal residence of the twelfth Earl of Airlie.

The position, on the boundary between the fertile plain of Strathmore and the glens running into the Grampian Mountains, was of potential strategic importance. The site, a precipitously sided promontory at the confluence of the Melgam Water and the River Isla and easily approached only from the E, is of great natural strength. The vulnerable E side has been cut through by a broad ditch, a fortification possibly pre-dating the C15 castle. This has been largely filled in but its now narrowed S end survives and returns to the S where it forms the beginning of a pathway cut through the steep slope of the ravine to the bank of the River Isla below.

38 The castle's 9 m.-high C15 E wall behind the ditch survives although now without parapet or battlement. Like the other buildings here it is built of warm red sandstone rubble. At the S end, a projecting tower-like rectangular buttress, its S face pierced by the outlet for the drain of a garderobe which

presumably stood at this corner of the wall-walk. The main (S) stretch of walling rises from a splay-topped projecting base. In this stretch, a pair of tall vertical slit windows to the ground floor. The entrance to the castle's courtyard is contained in a slightly advanced gatehouse tower standing at the join of the S two-thirds of the wall with the remainder. This tower is of four storeys, the W front's tall ground floor pieced by an archway, the top two storeys jettied out. At each of the upper floors, a small window, each placed slightly to the r. of the one below. The wall-head parapet is carried on block corbels, perhaps replacements of the 1790s when a balustrade (removed in 1956–7) was added on top. Also of the 1790s in its present form but doubtless replacing something similar is the top of the conical-roofed round turret projected on continuous corbelling at the SE corner, its internal stair providing access from the third floor and parapet walk to the roof of the tower. The pend entrance through the tower is formidable. To the E it presents a tall round-headed arch which has contained an outer door, its checks and hinges surviving. Behind, a lower pointed arch, the surround pierced with the slit for a portcullis. Behind this, a second pair of doors. N of the gateway the castle wall continues on the same line as that to the S but it rises higher, probably having been raised in the 1790s when a house was built behind. Certainly of the 1790s must be its battlement, the crenelles and merlons extravagantly wide.

Inside the courtyard, the gatehouse tower's first and second floors are on the same plane, projected on simple rounded corbels; also corbelled out to the N is a short half-gable containing a stair from the C18 house's upper floor to the first-floor room of the tower. At the bottom and top of the tower's second floor are rounded corbels which have supported the floor and lean-to roof of a narrow wooden outshot at this level. This has been entered from the tower by a round-headed door with chamfered jambs, now converted to a window and its head partly renewed. Boldly projecting string course under the third floor from which a S door opens onto the top of the wall-walk, from which an adjoining door gives access to the turret.

The S stretch of curtain wall is, on the courtyard side, thicker at the ground floor than above. At this ground floor, a pair of round-headed embrasures to its slit windows which are placed above stepped sills; cupboard between the windows. In the N window embrasure, a badly weathered STATUE, perhaps late medieval, of a bearded man, possibly a representation of St John the Baptist. It used to stand beside the castle's drive but its original setting and history are unknown.

The buildings in the courtyard's N range are quite domestic although their rear wall may be partly C15 or C16, as is the bottom of the front. The main block at the E is of two storeys and an attic above a half-sunk basement. The E five bays were built in 1790–4 to a design of *Richard Hogg*, the principal door placed at the centre. The W three bays, in the same unadorned manner, were added early in the C19 but the ground-floor entrance remained in its original position, by now off-centre. *Stewart Tod* shifted this door to the centre of the extended frontage and placed a small panel carved with the heraldic achievement of the Earls of Airlie above it. At the same time new dormer windows were erected, their scrolled tops rising to thistle and fleur-de-lis finials. All the basement openings are round-headed except for a small rectangular central opening with a chamfered surround which seems to be of the C15 or C16. It is now hidden by the double stair to the main entrance. This is the front's chief adornment, a Venetian door of the 1790s moved here *c.* 1960. W of the main block and at its basement level but fully exposed by the terracing of the courtyard here is a slightly recessed single-storey link of *c.* 1960, its ball-finialled parapet broken by a central balustrade. Above the door from the courtyard, a reused lintel inscribed 'L.M♥E.C/THE .LORD.DEFEND.HIS.FAMILY/16 60'. At the W end of the N range, a two-storey mid-C19 cottage. Gabled porch at the W bay of its front. At the cottage's back wall, a sturdy buttress, perhaps of the C16.

Inside the N range's main block are tunnel-vaulted ground-floor rooms, perhaps surviving from a C16 house on the site. The central room (now billiard room) was originally a kitchen, with a wide fireplace (partly infilled) in its W wall, an oven (now cupboard) to its N. As extended in the early C19 this block contained two virtually self-contained houses, one occupying the E five bays, the other the three to the W, each with its own entrance (the E at the principal floor, the W at the basement) opening onto a staircase. On the principal floor, the drawing room at the W is early C19 and a little higher than the other rooms. In the W wall, a chimneypiece of late C18 type with foliaged pendants under vases at the jambs and swags and the central relief of a vine on the lintel. It is flanked by niches, the N round-headed and with projecting blocky keystone and imposts. E of this, a dog-leg stair which rises from the basement the full height of the house. The house's centre room is the dining room which also serves as the entrance hall since the main door was shifted to its S wall *c.* 1960. Simple plaster panels on the walls. Another Adamish chimneypiece with urns at the top of the jambs and swags of roses issuing from a swagged urn on the lintel. Above, a carved and painted wooden overmantel of *c.* 1740, the lugged and swan-neck-topped frame enclosing the heraldic achievement of the Earls of Airlie. Immediately E is the 1790s staircase, unpretentious but not without elegance. The E room of the principal floor is the library formed *c.* 1960 from the space occupied by a staircase to the basement and a study. Bookcases along three walls, two with broken-pedimented centrepieces. Late C18 chimneypiece, the jambs bundle-shafted columns with Batty Langleyish Gothick capitals; on the lintel, a female head from which issue swags of roses. The first-floor bedrooms are plain but a short stair in the wall thickness leads from the E room down to the first-floor room (now bathroom) in the gatehouse tower. This is tunnel-vaulted; slit window in the N wall and a slightly larger opening to the E.

GARDEN of *c.* 1800 to the SE, the walls of rubble but higher and faced internally with brickwork at the taller centre of the W side where a greenhouse formerly stood. Wrought-iron S gate of 1906 decorated with stylized foliage. – SE of the garden, rubble-walled STABLES by *David A. Whyte*, 1813. Straightforward two-storey blocks serving as lateral wings to a taller centrepiece, its ground floor containing a broad Gothic carriage entrance, the upper floor a tall two-light pointed and Y-traceried dummy window flanked by a pair of quatrefoil dummy openings. The centrepiece's wall-head battlement rises higher at the chimney-topped centre. – At the S end of the drive's long curving avenue, GATES with ball-finialled GATEPIERS designed by *Stewart Tod* and erected in 1968 to commemorate the golden wedding of the twelfth Earl of Airlie and his wife. Beside the gates, a single-storey LODGE of *c.* 1865. Picturesque with broad eaves and bargeboards.

ARBIRLOT

6040

Small village in a rural parish.

ARBIRLOT FREE CHURCH, Main Street. Now church hall. By *John Milne*, 1854, a muscular buttressed and lancet-windowed oblong, the walling of squared and stugged masonry. The E gable's centre is slightly advanced, just hinting at a nave and aisles behind; its gabled bellcote has been removed.

ARBIRLOT PARISH CHURCH, Main Street. Rubble-walled kirk built on a T-plan in 1831–2 but enlarged to a cross in 1889, the later work's masonry squared and stugged. The original building, its corners with stepped angle buttresses, had Y-traceried pointed windows in the S side. Those of the outer bays now flank the S jamb added in 1889, its gable pierced by a pair of widely spaced tall lancets flanking a rose window; lean-to boiler house in the E inner angle. At the E and W ends, gabled porches and Tudor Gothic windows lighting the area; the gallery windows are each of three round-headed lights under a round-headed and louvred opening in the head of the gable. W bellcote with turret-buttresses at the corners and round-headed openings in the four faces; ball-finialled stone spire. On the E gable, a ball finial. The N jamb of 1831–2 projects from the N side, its N window of three tall lancet lights under a round-headed louvred opening. Built into the gable, a large GRAVESLAB commemorating David Ouchterlony †1738, one of what were presumably a pair of angels (souls) carved at the top still discernible. In the jamb's inner angle are three-sided outshots.

INTERIOR. Galleries of the 1830s at the E and W ends. The focus is now on the COMMUNION TABLE of 1926 in the S jamb, its front with linenfold panelling. – Behind, the ORGAN of *c.* 1900. – Early C20 routine Gothic PULPIT on the E side of the 'chancel'. – STAINED GLASS. In the 'chancel' two lights (the Sower; Dorcas) by *James Ballantine II*, 1913, originally in Arbirlot Free Church and moved here *c.* 1930. – Under the E and W galleries, two late C20 windows (the Adoration of the Magi; the Good Shepherd), examples of stylized realism. – In the N jamb, the three-light War Memorial window, strongly coloured and with a hint of Art Nouveau, by *J. S. Hamilton*, 1922. – In the E gallery, the E window (Obed, Ruth, Jesse, Boaz and David) is of 1938, erected as a memorial to the Rev. John and Mrs Christie. – Corresponding W gallery window (Our Lord and Children) by *Arthur Spiers*, 2000, realistic and strongly coloured but undisciplined.

Propped against the exterior of the church, large C18 GRAVE-SLABS carved variously with angels' heads, shields and emblems of death.

ARBIRLOT PRIMARY SCHOOL, 1.3 km. WSW. By *James Maclaren*, 1855. Single-storey, of squared and stugged masonry. Sprinkling of Romanesque detail, most emphatic at the round-arched and spire-finialled bellcote bestriding the roof. – Beside the school, a two-storey broad-eaved and bay-windowed SCHOOL HOUSE by *Aitkenhead & Mason*, 1875–6.

DESCRIPTION. L-plan village of single-storey terraced cottages, mostly harled and early C19 but many of the windows enlarged. The Parish Church occupies the inner angle, the former Free Church is set back at the NW corner. Also set back and opposite the Parish Church, the single-storey U-plan No. 20 MAIN STREET built as the Parish School *c.* 1800, a Venetian window in the pedimented gable of each wing. At the village's S end, an early C19 bridge, the main masonry of stugged ashlar but with vermiculated ashlar voussoirs to the round-headed arch.

THE GLEBE HOUSE. Originally Arbirlot Parish Manse and built in 1834–5. Two storeys, faced with cherry-cock-pointed rubble, the wall-head finished with a cornice and parapet. L-plan; in the inner angle, a flat-roofed porch dignified by Roman Doric columns *in antis*. Rubble-walled GARDEN and COURT OF OFFICES.

KELLY CASTLE. *See* p. 547.

6040

ARBROATH

Coastal town at the mouth of the Brothock Water, its origins as a burgh dating to 1178 when William I founded Arbroath Abbey and gave it leave to form a burgh with a weekly market and a port. The medieval burgh contained one principal street (High Street) leading from the harbour to the Abbey precinct and a shorter parallel street (Marketgate) to the W. By 1579 Arbroath was of sufficient consequence to be represented in Parliament and in 1599 was formally constituted a royal burgh whose merchants enjoyed the right to engage in foreign trade.

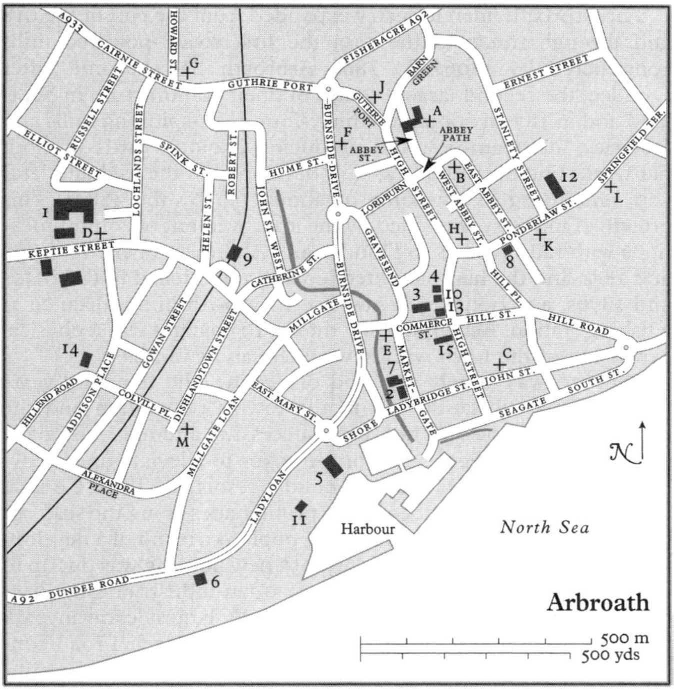

- A Arbroath Abbey
- B Arbroath Old and Abbey Parish Church
- C Arbroath United Free Church
- D Arbroath West Kirk
- E East Free Church
- F Inverbrothock Chapel of Ease
- G Knox's Church
- H Old Parish Church
- J St Andrew
- K St John's Methodist church
- L St Mary's Episcopal Church
- M St Thomas of Canterbury (R.C.)

- 1 Angus College
- 2 Arbroath Community Centre
- 3 Corn Exchange
- 4 Guildry Buildings
- 5 Harbour Visitor Centre
- 6 Ladyloan School
- 7 Public Baths
- 8 Public Library
- 9 Railway Station
- 10 Sheriff Court House
- 11 Signal Tower
- 12 Springfield Medical Centre
- 13 Trades Hall
- 14 Water Tower
- 15 Webster Memorial Theatre

In 1725–42 a new harbour was built at Arbroath whose ships traded with the American colonies, the Baltic, Scandinavia, France and the Netherlands. As significant was the establishment of industry begun in 1738–40 with the construction of factories for flax spinning and linen weaving. By 1760 a main linen stamping office had been established at Arbroath and by 1785 the town was the principal producer of canvas in Scotland.

The Arbroath linen industry expanded from the end of the C18 and through much of the C19, the first steam-powered mills constructed by 1806. By 1864 Arbroath had become, after Dundee, the second largest centre of linen manufacture in Scotland and in 1875 it contained thirty-four linen-spinning mills and factories, all steam-powered producing 450,000 yards of cloth per week. Engineering works also developed in the mid and later C19, employing a workforce of about 750 by the 1880s. This growth of industry was aided by the improvement of communications with railway lines to Dundee and Aberdeen opened in 1838 and 1850 and the harbour extended and remodelled in the 1840s and 1870s, a period which saw also its growth in importance as a fishing station. Accompanying these C19 changes was a physical expansion of the town with new streets and suburbs.

The C20 was largely a period of decline, the first fifty years marked by a substantial fall in the town's population and the closure of factories. A not very successful attempt was made during the Great Depression of the 1930s to alleviate unemployment and reinvent Arbroath as a holiday resort, the Town Council undertaking to construct concrete promenades along the seafront together with an open-air swimming pool. As a result of a development plan for the burgh agreed in 1953 new housing was put up to supplement schemes of the earlier C20, an industrial estate laid out and new factories opened, Scotland's largest caravan park formed on the W side of the town, and an inner relief road constructed, cutting off the town centre from the C19 developments. However, despite an increase in population to *c.* 23,000 by the end of the century, about the same level as a hundred years before, unemployment has remained resolutely high. The opening of new visitor centres at the Abbey and Harbour in 2001 and 2007 and the continuing gastronomic repute of Arbroath 'smokies' (cured haddock) are perhaps small signs of hope for future regeneration.

Arbroath.
View of town by John Slezer, 1693

ARBROATH ABBEY

Abbey Street

Now surrounded by the town, the tidy but ungainly ruin of one of the largest and most lavishly endowed of Scotland's medieval religious houses. Arbroath Abbey was formally founded by William I ('the Lion') in 1178, although preparations for its construction had perhaps begun a few years before, as an establishment of the Tironensian (reformed Benedictine) order, the first monks brought from Kelso Abbey (Borders). The monastery was dedicated to the newly canonized St Thomas Becket. p. 300

The choir, presumably the first part of the abbey church to be built, must have been substantially completed by 1214 when William I was buried there in front of the High Altar. The church was consecrated in 1232, a probable date for completion of the nave. The PLAN – an unaisled two-bay presbytery containing the High Altar, a three-bay aisled choir, N and S transepts and a nave of nine bays – was close to that of the slightly earlier Jedburgh Abbey (Borders) and St Andrews Cathedral (Fife), both Augustinian houses, the one slightly smaller, the other the largest church in Scotland. The cloister buildings, their E range running S from the church's S transept, were built on the standard quadrangular monastic plan, although oblong rather than the more usual square and with a Great Hall projecting from the W range. By the end of the C13 at the latest a wall had been constructed to enclose the abbey precinct containing ancillary buildings S and W of the church and cloister and a graveyard to their N.

In 1272 a gale leading to a fire, probably caused by lightning, considerably damaged the abbey church and led to partial collapse of the NW tower. The church was subsequently repaired, probably before the beginning of the Wars of Independence. In these the Abbey has achieved fame as the setting in 1320 of the fixing of the seals of the magnates and leading figures of Scotland to a letter addressed to the Pope and now known as the Declaration of Arbroath, an assertion of the independence of the Scottish Church and nation from English rule.

In the last years of the Wars of Independence, the Abbey was attacked by English forces in 1350 and 1379. Apparently more serious was the church's being struck by lightning in 1380 when the wooden roofs over the transepts and the central vessels of the choir and nave were destroyed, forcing the temporary dispersal of the monks among other religious houses. Repairs seem still to have been incomplete in 1395 when *William Tweeddale*, plumber, contracted to cover the choir roof with lead. An end to over a century and a half of damage and repair was signalled in the earlier C15 when Abbot Walter Paniter added a sacristy and treasury to the S side of the choir. In 1470 the monastic dormitory in the cloister's E range was said to have been remodelled. Also probably begun in the C15 and carried on in the first half of the C16 seems to have been a significant amount of work on the buildings to the W of the cloister, including a reconstruction of the Abbot's House, by then including the C13 Great Hall, as a lodging aloof from the monastic cloister.

At the Reformation the monastery was dissolved and the abbey church abandoned for worship. The abbey estates were granted to a succession of lay commendators until 1606 when the lands were constituted a temporal lordship held by James, second Marquess of Hamilton. The lordship was sold in 1642 to Patrick Maule of Panmure (later, first Earl of Panmure) but ownership of the monastic precinct itself was unclear. In 1580 it seems to have been regarded as the property of Esmé Stuart, Duke of Lennox, then the Commendator, who granted leave to the Town Council of Arbroath to remove stone and timber from the E range of the cloister for use in the erection of a new church in the burgh. However, in 1636 Charles I granted possession of the buildings within the precinct as part of the endowment for the bishopric of Brechin. With or without proper legal permission the church and monastic buildings had been extensively quarried by the late C17 when almost all the N side of the church had been removed as had been the cloister buildings except for the Abbot's House. After the abolition of episcopacy in the Church of Scotland in 1689 legal ownership of the abbey buildings reverted to the Crown which in 1753 granted a feu charter of the precinct exclusive of the abbey church itself to the Burgh of Arbroath. Subsequently, the Town Council granted individuals sub-feus or leases of much of the precinct land and buildings, the ranges adjoining the Gatehouse being let to various tradesmen and the church's sacristy, doubtfully the property of the Council, serving as a joiner's wood store by 1801. Some of the monastic buildings were partly demolished, either for the sake of their materials or because their condition posed a danger to passers-by. In 1780 the S wall of the chapter house was removed and, in 1800, the stone vault of the Gatehouse pend was demolished, nineteen years after the building's roof had been taken off.

Arbroath Abbey.
View from north-east by J. Hooper, 1790

Consolidation and repair of the abbey buildings as monuments to Scotland's history took place in the C19. In 1809, after the upper part of the S transept's circular window had fallen, Arbroath Town Council commissioned a report on the condition of the ruins of the abbey church from the engineer, *Robert Stevenson*, who recommended the carrying out of repairs and restoration at an estimated cost of £900. In 1815 work was begun by the Government and continued for some years, the House of Lords confirming its legal ownership of the abbey church in 1815. In 1835 the Commissioners of Woods and Forests instructed *Robert Reid*, architect to the Scottish Office of Works, to clear out rubbish and fallen masonry from the church's interior and provided an annual grant for repair of the its ruins whose maintenance still continues to be the responsibility of Government. In 1879 Arbroath Town Council acquired the Abbot's House and in 1905 granted H.M. Office of Works guardianship of its vaulted undercroft together with the Guesthouse Range, the Gatehouse, precinct wall and Regality Tower of the abbey precinct. After acquiring control over the whole of the Abbot's House in 1922, the *Office of Works* began an extensive reconstruction of the building nine years later followed by far-reaching work on the Guesthouse Range in 1937. A visitor centre N of the church's W end was built in 2000–1.

DESCRIPTION

At the corner of the Abbey's former precinct, at the junction of Abbey Park and Abbey Street, stands the four-storey REGALITY TOWER, its walls, like those of all the abbey buildings, of red sandstone ashlar. At the N and SW corners, tapering and sloping-topped angle buttresses and more buttresses of the same height and design along the outer face of the precinct wall, the appearance of all these suggestive of a mid-C13 date However, the tower's top stage, marked off by a string course, is finished at the N, W and S faces with boldly projecting moulded corbels, perhaps of *c.* 1500, which have carried a wall-walk; perhaps this top floor, with windows to the S, W and N, is an addition. At the ground floor of the tower, a plain doorway has been inserted, perhaps in the C18, in the centre of the W face. At the first floor, an off-centre round-headed S entrance and a fairly small rectangular window, also off-centre in the N wall. Above, a second floor doorway, also round-headed, in the centre of the S wall, and an off-centre window in each of the W and N faces. The tower's piended roof may be C18. Inside the tower, the two lower floors each contain a single room covered with a ribbed tunnel vault, the ground floor room originally entered by a trapdoor from the floor above. At the first floor and each of the rooms on the second and third floors, fireplaces flanked by moulded shafts; they are of *c.* 1500.

The PRECINCT WALL S of the Regality Tower was removed in the C18. The wall running E from the tower to the SW corner

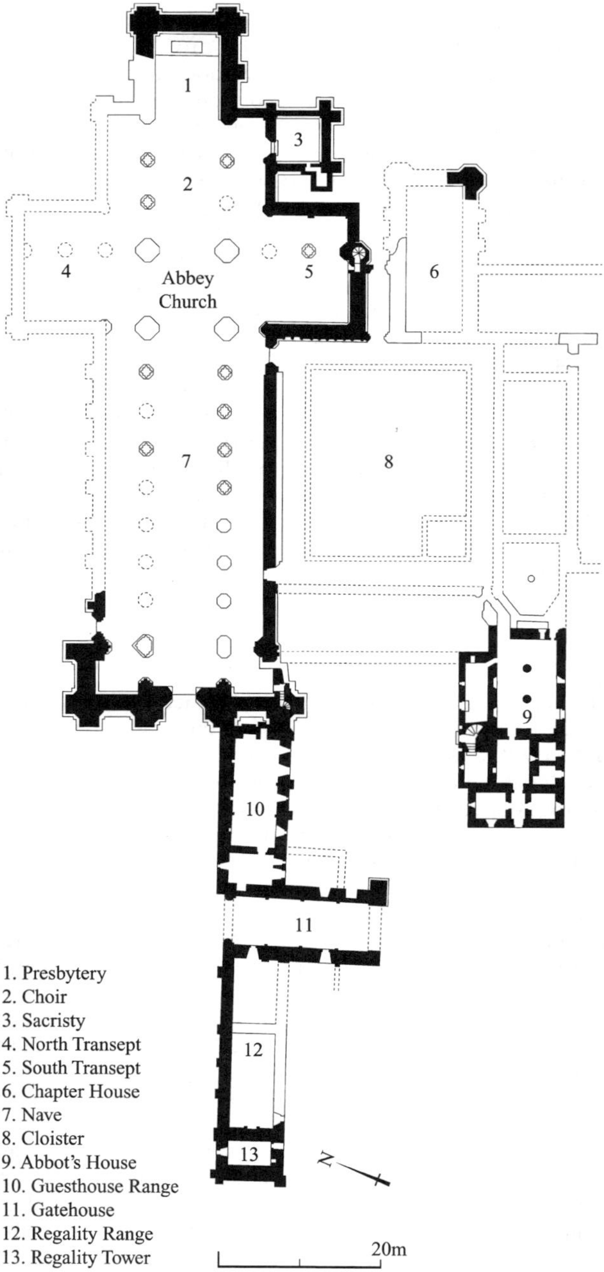

1. Presbytery
2. Choir
3. Sacristy
4. North Transept
5. South Transept
6. Chapter House
7. Nave
8. Cloister
9. Abbot's House
10. Guesthouse Range
11. Gatehouse
12. Regality Range
13. Regality Tower

Arbroath Abbey.
Plan

of the abbey church survives. Apparently it is C13 but its line must represent a change of mind from what was originally intended since it and the buildings constructed against its S side hide the base of the church's SW tower. Behind the W end of the present wall stood the REGALITY RANGE, traditionally and not improbably thought to have housed officials for the administration of the Abbey's estates. A roof raggle in the E face of the Regality Tower shows that this range was of three storeys and an attic in height. Probably also of mid-C13 origin, it has extended to the W side of the Gatehouse. Its ground floor contained two rooms. The E, entered from the Gatehouse's pend, was *c.* 8.5 m. by 5.5 m and covered with a ribbed tunnel-vault, the W (known as the Regality Courthouse), entered from the precinct to the S, *c.* 12.2 m. by 5.5 m. and with three bays of quadripartite vaulting.

About halfway between the Regality Tower and the W front of the abbey church the line of the precinct wall is broken by the GATEHOUSE. This is of two tall storeys, a long rectangle of *c.* 19.5 m. by 9.1 m. placed at right angles to the precinct wall and extending well clear of the adjoining ranges on the wall's S side. The N gable contains a broad pointed archway, *c.* 5 m. wide and 5.2 m. high, with bell-capitalled bundled shafts and a portcullis slot piercing its head. This much looks C13. So too may be the general design of the first floor where a large pointed window just W of the archway's centre is flanked on each side by two bays of blind cusped arcading which rises only half the height of the window. The window has been partly infilled *c.* 1500, this masonry blocking containing a stone-mullioned rectangular window of two lights under a circular opening. Also of *c.* 1500 and moulded like those of the Regality Tower's wall-head are the corbels which have been inserted either side of the window to support a walkway; a string course above the window perhaps supported the inner edge of a lean-to roof. At the same time the head of the gable was remodelled and given extravagantly tall gabled crowsteps.

The Gatehouse entrance opens onto a pend of four bays, its now missing quadripartite vaults springing from bell-capitalled clustered wall-shafts like those of the entrance archway. Halfway along the passage is an inner gateway, its jambs, surviving to the springing of the archway, broad and unadorned, their S faces checked for doors. Each side, a moulded 'ice-cream cone' corbel at the base of vaulting. In the pend's N bay, a pointed door to the Regality Range; a similar E door to the Guesthouse Range has been converted to a cupboard. In the two S bays, pointed doorways with chamfered surrounds. The pend's S entrance from the precinct is a simpler repeat of the N, the arch-head unsupported by shafts, and the large pointed first-floor window without the partial blocking of *c.* 1500 and not flanked by arcading. A sill course under the window continues round the hefty clasping buttress at the gable's SE corner. The head of the gable, like its N counterpart, is finished with tall crowsteps of *c.* 1500. Above the pend has been a hall lit from the windows in the gables and also from pointed openings in the side walls, the W wall's S window embrasure containing stone seats. In the SE corner, a door to a wall chamber; another door has opened into the Regality Range.

The line of the precinct wall E of the Gatehouse projects minimally to the N. Behind it is the Guesthouse Range (*see* p. 311) from which opens a small rectangular window in a chamfered surround with a circular shot-hole to its l., these perhaps insertions of the C16. Above, a mullioned-and-transomed two-light first-floor window, probably also an insertion.

The W FRONT of the church, even in its half-demolished state and with the base of its SW tower hidden by the precinct wall and Guesthouse Range, is a work of great presence. As built *c.* 1200 this was a powerful assertion of ecclesiastical power and monarchical patronage. It is symmetrical, the gabled centre (the nave) flanked by angle-buttressed towers significantly wider than the aisles behind. Originally, each tower's W front was identically treated. Above a splay-topped base, a tall double tier of pointed blind arcading, the shafts now missing except for their bases and bell capitals. The tall shafts which carried the upper tier of arches rose in front of the centres of the arches of the lower tier. Above, two tiers of paired tall and pointed single-light windows, the lower still mostly intact; between the tiers, a band of latticed enrichment. Above the level of the heads of the upper windows the tower's angle buttresses are finished with sloping tops. Over the corners of the SW tower, octagonal turrets, their lowest stage decorated with arcaded corbelling. Above the corners of the NW tower have been taller turrets, also octagonal, between which rose a low top stage added when the tower was repaired after 1272. Similarly treated is the surviving N face of the NW tower but without the latticed band under the upper windows.

Of the remains of the nave gable, the lowest stage is pierced by the processional entrance to the church. The door itself is set back in the wall whose outer part forms a porch, its entrance a simple round-headed arch, each of the ingoes containing a pointed recess whose arch-head has been carried on bell-capitalled shafts. The nave door is round-headed, the orders of its splayed surround carried on shafts, only their bell capitals surviving, and carved with chevron and bobbin enrichment. Above the door, the upper storey of the porch contains a gallery designed for use by a choir to greet the Palm Sunday procession on its return to the church. On the outer side, this gallery is open to the W through three pointed arches set in stonework slightly recessed from the main walling and surmounted by a trio of vestigial gablets originally surmounted by roofs supported on solid end walls and a pair of columns in the centre. Access to the gallery has been from a turnpike stair contained in the SW buttress of the SW tower and from there by a walkway across the interior of the tower. The gallery is divided into two aisles by a pair of bell-capitalled columns which support transverse stone beams. On the gallery's E side looking into the nave, six acutely pointed arches, their capitals carved with dentil enrichment. Above this gallery, the nave's W front bears a band of blind arcading under a huge circular window, only its bottom half now extant, which was probably filled with plate tracery.

Inside the church, the NAVE has been of nine bays, each of the flanking aisles beginning at the W with chambers within the towers, the N still largely intact. Tall pointed arches in their sides opened into the nave and others at the E to the aisles. Over each of the nave arches, an opening at the triforium level of the nave although the tower contained no floor behind. Each of these openings comprised a pair of pointed lights within a round-headed overarch. There appear also to have been openings above at the level of the nave's clearstorey.

The outer wall of the N aisle of the nave has been demolished except for the W bay adjoining the NW tower. In this bay, a door, the usual entry for laity into the church. It is pointed, the jambs with bell-capitalled shafts, mostly missing, alternating with engaged rolls; lavishly moulded arch-head. On the wall above the door, a blind arch whose head is carried on shafts standing on corbels from which spring also the bases of shafts formerly supporting a quadripartite vault over this bay of the aisle; presumably the aisles' other bays were also vaulted. The S aisle's side wall stands almost to the wall-head. Shafts for quadripartite vaulting are carried on corbels placed at the same height as in the N aisle's W bay. Between the shafts, pointed windows whose sills slope steeply down to a string course under the wall-shafts' corbel bases. Elaborately decorated but badly weathered pointed door from the cloister to this aisle's E bay. A round-headed door in the W bay has been built up.

Only the bases and lowest part of the pillars of the nave arcades survive. The pillars have been octofoil on plan, composed of bundles of keeled shafts with filleted rolls and hollows, and are similar to the probably slightly earlier piers of the nave arcades at Jedburgh Abbey (Borders) and Hexham Priory (Yorkshire). The pillars' bases continue the generally octagonal profile. Little evidence survives for the internal appearance of the nave's central vessel but its elevations were three-stage, the lower two probably like those at the NW tower's S side and surmounted by a clearstorey.

The CROSSING'S centre continues the line of the nave's central vesssel. Over it has been a square tower carried on 14 m.-high arches springing from bundle-shafted pillars. Of the crossing's N part and the N transept there survive only the bottoms of pillars and the foundations of walls. These show that the N TRANSEPT, like the S, extended for two bays beyond the N nave aisle and had a pair of lean-to side chapels entered through an arcade on its E side.

Much more remains of the S TRANSEPT. Externally, the lower parts of its W and S walls have been covered by the N and E ranges of the cloister (*see* below). Above, in the W wall a pair of immensely tall pointed windows. Corbelling under the wall-head's eaves. The raggle of the dormitory roof cuts into the S gable and partly blocks the W of a pair of windows, also pointed. The wall-head's corbelling continues under the head of the gable which is pierced by a circular window, presumably originally filled with plate tracery, its upper half a restoration of 1815. Octagonal buttress-cum-stair-tower at the gable's SE corner. Of the chapels which stood against the transept's demolished E side only the S end wall survives; in it a pointed window.

Internally the transept is lavishly decorated. Along its W and S walls as far E as the semi-octagonal respond marking off the transept proper from its E chapels is cusped and pointed blind arcading, the shafts missing but the bases and bell capitals in place. In the E bay of the arcading along the S wall, a round-headed and broader arch which contained a door to a stair which gave access to two passages at different levels along the transept's S and W sides. The lower, at triforium level, led to the monks' dormitory in the cloister's E range, and the upper passage opened onto doors in the ingoes of the windows; the W windows must have been crossed by temporary or permanent wooden bridges. Above the blind arcading at the bottom of the W wall, a plain band of masonry under the pair of windows, their ingoes with deep splays, their nook-shafts now missing. These openings are round-headed internally. This contrast with their external pointed appearance is seemingly the product of an innocent delight in the contrast of two forms rather than indecision as to what was currently in fashion. Along the S gable, above the lower level of blind arcading, another arcaded band whose arches have been carried on coupled shafts, now missing except for their bell capitals, the uncusped arch-heads tall and acutely pointed. This band runs under the triforium, its passage fronted by piers which have provided a backing for bell-capitalled nook-shafts, now largely lost, from which springs round-headed arcading. The large windows above are not quite as tall as those in the W wall. The partial blocking of the r. window is disconcerting but successfully hid the upper storey of the cloister's E range built against it.

The CHOIR has been of three bays. Except for the column bases of its aisles' arcades, there survives only part of the E and S walls of the S aisle. Shafts in the corner of the aisle show that it has been covered with stone vaulting. High up, above a string course continuing those of the S aisle of the nave, the S transept and the transept chapels, is the lower part of a window. At the E end of the S wall, a round-headed double piscina and an aumbry immediately to its W, both perhaps early C15.

About in the centre of the S choir aisle's S side, beside a blocked C13 window, is a door to the early C15 SACRISTY AND TREASURY. This is of two storeys and an attic. Externally, the S elevation has angle buttresses, the W with a large NW jamb, and a high-set door in its slit-windowed S face; surmounting the jamb, an octagonal turret topped by a stone-slabbed spire. In the S gable, a large pointed ground-floor window of four lights with intersecting tracery. String course under the first floor whose window is of simple design. At the wall-head, individual moulded corbels under a cornice formed by continuous corbelling. Above this, a recessed attic storey. In the E side, a two-light window. The N gable has risen above the S choir aisle, its first floor containing an off-centre rectangular door into the roof space above the aisle's vault. At the ground floor, originally covered by the vault of this bay of the aisle, a short and broad pointed three-light window above the entrance, also off-centre, whose pointed arch is enriched with mouldings. Inside, the ground-floor Sacristy is a tall square room, the walls faced with ashlar masonry of a greyer colour than the stone used in the rest of the abbey. It is well lit from the broad N window and tall S and E windows, the E's broad central mullion fronted by a wall-shaft from which springs a pair of hoodmoulds. Quadripartite vault springing from tall corner shafts, the two N with foliaged capitals, the S bearing shields, one displaying the coat of arms of Walter Paniter, Abbot of Arbroath from 1411 to 1449. The stonework of the N wall, the outer wall of the late C12 choir aisle, is unadorned. But round the W, S and E sides of the Sacristy the lower part of the walls is covered with pointed blind arcading, each of the cusped arch-heads marked off by a string course and filled with a pair of stones divided vertically by a central groove. The end bays of the S arcade do not conform to the common design but in each the pointed arch contains a round-headed arch, its surround carved with stylized foliage, in which is set a rectangular aumbry. Similar aumbry in the centre of the W wall, its surround with a roll-and-hollow moulding; the arch-head is covered with a shield on which the coat of arms of Abbot Walter Paniter was formerly discernible. The bay to its l. is occupied by a pointed door, slightly lower than the adjoining blind arches, which opens onto a tunnel-vaulted strongroom contained in the W jamb of the SW buttress. The surviving arcading shafts of the centre bays of the E wall are short and stand on corbels as if to allow space for a narrow table standing on the ledge below. Between the springing of the arches are outward projecting springers as if a vault had been intended to cover the bottom of this room below the level of the window sills. High up in the Sacristy's W wall, a hoodmoulded pointed door, presumably originally reached by a ladder, which opened onto a wall chamber and a stair contained in the SW buttress which leads to the Treasury above the Sacristy, its windows provided with stone seats. In the N wall, the door to the roof space above the church's choir aisle.

The late C12 PRESBYTERY projecting at the church's E end is of two unaisled bays. Of the N wall little more than footings survive except at its E end where there is evidence of blind arcading carried on bell-capitalled shafts, as also at the S wall. In the S wall the surviving lower parts of two windows rise above a string course which is placed just above the level of the choir's string course. The E wall's lowest stage also contains blind arcading with pointed arches carried on shafts whose bases and capitals survive, the capitals modelled variously with fluting, bell forms and foliage. Above, a window of three lights whose pointed arches spring from attached columns, some of their capitals fluted and others carved with stiff-leaf ornament. The bottom of a second tier of three openings survives. Probably there was a third tier, such as existed in the C12 at the E end of St Andrews Cathedral (Fife).

Sadly little apart from foundations remains of the CLOISTER. At the N cloister walk there survive the doors from the nave at its E and W ends (*see* above). So too do mutilated corbels which supported the beams of the roof. The N end of the E cloister walk ran beside the S transept's W wall from which projected a low stone bench above pointed blind arcading, vestiges of its shafts' bases and capital surviving. The arcading's two N bays incorporate rectangular recesses for the storage of books. The chapter house stood at the N end of the E range and projected boldly behind it. Its SE corner stands, an ungainly lump of masonry above a splayed base. The plan of other buildings has been established by excavation. The E range stretched far to the S, beyond the S range of the cloister, to form one side of a second courtyard from which it continued still further S. Its twin-aisled ground floor must have contained at least a parlour and warming house, and the first floor, whose N end abutted the church's S transept, contained the monks' dormitory and, at the S end, the latrines. In the cloister's S range was the refectory and, at its W end, the kitchen; in the inner angle of the S and W cloister walks stood a lavatory where the monks ritually washed their hands before entering the refectory. The W range may have contained stores, the abbot's lodging and guesthouse accommodation or a combination of these. A short part of its outer wall containing a blocked window survives at the N end of an extension to the Abbot's House.

The ABBOT'S HOUSE, projecting from the W end of the S range, has developed in several stages from the early C13, much of the evidence for its later history removed in a reconstruction of the 1920s and 1930s which attempted to restore its mid-C16 appearance. The first phase of development saw the construction of a two-storey building containing a twin-aisled vaulted ground floor under a tall first-floor hall. By about 1500 the building was extended W to provide an inner chamber for the abbot at this end of the hall, his former lodging in the cloister's W range probably given over to other uses. At the same time a lean-to extension was built on the house's N side containing further accommodation and an entrance and stair independent of the cloister. In the mid C16 the building was further enlarged by the erection of a narrow W block containing a first-floor gallery. Finally, the C13 hall was reduced to about half its original length, the area at its E end becoming an open platform with a view over adjoining gardens.

The walling is all of red sandstone rubble. The C13 main block's E end now forms a single-storey flat-roofed projection. In the main block's S side, a hoodmoulded and pointed blocked doorway, probably of the C13. To its W, a rectangular ground-floor window, perhaps of the C17. Then, a sturdy buttress, perhaps a C17 addition constructed when the original house's first floor was curtailed. Here the present E gable rises above the platform and is broken only by a couple of small windows. At each floor of the house's S side l. of the buttress, a mullioned-and-transomed two-light window. The lower openings may be C16. The very tall double-transomed first-floor r. window was formed or re-formed in the earlier C20. This block's late C15 W extension is of the same height but contains three storeys. At the S side's ground floor, a couple of doors, the r. with a circular opening above, the l. surmounted by a small rectangular opening. At the first floor, a pair of transomed windows of strongly vertical proportions. They are of the 1930s and replaced a mid-C18 Venetian window. Also of the 1930s in their present form are the two closely spaced two-light windows at the l. of the second floor.

The addition of *c.* 1550 lying across the house's W end has a monopitch roof and crowstepped half-gables to N and S. In the S, a small ground-floor window. The first and second floor's mullioned-and-transomed windows are of the 1930s. At the addition's W side the ground floor protrudes as a tall splay-topped base containing a central door inserted in the C20; to the l., a window perhaps C18, its plain surround checked for shutters. At the first floor, an array of six fairly tall transomed lights and six more at the second floor, all these openings with chamfered margins and probably mid-C16. In the N half-gable, a tier of windows, the ground-floor opening quite small, the first floor's with a transom and, to its r., a small horizontal opening.

The late C15 addition on the N side of the house projects slightly from the line of the W extension, its exposed end finished with crowsteps and containing a transomed window to the first floor and a decently sized window at the second. Except for the plain windows and doors at the ground floor this addition's N front was comprehensively remodelled in the 1930s when it acquired tall mullioned-and-transomed openings at the first floor and an irregular disposition of second-floor windows. Roughly in the centre of the first floor, a circular shot-hole. At this floor's l. end traces of a blocked door of *c.* 1550, presumably reached by a forestair.

The entrances to the undercroft of the C13 hall are at the E end. The UNDERCROFT is of three bays, the sturdy ribs of its twin aisles' vaults springing from the low and simple circular central columns and fat corbels along the side walls. At the S aisle's W end, a broad straight-lintelled fireplace, probably inserted in the late C15 when the undercroft became a kitchen. The round-headed window embrasures of this side have been partly built up, perhaps in the C16. In the E bay of the N aisle, a pointed door, possibly C13 but perhaps an insertion of *c.* 1500. It now opens onto an elliptically tunnel-vaulted store-room on the ground floor of the house's N addition. At the W end of this aisle, a late C15 door, a pendant hanging from its round-headed arch. This opens into a tunnel-vaulted passage which runs down the centre of the late C15 addition. Windows, perhaps to light the passage, from tunnel-vaulted stores either side but the stores' only access has been from the exterior. At the passage's W end, a round-headed door to the centre of three interconnecting tunnel-vaulted stores on the ground floor of the mid-C16 addition.

The r. entrance on the N side of the Abbot's House opens onto the foot of the mid-C15 addition's turnpike stair. At the first floor, E of the stair, a vestibule whose original entrance may have been only the blocked door at the E end of its N wall. Garderobe at the N end of the W wall. On a higher level to the S of the vestibule is the ABBOT'S HALL, its E end now represented only by the outside platform. The hall is of two-storey height, with pointed N windows in round-headed embrasures. Elliptical-arched embrasure to the tall S window, its present mullioned-and-transomed rectangular form perhaps dating from a C16 alteration. At the Hall's W end, a straight-lintelled fireplace with chamfered jambs, perhaps an insertion of the C16. High up, to the r. of the fireplace, has been an opening from a second-floor room so a floor seems to have been inserted at this level, perhaps in the late C16. At the end of this W wall, a door, its S jamb and lintel chamfered, into the Abbot's Chamber. The floor at the E end of the Abbot's Hall is covered with worn red tiles. These are probably C13 and were brought here in 1931 from the exposed former E end of the Hall. On the floor of the Abbot's Hall, a coped medieval GRAVESTONE, the top sculpted with a foliate cross, the S side with a sword, the carving badly weathered. Beside it, the worn and headless effigy of a cleric. Beside this, the torso of a C15 armoured knight, identified by an inscription as Alexander Gardin [Gardyne] which has formed part of an altar tomb. Against the E end of the Hall, the r. part of the front of a mid-C15 TOMB-CHEST decorated with blind arcading, the almost flat-topped panels containing relief figures of monks except at the l., originally the central panel, where there is the depiction of an angel holding a shield which bore the coat of arms of Abbot Walter Paniter.

W of the Abbot's Hall is the late C15 ABBOT'S CHAMBER. Straight-lintelled fireplace at the W wall. In the S, r. of the window, a pair of cupboards. On the plaster of the walls, fragments of painted decoration of *c.* 1500 imitating ashlar stonework above a frieze in reds and greens. On the E wall, a pair of early C16 oak PANELS, one carved with an angel holding a crucifix, the other with a thistle. They may originally have been part of a screen in the Abbot's House. In the centre of the N side, a round-headed door into the contemporary closet. Here, a fireplace, also with a straight lintel, at the S end of the W wall.

At the S wall's W end, an elliptical-arched recess as for a buffet. The arch of the recess to its E, containing the entrance from the Abbot's Chamber, is placed at a higher level.

The house's mid-C16 GALLERY stretching across the W end is well lit from windows in three walls, all in elliptical-arched embrasures. No fireplace. Cupboard at the N end of the S wall. In the second-floor room above the gallery, a row of joist holes in the E wall suggest there has been an attic above but its floor would have cut across the S window which looks original.

The GUESTHOUSE RANGE extending from the church's SW tower W to the Gatehouse is probably late C13. Its N side is formed by the precinct wall (*see* above). Ashlar-faced S front. At its ground floor, an irregular parade of stepped buttresses. Two pointed doors and one narrow pointed window, perhaps C13; the other ground-floor windows are rectangular and perhaps remodelled in the C16. Comfortably sized rectangular windows, perhaps all C16, to the first floor; one, just r. of centre, is surmounted by an arched hood. A lean-to roof has swept down from the range's W end to cover pointed doors (now blocked) to the Gatehouse pend's E side.

Inside the Guesthouse, two rooms, both covered with quadripartite vaulting. The E room is of three bays. At its E end, a cupboard. This is placed to the r. of the entrance to a mural garderobe reached by a short stair. At this wall's N end, a fireplace, perhaps C15, its hood carried on moulded corbels. Cupboard in this E bay's N wall and, in its S, a window, its stone seats C20 replacements. In the room's central bay are cupboards in the N and S walls, the S checked for a door; remains of stone seats in the embrasure of the S window. Pointed door to the W room. High-set small window in its N wall, a pointed window and door in the S; in the W, a recess, evidence of a blocked door to the Gatehouse pend.

GRAVEYARD. S of the abbey church and crowded with monuments, predominantly Victorian and of routine character. At the S end of its W wall, a couple of BURIAL ENCLOSURES of the mid or late C19 entered through Gothic arches; another with heavy Neoclassical gatepiers. – A handful of C18 and early C19 HEADSTONES. In line with the abbey church's crossing is one erected by David Simpson, ship-owner, to commemorate his wife, Jean Lyell, and their sons, Joseph †1822 and John †1824, the top of the W face bearing the relief of a sailing ship. – Some way E, the stone erected by George Greig, custom house boatman, to his wife, Catherine Findlay †1843, the top of the E face with the relief of a sailing boat. – N of the Simpson headstone, the cast-iron MONUMENT set up in 1830 by Andrew Duncan, ship-owner, to his wife, Margaret Rattray, and their daughter, Margaret. Square pedestal with Doric corner pilasters and entablature, the metopes decorated with rosettes; stepped top surmounted by a flaming urn. – On the graveyard's edge, in line with the Sacristy of the abbey church, a stretch of walling in which are set weathered tall slabs carved with the reliefs of a woman and man in C17 dress; they probably commemorate the Rev. Henry Philip, minister of Arbroath, †1627 and his wife, Isobel Paterson †1628. Above, a large sloping-ended stone which bears the date 1674 and the initials and coats of arms of Mr James Philip (grandson of the Rev. Henry Philip) and Margaret Graham, his wife. At the top, a segmental-headed stone bearing a relief of the Recording Angel, one arm resting on a balance, the other holding a trumpet, a skeleton trampled underfoot.

VISITOR CENTRE, by *Simpson & Brown*, 2000–1, pushing W from the N side of the abbey church's NW tower but a deferential introduction to the medieval building. It is formed of four parts stepping up to the E, the first single-storey under a shallowly piended roof, the second and third covered by monopitch roofs and with clearstorey lighting, the fourth of two storeys with a curved roof. Wall cladding of St Bee's red sandstone and Douglas fir. Inside, a foyer, café and exhibition area at the W and, behind, lavatories above which is a gallery. This is reached by a stone stair, a confident exhibition of craftsmanship inviting the visitor to make the ascent. From the gallery is a view over the abbey ruins to the E.

Inside the Centre, various fragments from the abbey ruins. GRAVE-SLAB of 1535 with the low relief of a monk. – Early C14 Frosterley marble (limestone) headless EFFIGY which was uncovered at the E end of the abbey church when rubbish was cleared from here in 1816. The figure is of a man clad in a mantle over a full-length robe his feet resting on a now headless recumbent lion. Clutching the mantle and robe are tiny human figures, several wearing chain mail and spurs. The effigy's position in the church suggests it may have been placed over the tomb of William I ('the Lion') but, if so and not the effigy of some other notable, it must have been erected about a century after his death. – Another C14 EFFIGY (also now headless) is of a bishop dressed in an alb and richly decorated chasuble, his r. hand raised in benediction, his l. apparently holding a now missing crozier. It was discovered in 1815 in the NW tower. Possibly this was a statue of St Thomas Becket, the Abbey's patron saint, and if so, probably replaced an earlier statue, perhaps one destroyed by the storm of 1272. – Fragment of a C17 TOMBSTONE bearing the relief of a skeleton who stabs an old woman with the dart of death.

CHURCHES

ARBROATH OLD AND ABBEY PARISH CHURCH, Abbey Path and West Abbey Street. Built as a chapel of ease in 1797 by *John Shanks*, mason, and *Alexander Macfarlane*, wright, it was originally a big and bare rubble box with two tiers of pointed windows in the long sides and a round opening near the top of each gable. This is still visible on three elevations but *Maclaren & Aitken* added a vestibule flanked by gallery stairs to the W side in 1878. This addition was remodelled in 1885 when it was given a simple Gothic front of coursed stugged masonry, the broad centre gable flanked by a parapeted S bay and, on the N, by a bell-tower, its corners chamfered, its slated spire roof with lucarnes.

INTERIOR. The only surviving late C18 decoration is a frieze of blind arcading. The church's compartmented ceiling, routine Gothic gallery around three sides and bench pews all date from the recasting of 1878 by Maclaren & Aitken who moved the position of the pulpit from the W to the E end. At this end is a simple Gothic COMMUNION TABLE of 1929. Behind and also Gothic but more elaborate, the PULPIT designed by *Aitkenhead & Mason* in 1875, now backed by a large ORGAN CASE of 1928.

STAINED GLASS. At the W end, a pair of two-light gallery windows (the Calling of St Peter and St Andrew; Our Lord Preaching from a Boat), clearly drawn and strongly coloured in a traditional manner, of *c.* 1955. – At the E end, also at gallery level, the outer pair of windows (Our Lord the Good Shepherd; St Paul) is by *The Abbey Studio*, 1938. – Between them, a pair (St Peter; St Elizabeth with St John the Baptist) by *A. Ballantine & Gardiner*, 1894. – Central rose window (Our Lord in Glory) of *c.* 1955.

ARBROATH UNITED FREE CHURCH, High Street. Built as an Episcopal church *c.* 1840 and reconstructed as High Street Free Church, *c.* 1860. Very plain red sandstone Gothic box.

ARBROATH WEST KIRK, Keptie Street. Originally St Margaret's Church. By *T. S. Robertson* of *Edward & Robertson*, 1878–9. Tall and boxy Gothic in red sandstone. Nave and aisles with transepts and a short chancel at the N end. At the S front, a gabled porch, its entrance's pointed arch springing from attached columns. In the inner angle of the nave and E aisle, a big square tower, its lower part of 1878–9, the tall belfry with its pinnacled battlement added (also to *Robertson*'s design) in 1903. Plain HALL at the NE, by *Hugh Gavin*, 1902–3.

Inside, nave arcades with pointed arches carried on leafily capitalled stone columns. S gallery. Stone chancel arch at the N end. – STAINED GLASS. In the E aisle, two windows (Tourism and Farming; Fishing and Weaving) by *John Blyth*, 1987. – The two windows in the W aisle (St Ninian and St Vigean; St Margaret of Scotland and St Andrew) are of 1980 and also by Blyth. – In the transepts, C20 glass from Ladyloan St Columba's Church and erected here in 1990. – The two brightly coloured mid-C20 expressionist outer lights (Agriculture, and Industry) of the chancel's N window were also formerly in Ladyloan St Columba's Church. The centre light (Our Lord as the Light of the World) is by *Gordon Webster*, 1974, its expressionism restrained.

EAST FREE CHURCH, Brothock Bridge and East Grimsby. Now a club. By *William Aitkenhead*, 1873–5. Free Style, built of stugged ashlar. Nave and aisles, all with double-pitch roofs. In the sides, round-arched windows. At the N front, parapeted transepts from which the nave's gable is marked off by squat octagonal turrets. Between these turrets stone spouts carry a stone balcony, its front pierced by quatrefoil openings. Below the balcony, a pair of three-light pointed windows.

ERSKINE UNITED PRESBYTERIAN CHURCH, Commerce Street. Secularized. By *James Maclaren*, 1851. Gothic of a type which just escapes the sobriquet of 'carpenter's'. Acutely pointed narrow windows in the rubble side walls. The ashlar-faced N front suggests (inaccurately) a nave and aisles behind. At the end of each 'aisle', a three-light window under a narrow lancet. The 'nave' gable is advanced with pinnacled buttresses. In it, a narrow lancet flanked by a pair of doors, the pointed head of each filled with an octofoil fanlight; four-light window above.

EVANGELICAL UNION CHURCH, Nos. 12–18 Keptie Street and Dishlandtown Street. Secularized. By *William Aitkenhead*, 1879. Two-storey building, the church (now housing) occupying the upper floor, the ground floor given over to shops (their shopfronts replaced in the C20). At the Keptie Street front, the church windows are each of three round-arched lights with acanthus-capitalled column-mullions, the stilted central lights rising into rectangular gablets surmounted by urn-topped pedestals. At the gable to Dishlandtown Street, a spired octagonal bellcote.

INVERBROTHOCK CHAPEL OF EASE, James Street. Disused. Economically elegant classical, by *Archibald Simpson*, 1827–8. Broad pilastered and pedimented five-bay S gable front, faced with stugged grey ashlar. In each of its three centre bays a door framed by a round-headed overarch, its blind 'fanlight' carved with an Empire garland. Tall round-arched windows at the side elevations which are of red sandstone rubble. The N gable is again pedimented but rubble-built and without pilasters. Projecting from it, a semi-octagonal apse lit by round-headed windows.

The interior was much altered in the later C20 when a floor was inserted at the level of Simpson's gallery to provide a ground-floor hall and a first-floor worship area. In the corridor which runs round the hall there survive the fluted Doric columns which supported the 1820s semi-octagonal gallery.

KNOX'S CHURCH, Cairnie Street and Howard Street. Originally Knox's Free Church. Late Gothic without frills, by *James Maclaren*, 1866–7, built of brownish-coloured stugged masonry. Nave and N transepts. The breadth of the S gable front is disguised by its centre being slightly advanced and marked off by low gabled buttresses. At the r., a blocky parapeted tower.

OLD PARISH CHURCH, Kirk Square. Secularized. Tall and austerely detailed Gothic, church by *John J. Burnet*, 1894–6, awkwardly attached to the W steeple which survives from the previous church which was burned down in 1892.

THE BUILDING NEWS, OCT. 25, 1895.

Arbroath, Old Parish Church.
Engraving, 1895

The steeple, designed by *John Henderson* and built in 1830–1,* is unarchaeological Georgian Gothic, faced with polished grey sandstone ashlar. Tower formed of two parts, each of two stages. At each corner of the lower part, a clasping buttress which rises into an octagon topped by a foliage-finialled

* The tower is the mid-C14 SW tower of the precinct of Arbroath Abbey but refaced and remodelled so that its appearance is entirely of the 1830s (with minor alterations of the 1890s).

pinnacle. At the W face of this part's lower stage, a depressed-arched recess, formerly a door but converted in the 1890s to a window of two cusped lights, the broad dividing mullion decorated with the base and canopy of an image niche. The upper stage of this lower part of the tower has an intake on the W face and, at a lower level, on the S; at the N face, no intake but a jumping string course. At each of the exposed faces, a hoodmoulded and transomed window of two narrow pointed lights. This stage is finished on each face with a corbelled-out block pediment. Behind these pediments rises the tower's intaken upper part, its chamfered corners surmounted by gableted and pinnacled buttresses. It begins with a clock stage. At each face, a shallowly projecting pedestal, the front panelled with pointed blind arches, topped by strapwork supporting a round clock face with a stone fleur-de-lis finial. The upper stage of this part is formed by the belfry. On each side, a steep gablet containing an opening, again of two pointed lights. Above, an octagonal stone spire with small lucarnes.

The steeple now appears as an unwanted appendage to the church, not even centred on the nave gable to which it is attached. The church itself, all of 1894–6, consists of a nave, a transeptal M-roofed double N 'aisle' or jamb and, placed in the NW inner angle, a short aisle parallel to the nave and ending in a semi-octagonal W 'chancel'. The masonry, in contrast to the grey ashlar of the steeple, is of brownish snecked rubble; slated roof. The style is First Pointed with a Scottish inflexion intended to evoke Arbroath Abbey. Three-bay nave, a tall and severely elegant box with paired lancet windows in the S side. In the E gable, a trio of lancets under a round window (a reminiscence of Dunblane Cathedral). The outer ends of each nave gable step up above the eaves, the stepping emphasized (except at the S end of the gable where the steeple does not allow room) by slender diagonally set buttresses. The sides of these steps have gablets, those of the E gable, whose main corners are chamfered, being scooped up to the square above corbels which look as if intended to carry statues. Paired lancets in the side walls of the N double 'aisle'. At the semi-octagonal chancel of the NW aisle, paired pointed lights (their hoodmoulds now without label stops) at the lower level; large windows above. Between this 'chancel' and the steeple, a low parapeted lean-to projection. Another low projection at the church's E end, partly serving to tie the church to the line of West Abbey Street from which it is angled as a result of Kirk Square and West Abbey Street not being at right angles to each other. This projection is simply detailed, with a tall parapet above a splayed string course which is broken by the finial of a hoodmoulded door. Rising above this projection at the inner angle of the nave and N double 'aisle', a semi-octagonal stair-turret, its roof poking up from within a parapet. At the SE corner, a porch with an angled corner joining its main fronts to Kirk Square and West Abbey Street. In each of these main fronts, a pointed and hoodmoulded entrance.

Parapet pierced by quatrefoils and with a tall image niche at the corner.

The interior's ground floor now contains offices which occupy part of the ground floor but leave the main structure untouched. The height of the nave emphasizes the E–W axis with the focal point provided by the organ which projects from a high but shallow pointed-arched recess. On the N side of the nave, huge minimally pointed arches springing from octagonal piers open into the double aisle, and a round-headed arch into the 'chancel' to its W. Round the walls, a high pine DADO of Late Gothic character up to the height of the aisles' gallery fronts. These GALLERY FRONTS are also Late Gothic in manner, the centre gallery bearing the arms of the Macdonalds carved by *Alexander Fletcher*, the E gallery the arms of the Allan Frasers of Hospitalfield carved by *James Peters*. The front of the 'chancel' gallery (the Town Council Gallery) is higher and more elaborate. Above it, a wooden 'rood beam' surmounted by a shield bearing the arms of the burgh of Arbroath topped by an angelic figure ('Faith') and flanked by statues of two knights. Under this gallery, a panelled session room.

At the W end of the nave, the ORGAN by *Brindley & Foster*, 1896, in a huge Gothic wooden case. – Immediately in front, three COMMUNION SEATS (for the minister and elders) also of the 1890s and Gothic, carved with figures of Apostles and, at the top, an angel. They form a reredos for the Lorimerian oak COMMUNION TABLE of 1913 whose splayed corners have tabernacle niches containing figures of saints. – To the S, the PULPIT of stained pine on a Brechin sandstone base, its corners with putti-carved corbels supporting empty image niches. – Brass eagle LECTERN, probably of the 1890s. – FONT designed by *Burnet* in 1897, of veined brownish cream and green marble. – STAINED GLASS in the three lights of the huge E window designed by *Edward Burne-Jones* and executed by *Morris & Co.*, 1895. Three tiers of figures (the Virgin Mary, Our Lord and St Elizabeth at the bottom, the prophets Elijah, Isaiah and Daniel in the centre row, and Abraham, Moses and David at the top). – In the other windows, some panes of frosted glass making free Late Gothic patterns.

Finally, a couple of curiosities. Over the NE gallery door, the head of a CROSS, its lower limb carved with a saltire. This looks like a medieval fragment. – The doors and walls of the gallery stairs are covered with stamped FABRIC.

ST ANDREW, Hamilton Green. Originally Inverbrothock Free Church. Lumpy Late Gothic, by *John Rust*, 1888–9. Broad grey ashlar front, the main entrance to the nave surmounted by a gablet carried on squat columns with big foliaged capitals. Each bay of the flanking aisles is covered by a double-pitch roof at right angles to that of the nave, giving a procession of gablets down the building's red sandstone sides. The hall to the N, also Gothic and of 1888–9, is almost lost behind a low extension of the later C20.

Inside, an open wooden roof over the nave, transverse vaults over the aisles which are marked off by slender cast-iron columns with big foliaged capitals. E gallery with a pierced cast-iron front. – At the N end, the Gothic pine PULPIT stands in front of an apse now containing the ORGAN (by *Wadsworth & Bros*, 1922). – This largely hides the apse's three STAINED GLASS windows (the Nativity, Crucifixion, and Ascension of Our Lord) by *William Pearce Ltd*, 1899. – In the E wall, three lights (Our Lord, St Paul, and St John) of 1890, and a two-light window (the Baptism of Our Lord) of 1926.

ST JOHN (Methodist), Ponderlaw Street. Built in 1772 but recast and extended in 1882. The C18 building was a rendered octagon, lit by two tiers of rectangular windows. The remodelling of 1882 altered the fenestration to a single tier of tall pointed lights, added a large stone-faced Gothic porch to the front and a vestry at the S. Organ chamber at the N of *c.* 1950. The low rubble-built hall at the SW was added in 1896.

Inside, a deep N gallery with a Gothic front and an outsize foliaged capital on its supporting cast-iron column. This, together with the pews and pulpit, is of 1882. – ORGAN by *E. H. Lawton*, 1902, its case of *c.* 1950. – STAINED GLASS. Behind the pulpit, one light ('Suffer the little children') by the *Abbey Studio*, 1950. – Another light ('Neither count I my life dear unto me') by the same firm, 1954, to its S.

ST MARY THE VIRGIN (Episcopal), Springfield Terrace. Dec with a varied display of Late Gothic tracery in the windows. It is by *John Henderson*, 1852–4, built of buff-coloured stugged sandstone masonry. Tall nave and a slightly lower chancel; shorter N aisle, its E bay (the Lady Chapel) lower, its NW inner angle with the nave filled by a steeple. The steeple's tower is angle-buttressed for its first two stages except at the SW where there is a stair-turret. In the N face, a big Gothic entrance, the label stops of its hoodmould carved with dragons. Above the entrance, a foliage-finialled gablet with high-relief male and female heads at the outer corners. The tower's second stage is slightly intaken. Large two-light belfry openings at the top stage whose walling forms a recessed panel at each face, the top of each panel with corbels to support the foliaged eaves cornice. Broached stone spire with gableted lucarnes.

Inside, a four-bay arcade separating the nave from the aisle, the pointed arches springing from sturdy sandstone columns. Tall stone chancel arch. The Lady Chapel has a broad angular arch into the chancel and a pair of pointed arches into the aisle. In the S wall of the E bay of the nave, a door from the vestry with a cusped head under a crocketed ogee hoodmould with a richly foliaged finial.

Expensive array of furnishings. S of the chancel arch, a stone PULPIT of 1854. Octagonal, each face having a pointed-arched panel. – Brass eagle LECTERN, probably late C19. – At the W end, a round stone FONT by *James Hunter*; it looks late C19. – Over the Lady Chapel altar, an oak REREDOS by *H. Hems & Sons*, 1903–4. Late Gothic, its five panels separated by buttresses with crocketed pinnacles, an octagonal canopy projecting over the broader and higher centrepiece.

In the chancel arch, a Perp oak SCREEN and HANGING ROOD CROSS by *Robert S. Lorimer*, 1919–21, the screen carved (by *W. & A. Clow*) with acorns and oak leaves and angels holding a shield. – In the sanctuary, Lorimerish oak PANELLING of *c.* 1930. – ORGAN by *Forster & Andrews*, 1871.

STAINED GLASS. Five-light main E window (the Crucifixion, with serried ranks of adoring angels) by *C. E. Kempe & Co. Ltd*, *c.* 1920. – In the sanctuary's N light, a sketchy and stylized depiction of Charity of *c.* 1930. – The sanctuary's S window (Dorcas) is by *Morris & Co.*, 1936, a warning of the aesthetic depth to which a once distinguished firm can fall. – In the nave's S wall the windows are all by *Mayer & Co.*, the two in the E bays (the Good Samaritan; Our Lord healing the Sick) of 1884 and much more richly coloured than the two to the W (the Women at the Tomb; the Raising of Lazarus) which are of 1892. – In the four lights of the nave's W window more glass (SS Paul, Peter, Andrew and John) by *Mayer & Co.*, 1885, crowded and richly coloured. – In the Lady Chapel's E window, two lights (the Presentation of Our Lord in the Temple) by *Christopher Charles Powell*, 1949. – The clearly drawn and light-coloured windows in the three E bays of the N aisle (Our Lord as the Good Shepherd with St John the Evangelist and King David; '*Caritas*' (Our Lady) with '*Sapientia*' and '*Industria*'; 'With Faith nothing is impossible') are all by *C. E. Kempe & Co. Ltd*, *c.* 1925–35. – In the W bay of this aisle, a window (Naomi, Ruth and Boaz) by *Christopher Charles Powell*, 1938.

ST PAUL'S UNITED PRESBYTERIAN CHURCH, Park Street and Gravesend. Now a shop. By *Aitkenhead & Mason*, 1887–8, reconstructing a piend-roofed box built for a 'Relief Methodist' congregation in 1825–6. Lumpy classical. Flattened lead dome over the SE corner where there are three-light windows with Composite column-mullions. Otherwise, two-light windows with Ionic column-mullions.

ST THOMAS OF CANTERBURY (R.C.), Dishlandtown Street. Georgian Romanesque survival, by *George Mathewson*, 1846–8. Broad box, the sides of red sandstone rubble, the W front of polished grey ashlar. The width of the front gable is broken up by a pair of battlemented octagonal turrets marking off the centre which is surmounted by a high parapet. At each turret, a crosslet opening at the second stage and, in each face of the third stage, a narrow round-arched opening set in a round-headed overarch which springs from attached columns. Across the breadth of the centrepiece, a diagonally buttressed gabled porch, its round-arched entrance under a stepped arrangement of round-headed lights. Above, a rose window. In the sides, tall and narrow round-arched windows. Lower and narrower chancel at the E end.

The interior is divided into a nave and aisles by arcades of round-headed arches carried on very slender cast-iron columns with bundled shafts. From these columns spring also transverse half-arches over the aisles and full arches over the nave, their spandrels pierced by circular openings. Above the entrance vestibule, a N gallery opening into the church through a Romanesque arch; above the gallery, a tunnel-vaulted ceiling. Another Romanesque arch at the S into the short low chancel, its tunnel-vaulted ceiling crossed by surface ribs springing from corbels. – Flashy REREDOS of oak and veined marble; it looks early C20. – STAINED GLASS. Three-light chancel window (SS Andrew, Thomas and Patrick), probably of the late C19.

Attached to the S side of the church is the contemporary PRESBYTERY, built of broached ashlar, with hoodmoulded and mullioned windows in its broad front gable. – To its S, a hall probably of the later C19, again with a broad front gable but built of polished ashlar and with simple round-headed windows.

WESTERN CEMETERY

corner of Forfar Road and East Muirlands Road

Laid out in 1867 and extended from *c.* 5.7 ha. to 8 ha. in 1874. ENTRANCE GATEWAY of *c.* 1870 at the SE corner. Classical, built of polished ashlar. Round-headed and console-keystoned arch, the piers' stonework channelled, with nook-shafts in the corners. Over the arch, a mutuled cornice topped by a rather small open segmental pediment which displays the portcullis coat of arms of the Burgh of Arbroath. Flanking the archway, rectangular pedestrian entrances, their piers also channelled and with anta-pilasters on their faces; urn finials over the outer ends. – Just to the N, a contemporary single-storey SUPERINTENDENT'S HOUSE, gentle Italianate, the walling of stugged ashlar.

MEMORIAL CHAPEL

On a low hill in the centre of the cemetery, one of Angus's weirdest flights of Victorian neo-medieval architectural fantasy, the sculpture-encrusted chapel designed by *Patrick Allan-Fraser* of Hospitalfield and built in 1875–84 as a memorial and mausoleum for his wife, Elizabeth, †1873 and her parents, Major John Fraser of Hospitalfield †1809 and Elizabeth Parrott †1851. On completion the chapel was gifted, together with an endowment for its maintenance, to the Burgh of Arbroath to be used for funerals of any and every denomination.

The chapel is faced with local red sandstone polished ashlar from Drumyellow and Brax quarries. Basically it is oblong in shape but with low aisle-like lean-to-roofed loggias along stretches of the N and S elevations where they project from the sides of tall flat-roofed and parapeted aisles. At the corners, towers or turrets, all of different design, the two W towers gripping the main W gable; between the E turrets, a tall two-storey vestibule and gallery across this end.

The entrance (E) front's vestibule and gallery covering the 32
nave gable is Free Style but conventional. Segmental-arched large doorway, the mouldings of its surround elaborately decorated, the central order with naturalistic bough and foliage enrichment. Inner and outer orders carved with bundled reeds. Shell decoration on the innermost ingoes. Above the entrance, a first-floor window of two rectangular lights; between them, a three-quarter-round tall column carved with spiralling enrichment and standing on a corbel carved with a trio of angels' heads. The column's capital, carved with doves, supports foliage-capitalled squat columns which carry the pedestal base of a large canopied image niche. In the niche, a statue of Our Lord in the Judgment Hall sculpted, like the rest of the principal carved work, by *James Peters*. The niche's panelled jambs are decorated with elaborate naturalistic foliate carving. Round the frieze of the domed canopy, a high-relief depiction of a funeral procession, the mourners dressed in ancient Scottish costume representative of the different social classes. The canopy's stone dome is patterned with tile decoration and topped by a large but plain cross. Behind the image niche and surmounting this central part of the front, a high parapet projected on foliaged corbels; under its cornice, a frieze carved with wreaths.

At the entrance front's N section, a splayed corner to the ground floor. Above, a square corner turret of two stages, the cut-out corners of the lower stage containing nook-shafts without either capitals or bases. A course of foliage-enriched continuous corbelling under the upper stage, its walling relieved by panels containing cruciform openings.

At the l. end of the vestibule and gallery's junction with the chapel's SE tower is corbelled out the lowest stage of a generously sized bowed stair-turret. Three upper stages, the lowest carried on continuous corbelling, the walling of the others broken only by moulded and vertically proportioned rectangular windows. Wall-head frieze carved with fern enrichment and a band depicting birds among foliage; corbelling under the eaves of the stone-slabbed low-spired octagonal roof. The E face of the SE tower abutting this stair-turret continues the line of walling of the E front's vestibule and gallery; at the ground floor, a segmental-headed recess. On the tower's splayed and chimney-topped SE corner, a tall image niche, its base a foliaged corbel on which stands a figure of Peace; stone-spired canopy carried on blocky corbels, its roof's lowest course enriched with a rope moulding, the finial a flaming urn. The tower's S face is of three stages, the tall top stage projected on a double tier of chequer-set corbels. Surmounting this and the W face, a rosette-studded cornice and high and sinuously pierced parapet. In the top stage's cut-out SW corner, a column composed of two sections, the lower bundle-shafted, the upper decorated with vertical strips of shallow-relief foliage; birds are carved on the capitals. The parapet's W corners hint at pugnacious purpose. On the SW, an angle-round but with a straight-splayed SW segment whose walling rises from an angel-sculpted corbel to break through the continuous corbelling of the S and NE segments to its own corbelling under the rounded top of the turret whose SE segment is pierced by a quatrefoil and rises to a high merlon. On the tower's NW corner, a diagonally set caphouse carried on heavy continuous corbelling and covered with a stone-slabbed pyramid roof.

The main part of the chapel's S side between the corner towers consists of a two-bay ground-floor loggia under a slabbed lean-to roof, the segmental-headed arches springing from corbels at the ends and, in the centre, a pair of squat columns whose capitals are carved with naturalistic foliage. Inside the loggia, a stone bench in front of the back wall (the side wall of the chapel's main S aisle) which is panelled with round-headed blind arcading. Rising behind and above the loggia is the chapel's two-storey narrow S aisle, its wall-head parapet projected on courses of rope moulding and continuous and individual corbelling. Behind this parapet, on the roof of the chapel's nave, are two pairs of dormer windows with elliptical-arched lights under shaped gable-heads which contain blank shields, the junction of the r. pair's gable-heads marked by a corbel carved with a couple of human faces. Serving as book-ends to the loggia are projections in the inner angles of the corner towers and S aisle. The r. of these is rectangular at the ground floor but then broached to carry an octagonal upper storey, its corners containing nook-shafts, its parapeted wall-head continuing that of the S aisle. High up in the inner angle, another projection, small and splayed. The book-end projection to the l. of the loggia is also of two-storey height; lean-to stone-slabbed roof, its slope rising to the W but halted by the intrusion of the SW corner tower's stair-turret. In the projection's S face, a tall elliptical-arched recess containing a stone bench backed by a pair of round-headed blind arches. The l. end of the recess's arch springs from a corbel carved with the head of a solemn angel.

At the W ends of both the S and N sides, in the inner angles with the W corner towers, are corbelled-out and conical-roofed fat round stair-turrets. The S turret is carried on continuous corbelling under a rope moulding. Below the eaves, a carved frieze and rosetted cornice; roof rising in two stages to a ball finial.

The chapel's W end is dominated by its corner towers. Between them, the gently bowed end of the chancel which contains a tall rectangular window, its moulded border decorated with fern enrichment and surmounted by a mound of carved foliage. Corbelling above the window supports a straight gable-head pierced by a crosslet window, its border also foliate; in the top of the gable, a round dummy opening. A rosetted finial surmounts the gable.

The W towers, containing the tombs of Major John Fraser and Elizabeth Parrott and of Patrick and Elizabeth Allan-Fraser, are both square, with identically treated lower stages.

The lowest is a tall, windowless corniced plinth which serves as the base of the second stage. Here, the W corners are cut out and filled with columns, their shafts carved with spiral enrichment and strips of foliage, the capitals with foliage, birds and beasts. At the open faces, rectangular unglazed window openings with chamfered jambs. Above, massive moulded individual corbels under a heavy balcony whose front is pierced by cusped dagger tracery, the splayed corners adorned by floral-decorated panels; poking out from below the panels of the W corners are the heads of snarling beasts. Inside each tower, these two lower stages form a double-height mausoleum covered by a groin-vaulted roof; over the tombs, ogee-profiled domes topped by cross finials.

The W towers' third stages share a family likeness but are more like half-brothers than twins. Both have rectangular windows with stone panels above but at the S tower the panels relieve the walling of both the S and W faces and are contained within elliptical-headed overarches, at the N there is a panel only on the W face and no overarch. The panels of the S tower are square and carved as sundials (the astronomical calculations made by the Arbroath meteorologist, *Alexander Brown*), the N tower's panel round and bearing a clock face. Surmounting the S tower is a parapet pierced by crosslet openings and carried on outsize moulded corbels. Over the S tower, a much spindlier pierced parapet but massive corner pinnacles and a crown spire, its design derived from the early C16 spire of King's College Aberdeen, provide a much more dramatic termination.

The general composition and appearance of the chapel's N front is a mirror image of the S but the central loggia is of three bays not two and the projection to its l. a substantial squat stair-tower, its lower stage square except for a canted NE corner, the upper octagonal and covered by a stone-slabbed roof. The E of the corbels under the parapet is carved with three ducks. In the centre of each pair of the nave roof's dormerheads are stones carved with the heads of animals.

INTERIOR. The main (E) entrance opens into the ashlar-walled vestibule. Groin-vaulted stone ceiling, the foliate ribs springing from fat corbels carved with birds and beasts set among more foliage and meeting at a central boss carved with the portcullis heraldic device of the Burgh of Arbroath. Rope moulding along the side walls. Beneath it, on the N wall, a pair of arches, one shouldered and serving as a window embrasure, the other rectangular and opening onto a gallery stair whose handrail, like those of the chapel's W stairs, is a carved inset in the walling. In the vestibule's S wall, a trio of round-headed arches, two blind and with carved ivy-leaf decoration, the r. moulded and opening onto a second vestibule which gives access to the chapel's SE stair. In the main vestibule's W side, the broad round-headed doorway to the chapel itself, its moulded surround carved with naturalistic foliage.

The ashlar-clad chapel interior is tall and relatively narrow, the focus on the stone bier at the W end of the nave and the narrower short chancel behind, its high-set crosslet window giving visual expression to the Christian promise of eternal life through the Crucifixion of Our Lord. Over both nave and chancel, a beamed wooden wagon ceiling. Stone-flagged nave floor with broad tiled borders. At the E end of the nave, over the entrance, the openings to a triforium gallery with a double row of columns (the concept perhaps taken from the W tribune in the church of Arbroath Abbey), their shafts carved with variegated spiralling and fluted designs, the capitals with deeply undercut foliage. They stand on pedestals bearing panels which display reliefs of birds; between the pedestals, panels depicting foliage. The columns support a straight lintel, its soffit also foliate, under a blind segmental arch-head studded with rosettes and surmounting the inscription DUST . THOU . ART . AND . UNTO . DUST . SHALT . THOU . RETURN. Below the pedestals of the columns, a band with the further inscription THE . GLORY . OF . THE . LORD . SHALL . ENDURE . FOR . EVER . The interior of the gallery is covered by a segmental-arched and compartmented stone vault, its ribs with foliate enrichment. On this side, the inner faces of the pedestals of the columned screen into the chapel bear panels depicting foliage.

Along the E two-thirds of the nave's side walls, blind arcading formed of single broad semicircular arch-heads placed between pairs and threesomes of pointed arch-heads, all springing from corbels carved with foliage, birds and beasts. Above, a line of continuous corbelling, also decorated with carved vegetation, and individual moulded corbels. Over this, on each side, panels displaying wreaths and yet more foliage. These are surmounted by three bays of triforium openings, each containing a fat bundle-shafted column between two pairs of thinner columns, all the capitals carved with naturalistic foliage, the column shafts of variegated designs except at the ends and on the N side where the shafts are plain; above the central columns, heavily corbelled bands of masonry. The end of this E part of the nave is marked on each side by tall barley-sugar columns. The S pair, their capitals again carved with birds and foliage, stand on a corbel decorated with a round panel displaying the branch of a pear tree; above, a pair of carved wreaths below a second and much taller panel with a relief of reeds. On the N side, a single column with a foliate capital and enriched shaft. It stands on a corbel whose face bears an oval panel depicting a pair of birds; above, a band carved with more birds among foliage and, above that, is the relief of a portcullis (for the Burgh of Arbroath) under the head of a man set among grapes.

The nave's W bay is longer than those to the E. Each side is occupied at ground-floor level by a segmental-arched transeptal shallow recess containing a seat and, at triforium level, by a gallery whose mourning occupants could look through a shouldered and enriched archway directly down to the coffin during a funeral service. Under the stone gallery fronts, bands of naturalistic foliaged sculpture. On the fronts themselves, panels carved with fruit, foliage and pious texts; under the N gallery's W end, a corbel depicting the head of a woman. Along the walls under the gallery openings, the inscription LIGHT . IS . SOWN . FOR . THE . RIGHTEOUS . AND . GLADNESS . FOR . THE . UPRIGHT . IN . HEART . THE . MERCY . OF . THE . LORD . IS . FROM . EVERLASTING . UPON . THEM . THAT . FEAR . HIM . In the centre of the nave's W bay is the stone BIER, its stumpy columns carved with foliage, its wooden top able to rotate so that a coffin could be turned through ninety degrees at the end of a service to let its head face the exit from the chapel before being carried to the grave.

From the nave two marble-clad steps ascend to the marble-floored narrower chancel, the steps flanked by splayed walls marking the entrance to this part of the chapel. Single bay to the W, its straight side walls containing rectangular doorways in foliate surrounds. These are the entrances to the mausolea under the W towers, a panel over the S door bearing the initials of John and Elizabeth Fraser, a panel over the N the initials of Patrick and Elizabeth Allan-Fraser. Rectangular window in the chancel's bowed W end wall. High over this bow, a foliate stone elliptical arch which supports a vertiginously placed balcony in front of the end's straight gable-head containing the crosslet window.

In the mausolea under the W towers, the identical sarcophagus TOMBS provided in 1884 to house the remains of Major John Fraser, his wife, their daughter Elizabeth and her husband, Patrick Allan-Fraser, the tops all carved with deeply cut foliage in which are set bronze relief portrait medallions of the deceased.

PUBLIC BUILDINGS

ANGUS COLLEGE, Keptie Street. Three distinct blocks, the two on the S side of Keptie Road built as Arbroath High School. The SOUTH WING is by *Carver & Symon*, 1895. Polite but gutless Jacobean. Barely projecting turrets mark off the three-bay centrepiece whose gable is topped by console-flanked panels, the lower containing a clock face, the upper carved with the burgh coat of arms; on top, a cartouche between strapwork scrolls which support a small pedimented finial. – WEST WING by *Angus County Council*, 1930. Stripped classical not quite daring to be Art Deco. – NORTH WING on the N side of Keptie Road, Modern-traditional on a budget, *c.* 2000.

Former ARBROATH ACADEMY. *See* PUBLIC LIBRARY, below.

ARBROATH ACADEMY, Seaton Road. By the Angus County Architect, *J.B. Yates*, 1960–2, and later extended. Flat-roofed curtain-walled boxes with brick used to give a look of permanence.

ARBROATH COMMUNITY CENTRE, No. 40 Marketgate and East Grimsby. The front block is a three-storey ashlar-fronted piend-roofed house of *c.* 1800. The pilastered doorpiece survives but the two ground-floor windows have been badly altered (one converted to a door). Behind, a big DRILL HALL added in 1897. In its gently bowed end to East Grimsby, a corniced door and two round-headed lights under an oculus.

Former ARBROATH HIGH SCHOOL. *See* ANGUS COLLEGE, above.

CORN EXCHANGE AND MARKET BUILDINGS, Market Place. Now subdivided into small units. Renaissance, by *Charles Edward*, 1852–5. Two storeys over cellarage, built of coursed brown sandstone; first-floor sill course and rusticated quoins. E front of nine bays, the two at each end and the three in the centre slightly advanced and pedimented. Round-headed ground-floor windows with rusticated surrounds. At the centre, a corniced projecting frame to the round-arched entrance, its keystone carved with a head. At the first floor, round-headed windows in the recessed third and seventh bays. The three windows of the centrepiece have pediments, the outer two triangular, the central one segmental. The centrepiece rises above the main cornice, its top part buttressed by scrolls; in its overall triangular pediment, a roundel containing a weathered shield. On the N elevation, round-arched ground-floor openings. Long but plain W extension of 1912. Blockily consoled and pedimented openings high up in the centrepiece which projects from its pedimented W gable.

GUILDRY BUILDINGS, Nos. 90–94 High Street. By *William Scott*, 1880–1. Laboured Italian Renaissance.

2 HARBOUR. Two approximately oblong compartments side by side, both faced with ashlar fronted by wooden rubbing posts. The inner (N) compartment is the WET DOCK (formerly Old Harbour) formed as a tidal basin in the second quarter of the C18, reconstructed by *James Leslie* in 1839 and converted to a wet dock in 1871–7. The outer compartment (the tidal NEW HARBOUR) was constructed to Leslie's design in 1839.

108 HARBOUR VISITOR CENTRE, Ladyloan. By *Baxter, Clark & Paul*, 2006–7. Assemblage of tall single-storey pavilions, their walls harled, boarded and with full-height glazing, the immense aluminium-covered roofs projecting like ships' prows.

Former LADYLOAN SCHOOL, Ladyloan. Disused. Simple Tudor, by *W. L. Moffat & Aitken*, 1874–6, built of squared red sandstone rubble. Single-storey, irregular H-plan, with shouldered-arched windows and a gableted bellcote on the SW gable.

POST OFFICE, No. 10 Hill Street. Now in other use. Jacobean Renaissance, by *H.M. Office of Works*, 1898–1900. Two tall storeys, built of yellow sandstone ashlar. Under the principal window of the first floor, a roundel containing a relief bust of Queen Victoria. On the overall parapet, the royal coat of arms in an Ionic aedicule. To the E, a garage extension of *c.* 1960.

PUBLIC BATHS, Nos. 22–36 Marketgate. Now housing. Plain Renaissance, by *Hugh Gavin*, 1913–15. At the centre, the round-arched entrance with concave jambs, flanked by vestigial pilasters. At the upper floor, the centre bay is treated as an Ionic-pilastered aedicule, the tympanum of its pediment carved with the burgh coat of arms. Converted to housing.

PUBLIC LIBRARY, Hill Terrace. The main block was designed by *James Black* in 1821 as Arbroath Academy but recast as the Public Library by *Hugh Gavin*, 1896–8. The shape is Black's. Two-storey piend-roofed rectangle of five bays by three, built of red sandstone ashlar. At the entrance (W) front, attached pier-like pilasters at the outer corners; the broad centre is slightly advanced with a pilastered and parapeted porch. String courses denote the level of the upper floor whose windows are linked by a sill course. Gavin converted the first-floor windows to niches, those of the front filled with statues (allegorical figures in the outer bays, Queen Victoria in the centre) and added a parapet. At the sides and rear, single-storey additions of 1896–8, partly altered and extended in 1936–8 by *Carver, Symon & Ross*. The main rooms of the interior are of 1896–8, with a grand stair to the first-floor art gallery.

In the forecourt, a gently stylized stone STATUE of a smirking Robert Burns by *Scott Sutherland*, 1958–9.

RAILWAY STATION, Keptie Street. Built in 1909–11. Tudor front block, with rinceau-patterned cast-iron brackets under its awning. The platforms behind are at a lower level and each is covered by a glazed double-pitch roof under which is a free-standing platform building.

SHERIFF COURT HOUSE, No. 88 High Street. Originally the Town House, it was designed by *David Logan* in 1803 and built in 1806–8. Two storeys and three bays of polished grey ashlar, the ground floor's stonework rusticated. At its advanced centre, a console-corniced door. The outer corners of the ground floor project as pedestals for paired Roman Doric pilasters at the upper storey whose status as a *piano nobile* is denoted by tall windows, those of the outer bays with balustered aprons and surmounted by panels almost like dummy attic windows. The first-floor centrepiece is marked off by paired Roman Doric attached columns supporting a fluted frieze with rosettes at its ends. These make a frame for a three-light window with Roman Doric column-mullions and a round-arched fanlight. Above the building's main cornice, balustrades at the outer bays. The centrepiece is finished with a tall attic-like parapet. At each end of the parapet, a pair of stumpy pilasters framing a cloth pendant; at the broad centre panel, a swagged clock face. The recessed plain N bay with a ground-floor pend to Market Place was added by *David Smith* in 1844.

SIGNAL TOWER, Ladyloan. Now a museum. Courtyard development of lighthouse keepers' houses and a signal tower built in 69
1813 to serve the Bell Rock Lighthouse *c.* 17.7 km. out to sea. *Robert Stevenson*, the designer of the lighthouse, was probably also responsible for this group. All of cream-painted ashlar. The entrance on the W side of the courtyard is flanked by a pair of identical buildings, each with a square pyramid-roofed two-storey centre block and single-storey piend-roofed wings. Their

doors and windows face the courtyard, all framed by segmental-headed overarches. On the N and S sides of the courtyard, lean-to verandas (now roofless) with cast-iron Roman Doric columns. The main range is the E. It builds up from low single-storey pedimented sheds at the ends through piend-roofed two-storey one-bay wings to the centre block. This is also piend-roofed and of two storeys but slightly higher. Three bays, the bowed centre with a semicircular portico. The bow rises above the eaves to form a round tower of three intaken stages, the lower two with rectangular windows set in tall and narrow round-headed overarches. The top stage is like a frieze, pierced with quatrefoils (alternate ones dummies) under a corbelled battlement.

SPRINGFIELD MEDICAL CENTRE, Ponderlaw Street. By *Campbell & Arnott*, 2004. Pleasantly informal grouping of harled and timber-clad blocks covered with shallow monopitch aluminium roofs.

TRADES HALL, No. 78 High Street. Now housing. By *David Hill*, 1814–15. Two tall storeys, the upper (originally containing the hall) exceptionally high, built of red sandstone ashlar. Front to High Street of three bays, the broad centre slightly recessed. Above the narrow first-floor windows of the outer bays, rectangular panels. The centre window of the first floor is of three lights with column-mullions and an overall segmental fanlight. Boldly projecting cornice topped by a parapet decorated with square panels at the ends and round-arched panels at the centrepiece. The four-bay side elevation to Commerce Street uses the same motifs but in a different arrangement, its first floor's two centre windows like those of the outer bays of the High Street front, its outer windows three-light under segmental fanlights but with plain mullions. At the W end, a short two-bay addition built in the late C19 when the building became the Sheriff Court; royal coat of arms above the entrance.

WATER TOWER, Keptie Hill, off Hillend Road. By *W. G. Lamond*, 1884–5, a formidable hilltop 'castle', built of rock-faced red sandstone ashlar. Battered and buttressed walls pierced by a few segmental-arched small dummy windows. At the N, a big round-arched entrance under a dummy box-machicolation whose crowstepped gablet is flanked by tall battlemented merlons. At the main wall-head, massive moulded corbels carry the battlement from whose sides project animal gargoyles. At the S end, a square tower which rises above the main block to its own corbelled battlement whose stone rainwater spouts are purposefully plain; corbelled out from this tower's SE corner, a round turret. Another battlemented tower but circular at the main block's NE corner.

WEBSTER THEATRE, High Street. Originally a public hall. Italian Renaissance, by *James Maclaren*, 1865–7. Ground floor with vermiculated rustication on the quoins. Attached Doric columns at the round-arched entrance whose keystone is carved with a human head. Over the entrance, a broad elliptical-arched canopy added during the theatre's refurbishment by *Angus Council* in 2007–8. At the first floor, Corinthian pilasters, their capitals badly weathered, and tall round-arched windows. Bracketed cornice and parapet, a pediment over the centre.

DESCRIPTION

Arbroath Abbey (*see* above) is the obvious starting point. To its W, on the opposite side of HAMILTON GREEN, St Andrew's Parish Church (*see* Churches, above).

HIGH STREET, starting from the foot of Hamilton Green and running parallel to East Abbey Street, is the undulating historic thoroughfare through the town, its general character Late Georgian and Victorian. Branching off downhill to the W at the beginning of High Street is JAMES STREET. On its S side, BRAICK'S WYND by *Baxter, Clark & Paul*, 1993, Neo-Vernacular housing with Scots and Postmodern touches. At the foot of James Street, Inverbrothock Chapel of Ease (*see* Churches, above).

High Street's first real incident is provided by the block of *c.* 1800 at Nos. 267–271 on the E side, a round-arched window in its broad wall-head gablet. Almost opposite, on the S corner of Church Street, No. 254, a tall commercial block by *Hugh Gavin*, 1909, its ground floor with a late C20 shopfront. At the two upper floors, channelled pilasters enclosing thin elliptical-headed arches in which are set shallow canted oriel windows, their glazing only just interrupted by panels at the level of the second floor, their tops decorated with anthemion and scroll cresting. Overall mutuled cornice with urns at the ends and, in the centre, a steep open pediment, its tympanum carved with a cartouche displaying a lighthouse. The adjoining No. 252 of *c.* 1860 is also three-storeyed but much lower. Still Georgian survival but with simplified blocky scrolls at the bottom corners of the window architraves and two-light windows in the outer bays. Then, on the E, a view up ABBEY PATH to Arbroath Old and Abbey Parish Church (*see* Churches, above). In EAST ABBEY STREET off Abbey Path, a neat early C19 villa (ABBEY LODGE) built of polished ashlar, its ground-floor windows aproned, a consoled cornice over the door.

On the SE corner of High Street and Abbey Street, a late C20 shopping development (Nos. 227–247), its small scale, recession from the street line and materials (brown brick and plate glass) breaking most accepted rules of townscape. It might matter less were the scale not to rise again and the street line be re-established at the early C19 three-storey Nos. 221–225 whose stugged ashlar walling is formed into panels by the polished stone lines of the window surrounds, first-floor band course, second-floor sill course, and strip quoins. Also of three storeys but much lower is the block at Nos. 215–219, probably early C19, its droved ashlar covered with a heavy coating of white paint. Beside it, Nos. 211–213, mid-Victorian Italianate, the cast-iron columned shopfronts intact. Opposite, No. 198, rebuilt in the late C20, and trying to fit in, the concrete blockwork walling being droved and the S block sporting an unhappily detailed version of a Georgian wall-head gablet. On the E side of High Street, at its S corner with Allan Street, No. 203, early C19, with a bowed corner, the upper floor's polished ashlar still visible. A little further S and on the W side, Nos. 184–186, again of the earlier C19 and of polished ashlar but still having its original shopfront with untapered simplified Doric columns; a large box dormer has been added to the roof. Still on the W side, No. 170 of *c.* 1860 with Ionic pier-mullions at the first-floor windows and, at the ground floor, fragments of the shopfront's original cornice carried on bracketed stiff-leaf capitals. On the E side of the street, at the corner with Kirk Square, No. 202, a tall late C19 block. At its splayed corner, a three-storey oriel topped by a slated octagonal spire.

KIRK SQUARE introduces a diversion to the NE. Its NE side is mostly filled by the front of the former Old Parish Church (*see* Churches, above). Beyond the church, on the corner of Hill Terrace and Academy Street, the Public Library (*see* Public Buildings, above). In front of it, a tall and ornate red-painted Late Victorian LAMPPOST, its base displaying the burgh coat of arms; it was made by *Walter Macfarlane & Co.* NE of the Public Library Academy Street becomes PONDERLAW STREET. On the r., No. 1, a three-storey house of *c.* 1800, built of droved ashlar. Corniced doorpiece. Unusually, the windows (unfortunately enlarged at the ground floor) get taller on each successive floor. At the house's l. end, a tiny single-storey outshot whose moulded door looks early C18. A little further up Ponderlaw Street, St John's Methodist Church (*see* Churches, above), its small forecourt bounded on one side by the hall. On the other side is the manse (WESLEY HOUSE), originally a single-storey cottage built, like the church, in 1772; the upper floor, its windows with bracketed sills, was added in 1868. At the early C19 No. 26 on the other side of the street, a pilastered and corniced frame to the door which has dummy sidelights and a segmental-arched fanlight. Further along, on the N, the Springfield Medical Centre (*See* Public Buildings, above).

SPRINGFIELD TERRACE (the NE continuation of Ponderlaw Street) begins on the r. with Nos. 1–1A, a mid-C19 villa, Georgian survival but the ground-floor windows two-light and the cornice over the door carried on heavy block consoles. Then on the S, St Mary's Episcopal Church (*see* Churches, above) and its substantial parsonical RECTORY designed, like the church, by *John Henderson* and built in 1852–3. NE of the church, more mid-C19 houses. The Georgian survival No. 3 has a console-corniced doorpiece but canted bay windows at the ground floor and two-light windows at the first. At No. 4, shallow rectangular bay windows and a strapworked parapet. At BELLEVUE, shaped pediments over the two-storey bay windows whose upper-floor level is marked by a string course which is carried across the centre on anta-pilasters. Opposite, on the N side of the road, the early C19 ABBEY BANK, a rendered villa with a segmental fanlight over the sidelit door; mid-C19 additions at the side and back.

High Street's progress SW of Kirk Square resumes on the E side with Nos. 163–165, built as the WHITE HART INN in 1821. The gable to Kirk Square is surmounted by a flat-topped and chimneyed pediment containing a Diocletian window. Over the centre of the five-bay front to High Street, a smaller version of the gable's pediment but raised on a pedestal (its ends panelled) and the Diocletian window now missing its mullions. The small windows of the three-storey Nos. 136–140 High Street suggest a possible C18 date. The block at Nos. 124–126, with pilaster strips at the corners, a second-floor sill course and plain frieze under the cornice, looks early C19. Are the unmoulded cornices over its first-floor windows replacements or later embellishments? The first-floor windows at the generally similar Nos. 118–122 are pedimented. The Late Georgian manner continues at Nos. 114–116 but this is now covered in cement render masquerading as ashlar. More straightforward early C19 ashlar-fronted architecture at Nos. 149–153 whose first-floor windows enjoy cornices and at Nos. 143–147 with only a second-floor sill course for ornament. Then the former ROYAL HOTEL, by *Charles Edward*, 1852. Over its first-floor windows, consoled pediments, alternately triangular and segmental; bracketed second-floor sill course. At the centre of the wall-head, Vanbrughian paired chimneys. The hotel's dentil cornice is continued across Nos. 125–127, a roughly contemporary block but with more sophisticated detail, the architraves of the windows of the upper floors enriched with anthemion decoration. The first-floor windows have cornices, the centre one carried on consoles and supporting a triangular pediment. The adjoining early C19 building (Nos. 121–123) is plainer, with strip quoins, sill courses and small cornices over the first-floor windows. Opposite, the former Royal Hotel, Nos. 104–108 of *c.* 1800 with rusticated quoins and a corbelled main cornice. Projecting over the central first-floor window, a carved eagle. Across the street, the former COMMERCIAL (now Clydesdale) BANK (Nos. 115–117) by *David Rhind*, 1863–4, a respectable but not very exciting palazzo; balustraded parapet above the cornice whose projecting lions' heads give the only hint of raffishness. Further on, the Late Victorian No. 93 is punchy but undistinguished Free Renaissance. More relaxed are the adjoining PRUDENTIAL BUILDINGS. Stripped Jacobean by *Hugh Gavin* in association with the Prudential Assurance Co.'s district surveyor, *J. H. Pitt*, 1915–16. At the splayed corner to Hill Street, a two-storey oriel window, a tall metal finial on its ogee dome.

On the W side of this stretch of High Street, the Guildry Buildings and Sheriff Court House (*see* Public Buildings, above) give touches of burghal pomp reinforced by a pair of late C19 LAMPPOSTS of the same design as the one outside the

Public Library (*see* above) and also by *Walter Macfarlane & Co.* Centrally placed in front of the Sheriff Court, a smaller but even more elaborate LAMPPOST, a crown over the light, which is inscribed TOWN HOUSE 1845. The pend under the N extension of the Sheriff Court gives access to MARKET PLACE in which are the former Corn Exchange and Market Buildings (*see* Public Buildings, above). Immediately S of the Sheriff Court, No. 86 High Street, a parapeted block of the earlier C19, its painted ashlar front divided into panels by strip quoins and string courses; the roof is piended to the front which has been given a Late Victorian wooden dormer. Beside it, the early C19 Nos. 80–84, built of red sandstone ashlar. At the first floor the outer windows are corniced, the centre one pedimented; overall pediment backed by a panelled parapet. On the corner with Commerce Street, the former Trades Hall (*see* Public Buildings, above).

COMMERCE STREET is mostly vernacular Georgian or Georgian survival in character. For the former Erskine United Presbyterian Church on its S side, *see* Churches, above. At the street's W end, a pair of banks. On the N is the grey ashlar Bank of Scotland (former BRITISH LINEN CO. BANK), by *David Cousin*, 1853–4, a sizeable but understated palazzo. At the W front, a Roman Doric-columned portico and first-floor windows with bracketed sills and consoled cornices; boldly projecting mutuled cornice. On the S corner, the Lloyds TSB Scotland (former TRUSTEE SAVINGS BANK), by *Hugh Gavin*, 1924. Single-storey free classical in red sandstone ashlar. Round-arched and key-blocked windows, a pediment over the entrance at the concave corner. To its W, on the corner of Brothock Bridge and East Grimsby, the former East Free Church (*see* Churches, above).

HILL STREET, laid out in 1806, continues the line of Commerce Street E of High Street. Its N side begins with the former Post Office (*see* Public Buildings, above). Opposite, the ashlar-faced ARBROATH MERCHANTS CLUB (No. 9) of the later C19. Two tall storeys and an attic. The ground floor is articulated by attached columns and, at the end bays, rusticated piers, all with lotus-leaf capitals. Three large windows lighting the first floor. Above, a stone gablet flanked by canted dormers. Further up, on the N side of the street, a two-storey terrace (Nos. 36–42) of *c.* 1820. The ashlar fronts (now painted) of its houses show individual traits. Nos. 36–38 form a double house, the doors (each with dummy sidelights and a segmental fanlight) paired under a single pilastered and corniced surround. Pilastered and corniced doorpiece at No. 40. No. 42 is swisher, its doorpiece with attached Roman Doric columns and its first-floor windows aproned. Projecting from its E gable, a late C20 Post-modern addition, clad in white-painted render and black wood under pitched slated roofs. In HILL ROAD to the E, a dry-dashed flatted block by the *Brunton Voigt Partnership*, 1995, the line of the boldly projecting slated roofs broken by gables; narrow V-shaped bay windows. Beyond, the former Grants

Shoe Factory (*see* Agricultural and Industrial Buildings, below). At the end of Hill Road, rusticated concrete pillars at the entrance to VICTORIA PARK which was laid out in 1897. Running S from the junction of Hill Street and Hill Road is WEST NEWGATE. On its E side, the late C18 NEWGATE HOUSE, a rubble-built three-storey laird's house, the wall-head rising in the centre where it is topped by a pediment. At the entrance, an early C19 doorpiece with squattish Ionic columns and rosettes at the ends of the frieze.

HIGH STREET S of Hill Street and Commerce Street begins with a couple of splay-cornered blocks. No. 85 on the Hill Street corner is late C19 with blocky North European Renaissance detail. On the corner of Commerce Street is the former BANK OF SCOTLAND by *Peddie & Kinnear*, 1865. Gentle Italianate with a bracketed main cornice. At the first floor, cornices over the outer windows; the three-light centre window has a segmental pediment, its tympanum carved with foliage and a rosette. A little further down, on the W side of High Street, the Webster Theatre and Arts Centre (*see* Public Buildings, above) followed by No. 60, early C19, with rusticated quoins and three-light first-floor windows in the outer bays; the ground floor was altered in the mid C20. Immediately opposite, No. 71, a three-storey palazzo of *c.* 1865, a carved shell in the head of the stilted round-headed arch of its entrance. At the ground and first floors, the windows are each of two stilted round-arched lights. Second-floor windows also bipartite but their lights are shouldered-arched. Only the stugged ashlar of the ground floor has escaped being covered with C20 cement. Workaday C19 vernacular follows on both sides of the street, broken by the deep forecourt of Arbroath United Free Church (*see* Churches, above) on the E. On the corners of John Street, Nos. 35–37 and 33, both buildings of 1830, with bowed quadrant corners. To the S, the last stretch of High Street to the shore, C19 vernacular with hints of fishertown which are taken up with a vengeance by the determinedly picturesque late C20 Nos. 18–22. Right at the end of High Street, on the E, THE OLD BREWHOUSE (the former SHIP INN), of two storeys and harled, the small windows suggesting an C18 date but it has been much tidied up in the C20 with cement dressings and brick chimneys. In the front wall, a panel bearing the relief of a ship. In SEAGATE and the one-sided OLD SHOREHEAD overlooking the harbour, fishertown vernacular, mostly of the C19.

W of High Street is MARKETGATE. Its E side, N of Ladybridge Street, is mostly pleasant but unexciting C19 vernacular but the harled No. 35A with a big chimneyed gablet may be late C18. The W side is dominated by the former Public Baths with the adjoining front block of the Arbroath Community Centre providing a ravaged Georgian contrast (for these, *see* Public Buildings, above).

LADYBRIDGE STREET leads to the harbour. At its W end, the ashlar-fronted SMUGGLERS TAVERN of 1830, quite smart with architraved first-floor windows and a bowed quadrant corner to East Grimsby.

THE SHORE, continuing the line of Ladybridge Street to the W, has houses only on its N side. They are restrained but prosperous. The early C19 tall No. 1 sets the tone. It is of three storeys and an attic, built of red sandstone ashlar. Three-bay front with a pilastered doorpiece, a plain string course above the first floor and a sill course linking the second-floor windows. No. 2, of *c.* 1800, also of three storeys and an attic, has been drydashed and given C20 dormers but the main architectural elements survive. At the ground floor, square windows denoting that floor's status as a basement although it contains the principal entrance. This is through a very tall Roman Doric-columned doorpiece which rises to the first-floor level: over the door, a fanlight, its glazing bars forming an oval pattern. No. 4 (HARBOUR HOUSE) is early C19, its front (now rendered) divided into panels by strip quoins, band courses and window margins. The consoled stone balconies with iron balustrades are mid-C19 additions. Adjoining ashlar-fronted tenement of *c.* 1800 at Nos. 6–9. Over the centre two bays, a chimneyed gablet containing a Venetian window with Roman Doric column-mullions. At the ground floor, pilastraded shopfronts (now with housing behind) of *c.* 1830, probably the date also of the bowed dormers. A couple of lower early C19 houses at the W end of The Shore, Nos. 10–12 (now drydashed) with an anta-pilastered doorpiece, No. 13 with an ashlar front and Ionic-pilastered doorpiece.

LADYLOAN curves SW away from the harbour. On its l. side, the Harbour Visitor Centre, Signal Tower and, further out, the former Ladyloan School (for these, *see* Public Buildings, above). Just beyond the school is the start of DUNDEE ROAD. On its N side, GAYFIELD, a short mid-C19 development comprising a plain three-storey tenement (Nos. 1–3) and a double house (Nos. 4–5), the double house having a pedimented centre with a round-arched dummy window at the first floor and pilastered paired doors; at the ends, giant pilasters. Prominently sited on the hill to the N is the WAR MEMORIAL by
96 *George Washington Browne*, 1920–1. Big slab-like cenotaph with battered sides and a Doric frieze. The polished ashlar masonry is channelled except at the inscription panel. Further out, on WEST COMMON a SCULPTURE ('Declaration of Arbroath') by *David Annand*, 2001, a bronze depiction of Robert Bruce and Abbot Bernard Linton holding aloft the sealed parchment of the Declaration of Arbroath of 1320 which asserted Scotland's independence, the result unfortunately kitsch.

MILLGATE LOAN goes N from the E end of Gayfield. Its r. side begins with mid-C20 local authority housing. High up on the l., the WINDMILL HOTEL, a big but bleak Jacobean villa of the mid C19. It is followed by the ST VIGEANS RESIDENTIAL HOME, an early C19 villa extended and much altered later in the C19 and again in the C20. The red sandstone garden elevation overlooking Millgate Loan has a full-height shallow bow in the centre. The entrance front (now rendered and partly overlaid by a glass and wood addition) is to COMMON BRAE. It is of three bays, the centre advanced with giant angle pilasters and a pilastered doorpiece; at the outer bays the windows (one still unaltered) are set in segmental overarches. Further down Millgate Loan and facing directly onto the street is a mid-Victorian double cottage (Nos. 68–70) dressed up with some Gothic touches; carved floral decoration at the wooden dormers. Beyond Common Brae, on the l. of Millgate Loan, the tall narrow-fronted NETHERCLIFFE HOUSE of *c.* 1860, with a Jacobean shaped gable, and the mid-C19 No. 62, with a Georgian survival console-corniced doorpiece but also with two-light windows and an iron-crested parapet.

ALBERT STREET'S S end is reached by Common Brae which climbs up the hill of High Common. In Albert Street, Nos. 5–6 are mid-C19 villas with gentle Jacobean detail. A little later and much fiercer is No. 3 with a pair of bowed oriel windows, both with bracketed eaves. One oriel is supported by a column and corbelling, the other by exceptionally heavy and deep corbelling. At Nos. 1–2 Albert Street, an L-plan double cottage of the mid C19. Rusticated quoins at the advanced gables which have crosslet 'gunloops' near their top and floriated iron finials. In COLVILL PLACE, plain Late Georgian and Georgian survival terraces of the earlier and mid C19. At its SE end, fronting Dishlandtown Street, St Thomas of Canterbury (R.C.) Church (*see* Churches, above). From Colvill Place's NW end, Princes Street leads to HILLEND ROAD off which a path runs across Keptie Hill past the water tower (*see* Public Buildings, above).

KEPTIE STREET on the N side of Keptie Hill is prosperous suburbia. Opposite the end of the path across the hill, a late C19 ashlar-fronted terrace (Nos. 17–25) of two storeys and an attic. The houses at Nos. 19–25 are each of two bays with, at the l. bay, a sidelit door under a broad pilastered basket arch whose head contains the first-floor window (its lower part blind). At the r. bay, a ground-floor bow window with a central column-mullion; on top of the bow window, a first-floor canted bay window under a canted dormer. No. 17, at the E end of the terrace, is more conventional. Again of two bays but broader than the other houses. At the l. bay, a three-light ground-floor window with Roman Doric column-mullions; at the r., a two-storey canted bay window. At the E side, a deep porch and an oriel window to its N. To the W of this terrace, late C20 housing (CAENLOCHAN GARDENS) occupying the front garden of CAENLOCHAN HOUSE, a big turreted and crowstep-gabled Baronial villa, by *William Aitkenhead*, *c.* 1865. Over the entrance, a battlemented tower with a diagonally set caphouse on one corner. At the E end of Keptie Street, Angus College (*see* Public Buildings, above) and Arbroath West Kirk (*see* Churches, above).

WEST KEPTIE STREET runs S from the E end of Keptie Street. On its W side, Nos. 7–9, an ashlar-fronted double house of the earlier C19. Battlemented main block of two storeys and two bays, with hoodmoulded windows and battlemented round corner turrets. At each end, a battlemented porch containing a Gothic entrance.

KEPTIE STREET'S curving E end mostly contains C19 domestic and small-scale commercial buildings. For the Railway Station, *see* Public Buildings, above. Just to its E, the WEST PORT BAR of the later C19, palazzo-like but the stonework badly weathered. Opposite, on the SW side of the street, No. 26, late C19 Italianate, the two-light windows having leafily capitalled thin column-mullions. On the corner with Dishlandtown Street, the former Evangelical Union Church (*see* Churches, above).

WEST PORT continues the line of Keptie Street towards the centre of the burgh. On its SW side, the late C19 No. 16. Ground-floor pub front with bulbous baluster-like columns. At the first-floor windows the architraves' bottom lugs are incised with floral decoration. On the wall-head, a pair of canted and pedimented stone dormers which flank an oval dormer.

MILLGATE leads NE from West Port. At its far end, on the SE side, the former Brothock Mill (*see* Agricultural and Industrial Buildings, below). On the NW side, WEAVERS CLOSE, a late C20 housing development, busy with Neo-vernacular and Neo-Mackintosh touches. At the NW, facing CATHERINE STREET, it incorporates a former mill (*see* Agricultural and Industrial Buildings, below).

AGRICULTURAL AND INDUSTRIAL BUILDINGS

ABBEY LEATHER WORKS, Palmer Street. By *A.E. Anderson* of Northampton, 1919. Neo-Georgian but with a hint of Jacobean at the advanced and gabled centre. C20 extensions.

BALTIC SPINNING MILL, Dens Road. Disused. Built in 1861. Four-storey-and-attic main block, of brownish-coloured rubble. It is of thirteen bays by three. At the front, the three centre bays and the two at each end are minimally advanced with rusticated quoins and acroterion-topped pediments. To the S and at right angles to the main block, a two-storey range with a chimneyed-pedimented gable at the front and a big round brick chimney at the back. NW of this range, a taller block, its pedimented W gable containing a four-light window with skinny Roman Doric pier-mullions.

BROTHOCK MILL, Burnside Drive and Millgate. Now offices. Built in several stages, all apparently of the mid C19 and constructed of coursed red sandstone rubble. At the NW, a tall weaving shed, its gable to Millgate with round-arched ground-floor openings and a circular window above. On its NE side, a three-storey piend-roofed block with a two-bay gable front. On the corner of Millgate and Burnside Drive, a three-storey-and-attic block of eight bays by three. At the long W front, round-arched ground-floor windows and one tall round-arched window rising through both the upper floors. At the S end, another block of three storeys but lower. The ground-floor windows are again round-arched and there are round-arched windows rising through the two upper floors at the end bays. To the S, a detached three-storey piend-roofed engine house, a tall square brick water tower on the NW corner of its roof.

DOOCOT, Steading Place. Now an electricity substation and with a door in the back (W) wall. Built as an appendage to Hospitalfield (q.v.) probably in the C17. Rubble-walled and of lectern type, a slabbed rat course along the back and the crowstepped ends; the original entrance was in the front wall.

GRANTS SHOE FACTORY, Hill Road. Now housing (MARINE COURT). Dated 1882 and built of stugged red sandstone. Main block of two storeys and fifteen bays, with rusticated quoins at the ends and sill courses joining the windows. Two asymmetrically placed doors (the E now a window) with rusticated jambs and 'keystones' at the lintels. Over the W door, a cartouche bearing initials and the date 1882. The lack of symmetry is reinforced by the prominence given an off-centre bay which is slightly advanced and contains a gently Gibbsian round-arched door under a two-light window with a Roman Doric pier-mullion and a bracketed sill. At the W end, a slightly advanced further bay rising above the rest as a small pyramid-roofed tower. W of this, a short single-storey range. Utilitarian but probably contemporary ranges at the back stretching along the E side of East Newgate.

MILL, Catherine Street. Now housing. The surviving mid-C19 block is of three storeys and an attic. Front of nine bays, the ends slightly advanced and with rusticated quoins. Ball finials on the gables which contain segmental-arched attic windows under oculi. The broad eaves and big piend-roofed dormers date from the mill's conversion to housing as part of the Weavers Close development (for the rest of which, *see* Description, above).

STEADING, The Steading. Now housing. Perhaps late C18 in origin but its present form is mid C19 and designed by *Patrick Allan-Fraser* as part of his improvements to buildings on the Hospitalfield estate. E-plan ranges constructed in red sandstone rubble. The middle range's E gable is crowstepped, contains a round-headed opening (now a window) and, under the gable-head, a triangular stone (sundial?) above a corbel carved as a human head. At this gable's NE corner, a conical-roofed round turret. S of the gable, a projection with a crowstepped half gable. Piend-roofed N and S ranges.

HOSPITALFIELD

off Westway

Victorian red sandstone Scottish Baronial fantasy from which peeps out an earlier laird's house. Despite the heavily detailed upper work and extravagantly vertical accents, the homespun lack of pretension of the residence of a landowner of modest means is still apparent. 62

After the Reformation the Hospitalfield estate, a former property of Arbroath Abbey, passed through various hands before its acquisition in 1664 by James Fraser of Kirkton, parish minister of Arbroath. Fraser was probably responsible for the erection of a low laird's house (thought to be the inspiration for the house of Monksbarns in Sir Walter Scott's *The Antiquary*) and, at right angles to it, a NW block containing farm and stable offices. In 1843 James Fraser's descendant, Elizabeth Fraser, heiress of Kirkton and Hospitalfield, married Patrick Allan, an artist, collector and architectural amateur. Known after his marriage as *Patrick Allan-Fraser* he completely remodelled the house, most of the work carried out in 1849–54. On Patrick Allan-Fraser's death in 1890, seventeen years after that of his wife, Hospitalfield with its contents and estate were left to endow a trust for the education of young men in painting, sculpture, wood carving, architecture and engraving.

The principal parts of the house form a Z, its N hinge occupied by a tower of exaggerated verticality built *c.* 1850, its walling of stugged ashlar. The top stage is shallowly projected on continuous corbelling and surmounted by a balustrade, a battlemented bartizan at the NW corner. Gripping the SW corner and rising from the ground, a turret whose tall two-storey rectangular crowstep-gabled top is set at a diagonal to the tower.

Immediately S of the tower, a short two-storey section of *c.* 1850 with a quatrefoil-pierced parapet. This joins to the two-storey and attic main block of the earlier laird's house. This house's principal features before the mid-C19 reconstruction were twin two-storey bows, probably late C18 additions, at its W front. They survive but hide behind Baronial additions. At the l. bow's first floor, a tall rectangular two-light oriel window of *c.* 1850. Splayed across the bow's N segment and filling its inner angle with the mid-C19 link to the tower is a high-set outshot carried on continuous corbelling. Above this corbelling the outshot's l. half forms a bowed and battlemented turret carried on further courses of continuous corbelling, the top course rope-moulded. At the outshot's r. half and at the same level as its turret, a rectangular projection, also on continuous corbelling; it fronts the N segment of the C18 bow and has its top on the same plane as the oriel window which it serves as a l. continuation. The r. continuation of the top of the oriel is provided by a segment-headed arch, its inspiration taken from Fyvie Castle (Aberdeenshire), in front of the recessed section between the bows. The r. support for the arch's springing is given by a high-level rectangular outshot on continuous corbelling which was added by Patrick Allan-Fraser to the front of the r. bow. Allan-Fraser also remodelled the straight section between the bows by adding an oriel-like rectangular projection pierced only by a single opening and supported on continuous corbelling which covers almost the whole of the ground-floor walling; at the top of the projection, above a rope moulding, a pair of armorial shields. Along the wall-head of this double-bowed section of the W front, a battlement of *c.* 1850 carried on massive moulded corbels. The battlement's base is formed by a cavetto cornice studded with foliate bosses and, in the centre, the head of a king and, at the splayed S corner, the initials of Patrick Allan-Fraser; above, a rope moulding. Behind the battlement, a pair of crowstep-gabled stone dormerheads.

Set back at the N end of the double-bowed section of the front is a single bay which contains the house's principal entrance, a sidelit door whose roll-and-hollow moulded surround of C17 character was probably renewed *c.* 1850. Covering this section is the heavily detailed head of a segmental arch, its l. side projected from the main walling on massive courses of continuous corbelling. As with the arch between the front's twin bows the entrance to Fyvie Castle was the inspiration but this second arch is placed higher than the first and surmounted by a high panelled parapet behind which is set another crowstep-gabled stone dormerhead. On the r. side of the arch-head, a splayed outshot across the inner angle with the projecting gable at the front's S end and joining to that gable's N tourelle; sticking out from the base of the tourelle's continuous corbelling is the half-length figure of a monk in allusion to the estate's medieval monastic ownership. At the ground floor of this three-storey end gable, a dummy double-keyhole gunloop and, to its r., a pair of round-headed arches, their central column with a foliaceous capital, which front a shallow recess containing a stone bench. Pair of first-floor dummy windows under a restless string course. Below the gable's chimney-topped and crowstepped gable-head are boldly modelled individual corbels under a string course, its centre carved with an angel's head. Overpowering the gable is its large conical-roofed round SW corner tower. On the N segment of its harled and jettied second stage and overlooking the approach to the house, a cusped niche containing the figure of a saint. Also harled is the tower's top stage marked off by a string course; quatrefoil opening at its W segment, a circular opening to the S. Stone dormer windows with shaped heads rise from the eaves.

On the house's S front, the l. bay beside the SW corner tower may incorporate C17 work at the first floor whose tall window with moulded margins is surmounted by an empty surround, perhaps intended for a heraldic panel; over the second floor window, a C19 shaped dormerhead inscribed JF/EP (for (Major) John Fraser of Kirkton and Hospitalfield and his wife, Elizabeth Parrott, parents of Elizabeth Allan-Fraser). Adjoining is a broad crowstepped and cross-finialled gable (the W end of the main W range), its upper part of *c.* 1850 but perhaps incorporating earlier work below. The small ground-floor windows' chamfered margins seem to be Victorian, possibly renewals. The roll-and-hollow mouldings to the first-floor windows may be C17. Roll-and-hollow mouldings also but of *c.* 1850 to the second-floor openings which are fronted by a boldly projecting stone balcony, its front pierced by quatrefoils.

its heavily moulded corbels carved as angels at the centre and ends.

To the r. of this gable the S range continues with an addition which is apparently all of *c.* 1850 and looks almost like a tower house in its own right. The addition's ashlar centrepiece is of three storeys, its ground floor windows small. At the first floor, a shallowly projecting rectangular oriel containing a two-light opening. On top of the oriel, rounded corbels support a cavetto cornice carved with depictions of plants, the cornice forming the base of a stone balcony, its parapet again pierced with quatrefoils. The balcony fronts a segmental-arched recess, its back wall pierced by a second-floor window; short balustrade over the walling above the arch. This centrepiece is set between a pair of unequally sized and differently detailed towers. The l. tower is bowed and conical-roofed. Top stages of stugged ashlar but the lower stages harled, the first floor jettied and with a roll-and-hollow moulded window and panel frame, both perhaps incorporating C17 stonework. The larger and taller r. tower has rounded corners and projects above its ground floor on continuous corbelling topped by a rope-moulded string course. Battlemented top stage, the corners of its square main part carried on continuous corbelling, the faces bearing stone sundials, the S and E set between foliage-decorated panels; at this stage, a NW jamb, also battlemented. At the E end of this 'tower house' centrepiece, a corbelled-out top floor; conical-roofed fat round turret at the NE corner. To the r. of this part of the S wing, a crowstep-gabled low two-storey section, constructed partly of Late Georgian brickwork and probably dating from *c.* 1800 but with some Victorian alterations. From this a screen wall, formerly fronted by a conservatory, joins to a now roofless Victorian two-storey fernery.

Pushing out from the tower at the N of the former laird's house range is the NE wing. This incorporates some walling of the C17 or C18 range of farm or stable offices on the site but now appears almost all of *c.* 1850. A forceful presence greeting the visitor passing along the drive from the N, the W gable is set between a pair of huge conical-roofed two-storey round corner turrets which sit on corbelling (both continuous and individual) placed just above the low ground floor of the wing. At the ends of the ground floor are low and sturdy sloping topped buttresses of *c.* 1850 but between them is earlier diagonally broached rough ashlar masonry which dates probably from the mid or later C18. This stonework is overlaid by a trio of Victorian cusped arch-heads enriched with ball ornament and springing from capitals, paired at the centre, without shafts. Two of these capitals have been left uncarved, two display heads of cattle, the other two crowned human heads. The r. arch contains a slit window, its chamfered surround mid-C19 work. Marking off the gable's upper floor is a rope moulding stretched between the corner turrets. At the first floor, a tall window of three lights, their surrounds with roll-and-hollow mouldings. Above, a battlement carried on individual moulded corbels under continuous corbelling which is decorated with carved human heads and an overall rope moulding. Set behind the battlement is a crowstepped gable-head pierced by a diamond-shaped dummy window.

The S side of the NE wing continues the mid-C19 display. In the centre of its ground floor, a pair of round-headed arches springing from foliage-capitalled bundle-shafted columns; above the central column, a panel displaying a tree. These front recesses, each containing a stone seat, the dividing wall between pierced by a quatrefoil as if to allow a pair of lovers the chaste expression of mutual infatuation. At the tall first floor, three bowed oriel windows, each carried on continuous corbelling under a rope moulding, the openings in roll-and-hollow surrounds. Along this side, a wall-head battlement above continuous corbelling which is ornamented with carved depictions of flora and fauna. The NE wing's N side, facing a service court, shows more evidence of its probable C18 origin with elliptical-headed cart or carriage doorways at the ground floor. A couple of gabled attic dormer windows of Neo-Jacobean character were added here *c.* 1850.

From the NW wing's W gable there extends a GATEWAY of *c.* 1850, its carriage entrance to the service court behind a segmental-headed arch under a shallow shaped and crowstep-topped gable. To the l. of the entrance, a fat tourelle, its conical roof with gableted and louvred openings. At the tourelle's front (W) segment, a clock face. Set back from the gateway's N side, a contemporary two-storey COTTAGE, the upper windows with gableted stone dormerheads. The service court is bisected by a two-storey block added *c.* 1850 to the NW wing's N side, its ground floor pierced by a second segmental-headed carriage entrance.

E of the house, a detached two-storey block built as an ART SCHOOL in 1901. At its S end, a contemporary brick-walled STUDIO.

WALLED GARDEN on the S side of the house. It is formed by two components, the S partly brick-faced and perhaps of *c.* 1800. The stone-walled N compartment may be of *c.* 1850 as certainly seems to be its doorway at the end of the N wall extending W from the house. The doorway's surround is moulded and with floral decoration carved in the top corners.

INTERIOR almost all of *c.* 1850. The principal entrance at the S end of the house's main block opens onto a stone-flagged and beam-ceilinged low ENTRANCE HALL, its W wall ashlar-clad, its N and S economically finished with pine panelling. At the E end, a pair of elliptical-headed stone arches. One is narrow and houses a cast-iron stove ('The Summerford'). The other and broader arch opens onto the ashlar-clad and beam-ceilinged Inner Hall which opens in turn to the Stair Hall. In the room N of the Entrance and Inner Halls is one jamb and a springer of a moulded stone archway, perhaps mid-C16, apparently discovered in the house or an outbuilding during the reconstruction by Patrick Allan-Fraser who placed it in its present position.

The Victorian Stair Hall's walls continue the ashlar cladding of the Inner Hall, a handrail for the stair carved in the stonework of the E side. Also on the E side, at the stair's first-floor landing, the seated figure of a monk reading a book (sculpted by *James Peters*). The E wall's adornment is further enhanced by an elaborate but slender Gothic lamp standard, the lower part of its two-tier shaft of stone, the upper of wood. This stands on a large stone corbel carved with the relief of a bird and foliage; figures of tortoises peep out from under the base of the lamp standard. On the stair's W side, paired pine barley-sugar balusters, the two in each pair having carving which spirals in opposite directions. The stair rises to the second floor, the upper flight recessed behind the plane of the lower's E side whose walling supports the line of the balustrade. Over the stair, a panelled and boarded wooden ceiling whose small hammerbeam trusses rest on rounded corbels carved with foliage designs. Set into the ceiling, a large rectangular glass panel to give top lighting.

From the stair's first-floor landing a broad corridor runs along the E side of the house's main range (the former laird's house). At its S end, the Dining Room with three windows overlooking the garden. The architectural treatment is mid-C19, mostly in the manner of *c.* 1700. Pulvinated friezes to the doorcases and walls covered with stamped leather depictions of flowers and vases to C18 designs, of Netherlands manufacture and brought here in 1850, the panels painted in green and gold. At the room's W end, an oak chimneypiece in a Jacobean Artisan Mannerist style, also of 1850 but not to Patrick Allan-Fraser's own design. Jambs formed of coupled columns with stylized square capitals; on the centre of the frieze, a recumbent lady; at the ends, terracotta portraits of the artists, John Philip, the close friend of Patrick Allan-Fraser, and Robert Scott Lauder under whom Allan-Fraser had studied. Mirrored overmantel, its broken pediment carried on volute-capitalled pilasters, their shafts deeply carved with fruiting foliage surmounted by the half-length figures, presumably emblematic, of a man holding a piglet and woman holding a book.

On the W side of the first-floor corridor and overlooking the entrance is the Drawing Room, its walls' wood panelling designed at the E side and S end to frame tapestries. At the N end, a plain classical chimneypiece of veined white marble. Trabeated ceiling, the ends of the E–W beams supported by panels carved with depictions of plants, these panels breaking the line of the cornice, itself decorated with stylized leaf ornament. In each of the ceiling's small compartments, the high relief portrait of a plant carved in the late C19 by *David Maver*.

At the N end of the first-floor corridor, an elliptical arch to its stepped continuation in the house's linking section between the old laird's house and the Victorian tower at the hinge with the NW wing. Occupying this tower's first floor is the

Ante-room of *c.* 1850. This is thriftily finished with door surrounds and a panelled dado of pine but near the E end is a pair of pilasters whose faces are panelled with cedarwood. At this end, a stone chimneypiece, its frieze with a rope moulding. Geometrically compartmented wooden ceiling with papier maché mouldings of Jacobean inspiration.

Off the Ante-room's W end is the Gallery, the largest and 64
most richly decorated of the rooms formed or remodelled by Patrick Allan-Fraser. Double height, it occupies the whole upper floor of the NW wing. Up to cornice height the walls are covered with oak panelling, the dado's round-headed blind arcading springing from fluted pilasters. Along the side walls, a high relief frieze of foliaged arabesque ornament, cherubs and hounds, the frieze rising to form a segmental-headed arch under the roof at each gabled end; in each side bay, a roundel containing initials of the forebears of Elizabeth Allan-Fraser (the Frasers of Kirkton and Hospitalfield and their wives on the N, the Parrotts of Hawkesbury Hall on the S). The doorpieces at the Gallery's E end have corniced friezes carved in relief with foliage, birds and hounds. On the wall above, large limewood reliefs of dead game birds hanging from leafy branches, these carved by *John Hutchison* in the 1850s. Above and between these and in the corresponding position at the W end are panels of stamped leather. The wall at the W end is pierced by a broad segmental-headed arch, its spandrels decorated with birds and foliage, the soffit carved with the Signs of the Zodiac. Along the side walls, corbels carved with the heads of men and women, a hound and a lion. From these spring the hammerbeam trusses which support the roof's compartmented and boarded ceiling. The large hammers are carved with fruits from which issue angels holding shields displaying coats of arms relating to the Frasers and their marriage alliances along the N side and to the Parrotts along the S. On the N pitch of the roof, a pair of dormer windows.

In the centre of the Gallery's N wall, a huge Neo-Jacobean alabaster chimneypiece, the elliptically arched fireplace opening framed by coupled columns whose bases are carved with reliefs of spiralling bands of ivy, their capitals with fruit and parrots (allusions to the strawberry (*fraises*) and parrot heraldic devices of the Fraser and Parrott families). On the centre of the chimneypiece's frieze and set among reliefs of honeysuckle foliage (carved by John Hutchison) is a figure of Puck, his ears pulled by two other diminutive boys (all these carved by *James Christie*). At the high overmantel, acanthus-capitalled pilasters from which spring a pair of chevron-ornamented arches. At the ends and centre of the arches, a trio of allegorical caryatids (also carved by Christie), the l. with a dove, the r. with a sickle and corn sheaf, representing Peace and Plenty.

Off the E end of the Gallery's N side, the Cedar Room on the first floor of the wing added *c.* 1850 to this block of former farm or stable offices. Walls and ceiling all panelled with cedarwood left unpolished so as to fill the room with its aroma, the dado detail repeating that of the Gallery. Moulded and dentilated stone cornice. Piercing the flat of the ceiling are two large rectangular glass panels, their borders engraved. Chimneypiece a version of that in the Ante-room but of cedarwood.

BELL ROCK LIGHTHOUSE. *See* p. 351.

SEATON HOUSE. *See* p. 670.

6040

AUCHMITHIE

Small former fishing village built on a cliff top overlooking the harbour.

ST PETER'S CHURCH (Episcopal). Formerly Auchmithie Parish Church. By *T. S. Robertson*, 1884–5. Romanesque, built of red sandstone squared rubble. Three-bay nave and a lower apsidal chancel; SE porch. On the SW gable of the nave, a bellcote with a pyramidal slabbed roof; the bellcote is projected on corbels carved with human heads. Moulded corbels under the chancel's eaves course.

Inside, the nave has plastered walls and a collar-braced roof, the chancel ashlar-clad walls and a boarded ceiling. Romanesque chancel arch.

HARBOUR. By *James Barron*, 1889–91; repaired and altered after storm damage, by *George C. Buchanan*, 1899. Roughly square basin, the stone piers partly utilizing natural rock outcrops.

SCHOOL. Dated 1859. Single-storey schoolroom with a birdcage bellcote on the SW gable, built of red sandstone. The adjoining two-storey schoolhouse is probably contemporary. At the SW, a small harled classroom extension of the earlier C20.

DESCRIPTION. At the SW end of the village, the school and St Peter's (Episcopal) Church. The main street, after a not very promising start, is made up of single-storey C18 and C19 cottages, mostly harled or pebbledashed. Almost in the centre of the village, a mid-C19 U-plan group of red sandstone cottages with a doocot over the pend in the centre of the NW range; in the open courtyard, a grey-brick round cistern. Set back from the SE side of the street, near the N end of the village and perched above the Harbour, the AUCHMITHIE HOTEL of 1885. It is harled, with gabled dormerheads.

MAIDEN CASTLE, East Seaton, 2.4 km. SW. The site is a coastal promontory with sheer drops on three sides at the S end of Carlingheugh Bay. This was fortified in the first millennium B.C. by a massive rampart fronted by a ditch to cut off the landward end.

ETHIE CASTLE. *See* p. 458.

AUCHTERHOUSE *see* KIRKTON OF AUCHTERHOUSE

BALGAVIES HOUSE

5050

2.7 km. WNW of Guthrie

Informally composed harled laird's house, the product of a not very orderly development from the C17 to the C20. The earliest part is the two-storey SE wing. Near the N end of its W side and now inside the house, its former external entrance, the lintel inscribed with the date 1691 and the initials TO and AS, presumably those of the owner and his wife responsible for its construction. Extending from this block's W side is the present main block, probably added in the C18, also of two storeys but higher. Five-bay front, the windows grouped 2:3. This block was enlarged *c.* 1935 by the addition of a gable-fronted bay at its l. end; projecting from this, a flat-roofed bay window. Extensive rear additions of the late C19 and earlier C20.

A path through woodland N of the house crosses the end of a small ornamental loch on a small BRIDGE of which one mid-C19 stone balustrade survives. The path leads to the ruins of the C16 BALGAVIES CASTLE, now consisting only of a pair of tunnel-vaulted chambers.

LODGE at the W end of the drive. Sizeable, in a mid-C19 picturesque manner, with bracketed broad eaves, bargeboards and mullioned windows.

BALINTORE CASTLE

2050

4.5 km. N of Bridgend of Lintrathen

Dramatically sited on the lower slopes of Cat Law, a towered and turreted Scottish Baronial mansion house (now derelict) designed by *William Burn* and built in 1859–60 for David

Balintore Castle.
View from south-west, 1860

Lyon, descendant of an Angus family, heir to a Jamaican fortune and a former Member of Parliament.

Almost square main block of three storeys above a basement, a single-storey and basement office wing extending N. Walls of forbidding dark grey stugged ashlar. The Jacobean aedicular entrance is placed at the l. of the W front in a slightly advanced one-bay projection, its crowstepped gable set between conical-roofed round turrets. To the r., a diagonal line of windows mark the ascent of the stair from the entrance hall to the principal floor's saloon. Above these but off-centre, a huge three-light Gothic window lighting the saloon. This bay's second-floor window, rising through the eaves to a shaped stone dormer-head, is mirrored by another in the r. bay. They frame this elevation's principal feature, a four-storey and basement tower, its bottom stage angle-buttressed, the top stage balustraded and with two-storey conical-roofed turrets corbelled out at three corners, a taller turret, also conical roofed at the NE.

At the main block's S corners, conical-roofed round towers of comfortably pacific appearance. The S elevation between them is symmetrical. Three bays with, at the outer bays, tall windows to the principal floor and shaped dormerheads over the second-floor openings. In the centre, a canted bay window under a crowstep-gabled rectangular top hamper. The E elevation, also placed between conical-roofed round corner towers, is of four bays and with shaped dormerheads over the second-floor windows. Symmetrical except that the two l. bays of the principal floor have been covered by a large canted oriel window (now fallen), probably original although Burn's drawings show a bay window in this position. Low office wing to the N, a small spire-roofed square tower on the W front the only excitement.

The interior was arranged around a double-height saloon in the centre of the main block. To the S was the drawing room, with the dining room in the house's SE corner and the library in the NE.

To the SE, at the foot of the former drive, a pair of single-storey octagonal LODGES contemporary with the house and presumably also designed by Burn, their rubble walls finished with parapets and pierced by round-headed windows. They flank a pair of gatepiers, their surmounting stepped pyramids topped by ball finials. Extending out from the lodges are short screen walls, each with a round-headed opening, which end against piers of the same design as the gatepiers.

5040

BALMADIES HOUSE

1.7 km. SW of Guthrie

Urbane villa-mansion house, its construction supervised by *George Sharp*, mason in Edinburgh, built in 1821 for Henry Stephens, the agriculturalist and author of the *Book of the Farm* (1844).

Two storeys above a basement which is windowless to the front. Three-bay façade of lightly broached ashlar. Slightly advanced and pedimented centre. Here a flight of steps rises to a portico of coupled Greek Doric columns, the entablature topped by a balustrade, the entrance door behind with sidelights and an overall elliptical-arched fanlight. Tall ground-floor windows, their architraves with entasis and surmounted by cornices. Band courses between the floors, that under the first floor reeded. A sill course joins the first-floor windows which are set in simply moulded architraves. Rubble-walled side and rear elevations, all of three bays; advanced centre at the rear.

Inside, a vestibule opens into a top-lit central stair-hall, its ceiling broken by an oval dome with a frieze of Greek key ornament at the bottom and a larger Greek key pattern round the cupola. Imperial stair to the first-floor gallery, the cast-iron balusters with anthemion decoration. The principal rooms, probably originally comprising a drawing room, library, dining room and bedroom, are all on the ground floor, well finished but without ostentation.

Immediately behind the house, a contemporary slab-roofed single-storey OUTHOUSE, a pair of doors in the W front. Was this a servants' privy?

STABLES, 0.15 km. W, probably of the same date as the house, a rubble-walled U open to the S. Built into the face of the E wing are some stones, probably from a C17 mansion house of Balmadies. One is carved with a thistle, fleur-de-lis and rose surrounding a weathered coat of arms. Below, a stone whose Latin inscription repels enemies and welcomes friends and strangers to the house. It is placed above a former lintel bearing the initials of Mr Alexander Pierson of Balmadies †1700 and Dame Margaret Murray, his wife, †1694. Below is a pair of skewputts, both carved with coats of arms, one also with the initials AB; under these, a pair of exceptionally squat balusters. In the gable of the W wing a triangular arrangement of flight-holes, so this contained a doocot. At the stables' N front are pavilions joined by linking ranges to a central two-storey coachhouse. Elliptical-arched carriage entrance at its ground floor; at the first, a tripartite opening, the outer lights dummies. – Late C17 corniced GATEPIERS to the W, their W faces with applied pilasters. In the stub walls extending either side further recollections of the previous mansion house. Each contains a small opening, the N circular, the S roughly rectangular; they are suggestive of gunloops but both are composed of several stones. Above the N, part of a stone carved with an inscription, perhaps a dormerhead. – WALLED GARDEN, probably of *c.* 1820, to the S. Slab-roofed lean-to outshot on the outer side of the N wall.

STEADING (MAINS OF BALMADIES), 0.35 km. W of the house, also of *c.* 1820. One two-storey rubble-built range of that date survives.

On the main drive to the house from the N, a rubble-built BRIDGE, probably also of *c.* 1820. Three-span, the round-headed arches springing from projecting imposts; circular panels in the spandrels. – At the entrance to this drive, early C19 GATEWAY with a pair of pedestrian entrances flanking the drive, each with a corniced and parapeted ashlar surround containing a round-headed arch springing from panelled imposts. On the drive's E side, the harled single-storey NORTH LODGE, also early C19, the W front of three bays articulated by ashlar anta-pilasters supporting the wall-head entablature and parapet. – WEST LODGE at the far end of the drive past Mains of Balmadies, also early C19 and single-storey but the walling of exposed rubble, the roof piended.

3060

BALNABOTH

1.7 km. NW of Glenprosen Village

Unpretentious and rambling yellow-harled mansion house formed in 1824 by Donald Ogilvy of Clova from several separate houses which had developed from the C16. The building is basically a U, open to the S. N range and E wing each of two storeys. The E wing's front is of five bays, the central door's surround Victorian but otherwise of C18 appearance. At the N range, the upper windows rise through the eaves into piend-roofed dormerheads, probably mid-C19 additions. The W wing was much altered and perhaps largely rebuilt by *David A. Whyte* in 1823–4. It is of two storeys and an attic but much taller than the other ranges and with large first-floor windows. E front of four bays, an oculus at the attic; the large splay-sided porch is probably an addition of the later C19. Extending W from the N end of this wing, a two-storey four-bay range, perhaps C18.

Just NW of the house, DAIRY of 1823–4 by Whyte, a conical-roofed circular building of one storey and an attic. – LODGE at the entrance to the drive, also of 1823–4 and designed by Whyte. Single-storey and broad-eaved, the E front of three bays, the centre projecting as a semi-octagon.

5060

BALNAMOON

1.8 km. ESE of Menmuir

Sizeable laird's house of modest pretension, the front block early C19 but incorporating a C16 tower, the NW wing C17.

A tower, probably at the SW corner of a barmkin enclosure, was built by the Collaces of Balnamoon in the C16, perhaps in 1584 (the date on a stone later built into a rear wing). A N wing was added to the tower in the C17, probably soon after 1632 when the estate was acquired by Alexander Carnegy, youngest brother of David, first Lord Carnegie (later, Earl of Southesk). Between 1812 and 1828 the house was remodelled and much extended in stages, the last designed by *William Burn* in 1825, for Alexander Carnegy's descendant, James Carnegy Arbuthnott, the C16 tower forming one end of a new S range. A NE wing, also built at the same time, was demolished in the 1970s.

The S-facing piend-roofed front block is, except for its porch, wholly early C19 in appearance. It is of two storeys above a fully exposed basement, the walling faced with render lined as ashlar; moulded band course under the ground floor. Small windows (one a dummy) to the basement. Very tall front windows at the ground floor, their status as the *piano nobile*'s openings further emphasized by cornices and cast-iron balconies. At first glance the front appears symmetrical with a seven-bay central section stretched between advanced ends. However, slightly closer inspection discloses that the symmetry is only approximate, the endearingly botched design probably the result of construction having occurred in stages (from W to E) with demands to economize increasing over the years. The front of the W section containing the remodelled C16 tower is of two bays, its side elevation of one with a three-light window to each floor. The E end section's front is of only one bay but its side elevation of three. The windows of the central section are grouped 3:4, the grouping presumably intended originally to be 3:1:3, the four l. bays belonging to one phase of construction, the other three part of a subsequent phase in which the r. openings were placed nearer than at first planned to the central door which originally was approached by a double stair. The discrepancy in the disposition of the openings is masked by the huge balustraded two-storey porch added *c*. 1860 at the middle of the main range, i.e. to the l. of the entrance but covering it. Entrance in the front of the porch with double doors under an outsize fanlight and flanked by niches. At the upper floor, the porch windows are set behind a screen of Roman Doric columns; in the centre, the large coat of arms of the Carnegy Arbuthnott family.

The C17 harled NW wing is three-storey but lower than the front block. Front of three bays, the tall stair window at the centre an insertion of the later C18 or early C19. Above this window, a stone panel of the earlier C17 displaying the Carnegy coat of arms, the surround pedimented and with caryatid jambs. The ground- and first-floor windows of the outer bays have C17 rounded margins, the second floor windows Late Georgian surrounds.

INTERIOR. The front porch, its ceiling with a leafy plaster rose, contains the l. part and landing of the early C19 stone entrance stair, both now with Neo-Jacobean wooden balusters of *c*. 1860. At the landing, a pilastered N wall (the former outside wall of the main block); towards its r. end, the early C19 entrance to the house. This opens into the early C19 entrance hall, now with an encaustic-tiled floor of *c*. 1860. The room is semi-octagonal, with round-headed niches in the splayed NE and NW sides. At the N end, elegant consoles supporting a Greek key lintel and segmental-arched fanlight over the doorway to the stair-hall. Here, a stair with cast-iron acanthus-decorated balustrades. From the stair-hall's E and W sides run passages off which open the S block's principal rooms. To the r. of the entrance hall is the dining room, now stripped of decoration except for a grey marble chimneypiece with columned jambs. At the house's E end and originally interconnecting with the dining room, a small library (also stripped of plasterwork). W of the entrance hall is the early C19 double drawing room, the E part (now dining room) with a prominently reeded chimneypiece of mottled brown marble at the E end and an elliptical-arched wood-grained archway to a recess at the W. From this recess, a door, also grained, into the principal drawing room formed in the first-floor hall of the C16 tower. This room's decoration is all of early C19 character, the plasterwork replicated in *Cunningham, Jack, Fisher, Purdom*'s restoration of the house in 1975–6. Chimneypiece of mottled grey marble. Anthemion and palmette cornice and an exuberantly swirling foliaged ceiling rose. In the house's NW wing, a stone stair with a distinctively detailed rounded newel of the C17.

GARDEN E of the house, its rubble-built N and S walls probably of the early C19. At the W end, a detached rubble-walled two-storey early C19 LAUNDRY. – N of the house, a double-courtyard red sandstone STEADING of the mid and later C19 (one building dated 1878), the N court now infilled with C20 buildings, the other now open to the S. – W of this, an early C19 FARMHOUSE, a rubble-walled two-storey box, a chimney at the centre of the piended roof. S front of three bays, the centre slightly advanced, the tall ground floor openings Gothic-arched and hoodmoulded.

BARNHILL *see* BROUGHTY FERRY

5030

BARRY

Small village of undistinguished C19 buildings. It is now joined to Carnoustie by late C20 housing but manages to retain a separate identity.

BARRY PARISH CHURCH. Originally Barry Free Church. By *James Maclaren*, 1888. Gothic, built of stugged grey masonry, the roof topped by a red tile ridge. Nave and SE tower. At the W end, broad transepts and, to their W, a session house. On the S side of the nave, low buttresses with blocky pinnacles. At the corners of the transepts, diagonal buttresses; a buttress in the centre of each transept gable. In each of the pointed windows of the nave, a round-arched light under a circled head. Main window of three lancet lights, the centre light under a plate-traceried trefoil. The hoodmoulded transept windows are each of two round-headed lights under a quatrefoiled head.

The SE tower is square. Angle-buttressed lower stage whose pointed door is surmounted by the carved emblem of the Free Church of Scotland (the Burning Bush). Tall belfry with chamfered corners. In each face, a hoodmoulded pointed and cusped opening. Battlement carried on arcaded corbelling from which project stone spouts. At the corners and above the spouts, octagonal pinnacles. Built into the S side of the porch to the session house, a stone from the church's predecessor inscribed FOR CHRIST'S CROWN/1843.

Inside, a ceiling whose braces spring from vaulting shafts and, at the transepts, from cast-iron columns. The nave opens into the transepts through two-bay arcades, the spandrels of the arches pierced by quatrefoils. – Plain PEWS of 1888. – At the W end, the PULPIT backed by the pipes of the organ moved here in 1954 from the former Barry Parish Church. – STAINED GLASS. In the N transept, a two-light window (an Angel Blessing a Knight) of 1914. – In the N side of the nave, one light (a Knight) of *c*. 1920. – In the S transept, one light of the E window was filled with stained glass (David) in 1888. – In the S wall of the nave, the E bay's window (St Paul) is of 1906. – The centre window of this wall (the Good Shepherd) was erected in 1888.

Propped against the E gable of the church, a mural MONUMENT with a moulded surround. It commemorates Grisell Durham †1664, the wife of David Alexander of Pitskelly ('Pitskellie') and bears their initials and two blank shields.

Uphill to the NE, the church's Tudorish MANSE of *c*. 1845.

PARISH CHURCHYARD. The site and shape of the FORMER PARISH CHURCH (built in 1800 and enlarged to a T-plan in 1818) are marked by a mound enclosed by a rubble retaining wall. – The graveyard MONUMENTS are generally C19. A few C18 HEADSTONES survive, most badly weathered but near the SE corner is a curly-topped one of 1762 commemorating John Cristall and his wife, Magdalen Ramsay. The sides are carved with flaming torches. At the centre of the front, a mantled shield bearing the initials JC and MR with an angel's head (the soul) above. – Immediately E of the site of the church, a headstone of 1795 to James Whitton displaying an angel's head with exceptionally large outstretched wings characteristic of contemporary gravestones in the immediate area (cf. Panbride Parish Church).

PANMURE GOLF CLUB, 0.6 km SW. Early C20. Low and quite picturesque Queen Anne, with broad mutuled eaves; low tower finished with a flattened ogee dome.

SCHOOL. Built in 1878. Single-storey rubble-walled school and a two-storey school house (now drydashed), both quite plain.

BARRY MILL, 0.7 km. NW. Straightforward late C19 rubble building with a lower bow-ended kiln at one end. Lean-to wheel house housing the wood and iron wheel which drives two pairs of stones.

BELL ROCK LIGHTHOUSE 7020

17.7 km. SE of Arbroath

Rising from a reef which is submerged by the sea at high tide p. 352
and a long-recognized danger to shipping on the approaches

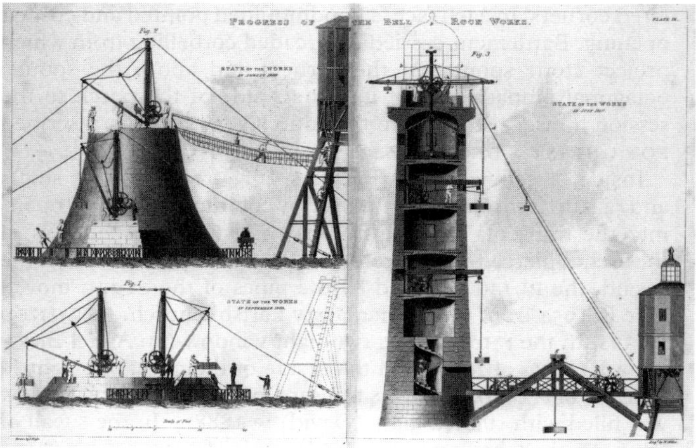

Bell Rock, lighthouse.
Elevation and section showing construction, *c.* 1810

to the Firths of Forth and Tay, the lighthouse designed by *Robert Stevenson* in consultation with *John Rennie* and built in 1807–11 at a cost of over £60,000. John Smeaton's Eddystone Lighthouse (Cornwall) was the prototype for its design and construction. 30 m. high circular tapering from a diameter of 12.8 m. at the base to 4.5 m. under the cornice, built of sandstone faced externally with granite ashlar painted white above the lowest courses. Small windows and a door placed high above sea level. Topping the tower, a lattice-sided walkway round a domed octagonal cast-iron and glass lantern.

3030 BENVIE

Quite rural, a handful of buildings near the graveyard of a medieval parish church.

GRAVEYARD. W entrance flanked by a pair of carved but weathered stones built into the enclosure wall. The l., perhaps the top of a dormerhead, bears the date 1637, the r. the impaled coats of arms of Scrymgeour and Kerr flanked by the date 1634; in the stone's top corners the initials I^{V}D and I^{L}C (for James [Scrymgeour], [second] Viscount Dudhope, and Lady Isabella Carr [Kerr], his wife). Inside the graveyard, the W gable of the former BENVIE PARISH CHURCH (the remainder demolished after the parish's union with Liff in 1753) still stands to a fair height but so covered in ivy that no feature is visible. At the Graveyard's E end, the HEADSTONE of John Marshal †1749. On its E face, a mantled coat of arms above emblems of death. Reclining cherubs on the E tympanum and top of the swan-neck pediment; an angel's head (the soul) on the W tympanum.

BENVIE FARM, 0.1 km. W. Farmhouse and steading built in 1810–12 by *James Scott & Co.*, masons, and *Robert Thompson*, wright. The harled house, which incorporated fabric of the early C18 Benvie Parish Manse, was largely rebuilt after a fire in the early C20 but to the Late Georgian design. Piend-roofed two-storey main block, the S front of five bays. Single-storey lateral wings, the W badly altered. Rubble-walled single-storey steading buildings behind, also piend-roofed.

BENVIE MILL, immediately N of the Graveyard. Forming an L, a rubble-built mill and mill house of the early C19. The mill itself is of two storeys and piend-roofed. Elliptical-arched cart entrance towards the W front's S end; small windows to the first floor. The water wheel and machinery survive inside. The mill house (SE wing) was originally single-storey but later given a broad-eaved upper floor, probably in 1865 (the date on the lintel of the E gable's basement door). Bargeboarded dormerheads over the first-floor windows.

GRAYBURN, 0.3 km. N. English Arts and Crafts villa, by *Patrick Thoms* of *Thoms & Wilkie*, 1905. Walls of crazy-paved rubble but with rendered heads to the gables; tall slated roof with bellcast eaves. Oriel window at the W gable. Projecting from the S front's advanced centre, a single-storey bow window. The SW corner of the ground floor originally formed a loggia-porch, the openings now infilled.

BIRKHILL *see* MUIRHEAD AND BIRKHILL

BRAIKIE CASTLE 6050

2 km. ENE of Kinnell

Derelict and roofless but largely intact tower house built in 1581 for Thomas Fraser of Braikie.

The crowstep-gabled four-storey-and-attic house is constructed of random rubble masonry composed of red sandstone and grey-coloured whinstone. L-plan, the jamb projecting from the N end of the main block's E side. In the S inner angle, a bowed stair-turret projected on continuous corbelling above ground-floor level. Wall-head chimney on the main block's E side; rounded turret, its conical roof now missing, also on continuous corbelling at the SW corner. The ground floor of both the main block and the jamb is pierced by slit windows and broad-mouthed oval gunloops. At the upper floors, comfortably sized windows with smaller round and rectangular shot-holes below their sills and also a few smaller windows. Despite the martial display of the walls, the roof is carried over the wall-head in a quite peaceful manner without battlement or parapet.

Roll-and-hollow moulding to the house's rectangular entrance at the W end of the jamb's S side. High up on the stair-turret, a moulded frame containing a panel on which a

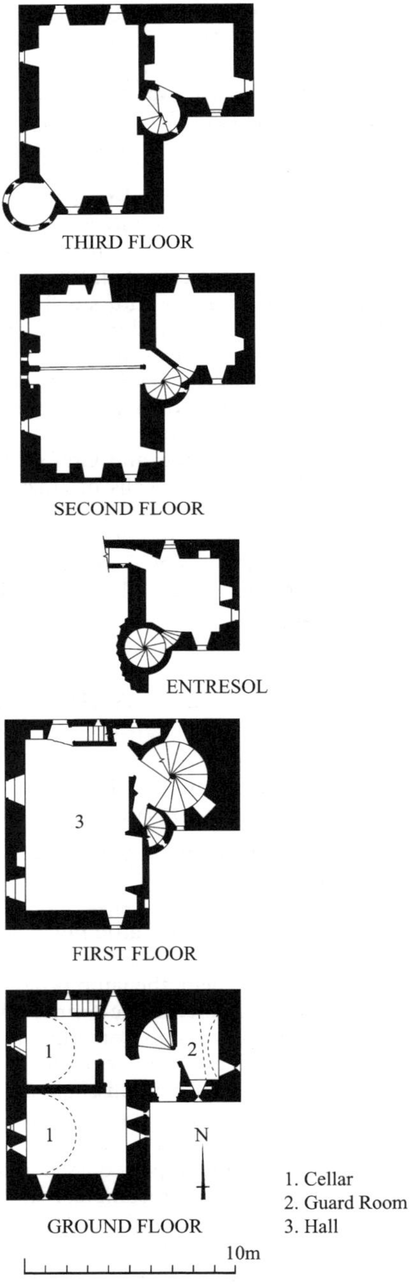

Braikie Castle.
Plan

shield displays the impaled coats of arms of Fraser and Kinnaird surmounted and flanked by the initials of Thomas Fraser of Braikie and his wife, C– Kinnaird; over the upper set of initials, the motto SOLI DEO CONFIDO ('In God alone is my trust') and, at the bottom of the panel, the date 1[5]81.

The entrance opens onto the foot of the jamb's stone turnpike stair to the first floor. Under the stair's E part, an elliptically vaulted guardroom lit only from gunloops in its S and E walls. In the main block a short vaulted passage along the N half of its E side, its end lit from a gunloop; doors in the W side and S end to the two cellars which occupy the rest of this block's ground floor. Both are covered with segmental-arched tunnel vaults. From the N, probably the wine cellar, a straight stair in the thickness of the N gable leads to the first-floor Hall. This, like all the rooms on the upper floors, is covered by a wooden ceiling, some of its beams bearing very faint traces of stylized painted decoration. Near the S end of the E wall, a broad rectangular fireplace with a simple roll-and-hollow moulding. The adjacent window to the S has been built up but its segmental-arched embrasure survives. Embrasures of the same design to the window in the E end of the S wall and the S end of the W. High-set horizontally proportioned window with a steeply sloping sill at the W wall's N end. In the W end of the N gable, a cupboard and, to its r., another window in a segmental-arched embrasure. In the embrasure's E ingo, the entrance to a straight stair in the thickness of the wall. This leads to an entresol room above the principal turnpike stair in the jamb. Near the top of this straight stair, a laird's lug or peephole into the Hall.

A secondary and tighter turnpike stair in the inner angle's turret gives access from the Hall to the floors above in both the main block and the jamb. On the second floor of the main block, a pair of rooms which have been separated by a clay stud-partition keyed for a plaster finish which has been painted with a decorative scene. More painted decoration has existed on the beams of the ceilings. In each room, an end fireplace and a close garderobe in the W side adjoining the partition wall.

BRECHIN 5060

Smallish burgh (population of about 7,650) boasting a cathedral but its character hesitant between that of a market town and an industrial centre, both functions now belonging to the past.

In the earlier C12 David I granted the Bishop of Brechin the right to hold a weekly market at his '*villa*' of Brechin, establishing it as a burgh of barony under the feudal superiority of the bishop. Subsequently the town acquired the position of a royal burgh, being represented in Parliament from 1479 and admitted to the Convention of Royal Burghs in 1555 although its status as a royal burgh was granted formal parliamentary

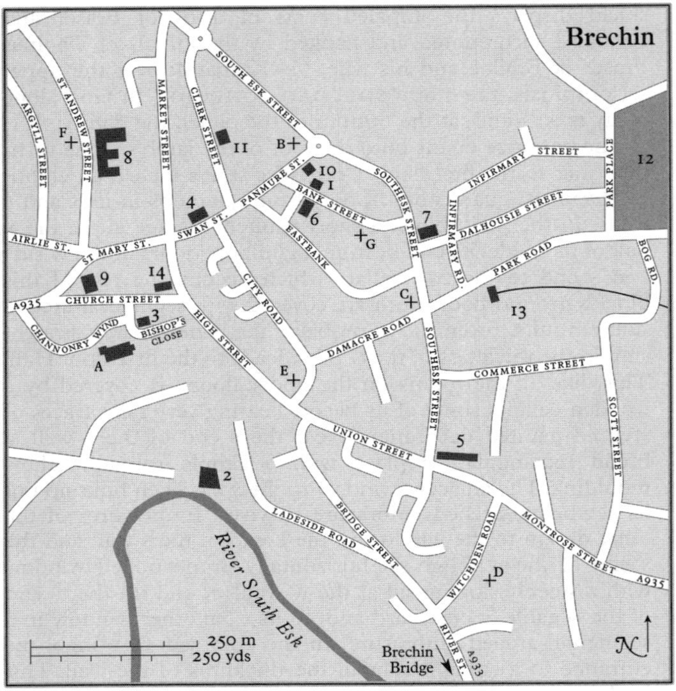

A Brechin Cathedral
B East Free Church
C Gardner Memorial Church
D Maisondieu United Presbyterian Church
E Protestor Church, Former
F St Andrew (Episcopal)
G St Ninian (R.C.)

1 Angus Council Office
2 Brechin Castle
3 Cathedral Hall
4 City Hall
5 Den Burn Works
6 Drill Hall
7 Library
8 Maisondieu Primary School
9 Mechanics' Institute
10 Parish Council Chambers
11 Post Office
12 Public Park
13 Railway Station
14 Town House

ratification only in 1641, four years before it was sacked and burned by the Marquess of Montrose's army.

In the C17 Brechin's importance was as a market for the sale of livestock and the produce of the glens to the W and it consisted of one main street (High Street) with the lesser streets of Castle Street and Church Street to the W. To the SE was a suburb beside Brechin Bridge over the South Esk. Industry began to develop from the later C18, linen weaving the principal occupation but a couple of distilleries, a brewery and a machine works had been established by the later C19. Much continued well into the C20 but most has now closed.

BRECHIN CATHEDRAL

Church Lane

Mostly of 1900–2, the re-creation of a C13 cathedral but incorporating medieval work, the W end memorable for its juxtaposition of a round tower of *c.* 1100 with the large and square tower of the C13 and C14.

History

A monastic foundation of *Céli Dé* was either already in existence or founded *c.* 972 when Kenneth II offered 'the great *civitas* of Brechin to the Lord'. From the establishment of the diocese of Brechin in the C12 or earlier this community served as the bishop's *familia* and its importance was marked by the erection of the Round Tower *c.* 1100, apparently followed a little later by the building of the first cathedral church on the site. In the earlier C12 the *Céli Dé* of Brechin had been transformed into the canons of a cathedral chapter, Pope Innocent III noting in 1250 that 'the brethren who have been wont to be in the church were called Kaledei and now by change of name are styled canons'. This change of clerical status was accompanied by the rebuilding of the cathedral on a larger, although still modest, scale. Work seems to have begun with the nave and transepts at the beginning of the C13, followed by construction of the choir completed by the mid century when the NW tower, perhaps an afterthought, was begun. The tower's upper stages were not completed until the episcopate (1354–84) of Bishop Patrick de Leuchars, perhaps a preliminary to the insertion of a new W window in the main gable of the nave.

After the Reformation the choir was abandoned for worship and quarried for building materials, the chancel arch blocked and the nave fitted up for Reformed worship. A thoroughgoing overhaul of the nave was undertaken in 1806–7 when the transepts and N porch were demolished and the aisles widened and heightened, their new roofs covering in the (blocked) medieval clearstorey windows, their side windows tall. Inside, a plaster ceiling was installed, galleries erected on all four sides and a new pulpit placed in front of the centre of the S gallery.

The reconstruction carried out in 1900–2 by *John Honeyman* of *Honeyman & Keppie* was an attempt to restore the appearance of the medieval cathedral and to provide a dignified setting for worship. The W five bays of the choir, where some stonework survived, were rebuilt, as were the nave aisles, their roofs lower than their Georgian predecessors (although higher than the medieval ones), allowing the clearstorey windows to be reopened. A new transept was added each side and a N porch erected on the foundations of the medieval porch. The interior was remedievalized in Edwardian good taste Gothic, rearranged along 'ecclesiological' lines and provided with new furnishings and stained glass. Subsequent alterations and additions have respected the Edwardian ethos.

Exterior

Except for the buff-coloured masonry of the Round Tower, the cathedral is all built of pinkish Ardovie sandstone, the polished ashlar of the Edwardian work looking very smooth in comparison with the weathered stonework of the surviving medieval parts.

7 The WEST FRONT, a disjointed composition of two very different towers flanking the main gable, displays evidence of the main pre-Reformation phases of the church's building history. The ROUND TOWER of *c.* 1100 on the r., now tenuously attached to the SW corner of the nave's S aisle, was originally free-standing. One of only two medieval circular towers in Scotland, the other being at Abernethy (Perth and Kinross), it is apparently of Irish inspiration. About 33 m. high, its external diameter is *c.* 4.65 m. at the base tapering to 3.7 m. at the corbelling under the eaves. Masonry of large squared blocks but laid in a gentle spiral rather than horizontal courses. No string courses or offsets. Only one small window in the SE segment and slightly larger belfry openings at the cardinal points, all rectangular. The entrance is in the W segment and placed about 2 m. above the ground. This is low and narrow (only *c.* 1.8 m. high and 0.56 m. broad) but sophisticated, constructed with a single stone for the sill, two others for the inclined jambs, and a fourth for the round-arched head, all carved with narrow inner and outer borders enriched with jewel-like pellet moulding. On each jamb, a small and weathered high relief of an ecclesiastic, one holding a crozier, the other a staff and open book. Over the arch and rising above its outer border, a depiction of the Crucifixion, Our Lord's legs, unusually, not crossed. On the sill, a shallower diamond-shaped relief; flanking the sill, a pair of crouching beasts. Two projecting stones flank the arch-head and may have been intended originally also to be carved. The tower is finished at the top with a two-course octagonal band studded with crude individual corbels which forms the base of a 5.7 m.-high spire, perhaps added in the C14 but repaired in 1683 after being 'blowen over'; the stone lucarnes look late C17. The spire's apex and ball finial were replaced by *William Nixon* of *H.M. Office of Works* in 1847.

The NORTH-WEST TOWER is much larger (7.6 m. square) and of greater height to the top of the spire (39 m. rather than 32.5 m.). It is ashlar-faced, of five stages each, except the third, marked off by a string course. The lowest stage is C13, the rest probably C14. Straight E–W buttresses at the S corners, the SE starting above the aisle roof; at the NW corner, an angle buttress. The NE corner is clasped by an octagonal stair-turret, its external door inserted in 1807. Small pointed windows in the faces of the lower stages. In each face of the belfry, a much larger opening of two cusped lights under a quatrefoil. Continuous corbelling under the tall battlement which was, at least partially, renewed in 1642 (the date on one of the E front's

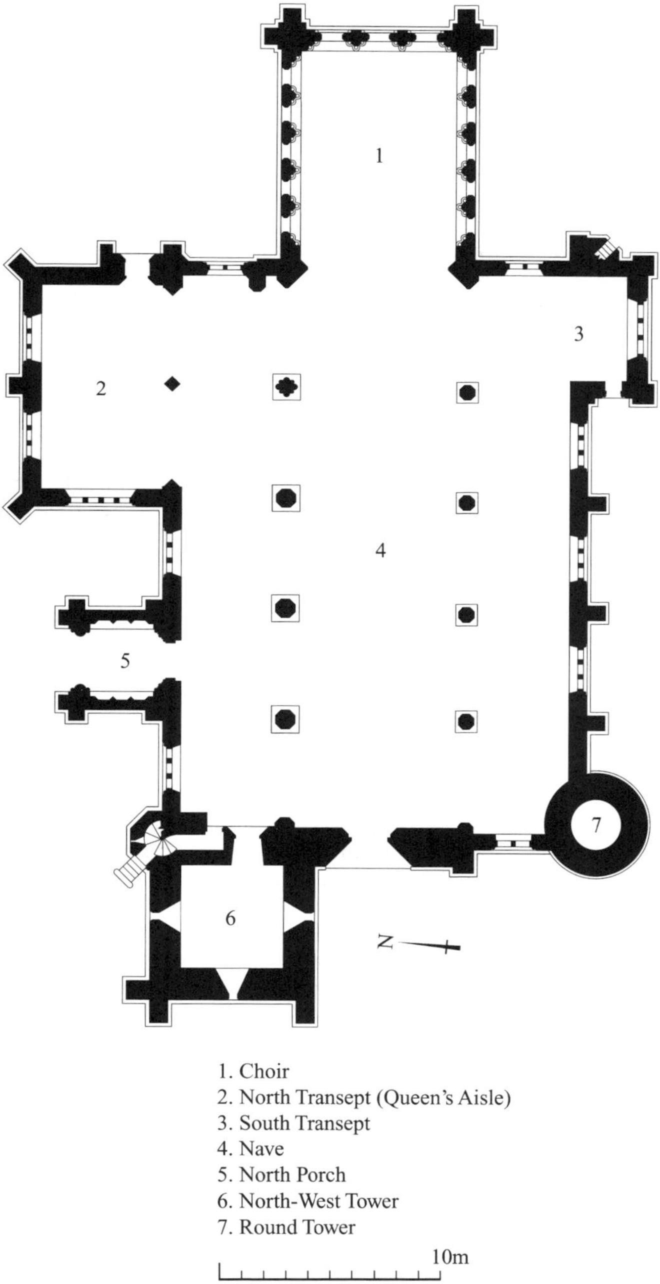

Brechin Cathedral.
Plan

merlons) and again in 1993. The inner side of the N merlon on the E front is carved with a human face, the centre merlon on the S with stylized decoration, both probably in the C17. Large clock faces (replacements of 1974 for a clock of 1807, itself replacing a clock erected in 1665) on the E and W fronts. Inside the battlement, an octagonal stone spire, with alternate faces having round-headed doors under crudely pedimental finials, perhaps of 1642. Above the doors are small lucarnes; larger lucarnes with angular pointed heads in the other faces.

The WEST GABLE OF THE NAVE is medieval but of two periods, the lower stage, built of rougher and more weathered masonry, of the early C13, the upper stage containing the great W window a C14 rebuild. The pointed and hoodmoulded W door has broad splayed sides, each embellished with five bell-capitalled shafts placed between roll mouldings, the orders in the head of the deeply filleted arch decorated with some chevron and nailhead enrichment (restored). To the r. of the doorway, above a construction joint,* a cusped pointed arch recess, its nook-shafts with bell capitals. Its hoodmould's label stops are carved as human heads, one much larger than the other; this carving, of fairly inept quality, may date from a post-Reformation repair. Set-back walling at the upper stage. In it, the large W window of four lights, the head filled with curvilinear tracery remarkably similar to the French-influenced S presbytery window of Melrose Abbey (Borders) and which provides an early C15 date for the work here. The W FRONT OF THE SOUTH AISLE is of 1900–2, its window of two pointed lights under a trefoil; bell-capitalled nook-shafts. The hoodmould's headstops are carved with the faces of a king and queen. Nailhead enrichment at the wall-head. The skewputt is carved with a dog carrying a stick.

The NORTH AND SOUTH AISLES of the nave are of 1900–2, built to the same width as the aisles of 1806–7 but lower in an approximation of the medieval height. Like the Late Georgian aisles but unlike the medieval aisles they are articulated by stepped buttresses. Detail all of 1900–2. In each bay a window of three stepped lights contained in a pointed arch with bell-capitalled nook-shafts. The hoodmoulds' label stops are carved with knots of foliage. Wall-head cornice of cavetto profile studded with genial grotesque heads; blocking course above. The CLEARSTOREY above is largely medieval, the squat hoodmoulded and pointed windows reopened in Honeyman's restoration. Unusually, they are aligned with the walling between the aisle windows rather than with the openings themselves. Moulded wall-head cornice with nailhead enrichment, largely of 1900–2 but copied from surviving C13 work on the N side.

* The position of this joint, at the same distance to the r. of the door as the NW tower's S face is to the l., led Dr J. S. Richardson to suggest that a SW tower balancing the NW tower was originally intended (*Transactions of the Scottish Ecclesiological Society*, xiv, pt. iv (1954), 17–18).

The NORTH PORCH in the second bay from the W was built by Honeyman in the position of the medieval porch removed in 1806. The general shape follows that of its predecessor but the detail is of 1900–2 and quite grand as befits what was intended to be the cathedral's principal entrance. It is sturdy, with angle buttresses, their octagonal spired tops with foliaged finials. Nailhead enrichment under the E and W parapets. The N entrance's ball-capitalled shafts support a pointed arch decorated with nailhead ornament, the hoodmould's label stops carved with knots of foliage. Inside, on each long side, a stone bench in front of hoodmoulded blind arcading, the attached columns with bell capitals and carrying cusped arches, their outer moulding with more nailhead enrichment. The door into the church has foliaged capitals to the columns and nailhead and chevron ornament.

The NORTH TRANSEPT ('QUEEN'S AISLE') bears little resemblance to its medieval predecessor. It is large and chapel-like, of two bays, the roof parallel to the nave's. Heavy diagonally set corner buttresses, those at the S rising from the aisle roof, each topped by a crocketed pyramidal pinnacle. At the N buttresses and the centre of the N wall are image niches surmounted by elaborate rib-vaulted canopies with human heads projecting from their corners and finished with crown finials. Battlement over the N side; stepped parapets at the gables. In the four-light W window and the two-light N windows, tracery of Scots Late Gothic character. Of the same inspiration is the E wall's rose window whose cusped loops spiral round trefoils surrounding a central sexfoil. Hoodmoulds with headstops over all the windows.

Honeyman's SOUTH TRANSEPT stands on the foundations of the medieval transept demolished in 1806. Projecting only a little and with clasping corner buttresses, it is integral with the S aisle's E bay, both sharing a roof set at right angles to the aisle's main roof and rising above it. Simple detail of 1900–2. Entrance in the W face, the door in a round-arched surround with bell-capitalled nook-shafts, the hoodmould's label stops carved as knots of foliage; over the door, an emblem of the Holy Trinity to which the cathedral is dedicated. In the transept's NW inner angle with the S aisle, a chimney whose upper two-thirds are projected on corbelling carved with foliage, a beast and a human head. In the S gable, a three-light window of C13 type, the tracery displaying quatrefoils under a trefoil, the nook-shafts with foliaged capitals, the hoodmould with male and female headstops. The walling of the E face of the transept and the aisle is continuous but their junction is marked by a sturdy stepped buttress. On the S side of the buttress, a small three-sided porch containing the stair to a boiler room, at the E end of the aisle, a window repeating the detail of the aisle's side windows.

The CHOIR, forming an unaisled and lower continuation of the nave, is a mixture of medieval and Edwardian work. Much shorter than its medieval predecessor (12 m. instead of

25.5 m.), it is of five narrow bays and rectangular-ended. In each side wall, five tall and splay-sided lancet windows linked by a sill course and a string course which jumps up over each to form a hoodmould. Bell capitals to the shaft-ringed columns. The three W windows on the N side are medieval and *in situ*. Of the S windows, one jamb of the westmost is medieval work *in situ*. The next window was in the fourth bay from the W but rebuilt here in 1900–2, the date also of the other side windows and most of the walling. Nailhead enrichment (a fragment at the W end of the N side medieval) on the cornices under the plain parapets. Just E of the centre of the S wall, a medieval CONSECRATION CROSS. The E gable is all of 1900–2. At the corners, gableted angle buttresses surmounted by spired octagonal turrets, their faces decorated with blind pointed arches. Just below the turrets, in the E inner angles, are (empty) image niches. In the gable, three equal-sized lancets covered by continuous hoodmoulding; foliage-capitalled nook-shafts and nailhead enrichment at the arches. Above, the side walls' cornice returns as a foliated string course under the head of the gable. In the head, a large rose window flanked by a pair of nook-shafted blind arches, all covered by continuous hoodmoulding.

Interior

The ROUND TOWER is self-contained.* Inside, no evidence of the external taper but a diameter of 2.3 m. for the full height. The semicircular wooden platforms and ladders were introduced by *William Nixon* in 1847.

On the NORTH-WEST TOWER'S ground floor, an ashlar-walled room (now vestry) covered by a stellar vault, its centrepiece a large round opening through which bells could be hoisted. The vault's ribs spring from attached columns (the shafts renewed in 1900–2) with stiff-leaf capitals, the SE with a crudely modelled face carved at the centre. The tight turnpike stair in the tower's NE turret gives access to the upper rooms. On the first floor a stone-slabbed floor and round-headed window embrasures in the thick walls. The W window was reopened by *A. B. Roger & Young* as part of their restoration of the tower begun *c.* 1989. Pointed window embrasures at the second and third floors, the second-floor windows with hinges for shutters. Just below the present third-floor level, a S doorway (with tusking at the jambs) into a wall passage. At the belfry, a narrow ogee-arched door. Under the NE corner of the spire, a corbel carved as a crouching dog. The corbels in the other corners are decorated with foliage. High up in the W wall, just above the top of the openings, a pair of unmoulded square corbels, their purpose uncertain. From the base of the tower and stair-turret, pointed doors into the nave's N aisle.

* A door into the church's S aisle was inserted in 1807 but blocked forty years later.

The NAVE'S C13 five-bay arcades are of different designs, the S arcade's probably later, constructed after the N had settled in alarming fashion. That arcade's piers, leaning dramatically outwards, are alternately octagonal and with clustered shafts of varying complexity, all with bell capitals and simple moulded bases of waterholding type perhaps re-cut in the C19. Octagonal respond at the W end, the E'S has clustered shafts. Another respond of the same size and also with clustered shafts at the E end of the S arcade but the pillars to its W are all octagonal and much slenderer than in the N arcade. The arcade also leans outwards but in much less pronounced fashion. Rubble walling (thicker at the N) in the spandrels and clearstorey whose squat windows are placed above the pillars rather than the pointed arches of the arcades. Chancel arch a larger version of the arches of the arcades. Above the arch, a change in the character of the masonry suggests that the church was roofed, presumably only temporarily, at a level just above the arcades before the clearstorey was built. Or is this the product of a post-Reformation rebuilding of the top of the nave gable? Also in this walling, evidence of a blocked round-headed high-level door into the choir. Open timber roofs of 1900–2 over the nave and aisles; something similar probably existed in the C13. The E bay of the S aisle is roofed at right angles to the rest, this roof continued into the S transept. The two E bays of the N aisle open into the N transept (Queen's Aisle) through a pair of arches of 1900–2, the capitals of their central pier and respond carved with naturalistic foliage; at the central pillar, the arches spring from a corbel carved as a bearded head. The arches contain a wrought-iron screen erected in 1951. In the transept's E wall, off-centre door, its hoodmould with male and female headstops. Hammerbeam roof over the transept.

In the CHOIR, the internal treatment of the lancet windows is either C13 work or a replica of it. Each window is placed between tall bell-capitalled shafts which carry an order enriched with dogtooth ornament. Between each pair of windows, another shaft, also with a bell capital, from which springs the hoodmoulding. The same treatment is repeated at the lancets of the E gable where Honeyman had no evidence of their medieval appearance.

FURNISHINGS arranged in Scoto-Catholic fashion. In the choir, an oak COMMUNION TABLE, polite Perpendicular Gothic of 1902. – Contemporary CHOIR STALLS in the same manner. – PULPIT on the S side of the chancel arch, also of 1902 and of oak, with metal figures of saints in tabernacled niches. – On the chancel arch's N side a brass eagle LECTERN, probably late C19. – FONT at the E end of the N aisle, its bowl C12 and decorated with round-headed blind arcading, the base C20. – Another FONT, in the N transept ('Queen's Aisle'), was provided in 1902. It is octagonal, of Corennie granite. – In the N transept, a simple COMMUNION TABLE of 1951. – Simple nave PEWS of 1902. – Hanging over the centre of the nave, a brass CHANDELIER, probably early C16 Flemish work, which was presented to the cathedral by Bishop Andrew Lamb in 1615. Foliage decoration on the arms and an angel finial. – Filling the W end of the nave, the ORGAN by *Peter Conacher*, 1878 (rebuilt by *John R. Miller*, 1900, and again in 1931 by *E. H. Lawton* and 1986 by *Rushworth & Dreaper*). It is in two sections flanking the W window, the polite Perpendicular Gothic ORGAN CASES designed by *Maclaren, Soutar & Salmond* in 1931. – Above the door into the NW tower at the W end of the N aisle, a large MORTIFICATION BOARD of 1683. – In the W bay of the S aisle, a bronze WALL MONUMENT to the Hon. David Wynford Carnegie, erected in 1925, its relief portrait by *William Lamb*.

STAINED GLASS. The choir's windows are all by *Henry Holiday*, 1901. The three E lancet lights show Christ as Prophet, Priest and King, the rose window above the *Agnus Dei* on a strongly coloured red background. In the side walls, effectively crowded and darkly coloured Scenes from the Life of Our Lord. – Flanking the chancel arch, two windows (the N depicting Isaiah and St John the Baptist, the S St Peter and St Paul) by *David Gauld*, 1901. – In the N transept, rose (E) window ('*Benedicite*') by *William Wilson*, 1953, and brightly coloured. – Also by Wilson, 1955, are the busy windows in the N wall (Daniel and Jeremiah). – The transept's mosaic-like four-light W window (the Annunciation flanked by depictions of Elijah and the Widow and Ruth and Naomi) by *Gordon Webster*, 1977–8. – In the N aisle, a war memorial window (Moses, Melchizedek and David) by *Douglas Strachan*, 1949, the colours uncharacteristically subdued and the composition disciplined. To its W, a window (Adam, Abraham and Isaac) by *William Wilson*, 1952.

The S transept's three-light S window (Our Lord Blessing Little Children) is by *Morris & Co.* from a design by *J. Henry Dearle*, 1906–7, a product of that firm's decline. – In the S aisle's side wall, a pictorial window (SS James, Matthew and Thomas) by *Hugh Easton*, 1952. – To its W, a small-paned window (SS Philip, Andrew and James) by *Herbert Hendrie*, 1932, with stylized hieratic figures. – Then, another window (SS Bartholomew, Simon and Jude) of 1952 by Easton. – The aisle's mosaic-patterned W window (St Paul before King Agrippa) is by *Gordon Webster*, 1978. – W window of the nave ('*Te Deum Laudamus*'), jewel-like by *William Wilson*, 1958. – The lights of the nave clearstorey are all, except the W window on each side, filled with brightly coloured figures of Scottish saints by Wilson, 1954–9.

In the ground-floor vestry of the NW tower, colourful but disciplined glass by *William Wilson*, 1956. In the S window, a depiction of Bishop Samson, first bishop of Brechin, and David I, reputed founder of the diocese. The W window (emblematic of the Holy Trinity) is based on the medieval seal of the cathedral chapter. The N slit window displays the Presbyterian Church of Scotland's symbol of the Burning Bush.

CARVED STONES. In the W bay of the S aisle, the 'ALDBAR STONE', believed to have been brought here from the graveyard of Aldbar Chapel, 3 km. SW of Brechin. It is probably of the C9 or C10, a cross-slab *c.* 1.75 m. high, the front carved with a ring-headed cross, the cross-shaft and head decorated with interlace, the ring and base with meander patterns. Reliefs of a pair of birds flank the top of the cross, a pair of ecclesiastics, each holding a book, the shaft. The back is more randomly composed. At the top, a pair of cloaked figures, possibly representing monks. Below them, a depiction of David killing a lion, accompanied by identifying symbols of a harp and a sheep. Just below, a mounted warrior with a short sword and round shield and, at the bottom, a horse or donkey. – Also in this bay of the aisle, a HOGBACK GRAVESTONE, probably of *c.* 1000 and an Irish-influenced local product. At one end is carved the stylized head of a grotesque beast reduced to little more than great staring eyes and a snout from which extend near-symmetrical curvaceous plant-like tendrils twining round fantastic animals near the other end. At this end, on either side, a pair of ecclesiastics. One of each pair holds a crozier. One of the others holds a book, the other a bell. – Also in this bay, fragments of medieval CARVED WORK found during restoration of the cathedral. Some, e.g. with chevron decoration, is Romanesque, probably of the C12.

On the E wall of the N aisle, above the font, is placed the 'MARY STONE', the carved fragment of a cross-slab, perhaps of the early C11, which was discovered in a garden near the cathedral. The head of the cross is intact. At the intersection of the arms, a roundel in a pelleted border, the roundel carved with a relief of the Virgin and Child and the inscription 's[ancta].MaRIa.m[ate]R.XR[IST]I'. On the top arm, a bird, probably representing the dove of the Holy Spirit; on the side arms, angels. The surviving top of the shaft is carved with a pair of saints, one identifiable by his emblem of the keys as St Peter, the other perhaps St Paul. Flanking the top arm of the cross, a pair of now headless angels (?), each holding a book; beside the l. figure has been added the incised date 1782. The top of the shaft is flanked by an eagle and a ferocious lion, symbols of the Evangelists St John and St Mark. – On the floor beside the font, a well-preserved GRAVE-SLAB of *c.* 1200 incised with a floriate-headed cross and, to one side, a pair of shears, perhaps for a tailor. – On the wall above, a weathered HERALDIC STONE displaying the arms of a bishop, perhaps George Shoreswood †1463.

CHURCHES

EAST FREE CHURCH, Panmure Street and Southesk Street. Disused. By *J., W. H. & J. M. Hay* of Liverpool, 1855–6. Typical individualistic Dec, the masonry of crazy-paved rubble. Sturdily buttressed six-bay box. At the S bay on each side, a taller window, its gable rising through the eaves in quasi-transeptal fashion. In the next bay on the E side, a gabled porch projecting from between the buttresses. At the centre of the S gable, a domineering steeple. Square tower with massive diagonal buttresses at the first two stages giving the appearance of a crouching weight-lifter. At the tower's lowest stage, the S entrance, its pointed arch's innermost order cusped, the hood-mould's label stops carved as two human heads, the l. a portrait of John Knox. Four-light window at the second stage, its hood-mould's label stops carved as male and female heads. Two-light opening in each face of the third (belfry) stage, the hood-moulds' label stops again carved as heads. These openings are set in angular gables with dragon gargoyles at their bottom corners, the gables' form determined by the splayed-foot broaching of the spire. On the spire, two tiers of stone lucarnes, the gabled lower lucarnes containing two-light traceried openings, the small upper lucarnes triangular.

NW of the church, a broad-eaved Dec HALL by *T. Martin Cappon*, 1895–7, a tall octagonal spired cupola-ventilator rising from the red-tiled ridge of its slated roof. Inside, STAINED GLASS SE window by *A. Ballantine & Gardiner*, 1897.

GARDNER MEMORIAL CHURCH, Southesk Street and Damacre Road. Built in 1896–8 and named to commemorate a son of the Rev. Alexander Gardner who had left money for an increase in church accommodation in Brechin. The architect was *J. J. Burnet* and this is the most elaborate of a series of churches* he designed between 1889 and 1900, all with nearly identical towers counterpointing low churches and halls, the style mixing Baronial, Romanesque, Scots Late Gothic, and Arts and Crafts elements. Here the church and hall form an L, its heel occupied by the tower, the church stretching W along Damacre Road, the hall N up Southesk Street, all built of stugged rubble with lightly broached dressings.

The church itself consists of a four-bay nave and slightly shorter N aisle, both with double-pitch roofs with bracketed and bellcast eaves. In the church's E gable, a stepped arrangement of three pointed lights. In the side elevations, paired broad lancets with splayed sides, those at the E bay of the nave with gently cusped lights. At the E end of the nave stands the tower. It is square with chamfered corners and a pronounced batter. Above the high base, two stages rise, unbroken by string courses, to the parapet. In the tower's S face, a small off-centre rectangular two-light window at the base and, above, a lancet like those of the nave. In the E face of the base, a window of two trefoil-headed lights. It is linked by a panel carved, like all the sculpture, by *William Vickers*, with the town seal of Brechin to the nook-shafted Romanesque window above. In each face of the belfry stage, a pair of two-light openings, their barely pointed surrounds each with two orders of nook-shafts, their

* The others are St Molio's Church at Shiskine (Arran), the Maclaren Memorial Church at Stenhousemuir (Stirlingshire) and Broomhill Trinity Congregational Church in Glasgow.

foliaged capitals of Celtic inspiration. Uncrenellated parapet projected on block corbels. Angle-rounds at the NW, SW and SE corners. Inside the parapet, a pyramid roof with tiny lucarnes and a plump weathercock. At the tower's NE corner, a round stair-tower with a tall parapeted and flat-roofed octagonal cap-house. At the tower's SE corner, a stepped and gableted buttress from which project the base and canopy of an empty image niche. At the NE corner of the tower, a low semi-octagonal protrusion, the stepping sills of the lancet windows in three of its faces disclosing the presence of a stair inside. At each of this protrusion's main corners, an attached column, its capital carved with the emblem of one of the four Evangelists. More carving (foliage) in the centre of each face of the cornice which is surmounted by a high parapet with a simple image niche at each corner.

N of the tower is the low T-plan hall range. The range's S bay is a porch, the entrance set between a pair of stepped and gabled buttresses, the upper part of each hollowed out to form an empty image niche. The entrance itself is a broad pointed arch, decorated with carved vines and a cusped outer order under an ogee hoodmould; iron gates of gentle Art Nouveau character. Flanking the entrance are low-set empty image niches. Above the entrance, a high, stepped parapet; at its centre, a gableted and tabernacled image niche, again empty.

N of the porch and continuing its roof is the hall proper. In the E front to Southesk Street, squat windows, each of three shouldered-arched lights containing small rectangular leaded panes. High parapet above a cornice studded with grotesques, alternately depicting humans and beasts set in foliage. Over a door at the N end the parapet steps up and has a projecting octagonal image niche. In the NE wing's gable, three stepped lancets under a continuous hoodmoulding. On the hall's W side the roof is cantilevered out over a 'cloister' walk. Half-timbering in the gable of the NW wing.

Access from the porch into the church is either through a door covered with embossed cloth into the E end of the aisle or via a vestibule to the S. In this vestibule, the stair to the nave's E gallery, its stone newel finished with a Romanesque capital. S of this vestibule, within the tower, a vestry under the gallery with a door into the nave.

The interior of the church is wonderfully light, the white plastered walls gently relieved by pale stone dressings. Elliptical arch marking off the gallery under the tower. Nave arcade with elliptical arches carried on round and octagonal pillars with small foliaged capitals. Heavy open wooden roof, the principal rafters supported on plain stone corbels. The importance of the W bay of the nave is emphasized by a tie-beam and queenpost truss, the beam's braces supported on attached columns, their capitals quite energetically foliaged. The very W end of the nave, the site of the communion table, is further distinguished by a cusped wooden arch.

Restrained FURNISHINGS (boxy pews; simple Wrenaissance choir stalls, pulpit and organ case) in a Presbyterian 'ecclesiological' arrangement with the communion table as the focus. – 1890s FONT at the aisle's E end, its quatrefoil-plan sandstone pedestal supporting an octagonal marble bowl. – Metal lantern-type LIGHT FITTINGS, also of the 1890s.

MAISON DIEU CHAPEL, Maisondieu Lane. Roofless fragment of the rubble-walled chapel dedicated to the Virgin Mary which formed part of an almshouse founded by Sir William de Brechin, lord of Brechin, in or shortly before 1267 when there was granted a charter in which the chapel is described as already in existence. There still stand a substantial part of the S wall and the S stub of the E gable. The S wall has been of at least six bays, with a splayed plinth. Pointed windows placed quite high and joined by a sill course which forms a hoodmould over the pointed door in the third bay from the E. Moulded entrance, its nook-shafts' bases and bell capitals surviving. Immediately outside the nook-shafts on each side, a narrow recess, the W's half-domed top extant. The windows' surrounds are also moulded and their hoodmoulds' label stops carved as human heads.

Inside, the windows are joined by a string course which forms a hoodmould over each and by a sill course which, although it rises as a hoodmould over the piscina, is interrupted by the S door. Deep splayed ingoes; near the windows' inner corners have been nook shafts, their surviving capitals of bell profile but with rings round them. Part of the S jamb of a taller window in the E gable is still visible. In the S wall, between the two E bays, a piscina with a stone shelf at the level of the springing of its pointed arch.

MAISONDIEU UNITED PRESBYTERIAN CHURCH, Witchden Road. Disused. Prominently sited and accomplished example of free Neoclassicism, by *George Washington Browne*, 1890–2. The general concept is of a two-storey rectangle of stugged masonry with a pedimented front (W) gable. But this front is broken by a projecting full-height polished ashlar centrepiece of three bays. At the centrepiece's ground floor, three doors framed by piers carrying a plain entablature. Above the entablature, a pedimented temple front with Ionic columns *in antis* behind which are two tiers of rectangular windows, the lower tall, the upper small and horizontal. At the church's SE corner, a tower, its stugged masonry rising unadorned to a Doric entablature. Above this, its stonework of polished ashlar, is a pedestal with urns at its corners which supports a tall octagonal belfry. At each of the belfry's pilastered principal faces, a round-arched opening. Above the belfry cornice, a low octagonal pedestal on which rests a dome topped by a ball-finialled stalk.

PROTESTOR CHURCH, City Road. Secularized. Church built for members of a small sect which had split from the Antiburgher Secessionists and opened in 1822. Front originally of six bays with pointed doors (now blocked) at the ends and tall pointed windows (partly infilled) in the two centre bays; the short upper windows of the intermediate bays lit galleries.

ST ANDREW (Episcopal), Argyle Street and St Andrew Street. By *Ross & Macbeth*, 1888. Very tall and bleak Early Geometrical cruciform, built of stugged pinkish sandstone. Clearstoreyed nave with sturdy buttressed aisles, high transepts, each with a rose window, and an unaisled chancel. The tower projecting from near the W end of the S side is stopped short of its intended height and finished with a pitched roof and weatherboarded gable, the appearance inappropriately cottagey.

Stone-faced interior. Open wooden roof with hammerbeams and kingpost trusses. At the nave arcades, squat columns with polished granite shafts and huge coarsely foliaged capitals. Tall chancel arch, its slender attached columns with polished granite shafts. From the choir a dizzying seven steps up to the sanctuary. At its S wall, a three-seater stone SEDILIA. – Routinely detailed stone REREDOS, probably of 1888, with three gableted recesses.

PULPIT designed by *Ross & Macbeth* and executed by *Harry Hems & Sons*, 1894. It is octagonal, of Painswick stone with Kilkenny marble shafts. Front carved with lumpy figures of Our Lord as the Good Shepherd flanked by St Andrew and St Ninian. – STAINED GLASS. E window (the Crucifixion) by *John Hardman & Co.*, 1888. – Contemporary W window (the Sermon on the Mount) by *Powell Bros* of Leeds. – In the aisle windows, undistinguished lights of the late C19 and C20.

ST NINIAN (R.C.), Bank Street. Originally Bank Street United Presbyterian Church. By *William Leiper*, 1873–5. Tall and austere early French Gothic. Four-bay nave, the broad-eaved roof swept over the flanking aisles. On each side of the N end of the nave, a higher and gabled bay suggestive of a transept but not projecting. The nave's N gable is marked off from the aisle ends by a buttress on the E and, on the W, by a slender octagonal tower, its spired roof covered with metal. At the tower's top stage, stilted arched belfry openings over each of which a string course rises in a gablet shape. In the main N gable, a pointed door under a tall two-light window, its nookshafts' capitals foliaged. Vesica in the apex of the gable.

Inside, the nave roof has elaborate bracing under the boarded ceiling which is stencilled with gold stars. In the aisles and at the E end, galleries supported on two tiers of columns, the lower with moulded capitals, the upper's capitals foliaged. Shallow but tall organ recess (now empty) at the W end. – STAINED GLASS. Two lights (the Good Shepherd, the Light of the World) in the S aisle, a two-light E window (St Paul and St John), all of *c.* 1895. They were originally in City Road United Presbyterian Church (now demolished) and moved here in 1922.

PUBLIC BUILDINGS

ANDOVER PRIMARY SCHOOL, Nursery Lane. Disused. Originally Tenements School. By *John Henderson*, 1859. Picturesque single-storey assemblage of bargeboarded gables, many of the windows with pointed lights. A strong vertical accent is provided by a clock tower, its steep fish-scale-slated roof with bracketed bellcast eaves and gabled dormer openings. On top of the roof, a square wooden cupola, its spired roof again fish-scale-slated and with a weathervane.

ANGUS COUNCIL OFFICE, Bank Street. Originally the Brechin Municipal Buildings. By *D. & J. R. McMillan*, 1894–5. Free Jacobean Scots Renaissance on a small scale but not without exuberance.

BANK STREET SCHOOL, Bank Street. Now in other use. The two-storey NW part on the corner of Martin's Lane was built as the East Free Church School in 1848 and could hardly be more austere. Jollier free Gothic SE extension by *William Fettis*, *c.* 1874, soon after it became a Board School, with a broad-eaved jerkin-head roof and big three-light transomed window.

BRECHIN BRIDGE, East Mill Road. Two spans of rough ashlar over the South Esk. The bridge of Brechin is on record during the episcopate (1219–*c.* 1246) of Gregory, Bishop of Brechin, and the shape of the obtusely pointed S arch, as seen from the E, may be of the early C13 although a later medieval date seems more likely and considerable repairs were carried out in 1648, perhaps the date of the simply moulded corbels under the E parapet above this arch. In 1786 *Alexander Stevens Sen.* was responsible for widening the bridge by about a third to the W, the extent of this clearly shown by a masonry joint on the S arch whose new work is round-headed. At the same time the N arch was rebuilt in segmental form. The W cutwater must be by Stevens and so too is probably the E. Both are triangular with sloping tops. At the centre of each parapet, both probably of 1786, a splay-sided pedestrian refuge, the E much shallower than the W.

BRECHIN CEMETERY, off Southesk Street. Laid out and the W approach across the narrow gorge of the Den Burn designed by *George Henderson*, 1856–7. On this approach, a stone BRIDGE of seven round-headed arches, the fronts of the piers, the arch-rings and the parapet all rusticated. – E of the bridge, the entrance GATEWAY built of rusticated hammer-dressed ashlar. Round-headed arch, its keystone carved with a high-relief death mask. The arch is set in a frame made up of corniced square gatepiers and a lintel on which sits the statue of a phoenix above the motto RESURGAM. Each side of the gateway, a concave quadrant of primitivist piers supporting a lintel. The N quadrant ends at a rusticated and corniced pier, the S at a two-storey LODGE built in 1875–6 when the cemetery was extended.

BRECHIN HIGH SCHOOL, Duke Street. Curtain-walled group by *Angus County Council*, 1967–70, and later extended in more brutalist fashion.

BRECHIN INFIRMARY, Infirmary Street. Dour, by *William Fettis*, 1868–9. Two tall storeys, an open pediment on the slightly projecting centrepiece.

BRECHIN LIBRARY, St Ninian's Square. French-influenced Free Style, by *J. McLellan Fairley*, 1891–3. Long single-storey ashlar-fronted main block. Mullioned-and-transomed windows, those of the reading room with round-arched central lights. At the E end of the principal (S) front, a gable carved with the burgh seal of Brechin. At the SW corner, a two-storey tower, its steep roof a quasi-pyramid. At the first floor the main block's parapet is carried across the tower as a band course which is projected at the centre on a pair of consoles to form a balcony. N of the tower, a two-storey caretaker's house, a steeply pedimented door in its semi-octagonal W front. At the library's E end, an impermanent-looking butterfly-roofed small addition of 1963–6. – Immediately SW of the library, an ornate late C19 cast-iron LAMP STANDARD.

CATHEDRAL HALL, Church Lane. By *William Fettis*, 1889, in best School Board manner, with rose windows in the steep gables, shouldered arched lights elsewhere, and a small Gothic cupola ventilator.

CITY HALL, Swan Street. By *Alexander Ross*, 1883. Two-storey ashlar-fronted block with ground-floor shops. Above, the style is Renaissance with block-consoled cornices over the windows but these are spaced with disconcerting asymmetry. Small block consoles under the wall-head cornice surmounted by a parapet with a fluted vase at each end.

DAMACRE CENTRE, Damacre Road. Originally a school. By *Ireland & Maclaren*, 1875. Plain except for a stepped gable at the centre of the main block and a cupola-ventilator with a tall octagonal spire.

DRILL HALL, Bank Street. Now in other use. The utilitarian hall block at the back was built in 1879–80. The front was added in 1897 by *T. Martin Cappon*. Quite small-scale, the detail Free Jacobean, with mullioned windows, those at the centre also with transoms and the outer bays' ground-floor windows corniced. The centrepiece rises to three storeys. Big round window at the second floor. Gable stepped up to a scroll-sided pediment broken by the stalk supporting its ball finial. Over the round-arched central entrance, the vigorously carved heraldic achievement of the Black Watch.

MAISONDIEU PRIMARY SCHOOL, St Andrew Street. Built as Brechin High School in 1875–7; *Aitkenhead & Mason* were the architects. At the centre of the main block's front, a tower which begins by being circular, is then corbelled out to an octagon, then further corbelled out to again become circular; tall slated truncated cone of a roof, its eaves extravagantly bellcast and with a projecting piended dormer fronted by a clock. On top, a spired round cupola. The rest of the school was completely remodelled and extended in polite but boring fashion by the *Forfarshire County Architect's Department*, 1927–30.

MECHANICS' INSTITUTE, St Mary Street and Church Street. 78
Tudor collegiate, by *John Henderson*, 1838–42, the Institute was built at the expense of William, Lord Panmure, the owner of

Brechin Castle, to house the town's Grammar School, Parish School and Burgh School, with a lecture hall and library on the floor above. Two tall ashlar-clad storeys, a string course between them, the first-floor windows taller than those below and transomed as well as mullioned. The W front's outer corners are buttressed by slim octagonal turrets topped by battlements filled with ball-finialled ogee domes. Battlement with crowstepped merlons, each decorated with a blind square panel. Nine-bay façade, with continuous window hoodmoulds at the outer three bays of each end. Three-bay centrepiece, the first floor of its two outer bays slightly advanced under a battlement, its corbelled angle turrets smaller versions of the turrets at the main corners. At the ground floor these bays are brought boldly forward, each with a straight parapet, an octagonal buttress-turret at the outer corner, and a narrow hoodmoulded blind arched window in the front. The centre bay is a slender tower, *c.* 26 m. high, its corners with octagonal buttress-turrets of the same type as at the main block's outer corners but with stepped diagonal buttresses projecting from their lower stages. At the tower's first stage, a high and narrow Tudor-arched entrance under the carved coat of arms of Lord Panmure. At the stage above, a very tall Tudor Gothic window of two lights, the top of its ogee hoodmould rising into the frame of a square clock face. Above, the belfry stage with a hoodmoulded tall two-light opening in each face. Cusped arcaded corbelling under the battlement, one broad merlon on each face. On the Institute's S side to Church Street, a full-height semi-octagon.

PARISH COUNCIL CHAMBERS, Panmure Street. Now Angus Council offices. Jolly free Scots Jacobean single-storey red sandstone block, by *D. Wishart Galloway*, 1897. Inside, the principal room has a coved ceiling with applied ribs. Neo-Jacobean wooden chimneypiece and doorcases. Original brass light fittings.

PICTAVIA AND BRECHIN CASTLE CENTRE, Haughmuir. By *Oliver & Robb*, 1999. Pair of pavilions, the W (PICTAVIA) a rotunda. Above the cast-stone base its walling is clad with vertically slatted timber with a strip of clearstorey openings; broad-eaved metal-ribbed roof. A short link joins to a cast-iron stone octagon (VISITOR CENTRE) whose slated roof is topped by an octagonal lantern. At right angles on the r., a line of buildings, the walls of timber above cast stone; prominent monopitch roofs of ribbed metal; the glazed N side opens onto a country park.

POST OFFICE, Clerk Street. Wrenaissance, by *H.M. Office of Works*, 1909. Piend-roofed ashlar box of two tall storeys with a deeply projecting mutuled cornice. Corniced ground-floor windows with straightforward architraves and pulvinated friezes. Lugged architraves at the first-floor windows. Studied asymmetry is provided by the end doors. The r. is narrow and corniced, its pulvinated frieze and architrave broken by a keystone. The l. is much broader and topped by an open segmental pediment boldly projected on consoles, the tympanum carved with foliage enclosing a crowned cartouche bearing the royal initials GVR (for *Georgius V Rex*).

PUBLIC PARK, Park Place. Not very formal layout of 1903. – Cast-iron FOUNTAIN by *Walter Macfarlane & Co.*, presented by Robert Duke of Bearehill in 1903. The concave-sided pedestal, each face with a large lion's head, supports a foliage-capitalled column surrounded by birds. On top, a lotus surmounted by another bird. – To the N, an octagonal BANDSTAND of 1908, also by *Walter Macfarlane & Co.* Ashlar base topped by a scrolly iron rail. Thin columns at each corner support the open roof, the soffit of its broad eaves decorated with Gothic panelling and rosettes. On top, a small metal dome with an iron finial. – To the N again, large WAR MEMORIAL of cenotaph type, by *Wright & Wrigley* of Wakefield, 1923.

RAILWAY STATION, St Ninian's Place. Opened as the terminus of the Aberdeen Railway Co.'s branch line from Bridge of Dun in 1847. U-plan platform. On its N side, the two-storey station building of 1847–8, with a piended platform roof. Italianate street front with round-arched doors and windows. Block brackets under the first-floor sill course; heavy moulded cornice. Lines to Forfar and Edzell were opened in 1895–6 and the station enlarged in 1897 by *Thomas Barr*, the Caledonian Railway's District Civil Engineer at Perth. Barr added the SW wing, its W (entrance) front plain except for a large round clock breaking up through the wall-head and a glass-roofed veranda whose iron cresting bears the name of the Caledonian Railway. Probably also of 1897 is the S platform's low range, the urinals in its gentlemen's toilet with stall partitions made from monolithic slate slabs. The cast-iron pillars and brackets of the platform awnings survive but the roofs themselves do not. S of the station, a large rubble-built SHED, probably of the late 1840s.

ST ANDREW'S CHURCH HALL, St Andrew Street. Built as a diocesan library, school and dwelling house in 1853 (the date, together with the weathered coat of arms and initials of Alexander Penrose Forbes, then Bishop of Brechin, on the E side). At the N, the former school (now hall). In each gable, a big Gothic window, the E blind, the W with reticulated tracery. The library and dwelling house on the S are in the parsonage Gothic manner of William Butterfield.

ST DROSTAN'S HOUSE, Infirmary Street. Built as an almshouse in 1879–80; *James Baxter* was the architect. Plain Tudor and now a bit altered and with a pair of bay windows added. Mature monkey-puzzle tree in the garden.

TOWN HOUSE, High Street and Church Street. Built in 1789. 72
Two-storey ashlar gable front to High Street, with rusticated quoins and a ball-finialled and Roman Doric columned birdcage bellcote. In the gable, a first-floor Venetian window; Late Victorian shopfront at the ground floor. Plain side elevation to Church Street, its central wall-head gable containing a panel bearing the date 1789.

DESCRIPTION

HAUGHMUIR leads in from the W. Set back on its N side, Pictavia and Brechin Castle Centre (*see* Public Buildings, above). CASTLE STREET continues its line. On the S side, the lodges and gateways of Brechin Castle (*see* below). On the N, the mid-Victorian Tudor lodge and gatepiers at the entrance to the grounds of BEAREHILL, a Late Georgian villa recast *c.* 1870 when it acquired shallow rectangular bay windows and a balustraded canted portico. Probably also of *c.* 1870 is the balconied second-floor Venetian window at the open-pedimented centre. Late Georgian single-storey wings, the front gable of each with a pediment containing a lunette, the N still with a three-light window, the S with a canted bay window of *c.* 1870. E of this Castle Street becomes urban. On the S, Nos. 21–23 of *c.* 1800, built of rough ashlar, No. 21 with cherry-cock pointing. Each has a single storey above a high basement but the cavetto splayed doors are placed at an intermediate level with their segmental-arched fanlight windows skied above them. Unassuming Late Georgian vernacular at Nos. 17–19. The contemporary No. 9 is rather grander with a semicircular dummy window in the central wall-head gablet. Then, housing of the later C19 on the S and of the later C20 on the N. At the end of the N side, the ashlar-fronted No. 4, of three storeys and an attic, its centre gablet containing an oval oculus under the date 1788. The street ends at a Y-junction dominated by the slim tower of the Mechanics' Institute (*see* Public Buildings, above).

CHURCH STREET leads downhill to the E, its houses mostly plain Late Georgian but the unity of character diminished by later intrusions and gapsites. At No. 37 of *c.* 1800, another cavetto splayed door. The adjoining single-storey No. 35 was built as a doctor's surgery in 1904. Over the Artisan Mannerist doorpiece, the medical emblem of a staff and snakes. At Nos. 18–22 on the N side, helpful inscriptions for the architectural historian (BUILT/1781; EXTENDED/1911). No. 18 on the E is of 1781, the capitals of its doorpiece's attached columns left in block. At No. 22, the extension of 1911, a broad corniced entrance with a lugged architrave, a curvy-topped surround to the first-floor window, and a curvilinear wall-head gablet. Pilastered doorpiece at the early C19 No. 25 opposite. It stands on the corner of CHURCH LANE which goes down past the Cathedral Hall (*see* Public Buildings, above) to Brechin Cathedral (*see* above). Church Street continues with another cavetto splayed door at the ashlar-fronted CASTLE VIEW (No. 17) of *c.* 1800 and the rubbly gable frontage of the rather earlier No. 15. At the street's NE corner and fronting High Street, the Town House (*see* Public Buildings, above). Outside, in an informal square in the centre of High Street, a large Late Victorian lamp standard by *George Smith & Co.*, of the *Sun Foundry*, with entwined dolphins round the shaft.

HIGH STREET's upper part, climbing N of Church Street, is mostly Georgian vernacular, the ground floors taken over by later shops. The two upper floors of the early C19 five-bay Nos. 4–8 are built of stugged ashlar, each with a centre window of two lights divided by a Doric column-mullion. At No. 7 opposite, of *c.* 1800, another cavetto splayed entrance but with a prominent keystone. The C18 group of Nos. 27–45 displays gables to the street. In this group the three-storey building at Nos. 39–43 seems to have developed from a set-back main block, perhaps of C17 origin, with a broad segmental arch at the first floor. This arch was cut across by the addition of the SE jamb, making the building L-plan. The resultant inner angle was filled in the late C19 by the addition of a two-storey block. In its pedimented gable front, a two-light first-floor window, the mullion provided by a very Artisan Mannerist version of a Corinthian column.

On the W side of High Street below Church Street the three-storey ashlar-fronted Nos. 38–40, probably of the late C18, with a central chimney gablet. The three-storey block at Nos. 42–44 also looks late C18. Its S bay rises a storey higher and contains a semi-elliptical arched pend to BISHOP'S CLOSE which runs W towards the Cathedral. Just inside the close, a fragment of the S jamb of an arched gateway which formed part of the long-demolished CARNOK'S TOWER, a gatehouse into the cathedral precinct which appears from its name to have been built by Bishop John de Cranach (1426–*c.* 1453). Just beyond, on the S side of the close, the CATHEDRAL MANSE, by *John Smith* of Aberdeen, 1850, the date on its plain rear wing. Jacobean L-plan W front, a ball finial on the gable of its advanced r. bay, the gablets of the other bays with spiky finials. The shallow rectangular bay window was added by *John Carver* in 1873.

In High Street S of Bishop's Close, the C18 No. 48, its chimneyless wall-head gablet looking as if it has been altered. Across the street, Nos. 51–55 of *c.* 1855, with a pilastered doorpiece, corniced first-floor windows, and a scroll-sided central decoration on top of the parapet. C18 gable fronts at No. 57 and the irredeemably altered No. 59. The two-storey rubble-built No. 61 has survived much better. Small first-floor windows and a chunkily crowstepped W gable. Ashlar band course under the eaves, the inscription on one stone ('David Lyon 1760') giving the bare facts of its building history. On the W side of the street, informal vernacular of the earlier C18 at Nos. 62–74, No. 66 now covered with a heavy coat of harling and its windows with cement margins, the crowstep-gabled Nos. 68–74 with chamfered margins to the first-floor windows but its slated roof replaced in corrugated iron. Nos. 65–69 on the E side, Neo-vernacular with exaggeratedly rubbly outshots towards the street, are outliers of a large housing redevelopment (by *R. W. Ritchie & Dick*, 1974) which stretches back to City Road. S of these a lumpy small former CINEMA by *S. B. Low*, 1926, followed by scrappy C18 and C19 vernacular until High Street's corner with City Road. Here is an unexpectedly smart early

C19 block (Nos. 111–115 High Street) of three storeys and an attic and five bays by three. Ground floor faced with rusticated V-jointed polished ashlar, forming a base for the upper floors' droved ashlar walling enlivened by polished dressings and rusticated quoins. At these upper floors, the centre bay is very slightly advanced with rusticated quoins and topped by an open-pedimented wall-head gablet containing a round-arched window. At the ground floor, a Roman Doric-columned doorpiece. Architraved and corniced first-floor windows; just architraves at the second floor. Immediately behind, at the foot of City Road, the former Protestor Church (*see* Churches, above).

UNION STREET to the E contains plain Victorian housing on the N side, unexciting housing of the later C20 on the S. At its E end, on the corner of Southesk Street and Montrose Street, the massive Den Burn Works (*see* Industrial Buildings, below).

SOUTHESK STREET was opened in 1837. Apart from the Den Burn Works its S stretch is very plain, largely Victorian and Edwardian. Halfway up, St Ninian's Square opens out to the E to make a not very formal civic space. Bordering the square are the Gardner Memorial Church on the W side, the Brechin Library on the N and the Railway Station looking into the SE corner (for these, *see* Churches and Public Buildings, above). Among the trees and grass in the centre of the square, a FOUNTAIN erected in 1877 as a memorial to the eleventh Earl of Dalhousie, originally sited outside the Mechanics' Institute but moved here in 1895. *J. M. Wardrop* was the designer, *John Rhind* the sculptor. Tall Late Gothic octagon of pinkish granite. At the lower stage, stepped and gableted corner buttresses; projecting from each face, a basin filled from a lion's head. The upper stage is open, the structure formed by a second tier of corner buttresses, their crocketed pinnacles rising above the parapet, and cusped round-headed arches at the front. Protruding from the parapet are half-round stone spouts. Above, an open crown spire, its ribs not curved but straight, topped by a crown with a ball-and-cross finial. Just N of St Ninian's Square, on the S corner of Bank Street, is No. 59 Southesk Street, dated 1858, an idiosyncratic little villa with an absurdly steep and narrow shaped gable at the centre of its front and an octagonal corner tower, now flat-roofed but probably designed for a spire.

BANK STREET climbing uphill to the NW, although neither formal nor prominently sited, was the Victorian choice for the positioning of several moderately important buildings of which there survive St Ninian's (R.C.) Church, the Drill Hall, Bank Street School and Angus Council Office (for which, *see* Churches and Public Buildings, above).

PANMURE STREET, opened in 1837, runs SW from Southesk Street, its NE view looking out to the gateway of Brechin Cemetery (*see* Public Buildings, above). At the street's start, the East Free Church and Parish Council Chambers facing each other (*see* Churches and Public Buildings, above). Beyond, the norm is of polite mid-C19 Georgian survival, quite accomplished at No. 28 which parades a pilastered doorpiece, cornices over the ground-floor windows, and a bowed corner to Bank Street. On the opposite side of Bank Street, another bowed corner at No. 26 but this is of *c.* 1900 and characteristic of that date with a shallow slated dome with bracketed eaves. Pedimented doorpiece and a chimney gablet on the mid-C19 No. 13 but its ground-floor windows have been enlarged to two lights. No. 10 on the SW corner of Martin's Lane, the burgh's former Post Office, is by *D. & J. R. McMillan*, 1895. Commercial Free Jacobean, with idiosyncratic Ionic pilasters at the shopfront. Just beyond, the CLYDESDALE BANK, its Baroque single-storey front block of *c.* 1900, with rusticated pilaster-strips and exuberantly carved capitals at the Ionic columns of the entrance. This fills the front garden of a villa of *c.* 1850, its Jacobean centre still poking up behind. On Panmure Street's N side, the NORTHERN HOTEL which has developed from 1842, the date of its NW end, a scroll-sided chimney on its bowed corner to Clerk Street. Of about the same date must be the NE part. Between them, gently Italianate infill of *c.* 1865 with round-arched windows, the ground floor now rather altered. In CLERK STREET to the N, the Post Office (*see* Public Buildings, above) some way up on the E side. On the W side, No. 3, mid-C19 Georgian survival remodelled by *Wardrop & Reid* in 1878. Pilastered entrance flanked by three-light windows; cornices over the first-floor windows, the centre ones carried on consoles.

SWAN STREET, the W continuation of Panmure Street, was widened to the N in 1863–4, the date of its tall block (the former ROYAL BANK OF SCOTLAND) on the corner with Clerk Street. This is by *Peddie & Kinnear*, austere except for foliaged capitals (carved by *Roddis* of London) at the column-mullions of its two-light windows. Further along is City Hall (*see* Public Buildings, above) followed by No. 5, a little Italianate palazzo of the later C19. Less convincedly Italianate and more overtly commercial is the architecture of Nos. 1–3, also of the later C19, with shouldered-arched windows and a rosetted frieze; at the splayed corner to Market Street, a balustraded stone balcony under the first-floor window, its cornice supported by heavy consoles. On Swan Street's S side, Late Georgian vernacular, mostly with C20 shopfronts. On the corner with High Street, the three-storey and attic Nos. 2–4 of *c.* 1815. Four bays, the two centre bays very slightly advanced under a rather steep pediment; another pediment on the gable to High Street.

ST DAVID STREET to the W starts, on its N side, with the DALHOUSIE HOTEL of 1879–80. Rather serious Italian detail. Huge consoles under the shopfronts' cornice; urns on the corners of the overall balustrade. The rest of the street is a fairly undistinguished jumble of the C19 and C20. Just beyond its end, in AIRLIE STREET, the ashlar-fronted No. 2 of *c.* 1835. At its recessed bowed corner, a first-floor window with a balcony projecting above a fluted apron. From here ST

Andrew Street leads N. In it, St Andrew's Episcopal Church and Maisondieu Primary School. In Maisondieu Lane, off St Andrew Street's E side, the ruin of the Maison Dieu Chapel (for all these, *see* Churches and Public Buildings, above).

INDUSTRIAL BUILDINGS

Den Burn Works, Montrose Street and Southesk Street. Victorian power-loom linen factory, the front block (converted to
111 housing in 1989) Italianate, by *Robertson & Orchar*, 1863–4, extended in the same manner in 1871. It is of four storeys and seventeen bays, built of stugged and coursed pinky sandstone, with rusticated quoins at the corners. At the ground floor, round-arched doors with projecting keystones and fairly small rectangular windows. Round-arched first-floor windows, the semicircular centre light with a consoled keystone and surmounted by a cornice and hoodmould. Large rectangular windows at the two top floors, the second floor's with a moulded sill course. In the centre of the second floor, under a round clock, panels carved with the name of the works and the dates of its construction. SW corner tower, its four lower stages only just projecting from the fronts of the main block. Rusticated quoins rising to the bracketed cornice, a continuation of the main block's. Above this cornice, a tall stage with anta pilasters at the corners and, in each face, a huge round-arched and key-blocked window. Another bracketed cornice under the eaves of the piended roof, its platform surrounded by metal cresting.

Behind the main block, the surviving front wall of nine bays of a single-storey WEAVING SHED of *c.* 1875, its S four bays removed in 1989. At the Southesk Street elevation, windows with lugged architraves and bracketed sills.

East Mill, East Mill Road. Flax (later jute) mill developed from the early C19. There survives a two-storey early C19 ten-bay block from whose W bay projects a three-stage tower, its pyramid roof crowned by the surviving base (containing clock faces) and Doric columns of a birdcage bellcote dated 1837.

BRECHIN CASTLE

off Castle Street

Mansion house of the Earls of Panmure (later Earls of Dalhousie) standing on the N edge of the gorge containing the River South Esk, self-assured but without bombast.

A castle of Brechin, probably on the present site, was in existence by 1303 when it was captured by Edward I. Presumably slighted during the Wars of Independence, it was again habitable in the C15 but was referred to disparagingly as *vetus castrum* ('the old castle') in 1527 when James V granted the lands of Brechin to his Secretary, Thomas Erskine of Haltoun, ordering him five years later to add a hall and other extensions to the castle. This work had been carried out by 1541 when Erskine was indebted to William Wood for 400 marks spent *pro reparatione castri et loci de Brechin* ('for the repair of the castle and place of Brechin'), perhaps a thoroughgoing reconstruction of the medieval building.

Patrick Maule of Panmure (later, first Earl of Panmure) bought the estate in 1634 and in 1686, after the erection of a new Panmure House (since demolished), his grandson, James, fourth Earl of Panmure, began a major repair and remodelling of Brechin Castle. *James Baine*, the King's Master Wright and Master Plasterer, was the contractor and apparently architect. This work was completed in 1691 but in 1696 the Earl began a much more extensive reconstruction to designs by *Alexander Edward*, the former Minister of Kemback (dispossessed in 1690 for his adherence to episcopacy) and amanuensis of Sir William Bruce. Edward's work began with the construction of a forecourt, its entrance flanked by pavilions (since demolished). In 1697 Edward continued with a range of office houses to the NE of the house. The next year he drew up plans for an extension of the existing NW wing to fill the whole inner side of his new forecourt and work was begun in August with *John Bachop* as mason and *William Walker* as wright. However, in 1701–2 Edward was commissioned by the Earls of Panmure, Mar and other nobles and lairds to undertake a tour of London, Paris and the Low Countries to 'view, observe and take draughts of the most remarkable Houses, Edifices, Gardings . . . and other curiosities of nature or art . . .' Following Edward's return, a further reconstruction, if not rebuilding, of the remodelled NW wing was begun, work not completed until 1711, three years after his death.

The fourth Earl of Panmure took part in the 1715 Jacobite rising. In consequence, his estates were forfeited but in 1764 were reacquired for the family by his nephew and heir, General William Maule, titular sixth Earl of Panmure in the Scottish peerage and from 1743 Earl Panmure of Forth in the Irish peerage. After General Maule's death in 1782 ownership of Brechin Castle passed his nephew, the eighth Earl of Dalhousie, and, five years later, to Lord Dalhousie's second son, William Ramsay Maule (later first Lord Panmure of Brechin and Navar) who, in 1795–7, employed *Alexander Laing* to remodel some rooms of the castle and to rebuild its courtyard's N wing. In 1853–63 Fox, second Lord Panmure of Brechin and Navar (from 1860 eleventh Earl of Dalhousie) carried out extensive work on the courtyard, extending its N range, rebuilding the E and remodelling the S, *John Henderson* acting as architect for the work until his death in 1862 after which *David Bryce* took over. The last major alterations on Brechin Castle were undertaken in 1903–4 by Arthur, fourteenth Earl of Dalhousie, and his wife, Lady Mary Heathcote-Drummond-Willoughby, who created a grandiose set of reception rooms on the first floor of the S range, fitted out by the decorators *Keeble & Co.* of London in the best antiquarian manner of the time.

EXTERIOR. The principal approach is from the W through a forecourt, its present appearance mid-C19. On the N and S are battlemented screen walls, lower on the S, the N ending in a low round tower under a witch's-hat roof. The E side is
49 filled by the castle's three-storey early C18 main block, its front a quietly imposing presence. This is faced with red sandstone ashlar, badly weathered and now partly covered with cement render. Eleven bays, the centre three slightly advanced as an urn-finialled centrepiece with rusticated corner quoins; projecting at each end of the front, a conical-roofed round tower. The hierarchy of floors within is manifested by the small windows of the bottom storey, the tall openings to the first floor's principal rooms and the smaller but decently sized windows of the bedroom floor above, all these with chamfered surrounds. Sill courses under the towers' first-floor windows but are these of 1702–11 or part of Alexander Laing's alterations of 1796–7? Probably of the 1790s are the band courses, with panels serving as aprons, under the first- and exceptionally tall second-floor windows of the centrepiece. Cornices over the central doorway and the centrepiece's first-floor windows. In the tympanum of the pediment, a huge heraldic achievement with two coats of arms, the l. those of the Maules, Earls of Panmure, the r. those of the Maules quartered with those of Hamilton (for Lady Margaret Hamilton, wife of the fourth Earl of Panmure), the remainder of the tympanum filled with carved motifs (shells and rosettes) taken from these coats. Splayed across each inner angle of the centrepiece and main block at the second floor is a heart-shaped panel pierced by a tiny round window lighting a closet behind. Only half-glimpsed because set well back on the centre of the roof is the cupola over the principal staircase.

The long S wing is plain, the windows of its early C18 W part with chamfered margins. Roughly in the centre, a square tower, its lower stages early C18, its top with a battlement carried on moulded corbels and bristling an addition of 1863 by David Bryce. The other ranges round the castle's service court are also of three storeys and plain, their character predominantly of 1853–63.

INTERIOR. ENTRANCE HALL in the centre of the W range, its size and wall panelling apparently of *c.* 1710. Across the centre, a screen of Ionic columns; a second and identical screen across the E end at the entrance to the GREAT STAIRCASE. The first of these screens is probably an early C19 insertion. The E occupies the position where Edward intended a screen but may be a replacement of the 1790s, as seems to be the cornice of dentils under tiny foliate enrichment. S of the Entrance Hall, the PRIVATE DINING ROOM created in the C20 by throwing together two early C18 tunnel-vaulted rooms (a porter's lodge and cellar). At the W end of the S wing, a SITTING ROOM, its early C19 marble chimneypiece with reeded jambs and frieze; rosettes at the ends.

E of the entrance hall is the early C18 Great Staircase to the first floor, its lowest flight aligned with the screen's central opening, its return to the S. At the l. of its lowest flight, the NW corner of the stair-hall rises to a capital-like stone carved with foliage and flowers. More foliage and flowers on the stair's scrolled tread-ends. Wrought-iron balustrade with open shields, scrolls and sparing leaf enrichment. Window-like opening, also with a balustrade, from the stair to the S range's first-floor GALLERY (*see* below). Over the stair, a high second-floor void finished with a plaster ceiling, its cornice probably of the 1790s; the ceiling's centre is cut out to admit light from the cupola above.

The house's principal rooms, occupying the W half of the S range, were formed *c.* 1860 but their decoration is of 1903–4. At the W end and with windows overlooking the river gorge to the S is the DRAWING ROOM divided by a screen of widely spaced Doric columns *in antis* into two mirror-image halves, their walls designed to be partly hung with tapestries of *c.* 1700 originally at Dalhousie Castle (Lothian) and moved here at the beginning of the C20. The exposed parts of the walls are covered with full-height panelling, copied like the chimneypieces and ceiling from the 'State Room' of 1606 from the demolished 'Old Palace' at Bromley-by-Bow (London) whose fittings had been moved to the South Kensington (now Victoria and Albert) Museum *c.* 1895 and of which the drawing room is essentially a double-length replica. The chimneypieces are, except for their heraldry, identical, each with a stone fireplace surround carved with birds and griffons and placed in an oak outer surround, its jambs' balusters with male and female terminal figures surmounted by Ionic capitals. Strapwork-topped aedicular overmantel of three compartments, the smaller two with niches containing figures of Peace and Plenty. At their inner ends, flanking the large central compartment, grotesque caryatids (their design derived from engravings by Hans Vredeman de Vries). In each centre compartment, a heraldic achievement, the W that of the Earls of Dalhousie, the E of the Earls of Panmure. Elaborately and richly moulded ceiling. In the strapworked compartments are roundels containing portraits of Joshua, Alexander and Hector (derived from Nicolas de Bruyn's engravings of the Nine Worthies* published at Antwerp in 1594), the moulds taken from the 'Old Palace's' ceiling. In the centre of each half of the ceiling, where the 'Old Palace' original had the Royal Arms of James VI and I, coats of arms of the Earls of Dalhousie and Panmure. The DINING ROOM to the E is simpler and finished in a late C17 manner with oak panelling and a marble chimneypiece.

N of the drawing room and dining room is the gallery. Full-height panelling. The design of the elaborate plaster ceiling is

* The Nine Worthies were three Jewish heroes (David, Joshua and Judas Maccabeus), three classical heroes (Hector of Troy, Alexander the Great and Julius Caesar), and three Christian heroes (Arthur, Charlemagne and Godfrey de Bouillon).

taken from the Globe Room of 1637 at the Reindeer Inn in Banbury (Oxfordshire). Richly strapworked geometric compartments containing motifs of mermaids and stylized foliage. On the S wall, an Edwardian Neo-Jacobean oak chimneypiece, the fireplace opening's surround with coupled Corinthian columns topped by cherubs' heads; more cherubs on the side panels of the frieze and a bowl of fruit in its centre. The overmantel contains a double tier of compartments, their carved reliefs probably reused C17 work, some showing a triumphal progress, others men with a machine.

In the W range's first-floor SITTING ROOM N of the centrepiece, a wooden chimneypiece, perhaps of the 1790s, its frieze with carved foliage of Rococo character. N of the Great Staircase, the stair to the second floor, its wrought-iron balustrade of *c.* 1700 with naturalistic flowering foliage.

PARKLAND. A formal landscape with radiating avenues was laid out by *Alexander Edward* after 1701 on the N side of the River South Esk. In the late C18 and earlier C19 this was extensively remodelled in less formal manner, only the West Avenue extending from the house surviving from the early C18 scheme, and belts of woodland planted along the W side of the river.

STABLES of 1806 NW of the house. A quadrangle, the principal S range faced with broached red sandstone ashlar. Here, two-storey pyramidal-roofed pavilions at the ends and centre are joined by single-storey links with overarched windows. At the end pavilions, delicate console-pedimented doorpieces; the centre pavilion's ground-floor window is Diocletian, its roof's ball finial topped by a griffon weathervane. Inside the courtyard, the N archway is set between Doric columns.

S of the castle, the IMAGE BRIDGE over the River South Esk was designed by *James Burn* in 1807. Three-span, the rubble piers standing on ashlar cutwaters. In the faces of the piers, niches containing statues. The original wooden arches with trellis-work balustrades were replaced by cast-iron girders *c.* 1890.

GARDEN SW of the castle, its walls of rubble faced internally with ashlar constructed in 1802 on a quatrefoil plan, a fifth (NW) lobe with a lower wall added in the late C19. Behind the vine house at the centre of the N side, a two-storey GARDENER'S HOUSE, also of 1802, its S front with rusticated quoins and a parapet. In front, the faceted stone SUNDIAL, probably of the C17, its base C19, brought here from the (demolished) Panmure House. At the N segment of the garden's NW lobe, the late C19 GARDEN ROOM, plain except for verandas at the ends. – Near the S end of the garden's W half, a pair of urn-finialled Roman Doric COLUMNS, perhaps of *c.* 1800.

At the end of the West Avenue, the WEST LODGE designed by *Brown & Wardrop* in 1852. Rope-moulded Tudor gateway under a stepped parapet and flanked by sturdy stepped buttresses. On the E side, a conical-roofed round tower. The similar but taller W tower contains the stair serving the crowstep-gabled lodge itself. – Just to the W, the OLD LODGE of *c.* 1800. Polished ashlar corniced gatepiers topped by pedestals. In the front of each, a rectangular panel under a quatrefoil panel. Battlemented links pierced by round-headed pedestrian gateways join to single-storey lodge houses, the front of each with an over-arched round-headed window and battlemented parapet.

ALDBAR CASTLE, 3.2 km. SW. The mansion house, C16 in origin but extended in 1649, 1800, *c.* 1820 and 1843–54, was demolished in 1965. Some estate buildings survive in the wooded policies.

GATEWAY of *c.* 1820 at the N end of the drive from the B9134. The carriage entrance is set between large battlemented gatepiers of broached ashlar, their fronts decorated with slender Gothic panels. Flanking them are pointed pedestrian gateways and roofless single-storey lodges, their front windows also pointed. Low convex screen walls join the lodges to piers which are miniature versions of those at the carriage entrance. – STEADING (MAINS OF ALDBAR) of *c.* 1860, 1 km. S of this. On the wall-head of the N range, crowstep-gabled 'dormerheads' but without windows. At the centre of this range, a square tower topped by a heavy and restlessly detailed battlement; rising higher at the tower's NW corner, a clock turret, its caphouse with a spired roof. – Rubble-walled GARDEN, perhaps of the early C19, immediately to the W. – At the S end of the E drive, the former ALDBAR SCHOOL built in 1850 by Patrick Chalmers of Aldbar as a memorial to his mother. It is an ashlar-faced T, the tail one storey with a gabled porch. Cross-bar at the S, its E end topped by a gabled bellcote. At the S side of the cross-bar, a stone-mullioned and Y-traceried two-light Gothic window and gabled porch with male and female headstops. The cross-bar's W end contains the single-storey-and-attic school house, a canted bay window on its S side.

ARDOVIE HOUSE, 3.4 km. S. Smart laird's house of the Speids of Ardovie. The two-storey main block was built in 1759 (the date on the skewputts). Ashlar-faced W front of three widely spaced bays, the centre carried up to a pediment pierced by a circular opening and with enjoyably exuberant and over-sized urn finials. The house has become a U by the addition of two later rubble-built rear wings, both joined to the main block by short curved links. The N wing is of two storeys and late C18, perhaps of 1776 (the date on a stone but it is not *in situ*), the S single-storey and early C19.

MURLINGDEN, 3 km. N. Early C19 harled two-storey villa, the S front originally of three bays with generous-sized full-height bows flanking a central Ionic portico; over the centre, a stepped parapet surmounted by the figure of a man. Extensive alterations in the mid C19 removed the portico, central parapet and statue, and extended the house W by one bay with a new entrance formed on that side. Of about the same date a single-storey-and-attic lateral E wing.

ST ANN'S COTTAGE, 3.5 km. W. Urbane single-storey villa of *c.* 1800, the rubble walling originally harled, the roof piended and broad-eaved. S front of five bays, the second and fourth formed as generous-sized bows flanking the segmentally fanlit entrance. Straight rear wings join the main block to a bowed N service range.

TEMPLEWOOD, 3.1 km. NE. Originally Cairnbank. Low-key ashlar-faced two-storey Tudor manor house of the 1830s. Asymmetrical composition of gable, bay windows and a gabled entrance porch. – Classical by contrast are the STABLES of 1825 to the E. Two storeys and piend-roofed. Main S range of eight bays, the centre four slightly advanced under a broad pediment, its tympanum containing a dummy oculus. At the centrepiece's ground floor, rectangular windows flank the carriage entrances which are surmounted by segmentally arched dummy fanlights; low horizontal windows to the first floor. In the outer bays, round-headed ground-floor windows and semicircular openings above.

KINTROCKAT HOUSE. *See* p. 570.

3030

BRIDGEFOOT

Hamlet, with a churchyard on the S side of CRAIGMILL ROAD and, on the N, two short rows of mid-C19 cottages (CRAIGMILL COTTAGES), one behind the other.

STRATHMARTINE PARISH CHURCHYARD, Craigmill Road. On the site of a church demolished after the union of Mains and Strathmartine parishes in 1799, a large granite Celtic CROSS erected to commemorate Sir John Ogilvy of Inverquharity and Baldovan in 1896. – To the E, some C18 HEADSTONES, mostly weathered, bearing trade symbols and emblems of death.

2050

BRIDGEND OF LINTRATHEN

Just the church and manse.

LINTRATHEN PARISH CHURCH. Disused. T-plan kirk, the main block of 1802–3 but altered in 1875 when the jamb was added. The S elevation, still substantially to the original design, is of five bays with pointed windows, their wooden Y-tracery probably of 1875. At the centre, a minister's door (now blocked), also pointed; above, an oval panel in a rope-moulded border. The 1875 alterations provided the present gabled bellcote and low session house at the W end, the horizontally proportioned and shouldered-arched gallery windows in the gables of the main block, and the N jamb, its side walls pierced by a double tier of windows with shouldered arches, its gable by pointed windows like those of the S front and possibly reused Georgian work. Built into the W gable, near its S end, the fragment of a CARVED STONE decorated with Celtic interlacing, perhaps of the C8 or C9.

The interior has been reorientated to the E and the end galleries removed. Gallery of 1875 in the N 'aisle'. Victorian PEWS.

W of the church, the harled former PARISH MANSE (now Melgam House). The main block is of 1795 and designed by *Samuel Bell*. Two storeys, the W front of three bays. In 1829 *David A. Whyte* added a wing to the centre of this front, the N inner angle of the main block and addition filled with a further extension in 1966. N wing probably originally early C19 and of one storey but raised to two later in the C19. Remarkably complete set of OFFICES (stable, byre, barn, gig house and pigsties), probably of *c.* 1795, to the E.

BALINTORE CASTLE. *See* p. 345.

BRIGTON HOUSE

4040

0.4 km. NW of Kirkton

Sizeable laird's house of the mid C18 whose front was extended and given a large centre bow in the early C19.

Main block of two storeys, the walling harled and with dressings of grey sandstone. The mid-C18 house, probably built for William Douglas who bought the estate in 1743 but almost certainly incorporating earlier work, consists of three parallel blocks. The principal front to the E was formed by these blocks' chimney-topped two-bay gabled ends, the centre block's slightly advanced and pedimented, its pair of diagonally set chimneys added in the earlier C19. Prominent keystones to all the windows, the central gable's smaller first floor openings linked by a sill course and its ground floor windows with Neo-Jacobean patterned glazing, perhaps introduced *c.* 1900.

At the symmetrical elevation of the house's N side, a slightly advanced and piend-roofed centre containing a round-headed and keystoned ground-floor window. Closely flanking the centre, a pair of first-floor windows like those of the E front and, below, a round-headed and keystoned door at the l. matched by the surround of the overarch to the r. window.

The S front is dominated by the broad full-height battlemented bow containing the console-corniced principal entrance, now surmounted by a stone sundial. This front's straight sections either side of the bow are each of two bays with tall ground-floor windows of the early C19. However, the part r. of the bow is C18, its first-floor windows now dummies, the r. window's lintel (probably not *in situ*) carved with the date 1629, perhaps that of the construction or remodelling of an earlier house on the site. The section of the front to the l. of the bow dates is an early C19 addition with a higher wallhead and higher-set first-floor windows.

The W elevation, like the E, is triple-gabled but with the S advanced considerably beyond the other two and with a battlemented two-storey bay window, perhaps an addition of *c.* 1840.

Projecting from behind the main house is a service court with, on its E and W sides, a pair of piend-roofed low two-storey blocks from which extend single-storey ranges joining to a third range closing the courtyard's N side, all these probably of the early C19. Inside, the principal rooms are early C19. The main door opens into a T-plan entrance hall, its S tail filling the front bow but with splayed sides and a Roman Doric columned screen to the cross-bar. In the cross-bar's N wall, a Tudorish Gothic archway to the stair-hall behind. The flying stair itself rises within an oval compartment, its curved wall with round-headed niches, its ceiling cupola with patterned and coloured glass. In the dining room E of the entrance hall, a coved ceiling and black marble chimneypiece of simple quality. Also early C19 is the high drawing room on the entrance hall's W side, its chimneypiece also of black marble and identical design. On the first floor, within the central bow, a splay-ended room, perhaps originally intended as the drawing room, its white marble chimneypiece of modest pretension.

N of the house, an early C19 detached rubble-walled and piend-roofed L of OFFICES (stables, byre and piggery), the E end of the S range and the NE jamb now roofless and with lowered walls. The S range has all been of three storeys, with low and horizontally proportioned windows in the outer sections. Slightly advanced and gabled centrepiece which contains a round-headed door between high-set windows, all with projecting keystones; dummy oculus to the top floor. Flanking the centrepiece are round-headed doors, also keystoned but their detail less emphatic than that of the similar openings in the house's E end. A little N of the centrepiece, a detached doocot, also early C19, between short and low lean-to wings. The doocot rises as a pediment-fronted tower with a large first-floor window and oculus above. Immediately W of the office court, a contemporary rubble-built coachhouse block of one tall storey with segmental-arched carriage entrances in the N side. – Rubble-walled GARDEN, probably also early C19, to the NW.

4030

BROUGHTY FERRY

A small fishing settlement in the vicinity of the medieval Broughty Castle until *c.* 1790 when the village of Broughty Ferry was laid out on a gridiron plan. By 1840 its population was nearly 2,000, limited employment provided by a fish-curing establishment, two ropeworks and a foundry, and the village was of 'clean and neat appearance' despite the streets still being unpaved. By then also the hillside behind had begun to be developed for villas whose occupants could commute to Dundee by the railway opened two

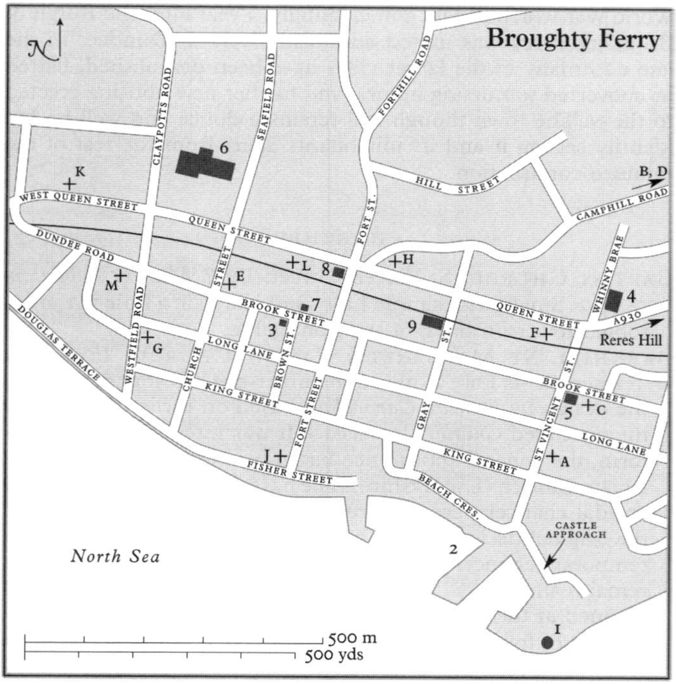

A	Baptist Church	L	St Mary (Episcopal)
B	Barnhill St Margaret's Parish Church	M	St Stephen's and West Church
C	Broughty Ferry Church		
D	Cemetery	1	Broughty Castle
E	Congregational Church	2	Broughty Ferry Harbour
F	New Kirk	3	Burgh Halls
G	Our Lady of Good Counsel (R.C.)	4	Eastern Primary School
H	Queen Street United Presbyterian Church	5	Former Eastern School
J	St James	6	Grove Academy
K	St Luke's and Queen Street Church	7	Police Station
		8	Post Office
		9	Railway Station

years before. Broughty Ferry served also in summer as a bathing resort although the Sunday incursions of inebriated Dundonian day-trippers annoyed the respectable inhabitants and their summer lodgers. The village became a burgh in 1864 and in the later C19 it acquired an array of churches and public buildings commensurate with that status. Also in the late C19 and early C20 came a far more intensive villa development of the ground to the N of Broughty Ferry itself and the lands of Barnhill and West Ferry to the E and W, some of the houses of grandiose size and opulence. The main villa-building period ended with the First

World War which began, coincidentally, a year after the Burgh of Broughty Ferry was united administratively to Dundee. In the late C20 many of the larger villas have been demolished, flatted or converted to nursing homes, and further new housing erected to the N. The town though still retains a douce and well-heeled identity setting it and its inhabitants apart from the rest of the Dundee conurbation.

CHURCHES

BAPTIST CHURCH, St Vincent Street. By *J. Murray Robertson*, 1881–2. Small, with simple Late Gothic detail; a little pyramid-roofed tower on the l. of the front gable.

BARNHILL ST MARGARET'S PARISH CHURCH, Invermark Terrace. Scots Late Gothic in hammer-dressed squared rubble, the design by *Duncan Carmichael* based on earlier sketches by the unrelated *Charles Carmichael*. It was intended to be cruciform, the general appearance based on the 1540s Biggar Collegiate Church (Lanarkshire). The nave, N porch and temporary apsidal chancel were constructed in 1894–5, the transepts (to the original design) added by *T. Lindsay Gray*, 1932, when the temporary chancel was rebuilt to their E, but the crossing tower remains unbuilt, as does the much longer choir and chancel planned at the E end.

Nave of four bays articulated by stepped buttresses. Ringed cross on the angle-buttressed W gable. This contains a large window, its round-headed lights surmounted by cusped loop tracery and grouped 2:2, the Y-traceried head also filled with cusped loop tracery; the inspiration came from the transept windows of Seton Collegiate Church (Lothian), also of the 1540s. Hoodmould over the window, its foliaged label stops, like the others at the church, rather small. Extending from the window, a sill course which is carried along the side walls of the nave and round the transepts. In the sides of the nave, hoodmoulded windows placed rather high, the N's label stops all foliate, some of the S side's carved with human heads. In each of these windows, three lights, the outer two pointed, the centre light's top formed by the bottom segment of the circle in its head, the design taken from the late medieval S choir window of the former Temple Parish Church (Lothian). Projecting from the penultimate bay of the N side, a crowstep-gabled porch, its stepped angle buttresses with crocketed pinnacles, the general appearance following that of the C15 porch at Whitekirk Parish Church (Lothian). In each side of the porch, a small pointed window. Pointed front entrance with bell-capitalled coupled shafts and a hoodmould whose head-stops are carved with the face of an owl and an animal. The entrance contains glass doors engraved in 1984, with a St Andrew's Cross and Crown of Thorns and the Celtic Cross of St John. Above the entrance, a tabernacled niche containing a figure of St Margaret of Scotland. In the gable of each transept, a pointed window of three round-headed lights under intersecting tracery, the hoodmould's label stops left uncarved. On the nave's E gable, a canopy sheltering a BELL cast by *A. & F. van Aerschodt* of the *van den Gheyn* foundry at Louvain in 1895. Projecting from this gable, the supposedly temporary chancel is low and harled with high-set square windows (two inserted by *T. Lindsay Gray* in 1979). Attached to its E end, a harled and flat-roofed extension containing a vestry, session room and choir room, also by Gray, 1979.

The interior of the porch is faced with polished ashlar and covered with a stone groin-vault, the heavy ribs meeting at a boss carved with the lion rampant of the Royal Arms of Scotland. Round-headed doorway into the church, the design derived from the C15 W door of Dryburgh Abbey (Borders) but its heavily moulded surround, instead of stylized floral decoration, is enriched with more naturalistic carving of St Margaret's daisy, the English rose and Scottish thistle (in allusion to St Margaret's ancestral and adopted countries). In this doorway, a solid oak outer door and a partly glazed inner door (by *James C. Ellis*) with linenfold panelling, the design based on the C15 screen doors in St Marnock's Church at Fowlis (q.v.).

The church interior is faced with stugged masonry; red mosaic tiles on the floors of the nave and transept passages. Open wooden roofs over the nave and transepts, their massive collars resting on heavy foliate rounded corbels; those in the nave bear carved and painted shields displaying the coats of arms of European royal families descended from St Margaret. Chancel roof with radiating rafters. On the chancel walls, oak PANELLING of 1954. – Simple PEWS, also oak, of the 1890s in the nave and of the 1930s but to the same design in the transepts. – COMMUNION TABLE, again of oak, by the *Lord Roberts Workshops*, 1970. – To its l., octagonal stone PULPIT of *c.* 1912, designed by *Charles Soutar*, the faces carved with foliage and shields bearing the IHS and symbols of the four Evangelists. – To the r., a stone FONT by *David Tocher* from *Charles Carmichael*'s design, 1887, which stood in the church's iron predecessor.

STAINED GLASS. Strongly coloured and accomplished W window (Our Lord Bearing the Cross; the Resurrection), 1933. – In the nave's sidelights, figures of the Blessed Virgin Mary and saints associated with Scotland. Five of these are of 1884–5 and were in the church's pedecessor. The other two must be of *c.* 1895. – The S transept's S window (Scenes from the Life of St Margaret) is by *J. T. & C. E. Stewart*, 1933. – The corresponding window in the N transept (SS Columba, Andrew and Kentigern) by *Herbert Hendrie*, 1937, is an essay in brightly coloured Modernist realism.

BROUGHTY FERRY NEW KIRK, corner of St Vincent Street and Queen Street. Originally Broughty Ferry East Free Church. By *Andrew Heiton Jun.*, 1864–5. Dec, built of stugged Carmyllie stone. Nave and aisles, their roofs running at right angles to the nave and ending in buttressed gables; W transepts. Porches at the E end and, intended as the base of a steeple, at the W bay of the N side. Crowded detail, the label stops of the hoodmoulds over the doors and windows carved with human heads. Big leafy capitals to the columns of the N door. Loop tracery in the round W window.

Inside, the collars of the nave roof are pierced by quatrefoils and spring from corbelled wall shafts. E gallery, its front with quatrefoiled panels. – PEWS of 1865. – At the W end, the Gothic PULPIT, also of 1865. It stands in front of an ORGAN (by *Gray & Davison*) introduced in 1894.

HALL at the W end, simple Gothic by *Maclaren, Sons & Soutar*, 1914. It is joined by a flat-roofed link to a drydashed second hall of 1959–60.

CONGREGATIONAL CHURCH, Brook Street. By *James Maclaren*, 1864. A box, the rubble-built sides pierced by paired lancet windows. Front (S) gable of squared and stugged masonry. Pinnacled buttresses divided it into a 'nave' and 'aisles'. The upper part of the 'nave' walling is intaken above a pierced parapet which is interrupted by the pointed centre door, its gablet pierced by a quatrefoil. Above the door, a hoodmoulded window of three pointed lights, their heads filled with foiled circlets. At the ends of the 'aisles', paired narrow lights, their heads cusped.

OUR LADY OF GOOD COUNSEL (R.C.), Westfield Road. Nave and tower by *T. Martin Cappon*, 1904, the chancel an addition of the later C20. Cappon's work is simple Gothic, the walls of glazed red brick, the windows' curvaceous hoodmoulds of red sandstone. The W gable of the nave is divided by two buttresses. In the centre compartment, three small windows under a tall three-light window. Battlemented NW tower, the ogee-arched hoodmould of its entrance rising to the corbel base of a canopied niche containing a stone statue of the Virgin and Child; large paired belfry openings. Buttressed N aisle E of the tower, the nave roof swept over it to end in bracketed broad eaves. On the S side of the nave the W three bays are unaisled but buttressed. At the W bay, a broad segmental-arched door; paired tall windows to the E. At the four-bay chancel, a flat roof over the central vessel; monopitch roofs over the aisles.

QUEEN STREET UNITED PRESBYTERIAN CHURCH, corner of Queen Street and Camphill Road. Secularized. By *Maclaren & Aitken*, 1875–6. Geometric, of khaki-coloured stugged masonry with dressings of polished white ashlar. Nave and aisles, the roof over each aisle bay at right angles to that of the nave, the gables of the centre bays containing two-light windows with circled heads under rose windows. At the W gable of the nave, three pointed lights with circled heads; large rose window above. Semi-octagonal apse at the E end. SW steeple, its gableted angle buttresses stopped below the belfry stage. At the belfry's canted corners are pinnacled buttress-like triangular projections topped by big stone spouts. The belfry is finished with a stone parapet decorated with Gothic arched panels. Broached spire.

ST AIDAN'S PARISH CHURCH, Brook Street. Originally Broughty Ferry Church. Simple Gothic, by *James Black*, 1824–6. Rubble rectangle with a W tower, its top two stages and spire added by *Charles Edward*, 1858. The organ chamber on the church's S side was provided in 1875 by *Maclaren & Aitken*.

At the N front, two large pointed and Y-traceried windows. This front's central gablet containing a wooden-traceried rose window looks a late C19 alteration. Projecting from the centre is a porch of three bays, the outer two parapeted and with paired lancet windows, the advanced and gabled centre bay containing a pointed door. At the E gable, a small pointed gallery window with a roundel above; piend-roofed vestry. The S elevation is overlaid by the addition of 1875. Broad centre gable containing a pair of round-headed windows under a large circular opening. At the flanking bays, tall pointed windows. At this front's W end a session house added in 1858.

The four stages of the W tower are marked off by string courses. At each of the W and N faces of the lowest stage, a rectangular door with a small pointed window above looking like a skied fanlight. A sizeable pointed window at each exposed face of the second stage. Above this is work of 1858. Low third stage pierced by paired belfry openings. At each face of the top stage, a round clock face under an angular hoodmould. Slated broach spire with big lucarnes.

ST JAMES, Fort Street. Originally Beach Church. Humble and cheap Romanesque, by *T. S. Robertson*, 1890. Nave and an E aisle, the roofs of its two bays at right angles to that of the nave. Gabled porches at the ends. On the S end of the nave, a bell-cote, its pyramidal roof covered with stone slabs. At the N end, a HALL in the same manner, dated 1896.

ST LUKE'S AND QUEEN STREET CHURCH, West Queen Street. Originally St Luke's Free Church. Early French Gothic, by *Hippolyte J. Blanc*, 1884–5, built of red sandstone, the main walling hammer-dressed, the dressings of polished ashlar. Nave with low aisles, transepts and a semi-octagonal E apse; SW porch and NW stair-tower. The inner angles of the buttresses at the transepts and the W end of the nave contain carved snarling beasts. At each bay of the buttressed aisles, small paired lancets, their label stops carved as foliaged balls. The hoodmoulded windows of the nave's clearstorey are each of three steeply pointed lights. At each transept gable, three tall lancets and a small quatrefoil opening above. The apse windows are simple, their hoodmoulds linked by a string course. Over the crossing, a tall octagonal slate-spired ventilator. The boldly projecting and stoutly buttressed SW porch was intended as the base of a tower. Stiff-leaf capitals at the attached columns of the doorway. In the W gable, a pointed door flanked by small windows, all linked by hoodmoulding. Above, two tall Y-traceried two-light windows flanked by smaller blind arches, all with bell-capitalled attached columns; a vesica in the top of the gable.

INTERIOR. Terrazzo-floored W vestibule entered from the porch through a pair of segmental-headed overarches. An answering pair of arches on the N of the vestibule gives access to the gallery stair. Over the vestibule a W gallery, the tops of its moulded panels filled with gilded Anaglypta. The nave is separated from the passage aisles by arcades, the pointed arches carried on piers of polished granite; above the arcades, the walls up to the level of the clearstorey windows are covered with floral-patterned brown tiles. The ribs of the nave's tunnel-vaulted boarded ceiling spring from vaulting shafts, their supporting corbels carved with beasts and foliage. Taller two-bay arcades to the transepts. Pointed chancel arch, its nook-shafts again of polished granite. In the chancel, ashlar-clad walls above a panelled dado; boarded ceiling. – PULPIT of the late C20 to the l. of the chancel arch. – Circular Victorian GASOLIERS. – STAINED GLASS. The five apse windows (Enoch, Ruth, the Good Shepherd, the Virgin Mary and St John) are of 1884, executed by *Morris & Co.* from designs of 1873–80 by *Edward Burne-Jones*. – ORGAN on the S of the chancel, by *Gray & Davison*, 1895.

ST MARY (Episcopal), Queen Street. Austere Gothic in sneck-harled rubble. The nave and chancel are of 1858 by *G. Gilbert Scott* who added the S aisle in 1870. The transeptal organ chamber on the N of the chancel was enlarged in 1887. In 1911 *Robert S. Lorimer* extended the nave one bay to the W and the chancel by another to the E.

Angle buttresses at the gables; hoodmoulds over the windows, their label stops left in block. On the W end a gableted bellcote. It was designed by Scott and reused by Lorimer as was the E window of three stepped lights but this was placed higher than originally intended. At the W gable of the nave, two tall windows under a foiled roundel, again by Lorimer repeating Scott's design. Two windows with a vesica above in the aisle's W gable. At its E gable, two windows under a foiled roundel. Halls under the church, their windows with shouldered arches.

Inside, scissor-truss roofs over the nave and chancel, the chancel ceiling's plasterwork stencilled in blue and gold. Nave arcade to the S aisle, the pointed stone arches carried on octagonal pillars. The chancel arch and the arch from the chancel into the chapel occupying the aisle's E bay spring from tall wall-shafts, the small corbels at their base carved as human heads. The three lights of the sanctuary's E window are framed by polished marble shafts carrying stilted arched hoodmoulds.

CHANCEL SCREEN designed by *Robert S. Lorimer* and executed by *W. & A. Clow*, 1919–21, of fumed oak, in a Late Gothic manner. On the centre of the beam, angel supporters hold a shield bearing the lily emblem of the Virgin Mary. – Oak PULPIT of 1915, again by *Lorimer*, its faces panelled with ogee arches, their tops decorated with foliage, symbols of the Evangelists, an angel and beasts. – Late C19 brass eagle LECTERN by *Hart, Son & Peard*. – CHOIR STALLS and BISHOP'S

THRONE of 1911, also by *Lorimer*, the stalls with linenfold panelling, the back of the throne carved with the coat of arms of the diocese of Brechin. – Oak REREDOS of 1917, again designed by *Lorimer*, the carving by *W. & A. Clow*, the painted decoration by *John Duncan*. Framework carved with plenty of foliage and fruit. At the base, birds and a gilded chalice under the central panel, shields bearing emblems of the Passion under the side panels. The broad centre panel is painted with a depiction of a youthful Christ the King, the side panels with the four archangels. – Plain PEWS of the later C19 in the nave and side aisle. – ORGAN by *Brindley & Foster*, 1887, and enlarged by the same firm in 1892; it was rebuilt by *H. Hilsdon*, 1916, and later by *J. W. Walker & Sons*.

STAINED GLASS. The chancel's small-paned three-light E window (the Crucifixion, with Our Lady and St John) is of 1880, the quite strongly coloured figures set against heavy clear glass. – In the sanctuary's N and S windows, brightly coloured panels (the Crucifixion; Christ the King) of *c*. 1911. – In the N wall of the nave, the E window (Our Lord with Martha and Mary) is by *Ward & Hughes*, 1874. – To its W, a very pictorial window (the Good Samaritan; Our Lord and St Peter) by *C.H. Burckhardt*, 1874. – Also of 1874 and by *Burckhardt* the next window (the Massacre of the Innocents; Rachel Weeping for her Children). – The nave's very brightly coloured W window (Our Lord blessing Children; a massacre of women and children) was designed by *Joseph Cattermole* and executed by *Scott* of Carlisle, 1858. – Probably also of 1858 the roundel above (the Presentation of Our Lord in the Temple). – The E window of the chapel at the end of the S aisle (St Margaret of Scotland and St Cuthbert) is a characteristic work by *William Wilson*, 1961. – In the chapel's S wall a sentimental window (St Margaret of Antioch and the Virgin Mary) of *c*. 1900. – W of this, in the S aisle, a window (Our Lord and the Samaritan Woman; Our Lord and Little Children) by *Clayton & Bell*, 1872, strongly coloured but disappointing. – Then, a bright narrative work (Abraham and Isaac; the Risen Lord Appearing to St Mary Magdalen) by *C. H. Burckhardt*, 1872. – Beside it, a window (Acts of Mercy) of 1880 by *Ward & Hughes*. – The W window of this side (Our Lord and Martha; Our Lord and the Disciples) is by *J. B. Capronnier*, 1883. – The aisle's neo-medieval end window (Ruth and Naomi) is of *c*. 1875.

Outside the W end of the church, a MONUMENT of 1905 to Bishop Hugh Willoughby Jermyn, a Celtic cross carved with interlaced work.

ST STEPHEN'S AND WEST CHURCH, Dundee Road. Originally St Stephen's Church. Uninventive Dec, by *Edward & Robertson*, 1871. Memorably ugly plentifully buttressed exterior, the stonework stugged, the roof of grey slates banded with green fish-scale slates. Nave with tall aisles, transepts and a short low chancel. At the N end, a gabled porch, the columns of its arched entrance with stiff-leaf capitals. NE steeple, the angle-buttressed tower rising to a top which is broached as if for a spire but instead carries a circular belfry, its louvred pointed openings nook-shafted; above the belfry, a tall slated witch's-hat spire with one tier of bargeboarded wooden lucarnes. Disappointingly small weathervane. – To the SW, a large Gothic HALL of 1894, its grey sandstone walling enlivened by red sandstone dressings.

INTERIOR. Pointed stone arches with stiff-leaf capitals to the aisles, transepts and chancel. Galleries in the aisles and across the N end of the nave. Boarded pointed tunnel vault over the nave. – PEWS of 1871.

Overpoweringly lavish and complete collection of STAINED GLASS, all by *Morris & Co.* and, except where stated, from designs by *Edward Burne-Jones*. The chancel's three-light S window (the Martyrdom of St Stephen) is of 1894 from a design of three years earlier. – In the W transept, the S window under the gallery (the Miraculous Draught of Fishes) is of 1903 using a design of 1876. – This transept's three-light W window (the Ascension) of 1906 is from designs by *Burne-Jones* (the Angels in the sidelights) of 1874 and *Henry S. Dearle* (the centre light) of 1903. – N window of the transept (Our Lord Stilling the Waves) of 1915 from a design of 1911 by *Dearle*. – In the W aisle under the gallery, S window (Our Lord in the Carpenter's Shop; the Baptism of Our Lord) of 1897 using designs of 1874. – To its N, a window (the Calling of St Peter; the Penitent Woman Washing the Feet of Our Lord) also of 1897, the designs dating from 1875–7. – In the E transept's S side, under the gallery, a window (Our Lord Preaching from a Boat) of 1903, the design of 1876. – In the E gable of this transept, a
26–28 three-light window (the Crucifixion, with Our Lady and St John) of 1914 from designs of 1872–7. – In the transept's N wall, a window (Our Lord Walking on the Water) of 1915 from a design of four years earlier by *J. Henry Dearle*. – In the side wall of the E aisle, under the gallery, the S window (the Last Supper; Our Lord Blessing Children) is of 1895 from designs of 1872–4. – To its N, another window (the Adoration of the Magi; the Anunciation to the Shepherds) of 1895, using designs produced in 1873. – The great four-light N window (Sarah, Rebecca, Miriam, Deborah, Ruth, Hannah, Abigail and Esther, with the Nativity of Our Lord in the foiled circlet at the head) of 1913 using *Burne-Jones* designs of 1874–92 and one (for Deborah) by *J. Henry Dearle* of 1907. – In the W transept at gallery level, a four-light S window (the Archangels Gabriel, Michael, Raphael and Uriel) of 1914, from designs produced by *William Morris* and *Ford Madox Brown* in 1862. – In the W gable, a rose window (Christ the King), also of 1914, the design adapted from one of 1865. – In the gallery over the W aisle, a window (Samuel and Eli; Ruth and Boaz), again of 1914, the designs produced in 1876–9. – Beside it, another window (David Lamenting the Death of Absolom; Daniel in the Lions' Den) of 1914, from designs of 1875 and 1896. – In the gallery of the E transept, a four-light S window (Jeremiah, Isaiah, Ezekiel and Daniel) of 1914, the designs of 1875. – Rose

window in the transept's gable (*Dies Domini*), also of 1914 from a design of 1875. – In the gallery above the N aisle, the S window (Moses in the Bulrushes; Abraham and Isaac) is of 1914 from designs of 1874–9. – Beside it, yet another window (Noah Building the Ark; the Expulsion from Eden) of 1914, from designs of 1874–7. – In the vestibule, two lights (Angels) of 1919, the designs produced in 1878.

PUBLIC BUILDINGS

BARNHILL CEMETERY, corner of Nursery Road and Strathmore Street. Opened in 1869, the date of the Neo-Jacobean LODGE (by *James Maclaren*) and Gothic GATEPIERS at the SW corner, and containing an array of prosperous Victorian monuments mingled with shrubbery and trees. At the NE corner of the S compartment, the MAUSOLEUM of George Gilroy of Castleroy, a partner in the textile firm of Gilroy Bros, owners of the Tay Works in Dundee. It is by *J. Murray Robertson*, 1892, a sturdily buttressed and crowstep-gabled polished ashlar oblong. In the S gable, a hoodmoulded Tudor Gothic door under a shield displaying the Gilroy coat of arms. Tunnel-vaulted interior. Round the mausoleum, wrought-iron railings decorated with flowers and finials of lions holding shields at the outer corners and dolphins (the heraldic device of the Gilroys) flanking the steps to the entrance.

BROUGHTY FERRY RAILWAY STATION, Gray Street. By *Grainger & Miller*, 1838. On the S platform, a bargeboarded L-plan grey sandstone building, the main block of one storey, the NE jamb of two. Filling the long inner angle, a double-pitch canopy, its W and N sides on cast-iron columns whose fluted capitals support four-way brackets; quatrefoils piercing the spandrels.

BURGH HALLS, Brook Street. Two-storey villa of the earlier C19, extended to the E as the municipal buildings soon after Broughty Ferry became a burgh in 1864. Prominent clock suspended from a balcony. Further additions by *Alexander Johnston*, 1897.

DUNDEE COLLEGE GARDYNE ROAD CAMPUS, Gardyne Road. By *Thoms & Wilkie*, 1972–5. Four-storey main building and lower wings, their alternating bands of concrete blockwork and glass well mannered but unexciting.

Former EASTERN SCHOOL, corner of St Vincent Street and Brook Street. Now in other use. Single-storey symmetrical Free Jacobean, of 1874–5.

EASTERN PRIMARY SCHOOL, Whinnybrae. By *James H. Langlands*, 1911. Tall and cheerless, making education appear an industrial process. At the main ranges, in each of two tall storeys, windows whose verticality contrasts with the horizontal bands at the five-storey corner blocks. On the roofs, ventilators finished with lids surmounted by domes.

GROVE ACADEMY, Queen Street. Undistinguished and plain building of 1889 by *James Maclaren & Sons* who extended it E in 1897. Brown brick W addition (The Centenary Building) of 1989. To the N, a very large N extension by the *Holmes Partnership*, 2005–9, the walls faced with blockwork, render and yellow brick. Concave W side, a red drum tower giving a modicum of panache.

HARBOUR, Castle Approach. The E dock is by *Thomas Grainger*, 1847–51, constructed to serve the ferry carrying passengers to or from the Edinburgh & Northern Railway's terminus at Tayport (Fife), its E pier abutting the rock on which stands Broughty Castle. Roughly rectangular basin, the piers built of hammer-dressed ashlar, the buttressed NE wharf now mostly covered with concrete. Ramp on the inner side of the broad NW pier. – Some way to the W, the WEST PIER by *David Cunningham*, 1872. Its NE part is of coursed rubble. At its S end and angled to the E, a return section originally of wood but now of concrete. – Further E, the utilitarian LIFEBOAT HOUSE, by *W. T. Douglass*, 1909.

MONIFIETH HIGH SCHOOL, Wemyss Crescent. By *Tayside Regional Council*, 1977–80. Brown brick boxes, their corners chamfered, the wall-heads sloped.

POLICE STATION, Brook Street. Dated 1848. A small Neo-Jacobean former school.

POST OFFICE, Queen Street. Now in other use. By *W. T. Oldrieve* of *H.M. Office of Works*, 1907–8. Ashlar-fronted, of two storeys, with an English Baroque segmental-pedimented entrance.

PUBLIC LIBRARY, Queen Street. A drily detailed single-storey version of the *Petit Trianon*, by the Dundee City Architect, *James Thomson*, 1923.

RERES HILL, Monifieth Road. Small piece of wooded parkland. The ashlar GATEWAY designed by *T.S. Robertson* was erected in 1887 to commemorate Queen Victoria's Golden Jubilee. Round-headed arch between circular turrets with stone-slabbed conical roofs, their corbelled-out top stage decorated with panels containing alternating roses and thistles. The rope moulding surmounting this stage continues above the central archway whose spandrels bear shields carved with the royal arms of Scotland and the United Kingdom. Above the archway, a battlement whose large central panel contains a relief portrait of Queen Victoria. Behind, a drinking fountain in the same manner.

SCHOOL, corner of Dundee Road and Claypotts Road. Now in other use. Mid-C19. Single-storey, with bracketed broad eaves.

VOLUNTEER DRILL HALL, Church Street. Nightmare free Baroque of *c.* 1875, a huge round window in the centre of the open pedimented ashlar front.

DESCRIPTION

MONIFIETH ROAD is the entry from the E. On the N Reres Hill (*see* Public Buildings above) is an introduction. A little further on, Nos. 47–53, a pair of single-storey-and-attic Voyseyish double houses by *Gauldie, Hardie & Sharp*, 1930. Harled, with red Rosemary-tiled roofs presenting M-shaped double gables to the front. A little further on, on the S side's corner with Taymouth Place, Nos. 20–24 Monifieth Road, a two-storey-and-attic tenement by *Maclaren & Aitken*, 1869, in the manner of F. T. Pilkington and faced with hammer-dressed ashlar. Canted corners and a corbelled wall-head cornice under the attic's bargeboarded dormer windows; steeply pedimented Jacobean doorpiece. Calmer is the mid-C19 short single-storey terrace of Nos. 8–12, rubble-built and with rusticated quoins, Nos. 10–12 forming a bay-windowed double cottage, No. 12's skewputt carved with a lion. At Monifieth Road's W end, the diagonally opposed presences of the Eastern Primary School and Broughty Ferry New Kirk (see Churches, above).

ST VINCENT STREET, passing under the railway line to the S, leads to Broughty Ferry Harbour (*see* Public Buildings, above) and Broughty Castle (*see* below). On the E corner with KING STREET, LINKS HOUSE (No. 357 King Street), an early C19 villa of two storeys over a basement. Three-bay front, the ashlar stonework badly weathered, with a fanlit door in a Roman Doric-columned surround and a first-floor sill course. In BEACH CRESCENT at St Vincent Street's S end, Nos. 41–47, a double house of *c.* 1840 which was converted to flats about twenty years later. Two storeys and an attic above a high basement. Six-bay front of polished ashlar, the ground-floor windows corniced, consoled pediments over the end doors, moulded architraves and a sill course at the first-floor windows. Beach Crescent ends at the W with the two-storey and harled FERRY HOUSE of *c.* 1800 but rather altered. It is L-plan with a sidelit entrance under a huge semicircular fanlight at one end of the NW wing's elevation to GRAY STREET. Adjoining is the contemporary No. 22 Gray Street, also harled and with a corniced doorpiece. At Gray Street's N end, Broughty Ferry Railway Station (*see* Public Buildings, above).

FISHER STREET continues the curvaceous line of Beach Crescent along the shore. Off its N side, a single-storey double cottage (Nos. 6–8) clad in render lined in imitation of ashlar, presumably built in 1823 (the date cut over the door of No. 6). Nos. 183–195 Fisher Street is a terrace of three cottages of *c.* 1800, now harled or drydashed. Further along, BAROMETER COTTAGE of 1812, its walling of sneck-harled rubble. Standing like a sentry box beside the entrance is a stone case (dated 1859) containing the barometer from which it takes its name. To the NW, a two-storey-and-attic rubble-walled early C19 terrace (Nos. 61–83), its mixture of houses and tenements characteristic of Broughty Ferry's Late Georgian domestic buildings.

FORT STREET leads N from Fisher Street. On the r., No. 34, perhaps late C18, a two-storey rubble-built house, the door set in a lugged and corniced architrave. On the corner of King Street, THE EAGLE INN, harled and of two storeys, the main block late C18 but altered, the E wing a mid-C19 addition. The

S gable's carved and gilded sign (of an eagle) is by *James Law*, *c.* 1860. Fort Street's scale increases with a Free Jacobean commercial block of *c.* 1900 at Nos. 84–86. This is of two tall storeys and an attic, the wall-head parapet over the outer bays scooped up to the base of a steep central pediment over three mullioned-and-transomed first-floor windows. The ground floor's Artisan Mannerist Ionic pilasters survive from the original stylish shopfronts. In BROOK STREET off Fort Street's W side, the MASONIC HALL by *H. & F. Thomson*, 1911. Not large and with shops at the ground floor but its ashlar-clad authoritarian Beaux Arts classical shows the cold self-assurance of good breeding. At the top of Fort Street, the former Post Office (*see* Public Buildings, above).

QUEEN STREET is Broughty Ferry's most public and traffic-heavy thoroughfare. Together with the railway line it serves to divide the tight-knit Late Georgian gridiron of the planned village beside the Firth of Tay from the more informal layout of the Late Victorian and C20 villadom on the hillside behind. On its S side, W of the Post Office, St Mary's Episcopal Church (*see* Churches, above). Opposite, the single-storey-and-attic white-rendered BRAE COTTAGE. As first built for a shipmaster, Andrew Finlay, this was a simple oblong, its front of three bays. About 1830 it was lengthened at both ends, the E extension with a front bow, the W with a semi-octagon.

Near Queen Street's W end, the beginning of CHURCH STREET. On its W side, the former Volunteer Drill Hall (later Regal Cinema) for which, *see* Public Buildings, above. At the S end, JAMES PLACE overlooking the Tay. Here is a two-storey-and-attic terrace (Nos. 1–13) of *c.* 1840. Front of polished ashlar, a band course above the ground floor, sill course linking the first-floor windows; bowed quadrant corners at the ends. No. 3's bay window is presumably an addition. At the NW end of James Place, WESTFIELD ROAD running to the N. On its NE corner with King Street, a late C18 two-storey rubble-walled double house (No. 18 Westfield Road and No. 9 King Street), the entrance to one dwelling by an anta-pilastered and corniced door at the front, the entrance to the other by a console-corniced first-floor side door. Further up Westfield Road, the Church of Our Lady of Good Counsel and, on the corner of Dundee Road, St Stephen's and West Church (*see* Churches, above).

DOUGLAS TERRACE continues the line of James Place beside the shore, its houses of *c.* 1840 all on the N side and set back. Nos. 1–8 are bay-windowed and broad-eaved ashlar-faced double houses (now rather altered) with cast-iron anthemion-balustraded balconies. At Nos. 9–12, a bay-windowed short terrace. No. 23 (WEST BEACH) was built and presumably designed by *George Mathewson* *c.* 1838. It is a single-storey-and-attic *cottage orné* with steeply pitched gables and broad eaves. Triangular bay windows topped by latticed parapets. In DUNDEE ROAD behind, a pair of large villas (Nos. 74–76) with fretted bargeboards.

VILLAS

ALBERT ROAD. BROOMFIELD (No. 3) is of 1865. Italianate, the symmetrical S front with canted bay windows at the ground floor and elliptical-arched and keystoned lights to the first-floor openings. Four-stage E tower over the entrance, its roof a lead-covered truncated pyramid, the flat top surrounded by iron cresting.

CAMPHILL ROAD. CARBET CASTLE, the huge Victorian mansion of the textile manufacturer, Joseph Grimond, was demolished in the 1920s and the site is now occupied by CAMPHILL CASTLE, a block of flats by *Ron Valentine*, 1997–8. Nearby, Carbet Castle's former LODGE (No. 7 Camphill Road) by *T.S. Robertson*, 1874, a single-storey L, the inner angle containing a round tower over the entrance which is surmounted by a heraldic panel bearing the Grimond coat of arms. At the tower's heavily corbelled top stage, quatrefoil openings recessed in circular surrounds; fish-scale-slated conical roof with iron-finialled lucarnes and a tall weathercock. Heavy Gothic GATEPIERS with nook-shafts of polished pink granite and capitals carved with stiff-leaf foliage; grey granite pyramidal tops. – ST MARGARET'S (No. 18). Mid-C19 with bracketed broad eaves and a low Italianate tower, the surrounds to the windows of its top stage with shells carved in their round-arched blind heads. – CRAIG-GOWAN (No. 42) on the E corner of Whinny Brae, by *Maclaren & Aitken*, 1878. Blowsy French Renaissance. At the SE corner, a pavilion-roofed low tower with elaborate iron cresting. On the house's S side, a full-height canted bay window enjoying the view over the Tay.

CRAIGIEBARN ROAD. The two-storey-and-attic CRAIGIEBARN HOUSE, by *Maclaren, Soutar & Salmond*, 1911, is relaxed and multi-gabled English Arts and Crafts, the walls of flush-pointed rubble and harl, the roofs covered with red Rosemary tiles and with neat piended dormers.

DUNDEE ROAD. No. 36 is a harled Neo-Jacobean broad-eaved and gabled villa of *c.* 1830, the principal windows hoodmoulded; tactful additions by *Mills & Shepherd*, 1905. – FORT WILLIAM (No. 34, now Royal Tay Yacht Club), an idiosyncratically smart white-harled and broad-eaved villa built in 1839 for Captain James Neish and named after his ship. It consists of three parallel blocks side by side, the broader centre block of two storeys above a basement, the piend-roofed E and W blocks a storey lower and with S ends projecting as canted bays overlooking the Tay. At the ground floor of the centre block's S gable, a screen of Ionic columns *in antis* under a guilloche-pierced parapet; behind the parapet, a first-floor round-headed window flanked by rectangular sidelights. Plain single-storey and basement E wing, an addition of the later C19, as is the W porch. Inside, on the ground floor, a central hall with pilasters at the N and S ends and divided by ceiling beams into two compartments, the S originally a small room, the narrower N compartment with a cupola-topped octagon in the centre of the ceiling and with Ionic columns framing the doors to W and (now blocked) E. The SE ground floor room was the drawing room (now bar and much altered). The SW room is the bow-ended dining room with a black marble chimneypiece, an egg-and-dart cornice and ceiling rose. – THE LODGE (No. 69) was designed by *Andrew Heiton Jun.*, *c.* 1860, as the lodge to Fernhall (demolished), the house of the flax-spinner, John Sharp. Single-storey Gothic L, the roofs of both wings with iron cresting. In the inner angle, a fish-scale-slated conical-roofed round tower containing the nook-shafted entrance.

FAIRFIELD ROAD. RED COURT (No. 17) by *Hippolyte J. Blanc*, 1886. Jacobean Renaissance, the masonry of bullnosed red sandstone.

RALSTON ROAD. SUNNINGDALE (No. 2) is by *Donald Ross* of *Thoms & Wilkie*, 1933, a quite small two-storey villa, its style Art Deco with a vengeance but the original metal-framed windows now replaced. Symmetrical S front, its recessed centre fronted by a canopied first-floor balcony. Shutters to the windows of the end bays whose wavy wall-heads are covered with red tiles.

RERES ROAD. RERES HOUSE, a large villa of 1849 with exuberantly carved bargeboards. It forms an L with a contemporary NE coachhouse wing.

STRATHERN ROAD. NORTHWOOD (No. 118), a very large but not over-ostentatious free Jacobean villa by *G. S. Aitken*, built (as Corona) for the ship-owner, Robert Mudie, in 1880 and doubled in size by *Robert Gibson* for another ship-owner, William Thomson, in 1911. The principal front faces S. The E half is of 1880, rectangular bay with a guilloche-pierced parapet at the l. At the r., a two-storey canted bay window projects from a broad gable, its head carried on very tall moulded corbels. This front's W half is of 1911, the join marked by a diagonally placed gable fronted by a semicircular Roman Doric portico. To the l., a broad rectangular bay window, very like that of 1880 to the E, and a narrow canted bay window. Domed round turret on the SW corner. At the house's E end, a conservatory, perhaps also of 1911. At the E end of the N side, a square tower of 1880, English Jacobean Renaissance in manner, with tall urns on the crowning balustrade. Beautifully finished and expensive INTERIOR in the same Neo-Jacobean manner.

VICTORIA ROAD. AYSTREE HOUSE (No. 26) on the corner with Albert Road is by *C. Ower & Co.*, in association with *C.G. Soutar*, 1903. English free style, the walls of hammer-dressed stonework and render with half-timbering in some gable-heads, the roof covered with red Rosemary tiles. At the S front, a two-storey canted bay window projecting from a shaped gable. A second S gable of exceptional breadth, its slightly advanced centre containing five-light windows to the ground and first floors, the intervening panel carved with swagged ornaments. Above the W side's porch, a parapet of pierced strapwork; swan-neck pediment over the entrance. Conservatory at the house's E end. Conversion to flats by *James F. Stephen*, 2011.

Glen Clova (p. 1)
Arbroath, harbour (p. 326)

3. Menmuir, Brown and White Caterthuns, forts, Iron Age (p. 608)
4. Aberlemno, Pictish slab, probably C7 (p. 288)

5. Glamis, Kirk Wynd, Pictish slab, probably c7 or c8 (p. 499)
6. Aberlemno, Pictish slab, probably c8 (p. 288)

7. Brechin Cathedral, NW tower and W front, C13–C14; Round Tower, *c.* 1100 (p. 358)
8. Restenneth Priory, tower, C11–C12 (p. 660)
9. St Vigeans Church, C12, enlarged, C15, reconstructed, 1871–2 (p. 666)

10. Arbroath Abbey, W front, C13 (p. 304)
11. Fowlis, St Marnock, panel from rood, C15 (p. 488)
12. Fowlis, St Marnock, sacrament house, C15 (p. 488)

13. Dundee, City Churches, W tower, C15, and The Steeple Church, by Samuel Bell, 1787–9 (pp. 86, 87)
14. Kirkton of Auchterhouse, Auchterhouse Church, 1630, reconstructed, 1775 (p. 574)
15. Dun Church, pulpit, 1615 (p. 439)

DUN PRIMARY SCHOOL
1850 2005

[cut off]. Dundee, St Andrew, by Samuel Bell, 1772–4 (p. 95)
[cut off]. Glamis Parish Church, 1792–3 (p. 497)
[cut off]. Cortachy Church, pulpit, 1828–9 (p. 427)

19. Montrose, Old Parish Church, steeple, by James Gillespie Graham, 1832–4 (p. 620)
20. Montrose, St John, by William Smith, 1827–9 (p. 621)
21. Dundee, St Andrew's (R.C.) Cathedral, by George Mathewson, 1835– (p. 155)

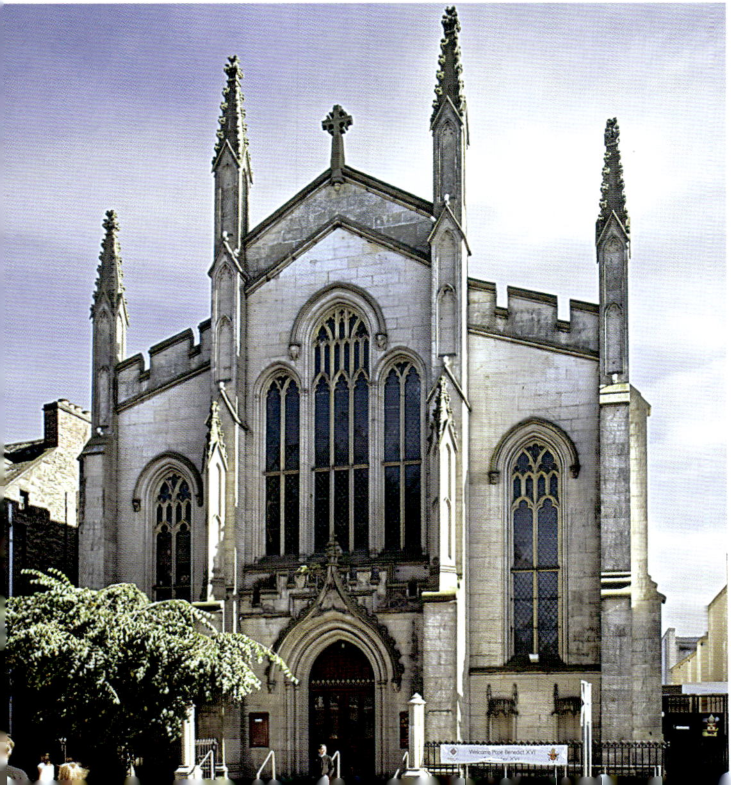
Welcome Pope Benedict XVI

ST MARY'S
Catholic Church
LOCHEE

West Bell Street

Dundee, St Mary (R.C.), by J.A. Hansom, 1864–6 (p. 242)

Dundee, St Mary Magdalene (Episcopal), by Edward & Robertson, 1867 (p. 215)

Dundee, St Salvador (Episcopal), by G. F. Bodley, 1858–74 (p. 230)

s mary

INRI

s john
who died 27th august 1877

. Dundee, Cathedral Church of St Paul (Episcopal), by G. Gilbert Scott, 1852–5 (p. 84)

–28. Broughty Ferry, St Stephen's and West Church, stained glass, by Morris & Co., 1914 (p. 394)

. Dundee, McCheyne Memorial Free Church, by Pilkington & Bell, 1869–70 (p. 154)

30. Kirriemuir, St Mary (Episcopal), by J. Ninian Comper, 1904–5 (p. 581)
31. Dundee, St Mary Our Lady of Victories (R.C.), E front, by T. Martin Cappon, 1900–2 (p. 228)
32. Arbroath, Western Cemetery, Memorial Chapel, by Patrick Allan-Fraser, 1875–84 (p. 321)
33. Kirriemuir, St Anthony (R.C.), by James F. Stephen, 1985–7 (p. 581)

34. Inverquharity Castle, c15 (p. 543)
35. Edzell Castle, c16 (p. 448)

. Inverquharity Castle, Great Hall, c15 (p. 545)
. Broughty Ferry, Claypotts Castle, c16 (p. 404)

38. Airlie Castle, c15 (p. 292)
39. Dundee, Mains Castle, c16 (p. 277)

0. Cortachy Castle, c16–c19, remodelled, 1948–51 (p. 427)
1. Dundee, Dudhope Castle, c17, remodelled, late c18 and 1985–8 (p. 223)

42. Glamis Castle, Great Tower, C15, remodelled, early C17 (p. 503)
43. Glamis Castle, Great Hall, C15, remodelled, early C17 (p. 510)
44. Glamis Castle, Chapel, 1679–88 (p. 510)

5. Glamis Castle, sundial, late C17 (p. 503)
6. Edzell Castle, garden, early C17 (p. 452)
7–48. Edzell Castle, garden, wall panels ('GEOMETRIA' and 'MUSICA'), early C17 (p. 454)

49. Brechin Castle, by Alexander Edward, 1698–1711 (p. 380)
50. House of Pitmuies, *c.* 1730, remodelled, late C18 and early C19 (p. 535)

1. House of Dun, by William Adam, 1730–42 (p. 526)
2. House of Dun, Saloon, plasterwork by Joseph Enzer, 1741–2 (p. 530)

53. Stracathro House, by Archibald Simpson, 1827 (p. 671)
54. Dundee, Camperdown House, by William Burn, 1820–6 (p. 275)
55. Stracathro House, Inner Hall, ceiling, 1827 (p. 672)
56. Dundee, Camperdown House, saloon, 1820–6 (p. 275)

57. Downiepark, s front, *c*. 1805, with portico of 1819 (p. 437)
58. Dunninald Castle, by James Gillespie Graham, 1823–4 (p. 440)

. The Guynd, 1817 (p. 518)

. Dunninald Castle, dining-room ceiling, 1823–4 (p. 441)

1. Kinnaird Castle, by David Bryce, 1854–60, remodelled by Kelly & Nicol, 1920s (p. 551)
2. Arbroath, Hospitalfield, by Patrick Allan-Fraser, 1849–54 (p. 337)
3. Kinnordy House, by Wardrop & Reid, 1879–81 (p. 562)
4. Arbroath, Hospitalfield, Gallery, 1849–54 (p. 343)
5. Kinnordy House, Inner Hall, 1879–81 (p. 563)

66. Glamis Castle, Gladiator Gate, by Alexander Craw, 1680–1 (p. 513)
67. House of Dun, stables, W range, mid-C18 with early C19 cupola (p. 527)
68. Stracathro House, stables, by Archibald Simpson, *c.* 1830 (p. 674)

69. Arbroath, Signal Tower, probably by Robert Stevenson, 1813 (p. 327)
70. Dun, Bridge of Dun, by Alexander Stevens Sen., 1785–7 (p. 439)
71. Montrose, The Tower, by William Middleton, 1841 (p. 630)

2. Brechin, Town House, 1789 (p. 373)
3. Montrose, Town House, 1763–4, remodelled by William Smith, 1819 (p. 629)
4. Montrose, Montrose Academy, by David Logan, 1815–16 (p. 625)
5. Dundee, High School of Dundee, by George Angus, 1829–35 (p. 108)

76. Forfar, Sheriff Court, by Brown & Wardrop, 1868–71 (p. 477)
77. Dundee, Sheriff Court, by William Scott, 1861–3 (p. 115)
78. Brechin, Mechanics' Institute, by John Henderson, 1838–42 (p. 371)
79. Montrose, Montrose Museum, by John Henderson, 1837–42 (p. 626)

PANMURE PLACE
MUSEUM

Dundee, Central Reading Rooms, by James Thomson, 1909–11 (p. 106)

Dundee, The McManus, Dundee's Art Gallery and Museum, front block by G. Gilbert Scott, 1865–8 (p. 111)

Dundee, Royal Exchange, by David Bryce, 1853–6 (p. 114)

83. Dundee, Nethergate, Nos. 135–139 (Morgan Tower), *c.* 1795 (p. 171)
84. Dundee, Castle Street, Exchange Coffee Room, by George Smith, 1828–30 (p. 125)
85. Dundee, Magdalen Yard Road, No. 43 (The Vine), 1836 (p. 175)
86. Montrose, Panmure Terrace, *c.* 1850 (p. 641)
87. Dundee, Springfield, 1830–51 (p. 179)

88. Dundee, Murraygate, Nos. 35–39 (former British Linen Co. Bank), by David Cousin, 1868 (p. 132)
89. Dundee, Meadowside, General Post Office, by W.W. Robertson, 1895–8 (p. 107)
90. Dundee, corner of Commercial Street and Murraygate, late C19 (p. 129

Optical
Express
Optical
Express

1. Dundee, High Street, former Clydesdale Bank, by William Spence, 1875–8 (p. 127)
2. Dundee, High Street, Nos. 3–4 (The Royal Bank of Scotland), by George Washington Browne, 1897–9 (p. 124)
3. Dundee, Princes Street, former Dundee Savings Bank Eastern Branch, by Johnston & Baxter, 1914–15 (p. 203)

94. Dundee, Albert Square, statue of Queen Victoria, by Harry Bates, 1898–9 (p. 114)
95. Carnoustie, war memorial, by Bruce, Son & Morton, with sculpture by Thomas Beattie, 1925 (p. 420)
96. Arbroath, war memorial, by George Washington Browne, 1920–1 (p. 334)

ANCRUM·ROAD·PUBLIC·SCHOOL
Ancrum Road
Primary School

7. Dundee, Ancrum Road Primary School, by James H. Langlands, 1905–7 (p. 244)
8. Dundee, University of Dundee, Carnegie Building, by Rowand Anderson & Paul, 1908–9 (p. 161)
9. Dundee, University of Dundee, Tower Building, by Robert Matthew & Johnson-Marshall, 1957–61 (p. 159)

100. Dundee, Ninewells Hospital, by Robert Matthew, Johnson-Marshall & Partners, 1963–74, extended by Keppie Architects, 1995–9 (p. 187)
101. Dundee, Ninewells Hospital, Maggie's Centre, by Frank Gehry, 2001–3 (p. 187)

02. Dundee, University of Dundee, Queen Mother Building, by Page & Park, 2003–6 (p. 163)

03. Dundee, University of Dundee, Main Library, extension, by Austin-Smith:Lord, 2005–7 (p. 162)

104. Dundee, Cowgate, Wishart Place, by James F. Stephen, 1996–2000 (p. 202)
105. Dundee, Dundee Technology Park, Hillcrest Housing H.Q., by Nicoll Russell Studios, 2009–10 (p. 188)
106. Dundee, Camperdown Dock, Storm Water Tank, by Nicoll Russell Studios, 2002 (p. 146)

)7. Dundee, Dundee Contemporary Arts, by Richard Murphy, 1997–9 (p. 165)

)8. Arbroath, Harbour Visitor Centre, by Baxter, Clark & Paul, 2006–7 (p. 326)

)9. Dundee, Dundee College Kingsway Campus, The Space, by Nicoll Russell Studios, 2000–2 (p. 271)

110. Dundee, Victoria Road Calender, by Robertson & Orchar, 1874–5 (p. 238)

111. Brechin, Den Burn Works, by Robertson & Orchar, 1863–4 (p. 378)

12. Dundee, Tay Works, s block, by Joseph Lindsay, 1865 (p. 264)
13. Dundee, Camperdown Works, High Mill, by George A. Cox, 1857–68 (p. 250)

114. Dundee, Camperdown Works, Cox's Stack, by George A. Cox and James Maclaren, 1865 (p. 252)

– HERMON LODGE (No. 48) by *Edward & Robertson*, 1872–4. Germanic, the SW circular corner tower with a truncated conical roof, the flat top ringed by cresting. Domed conservatory at the E end added by *Charles Stuart* in 1910.

BROUGHTY CASTLE

Castle Approach

Late C15 tower house on the shore of the Firth of Tay, remodelled together with its barmkin wall as a Victorian gun battery.

In 1490 James IV granted the *rupem de Bruchty* ('the rock of Broughty') to Andrew, second Lord Gray, allowing him and his heirs *plenariam potestatem ad edificandum et in alterum erigendum castrum ac fortalicium super dictam rupem, cum propugnaculis, vectibus ferreis* le machc[o]ling, *et* drawbriggis *ac omnibus aliis munitionibus necessariis* ('fullest power to build and otherwise erect a castle and fortalice on the said rock, with battlements, iron bolts, machicolation and drawbridges and all other necessary fortifications'). The tower was apparently completed by 1496 (the date formerly visible on it). In 1547, during the Duke of Somerset's invasion of Scotland, Broughty Castle was handed over to the English who attempted to strengthen its apparently inadequate defences by heightening the barmkin or enclosure wall and digging a ditch on the landward side. Later that year the tower was damaged in an unsuccessful attempt by the Regent Arran to capture it, and the next year the English constructed a new fort on Balgillo Hill (or Forthill) to the S. In 1550 both Balgillo Fort and Broughty Castle fell to Arran, the last active military action apparently experienced by the castle.

In 1666 Patrick, eighth Lord Gray, sold Broughty Castle to David Fothringham of Powrie and by 1787 the tower was a roofless ruin and the walls of the enclosure served as a quarry. Broughty Castle was sold to the Edinburgh and Northern Railway in 1845 and nine years later, during the Crimean War, was acquired by the Government. In 1860–1, as the result of apprehensions of imminent war with France and the consequent need to strengthen Britain's coastal defences, *R. Rowand Anderson* was employed to restore and enlarge the late C15 tower as a magazine and barracks and to reconstruct the enclosure as an artillery battery. Further alterations to the enclosure were carried out in 1889–91. The castle's garrison was removed in 1932 but restored in 1939 for the duration of the Second World War. In 1949 Broughty Castle was leased to the City of Dundee Council which opened it as a museum in 1969.

The site is a roughly square-shaped low hill sticking as a peninsula into the Firth of Tay. The surrounding rubble-built ENCLOSURE WALL is almost all of the later C19. Protruding from the SW corner is a polygonal bastion of 1860–1, its sides pierced by square gun-ports with chamfered margins, the jambs splayed back internally to large slits which were blocked by brickwork when the interior of the bastion was remodelled

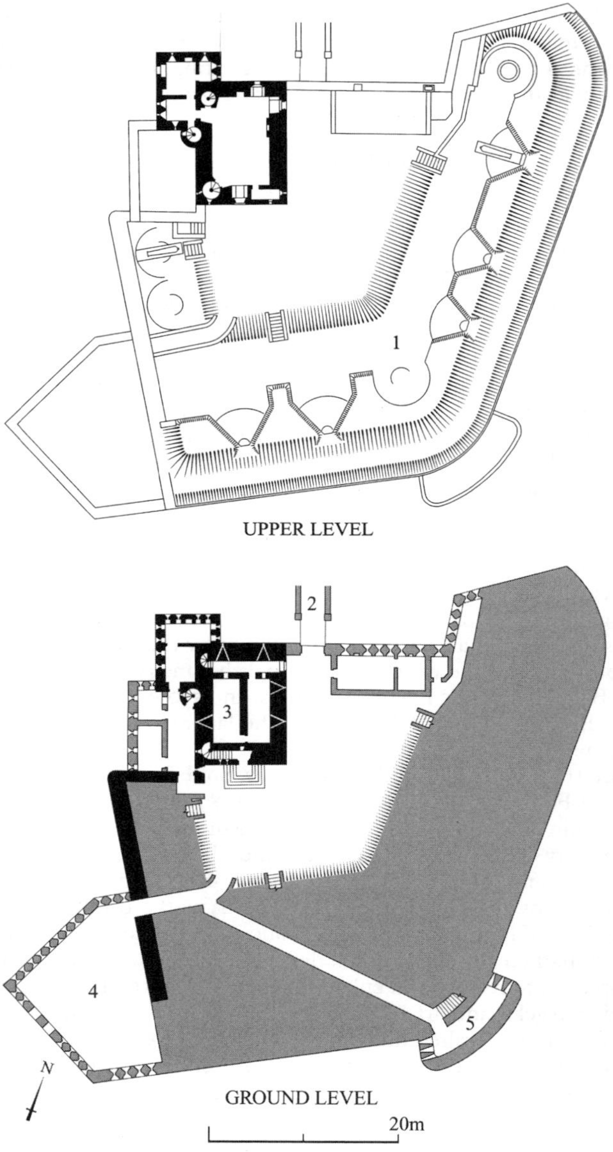

1. Gun Platform
2. Drawbridge
3. Tower House
4. Bastion
5. Caponier

Broughty Castle.
Plans

in 1889–91. Towards the N end, a (blocked) door, its margin rounded. The short main W curtain wall to the N may be late C15 or C16. In it, two plain windows, both built up. N of this and set back, the slightly higher external walls of the buildings in a small courtyard formed in 1860–1 against the W side of the tower. At the courtyard buildings' W side, large oval gun-loops splayed back internally to round gun-holes. At the N side of the courtyard, small gunloops, their design repeated at the ground floor of the contemporary NW jamb which Anderson added to the tower house. On the N side of the main enclosure, E of the tower house, a ramped approach to a drawbridge of the 1860s. Segmental-arched gateway into the enclosure. In the wall E of the gateway, square gunports of the same type as those at the SW bastion. Like them they are of 1860–1, as are the gunports in the W side of the NE bastion which Anderson designed to provide enfilading fire to cover the approach to the gateway.

On the E side of the enclosure, a retaining wall of 1860–1 behind which was an earthen gun platform formerly surmounted by an earth parapet; the 68-pound guns placed here in the C19 fired over the parapet and the 10-inch shell guns through its embrasures. At the obtusely angled SE corner of the embrasure, a caponier with gunloops for muskets placed at two levels provided flanking fire along the enclosure's E and S sides. A long horizontal slit at the upper level was inserted in 1914–15 to allow a Maxim gun to cover the shore below. The S side of the curtain was, like the E, primarily a retaining wall for the gun platform behind.

The 1490s TOWER HOUSE at the NW corner of the enclosure is a straightforward four-storey-and-attic rectangle (*c.* 9.3 m. by 13.4 m.), its rubble walls rendered since the 1860s. At the ground floor, gunloops. At the E wall they are of inverted keyhole type and of the 1490s. Those of the N, W and S walls may have been altered or inserted in the C16. Anderson provided the gunloops with checks for flash covers and redents in their internal splays, converting them to baffled flash-proof vents to safeguard against an explosion in the magazine inside the tower. At the N end of the tower's E side, a round-arched door; pointed door in the S gable. Both owe their present appearance to Anderson's work of the 1860s but are in the position of earlier openings, the S certainly of the 1490s, the E probably an insertion of the C16 or C17. At the upper floors, comfortably sized windows, their margins chamfered. The N windows, the third-floor one round-headed, were inserted by Anderson. The plan of the wall-head battlement, with a bowed projection at the centre of each side and minimally projecting square bartizans at the corners, is of the 1490s and its corbels are almost all of that date except on the W side where they are of 1860–1. The battlement itself is of the 1860s, its unsplayed crenelles narrower than would have been those of its medieval predecessors. Inside the battlement, a crowstep-gabled attic of 1860–1. Of the same date is the present crowstepped caphouse over the SW corner. On the SE corner, a brick-built defence post of 1942 designed by *H.M. Office of Works*.

The rubble-walled NW jamb was added by Anderson in 1860–1. Its defensive appearance is serious. Gunloops at the ground floor. Above, a mixture of large windows and slits. Corbelled ashlar battlement with angle-rounds and cannon spouts.

Inside the C15 tower the S entrance opens onto a lobby in the wall thickness. Short straight flight of steps to the W giving access to a turnpike stair in the SW corner of the tower and rising to the caphouse. Behind the entrance lobby and separated from it by a wall of 1860–1 are two stores, now reached from a passage inserted by Anderson which runs from the NE entrance to a service stair in the NW corner of the tower; this stair rises to the first-floor hall. Over each store, a tunnel vault, that of the W store irregularly shaped, perhaps as the result of settlement but possibly because it was originally intended to cover this floor with a single vault and a change of mind took place during construction but after the W end of the vault had been begun. A single room on each upper floor of the C15 tower, all remodelled in the 1860s.

The INTERIOR OF THE ENCLOSURE S of the tower house is mostly of 1889–91 when the ground level was raised. Two circular gun emplacements on the S side.

Outside the enclosure, to the E, a surviving two-storey block of the SUBMARINE MINERS' DEPOT built in 1886–7. A N stair gives access to a balcony supported on cast-iron columns along the W side. At the S end, a single-storey store, its entrance segmental-arched.

CLAYPOTTS CASTLE

corner of Claypotts Road and Claypotts Gardens

37 Now in a suburban setting, the idiosyncratic C16 laird's house built for the Strachans who held the lands of Claypotts from the beginning of the C16 until 1621, the walling of red sandstone rubble, formerly harled, the roof covered with stone slabs.

The house is Z-plan. Three-storey-and-attic rectangular main block, *c.* 10.6 m. by 7.6 m. Attached to the NE and SW corners are round towers, each *c.* 6.4 m. in diameter and of about the same height as the main block but containing an extra floor; rising from the ground in the inner angles of the towers and the long sides of the main block are slimmer bowed stair-turrets. All-round display of wide-mouthed oval gunloops at the sparsely windowed ground floor. At the NE stair-turret, no gunloop but a notch has been cut in the masonry to allow the gunloop in the SE face of the adjacent corner tower to defend the main block's E side with raking fire. Low down at the ground floor of the main block's E elevation, a small opening looking like the base of a garderobe

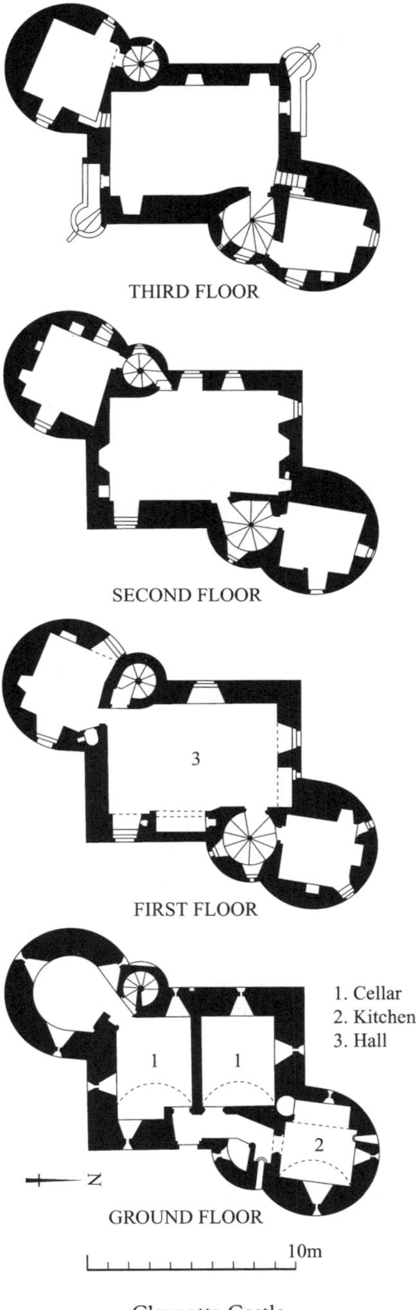

Claypotts Castle.
Plans

chute but, inside the house, there is no garderobe in this position.

At the crowstep-gabled main block's upper floors, a not very regular disposition of windows of varying size, one at the E side's first floor high-set and of horizontal proportions. The attic windows have risen into stone dormerheads, now missing. Wall-head chimney in the centre of the W front. Below it, at the ground floor, the house's segmental-arched entrance under the moulded frame for a missing heraldic panel. Below the slightly recessed heads of the N gable's S W half and the S gable's E half, attic doors onto balconies which end at angle-rounds at the outer corners, all carried on continuous corbelling; prominent stone spouts drain the walks of the balconies but the parapets above have been removed.

At the round SW tower, chamfered margins to the windows, some low and horizontally proportioned. Sitting on top of the tower is the rectangular and crowstep-gabled ashlar-faced attic, placed at a slight diagonal to the main block. Its awkward relationship to the tower below suggests it was an afterthought. For the most part it is slightly set back from the curved face of the walling below but the corners are projected timidly on three courses of continuous corbelling. Rising from the wall-head of this attic's S face, an aedicular stone dormer window, its jambs with three-tier attached columns, the segmental pediment carved with a sunburst; pinnacles over the ends. This face's E skewputt bears a blank shield, the W the date 1569, probably that of completion of the main block, this tower and its stair-turret. Catslide roof to the turret but crowsteps above its N segment.

The NE tower is generally similar to the SW although, two-thirds of the way up, a change in the stonework may indicate that its construction took place in two stages. The attic storey is also a crowstep-gabled rectangle but built of rubble and set at a more pronounced diagonal to the main block than the corresponding feature at the SW. Moreover, it sits more confidently on top of the round tower, all projected clear of the curved walling below and carried on four courses of continuous corbelling. On the front face's l. skewputt, the date 1588 (the numeral 5 upside down), on the r., the initials and coat of arms of John Strachan. Straightforward catslide roof over the adjacent stair-turret which is slenderer than the corresponding turret at the SW.

INTERIOR. The entrance opens into a vestibule-passage. On its E side, a pair of doors, like all the doors in the house with chamfered jambs. These open into tunnel-vaulted cellars, the S subdivided by C20 partitions. Off the N cellar, an irregularly oval-shaped room in the NE tower, also tunnel-vaulted and perhaps originally the wine cellar; beside its doorway, the entrance to a tight turnpike stair in the adjoining turret. Near the vestibule-passage's S end, the entrance to a larger and more comfortable turnpike in the SW stair-turret and, piercing the walling of that turret's W segment, an inlet for water. The vestibule-passage's S door opens into the house's tunnel-vaulted rectangular kitchen in the SW tower. The kitchen's E end is filled by an elliptically arched fireplace, a bread oven in the N jamb, a shot-hole (blocked) in its back. At the E end of the S wall, a slop drain.

The upper floors are unvaulted. Above the kitchen and entered from the SW stair is a room, perhaps intended for guests. It is also rectangular and with a smallish fireplace at the S end of the E wall. In the room's S side, a recess and a high-set and small horizontal-shaped window; larger window in the room's SW corner.

The first floor of the main block is occupied by the hall, its S end, entered from the main stair, formerly divided off by a screen, its position disclosed by traces in the plasterwork. In the screens passage's S wall, a good-sized window in a segmental-arched embrasure and a large serving recess, a small window in its back. At the hall's NE corner, the doorway from the N stair to the room's dais end which is lit by a large S window, its embrasure also segmental-arched and with a cupboard in its S side. S of this window, the hall fireplace, a salt-box in its S jamb; the fireplace lintel is missing and the opening now rises to the elliptical-headed relieving arch above. Opening off the hall, in the NE tower, a well-lit chamber which has had a N fireplace; cupboard in the E wall.

On the second floor of the SW tower and also entered from the S stair, a room whose walls are again straight-sided but not at right angles to each other. One of its two windows is high-set and horizontal; no fireplace. In the NE tower, at a level intermediate between the main block's first and second floors, a roughly rectangular room entered from the N stair. N fireplace; cupboards in the N and E walls. The room above is also entered from the N stair and with no direct communication with the main block. The second floor of the main block has contained two rooms, the dividing partition now missing, each with a roll-moulded fireplace in the gable. In the S room, a narrow recess, possibly to house a close stool, beside the fireplace. In the N room, a cupboard W of the fireplace.

In the SW tower, at an intermediate level between the main block's second floor and attic, a nearly rectangular room; W wall cupboard but no fireplace. The attic of the main block now contains a single room without either fireplace or wall cupboards. Formerly it was lit from dormer-headed windows (now built-up) in the side walls. The original A-framed wooden roof structure survives almost intact. In each gable, a door to the external balcony. Also in the N gable, at a higher level and originally reached by wooden steps, a door into the NE tower's attic room. In the S gable, steps in the wall thickness rise to the SW tower's attic room, a fireplace in its W wall.

CAMPERDOWN HOUSE *see* DUNDEE: ARDLER AND DOWNFIELD

5060

CARESTON

Isolated church and manse of a rural parish.

CARESTON CHURCH. Small rubble-walled kirk of 1636, remodelled in 1808 and again in 1905 by *D. Wishart Galloway*.

The C17 church was a T, the N jamb containing the laird's pew above a burial vault and facing the pulpit at the centre of the S wall. In this were placed the nave's principal windows and doors supplemented by a small window placed high in each gable; at the jamb, a large N window and a W entrance. In the alterations of 1808 the jamb, cut off by a lath-and-plaster partition, was converted to a vestry and heating chamber, the pulpit moved to the E end of the nave where the C17 window was built up and two Gothic windows inserted, the S doors were blocked and a new entrance made in the W gable which opened into a vestibule across this end of the church. In his reconstruction of 1905 Galloway made a chancel at the E end of the nave, restored the laird's pew in the jamb, rebuilt the S wall of the nave, built up the W door and formed a new window at this end, and added a NW porch joined to the jamb by a heating chamber.

The church, as remodelled in 1905, consists of a largely Edwardian nave and 'chancel', although of C17 dimensions, and a C17 jamb. On the nave's W gable, a birdcage bellcote of 1636 but the hoodmoulded two-light window below is of 1905. The S elevation is all of 1905. Lighting the nave are two pairs of depressed-arched windows; smaller 'chancel' window at the E end. On the SE corner a SUNDIAL, its inscription recording the church's remodelling in 1808. Of that date is the stone cross on the E gable. Also of 1808 the pair of quite narrow depressed-arched windows but their depth was curtailed in 1905. Between them, a smaller rectangular light in a roll-and-hollow surround is of 1636 but reopened and restored in 1905; above, a circular opening (blocked), probably inserted in 1808 to ventilate the roof-space when the church's interior was ceiled. In the S side, E of the jamb, a single chancel window of 1905.

The jamb's exterior was relatively unaffected by the C19 and C20 alterations. Finial on the N gable bearing the date 1636. In this gable, a window of three narrow lights, the stone mullions replacements of 1905, the angular pointed heads cut into a single lintel whose horizontal bead moulding is suggestive of a hoodmould. The entrance to the jamb is on the W side, a rectangular door with a roll-and-hollow moulding and surmounted by a panel bearing the impaled coats of arms and initials of Sir Alexander Carnegy of Careston and Balnamoon, builder of the church, and Dame Giles Blair, his wife. In the jamb's W inner angle with the nave, the gabled porch and heating chamber of 1905, the round-headed N entrance under a hood-mould. A second doorway, its roll-and-hollow moulding of C17 derivation, opens into the church; above, a panel commemorating the Edwardian restoration.

The church's INTERIOR is mostly of 1905, the walls of exposed rubble, both nave and jamb covered with open kingpost and scissor-truss roofs which intersect at the crossing. The opening to the laird's pew is a round-headed arch reconstructed in 1905 reusing the stones of an arch, presumably in that position, which were discovered under the floor of the church. The arch contains the early C17 front of the LAIRD'S PEW. Standing on a low stone wall this is an oak frame which consists of a pair of widely spaced barley-sugar columns supporting a long entablature, the frieze carved with arabesques of fruiting foliage, winged hearts and, at the ends, angels' heads; egg-and-dart enrichment under the cornice. – The FURNISHINGS of the nave and chancel are all of 1905, the pine pews boxy. Flanking the chancel steps, the lectern and pulpit and, in the chancel itself, choir stalls and the communion table, these all of oak in best restrained Gothic good taste. – STAINED GLASS. Strongly coloured and jewel-like. The central window at the E end (Christ the King) is of *c.* 1910, the flanking lights (the Nativity of Our Lord; the Man of Sorrows) by *Henry Holiday*, 1919–20.

MANSE to the W. Plain two-storey rubble-walled house built by *James Duirs*, mason at Laurencekirk, in 1802–3. The front was altered in 1836–7 by *James Ross* who gave it corniced two-light windows.

CARESTON CASTLE

0.5 km. S

Large rubble-built mansion house which has developed from the late C16 to the late C19, the dignified exterior hardly hinting at the exuberant heraldic display within.

The lands of Careston were acquired by Sir Henry Lindsay of Kinfauns (later, thirteenth Earl of Crawford) in the later C16, and by 1592 he had built 'the new place of Carraldstone', a substantial L-plan residence, the main block *c.* 23.2 m. by 8.8 m., the jamb *c.* 7.0 m. by 5.7 m., tenuously attached to the SW corner from which it projects to both S and W. Bowed turret in the jamb's N inner angle with the main block; semicircular stair-tower on the main block's N side. By 1612 the Lindsays were in financial difficulties and Sir Henry and his eldest son, John, disposed of Careston to Adam Rae, a merchant burgess of Edinburgh. After passing through various hands the estate was acquired in 1623 by Sir Henry Lindsay's nephew, Alexander Lindsay, second Lord Spynie, who carried out some internal alterations to the house before selling the property four years later. About 1630 it was bought by Sir Alexander Carnegy of Balnamoon who seems to have further remodelled the interior soon after. Sir Alexander's grandson, James Carnegy of Balnamoon, was probably responsible for a recasting of the house *c.* 1700 when the S front was made a symmetrical U by the addition of a SE wing to balance the SW and the interior again altered. In 1707 James Carnegy's son, Alexander, sold Careston to John Stewart of Grandtully who seven years later added a swaggering coat of arms to the front. However, in 1720 the Stewarts sold the estate to Major George Skene of that Ilk and it was held by his descendants until 1871. The principal alteration to the house during the period of Skene ownership was the addition, *c.* 1790, of a grandiose stair-hall at the rear and the embellishment of the C16 N corner turrets and stair-tower in Georgian Gothic style. Further additions at the back and a loggia across the front of the main block were built *c.* 1880 after the house's acquisition by John Adamson, an entrepeneur and owner of the Erichtside Linen Works at Blairgowrie.

The U-plan principal front faces S and, despite the different stages of its development, appears surprisingly unified. Four-storey main block of five bays, the top floor's windows rising through the eaves to pilastered and pedimented wooden dormerheads, mid-C19 replacements for C17 stone pediments. The first- and second-floor windows are all set in rusticated surrounds of *c.* 1700; above the first floor's central opening the huge coat of arms of the Stewarts of Grandtully under the date 1714, presumably that of its erection. Fairly small windows to the ground floor, perhaps of the mid C17; the plain central entrance may be an C18 insertion. In front of the ground floor, a late C19 loggia, its elliptical-headed arches carried on sturdy columns. Protruding from the ends of the main block are the wings, the SW late C16, the SW of *c.* 1700 but both of now identical appearance; presumably the SW was remodelled when the SE was built. Each is of four storeys, its wall-head above that of the main block but the roof ridge at the same height. In the inner side wall of each, a plain door and window at the ground floor, the door covered by the loggia, the window the lowest of a tier, the SW wing's top-floor openings blind. At each wing, a two-bay front gable; in its head, a pedimental arrangement of three circular lights. Blocked openings in the W side of the SW wing, its second-floor window's rusticated surround of the same design as those to the front windows of the main block, the third-floor window framed by pilasters which seem to have supported a pediment above the wall-head. At the back of the SE wing and filling its N inner angle with the main block, a simply detailed piend-roofed two-storey jamb. A lean-to C19 extension in the inner angle of the SW wing and main block hides the corbelled base of a late C16 stair-turret. This is pierced just above second-floor level by a window of *c.* 1700 and, above this, an earlier opening whose rope-moulded surround returns at lintel level round the turret and is carried under the jettied walling of the top stage. The turret's original roof, probably of conical form, was replaced *c.* 1790 by a flat one surrounded by an unconvincingly martial tall-merloned battlement. The upper windows of the main block's gables are unencumbered by the house's late C19 additions. The second floor's are of *c.* 1700, the third floor's in pedimented aedicular surrounds, probably of the earlier C17. The gables' heads, the W crowstepped, are pierced by round windows under quatrefoil panels, embellishments of *c.* 1790. So also are the quatrefoil-panelled top stages of the N corner turrets whose 'battlements' are similar to those of the W stair-turret but carried on moulded corbels. A similar top stage now crowns the top of the C16 stair-tower which pokes up above the late C18 and C19 rear additions.

INTERIOR. The house's principal entrance until the C18 was in the E side of the SW wing. This opens onto the foot of the stair which occupies that wing's bottom stage. A tunnel-vaulted passage runs from this stair along the S side of the main block. On the passage's N side, a pair of tunnel-vaulted stores, the W formerly with a stair to the first floor in the thickness of its W wall and presumably the house's wine cellar. A third cellar, in the centre of the house, has been altered to form a passage from the main block's C18 front entrance to the stair-hall of *c.* 1790 behind. In the stair-hall, an imperial stair. The E end of the ground floor of the main block contains the late C16 kitchen, also tunnel-vaulted. Off the kitchen's NW corner, a late C16 turnpike stair in the N stair-tower.

The SW wing's principal stair leads to the first floor. It is scale-and-platt, the risers with simple mouldings. On the stone newel's corner faces are rope mouldings, the E corner's with a human head carved at the top. Over the first-floor landing, a single course of continuous corbelling which carries a stilted semicircular tunnel vault. At the landing's N end, a pair of doors, the l. to the turnpike stair in the turret in the NW wing's inner angle with the main block. Over the doors is carved a large oval panel set in a border of drapery and with figures of male and female trumpeters at the base. The oval contains a central circular shield displaying the Carnegy coat of arms. Round this shield are eight others, the l. group displaying the coat of arms of the mid-C17 owner of Careston, John Carnegy of Balnamoon, surmounted by those of his mother and grandmothers, the r. those of John Carnegy's wife, Helen Ogilvy, under those of her mother and grandmothers. The r. door opens into an ante-room formed probably *c.* 1700 from the SW corner of the house's C16 Hall; to its N was a small room, now subdivided to provide a passage to the house's late C19 NW extension and a store. E of the ante-room is the DRAWING ROOM (the mid-C17 outer chamber and dining room of *c.* 1700) formed in the E two-thirds of the C16 Hall. On the walls, high-quality wooden panelling of *c.* 1700 under a broad mutuled cornice; similar cornices to the doorcases. At the room's E end, a huge stone chimneypiece, perhaps erected by Alexander, Lord Spynie, in 1623 or soon after, its design, like those of all the house's remarkable array of chimneypieces of the earlier C17, derived from engravings published in the second volume of Jacques Androuet du Cerceau the elder's

Livre d'architecture of 1561.* The frieze under its bold cornice is ornamented with a sort of egg-and-dart moulding; pedestals flank the jambs. The fireplace opening was contracted *c.* 1700 and given an inner chimneypiece in the same style as the room's doorcases. Above, a massive overmantel, also of stone and elaborately carved. At the bottom corners are sphinxes, each ridden by a naked boy who holds aloft with one hand a tall trophy-bedecked spear. Pedestals on the heads of the sphinxes support large upstanding female nudes, each covering her *pudenda* with one hand whilst the other holds one end of a fruiting swag whose inner end is supported by one horn of a satyr's head at the centre of the frieze. Below this head, an oval panel carved in high relief with the Royal Arms of Scotland. Below, a strapwork-surrounded panel inscribed

THIS.HONORIS.SINGE.
AND.FIGVRIT.TROPHE.BOR·
SVLD.PVSE.ASPYRING.SPRE
ITS.AND.MARTIAL.MYND
TO.TRVST.YAIR.FORTVNE
FWRTH.&.IN.HIR.SCORN
BELEIVE.IN.FAITHE.
OVR.FAIT.GOD.HE S.ASSINGD

To the E is the DINING ROOM (the C16 and early C17 inner chamber and drawing room of *c.* 1700). The main entrance is at the S end of the drawing room's E wall. This opens onto a square alcove covered with a stone groin-vault whose ribs meet at a central pendant. This work seems to be early C17, probably of 1623, the date on an aumbry in the alcove's SW corner. Over the door from the drawing room has been placed the stone head of a dormer window's pediment, probably originally on the S front of the house, the tympanum carved in high relief with a pair of reclining figures. On the walls of the main part of the dining room, panelling of *c.* 1700. At the W wall, a stone chimneypiece, perhaps of 1623. At the jambs, stolid-looking satyrs stand to attention, each balancing on his head a scroll which supports one end of the cornice. As in the drawing room, the fireplace opening has been contracted *c.* 1700 and a second chimneypiece introduced, its frieze carved with delicate foliage, its cornice with egg-and-dart enrichment. Above the early C17 chimneypiece's cornice, a frieze bearing Jacobean enrichment and surmounted by a second cornice which serves as a base to the overmantel. This is carved in high relief. At each end a naked man stands between two large jars from which issue intertwined snakes. Above, a frieze adorned with rope-moulded roundels. In the centre of the overmantel, a strapwork-framed panel carved with the coronet-topped coat of arms of the Ogilvys, Earls of Airlie. It is of a greyer stone

* As first pointed out by Professor Ian Campbell.

than the rest and probably replaced some other coat of arms. Presumably it was erected after 1642 when John Carnegy, second of Balnamoon, married Helen Ogilvy, daughter of James, first Earl of Airlie, and perhaps after 1657 when he succeeded his father and before his own death in 1662.

The rooms on the floor above were partly remodelled *c.* 1700. In the SW wing, a bedroom whose coved ceiling is painted with the depiction of a sunburst. The W room in the main block also has a coved ceiling; panelling on the N wall, dadoes at the others whose plasterwork was probably intended to be covered with tapestries. The stone chimneypiece at the N was apparently introduced by Sir Alexander Carnegy of Balnamoon and may date from *c.* 1640. At the jambs are columns with splayed bases and capitals carved with stylized foliage; they support scrolls under the cornice. As elsewhere in the house the fireplace opening was contracted *c.* 1700 and given an inner chimneypiece with a pulvinated frieze and dentilated cornice. The original overmantel survives intact. Double-lugged central panel with figures of full-length angels at the sides and human heads at top and bottom. Inside the panel, figures of sportive boys around a bay-leaf roundel which encloses the strapwork-framed circular coat of arms of Blair of Balthayock (for Giles Blair, wife of Sir Alexander Carnegy). The main block's centre room (subdivided) has also been fitted up with a dado, the walls above intended for tapestries; the door is dated 1702. In the present corridor carved out of the room's N end, another stone chimneypiece of *c.* 1640, the jambs' columns with fleur-de-lis capitals, the fireplace opening contracted *c.* 1700 and given a surround like that in the W room. High overmantel carved in relief with a pair of full-frontal three-quarter-length figures of a man and woman, naked except for aprons of fig-leaves (so probably representing Adam and Eve), and standing on pedestals. In the centre, an armorial panel whose first and third quarters display the coat of arms of Blair of Balthayock. Consoles on the frieze above. In the room to the E, another stone chimneypiece of *c.* 1640, the jambs' columns with foliaged capitals, the fireplace opening contracted *c.* 1700 in familiar fashion. At the ends of the overmantel are figures of sidewards-facing gentlemen and forward-looking ladies, all in C17 dress. The grey stone central panel is probably a replacement of the later C17 and bears the coat of arms of Ruthven of Gowrie, probably in allusion to Jean Ruthven, grandmother of Helen Ogilvy, wife of John Carnegy, second of Balnamoon.

Behind the mansion house, a late C17 GATEWAY, the ashlar piers of banded masonry and joined by a wrought-iron overthrow. Extending from the gatepiers are screen walls pierced by shot-holes. These link to a pair of piend-roofed PAVILIONS, probably C18, the E a former coachhouse, the W stables. – Crowstep-gabled lectern DOOCOT beside the N drive, 0.35 km. NE of the mansion house. Pair of high-set windows (later insertions) in the front wall. These flank the central doorway, its lintel bearing the date 1672, which has been surmounted by an armorial panel. – At the end of the drive, the NORTH LODGE of *c.* 1800, a small single-storey half-octagon. Pedimented front (N) gable containing a large Venetian dummy window. – SOUTH GATES of *c.* 1830 at the end of the S drive, formerly at Stracathro House (q.v.) and re-erected here in 1957. Four panelled ashlar gatepiers, the taller inner pair with vase finials; wrought-iron gates.

5040

CARMYLLIE

Church and former manse by themselves looking over open fields to the S.

CARMYLLIE PARISH CHURCH. T-plan kirk, the cross-bar's E and W ends of *c.* 1609 when the parish of Carmyllie was formed, the taller tail, its S end bisecting the cross-bar, a replacement by *Maclaren & Aitken*, 1873–4, for an 'aisle' constructed in 1836.

The early C17 cross-bar is an ashlar-faced oblong. In the S side of its W part are blocked openings – a rectangular window and, to its W, an elliptical-arched window above a roll-and-hollow-moulded door surround; to its l., the moulded surround of a rectangular window. On the W gable, a birdcage bellcote, its corners with ball finials, the pyramidal roof with a scrolled finial topped by a weathercock. In the gable, a stone bearing a shield set between the initials of Mr Alexander Ochterlony, minister of Carmyllie from 1666 to 1683, and his wife, Helen Mudie. The gable's three-light Gothic window was inserted in 1902, a replica of the E gable's window of 1874. In this W part's N side, a blocked C17 or C18 window. At the E gable, a pair of C17 skewputts carved with human faces. Evidence of a blocked door and former porch at this end but now the only opening is the 1870s window.

The S tail of 1873–4 is a large but routinely detailed buttressed Gothic interloper, its walling of stugged ashlar. In the S gable, a plate-traceried rose window above a metal sundial.

Inside, utilitarian braced roofs over the cross-bar, a collar-braced roof over the tail. Victorian N gallery over the N vestibule. This faces the Jacobean-Gothic PULPIT of 1874 at the centre of the S wall. In front, a COMMUNION TABLE of 1951. – On the S wall, a fragment of WOODWORK from the C17 pew of the Ouchterlonys of The Guynd. Under a cornice, the heads of four round-arched compartments and the initials IO and KM (for John Ouchterlony and Katherine Maule, his wife) flanking the date 1657. – Late C19 two-manual ORGAN installed here in 1953.

STAINED GLASS. Flanking the pulpit, a pair of lushly coloured windows (Ruth and Boaz; St Paul) by *Stephen Adam*, 1907–8. – In the rose window over the pulpit, a depiction of Our Lord as the Good Shepherd, by *Stephen Adam & Son*, 1902. – In the cross-bar's E window, a strongly coloured panel (St Columba) by *Horatio John Greensmith*, *c.* 1935. – In the N 'aisle's' W side, a window (St Andrew) of 1900, realistic but wooden. – In the E side of the 'aisle', a window erected in 1991 which incorporates imported glass of *c.* 1900 (the Holy Family).

GRAVEYARD. SE of the church a few C18 HEADSTONES, one displaying the crowned hammer of the smiths. Another, of 1788, was erected by James Mitchel to commemorate his wife and son, the top of its W face carved in relief with a woman holding a baby in her arms and flanked by angelic trumpeters. – Immediately S of the centre of the church's S side, the large headstone of 1810 to James Kyd and his wife, Marion Dall, the E face with the relief of a plough. – To its W, the headstone erected in 1805 for David Kyd and Agnes Morgan, his wife. On the E face, reliefs of a plough, sock and coulter, and swingletrees. Inscription:

Let Marble Monuments record
Their fame who distant land explore
This humble stone points out the place
Where Sleeps a virtuous ancient race
Their Sire possessed ye neighbouring plain
Before Columbus Crossed the main
And tho' ye world may deem it strange
His son contented seeks no change
Convinc'd wherever man may roam
He travels only to the Tomb

Harled two-storey former manse (CARMYLLIE HOUSE) to the E. Built in 1820 and quite plain. Front of three bays, a full-height bay window added at the l. later in the C19. – BEE-BOLLS, probably of the early C19, in the garden wall to the E.

THE GUYND. *See* p. 518.

CARNOUSTIE

5030

Small burgh which began *c.* 1810 as a planned gridiron village laid out on lands recently acquired by George Kinloch (his name perpetuated in Kinloch Street). The railway arrived in 1838 but expansion and a measure of prosperity came in the second half of the C19 with the opening of linen mills and the development of the links beside the shore for golf, a sport for which the town is still well known. Carnoustie acquired the status of a police burgh in 1889.

CHURCHES

CARNOUSTIE PANBRIDE CHURCH, Arbroath Road. Originally Panbride Free Church, it was built in 1854–5 to a design by

James Maclaren, repaired by *James P. Bruce* of *John Bruce & Son* in 1887–8 after a fire, and enlarged by Bruce, 1901, all the work in an unexciting Gothic style. The church built in the 1850s was cruciform and with a SW tower. Front to the W where the gable contains a pair of very tall lancet windows; above, a relief of the Free Church of Scotland's emblem of the Burning Bush surmounted by a gableted canopy. Tower of two stages, the lower containg the hoodmoulded entrance. The upper stage is a tall octagonal belfry. In alternate faces, pointed and cusped openings and quatrefoil panels. At the E gable, two tall lancets and, near the apex, a small lancet.

Bruce's enlargement of 1901 involved the extension of the original S transept to form a new nave with an aisle on its W side. The clearstorey windows of this nave's W side and the upper windows of its E side rise into gablets. At the SE corner, a bowed projection containing a stair to the gallery. In the S gable, the new main entrance, the hoodmoulds of its door and flanking windows linked by a string course. Above, a three-light window, the arcs of the mullions of the centre light intersecting at the head. In the apex of the gable, a small window of three pointed lights. At the N end of the church, additions of 1882 and 1932 (by *Bruce, Son & Morton*).

The interior is mostly of 1901. Ceiling with pendants hanging from its wooden ribs. S gallery. Communion table at the N end. – STAINED GLASS. In the W transept, one light (St Matthew) of 1897. – In the E transept, one light (Ruth and Boaz) by *Stephen Adam*, 1908. – Another window (the Virgin and Child) is of 1937 in the manner of Douglas Strachan with blues and purples dominating. – In the N gable, two lights (the Good Shepherd; Hope as an anchor of the Soul) of *c.* 1895.

CARNOUSTIE PARISH CHURCH, Dundee Street. Thrifty Early Christian by *P. Macgregor Chalmers*, 1900–2, built of stugged Carmyllie masonry, its khaki colour made no more appealing by being badly weathered and patched with cement. Nave with clearstorey windows above the roof of the W aisle. The E aisle is taller, of two storeys and covered by a continuation of the nave roof. Transeptal N block containing the chancel with an organ chamber on the W and a chapel on the E. SE tower disappointingly finished with a flat roof instead of the intended spire. Except at the S (entrance) front and the tower, the detail is of the simplest with splayed surrounds to the small round-arched windows. The S front is economical but bolder. At the nave gable, three broad sloping-topped buttresses, the central buttress surmounted by a canopied image niche, its pedestal unfinished and without a statue. Two tall round-arched windows, their nook-shafts without capitals. At the tower, a double entrance, its round-arched doorways framed by simple moulded arches which spring from a central attached column and responds. At the second stage, above a sloping offset, tall and narrow round-arched windows, their nook-shafts with cushion capitals. Small round-arched openings above.

Inside, the walling is of grey stugged masonry, the open wooden roofs of kingpost-truss construction. Nave of five bays, the S bay separated from the tower vestibule on the E and the end bay of the W aisle by walls pierced with round-arched entrances. At the other four bays, arcades with unmoulded round-headed arches carried on cushion-capitalled columns, the capital of the N column of the E arcade decorated with light fluting. But the arcades do not correspond to each other, the arcade into the W aisle being low, that into the E tall to allow for a gallery. The lack of balance is less disconcerting than expected because of the strength of the visual thrust towards the two-bay chancel. This, narrower than the nave, is entered through a tall round-headed arch, the capitals of its responds with simply carved cushion capitals. On each side of the chancel's S bay (the choir), a plain round-headed arch, the W containing the organ, the E opening into a side chapel whose S entrance from the aisle is through a pair of round-headed arches which share a central column with a massive square capital but die into the walls at their outer ends. The chancel's E bay (the sanctuary) is marked off by attached columns. High up on the chancel walls, panels carved with eucharistic texts.

FURNISHINGS. In the E aisle, GALLERY FRONTS panelled in a simple Arts and Crafts manner. – Boxy oak PEWS. – On the W side of the chancel arch, an oak PULPIT on a stone base. The pulpit is decorated with Romanesque arcading and a floriated cross, its shaft flanked by emblems of the Apostles. Under the cornice of the pulpit, Neo-Romanesque corbels and, at the corners, angels' heads. – Octagonal stone FONT with a round-arched panel on each face. – In the chancel, oak CHOIR STALLS, quite simple except for little panels carved with interlacing. – In the sanctuary and raised by a few steps, the COMMUNION TABLE, again of oak and panelled with Romanesque arcading containing reliefs of angels, vines and a cross on an interlaced background. – Behind the communion table, simple Gothic oak PANELLING introduced in 1930. – ORGAN by *H. S. Vincent*, 1902; rebuilt by *John Lightbown*, 1989.

STAINED GLASS. In the roundel high up in the N wall of the sanctuary, a bitty design (the Maries at the Empty Tomb) by *Alexander Strachan*, 1930–1. – Under the gallery of the E aisle, the two-light N window (Our Lord healing the sick) is of 1912, accomplished in pale colours. – More garish is the adjoining window, also of two lights (Our Lord and a disciple; St Ninian and St Columba) by *The Abbey Studio*, 1953. – To the S, one light (Our Lord with women) of the mid C20. – The two tall lights of the S window of the nave (Our Lord Washing the Disciples' Feet, the Agony in the Garden and the Ascension; Our Lord and the Centurion, the Valley of the Shadow of Death, and the taking up of Elijah) are by *Margaret Chilton* and *Marjorie Kemp*, 1923, unusually powerful for those artists. – In the W aisle, three lights (Ruth; St Luke; Our Lord and a boy) of 1956–8, all by *Douglas Hamilton*.

CARNOUSTIE UNITED PRESBYTERIAN CHURCH, Dundee Street. Now a bar. By *Robert Baldie*, 1872–3. Tall buttressed and lanceted box. The effect of the front gable's division by buttresses into a 'nave and aisles' is now obscured by a two-storey C20 addition and the bellcote has been removed.

CHURCH OF THE HOLY ROOD (Episcopal), Maule Street. Unfussy Gothic, by *Alexander Ross*, 1880–1, the chancel (intended from the start) added by *Ross & Macbeth* in 1893–4. Walling of stugged Carmyllie stone, the roofs covered with green Cumberland slates. Angle-buttressed nave and chancel. In their side walls the windows are each of two cusped lights. E and W windows of three stepped lights with circled heads. Transeptal vestry on the N side of the chancel. On the S side of the nave, a porch with heavy clasping buttresses. Entrance arch springing from columns with big foliaged capitals; in the arch-head, a blind stone quatrefoil. At the SW corner of the nave, a round tower with pointed belfry openings and a tall conical slated roof, a free quotation from Brechin Cathedral.

Inside, walls of stugged Arbroath stone; braced kingpost roof. Pointed stone chancel arch (formerly containing a wrought-iron and brass screen). – Octagonal PULPIT of Caen stone with marble columns at the corners. It is of 1895. – Low oak CHOIR STALLS of 1938. – The Gothic REREDOS, introduced in 1906, is of oak with touches of gilding. Carved emblems in its panels were removed in 1939 when the ogee-arched centre compartment was painted by *James Bell* with a scene of Our Lord and the Disciples on the Road to Emmaus. – ORGAN By *John R. Miller*.

STAINED GLASS. The three-light E window (the Crucifixion with Our Lady and St John) is of 1895. – In the S wall of the nave, the window at the E end (St Peter and St Paul) is of *c.* 1900. – Then a window (Angels of Paradise) by *Morris & Co.*, 1906, from a design by *Edward Burne-Jones* prepared in 1881. – To its W, a two-light window (scenes from nature) by *Patrick Ross-Smith*, *c.* 1990. – Two of the windows in the N aisle are filled with stained glass. The E (the Archangels Michael and Gabriel) is by *John Duncan*, 1937, mosaic-like and clearly drawn. The other (Angels) is of *c.* 1930 and well-coloured. – Main W window (Adoration of the Magi) of 1924–5 by *Morris & Co.*, adapting a design by Burne-Jones.

ERSKINE UNITED FREE CHURCH, Kinloch Street. At the S, the stone-walled Secession Church built in 1810 and looking like a cottage. It is incorporated in a large hall extension of 1990. This is couthy with drydashed walls, slated roofs and a small turret-like pyramid-roofed cupola with a cross-and-dove weathervane.

Former ST ANNE (R.C.), Dundee Street. Built in 1927–8 and now housing. Small, of hammer-dressed ashlar, the windows round-arched. Nave with shallow buttresses and a SW porch; one-bay chancel.

ST ANNE (R.C.), Thomas Street. By *James F. Stephen*, 2000. Large and harled, a nave and aisles under shallow-pitched and broad-eaved metal roofs, the S gable, clad in the same metal sheeting, rising above and behind a long low vestibule.

ST BRIDE'S HALL, Maule Street and Carlogie Road. A former mission church, by *James Maclaren & Sons*, 1900–1. Sturdy plain Gothic, built of stugged coursed masonry, the broad-eaved roof covered with green Vermont (USA) slates and with a red-tiled ridge. Nave and N aisle under a single roof; NW porch. Lower chancel at the E end with, on its N side, a vestry and a blocky gabled 'bellcote'.

PUBLIC BUILDINGS

BURNSIDE PRIMARY SCHOOL, Thomas Street. By *Mackie Ramsay Taylor*, 2007–8. Large and informally composed, of two storeys, the walls of yellow render, reconstituted red stone and timber cladding, the shallow-pitched roofs of ribbed metal.

CALEDONIA GOLF CLUB, Links Parade. Built in 1889 and extended W in 1891–2. Low single-storey clubhouse. U-plan front with bargeboarded gables at the advanced ends and, across the centre, a veranda which rises into two bargeboarded gables. At the NW corner, the purposeful low square tower added in 1891–2, a conical-roofed round caphouse on its NW corner. C20 W addition.

CARNOUSTIE ACCESS OFFICE, High Street. Originally Municipal Buildings. By *John Bruce & Son*, 1897. Free Jacobean Renaissance. Bowed quadrant corner under a fish-scale-slated dome; over the entrance a stone balcony supported on heavy unmoulded consoles.

CARNOUSTIE HIGH SCHOOL, Shanwell Road. Curtain-walled, by *jmarchitects*, 2007–9. Assemblage of three-storey rendered boxes in a Modern Movement manner eschewing Postmodern tricks.

CARNOUSTIE LEISURE CENTRE, Links Parade. The W part (originally a concert hall) is by *Allan & Friskin*, 1934. Unelaborate Art Deco; harled with cement dressings. E extension of 1992, shedlike despite a few Postmodern touches.

CARNOUSTIE YACHTING AND RUGBY CLUB, Links Parade. Begun in the early C20. Harled pavilion, its veranda's cast-iron columns with decorative spandrels. Later additions include a diminutive clock tower.

In front of the club, a round FOUNTAIN erected in 1906. Urn-topped red granite pedestal surrounded by a peristyle of grey granite columns.

PANMURE COMMUNITY CENTRE. *See* Description, PANMURE WORKS, below.

PHILIP HALL, Dundee Street. The hall of Carnoustie Parish Church (*see* Churches, above), by *Bruce, Son & Morton*, 1927. Single-storey L-plan, harled with cement dressings, the round-headed windows giving it the look of a diminutive Georgian kirk.

ST BRIDE'S HALL. *See* Churches, above.

95 WAR MEMORIAL, Dundee Street. By *Bruce, Son & Morton*, 1925. Curved ashlar screen wall. At its ends, piers with wreaths carved on their fronts. At the centre, a pedestal on which stands a large stone statue by *Thomas Beattie* depicting a soldier of the Black Watch with bowed head and one hand holding a bonnet and rifle, the other placing a wreath on a cross.

DESCRIPTION

BARRY ROAD, the entry from the W, is bordered by large late C20 housing developments. At its end the approach of the older core of the burgh is signalled by late C19 terraced cottages. Then the road jinks l. to join the top end of BROWN STREET whose E side is filled by the mid-C19 CORNER HOTEL, trim in white harling with black-painted margins, the corner to Dundee Street gently bowed.

DUNDEE STREET starts off with plain Late Victorian cottages, the only touch of frivolity provided by the bargeboards of the STAG'S HEAD BAR. Further E, the former St Anne's (R.C.) Church, the former Carnoustie United Presbyterian Church and Carnoustie Parish Church on the N side and Philip Hall on the S (for these, *see* Churches and Public Buildings, above). Then, on the N, some seaside fun at the late C19 Nos. 46–52 whose first-floor windows enjoy big cast-iron balconies and anthemion friezes; a conical-roofed turret at the SE corner. The ensuing late C19 single-storey-and-attic terraced cottage-villas have canted bay windows and bargeboarded dormers but their character is determinedly sober. The scale then rises to two storeys and housing gives way to Late Victorian commercial buildings, but the character quickly changes again on the N side at the former POLICE STATION (Nos. 126–128). This is a mid-C19 broad-eaved double house, the l. part two-storey and gable-fronted with a consoled stone canopy over the first-floor window (the ground-floor window may once have had a canopy too) and a slated canopy on wooden consoles over the door, the r. part single-storey. Immediately to the E, a municipal garden containing the war memorial (*see* Public Buildings, above), followed by C19 and C20 commercial buildings. On the corner with Queen Street, a block (No. 108) by *David Fraser*, 1899. At its canted corner, an oriel window which is carried up as an octagonal turret, its fish-scale-slated ogee dome topped by a weathervane.

PARK AVENUE is a diversion to the S from which a footbridge over the railway gives access to LINKS PARADE which contains an assembly of the Carnoustie Leisure Centre and sports clubs (*see* Public Buildings, above). Among them is BRUCE COURT, a former hotel (now housing) by *David Fraser*, 1891, looking like a tall and thriftily detailed broad-eaved villa; fairly tactful late C20 W extension. To its E, DALHOUSIE COURT, a large harled blocks of flats of 2005, generally traditional in manner but with glazed corners and balconies in a not very successful attempt to add interest. Immediately E of the Caledonian Golf

Club is SIMPSON'S GOLF SHOP of 1883, a piend-roofed red brick pavilion with a domed octagonal jamb at the SW corner. On the S side of Links Parade, the CARNOUSTIE GOLF HOTEL, by *Wellwood Leslie*, 1999, a very large three-storey harled presence, traditional in manner but without flair or wit.

HIGH STREET continues the generally commercial character of the E end of Dundee Street. The YOUNG MEN'S CHRISTIAN ASSOCIATION at No. 94 is by *C. & L. Ower*, 1881, with Flemish Gothic touches. Further E, on the S side, the 'Tyrolean'-finish rendered former FAIRWAY GARAGE by *Bruce, Son & Morton*, 1925, its tall ground floor builder's *moderne*, the upper storey cottage-domestic. Opposite, Nos. 46–48, a tall red sandstone villa of *c.* 1870, with a two-storey canted bay window scooped up to the square under the eaves; fretted bargeboards. The blocky Jacobean building (Nos. 30–32) on the W corner of Lochty Street is by *James P. Bruce*, 1901. Canted corner with a two-storey oriel rising above the broad eaves as a low turret under a flattened ogee dome topped by an Art Nouveauesque finial. Across Lochty Street, the Carnoustie Access Office (*see* Public Buildings, above). Near the E end of High Street's N side, the mid-Victorian former CLYDESDALE BANK (No. 2B). Heavy villa style, the round-arched ground-floor windows giving something of an Italianate look.

DALHOUSIE STREET is a diversion to the N. On its NE corner with WILLIAM STREET, the red sandstone PARKLANDS (No. 1 William Street) by *James P. Bruce*, 1900. Symmetrical free Queen Anne, the end bays slightly advanced under pediments pierced by foliage-framed oculi and with single-storey canted bay windows; modillioned wall-head cornice. On the corner with Maule Street, No. 16 Dalhousie Street is an Arts and Crafts villa of generally English inspiration, by *Swanston & Legge*, 1897. Ground floor of hammer-dressed grey stone, the porch of red brick with fluted wooden piers. Harled upper floor with half-timbering in the gables. Jettied out over a canted bay window is a rectangular gabled projection. Voyseyish battered chimneys. To the W in MAULE STREET, the Church of the Holy Rood (Episcopal), for which, *see* Churches, above. Beside it, its 1880s RECTORY, quite pretty small-scale parsonical Gothic.

CHURCH STREET continues the line of High Street to the E. On its N side, the gardens of C19 villas whose fronts are to William Street; on the S side, some plain C19 low housing. At the E end of Church Street, on its N corner with CARLOGIE ROAD, EARLSTON COURT, a weirdly detailed broad-eaved housing development by the *Brunton Voigt Partnership*, 1995, the single-columned porticoes in the inner angles of its sawtoothed front especially disconcerting. It is a powerful argument for a rediscovery of the principles of the Modern Movement. Higher up Carlogie Road is St Bride's Hall (*see* Churches, above). At the S end of Carlogie Road, on the corner with Ireland Street, Nos. 1–3, a double villa of the later C19. Hoodmoulds over the outer ground-floor windows, consoled canopies over the doors; bargeboards with bold foliage carving.

PANMURE WORKS, Kinloch Street and Panmure Street. Surviving parts of a former power-loom factory for the manufacture of linen. The two-storey calender shop at the S is of 1857 to a design by *Robertson & Orchar*. Twenty-one-bay S front, the windows segmental-arched. Rusticated quoins at the end corners and at the corners of the slightly advanced three-bay centrepiece which is topped by a pedimented pedestal flanked by scrolls and vases. More vases on the gables. At the N, fronting Kinloch Street, a parapeted office block (now PANMURE COMMUNITY CENTRE) added in 1864–5. Two tall storeys, with round-arched first-floor windows and an Italianate tower.

4050

CARSE GRAY

1.9 km. N of Lunanhead

Unpretentious harled and crowstep-gabled laird's house, the product of several stages of development, all given some semblance of unity by a reconstruction carried out in 1854 when the house's chimneys were rebuilt in panelled and corniced form and topped by diagonally set stacks.

The building forms a fairly regular U, the courtyard open to the S. The earliest part is the E range, perhaps dating from soon after 1598 when the lands of Carse, formerly the property of the Archbishops of St Andrews, were granted to William Rynd of Carse, probably the former tenant of the estate. This is oblong except for a stair-tower projecting from near the S end of the W front, the N and S walling of its upper floor jettied out; at the foot of the stair-tower's N face, the C16 or C17 entrance, its rounded jambs, composed of several blocks of stone and with prominent pointing, perhaps renewed in the 1850s, as seem to have been the similarly treated windows of this range's W front. The openings in the S gable and E side are probably all of 1854, a couple at the E of two lights.

The N range of the house is double pile. The S block, facing the courtyard, probably incorporates C16 or C17 work, perhaps including a kitchen, but the appearance is largely mid-C18, apparently as remodelled by Captain Charles Gray who acquired the estate in 1741. The slightly lower but longer N block is probably all of 1854. At the S end of the S block's front, an unusually broad doorway, its rounded jambs perhaps C16 or C17 work but renewed in the mid C19. Flanking the doorway, a pair of small windows, also probably of the C16 or C17, and, above, a panel carved, probably in 1854, with the Gray coat of arms. The other S windows are all of Georgian character, those of the first floor very tall. The back block's N elevation, a very large porch below its tall stair window removed in the late C20, is now quite plain. Two-light first floor windows in the gables. The house's W range, also two-storey but a little lower than the main E and N ranges, seems all to be of 1854, Georgian survival in manner. In the inner angle with the N range, a full-height outshot containing an entrance and, to its S, a battlemented single-storey small addition, perhaps of the early C20.

The interior was comprehensively remodelled in the mid C19 and some further alterations made in the C20. Of C16 or C17 work the only substantial survivor is the stone turnpike stair in the E range's stair-tower. This range's original first-floor hall became a billiard room in the 1850s when the principal room of the N range's S block was the drawing room and the room in the Victorian block behind the dining room, both these subdivided in the C20.

In woodland NE of the house, a tall square and piend-roofed WATER TOWER of the mid or later C19. – N of the house, a crowstep-gabled STABLES COURTYARD of *c.* 1860. – At the E end of the drive, a picturesque single-storey bargeboarded LODGE dated 1863, and contemporary urn-topped GATEPIERS.

CLAYPOTTS CASTLE *see* BROUGHTY FERRY

CLOVA

3070

Church and hotel standing in Glen Clova.

CLOVA CHURCH. Built in 1728 but completely remodelled in 1855 by *Davidson*, wright in Kirriemuir, who shortened the building and heightened the walls by 0.9 m. It is a humble oblong, built of whinstone with dressings of stugged red sandstone. Birdcage bellcote on the E gable. At the W end, a C20 wooden porch.

Equally unpretentious interior. ENCAUSTIC TILES in the central aisle and sanctuary and boxy PEWS, all probably of 1855. – Quite elaborate red sandstone Gothic FONT of 1896. – STAINED GLASS E window (the Lamb of God) of 1968.

GLEN CLOVA HOTEL. Late C19, white-harled, with bargeboards to the gables. Large monkey-puzzle tree in front. – To the W, a mid-C19 single-storey rubble-built MILL, a water wheel at the E gable.

ROTTAL LODGE, 5.5 km. SE. White-harled two-storey shooting lodge. Originally mid-C19, the S façade of three bays, but given a bow-fronted extension at each end in 1911 and 1936.

COLLISTON

6040

Small L-plan village, mostly of the C19, the two-storey three-bay fronted COLLISTON INN a presence on the S approach. The church presiding over the T-junction at the N end.

COLLISTON PARISH CHURCH. Angle-buttressed cross, the E end minimally projecting. The nave was designed by *James*

Maclaren and built in 1870–1, the broad transepts and E gable added in the same manner by *Maclaren & Aitken*, 1876. Simple Gothic, the masonry of squared red sandstone. Bellcote on the W gable whose window is a stepped arrangement of three cusped and pointed lights under quatrefoils. The nave's side walls and the gables of the transepts are pierced by pairs of cusped lights under circular openings, also cusped. Single lights in the transepts' side walls. Gabled porch at the W end of the nave's S side. In the W side of the S transept, a doorway with a shouldered arch, an insertion of *c.* 2000 to provide disabled access.

MANSE (now The Beeches) of *c.* 1875 to the W. Also of red sandstone, two-storeyed and Neo-Jacobean.

COLLISTON CASTLE

1.5 km. NE

C16 laird's house of marked but modest pretension, altered in the C17 and C18 and again in the late C19 when a large addition was built.

In 1545 Cardinal David Beaton, Archbishop of St Andrews, granted the lands of Colliston in feu ferme to John Guthrie and Isobel Ogilvy, his wife. The harled main part of the present house may have been built at the time but a date later in the C16 is more probable, perhaps 1583 as borne on a stone now on a stair-turret. It is Z-plan with towers at the NW and SE corners. Crowstep-gabled main block of three storeys and an attic. At the ground floor of its S front, three oval gunloops, the r. under a slit window, all these C16. The ground floor's two comfortably sized windows have been inserted, the l. perhaps in the C18, the centre opening formed in 1893 when a C17 or early C18 door in this position was built up. Above the l. window has been placed, probably in 1893, a weathered dormerhead, probably originally from the house but which had been built into the walls of a neighbouring farm steading. Its arched head is ornamented with scrolls rising from human figures at the bottom corners; at the centre of the head, a figure of Diana, symbolic of Chastity. Over the centre window, the curly-headed stone which had surmounted the door in this position before 1893. Its central panel is carved with the Royal Arms of James VI flanked by small panels bearing the motto LAVS DEO under the date 1621 and the initials of Henry Guthrie, fourth of Colliston, and Jean Lindsay, his wife. To the r., more early C17 carved stones, probably originally from the house but which had also been built into a farm steading. One is a lintel, now topped by a couple of finials, inscribed LAV.DA.SION.SALVATOREM, another a dormerhead decorated with a rose flanked by thistles, the choice of flowers suggesting a celebration of the Union of the Crowns of England and Scotland in 1603. At the first floor, three tall windows, the outer in roll-and-hollow moulded surrounds and C16, the centre opening's plain surround suggesting it may be an insertion, perhaps of the C18. Between the two l. windows, a stone bearing the coat of arms and initials of George Chaplin, a Jamaica merchant, and the date 1721, the year in which he acquired the estate of Colliston. Tiny window at the l. end of this floor. The main block's second floor has been much altered, probably first in 1621 when the windows may have been formed in walling slightly jettied above and below a jerky string course; over these windows were probably the dormerheads now built into the wall below. If so, the dormerheads were removed in the C18 or early C19. A third alteration took place in 1893 when *Hay & Henderson* added an ashlar battlement with widely spaced crenelles. Behind the battlement, a trio of gabled dormers, also of 1893.

The SE corner tower's two lower floors are round. Above projects a rectangular top floor placed at a diagonal to the main block and carried on continuous corbelling, one course ornamented with herringbone enrichment, two others with diagonal grooves. This storey was remodelled in the C17 or C18 when it was lowered to the height of the main block's wall-head and given a catslide roof. In 1893 Hay & Henderson restored its likely original height and gave it a crowstep-gabled double-pitch roof. Supported on continuous corbelling in the tower's SW inner angle with the main block is a conical-roofed stair-turret which ascends from the first floor. In 1893 it was heightened to rise above the wall-heads of both the main block and the SE tower. At the tower's ground floor is the house's C16 entrance placed in a roll-and-hollow-moulded surround. To the r., an oval gunloop; another in the SE segment. Small former stair window to the E. Facing SW is a large first-floor window, its surround also with a roll-and-hollow moulding; under the ends of its sill, a couple of cows' heads carved in relief. Directly above, a smaller second-floor window, again in a roll-and-hollow-moulded surround. Also at this level are circular shot-holes; small window to the SE. The stair-turret is pierced by small windows (lighting the former stair inside), shot-holes and, at the top, a W-facing oval gunloop. Set into the turret but not necessarily *in situ* or belonging together are two carved stones. The lower is horizontal and bears the date 1583 and the motto LAVS.DEO, the upper is a heraldic panel which displays the coats of arms and initials of John Guthrie, third of Colliston, who held the estate from 1580 to 1620, and Marion Falconer, his wife.

The NW tower, round for its full height, is plain. Small windows except at the ground floor where a pointed opening has been inserted, perhaps in the early C19. Also at the ground floor are C16 gunloops. This tower, formerly finished, perhaps in an C18 remodelling, with a catslide roof over the second floor, was heightened to four storeys and given a corbelled parapet in 1893.

Across most of the back of the house and projecting to its E is the addition designed by *Hay & Henderson* in 1893 for John

Peebles Chaplin to replace an earlier and smaller wing in this position. Harled and crowstep-gabled like the main block, it is of three storeys, the style unassertive Baronial, a parapeted three-storey bay window at the E elevation the main feature. On the exposed S side, a stone inscribed with the date 1893 and the initials of John Peebles Chaplin and Caroline Watson Copley, his wife. Above, a steep triangular dormerhead, the face ornamented with a diaper pattern. It is probably early C17 and originally belonged to the house but, like the other carved dormerheads, had been built into a farm steading. Behind the addition, a court of offices, also of 1893, bounded by screen walls enlivened by crosslet arrowslits and with battlemented round towers at the N corners.

The door at the SE tower opened originally onto the foot of a stair (removed in the C17 or C18) which rose to the first floor. Across the S side of the main block, a passage with a couple of tunnel-vaulted stores off its N side and the house's C16 kitchen, also vaulted, at its W end. In the C17 or early C18 when a new entrance (now a window) was made in the S side of the main block, the centre store was converted to a hallway giving access to a new stair added to the house's N side. This hall was remodelled in 1893 when its S wall was removed, opening it into the passage. Occupying the first floor of the main block is the drawing room. Probably originally, as now, a single room, it has been divided, perhaps in the C18, into two with a fireplace at each end. Chimneypieces in a late C18 manner, one with a figure of Hope on the lintel, the other with the depiction of a fanciful castle.

3050

CORTACHY

Handful of houses outside the gateway at the N approach to Cortachy Castle (*see* below).

CORTACHY CHURCH. By *David Paterson*, 1828–9. Relatively tall Gothic and pinnacled buttressed box faced with stugged red sandstone ashlar, the dressings of broached stone. The battlemented side walls contain hoodmoulded large Perp three-light windows; five-light windows in the gables. Depressed-arched doors in the outer bays of the side. One of the S buttresses bears a strapwork-bordered SUNDIAL of 1675 carved with the face of a humanoid sun and the initials KC. The low N vestry was added in the late C19.

At the church's E end, the AIRLIE MAUSOLEUM, also of 1828 and designed by Paterson but built of polished grey sandstone ashlar. It is semi-octagonal and chancel-like, buttressed and battlemented, the Gothic openings with hoodmoulds. On the N side, a dummy window filled with two sculpture fragments. At the top, an arched stone, possibly a dormerhead, bearing three coats of arms (one those of Ogilvy), initials and the date 1614. The fragment below is the head of an aumbry, probably a C15 or early C16 sacrament house, the jambs topped by pinnacles. The ogee arch's naturalistically foliaged crocketing rises to a finial carved with the head of Our Lord flanked by angels.

The church's INTERIOR is of 1828–9. Shallow vault of Late Gothic character. E gallery, its front in a Late Georgian Gothick manner. – Simple PEWS with a quatrefoil panel on the end of each. – Tall PULPIT at the W end, also Gothick, the canopy 18
surmounted by a crocketed crown spire, the ogee-arched flying buttresses meeting at large foliaged finials.

GRAVEYARD. Several C18 HEADSTONES. Just S of the Airlie Mausoleum's E end, the stone erected to David Watt in 1742, its curvaceously topped W face with ball-finialled attached columns, a shield bearing a plough and, in the tympanum, the relief of a pair of angels' heads (souls). At the bottom of the E face, emblems of death. – To the W, the stone erected in 1786 to Margaret Smith, the face with a shield displaying a horse-shoe; reminders of mortality at the bottom, an angel's head in the curly top. – To its SW, the headstone erected in 1779 by James Thomson, gardener, its W face with a mantled shield under a panel carved with plants; fir-cone finials at the top.

CORTACHY SCHOOL. Plain single-storey Board School of the late C19.

AIRLIE MEMORIAL TOWER, Tulloch Hill, 2.4 km. NW. Rising *p. 428*
among trees, a craggy Baronial landmark designed by *T. Martin Cappon* and erected in 1900–1 to commemorate the eleventh Earl of Airlie who had been killed in the South African War. Massive square tower, its battered base broached to support the tall second stage. The top stage is lower, projected on corbels and crowned by a corbelled-out balustrade; conical-roofed circular caphouse at one corner.

HOUSE OF THE GLENS, 0.8 km. W. Built in 1862 as the factor's house for Cortachy Castle. Two storeys, harled and crowstep-gabled Scotstyle, with rounded corners corbelled to the square under the eaves. In the inner angle a bowed projection containing the entrance, the rectangular upper floor corbelled out and diagonally set.

CORTACHY CASTLE

0.3 km. SE

White-harled edifice rising from parkland beside the South Esk. 40
The lands of Cortachy were granted to Thomas Ogilvy of Clova in 1473 and a charter signed here in 1545 suggesting the existence of a laird's house by that date. In 1625 the lands were sold to James, seventh Lord Ogilvy of Airlie (later, first Earl of Airlie), whose principal seat, at the time, was Airlie Castle. However, in 1640 Airlie Castle was destroyed by a Covenanting force led by the Earl of Argyll and not subsequently reoccupied until the 1790s, Cortachy becoming and remaining the principal residence of the Earls of Airlie.

Cortachy, Airlie Memorial Tower.
Engraving, 1903

The house seems to have been begun in the early C16 as an L, its main block running E–W, the jamb projecting N from the W end and with a stair-tower in the inner angle but also with a tower and stair at the outer SW corner. In the early C17 the main block was extended E and another tower built at the SE corner. In 1787–90, after David, Lord Ogilvy (titular Earl of Airlie) had received a free pardon for his part in the 1745

Jacobite rising and returned from exile in France, the mason-architect, *Richard Hogg*, carried out building work at Cortachy, including the construction of a sizeable addition to the end of the NW jamb. David Ogilvy (from 1829, Earl of Airlie) succeeded to the estate in 1819 and in 1820–1 employed *R. & R. Dickson* to remodel the house, adding a crenellated W porch and battlements and replacing the original stair in the inner angle of the C16 house with a new one. Probably a little later an additional wing was built behind the S range and extending E of it. Much more extensive was the huge addition added to the house's W side in 1870–3 by *David Bryce*, most of this work removed in a further remodelling carried out in 1949–51 by *Philip Tilden*.

The exterior is all harled, with dressings of polished red sandstone. The C16 and C17 main range faces S. At the ground floor a not very regular disposition of three windows, the centre small and probably C16, the other two enlarged in the late C18 or early C19. The first floor is of four bays, the three l. windows in the side of the C16 house, the r slightly further apart and belonging to the early C17 extension. Now very tall and with roll-and-hollow mouldings, these openings date from the 1870s when the original first and second floors were thrown into one. At the top floor four windows, all with roll-and-hollow mouldings but probably of 1820–1. They are aligned with those below but the centre two are quite small, the end ones set at a higher level and topped by the bartizan-like ends of the wall-head battlement which was added in 1820–1.

At either end of this S range is a tower. The SE tower is early C17 in origin, fat and round, *c.* 5.8 m. in diameter, and with a bowed stair-turret in the SW inner angle. The battlement carried on arcaded corbelling is of the 1820s, the fish-scale-slated conical roof of the 1870s. Also of the 1870s the stair-turret's timidly jettied top floor and slated roof. The less altered SW tower is largely early C16. It is of four storeys, the lower three of a near-circular shape, the top corbelled out to a crowstep-gabled and diagonally set rectangle, its SSW face carried on a Gothic arch, the corners on continuous corbelling. In the tower's SW segment, a splayed gunloop at the ground floor. Tier of small stair windows in the NW segment and the other openings also quite small. On the top floor's SE face a large SUNDIAL by *Harber Designs* erected in 2002 to commemorate the Golden Wedding of David, thirteenth Earl of Airlie, and Virginia Ryan.

The W elevation is now U-shaped, the hollow centre formerly more than filled by Bryce's addition which projected boldly from it. The three r. bays are formed by the house's early C16 NW jamb but its wall-head battlement is of 1820–1, the present appearance of the rest of 1948–51. The remainder of this front is all by Tilden although some of the structure is of the 1870s but recast. Battlement over the recessed centre; crowstepped gable on the NW wing. At the NW corner, a square tower which supports a conical-roofed circular top stage. N elevation also mostly of 1948–51, with castellated and Scots manorial features and, at the W end, a battlemented single-storey outshot. Behind and projecting E of the C16 and C17 main range, a three-storey-and-attic wing, originally of the earlier C19 but remodelled by Tilden who removed its wall-head battlement and gave it a crowstepped gable and catslide dormers. Its E gable contains the house's principal entrance formed in 1949–51, the doorway with a lugged architrave and surmounted by a pedimented frame containing the heraldic achievement of the Earls of Airlie.

The INTERIOR is largely of 1949–51 but at the heart of the house is the STAIR-HALL designed by *R. & R. Dickson* in 1821. In it, a stair rises from the first floor to the top of the house, the cast-iron balusters decorated with quatrefoils. On the S of the stair-hall is the drawing room formed by David Bryce in the 1870s from the C16 hall. Jacobean plaster ceiling dated 1873, modelled on the early C17 ceiling in The Old Mansion House at Auchterhouse (q.v.), also a property of the Earls of Airlie and the seat of their progenitors, and, like that, with prominent pendants. The decoration in the compartments includes flowers, the lion passant heraldic motif of the Ogilvies of Airlie, and the coroneted and monogrammed initials of BA (for Blanche, [Countess of] Airlie). White marble Adam Revival chimneypiece, probably also Late Victorian. A segment of the house's SW tower intrudes into one corner and, above the door into the tower's first-floor room, a small balcony marks the position of the main range's original second floor.

The DRAWING ROOM, as formed in 1873, was L-plan but the NW jamb, its ceiling a continuation of that in the main part of the drawing room, was partitioned off in the late C20 to form a library. Veined marble chimneypiece of late C17 type but probably of 1873. E of the drawing room is the KING'S ROOM (dining room) occupying the early C17 extension of the S range. Its present height and character were given it in the 1870s. Walls covered to half their height with oak panelling. The chimneypiece is of Jacobean Renaissance inspiration with putti on the jambs and cherubs' heads atop the scrolls which flank the overmantel. This is carved with the macabre relief of a cherub hammering a bolt into a lady's head. Above the overmantel, a heraldic achievement bears the quartered arms of Ogilvy of Airlie and Stanley of Alderley (for Blanche Stanley, Countess of Airlie). In the SE tower's first-floor room, a plain moulded stone chimneypiece of the C17. In the SW tower, the first-floor room is an irregularly shaped heptagon. Off its NW side, a tight turnpike stair from the ground to the second floor. Near the foot, a blocked door which has given access to the exterior. In the tower's ground-floor room, a gunloop under a small horizontal-shaped light. The doors from the turret's stair to the drawing room's balcony have panels carved with depictions of mounted warriors, perhaps C18 work.

POLICIES. Extensive and well-wooded parkland setting for the house. The grand approach is from the N where the drive enters the grounds from the village of Cortachy at THE GREY LODGE of *c.* 1820. Pair of mirror-image single-storey Tudor-style pavilions, the walling carried up to form parapets fronting the road. At the outer corners, octagonal turret-buttresses. Between the lodges, the gateway, a tall and broad round-headed carriage entrance between more turret-buttresses and flanked by parapeted pedestrian entrances. – Just SW of The Grey Lodge, Cortachy Church (*see* above) and, beyond that, 'THE GOLDEN GATES', delicately decorative wrought-iron gates, probably C17 Italian, set between late C19 ball-finialled gatepiers.

SE of Cortachy Castle is the DAIRY COTTAGE of the mid or later C19. Long crowstep-gabled and ball-finialled single-storey principal range fronted by a loggia, an oriel window set in a crowstepped gable at one end, at the other a slightly projecting jamb, the jettied upper floor containing a window under a steep pediment. – HOME FARM to the SE, the rubble-walled main buildings designed by *David Paterson*, 1829. The E range consists of two-storey pyramidal-roofed square pavilions joined by single-storey links (their windows enlarged) to a two-storey farmhouse in the centre. At the W range, two-storey pavilions, also pyramidal-roofed at the ends but piend-roofed at the centre, joined by slightly recessed and lower links, some of the windows enlarged and a couple heightened to rise into dormerheads. – Immediately to the S, the late C18 STABLES, the S range mostly built of whinstone rubble with red sandstone dressings but the centrepiece of red sandstone with some cherry-cock pointing. At each end, a two-storey square pavilion, its front pierced by a segmental-arched carriage entrance. Recessed links, of two storeys but lower, to the centrepiece. This, set slightly forward of the links but not to the line of the end pavilions, is a tall two storeys and attic with an elliptical-arched broad pend entrance at the ground floor, a round-headed dummy window with projecting keystone and imposts at the first floor. The attic forms a pediment which contains a double tier of rectangular flight-holes set in a semicircular arch. Behind, plain rubble-built E and W wings, the W with elliptical-arched carriage openings in the outer wall. A screen wall closes the N side of the courtyard.

At the end of the W drive, 0.4 km. SW of Cortachy Castle, THE RED LODGE of 1859. Single-storey and picturesque in stugged red sandstone masonry, with hoodmoulds over the windows and bracketed broad eaves. T-plan, with splayed projections across the inner angles. Corniced GATEPIERS with belted ball finials. – At the convergence of the W and S drives, the GARDEN, its N side bounded by a brick wall of 1857 surmounted by swagged urns and, at the W end, stone acorns. At the wall's N end, a contemporary GARDENER'S HOUSE, also of brick and broad-eaved. A pair of pointed gateways in the wall flank a long lean-to brick shed, probably also of 1857, on the wall's outer side. – Straddling the S drive is AIRLIE LODGE built in 1889, a tall battlemented gatehouse flanked by single-storey crowstep-gabled wings. The gatehouse's pointed archway, containing an iron yett and dummy portcullis, is surmounted by a crowstepped hoodmould, its top containing the heraldic achievement of the Earls of Airlie under the monogram MA (for Mabell, Countess of Airlie). At the SE corner of the gatehouse, a round tower, its upper stage jettied out on continuous corbelling, its conical roof covered with fish-scale slating. – At the end of the drive, a late C19 BRIDGE over the Prosen Water, its parapets of bull-nosed ashlar, the roadway carried on cast-iron Tuscan columns.

DOWNIEPARK. *See* p. 437.

7050

CRAIG

Hamlet on a hillside overlooking Montrose Basin.

CRAIG PARISH CHURCH. Now housing (KIRKTOWER HOUSE). Suave Gothic, by *Richard Crichton*, 1796–9. The church comprises a nave, tall aisles and a W tower, the walls of rubble formerly harled. In the nave's battlemented E gable, a window of three stone-mullioned and transomed lights with simple tracery in the head. The aisles' side windows contain wooden Y-tracery. Against the E end of the N side, a small boiler-house addition, probably of the early C20. Beside it, a harled MAUSOLEUM of 1815, its N parapet carried on corbels and with obelisk finials on the corners.

Standing against the nave's W gable, also battlemented, is the tower. Its lowest stage is oblong. At the long W face, a broad centrepiece marked off by pairs of tall bundle-shafted attached columns, their quasi-Egyptian capitals carved with stylized foliage. These support an entablature above whose ends rise short parapets panelled with Gothic dummy arcading. At the inner end of each parapet and aligned with the columns below, a pair of drums flanking a panel in which is sunk a diamond shape. In this stage's W face, a huge pointed entrance in a cavetto-splayed surround; above, a long panel inscribed 'Enter His Gates with Praise'. In the S face is a second entrance under a quatrefoil opening, both contained in a tall pointed overarch. The tower's upper stages are square, their N and S sides set back from the first stage's ends. They rise between giant pilaster-like clasping buttresses, their capitals panelled with blind Gothic arcades. Crocketed finials on the corners of the wallhead battlement. A quatrefoil-traceried round window in each face of the second stage. At the top stage, tall pointed two-light windows, their column-mullions and end shafts with capitals of stylized foliage, their aprons ornamented with diamond panels, their heads with concave-sided diamond-shaped dummy openings.

In the tower's N inner angle, an outshot with a Gothic dummy window to the front and a parapet whose simple

Gothic panelling repeats that of the parapet over the bottom stage of the tower.

CHURCHYARD. At the entrance, Tudor Gothic octagonal GATEPIERS and a wrought-iron overthrow, probably of *c.* 1800. – Just N of the church, the detached MAUSOLEUM of the Hoyer Millars of Rossie Castle, very tall and seriously Gothic.

KIRKTON HOUSE, the former Craig Parish Manse, to the E was built in 1805, the masonry covered in pink harling. Two-storey piend-roofed main block with a taller central bow and hood-moulds over the first-floor windows. Turret-buttresses at the corners; wall-head parapet with Gothic blind arcading. Mid- and later C19 additions of one and two storeys at the ends. – Rubble-built OFFICES, probably of 1805, to the W.

CEMETERY, Todd's Hole, 2.1 km. S. On the site of a medieval chapel dedicated to St Skae or Skeoch, a rubble-walled graveyard containing some C19 HEADSTONES. – Two BURIAL ENCLOSURES. One, of *c.* 1840, is rubble-walled and plain. The other, of the Keiths of Usan and probably built in the earlier C19, is of polished ashlar. Rusticated quoins at the corners of the S front which contains the Roman Doric pilastered and pedimented entrance.

THE CRAIG

0.4 km. N

Early C16 frontal display of status masking unshowy domesticity behind.

In 1535 James Beaton, Archbishop of St Andrews, granted the lands of Craig together with *turre et fortalicio super eisdem constructis* ('the tower and fortalice built on them') in feu ferme to David Wood, one of James V's closest advisers and later his Comptroller and Coroner of the shires of Forfar and Kincardine. Mention of the construction of the buildings, unusual in charters, suggests that they were of recent date, probably replacing a grange. The lands had reverted to the diocese of St Andrews by 1620 when Archbishop John Spottiswood granted them to James Carnegie, second son of David, Lord Carnegie (later, first Earl of Southesk). From the C17 to the C20 the estate was held successively by the families of Carnegie, Scott, Ross, Macdonald and Hoyer Millar, all of whom seem to have carried out alterations to the buildings, leaving a puzzling array of disparate features which makes a coherent account of the house's development difficult if not impossible.

The first building reached on the approach from the S is the GATEWAY, little altered though partly demolished. This is of *c.* 1530 and, like all the buildings at The Craig, of rubble construction. It consists of a screen wall pierced by a simply moulded central archway and finished with a tall parapet, perhaps originally the front wall of an upper storey, carried on individual double-moulded corbels except at the centre where the parapet is of bolder projection and the corbels triple-moulded. To the r. of the archway has been inserted, perhaps in the C18, a second round-headed entrance (now blocked) which served a coachhouse behind. At each end of the screen wall, a boldly advanced round tower and, in the inner angle, continuous corbelling which has supported a bowed turret. The end towers themselves have been of at least three storeys. The W tower's ground floor contains wide-mouthed oval gun-loops surmounted by horizontal sighting slits. At this tower's E segment, a first-floor window (now blocked) and in its SE segment a large second-floor shot-hole. The SE tower is more ruinous but one jamb of an upper window survives in the S segment. Inside the gateway is a large OUTER COURTYARD, *c.* 50 m. (N–S) by 23 m. (E–W). Along the N end of its E side, a two-storey COACHHOUSE range. It may be C18 but some of the W openings have chamfered margins, probably reused from elsewhere in the complex. In the N gable, a segmental-arched brick-built garage opening of the C20. The rest of the court-yard's E and N sides are bounded by walls broken only by garden gates, the N gate a round-headed arch on the axis of the complex's main S gateway and probably designed in conscious imitation of it. The wall on the outer courtyard's E side, also broken by a gate, probably of the C19, is higher and with an intake in the masonry, perhaps evidence of a C16 parapet walk. This wall extends for only about half the length of this side of the courtyard, its line continued by the E face of a tower standing at the SE corner of an INNER COURTYARD opening to the W of the outer courtyard and once bounded on all sides by the mansion house.

The early C16 showfront of the MANSION HOUSE faced S but is now largely hidden except from close view by the S wall of the garden and a high yew hedge planted close to the house. This SOUTH RANGE is represented by a screen wall stretched between and on the same plane as the S faces of a pair of nearly identical and almost square towers, their corners rounded. The wall has fronted a two-storey lean-to range, now removed and its S window openings built up. Each tower is of three storeys with a crowstep-gabled attic (the E tower's roof ridge running N–S, the W's E–W) set behind a tall parapet carried on individual double-moulded corbels and drained by large stone spouts. Unusually there is no pretence of serious defensive purpose. Not only are the towers' fronts flush with the outer wall of the courtyard so unable to provide a raking gunfire defence but they are unprovided with gunloops or shot-holes. In the S face of the W tower a ground-floor slit window; there may have been a corresponding opening at the E tower but a door has been inserted here. Above, in the W tower's S side, a generously sized first-floor window (blocked) and another, perhaps a C20 insertion, at the second floor. In this tower's W face another slit window to the ground floor and a blocked opening at the first. In the E tower's E face to the outer courtyard a ground-floor slit window and, at the first floor, a slightly larger opening with a chamfered surround. At this tower's S face the presence of a blocked ground-floor door is marked by a relieving arch and, inside the tower, by an elliptical-arched recess. At the E end of the second floor, another door, its surround chamfered, presumably gave access to the mansion house's now missing E range. The present ground-floor entrance in this tower's W face is clearly a later insertion but its first-floor door, the surround also chamfered, seems to be C16. It has opened into the lost living accommodation of the S range and faces another door (now converted to a window) in the corresponding position at the W tower. These doors perhaps served a first-floor gallery, *c.* 2.7 m. wide but 14.6 m. long. Of the house's EAST RANGE even less survives, only one jamb and the springing of a ground-floor archway attached to the E tower's NE corner; the hinges for this archway's door are still on the tower's S face.

Crowstep-gabled two-storey and attic NORTH RANGE, its masonry partly covered by harling. From the thickness of a wall between the present drawing room and dining room and from the different floor levels of ground-floor rooms it may be deduced that it was built in two phases, both perhaps of the C16. The E part, perhaps the earlier, extended one bay W of the present oriel window on the S elevation, the slightly shorter W part occupied the remainder of this range. At the ground floor of the S front are three doors, the r. rectangular and not original although perhaps C16 or C17 and with a chamfered surround, the surrounds of the other two (each belonging to a probable different phase of construction) also chamfered but with shouldered arches, perhaps a conscious archaism. Beside each of these arched doors, a slit window. In front of the E end of this front is a Victorian brick-built and harled two-storey lean-to addition, its ground floor a loggia. To its E and of about the same date, a first-floor wooden canted oriel window supported on stilts. To the r. of this, a large window with a chamfered margin, perhaps of the C16, and further r., a smaller window, also with a chamfered surround, but looking like a Victorian insertion. At this range's E gable the ground-floor masonry is thicker than that above so as to support the thrust of vaulting inside. In this E gable, a fairly small and squarish window which has probably been enlarged but the relieving arch above shows that there was originally an opening in this position. At the first floor a (blocked) slit window, perhaps originally lighting a closet or garderobe, to the l. and, off-centre to the N, a large window with a chamfered surround probably of the C16. Just below the present attic a blocked slit window. In the head of the gable, a pair of decently sized attic windows, probably of the earlier C20. At the E half of this range's N (garden) front, the walling is intaken at progressively but seemingly arbitrary higher levels towards the centre. Slit window at the E end of the first floor. To its r., a couple of large Georgian windows and between them, at the ground floor, a pointed door, probably of the C19. Further r., a small opening high up at the first floor. The walling W of this has been partly rebuilt in harled brickwork in the late C18, probably for Hercules Ross who had made a fortune as a naval purser during the American War of Independence and bought the estates of Craig and Rossie Castle in 1783. In this walling, a first-floor Venetian window, the central light placed between Roman Doric half-columns, the jambs formed by half-pilasters. Below but not centred on the window, a doorway, perhaps a Victorian insertion, which has been covered by a round-headed brick porch or canopy. The ground-floor window to the r. is probably also C19 but at the first floor is a C16 or C17 slit window, perhaps originally to a garderobe. At the attic, three catslide-roofed dormer windows of the earlier C20. This range's W gable puzzlingly suggests it was constructed in two stages but such a development is at odds with the interior. As far up as an intake under the gablehead the walling of the N third is thicker than the rest, whilst projecting from that S two-thirds is a row of moulded corbels, apparently only for meaningless decoration. In the gable's N third, a first-floor door, presumably inserted in the C18 or C19; to the r., a large window, probably of the C16. In the gablehead, a pair of small C16 or C17 windows.

The WEST RANGE appears to be largely of the early C17, perhaps built or rebuilt soon after 1620 when the estate was acquired by James, Lord Carnegie, for his second son. Roughly in the centre of the E (courtyard) elevation, the original entrance to this range (now a window), its surround chamfered. To its l., a ground-floor window of horizontal proportions, probably widened, and, to the r., the house's present entrance, a Late Victorian shouldered-arched doorway. Three first-floor windows, all probably C17 and with chamfered margins, and one second-floor window which rises through the eaves to a catslide dormerhead. Above the C17 entrance, a tall C18 stair window. Below this opening has been placed a corniced panel carved with an ogee arch, perhaps the surround for a coat of arms but now containing a strapwork-framed stone bearing the date 1637. Between the first-floor windows to the l., a tier of panels placed here in the mid C19. The top two are carved with a lion rampant and the eagle coat of arms of the Carnegies, the bottom with the monogram SDC, perhaps for Sir David Carnegie; all seem to be C17. The range's W elevation is without pretension. The garden level outside has been raised so that the ground-floor windows now appear as basement openings, the S partly blocked, the centre a slit and the N an C18 insertion. At the first floor, a sizeable C17 window at the r., a tiny central opening and a Victorian oriel window at the l. There have been four C17 second-floor windows, one now blocked, the end windows now rising through the eaves to catslide dormerheads.

INTERIOR. Three of the four ground-floor rooms of the N range are entered from the courtyard and their floors are placed a few steps below its level. All are tunnel-vaulted. The E room has been the kitchen; very wide elliptical-arched fireplace at the E end, now partly built up but still with evidence of an oven in the W side. E window, apparently in its original position but enlarged. The present entrance, at the W end of the S side, cuts into the vault; it replaced an earlier doorway at the centre of this wall. The adjacent room has been a store. Cupboard in the N wall. Here also projects the curved bottom of a stair which rises as a straight flight within the wall thickness but curves again where it reaches the first floor. The two rooms to the W are placed at a slightly higher level. The second of these is entered from the W range. Like the two to its E, the S doorway has a shouldered arch. Fireplace in the W side, probably a C19 insertion.

The house's entrance hall is now in the W range. Beside it, a Georgian cantilevered stair. The principal first-floor rooms are in the N range. At its W end, the drawing room, its E chimneypiece of mid-C18 character with consoled jambs and a swag of fruit carved on the lintel; it was imported in 1997. The ceiling was painted by *Richard Jordan* in 2005 with designs of beasts and birds in the manner of *c.* 1600. In the E wall, a door made up of early C17 carved panels, the centre with a scene depicting crowned human figures (the Adoration of the Magi?). The dining room and breakfast room to the E seem to have been formed from the hall of the first house here. The study at the E end may have been that house's private room.

DUNNINALD CASTLE. *See* p. 440.

DOWNIEPARK 4050

1.7 km. SE of Cortachy

Idiosyncratically smart harled mansion house built *c.* 1805 for Lieutenant-Colonel William Rattray on his return from service in the Honourable East India Company's Bengal Artillery. Piend-roofed main block, its entrance (N) front of three bays, the outer of two storeys above a basement, the centre rising a storey higher and finished with a parapet. At the centre, the sidelit and segmentally fanlit entrance to the principal floor approached by a broad flight of steps. At each end of the main block, a single-storey one-bay link, overlaid by accretions on the N side, to a piend-roofed pavilion, also single-storey, its front pierced by a single three-light window.

At the S front the basement is fully exposed. This elevation 57
is individualistic, the main block's centre forming a semicircular bow fronted by a Roman Doric-columned portico added in 1819, also semicircular and with a flat roof serving as a balcony to the principal floor. The outer windows of that floor are Venetian, their sidelights dummies, set in round-headed overarches. Lower first-floor windows joined by a sill course which runs under the openings at the centrepiece and extends to but not beyond the outer bays' tripartite windows, their outer lights dummies. Mutuled cornice under the eaves of the outer bays and carried across the centrepiece where it supports

the jettied top floor. Round-headed windows to the single-storey links which are here set back from the main block. Each of the end pavilions contains a three-light window and is finished with a pediment, its base formed by a quatrefoil-studded frieze, a segmental-arched dummy opening in the tympanum.

INTERIOR. The front door opens directly into a stair-hall. The flying stair, its cast-iron balustrades with anthemion ornament, rises along the E, N and W sides. On the S, opposite the entrance, a first-floor Roman Doric-columned screen opens onto the bedroom landing. Below it, another screen but, reversing the expected hierarchy of orders, its columns are Corinthian with eagles nestling in the capitals' foliage; the openings to the inner hall behind are round-headed arches. On the inner hall's ceiling, an acanthus-leaf rose in a surround of swagged husks. Doors from the inner hall, their surrounds' reeded jambs topped by corn sheaves, open to the principal rooms. Plain sitting room in the house's SE corner. At the SW is the dining room, the walls plaster-panelled and with a bowed sideboard recess at the N end. The N and S ends of the central drawing room are bowed. White marble chimneypiece with reeded jambs and lintel, reliefs of female dancers carved at the ends. The first-floor room above has a bowed S end and, at the N, a bed recess, also bow-ended.

STABLES axially sited 0.15 km. N. Pair of S-facing ranges built of red sandstone rubble and dated 1805. At each, a three-bay centrepiece, the ground-floor windows surmounted by large quatrefoil dummy openings. At the ends are pavilion-roofed blocks with basket-arched carriage openings at the ground floor and, at the first, Venetian dummy windows flanked by single-light windows, also mostly dummies. Rear wings dated 1812.

6060

DUN

Rural parish church sitting on the edge of the parkland of House of Dun.

DUN CHURCH. By *Robert Dalgarno*, 1832–4. Broad Gothic rectangle of cherry-cock-pointed rough ashlar. Windowless N side; tall pointed windows in the S. Smaller windows in the W gable from which protrudes a piend-roofed session house. The E gable's tall windows flank a slender square tower. At its lowest stage a Tudorish entrance set between battlemented octagonal turret-buttresses; over the door a corniced TABLET commemorating William Henry Kennedy-Erskine of Dun †1870 and bearing the crest of the Erskines of Dun. Above, a tall Y-traceried two-light dummy window. At each face of the tower's top stage, a round-headed belfry opening; pinnacles on the corners of the wall-head's cornice.

INTERIOR. Panel-fronted GALLERY on wooden Roman Doric columns round three sides. On the centre of its E front,

a carving, probably C17, of a pair of hands holding a scroll inscribed LAUS DEO. – Boxy PEWS. – Early C17 PULPIT at 15
the W end, its base C19. The body is formed of a panelled rectangle from which extends a box-fronted projection; on the panels, floriated geometric designs. The back is divided into two tiers of fluted panels, the upper tier's centre panel bearing the date 1615 and the coat of arms and initials of John Erskine (Minister of Dun from 1614 to 1621). The front of the canopy is carved like a drapery pelmet; urn finial. – On the pulpit and elsewhere in the church, early C19 ornamental cast-iron LAMP BRACKETS for gas lighting.

BRIDGE OF DUN, 1.6 km. S. By *Alexander Stevens Sen.*, 1785–7. Very smart ashlar-faced bridge over the River South Esk. 70
Crossing the water are three spans, the outer arches elliptical, the centre taller and segmental-headed. The roadway slopes gently up over the outer spans to a flat centre. Corbelled straight parapets following the line of the road. Flanking the central arch are keel-shaped cutwaters from which rise very tall and elegantly slender bundle-shafted columns to carry, at parapet level, individual entablatures, their friezes with triglyphs and quatrefoil-decorated metopes; above the entablatures, keel-shaped pedestrian refuges. At the ends of the bridge, sturdy piers with obelisk finials. From these, rubble-built approach walls ornamented with crosslet 'arrowslits' curve outwards to end at quatrefoil-plan stumpy piers, their pinnacles of general obelisk type but also quatrefoil on plan.

BRIDGE OF DUN RAILWAY STATION, 1.4 km. S. Opened in 1848. Office building of one tall storey with a wooden valence platform which covers the S platform.

BROOMLEY, 1.4 km. SE. Mid-C18 laird's house, the walling of red sandstone rubble. Two storeys above a half-sunk basement. W front originally of five bays, the central door in a cavetto-moulded surround. About 1790 a full-height splay-sided addition was built covering the two r. bays. Lower long two-storey harled SE wing, also an addition and perhaps of the earlier C19. – Mid-C19 LODGE, with bracketed broad eaves, at the entrance to the N drive.

HOUSE OF DUN. *See* p. 524.
LANGLEY PARK. *See* p. 590.

DUNNICHEN 5040

Church and manse standing at the gateway to the former Dunichen House (demolished, 1966, and a bungalow built on the site).

DUNNICHEN CHURCH. Rubble-walled oblong of 1801–2, the roof's original flagstone covering replaced by slates in 1817. Tall Gothic windows in the S side. Birdcage bellcote on the W end. Originally, each gable contained a pointed door under a short window, also pointed, but the head of the W door was built up when it was enclosed in the off-centre session house added to this end in 1883.

Inside, the bow-fronted PULPIT of 1802 stands at the centre of the S side. – In front, a Neo-Jacobean COMMUNION TABLE with a vine leaf-decorated frieze, of *c.* 1920. – Five-sided GALLERY along the ends and N wall, the panelled front projected on brackets, the main structure supported on beams carried on cast-iron columns.

GRAVEYARD. Some C18 and early C19 HEADSTONES. S of the church a stone of 1774 commemorates David Espline, the top of the W face carved with a book and bone. Below, a pair of angels' heads (souls) above a shield bearing Espline's initials, the date and the tools of a wright; at the bottom, emblems of death. – Further S, the stone erected in 1823 by Alexander White in memory of his father David, the W face's swan-neck pediment with the relief of a sailing ship; below, a shield displays a coat of arms.

Immediately W of the graveyard, a cast of the DUNNICHEN STONE now in the Meffan Museum at Forfar, a sandstone slab incised, perhaps *c.* 600, with 'flower', 'double-disc and Z-rod', 'comb and mirror' symbols.

MANSE S of the church. Built in 1814–15 and two-storey. Straightforward rubble front of three bays, rendered gables and rear. Single-storey offices at the back.

7050

DUNNINALD CASTLE

1.5 km. S of Craig

58 Designed by *James Gillespie Graham*, a castellated asymmetrical Tudor-Gothic small-scale mansion house. It was built in 1823–4 for Peter Arkley who had bought the estate in 1811.

Two-storey-and-attic main block, the walling of cherry-cock-pointed ashlar, the windows all hoodmoulded and containing Gothic-patterned glazing, the ground floor's taller than the first floor's; all round, a wall-head battlement projected on moulded individual corbels. At each of the NW, NE and SE corners, a slender square tower of three storeys, its pointed slit windows decreasing in size from the ground floor to the second, its wall-head battlement also carried on corbels. Also of three storeys but taller is the fat round tower at the SW corner, its round-headed windows also decreasing in size from the ground floor up, the two bottom stages' with hoodmoulds; arcaded moulded corbelling under the crowning battlement. Rising above, in the tower's NW inner angle with the main block, a slim turret, its lowest stage square and containing a hoodmoulded narrow window, the upper stages broached to an octagon and pierced by pointed slits like those of the house's other turrets. Tall battlement, again on moulded corbels.

The main block's W front between the corner turrets and tower is of six bays, the third bay from the N much broader and taller than the rest. In the two bays l. of this 'centrepiece' are rectangular windows, pointed ground-floor openings in the three bays to the r. At the 'centrepiece' a porch between octagonal clasping buttresses, its Tudor-arched entrance flanked by bell-capitalled skinny columns. Over the porch a rectangular oriel window containing three Gothic lights, the surmounting battlement carried on continuous corbelling.

The main block's N elevation is of three bays, each containing ground- and first-floor windows of equal width, the l. bay's decently sized and rectangular, the centre's narrow and pointed, the r.'s each of three mullioned lights. The S elevation is two-bay, one of the ground-floor windows pointed, the other rectangular, both first-floor openings rectangular.

Extending E of the main block to enclose a rear service courtyard are lower two-storey battlemented wings, the N ending with a short stretch of screen wall, also battlemented, the line of the shorter S wing continued by a piend-roofed single-storey range which returns along the courtyard's E end. Inside the courtyard, low additions of the 1890s against the main block's E side. A low battlemented wall extends N from the service court's NE corner to a square bastion equipped with stone cannons whose spouts poke through the crenelles of its battlement.

INTERIOR. The porch's entrance opens into a small vestibule covered with a plaster rib-vault. In front and stretching the full depth of the main block, a much broader and longer HALL, its single-storey W two-thirds also covered with a flattish vaulted plaster ceiling, the ribs springing from foliaged corbels and meeting at bosses, also foliaged. In the hall's N and S sides are delicately detailed narrow Gothic niches whose crocketed and foliage-finialled ogee arches enclose panelled recesses. Beside each niche, a four-centred arch, the N containing the door to the dining room, the S the entrance to the Cloister. At the hall's E end, a broad arch, its soffit enriched with Gothic plaster panelling, opens onto the two-storey inner hall containing the imperial stair to the first floor, its cast-iron balustrade also Gothic. Over the stair, more ribbed plaster vaulting. Lighting the half-landing, a three-light mullioned-and-transomed Gothic window with a quatrefoiled head; in the lights are set STAINED GLASS panels of 1890 displaying the coats of arms of Arkley, Stansfeld and Smyth (the last two for Captain John Stansfeld and Charles Smyth, the husbands of the Arkley co-heiresses of Dunninald at the end of the C19).

The DINING ROOM continues the Gothic manner, the doors with pointed panels; more Gothic panelling at the E end's broad-arched shallow sideboard recess. *Trompe l'œil* painted 60
Gothic panelling on the walls and ceiling, including a central rose formed by radiating arches. Columned chimneypiece of black marble veined with yellow on the S side. S of the hall, THE CLOISTER (a narrow corridor) covered with plaster

sexpartite vaulting, the ribs meeting at heavy foliaged bosses, a three-light Gothic mullioned-and-transomed window at its end. Off the W side, the oblong DRAWING ROOM with a foliate frieze and white marble Gothic chimneypiece. At the S end, double doors to the circular LIBRARY (now Round Drawing Room). Gothic bookcase recesses in the E and W walls, foliate frieze and a plain chimneypiece of veined grey marble. At the first floor, the room above the W porch (now Porch Room) was originally the BILLIARD ROOM, its chimneypiece of black marble veined with yellow. In the OAK ROOM on the house's N side, a late C19 chimneypiece with carved figures.

E of the house, an avenue (the BEECH WALK) with, at its N end, very tall channelled, corniced and urn-finialled GATE-PIERS of *c.* 1700, each of their faces bearing a channelled pilaster. – SE of the house, a GARDEN of the earlier C19, its walls mostly of rubble but the N two-thirds of the E wall and the N wall's internal facing brick-built. In the N side, a segmental-arched brick gateway, its stone finials in the form of acorns. It now contains wrought-iron GATES by *James Brown*, 1906, decorated with roses, thistles, pheasants and birds of more malevolent aspect. Less exuberant the GATES of 1907 and also by Brown in the W wall of the lower (S) garden. Also in this wall, an Edwardian oval relief of a cherub playing the pipes.

The NORTH LODGE at the end of a former drive was built in 1891. Battlemented and with mullioned windows, a Gothic door and a square NW turret. A gateway, also battlemented and set between octagonal turret-buttresses, joins the lodge to a screen wall, again surmounted by a battlement and with an octagonal turret at its E corner.

STABLES, immediately E of the park, built in 1797. Quadrangular, some of the ranges remodelled in the late C19. The main two-storey frontage is to the S, its broad and tall centre and end bays pedimented and with openings set in round-headed overarches. In the centre of the courtyard, a pavilion-roofed square building, its S front with a round-headed dummy window and a gablet pierced by four tiers of flight-holes serving the doocot inside.

3040

EASSIE

Little more than a farm and a graveyard containing the ruins of the former Parish Church.

PARISH CHURCH. Roofless rubble-built rectangular kirk abandoned after the construction of Eassie and Nevay Parish Church (*see* p. 443) in 1833. It is probably late C16 or C17. Simple birdcage bellcote on the W gable in which is a gallery door under a horizontal rectangular fanlight. In the S wall (its W end missing), two doors and three windows, all with chamfered margins, one door lintel inscribed '17 Mr J. O. Mnr. 53', the initials those of James Ogilvy, Minister of Eassie and Nevay from 1752 to 1802. In the E gable, a large rectangular window, the margins checked for shutters. A door (now robbed of jambs) has been inserted at the N end of this gable. Windowless N wall.

Inside, at the SE corner and now covered by a glass shelter, a CROSS-SLAB of the C8 or C9. The front is carved with a cross decorated with interlacing and key pattern; at the corners of the crossing, rings looking like settings for jewels. Above the arms, the figures of two angels (the r. angel mutilated). Below the l. arm of the cross, the figure of a warrior armed with a spear and shield. Under the r. arm, three animals; the top animal is a stag, the one below may also be a deer, the bottom animal (now missing its head) a hound. On the back of the cross, symbols including a 'Pictish beast' and a 'double disc and Z-rod'; also, cloaked figures, a tree in a pot and three cattle. – Propped up in the NE corner of the church, a HEADSTONE to the Rev. Alexander Finlayson †1731. In its open pediment, a mantled shield. Round the inscription panel, a border carved with climbing pot plants and, at the top, angels' heads (souls). At the bottom, reminders of death.

EASSIE PRIMARY SCHOOL. *See* p. 444.

EASSIE AND NEVAY 3040

The centre of a parish formed in 1600 by the union of the medieval parishes of Eassie (q.v.) and Nevay (*see* p. 571). Just the church, school and hall and a couple of small houses. Immediately to the W, at Balkeerie, a small group of C19 and C20 houses with Balkeerie House and its steading at the W end.

PARISH CHURCH. By *David Paterson*, 1833. Broad box, the N wall built of rubble, the others of hammer-dressed ashlar masonry. On the W gable, a bellcote composed of a battlemented Tudor arch between two battlemented buttresses. This gable contains the entrance, a pointed door under a rectangular hoodmould; blind quatrefoils in the spandrels. High up in the gable, two smallish hoodmoulded windows, each of two main lights with four narrow lights above. In the N wall, three hoodmoulded windows, each of two lights with a quatrefoil in the head. One window of the same sort but without a hoodmould in the centre of the S wall. At the E end of this side, a built-up rectangular door. At the W end, a rectangular window with splayed jambs, probably of 1915 when *Thoms & Wilkie* inserted the adjoining horizontal two-light window. At the E gable, ogee-profiled skews. In the gable, a Tudor-arched window of four main lights under eight narrow lights. Above the window but within its ogee-arched and foliage-finialled hoodmould, a quatrefoil panel.

Inside, a deep W gallery.

EASSIE PRIMARY SCHOOL. Built in 1929. – Beside it, the mid-C19 OLD SCHOOL HOUSE, a broad-eaved school and school house, some of the windows much enlarged.

W.R.I. HALL. Built in 1927. White-harled, with half-timbering in the gables; a small cupola-ventilator on the roof.

BALKEERIE HOUSE. Early C19 two-storey-and-attic house of three bays, with a pilastered doorpiece. The dormer windows are additions.

FORT, Denoon Law, 1.5 km. SE. Occupying the summit of a steep hill, a large grass-covered fort of the first millennium B.C. The defences surrounding the hill's flattish summit form a rough oblong, *c.* 131 m. by 85 m., with a rampart up to 15 m. wide and standing in places to a height of over 4 m. Curved round the NE end are three much less substantial ramparts, possible evidence that originally the fort covered a larger area and was later contracted at this end.

6060

EDZELL

Respectable but dour village, originally known as Slateford, which was redeveloped and expanded after 1839, its High Street's houses mostly Victorian or Edwardian and many long used as bed and breakfast establishments for tourists. At each end, a hotel (the GLENESK HOTEL by *David Fraser*, 1896, and the PANMURE ARMS, Victorian in origin but remodelled and extended by *T. Martin Cappon*, 1895–7 with half-timbering but eschewing frivolity).

EDZELL LETHNOT PARISH CHURCH, Lethnot Road. By *David Neave*, 1818. Tall rubble-walled three-bay box, stone Y-tracery in the pointed windows. Battlemented W tower, its openings hoodmoulded. Within the battlement, an iron crown spire topped by a metal bellcote, probably of the late C19. Flat-roofed vestry at the E by *William Fettis*, 1895. Lean-to session house in the NW inner angle, its present form the result of work by *C. G. Soutar*, 1938.

The interior was remodelled by *D. Wishart Galloway*, of *Maclaren, Soutar & Salmond*, 1901–2, who designed a Neo-Jacobean plaster ceiling, W gallery and simple pews and pulpit at the E end. – ORGAN by *J. J. Binns*, 1912.

In the vestibule, a crudely shaped C13 round FONT BOWL. It came from the demolished Navar Parish Church. – BELL of 1701, from Lethnot Parish Church.

OLD PARISH CHURCHYARD, 1.7 km. W. Of the church demolished after the erection of a new church in the village of Edzell in 1818 there remains only the LINDSAY AISLE, a laird's 'aisle' and mausoleum built by Sir David Lindsay of Edzell (ninth Earl of Crawford) *c.* 1549. It is a humble rectangle of sneck-harled rubble, the broad eaves of its slated roof presumably dating from a repair of 1881. Rectangular S window (partly blocked). At the N end, the aisle's entrance into the missing church, its round-headed arch springing from imposts, the jambs chamfered. Inside, below the S window, a segmental-arched recess, perhaps intended to contain a rather small effigy. At the E end of the S wall, an ogee-headed aumbry, a beaded moulding round its arch.

In the surrounding graveyard, a fair number of early and mid-C18 HEADSTONES carved with mantling and shields bearing trade emblems or initials, with reminders of death at the bottom and angels' heads (souls) at the top, several with torches at the sides. – Beside the NE entrance, a crowstep-gabled STORE of *c.* 1900, its upper floor jettied, the NE corner rounded.

DALHOUSIE MEMORIAL ARCH, High Street. Erected in 1888 to commemorate John, thirteenth Earl of Dalhousie and his wife, Ida, who had both died the year before. It was designed by *Hay & Henderson*. Crowstepped gable containing a broad pointed arch which springs from between saddleback-roofed towers. At the sides, pedestrian gateways with pointed arches.

DRINKING FOUNTAIN, High Street. At the street's N end, a garishly painted late C19 fountain by *George Smith & Co.*, of the *Sun Foundry*, its octagonal pillar rising between entwined dolphins.

EDZELL PRIMARY SCHOOL, High Street. Built in 2004. Brick-walled and piend-roofed, mostly of one storey but with a higher hall making a welcome vertical counterpoint.

GANNOCHY BRIDGE, 2.1 km. N. Single ashlar arch over the North Esk, built in 1732. In 1795 it was widened to the SE, that side having, below its parapet, a more assertive string course than the 1730s one which survives on the other side.

INGLIS MEMORIAL HALL, High Street. Built as a memorial to the Rev. Robert Inglis. By *C. & L. Ower*, 1896–8. Scots Renaissance, with crowstepped gables, small angle-rounds, and mullioned-and-transomed windows. At the centre of the front, a dottily detailed tower. Its lowest stage is a porch, its round-headed arches springing from piers inlaid with panels of polished granite. At the front piers, granite-columned nook-shafts and Composite pilasters, those of the principal face with upside-down volutes framing boys' heads. In the porch's broken segmental pediment, mosaic work by *Salviati* giving the hall's name on a background of thistles. Above the porch rises a round tower, its transomed first-floor windows surmounted by steep triangular pediments. On top of this, an octagonal stage with alternating clock faces and curved balconies. Finally, a rather dumpy octagonal spire with stone lucarnes.

Inside, on the S of the entrance hall, a board room, its windows filled with stained glass (thistles) by *William Meikle & Sons*, the firm responsible for all such work in the building. Also original is this room's brass gasolier. Behind, the main hall with a large W gallery and a small gallery over the stage at the E end. More thistle-decorated stained glass in the windows. On the N side of the building, the library, its stained-glass windows a display of improving maxims on a background of thistles. Behind, a small hall, again with stained-glass thistles in the windows.

Former SCHOOL, Lethnot Road and Church Street. By *D. Wishart Galloway*, 1901–2. Sturdy Free Renaissance, with an ogee-roofed octagonal cupola.

EDZELL CASTLE

1.6 km. WNW

Red sandstone palace, roofless but far from gloomy, rising among fields.

An earlier castle, a motte and bailey, probably dating from the C12, stood *c.* 0.4 km. S, immediately beside the Old Parish Churchyard. This was first held by a family which took its surname from its lordship of Glenesk and then by the Stirlings of Glenesk whose line ended *c.* 1350 with two co-heiresses, one of whom, Katherine, married Sir Alexander Lindsay, bringing him the lands of Glenesk and Edzell. Their descendant, David Lindsay of Edzell (from 1542 until his death in 1558 also ninth Earl of Crawford) inherited the property in 1529 and probably soon after began the construction of a new residence on the present site. That was a tower house which stood at the SW corner of a barmkin against whose walls stood ancillary buildings, probably largely of wood, including a kitchen. In the mid C16 David Lindsay decided to replace these ancillary buildings with a quadrangular palace containing the castle's principal rooms, the tower house taking on the status of a private lodging. The new W range* appears to have been completed by the 1550s.† Work on the other ranges was begun by David Lindsay's son, Sir David Lindsay, Lord Edzell, in the later C16 although they seem never to have been completed as intended. In 1604 Sir David constructed the walled garden S of the castle courtyard, a magnificent display of pride in his personal virtues and family's standing.

In the mid and late C17 the Lindsays of Edzell became increasingly embarrassed financially. Finally, in 1714, the last David Lindsay of Edzell sold his properties of Edzell and Glenesk to James Maule, first Earl of Panmure. Panmure joined the Jacobite rising of 1715 and, subsequently, his peerage was attainted and estates forfeited. Edzell Castle was partially dismantled, damage to its fabric increased by its being garrisoned by a force of soldiers from Argyll loyal to the Hanoverian government in 1746. In 1764 the castle's woodwork and roofing materials were stripped and sold. The forfeited estates of the Maules of Panmure were bought back by that family in 1782 but Edzell Castle remained a roofless ruin, further damaged by a gale in 1838. After inheriting the estate in 1852, Fox Maule, second Lord Panmure (later, eleventh

* Really NW but for convenience of description the NW side is given as W, the NE side as N, etc.

† Robert William Billings, *The Baronial and Ecclesiastical Antiquities of Scotland*, ii (1845–52) and Lord Lindsay, *Lives of the Lindsays*, i (1849), 347, reported the coat of arms and initials of David Lindsay of Edzell, together with the date 1553, as being on a carved stone above the castle's principal entrance. David MacGregor Peter, *The Baronage of Angus and Mearns* (1856), 199, wrote that a heraldic stone, now against the N wall of the garden, bore the date 1555.

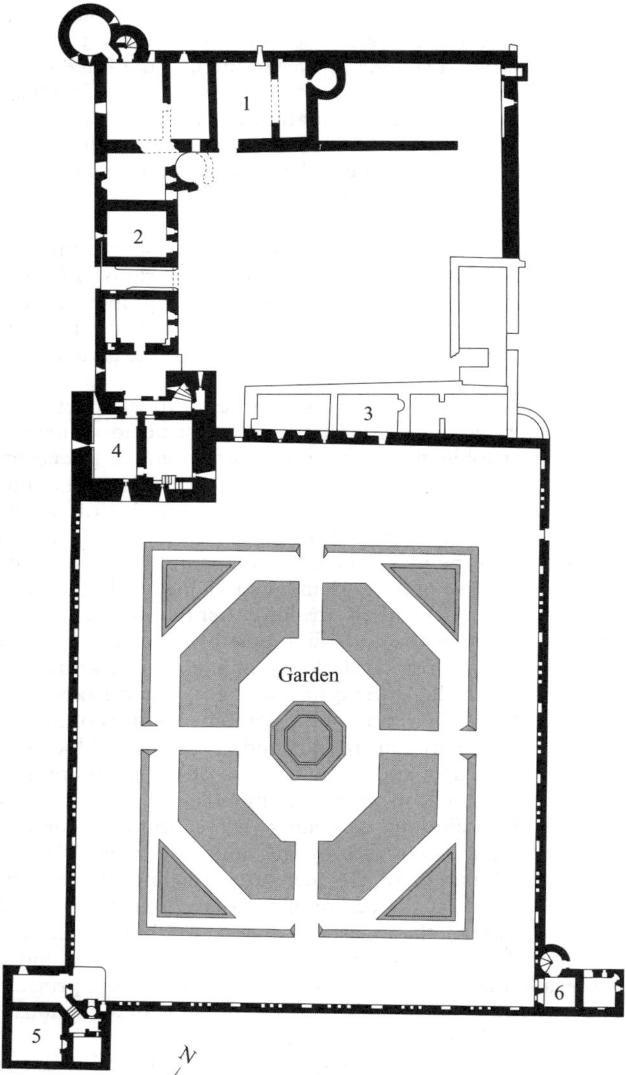

1. North Range
2. West Range
3. South Range
4. Tower House
5. Bath House
6. Summer House

Edzell Castle.
Plan

Earl of Dalhousie), carried out repairs and a custodian's lodge was built beside the castle in 1901 but by 1930 the ruins were again 'in a very bad state'.* However, in 1932 the fifteenth Earl of Dalhousie gave custody of the walled garden to *H.M. Office of Works* which undertook its restoration and replanting a few years later. H.M. Office of Works took over the responsibility for the castle itself in 1936. Since then admirably conservative repair and restoration have been carried out.

The SITE of the castle has been chosen for comfort rather than defence. It is flattish land, sheltered and overlooked from the W and N by the steeply rising slopes of Drummore Hill and the Hill of Edzell but with open views to the S and E. On this the castle buildings surround a N courtyard, the garden a rectangular S enclosure.

The TOWER HOUSE at the SW corner of the N court, like all the other buildings of the castle, is constructed of local red sandstone rubble, with long-and-short quoins at the corners. It is of four storeys and an attic, L-plan, the main block *c.* 13.5 m. by 10.4 m., the NE jamb *c.* 4.7 m. by 1.8 m., its E face flush with the gable of the main block. All round the wall-heads of both the main block and the jamb, a wall-walk, only the lowest course of its battlement surviving, projected on two tiers of chequer-set corbels, the lower tier purely decorative but the appearance of the corbelling possibly intended to suggest a *fess chequy*, the principal charge of the coat of arms of the Lindsays of Edzell. At the centre of the N, W and S faces of the main block and the centre of the combined E faces of the main block and jamb are half-rounds and, at the main block's NW, SW and SE corners and the N corners of the jamb are angle-rounds, all carried on individual moulded corbels above two courses of continuous corbelling, the continuous corbelling under the rounds cut into by the house's corners. The wall-head's combination of chequer-set corbelling, angle-rounds and half-rounds at the centre of each face is strikingly similar to that of Craignethan Castle (Lanarkshire) built in the 1530s and probably contemporary with this house. Set behind the wall-walk, the main block's attic, a chimney-breast projecting at each crowstepped gable, and the remains of a caphouse at the head of the stair in the jamb.

The tower house's masonry below the wall-head rises sheer except for tusking low down on the E side, perhaps marking the position of the original barmkin's S wall a little beyond the S side of the late C16 range. At the ground floor of the main block, irregularly disposed wide-mouthed gunloops, similar to those at Craignethan Castle, in the E and W walls of the main block and the N face of the jamb. They are perhaps primarily for show since such a naturally weak site was chosen for the castle. At the W end of the main block's N face a small roughly

* According to W. Douglas Simpson, 'Edzell Castle', *Proceedings of the Society of Antiquaries of Scotland*, lxv (1930–31), 119.

rectangular vertical gun-slit, perhaps altered when the W range was built (perhaps partly blocking an earlier and wider opening). Small rectangular opening, grooved for glazing, E of this face's door. In the jamb's W face, a much taller inverted keyhole slit for covering fire to defend the entrance. This entrance, set unusually far from the jamb, and not directly below that N half-round, is round-headed and roll-moulded. At the floors above, rectangular windows, quite large at the first and second. All have chamfered margins except at the W elevation where the surrounds have roll-and-hollow mouldings. Are these original or were they remodelled when the W range was built in the mid C16? At this face, under the small first-floor l. window and the close-set second-floor openings, also near the N end, are moulded oval shot-holes, paired at the second floor, with stepped or redented ingoes, perhaps work of the 1550s rather than of twenty years earlier. There may have been another shot-hole under the r. first-floor window but masonry below its sill is missing. At the jamb, quite large slit-like windows light the stair. Elsewhere in the tower, a sprinkling of small windows lighting garderobes and wall closets.

The tower house's entrance is doubly checked for a door backed by a missing iron yett. It opens into a passage along the N side of the main block. In the wall at the passage's W end, a recess, perhaps for a lamp. S of the passage and at a lower level is a pair of cellars; their N entrances share a central jamb and cut into the rough ashlar of their tunnel vaults. The small door at the S end of the wall between the cellars may be an insertion. At the E cellar's S end are stone steps up to the entrance to a straight service stair to the first floor which is contained in the wall thickness. Near the E end of the ground-floor passage, a diagonally set round-headed squinch arch provides a visual nudge to a visitor to turn l. to mount the main stair in the jamb. Under the stair, at the end of the passage, a small porter's room lit only from a N gunloop.

The main stair is a well-lit and broad turnpike which has risen the full height of the house. On the first floor it intrudes into the NE corner of the HALL. Joist holes at the E end of the N side of the hall and in its E gable show that there has been a 2 m.-high screens passage. In this gable, a small fireplace to heat the passage or, perhaps, to warm food before serving. In the thickness of the gable, a garderobe at the N end; S of the fireplace, steps up to a lobby at the head of the service stair from the cellar below. In the hall's N wall, a large corniced fireplace with a roll-and-hollow-moulded surround. Pushing out beside it is the canted corner of a closet, probably originally contained in the wall thickness of the house's SW corner but later, perhaps in the early C17, extended to encroach on the floor space of the hall. It has been shelved and possibly was a charter room. Lighting the closet is a fair-sized window above a circular shot-hole. Two large windows in the hall's S side, the E in a round-headed embrasure and with window seats, the W's embrasure elliptical-headed. Another large window faces

W, its entrance segmental-arched. Just above the tower house's first-floor level, a narrow door, presumably inserted in the 1550s, opens off the main stair to the first floor of the castle's W range.

The wooden floors of the tower house's upper storeys are missing. The second floor has contained two rooms, each with a small fireplace in one of the gables. In the S wall, a pair of side-by-side garderobes, one for each room, the entrance to the W garderobe surmounted by a small window. The W room has contained a NW closet very like that in the same position on the floor below and presumably also enlarged. At the third floor, only a W fireplace. At the E end, a fairly small window whose segmental-arched embrasure contains stone seats. To the N, a rectangular recess. The attic has been lit from windows in the gables. Fireplace towards the W end of the N side.

The mid-C16 WEST RANGE between the tower house and the W gable of the N range has been of two storeys and, over the section S of the castle entrance, an attic. The W front stands almost to the wall-head, the E elevation to the castle's courtyard is more fragmented but still substantial. The ground floor of the front is pierced by three wide-mouthed gunloops, smaller but of similar appearance to those of the tower house. Of these, two are to the l. and one to the r. of the off-centre round-headed entrance. The S end of this front is divided visually from the rest by a large wall-head chimney containing the flue of the kitchen fireplace. In this S section, a small first-floor window with a chamfered surround and, above, the bottom of a dormer window, its surround also chamfered. N of this the first floor is of four bays, the windows grouped 2:2 and with roll-and-hollow-moulded surrounds. In the centre of the S pair above the entrance, the moulded frames for four missing heraldic panels arranged as an H laid on its side.

The entrance, checked for a single door, opens onto a tunnel-vaulted transe, its side walls with stone benches for most of their length; lamp recess on the S near the doorway. At the range's S end has been a lobby which sheltered the entrance to the tower house. Most of the ground-floor masonry of the lobby's E wall has been removed so that a segmental relieving arch over its doorway now looks like a tall entrance. The first-floor room over the lobby is entered from the tower house's main stair. In this room's N wall, a window looking into the adjoining probable bedchamber in the W range and possibly intended as a serving hatch for food prepared in the W range's kitchen and brought up the tower-house stair for consumption in the bedchamber. The attic room above has been entered from the W range's room to its N. Adjoining the ground-floor lobby is a tunnel-vaulted kitchen, entered both from the lobby and also from the courtyard. Square windows, one at a high level, to the courtyard. Filling the W end, a wide segmental-arched fireplace, an oven in its S ingo. N of the entrance transe the ground floor contains two tunnel-vaulted rooms, the S apparently a store, the N (with a small fireplace at the W end) perhaps a guardroom. On the first floor, over these rooms and the transe, were two rooms, both with fireplaces in the E wall, the larger (N) room probably the 'outer chamber of dais' mentioned in an inventory of 1573,* the smaller a bedchamber with a close garderobe in the SW corner. These rooms are reached by a stair contained in a now ruinous polygonal tower which projected into the courtyard at the N end of the range. The tower probably dated from the later C16 and was built as part of the N range although a stair approximately in this position must have been provided in the 1550s. The lower part of the l. jamb of the tower's courtyard entrance survives and shows that it was classical of a sort with a column and fluted pilaster on the outside of a rope moulding.

Rising flush at the end of the W range is the NORTH RANGE's crowstepped and chimney-topped three-storey gable containing large roll-and-hollow-moulded windows. Projecting from its NW corner, a round tower of four storeys. In the tower's E inner angle, a bowed stair-turret which must have been an afterthought during the construction of this range since it blocks a gunloop at the ground floor of the tower. Both tower and turret have been finished with a battlement carried on moulded individual corbels. At the tower, wide-mouthed gunloops like those of the tower house and W range. Only the W half of the N range seems to have been completed as intended and its S wall is now missing.

The N range's ground floor has contained three tunnel-vaulted rooms, the W, off which is the service stair to the upper floors, probably a wine cellar. The E room has been a kitchen, its end occupied by the fireplace, a circular oven projecting behind it. Recess, perhaps a salt-box, in the fireplace's N ingo. In the N wall, W of the fireplace, a large slop drain. The first floor is filled by the castle's great hall, a huge room of *c.* 15.2 m. by 7.3 m., its principal approach originally from the stair-tower in the inner angle of the W and N ranges. Fireplace in the N wall, a little E of centre but centred if allowance is made for a screens passage at the W end. Over the missing screens passage has been a minstrels' gallery entered from a door off the NW service stair. At the N wall's E end there survives the top of the round-headed arch of a buffet recess. At the E gable of the great hall have been closets which flanked the projecting flue of the kitchen fireplace. They have contained doorways to the intended adjoining room to the E but these openings have been blocked and a gunloop inserted in the N, presumably when it was decided to postpone or omit the construction of an upper floor over the N range's E half. The second floor of the N range's W half has contained two rooms. In the NW round tower, a room at each floor, the lowest with a tunnel vault although a domical vault might have been expected, the top with a fireplace.

The E half of the N range seems to have been intended as one wing of an L-plan building, the other wing forming the

* National Library of Scotland, Acc. 9769/4/1/84.

courtyard's EAST RANGE. This building stands to a height of about one-and-a-half storeys, apparently all that was constructed, but tusking at the E gable of the N range's W half shows that it was intended to be of three storeys. At the NE corner, just above the level of the completed lower parts of the first-floor windows, are rounded corbels, probably for a battlement.

The courtyard's SOUTH RANGE, probably of the later C16, has contained four rooms, their foundations visible, the masonry suggesting two phases of construction. Only the S wall stands above the lowest courses; in it, chamfered windows and a door to the garden.

46 The GARDEN S of the courtyard is a rectangle, *c.* 43.6 m. by 52.4 m. but with the castle's tower house intruding on the NW corner. Projecting from the S corners are a summerhouse at the SE and the foundations of a bath house at the SW. On the N side the garden was bounded by the S range of the castle courtyard, on the others by walls. Externally, these are constructed of large blocks of rubble and finished with a cornice surmounted by a cope. At the NE corner, remains of an angle-round carried on continuous corbelling containing downward-pointing shot-holes. On the E side, the cornice steps up in suggestion of the low merlons of a battlement, these surmounted by segmental pediments decorated with abstract and floral designs, including representations of thistles. Near this wall's N end is the garden's principal entrance, a roll-moulded rectangular doorway. Above, a moulded frame topped by a steep broken pediment, the frame containing a panel carved with the impaled coats of arms of Sir David Lindsay, Lord Edzell, and his wife, Dame Isabel Forbes, together with the date 1604, probably that of the garden's completion; the same pedimented framework and panel are repeated on the inner side of the gateway.

Inside the garden, the N wall is unadorned, broken only by the windows of the castle's S range and, at the W end, an unobtrusive gateway from the courtyard. Each of the garden's W, S and E walls is partly faced with ashlar in which is carried out the heraldic and iconographic scheme of decoration which makes the garden of Edzell a uniquely accomplished proclamation of Sir David Lindsay's lineage and learning. These walls have been divided into 3 m.-wide bays by Doric pilasters, their tall shafts now missing but the dogtooth-ornamented bands which cross them halfway up still in place. Over the centre of each bay of the E wall, a segmental-pedimented stone, its face containing a round-headed recess above a cushion-like base and probably intended to house a bust, the pediment's tympanum carved with a blank scroll. Similar recesses also at the S wall but now without pediments. The W wall has no recesses and is finished with a plain cornice. Alternate bays of the W, S and E walls contain the *fess chequy* armorial charge of the Lindsays of Edzell formed by chequer-set bands of alternating square panels flush with the walling and square recesses, the panels probably originally painted blue and the recesses' dished bases planted with silver flowers to provide the correct heraldic colouring of *azure* and *argent*, the surrounding red sandstone the *gules* ground of the coat of arms of the Lindsays of Edzell. At the top of each of these heraldic bays is a band carved with three mullets (stars), the heraldic charge of the Stirlings of Glenesk from whom the Lindsays had inherited Edzell; at the centre of each mullet, a round hole in the wall, perhaps intended as a nesting box. In each intermediate bay of the three pilastered walls is a sizeable rectangular horizontal recess, *c*. 0.9 m. by 0.6 m., its base ditched for planting. Above, a panel carved in relief and with its head flanked by stones pierced by round holes, perhaps also meant for nesting boxes. The reliefs on the panels proclaim the influences which had combined to make Sir David Lindsay of Edzell an exemplar of learning and virtue. The W and E walls seem intended to be read from r. to l. and the walls themselves in a sequence from the W via the S to the E.

The panels of the W wall are rectangular, the centres of their sides decorated with scrolls, their heads with foliage. Each is carved in vigorous but lumpy manner with a female figure emblematic of one of the Cardinal Virtues and identified by its Latin name. The derivation of the designs may be from German woodcuts. At the l. end of the wall is Temperance (TEMPERANTIA) diluting a cup of wine with water. Then, Strength (FORTITUDO) breaking the head off a column. Next, Prudence (PRVDENTIA), the figure with a serpent (emblem of wisdom) coiled round one arm and holding a mirror to reflect her face, the action symbolic of self-knowledge. Three of the last four of these Virtues are specifically Christian and it is possible that originally the sequence culminated with the Christian Virtues. The first of these four is Charity (CARITAS), the main female figure holding naked children in her arms while others cling to her skirt.* Then, Justice (JUSTITIA) carrying her emblems of a sword and scales followed by Hope (SPES) accompanied by an anchor and spade. The last figure is Faith (FIDES) trampling a serpent and holding a chalice and the shaft of a cross whose head has weathered away.

The panels, also rectangular but larger, on the S wall symbolize the Seven Liberal Arts and are arranged, from l. to r., in the order in which they were studied by scholars. Each contains an emblematic female figure set in a pilastered and round-headed frame, the designs also probably derived from German woodcuts but the carving more accomplished. At the l., a panel depicting Grammar (GRAMMATICA), the original inscription largely lost and a later inscription incised on the l. pilaster labelling the figure as EDUCATOR. Tucked into her girdle is a birch, seated beside her a boy. Next is Rhetoric

* This panel had been built into the S wall and was placed here after 1932. In 1930 the four S places on the W wall (from r. to l.) were occupied by panels depicting Faith, Justice, Hope and an empty space.

(RHETORICA), also seated, a scroll in one hand, a *caduceus* (symbol of Eloquence) in the other. Another seated figure, Dialectic (DIALECTICA) follows, one of her arms encircled by a serpent (symbol of the wiles of dialectic), a swallow (symbol of chatter) on her head, a pair of frogs (symbolizing garrulity) at her feet. Behind her l. shoulder, the small figure of a mantled philosopher, probably Aristotle; another figure, probably of Zeno, was formerly discernible behind her r. shoulder. Then, Arithmetic (ARITHMETICA), a well-preserved studious-looking lady engrossed in making a calculation on a tablet. Next,
48 Music (MUSICA), the now headless figure playing a lute; other musical instruments float in the background. There follows
47 Geometry (GEOMETRIA), the full-bosomed figure with one foot resting on books and measuring a serpent-entwined globe with a pair of calipers; below are compasses, a setsquare and a bevel-stock. Over the entrance to the bath house at the wall's W end (*see* below) is the recess for a missing panel which presumably depicted Astronomy.

The panels (some now replicas) on the garden's E wall are rectangular but contain central ovals on which are depicted the Planetary Deities identified by their astronomical signs, their designs, except for that of Saturn, taken from a series of engravings produced at Nuremberg in 1528–9 by an artist known from his initials as Meister I. B., the carving the most graceful of the three sets of panels at Edzell. In the engravings and in most of the panels here, each of the Planetary Deities except the Sun and Moon was accompanied by a 'day house' and a 'night house' consisting of the constellations corresponding to zodiacal signs; the Sun and Moon, rulers of the Day and Night, were accompanied only by a 'day house' and a 'night house' respectively. The S panel, over the entrance to the summerhouse (*see* below) is carved with a relief of Diana (emblematic of the Moon and, in medieval thought, the patron of Infancy) holding in one hand a crescent moon, in the other a spear. She stands on a badly weathered object shown in old drawings and the Nuremberg engravings as a lobster, presumably intended to identify the zodiacal sign, *Cancer* (a crab) of the Moon's 'night house'. Next, on the garden wall itself, a panel with thistles at the outer corners, the central oval containing the figure of Mercury (patron of Childhood) shown as a youth wearing a sword, winged helmet and sandals and holding a *caduceus*. By his feet were small figures, now weathered away, of his 'day house' (*Virgo*) and 'night house' (*Gemini*). To the N, a panel with roses at its corners. On the central oval, a relief of Venus (patron of Adolescence) holding in one hand a (mutilated) heart and, in the other, a dart. Above her r. hand is a stylized balance, the zodiacal sign of her 'day house' (*Libra*); crouched at her feet is her 'night house' of *Taurus* (a bull). Then, a panel with fleurs-de-lis in the corners. In the oval, a figure emblematic of the Sun (patron of Youth) shown striding away, his head half turned to look back. He carries a flaming torch and a shield bearing the symbol of the Sun in Glory. At his feet the crouching lion (*Leo*) of his 'day house'. In the panel beyond, a representation of Mars (patron of Middle Age) clad in a mixture of medieval and antique armour and with a sword, shield and halberd, the last bearing the initials IB, those of the artist of the Nuremberg engraving from which the design was taken. At his feet, a ram emblematic of his 'night house' (*Aries*). No emblem of his 'day house' (*Scorpio*) is now visible and it may never have existed here. The next panel depicts Jupiter (patron of Old Age) holding a sword and shield. On the shield, a kneeling archer to represent his 'day house' (*Sagittarius*). There used to be seen behind the main figure a depiction of two fishes for Jupiter's 'night house' (*Pisces*). The last of the panels before the gateway shows Saturn (patron of Senility and cripples), one-legged (the other replaced by a wooden limb), carrying a scythe in one hand and with the other holding a child whom he is about to devour. At his feet, a goat emblematic of his 'day house' (*Capricorn*); his 'night house' (*Aquarius*) has been omitted. Between this bay of the E wall and the next is the pedimented gateway (*see* above), clearly designed as a ceremonial exit from the walled garden to the less formal open landscape beyond. N of the gateway, two more bays of the garden's E wall, treated like the other main bays but the N's oval panel is uncarved. Perhaps it was painted with a depiction of the 'crystal heaven' or eighth firmament containing, according to medieval cosmogony, the fixed stars.

LAYOUT AND PLANTING of the garden were undertaken in 1934–8, the design by *James S. Richardson*, Inspector of Ancient Monuments for Scotland, with advice from *Sir John Stirling-Maxwell*, Chairman of the Ancient Monuments Board for Scotland. Excavation had found some evidence of a central feature where a large yew bush has now been planted. All the rest is conjectural. In the *fess chequy* wall recesses are blue and white lobelias, marigolds in the larger horizontal recesses, the colours those of the armorial charge of the Lindsays of Edzell. The ground is laid out as a lawn and flower beds.

Outside the garden's SW corner are the foundations of a BATH HOUSE which were uncovered by excavation in 1855. Probably built *c.* 1604 it has been L-plan, the main block standing against the S wall of the garden, the jamb against the W. In the garden's W wall, a roll-moulded door and adjoining window sharing a central jamb. Above, the S panel (Hope) of the Cardinal Virtues (*see* above); to its r., the lower part of an oval surround for a window or a panel has been built into the wall, perhaps as part of the repairs carried out in the early 1850s. Also not *in situ* are the capital and base of a pilaster placed in the inner angle of the main block and jamb. At the W end of the S wall of the garden, a rectangular opening, its sill serving as the head of a circular ashlar-walled well-shaft which could be reached from either side of the wall. To the l. of the well-shaft, a low-set roll-moulded window above a slop drain. The bath house's main block S of the garden wall has contained three rooms; in the jamb are steps down to a door which opened onto parkland W of the castle.

Projecting E from the garden's SE corner is a two-storey crowstep-gabled SUMMERHOUSE, also of *c.* 1604. Again it is L-plan, the broad NW jamb in the inner angle with the E wall of the garden containing a stair to the upper floor; at the SE corner, a rounded turret carried on continuous corbelling. In the main block, a simply moulded N door and ground-floor windows to the N and S. The unmoulded door into the jamb looks like an insertion, perhaps of the mid C19. More elaborate mouldings at the first-floor openings, each gable containing an identical window surmounted by a concave-sided and flat-topped pedimental head, the sides of the E embellished with scrolls, the tympana carved with foliage and the initials of Sir David Lindsay, Lord Edzell. The summerhouse's W front is formed by the E wall of the garden and contains the first of the panels depicting the Planetary Deities (*see* above) but flanked by a pair of vesica openings and surmounted by a pedimented recess; above this the wall is carried up as the summerhouse's upper floor. In this bay of the garden wall, instead of a big horizontal recess, there are a simply moulded door and window. Under the S and E windows of the first floor are trios of closely spaced shot-holes, the outer two circular, the centre diamond-shaped; at the SE turret, three large round shot-holes. Deep-set and redented circular shot-hole in the E face of the stair-tower. Less decorative but perhaps of more serious murderous intent are the downward-pointing small shot-hole covering the summerhouse's N entrance and the four smallshot-holes in the SE turret.

Inside the summerhouse, two ground-floor rooms, the tunnel-vaulted E room entered from the N and with no communication with the building's other rooms. The W room, entered from the garden, is square and covered by a quadripartite vault, its heavy moulded ribs meeting at a mutilated pendant. The stone bench round the walls and stone round table in the centre of the room probably date from the 1850s repairs. From this room, a turnpike stair in the jamb rises to the first-floor room which occupies the whole of the main block. Fireplace in the E gable and a cupboard at the E end of the N wall; closet in the SE turret.

In the summerhouse are CARVED STONES AND WOODWORK brought here from elsewhere in the castle complex and beyond. In the ground floor's E room, the original carved stone panels of the Planetary Deities from the garden's E wall. In the main block's first-floor room are C16 oak panels, perhaps formerly in the castle's chapel which is on record in 1573. They are carved with stylized depictions of the Annunciation, the Virgin and Child, the Crucifixion, foliage and a grotesque head issuing from among leaves. Also in this room are the central boss and one arm of a free-standing stone cross, probably of the C9, formerly in Edzell Old Churchyard. The front of the boss is carved with interlacing and of the arm with a repetitive key pattern. The back of both boss and arm are decorated with spirals disposed in circular shapes.

Placed against the N wall of the garden are FRAGMENTS of heraldic stones. One is a cracked slab bearing a pair of badly weathered shields, one bearing the arms and flanked by the initials of David Lindsay of Edzell, the other with the coat of arms of his wife, Margaret Wishart. It must date from between 1595 when they married and his death in 1646 and was formerly at the demolished Auchmull Castle 5.4 km. away. – Three originally separate fragments have been combined to form a not very satisfactory whole. One is carved with part of the lion rampant supporter of the coat of arms of the Earls of Crawford and may be of the later C16. Another bears the impaled coats of arms of Lindsay and Campbell of Cawdor for David, ninth Earl of Crawford, and his second wife, Catherine Campbell. Presumably it dates from between 1549 when they married and her death in 1578 and came from either the N or, more likely, the W range of the castle. The third fragment, part of a segmental dormerhead, is carved with the plumes of a helmet, the opening letters of the motto of the Earls of Crawford ('Endure fort') and the initials D^E^L, perhaps for David, Earl Lindsay (i.e. David Lindsay, Earl of Crawford). It was said in the mid C19 to have borne the date [15]55.* – Almost complete is a triangular dormerhead, its sides decorated with scrolls, the tympanum with a shield bearing the coat of arms of Lindsay, the date 1664 and the initials IL, IL, for John Lindsay of Edzell and his wife, Jean Lindsay.

VISITOR CENTRE 0.1 km. E of the castle, dated 1901 and built as a custodian's house. Superior cottage in a late C16 Scots manner.

DOOCOT 0.4 km. ESE of the castle. Probably mid-C16 and *c.* 6.5 m. square, built of harled rubble. Saddleback roof with a cavetto cornice whose moulding continues at the gables' crowsteps. At diagonally opposite (NW and SE) corners are the lower parts of angle-rounds timidly projected on continuous corbelling; their upper parts have been cut down and they are now covered by the main roof. Round the walls, a moulded rat course which jumps up at the centre of each face, presumably over the frame for a panel; one frame, at the N gable, survives. In the gables, flight-holes above projecting stone perches. The original entrance was at the W; a second door has been inserted in the E gable. Inside, stone nesting boxes.

DOULIE TOWER, 3.6 km. N of Edzell. Folly built in 1796 beside a woodland path from The Burn (Aberdeenshire) along the top of the steep E bank of the River North Esk. It is a rubble-walled and battlemented round tower, the two stages delineated by a band course. At both stages, angular Gothic openings to the S, tall at the ground floor, dummies at the upper. Short and

* David MacGregor Peter, *The Baronage of Angus and Mearns* (1856), 199.

lower screen walls extend E and W, each with a Gothic doorway under a round dummy window.

DUNLAPPIE, 1.6 km. SW. Grey sandstone villa designed by *Thoms & Wilkie* in 1901, and extended in 1924. Two-storey double-pile main block, the manner gentle Scots Jacobean with crowstepped gables and shaped dormerheads over the upper windows of the N front. NE corner splayed at the ground floor and corbelled to the square above. Loggia-like porch. At the W elevation, a two-storey canted bay window fronting the l. gable and, at the broader gable to the W, a much longer but single-storey bay window, its ends also splayed. The roof sweeps down over the SW back wing whose first floor is relegated to attic status. The SE addition of 1924 is also Scots domestic, with a pair of battlemented and canted two-storey bay windows on the E side.

Inside, a panelled entrance hall with a compartmented plaster ceiling of Jacobean character. Ionic-pilastered wide elliptical arch to the stair-hall behind. Off the stair-hall's W side, the dining room, also panelled and with a Jacobean plaster ceiling. At its N wall, Artisan Mannerist Corinthianish pilasters frame the chimneypiece and mirrored overmantel. Unambitious Late Georgian Revival husked plasterwork on the ceiling of the drawing room in the house's NE corner. Beamed ceiling to the Billiard Room in the wing of 1924.

LUNDIE CASTLE. *See* p. 603.

6040

ETHIE CASTLE

2.8 km. N of Auchmithie

Large but low-key manor house, its walling all of red sandstone rubble. It has developed from the C16 to the late C19.

The house was probably begun *c.* 1530 for David Beaton, Abbot of Arbroath (later, Cardinal Archbishop of St Andrews). In 1555 the estate was acquired by Sir Robert Carnegie of Kinnaird and in 1596 passed to his grandson, John Carnegie, who was created Earl of Ethie in 1647 (the title changing to Earl of Northesk in 1666) in whose family it remained until the early C20.

The earliest part is at the SW corner. This was L-plan with a three-storey crowstep-gabled main block and a short NW jamb. Probably there was a rectangular barmkin enclosure on the N with ancillary buildings, perhaps of wood, along its other sides. Perhaps in the mid C16, a stone-built screen wall containing the courtyard's entrance was erected along the barmkin's W side. In the late C16 or earlier C17 the original house was extended with a sizeable wing across its E end and a detached range, perhaps partly intended as a jointure house but also containing a large kitchen, built on the courtyard's N side. Probably in the early C18 a W range was built behind the courtyard's W screen wall. In 1891–2 *R. Rowand Anderson* further remodelled the house, adding two further storeys to the early C16 house's jamb to make a tall tower, the only display of real pretension.

The main front faces W. Roughly symmetrical in a C17 manner with the two-storey W range stretched between the taller gables of the N and S ranges. At the centrepiece, quite small ground-floor windows and tall first-floor openings, probably enlarged in the earlier C19, all these with chamfered margins. In the centre bay, the C16 courtyard entrance (now the principal entrance to the house) with a roll-and-hollow-moulded surround; the coat of arms above is a late C20 replacement. At the front's l. end, the N range's three-storey gable, its S slope crowstepped, its N with a straight skew, the first-floor window also probably enlarged. At the gable's N corner, a conical-roofed four-storey tower, its top floor jettied. To the r. of the front's centrepiece, the early C16 house standing on a splay-topped base. Its jamb now serves as the lower part of the tower formed in 1891–2, the Victorian upper floors' masonry squared and stugged. The ground-floor window looks C17. At the tower's wall-head, a dentilated cornice topped by a balustrade. Projected on continuous corbelling from the tower's NW corner is a tall conical-roofed round turret, its upper stages jettied. At the S end of the house's W elevation, the crowstepped gable of the main block of the early C16 house. The ground floor's low window with a chamfered margin is probably a C17 insertion or alteration. Higher up, at the r. of the gable, a small stair window. Tall first-floor window, also in a chamfered surround but it may be of the earlier C19, a disturbance in the adjacent masonry suggesting that there may have been an earlier opening further N. To the l. of this window, a blocked slit window, probably of the C16.

At the S elevation of the early C16 house, three ground-floor windows, all with chamfered margins. The l. is quite small but seems to have been restored, perhaps in 1891–2. The central opening is smaller still and probably original. The r. window is now of two lights and Victorian in appearance but the upper parts of its jambs look earlier, and perhaps there was a low horizontally proportioned opening here originally. Three first-floor windows grouped 1:2, the W probably C17. The other two have both been deepened in the early C19 and the position of the l. shifted to the r. The three second-floor windows rise through the eaves, their present appearance of 1891–2 when Anderson heightened the centre window and gave them all Neo-Jacobean pedimented dormerheads carved with the coat of arms, crest and coronet of the Earls of Northesk. The early C17 extension at the E end of this block begins with an advanced and crowstepped broad gable, the upper floors jettied, the windows all of the 1890s and with chamfered margins. Set slightly back from the gable, at the house's SE corner, a crowstep-gabled square jamb containing a stair. The attic window of the jamb's S side is surmounted by a semicircular dormerhead bearing the initials $I^{S}C$ and $M^{D}H$ (for Sir John

Carnegie of Ethie (later, Earl of Ethie and Earl of Northesk) and Dame Magdalen Hallyburton, his wife) together with the date 1627, perhaps that of the addition's construction. At the addition's principal E elevation, a large central chimneystack jettied out from the wall. The second-floor windows rise into pedimented dormerheads of C17 type, the r. apparently a replacement but the l., perhaps of 1655, bearing the initials I[E]E (for John, Earl of Ethie) and the date 16–5. At the N end of this wing, an 1890s addition and, projecting in its NW inner angle with the house's low E range, a stair jamb whose design Anderson took from the C17 addition's SE jamb but with a bowed turret with a half-conical roof in the E inner angle.

The house's N range is informal, its W part consisting of the late C16 or early C17 three-storey block whose gable faces the approach. The range continues to the E with a two-storey extension, a bowed stair-tower at the centre of its S front, and a single-storey addition beyond, both of these C19. Single-storey passage additions of the C19 serve to link the inner sides of the ranges round two courtyards.

INTERIOR. At the house's SW corner, the ground floor of the main block of the early C16 house survives, the rooms probably all originally cellars or stores. The W is tunnel-vaulted. In the W side, a C17-style chimneypiece, probably inserted in 1891–2. In the wall thickness of the SW corner, a narrow stair to the first floor so this room was probably the original wine cellar. Over the centre room (now Chapel), a pointed tunnel vault. Another pointed tunnel vault over the vestry to the N in an early addition to this house. E of the Chapel, another cellar, its tunnel vault semicircular. In the centre of the house's N range, the Tudor Kitchen, the house's late C16 or early C17 double-height kitchen; at its E end, a huge segmental-arched fireplace, the surround chamfered. The room was probably originally vaulted. On the first floor, the SW room was the hall of the early C16 house. Compartmented plaster ceiling of *c.* 1630, imperfectly aligned with the shape of the room. The walls' panelling is in a late C17 manner but probably of the 1890s. Behind it, at the E wall's N end, a window which has been blocked by the construction of the early C17 SE addition. In the other principal rooms, ceilings and panelling of the 1890s, all in C17 style.

SE of the house, a battlemented and Gothic-windowed octagonal FOLLY built in 1907, the walls clad externally with boulders; forestair to the flat roof. Inside, the walls are studded with pebbles. On one wall, a panel bearing the coroneted coat of arms and initials of David John, [tenth] Earl of Northesk.

Immediately E of the house, a GARDEN with rubble walls, their present form of 1784, on the N and E sides. In the E wall, corniced GATEPIERS, their stepped tops surmounted by ball finials, the elaborate wrought-iron gates decorated with foliage, the overthrow's top a coronet. The gates open onto a further WALLED GARDEN. In its SE corner, a two-storey-and-attic GARDEN HOUSE of 1674, the first floor reached by a forestair.

FARNELL

6050

Hamlet on the S edge of the parkland of Kinnaird Castle (q.v.).

FARNELL PARISH CHURCH. Gothick, an early and sophisticated example of the style applied to Georgian churches in Scotland. *James Playfair*, who produced working drawings and estimates of the cost in 1788–9, was probably the architect but the church was not built until 1806, twelve years after his death. Ashlar-walled oblong, with slender stepped buttresses along the battlemented four-bay sides. At the N side, pointed three-light dummy windows with splayed ingoes at the centre bays; at the ends, doors under large crosslet dummy arrowslits. In the S side away from the approach, just a narrow window in each of the two centre bays. Each gable is in the shape of a pointed arch, its head formed by a curved parapet like a screen wall which hides the straight pitches of the roof and is surmounted by crenelles whose curved tops describe outer arcs aligned with those of the curved sides of the arch itself. In the E gable, a four-light window with intersecting tracery. The W gable's main window is also of four lights but narrower and flanked by two-light openings. Near the head of this gable, a tabernacled Gothic recess containing the church bell. Projecting from the gable is the flat-roofed session house added by *D. Wishart Galloway* in 1929.

Inside, a quadripartite-vaulted plaster ceiling, the main ribs springing from corbels modelled as feminine angels. Pine PEWS of 1852 installed when the pulpit was shifted from the centre of the S side to the E end and the E and N galleries removed. – WEST GALLERY of 1806, carried on cluster-shafted columns; pine front, its panels decorated with alternating stars and quatrefoils.

GRAVEYARD. S of the church, a railed burial enclosure. In its N side, a large MONUMENT to David Carnegy of Craigo, Minister of Farnell, †1672, his first wife, Helen Lindsay, †1656 and ten of their children. Aedicular, the fluted pilasters with exceptionally heavy capitals surmounted by ball finials. These flank a semicircular pediment carved with a coat of arms. – A few C18 HEADSTONES. One, to the W of this enclosure, of 1767 to Thomas Spence and Helena Mathew bears on the W face a pair of angels' heads (souls) above a shield which displays a ploughshare and coulter; emblems of death at the top of the E face. – On another, S of the enclosure, erected by David Oeikinheid to his children, John, James and Robert, †1699–1714, a large angel's head and initials on the W face; emblems of death again on the E.

Former PARISH MANSE, W of the graveyard. Two-storey rubble-walled main block of *c.* 1795, the three-bay W front with a central gablet and later porch. To the E, two L-plan office buildings, perhaps early C19. – At the entrance to the garden, small but smart corniced and ball-finialled GATEPIERS of *c.* 1800, their masonry with V-jointed rustication.

FARNELL SCHOOL, N of the church. Now housing and a shop (House of Farnell). Main block built in 1855 incorporating earlier work. Stone-mullioned three-light windows to the E and mullioned-and-transomed windows in the gables. W wing of 1875, the tall windows rising through the eaves to decoratively bargeboarded gabled dormerheads. More bargeboards on the S porch.

FARNELL CASTLE

0.3 km. W

Red-harled C15 manor house of the bishops of Brechin, altered and extended in the late C16 and later used as an almshouse before its restoration in 1966.

The building is a three-storey oblong, the crowsteps of the E and mid gables gableted, one of the E skewputts inscribed with a crowned M (for *Maria*), the other with JM (for *Jesus Maria*). Possibly the mid gable marks the original end of the building and the part to its W is a C16 addition. At the E gable, brackets to support a first-floor wooden gallery whose roof beam has been carried on corbels at the gable's head; sloping stone roof ridge above. At the E end of the N side is a full-height projection which enclosed the drains from garderobes at the upper floors. Quite small ground-floor windows. The first-floor openings seem to have been enlarged. Roughly at the centre of the S front, a bowed stair-tower under a crowstep-gabled rectangular top; this was probably added by Archibald, fifth Earl of Argyll, who acquired the estate in 1566, or the next owner, James, fifth Lord Ogilvy of Airlie, *c.* 1580. Round shot-hole under one window at first-floor level and another to the l. of the entrance. At this side's W end, a rubble-built and battlemented ground-floor protuberance of uncertain purpose. Tusking at the house's SE corner indicates that a wall, perhaps for a barmkin enclosure, has extended S.

KINNAIRD CASTLE. *See* p. 551.

4060

FERN

Rural hamlet.

PARISH CHURCH. By *Carver & Symon*, 1883. Broad buttressed Gothic box with a NE vestry. S tower, with an angle-buttressed lower stage. At the belfry, chamfered corners and two-light openings. Corbelled parapet, a purposeful stone spout projecting from the centre of each face. Inside the parapet, a saddleback-roofed caphouse.

Inside, a collar-braced roof, the spandrels pierced. Bench PEWS facing the pitch-pine Gothic PULPIT at the E end. – STAINED GLASS. In the E gable, l. of the pulpit, a late C19 two-light window (the Baptism of Our Lord; Moses), strongly coloured and realistic. – To the r. of the pulpit, two lights ('Consider the Lilies') by *A. Ballantine & Son*, 1909. – Also by Ballantine and of 1909 the three-light window (Our Lord in Glory Adored by Angels) high up in the centre of the gable. – In the S wall's E end, a lushly coloured window of 1924 (Isaiah). – Beside it, the First World War memorial window of *c.* 1920 (Our Lord Holding the Crown of Life) and, to its W, a more sketchily drawn mid-C20 depiction of the Nativity of Our Lord. – In the W gable, an accomplished three-light window (Our Lord with St John the Baptist and St John the Evangelist, a small figure of the Sower at the bottom) by *C. E. Kempe & Co. Ltd*, 1933. – In the vestibule, a BELL cast in Flanders in 1506.

Propped against the S wall of the church, the worn fragment of a GRAVE-SLAB, perhaps of *c.* 1700, crudely carved with two angels trumpeting over a skeleton. – A few C18 HEADSTONES decorated with heraldry and emblems of death but most of the monuments are C19 and unremarkable.

To the S, a plain harled MANSE of 1808.

OLD SCHOOL HOUSE. Now a private house. Bargeboarded school and school house of 1859, incorporating earlier work.

SCHOOL. Dated 1897. Quite aggressive with crowstepped gables and bull-nosed masonry; small cupola.

AUCHNACREE, 2.9 km. N. Harled two-storey shooting lodge built in 1836 but extended later. On the E front, a multiplicity of steeply gabled dormerheads. – To the W, a mid-C19 rubble-built and crowstep-gabled group of OFFICES, one building topped by a cupola containing a clock.

EASTER OGIL, 3.1 km. W. Built for James Forrest, a Kirriemuir banker and merchant, *c.* 1850. Steeply gabled Elizabethan manorial style. The battlemented tower with a spire-roofed square caphouse on one corner is a Late Victorian addition.

NORANSIDE. *See* p. 651.

VAYNE CASTLE. *See* p. 681.

FERRYDEN 7050

Former fishing village and, until the opening of the first Bridge of Montrose in 1796, the S end of a ferry across the South Esk. At the W end, overlooking a late C20 Oil Service Base, plain C19 housing. Also C19 but more picturesque is the fishertown vernacular of the buildings at the E end of the village.

INCHBRAYOCK PARISH CHURCH, Church Road. Originally Craig Free Church. By *John Greig*, 1844, but recast in 1898 by *John Sim*. As first built it was a rubble-walled M-roofed double-pile with an E steeple. In the 1890s remodelling the walls were heightened by *c.* 1.8 m., the church's E bay made a quasi-transept, and the side windows enlarged as mullioned-and-transomed rectangular openings. The main elevation is the E (now harled and the dressings largely renewed in cement). A pair of round-arched Y-traceried windows flanking the tower appear to be of 1844 but the round lights and gablets above are of 1897. The faces of the tower's two stages are panelled and the detail 'Saxon' of an unarchaeological Late Georgian type. Rising within the battlement, an octagonal slated spire topped by a dove weathervane.

INCHBRAOCH CEMETERY. *See* Montrose: Cemeteries.

HALL, Beacon Terrace. Mid-C19. Tall single storey, a spiky finial on the gable front.

INCHBRAYOCK PARISH CHURCH HALLS, Brownlow Place. Lanceted Gothic, built in 1876 and extended, 1884.

INFANT SCHOOL, Rossie Terrace. Only the bell-tower survives of the school built by Miss Ross of Rossie in 1838. Small lower stage with round-arched dummy openings in the E face. The spire-topped belfry above is like a large birdcage bellcote, with pilastered corners and round openings (dummies except at the E).

SCHOOL, Usan Road and Hillview Crescent. Now in other use. Built in 1879, the main windows mullioned.

FISHERIES LOOK-OUT TOWER, Seaton of Usan, 2.5 km. S. Tall mid-C19 harled square tower with a high battlement above a dentillated cornice. Windows, each of two round-headed lights except for the circular opening at the top stage of the E face.

INCHBRAOCH VIADUCT, W end of the village. By *Thomas Bouch* for the Dundee and Arbroath line of the North British Railway, 1881. Seventeen-span, of brick, the arches round-headed except for the longer one at the S which is segmental. Metal railing instead of a parapet.

LIGHTHOUSE, Scurdie Ness, 1.6 km. E. By *D. & T. Stevenson*, 1868–70. Tapering round tower built of white-painted brick, a cantilevered railed walkway around the cupola light. – Contemporary KEEPERS' HOUSES of one and two storeys. – To the W, two conical BEACON TOWERS designed by *David Hutcheon*, 1819, and built of whitewashed rubble. The more complete E tower has a drum base and stands by the shore, the W surmounts the cliff behind.

INCHBRAYOCK HOUSE, 0.5 km. S. Rendered two-storey villa of 1813. S front of three bays, the slightly recessed centre containing the entrance. Originally this was fronted by a portico but it is now set in a cast-iron surround of *c.* 1998, its design based on the N elevation's veranda. Asymmetrical W elevation with a two-storey bow at the l. N front of three bays, the r. pedimented, the slightly set-back centre with a single-storey bow circled by a cast-iron veranda.

USAN HOUSE. *See* p. 680.

FINAVON CASTLE

4050

1.9 km. E of Oathlaw

Mansion house designed by *Carver & Symon* and built in 1864–7 for David Greenhill Gardyne who had just inherited the estate. Bay-windowed and crowstep-gabled Baronial but with Gothic touches, more suggestive of an institution than domesticity. At the SW corner, a tower with a corbelled tall battlement; at the tower's SE corner, a round turret topped by square bartizans within which rises a slated conical spire.

THE COACH HOUSE, 0.1 km. W on the N side of the rubble and brick WALLED GARDEN, is contemporary, also with Gothic touches but eschewing overt Scottishness. NE corner tower with a Frenchy roof.

OLD FINAVON CASTLE, hidden in woodland 0.2 km. E, is perched above the confluence of the Lemno Burn and a tributary. Only fragments survive of what was apparently a notable residence for three centuries. From *c.* 1400 it was held by the Lindsays (later Earls of Crawford) and then by a cadet branch of that family, the Lords Spynie, before passing in 1672 to James Carnegie of Finavon, a younger son of the second Earl of Northesk, who, within a few years had made 'a most excellent house; fine roomes and good furniture, good yards, excellent planting, and inclosures and avenues'.*

The surviving buildings seem to have stood in the SE corner of an enclosure. They comprise a rectangular block, probably of *c.* 1400 and originally of two storeys, which probably contained a first-floor hall above storage, and, against its N side and projecting to the E, an L-plan tower of *c.* 1600. The S block is now reduced to little more than foundations but its ground-floor plan was disclosed by a mid-C20 excavation. It has been *c.* 17.4 m. by 10.1 m. externally, the 3 m.-thick walls faced with squared rubble. Piercing the W gable was a ground-floor gunloop. Probably there was another in the corresponding position at the E end but, if so, this was later enlarged to a door. The C14 entrance to the ground floor was a N door from the courtyard, its surviving chamfered jambs probably insertions of *c.* 1600 when it was covered by the jamb of the tower. Inside, the ground floor seems to have been unvaulted. Roughly in its centre, a well and, to its E, a drain running from the SE corner to the N entrance and with a catch-pit or sump at its centre. The first floor is now wholly lost.

The roofless tower of *c.* 1600 is far more striking. Main block of *c.* 5.6 m. by 5.3 m., its N and E walls standing to the full four-storey-and-attic height. The N gable is topped by a large chimney. Crowsteps along the W slope of the roof whose E slope is hidden by a round turret projected on continuous corbelling at the NE corner. The lower parts of the turret's comfortably sized windows survive, together with paired

* Description of 1684–5 by John Ochterlony of The Guynd, quoted in Alexander J. Warden, *Angus*, ii (Dundee, 1884), 266.

shot-holes; more shot-holes between the corbelling. The only opening in the gable itself is an oval gunloop at the ground floor. The main block's E side rises to its wall-head's cavetto cornice but is riven by a central fissure descending through a stack of windows, their surrounds with chamfered jambs. Near the bottom of this side but r. of centre is a gunloop, the surround now eroded but probably originally of oval form. Oval gunloop at the centre of the base. The S gable of the main block has mostly fallen but, towards the W end of its base, another oval gunloop below a horizontal window. The tower's SW jamb, *c.* 7.0 m. by 5.2 m., has been largely demolished but enough remains of its N wall to show that it has risen the full height of the main block. Inside the jamb, the lower part of a scale-and-platt stair survives. Beneath it has been a vaulted room, probably a guardroom or store.*

The jamb has been entered from a door in the N wall of the earlier block and has a door in its E side, its straight-lintelled head intact, to the main block of the tower. In this main block, tunnel vaults over the ground and first floors, the ground floor's running E–W, the first floor's N–S. The ground-floor room has been a store. The first-floor room was a kitchen whose fireplace occupied almost the full width of the N gable, its W ingo containing a cupboard, its E a slop drain. The upper floors have each contained a single room with a N fireplace. Joist holes show that they were covered by beamed ceilings.

Extending N from the tower's E side, a short and ruinous stretch of the BARMKIN WALL. It contains a pair of wide-mouthed oval gunloops, probably of *c.* 1600.

4050

FORFAR

A royal burgh since *c.* 1160 and the county town of Angus. A linen industry developed from the mid C18 and continued into the C19 although the mills later turned to the manufacture of jute and, in the late C20, of artificial fibres. Forfar is still an administrative centre and the small metropolis of the surrounding area.

CHURCHES

CONGREGATIONAL CHURCH, Osnaburg Street. Rubble-walled block built in 1836 and, at first sight, looking like a two-storey-and-attic tenement. Utilitarian domestic ground floor, a corniced doorpiece at the front gable the only decoration. The tall first-floor side windows disclose the presence of a hall or church inside. In the gable, an attic window of three round-headed lights, the detail badly weathered.

* But identified as a pit prison by W. Douglas Simpson, 'Finavon Castle', *Proceedings of the Society of Antiquaries of Scotland*, lxxxix (1955–6), 406.

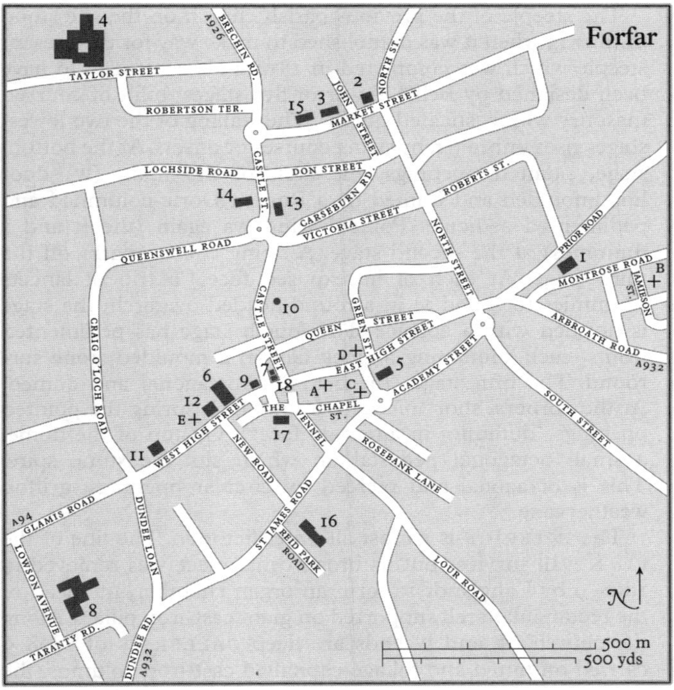

A	East and Old Parish Church
B	Lowson Memorial Church
C	St James
D	St John (Episcopal)
E	St Margaret
1	Angus Music Centre
2	Auction Mart
3	County Buildings
4	Forfar Academy
5	Forfar Academy (Former)
6	Forfar Library
7	Kingdom Hall
8	Langlands Primary School
9	Meffan Institute
10	Mercat Cross
11	Police Headquarters
12	Post Office
13	Queen's Own Yeomanry Depot
14	Reid Hall
15	Sheriff Court
16	Strathmore Primary School
17	Swimming Pool
18	Town and County Hall

FORFAR EAST AND OLD PARISH CHURCH, East High Street. The body of the church was built in 1788–91 to a design by *Samuel Bell* based on a plan by *James Millar*, mason at Bridgeton. It is a large rubble-built box with pointed windows whose mullions and plate tracery presumably date from the alterations made by *James H. Langlands* in 1898–9. Langlands also widened the church to the N where its new side wall rises into gablets. Probably also of the 1890s are the gableted and spired metal ventilators on the roof. At the E end, a plain session house of *c.* 1880.

The steeple of the previous parish church on the site stood until 1813 when it was demolished to make way for the present steeple which was completed in 1814 and seems also to have been designed by Bell.* Tower of five stages, built of coursed masonry with rusticated quoins. The walling of the two lowest stages rises unbroken by string courses or offsets. At the bottom stage, pointed openings, the arch of the main (W) door hoodmoulded and framed by a Roman Doric-columned and pedimented aedicule. Pointed windows again (the N and S dummies) at the second stage. A string course marks off the third stage. At each of its exposed faces, a trio of lancets (dummies to N and S) in a round-headed overarch; the stage is finished with a cornice. The fourth stage has pedimented fronts, each containing a clock face in a moulded stone surround. The fifth stage (the belfry) is octagonal and domed. At the corners, short pilasters from which spring the pointed openings (dummies in alternate faces). On top of the dome, a small octagonal pedestal on which sits the stone spire. This is octagonal and pierced by circular openings; griffon weathervane.

The INTERIOR is almost all Late Victorian. The line of the C18 N wall survives but its broad centrepiece was removed in 1898–9 by Langlands to form an organ chamber, the head of the rectangular arch supported on giant cast-iron pillars. Along the church's E and W ends are deep GALLERIES of 1898–9 carried on fluted and foliage-capitalled cast-iron columns, the panelled fronts of Georgian inspiration, each with a central clock face. In the area, bench PEWS by *Robert Blackadder*, 1900. These face the contemporary PULPIT at the centre of the S side and also designed by Blackadder. It is roomy and Gothic, the back triple-gabled. In front, an oak COMMUNION TABLE of 1897, the frieze carved with vine decoration. – Huge ORGAN projecting from the N wall, by *Forster & Andrews*, 1898–1900, the Wrenaissance case designed by Langlands, its woodwork executed by *Alexander Bain*.

STAINED GLASS. In the S wall and flanking the pulpit, a pair of two-light windows (Abraham and Isaac; St Paul Preaching at Athens) designed by *Henry Holiday* and executed by *James Powell & Sons*, 1887. – These are, in turn, flanked by a pair of First World War memorial windows (Angels and a Christian Knight Receiving the Crown of Life) by *James Ballantine II*, 1920–2. – The W gable's S window (Moses Striking the Rock) is late C19. – Beside it, a realistic window (Our Lord) by *A. Ballantine & Son*, 1917. – The N window of this gable (St Andrew) is by *Douglas Hamilton*, 1949, an example of brightly coloured modernistic realism. – In the first-floor room of the

* Both an inscription on the church and *The Scots Magazine* for 1814 record that *Patrick Brown* of Lochee (in Dundee) was architect of this work. However, in 1790 *Samuel Bell* had been asked to inspect the old steeple and receive instructions for construction of a replacement and the steeple built in 1813–14 is to an unexecuted design by Bell for the steeple of St Rule's Parish Church at Monifieth. Probably Brown was the executant architect or contractor rather than the designer.

session house, a strongly coloured round window (the Burning Bush) of 1866, formerly in Forfar East Free Church.

CHURCHYARD. Immediately S of the church, the GRAVE-SLAB of George Woo[d] †1642. At the top, angels trumpet to an upright skeleton. Below this, two panels. The l. is carved with a relief of two savages with cudgels in their hands; they flank a tree from which rises a figure. The r. panel bears the relief of a hunting horn hung from a tree. – Immediately beside it, the worn GRAVE-SLAB of (among others) Charles and John Mil, dated 1648, the carved decoration including a pair of skulls and crossbones. – To its S, another weathered stone displaying a tree at the top and a skull at the bottom. It commemorates James Wood †1607. – Just S of the church's E end, the HEADSTONE of 1778 to William Boath and his wife. Well-preserved carving of a cartouche with reminders of death below and an angel's head (the soul) above. – Another angel's head on the HEADSTONE erected in 1782 by John Cob, tailor, to his wife, Babie Deuchars. This stands roughly opposite the centre of the church, at the top of the graveyard's steep slope to the S. – Further down the slope is the HEADSTONE erected to his father by David Suttie, tailor, in 1804. Front carved with yet another angel's head above crude but still crisp foliage. – Adjoining on the W, a rather similar late C18 HEADSTONE to members of the Samson family. – S of this, a HEADSTONE of 1777. It is badly worn but still visible are the wings of an angel's head above an hourglass, skull and crossbones. – To its W, a big GRAVESLAB of the mid or late C17 to Patrick Suttie †1655 and other members of his family. Marginal inscription; another inscription on a shield in the centre.

CHURCH HALL at the bottom of the churchyard, bordering Chapel Street. It is by the Forfar Burgh Surveyor, *Alexander P. Rough*, 1911–12. Rubble-built Neo-Georgian but with a couple of round-arched openings and boat-shaped chimneyed gablets at the ends.

FORFAR EAST FREE CHURCH, Green Street. Secularized. Built in 1851–2. Rubble-built box with narrow pointed lancets in the side walls. The front is more ambitious, a tall screen divided into a 'nave' and 'aisles' by two-tier buttresses, their lower parts with sloping tops, their upper parts flying buttresses. The 'nave' gable is flanked by the horizontal battlements over the 'aisles'. Elaborately traceried 'nave' window of four lights.

FORFAR FIRST FREE CHURCH, Little Causeway. Now in commercial use. Broad Tudor Gothic box, built in 1843–4. Sides of red sandstone rubble pierced by Y-traceried pointed windows. The front, of polished grey ashlar, is divided into a 'nave' and 'aisles' by pinnacled buttresses. Above the broad door, a four-light window with Flamboyant tracery, the hoodmoulds' label stops left in block. Inside, a floor has been inserted at gallery level.

LOWSON MEMORIAL CHURCH, Jamieson Street and Montrose Road. Built by his family to commemorate John Lowson Jun., a Forfar mill-owner, the church is perched prominently on ground which rises above the neighbouring streets. It is prosperous Scots Gothic by *A. Marshall Mackenzie & Son*, 1912–14. The masonry of the walls is of purplish-coloured squared and hammer-dressed rubble, the roofs covered with small green slates. Clearstoreyed nave with very slightly shorter aisles, a minimally projecting SW porch, transepts and a chancel. In the inner angle of the chancel and S transept, a vestry. Over the crossing, a tower surmounted by a spire.

At the crowstepped gables of the chancel, transepts, nave and porch, diagonal buttresses, their stepped tops surmounted by crocketed pinnacles. Straight buttress poking out to the N from the W end of the N aisle. At the aisles, cavetto cornices carried on simple moulded corbels. Along the long sides of the nave, transepts and chancel, corbels of the same type support parapets. At the W end of the nave, below the top of the gable, a shallowly crenellated battlement boldly projected on double-moulded corbels. Square-section lead downpipes, their hoppers decorated with rosettes.

The six lights of the nave's W window are divided 3:3 by a broad centre mullion. Each half of this window is hoodmoulded and contains three pointed lights which rise in height towards the centre. The r. half is copied from the C13 E window of the Lady Chapel at Dunblane Cathedral and the l. half is its mirror image. The result is idiosyncratic. In the W end of each aisle and the gable of each transept, a similar but simpler version of this window under a pair of rectangular openings ventilating the roof space. The SW porch is gabled and built of ashlar lightly dressed with diagonal broaching. Its outer entrance consists of a broad arch with a roll-and-hollow moulding. Inside, ribbed vaulting. Round-arched door into the church. At the W bay of the N aisle, a plain rectangular door. The nave's clearstorey windows, each of four lancet lights in a semicircular arch, quote from the C14 clearstorey windows in the nave of Sweetheart Abbey (Dumfries and Galloway). The side windows of the aisles and transepts are small, each of a single pointed and hoodmoulded light. Immediately below them, a string course which is carried also across the transept gables and round the chancel. The low vestry, looking like a miniature chapter house, has an octagonal roof but its walls project from the church to form only a little more than a semi-octagon. In the walls, rectangular windows. At the E gable of the chancel, a seven-light window copied from the early C16 E window of Greyfriars Church in Aberdeen, the tracery intersecting but the arcs not all reaching to the top so that there are three large openings at the head. Below the transom, each light is topped by a flattened ogee arch.

The square crossing tower is sturdy and plain, its general appearance rather like that of the tower at the C14 St Monans Parish Church (Fife). In each face, two narrow pointed and hoodmoulded windows with cusped heads. At the NE corner, a stair-tower, its lower part a rounded conical-roofed projection in the inner angle of the chancel and transept, its upper part rising from inside like a massive diagonal buttress topped by a octagonal caphouse roofed with a stone spire. The tower's parapet is carried on simple moulded corbels. Inside it, the octagonal stone spire. It has four tiers of gabled and louvred lucarnes, those of the lowest tier very tall, the size of the others progressively diminishing. On top, a small metal weathervane.

Inside, the walls are ashlar-faced, the ceilings boarded with oak. The W bay of the nave forms a narthex, divided off by a big oak and glass screen topped by an organ and choir gallery. The ceiling over this narthex and the four bays of the nave proper is a tunnel vault with surface ribs, the vault's line broken by small transeptal vaults over the clearstorey windows. Nave arcades opening into the passage aisles through chamfered semicircular arches springing from round pillars. At each side of the crossing, a pointed stone arch. Over the crossing, an elaborate late medieval vault. Pointed tunnel vaults with surface ribs over the transepts and chancel. Each of the side walls of the chancel is panelled with a round-headed blind arch.

The original furnishings, the woodwork all of oak, survive, as does their ecclesiological arrangement. – In the nave, boxy PEWS. – On the N side of the chancel arch, an exceptionally long wooden PULPIT, its cornice carved with vines, standing on a stone base. – On the S of the chancel arch, the stone FONT, its circular stem supporting an octagonal bowl, its faces panelled with shouldered round-headed arches; this bowl is copied from that of the medieval font from Restenneth Priory which is now in St John's (Episcopal) Church (*see* below). – In the centre of the chancel, the COMMUNION TABLE, its cornice repeating that of the pulpit. – Against the side walls of the chancel, long ELDERS' STALLS, with fleur-de-lis finials at their fronts and simply panelled backs. – LECTERN with simplified Gothic carved decoration. – ORGAN by *Watson & Conacher*, its case in a Late Gothic style, decorated with carved foliage. – The LIGHT FITTINGS are pendant brass rings with applied fleurs-de-lis and pierced by quatrefoils. – Above the communion table, a SANCTUARY PENDANT, its general appearance that of a sanctuary lamp or thurible. It is of silver, with an encircling silver-gilt band studded with cherubs' heads.

STAINED GLASS all by *Douglas Strachan*, 1914, the draughtsmanship on a small scale and crowded but not undisciplined. The E window depicts *Te Deum*, strong dark blues and reds the dominant colours. The N transept window (Creation) is much cooler in blue, purple, grey and yellow. S window (Revelation) fiery in reds and oranges. In the W window, mostly plain glass but there are two tiers of dark-coloured stained-glass scenes from the lives of Scottish saints.

The church forms the N side of an informal courtyard which is open to Jamieson Road to the W. In the centre of the courtyard, a lawn with a large cedar. On the E side, the single-storey CHURCH HALL, also of 1912–14 and by *A. Marshall Mackenzie & Son*. It is built of the same materials as the church. T-plan with an E jamb and crowstepped gables. At the parapeted W side, a round-arched door at the N bay and a square porch at the S; between them Y-traceried two-light windows. In the N and S gables, tripleted lancet lights; tall rectangular windows in the gable of the jamb.

On the S side of the courtyard is the MANSE, again by *Mackenzie & Son*, 1912–14, and using the same materials. Crowstepped gables. At the N end of the W front, a boldly projecting bay window topped by an attic storey corbelled out to the square.

ST FERGUS (R.C.), Glenogil Terrace. Church and priest's house, by *James Parr*, 1963, both with walls of brown brick. At the church, a band of clearstorey glazing; SW porch with assertive timber-clad uprights. The shallow-pitch ribbed metal roofs were added *c.* 1985.

ST JAMES, St James Road. Disused. By *James Brewster*, 1835–6, it was built as a chapel of ease. Big rubble-walled box, the front divided into a 'nave' and 'aisles' by flattened buttresses and a stepping of the gable. In this front, simple Romanesque openings, the 'nave's window tripartite with an extravagantly stilted centre light. In the top of the gable, a round light.

At the E end, a HALL by *T. R. Soutar*, 1913, built of hammer-dressed masonry.

ST JOHN (Episcopal), East High Street. 1879–81, by *R. Rowand Anderson* and characteristically austere First Pointed, built of local purplish-coloured squared rubble with dressings of buff Polmaise (Stirlingshire) stone. Three-bay chancel at the N (liturgical E) end, nave of five bays, the S (liturgical W) bay shorter than the others which have a W aisle. At the SW corner, the base of a tower, its W face flush with the wall of the W aisle. In the front (S) gable, three lancets. Very tall centre light; over the two outer lights, vesicas containing the emblem (an eagle) of St John the Evangelist and the coat of arms of the diocese of St Andrews. Rising between the windows to just above the level of their sills, low gableted buttresses; another buttress to the r. Set back on the l. of the gable, the inner angle partly filled by a bowed projection, is the lower part (*c.* 12.2 m. high) of Anderson's intended but unfinished 49.7 m.-high steeple. In the S face of this tower, a pointed door framed by pinnacles and a crocket-finialled gablet. In the gablet, a trefoil containing a panel carved with the high relief of an angel holding a scroll. Above, a rose window. In the side walls of the church, two-light windows, their hoodmoulds' label stops carved with foliage. Flattened buttresses along the E side facing Green Street. At the rear, a plain low HALL by the Rev. *Edward Sugden*, *c.* 1890.

Inside, the walls are tiled, the red tiles of the nave now painted cream, the polychrome of the alternating bands of red tiles and alabaster in the chancel still exposed. Flooring of encaustic tiles by *William Godwin*, the decorative scheme becoming richer in the choir and still richer in the sanctuary where gold is the dominant colour. Over the nave, a kingpost roof, the kingpost's struts well above the tie-beam. It is carried on stone wall-shafts. The chancel is covered with a polygonal boarded ceiling, its painted decoration of sacred emblems and the figures of saints introduced by *Tarbolton & Ochterlony* in 1947. The W arcade has pointed arches springing from compound piers without capitals. The aisle itself was altered in 1974–5 by *F. R. Stevenson* who partitioned off most of its W side in the three S bays to provide vestry accommodation and formed a Lady Chapel at the N end. The stone chancel arch is carried on corbelled wall-shafts. Opening from the W side of the chancel's S bay is the organ chamber. On the E side of the sanctuary, three-seat SEDILIA, the cusped arches springing from shafts of honey-coloured marble. In the chancel, a panelled oak DADO by *Tarbolton & Ochterlony*, 1947, in a routine Gothic manner. – The oak CHOIR STALLS and PULPIT are by *Anderson*, 1879–81. – Brass eagle LECTERN given by the Earl of Kintore in 1880; it cannot be much earlier. – Wooden REREDOS over the High Altar by *Willis & Jones*, 1905. Five gableted compartments, the centre framing the altar cross. In the flanking compartments, reliefs of Our Lord as the Good Shepherd and blessing little children; in the end compartments, A and Ω. – ORGAN by *Conacher & Co.*, 1880–1. It was rebuilt by *Rushworth & Dreaper* in 1951 when it acquired a new case, the simple frame topped by the figure of a trumpeting angel. – Early C20 pine SCREEN to the Lady Chapel in a Lorimerian Late Gothic manner. – At the W end of the nave, the FONT. The octagonal stone bowl, each face decorated with a shouldered round-arched panel, is probably C13; it came from Restenneth Priory (q.v.).

STAINED GLASS. In the chancel's five-light N window of *c.* 1890, strongly coloured and rather crowded depictions of scenes from the life of Our Lord, with the Nativity, Crucifixion and Ascension in the centre light. It may be the work of *John Hardman & Co.* – Also of *c.* 1890 and perhaps by Hardman is the two-light window (the Last Supper; Moses Striking the Rock; the Israelites Gathering Manna) in the W wall of the chancel. – In the chancel's S wall, three windows, the two in the N bays (the Annunciation and the Visitation of Our Lady) by *C. E. Kempe*, 1907, the third (the Adoration of the Shepherds) by *C. E. Kempe & Co. Ltd*, *c.* 1925. – In the E wall of the nave, at the N bay, a window (St Mary Magdalene, St Peter) of 1881 by *Morris & Co.* from designs by *William Morris* and *Edward Burne-Jones*, realistic and bad. – Also realistic but insipid the next window (St John the Evangelist, St Agnes) of 1946. – Much better the strongly coloured glass by *J. H. Powell* of *John Hardman & Co.*, 1884, in the window to the S (Arannah the Jebusite Offering his Threshing Floor to King David; the Jewish elders Appealing to Our Lord on Behalf of the Good Centurion). – Then a colourful but grimly realistic window (St Columba's Last Address to his Monks; St Margaret of Scotland Teaching her Children) by the *British & Foreign Glass Co.*, 1906. – In the S bay, one light (Our Lord with Little Children), a disappointing work by *J. H. Powell*, 1885. – In the N bay of the Lady Chapel, a two-light window (an Angel Ministering to Our Lord; an Angel with the Maries at the Tomb) of *c.* 1890. – In the window of the chapel's S bay, a stylized nature scene by *Septimus Waugh*, 1992.

ST MARGARET'S PARISH CHURCH, West High Street. Originally Forfar First Free Church. Thrifty Gothic, by *Mackenzie & McMillan* of Aberdeen, 1879–81. Broad nave; projecting from its sides, processions of gables over the aisles. The nave's front gable is flanked by a transeptal projection on the l.; on the r., three stages of an incomplete tower which was intended to be finished with a spire. In the front gable, a four-light window with a big rose in its head. Below the window, the entrance whose gablet's bottom ends are carved with foliage.

Inside, boarded roofs, each bay of the aisles having its own roof at right angles to the nave roof. The barely pointed arches of the nave are carried on cast-iron columns which have foliaged capitals under the galleries as well as at the springing of the arches. The galleries, their fronts panelled with blind Gothic arcading, are carried round three sides. – Pitch-pine PEWS of 1879–81 with columns supporting the arm-rests which rise to the back where they end in scrolls. – PULPIT of light-coloured wood, made in 1988. – Behind the pulpit and also of 1988, the ORGAN CASE constructed when the ORGAN (by *Henry Willis & Sons*, 1903; extended by *J. Simpson & H. S. Vincent*, 1910–11), formerly in St Kessock's Church at Callander, was rebuilt here.

At the rear of the church, a plain HALL of 1879–81, with a central chimneyed gablet. The hall was extended E in 1929.

PUBLIC BUILDINGS

ANGUS MUSIC CENTRE, Montrose Road. Originally East Town End Burgh School. By *George Milne*, 1844; single-storey, of stugged ashlar. Asymmetrical composition, with open-pedimented gables with circular openings in the tympana; most of the windows are round-headed. Tactful E addition of the later C19.

AUCTION MART, Market Street. Now in other use. Dated 1872. Stugged masonry octagon, a horse-finialled weathervane on the slated spire roof. The entrance is contained in a pilastered aedicule, its pediment topped by a ball finial.

CEMETERY, Newmonthill. Laid out by *George Henderson* and opened in 1850, presumably the date of the LODGE, a *cottage* thriftily *orné* with broad eaves and hoodmoulded windows. – At the highest point of the Cemetery, the PEEL MONUMENT erected in honour of Sir Robert Peel in 1850–1; it was designed by *James Maclaren*. Square on plan, built of polished ashlar, with channelled rustication at its solid pedestal. This pedestal's S corners are canted and panelled; projecting from the N corners, large consoles, the effect reminiscent of the entrance to St Stephen's Church in Edinburgh. The pedestal supports an open-centred upper stage enclosed by tall semicircular arches springing from corner piers. Breaking forward at each front, a Corinthian-columned portico with anthemion finials on the pediment. Stone sphinxes sit in the E and W porticoes. Above is an attic stage topped by acroteria and a balustrade with round-headed arcading. Inside the balustrade, a stepped pyramid roof, its crowning vase now missing, as is the bust of Peel (by *William Anderson*) which the monument formerly sheltered. – In the rest of the cemetery, an extensive collection of prosperous Victorian funerary MONUMENTS. The largest and showiest, to the S of the Peel Monument, is a tall Corinthian-urn-topped column erected *c.* 1860 to commemorate members of the Meffan family.

COUNTY BUILDINGS, Market Street. Built as a prison in 1842–3; *David Smith* was the architect. Symmetrical block, its castellated manner neither frivolous nor frightening. The prison was converted to offices by *John Carver* in 1884 when the windows were altered and enlarged. At the rear, an addition of 1933, with a steep central pediment and a pair of boat-shaped dormers. Further extension of 1950 behind.

Former EAST TOWN END BURGH SCHOOL. *See* ANGUS MUSIC CENTRE.

Former FORFAR ACADEMY, Academy Street. The original two-storey block, at the E end of the site, is unassertive Greek Revival by *David Logan*, 1815. Ashlar front of five bays, the ends advanced. At the three-bay centrepiece, fluted Doric columns. The entablature is without triglyphs; panelled parapet, carried up slightly higher at the end bays. Set back at each end, a single-storey Greek Doric aedicular porch, its entablature correctly triglyphed. The building was given a recessed two-storey extension at each end in 1904–7. Each of these wings is piend-roofed, built of rougher ashlar than the original building, and has sill courses but the E wing is of four bays and the W of six.

To the SW, a detached free Wrenaissance block by *Gavin & Soutar*, 1909–10. U-plan front, the ends with rusticated pilasters at the corners and open pediments, each containing a keyblocked circular opening above a swag of thistles; tall round-arched windows below. At the recessed central section, two tiers of rectangular windows. Entrance in an aedicule whose giant Corinthian columns carry a bold open pediment.

FORFAR ACADEMY, Taylor Street. By the Angus County Architect, *J. B. Yates*, 1965. Low, with much enamelled steel curtain walling.

FORFAR LIBRARY, West High Street. A late C20 supermarket; converted to a library in 1988. Undistinguished, in brown brick.

KINGDOM HALL, Nos. 117–119 Castle Street. Originally Post Office. By *George Morham*, 1897–8. Pompous but blowsy Renaissance.

LANGLANDS SCHOOL, Taranty Road. By *Mackie Ramsey Taylor*, 2008–9. Single-storey, the walls faced with render or blockwork, the pitched roofs metal-covered. Double-height hall set back at the NE.

MEFFAN INSTITUTE, West High Street. By *Tait Conner & Henry Mitchell* of Glasgow, 1898. Plain two-storey building, the walling of stugged grey ashlar. Four-bay front with mullioned-and-transomed two-light windows. In the r. bay, the entrance with a semicircular pediment, its tympanum glazed as a fanlight. The ends of the overall parapet are swept up. On the roof, a Roman Doric-columned and ogee-roofed cupola surmounted by a weathervane.

MERCAT CROSS, Castle Hill, off Canmore Street. The cross, originally placed in front of the Tolbooth (on the site of the present Town and County Hall) was built in 1683–4. *Alexander Adam* was the contractor and perhaps the designer. It was rebuilt on Castle Hill in 1799. The finialled shaft of the cross itself is now missing. What survives is the structure on which the shaft stood. This is a battlemented octagonal tower, *c.* 6 m. high; on its sides, panels carved with the coat of arms of the burgh of Forfar (a castle), a thistle, and the monogram CR (for *Carolus Rex*).

POLICE HEADQUARTERS, West High Street. By the Angus County Architect, *J. B. Yates*, 1969.

POLICE OFFICE, Chapel Street and The Vennel. Now in other use. Three-storey mid-C19, its canted corner with a shaped pediment. At this corner, a segmental-arched door under a badly weathered carving of the coat of arms of the burgh of Forfar; above the carved panel, an inverted keyhole 'gunloop'.

Former POST OFFICE. *See* KINGDOM HALL.

POST OFFICE, West High Street. Opened 1971. Slate-hung above a ground floor of artificial stone.

QUEEN'S OWN YEOMANRY DEPOT, Castle Street. Originally Employment Exchange. By *H.M. Office of Works*, 1937. Neo-Georgian made authoritarian by concrete-block walling and a heavy rusticated doorpiece.

REID HALL, Castle Street. Built at the expense of Peter Reid, confectioner and Provost of Forfar, and gifted by him to the burgh. Flemish-Baronial, by *Brown & Wardrop*, 1869–71. Tall H-plan block, the transepts projecting minimally at the ends, all built of coursed and stugged masonry. Gables finished with large pedimented crowsteps. Tall lancet windows in the buttressed sides. The architectural interest is concentrated at the E front which is divided into a 'nave' and 'aisles' by sturdy offset buttresses whose tops slope into continuous corbelling under the fat conical-roofed turrets which flank the crowstepped 'nave' gable. In the lower part of this gable, narrow rectangular windows set in pointed overarches whose hoodmoulds' label stops are carved with human heads. Above, a pair of blind quatrefoils set in dummy roundels; on the quatrefoils, shields carved with the heads of a man and a woman. An upper storey containing a gallery is demarcated by a string course continuing the top stage of the corbelling under the turrets. At this storey, the carved coat of arms of the burgh of Forfar above a pair of mullioned-and-transomed windows, whose pointed heads contain plate-traceried cinquefoils. Corbelled out from the top of the gable is the diagonally set base of an iron weathervane. The hall was gutted by fire in 1941 and reconstructed in 1950–6 when low outshots were added at the sides.

REID PARK, off Hillside Road. Another gift of Peter Reid to the Burgh of Forfar, it was laid out in 1895–6. At the entrance, a crowstep-gabled LODGE dated 1895. – To the N and S of the lodge, brick-built PAVILIONS of *c.* 1900, the N (occupied by a bowling club) with a veranda across the front. – To the W, on a tall grey granite pedestal, the small seated bronze STATUE of Peter Reid by *George Webster*, 1898; originally it stood in Castle Street. – In the centre of the park, an octagonal BANDSTAND of *c.* 1900, its roof carried on slim cast-iron Composite columns from which spring big foliaged spandrels. Around the eaves, a cast-iron pelmet; on top of the roof a crown spire composed of foliaged iron ribs.

Former SHERIFF COURT, Castle Street and Buttermarket. A confident classical assertion of civic status, by *David Neave*, 1823–4. Basically this is a free-standing piend-roofed two-storey block of five bays by three but with the S end bowed. Masonry all of polished ashlar, the windows linked by sill courses. At the principal (W) front, a build-up from narrow slightly recessed ends to the projecting Ionic columns which mark the three-bay centrepiece. Over the outer bays the entablature is finished with a blocking course which is carried up higher over the second and fourth bays and becomes a panelled parapet above the central bay. At the centrepiece, corniced ground-floor openings and first-floor windows with moulded architraves. The E front is a simplified version of the W, its slightly advanced three-bay centrepiece marked off by Ionic pilasters. The S end, almost squashed against the Town and County Hall (*see* below) is quite plain. At the bowed N end, prominent in the view along Castle Street, giant Corinthian columns and a bowed chimney.

The interior was converted to offices for Forfar Burgh Council *c.* 1870 after the construction of a new court house (*see* below) but the entrance hall is of the 1820s with marbled Ionic columns *in antis* forming a screen to the stair behind.

SHERIFF COURT, Market Street. Tudor-Baronial mixture, by 75
Brown & Wardrop, 1868–71. Two tall storeys and an attic, built of coursed squared masonry. U-plan principal (S) front of seven bays. At the advanced ends, crowstepped gables from whose corners are corbelled out diagonally set crocketed pinnacles; at the base of the pinnacles, projecting stone griffons. Between these ends, the main range, its four outer bays battlemented, its centre rising into a crowstepped gable topped by a corbelled-out foliaged pinnacle. At this centre, the principal entrance which is flanked by buttresses supporting the ends of

an urn-topped stone balcony whose front is pierced by quatrefoils; more griffons at the corners of the balcony. Behind the balcony, a window surmounted by a carving of the royal coat of arms.

At the E and W elevations, bargeboarded dormer windows. Near the N end of the W side, a round tower, its top stage surmounted by arcaded corbelling under a rope-moulded string course from which project yet more griffons. Conical slated roof. At the back of the building the height drops and the character becomes one of plain domesticity.

Inside, a flat hammerbeam roof over the first floor's central Court 1.

STRATHMORE PRIMARY SCHOOL, St James Road. School and school house, by *David Smart* adapting a design by *James Anderson*, 1870–2. Picturesquely gabled and gableted Tudor, the windows hoodmoulded. Bellcote on the school.

SWIMMING POOL, The Vennel. By *Hippolyte J. Blanc*, 1909–10. Utilitarian except for the Jacobean Renaissance front gable which is built of hammer-dressed masonry and divided by pilasters into a 'nave' and 'aisles'. On top of the pediment, a semicircular pediment broken by a pinnacle. In the front of the 'nave', a round-arched and keystoned window. The building was extended to the SE by the Burgh Surveyor, *A. Waterston*, in 1911, the roof of the outshot topped by a cupola.

TOWN AND COUNTY HALL, The Cross. By *James Playfair*, 1786–8. Piend-roofed two-storey rectangle, built of local Craignathro stone, the S front's masonry of stugged ashlar above a base of cheese-like rustication, the other elevations of rubble. The S front is of four bays with the centre two slightly advanced under a pediment, its tympanum containing a circular clock face in a moulded stone surround. Ground-floor openings (doors in the outer bays, windows in the inner) all round-arched. Above the ground floor, a simple moulded string course. At the first floor, tall rectangular windows with projecting aprons.

The E and W elevations seem originally to have been identical, each of three bays with round-arched ground-floor openings (the centre one a door) and rectangular windows above. The W elevation has remained unaltered but at the E the N first-floor window has been built up, the ground-floor opening is now rectangular, and the centre door has been converted to a window.

At the back (N), the building originally contained prison cells and is of three storeys in the height of the two storeys of the rest. Five-bay elevation with fairly small windows at the upper floors, two of those at the first floor enlarged as bipartites. At the ground floor, broad segmental arches (now filled in) apparently to a loggia.

The interior was recast in 1840–1 by *David Neave*. First-floor hall with a coffered ceiling and console-corniced window architraves. At the W end, a gallery, its centre supported on leafy consoles springing from Corinthian columns. The three

STAINED GLASS windows (the arms of the county of Angus; St Michael the Archangel; the arms of the Burgh of Forfar) are by *Alexander L. Russell*, 1951–2. Contemporary window (the arms of the three armed services) also by Russell at the top of the staircase.

WELLBRAE PRIMARY SCHOOL, Victoria Street and Wellbraehead. The original part, built in the later C19, is on the N facing Victoria Street. Plain U-plan front with a spired cupola-ventilator. The school was doubled in size by *Gavin & Soutar*, 1912. The extension is again single-storey but its masonry is hammer-dressed and with dressings of bright red sandstone. Mullioned-and-transomed windows; pagoda-ventilators.

WHITEHILLS HEALTH AND COMMUNITY CARE CENTRE, Station Road. By *MRT Architects*, 2003–5. Large but low piend-roofed pavilions extending from a taller central rotunda, its walling rendered above a masonry base, its oversailing roof, like those of the pavilions, covered with ribbed metal.

DESCRIPTION

GLAMIS ROAD, the entry from the SW, begins with late C20 housing but also, on the l., two sizeable mid-Victorian villas, BENHOLM, Tudorish with gables and gablets, and the parsonical BARON HILL. Set back on the r. in ANDREW SMYTH GARDENS is the early C19 BRIAR, a two-storey villa, its main (W) front with a Doric-columned porch and corniced windows. Projecting from the N gable, a canted bay window topped by a balconied bow, perhaps an early addition. Balustraded parapet and a piended platform roof, its iron cresting a Victorian embellishment; Victorian wing at the back. A little further on in Glamis Road, housing of the later C19. Set back on the r., Langlands School (*see* Public Buildings, above).

WEST HIGH STREET's beginning raises the scale a little with a long two-storey block of 1896–1900. Canted corners, the SW to Craig o' Loch Road with a pediment, the NE with a shallow rectangular oriel. This block is followed by the Police Headquarters (*see* Public Buildings, above). Two-storey late C20 box of the BANK OF SCOTLAND. Then, St Margaret's Parish Church (*see* Churches above).

LITTLE CAUSEWAY opens off West High Street to the S to form a cobbled square. In the centre of this square, a classical pink and grey granite FOUNTAIN erected in 1911 as a memorial to James Webster. Most of the houses are of two storeys and rendered, their present plain appearance dating from the C19. The harled house at Nos. 7–8 on the S side of the square is late C18 and rather grander, with a lugged architrave to the door and, at the W bay, a pend arch with rusticated pilasters and lintel. Also on the S side is the L-plan No. 4, C17 in origin but with windows and doors of Late Georgian dimensions. To the E, the former First Free Church and, across the street, the

Congregational Church (for these, *see* Churches, above). On the E side of OSNABURG STREET, the rubble-built three-storey OSNABURG BAR of 1827. Its SW corner is bowed but, just below the eaves, brought to the square with a heavy corbel supporting the top of the walls. Bowed projection, also of three storeys but lower, at the SE corner. To the SE, at the bottom of THE VENNEL, the Swimming Pool and, on the corner of CHAPEL STREET, the former Police Office (for these, *see* Public Buildings, above). In front of the Police Office, a Late Victorian cast-iron LAMP STANDARD by *Walter Macfarlane & Co.*, its baluster stem decorated with acanthus leaves.

WEST HIGH STREET NE of the entry into Little Causeway is largely workaday vernacular of the C18 and C19 but jolted by the late C20 Post Office and Forfar Library (for these, *see* Public Buildings, above). On the r. side, the C18 Nos. 15–17 with an off-centre chimneyed wall-head gablet, and the early C19 Nos. 11–13 with moulded architraves at the first-floor windows and a bowed corner to the E entry into Low Causeway. Across this entry, Nos. 7–9 West High Street (originally, UNION BANK), a tall plain palazzo by *William Railton*, 1868. Segmental-arched first-floor windows, their key blocks carved with roses and supporting cornices at the outer bays and a segmental pediment at the centre. Asymmetrical ground floor with, at the l., round-arched and rusticated doorways paired under a cornice; at the r., a corniced two-light window with pilaster-mullions. Opposite, the Meffan Institute (*see* Public Buildings, above).

THE CROSS, the NE continuation of West High Street, begins with the QUEEN'S HOTEL of 1885 whose bowed corner rises to form a low round tower under a witch's-hat roof. At the asymmetrical front elevation, an off-centre chimneyed gablet and a muscularly corbelled triangular oriel. Then, mid-C19 Georgian survival with pilastered shopfronts at Nos. 8–11. This is followed by tall Victorian bank buildings. The former NATIONAL BANK OF SCOTLAND is by *David MacGibbon*, 1862. At its centre, a full-height central bay window with its two lower floors canted and the top corbelled to the square under a corbelled and crowstepped gablet. More crowsteps at the gabled porches; over the ground-floor windows, segmental-arched panels carved with foliage. The National Bank's hammer-dressed masonry contrasts with the polished ashlar of its adjoining and taller rival, the former BRITISH LINEN CO. BANK (No. 5) of 1895–6, by *Kinnear & Peddie*. North European Renaissance with a shaped gable. At the rusticated ground floor, an Ionic-pilastered entrance whose pediment is broken by a cartouche which displays the initials of the bank. The N side of The Cross is filled by the Town and County Hall; behind it, in the middle of the Y-shaped S end of Castle Street, the former Sheriff Court (for these, *see* Public Buildings, above).

CASTLE STREET is the principal road leading N. Its W side begins with the late C18 Nos. 1–5, rubble-built but symmetrical, with a central gablet, and the Late Georgian Nos. 7–11, the ashlar front divided into horizontal bands by sill and lintel courses. Rather more assertive is the Late Victorian Renaissance block at Nos. 17–21. Then, the ROYAL HOTEL of *c.* 1840, with architraves at the windows of the first floor and bracketed sills under those of the second.

The E side of Castle Street starts with the two-storey block of Nos. 10–14, built of cherry-cock-pointed squared and coursed rubble, the small first-floor windows suggesting a late C18 date. The scale rises at Nos. 16–22 of *c.* 1870, the outer windows of the second floor topped by gableted dormerheads with wrought-iron finials; a chimney corbelled out from the broad centre gablet. Plain but unaltered shopfronts under a cornice carried on foliaged consoles. The adjoining three-storey block (Nos. 24–26) is by *T. R. Soutar*, 1909. Projecting shopfront, the plate glass held by very slender cast-iron columns; banded pilasters at the corners. At the upper floors, superimposed Doric pilasters and a canted centre bay jettied over the shopfronts. The wall-head is surmounted by a ball-topped balustrade behind which pokes up a steep centre gablet pierced by a bullseye window. Across Queen Street, the mid-C19 Nos. 28–36 Castle Street, with a bowed corner. At the first-floor windows, lugged architraves, the centres of the lintels rising into semicircles; bracketed sills under the second-floor windows. There follow plain and rather altered C19 buildings of two and three storeys. Then, Nos. 60–66 dated 1891. The main block is of three storeys, its eaves cornice topped by a low scroll-sided plinth supporting a rather steep pediment from which rises a chimney; at the ends, pedestals carrying stylized urns. Short two-storey-and-attic part to the N, with a Jacobean aedicule containing a monogram.

On the W side of Castle Street between Myre Road and Manor Street, two minor blockbusters. The first is the CLYDESDALE BANK BUILDINGS by *A. H. L. Mackinnon*, *c.* 1900. Two storeys, of polished red sandstone ashlar, channelled at the ground floor. At the S end, a tall parapet topped by urns. N of this parapet are balustrades flanking a parapet which is swept up to the tall semicircular pediment of an Ionic-pilastered aedicule containing the bank's coat of arms; the pediment is broken by an obelisk. It looks as if a further section to the N were intended to balance the S end but the space is occupied by the late C19 Nos. 79–83 Castle Street which displays steeply pedimented gablets and, on the E front, a terracotta plaque bearing a portrait of Queen Victoria and an inscription recalling her Diamond Jubilee of 1897, perhaps the date of the building.

MANOR STREET is a diversion to the W. On its S side, buildings whose fronts face over big gardens running down to Myre Road. At the E end, the early C19 Nos. 1 and 7, both with corniced doorpieces. Further along, the former Manor Works, now Manor Court (*see* Industrial Buildings, below). On the N side of Manor Street, the harled Nos. 2–6 with small windows and a centre gablet looks late C18. The adjoining No. 10 was originally Forfar Parish Manse, begun in 1619 but its present appearance late C18 with a centre gablet; the r. windows have been enlarged in the late C19 or C20.

In Castle Street, opposite the opening into Manor Street, a Georgian survival building (Nos. 74–80) of *c.* 1860, built of stugged ashlar, a consoled cornice above its shopfronts. Further N, the former MASONIC HALL (Nos. 98–102) by *James Hutton*, 1880. Over the entrance, a cornice on paired chunky corbels. Hoodmoulds above the first-floor windows, that at the centre forming a segmental pediment whose tympanum is carved with thistles supporting a book, its open pages displaying masonic symbols. The second-floor windows have gableted dormerheads; dragon gargoyles project from the broader dormerhead at the centre. Opposite, the former Post Office, now Kingdom Hall (*see* Public Buildings, above). Off Canmore Street to the E, steps up to Castle Hill, the present site of the Mercat Cross (*see* Public Buildings, above).

Further N, on Castle Street's E side, the two-storey No. 128. Free Queen Anne of *c.* 1905, harled with (painted) ashlar dressings. The heavy keystone of the round-arched door supports a canted oriel roofed with a half-dome. The main cornice carries a parapet at the outer bays but, at the centre, rises to form an open pediment. Across Victoria Street, the mid-C19 STAG HOTEL, its canted corner corbelled to the square under the eaves; on the S front, a central chimneyed gablet. Just to its N, the Queen's Own Yeomanry Depot and N of that, on the opposite side of the road, the Reid Hall (for these, *see* Public Buildings, above). MARKET STREET runs E from Castle Street's N end past the Sheriff Court and County Buildings to the Auction Mart (for all these, *see* Public Buildings, above).

EAST HIGH STREET begins back at The Cross. On its S side, No. 2, perhaps of the mid C18, built of rough ashlar, with shouldered architraves to the windows of the two upper floors, the second-floor windows smaller than those of the first. Pend under the building's W end. Plain early C19 buildings follow. More ambitious is the three-storey L-plan block at Nos. 20–26 designed by *David Mackenzie* in 1832. Corniced windows at the first floor (the dressings crudely renewed in cement) and a second-floor sill course. The pseudo-classicism of the C20 wooden shopfront at No. 20 compares badly with the original pilastered stone fronts at Nos. 24–26. Small gablet at the centre of the NE wing. Beside this, a flight of steps up to the graveyard of the East and Old Parish Church (*see* Churches, above) which sits in aloof seclusion from the life of the street. On the N side of East High Street, a tall and bare Baronial building (Nos. 37–39) dated 1871. A little to the E, another tall block (No. 53) but slightly earlier and its style Georgian survival going Italianate, with round-arched doors and Ionic aediculed two-light first-floor windows. On the S side of the street, the ashlar-fronted No. 52 built in 1826. Three storeys above a rock-faced basement. Sill courses at the upper floors whose windows are architraved, those of the first floor corniced. In ALBION

PLACE, a lane on its W, a rendered house, probably early C18 in origin, which was reconstructed *c.* 1772 and again fifty years later, its fanlit tripartite doorpiece contained in a segmental-headed arch. The S side of East High Street continues with a late C20 commercial block jazzed up with fully glazed triangular bay windows and oriels. The ROYAL BANK OF SCOTLAND opposite, by *Dick Peddie & McKay*, 1969, is a comparatively self-effacing but equally inappropriate polished granite box. Beside it, CHAPELBANK HOUSE (No. 69), a broad-eaved mid-Victorian villa followed by St John's (Episcopal) Church (*see* Churches, above) on the corner of Green Street. Further down GREEN STREET, the former East Free Church (*see* Churches, above). Opposite St John's Church COUTTIE'S WYND leads off East High Street to the S, angling past No. 13. This is an early C19 two-storey double-pile house, the back (N) block shorter than the front; in the inner angle, a triangular-shaped crudely battlemented extension. At the S front of the house, an architraved doorpiece with a fluted frieze. Central wall-head chimney; moulded roundels at the fronts of the skewputts. At the foot of Couttie's Wynd, No. 21 ACADEMY STREET, an early C19 ashlar-fronted house of a single storey over a basement. To its E, the N side of Academy Street is occupied by the former Forfar Academy (*see* Public Buildings, above). ST JAMES ROAD continues the line of Academy Street to the SW. On its N corner with Chapel Street, the former St James's Church (*see* Churches, above). NEWMONTHILL leads SE uphill to the Cemetery (*see* Public Buildings, above). Further along St James Road, the St James Works (*see* Industrial Buildings, below).

The E end of High Street is a pleasant but not very distinguished C18 and C19 vernacular medley. In this, the late C18 former MASONIC LODGE (Nos. 100–102) stands out. At its upper floor, a large dummy Venetian window flanked by two big windows to light the hall inside. At the very end of East High Street, the COACH HOUSE HOTEL of 1885, with heavy gableted stone dormerheads and a pyramidal roofed oriel on the canted corner to South Street. Further E, in MONTROSE ROAD, the Angus Music Centre (*see* Public Buildings, above) and the Lowson Memorial Church (*see* Churches, above).

INDUSTRIAL BUILDINGS

MANOR WORKS, Manor Street and Myre Road. Now housing (Manor Court). Built as a textile mill in 1863. Steeply sloping site so that it is of two storeys to Manor Street and three to Myre Road. Main block of thirteen bays with the three at each end slightly advanced with rusticated quoins and urns on the outer corners; stone vases at the tops of the gables. Segmental-arched windows. At each end, a slightly recessed full-height three-bay wing with rectangular windows and bowed projection.

MILL, South Street and Strang Street. Disused. Built in the later C19. The weaving shed ranges were altered in the C20. Two-storey main block with round-headed first-floor windows and an Italianate tower at the SE corner.

ST JAMES WORKS, St James Road. Disused. Extensive but plain linen factory of the later C19. Bellcote on the gable of one building. At the NE end, a single-storey classical block dated 1877.

2050

FORTER CASTLE

5.1 km. NW of Kirkton of Glenisla

Tower house, its construction for James, sixth Lord Ogilvy of Airlie, completed by *William Stanness*, mason in Dundee, in 1608. Burnt out and partly demolished by followers of the Earl of Argyll in 1640, it was restored by *Nicholas Groves-Raines* in 1990.

Built of sneck-harled rubble, it is an L, the jamb projecting to both W and S. Main block of three storeys and an attic, *c.* 11.9 m. by 7.9 m. The jamb, *c.* 6.4 m. square, its wall-head only a little higher, contains one further storey but its floor levels, except at the ground floor and the attic, are placed slightly below those of the main block. At the main block's NW, NE and SE corners, conical-roofed round turrets on continuous corbelling, the NW and SE of one storey, the NE of two. The lower parts of the NE and SE are early C17 but their upper parts and roofs are conjectural reconstructions; the whole of the NW is conjectural. Below all the house's principal windows are circular shot-holes, mostly restored or mutilated.

In the main block's SW inner angle with the jamb, a bowed stair-turret projected on continuous corbelling rises to the jamb's wall-head above which it is finished with a conical roof, its top part and most of the windows conjectural. The elevations of the main block are a mixture of original and 1990 work. The ground floor is lit only from slit windows, all original. On the W elevation, much of the walling including the large wall-head chimney is substantially original. Large first-floor window towards the N and tiny openings at sill and lintel level to its l., all these original. So too are the small second- and third-floor openings but the attic's stone gabled dormer window rising from the wall-head is of 1990. Just a couple of small windows in the N gable, its crowsteps and chimney provided in 1990. The main block's E side was largely intact before the restoration. In it, one decently sized first-floor window and, at the second floor, a pair of regularly disposed but smaller windows with a couple of slit openings between. The wall-head's pair of gabled dormers is of 1990. The main block's S gable is also largely original and with a large first-floor window. Off-centre and smaller second- and third-floor openings and slits at the l. Two tiny attic windows, the r. pre-dating the restoration, the l., at a slightly higher level, partly original and partly of 1990. Again the gable's crowsteps and chimney are of 1990.

The S end of the jamb's E gable projects clear of the main block. In it, a tier of small windows, all original. The crowsteps on top are of 1990. In the S side of the jamb, a tier of openings slightly to the l. of centre, the first-floor window of decent size and with holes for a grille in its surround, the others smaller. All these are original but the gabled dormer on the wall-head is of 1990. In the W gable, small first- and second-floor windows aligned above each other at the l., a third-floor window at the r., all original. The gable's crowstepped and chimneyed top was rebuilt in 1990. The jamb's N side contains the entrance. The windows to the floors above form a diagonal line. At the wall-head, another gabled dormer of 1990.

Inside, tunnel-vaulted rooms on the ground floor. On the first floor the Great Hall, its beamed ceiling decorated in a Scots Jacobean manner by *Jenny Merredew*, *c.* 2005.

WELL to the N, its enclosing rubble wall of 1990.

FOWLIS

3030

Small village, most of the housing late C20 but, in SMIDDY BRAE curving S from St Marnock's Church up to Fowlis Castle, a rubble-built L-plan MILL and SMITHY of the 1840s.

ST MARNOCK'S CHURCH, Kirk Road. Built as a parish and collegiate church* by Andrew, first Lord Gray, in 1453, the chancel was partitioned off as the Gray family's burial vault after the Reformation but reopened into the nave in *T. S. Robertson*'s restoration of 1888–9.

Externally, the church is a long unaisled rectangle, *c.* 26.8 m. by 8.5 m., the ashlar walling and splay-topped base course all C15. Gableted bellcote of 1889 on the W gable, a contemporary floriated cross on the E. The gables' skewputts are original and still bear their heraldic display of the coats of arms of Gray (NW and SE), Wemyss of Reres, for Elizabeth Wemyss, wife of the first Lord Gray (SW) and the Royal Arms of Scotland (NE). A little E of the centre of the N side, a single-light pointed and cusped window which originally lit the space between the pulpitum and rood screen. Like all except one of the side windows, its surround is checked for shutters, probably a Georgian alteration. At this side's W end, a round-headed door, its surround chamfered. The W gable's window is pointed, of four cusped lights; in the head, a pair of cusped vesicas flanking a mouchette. The doors and windows in the N side are a mixture of the elaborate and the utilitarian. The door at the W

* Foundation of a collegiate church was certainly intended by 1450 and a college of canons was in existence by 1511 when its reconstitution gained papal approval. A few years later the college seems to have comprised a provost and at least six canons.

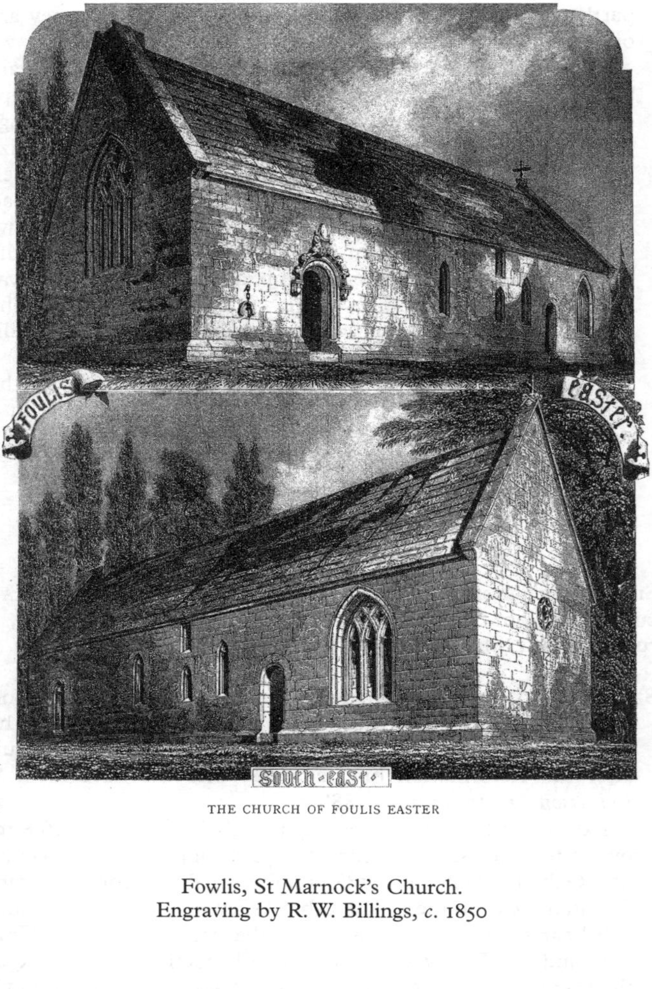

Fowlis, St Marnock's Church.
Engraving by R. W. Billings, *c.* 1850

end, presumably intended as the access for the Lords Gray and their retinue, is a show-off. Round-headed, with a filleted roll-and-hollow moulding under a crocketed ogee-arch. The weathered label stops were carved with the heads of angels bearing shields. The r. angel, wearing a string of pearls, has lost his shield, the l. angel is now headless but the shield survives to display the impaled coats of arms of Gray and Wemyss. Under the top of the hoodmould, a shield, its coat of arms obliterated. The hoodmould's finial has been carved as a helmet from which rises the swan crest of the Wemyss family; flanking the helmet, the lion rampant supporters of the Grays. E of the door, a fairly tall and pointed one-light nave window, its cusped head apparently original. An identical window but its head a C19 restoration at the W end of the chancel. Between these two but placed closer to the E than the W, a double tier of windows opposite the window in the church's N wall. The lower is a repeat of the N opening, the upper, originally lighting the rood loft, is rectangular. Beside the window lighting the chancel's W end is a round-headed door, its surround chamfered; this was the principal access for the canons to their choir. The E window of the church's S side, the main light for the altar inside, is quite large and pointed, of three lights under a head pierced by trefoils, the tracery all restored in the C19; filleted roll-and-hollow surround. In the E gable, only a small round window, its cast-iron tracery probably dating from repairs of 1842.

INTERIOR. Originally the parish church occupied the nave and the collegiate church the choir, the two parts separated by a pair of screens surmounted by a rood loft. The 1.5 m.-deep space between the screens contained a pair of small sacristies either side of a central passage whose W entrance from the nave was flanked by a pair of altars, probably backed by altarpieces painted with depictions of the Nativity and Resurrection of Our Lord. Behind the rood loft the line of the E screen was continued up to the ceiling by a rood screen which served as a reredos, painted with a scene of the Crucifixion, behind the loft's central altar facing the nave. The High Altar at the E end of the choir probably stood *c.* 1.5 m. clear of the E wall and in front of a tall altarpiece, light on the altar coming from the large window at the E end of the church's S side. Behind the altarpiece may have been a small reliquary chapel lit from the round window in the E gable. Altered after the Reformation, the interior was recast in 1888–9 by *T. S. Robertson* who covered it with a decoratively detailed collar-braced roof of red pine. The W bay serves as a vestibule, separated from the nave by a routine Gothic SCREEN of 1889. This contains a pair of late C15 doors with linenfold panels at the bottom and traceried arcading at the centre; crocketed pinnacles at the open tops. Originally they were in the medieval screen between the nave and chancel, its position indicated by the N and S walls' pairs of moulded corbels which supported the rood loft; on the N wall, another corbel to the W and at a lower level was probably a support for the stair to the loft. – Two STOUPS, both late C15, with round-headed recesses, and in unusually good condition. One, just E of the vestibule screen and intended to serve the S door, has a straight-faced bowl carved with a shield, now plain but presumably intended to be painted with a coat of arms. The other is beside the N door. Its bowl's sides are gently bowed and carved with rosettes, the front with a fleur-de-lis. – Octagonal stone FONT, also of the later C15, in the vestibule, its faces carved with scenes (their tops broken off) of the Life, Passion, Death and Resurrection of Our Lord. Shields on the splayed base bearing the coats of arms of Gray and Wemyss (for Andrew, first Lord Gray, and Elizabeth Wemyss, his wife).

Plain boxy PEWS of 1889 in the nave. In the chancel, a contemporary COMMUNION TABLE and simple Gothic PULPIT.

– ORGAN by *Walker*, *c.* 1970, and rebuilt here by *A. F. Edmonstone* in 2004. – At the N end of the E gable, a late C15 SACRA-
12 MENT HOUSE, its foliage-enriched ogee arch flanked by rosetted pinnacles. Over the arch is carved a half-length figure of Our Lord as *Salvator Mundi* holding an orb and flanked by wingless angels, one holding the Cross, the other the scourging post. The sacrament house's crowning cornice is decorated with foliage. Above this has been placed a stone whose sloping front is carved with a depiction of the Annunciation, also of the later C15 but probably not originally in this position. – At the centre of this gable have been placed eleven PANELS, ten painted with figures of Saints, the centre with Our Lord, his r. foot standing on an orb. A flag at the r. panel (St Ninian) displays the coat of arms of the Lords Gray. These panels probably formed part of the front of the medieval rood loft.

Towards the E end of the N wall is a large fragment of the church's late C15 ALTARPIECE, its upper part painted with Our Lord set between smaller full-length figures of St Catherine of Alexandria on the l. and, on the r., St John the Baptist and the Blessed Virgin Mary suckling the Infant Jesus. The centre of the panel has lost its decoration, perhaps a strip of decorative carving, but at the bottom survive richly dressed representations of two Evangelists, a female martyr, St Mary Magdalen, St John (all now headless) and, in the centre, the Virgin of Pity holding the body of the dead Christ. – A little W of the centre
11 of the N wall, a large and remarkably well-preserved PANEL, also of the later C15. Originally it formed a major part of the rood surmounting the chancel screen and the curved line of paintwork at its top shows that it was designed to fill the head of the tunnel-vaulted roof, presumably wooden, which originally covered the church. The panel is painted with a scene showing the Crucifixion of Our Lord flanked by the two thieves, the soul of the l. being carried by an angel to Heaven, the soul of the r. being taken to Hell by a demon. Gathered at the foot of the cross, together with the Holy Women and St John, is a crowd of richly garbed spectators including horsemen, Caiaphas and Herod. The inspiration seems to be Flemish or German although the artist may have been a Scot. At the bottom of this panel has been placed a beam, probably from the medieval chancel screen, painted with an inscription recording the church's erection and dedication to St Marnock by Andrew, Lord Gray, and his wife in 1453. – Near the S wall's W end, five panels, apparently also from the rood screen and painted with fragments of the Crucifixion scene.

STAINED GLASS. In the E gable's roundel, a brightly coloured late C19 window. At its centre, the coat of arms of the Lords Gray. – In the S window of the chancel, a window (the Last Day) of *c.* 1870, the central figure of Our Lord flanked by trumpeting angels. – Further W, a modernistic window (St Andrew) by *Margaret Chilton* and *Marjorie Kemp*, 1930.

GRAVEYARD. In the NW corner, a two-storey broad-eaved SESSION HOUSE of 1841, the upper floor entered from a forestair. – W of the church, the HEADSTONE of Andrew Mar: †1717, its E face carved in shallow relief with emblems of death. – Immediately to its S, the stone erected in 1735 by John Lyon to commemorate his parents and wife, the E face with a mantled coat of arms set in a baluster-pilastered aedicule, an angel's head (the soul) in the round-headed pediment. – Another mantled coat of arms on the stone erected by Margaret Petrie to her husband, Patrick Donald, †1764, but with angels' heads on both faces. – S of the church, near the W door, the GRAVE-SLAB of 1665 to Agnes Falkener carved with a pair of shields and a panel bearing a skull and crossbones. – S of this, a plain medieval monolithic stone CROSS, *c.* 1.9 m. high. – Just to its E, several C18 HEADSTONES adorned with angels' heads and reminders of mortality. Among them is the stone to Agnes Beig †1763 erected by her schoolmaster husband. At the top of the W face, trumpeting cherubs flank an angel's head. Another angel's head on the E face; below, set between torches, is a pair of scholars holding an open book. Also in this group, a stone of 1746 on which a floating angel trumpets news of the Resurrection. At the group's SE corner, the GRAVE-SLAB of Margaret Crichtone †1712, the base carved in shallow relief with emblems of death and another angel's head.

FOWLIS CASTLE, off Smiddy Brae. Rubble-walled three-storey-and-attic tower house of the Lords Gray, perhaps built *c.* 1500 but half-ruinous by 1862 when the shell was restored by *Hugh Robertson* for Patrick Keith Murray of Ochtertyre who then owned the Fowlis estate. The lands of Fowlis had been held by the Grays (in succession to the Mortimers) since 1377 and the naturally defensible site beside the steep banks of a burn was enclosed by a massive wall, the courtyard entered through a gatehouse tower, until the late C17 or C18. The surviving house seems to have been the main residence inside this courtyard and stood at its SW corner. However, after their construction of Castle Huntly (Perth and Kinross) in 1453, that house was the principal seat of the Grays and Fowlis Castle probably served as a jointure house, the surviving building perhaps intended only for occasional occupation. It is a crowstep-gabled three-storey and attic oblong, *c.* 12.3 m. by 7.0 m., but with a massive chimney, which rises with offsets, projecting from a little E of the centre of the S side. In the chimney's W inner angle, a round stair-tower, perhaps original but possibly an addition of 1640 when the house seems to have been remodelled;* the stair-tower's conical roof is an addition of 1862. The original entrance (built-up early in the C19 when the ground-floor doors were inserted) was in the W gable. Cavetto cornice under the eaves; skewputts at the corners, the E carved as heads. The gabled dormer windows, of brick at the front and tile-hung at the rear, are of 1862, as is the plain two-storey-and-attic NW wing.

* A stone bearing that date, probably from a dormerhead, was recorded by David MacGibbon and Thomas Ross, *The Castellated and Domestic Architecture of Scotland*, v (1892), 275, as having been reused in a nearby house.

Inside the main block, a broad segmental-arched kitchen fireplace at the ground floor.

5040

FRIOCKHEIM

Village laid out in 1811 by John Anderson, Provost of Arbroath, who had acquired a feu of part of the lands of Friock for the erection of a flax-spinning mill. The name was changed from Friockfeus to Friockheim in 1824 and by 1841 the village had a population of 805, almost all weavers and spinners. The housing, now predominantly of the mid and later C19, formed a triangle bounded by Gardyne Street, its buildings mostly two-storey, on the S, and the largely single-storey cottages of Millgate on the NW and Union Street on the E. Some of these were rebuilt in the C20 when the village expanded to the W and N.

FRIOCKHEIM AND KINNELL PARISH CHURCH, corner of Millgate and Gardyne Street. Opened as a chapel of ease in 1835 but enlarged with a NE jamb in 1841 and reconstructed by *William Aitkenhead* in 1881–2, the appearance now generally Late Victorian. It is rubble-walled, the short main block with tripod finials on the gables. Front (W) gable with a double tier of windows in Jacobean Renaissance surrounds. Projecting from the gable is a tower which contains the entrance, its four-centred arch-head filled with a fanlight and set in a corniced rectangular surround, the spandrels decorated with rosettes. At the tower's second stage, narrow round-headed and keystoned dummy windows, the W under a tall crosslet dummy-slit. The top (belfry) stage's E and W sides' openings are each of two round-headed lights; in the N and S the faces of a clock (by *James Ritchie & Son*, 1885). Topping the tower, a pyramidal roof with dragon weathervane. NE jamb in the same manner. In its NE inner angle with the main block, a two-storey outshot containing a stair to the galleries. Across the church's E end, a HALL added in 1910.

FRIOCKHEIM PUBLIC SCHOOL, Eastgate. Disused. Built in 1875. Squared-rubble U, a pair of round-headed windows in the advanced and bargeboarded ends.

MASONIC LODGE (BRUCE LODGE NO. 593), Gardyne Street. Built as Friockheim Congregational Church *c.* 1845 but converted to a masonic hall in 1885. Oblong, now drydashed and the rectangular windows looking C20. Projecting from the centre of the front gable, a corniced door; above this a slender tower topped by pinnacles.

PARKGROVE CREMATORIUM, Douglasmuir, 2.4 km. SE. By *Inglis & Carr*, 1993. Tall single storey, the drydashed and blockwork walls supporting a prominent slated piend roof which extends over the entrance to cover a large porch. Diagonally set chimney, its detail of Ægypto-Greek inspiration, at the back. Inside, the broad chapel is covered by an elaborately braced single-span roof. Fully glazed S wall, a strip of clear-storey windows at the N.

MIDDLETON. *See* p. 609.

GAGIE HOUSE

4030

2.7 km. NNW of Murroes

Two-storey laird's house, the property of the Guthries from the C17 until the C20, the walls covered in white harling and with dressings of grey sandstone. The shape is an irregular T whose tail comprises the earliest part of the house, probably built soon after 1610 when the lands of Wester Gagie were acquired by Walter Guthrie, the second son of Alexander Guthrie of that Ilk. Extending from the back of the cross-bar this projects considerably to the S. The S gable is gripped by tall conical-roofed round corner turrets carried on continuous corbelling, the E turret with a small S window whose sill is pierced by a round shot-hole. The gable's pair of ground-floor windows with chamfered margins are perhaps early C19, the off-centre window to the first floor, also in a chamfered surround, probably early C17. Large Late Georgian windows in the E side, the first floor's with a piend-roofed dormerhead. At the S end of the tail's W side, a crowstep-gabled full-height addition, probably of the earlier C19, its upper floor jettied. Two-light ground-floor window; steep pedimental head to the first-floor opening. At the bay N of this addition, another two-light window at the ground floor and a first-floor window which rises into a gabled dormerhead, both openings probably early C19 in their present form. Between them, a stone carved with a shield bearing the coat of arms and initials of Isabel Leslie, wife of William Guthrie, first of Gagie.

In the SW inner angle of the tail and cross-bar of the T, a battlemented two-storey porch, probably of the early C19 but remodelled by *James Maclaren & Sons* in 1893–4 when it was given a Neo-Jacobean Renaissance doorpiece whose segmental pediment bears the heraldic achievement of the Guthries of that Ilk. The cross-bar's W part seems to be Late Georgian but remodelled in 1893–4 when the ground-floor windows were enlarged to two lights and a conical-roofed round turret added to the W gable whose piended roof was masked by a crowstepped gable containing a dummy double-keyhole 'gunloop'. The E part of the cross-bar is shorter and the rubble walling exposed. It is mostly Late Georgian but with some discreet additions of 1973 by *France Smoor*.

Inside, the principal rooms have good-quality but simple finishings of the 1890s.

S of the house, a drystone-walled GARDEN, perhaps of C17 origin. – Against the E wall stands a SUMMERHOUSE, its monopitch roof sloped down to the E, its parapet bearing the badly weathered date of 1762. Façade of polished ashlar with paired Roman Doric pilasters at the ends and a single pilaster in the centre, all crossed by a band course which forms imposts at the springing of the pair of round-headed arches between them; the pilasters carry a Doric entablature with a mutuled cornice under a tall parapet surmounted by urns. – At the top end of the garden's central path on the axis of the house's tail, an early C20 octagonal marble FONT in a Perpendicular Gothic manner. – Further S along the path, a SUNDIAL of 1766, a gently bulbous stone pillar, its flat top covered by the metal dial-plate. – Just SE of the garden's NW part, its dwarf walls with arrowhead railings of *c.* 1760, a second SUMMERHOUSE. This is of 2002–3, designed by *France Smoor*, with cast-iron columns and an octagonal bellcote under a tall slated spire.

STABLES AND COACHHOUSES W of the house. A rubble-built range, perhaps begun *c.* 1700, the original height shown at the E gable by the two small rectangular windows above a cartshed entrance. This was raised in 1759 when a double-pile coachhouse was built, the keystone of one of its pair of segmental-arched openings carved with human heads. The spired octagonal cupola was added by *France Smoor* in 1982.

6060

GALLERY HOUSE

1.4 km. NE of Logie Pert

Unshowy but not unsophisticated laird's house built in 1677–*c.* 1680 for Sir John Falconer of Balmakelly, Master of the Mint; *Thomas Wilkie*, mason in Edinburgh, was the builder and perhaps the architect.

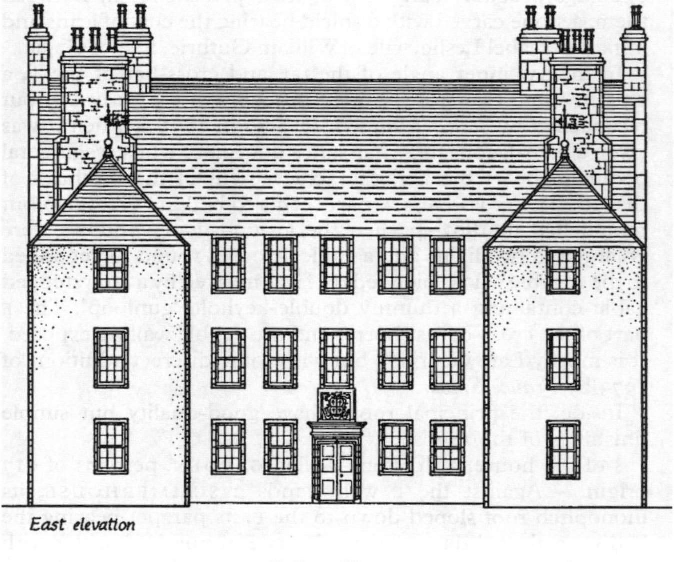

Gallery House.
Front (east) elevation

The house is U-plan, built of harled rubble with dressings of pink and white sandstone. Main block of three storeys; the pavilion-roofed square E wings contain the same number of floors but are slightly lower. To the E approach, the main block displays a regular five-bay front, the windows all of the same height; originally with casements they now contain sashes. Central door in a corniced surround, the space between its top and the first-floor window sill filled by a moulded frame, apparently of the late C17 but containing a late C18 panel which displays the coat of arms of David Lyall, a Gothenberg merchant who acquired the estate in 1787. The front of each wing is of a single bay; ground- and first-floor windows of the same size as the main block's but the second-floor openings are lower. On the S wing, a wrought-iron weathervane pierced with the initials I^{S}F and B^{D}I (for Sir John Falconer and Dame Barbara Jaffray, his wife); the N wing's weathervane bears the initials WL and IC (for William Low, a Dundee jute manufacturer who owned the house in the early C20, and his wife) and the date 1915. Immediately behind each wing, a large chimney rises from the wall-head of the main block. Extending S from the SE wing, a plain mid-C18 two-storey-and-basement service range. Regular three-bay elevation to each gable of the main block. Its W elevation is also symmetrical and of five bays but with the outer bays' windows grouped 2:2 either side of the stair windows which are of the same height as the others but placed between the floor levels to light the half-landings inside.

INTERIOR. A spine wall divides the main block into two parts. In the centre of the E part, the entrance hall with a stone segmental arch to the stair-hall in the centre of the W part. Stone stair with a solid newel and moulded treads. The SE wing originally contained the kitchen, later altered and with a door formed through the large W fireplace. This room's floor is above the level of that of the main block to allow height for a tunnel-vaulted cellar below. The two principal ground-floor rooms are in the house's W part. In the SW room, perhaps the C17 Low Dining Room, a dado of bolection-moulded pine panelling. The NW room, perhaps the C17 family bedroom, contains similar but full-height panelling; china cabinet in the centre of the E, perhaps dating from an C18 or early C19 alteration. At the first-floor stair landing, doors in chamfered stone surrounds to the house's NW and SW rooms and the Long Gallery which fills the full length of the E part. The Gallery's W wall originally contained a pair of chimneypieces. The SW room was the C17 High Dining Room. The lugged surrounds of the wooden doorcase and chimneypiece are both perhaps early C18 but the chimneypiece's low overmantel, its frieze adorned with Gothick pendants, looks a late C18 embellishment. The walls' heavy cornice above a florally decorated frieze is of *c.* 1680. So too is the richly modelled plaster ceiling. This is of geometric pattern with long rectangular end panels containing swags of foliage hanging from ribboned knots. The centrepiece is an oval set in a vine-leaf border. Surrounding this, four panels, the inner sides curved, each containing an eagle rising from knotted branches. On the second floor, the W wall of the main block's NE room retains full-height late C17 panelling; a single panel above its E door whose lugged surround looks early C18.

GARDEN immediately N of the house, probably of the mid or later C18, its walls of rubble faced internally with brick. S gateway, its masonry rusticated; over it, statues of falcons. Statue of a recumbent dog on the N wall. – Plain ashlar-fronted oblong COACHHOUSE to the NW, dated 1743 on a keystone. Elliptical-arched carriage doors at the end bays; loft above, its l. window heightened with a C19 dormerhead. – Mid-C19 GATEWAY at the W end of the drive, the stone piers with vermiculated rustication and carrying ball finials.

5040

GARDYNE CASTLE

1.8 km. S of Guthrie

Substantial laird's house of modest but endearing pretension which has developed in stages from the C16 to the C20.

The site, on the edge of a steep bank, offers a modicum of natural defence and may well have been occupied by the medieval residence of the Gardynes of that Ilk. The earliest (E) part of the present house was apparently built for Patrick Gardyne in the 1560s. Constructed of large blocks of rubble masonry and presumably originally harled, this is of three storeys and an attic. Main block of *c.* 8.8 m. by 7 m. with round turrets at the E corners and, projecting from the NW corner, a circular stair-tower of *c.* 3.5 m. diameter; originally there may also have been a turret on the SW corner. Pair of quite tall slit windows with chamfered margins at the ground floor of the S side. At the N end of the E gable a small ground-floor window and, in the ground floor of the N side, a pair of splay-mouthed horizontal openings containing round shot-holes, all these probably of the 1560s. Another shot-hole, at the S end of the W gable, has been covered by the later extension at this end of the original house. At the S side's first floor, two tall windows, their moulded surrounds appearing C17 rather than of the 1560s; probably also of the same date is the E gable's first-floor window (converted in 1910 to a door opening onto an iron balcony). Between the two S windows, a worn panel, perhaps not *in situ*, with baluster-carved jambs supporting an ogee arch topped by sculpted acorns. Within this framework, remains of the coat of arms of the Gardynes of that Ilk; surmounting cornice bearing the date 1568. The roll-and-hollow-moulded surround of the small first-floor window on the N side looks original; tiny slit opening to its r. At the second floor, a pair of S windows, both in moulded surrounds like those of the openings below and also probably C17. Off-centre attic window in the crowstepped E gable. Also at this level are the ashlar-clad round turrets carried on continuous corbelling pierced by downward-pointing shot-holes. In the lower part of the walling of the turrets, more shot-holes, here in splay-mouthed horizontal surrounds like those in the N side of the main block. All this seems of the 1560s but are the upper parts of the turrets of the same date or do they date from a C17 remodelling? These contain smallish windows and, above, battlements, each carried on a single course of continuous corbelling studded with barely projecting stylized cannon spouts. Within the battlements rise conical stone-slabbed roofs surmounted by fat finials and fronted by dormer windows with pointed pedimental heads, also topped by finials; these roofs are similar to the C17 roof over the stair-tower at Scotstarvit Tower (Fife).

The NW stair-tower seems to have been built in two stages. The first, probably of the 1560s, produced a round tower rising to the second floor of the main block, the walling pierced at various levels by shot-holes contained, as elsewhere, in splay-mouthed horizontal surrounds. In the NW segment, a couple of windows in roll-and-hollow-moulded surrounds; smaller but similar window at the top of the N segment. In the E inner angle, continuous corbelling at the house's second-floor level carries a bowed turret containing a secondary stair to the attic of the main block. This stair serves also as the access to a caphouse over the main stair, its present form probably an afterthought of the late C16. This is a crowstep-gabled rectangle on continuous corbelling carried rather timidly clear of the rounded structure below. Window in the N gable, its surround also with a roll-and-hollow moulding.

The C16 house was more than doubled in size by the construction of a W addition. This addition and the original house are now of the same height and width and share a continuous moulded wall-head cornice along the S front. This addition seems to have been built in two stages. The walling of the ground floor and lower part of the first floor is constructed of roughly squared and coursed rubble masonry (fragments of harling still adhering) and perhaps belonged to a C17 extension of the original house, at least one storey and an attic in height. Above, the walling is of rough ashlar but incorporates one moulded jamb of an opening probably of the C17 and apparently reused here as a useful piece of stonework. This second stage appears to date from 1740.* The extension's S front is of three bays, the openings grouped 2:1. At the ground floor, a pair of roughly formed smallish windows, probably C18, in the l. bays. In the masonry to their r., the moulded stonework of a window, probably of the C17, but was there a window here which was built up in the C18 or is this also dressed work from elsewhere and reused in the C18 reconstruction of the ground floor? The r. bay contains the C18 entrance to the house and, above, a large panel displaying the mantled and crested coat

* As stated by David MacGibbon and Thomas Ross, *The Castellated and Domestic Architecture of Scotland*, ii (Edinburgh, 1887), 497.

of arms of the Lyells of Gardyne who owned the estate from the late C17 to the mid C20. Tall windows to the first floor, decent-sized but smaller openings at the second.

The house was further enlarged at the end of the C19 with a crowstep-gabled block N of the C17 and C18 W extension. Then, in 1910 *Harold O. Tarbolton* added a two-storey extension across the W end of the house and projecting to its N, the stonework of stugged red sandstone ashlar. Slightly advanced S front of two bays, in an unshowy Scots C17 manner deferential to the house's earlier architecture.

INTERIOR. On the ground floor of the C16 house and entered through a door with chamfered margins is a store. It is covered by a high tunnel vault of ogee profile which is probably an insertion or afterthought but presumably also C16. Elliptical-arched embrasures to the E and S windows; pair of shot-holes in the N wall. At the S end of the W wall, a recess, its back containing another shot-hole. There is thought to be a cellar below the early C20 concrete floor. In the house's C17 and C18 W extension, a ground-floor dining room formed, probably in 1910, from the C18 entrance hall and adjoining room. At the W end, a basket-arched stone chimneypiece of 1740 but its moulded wooden surround, the design of early C18 inspiration, is of 1910.

The C16 stair from the ground floor is a comfortable turnpike, the steps' wooden covering probably of 1910. On the first floor, the house's E room is the C16 HALL (now DRAWING ROOM), its floor level raised slightly above the original, its ceiling considerably lower. The S and E window embrasures are elliptical-arched and apparently C16, the small N window also C16 and, unusually, with a roll-and-hollow-moulding on the inner as well as the outer face of its surround. Roll-and-hollow moulding also to the W end's stone chimneypiece, now with an outer surround of 1910. In the house's W extension are two first-floor rooms (both now bedrooms), the W with painted pine panelling of *c.* 1740 and a double-lugged overmantel but the chimneypiece below is Edwardian. The second floor of the C16 house contains two rooms, their present form and floor and ceiling heights of *c.* 1740. Also of *c.* 1740 their stone chimneypieces, the E room's basket-arched and with a thistle carved on the keystone, the W's rectangular and with a rose on the keystone. Contemporary pine panelling. The E room's E corner cupboards contain C16 stone corbelling under the gable's turrets. Below the N corbelling, part of a moulded stone, perhaps a fragment of the C16 hall's cornice.

The main turnpike stair rises above the present second floor to a landing with silhouette wooden balusters, probably at the level of the C16 second floor. A doorway from this landing to the main block has been built up, probably in the remodelling of *c.* 1740. Access to the main block's present attic is by a tighter turnpike stair in the turret on the main stair-tower's E side. Rising above the floor at the E end of the attic's N wall is the head of the late C16 doorway from the landing to the former second-floor level. This is of stone with a roll-and-hollow-moulded surround surmounted by a half-dome topped by a ball-finialled stalk. Doors at the ends of the room's E gable open onto steps down into the corner turrets. In each of these turret rooms, shot-holes in the walls and in horizontal slits in the floor. Both are lit by a double tier of windows. Over these rooms, conical roofs rising into domical ashlar vaults.

Steps off the stair-turret's turnpike give access to a room in the caphouse over the main stair-tower. This may originally have been the laird's study. Its bowed ashlar doorpiece is distinctly smart with a roll-and-hollow moulding under a rope-moulded cornice. In the S wall of the room, a narrow stone chimneypiece, also with a roll-and-hollow moulding.

GLAMIS *3040*

Couthy estate village on the edge of the park of Glamis Castle.

GLAMIS PARISH CHURCH, Kirk Wynd. Built in 1792–3, a rubble-walled box with a W steeple; alterations were made and an E apse added by *George Bennett Mitchell & Son*, 1933–4. 17

The N side originally had two tiers of rectangular windows. Several of these were blocked in the 1930s when a pair of tall round-headed and Y-traceried two-light windows, copies of C18 windows in the S side, were introduced. Also of the 1930s is the splay-sided apse at the E gable, again with round-headed windows, the centre one of three lights with intersecting tracery. High on the gable wall, a medieval stone carved with a pair of human heads under a canopy. At the ends of the S side, two tiers of rectangular windows. At the centre of this side, the minister's vestry flanked by a pair of Y-traceried round-headed windows and surmounted by the head of a third (dummy) window.

The W gable is windowless; blocked door immediately S of the steeple. This projects boldly. At the two lower stages, unbroken by string courses, a hoodmoulded round-headed door (enlarged in the 1930s) under a fairly small window, also round-headed; the panel carved with the Church of Scotland's emblem of the Burning Bush is probably of 1934. Above these two stages, a mutuled cornice under the ashlar-clad and corniced clock stage. Then, an octagonal belfry, the openings (dummies in alternate faces) again round-headed. Octagonal stone spire, its weathervane in the form of a salmon.

Tenuously attached to the SE corner of the church is the STRATHMORE AISLE built *c.* 1480 by Isabella Ogilvy, widow of Patrick Lyon, first Lord Glamis, and apparently designed as a transeptal chapel above a burial vault. Probably it was attached to the S side of the chancel of the medieval parish church. The Aisle is an ashlar-walled rectangle, the gables topped by heraldic beasts (a lion and a griffon) bearing shields. Boldly projecting splay-topped string course along the W side and S gable. The S door is an insertion, possibly of 1742 (the date, together with the initials ES for Earl of Strathmore, on its lock) but with a roll-and-hollow moulding suggestive of a C16 or C17 date. It has curtailed the depth of the window above. This is of three cusped lights, the heads of the outer openings containing foiled openings (their stonework renewed). Above the window but off-centre, a foliaged corbel, perhaps C17 and not *in situ*, under a sundial of 1771. On the N side of the Aisle, a battlemented Georgian Gothic addition of the earlier C20.

The interior of the church originally had galleries along the N side and the E and W ends, the pulpit standing at the centre of the S side. In the reconstruction of 1933–4 the existing galleries were removed, a new W gallery erected, and the E end converted to a chancel entered through a round-headed arch and with an organ chamber on its N and a vestry on the S. The WEST GALLERY FRONT and FURNISHINGS are all of oak in a politely expensive Late Gothic manner with the occasional Celtic touch, much of the carving executed by parishioners who formed a *Carving Guild* for the purpose. – ORGAN by *J. J. Binns, Fitton & Haley Ltd.* – STAINED GLASS. Two windows in an accomplished small-paned modern realist manner. The one at the E end of the S side (St Andrew and St Fergus) is by *Herbert Hendrie*, 1939. The corresponding window in the N wall (Scenes from the Life of Our Lord and Our Lady) is of 1969 by *Gordon Webster*.

The two-bay interior of the Strathmore Aisle is covered by sexpartite vaulting, its foliage-surrounded bosses and corbels carved with shields, some plain, others displaying, severally or impaled, the arms of Lyon (a lion rampant) and Ogilvy (a lion passant). The W two-thirds of the N end is occupied by the (blocked) round-headed arch, its position unrelated to the vaulting, which presumably gave access from the medieval church. The arch's W end springs from a low semi-octagonal respond. The E end is supported by an octagonal pier, its capital carved with a fruiting vine and a shield bearing the Lyon coat of arms, the walling E and N of the pier hollowed out to allow space for it. Was a second arch to the E originally intended but left unexecuted, the E–W breadth of the chapel curtailed from what had been first planned? Above the arch, a blocked rectangular window. E of the arch and set above the top of its pier, a blocked doorway, its jambs chamfered, which presumably gave access to a room or stair in the wall thickness. Near the N end of the E wall, a SACRAMENT HOUSE with an ogee-arched roll-and-hollow-moulded and crocketed surround; above each end, a shield, the l. defaced but apparently bearing the Lyon lion rampant, the r. with the impaled arms of Lyon and Ogilvy. At the S end of this wall, a segmental-headed door of the earlier C19 into the E addition. The C15 window in the S end has been shortened to allow the insertion of the later door below.

GRAVEYARD. At the SW corner, a piend-roofed SESSION HOUSE of *c.* 1840. – Set into the wall just to its E, a STONE, perhaps of the C17, carved with a skull and crossbones. –

Exceptional number of C17 GRAVE-SLABS carved variously with one or two angels' heads (souls), shields and reminders of death (skulls, crossbones, hourglasses and crossed sexton's tools). – Similar motifs, often accompanied by trade emblems, on the C18 HEADSTONES which are carved in fairly high relief with rustic Baroque exuberance. Well-preserved ones stand S of the centre of the church. Among them, one of 1777 erected by James and John Wightman to their parents which displays a weaver's shuttle and loom. Another, also of 1777, commemorating Thomas Farquharson, mason in Ballindarg, has extravagantly capitalled fluted Corinthian pilasters flanking a shield which bears three castles and a mason's tools. – Large stone to James Doig, brewer in Glamis, †1777, the shield bearing a brewer's shovel and mash-oar. – E of these, a stone erected by Thomas Cathro to his wife, Jean Proctor, †1761, the shield bearing swingletrees and socks and coulters, the emblems of a farmer. – To its N, a headstone of 1769 erected by David Lindsay to his wife and daughter, carved in exceptionally high relief, its fluted Corinthian pilasters again with extravagant capitals, the shield bearing the three castles and dividers of a mason.

DESCRIPTION

KIRK WYND leads W from the gates of Glamis Castle (*see* p. 500) and Glamis Parish Church (*see* above). On the N side, the MANSE. Main block built in 1798, of two storeys with tiny gable windows lighting the attic. Front of rough ashlar; urns on the ends of the wall-head. The front was altered in the later C19 when the entrance was moved to the W bay from the centre which was given a two-light window, a bay window was added at the E and a wall-head chimney erected. Single-storey piend-roofed lateral wings of *c.* 1830. In the front garden, a very large PICTISH STONE, probably of the C7 or C8. The slab's roughish 5
E side is incised with a snake, a salmon and a mirror. On the W face, the relief of a cross with hollows at the intersection of the arms and interlaced decoration. In the corner compartments of the slab are carved a lion, a centaur holding axes in both hands, a cauldron standing on human feet with, below, two warriors fighting with axes, and a dog's head above a 'triple-ring' symbol (perhaps a cauldron seen from above). After the Manse Kirk Wynd curves to the SW. On the N, at the start of the curve, a plain mid-C19 U-plan STEADING. A two-storey cartshed forms the centre range, its piended roof covered with stone slabs. The other ranges are single-storey. Across the street, a rubble-built and slab-roofed terrace of single-storey cottages (now the ANGUS FOLK MUSEUM), their small windows indicating an C18 date. Large roof-lights at the back provided in *T. H. Thoms*'s restoration of 1957 for the National Trust for Scotland.

FORFAR ROAD goes S from the end of Kirk Wynd. On its E side, the two-storey MASONIC LODGE NO. 99, built as the

Masons' and Gardeners' Hall *c.* 1830. Three-bay front of droved ashlar, with horizontal-paned windows and an architraved door. Further S, a rubble-built small MILL of the earlier C19.

THE SQUARE is the village's oblong central space. At the E end, the gable of a harled two-storey house, C19 in its present form but with a corner sundial bearing the date 1768. On The Square's N and S sides, two-storey terraced houses of the C18 but much restored in the C20, built of harled or painted rubble. The date 1765 appears over the W ground-floor window of the N terrace. This end of that terrace is now part of the STRATHMORE ARMS HOTEL whose taller main block, set back from the building line, is of the early C19.

MAIN STREET leads W from The Square. At the start of its N side, a harled and thatched cottage. Its datestone of 1745 is not *in situ* but not necessarily inaccurate. Then, on both sides, plain two-storey rubble-built houses of the later C18, some of the originally small windows enlarged. Inoffensive Victorian intruder at No. 12. Dates of 1765 and 1769 on the door lintels of Nos. 11 and 18. No. 19 at the W end of the N terrace is of the later C19, with gableted dormerheads and a two-light ground-floor window. The end building of the S terrace (CORNER HOUSE) is a three-storey late C18 tenement. Three-bay N front, the roof piended at the W end. Full-height three-bay S wing, its roof also piended at the S end. Two-storey S addition, perhaps of the early C19. Immediately W of the Corner House, a cast-iron Victorian PUMP by the *Glenfield Co. Ltd* of Kilmarnock. It is a dome-topped fluted column, a lion's head on the capital. More utilitarian-looking ashlar pier PUMP, perhaps of the earlier C19, beside it.

DUNDEE ROAD runs S. At the top, on the W side, GLAMIS PRIMARY SCHOOL. Dumpy Jacobean school and school house of 1839. Further S, on the E side, the STRATHMORE ESTATES OFFICE of *c.* 1840. Single-storey, with broad piended roofs and horizontal-paned windows.

GLAMIS CASTLE

1.3 km. N

Fantastic array of tower and turrets, the most exuberant display of baronial status in Scotland although its former almost vulgar gaudiness has been toned down by the removal of harling from the rubble walls and of paint from its abundant sculptured heraldry. The castle now rises from well-tended parkland.

The earliest member of the Lyon family on record and the first to hold the lands of Glamis was John Lyon who was named as one of the auditors of the accounts of the King's Chamberlain in 1369 and appointed Keeper of the Privy Seal two years later. In the 1360s and 1370s he acquired various estates, by far the most significant the lands of the thanage of Glamis which he was granted by Robert II in 1372. In 1376 he married the King's daughter, the Princess Joanna, after which he was appointed

Chamberlain of Scotland and knighted. The chief residence on these lands probably stood on the site of the present house, an extensive promontory at the confluence of the Glamis Burn and the Dean Water. Here, in 1435, the first Sir John Lyon of Glamis's grandson, Patrick (from 1445, first Lord Glamis), began construction of the Great Tower, a very large three-storey-and-attic L-plan tower house. After his death in 1459 the work was completed, apparently following an interval, by his widow before her own death in 1484. Probably at about the same time there was built a detached oblong block containing a first-floor Great Hall and standing S of the Great Tower and extending beyond it to the E. In 1537 the estate and castle of Glamis were forfeited as a result of the supposed treason of John, seventh Lord Glamis, and his mother and held by the Crown for the next five years. Perhaps at that time but more probably after the restitution of the property to the Lyon family in 1542, the Great Tower and SE hall block were united by the erection of a short link containing a stair, the house becoming Z-plan, and the hall block was remodelled to contain two suites of rooms above a kitchen.

A thoroughgoing remodelling of the Great Tower was undertaken in the early C17 by Patrick, ninth Lord Glamis and, from 1606, first Earl of Kinghorne, †1615 and completed by his son, John, second Earl of Kinghorne. In this work the dumpily proportioned C15 tower house was heightened by a further two storeys, embellished with carved detail and a swaggering bowed stair-tower erected in the SW inner angle as the chief feature viewed on the approach and an effective disguise for the disparity in size between the main block and jamb. The medieval hall was lavishly decorated with plasterwork.

Patrick, third Earl of Kinghorne (from 1677, Earl of Strathmore and Kinghorne), was only two when he succeeded his father in 1646. On attaining his majority in 1660 he first turned his attention to the repair and remodelling of Castle Huntly (Perth and Kinross) before beginning work at Glamis Castle in 1669. Initially he carried out repairs and tidied up the immediate environs, removing outbuildings as a preliminary to making a formal courtyard in front of the house. There followed the construction of additions behind the castle's SE wing and at the NE corner of the Great Tower, this last containing a first-floor library and second-floor chapel. Most important was Earl Patrick's decision 'to order my building so as the frontispiece might have a resemblance on both syds, and my great hall wch is a rowme that I ever loved haveing no following was also a great inducement to me for reering up that quarter upon the west syde'. Consequently he added a NW wing roughly balancing and of the same height as the house's SE wing and also with a round tower at the outer corner. Inside this new wing he placed a first-floor suite of family rooms consisting of the 'Family Drawing Roum and Dining Roum', 'My Lady's Chamber' and, in the round NE tower, the 'Closet of My Lady's Chamber'. The second floor, entered from the Great Hall of the Great Tower, contained a state apartment comprising the 'High Dining Roum', 'Withdrawing Roum', 'fine

Bed Chamber' in which stood the state bed, 'Closet of the fine Bed Chamber' and, in the round tower, the 'Closet of the Withdrawing Roum'. At about the same time were built single-storey-and-attic ranges extending out from both wings. Work was complete by 1701 when *John Sharres* contracted 'to cast and harle the said noble Earles Castle of Glamiss old and new work thereof with lyme on the frontispiece and round the same'.

Designs, one by *John Carr* of York, for remodelling the Great Tower and wings in a picturesque Tudor or castellated manner were prepared in 1763. In 1773–6 the service ranges E of the house were extended round a courtyard, this work including the erection of a double-height kitchen under a library E of the late C17 Chapel Block. In 1775 the late C17 NW wing was demolished but its rebuilding was halted the next year by the death of the ninth Earl of Strathmore and Kinghorne. In 1798, when the tenth Earl had attained his majority, work resumed on the NW wing which was completed in 1801, probably to a revised design and containing a double-height first-floor drawing room; the SE wing was remodelled externally to correspond. The NW wing's drawing room was converted to a dining room in 1850–2. In the 1860s designs were obtained from *Brown & Wardrop* for extensive alterations and additions to the C18 service ranges E of the main house but only a little of what was projected was carried out at the time and further work on a less ambitious scale was not executed until 1889–1901 to designs by the Glamis estate architect, *James A. Ferguson*. In 1903 the 1770s library was lavishly remodelled as a billiard room, the last important remodelling of one of the house's principal rooms.

The APPROACH is from the S. At the entrance to the drive, the QUEEN MOTHER'S GATES erected in 2008. Banded and corniced GATEPIERS by *James F. Stephen*, bearing the names and coats of arms of the burghs of Angus; surmounting the piers are stone statues of snarling lions. Over the footgates at the sides, coats of arms including those of the Bowes-Lyons, Earls of Strathmore and Kinghorne. On the spear-headed cast-iron GATES themselves (designed by *Lachlan Stewart* of *Anta Architecture*), the coat of arms of Queen Elizabeth the Queen Mother. The 1.3 km.-long drive, bounded by an avenue planted with a mixture of oak, ash, horse chestnut and sycamore, leads directly to the castle. About halfway along, on the W, a crowstep-gabled two-chamber lectern DOOCOT, its back wall rising as a gabled screen. In the front, a pair of doors and two gabled dormers containing flight-holes. In the late C17 the drive passed through two gateways before reaching a third which stood at the apex of a triangular space pushing into the centre of the S side of the walled Inner Court in front of the castle. In each corner of this court stood a statue of one of the four C17 Stewart kings of Scotland. On either side of the court and divided from it by dwarf walls surmounted by iron railings were gardens, the W the Fountain Garden with, unsurprisingly, a fountain centrepiece, the E the Dial Garden with a sundial in the centre. On the gardens' s side were walls which continued the line of the Inner Court's s wall, each ending at a round tower. These gateways and walls were removed in the 1770s and the castle now rises from a sweep of gravel set among lawns. However, standing at the end of the drive, just s of the former s side of the Inner Court, are two of the more than life-size lead STATUES of the Stewart kings (Charles II and James VII now missing) which stood in that courtyard. They were made by *Arnold Quellin* in 1685–6, James VI in royal robes and holding an orb and sceptre, Charles I dressed in armour, his hand on his sword; originally they were 'coloured over after the manner of brass'. Marking the former outer s corners of the gardens which flanked the Inner Court are the EAST AND WEST ROUNDS, early C19 replacements for the late C17 dairy and still house which stood in these positions. Like their predecessors they are circular. Each is a rubble-built roofless two-storey battlemented tower with a door and couple of dummy windows to the ground floor and openings of upright ovals at the first floor. On the lawn between the East Round and the castle, the late C17 stone SUNDIAL which stood in the former Dial Garden 45 here. It is *c.* 6.5 m. high and displays a multitude of dial faces. From its octagonal base rise alternating barley-sugar shafts and lions rampant (the heraldic motif of the Earls of Strathmore and Kinghorne) who hold dials. These are sheltered by a domed canopy above which is placed a multi-faceted globe, all the faces dials. Tall scrolled topknot rising into a coroneted fleur-de-lis finial.

The approach to the house is focused on the early C17 great 42 bowed STAIR-TOWER filling the inner angle of the L-plan Great Tower, its ashlar masonry a smooth contrast to the rubble walling of the rest of the house, now stripped of harling. At its lowest stage, the house's principal entrance, its surround with foliate-capitalled fluted pilasters and cornice surmounted by the heraldic achievement of the royal arms of Great Britain. Above, a round niche containing a bust (formerly 'coloured over after the manner of brass') of Patrick, third Earl of Strathmore and Kinghorne; it too is by *Quellin*, 1685–6. To the l. of the entrance, a tier of windows in roll-and-hollow-moulded surrounds and surmounted by panels carved with heraldic achievements. The top three panels, their surrounds all chamfered, display the impaled coats of arms of the sixth, seventh and eighth Lords Glamis and their wives; probably they were erected by the first Earl of Kinghorne on his construction of the stair-tower at the beginning of the C17. The frame of the lowest panel is rounded and the achievement bears the impaled coat of arms of Patrick, third Earl of Strathmore and Kinghorne, and Helen Middleton, his wife; it must date from after their marriage in 1662 and probably before his death in 1695. To the r. of the entrance is a second tier of openings, all in roll-and-hollow-moulded surrounds and placed under panels with chamfered surrounds and displaying the coat of arms of the Lyons, Earls of Kinghorne, by itself and impaling the arms

Glamis Castle.
Perspective elevation by J. Slezer, 1686

of the wives of the first and second Earls of Kinghorne; the bottom panel of this tier is again later than the others since it bears the impaled coats of arms of John, fourth Earl of Strathmore and Kinghorne, and his wife, Elizabeth Stanhope, and probably dates from between his succession in 1695 and death in 1712. In this tier the panel over the second window up is placed across a band inscribed BVILT * BY * PATRIK * LORD * GLAMIS * AND * D[AME] * ANNA. This inscription and the accompanying heraldic panels, except the lowest which seem to be afterthoughts, provide evidence that the stair-tower was at least partly completed between 1595 when Patrick, ninth Lord Glamis, married Anne Murray and 1606 when he was created first Earl of Kinghorne, and of its further embellishment with heraldry *c.* 1620 by John, second Earl of Kinghorne, after his marriage to Margaret Erskine in 1618. The heraldic panels rise only to a string course which marks off the stair-tower's low stages from those above. At these, window openings, also with roll-and-hollow mouldings, continue the vertical lines of the tiers below. At the top stage of the tower, directly over the entrance, a half-round turret projects on continuous corbelling, its windows set in moulded surrounds and now partly blocked by a corniced clock face dated 1811. Behind, at the hinge of the Great Tower's main block and SE jamb, a domed cupola.

The GREAT TOWER, its roof's iron cresting a replacement of 1925–6 for cresting erected in 1684, serves as a not unobtrusive backdrop to the stair-tower. Its two stages of construction, in the C15 and beginning of the C17, are evident from a change in the masonry above the three lower storeys. The ground floor of both the main block and SE jamb project under splay-topped intakes and are pierced by smallish windows in roll-and-hollow surrounds; like all the openings of the Great Tower they seem to have been remodelled in the early C17. Above the ground floor, the main block's S front is near-symmetrical. At the first floor, a pair of fairly small windows flanking a large one, all in chamfered surrounds; at the second floor, a huge window, its roll-and-hollow-moulded surround topped by a pedestal whose concave sides are filled with scrolls and which carries an ogee-arched pedimental head flanked by scrolls and with a coronet finial; in the head, the initials P^E^K (for Patrick, first Earl of Kinghorne) and, on the pedestal, those of his wife, Dame Anne Murray, giving a likely date for this work of between 1606 when he was granted the earldom and his death in 1615. Two much smaller openings at the third floor. The r.'s surround is chamfered. The l. is set in a roll-and-hollow-moulded surround and linked vertically to the taller fourth-floor window by a panel carved with a shield bearing the lion rampant coat of arms of the Lyons, Earls of Kinghorne, and framed by flattish fluted consoles. This principal window at the fourth floor is set between fluted Doric pilasters with torch-like finials and rises through the eaves; surmounting its lintel, a conical-roofed round turret carried on continuous corbelling, its windows' surrounds with roll-and-hollow mouldings. Similar turrets also at the W gable of the main block but with oval dummy openings directly under the eaves; the S of these is early C17, the N a replacement of *c.* 1800 for a two-storey rectangular turret like that at the main block's NE corner. The gable-head between these was remodelled *c.* 1800. Before, it was finished with a pair of chimneys flanking a small bowed bartizan. Now the centre rises a full storey above the eaves to a circled stone balustrade whose bowed centre is projected on continuous corbelling and finished with an open-sided and dome-topped cupola, its design copied from the early C17 cupola on top of the S gable of the jamb. Tier of windows at the centre of the gable. The second-floor opening was blocked in the late C17 by the addition of the NW wing but its flat-topped pedimental head survives; it is carved with a coronet over the monogrammed initials of Patrick, first Earl of Kinghorne, and Dame Anne Murray, so probably dates from between 1606 and 1615. Third-floor window in a roll-and-hollow-moulded surround, the date 1606 carved under the scroll-sided pedimental head. Corniced window at the fourth floor, its curvaceous pediment containing a shield. The attic window, also corniced, is surmounted by an aedicule, its cornice carried on broad fluted pilasters, which is carved with the lion rampant coat of arms of the Lyons and the initials P^E^K (for Patrick, [first] Earl of Kinghorne).

Tying together the S front of the Great Tower's main block, the W side of its jamb and the N end of the SW wing is a broad band marked off by two string courses and studded with panels, the intervening stair-tower circled by the narrower inscription band recording its erection. The three panels of the band along the main block are carved with heraldic achievements displaying the impaled coats of arms of the second, third and fourth Lords Glamis and their wives. On the jamb, the central panel bears the impaled coats of arms of Patrick, first Lord Glamis, and Isobel Ogilvy, his wife, and the r. panel the coat of arms of the Lyon family. All these are probably early C17 but at the band's l. end is a panel displaying the impaled arms of John, fourth Earl of Strathmore and Kinghorne, and Elizabeth Stanhope, his wife, and above, the band's upper string course is a semicircular pediment carved with coroneted drapery and flanked by the fourth Earl's and Countess's weathered initials, together with the date 169-. In the narrow W side of the jamb, above this band, windows whose roll-and-hollow-moulded surrounds are probably early C17. The jamb's S gable is treated almost identically to the W end of the main block but the round turret's oval windows under the eaves are open, the base of the SE turret is pierced by a shot-hole and the wall-head's pierced parapet is of *c.* 1800, a replacement for iron cresting.

The W front of the short mid-C16 LINK between the Great Tower's jamb and the SW wing is flush with the W walling of both jamb and wing and continues their splay-topped ground-floor projection. A semblance of unity with the wing is given to the link by their common height and the arcaded wall-head cornice and battlement added to both *c.* 1800. Otherwise the link's detail is mid-C16. At the ground floor, a blocked door and window, both with roll-and-hollow mouldings, as has the first-floor window over the door; small window to its r. At the second floor another pair of windows with roll-and-hollow-moulded surrounds and oval gunloops in their sills; they are linked vertically to the openings above by the heraldic panels of the band which is continued from the jamb.

The general shape of the SE WING is C15, its detail of the mid C16 and of *c.* 1800. In the splay-topped projecting ground floor, recesses containing large Late Georgian dummy crosslet 'arrowslits'. The first floor's pair of tall windows with roll-and-hollow mouldings are of *c.* 1600, as are the smaller openings above. Over these, a pair of low and horizontally proportioned openings in bow-ended surrounds. These are of *c.* 1800, as is the wall-head cornice and battlement and the SW corner's turret which is carried on continuous corbelling. In the turret's SW segment, a window in a projecting roll-moulded surround under a small oval opening; above a string course are vertical dummy recesses, their tops and bottoms rounded. Slated conical roof with a pronounced bellcast profile. The wing's longer S side is similarly treated but with no projection at the ground floor whose crosslet 'arrowslits' serve as windows. The upper floors' main openings are grouped 2:1 with, to the r. of the W pair, small closet windows. Chamfered surrounds at the first floor and more elaborate mouldings at the second, these probably mid-C16. At the wing's SE corner, a conical-roofed and sturdy four-storey tower (the GREAT ROUND). Above its splay-topped projecting base, inverted keyhole gunloops suggestive of a C15 date. The roll-and-hollow mouldings to the windows of the upper floors and small oval dummy openings under the eaves may date from a C17 remodelling.

The NW WING of *c.* 1800 is, for the most part, a carefully executed replica of the SE wing but the projecting base of its NE tower is not splay-topped. At the back the wall-head of the N side is topped by a balustrade, of the E by a parapet. These two rear elevations are partly hidden by a two-storey battlemented coachhouse addition, probably of the earlier C19, which extends E from the wing's NW tower; segmental-arched carriage entrance in the N side. At this addition's E end, a short single-storey stable block, also probably of the earlier C19. Behind this rises the N side of the Great Tower. A couple of windows at first floor. Single second-floor window in a chamfered surround, its original depth apparently curtailed and with a round shot-hole below. Above a stair window at the r. end of this elevation, a row of individual corbels which originally supported the tower's wall-head battlement but now carry the walling of the C17 fourth floor and attic, the windows of both storeys regularly spaced, the attic windows rising into crowstep-gabled dormerheads, the central gablet containing a garret light above the attic window. Projecting on individual corbels from the NE corner of the Great Tower is a rectangular two-stage crowstep-gabled turret, its top floor further projected on corbels. This extends back along the tower's E side until halted against a two-thirds gablet whose N end consists of a small bowed bartizan between two chimneys, its S of a crowstepped roof slope. At this E elevation the only hints of ostentation are given by the elliptical heads of the first-floor windows of the castle's Crypt (Laigh Hall) and the huge second-floor window to the Great Hall.

Against the E end of the Great Tower's N side is the four-storey late C17 CHAPEL BLOCK, quite plain except for stone mullions and transoms to the second-floor windows and the crowstepped dormerheads over its top floor's openings. The KITCHEN BLOCK of 1773–5 at its E end continues the height of the Chapel Block but contains only two very tall storeys, the ground floor's windows pointed, the first floor's rectangular. E of this, a lower three-storey block, its second-floor windows rising into thistle-finialled gabled dormerheads. It is probably of the 1770s but was heightened in 1867. E of this, a range also of three storeys but lower, its top three windows also with gabled dormerheads; its E three bays are by *Brown & Wardrop*, 1869, the l. two of 1900 by *James A. Ferguson* but in the same manner. In front, a battlemented single-storey outshot of 1900. At the end of this range, a broad crowstepped gable of 1900, a conical-roofed round turret at its NW corner, a round tower, also conical-roofed, at the NE.

The N range E of the Great Tower formed one side of a couple of SERVICE COURTS. On their S side, E of the main SE wing, a three-storey-and-attic tepidly Baronial block designed by *James A. Ferguson* in 1891. Slightly set back to the

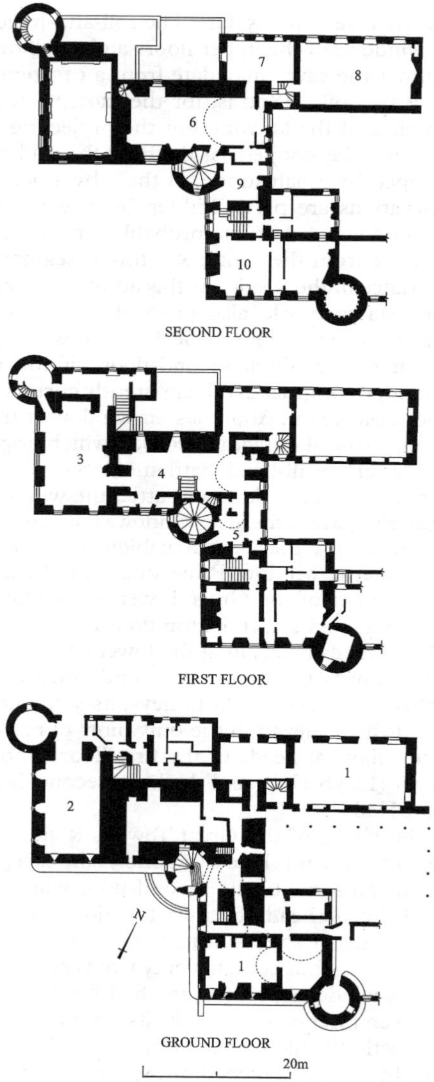

1. Kitchen
2. Coach House
3. Dining Room
4. Crypt
5. Duncan's Hall
6. Great Hall
7. Chapel
8. Billiard Room
9. King Malcolm's Room
10. Queen Mother's Sitting Room

Glamis Castle.
Plan

E, a two-storey late C18 range remodelled in quiet Baronial fashion in 1891. In front of these SE ranges and the earlier SE wing is the DUTCH GARDEN laid out in 1891–3 to a design by *Arthur Castings*, the entrances on the S side and at the W end flanked by stone lions rampant (the armorial motif of the Earls of Strathmore and Kinghorne) carved by *James Law* in 1869 and originally at the Walled Garden but moved here in 1925. In the garden's centre, a STATUE of Mercury.

INTERIOR. The main entrance opens onto the foot of a broad turnpike stair of the early C17, its stone newel hollow so as to allow hot air to rise within it from a stove at the base and escape through openings at various levels. The staircase walls were stripped of plaster in *James A. Ferguson*'s 'antiquing' alterations of 1896.

In the Great Tower's jamb, E of the entrance, a tunnel-vaulted ground-floor lobby, probably originally a store. Off its S side, the mid-C16 scale-and-platt stair filling what was originally the gap between the Great Tower and SE wing and serving the upper floors of the remodelled wing. On the ground floor of the originally detached C15 SE wing, placed a few steps below the entrance level, two rooms. The E is a tunnel-vaulted store, its N entrance originally from a courtyard but now off a passage. The W room was formed in the mid C16 by throwing together two C15 rooms, probably also stores, to make a kitchen, its side walls thickened to carry a new segmental-arched tunnel vault at right angles to that of the E room. At the E end of the N wall, the blocked doorway which formerly opened onto the C15 middle room; a wide-mouthed gunloop was inserted here in the mid C16. Filling the kitchen's W end, a vast segmental-arched fireplace. Off the N side of the lobby in the Great Tower's jamb, a passage through the thickness of the main block's S wall. Contained in the thickness of the passage's E wall is a well-shaft which rose to the level of the second-floor of the Great Hall. On the passage's W side in the thickness of the main block's S wall, a straight stair rises to the first-floor Crypt (Laigh Hall), its head gently curved and with a small window now opening onto the C17 main stair.

The ground floor of the NW wing is occupied by the COACH-HOUSE of *c.* 1800, its principal entrance from the N. It is covered by a brick vault inserted in 1850–2 by *Thomas Liddell* to strengthen the floor of the Dining Room above. In the N range, the cove-ceilinged double-height kitchen provided in the 1770s. In the S wall, an elliptical-arched recess containing hot plates and a central oven of 1851–2 (by *W. & P. Steele*). More recesses, apparently C18, at the E end, the centre elliptical-arched, the other two rectangular, all with bold voussoirs and V-jointed rustication.

A straight flight of steps off the C17 main stair leads through the S wall of the Great Tower's main block to the CRYPT (Laigh Hall) which occupies the block's first floor. This is a mezzanine which divides the lower of the two high vaults of which the principal part of the main block was originally constructed.

Over the Crypt, a semicircular tunnel vault, its stonework of thin ashlar blocks from which plaster was stripped in 1896. Window at the W end of the S side; at its ingoes, doors to wall chambers. A pair of windows at the room's E end, the S equipped with stone seats. At the W end, beside a round-headed buffet recess, the entrance to the castle's DINING ROOM, originally formed *c.* 1800 as the Drawing Room and converted to its present use by *Thomas Liddell* and *James Anderson* in 1850–2. This is double-height. At the N end, a huge, almost full-height sideboard recess with pilastered jambs; ovals and lozenges ornament its lintel's frieze. Round the room, a high dado with a strapwork frieze. In the centre of the E side, a vast wooden chimneypiece, the overmantel framed by paired pilasters and carved with the heraldic achievement of the Lyons, Earls of Strathmore and Kinghorne. Pilastered and corniced surrounds with fleurs-de-lis finials at the main windows. Higher up, a second tier of smaller and square openings containing heraldic stained glass (by *John Brown*). Compartmented plaster ceiling decorated with pendants, roses and thistles; lions' heads on the frieze. In the Great Tower's jamb, S of the Crypt, is DUNCAN'S HALL covered with a C15 semicircular tunnel vault. The W wall's round-headed fireplace seems an insertion.

The second floor of the Great Tower's main block is filled
43 with the GREAT HALL, a magnificent double-height space remodelled in the early C17 by the first and second Earls of Kinghorne. The shape of its semicircular tunnel-vaulted ceiling is C15, its plasterwork bears the date 1621. This is composed of geometric compartments and, along the centre, a line of foliage-modelled pendants. The compartments contain floral and foliage motifs, together with the lion rampant armorial device of the Lyons, portraits of David, Joshua, Hector and Alexander (i.e. four of the Heroes or Worthies of biblical and classical Antiquity), the casts later reused at Muchalls Castle (Kincardineshire) and Craigievar Castle (Aberdeenshire), and coroneted shields bearing the monogrammed initials of Margaret [Erskine], Countess of Kinghorne (wife of John, second Earl of Kinghorne); in the central compartment are the Royal Arms of Great Britain. In the centre of the S wall, a huge stone chimneypiece, the jambs with panelled pilasters, the cornice-mantel enriched with foliage. Overmantel ornamented with plaster thistles which border a panel bearing the Royal Arms. At the sides of the overmantel, paired Atlantes and caryatids. Above the overmantel, a strapworked frieze.

N of the Great Hall's E end is the CHAPEL, added in 1679–83
44 and decorated in 1688. It is a straightforward oblong, *c.* 9 m. by 5.5 m. FURNISHINGS of 1866 replacing box pews, and an almost square altar surrounded on three sides by a heavy communion rail. The walls are wood-panelled. The pair of panels on the lower part of the ends of the E wall are of 1866, decorated with fleurs-de-lis in a diaper pattern. The other panels are of 1688, all painted by *Jacob de Wet* and with inscriptions lettered by *William Rennie*. The artistry is decidedly pedestrian.

On the E wall, above the altar, is a depiction of the Crucifixion derived from an early C17 engraving by Boetius Adam a Bolswert. At this wall's N end, a portrait of St John, the inscription at the bottom, as on the other panels depicting Apostles, relating the manner of his death; at the S end of the wall, St Peter. On the S wall, two tiers of panels, each of the upper containing the figure of an Apostle, the lower a scene from the Life of Our Lord. They begin at the E with St Andrew and St Thomas above a representation of the Last Supper. Then (W of a door which originally opened onto a vestry and now to a stair placed here in the later C18) St James the Less above a view of the Risen Lord, a spade in his hand, his face a portrait of Charles I, appearing to St Mary Magdalen, the design also derived from an engraving by Bolswert. Above the Chapel's corniced broad doorway from the Great Hall, a horizontal panel showing the Nativity of Our Lord. At this wall's E end, St Philip but with no panel below. On the W end wall, St James the Great and St Bartholomew at the upper tier. At the lower, a depiction of Our Lord as *Salvator Mundi*, the panel apparently cut to fit the space and probably not *in situ* and perhaps not by de Wet. Above this, a STAINED GLASS roundel of St Michael the Archangel by *Heaton, Butler & Bayne*, 1870. The upper tier of portrait panels continues along the S wall, beginning at the W with St Judas Thaddeus followed by St Matthew and St Simon and ending with St Matthias. Between these, mullioned-and-transomed windows which contain small-scale STAINED GLASS scenes emblematic of the Ministry of Angels, by *C. E. Kempe*, 1882–3. On the S wall, beside the main door, tabernacle-framed PAINTINGS of saints. The Chapel ceiling is divided into large and small panels, all painted by de Wet. On the small panels, depictions of angels and various symbols (the sun, moon and stars, the IHS monogram, dove, burning heart, and the eye, ear and hand of God). The larger panels have fifteen Scenes from the Life of Our Lord, all derived from a series of engravings by Boetius Adam a Bolswert first published in a devotional book produced at Antwerp in 1622 and later bound in Bibles and copied by F. H. van Houe for a Bible published at London in 1680. They are arranged in three rows, each reading chronologically from W to E, the N row of scenes referring to the Birth and Childhood of Our Lord until his Baptism, those of the centre row to his Ministry and those of the S row to his Passion.

E of the Chapel is the double-height BILLIARD ROOM, originally the 1770s Library but recast in 1903 for its present use. Along the S wall are bookcases. At the E end, a Neo-Jacobean chimneypiece formerly at Gibbside (County Durham) and perhaps dating from *John Dobson*'s alterations to that house in 1856. At the jambs caryatids rise from pedestals whose fronts are carved with lions; rinceau ornament with dragons' heads and a central angel on the lintel of the fireplace. The overmantel is divided by slender attached columns into three panels, each bearing the coat of arms of one of the ancestors of Mary Eleanor Bowes, heiress to Gibbside and wife of John, ninth Earl of Strathmore and Kinghorne. Neo-Jacobean coved and compartmented ceiling ornamented with small foliaged pendants, heraldic motifs and the initials, singly and in coroneted monograms, of Claude and Frances, thirteenth Earl and Countess of Strathmore and Kinghorne, together with the date 1903.

On the second floor of the Great Tower's SE jamb, KING MALCOLM'S ROOM which was remodelled *c.* 1620. Compartmented plaster ceiling, enriched with lions rampant, the coroneted and monogrammed initials of John, [second] Earl of Kinghorne, and his wife, Margaret [Erskine], and heads of Heroes or Worthies of biblical and classical Antiquity. The chimneypiece, of wood and embossed leather, with scenes showing figures in Jacobean dress and the Crowning of Our Lord with Thorns looks a mid-C19 embellishment. Above, an early C17 plaster overmantel, its floral-decorated border surrounding a heraldic achievement which displays the impaled coats of arms of Lyon and Erskine over the initials I.L.E.K and M.C.K. (for John Lyon, [second] Earl of Kinghorne, and Margaret [Erskine], Countess of Kinghorne). In the SE wing, the W room (the QUEEN MOTHER'S SITTING ROOM) contains a heavy Neo-Jacobean chimneypiece and overmantel, probably of the mid C19.

The PARKLAND planting is predominantly of the late C18 and earlier C19. Except for the straight avenue along the main drive from the S it is relatively informal, with broad belts of trees along the banks of the Dean Water and Glamis Burn. W of the house, the EARL JOHN BRIDGE over the Dean Water, a single segmental-arched humpbacked bridge constructed of red and grey rubble masonry; an inset panel inscribed J^{E}S.1697.E^{C}S, the initials those of John, fourth Earl of Strathmore, and his wife, Elizabeth [Middleton], Countess of Strathmore, provides a date for its erection.

A straight walk formed in 1907–10 runs E from the Dutch Garden directly S of the house (*see* above). On the walk's N side, the PRIVATE GARDEN in which stands a crowstep-gabled lectern DOOCOT, perhaps of the C18. On the wall's S side, the ITALIAN GARDEN formed in 1907–10 by *Arthur Castings*, its principal architectural feature a square PAVILION against the S boundary's yew hedge. Elliptical-arched openings in three sides; corbelled eaves to the pyramidal slated roof. At the S side, a long stone bench, the centre of its back surmounted by a red sandstone panel carved in relief with a half-length female figure rising from between branches of foliage. – At the end of the E walk, on the W bank of the Glamis Burn, the PRINCESS MARGARET MEMORIAL designed by *Michael, eighteenth Earl of Strathmore and Kinghorne*, and erected in 2006, a Postmodern Neoclassical pedimented aedicule which frames a round-headed arch containing a corniced Late Georgian pedestal surmounted by a terracotta swagged vase. – Just N of this, a bridge over the Glamis Burn gives access to a winding walk through the PINETUM of *c.* 1865. – At its N, the iron EARL

MICHAEL BRIDGE over the Dean Water, designed by *David Waterston* in 1898 and restored in 1996, its balustrades with scrolls set between alternating barley-sugar and plain uprights, the latter topped by fleurs-de-lis, thistles and roses. Corniced ashlar GATEPIERS, perhaps of the 1860s, at the ends. – N of this, the large brick-walled GARDEN formed in 1866–8 to a layout designed by *Archibald Fowler*, the E, W and S walls surmounted by lions holding shields. The GATEWAYS were designed by *Brown & Wardrop* in 1866, with banded ashlar gatepiers, their stone lion finials carved by *M. W. Stephens*, *c.* 2000, replicas of finials erected here in the 1860s but moved to the Dutch Garden (*see* above) in 1925. The wrought-iron gates were made by *Alexander Sinclair* in 1868. – NE of the walled garden, a barge-boarded single-storey and attic substantial COTTAGE of *c.* 1868. – SE of the walled garden, BRIDGE over the Dean Water, by *W. & R. Blackadder*, 1866, a single segmental-arched ashlar-faced span with rusticated voussoirs. At the ends, battlemented piers from which project cannon spouts.

Now on the edge of the parkland are the late C17 gateways removed from the main drive and rebuilt here in 1775. At the S end of the SE drive, beside Glamis Parish Church, the KIRK GATE. Gatepiers of rusticated stonework, each surmounted by one sloping side of a pediment, its centre broken by the line of the drive; ball finials. – Just W of the Queen Mother's Gates (*see* above) at the entrance to the main drive, the SATYR GATE built by *Alexander Craw*, mason, in 1681 and which originally stood near the drive's S end. It is of polished ashlar, the tall fluted and banded corniced piers surmounted by octagonal finials, replacements for stone eagles. Between the piers, a round-headed archway beneath a downward-curving elliptical head topped by foliage cresting and a central coronet. Flanking the archway is a pair of panels, each carved in relief with a satyr. Flanking the gatepiers are tall and narrow strips of walling on which stand lion supporters, each holding a shield carved with the lion rampant device of the Lyons, Earls of Strathmore and Kinghorne. From these extend lower battlemented screen walls, perhaps of *c.* 1800, containing hood-moulded openings, the two-light windows dummies, the doorways at the inner ends serving as footgates. At the screen walls' outer ends, badly weathered lion supporters hold shields displaying the Lyon coat of arms; beyond these the walls are swept down to lower piers. The wrought-iron gates themselves, decorated with foliage and the heraldic achievement of the Bowes-Lyons, Earls of Strathmore and Kinghorne, were erected in 1931 to celebrate the Golden Wedding of the fourteenth Earl and his wife. – At the W end of the W drive, 0.8 km. from the castle, the GLADIATOR GATE built in 1680–1 and 66
also by *Craw*; originally it stood near the N end of the main drive. Like the Satyr Gate it is of polished ashlar. Tall corniced piers, the W face of each fronted by a pilaster, the E by a lower pier surmounted by a crouching lion. On the top of each pier, a ball finial decorated with fruit embellishment. Originally

there were narrow strips of walling either side on which stood figures of more than life-size naked gladiators. These figures now stand on top of battlemented screen walls of *c.* 1800, very like those flanking the Satyr Gate.

PICTISH STONE (ST ORLAND'S STONE), Cossans, 3.6 km. NE of Glamis village. Tall (almost 3 m. high) slab of the C8 or C9. One face is carved in relief with a ringed cross decorated with spiral and interlace patterns. At the intersection of the arms, an empty circular recess, perhaps originally containing a metal plaque. Intertwined fish monsters flank the shaft. The other face is bordered by a pair of etiolated fish monsters. The upper half bears reliefs of a 'crescent' and 'double-disc-and-Z-rod' symbols and, below, an irregularly shaped recess as if a third symbol had been excised. On this face's lower half are reliefs of scenes. At the top, a pair of riders and, below, another pair but accompanied by hounds. Beneath these, a long boat carrying five men and a large sack. At the bottom, an ox confronted by an angry feline creature.

PICTISH STONE, Hunter's Hill, 0.7 km. E. Perhaps of the C8. The front is carved in relief with a cross decorated with panels of interlacing. Flanking the head, an angel and a bird-headed man. Either side of the shaft are animals and, on its l., 'triple-disc' and 'flower' symbols. Roughly finished back incised with animal, serpent and 'mirror' symbols.

GLAMIS HOUSE, 0.8 km. W. Early C19 piend-roofed house of marked but modest pretension. Semi-octagonal porch at the centre of the two-storey main block's N front. Single-storey wings, also piend-roofed.

GLENISLA *see* KIRKTON OF GLENISLA

GLENLEE PARISH CHURCH *see* INVERMARK

GLENPROSEN VILLAGE

3060

Church and a handful of houses at the meeting of Glen Tairie and Glen Prosen.

GLEN PROSEN CHURCH. Humble whitewashed rubble box built by *Alexander Milne*, mason, in 1802. Pointed windows in the W wall and S gable. The small gabled bellcote on the N gable looks Victorian. Attached to this end, a granite-walled porch added by *B. N. H. Orphoot* in 1920; bellcast roof and, in the gable, a cross picked out with slivers of slate.

The interior was remodelled by *Robert S. Lorimer* in 1900. Kingpost truss roof. Boxy PEWS. At the S end, a 'chancel', its oak panelling decorated with fruiting foliage. Small COMMUNION TABLE, its front with linenfold panelling. It stands in front of the PULPIT whose front panel is carved with a crowned vine (a bird among its leaves) and cross, the back with more linenfold panelling and a vine-decorated pierced frieze. – STAINED GLASS. Two windows (St Agnes; Charity) of 1900 flanking the pulpit, the figures set in obscured glass. – In the W wall, three lights, the principal subjects (the Nativity, Baptism and Ascension of Our Lord) also set in obscured glass, by *Margaret Chilton*, 1928.

GLENPROSEN LODGE, 4.1 km. NW. Pink-harled and decoratively bargeboarded mid-C19 shooting lodge.

LEDNATHIE HOUSE, 2.2 km. S. Early C20 harled villa of two storeys. Scotstyle, the S front's advanced and crowstep-gabled centrepiece pierced by an oculus; from it projects a small porch

BALNABOTH. *See* p. 348.

GREYSTANE *see* DUNDEE: ARDLER

GUTHRIE 5050

Handful of C19 cottages near the church and former manse.

GUTHRIE CHURCH. Gothic-windowed oblong kirk of 1826 built of red sandstone, rubble at the E end and side walls but the front (W) gable is faced with droved ashlar. This gable, surmounted by a Roman Doric-columned and domical-roofed birdcage bellcote, contains the pointed entrance and a pair of windows; high up, a quatrefoil dummy opening between a pair of crosslet 'arrowslits' which serve to ventilate the roof-space above the ceiling. At the S side and E gable, broad windows, those of the E end enlarged in 1879. A piend-roofed vestry was added at the centre of the N side in 1961.

Inside, plain boxy PEWS of 1826 and, at the E end, the PULPIT which was remodelled in 1962 when its canopy was removed and it was encased in oak. – STAINED GLASS in the W windows, the S (the Good Shepherd) old-fashioned realism of 1920, the N (the Sower), also brightly coloured but the realism stylized, by *William Blair* and *John Blyth*, 1970. – On the W wall, a bronze TABLET commemorating the Rev. William McConnachie with a half-length relief portrait; a replica of the tablet in Lauder Parish Church (Borders), it was erected in 1935.

S of the church's W end is the GUTHRIE AISLE. Now detached, this was a transeptal chapel added to the medieval church, probably *c.* 1470,* by Sir David Guthrie who was reported to have enlarged the parish church with a view to its becoming collegiate, a status granted by the Pope in 1479 when a college consisting of a provost and four canons was established here. The chapel is a simple rubble-walled oblong which has opened to the church through a round-headed arch. This

* There is a dendochronological date of 1464 for the roof timbers.

has been built up, perhaps in 1681 when the parish church was rebuilt. In the blocking, a door whose straight lintel has headstops at the ends and a centre tweaked up to form a tiny pointed arch with a foliate finial. Above this door, the empty frame for a heraldic panel. Towards the N end of the Aisle's W side, a rectangular window with a moulded surround and, near the S end, a rectangular door, its surround also moulded. In the S gable, a three-light window, again rectangular and with a moulded surround; the mullions have been renewed, probably in 1881 when the Aisle was restored.

The interior of the Aisle is still covered by its C15 roof, with wall-posts and sole-pieces at the base and collars serving as horizontal ties to the rafters. Formerly it was hidden by a tunnel-vaulted oak ceiling painted with depictions of the Crucifixion and Last Judgment but this has been removed and is now in the National Museum of Scotland. – Set into the floor is a C17 GRAVE-SLAB, the ineptly carved shield at the base displaying two coats of arms. – Propped against the W wall, another SLAB which commemorates William Aire †1630 and his wife Besse Scrymgeour †1628, one of its shields bearing a maltster's shovel and tongs, the other a lion rampant. – Circular stone bowl of a FONT, perhaps of the C13.

GRAVEYARD At the W entrance, a gabled GATEWAY with stumpy obelisk finials on the apex and ends. It contains a segment-headed arch under a panel carved with the date 1639, the Guthrie coat of arms and the initials CBC or GBG. – At the churchyard's SE corner, the BURIAL ENCLOSURE of the Guthries of Guthrie formed in the later C19, the battlemented E wall rising at the centre into a cross-finialled gable containing a coat of arms.

MANSE (now Kirkton House) to the S. Villa-like by *James Maclaren*, 1861.

GUTHRIE CASTLE

0.5 km. W

C15 tower rising boldly above a Victorian Baronial manor house.

The lands of Guthrie were acquired by David Guthrie of Kincaldrum in 1466 and a tower house built probably soon after. About 1760 a detached house was put up SE of the tower. In 1818 this was attached to the tower by the construction of a linking wing. In 1848 John Guthrie of Guthrie employed *David Bryce* to remodel the C18 house and add sizeable extensions to its N and E and also on the S side of the C15 tower. The masonry is all of buff-coloured rubble, the earlier work at least originally harled.

The C15 tower is of three storeys and an attic. L-plan, the main block *c.* 12.2 m. by 9.4 m. and with a small SE jamb. Architecturally it is austere and most of the windows have been enlarged in the C18 or C19. At the wall-head, carried on moulded corbels, a battlement with angle-rounds, all of the mid C19. Also of the mid C19 are the gabled dormer windows of the crowstep-gabled attic and the tall upper stage of the jamb rising to a high pyramidal roof.

The addition of 1818 is clearly visible towards the W end of the building's S front where it appears as a two-storey three-bay block, its ground floor with a rectangular bay window, its wall-head parapet with shaped Neo-Jacobean merlons. Bryce's reconstruction and extension of the C18 block were extensive but low-key despite their use of much of the vocabulary of the Scottish Baronial style – conical-roofed round turrets, canted bay windows corbelled to the square at the upper floors and crowstepped gables.

The Neo-Jacobean entrance of 1848 adjoining the C15 tower on the house's N side opens into Bryce's Stair Hall, its walls covered with oak panelling for two-thirds of their height. Stair of Jacobean character. Off the Stair Hall's W side and occupying the ground floor of the C15 tower is the Library formed in 1848 by throwing together two cellars. Compartmented Neo-Jacobean plaster ceiling with rather small pendants at the intersection of some of the ribs. Lugged stone chimneypiece of late C17 derivation at the N wall. In the S wall, double doors to the Drawing Room, also of 1848 and occupying the ground floor of Bryce's addition on the S side of the tower. Similar but more elaborate ceiling. White marble chimneypiece of Louis XV inspiration. On the tower's second floor, the C15 Tower Room (the medieval Upper Hall). This is double-height and tunnel-vaulted. Fireplace in the N end of the W wall.

WALLED GARDEN N of the house, apparently formed in the early C17 but its present ashlar walls probably of the later C18. D-shaped, the N wall curved. At the centre of the S side, an early C19 portico of paired Roman Doric columns, the entablature's frieze with arcaded decoration. It is surmounted by a stone inscribed with the initials of William Guthrie of Guthrie and the date 1614. At the garden's N end, a garden house and, at the W, a two-storey Gothic-windowed apple store, both Late Georgian. In the E wall, a late C18 Tudor-arched entrance between tall bundle-shafted and pinnacled column-buttresses. – W of the Walled Garden is the WILD GARDEN laid out in 1925. Its entrance is provided by a round-headed archway surmounted by a small stone bearing the date 1601 and with a probably contemporary thistle finial. In the archway, a pointed wrought-iron YETT, probably of the C15 and originally in the mansion house's tower.

WEST GATEWAY of 1838, at the S end of the drive from the SW, constructed as a combined gateway and railway viaduct. It is built of polished red sandstone ashlar. Hoodmoulded Tudor arch in a battlemented surround, its cavetto cornice decorated with rosettes, the central merlon carved by *G. Mill* with the heraldic achievement of the Guthries of Guthrie. At each end of this central section, a tall octagonal turret, its battlemented top stage with pointed openings, the cavetto cornice with grotesque heads. From these concave screen walls step down and end against battlemented low square turrets. Inside the gateway, an early C19 single-storey ashlar-faced and broad-eaved LODGE, its windows and door in four-centred over-arches. – At the end of the E drive, the EAST GATEWAY of *c.* 1840. Broad carriage entrance flanked by a pair of Tudor Gothic footgates, each contained in a parapeted ashlar frame-work with octagonal turret-buttresses at the corners, their faces with slit-and-crosslet dummy openings. Curved screen walls extend to lower turret-buttresses, also with crosslet dummy openings.

TURIN HOUSE, 3.1 km. NW. Mansion house by *James Maclaren*, 1870, but rebuilt on a slightly more elevated site, *c.* 1927. W and S elevations dressed up with a variety of gables in the Tudor manorial manner of William Burn.

BALMADIES HOUSE. *See* p. 346.

GARDYNE CASTLE. *See* p. 494.

5040

THE GUYND

1.7 km. ESE of Carmyllie

59 Villa-mansion house built in 1817 for John Ochterlony of The Guynd whose family had held the estate from the early C17.

Walling all of rubble, formerly harled, and with polished ashlar dressings. Main block of two storeys above a sunk basement. S (entrance) front of five bays, the centre three minimally advanced under a parapet, its ends fluted, its centre panelled; balustrades over the front's outer bays. At the centre of the ground floor, a parapeted portico of coupled Roman Doric columns, their capitals badly weathered; delicately detailed cast-iron fanlight above the entrance. The bandcourse under the first-floor windows is carried the full length of the main block. So too are a sill course under the ground-floor openings and a string course above the basement; at the windows of the end bays these cut across the bases of rectangular overarches to suggest aprons. Minimally recessed from each end of the main block is a single-storey-and-basement pavilion which presents to the S a single pediment-surmounted bay, its window set in a rectangular overarch like that at the end bays of the main block. At each end, a generous-sized bow, the E now approached by a utilitarian stair.

INTERIOR. Entrance hall with an egg-and-dart ceiling cornice under a band of quatrefoiled circles. A broad corniced doorcase at each side wall. The N end is splayed, its side walls with round-headed recesses and, at the outer ends, Ionic attached columns. At the centre, a pair of columns, also Ionic, frame the opening to the stair-hall. Here, a flying stair, its cast-iron balusters decorated with elongated quatrefoils. Over the stair, a cupolaed dome. On the first-floor landing's N side, a broad elliptical arch.

Off the W side of the entrance hall is the library, its E and N walls with round-headed recesses containing bookshelves. Between the N recesses, a severe chimneypiece of veined white marble. Elaborately foliaged deep cornice to the ceiling. The W wall is filled by a broad segmental arch opening into the bow-ended drawing room which occupies the house's W pavilion. Another white marble chimneypiece, also severe and flanked by round-headed recesses. Off the E side of the entrance hall is the dining room. At its E end, an Ionic-columned screen under an anthemion and palmette frieze; the screen's centre forms a sideboard recess, the narrow ends frames for a pair of doors. Wooden chimneypiece with wooden Ionic columns at the jambs and a mean entablature. Inside this framework, a Neoclassical black marble surround to the fireplace opening.

Immediately behind the mansion house, the very plain single-storey STABLES, also of the early C19. – 0.3 km. S of the house, a rubble-walled early C19 GARDEN. Over its W entrance, a re-set stone bearing the date 1664. – Just W of the garden, THE OLD GUYND, an early C19 two-storey *cottage orné* with segmental-headed windows in the W front, a Venetian window at the S end and a large Gothic opening at the E jamb. It may incorporate some of the structure of the C17 mansion house. – TEMPLE, 1.3 km. ESE of the mansion house and overlooking the Elliot Water. Ionic-columned domed rotunda of 1853. – LODGE at the NW end of the main drive. Single-storey T of *c.* 1840. Consoled cornice over the door; cornices but without consoles also over the windows which contain horizontal-paned glazing.

HATTON CASTLE 3040

0.6 km. ESE of Newtyle

Perched on a hillside, the pink-harled mansion house built in 1575 for Laurence, fourth Lord Oliphant, unroofed *c.* 1720 and restored in the 1980s. It is Z-plan, the jambs each projecting from two sides of the main block and well provided with gunloops to afford, at least symbolically, raking fire to protect the main block from attack. Despite this martial vocabulary, amply supplemented by shot-holes, the house appears peacefully domestic.

Main block, *c.* 20.4 m. by 7.3 m., of three storeys and an attic. At the S front, quite comfortably sized ground-floor windows with chamfered jambs, the r. two placed directly above splayed oval gunloops, the l. beside a gunloop. At the first floor three large windows, not aligned with the ground floor's; like almost all the main windows they have rounded margins. Below are circular shot-holes, each with a small vertical slit at the top, a characteristic of all the shot-holes at the house. Three windows also to the second floor, the r. aligned with the window below, the other two smaller and set higher but not at the same level as each other, the l. of these a 1980s restoration. Beneath these windows are more shot-holes. In the r. bay an attic window rises through the wall-head to a curly pedimented head bearing the initials of Roderick Oliphant and his wife who undertook the house's 1980s restoration; there was clear evidence of a window in this position but its form is late C20 conjecture. Also late C20 the pair of catslide-roofed dormer windows to the l. Towards the W end of this elevation, a massive wall-head chimney. The crowsteps on the S pitch of the E gable were provided in the late C20, as was the present appearance of the large chimney to which they ascend and from whose N side a short pitch descends before being halted against the house's SE jamb. Projecting from this gable, at the S end of the ground floor, is a shallow stone basin placed outside the aperture of a water inlet which served the kitchen; tiny window to its r. Another tiny opening at the S end of the first floor but quite comfortably sized windows to the second floor and attic, both with shot-holes below.

The NE jamb, *c.* 6.4 m. by 4.3 m., is of four storeys. The S gable, its crowsteps replaced in the 1980s, is pierced only by an oval gunloop. Another gunloop to the ground floor of the E face. Below both this face's first- and second-floor windows are shot-holes. Third-floor window directly under the eaves. The N gable's ground-floor window is a late C20 insertion. The gable's upper windows are C16, those of the first and second floors provided with shot-holes. In the jamb's W face a third-floor window was inserted in the 1980s when a sizeable first-floor window was blocked. Its position abuts a late C20 narrow splayed outshot formed in the inner angle with the stair-tower to the W. In this outshot, tiny windows and, at the ground floor, an oval gunloop. At the base of the conical-roofed circular stair-tower, its top rebuilt in the 1980s, a pair of oval gunloops which face W and NW. Window at each of the upper floors, variously to the W, N and NW, the top one of the 1980s.

The N wall of the main block is pierced by a pair of ground-floor slit windows, one of them tiny; oval gunloops below. At the first floor, a large window at the l. and another but horizontally proportioned at the r., both with shot-holes below. Fair-sized late C20 windows, also above shot-holes, to the second floor; at the attic, a pair of catslide-roofed dormers. In the main block's E gable, its crowsteps late C20, a tiny ground-floor window and, to its r. and at a lower level, an oval gunloop. Just below first-floor level, a tiny stair window at the r. The window of the first floor itself is large and again placed above a shot-hole. Another shot-hole under the second floor's comfortable-sized window; smaller window lighting the attic.

The E gable of the main block, its crowsteps again replacements of the 1980s, is pierced at the ground floor by a tiny window and, some way to the r. and at a much lower level, by a gunloop. Large first-floor window with a shot-hole below; tiny stair window to the r. Another shot-hole under the second-floor window. Decently sized attic window.

Filling the main block's NW inner angle with the SW jamb is a bowed turret, much restored in the 1980s, which contains a stair (reinstated in the 1980s) from the first floor to the top of the house. At the turret's ground floor, oval gunloops facing N and W and a comfortably sized window, perhaps a C17 insertion. Small stair windows at the rebuilt upper stages. The SW jamb itself is *c.* 4.3 m. square. In its W face a tiny horizontal window above an oval gunloop. The windows to the upper floors are all placed above shot-holes, the first floor's with a pair in its sill. At the jamb's S gable, also given crowsteps in the late C20, another oval gunloop at the ground floor. Window to the stair's half-landing with a chamfered margin; shot-hole below. At the top floor, a small window placed at the r. of the gable. The jamb's E face contains the entrance to the house, a roll-and-hollow-moulded door with, to its l., an oval gunloop; further l. and at a higher level, a window which lights the half-landing of the main stair inside. At first-floor level but curiously unrelated visually to the entrance is the large moulded frame for a missing heraldic panel. Above and slightly to the l. of this, two windows, one to each of the jamb's top floors, the upper window a late C20 restoration, both with shot-holes below.

INTERIOR. The entrance opens onto the foot of the main stair to the first floor. Under the stair, an L-plan room, perhaps for a porter, both its limbs covered with tunnel vaults. To the N a doorway to the tunnel-vaulted passage which runs along the ground floor of the main block. On the passage's N side, doors in chamfered surrounds open into a pair of tunnel-vaulted cellars. In the thickness of the W cellar's W wall, a straight stair (restored in the 1980s) to the first floor from which a turnpike stair ascends to the top of the house. At the passage's E end, the C16 kitchen, also tunnel-vaulted. Almost all of the E wall is filled by a huge elliptical-arched fireplace, a tiny window in its back. To the r. of the fireplace, the water inlet from outside; slop drain in the room's NW corner. Two doors in the N wall. The r. opens into the C16 larder, its N window inserted when it became a kitchen in the 1980s, the l. onto a comfortable turnpike stair serving all the upper floors.

The ceremonial approach to the first floor is by the SW jamb's scale-and-platt stair, the flights covered by tunnel vaults. On the first floor the W two-thirds of the main block are occupied by the hall. The stone-flagged floor and beamed ceiling are late C20 restorations. Huge fireplace in the S wall, its position original, its rectangular stone surround with a roll-and-hollow moulding of the 1980s. To the E is a chamber with a N fireplace. Off it, a small room, possibly intended as a charter room rather than to house a close stool, in the wall thickness of the house's SE corner. Bedchamber in the NE jamb, a fireplace in its S wall. In the W wall, a cupboard formed in the embrasure of a blocked window and, to its S, a tall recess, perhaps intended for a close stool. The second floor of the main block now contains three rooms, each with a fireplace, the E room with a laird's lug to the hall.

7060

HILLSIDE

Sprawling village, formerly the site of substantial Victorian villas, their ground mostly developed in the C20 for less ostentatious housing.

HILLSIDE CHURCH, Old School Way. Gothic, by *Alexander Grieve*, 1869–70. Tall oblong, the walls of stugged masonry, a gableted bellcote on the N end. Lancet windows in the sides. In the S gable, a hoodmoulded window of four Scots Late Gothic lights under a roundel containing a quatrefoil opening; three-light S window, also hoodmoulded and surmounted by a quatrefoil-pierced roundel. Tall porch at the E side's S end, its gable with set-back buttresses and topped by a bellcote with a steep pyramidal roof; hoodmoulded door in the N side. At the N end of the church's E side is a smaller porch with a fleur-de-lis finial to the gable.

Inside, Gothic PEWS face the mid-C20 Lorimerian COMMUNION TABLE at the N end. – Tall late C19 PULPIT in the NE corner, Gothic but supported on barley-sugar columns which give it a Jacobean flavour. – ORGAN at the NW, by *Ingram & Co.* – STAINED GLASS. N window, a clearly drawn memorial to Allan James Dickson, killed in the First World War, by *James Ballantine II*, 1919. In the l. light, a student and preceptor, in the other two lights, a Christian Knight Armed for the Fight and Being Received into Heaven. – S window (emblematic figures of Justice, Charity, Hope and Virtue) of *c.* 1920, rather in the manner of Morris & Co.

SCHOOL, Old School Way. Now housing. Built *c.* 1875. A double pile, the gable of the shorter W block with overlapping skews tweaked up at the top to a cross. E block perhaps a slightly later addition with a hoodmoulded two-light window in the N gable.

MONTROSE WATERWORKS FILTER HOUSE, 1.1 km. N. Built in 1870 and extended, 1880. Two storeys, the gables stepped. First-floor windows of three round-headed lights set in overarches, rectangular at the sides and segmental-headed in the E gable.

SUNNYSIDE ROYAL HOSPITAL, Hospital Road and Marykirk Road. Opened in 1857 as a replacement for the Montrose Lunatic Asylum, its hillside situation allowing the patients fresh air and extensive views to the S. Extended later in the C19 and C20 by additional detached blocks, the complex is now (2010) largely disused.

Built into the hillside, at the centre of the hospital, is the MAIN BUILDING, the original asylum designed by *W. L. Moffatt* and built in 1856–7. It is of three storeys above a fully exposed basement, the walls faced with brownish stugged ashlar masonry. The style is Tudor of an economical variety, the windows mullioned and transomed except at the basement where they are small and arched. Breaking the length of the façade is an advanced centrepiece of five bays, its centre three with shaped gables to the front, the end bays at right angles and their gables, also shaped, facing E and W; depressed arch to the main entrance. Each side of this, a four-bay link to another advanced and shaped gable and then a five-bay link to the broad gables, also advanced and shaped, of the end bays. Plain side elevations, also with advanced and shaped gables to avoid monotony. Added to the rear in 1882 was a Gothic-windowed Recreation Hall, its roof surmounted by a square louvred ventilator topped by a flèche. Inside, the T-plan first-floor Hall itself has boarded ceilings rising as half-vaults from the cross-bar and tail's side walls before forming broad tunnel vaults over the centres of the limbs, the structure, with barley-sugar kingposts, a display of carpentry. Immediately behind the main block, a BOILER HOUSE of the earlier C20, a tall round chimney its main feature. Behind the boiler house, WORKSHOP range of *c.* 1900. Discreet Jacobean detail at the single-storey and attic S block whose centre is carried up as a muscular rectangular tower, its parapet carried on heavy moulded corbels. E of the workshop, a large and lumpy harled LAUNDRY block of c. 1930. Behind these, a late C19 single-storey quadruple-pile STABLE BLOCK. Its S front is symmetrical, the end ranges gabled, the centre two piend-roofed.

The HOSPITAL or infirmary, W of the main block, was built in 1888–91 to a characteristically Free Jacobean design by *Sydney Mitchell & Wilson*, the main elevations of bullnosed ashlar, the rear of greyer-coloured rubble. It consists of a line of four two-storey-and-attic pavilions, the centre two with shaped gables and canted single-storey bay windows, the outer two piend-roofed and with canted gables facing S, E and W, all surmounted by cupolas. They are joined by single-storey-and-attic links. A few shoddy-looking late C20 extensions. On the lawns in front of the main block and hospital, picturesque single-storey PAVILIONS of the early C20. – BOATH HOUSE, downhill to the S of the main building, by *J. A. Ogg Allan* and built in 1932–5 as a nurses' home. Of two storeys and an attic and three storeys, harled with grey stone dressings, it hesitates between Neo-Jacobean and Neo-Georgian but is unequivocally institutional.

NORTH ESK VILLA, NE of the main building, is a detached villa built in 1902–4 to house sixty women patients. Two and three storeys and with crowstepped gables, those of the main block panelled with giant ogee-headed overarches; single-storey curvaceously parapeted bay windows. OCCUPATIONAL THERAPY building to the E, built in 1971, a procession of monopitch-roofed two-storey blocks and flat-roofed linking sections. Immediately to the S, CARNEGIE HOUSE, a villa-like block to house private patients, by *William Kelly*, 1895–9. Large but plain, faced with stugged and squared purple-tinged masonry of Brechin stone. Symmetrical front, the main block joined by broad-eaved lower links to slightly advanced end wings. At the centre, an elliptical-arched entrance in a rectangular surround, the spandrels bearing reliefs of a male and female head in foliage-enriched roundels. The head of the entrance is framed by an aedicule, its Ionic columns standing on corbels, the pediment's tympanum carved with a floral-decorated panel. Inside, the W part of the ground floor was allotted to female, the E to male patients, both parts containing parlours and drawing rooms, the E also a billiard room. On the first floor, above the entrance hall, was a dining room, the panels of its beamed ceiling painted with the Signs of the Zodiac; chimneypiece of Jacobean character. Downhill to the E, ANGUS HOUSE by *J. A. Ogg Allan*, 1936–9, large but low, on a butterfly plan, and intended to accommodate elderly patients. – At the end of the E drive, CARNEGIE LODGE. Picturesque of 1900, the ground floor of hammer-dressed purplish sandstone, the upper floor half-timbered and oriel-windowed. Red-tiled roof ridge.

KINNABER HOUSE, 1.9 km. E. White-harled three-storey laird's house built for the Fullertons of Kinnaber in the 1680s and remodelled and enlarged *c.* 1790. The E-facing main block is of five bays, the tall first-floor windows deepened in the late C18, the moulded centre door hidden behind a C20 porch which overlays the three r. bays. Full-height round tower at the N corner. In this block's W face, a moulded surround for a missing armorial, the lintel inscribed with the date 1686. NW jamb added *c.* 1790, a round tower at its NW corner balancing the main block's NE tower. In the jamb's S face and the W face of the main block are three-light first floor windows, both of *c.* 1790. – Immediately N, a double-pitch-roofed and ball-finialled whitewashed DOOCOT of the late C16 or C17.

ROSEMOUNT STABLES, Rosemount Road. Surviving appendage of the demolished Rosemount House. Single-storey and attic ranges of *c.* 1860, the dormerheads of the upper windows with open pediments. In the centre of the S range, an Italianate square clock tower with rusticated quoins at its corners and a shallow pyramidal roof. Keystoned round-headed entrance at its lowest stage. Aproned rectangular window at the first floor and, above, a round clock face. At each face of the top stage, an opening of three round-headed windows fronted by a stone balcony. At the stables' N range, perhaps added in the late C19, a tall red brick chimney. – GARDEN to the S, its brick walls perhaps constructed in the early C19. – Mid-C19 broad-eaved WEST LODGE at the end of the drive, its W gable bowed.

HOSPITALFIELD *see* ARBROATH

6050

HOUSE OF DUN

0.5 km. ESE of Dun

Confidently poised above the Montrose Basin, the most important C18 mansion house in Angus. It was designed by *William Adam* and built in 1730–42 for the judge and landowner, David

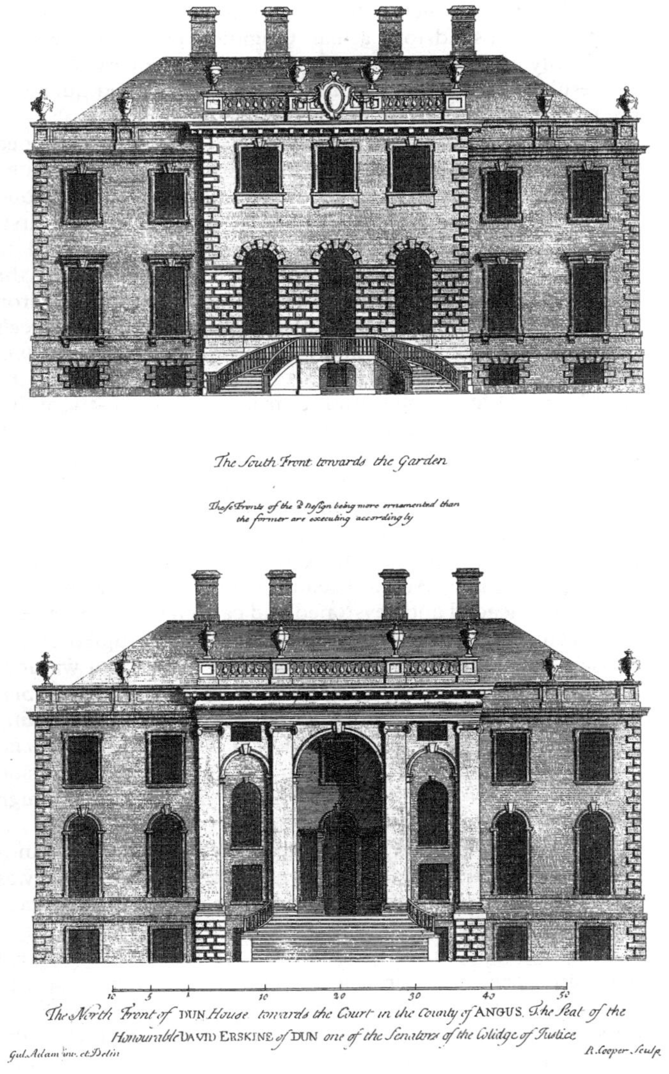

House of Dun.
Elevations, *c.* 1740

Erskine, Lord Dun, the interior partly recast in the early C19. It is now the property of The National Trust for Scotland which employed *Cunningham, Jack, Fisher, Purdom* (from 1988 the *Jack, Fisher Partnership*) to carry out restoration of the exterior and some internal alterations in 1985–9 before opening the house to the public.

The house is a piend-roofed oblong, of two storeys and an attic over a basement which is fully exposed at the ends. Masonry all of local red sandstone ashlar. Originally polished, it weathered badly and, as a result, was cut back in the early C20 and the resultant new surface lightly stugged. Rusticated quoins at the corners and a belt course above the basement.

51 The seven-bay entrance front faces N. The end bays, topped by wall-head parapets, are straightforward. Tall round-headed ground-floor windows (lighting a mezzanine as well as ground floor) with projecting imposts and keystones. Rectangular first-floor windows in lugged architraves. Awkwardly related to these bays is the three-bay centrepiece which contains the entrance, fronted by a broad flight of steps, their lyre-back iron railings probably early C19 replacements. The centrepiece's design is clearly derived from the one produced by *John Erskine, sixth and eleventh Earl of Mar*, in 1723 for a house on this site. Like Mar's design for the entrance front, it is a quasi-triumphal arch with giant fluted Ionic pilasters between the bays.* In each of the narrow outer bays, a giant round-headed and keystoned overarch carried on half-pilasters contains the low ground-floor window and tall round-headed opening above which lights the half-landing of a stair; squashed between the top of the overarch and the wall-head entablature, a small horizontal window. At the broader central bay, a giant arch, also round-headed and keystoned and carried on half-pilasters. This fronts a deep recess whose back wall is occupied by the house's Venetian principal entrance under a first-floor window. Along the wall-head of the whole centrepiece, a full entablature, the frieze incised with the date 1730; the surmounting balustrade was shown in Adam's design illustrated in *Vitruvius Scoticus* but apparently not executed in the C18, this omission rectified in the 1980s by the *Jack, Fisher Partnership* although the urn finials remain unexecuted.

The E end's elevation is regular, of five bays, the N ground-floor window a dummy. In the early C19 a French window was formed at the centre of the ground floor to give direct access to the walled garden.

The S (garden) front is architecturally less ambitious than the N and, perhaps, more successful. Also of seven bays, with rusticated quoins at the outer corners and the ends of the three-bay centrepiece. This is slightly advanced and higher, the wall-head finished with a mutuled cornice. The surmounting balustrade, like that of the N front, is illustrated in *Vitruvius Scoticus* but apparently not executed until the 1980s, also without the intended urn finials but with a central panel which contains a cartouche bearing the coat of arms of Erskine of Dun and is flanked by drapery swags. All the basement windows are small, of horizontal proportions and in Gibbsian surrounds. At the outer bays of the ground floor, corniced windows in

* Mar's design was for a front of only three bays, all part of the triumphal arch and W-facing to receive afternoon sun throughout the year.

lugged and keystoned architraves, the ends of their sills supported on block consoles; first-floor windows in double-lugged architraves. Tall parapets at the wall-head. The centrepiece's ground-floor masonry, much restored in the 1980s, has V-jointed rustication from the sill level of the windows to the springing of their semicircular arch-heads; at these heads, projecting voussoirs. The centre of these openings is a French window fronted by a perron from the garden terrace. First-floor windows in double-lugged architraves like those of the outer bays but with aprons.

The W elevation is of six bays, quite straightforward and with no attempt to disguise the existence of mezzanine floors at the ends. This fronts the house's Stable Court and from its corners extend convex screen walls, probably of the C18, to join the house to its N and S ranges. These are C19. At the E end of the N range, the former kitchen built in 1859. Height of two storeys but only containing one, the interior top-lit and with a large E fireplace. At these ranges' W ends are cartsheds, probably of the earlier C19, each of one tall storey. Across their ends are piend-roofed low two-storey blocks, perhaps C18, the W face of each containing elliptical-arched carriage entrances under first-floor windows. Between them are the much taller two-storey piend-roofed mid-C18 pavilions of the courtyard's W range, each with a forestair to the first floor at the E elevation. At the W front of each, a round-headed central door in a Gibbsian surround, the N pavilion's a 1980s restoration, with a large loft door at the centre of the first floor. Between them is the entrance to the courtyard, a keystoned and round-headed arch under a pediment, its ends topped by ball finials. Over the pediment, a pedimented and ball-finialled early C19 cupola 67
housing a clock. In front of the S pavilion, a stepped MOUNTING BLOCK.

The house's INTERIOR juxtaposes magnificence and domesticity. The principal floor is bisected by the Entrance Hall and Saloon providing a vista from the front door to the garden door and its view over Montrose Basin. On the E side of these was placed a state apartment (drawing room, bedroom, dressing room and closet) stretching back from the Saloon and intended theoretically to be occupied by the King or some other visitor of royal or vice-regal status. On the W was a family apartment (parlour, with Lord Dun's dressing room and charter room to its N and, to its S, the family bedroom, Lady Dun's dressing room and closet from which a stair in the house's SW corner led down to the nursery below).* The basement contained the nursery, kitchen and domestic offices, the first floor a library, bedrooms and closets and the attic further bedrooms.

* Some of these rooms must have been designed for occupation by an ideal or future family rather than the Erskine family as it existed when the house was built. Of Lord Dun's children one had died in infancy long before and the other two were born in 1709 and 1712 and so had left the nursery before construction began. Lady Dun died in 1736, six years before the building's completion.

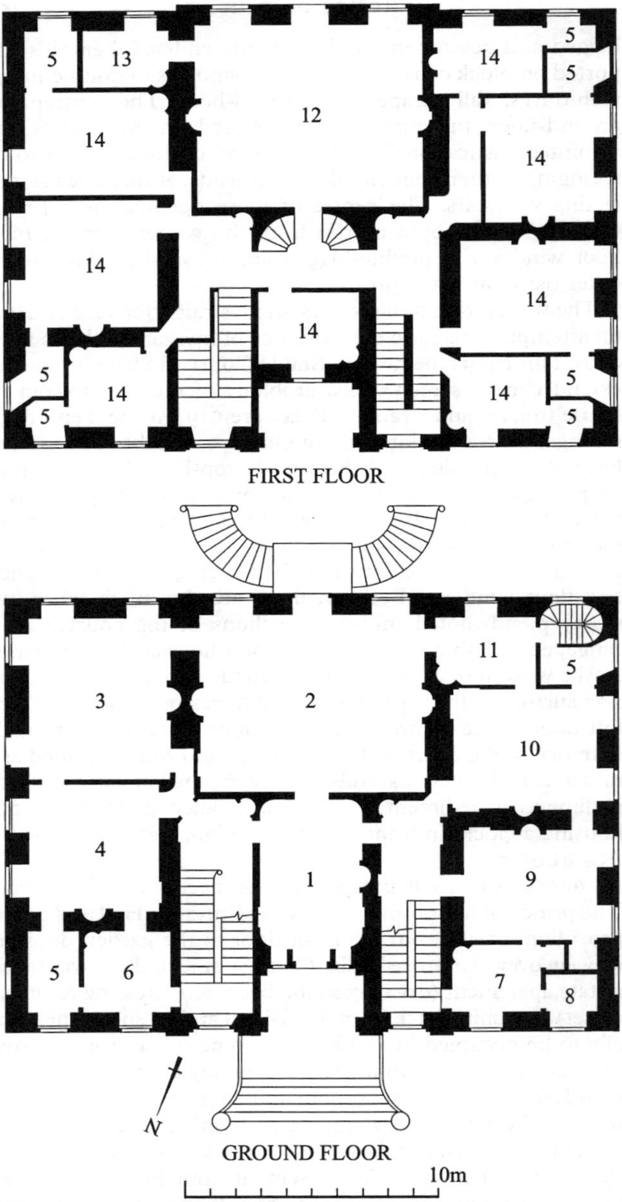

1. Entrance Hall
2. Saloon
3. State Drawing Room
4. State Bedroom
5. Closet
6. Dressing Room
7. Lord Dun's Dressing Room
8. Charter Room
9. Parlour
10. Family Bedroom
11. Lady Dun's Dressing Room
12. Library
13. Library Closet
14. Bedroom

House of Dun.
Plans

The ENTRANCE HALL was originally a straightforward rectangle. Egg-and-dart cornice and foliate rose at the ceiling. The N (main entrance) and S (Saloon entry) doors are each framed by tall panelled pilasters and surmounted by a round-headed and keystoned fanlight. On the W side, a trio of pilastered panels, also round-headed and keystoned, the outer two containing doors (the r. a dummy), the centre slightly advanced and possibly intended for a stove. Over the doors, stucco baskets of fruit and sprays of foliage modelled, like all the C18 plasterwork, by *Joseph Enzer* in 1741–2. On the centre panel, a stucco pendant of flowering and fruiting foliage. The E wall may have been treated similarly in the C18 but in the early C19 it was opened to the Principal Stair by the insertion of a broad elliptical arch.

The SALOON behind the centrepiece of the house's S front is both banqueting hall and the introduction to the state apartment. Its size (*c.* 9.5 m. by 7 m.) is not disproportionate to that of the house, the seat of a laird rather than a royal palace, but its height (*c.* 5.5 m. instead of the 4.2 m. of the other principal rooms) and the richness of its decoration make it an unexpected assertion of status. The general design is straightforward enough, an oblong whose S side is pierced by three windows, the N by a central door (the door itself a replacement of 1795 by *William Hill*) between large panels. At each of the E and W ends, a pair of lugged-architraved doors set in round-headed overarches and flanking a basket-arched chimneypiece of veined grey marble which is placed in a broad centre bay marked off by Corinthian pilasters. Cornice with rosettes between foliaged modillions; deep cove to the ceiling above. It is Enzer's stuccowork which makes this exceptional. On the flat of the ceiling a Greek key border encloses a large panel, its corners with reliefs of shells from which extend tendrils of foliage in a Rococo manner. At the centre of the long sides are heads of Bacchus and Apollo, the gods of wine and of poetry and music, appropriate for a banqueting hall. At the N wall's outer bays simple rectangular surrounds enclose panels with rosettes in their cut-out corners. On this door's keystone, the head of a bearded man from which extend swags and pendants of fruiting foliage of the same character as those in the Entrance Hall. On the centre of the cove above the main cornice, the huge heraldic achievement of Erskines of Dun. It is flanked by segmental-arched recesses, their soffits decorated with branches of foliage issuing from shells, each containing the figure of a lion holding a shield which displays an upright sword (the coat of arms of Dun). Above each recess the cove is ornamented with a framework of drapery topped by a shell and enclosing a human head. Above the windows of the S wall, segmental-arched recesses like those of the N but containing busts. On the cove above, reliefs of gardening tools and flowers at the E end and of musical instruments at the centre and W end, apparently in celebration of the innocent domestic pursuits of the inhabitants of the house, a balance to the proclamation of the family's status opposite, the design based on an engraving by Watteau, the relief of a violin an actual instrument encased in stucco.

Celebration of the family seems to continue at the Saloon's W end behind which lies the family apartment. The overmantel
52 of the chimneypiece is filled with a figure of Neptune standing in a chariot drawn by a pair of sea horses with the figure of a conch-blowing Triton (Neptune's son) between them. This depiction of the sea god may well allude to Lord Dun's rights over salmon fishings in the Montrose Basin. On the frieze under the main cornice, a trophy of arms extending horizontally from a human head. In this wall's outer bays, stuccoed overdoor decoration depicting swagged vases overflowing with shells and foliage, i.e. the fruits of the sea and garden. On the ceiling cove, a further nautical allusion, the relief of a dolphin being strewn with flowers by small boys or wingless putti, two holding torches, one of these also grasping a navigator's lead weight to which another points a staff. This is set in an elliptical-arched surround formed by the representation of hounds hunting a stag, probably in allusion to the outdoor leisure pursuits of the lairds of Dun. At the room's other end, behind which lay the state apartment, the stuccowork's iconography seems likely to be a celebration of royal power. Over the chimneypiece, a figure of Mars, the god of War, standing on the crown, orb, sceptre and sword symbols of kingship placed among cannon, furled standards and shields which bear armorial emblems of Great Britain, Scotland, France and the Holy Roman Empire, a squashed-looking lion peering out from beneath them. On the frieze under the main cornice, a horizontal trophy as at the E end but extending from a helmeted head of Minerva. In the cove above, another representation of Minerva, goddess both of War in defence of Justice and also of Peace, sitting among cannons and standards, a pair of shackled captives at her feet. The symbolism seems to relate to warfare leading to peace, perhaps linked to the dual role of the King as warrior and peacemaker.

The S door at the Saloon's E end now opens into the house's DINING ROOM. This was formed in the early C19 from the C18 cove-ceilinged State Drawing Room and half of the State Bedroom whose S wall was replaced by a screen of Corinthian columns *in antis* under a frieze (executed by *Alexander Reid*, 1816) of husked swags surmounted by crossed corn sheaves. The basket-arched C18 chimneypiece of the State Drawing Room at the W wall is in place. It is of white marble veined in black and grey. Scroll-sided overmantel of the same marble framing a mirror. Above the foliaged cornice, a large stucco work panel. It shows oak twigs as the background to a shield with shells at its top and bottom and a central display of flowers and leaves. In the room's early C19 end wall, a jib door to a service room formed at the same time from the N half of the State Bedroom which has been cove-ceilinged and partly panelled. On its N wall, above the missing chimneypiece, stucco swags and a pendant of flowering and fruiting foliage. Some C18 panelling in the low KITCHEN behind which has been formed by throwing the C18 state apartment's Closet and Dressing Room into one.

On the W side of the Entrance Hall is a lobby (STONE HALL), its S end semi-octagonal and with round bowl-shaped niches in two walls. This gives access to the scale-and-platt back stair to the S and, on the W, to the C18 Lord Dun's Dressing Room (later converted to a lavatory) and Parlour. The cove-ceilinged PARLOUR was the principal room of the C18 family apartment. Each wall is symmetrically treated. At the S, two doors (the l. a dummy) under stucco cartouches decorated with foliage and human heads. Between them the slightly projecting chimney-breast, the present simple stone chimneypiece brought here in the 1980s from the former State Bedroom; the Parlour's original chimneypiece had been removed on the house's conversion to a hotel in 1950 when this room became a bar. In the centre of the E wall, above the door from the Stone Hall, a stucco relief of an eagle holding a cartouche bearing a human head; foliate branches extend from the cartouche. Between the W wall's two windows, a stucco panel, its head filled with a diaper design of small rosetted panels from which hangs a pendant cartouche displaying the relief of a trumpeting cherub. At the N end, a trio of doors (two dummies) under a basket and swags of fruiting and flowering foliage. The W door opens into the small and low panelled CHARTER ROOM. S of the Parlour was the C18 Family Bedroom and, to its S, Lady Dun's Dressing Room with a door to the Saloon and the Closet with a stair down to the Nursery. In the early C19 these three rooms were thrown together to form a pleasant but plain LIBRARY with two of the W windows blocked to form round-headed recesses. At the N end, an early C19 white marble chimneypiece with reeded jambs; oval panels at the ends of the lintel, also reeded, and, in its centre, a roundel carved with the crest and motto of the Erskines of Dun.

The PRINCIPAL STAIRCASE on the E of the Entrance Hall rises from the ground to the first floor. At the bottom the stair-hall's SE corner is splayed and contains a bowl-shaped circular recess like those in the Stone Hall. The stair itself is well finished but not ostentatious, with turned balusters and scroll-ended treads. At the first-floor landing the walls form a half-octagon at the S, also with bowl-shaped recesses. From the landing a balcony returns N to give access to the NE room. The principal first-floor room is the Library (now OLD LIBRARY) placed above the Saloon and, because of that room's height, raised above the level of the rest of the first floor and approached by a divided stair of two short curving flights. Like the Saloon it has a fireplace at each end but the chimneypieces are of stone and simply moulded. Partitioned in the C19 to form two bedrooms and a common lobby, in the 1980s it was restored as a single room plainly finished in a mid-C18 manner. The C18 bedroom to the N (now PORCH

ROOM) was opened to the central passage in the 1980s when its S wall was removed leaving the NW corner fireplace looking somewhat inconsequential.

The E-facing rooms of the first floor are mostly early C19 in their present form. At the house's NE corner MR ERSKINE's DRESSING ROOM formed from an C18 bedroom and two closets, the E window which lit the SE closet with a deeply splayed N ingo, the E of the two N windows built-up. The central bedroom (MRS ERSKINE'S BEDROOM) retains its C18 size and shape. N chimneypiece of grey-veined marble with a mirrored overmantel, also marble-framed and with block scrolls at the bottom corners. It is probably identifiable with the 'Dove Colour Chimney & Glass frame' supplied by William Adam in 1742 and was perhaps moved here in the early C19 from the Family Bedroom on the ground floor. The DRESSING ROOM and BOUDOIR to the S are again early C19, formed from an C18 bedroom and two closets. At the Boudoir's W wall, an C18 basket-arched stone chimneypiece now set in an early C19 wooden frame, its jambs composed of fluted Doric half-columns.

The RED BEDROOM and DRESSING ROOM occupy the house's SW corner. Although William Adam's engraved plan in *Vitruvius Scoticus* shows two bedrooms and two closets in this position, the panelling, grained in imitation of cedarwood, seems to be C18 as do the simple stone chimneypieces. S of these, the TAPESTRY ROOM retains its C18 stone chimneypiece and part-panelling, the walls otherwise covered with C17 Flemish tapestries moved here from the Principal Staircase in 1989 but which may have hung here formerly. The room in the house's NW corner (MISS MILLICENT'S ROOM) was formed in the C19 from an C18 bedroom and two closets.

The basement is mostly occupied by domestic offices and servants' rooms. In the NW corner, the groin-vaulted C18 KITCHEN. In its E side, a broad basket-arched fireplace with a hot-plate recess to its l. and the round opening to an oven on the r., all much restored. S of the central E–W passage, THE HOUSEKEEPER'S ROOM AND BEDROOM. The larger Housekeeper's Room was the C18 Nursery with built-in beds (later converted to cupboards) along the E wall. Partition wall of simple C18 panelling between this and the Bedroom to the N which was formed in the C19 from a couple of closets and the stair to the ground-floor family apartment. In both rooms, simple C18 stone chimneypieces. At the centre of the basement's N side, the C18 Laigh Hall (now OLD LAIGH HALL) or servants' hall, covered with a semicircular tunnel vault. Off the central passage a second at right angles leads to an C18 bedroom and closet (now a single room, the GUN ROOM) and Second Table Room (now ROD ROOM) or upper servants' dining room. Each side of the passage, a tunnel-vaulted cellar, the W the WINE CELLAR, its stone bins probably C18.

The TERRACED GARDEN S of the house was laid out in the 1730s or 1740s. A long walk below the top terrace ends with contemporary ball-finialled GATEPIERS. – WALLED GARDEN E of the house, probably also of the 1730s or 1740s, the rubble walls with brick copes.

WEST LODGE at the end of the main drive, 0.6 km. S of the house. An early C19 piend-roofed single-storey lodge, the windows now altered. Contemporary corniced GATEPIERS, alternate courses of their V-jointed masonry carved with rosettes and vermiculation. – Just E of these, EAST LODGE of the earlier C19. Also single-storey but with a mild Jacobean flavour. Heavy classical porch at the E end; broad bow pierced by a window of three pointed lights at the E end of the N side. Contemporary GATEPIERS with verticulated masonry.

A WOODLAND WALK W of the house was laid out along the steep banks of the Den of Dun in the early C19. Built into the W bank, 0.5 km W of the house, an C18 ICE HOUSE containing two tunnel-vaulted chambers, the inner much deeper and higher than the outer. – This lies just outside the large WEST WALLED GARDEN formed in the C18, the rubble walling partly faced with brick. Just N of the walled garden, a two-storey rubble-built Late Georgian house. A similar but mid-C19 house backs onto the garden's W side. – Inside the garden, roughly at the centre of the W side, a free-standing ARCHWAY, the round-headed opening, *c.* 3 m. wide, with a roll-and-hollow moulding and checked for doors. It may be C17 and perhaps a surviving portion of an outer courtyard of the former House of Dun which stood on or near this site.

Immediately S of the West Walled Garden is the OLD DUN PARISH CHURCHYARD. In it, a MAUSOLEUM of *c.* 1835 incorporating part of the fabric of the former medieval Dun Parish Church. Walls surmounted by battlements, carried at the sides on moulded corbels. At the W gable, paired pointed doors, their hoodmoulds with pendant label stops, pinnacled angle buttresses and an urn finial. The E gable-head is of ashlar rather than rubble. In this gable, a rectangular door under a window, also rectangular, both with chamfered surrounds and perhaps inserted in 1716 when the 'Quire' walls of the church were heightened. – Several weathered C17 GRAVE-SLABS. – S of the Mausoleum curvaceously topped C18 HEADSTONES carved with angels' heads (souls) and shields bearing trade symbols.

HOUSE OF GRAY

3030

0.9 km. S of Liff

Standing on a gently sloping hillside and looking across the River Tay to Fife (the view now blocked by recent planting), a classical mansion house of restrained exuberance. It was designed for John, ninth Lord Gray, in 1714 and completed in 1716. The wall-ing's warm red sandstone is now covered with dazzling white paint; the internal finishings, including a wealth of panelling, were removed in the later C20.

Piend-roofed main block of two storeys above a fully exposed basement, the appearance of the almost identical N and S fronts remarkably similar to those of the main block of Strathleven House (Stirling and Central Scotland) built in 1708. As at Strathleven, the principal elevations are each of seven bays with a slightly taller advanced and pedimented centrepiece, its corners, like those of the ends, with rusticated quoins. Also as at Strathleven the pediment of each front's centrepiece contains a pair of oculi flanking a (now weathered) heraldic achievement. Low and horizontally proportioned basement windows joined by sill and lintel courses, the latter moulded. Tall ground-floor windows denote the *piano nobile*. At the ground floor of each centrepiece, a door opening set in a segmental-pedimented and moulded architrave (also as at Strathleven), the pediment's tympanum carved with a shield between bunches of grapes. Flight of stone steps, now missing their balustrades, to the S entrance. The corresponding N opening, although having the depth and appearance of a door, does not have steps for access and is shown in William Adam's engraving of the earlier C18 in *Vitruvius Scoticus* as a window.

The first-floor windows of the centrepieces are more grandly treated than those at Strathleven. Here they are elliptical-headed and surmounted by now badly weathered floral swags, those of the S front's outer bays with shells at the centre, the ends of this front central swag hanging from grotesque heads. Round the main block, a moulded eaves course; rising from the centre of the roof, a pair of chimneys, the ashlar masonry of their narrow N and S ends channelled. Piend-roofed dormer windows, perhaps of the earlier C19, have been added to the N elevation.

At each end of the main block, slightly recessed from its S front and set well back from the N elevation, is a square full-height pavilion-like stair-turret, its wall-head's eaves course, corners' rusticated quoins and the sill and lintel courses of the basement windows (some later converted to doors) like those of the main block. The turrets' ogee roofs are probably more steeply profiled replacements of the C19, the likely date for their present tall double-ball-and-spike finials. Splayed C19 outshot in the N inner angle of the W pavilion and main block.

Extending laterally from each pavilion and set well S of the front wall of the main block is a piend-roofed single-storey-and-basement wing, its S front of four bays. At the back of each wing, a semi-octagonal stair-turret, its ogee roof, like those of the turrets at the ends of the main block, probably heightened in the C19. At the front of each wing, sill and lintel courses like those of the main block and stair-turrets and, rising from its roof, a chimney whose stonework detail repeats that of the main block's chimneys. These suggest that the wings are contemporary with the main block and its stair-turrets but the wings' corners have strip quoins and the eaves courses are unmoulded. Could it be that the design, both of House of Gray and Strathleven House, did not originally include the wings and that they were added as afterthoughts to provide extra accommodation, if they were not actually built a few years after the rest of the house?

The interior has been stripped out but originally* the ground floor of the main block contained a very grand state apartment. From the large entrance hall behind the centrepiece of the S front was entered a dining room which occupied the full depth of the main block's W end. This opened to a drawing room in the centre of the N front, behind the entrance hall. Off this were a bedchamber with, to its S, a dressing room and closet.

HOUSE OF PITMUIES 5040

0.8 km. S of Guthrie

Georgian laird's house accompanied by a complement of appendages, making the delectable centrepiece of a small estate.

The three-storey main block of the MANSION HOUSE was built 50
for the Ogilvys of Pitmuies, *c.* 1730. This is harled, with dressings and a base course of grey sandstone ashlar. W front of five bays, the second-floor windows low and of horizontal proportion. Advanced and pedimented centre, its first- and second-floor windows separated only by a cornice. In 1768 the estate was acquired by James Mudie who seems to have been responsible for remodelling the house soon after when the first-floor windows of the outer bays were probably deepened and a three-light opening placed under each pair. Also of the late C18 or more likely the early C19 was the addition at the centre of a boldly projecting Ionic portico (now porch) flanked by narrow sidelights framed by attached Ionic columns; at the centre of the portico's parapet and over the sidelights are fluted panels. At the same time was added to the ends piend-roofed pavilions, each of a tall single storey in height and with a bow front faced with droved red sandstone ashlar, the N pavilion perhaps begun as an addition of 1770 (the date on a segmental-arched doorway in its rubble N side) but remodelled when the S was built. Behind the S pavilion, a wood and glass octagonal conservatory added by *W. Schomberg Scott* in 1968. This occupies the inner angle of the main house and a two-storey wing, its present appearance plain Georgian except for a pair of gabled dormerheads on the N side but perhaps incorporating stonework of an earlier house. Joining to this wing are single-storey rubble-walled and slab-roofed ranges of the late C18 or early C19, which form the E and N sides of a service court; two-storey pavilion in the centre of the N range.

Inside the house's main block, a central entrance-cum-stair-hall, the early C18 stair with carved and twisted balusters. To the l., the present dining room formed in 1968, an elliptical-arched and pilastered sideboard recess on the E side. Morning

* If the plan illustrated in *Vitruvius Scoticus* is to be trusted.

room (former dining room) r. of the entrance hall, its decoration of *c.* 1800, the sideboard recess with a screen of fluted Ionic columns *in antis*. Simple wooden chimneypiece with fluted jambs and lintel, rosetted panels at the ends. Much higher the bow-ended drawing room in the S pavilion, its smart decoration also of *c.* 1800, perhaps enhanced about a century later and restored in the 1960s. Pine chimneypiece of Adamish type with pendant foliage on the jambs and, on the lintel, urns linked by drapery swags to the centre panel enriched with a saltire of a torch and *fasces*.

GARDEN to the E and extending N and S of the house, formed in the late C18 and bounded by rubble walls. On the N side, a single-storey building with small windows to the N and the date 1775 carved on a stone in the W gable. On the garden's S side, a dwarf wall containing an entrance with corniced and urn-topped gatepiers. – Immediately S of the garden, a two-storey early C19 WASHHOUSE. Rubble-walled oblong with Gothic first floor windows in the N gable and a crosslet opening in the W side. Single-storey outshot, perhaps an addition, at the S end. – DOOCOT to its W, its rubble walling formerly harled. Probably built in the early C17, it is of lectern type, with crowstepped gables and a projecting stone-slab rat course. In the N side, a panel carved with the impaled coats of arms of Ogilvy and Guthrie (for David Ogilvy and his wife, Nicola Guthrie, heiress of Pitmuies) together with the date 1643, perhaps that of the doocot's erection. Flight-holes under the eaves of the S side. This front has been dressed up at the beginning of the C19 by the addition of battlemented circular corner towers, each with a crosslet dummy opening, and the recasting of the entrance in Gothic form. Stone nesting boxes inside.

Late C18 HOME FARM just N of the mansion house and garden, ranges of its courtyard steading rubble-walled and slab-roofed, an iron weathervane on the NE gable pierced by the initials JM (for James Mudie of Pitmuies) and the date 1770. Lattice glazing, probably early C19, in the windows. Segmental-arched cartshed openings at the W range. The detached and lower E range is perhaps an early C19 addition. – Just N of the steading, a rubble-built BRIDGE over the N drive. Single segmental arch, one keystone bearing the date 1819.

In the garden of the North Lodge beside the A932, the surviving lower two-thirds of a much worn upright SLAB, perhaps of the C9, each face carved in relief with the shaft of a cross standing on a scroll-decorated base. Below the cross on the W face, a pair of hound-like beasts with extravagantly long and intricately curled tails.

4040

INVERARITY

Nondescript L-plan hamlet of rendered and cream-painted C20 cottages, the late C19 school at the hinge, the church by itself a little to the E.

INVERARITY KIRK. Built in 1754–5. White-harled oblong with ashlar strip quoins at the corners and overlapping skews. On the W end, a birdcage bellcote, its spired roof with bellcast eaves and a ball finial. In the S wall, three round-headed and keystoned windows, the centre shorter than the other two. Double tiers of rectangular windows in the gables and back wall. End porches added in 1854.

Inside, a panel-fronted GALLERY along the N wall and E and W ends. – Boxy bench PEWS. – At the centre of the S side, a late C20 PULPIT. – STAINED GLASS. In the window behind the pulpit, depiction of a trinity of three geese over Angus, *c.* 2000. The design was based on a drawing by *Barbara Robertson*, the cartoon drawn by *John Lindsay* and the window executed by *Aileen M. Ogilvie* of *Stained Glass at Sa'ty Dyke*.

GRAVEYARD. Immediately S of the church, several C18 TABLE STONES. The top of one (commemorating Thomas Mill, tenant in Corbiemill, †1765) is carved with reliefs of two upright angels flanking a Greek cross, its central boss carved with a roundel which contains a sock and coulter. – Another, to William Ker †1768, has an egg-and-dart border. At the head, a pair of angels' heads (souls) and, at the foot, emblems of death. – Immediately E of the church, the HEADSTONE erected in 1772 by David Ramsay, watchmaker in Forfar, to commemorate his sister, Margaret. On the W face, bold carving of flaming torches and a pair of angels' heads. These frame a helmed and mantled shield which bears an array of watchmaker's tools and a human hand.

DOOCOT, Fothringham Home Farm, 0.7 km. E. Probably late C18. Tall white-harled cylinder with circular dummy openings near the top. Wrapped round the base, a veranda on timber posts to provide shelter for cattle. Truncated conical roof with bellcast eaves and surmounted by a lantern containing the pigeon entries.

LOUR HOUSE. *See* p. 600.

INVERKEILOR 6040

Dour little village of C19 and C20 housing, the parish church on its N edge.

INVERKEILOR CHURCH, off Kirkton Road. T-plan kirk, built of red sandstone rubble, the product of several stages of development. The medieval church on the site probably consisted of a nave and chancel. The chancel seems to have been rebuilt in the 1630s when it was taken over by the Carnegies of Ethie (later, Earls of Northesk) as their burial place. In the late C17 or early C18 the nave was rebuilt or reconstructed, its long and skinny dimensions (*c.* 24 m. by 6.1 m.) suggesting that it stands on medieval foundations. At the end of the C18 or beginning of the C19 a transeptal jamb (the Anniston Aisle) was added on the N side of the nave to house the family and dependants of the Raits of Anniston. Repairs were carried out by *James Maclaren* in 1862 and in 1880 he heightened the walls of the church, gave it a new roof and refurnished the interior.

The exterior is unpretentious. Gabled bellcote, probably of 1880, on the W end. Above this gable's central buttress, perhaps added in the repairs of 1862, a window of three rectangular lights, probably of the late C17 or early C18 but perhaps of 1805 when a gallery was erected at this end; the pointed dummy arch-head of the central light bears the date 1862 so presumably belongs to the alterations of that year. In the top of the gable, a quite broad cusped and louvred round-headed opening, probably of 1880, ventilating the roof-space inside. The S front is nearly symmetrical. Low gabled buttresses, probably Victorian, mark off a centrepiece where a pair of pointed windows, their ogee-headed lights topped by cusped daggers, flank a high-set circular window, all these openings Victorian and probably of 1880. Each side of the centrepiece is a pointed window, also Victorian. At the W end, a sturdy low buttress, perhaps of 1862. To its r., a door flanked by quite small windows, all rectangular and with chamfered surrounds; they are of the late C17 or early C18. Above the door a heraldic stone bearing the impaled coats of arms of the Raits of Anniston and, perhaps, Lyon of Brigton and, above that, a two-light window, probably of 1880, which rises through the eaves to a gabled dormerhead. At the nave's E end, a sloping-topped buttress, perhaps of 1862, with an earlier heraldic stone above. To the l. of this buttress, another smallish rectangular window and door of the late C17 or early C18; above the door a Victorian window rising through the eaves to a gabled dormerhead.

In the nave's N wall W of the Anniston Aisle, just two smallish rectangular windows and a date stone of 1799, perhaps referring to the addition of the Aisle. The Aisle itself is two-storey and L-plan. In the main block's piend-roofed N gable, a rectangular ground-floor window and, above, a broad pointed window of three angular lights, perhaps altered in the later C19. Two-light rectangular gallery window in the E face. The slightly lower NW jamb containing the gallery stair is a Victorian addition, the ground floor bowed, the upper corbelled to the square; in the W face, a large pointed window, probably Victorian.

The early C17 chancel is short. Intake at the head of the E gable. In the S side, a pair of quite small and high-set windows, their surrounds with roll-and-hollow mouldings. Above, three panels, also in roll-and-hollow-moulded surrounds. The centre panel bears the date 1636 and the initials and impaled coats of arms of John Carnegie of Ethie (later, first Earl of Northesk) and his wife, Magdalen Haliburton. On the l. panel, the relief of a skeleton, on the r. two trumpeting angels (the head of the r. now missing) trampling emblems of death and holding a shield.

Interior mostly of 1880. The collar-braced roofs over the nave and jamb intersect at the crossing. – PULPIT of 1880 with a tall gabled back. – Simple PEWS and NORTH and WEST GALLERY FRONTS also of 1880. – The EAST GALLERY was erected for occupation of the Carnegies of Ethie (later, Earls of Northesk) in 1635, the date carved on it together with the initials and impaled coats of arms of Sir John Carnegie of Ethie and Dame Magdalen Haliburton, his wife. Exceptionally tall foliaged capitals to the pilasters of the front. Above the pilasters are stars set between basket-arched panels; abstract motifs decorate the frieze. – STAINED GLASS. The three windows behind and above the pulpit (the Raising of Jairus's Daughter; Our Lord and Little Children; the Good Shepherd) are of *c.* 1885. – In the E ingo of the l. window behind the pulpit, a GRAVE-SLAB dated 3 September 1631, and bearing the initials of Dame Eupham Maklene and her husband Mr John Durie, Minister of Inverkeilor, †1631 together with a shield bearing the Durie coat of arms; above, the relief of a skull and bone. – In the window's W ingo, a STONE with the date 2 February 1628 above a shield bearing the Ramsay coat of arms of a double-headed eagle flanked by the initials IR and (monogrammed) MDR and DIM; below, a skull. – On the N wall, MONUMENT to Elizabeth Beattie †1661, the first wife of the Rev. John Rait, and their son, John, †1675. Below the inscription are two panels, one carved with two angels standing above a recumbent skeleton, the other with an upright and lively-looking skeleton standing between the angels.

GRAVEYARD. N of the church's W end, the early C19 BURIAL ENCLOSURE of the Raits of Anniston, its back wall of V-jointed red sandstone ashlar surmounted by a scroll-sided block pediment. In this, a recess for the marble MONUMENT to John Rait †1823 and his wife, Elizabeth Guthrie, †1814, with the relief of a lady on a chaise longue clasping her dying husband, both in early C19 dress; it is signed by *M. W. Johnson* of London. – To the W, another ENCLOSURE of the earlier C19, its polished ashlar and parapeted W wall divided by buttresses into three compartments, the centre one bearing an inscription to George Mathew, late tenant in Courthill, †1830. – Several C18 HEADSTONES carved with the standard motifs of angels' heads (souls), shields and emblems of death. – S of the church's W end, a large stone of 1785 bearing a relief of a sailing ship. It commemorates Edward Browning who lost his life at sea. – Immediately E of the church, the TABLE STONE erected by Robert Anderson to his wife, Elizabeth Young, †1744, carved with a pair of angels' heads surmounting a shield with trade emblems; reminders of mortality at the base. – Immediately S, a pair of small and crudely executed but well-preserved HEADSTONES of 1738–9, one, erected by Robert Milne to his father Patrick, a miller, and his wife, Janet Anderson, carved with a solemn angel's head above a shield which displays a miller's rind and picks; floral decoration on the jambs, an hourglass, skull and crossbones at the base. The other, a more cheerful angel's head at the top, commemorates John Cant.

Former MANSE to the S. Harled two-storey main block of 1795, its W front of three bays, the canted bay windows added by *James Maclaren* in 1866–7.

INVERKEILOR FREE CHURCH, Station Road. Now Church Hall. Oblong of red sandstone rubble masonry, designed by *David Reid* and built in 1843 but heightened by 1.2 m. five years later. Round-headed side windows. Above the front (E) gable, a semicircular-headed bellcote in a simplified Baroque manner; small louvred round opening below. Extending across the gable is a porch added in 1957.

INVERKEILOR PRIMARY SCHOOL, Station Road. Mid-C19 two-storey school house and school, its front gable with a blocky birdcage bellcote, joined by a tall single-storey range added by *William Aitkenhead* in 1880. Late C20 Neo-vernacular harled S extension.

ABBEYTHUNE, 1.7 km. S. Two-storey piend-roofed red sandstone mansion house built for a naval officer, Captain Robert Scott, in the early C19. The S front's walling is of cherry-cock-pointed rough ashlar. Tall ground-floor windows to denote the principal floor. Façade of three bays, the entrance set behind a parapeted grey stone Greek Doric portico. The house's sides and rear are of rubble. At the E side, the end bays are slightly advanced under chimney-topped pediments. At the centre of the W side, a large full-height bow fronted by a veranda of cast-iron trellis-work and anthemion panels. – Contemporary two-storey STABLES immediately E of the house, built of red sandstone rubble, the centre of the three-bay S front slightly recessed.

ANNISTON, 1.1 km. SE. The mansion house designed by *James Playfair* and built in 1785–6 has been demolished. Its WALLED GARDEN of *c.* 1790 survives, as does THE OLD COACHHOUSE to its SE, also of *c.* 1790 and consisting of a pair of tall single-storey pavilions containing round-headed carriage entrances. Joining the pavilions is a lower range from which projects a late C20 piend-roofed outshot added on the building's conversion to a house.

LAWTON HOUSE, 2.9 km. W. Ashlar-faced late C18 laird's house. The main block is of two storeys over a basement. Front of three bays with a columned and corniced central doorpiece. Slightly recessed lateral wings, each of one tall storey and with a round-headed overarch over the single front window.

KINBLETHMONT. *See* p. 550.

WEST NEWTON HOUSE. *See* p. 681.

4080

INVERMARK

Place-name at the confluence of the Water of Mark and the River North Esk. It marks the position of Glenlee Parish Church, its adjacent former manse (of 1803 but altered in the late C19), the nearby Invermark Castle and the slightly more distant Invermark Lodge and former Lochlee Parish Church at Kirkton.

GLENLEE PARISH CHURCH. Originally Lochlee Parish Church. Built in 1802–3 but repaired and enlarged in 1824, the likely date for its having acquired a Gothick appearance. It is an oblong, now drydashed, with a spikily finialled small birdcage bellcote on the W gable. In the centre of the S front a pair of broad three-light windows with intersecting tracery; flanking doors, their pointed heads dummies, under quatrefoil openings. Small pointed arch-head windows in the gables. The N wall is windowless.

The interior seems to have been remodelled *c.* 1860 when N and E galleries were removed and the pulpit's position shifted from the S side to the E end. – Late Georgian WEST GALLERY, its front panelled. – PULPIT also early C19. Fluted pilasters at the back support the domed and urn-finialled hexagonal canopy.

LOCHLEE PARISH CHURCH, Kirkton, 1.5 km. W. Roofless remains of the former parish church, perhaps dating from the late C16 or early C17 but repaired *c.* 1730 when a bellcote (now missing) was added to the E gable. It has been a rubble-walled rectangle of which the gables and most of the windowless N wall still stand. Door in the E gable. At the W gable, a scarcement, perhaps to support a gallery; above, a pair of widely spaced small square windows.

In the GRAVEYARD, several C18 HEADSTONES. S of the church's W end, David Christi son †1767, an angel's head (the soul) in the curly top. – Further S, another angel's head at the top of the stone to Daniel Christison †1751; emblems of death at the base. – More reminders of mortality but crudely incised on the stones commemorating Al Brown †1732 and Donald McDonel †1733 and others to the E.

QUEEN'S WELL, 3.6 km. NW. A 6 m.-high granite crown spire rising from the ground to cover a white sandstone basin inscribed 'Rest, travellers on this lonely green,/And drink and pray for Scotland's Queen.' It was erected *c.* 1863 to commemorate the visit here of Queen Victoria and Prince Albert in 1861.

INVERMARK CASTLE, 0.4 km. W. Roofless but substantial ruin of a rubble-walled tower house of the Earls of Crawford, the principal seat of their barony of Glenesk. It seems to have been built in two stages. The first can be dated to between 1511 when the only building noted in the barony was 'le alehous de Glenmark' and 1554 when a charter mentions *Glenmark cum brasina, turre, fortalicio et manerie de Invermark* ('Glenmark with the brewhouse, tower, fortalice and manor of Invermark'),* the second probably to *c.* 1600.

The house is oblong, *c.* 11.7 m. by 8.2 m., the corners rounded but corbelled to the square at the eaves. Originally it was of three storeys with a wall-head parapet projected on corbels, some of their stubs still visible in the stonework. In the second stage of development the building was heightened by one additional floor and an attic and given a tall round SE turret supported on continuous corbelling.

* *The New Statistical Account of Scotland*, xi (1845), 194, gives a date of 1526 for the castle's erection but without citing a source for this assertion.

Formidable array of crude horizontal gunloops all round the ground floor but no windows at this level. As first built the E and N walls were without first- and second-floor openings. At the W end of the S front's first floor, a round-headed door, the front of its chamfered surround with grooves and holes for a wooden drawbridge which gave access to the tower from a detached range of buildings (removed in 1803) to the S. The doorway contained a wooden door (now missing) and, behind it, an iron yett, still in place. Towards the E end of this side, one large and one smaller window, both with chamfered surrounds. At the second floor, a symmetrically disposed pair of fairly small windows. In the W gable, a slightly off-centre first-floor window of the early C16 was blocked *c.* 1600 when a large central window was inserted. At this gable's S end, one small stair window above ground-floor level and, at the E end, a tier of small openings lighting a second stair. The third floor added *c.* 1600 has quite small windows on all sides. So too does the attic, its openings at the long sides piercing large wall-head chimneys. At the S chimney, an upper window ventilating the roof-space and a panel recess above; another panel recess above the N chimney's attic window.

The SE corner turret is of two storeys, the lower entered from the main block's third floor, the upper from the attic. At the lower floor, round shot-holes in the NE and SW segments; in the SE, a double gunloop looking like a pair of pince nez. At the upper floor, an oval gunloop.

Inside, from beside the first-floor entrance a turnpike stair in the SW corner leads down to the ground floor which is occupied by a tunnel-vaulted store lit only from gunloops. On the first floor, two rooms, the larger hall at the W with a S fireplace. The fireplace of the E room is in the E gable which also contains a buffet recess. Pair of garderobes, one for each room, in the N wall. Stone seats in the ingoes of the S windows. NW stair (now missing) from the first floor to those above which have been similarly arranged.

INVERMARK LODGE, 0.9 km. ENE. Large multi-gabled shooting lodge, by *Burn & Bryce*, 1847. Veranda at the centre of the S front, a conical-roofed tower at the NE.

4050

INVERQUHARITY CASTLE

1.9 km. SW of Memus

L-plan tower house built for the Ogilvys of Inverquharity in the C15 and restored in the 1970s.

The lands of Inverquharity were acquired in 1403 by Walter Ogilvy of Carcary, later lord of Lintrathen and progenitor of the Earls of Airlie, who granted them to his younger brother, John, in 1420. In 1444 James II gave licence to John Ogilvy's son, Alexander, 'to fortifie his house and to strenth it with ane Irne yet', the date of this licence approximating to that of the tower's construction, perhaps of its completion. Alexander Ogilvy's descendants continued to make Inverquharity their principal residence until *c.* 1680 when they built a new house at Kinnordy 5.4 km. to the SW. Thereafter, Inverquharity Castle seems to have been unoccupied although still roofed but the jamb was demolished, probably serving as a quarry for stone for new farm buildings.* In 1970–2 the main block was restored and a new NE jamb built on the foundations of the old; *Cunningham, Jack, Fisher, Purdom* were the architects.

The site is the edge of a bank which slopes steeply to the NE towards the River South Esk. Probably the tower stood originally at the NW corner of an enclosure, its other sides bounded by service buildings.

The main block is oblong, *c.* 13.5 m. by 10 m., the walling of ashlar but the lowest courses irregular, perhaps evidence of foundation problems encountered during construction. It is of four storeys but the second floor is double-height and with windows at two levels. At the NW, SW and SE corners are angle-rounds, each projected on three courses of continuous corbelling above which are tall triple-moulded individual corbels supporting another course of continuous corbelling under their battlements. The battlements continue along the ends and sides of the main block where they are supported by individual corbels, also triple-moulded, placed between continuations of the top course of the continuous corbelling under the angle-rounds and the continuous corbelling under their battlements. At the N end of the exposed stretch of the E side the battlement is taller and projected on quintuple-moulded individual corbels, the course of continuous corbelling below dropping to take account of their greater depth; machicolations between these corbels. These machicolations defend the ground-floor entrance directly below, a pointed door which contains the iron yett mentioned in the licence of 1444. Almost directly above the door, a tall second-floor window, like all the other C15 windows, in a chamfered surround and with an iron grille. In the main block's S face, a small and narrow window almost at the centre of the ground floor; another narrow but larger window at the first floor and a third, placed further l., at the upper stage of the second floor. In the main block's W side, randomly disposed windows to the first and second floors, the second floor's l. opening an insertion of 1970–2; at the N, slit windows light a stair. Randomly disposed and variously sized windows also at the N elevation, the opening to the second floor's upper level tall and narrow. In the E half of this N gable, drainage outlets at the ground and first floors and, at the second floor, a sloped stone which projects so as to throw water from a slop drain clear of the main walling. The thin-walled third floor (its masonry's thickness *c.* 0.9 m. rather than 34

* There is a persistent tradition that the jamb was destroyed by the Lindsays after their defeat of the Ogilvys at the Battle of Arbroath in 1446 but the house's continued occupation until much later makes this unlikely.

the 2.1 m. of the lower floors) is set behind the main block's battlements. Large chimneys at the N and S ends which are finished with gabled crowsteps. On the W side a pair of stone-gabled dormer windows. In the centre of the E side, a caphouse over the main stair, its steeply pitched roof's crowsteps also gabled.

The NE jamb, except for short W stubs of medieval ashlar N and S walls which rise to the wall-head of the main block, is almost all a reconstruction of 1970–2 and rubble-walled. In the S stub wall, C15 slit windows lighting the main stair inside. The jamb is of four storeys but lower than the main block and with the top floor's N and S windows rising through the wall-head to gabled dormerheads. In the E gable, a round-headed door to the first floor. It is approached by a stone forestair whose base serves as a porch to the ground-floor room, its entrance also round-headed.

INTERIOR. The main block, like that of a few other C15 tower houses, e.g. Cessford and Neidpath Castles (Borders), Cawdor Castle (Highland and Islands), Glamis Castle (q.v.) and Scotstarvit Tower (Fife), was constructed as two double-height vaults, one above the other, the lower containing ground-floor storage and a first or entresol floor serving as a lower hall, the upper vault containing the second floor's Great Hall. The main stair, contained in the wall thickness of the E side of the main block, rises the full height but seems originally to have had no door to the first floor which, instead, was reached by a NW stair from the Great Hall above.

The door in the E face of the main block opens onto a mural lobby covered with an elliptical-arched tunnel vault. At the lobby's N end, the entrance to the house's main turnpike stair. On the lobby's W side is a round-headed doorway with a chamfered surround; it seems an insertion, probably of the C16. This door gives access to the ground floor's single room, originally a store, perhaps divided by wooden partitions. It is lit from small N and S windows with deep embrasures; cupboard in the N wall. Massive stone corbels support the floor above. At the room's S end, a 1970s stair in early C18 style to the first floor. Originally, there was presumably a ladder or wooden stair, perhaps with a trap door, to the first floor. Near the N end of the room's E side, another round-headed door, its surround chamfered, opens to the jamb's ground-floor room. Set at a slightly lower level, this is mostly of 1970–2 but the massive stone corbels at the W end to support the floor above are medieval. So too is the well (much restored in the 1970s) in the SW corner and a cupboard above. At the E end, a stone chimneypiece, probably C17, carved in a vigorous but naïve manner with grapes; it was imported in the 1970s from a farm steading in Fife.

The first (entresol) floor of the main block is filled by the LAIGH HALL, covered by the segmental arch of the house's lower tunnel vault containing this and the floor below, its ashlar stonework of high quality. No fireplace but comfortably sized windows to the S, W and N, the bottom of the W opening's embrasure showing rough masonry, perhaps an indication of the former presence of stone window seats. In the E wall is a doorway to the main stair but this is roughly formed and clearly an insertion unlike the stair's small lobby at this level and its door into the jamb. At the N end of the Laigh Hall's W wall, a C15 door to a second turnpike mural stair, apparently originally the sole connection between this room and the Great Hall above.

Just below second-floor level, a spur off the main turnpike stair, also in the thickness of the main block's E wall, ascends N by a straight flight of steps to a second-floor L-plan wall passage, both the spur and passage with simple stone cornices. The passage's E side now contains a door to the jamb. This was inserted in the 1970s in place of what seems to have been a C15 service hatch, so perhaps the jamb originally contained a kitchen at this level. Over the passage's NW jamb, also in the wall thickness, a segmental-arched tunnel vault; the jamb is lit by a pair of windows, their embrasures also segmental-arched, the E window's sill with a slop drain. Off the passage's S side is the double-height GREAT HALL, its stone-flagged door 36
restored in the 1970s. Semicircular tunnel vault of ashlar masonry, its W half constructed of carefully graded stones, the E of much smaller stones and ungraded. At the room's W end a pair of doors, their surrounds chamfered. The r. is the entrance from the wall passage off the main stair, the l. the entrance to a segmental-vaulted mural lobby, a window in its N side. Originally this gave access to a stair in the house's NW corner which descended to the Laigh Hall. The lobby's opening to the stair was blocked in the late C16 or early C17 when a new access was formed in the NW corner of the Great Hall itself, the stairhead enclosed in a corniced rectangular outshot. This is placed at the end of the site of a screens passage whose position is indicated by slots in the stonework of the E wall and one joist hole in the W; over the joist hole, a seemingly inconsequential corbel, its purpose uncertain. Also in the E wall's stonework, a raggle marking the position of a former stair to a minstrels' gallery above the screen. Immediately S of the screens passage, a door in the W wall opens to a mural chamber, its floor's flagstones medieval but reused. Near the S end of the Great Hall are good-sized windows to E and W, each set in an elliptical-arched embrasure and provided with stone seats. At the S wall, a moulded and elliptically arched large fireplace. High up in each end wall, a window above a steeply sloping sill.

Near the top of the main turnpike stair, a short curved spur leads to the third floor of the main block. At its end, a W door to the Upper Hall and, at the N, a garderobe and door to the N room on this floor. Of the two third-floor rooms, the S is the C15 UPPER HALL (now a bedroom), its windows placed high in the S, E and W walls, the ceiling originally faceted but now a simpler coved replacement of the 1970s.

At the S end, a moulded stone chimneypiece with a corniced tall lintel; in its W side, a cupboard, perhaps a salt recess or oven. At the room's N end a dog-leg partition (renewed) between it and a bedchamber (now bathroom), the recess at the bedchamber's W end perhaps intended for a bed. High-set windows in the N and W walls of the bedchamber. At its N end, a moulded stone chimneypiece, its corniced tall lintel formed of voussoirs.

The top of the main turnpike stair is enclosed in the caphouse at the centre of the main block's E side. From the caphouse's S side, a door onto the broad parapet-walk. Steps from the parapet-walk to the N door of the caphouse. This opens to a small room above the stair, comfortably equipped with a tall S window and E fireplace.

6060

KEITHOCK

2 km. SW of Stracathro

Dignified classical small mansion house built *c.* 1805 for Patrick Bowie who had bought the estate in 1802. The Georgian house covers the front of the late C17 residence of the Edgars of Keithock, its exposed gables remodelled at the same time.

The main house is a two-storey rendered triple pile, its N and S blocks (the N late C17, the S of *c.* 1805) of the same size and height and both with pedimented gables topped by chimneys. The Late Georgian S (entrance) front is of three bays, the centre minimally advanced under a pediment fronting a parapet whose line is continued by balustrades along the wall-head of the outer bays. At the centre, a portico of paired Doric columns in front of the side-lit entrance; three-light window above. The outer bays' ground-floor windows are also of three lights, the first floor's openings single. Sandwiched between the N and S blocks is the narrower and slightly lower middle block whose ends project as bows, the E smartly clad with attached Roman Doric columns framing the ground-floor windows and with aprons of silhouette balustrades under the windows of the first floor; on the wall-head, a high balustrade. Plain office wing at the rear.

Inside, the vestibule opens onto the inner hall; at its end, a screen of Roman Doric columns to the stair. The principal rooms are well but simply finished. In the N wall of the dining room at the E of the centre block, the C17 front entrance surmounted by a stone displaying the arms and initials of David Edgar and his wife together with the date 1680, presumably that of the late C17 house's erection.

LODGES at the E end of the drive, probably also of *c.* 1805. Single-storey ashlar-faced and piend-roofed rectangles; mutuled cornices and low parapets at the wall-heads. Between them, corniced GATEPIERS of V-jointed ashlar.

KELLY CASTLE

6040

0.8 km. SE of Arbirlot

C15 tower house standing in one corner of a barmkin enclosure whose present picturesque service ranges are largely of the C17.

The lands of Kelly were held by the Ochterlonys of that Ilk from the C15 until the early C17 when they passed to the Irvines of Cuthlie and Drum. In 1675 the estate was acquired by George, second Earl of Panmure, who granted it a few years later to his younger brother, Harry Maule. Forfeited to the Crown after the Jacobite rising of 1715, Kelly Castle was later bought, together with most of the forfeited estates of the Earls of Panmure, by General William Maule. The house had been abandoned by the mid C19 but in 1863–4 was restored by *James Maclaren* for John Shiell who was then tenant of the property. It remained in the hands of the Maules (later, Maule Ramsays and Earls of Dalhousie) until the mid C20.

The tower, probably identifiable as the *mansionem* occupied by William Ochterlony in 1468, is a T, its walls built of red sandstone rubble. Crowstep-gabled four-storey-and-attic main block, the taller jamb projecting from the centre of the N side. Cutting into the main block's W gable, a bowed SW corner turret, the top course of its supporting continuous ashlar corbelling jumping up to suggest a battlement; small moulded windows, perhaps of the C15 but possibly restored in the 1860s. At the main block's SE corner, cutting across the E gable and also carried on continuous corbelling, a two-storey-and-attic crowstep-gabled square turret, the moulded surrounds to its windows of the 1860s in their present form. At this turret's SW corner, a two-storey tourelle, its upper floor jettied. The S windows of the main block's S front all have roll-and-hollow mouldings, probably dating from the 1860s. Also of the 1860s is the narrow first-floor door at the l. end which opens onto a flight of stone steps down to the garden. At this front, a crowstep-gabled Victorian dormer window. In the main block's W gable at second-floor level, what seems to have been the frame (now badly weathered) for a missing heraldic panel. Also in this gable, tall windows, some, if not all, of their roll-and-hollow-moulded surrounds renewed in the 1860s. The N jamb was largely recast in the C18 or C19, its stonework giving confused evidence of blocked openings and altered floor levels.

The E inner angle of the C15 main block and its jamb was filled in the C17 or C18 with a single-storey addition which was extended later, probably in the C18. This block was remodelled and given a long N wing, perhaps in the C18, and again recast by *Peddie & Forbes Smith* in 1914, the infill block and wing now stepping down from three storeys at the S end to a single storey at the N, all in a manner sympathetic to the earlier work of the complex.

The W inner angle of the original main block and jamb was given a porch-cum-staircase addition in 1701 by *James Thomson*, mason in Edinburgh. To the W it presents a half-gable, its present crowsteps of the 1860s, stopped against the section containing the entrance, this section's battlement also of the 1860s. The doorway's moulded surround is surmounted by a pediment, its cornice's horizontal corona extending beyond the cymatium of the sloping sides in a manner characteristic of the contemporary works of James Smith. Over the entrance the much restored moulded frame of a lost heraldic panel. N of the C15 jamb is a three-storey rubble-walled addition, probably of the early C17, most of the openings with roll-and-hollow surrounds. High up in the wall, the weathered frame for another heraldic panel. Also in this wall, a shot-hole under what may be a blocked window but is perhaps the remains of a panel frame. At the top floor a pair of tall windows rise through the eaves to pedimented stone dormerheads, one segmental-headed, the other semicircular, both C17 but restored in the early C21. Between them, a large bell-surmounted pedestal added in the C19 or early C20.

The C15 tower and its N additions form the E side of a courtyard. The courtyard's N and S ranges are each of two storeys and probably date from the C17. Chamfered surrounds to the ground-floor windows; the upper floor's openings are mostly set in roll-and-hollow surrounds, some probably C17 although others may be of the 1860s. In the N front of the S range, a segmental-headed carriage doorway, perhaps an C18 insertion. At this range's outer (S) elevation, five regularly disposed first-floor windows, all with roll-and-hollow mouldings. Towards the E end of the ground floor, a pair of large horizontal windows (now blocked), perhaps C17.

The outer face of the two-storey W range provides a pleasantly semi-formal approach to the courtyard, its form generally C17. Central carriage entrance, its basket arch of the 1860s as is the crowstepped gablet above. Flanking this is a pair of widely but unevenly spaced bowed turrets, the tall upper stage of each carried on continuous corbelling. The fatter S turret encircles the outer corner of the S range's crowstepped gable and is covered with a conical roof; at its upper stage, a large blocked door. In the S range's gable, a tall window in a roll-and-hollow moulding, a shot-hole below. Beyond this gable, in the S section of the W range, a window, its surround also with a roll-and-hollow moulding. To the l. of the entrance, a section containing two small unmoulded openings to the ground floor and one taller but narrower first-floor window in a roll-and-hollow-moulded surround. The N turret at the l. of this section is semicircular, its roof bowed to the front. Set well back beyond the turret is the crowstepped W gable of the courtyard's N range.

INTERIOR. On the ground floor of the main block of the C15 tower, a tunnel-vaulted cellar and kitchen, the kitchen's segmental-headed W fireplace now with a sizeable window in the back of the chimney-breast.

Inside the C17 entrance to the porch on the W side of the jamb of the C15 tower, a scale-and-platt stair with moulded stone treads rises to the first floor. Here, a window with a chamfered margin in the original outer wall of the tower's jamb. To its r., a door to a Victorian passage along the W end of the tower's main block and another door to the house's main stair in the jamb. This is a turnpike with moulded treads and ascends round a solid oval stone newel. E of the passage and occupying the remainder of the main block's first floor, the DINING ROOM. This is now almost all of the 1860s. Trabeated ceiling, a small plaster rose in its central compartment. Between the brackets of the cornice, semicircles containing foliage ornament. At the room's W end, a sideboard recess with a shouldered arch, at the E, a C17-style stone chimneypiece with a simple roll-and-hollow moulding. At the W end of the first floor of the courtyard's S range, a long cove-ceilinged LIBRARY. At its E end, a panelled oak chimneypiece of 1864, its elaborate overmantel of vaguely Jacobean Renaissance inspiration, the central oval containing a painted portrait of Fox Maule Ramsay, eleventh Earl of Dalhousie, above his armorial achievement; at the centre of the top, an earl's coronet, and, at the ends, the griffon and greyhound supporters of the Dalhousie coat of arms, each holding a shield which displays the eagle heraldic device of the Ramsays. On the first floor of the C17 extension N of the tower, a room with a C17 roll-and-hollow-moulded chimneypiece. In this room's thick W wall survives one roll-and-hollow-moulded jamb of an elliptical-arched door.

The DRAWING ROOM of 1864 occupies the whole second floor of the tower's main block. Neo-Jacobean geometrically compartmented ceiling adorned with small pendants. In the three main compartments, elaborate ceiling roses with shell enrichment (shells were the heraldic device of the Maules) and displaying small shields. In the centre of the ceiling the shields encircle a series of dates (1449, 1614, 1697 and 1864) and bear the initials of the then occupants (Oliphant, Irvine, Maule and Shiell). The similar rosettes of the other compartments are without dates and only one shield bears an initial (G for Grassick, the family who acquired the house at the beginning of the C21). The stone chimneypiece is of 2003 but in a late C17 manner.

Rubble-walled GARDEN, perhaps of *c.* 1865, to the S and E of the house.

DOOCOT, probably C17, in woodland beside the main drive from the W. Oblong, the rubble walls still with plentiful traces of their former harled overcoat; single rat course and a double-pitched roof. Stone nesting boxes survive inside. – At the end of the drive, banded and corniced GATEPIERS of late C17 inspiration, erected *c.* 1865. They are topped by stone eagles.

KILRY

2050

Just the church, manse, hall and a handful of cottages in Glen Isla.

KILRY CHURCH. Built in 1876–7. Lancet-windowed oblong, the walls now drydashed and with red sandstone dressings; bracketed broad eaves. At the S side's W end, a gabled wooden porch. In the W gable, the broad pointed entrance under a circular window; steeply gableted bellcote. Chancel-like low vestry at the E end.

Simple interior, the pews originally facing the E end. – STAINED GLASS. In the N wall, a window (the Good Shepherd), pictorial of 1919. – Contemporary First World War memorial window (a Christian Knight) in the S wall.

E of the church, the contemporary two-storey broad-eaved MANSE, also now drydashed.

6040

KINBLETHMONT

3.4 km. SW of Inverkeilor

Large but architecturally unambitious house designed by *William Spence* and built in 1856–9 for William Fullerton Lindsay-Carnegie; it was reconstructed internally in 1888 by *Sydney Mitchell & Wilson* after a fire. Two-storey main block, the walling of stugged masonry. At the W front, an off-centre three-storey gabled tower over the entrance, its top stage projected on continuous corbelling. Over the doorway the coat of arms of Fullerton Lindsay-Carnegie. In the tower's S inner angle and also carried on continuous corbelling, a round turret whose fish-scale-slated conical roof is now bereft of its cast-iron finial. Broad crowstep-gabled end bays, the r.'s canted bay window removed in 1888. The four-bay S elevation was originally symmetrical, the crowstepped ends with two-storey rectangular bay windows of shallow projection; at the centre bays, two-light ground-floor windows and single openings under crowstep-gabled dormerheads above. In 1888 the l. rectangular bay window was replaced by a larger canted bay of the same size as formerly at the S end of the W front but its mullioned-and-transomed appearance and pitched roof characteristic of Sydney Mitchell & Wilson's work.

INTERIOR of 1888 in a mixture of C17 and early C18 manners. Entrance hall in late C17 style but, behind, a Neo-Jacobean compartmented ceiling over the broad passage and the same style continues to the stair at the N. Doors with late C17 detail from the passage. One, at the W end, opens into the SW drawing room, its chimneypiece and swagged cornice reminiscent of C18 work. In the house's SE corner, the dining room whose walls' painted panelling is delicately detailed and adorned with carved festoons. – In an internal covered courtyard, the large fragment of a PICTISH STONE, perhaps of the C6 or C7. Its face is incised with symbols depicting an amiable-looking 'Pictish beast', a 'crescent and V-rod' and, at the broken edges, part of a 'mirror and comb' and 'wheel'.

S of the mansion house, a rubble-walled GARDEN, perhaps of the mid C19. – In woodland just E of the house, remains of the ground floor of a rubble-built LAIRD'S HOUSE of *c.* 1600. These consist of a pair of tunnel-vaulted cellars, the E end of the S demolished, its W end with a slit window. Round gunloop in the N wall of the N cellar.

KINGOLDRUM *see* KIRKTON OF KINGOLDRUM

KINNAIRD CASTLE 6050

1.7 km. N of Farnell

Huge Franco-Scottish Baronial Victorian edifice encasing a late C18 mansion, itself incorporating an earlier house. 61

The lands of Kinnaird were acquired by Duthac Carnegie, progenitor of the Earls of Southesk, in 1410, apparently through his marriage to Mariota de Kinnaird, one of three co-heiresses of the estate. The earliest part of the present house was probably built by Duthac's son, Walter Carnegie of Kinnaird, in the later C15 and completed before his death in 1479. In 1555 Sir Robert Carnegie, fifth of Kinnaird, employed *John Hutton* and *William Welsh*, masons, to more than double the size of the building by the addition of a SE jamb or wing and the construction of a large extension to the N. In the early C17 a further addition seems to have been built for Sir David Carnegie, eighth of Kinnaird, and, from 1633, first Earl of Southesk. This apparently included an additional N jamb, making the house an inverted F-shape, and probably also the extension or remodelling of various buildings which formed a court to the E. Schemes for further enlargement and remodelling of the house were prepared for the fourth Earl of Southesk by *Sir William Bruce* and *Alexander Edward* in 1698 but the Earl's death the next year leaving a seven-year old heir precluded work being carried out. The fifth Earl joined the Jacobite rising of 1715, was subsequently exiled and attainted and his estates and titles forfeited.

In 1764 Sir James Carnegie of Pittarrow, a descendant of the first Earl of Southesk and, from 1730, heir to the attainted earldom, bought most of the Southesk estates, including Kinnaird. His son, Sir David Carnegie, referred disparagingly to Kinnnaird Castle in 1779 as the 'uncouth mansion of this ancient place'. Nine years later he began a major remodelling of the house to designs by *James Playfair*, such of the earlier house as was retained becoming unrecognizable. When work was completed in 1793 Kinnaird Castle appeared as a magnificent castellated building containing a set of state rooms fully appropriate to the status of a nobleman, aptly described in 1813 as 'a noble Mansion lately built in a superb and princely style . . .'* In 1855 the forfeited earldom of Southesk was restored to Sir David's grandson, Sir James Carnegie, an event accompanied by the Earl's thoroughgoing Franco-Baronial recasting of Kinnaird Castle in 1854–60 to designs by *David Bryce*.

* Nicholas Carlisle, *A Topographical Dictionary of Scotland*, i (London, 1813).

A fire in 1921 gutted the W and S ranges of the house. In ensuing repairs by *Kelly & Nicol*, *c.* 1922–6, the exterior was restored to its appearance before the fire with the exception of Bryce's high Frenchy roofs over the main elevations' towers which were omitted, sadly depriving the house of much of its architectural panache. Internally, some of the principal rooms in the W range were re-fitted in simplified form, others left stripped out. The S range remained a shell until 2009 when *Lachlan Stewart* of *Anta Architecture* re-fitted it to form a self-contained house.

EXTERIOR. The external treatment, except for Kelly & Nicol's removal of the tower roofs, is almost all Bryce's but the house's general shape is still what it became in the late C18. Playfair's main block was a three-storey battlemented oblong, its W-facing principal or entrance front of seventeen bays, the centre three forming a slightly advanced and taller centrepiece fronted by a boldly projecting *porte cochère*; at each end, a rectangular corner tower, also slightly taller. End elevations of three bays between corner towers.

In the remodelling of 1854–60 Playfair's rendered walling was encased in stugged masonry and the house's austere castellated dress replaced by more freely composed and extravagant Franco-Baronial garb. Bryce shifted the position of the principal entrance to the N end of the main block whose corner towers were heightened to four storeys and an attic. In the N face of each, a mullioned-and-transomed canted oriel window supported by a central buttress from whose top extends continuous corbelling, one course carved with foliage enrichment; over each oriel, a stone-slabbed roof. Above, a window of Jacobean Renaissance character with an aedicular surround and fronted by a stone balcony supported on huge brackets. At the wall-head, arcaded corbelling under a rope-moulded cornice below the battlement which is drained by dragon-shaped stone gargoyles. The E tower has a French pavilion roof with small gableted wooden dormers and iron cresting, a 1920s version of Bryce's work. The W tower's battlement is of the 1920s and the 1850s French pavilion roof was not replaced after the fire in 1921. On the towers' inner corners, tall tourelles carried on continuous corbelling, the top course with guilloche enrichment. Panels on the towers and elsewhere on the house's N and W fronts bearing the coats of impaled arms of various Carnegies of Kinnaird and Earls of Southesk and their wives from the C15 to the C20, the NW tower with those of the eleventh Earl of Southesk and Princess Maud of Fife, the date 1923 that of their marriage and also marking the house's restoration. The N end of the main block between the corner towers is now of four bays, the windows grouped 1:2:1, the centre openings occupying the place of a single late C18 window. In the outer bays of the ground floor, fairly low mullioned-and-transomed four-light windows. These flank the entrance porch. Projecting in front, a Neo-Jacobean *porte cochère*, its corners with coupled Roman Doric columns, the bottoms of their shafts with spiral decoration, their necking with lozenge ornament. These carry the entablature, its cornice supported on console-metopes. Above, a balustrade, the panelled corner dies surmounted by rosetted urn finials, the front's centre panel inscribed PERFECT.LOVE/CASTETH.OVT.FEAR. Above the *porte cochère*, a pair of close-set windows surmounted by a large aedicular frame with scrolls at the sides and a semicircular shell-carved pediment; in this, the huge heraldic achievement of the Earls of Southesk leaving little doubt as to the ownership of the house. Flanking this are windows, also in aedicular surrounds, their semicircular pediments carved with shells. The second floor, marked off above and below by restless string courses, contains shoulder-arched windows. Balustrades surmount the wall-head over the outer bays. Above the two centre bays, a pair of crowstepped gables, each containing a small window in an aedicular surround, its character also Neo-Jacobean.

The main block's W front is *c.* 50 m. long between the corner towers whose W faces are treated like those at the N but without turrets in the inner angles. Because of the length of the block between them, the loss of the vertical emphasis of Bryce's Frenchy roofs is the more regrettable. High up on the N face of the SW tower, a keyhole gunloop, probably of the later C15. Bryce brought the adjoining bay at each end forward from the building line of the main block and topped it with a crowstepped half-gable. The l. contains mullioned-and-transomed three-light windows at the ground and first-floors and a shoulder-arched opening under a heraldic cartouche at the second. In the r. of these bays, a tall two-light and double-transomed window rises into the second floor like the windows of the two bays to its l. Running the full length of the W front between these end bays is a stone-balustraded first-floor balcony carried on moulded brackets. From this, at the ends of the front's centrepiece (the position of Playfair's centrepiece and *porte cochère*), a pair of L-plan stairs down to the garden.

The W front's centrepiece is provided by the late C18 tower as heightened and remodelled by Bryce but without his tall French pavilion roof, destroyed in the fire of 1921 and not subsequently replaced. At the ground floor, a tall five-light window flanked by narrow shoulder-arched recesses. Rising from the balcony above and topped by a balustrade, a large two-storey canted bay window, the lights all transomed; between this bay window's first- and second-floor openings, the huge heraldic achievement of the impaled coats of arms of Bryce's client, the ninth Earl of Southesk, and his wife, Lady Elizabeth Murray. Flanking the bay window, a pair of armorial panels. Three shoulder-arched windows at the third floor of the tower, its front corners gripped by large two-stage tourelles carried on continuous corbelling, one course with guilloche enrichment; rope moulding under the upper stage of the turrets which is carried across the tower under a course of arcaded corbelling; the battlement above is a 1920s replacement for a straight parapet. At the SE corner of the tower, a tall open-windowed and pilastered circular caphouse, its appearance and that of the tourelles, since the loss of the tower's Victorian roof, more starkly assertive than originally intended.

The W front's elevations between the ends and centrepiece owe much to the late C18's uniform disposition of windows but Bryce gently subverted this regularity to produce asymmetry and he replaced Playfair's wall-head battlement with a balustrade. To the l. of the centrepiece, at the ground and first floors, a regular six bays, the taller first-floor windows denoting the *piano nobile*. The ground floor's two-light mullioned-and-transomed openings are set between buttresses. Jacobean Renaissance surrounds to the first floor's single-light windows, their rosette-finialled semicircular pediments containing cartouches carved with flora and fauna. At the second floor, the windows of the two l. bays are shoulder-arched and aligned with those below. To the r. and not quite centred on the walling between the two centre windows of the ground and first floors, a rectangular oriel, one course of its continuous corbelling carved with egg-and-dart ornament; above the oriel, a crowstep-gabled attic, a 1920s replacement of a pavilion roof which rose from the wall-head of the oriel and was fronted by a segmental-pedimented dormer window, now subsumed into the attic. Another oriel window to the r., also not quite centred between the lower windows of the two r. bays. It is now finished with a balustrade, the 1920s replacement for a battlement above which rose a pavilion roof like that over the l. oriel. Between these two oriel windows, another heraldic panel.

To the r. of the centrepiece, the ground- and first-floor windows of the three first bays are treated like those of the bays to the l. Over the l. bay, a shoulder-arched second-floor window and, to its r. and not quite centred between the windows of the second and third bays of the lower floors, an oriel window, its 1850s design identical to that of the oriel windows to the l. but in the 1920s given a battlement and deprived of its pavilion roof. To the r., dividing this part of the elevation into two sections, is a fat tourelle, its upper stage jettied, the base carried on continuous corbelling, one course carved with guilloche enrichment. In the two bays to the r., narrow dummy windows to the ground floor, perhaps intended to indicate the presence of the castle's earliest part behind. Above, very tall double-transomed first-floor two-light openings of two-storey height.

The S end of the main block is near-symmetrical. The faces of the corner towers are treated relatively simply, balcony-fronted and aedicule-framed second-floor windows their chief embellishments; battlemented wall-heads, the surmounting pavilion roofs removed in the 1920s. In the inner angle of each tower, a conical-roofed tall tourelle projected on continuous corbelling, one course with guilloche enrichment. Set back between the towers, the three-bay end of the main block, its outer bays crowstep-gabled. At the ground floor, three-light mullioned-and-transomed windows, the centre openings of two converted to doors in 2009. At the first floor, the window of the l. bay is also of three lights but very tall and double-transomed. It rises into the second floor where it is surmounted by a panel carved with entwined Ss (for Southesk). Small Neo-Jacobean aedicule-framed attic window in the gable. Fronting this bay's ground floor, a stone bench on which visitors could sit awaiting admission to the Earl of Southesk's business room on the first floor of the SW tower. Similarly treated r. bay but with distinct first- and second-floor windows. In the centre bay, smaller windows to the first and second floors and, between them, a low mezzanine opening.

E of the main block's S end is the S side of the service court. Balustraded W section of two bays. Boldly projecting from it is a conservatory also of the 1850s but the glazing now largely lost. The conservatory's framework consists of stone piers and a cast-iron roof structure, the beams pierced by circles; strap-work decoration on the parapets. This section of the service court's S side ends at a square tower, also of two storeys but taller, its upper floor jettied; steeply pedimented attic dormer, the pavilion roof behind dating from the 1920s, lower than the Victorian original and without its iron cresting.

The service court's E range, formerly containing stables and coachhouses, is also of the 1850s. Single-storey-and-attic, the ground floor much altered but still with a couple of elliptical-arched carriage entrances. At the attic, a procession of stone-gabled dormers rising from below the wall-head and, above, a sill course which jumps up between the openings as an eaves course. In the centre of the range, a moulded round-headed archway, the entrance for carriages and carts to the courtyard beyond. At each end, a broad crowstepped gable which contains a three-light attic window; beyond, a round tower, its fish-scale-slated conical roof fronted by a gabled dormer window. The courtyard's W side is filled by the back of the main block. Architecturally utilitarian but the unrendered reddish stone of its S half suggests that this represents the house before it was remodelled by Playfair and that it was then utilitarian.

At the E end of the N service range, a three-storey block, its top-floor windows rising into aedicular stone dormerheads. Projecting slightly to its r., a wing, also of three storeys, whose crowstepped N gable is set between fat tourelles. At the gable's first floor, a parapeted canted oriel window. In the ground floor of the wing's W side, a pair of mullioned-and-transomed two-light windows; taller first-floor window, also of two lights. Minimally jettied second floor, its windows rising through the wall-head into a Neo-Jacobean aedicular dormerhead. On the centre of the wall-head, an elaborately detailed Neo-Jacobean chimneystack, its corners with two-tier banded columns, its front bearing a panel displaying a large monogram. Joining this wing to the N end of the main block is a three-storey-and-attic section, its central ground-floor window of three transomed lights, the second-floor windows rising through the wall-head into Neo-Jacobean aedicular dormerheads.

INTERIOR. The layout of the principal rooms is of the 1850s, at the principal floor largely adhering to the late C18 planning. However, the decoration is mostly of the 1920s, a thrifty reinterpretation of Bryce's work. The front door opens onto a Vestibule, quite plain except for egg-and-dart enrichment under the mutuled ceiling cornice. At the W end of the room, a door to the Inner Hall. This is also plain and with egg-and-dart enrichment under a heavy dentilated cornice. On the E side, a canopied stone chimneypiece survives from the 1850s, its hood carved with the crest of the Earls of Southesk. Beyond the Inner Hall is the Lower Gallery along the W side of the main block. It is divided into two parts, the N with a canopied stone chimneypiece like that of the Inner Hall and also of the 1850s, the hood with the coroneted coat of arms of the Earls of Southesk. The S part's E side opens onto the principal staircase. At this part's S end, a 1920s chimneypiece of late C17 inspiration. A door at this end opens into the Billiard Room which Bryce formed in place of the late C18 entrance-cum-stair-hall. S of the Billiard Room are tunnel-vaulted cellars, survivors of the late C15 castle. A turnpike stair formerly projected from that house's NE corner; beside its site, an inverted keyhole gunloop.

The entrance to the principal staircase from the Lower Gallery is through a wooden screen of the 1920s. Both this and the contemporary staircase itself, also of oak, are in a sort of early C18 manner, a cheaper version of Bryce's Neo-Jacobean work. Lighting the stair, a large mullioned-and-transomed window still with some panes of 1850s obscured glass patterned with small foliate crosses.

At the first floor, the stair gives access to the Upper Gallery which runs behind the principal W-facing rooms, its finishings, an oak dado the main feature, all quite simple and of the 1920s. Off the Gallery's N end is a set of family rooms. The N of the public rooms is the Dining Room, formed here by Bryce from Playfair's Drawing Room, its dentilated cornice of the 1920s. So too is the wooden chimneypiece, the jambs displaying the crest of the Earls of Southesk and the half-figure of a knight in armour, the lintel the coroneted coat of arms of the Southesks. In the centre of the W front is the bay-windowed and cove-ceilinged Central Drawing Room formed by Bryce from the upper part of Playfair's stair-hall, its character now also of the 1920s. Wooden chimneypiece in a late C17 manner displaying a coroneted panel bearing intertwined Ss flanked by oak leaves. Bryce had provided double doors (now built up) in the S wall which opened to the South Drawing Room, an 1850s remodelling of Playfair's Dining Room occupying the place of the inner chamber of the C15 Kinnaird Castle. The room is now stripped out. At the W end of its N wall, the doorway (built up) which opened from Playfair's stair-hall. At this wall's E end, a cupboard, perhaps C15. The 1850s doorway in the centre of the S end opens into the double-height Library, formed by Playfair in place of the C15 hall and remodelled by Bryce in the 1850s but now stripped out and open to the building's roof. The fireplace in the centre of the E side is flanked by a pair of tall round-headed recesses, presumably intended as bookcases. Off one corner of the Library is the house's SW tower. This contained the late C18 cabinet, the C19 business room, its brick tunnel vault (a fire precaution) probably of the 1850s but perhaps late C18. Part of the house's late C18 external wall finish is here exposed, the stonework faced with a mixture of droved ashlar and render. Above was the castle's muniment room. Also in the SW tower, a C19 stair from the ground to the first floor providing access for visitors to the business room without entering any other of the house's rooms.

PARTERRES are laid out to the W and S of the house. At the N end of the W garden, a lead STATUE of a scantily clad Flora, probably C17 and of Italian provenance. On the axis of the W front's centrepiece, a bulbous baluster SUNDIAL of 1675, the gnomon bearing the coroneted coat of arms of the Earls of Southesk. At the end of this path, banded and corniced ashlar GATEPIERS by *David Bryce*, *c.* 1860, with scrolled supports at the sides and urn finials.

Brick-walled GARDEN of 1790, 0.3 km. E.

0.7 km. W, the GRAVEYARD of the former KINNAIRD CHURCH which was demolished after the union of that parish with Farnell in 1772. A few TABLE STONES AND HEADSTONES still stand. Among them, the headstone erected in 1761 by Isoble Stewart to her husband, James Fouller, a pair of angels' heads (souls) above a mantled coat of arms on the W face; on the E, emblems of death. – To the E, headstone of 1769 to Thomas Millar, its E face with a worn angel's head above a shield displaying a saltire.

BURIAL ENCLOSURE of *c.* 1695, 0.8 km. S and approached by a straight path from near the loch SW of the deerpark. High rubble walls, the W side with a pair of low stepped buttresses and, at its corners, diagonally set and ball-finialled stugged ashlar buttresses, all these perhaps added in the later C19 when the ninth Earl of Southesk carried out repairs. In the centre of this side, the late C17 entrance set between corniced gatepiers of channelled ashlar, their faces with applied banded pilasters; tall flaming urn finials. Flanking the entrance, a pair of rectangular moulded frames. Their heraldic panels (now badly weathered) used to display the arms of the Earls of Southesk and the coat of impaled arms of Southesk and Maitland for Charles, fourth Earl of Southesk, and his wife, Lady Mary Maitland, providing a probable date for the enclosure of between 1691 when they married and his death eight years later.

SW of the burial enclosure and 1.7 km. S of Kinnaird Castle, the two-storey mid-C19 SCHOOL HOUSE, originally the South Lodge and later used as the Farnell parish schoolhouse. Jacobean with gablet dormerheads, a gabled E porch and a canted bay window to the S; horizontal-paned glazing in the windows.

– Contemporary single-storey-and-attic CARCARY LODGE, 0.9 km. S of the mansion house, the gables' bargeboards decorated with zigzag patterns, those of the porch and dormerheads curvaceously shaped.

MONTROSE'S VIEW in woodland, 1 km. NW of Kinnaird Castle, is an octagonal wooden summerhouse said to have been designed by *Agnes Murray, Lady Carnegie*, *c.* 1800. Between the tree-trunk uprights, decoratively patterned wattle walling; Gothic openings. Slated spire roof.

TEMPLE, near the bank of the River South Esk, 1.7 km. NW of the mansion house. Perhaps designed by *James Playfair*, this is of *c.* 1790, a domed circular drum surrounded by a Roman Doric peristyle. The statue of Flora which used to surmount it is now in the garden W of the house (*see* above).

On the N drive, 1.5 km. NW of the house, FOREBANK HOUSE, a two-storey farmhouse of *c.* 1860 with prettily carved bargeboards. – NORTH LODGE, 2.3 km. NW of the house at the entrance to the drive from Brechin, designed by *David Bryce* in 1861. Channelled and corniced gatepiers with coronet finials. To the N, a low round tower, its tall conical roof with fish-scale slating and bellcast eaves. Fatter but similar tower to the S which displays a panel bearing the date 1861 and the coroneted Southesk coat of arms. This tower forms the NW wing of a single-storey-and-attic lodge, its first-floor windows with pedimented stone dormerheads, the gables with gableted crowsteps; on the E side, a canted bay window.

6050

KINNELL

Little more than the church and manse preluded by the bridge.

KINNELL PARISH CHURCH. Disused. Prominently sited gaunt Gothic church, by *William Scott*, 1855, the walling of squared masonry. Angle buttresses at the corners. The S gable's centre is slightly advanced to suggest a stepped tower and was topped by a bellcote (now removed). Low semi-octagonal vestry at the E end. MEMORIAL TABLETS on the E gable. The l. is dated 1719 and commemorates members of the F- family. Angel's head (the soul) at the top, reminders of death at the bottom; in between, a shield bearing initials. – The r. is to the Rev. James Thomson Jun., Minister of Kinnell, †1681. Framing the inscription, a scroll-sided border; at its top an angel's head flanked by the heads of mythical beasts, at the bottom bones, an hourglass, skull and crossed mattock and spade. (Inside, on the church's N wall, MONUMENT to the Rev. James Thomson Sen., Minister of Kinnell, †1690. Moulded frame, an angel's head at each corner. Below the inscription, an hourglass flanked by two shields, the l. with the impaled coats of arms of Thomson and Collace (for Mr James Thomson and Margaret Collace, his wife), the r. with the coats of arms, also impaled, of Thomson and Graham, presumably for James

Thomson's son and successor, David, and his wife, Catherine Graham.)

In the GRAVEYARD, a few C18 HEADSTONES with angels' heads and mantled shields S of the church.

Piend-roofed two-storey MANSE of 1814 to the S, a Victorian bay window added at the l. of the front.

BRIDGE over the Lunan Water. Erected in 1819, a rubble-built gently humpbacked bridge of two segmental-headed arches.

BRAIKIE CASTLE. *See* p. 353.

KINNETTLES HOUSE 4040

0.6 km. NE of Kirkton

Designed by *Peddie & Kinnear* in 1865, a crowstep-gabled Scottish Baronial villa-mansion built for James Paterson, merchant in Dundee, the hillside site looking across the broad valley of the Kerbet Water. The house, built of buff-coloured stugged ashlar, stands on a terrace extending to its E and W, the battered retaining wall with rounds at the corner and at the top landing of the double stair down to the front lawn.

The approach is from the E. Here, L-plan service wings extend N and E from the main block. The NE wing is of two storeys. In the centre of the E side, a stepped buttress topped by a round turret carried on continuous corbelling. At the top of the turret, a lantern, its ball-finialled conical roof carried on round-headed arches springing from primitivist columns which stand on a rope-moulded base. In the E side's r. bay, an inserted late C20 garage door. At the r. of the S front, a crowstepped gable containing the Paterson coat of arms set

KINNETTLES HOUSE, NEAR FORFAR, SCOTLAND.—Messrs. Peddie & Kinnear, Architects.

Kinnettles House.
View from south-east

in an aedicule, its attached columns with elided capitals, the pediment carved with a sunburst. In the inner angle of the NE and N wings, a round tower under a spire-roofed square top storey carried on continuous corbelling. S of this, the N wing is of three storeys, its E front of low-key domestic appearance except for a heavily moulded string course under the second-floor windows which rise into gablet dormerheads. Along the roof ridge of this wing, as also on the main block, decorative cast-iron cresting.

S of the N wing is the main block, its E end's N bay with a starkly vertical four-stage square tower over the entrance. The tower's wall-head is crowned with a boldly corbelled parapet studded with stone cannon spouts and breaking into battlemented rounds at three corners; at the fourth (SW), a taller round turret, its stone-slabbed conical roof rising from a circle of gablets over the attic windows. Above the entrance itself, a rope-moulded string course which jumps up over a panel carved with the Paterson coat of arms. This is surmounted by a square panel bearing James Paterson's monogrammed initials; above that, a window in a steeply pedimented Neo-Jacobean aedicular frame. S of the entrance tower, a recessed one-bay link fronted by a single-storey bowed projection. The link joins to a crowstepped gable containing a mullioned window at each floor. Corbelled turret in the gable's inner angle with the cut-out S corner of this end of the main block, the turret's conical roof covered with fish-scale slating.

At the S front the main block's basement is fully exposed. Here, the architecture is relaxed, suggesting but gently subverting symmetry. The general concept, l. of the recessed and turreted SE corner, is of a centrepiece recessed between crowstepped gables. At the E of these gables, a rectangular basement, its top broached to support a semi-octagonal two-storey bay window, the upper floor's corner projected on continuous corbelling, its attic storey corbelled out to a rectangle. The l. gable is gripped by round turrets, their conical roofs fish-scale-slated, their wall-head friezes decorated with circles. Projecting from it, a two-storey-and-basement bow on which sits the heavily corbelled rectangular attic set at a higher level than the equivalent storey of the r. gable. Between these gables, the two-bay centrepiece, the ground-floor openings (the l. a panel) above a balcony, its stone front decoratively pierced; under the balcony, a small late C20 glass-fronted addition. The first-floor windows rise through the eaves and are topped by steeply pedimented Neo-Jacobean gablets.

The main block's corner-turreted E end is asymmetrical but plain. Two-part composition. The r. is crowstep-gabled and with an exceptionally restless first-floor string course; l. of the gable, balancing its r. turret, a first-floor opening under a segmental-pedimented dormerhead. The l. part of this end is a full-height canted bay containing mullioned openings at both floors and finished with a plain parapet and slated spire roof, a gableted wooden dormer on its W face.

The INTERIOR is finished in an unexciting Neo-Jacobean manner with compartmented plaster ceilings in the principal rooms; columned screen dividing off the drawing room's E end. These rooms (dining room at the SE, drawing room to its W and with double doors from its N side to the W-facing library) are arranged in an L on the S and W sides of a stair-hall, its wooden stair rather spindly in character, reached from the entrance vestibule by a straight flight of steps.

STABLES to the NE, also by *Peddie & Kinnear*, 1865. Near symmetrical S front with broad single-storey advanced, crowstepped and ball-finialled gables at the end bays; in the centre, a narrower advanced gable, also crowstepped and ball-finialled but of two storeys, the upper floor jettied on continuous corbelling and containing a pedimented window; round-headed entrance at the ground floor, the ends of its rope-moulded hoodmould carved as outsize knots. Conical-roofed round turret in the centre gable's W inner angle. Gableted dormers at the intermediate bays, the r. with carriage entrances at the ground floor. – Rubble-walled GARDEN, also of the 1860s, to the E, its W entrance under a rope-moulded hoodmould. – Crowstep-gabled single-storey LODGE at the end of the drive from the SW. It is of 1867 and also designed by Peddie & Kinnear. At the W front, a gabled porch, its round-headed entrance again under a rope-moulding with outsize knots. Gable to the r. at which is a catslide-roofed canted bay window. Contemporary GATEPIERS (a couple renewed) with rope-moulded friezes and Neo-Jacobean finials.

KINNETTLES PARISH CHURCH *see* KIRKTON

KINNORDY HOUSE 3050

2 km. NW of Kirriemuir

Large but low-key mansion house designed by *Wardrop & Reid* and built for Leonard Lyell (later Sir Leonard Lyell and first Lord Lyell) of Kinnordy in 1879–*c.* 1881.

The estate of Inverquharity and Kinnordy had been acquired in 1782 by Leonard Lyell's great-grandfather, Charles Lyell, who had made a fortune as a naval paymaster. After his purchase of the estate he had virtually rebuilt the existing house at Kinnordy as a sizeable but unpretentious H-plan mansion, a canted bay at the centre of the S front its principal feature. In 1877 Leonard Lyell inherited the estates of Pitmuies and Arbikie near Friockheim, together with a substantial amount of money and investments, from his cousin, John Mudie, and seems to have decided almost immediately to build a new house on the Inverquharity and Kinnordy estate. In May 1878, Wardrop & Reid produced designs for the restoration of the C15 Inverquharity Castle and the construction of a huge E extension to it. However, by April 1879, it had been decided, instead, to rebuild Kinnordy House, incorporating some of the structure of the existing late C18 house. Work was begun in 1879 and largely complete by 1881 although the house seems not to have been finished internally until a little later.

The style is Free Jacobean manorial, with just enough in the way of crowstepped gables and towers to make clear that this is a native Scot. Masonry (all Victorian except for some earlier work visible at the N end) of dark red stugged ashlar sandstone.
63 Main block of two storeys and an attic above a high and fully exposed basement. The entrance is on the E side placed in a conical-roofed round tower, its upper storey jettied. A straight section of walling, cutting across the curve of the tower, contains the aedicular doorpiece, its thin pilasters banded, the frieze's blank shields perhaps intended for heraldic carving; above the cornice, a square panel framed by strapwork scrolls and containing a shield, also blank. The tower's walling directly above the entrance is also straight and contains a window whose moulded surround is topped by a concave-sided pedimental stone bearing the initials LML (for Leonard and Mary Lyell*). To the r. of this tower, a crowstepped gable, its upper windows with moulded surrounds under pedimental tops like that of the tower's window over the entrance. At its N end the E elevation of the main block is finished with a slightly recessed section, plain except for a gabled dormer window rising from the wall-head and, at the NE corner, a fish-scale-slated conical-roofed turret projected on continuous corbelling. S of the entrance tower the main block's E elevation indicates the house's internal planning. Two mullioned-and-transomed windows, the N very large, express the position of the Inner Hall and the rise of its stair to the principal floor. Above are first-floor windows which rise through the wall-head into Neo-Jacobean gabled dormerheads, the finial of one carved as a star and of another as a thistle; the third finial, perhaps shaped as a rose or fleur-de-lis, is now missing. The S end of the E elevation is provided by the taller side of one end of the S range, quite plain except for the wooden gable of a dormer window and crowsteps to the N and S gables.

The S range, overlooking the terraces of a former flower garden, contains the house's principal rooms. Near-symmetrical U-plan, the shape reminiscent of the entrance front of the late C18 house but the crowstep-gabled end bays much less boldly advanced than had been that house's wings. At each of these, a broad two-storey-and-basement canted bay window covered with a sloping roof, the basement's low window openings simply mullioned, those of the principal and first floors taller, the principal floor's the tallest and also transomed. Between these ends the elevations of this range's basement and principal floors are five-bay. At the centre, a very broad two-storey canted bay window almost completely filled with glazing set in mullions and transoms at the principal floor; this is flanked

* Leonard Lyell had married Mary Stirling in 1874.

at the principal floor by a pair of tall windows, also with mullions and transoms. In the end bays, quite straightforward single-light windows but the r. of these bays is minimally advanced and with a jettied and gabled top floor. Between this gable and the projecting W end the range's top floor is also jettied and its windows rise into pedimental Neo-Jacobean dormerheads, the alternately segmental-arched and triangular tops carved with the initials of Leonard Lyell, his wife Mary, and their children, Charles Henry, Mary Leonora and Eleanor Katherine.

The W elevation, also overlooking a terrace but the garden here relatively narrow and bounded by the Moss Burn, is divided into two main parts. The S, with crowstepped N and S gables, is taller and of five bays. Projecting from its centre, a conical-roofed round tower, its top floor slightly set back above a moulded string course; roll-and-hollow mouldings to the windows of the principal floor. To the l. of the tower, French windows from the principal floor onto a balcony carried on heavily moulded stone corbels and with a wrought-iron balustrade; the balustrade continues down a stone stair which winds round the tower on its descent to the garden. The part to the N is of three bays and symmetrical. At the centre, a two-storey canted bay window, its lights at the principal floor mullioned and transomed. Single-light windows in the outer bays, the principal floor's also with mullions and transoms. At the top floor the windows rise into gabled dormerheads with star, rose and fleur-de-lis finials.

N of the main block the W elevation continues with a short two-storey rough ashlar fragment of the late C18 house; at the upper floor, a three-light window. To the N, more of the late C18 W wing but here of only one storey. These fragments form the W side of a service court, its plain S side of 1879–81. The court's N side is bounded by a late C18 range. Single-storey but with a pedimented two-storey 'centre' containing an elliptical-arched pend and, at the N elevation, a round-headed first-floor window. On the court's E side, a parapeted single-storey range of 1879–81 extending N from the main block to a taller pavilion with crowstepped gables to the E and W.

INTERIOR. The E entrance door opens into a small circular lobby. Beyond, an austere ENTRANCE HALL, the N wall's stone chimneypiece of late C17 derivation, the plaster ceiling simply compartmented. At the S end double doors with round-headed panel open to the double-height INNER HALL containing the stair to the principal floor. High panelled oak dado in which fluted pilasters frame the Entrance Hall's doors, their woodwork on this side of elaborate Neo-Jacobean character. Neo-Jacobean also the W wall's stone chimneypiece set in an Artisan Mannerist surround with superimposed pilasters. Of the same character is the cove-sided plaster ceiling, its beams springing from corbels modelled as lions' heads; swagged ox skulls on the frieze between them. The panels of the flat are enriched with fruiting foliage and small pendants; strapwork ornament at the ends. All this plasterwork, as elsewhere in the house, was 65 executed by *William Campbell & Son*. Continuing the Neo-Jacobean theme is the stair to the principal floor, executed, like the rest of the joinery, by *Davidson & Herald*. It is L-plan, the first flight rising S along the E wall, the second flight returning W against the S end. The balusters' pilasters are either fluted and banded with panels or topped by human heads between volutes. Newel posts carved with strapwork and surmounted by square urns with voluted tops.

At the head of the stair a round-headed arch, its keystone modelled as a grotesque head, the soffit enriched with geometric panels, opens into a LONG GALLERY running along the N side of the S range. At the Gallery's E end, another arch of the same design opens at the N to the stair to the first or bedroom floor. This continues the Neo-Jacobean character of the lower stair but the soffit of the landing has more delicate detail and some foliage enrichment. Over the Long Gallery, a Neo-Jacobean ceiling from which hang pendants; the ceiling's compartments are enriched with strapwork and shell and foliage decoration. Walls with an oak dado and plaster frieze decorated with cornucopia. On the Gallery's N side, overlooking an internal courtyard, a mullioned-and-transomed window with geometric-patterned Neo-Jacobean glazing.

The principal rooms of the house open off the S side of the Gallery and, at its far end's return to the N, off the W side. The S-facing rooms begin at the E with a lobby which opens to a self-contained set consisting of a Study, small Sitting Room and lavatory. In the bay-windowed STUDY (now Billiard Room), a white marble chimneypiece, the pilastered jambs enriched with foliage and cherubs, the capitals' volutes with eagles, the lintel with lions' heads at the ends, more foliage and a shield in the centre. Adam Revival wooden chimneypiece in the adjoining Sitting Room.

W of this set, a widely spaced pair of doors, smartly panelled in Neo-Jacobean style and set in pilastered surrounds, opens from the Long Gallery to the LIBRARY. This is large and high, its S side largely glazed, with mullioned-and-transomed three-light windows flanking the shallowly projecting central bay window, its S front of five lights and with single lights at the splayed sides. Bookcases rise to about half the height of the walls at the E and W ends, the bases of their Corinthian-pilastered uprights Neo-Jacobean but otherwise treated in a Georgian manner with rinceau enrichment on the friezes. Lower and plain bookcases along the N wall. Between them, a large wooden chimneypiece, Artisan Mannerist in style with a pair of shell-headed round-arched panels between attached Corinthian columns; face-to-face griffons on the frieze. The Library's plaster wall frieze is ornamented with arabesques, mermaids, griffons and birds. The ceiling is in the usual Neo-Jacobean manner with compartments radiating from pendants, the larger compartments modelled with foliage and some displaying panels with grotesque faces. At the Library's W end, a door, also Neo-Jacobean, into the BOUDOIR whose other doors (from the Long Gallery on the N and the Drawing Room on the W) are more Georgian in inspiration. However, the ceiling is again Neo-Jacobean, its main compartments containing roses, their borders with fleurs-de-lis and floral finials and meeting at foliaged bosses.

In the house's SW corner is the DRAWING ROOM, lit both by a canted bay window at the S end and by a pair of windows in the W side. The compartmented ceiling enriched with fruiting foliage is generally of Jacobean character but its frieze, decorated with birds among foliage which sprouts from vases, is Early Georgian in manner. The woodwork of the dado, shutters and door cases is, however, influenced by Late Georgian work, as is the E wall's white marble chimneypiece, the jambs carved with leafy pendants dropping from the rosettes at the ends of the lintel, the lintel's centre bearing a panel with swagged drapery. To the N of the Drawing Room and serving as an ante-room to it is the INDIA (now CHINESE) PAPER ROOM. This is entered from the N end of the Long Gallery through double doors in a lugged-architraved surround and from the Drawing Room through another door, its surround also with a lugged architrave. In the Chinese Paper Room's W side French windows open onto a balcony with a stair down to the garden. On the walls, C18 Chinese wallpaper painted with depictions of flowering trees and birds, the plaster above the paper painted in the same manner in the later C20 by *Sophie, Lady Lyell*. Simple wooden chimneypiece of early C18 character.

Outside the Chinese Paper Room the Long Gallery returns to the N. In the E wall of this return, a two-light mullioned and transomed window to the internal courtyard, at the N an off-centre Neo-Jacobean doorway; despite its quite grand appearance it gives access to service quarters. At the return's W side, the entrance to the DINING ROOM, its surround with a lugged architrave. At the Dining Room's W side, a canted bay window, the lights mullioned and transomed, flanked by single-light openings. Wooden dado, doors and chimneypiece in a Neo-Jacobean Artisan Mannerist style.

THE BELL GATE E of the house is probably late C18 and perhaps moved here from a courtyard behind the house. Fluted and corniced gatepiers flank a round-headed and keystoned arch under a concave-sided and flat-topped pedimental feature surmounted by a wrought-iron frame which contains a small bell. Decorative wrought-iron gates hang in the archway. – Immediately behind this gateway is the rubble-built rhomboidal WALLED GARDEN, also probably late C18, the N and E walls faced internally with brickwork. In the garden's SE corner, the MUSEUM AND OBSERVATORY, again probably of the late C18. The Museum is also a rhomboid, of two storeys and battlemented; tall pointed windows in the main faces. From its SE corner rises the tall circular Observatory tower, its stonework ringed with band courses. Windows only at the top stage which is finished with corbels supporting a decoratively balustraded wrought-iron balcony. Inside the balcony, an octagonal cupola surmounted by a circular lantern, its lead dome topped by a weathercock.

The HOME FARM NE of the walled garden is also probably late C18, the steading's two-storey W front of red sandstone ashlar. Broad centrepiece slightly advanced under a pediment, its base line broken by the keystoned arch of a round-headed loft door set between a pair of circular openings. At the ground floor, a basket-arched cart opening (now built up). N range also of two storeys with a central square tower, its pavilion roof topped by a louvre-sided ventilator. Farm cottages of the later C19 with gabled wooden porches.

LODGE of *c.* 1880, 0.7 km. SE of the house at the end of the drive. Picturesque and piend-roofed. At the advanced and gabled centre of the SW front, an oriel window of late C17 inspiration above a boldly projecting piend-roofed portico. Contemporary GATEPIERS, corniced and ball-finialled.

2040

KINPURNIE CASTLE

1.3 km. SW of Newtyle

Along the N slope of Newtyle Hill, a hugely strung-out free C17 Scotstyle villa designed by *Thoms & Wilkie*. It was built in 1907–8 but remodelled and enlarged two years later. The client was Sir Charles Cayzer, the ship-owner and founder of the Clan Line, most of whose nine children had already married and produced a quantity of progeny for some of whom at least accommodation during school holidays was required.

The walls are all harled above a base course of bull-nosed red sandstone, the dressings of polished grey sandstone. Main block of two storeys and an attic. The entrance is at the three-bay W end. At this elevation's ends, full-height bows, each containing three ground-floor windows and a two-light window to the first floor. Timidly projecting attic carried on small individual corbels. Originally these corbels supported battlements through whose central crenelles rose windows topped by shaped dormerheads and fronting conical roofs. In the alterations of 1910 Thoms & Wilkie heightened the attic walls to a full storey under new battlements within which rise new and taller conical roofs. Above the surrounds of the attic windows are the reused former dormerheads now appearing as panels on the walling; they are decorated with reliefs of birds and the date 1907. Between the end bows, a battlemented ashlar *porte cochère* of 1910, its angle buttresses topped by rounds. Round-headed openings in the sides of the *porte cochère* and segmental-headed windows at the front which bears a panel displaying the Cayzer crest of a sea lion. Originally the centrepiece of this elevation rose to a chimney-topped crowstepped gable. In the alterations of 1910 the wall-head was raised and the chimney rebuilt, the new walling carried on a

Kinpurnie Castle.
Entrance (west) front as first completed, 1908

round-headed arch in front of the attic window. Behind the *porte cochère*, the round-headed and moulded doorpiece of 1907–8, its jambs with foliage-capitalled columns, the arched head carved in relief with fruit and flowers, including roses and thistles in homage to Sir Charles Cayzer's native and adopted homelands. Over the door are boldly moulded corbels which supported a stone balcony until its replacement by the *porte cochère*, the centre corbel carved with a lion's head.

The main block's N elevation, the view from the ground-floor rooms across Strathmore to the hills beyond now blocked by trees, is informally composed, the main elements a couple of canted bay windows and, at the E end and flush with the walling of this side, a four-storey oblong tower whose comfortably sized windows and battlement's small crenelles make its appearance quite pacific; a conical-roofed round turret at the tower's SE corner. On the tower's balustraded bay window, between the openings to the ground and first floors, a shield displaying the Cayzer coat of arms.

The main block's S elevation is domestic, the centre slightly recessed between a pair of crowstepped gables, the l. topped by a chimney, the r. with a canted bay window at the ground floor and a chimney on one side. At the centrepiece, broad three-light stone-mullioned stair windows.

E of the main block, a slightly lower service wing above a basement, its N front's first-floor windows rising through the eaves to large shaped dormerheads carved with floral motifs. A chimney sticking through the N roof slope marks the line of the wing's original E gable beyond which was a low L-plan washhouse and laundry range. On the S side, the service wing's roof sweeps down over the first floor whose windows are dormers. A projecting crowstep-gabled kitchen block originally provided the visual termination to this side's E end. In 1910 the service wing was extended E. The addition's N elevation first quotes the earlier work until it is halted against a crowstep-gabled tower, its ground- and first-floor N windows linked vertically by ashlar panels; curvaceously headed surrounds to the first-floor and attic openings. Corbelled out under the attic along the exposed N and E faces is a balustraded stone balcony; angle-round at the SE corner. To the S the addition presents a large crowstepped gable with a conical-roofed angle turret at its r. corner. A short low block extends further E and returns to the N as a battlemented single-storey range of stores.

INTERIOR. The W entrance opens onto a small vestibule, its walls oak-panelled (like all the house's panelling, by *Methuen, Hyslop & Co.*), the tunnel-vaulted plaster ceiling (executed, as are all the ceilings in the main rooms, by the *Bromsgrove Guild*) with plaster roses, thistles, oak leaves, etc. The oak panelling and tunnel vault, now compartmented and with the centre panel modelled with the same motifs as in the vestibule, continue into a passage to the E. On the l. of the passage, the DRAWING ROOM, its W end bowed. Shallow canted bay window at the N wall. At the E end, a white marble chimneypiece, its jambs with decorously clothed caryatids clutching flowers. The spandrels of the round-headed fireplace opening are decorated with flowing foliage; keystone now bearing the Cayzers' sea lion crest. The chimneypiece was brought here from another of Sir Charles Cayzer's houses, Ralston, near Paisley (Renfrewshire), and probably dates from 1864 when *Campbell Douglas* extended that building. Plaster ceiling dated 1908, its outer border decorated with thistles. In the centre, a pair of foliaged circles contained in borders whose floral enrichment includes roses, thistles and acorns. Between the circles, reliefs of flowers, corn and birds. S of the passage, a SITTING ROOM (originally Billiard Room), its W end also bowed. At the E end, a late C18 chimneypiece brought here in the later C20. It is of white marble with touches of honey-coloured veining. At the jambs, leafily capitalled pilasters surmounted by urns; swagged and rosetted centre panel. On the plaster ceiling, a bow-ended panel, its border enriched with rinceau ornament. In the centre, a pair of reliefs, one depicting birds and a squirrel set among grapes, the other an owl with a mouse in its talons and set among corn sheaves. On the ceiling's E end, reliefs of fruit and foliage.

At the passage's E end is the INNER HALL, designed as a living room as well as for circulation, its windows placed to enjoy the N view. High oak-panelled dado. In the room's W side, a simple chimneypiece, also of oak and decorated with small-scale carving of rosettes and foliage. At the S end, a trio of round-headed arches, the l. two to a lobby, the r. to the main staircase, its walls partly panelled. Large S window to the half-landing with obscured glass containing stained-glass panels, some with blank shields and others with shields bearing the Cayzer coat of arms; stained-glass depictions of pendants, some bearing the Cayzer crest, which hang from ribbons. Over the top of the stair, a simple compartmented ceiling.

Off the Inner Hall's E side, the DINING ROOM, a canted bay window at its N end. In the W wall, another imported late C18 chimneypiece, of white marble with insets of honey-coloured veined marble. On the jambs, pendants of fruiting foliage hang below leafy consoles. The central panel of the entablature's frieze is carved with the relief of Cybele in a chariot drawn by lions; egg-and-dart cornice. The plaster ceiling is divided into three compartments by heavy beams, their soffits modelled with oak leaves and acorns, their sides with birds; in the central compartment, birds and a squirrel among fruiting foliage. Just off the Inner Hall, to the SE, is the SMALL DINING ROOM (originally Morning Room), a canted bay window at its S end. At the E side, an inglenook in which is placed an C18 white marble chimneypiece, also imported, carved in high relief with cherub terms who garland the head of a god; consoles at the sides.

GARAGE AND CHAUFFEUR'S HOUSE, 0.1 km. NE. Also harled and in a free C17 Scots manner; of two storeys. As originally built in 1908 to a design by *Thoms & Wilkie*, the S front was of four bays and asymmetrical, the three E bays containing segmental-headed garage doors grouped 1:2, the first-floor window above the l. of these bipartite and rising through the eaves into a pedimented dormerhead carved with the Cayzer coat of arms, the two first-floor windows to the r. with semicircular dormerheads. At the l. of this front, a door opened onto the stair to the upper floor and there was a small first-floor window above. In the later C20 the building was extended W with another garage door at the ground floor; the first floor became symmetrical, a pair of new windows with semicircular dormerheads at the l. matching the earlier ones to the r. – To the S, a single-storey and crowstep-gabled GARAGE of *c.* 1990. On the roof, a domed octagonal lantern with a clock (by *Victor & Sons*) and sailing ship weathervane. – Large WALLED GARDEN of 1908, 0.2 km. E of the house.

LODGE, 0.1 km. NE of the house, at the entrance to the drive, again of 1908 and by *Thoms & Wilkie* in free C17 Scotstyle. Harled and crowstep-gabled, of two storeys. Big single-storey bow projecting from the W gable; conical-roofed bowed stair-tower on the N side. – Contemporary GATEWAY, its circular piers of hammer-dressed ashlar and with foliage-finialled conical tops at whose base are carved lions. Wrought-iron gates decorated with roses and thistles. Over the footgate at one side, a swan-necked top bearing the Cayzer crest flanked by the initials CWC (for [Sir] Charles William Cayzer) and the date 1908.

5050

KINTROCKAT HOUSE

3.4 km. W of Brechin

Unpretentious small mansion house. The main block is of 1721. Two storeys over a partly exposed basement. S front of three bays, the centre minimally advanced under a pediment, its tympanum pierced by a dummy roundel; broad flight of steps up to the entrance. Contrasting with the harled walling are the door and window openings' surrounds of dressed stone which are linked at all the floors by sill and lintel courses; modillion eaves cornice. Piend-roofed dormer windows, perhaps early C19 additions. Set well back from the front of the main block and probably of the later C18 are one-bay links, each of a tall single storey and with sill and lintel courses across its front, which join to the front gables of contemporary two-storey NE and NW wings. At each, a ground-floor window from which extend sill and lintel courses; first-floor window in a round-headed overarch, a band course at the level of its springing extending across the gable. At their N end the wings are linked by an ashlar-fronted stables range of *c.* 1800. This consists of three two-storey pavilions joined by single-storey sections. At each of the piend-roofed and parapeted end pavilions, a slightly advanced centre whose ground-floor window is set in a round-headed overarch. The two-bay central pavilion is surmounted by a pediment containing a circular dummy window. Elliptical-arched carriage openings at the ground floor. Inside the main block, the entrance hall opens through a pair of round-headed arches to the stair behind.

Rubble-walled GARDEN, perhaps late C18, to the E of the house. – Early C19 LODGE at the N end of the drive, a single-storey ashlar-faced square box, its pyramidal roof rising to a central chimney. In its N wall, a window of two Gothic lights flanked by crosslet dummy 'arrowslits'. On the W side, a veranda, its log posts rebuilt in brick.

3040

KIRKINCH

Informal group of houses, mostly of the later C20, with Nevay Churchyard rising as a mound in the centre.

NEVAY CHURCH. The roofless remains of a rectangular rubble-built C17 kirk which fell out of use after the construction of Eassie and Nevay Parish Church (for which, *see* Eassie and Nevay) in 1833. There survive most of the E and W gables, two-thirds of the S wall and the lower part of the N wall, the last now topped with slabs of which three are badly weathered grave-slabs. In the W gable, a round-arched door with chamfered margins under a small roll-and-hollow-moulded round-arched window; above the window, a worn stone (probably not *in situ*) carved as a human head. At the top of the gable, what looks like the base of a bellcote. No openings are now visible in the N wall which may have been windowless. In the E gable, a rectangular window with chamfered margins. In the S wall, at the E end, the sill and one jamb of a blocked window. In the centre of this wall, a narrow window flanked by two doors, all with chamfered margins. The lintel of the W door is inscribed .16.DN.95., the initials probably those of David Nevay of Nevay, the date likely to be that of the construction of the building.*

Inside, a couple of joist holes for a W gallery. – MONUMENTS. In the external openings of the S doors have been placed grave-slabs, probably C17, the W bearing emblems of death and an angel's head (the soul). – Inside the church and set into the W of these doors, a headstone to Andrew Doog †1750. At its bottom, a very crudely incised bone and a skull displaying a fine set of teeth. – Near the W end of the S wall, the grave-slab of Johne Makein (?) †1597, with a skull and crossbones.

GRAVEYARD. SW of the church, a TABLE STONE erected to David Black †1751. Carved at the top, a pair of angels' heads; at the bottom, an hourglass, skull and crossbones, and a recumbent skeleton. – Just to the SE, a half-buried SLAB, perhaps C17, with a carved skull at the top. – SW of this, a couple of HEADSTONES (to John Doig †1780 and David Ross, erected in 1759), each displaying a mantled shield and an angel's head. – To the S, the HEADSTONE of 1818 to Peter Hutchison, the front with orderless fluted pilasters and an angel's head. – Adjoining TABLE STONE to Jean Paterson †1776, carved in high relief with a mantled shield and reminders of death. – To the E, several C18 HEADSTONES with mantled shields and angels' heads.

KIRKTON 4040

Tiny T-plan village begun in 1813.

KINNETTLES FREE CHURCH. Now Duncan Hall. Built in 1846, a lancet-windowed rectangle of stugged masonry; N porch.

* But a stone bearing the date 1651 was noted in Alexander J. Warden, *Angus*, iii (1882), 205.

KINNETTLES PARISH CHURCH. Now housing (KIRKHOLM). By *Samuel Bell*, 1811–12. Rubble-walled oblong; on the W end, a birdcage bellcote with a steeply pyramidal stone roof. In the church's S side, a pair of tall pointed windows and, in each end bay, a double tier of smaller segmental-headed windows. Originally, each gable contained a pointed door under a segmental-headed gallery window and, above, a small circular dummy opening; a porch was added to the E gable in the late C19.

DESCRIPTION. At the W end of the village, on the S side of the B9127, the former KINNETTLES FREE CHURCH MANSE of 1846 but enlarged to an L in 1870. Curvaceously bracketed cornice over the entrance. Then the former Kinnettles Free Church (*see* above) followed by a short Neo-Jacobean cottage terrace of 1871. U-plan front of stugged masonry, the gabled end bays containing hoodmoulded two-light windows. At the centre and in the inner angles, gabled porches, the doors surmounted by jumping hoodmoulds. At right angles to this group and running S towards Kinnettles Parish Church (*see* above) are KIRKTON COTTAGES built in 1813. Single-storey four-bay double houses. At each, the end windows are set in segmental-headed overarches tweaked up to a point at the centre; between them, paired doors under a single long hoodmould. Battlemented screen walls link each double house to the next.

DOOCOT, 0.3 km. E. Lectern doocot probably of the C17. Rubble walling, formerly harled. Projecting rat course all round and another, at a higher level, along the back (N) wall. Chamfered surround to the S door. Now roofless but stone nesting boxes survive inside.

BRIGTON HOUSE. *See* p. 385.
KINNETTLES HOUSE. *See* p. 559.

KIRKTON OF AIRLIE

3050

Church, former manse and a handful of altered C19 cottages.

AIRLIE CHURCH. Drydashed T-plan kirk, the body built in 1781–3, the N jamb of 1892–3. The main block is an oblong. In the S side, lowly placed rectangular windows at the end bays and, between them, three taller round-headed windows, the sill of the centre opening inscribed 17 M^{r} IS MNr. 81, the initials those of Mr James Stormonth, minister of Airlie from 1780 to 1809. On the W gable a birdcage bellcote, the uprights consisting of columns superimposed on piers, the roof of ogee profile, the weathervane dated 1783. Ball-finialled E gable. Attached to these ends additions of *c.* 1850 housing staircases to the galleries. In the N side, a high-set gallery window at each end; projecting from the centre is the jamb added by *Alexander Johnston* in 1892–3, the windows round-headed. Built into the W gable is a medieval stone carved in high relief with the figure of a saint. Interior recast in 1893 by *John Carver* who provided new GALLERIES and PEWS. In front of the E gallery stands the contemporary PULPIT (to the N) and a fairly ornate Gothic COMMUNION TABLE of 1895. – In the N jamb, ORGAN by *Brindley & Foster*, 1884. – STAINED GLASS window (St Andrew) of 1898 in the S wall.

In the mid-C19 E outshot, a now headless medieval stone STATUE, perhaps representing a saint. It came from the medieval parish church. – Built into the N wall, a SACRAMENT HOUSE of the C15 or early C16, the jambs formed as banded and foliage-finialled piers, the door's ogee arch with a fleur-de-lis finial. The arch-head is flanked by a ringed cross on the l. and the *Arma Christi* (the pierced hands, feet and heart of Our Lord) on the r. At the back but probably not *in situ* a stone bearing the arms of the Fentons of Baikie.

GRAVEYARD. SW of the church, a pair of BURIAL ENCLOSURES, both probably of the C17, the W's front wall with a sloping cope. The S entrances are set in roll-and-hollow-moulded surrounds, the lintel of the W recording that it was built by William Malcolm in 1609. On each side of this entrance, a stone incised with a skull and bone. To the r., a stone inscribed PVLVIS.ET/VMBRA.SVMVS ('We are dust and shadows') and another with the initials W^{M}M and GM (for Mr William Malcolm, minister of Airlie from 1590 to 1636, and his first wife, Grisel Mather †1609). To the l. of the entrance, a stone inscribed DISCE.MORI.VT/BENE.MORIARIS ('Learn to die that you may die well'). – Standing against the W end of this enclosure are a couple of GRAVE-SLABS. One, erected in 1736 to James Nicol, has a pair of angels' heads (souls) at the top, the other, to Isobel Watson †1695, bears a helmed and mantled shield and emblems of death. – Some other but weathered C17 and C18 stones, bearing variously angels' heads, shields and reminders of mortality.

Former MANSE, now also drydashed, to the SE. Built in 1791–2, it was originally quite plain and of two storeys but in 1891 *John Carver* gave it gabled dormer windows and a piend-roofed long porch at the centre of the three-bay front.

SOUTERRAIN, Barns of Airlie, 0.7 km. W. Earth and grass-covered underground storage chamber constructed *c.* 100 A.D. and remarkably intact. It is banana-shaped, *c.* 19 m. long, 2 m. broad and 1.8 m. high, the walls composed of a base of massive boulders supporting courses of stone slabs and smaller boulders corbelled inwards to carry the roof slabs, one a reused stone indented with eight cup marks of Neolithic date. The present entrance is through a hole in the roof at the chamber's E end but a blocked narrower passage has led up from here to the surface of the ground.

STANDING STONE, Airlie, 2.1 km. S. On a low hill commanding an extensive view to the S, an upright slab erected probably in the second millennium B.C.

AIRLIE CASTLE. *See* p. 292.

3030

KIRKTON OF AUCHTERHOUSE

Informally laid out small village.

14 AUCHTERHOUSE CHURCH. Church consisting of a nave, chancel and W tower, built on medieval foundations and incorporating some medieval work in 1630 and largely rebuilt but reusing old materials in 1775. The nave walls, mostly of 1775, are of cherry-cock-pointed greyish ashlar. Except for one window towards the N end of the W gable, perhaps an insertion, the only openings are in the S wall. Rectangular windows, their surrounds checked for shutters. The main entrance, placed one bay from the W, has a segmental-arched and keystoned head, its roll-and-hollow moulding looking C17. This springs from bell-capitalled attached shafts, probably archaizing work of 1630 rather than reused C15 material. The square W tower may be substantially of 1630. At the bottom stage, a W door under a dummy fanlight. The walling of the upper stage is intaken. S door reached by a forestair. Above are rectangular openings, the top serving a belfry. Wall-head cornice carried on rounded corbels and surmounted by a square low platform supporting the round spire which rises in two stages, both bellcast, to a ball finial and gilded weathercock.

The chancel seems all to be of the earlier C17. In its S side a pair of windows, each of two angular pointed lights, flanks a rectangular moulded door. Built into the E gable are carved stones. One is a sundial, probably of the C17. Another is incised with the date 1630. The third bears a fleur-de-lis and the eroded inscription *Ave Maria*; it is probably C15.

The interior was recast by *Robert Blackadder* in 1881 and refurnished in 1910 by *James W. Mackison* who provided the beamed ceiling. Attention is now focused on the chancel, its E end partitioned off as a vestry, which from the C17 to the C19 housed a laird's loft above a burial vault. This is entered through a pointed arch with simply chamfered responds; it is perhaps C15. Inside the chancel which is raised by three steps above the level of the nave, PANELLING of 1910, the wood reused from the church's Georgian pews. In pride of place is the COMMUNION TABLE and, on the N side of the chancel arch, the PULPIT, both routine Gothic of 1910. In front of the pulpit, the upper part of the shaft and the base of the bowl of an octagonal stone FONT, perhaps of *c.* 1500. – STAINED GLASS. W window (Christ the Shepherd-King) by *Alexander L. Russell*, 1952. – In the S wall, a two-light window (Our Lord the Good Shepherd; Our Lord the Light of the World) of *c.* 1915, brightly coloured and realistic. – Late C18 CLOCK at the W end, by *James Ivory*, the case with Chinoiserie decoration.

GRAVEYARD. The GATEWAYS at the N, S and E incorporate fragments of late medieval stone window tracery, presumably from the previous church on the site. – A few weathered GRAVE-SLABS of the C17 and C18, carved variously with angels' heads (souls), trade emblems and symbols of death. – Some way S of the church, the classical MONUMENT to the parish schoolmaster, James Spence †1813, the pedestal surmounted by a truncated pyramid, its urn finial decorated with human faces from which hang swags.

THE OLD MANSION HOUSE

Auchterhouse, 1.1 km. SW

Manorial laird's house formerly the centre of the barony of Auchterhouse held successively by the Ramsays and Ogilvys, hereditary Sheriffs of Angus, before passing by marriage to the Earls of Buchan in 1478.

The house forms a U, its harled ranges enclosing a courtyard bounded by a screen wall on the E. The S range is the principal block, its E third of three storeys, the W of two and an attic but standing to the same overall height. Of these parts the E is probably C15 or C16, an oblong of *c.* 11.3 m. by *c.* 6.7 m. Tiny windows at the ground floor. Comfortably sized openings, probably enlarged in the C18 or C19, at the upper floors, the walling of the second floor's S face slightly recessed. A gabled rectangular SW jamb, its upper floors jettied out, was added to this block in the late C16 or more probably the early C17. Entrance with a moulded surround at its S face. Small windows except for a S top floor opening, probably a Georgian enlargement, which is flanked by a pair of shot-holes; another shot-hole in the E face.

In the early C17, perhaps at the same time as the addition of the jamb to the S range's E part, this range was extended W by *c.* 16.8 m., the extension's S face on the same plane as the earlier part but its N side slightly projecting. On the S, a massive stepped chimney which rises from the ground a little l. of centre. Exceptionally large windows to the ground floor, the l.'s moulded surround and that of the adjoining door apparently C17, the surrounds to the others Georgian as are those of the smaller first-floor openings. A trio of gabled dormers at the attic was added by *Mills & Shepherd* in 1923, the l. incorporating a stone inscribed with the date 1703 and the initials of Patrick Lyon of Auchterhouse and his wife, Margaret Campbell, who then owned the estate. Massive buttress at the house's SW corner, dating probably from an C18 repair.

The house's three-storey and attic W range, slightly recessed from the gable of the S, has been built in two stages. The first, probably of the mid C17, provided a two-bay section. The second, of three storeys and mid-C18, extended this by a further two bays; wall-head chimney to mark the join of the two parts. The plain single-storey N range may also be of mid-C18 origin but was altered in the mid C19.

INTERIOR. In the house's earliest part at the E end of the S range, a couple of tunnel-vaulted rooms (originally stores, the l. now the entrance hall). On the first floor above the E of these, the library with a compartmented plaster ceiling of the early C17. There was no direct access from the ground floor of the S range's E part to the W until 1923 when a round-headed doorway and short stair were provided from the present entrance hall to the Reception Hall (the C17 inner chamber). Elaborate plaster ceiling with pendants and compartments containing floral and foliage motifs. In the adjacent and larger drawing room (the C17 laird's hall or outer chamber) a very similar ceiling, its decorative motifs including the monogrammed initials of James [Erskine] and Mary [Douglas], Earl [*jure uxoris*] and Countess [*suo jure*] of Buchan. Further lavish decoration on the plaster overmantel of the moulded stone chimneypiece. This has Artisan Mannerist Corinthian columns at the ends. Between them, an elaborate display of stylized Jacobean motifs and two sets of the coroneted initials of Mary [Douglas], Countess of Buchan. Centre panel displaying the impaled coats of arms of Erskine and Douglas under the initials IEB (for James [Erskine], Earl of Buchan. The heraldry and initials provide a likely date for the plasterwork and probably also the construction of the S range's E part of between 1617 when the Earl and Countess married and 1628 when she died. Further early C17 plaster ceilings in two rooms above.

The WALLACE TOWER immediately S of the house is the surviving fragment of the mansion's predecessor, apparently a castle of enclosure, possibly of the C13. The tower may have been the keep or lord's lodging. It is oblong, *c.* 12.5m. by 9.1m., with 2.4m.- thick rubble walls which stand up to *c.* 4m. high at the N and W but only to *c.* 1m. at the other two sides. The ground floor has been lit by a small N window, entered from an arched W doorway and covered by a tunnel vault, its springing evident inside at the N wall; round-headed deep embrasure to the window. The original height and appearance of the tower above the ground floor can only be conjectured. – C17 rubble-built double-chamber lectern DOOCOT, 0.1 km. N of the house, on the E side of the Auchterhouse Burn. In the E front, a pair of doors, the empty frame for a heraldic panel, and catslide-roofed dormers containing flight-holes. Rat course along the back wall and ends. – At the entrance to the short drive, a harled single-storey LODGE, of early C19 origin but extended and remodelled by *Mills & Shepherd*, 1923. Scrolled skewputts and, at the window of the W gable, a reused pediment, probably C17 and originally belonging to a dormerhead.

CROSS-SLAB (MARTIN'S STONE), Balluderon, 3.2 km. E. Fragment of a slab, probably of the C9, one face carved in relief. It bears the base of a cross (the rest broken off) on which is displayed a horseman. Below, another horseman and 'Pictish beast' and 'serpent-and-Z-rod' symbols.

MONUMENT AND CAIRN, West Mains Hill, 2.9 km. W. Tall conical stone pillar erected by *William Mackison* in 1887 to commemorate Queen Victoria's Golden Jubilee. It stands on a mound of *c.* 20 m. diameter and 2.5 m. high which was formed at the beginning of the second millennium B.C. as a Bronze Age burial cairn. This consisted of a central slab-sided and roofed double cist of *c.* 1.5 m. by 0.6 m., containing three cremations and a bronze dagger. The slabs' joints had been sealed with clay and the cist was surrounded by a packing of rough stones. Over this had been placed a layered mound of earth taken from the valley below and mixed with wood ash, possibly associated with the cremations, and this in turn was covered with a low pyramid of stones. The top finishing is a layer of earth in which grow grass and heather.

KIRKTON OF GLENISLA *2060*

Strung-out handful of houses, mostly of the C19.

GLENISLA PARISH CHURCH. Rubble-walled oblong kirk of 1821, a birdcage bellcote on the W end. A hearse house was added to the N side, probably in the mid C19. In the W gable, two quite small rectangular gallery windows. S front of four bays with end doors surmounted by windows, also rectangular; in the centre, a pair of large pointed windows.

The fairly large rectangular opening in the E gable probably dates from alterations of 1885 by *John Carver* who moved the pulpit from the S side to this end. Inside, a canopied PULPIT of 1821. – PEWS of 1885.

FORTER CASTLE. *See* p. 484.

KIRKTON OF KINGOLDRUM *3050*

Scrappy small village, the houses dating from the C19 to the early C20.

KINGOLDRUM CHURCH. By *David Mackenzie*, 1840. Red sandstone rectangle with flat-roofed porches attached to the ends of the S side. On the W gable, a spikily pinnacled and spired bellcote, its openings elliptical-arched. Metal roof ventilator, probably Victorian. Segmental-headed windows in the S side; at each porch, a round-headed S window. – Standing against the S wall, a medieval GRAVE-SLAB carved with a ringed cross and a sword and very similar to a stone now built into the offices of the former Parish Manse at Ruthven (q.v). – Also here, a rough stone BASIN, probably the bowl of a medieval font.

Simple interior, the position of the pulpit moved from the S side to the E end in 1957. Victorian PULPIT and COMMUNION TABLE brought here from the former Whitburn Free Church (Lothian) in 1967 when the PEWS were made.

BURIAL ENCLOSURE S of the church built for the family of John Farquharson of Baldovie, probably in the early C19. Neo-classical, faced with grey ashlar. Principal front to the N where the masonry of the end bays is V-jointed and pierced by slit windows. Centre slightly advanced between anta-pilasters. It bears the inscription panel and is surmounted by an urn.

Harled former MANSE of 1792 to the NE. Two storeys and an attic, the gabled dormers probably added as part of *David Bryce*'s alterations in 1863–4. Three-bay front with tripartite windows at its ends.

ASCREAVIE HOUSE, 2.2 km. N. Mid-C19 version of an Elizabethan manor house, with pedimented dormerheads over the first-floor openings and a large canted bay window at the l. end of the S front. Crowstepped gables to show it belongs to Scotland.

BALFOUR MAINS, 0.5 km. S. Plain rubble-walled farmhouse of *c.* 1840. Three storeys, the second-floor windows with gablet dormerheads. At the SE corner, a surviving fragment of BALFOUR CASTLE which was built for the Ogilvys of Balfour, probably in the early C16. This consists of a six-storey round tower, *c.* 5.5 m. in diameter and 17 m. high, constructed of large blocks of rough rubble crossed by string courses, one jumping up over a pair of windows, their positioning unrelated to the floor levels inside. Projecting base in which are set oval gunloops facing E and W; another gunloop (facing NW) at the first floor. Variety of windows at the upper floors, some slits and others of quite good size; a large S-facing one has been built up. A door in the S segment, probably a later insertion, opens into the ground floor's tunnel-vaulted circular room. It was reached from the first floor of the missing main block by a stair on the N. Of the main block there survives only a stub of wall at the tower's NE segment. It contains one jamb of a large upper window. Two wings of the house were said to have been demolished *c.* 1838 so perhaps it was Z-plan, the surviving tower forming the SW jamb.

3050

KIRRIEMUIR

A burgh of barony from 1495, the town developed from two small settlements, the Kirkton around the Parish Church and the Milltown beside the Gairie. Population growth took place in the second half of the C18 when linen weaving was introduced, and linen manufacture continued as the principal industry through the C19, with power-loom factories (later converted to jute-weaving) being built from *c.* 1870. The town, although small, retains an industrial base but serves also as a local shopping centre.

CHURCHES

ANTI BURGHER CHURCH, Seceders' Close and Church Lane, off Glengate. Now Seceder Hall. Harled two-storey box built *c.* 1773.

KIRRIEMUIR FREE BAPTIST CHURCH, Nos. 12–16 Bank Street. Built as an Original Secession church in 1891–3, the architect was *James Chalmers* of Glasgow. The ground floor of the building is occupied by shops. The church itself is placed on the upper floor whose ecclesiastical character is made clear by tall buttresses and pointed windows; plate-traceried rose in the head of the two-light centre window.

NORTH FREE CHURCH, Glengate and St Malcolm's Wynd. Disused. Tudor, by *William Paterson*, 1846. Built of local red sandstone, it is L-plan with the jamb projecting at the NW. Two-storey main block with rectangular windows at the ground floor and Tudor Gothic openings above. The S gable is dressed up to suggest a nave and aisles behind, the centre being slightly advanced and with pinnacles on its corners. Corbelled out from the top of this gable, an octagonal bellcote whose Roman Doric columns support an ogee roof topped by a ball-and-spike finial. Near the top of this gable and in the gable of the jamb, round-arched louvred openings. Tudor Gothic windows at the jamb whose NW corner has been removed to improve sightlines for traffic.

OLD PARISH CHURCH, off High Street and Bank Street. Economical but urbane classical, by *James Playfair*, 1786–8. The church is a broad rectangle, built of local red sandstone rubble partly covered in cement lined out as ashlar, the W steeple faced with ashlar masonry. Long two-storey S elevation of seven bays, the ends slightly advanced under parapets, each with a fluted centre panel. At the ground floor, rectangular windows and, in the end bays, doors (the E now built up). Above, round-headed gallery windows, the W still sash-and-case. Originally, the N side was quite plain and the starkness has been only slightly relieved by the insertion of three windows under the gallery in 1884. Pedimented E gable containing three round-headed windows (the centre larger than the other two) at the upper level. This end was overlaid in 1905 by *Gavin & Soutar*'s addition of a hall which was extended by two W wings in 1914 and to the E in 1968.

The W gable is the showfront. Overall pediment, an oculus in its tympanum. Below the pediment, five bays, the ends very slightly advanced. Round-headed windows at the upper level, the centre three linked by a sill course. At the ground floor, five doors, those of the outer and central bays all originally corniced and with dummy fanlights; the centre door has lost its cornice. Above the gable is the steeple. Its lowest stage is a corniced belfry, a circular opening in each face. Then, an offset clock stage with cut-out corners; the clock is a replacement of 1897. Above this, the octagonal stone spire, its flattened top surmounted by a dragon-finialled weathervane.

The interior is divided into a nave and aisles by cast-iron columns of two superimposed orders, the lower Tuscan, the upper with fluted capitals. Over the aisles, flat ceilings; a basket-arched ceiling over the nave. In the aisles and across the W end of the nave are galleries supported on the lower tier of columns.

The C18 furnishings have been replaced. Pine PEWS of 1870–1 in the main area, of 1876 in the galleries. – Mid-C20 COMMUNION TABLE and PULPIT at the E end. – The ORGAN (by *Makins Organs Ltd*, 1988) is an electronic replacement but pipes of the organ of 1875 survive in the W gallery.

Comprehensive display of STAINED GLASS. The main E window, of three lights (the Last Supper) is of 1884. – Of the same date the windows (the Annunciation to the Shepherds; the Maries at the Tomb) in the E wall at the ends of the N and S galleries. – Under the N gallery, three lights (the Sower; St Michael; the Calling of St Peter) by *William Wilson*, *c.* 1950–62, characteristically colourful in a modern-realistic manner. – Five windows under the S gallery. Three (Our Lord and Little Children; the Baptism of Our Lord; the Nativity of Our Lord) are of *c.* 1950–9 and also by Wilson. – They alternate with two windows (the Raising of Jairus's Daughter; the Finding of Our Lord in the Temple) by *A. Ballantine & Son*, 1915–16. – In the S gallery, five windows (Scenes of the Passion, Crucifixion and Resurrection of Our Lord) by *William Wilson* and his partner and successor, *John Blyth*, 1967–73.

GRAVEYARD. At the W entrance from High Street, corniced GATEPIERS, probably of 1788. – MONUMENTS. Placed against the E end of the church's S wall, a well-preserved but half-buried slab commemorating David Walker †1655, with a marginal inscription which continues on the centre of the stone. – Just to its SE, two slabs to Janet Cudber †1655 and Alexander Cudber †1674, both carved with reminders of death. – Similar slab to William Doig †1686 further to the SE. – S of the church hall, a hog-backed slab to Alexander Wood †1666, his wife, Margaret Adam †1668, and Androv [*sic*] Wood †1679 and his wife. It bears their initials flanked by shields, skulls and bones. – Just SE of the hall, a HEADSTONE erected by James Don in memory of his uncle, James Thomson †1744. On its front, idiosyncratically detailed thin columns which frame a shield under tasselled mantling; two angels' heads at the top. At the bottom of the back, small emblems of mortality.

ST ANDREW, Glamis Road. Originally South United Free Church. By *Thoms & Wilkie*, 1901–3. Blocky Late Gothic with a squat NW steeple and NE porch, built of red sandstone with buff-coloured dressings. At the front (N) gable, broad and shallow buttresses with Gothic-arched panels below their sloping tops. In the gable, a lower tier of segmental-arched windows, each containing two rectangular lights under a dummy fanlight. Above, three pointed windows, each of three round-headed lights under simplified Gothic tracery. These upper windows are linked by a hoodmould which rises to a foliaged finial at the centre; label stops carved with foliage and cherubs' heads. Behind, plain side elevations with segmental-arched clearstorey windows. Rectangular lights in the side aisles which run back to flush transepts. In each transept gable, a two-light traceried window like that of the N front.

The NW steeple has low diagonal buttresses. Foliaged bosses carved on the splayed soffit of the N entrance arch. Round-headed W window. In each face of the belfry, a two-light opening containing loopy tracery; foliaged label stops to the hoodmoulds. Griffons at the corners of the battlement and, within it, a small slated pyramidal spire.

Inside, a queen-strut roof over the nave. The long N bay is unaisled and may have been intended for a future gallery. The aisled bays to the S have minimally pointed arcades carried on red sandstone columns. The taller arches into the transepts spring from corbelled responds at their S. In the nave's S wall, a round-headed arch springs from foliaged corbels and opens into the recess which houses the organ. The combined ORGAN CASE and PULPIT (by *Thomas Justice & Sons Ltd*) are of 1903 in the same Late Gothic manner as the rest of the church, the organ rebuilt by *Ronald Smith*, *c.* 1990.

ST ANTHONY (R.C.), St Mary's Close, off Roods. How to make the most of a modest budget without tricks, it is by *James F Stephen*, 1985–7. Hexagonal plan with short sides at the SW entrance and behind the altar at the NE but covered with a lozenge-shaped roof, its beams projecting boldly, which sweeps up from the entrance to a high point above the altar. Laminated timber construction, the lower part of the walls clad in local sandstone rubble, the upper parts glazed or clad in wood or slate.

The entrance opens into a porch whose NE wall is curved at the back of the church itself. Over the church, a boarded pine ceiling. Simple but chunkily detailed ALTAR RAIL and LECTERN of 1987, the light-coloured wood enlivened by touches of green-painted metal. – Rocky stone ALTAR by *Church Bros.* 33
1987. – In the large window behind the altar, STAINED GLASS (stylized depiction of Local Scenery) by *Daniella Mayes*, 1987. – Stained-glass PANELS in the SW corner (the Virgin and Child) and in the passage from the porch to the sacristy were made by *Sadie McLellan*, *c.* 1950, for the previous St Anthony's (R.C.) Church. – At the ends of the church's back wall, two MOSAIC PANELS (Miracles in the Life of St Anthony of Padua) by *Walter Pritchard*, *c.* 1950, also from the former church. – STATIONS OF THE CROSS. White-painted figurative outlines on wooden panels, by *Anne Myles*, 1987. – Wooden STATUE of Our Lady begun by *James Stewart* and completed after his death by *Mrs Scott Laidlaw*, 1987. – Stone STATUE of St Anthony of Padua by *Bruce Walker*, 1987.

ST MARY (Episcopal), West Hillbank. 1904–5 by *J. Ninian Comper* 30
and one of the last of his works designed on the principle of 'unity by exclusion', i.e. inspired by the perfection of North European Late Gothic to the exclusion of all other influences. For its design Comper claimed a rigid exclusivity of historical and regional influence. He wrote* of the thinking behind his design:

> . . . the building ought to bear the stamp of a Christian Church; more particularly here in Scotland it should visibly express the claim which the Episcopal Church makes to be historical and national.

* In *The Scottish Chronicle*, i (1905), 325.

To model the building on English, or Italian, or even directly on French work would be to contradict this; rather the neighbouring fragments and ruins of the latest Christian Churches of the middle age have been taken as a guide, so far as guidance in style has been sought for at all. There is, indeed, no later nor nearer manner in which to build. That is not to say that the Church is made to look like a sixteenth century building; its details will tell its modern story as the details of old buildings tell their history to the instructed eye.

So the starting point for the design was Late Gothic of a specifically Scottish character. With this was coupled Comper's desire to use local materials, a wish partly frustrated by his discovery that 'the red sandstone of Forfarshire has a tendency to flake, and the slates are difficult to procure, and are very heavy'. Consequently, although local red sandstone was used for the rubble walling, the dressings are of red Dumfriesshire stone and the slates are West Highland from Ballachulish, the use of these materials found satisfactory by Comper who proclaimed that 'local colour is not sacrificed in the use of either'.

For the plan Comper claimed no specifically Scottish character but referred to meeting the needs of 'an ordinary parochial church to-day', the most important of these identified by him as the requirement 'to emphasise the altar as the holy table, no less than the place of Sacrifice'. The building consists of a two-bay chancel with a sacristy on its S side, and a taller and broader four-bay nave with a SE porch and N aisle; on the N side of the aisle, a choir vestry, originally of two bays but later doubled in length to the E. A fifth nave bay is provided by the W tower whose side walls continue the lines of the S side and N arcade of the nave.

The chancel's E gable is diagonally buttressed. In its large five-light E window reticulated tracery combines with loop forms to produce a Late Gothic variant of the W refectory window of Dunfermline Abbey (Fife). In the N and S walls of the chancel, steeply pointed windows, each of three cusped lights, the sidelights surmounted by dagger tracery, the centre lights rising to the window heads. The sacristy on the S of the chancel is flat-roofed and simple, its rectangular windows containing untraceried cusped lights. Rising from the sacristy's NW corner, in the inner angle of the chancel and porch, a round turret with a conical slabbed roof and, on its N side, an octagonal chimneystack, almost Gaudiesque in character.

The nave roof is carried down over the N aisle and so extends beyond the tower on that side. On the E gable of the nave, a bellcote containing a sanctus bell. On the nave's S side, the E bay is covered by the two-storey crowstep-gabled porch, its general appearance reminiscent of the C15 porch at St Michael's Parish Church, Linlithgow (Lothian), but with the addition of diagonal buttresses (possibly a quotation from the transeptal chapels of the same church) and with the Linlithgow porch's first-floor oriel window replaced by a dummy image niche. This 'niche' is composed of ashlar panelling applied to the rubble walling but without a recess to shelter the statue of the Virgin and Child. The statue stands on a corbel which serves as the finial of the hood-mould over the porch's ogee-arched entrance. The three bays of the nave W of the porch are marked off by stepped and pinnacled buttresses. In each bay, a big four-light steeply pointed window, each pair of lights topped by flame-like curvilinear tracery; in the head of each window, a large tracery fleur-de-lis, the emblem of the Blessed Virgin Mary to whom the church is dedicated.

The tower forms a W continuation of the nave. At its E corner, angle buttresses, the E part of the S buttress rising from the wall-head of the nave. They have gablets below their tops which slope into the walling below the battlement (cf. the buttresses of the NW tower of Brechin Cathedral, q.v.). Similarly detailed angle buttress at the NW corner. At the SW corner, a round stair-turret rising above one low offset to a crenellation. The tower itself is finished with a corbelled tall battlement, powerfully detailed with stepped merlons at the corners and the centre of each face. In each of the tower's N and S elevations, a window identical to those at the nave and, higher up, a small opening of two round-headed cusped lights. At the W front and approached by a broad flight of steps, a steeply pointed arch of the same breadth and rising to the same height as the window. This arch contains the tower entrance. The doorway itself has a depressed arch; above it the head of the main arch is filled by four cusped lights under a quatrefoiled tracery head. Over this entrance, a mullioned-and-transomed circular window containing four trefoil lights. The tower's belfry stage is marked off by a string course. In each face, a large square opening containing reticulated tracery just like the C15 belfry opening in the E face of the crossing tower of Iona Abbey (Argyll).

The narrow N aisle is lit from a window in each gable. The W window is of two round-headed cusped lights under loop tracery. Rectangular E window containing three cusped lights.

INTERIOR. The main entrance is from the W into the tower which contains a baptistery with a beamed wooden ceiling. Broad pointed stone arch into the nave whose boarded roof is a pointed tunnel vault with surface ribs. Monopitch roof over the N aisle and a double-pitch roof over the chancel, both with the principals exposed. The nave's N arcade has keel-shaped piers without capitals from which spring pointed arches. Taller arch into the chancel where the altar is raised only one step above the choir, in accordance with the medieval precedents championed by Comper and also to allow enough space above for the large E window designed to flood the altar with light.*

The upper storey of the porch at the E bay of the nave is an organ chamber from which the ORGAN (by *C. & F. Hamilton*, 1906) projects on a cantilevered wooden balcony into the S side of the church.

FURNISHINGS all of 1905 and designed by Comper. – Corbelled out in the inner angle between the chancel arch and the E bay of the nave arcade is the stone PULPIT. Semi-octagonal, with Gothic panels on the sides. On the corners, three coats of arms, the centre bearing the crowned monogram of the Blessed Virgin Mary, the other two the arms of Douglas, one to commemorate Canon James Douglas to whom the pulpit was a memorial, the other for the burgh of Kirriemuir (a burgh of barony whose superiority was held by the Douglas family). The pulpit is entered through an arched doorway from a sloping-roofed porch reached by a stair in the thickness of the chancel wall. – Simple stone HIGH ALTAR, with angel-topped riddel-posts between which run the rails for curtains at its back and sides. – Boxy oak PEWS. – Octagonal FONT of red sandstone with simple Gothic panelling on the sides.

STAINED GLASS. Extensive scheme, all except one window by *Comper*. In the chancel, E window (First World War memorial, depicting the Risen Christ as a beardless youth flanked by figures of SS Columba, Michael the Archangel, George and Patrick; the Virgin and Child in the tracery at the top), the outer lights filled in 1920, the two outer and the tracery in 1927, all in strong colours with blue predominant. – In the N wall of the chancel, the E window of 1928 is a memorial to Vice-Admiral John Drummond and its subject (St Margaret of Scotland in a boat, St Stephen of Hungary at the stern, St John the Evangelist in the prow) alludes to the legend that the progenitor of the Drummonds was a Hungarian who accompanied St Margaret to Scotland; the W window (St Anne with Our Lady as a Child; in the sidelights, Sarah with the Child Isaac, and St Elizabeth of Hungary) of *c.* 1940. – In the S wall of the chancel, E window (St Barnabas and St Margaret of Scotland, David, King of Israel, and St David, King of Scots) of 1924, and a small W window (St Susanna) of 1942. – The E window of the N aisle was erected in 1905 as a memorial to Comper's father, the Rev. John Comper. It depicts the Virgin and Child with, on the l., the Rev. John Comper and St John the Evangelist, and, on the r., St Ninian (a portrait of Bishop Alexander P. Forbes who had ordained Father Comper). – The W window of this aisle (the Presentation of Our Lord in the Temple) is a sentimental production of 1948. – In the nave's S wall, at the E end, a colourful window (SS Martin, Andrew,

* Comper also intended the E window to illuminate the altar sufficiently to permit the following of 'ancient precedent' by the introduction of a chancel screen which, 'with ample light behind it' would become 'transparent', allowing a view of the altar to worshippers in the nave (*The Scottish Chronicle*, i (1905), 325).

Dionysus (Denis) and Quintin) of 1920. – Even stronger in colour and powerfully drawn is this wall's other window (Our Lord on the Cross, and Our Lord in Glory) which is by *William Wilson*, c. 1955. – Over the W door to the baptistery, a light ('Suffer little children') by Comper, 1929.

SOUTH CHURCH, Glamis Road. Now church hall. Built as a chapel of ease in 1836, it is a tall box, the walls constructed of local red sandstone rubble. Four bays, with tall pointed two-light windows in the S front and gables. At the front, gabled porches with spiky pinnacles. In the back (N) wall, a double tier of windows, the lower rectangular, the upper short and pointed. The ashlar eaves course returns across the gables to form rudimentary pediments. – To the SW, a plain Tudorish HALL by *Hugh Gavin*, 1900.

WEST UNITED PRESBYTERIAN CHURCH, Glengate. Now Boys' Brigade Hall. Opened in 1853. Plain Gothic box, its gable front divided into a 'nave' and 'aisles' by pinnacled buttresses and its windows hoodmoulded. In the centre of the front, a Tudor door under a window of three stepped lights; small rose window above.

PUBLIC BUILDINGS

BOYS' BRIGADE HALL. *See* Churches, above: West United Presbyterian Church.

CEMETERY, Cemetery Road. Opened in 1858. At the N end, WAR MEMORIAL by *John Kinross*, 1921–2. Tall granite pedestal with Ionic columns at the corners. It is surmounted by the granite statue of a kilted soldier by *Henry Hutcheon*.

PARK, Hill of Kirriemuir, off West Hill Road and Hillbank Terrace. Playing fields without formal planting. On the W side, the BARRIE PAVILION by *Frank Thomson*, 1930, the gift of Sir James Barrie to his native town. Harled, with dressings of local grey stone. Single-storey broad-eaved piend-roofed pavilion. On the E side the entrance is contained in a semi-octagonal projection which rises above the eaves as a full octagon, its roof topped by a metal drum which houses a camera obscura. At the back of the pavilion the surrounding terrace rises and breaks forward as a semi-octagon on which stands a stone pedestal, its top covered by a metal plate which indicates the height of the surrounding hills. – STANDING STONE, 0.4 km. E, on the ridge of the hill and with extensive views to the Grampians, a craggy 2.7 m. tall pillar erected probably in the second millennium B.C.

POLICE STATION, Reform Street. Built in 1895–6. Symmetrical Scots C17 style, the bull-nosed ashlar walling of red sandstone. Swan-neck pediments over the doors; a scroll-supported chimney on the central gablet.

POST OFFICE, Reform Street. Joyless Georgian survival, by *David Waterston*, 1896.

SECEDER HALL. *See* Churches, above: Anti-burgher Church.

SOUTHMUIR PRIMARY SCHOOL. *See* WEBSTER'S HIGH SCHOOL, below.

TOWN HALL AND LIBRARY, Reform Street, The Town Hall is by *C. & L. Ower*, 1885. Flemish, with a big Dutch gable. Over the entrance, paired heavy consoles support a stone balcony in front of a three-light window; above the window, a fanlight with a stilted round-headed arch. The Library, added to the W by *Leslie Ower & Allan* in 1913, is a less assertive version of the Town Hall, again with a Dutch gable but also with a low conical-roofed round tower at the corner with Rosefield Road.

TOWNHOUSE, High Street. Two-storey L-plan building of local red sandstone rubble. The general shape and a little of the detail date from 1604. The main block's E gable has rounded corners corbelled to the square at the first floor which may originally have supported another storey. On the bowed front of the jamb's N gable, a bowed C17 panel suggesting that this gable is also of 1604. However, the bowed W gable of the main block looks more likely to date from the alterations made in 1835. The building was remodelled in 1862–3 by *John Carver* who added a low tower in the inner angle. Rising inside the tower's heavy battlement, a fish-scale-slated spire. Also of 1862–3 is the steeply pedimented dormerhead over the first-floor window of the jamb's gable; it bears little pedestals which give it a crowstepped look.

TRADES HALL. *See* Description, below.

WEBSTER'S HIGH SCHOOL, Prosen Road. By *Angus County Council*, 1954, the walls of brick and render with metal-framed horizontal glazing; shallow-pitched corrugated metal roofs. At the NW, a late C20 SPORTS CENTRE, faced with red 'Fyfestone' blocks, the low pitched roofs also of corrugated metal. The High School was extended and remodelled in 2000–1 and SOUTHMUIR PRIMARY SCHOOL built at its SE end.

DESCRIPTION

GLAMIS ROAD is the main approach from the S. Its first prominent incident, on the l. side, is the early C19 white-painted NEWTON HOTEL, its broad gable front crossed by lintel courses. Just to the N, the mid-C19 Nos. 47–49, constructed of red sandstone, the dominant building material of the street and the town. Panelled aprons between the lintel course joining the ground-floor windows and the sill course under the windows of the first floor; rusticated quoins. Then, plain C19 two-storey houses. Near the top of Glamis Road, on the r., St Andrew's Church. Almost opposite, the former South Church in front of Southmuir Primary School (for all these, *see* Churches and Public Buildings, above). On the corner of Glamis Road and Forfar Road, Nos. 2–6 Glamis Road, an early C19 block with a quadrant corner and wall-head chimneys. On the l. side of Glamis Road, No. 7 (WINDOW IN THRUMS COTTAGE), a late C18 cottage, the walls of white-painted rubble, the roof originally thatched but now slated. The road now twists and becomes BELLIE'S BRAE, its steep descent to the Gairie Burn overlooked by Webster's High School (*see* Public Buildings, above). At the foot of Bellie's Brae, the Gairie Works (*see* below) past which the road climbs up to the N.

HIGH STREET's effectual beginning is provided by Nos. 1–3 Bellie's Brae on the l. side of the road, late C19 commercial Renaissance with a canted corner to Cumberland Close. In CUMBERLAND CLOSE, CROFTHEAD and PIERHEAD to the W of High Street, C19 venacular housing spruced up in a restoration scheme of 1994, which included the construction of some new buildings, one with a twee conical-roofed tower. On the N side of Cumberland Close, at its E end, a late C20 extension to a building which faces High Street. Built into the extension is a door lintel inscribed J7.DW IS 65. On the E side of High Street, opposite the entrance to Cumberland Close, the Townhouse (*see* Public Buildings, above), a dumpy civic presence. E of the Townhouse is the entrance to the graveyard of the Old Parish Church (*see* Churches above) and to the plain red sandstone C18 and C19 housing in KIRK WYND on the S of the graveyard. The early C19 No. 1 Kirk Wynd has a reused door lintel inscribed I.F. 16 88 B.F. At the C18 Nos. 2–4 opposite, small windows and a front slightly angled to a bend in the street. In High Street N of the Townhouse, a small and not very formal square in which was erected in 1994 a bronze STATUE of Peter Pan (in tribute to the playwright and novelist, Sir James Barrie, a native of Kirriemuir); it is by *Alistair Smart.** On the W side of the square, Nos. 35–37 High Street of *c.* 1800. At the centre of the ashlar front, a pilastered and chimneyed gablet containing a pointed window with projecting keystone and imposts. No. 39 is late C18 with a rendered gable front containing a small round window to light the attic. Also of three storeys and an attic and gable-fronted is the adjoining early C19 building (Nos. 41–42) with a pointed window to the attic. On the N side of the square, the four-storey ashlar-fronted and quadrant-cornered Nos. 16–18 High Street (formerly the Commercial Hotel) of *c.* 1840.

BANK STREET goes E from the N side of the square. The block (Nos. 2–8) at the beginning of its S side was built in 1815, its ground floor occupied by shops (the shopfronts now C20). The first floor contained the TRADES HALL whose presence is disclosed by very tall windows and the remains of a late C19 metal ventilator on the roof. E of the Trades Hall, the Kirriemuir Free Baptist Church at Nos. 12–16 Bank Street (*see* Churches, above). On the N side of Bank Street, an ashlar-faced tenement (Nos. 7–9) of *c.* 1995, Neo-vernacular with a bargeboarded gable over the jettied upper floors of the two centre bays. The Bank of Scotland (originally CITY OF GLASGOW BANK) is by *John Carver*, 1862. Restless Scots Jacobean, with heavy corbels supporting a narrow triangular

* A bronze statue by Smart was erected in Glengate in 1968. This was later damaged and replaced by a cold concrete cast in 1983. The statue was recast in bronze and unveiled on the present site in 1994.

oriel at the r. bay and steeply pedimented dormerheads. Much calmer is the adjacent Late Georgian block (Nos. 13–17), its central chimneyed gablet containing a round-arched attic window. Also at the centre, the round-arched entrance into a tunnel-vaulted pend. THE ROYAL BANK OF SCOTLAND is of *c.* 1840. Two-storey five-bay front of stugged grey ashlar, the first floor marked off by a band course. Piered portico renewed, like the dressings, in cement; aprons under the ground-floor windows. Then, the two-storey THRUMS HOTEL, its main part early C19, the stugged ashlar masonry painted bright white.

High Street to the N of Bank Street forms another small square. On the W side, a rendered low block (Nos. 43–44) with splayed margins to the first-floor windows; it looks late C18. Much taller is the adjoining former BRITISH LINEN BANK (Nos. 45–47) designed by *George Angus* in 1839 and executed in 1841–3. Built of grey sandstone ashlar, polished at the ground floor, stugged at the two upper storeys. At the corniced ground floor, aproned windows and a central entrance framed by Ionic columns *in antis*. Architraved first-floor windows, the outer openings aproned and corniced, those of the slightly recessed three centre bays linked by a sill course. Another sill course under the second-floor windows. Parapet above the wall-head cornice. On the E side of the square, Nos. 12–14, probably early C19, the second floor's windows smaller than those of the first. At Nos. 9–10 a pompous but blowsy Late Victorian Renaissance block, the grey-buff stonework badly weathered. On the square's N side, the former OGILVY ARMS HOTEL of *c.* 1900, built of red stone with buff-coloured dressings. Not large but heavily detailed, with big cast-iron columns to the ground-floor shopfronts (now partly built-up), segmental-arched lights at the first-floor windows, and second-floor windows rising to segmental and triangular stone pediments. Then the street jinks and the winding GLENGATE begins. Straightforward early and mid-C19 buildings containing flats above shops interrupted by the former North Free Church on the corner of St Malcolm's Wynd. Opposite, the former West United Presbyterian and Anti-burgher Churches (for all these, *see* Churches, above).

ST MALCOLM'S WYND'S N side is filled by a housing development, 1996. A round corner tower and a couple of gablets attempt to give it interest. On the S side of the street, the two-storey AIRLIE ARMS HOTEL of the earlier C19 made conspicuous by a thick application of white harling. ROODS leads N and is well worth exploring for the two churches sited off its W side, St Anthony's (R.C.) in ST MARY'S CLOSE and St Mary's (Episcopal) in WEST HILLBANK (*see* Churches, above).

REFORM STREET is an E continuation of St Malcolm's Wynd. On the S side, the Post Office followed by the Police Station; at the E end of the N side, the Town Hall and Library (for these, *see* Public Buildings, above). BRECHIN ROAD makes a long exit to the E. At its start, on the S side, early C19 vernacular housing which fronts onto LILYBANK. BARRIE'S BIRTHPLACE (Nos. 9–11 Lilybank) stands out as a result of the thick cream harling applied by the National Trust for Scotland to give the birthplace of Sir James Barrie a cleaner and couthier appeal than it had during the writer's lifetime. Further out, on the l., ABERGELDIE, a Jacobean villa of *c.* 1860 and, on the r., the red sandstone LISDEN, built for Robert Forrest, a local lawyer, in 1872–3. It displays turrets and iron cresting. Late C20 additions at the E for its present use as a nursing home.

GAIRIE WORKS, Bellie's Brae. Low but very extensive complex, originally a linen factory but later used to make jute products. The main buildings, at the W of the site, are by *Robertson & Orchar*, 1869. Weaving and finishing sheds constructed of stugged and squared red sandstone; large weathervanes on the cupola-ventilators. Plain villa-like office. To the E, two engine sheds, the N of 1895 with tall windows and an elaborate cast-iron external stair, the S probably of 1915. More C20 additions to the E.

BALLINDARG HOUSE, 3.4 km. SE. Laird's house built in two stages. The earlier is at the NE, an C18 two-storey L-plan building, its E front of three bays and quite plain. In the early C19 a piend-roofed block, also of two storeys, was built across the S gable and the side of the rear wing. This is much smarter. Three-bay S front faced with stugged ashlar, the outer first-floor windows tripartite, the l. with dummy sidelights; anta-pilastered and corniced doorpiece. – W of the house, beside a mill lade, a pair of scroll-decorated CARVED STONES bearing the date 1758, possibly from a well-head. – Urn-finialled and corniced GATEPIERS, probably early C19, to the S and smaller versions of these to the N. – GARDEN, its rubble walls perhaps early C19, NW of the house.

L-plan former STEADING (MAINS OF BALLINDARG) N of the garden. Early C19 cottage range at the N, an urn finial on the E gable. At the W end, a slightly larger house, mid-C19 in its present form, with an advanced centre to the W front. The N part of the steading's SE range (converted to housing, *c.* 1990), its S front with elliptically arched cartshed openings, is probably roughly contemporary. At its S end, an ashlar-faced two-storey block. Urn finial on the N gable; on the S, a ball-finialled birdcage bellcote of comfortable girth. In the S end, a carriage entrance, its keystone carved with the date 1761; above, a round-headed window.

BALLINSHOE CASTLE, 3.2 km. SE. Roofless remains of an engagingly modest C16 laird's house, the rubble walls constructed of large blocks of red sandstone. Crowstep-gabled three-storey oblong main block, *c.* 8.2 m. by 6.7 m., the openings with chamfered margins. Of a stair-tower at the NE corner there survives only the inner side which contains doors to the rooms in the main block. Also surviving but fragmentary is a second-floor SW corner turret carried on continuous corbelling pierced by downward-pointing shot-holes; another shot-hole in the SE segment of its walling. Round shot-holes in the ground floor of the N gable and E side have flanked the stair-tower. Ground-floor slit openings in the W side but, at the E, a comfortably sized window. Decent-sized first- and second-floor windows in the sides and S gable, several with shot-holes below, at others the masonry in this position now missing. The interior has been unvaulted. Fireplaces in the S gable at the first and second floors, each apparently containing a single room.

KINLOCH MAUSOLEUM, New Kilrie, 2.8 km. S. Within a dry moat and rubble-walled enclosure, the mausoleum of the Kinlochs of Kilrie and Logie, built *c.* 1800. Octagon of polished red sandstone ashlar with pilastered corners. In each face, a round-headed arch, blind except for the W which contains the entrance. Wall-head entablature and parapet. Stone domed roof topped by a circular pedestal bearing a swagged flaming urn.

KINNORDY HOUSE. *See* p. 561.

LOGIE HOUSE. *See* p. 599.

6060

LANGLEY PARK

1.9 km. E of Dun

Mutilated ashlar-clad Georgian mansion house. As first constructed in the later C18, it was a piend-roofed building of three storeys, the W front of seven bays with the centre three slightly advanced under a pediment. At the S elevation, also of seven bays, a broad centre containing a three-light window to each floor. About 1820 a two-storey bow was added across the two S bays of the front and a Roman Doric portico to its centrepiece. Then, in 1949 the house was remodelled, its height reduced from three to two storeys and the S front's portico not replaced. It now appears Neo-Georgian.

GARDEN of *c.* 1800 to the E, its walls partly of rubble and partly of brick. – To the W, a quadrangular rubble-built STEADING, also of *c.* 1800. S-facing two-storey main range. At its centre and ends, taller pavilions with wall-head battlements carried on moulded corbels. In each outer face of the end pavilions, a giant round-headed overarch containing a double tier of openings, the upper window also round-headed, flanked by crosslet dummy 'arrowslits'. Similar treatment at the central pavilion but here are tall crosslet 'arrowslits' at the ground-floor and more decorative ones above. The linking sections are plain except for mid-C19 gablet dormerheads and, in the end bays, pointed openings containing the ground- and first-floor windows. At the centre of the N range, a battlemented square tower, its top stage designed to serve as a doocot and with a boldly projecting rat course. The steading is being converted to housing (2010). – Piend-roofed single-storey MID LODGE, also of *c.* 1800, halfway along the drive from the S. Polished ashlar front of three bays, the taller parapeted centre with a round-headed overarch containing the entrance. Late C20 additions at the back. – At the S end of the drive, a slightly later LODGE, also of one storey and ashlar fronted, the ends bowed.

LETHAM

5040

Dour village laid out in 1788 by George Dempster, proprietor of the Dunnichen estate, a square in the centre.

CHURCH, off The Square. Now a house. Built at the beginning of the C19 by James Hawkins, an advocate and heir to the Dunnichen estate, as a church in which he could proclaim his belief in the doctrine of universal salvation. Rubble-walled oblong with a tall and battlemented W tower. Rectangular windows in the sides of the main block, the S very tall. W entrance in the bottom stage of the tower, its corniced entablature a replacement of 2009–10 when it was carved with the date 1810. Hoodmoulded two-light windows at the tower's second stage, the W's king and queen headstops renewed in 2009–10. Two-light windows also at the third but without hoodmoulds. At the top stage, a panel in each side, the W with a clock face. Discreet E extension of 2010.

LETHAM CHURCH, Dundee Road. Originally Dunnichen Free Church, it is by *William Paterson*, 1845. Simple rectangle of snecked and squared masonry, the windows and doors round-headed. Astride the S gable, a birdcage bellcote with would-be Doric columns. The large session room protruding from the centre of the W side was added in 1852. Simple interior, partly altered in the C20. – STAINED GLASS. Abstract-patterned glass of the later C19 in the E windows. – One Late Victorian light (the Good Shepherd) in the S gable.

LETHAM PRIMARY SCHOOL, Braehead Road. By *T. R. Soutar*, 1911. Free Jacobean Renaissance main block of one tall storey. E front of nine bays, the windows of the second, fifth and eighth tall and bipartite with mullions and transoms and rising through the eaves into gablets, the centre semicircular, the outer triangular. Ogee-domed square cupola on the roof. Gabled porches, one for boys, the other for girls, are set back at the ends. Postmodern blockwork-walled addition of *c.* 1995 at the N.

GRAVEYARD, Chapelton, 2.3 km. NNE. Rubble-walled graveyard, the lintel of the S entrance bearing the date 1669. Inside, two rows of C17 and C18 HEADSTONES, the earlier with emblems of death at the top, the later with angels' heads (souls) at the top and reminders of mortality at the bottom.

6040

LETHAM GRANGE

2 km. E of Colliston

Late Georgian mansion (now hotel), an epitome of restrained classicism, given an opulent Late Victorian Baroque makeover. It is now a hotel, the surrounding parkland given over to golf courses and housing.

Between 1803 and 1822 Alexander Hay, a merchant and manufacturer and sometime Provost of Arbroath, put together an estate consisting of the adjoining lands of Letham, New Grange and Peebles. In 1827–30 his son, John, a bachelor and noted sportsman, employed *Archibald Simpson* as architect of a new mansion house which he christened Letham Grange. After John Hay's death the estate was sold in 1877 to James Fletcher of Rosehaugh who had made a fortune as an importer of alpaca wool. In 1881–5 Fletcher carried out a major remodelling and enlargement of the house to designs by *John Robertson* but modified by *John Rhind* when Robertson fell too ill to continue the work.

The house is all faced with lightly stugged ashlar masonry but Simpson's work has weathered to a buff colour, Robertson's and Rhind's to grey. The 1820s main block was of two storeys. E-facing entrance front of five broad bays, the centre three articulated by giant Roman Doric columns which support a pediment topped by a fluted finial. Projecting E from each end of the main block, a long single-storey wing. At the W (garden) front, a bowed two-storey centrepiece fronted by a semicircle of Roman Doric columns and originally surmounted by a dome. Restrained detail, the tall ground-floor windows with aprons, architraves and cornices; wall-head entablature.

The 1880s remodelling overlaid but did not obliterate Simpson's work. At the centre of the E front, a heavily detailed single-storey porch with a screen of Roman Doric columns *in antis* and surmounted by an urn-finialled balustrade. Balustrades of the same design and also with urn finials were added to the wall-heads, only the front pediment left unembellished except for urns at the ends. Simpson's wings were heightened to two storeys and an attic, their round-headed dormers imparting a French Second Empire flavour. Full-height bowed quadrants were added in the wings' inner angles with the main block and two-storey bow windows to the wings' W bays and single-storey outshots in their W inner angles. The main block's W front was enlivened by the addition of single-storey bow windows to the penultimate bays. The most striking alteration was the removal of this front's central dome and the erection of a tower behind the bowed centrepiece. This is square and of two stages, each with three-light windows in every face, the openings of the lower stage round-headed, those of the upper recessed between console-mullions. At the corners, giant pilasters with fluted capitals; above the wall-head's entablature, a balustrade of the same design as elsewhere but, exceptionally for the 1880s embellishments, without urn finials. Filling the

SW inner angle of the main block and the NW wing, a very large conservatory of *c.* 1900 which replaced a much smaller one of the 1880s.

The INTERIOR is almost all of the 1880s, presumably designed by Rhind and Neo-Jacobean in style. Inside the main entrance, a vestibule opens through a screen into the INNER HALL. Here, a leafy cornice and compartmented ceiling. From the Inner Hall's W end a corridor runs N–S behind the principal rooms along the W (garden) front which interconnect through double doors to form an enfilade. The N of these is the DINING ROOM (now ROSEHAUGH RESTAURANT), a bow window in the centre of its W side. Like the others it is expensively finished. Oak-panelled dado executed, as were all the decorative woodwork and chimneypieces, by *Howard & Sons* of London, its rinceau frieze studded with human heads and figures of animals and reptiles. Compartmented oak-lined ceiling with pendants at the intersections of the ribs and, in the centre, a large boss enriched with cherubs' heads set among foliage. The 1880s oak chimneypiece, its caryatid jambs supporting a heavily moulded overmantel, had been replaced before *c.* 1900 by a simpler one without an overmantel. This second chimneypiece was in turn replaced in the 1970s by one from elsewhere in the house, possibly the one originally designed for this room. It is also of oak, the date of 1650 on the lintel unlikely to be genuine. At the jambs, pudgy half-naked caryatid child musicians, one a violinist, the other a piper. Overmantel with a mirror framed by attached Ionic columns embellished with vines and corn sheaves supporting an entablature, its frieze enriched with more foliage and cherubs.

At the centre of the house's W front, the MORNING ROOM (now BRASSERIE), its bowed W end on the axis of the entrance and Inner Hall from which it is entered through a delicate screen, the bottom panels carved with swagged lions' heads. Restrained decoration. High dado, also of oak. Chimneypiece of late C17 derivation surmounted by the dado's frieze whose central panel is carved with a satyr's head. The wall's cornice, possibly a survivor from the 1820s, superimposes mutules over egg-and-dart enrichment. The decoration below is of the 1880s, the wallpaper embossed with vines. The ceiling is also papered but the embossed decoration is in shallower relief, with small rosetted compartments flanked by human heads. The S of the three rooms along this front is the 1880s DRAWING ROOM (now BAR), a bow window at the centre of its W side. Shallowly compartmented ceiling with a modillion cornice. Artisan Mannerist chimneypiece with floral decoration on the jambs' Ionic columns; mirrored overmantel, the centre topped by a pediment. The door at the S end, originally onto a flight of steps descending from a terrace, now opens into the large double-height cast-iron and glass CONSERVATORY of *c.* 1900, its roof supported by slender columns. Externally, the door retains its 1880s appearance, with heavy pilasters supporting a balustraded entablature.

At the main corridor's S end, beside the conservatory, is the main STAIR HALL, the stair top-lit from the glazed centre of the ceiling. Along the S side of the house, three rooms, now interconnecting. The first, originally with doors from a corridor to its N and the Conservatory to its W, was the 1880s LIBRARY (now OAK BAR), its S end filled by a bow window. Delicately panelled dado and simple compartmented ceiling. One corner is now occupied by a bar gantry made up of reused Neo-Jacobean woodwork including a pair of caryatids, presumably from a chimneypiece. The small room at the centre of this side was the 1880s SMOKING ROOM and originally entered only from the Billiard Room to its E. High oak dado, its panels with scallop-shell tops, the cornice studded with lions' heads. Wallpaper frieze heavily embossed with depictions of fruit. The 1880s BILLIARD ROOM beside it occupies the full width of the SE wing. Oak dado of the same design as the Smoking Room's, embossed paper on the cavetto cornice, simply compartmented ceiling and elaborate panelled door. Of similar Neo-Jacobean character the chimneypiece, its stair jambs carved with human faces above flowers and fruit; at the top of each jamb, a corbel carved as a snarling lion holding a shield. The chimneypiece's lintel is of oak, its panels with rinceau ornament and a central cartouche. At the surmounting entablature the frieze is carved with shields, the cornice with lions' heads. Round the fireplace opening, tiles of Persian design depicting flowers and horsemen.

DOOCOT to the N of the house, probably late C16 or early C17. Of lectern type, a crowstep-gabled rubble rectangle with a boldly projecting rat course constructed of stone slabs. – HOME FARM, 0.4 km. NE. Rubble-built steading of 1895–6. At the W range a gabled centrepiece topped by a weathervane and containing segmental-arched cart doors under a circular dummy window. Parallel ranges at right angles behind, each covered with a piended roof.

WEST GATEWAY at the entrance to the drive from the NW, built in 1890, of bull-nosed red sandstone rubble. Pair of three-storey round towers, their stages marked off by string courses. Hoodmoulded windows to the first floor, crosslet dummy arrowslits to the second; wall-head battlement on moulded corbels. Between them, a round-headed arch under a corbelled parapet. – EAST LODGE at the end of the former E drive. By *Alexander Ross*, 1887. Single-storey, of polished ashlar, it is determinedly Neoclassical with a hint of Egyptian. – Contemporary GATEPIERS in the same manner.

5060

LETHNOT

Just the abandoned church of a rural parish.

LETHNOT PARISH CHURCH. Roofless rubble-built box of 1827, a birdcage bellcote on the W gable. Main front facing S, its openings all round-headed and rather narrow. In the centre, tall windows flanked by doors; at each end and set much higher, a window. Two rectangular windows in the N wall and one in each gable.

Inside, two MONUMENTS on the N wall. One, to the Rev. John Row, is dated 1747, aedicular with attached Tuscan columns and anthemion finials on the pediment. The other has a well-lettered inscription commemorating George Davidson †1760 set in a pie-crust border and with an angel's head (the soul) at the top.

S of the church, several mid-C18 HEADSTONES, vigorously carved with shields, mantling angels' heads and reminders of death. – Also a grander GRAVE-SLAB, probably the top of a table stone, to James Black †1750, with a high-relief angel of the Resurrection attempting to bestir the mantled helmet which surmounts its coat of arms.

LIFF

3030

Described in 1884* as 'a small straggling hamlet', Liff has become a respectably sized village with the erection of late C20 and early C21 housing filling in the earlier L-plan formed by Church Road and East Road to form a rectangular development.

LIFF CHURCH, Church Road. Originally Liff and Benvie Parish Church. Crowstep-gabled Tudor Gothic box with an E steeple, by *W. M. Mackenzie*, 1838–9. Identically treated N and S sides, with tall mullioned-and-transomed two-light windows under hoodmoulds. In the W gable, a pair of windows of the same design but without hoodmoulds and surmounted by a round opening. At the church's E end, a pair of doors under gallery windows, all hoodmoulded; headstops at the doors. These flank the steeple. Tower of three stages, the first containing the entrance, the second a tall two-light window, the hoodmoulds of both with headstops; at the third stage, a hoodmoulded belfry opening in each face. The wall-head battlement's stepped merlons support pinnacles at the corners. These are tied by flying buttresses to the stone spire; at each of its faces, a lucarne. Beside the entrance, a badly weathered late medieval octagonal FONT BOWL.

Inside, on the N wall of the vestibule under the tower, the PLASTER CAST of a stone of the earlier C10, carved with the relief of an aged horse plodding uphill, its elderly rider quaffing from a drinking horn whose tip is modelled as a bird's head. The original was unearthed at Bullion (Dundee) in 1934 and is now in the National Museum of Scotland. – On the vestibule's S wall, a floral-bordered GRAVE-SLAB, probably the top of a table stone, of 1742 and commemorating James Cock, weaver in Locheye [Lochee] and progenitor of the Cox family

* By *The Ordnance Gazetteer of Scotland*, ed. Francis H. Groome, iv (1884), 177.

of linen and jute manufacturers, and his wife, Isobel Doig; it was brought here from the churchyard at Invergowrie (Perth and Kinross) in 1914. At the centre, framed by mantling which spills down from a helmet, is a tablet bearing their initials and the date, all this flanked by dowsed torches. At the top of the slab, an angel's head (the soul) under a crown flanked by a pair of weavers' shuttles set between angelic trumpeters; at the base, reminders of death and, in the centre, a boy who holds a sword and scales, emblems of Justice.

In the church itself, a Tudor-Gothic ventilator-rose on the ceiling. – U-plan GALLERY carried on octagonal pillars. Square panels at its front whose top displays shields bearing the coats of arms of the Lords Gray and the Duncans of Camperdown; figures of angels at the centre and ends. – Boxy PEWS of 1839, the front ones hinged so that they can be converted into communion pews surrounding long tables. – Sanctuary enclosure at the W end, its RAILING designed by *Ian Dalgetty*, 1932. In it, a COMMUNION TABLE (by *Thomas Justice & Sons Ltd*, 1922) fronting the late C19 PULPIT which is backed by the stencilled pipes of the ORGAN (by *Alexander Young & Son*, 1880). – STAINED GLASS. Four-light W window (Moses; Our Lord; St John the Evangelist; St Paul), Glasgow-style by *J. & W. Guthrie*, 1893.

GRAVEYARD surrounding the church. At the NE corner, a HEARSE HOUSE built in 1875–6. In its E gable to the road, a large round-headed entrance for the parish hearse. Above, a decorative date panel (inscribed 1876) and a wrought-iron foliage finial. – At the graveyard's E end, WAR MEMORIAL of 1920, a fluted Doric column with rosetted necking, surmounted by a panelled and ball-finialled sundial-like square block. – N of the church's W end, the BURIAL ENCLOSURE of the Watts and Websters of Balruddery. Its E side is formed by the large MONUMENT to Katherine Webster, wife of Isaac Watt of Logie, designed by *David Neave* in 1809. Portico-like ashlar aedicule with Roman Doric columns *in antis* framing the inscription tablet under a frieze carved with swagged drapery. On top of the monument, a reeded panel with an upside-down fan at the centre; urn finial now on the ground. – W of the church, the crisply carved HEADSTONE erected in 1785 by George Langlands and Margaret Finn to nine of their children, the E face's roundel carved with a mantled shield bearing a weaver's shuttle; angel's head (the soul) at the top, emblems of death at the base. – Some other C18 HEADSTONES behind, including one (to James Wightone, shoemaker, †1725) with a crowned last and another with a shuttle. – Just to the N, weathered C17 GRAVE-SLABS carved with reminders of mortality.

LIFF PRIMARY SCHOOL, East Road. Two buildings, the first (originally the parish school) by *David Neave*, 1828. Quite simple, with a two-storey piend-roofed S-facing school house and, forming a NW wing, the single-storey schoolroom, originally of three bays but extended N by *James Salmond*, 1873. The second building, to the N, is by *James H. Langlands*, 1897–8.

Walls of hammer-dressed rubble, the roof broad-eaved and bargeboarded. Rear additions in a tamer harled version of the original manner, *c.* 2000.

ROYAL DUNDEE LIFF HOSPITAL, 0.9 km. E. Originally Dundee Royal Asylum (a replacement for the Asylum of 1818–20 in the centre of Dundee), designed by *Edward & Robertson* and built in 1877–82 to house 400 patients but mostly converted to housing at the beginning of the C21. The wards were contained in a large building, its style thrifty but not unfriendly Baronial, the walling of khaki-coloured sandstone rubble. This is predominantly two-storey and U-plan but with the corners clasped by projecting pavilions and, in the N inner angles, four-storey crowstep-gabled towers with conical-roofed round corner turrets. The 183 m.-long S range's S front is punctuated by two-storey-and-attic gabled projections fronted by bay windows under two-light openings surmounted by pediments broken by finialled pedestals. This range's three-storey-and-attic advanced centrepiece is formed by a broad bay-windowed and balustraded middle flanked by turreted gables. In the N pavilions' S inner angles, conical-roofed low towers and, at their N corners, fat round turrets, also with conical roofs. Single-storey wings run N from these pavilions and return E and W to suggest a N range. In the space between, a detached two-storey administration block, dated 1880, its advanced and gabled centrepiece with rounded corners, the Roman Doric pilastered and corniced entrance surmounted by a panel carved with the coat of arms of the Burgh (later, City) of Dundee. In the courtyard between this block and the main building, garages of *c.* 2005. – Down the steep hillside S of the main building, a wooden PAVILION of *c.* 1900, with touches of half-timbering at the gables. – Further S, GOWRIE HOUSE, a large but low-key red sandstone Baronial villa, by *T. S. Robertson*, 1898–1901, designed as an asylum for private patients. – At the entrance to the hospital's drive from the NE, a solid-looking Baronial single-storey LODGE of *c.* 1880. – Just to its W, an early C20 SHELTER, with wooden walls and a tree-trunk veranda.

LOSSIE HALL, 0.6 km. NE. Single-storey-and-attic Arts and Crafts villa, by *Thoms & Wilkie*, 1903. Harled walls under high slated roofs. Asymmetrical W front, its l. section M-roofed with a large canted bay window to the r. of the entrance whose door is set in a curvaceously moulded surround of C17 inspiration. Another big bay window at the S gable.

FORT, BROCH AND SOUTERRAIN, Hurly Hawkin, 0.1 km. W. Steep-sided roughly triangular promontory whose N end has been cut off, probably in the late first millennium B.C., by a rampart behind a pair of ditches. The inner ditch was later filled in and, perhaps in the early centuries of the first millennium A.D., a large stone-walled curved souterrain, *c.* 2.1 m. wide, formed here. Also in the early centuries of the first millennium but probably a little before the formation of the souterrain the fort's rampart was overlaid by the construction of a broch of *c.* 12 m. diameter, its massive wall *c.* 5.2 m. thick and incorporating chambers and possibly a stair. Perhaps originally *c.* 4 m. high, the broch now rises to only 1 m. Inside was a central hearth. A series of post-holes suggest that it was ringed by lean-to structures.

HOUSE OF GRAY. *See* p. 533.

LINTRATHEN *see* BRIDGEND OF LINTRATHEN

7060

LOGIE

Remains of the former parish church in a roughly circular graveyard beside the River North Esk, the former Logie Pert Free Church on higher ground to the S.

LOGIE PARISH CHURCH. Medieval church which was abandoned after the union of the parish with Pert in 1647 and converted to a mausoleum for the Carnegies and Macpherson Grants of Craigo in 1857. It is now a short rubble-walled roofless rectangle. The W gable containing the entrance is wholly Victorian Gothic. On it a pair of shields, the l. bearing the arms of the Carnegies of Craigo, the r. the arms of the Macpherson Grants who succeeded to the estate in 1856. Some medieval work survives in the S wall. Towards its W end, a pair of narrow lancets, perhaps C13. Roughly in its centre, a round-headed chamfered doorway, probably an insertion of the C15 or C16, and, at the E end, a contemporary three-light window in a rectangular surround, its intersecting dummy tracery perhaps an embellishment of 1857. In the E gable, a stepped arrangement of three narrow lancets, probably C13. (Inside, on the S wall, mutilated remains of two medieval PISCINAS. Also, a SACRAMENT HOUSE, perhaps of *c.* 1500, the door set in an ogee-arch with a fleur-de-lis finial flanked by a pair of circlets.)

GRAVEYARD. Most of the HEADSTONES are Victorian but just S of the church's W end is one erected to Robert Findlay †1742, the curvaceously topped W face decorated with reminders of death, the E with a pair of angels' heads above a shield and a third head poking out of the swan-neck pediment. – Beside it, John Miln †1730, carved in high relief with flaming torches which flank a mantled shield bearing the tools of a wright and the date 1748. – Also of 1748 and similar, the stone now inscribed to William Wilson to the N but its shield bears a weaver's shuttle.

LOGIE PERT FREE CHURCH, Denhead, 1 km. S. Secularized and altered. Cheaply detailed Romanesque rectangle of 1844, the walling of cherry-cock-pointed rubble. Pyramidal-roofed birdcage bellcote added in 1851.

SCHOOL, 0.6 km. W. Now a house. Single-storey school of *c.* 1800, the clay-built walls rendered and covered with a piended roof, its Welsh slates and off-centre brick chimney dating probably from late C19 alterations. S front of six bays.

At the E end, a corrugated iron bellcote-topped porch and vestry added *c.* 1930 when this became a United Free Church.

CRAIGO, 1.8 km. W. The mansion house, built in 1767 and enlarged in 1790, was demolished in 1967. There survive the mid-C19 STABLES, a broad-eaved U-plan of offices. In the centre, a free-standing square tower, gently Italianate in manner, also with broad eaves and a shallow pyramidal roof. The top stage is a doocot, with a single tier of round-headed pigeon entries. – Ashlar-faced LODGE at the W end of the drive, also mid-C19 but in a gabled and bay-windowed Jacobean manner.

LOGIE HOUSE

3050

2.1 km. S of Kirriemuir

Laird's house built for John Wishart of Logie *c.* 1540 but extended and remodelled in the late C17 and again in the early C18 and subsequently.

The walling is all harled and with cement dressings. C16 oblong main block of three storeys and an attic, a bowed stair-tower projecting at the NE corner, its NW segment pierced by a shot-hole. Regularly windowed N elevation, probably recast in 1691 (the date, together with a Latin motto, on one lintel). The S front's E bay is slightly recessed. In it, three-light windows, perhaps Late Georgian. Projecting from the W end is a lower three-storey wing, perhaps a late C17 addition. Roll-and-hollow-moulded door in its E side. At this wing's S gable, a large stepped chimney-breast surmounted by an ashlar chimney; at the top of the breast a PANEL carved by *Bruce Walker* in the early C21 with a relief of birds among grapes. The main block's W gable was dressed up in the early C18 like a piece of stage scenery facing the main approach. Symmetrical façade of three bays, the centre occupied by a pilaster-like chimney-breast. Sill course joining the first-floor windows, their lintels inscribed with the date 1722 and the initials of David Kinloch of Logie and Isobel Oliphant, his wife. Corbel course under the gable-head to give a pedimental effect, the top of the chimney-breast panelled with dummy windows.

Service courtyard behind the house, the unassuming one- and two-storey ranges C18 and C19, the E with catslide-roofed dormers. C19 N range, a turret over its W end. Its elliptical-arched entrance to the courtyard was inserted as part of *Nicholas Groves-Raines*'s alterations of *c.* 2000. Inside the courtyard, C19 verandas along the E, W and S sides. The line of the E range is continued N by a screen wall on which has been placed a dormerhead bearing the date 1688.

INTERIOR. The ground and first floors of the SW wing now contain a stair formed *c.* 2000. On the N side, a ground-floor door in a chamfered surround to a tunnel-vaulted passage along the S side of the C16 main block. On the passage's N side, a tunnel-vaulted store (now dining room). At the E end of the passage, a door and small window into the kitchen. This is covered by an elliptical-arched tunnel vault. Part of the arch of its E fireplace is exposed. Off the kitchen's NE corner, the C16 stair to the floors above, its lower flight straight before it continues as a turnpike.

The whole first floor of the main block is occupied by the drawing room formed *c.* 2000 from three rooms, the E two perhaps taking the place of a C16 hall, the W of an inner chamber. Its character is now predominantly of mid-C18 inspiration with (plaster) panelled walls and a ceiling enriched with fruiting foliage in a Rococo manner. Stone W chimneypiece, also carved with reliefs of fruiting foliage but in early C17 style. The W end of the room, divided off by a broad rectangular archway, contains a wooden chimneypiece of early C18 derivation, the overmantel with a broken pediment. From this room's SW corner, a secondary stair, perhaps formed in the late C17, to the second floor. On this floor, in the SW wing, a room with early C18 panelling and a moulded stone chimneypiece, its wooden frieze and mantelshelf early C19 additions.

E of the house, an ornamental LOCH fed from the Gairie Burn by an artificial WATERFALL, its top step inscribed with the initials IC (or IG) and MD and the date 1666, presumably that of its construction.

Rubble-built two-storey STABLES of the early or mid C19 N of the house. W front with a parapeted three-bay centrepiece. In each of the broad and gabled end bays, an elliptical ground-floor carriage entrance and, above, a loft door under a roundel. – N of the stables, the GARDEN, its long rubble-built N wall perhaps of *c.* 1800.

6060

LOGIE PERT

Handful of houses around the former parish church.

LOGIE PERT PARISH CHURCH. Now housing. Rubble-walled high box built in 1840. On the W gable, a cast-iron birdcage bellcote, its roof of ogee profile. Segmental-arched tall windows and, in the gables, rectangular doors; large dummy oculus in the head of the W gable. Vestry at the centre of the N side.

LOGIE PERT FREE CHURCH. *See* Logie.

GALLERY HOUSE. *See* p. 492.

4040

LOUR HOUSE

3.2 km. NE of Inverarity

Unpretentious rubble-walled three-storey laird's house which has developed from the C16. The earliest part seems to be the two-bay S section of the W-facing main block. This has been remodelled and extended N by a further three bays, the addition's W windows more widely spaced than those of the earlier part. Likely although approximate dates of 1688 and 1699 for this enlargement are provided by the lintels of two roll-and-hollow moulded ground-floor windows. Perhaps of the early or mid C18 is the Venetian door at the centre of the front. In a further alteration, of the early C19, the front's two r. first-floor windows were enlarged and additions built at the back.

Quadrangular STEADING AND STABLES immediately NW, mostly of the C18 but altered and enlarged in the C19. Over the S side of the entrance archway has been placed a weathered heraldic stone bearing the initials AB and MS (for Alexander Bruce of Kincaldrum and his wife) and the date 1738; it came from the graveyard of the demolished Meathie Church which stood 1.2 km. W.

C17 DOOCOT 0.2 km. W of the house. Rubble-built, of lectern type, with a rat course which steps down at the gable and with skewputts carved as human heads. – TEMPLE on Hill of Lour, 0.6 km. W, a round lookout tower of the C18, the walling also of rubble. It was given a wall-head battlement in the earlier C19.

LUNAN

6050

Just the Parish Church standing on the edge of the grounds of Lunan House and its steading.

LUNAN PARISH CHURCH. Disused. Red sandstone oblong designed and built by *Robert Dalgarno* in 1844. On the W gable a birdcage bellcote (now without its bell) with a round-headed arch in each face and a shallow pyramidal roof. High up in this gable, a quatrefoil dummy opening above the gabled W porch, its windows round-headed and hoodmoulded. In the church's S side, four windows, also round-headed and hoodmoulded, and, in the centre, a grey stone TABLET, probably C17 or C18, bearing the relief of two angels holding a panel inscribed with initials.

At the graveyard's entrance, corniced ashlar GATEPIERS, probably contemporary with the church.

BRIDGE over the Lunan Water, S of Lunan Parish Church. Erected in the C18 and rubble-built. Pair of segmental arches and, in the centre of each side, a sloping-topped triangular cutwater.

LUNAN HOUSE. Two-storey piend-roofed laird's house built in 1825, the walls of cherry-cock-pointed rubble. Parapeted S front of three bays with giant piers at the outer corners; at the centre, a Tuscan-columned portico under a three-light window. Rear wing in the same manner added in 1850. Late C20 extension to the NE built for the house's present use as a care home.

LODGE of the earlier C19 at the W end of the short drive. Single-storey and rubble-built, the piended roof with broad eaves, the windows hoodmoulded. – LUNAN HOME FARM to the E, the steading's S range mid-C19, its centre tower topped by a tall slated spire with bellcast eaves.

DOOCOT, Nether Dysart, 1.6 km. NE. Harled lectern doocot with a single rat course, probably dating from the C17.
RED CASTLE. *See* p. 658.

4050

LUNANHEAD

Small village, with some C19 cottages along the B9134, the rest of the housing C20.

ST MARGARET'S CHURCH (Episcopal). By *William L. McLean*, 1906–7. Humble rubble-walled Gothic in the manner of forty or fifty years earlier. Nave and small N chancel; bellcote on the S gable. – STAINED GLASS N window (the Crucifixion) by *A.O. Hemming & Co.*, 1913.

CARSE GRAY. *See* p. 422.
PITSCANDLY HOUSE. *See* p. 657.
RESTENNETH PRIORY. *See* p. 660.

2030

LUNDIE

Rural hamlet, the houses mostly C19, standing E of the church.

LUNDIE CHURCH. Probably dating from the C12 but remodelled in the 1780s and 1840s, the nave is an oblong of broached and squared masonry. In the S wall symmetrically disposed doors (the W now covered by a broad-eaved gabled porch of the late C19) and windows, the openings all pointed. The window margins are chamfered up to the block imposts which support the springing of the moulded arch-heads. A stepped buttress against the centre of the W end whose gable-head is intaken. A chimney of the 1840s rises against the centre of the N wall. To its E, a round-headed window, probably of the C12. On the E gable, a birdcage bellcote surmounted by a weathercock, perhaps of the 1780s.

Built against the church's E end in place of the former chancel is the MAUSOLEUM of the Duncans of Lundie, erected in 1787–9 to a design by *Robert Mylne* and converted to a vestry in 1892. It is square, the walls of droved ashlar, and finished with a cornice and blocking course. In each exposed side, a large round-headed recess, the S wall's serving as an overarch for the pilastered and fanlit entrance. The roof is a stone saucer dome topped by a plug-like drum finial.

The church's interior was recast in 1892 by *T. S. Robertson* who lined the walls and ceiling with pine boarding. The focus is on the COMMUNION TABLE at the E end with the PULPIT to its N, both of 1892. In front of the pulpit, a circular stone FONT, perhaps contemporary. – STAINED GLASS window (St John the Evangelist) in the S wall of the 'chancel', made by *Morris & Co.*, 1897, from a design by *Edward Burne-Jones* first used for a window in the Albion Congregational Church at Aston-under-Lyme (Lancashire) two years before. – On the N wall, a carved stone FRAGMENT. It has been the head of a crocketed arch with stumpy pinnacles at the centre and ends. It seems to be C15 or early C16 work and perhaps part of a sacrament house.

GRAVEYARD. Fair number of C18 HEADSTONES. S of the church one erected in 1730 by Colin Crookshank and Elizabeth Gellatly to their children, the swan-neck pediment containing the high relief of a cow and calf. – To its W, the headstone of 1759 erected for the children of Donald Richie, tailor, and Isabel Gibbins, its carved decoration crude but vigorous and exceptionally well preserved. The top of the E face is carved in high relief with a depiction of Abraham about to sacrifice Isaac, the top of the W with Adam and Eve and the Serpent above a shield bearing a tailor's shears and iron; below, emblems of death.

LUNDIE MILL, E end of the hamlet. Rubble-walled mill built in 1837. Four-storey main block at the W. Two-storey E wing with a couple of segmental-arched cart entrances and low first-floor windows. Brutally but effectively converted to housing in the late C20.

LUNDIE CASTLE

5060

3.6 km. W of Edzell

Late C19 mansion house, its architecture an earthbound Victorian version of the Late Georgian castle style. It is of two storeys, the walling of coursed rubble under a corbelled ashlar battlement. At the corners of the SE front, round towers, their conical roofs set back behind the battlements, and at the W corner a square tower, its roof a steep pyramid, all these of the same two-storey height as the main block. Three-storey square tower over the house's entrance at the l. end of the NE elevation. In the principal rooms, Neo-Jacobean oak panelling and plaster ceilings.

WALLED GARDEN to the S, with a lean-to glasshouse range along the N side, its centrepiece taller and dome-topped.

MAINS CASTLE *see* DUNDEE: ARDLER

MARYTON

6050

Isolated former church of a rural parish, its Free Church competitor some way apart.

MARYTON FREE CHURCH, Burnhead, 2.2 km. NW. Now housing (THE KIRK). By *David Bryce*, 1857. Buttressed oblong built of squared red sandstone rubble, originally with lancet windows in the side walls. Hoodmoulded tall window of three lights in the E gable. In the W gable, a pair of low bipartite windows under a hoodmoulded large circular light. NW tower of two stages, the lower with a round opening in the W face and a bipartite window in the N; circular windows at the upper stage. Pyramidal slated roof. The church was rather altered in its late C20 conversion to a house when various outshots were added.

MARYTON PARISH CHURCH. Now housing. Oblong Gothic kirk of 1791–2, the walls of red sandstone rubble. On the W gable, a bellcote with round-headed side panels and corner pilasters; it is surmounted by a stepped base on which stands an elegant elongated urn finial. In the gable, a round-headed door (now window) under a pointed gallery window with a quatrefoil dummy opening above. S side of four bays, the outer containing doors, the W round-headed, the E broader and elliptical-arched, under pointed window heads which light the galleries. Stone Y-tracery in the central windows. At the E gable a pair of tall and narrow pointed windows flank a shorter opening, also pointed, with a small pointed light above. Late C20 rectangular windows were punched through the originally windowless N side on the church's conversion to a house.

GRAVEYARD. E of the church, C18 and C19 HEADSTONES, some of the earlier with emblems of death and/or angels' heads (souls). Quite far E, the stone of 1748 to James Orr, the curved top of the W face carved with a pair of full-length angel trumpeters. In the top of the E face, an angel's head and, in the centre, a panel with a helmed and mantled coat of arms above the figure of a recumbent corpse; reminders of mortality at the base.

OLD MONTROSE, 1.5 km. NW. Rambling small mansion house of *c.* 1845 in a crowstep-gabled Scots manorial style. – To the N, a large brick-walled GARDEN, probably contemporary with the house, its N wall mostly missing. – At the end of the N drive, cone-topped circular GATEPIERS, their masonry V-jointed. They may be late C17.

The STEADING to the W has been mostly rebuilt in the later C20 but the two-storey W range of 1831 survives. It contains cartsheds with elliptical-arched entrances. At the NE corner, a low round-headed gateway in a pedimental gable above which rises a three-stage octagonal tower, its roof surmounted by a round cupola with a ball-finialled dome, its weathervane perforated with the date 1771.

5050

MELGUND CASTLE

2.5 km. E of Aberlemno

Dignified and without ostentation, the large mid-C16 rubble-walled house built for Marion Ogilvy, *maîtresse en titre* of Cardinal David Beaton, Archbishop of St Andrews and Chancellor of Scotland.

The estate of Melgund (then, North Melgund), acquired by Beaton in 1542, was the next year settled by him on Marion Ogilvy in life rent and their eldest son, David Beaton, in fee. Construction of the house was under way in 1543 and it was presumably habitable by 1545 when a charter was signed here. Although the stonework provides clear evidence that it was built in a single phase of work, the building is divided visually and, to a large extent functionally, into two parts, a long hall block (perhaps intended for David Beaton's occupation) and a W tower (perhaps for Marion Ogilvy), the division emphasized by *Benjamin Tindall*'s 1990s restoration and harling of the tower whilst leaving the hall block roofless and with its masonry of local red sandstone exposed.

The tower is a four-storey-and-attic L, the main block *c.* 11 m. by 9.1 m., the NE jamb *c.* 4.6 m. by 4.3 m., and with a narrow 4 m.-long projection in the W inner angle. Small slit windows to the main block's ground floor, lighting wall chambers at the W end of the S side. At the upper floors are rectangular windows with chamfered jambs, the largest at the first floor to denote its status, this emphasized by the coats of arms of Marion Ogilvy on the lintel of the W window and of David Beaton on the lintel of the S. Shot-holes at the W corners of the ground and first floor. Quite comfortably sized windows to the jamb, small lights at the inner angle's projection. All round the wall-heads continuous corbelling fronted by individual moulded corbels; discreet angle-rounds at the corners. The battlement above was provided in the 1990s restoration, as were the crowstep-gabled caphouse over the jamb and the roof of the main block. In front of the jamb's E face, a stone porch in the position of an earlier vestibule whose foundations were uncovered in an excavation of the 1990s.

The 21 m.-long hall block has been of two storeys and an attic and double-pile, the S part of the same width as the tower, the narrower N part the width of the jamb and continuing the line of its N wall; a round tower of *c.* 3.6 m. diameter at the NE corner. The S wall, E gable and NE tower still stand to the wall-head and the central internal E–W spine wall survives to about the same height but the N part, except for an E stair and fragment of the E end of the N wall, has been demolished. Slit windows and one larger (kitchen) opening at the ground-floor of the S part's S side and end. E doorway to the N part. Wide-mouthed gunloops at the ground-floor of the NE tower. Large first-floor windows in the centre and E end of the S wall and others in the E gable and the NW segment of the NE tower whose other first-floor openings are slits. To the l. of the central S window is a pair of smaller horizontally proportioned and high-set windows, their lintels at a level with that of the central window. The wall-head's missing battlement has been supported by heavily moulded individual corbels under a moulded cornice. In the spine (present N) wall's exposed N face, doorways and, at the first floor, fireplaces and the stumps of cross-walls.

INTERIOR. The principal entrance, in the E face of the tower's jamb, opens onto a lobby at the foot of the jamb's stair. From the lobby, a short passage in the inner angle's projection. In the S side of the passage, a couple of cupboards, the larger's surround checked for doors. Off this passage is a pair of tunnel-vaulted cellars which occupy the ground-floor of the main block. Cupboard in the E cellar's N wall. The corners of the W cellar are hollowed out to form small chambers, their outer sides pierced by gunloops. The main stair in the tower's NE jamb is a comfortable turnpike, the soffit of one of its treads carved with the coat of arms and initials of Marion Ogilvy. Two doors at the first floor. The lintel of the E (into the tower's main block) bears the Ogilvy coat of arms, the W (into the hall block) the arms of Beaton.

The tower's first-floor Hall was originally self-contained but a doorway was inserted in its SE corner, perhaps in the C17, to provide direct access to the house's hall block. In the N wall adjoining the entrance from the stair and sharing its l. jamb, is a door into a garderobe in the projection of the tower's inner angle. At the garderobe's W end, a door into a second chamber, perhaps a charter room. The Hall's W corners, like those of the cellar below, contain chambers, each with gunloops in the outer faces (the N gunloop later enlarged to form a window). Large windows in the W and S walls, their ingoes equipped with stone seats. Also in the W side and near its S end, the Hall's fireplace, quite small and with a simply moulded rectangular surround. Each of the upper floors of the tower contained originally a single room covered with a beamed ceiling and provided with a fireplace and one or two decent-sized windows.

E of the tower, the hall block. Its N part (now demolished) contained a vaulted ground-floor passage which stretched from the tower's jamb to a second stair at this block's E end. Off the S side of the passage and entered from it have been five tunnel-vaulted rooms, the vaults over the three E rooms now fallen and their supporting cross-walls reduced to stubs. Four of these rooms were cellars. The W was the house's kitchen, its W fireplace 3.7 m. wide. Remains of a circular oven in the wall to the l. of the fireplace. There has been a slop drain under the S window.

The principal access to the hall block's first floor was from the stair in the tower's NE jamb. Occupying the W three-fifths of the block's S part is the HALL. Pair of horizontal windows in the S wall and placed high, probably to allow room for a buffet below. At this wall's E end and lighting the dais end of the Hall, a larger and vertically proportioned window. In the N wall and r. of centre is the fireplace, its jambs with bundle-shafted columns, the head elliptically arched. The top of the chimney-breast is finished with a moulded stone cornice. Joist holes show that the room has been covered by a beamed wooden ceiling. Off the dais end of the Hall, a smaller but still sizeable inner chamber lit by windows in the S and E walls. The fireplace has been positioned in the centre of the W wall. Off the room's NE corner, a door to the adjacent secondary stair of the house, a turnpike which has risen from the ground floor to the hall block's attic.

On the evidence of stubs of walling and fireplace recesses it can be deduced that the hall block's N part contained three first-floor rooms, the E entered from the inner chamber, the centre room from the hall. The W room had no direct communication with the S part of the hall block and was entered from the principal stair. It may have been intended for a guest.

MEMUS

4050

Small village, the houses mostly C20.

MEMUS CHURCH. Originally Memus Free Church. Built in 1843 but remodelled by *Carver & Symon* in 1900. Rectangular-windowed box built of stugged and squared red sandstone ashlar. Dating from the alterations of 1900 is the treatment of the S gable with a corniced doorpiece set between giant pilasters supporting the segmental-pedimented bellcote.

Georgian survival two-storey MANSE of 1845 to the N, its prettily Gothic detailed wooden porch an embellishment of the later C19.

MENMUIR

5060

Hamlet composed of little more than the church, manse and school.

PARISH CHURCH. Disused. Tudor, by *David Smith*, 1842. Ashlar box; on the W gable, a rectangular bellcote with a spiky stone finial. Two-light Y-traceried and transomed four-centred arched windows. Part of the E half of the N wall incorporates the C17 burial vault of the Carnegys of Balnamoon. Elliptical arch under a moulded frame containing a heraldic panel, the owners of the impaled arms identified by the initials [S.A.]C. and D.G.B. (for Sir Alexander Carnegy and Dame Giles Blair, his wife) carved at its sides and bottom. On the S wall of the church, a large MONUMENT dated 1717, erected by Alexander and George Fairweather, James Don and Alexander Smith to the memory of their ancestors and to commemorate themselves, their wives, children and posterity. Above the inscription panel, an oval tablet containing four mongrammed cartouches; below the panel, emblems of death. The gabled surround has been renewed in cement but the stone angel's head at the apex looks original work. The inscription's lettering has been re-cut, perhaps in 1809 when mention of Thomas Don was added.

GRAVEYARD. S of the church, a fair number of C18 HEADSTONES carved with heraldry and/or reminders of death and angels' heads (souls), the earliest of this group dated 1714 and two-thirds buried. – Right at the S edge of the graveyard and half-buried on edge, a stone SLAB which may be late C17, crudely carved with a pair of trumpeting angels who flank an angel's head; below is a very dead corpse.

Two-storey MANSE to the S. Pink-harled L-plan, the N wing built in 1798–9, the S added in 1826.

SCHOOL. Built in 1907 and very plain.

3 FORT, Brown Caterthun, 3.2 km. NE. One of a pair of neighbouring hilltop forts, probably first occupied in the C5 B.C. Successive stages of development have surrounded the roughly oval site with approximately concentric rings of fortification. The earliest structure, enclosing an area of 2.3 ha., seems to have been a 4.5 m.-wide wall which still stands to a height of 1.3 m. This was constructed of boulders and cobbles and topped with turf into which was set, probably a little after its original erection, a wooden breastwork later detroyed by fire and replaced by a further turf topping. Nine entrances break the line of the wall and of the two terraces which front it, the upper terrace formerly surmounted by a wooden palisade. A second stage of development, probably also of the C5 B.C., saw the construction of a less regularly shaped outer rampart at a distance of between 15 m. and 40 m. from the earlier wall and its accompanying terraces, enclosing a total area of *c.* 6 ha. This rampart, 3.5 m. wide and now standing 0.8 m. high but originally much taller, was constructed of earth laced with timber. Some time in the C4 or C3 B.C. the fort's enclosed area was again increased and a new glacis-style outer rampart constructed. This is up to 3.5 m. wide at the base and now rising to only 0.6 m., a little less than half its likely original height; breaking the rampart are several entrances. Further defence is provided by an accompanying outer ditch cut in the rock of the hillside. An incomplete rampart and ditch further downhill to the SW may represent an earlier but abandoned intention to have these defences enclose a yet larger area. The fort's final stage of development took place after 350 B.C. Instead of yet further enlarging the area enclosed by the defences, this comprised the fortification of a very much smaller enclosure (only 0.4 ha. in extent) at the centre of the complex by the erection of a double palisade, the slots for its uprights set *c.* 1 m. apart, and accompanying ditch.

3 FORT, White Caterthun, 2.1 km NE. Hilltop fort, its defences begun probably in the C5 B.C. and all dating from before the end of the first millennium B.C. but the dating and chronology largely conjectural. The earliest work seems to have been the erection of a rampart, broken by at least nine entrances, which encloses an oval area of *c.* 5.8 ha. Outside but partly overlying this was later constructed a roughly concentric double rampart with a central ditch. About 25 m.–30 m. beyond the double rampart's NW segment are stretches of a ditch and outer bank, possibly an unfinished attempt to supplement the defences of

one or other rampart. At the fort's N end, a roughly oblong annexe, perhaps an addition of the late first millennium B.C. Inside the main enclosure, the flat top of the hill, also oval-shaped and *c.* 1 ha. in extent, has been surrounded in the probable last major phase of the fort's development by two massive stone walls, the inner timber-laced, *c.* 12 m. thick and still standing up to a height of 3 m., the outer *c.* 6 m. thick and containing in its NW segment a boulder incised with about 70 cup marks; neither is broken by any obvious entrance into the enclosure. The outer of these two walls is surrounded in turn by a ditch. Inside the enclosure, near its W end, a cistern cut in the rock.

BALNAMOON. *See* p. 348.

MIDDLETON *5040*

1 km. SW of Friockheim

Harled laird's house, perhaps of late C17 origin, remodelled and enlarged by *David Mackenzie* in the early 1840s, the earlier work with dressings of grey sandstone, the later dressings of red stone. The three-storey main block seems to be late C17 or early C18. Front of five bays, the windows with chamfered margins, tall at the first floor to denote a *piano nobile* and small at the intermediate bays of the second. The mid-C19 remodelling added a heavy-jowelled ball-finialled Jacobean porch, strap-work tops to the intermediate bays' first-floor windows, a heraldic panel over the central opening, ball-and-spike-finialled gablet dormerheads containing blank shields over the second floor's end windows and a large cross-finialled gablet with a shield bearing the Gardyne device of a boar's head at the centre. Also of the 1840s is the wing containing a first-floor drawing room at the main block's S end, its broad W gable with a two-storey canted bay window. At the N end of the main block, a two-storey wing, probably of the later C18 but its W front remodelled in the 1840s with gablet dormerheads added above the first-floor windows. Projecting from the back of the main block, a pair of harled long single-storey wings of the late C17 or early C18 which enclose the N and S sides of a service court, its E end bounded by a screen wall, probably of the 1840s, surmounted by a birdcage bellcote. Built into the N wing's E gable is a worn triangular stone, probably an early C17 dormerhead, which bears the initials ES. – On the lawn in front of the house, a stone SUNDIAL in a sort of Tudor-classical manner. It bears the initials TG (for Thomas Gardyne of Middleton) and the date 1836. – E of the house, a rubble-walled GARDEN laid out by *George Henderson* in 1843. In the centre of its W side, a square single-storey PAVILION of the 1840s with quatrefoil windows in the sides and a stone-slabbed pyramidal roof.

NORTH LODGE at the end of the avenue on the main approach to the house. Piend-roofed single-storey, of the earlier C19, its gabled W portico with tree-trunk columns. – S of the house, the white-harled and broad-eaved GARDENER'S COTTAGE, also of the earlier C19 and single-storey, its windows round-headed, a bow at the centre of the E side. – At the end of the S drive, the harled mid-C19 SOUTH LODGE with wavy barge-boards and a W veranda, its columns with lotus-bud capitals.

4030

MONIFIETH

Small town, now a suburb of Dundee. It began as a village to the E of Monifieth (now St Rule's) Parish Church and, as late as the earlier C19, was said to have consisted of 'a number of turf huts, for they hardly deserve the name of houses, thatched and with small windows . . .' The establishment of industry, beginning in 1811 with the erection of the Monifieth Foundry and followed by a factory making carts and ploughs, a spinning mill and jute works, accompanied by the opening of the railway line to Dundee and Arbroath in 1839, brought about the village's redevelopment and expansion along the main street while the high ground to the N came to be occupied by villas looking S over the Tay to Fife. In 1895 Monifieth became a police burgh.

CHURCHES

HOLY TRINITY (Episcopal), Panmure Street. By *Mills & Shepherd*, 1909, and looking more like a bungalow than a church. Nave with a SW porch and NW vestry, chancel and NE sacristy, the walls harled, the broad-eaved roofs covered with red Rosemary tiles. At each bay of the nave, marked off by plain buttresses, is applied half-timbering and a rectangular window of three cusped lights. At the half-timbered W gable, a four-light rectangular window. Another rectangular window but of two lights in the S side of the chancel. In the E gable, three small lancets. Half-timbered and gabled porch.

Inside, an open wooden roof over the nave. Above the W vestibule a gallery containing the stencilled pipes of the ORGAN (formerly in St John's Episcopal Church at Forfar and rebuilt here in 1909 by *Allan Watson*). – Round-headed chancel arch, its oak SCREEN of simplified Gothic character erected *c.* 1950. – On the chancel's E wall, simple oak PANELLING of 1921. – Sub-Lorimerian oak COMMUNION RAILS made by the *Lord Roberts Memorial Workshops* in 1939. – Mid-C20 STAINED GLASS in the three lancet lights of the E gable (Our Lord flanked by St Peter and St John the Evangelist).

MONIFIETH FREE CHURCH. *See* Murroes.

MONIFIETH SOUTH CHURCH, Hill Street. Originally Monifieth South Free Church. By *James Maclaren*, 1871–2. A lumpy Gothic rectangle. Porch across the chunkily bellcoted S gable.

The conical-roofed SE tower was added in 1884. At the N end, plain Gothic transepts, by *Charles G. Soutar*, 1904.

Inside, the collar-braces of the nave roof are pierced by arcading. Pairs of pointed arches open into the transepts. Gothic fronted S gallery of 1884. Victorian PEWS. – At the N end, the PULPIT of 1872 and the ORGAN by *Allan Watson*, 1926. – STAINED GLASS. Behind the pulpit, two lights with flower-decorated panels and a roundel depicting a Dove, probably of the 1870s. – In the E side, a light (the Good Shepherd) of 1904, colourful but bad. – In the W wall, a window (Our Lord and disciples) of 1925.

PANMURE CHURCH, Panmure Street. Disused Economical Gothic, by *T. Lindsay Gray*, 1936. Nave and transepts, the walls harled and with dressings of glazed red brick. – At the rear, a simple stone-built HALL, by *James Foggie & Son*, 1898–9.

ST BRIDE (R.C.), Brook Street. By *Brocks Bros*, 1983–4. Of red brick under a stepped-pyramidal concrete-tiled roof topped by an octagonal spirelet. – STAINED GLASS. Very colourful designs incorporating Scenes of Local Life, by *Gail Donovan*.

ST RULE'S PARISH CHURCH, Church Street. Originally Monifieth Parish Church. By *Samuel Bell*, 1812–13. Gothic windowed box of squared and stugged masonry, a tower at the W end. At the S side wall, large hoodmoulded Y-traceried two-light windows linked by a sill course. At the N side and the gables, two tiers of windows, the W gable's hoodmoulded. The windows were subdivided by wooden mullions and tracery in *Edward & Robertson*'s alterations of 1873. The E gable is largely overlaid by a vestry which was heightened to two storeys in 1954. Built into the top of the gable, stones carved with coats of arms and initials reused here from the Durham of Pitkerro Aisle which had been added to the previous church *c.* 1630 and was demolished in 1812. Among them is a scroll-sided and foliage-finialled C17 dormerhead. On top of the church, ogee-roofed square ventilators.

W tower of three stages, with hoodmoulded pointed openings, the windows (dummies at the S face) with Y-tracery, the belfry openings overlaid by clock faces. Plain parapet. Inside, along the N, E and W walls, a semi-octagonal panel-fronted GALLERY of 1812–13 on Roman Doric columns. – PEWS of 1873. – PULPIT and COMMUNION TABLE of the earlier C20.

STAINED GLASS. In the S wall, a pair of large two-light windows flanking the pulpit, strongly coloured with large figures of Our Lord, St John the Evangelist, St John the Baptist and St Paul against a background of lush foliage, both by *Morris & Co.*, the r. window of 1877 and incorporating designs by *Edward Burne-Jones*, the l. of 1902. – Also by Morris & Co. and using designs of Burne-Jones, a window of 1901 at the W end (St Mary Magdalene at the Empty Tomb; the Risen Lord Appearing to St Mary Magdalene). – At the E end, another Morris & Co. window (of 1902) with Burne-Jones designs (Our Lord as the Sower; Our Lord Stilling the Waters). – In the N wall, a pair of Second World War memorial windows

(Angels Holding a Laurel Wreath over a Dead Knight; a Knight Entering Heaven), examples of Modernist realism, by *John M. Aiken*, 1948.

GRAVEYARD. S of the church, a fair number of C18 HEADSTONES carved with angels' heads (souls), some with downcast wings; a few of the stones also bear emblems of death and/or shields. The most endearing is the stone to the SE of the church erected in 1784 by Thomas Findlay, weaver, and Elizabeth Neish, his wife, to their children, the front carved with two angels' heads flanking a pair of shroud-wrapped babies; above, a weaver's shuttle.

S of the churchyard and looking like a church in its own right, a Gothic HALL, by *T. S. Robertson*, 1882, a flèche on the roof.

PUBLIC BUILDINGS

ASHLUDIE HOSPITAL, Victoria Street. Ashludie itself, a large but weakly detailed Jacobean villa by *James Maclaren*, was built in 1866 for Alexander Gordon, the owner of a flax-spinning mill in Arbroath. It was converted to a sanatorium by the Dundee City Architect, *James Thomson*, in 1916. Large but plain rear extension by the Dundee City Engineer, *George Baxter*, 1928. Big but low detached block to the S by Baxter's successor, *David B. McLay*, 1931. – W of the house, a WALLED GARDEN of the 1860s, its low S wall built of stone, the other walls higher and of brick. – LODGE at the entrance from Victoria Road, contemporary with the house and also Jacobean.

INVERTAY HOUSE, Maule Street. Originally Monifieth School and now council offices. Single-storey front block, by *James Maclaren*, 1878. Jacobean, with stepped and shaped gablets, some with bartizans. Rear extension of 1898, heightened to two storeys by *James Munro*, 1907, its shallow U-plan S front in the same manner as the original school.

MONIFIETH HIGH SCHOOL. *See* Broughty Ferry.

SOUTH CHURCH HALLS, High Street. The small hall at the E was built in 1858. Rectangular windows; gabled bellcote on the gable front. In 1909 *Maclaren, Sons & Soutar* added the W hall and linking porch. This hall's front is a broad gable containing tripleted but individually hoodmoulded pointed windows, the centre lights taller than the others. Depressed arch entrance to the porch.

WAR MEMORIAL, corner of Maule Street and Albert Street. By *Charles G. Soutar*, 1921, a battered pier of grey granite. A rectangular recess in the stepped top contains the bronze statue (now painted) of a knight.

DESCRIPTION

PANMURE STREET carries the A930 into the E end of the town. On the N, Panmure Church followed at a distance by Holy Trinity Episcopal Church (*see* Churches, above). TAY STREET leads off to the S. On its E side, the two-storey PANMURE HOTEL, by *Johnston & Baxter*, 1898, plain except for an ogee-roofed tower at the SW corner. In BROOK STREET running W from Tay Street, St Bride's R.C. Church (*see* Churches, above).

HIGH STREET continues the line of Panmure Street. On its N side, the South Church Halls (*see* Public Buildings, above). Then the road becomes MAULE STREET. On the S, Invertay House (*see* Public Buildings, above). On the N the hall of St Rule's Parish Church and in CHURCH STREET which runs off to the N, the church itself (*see* Churches, above). NE of the church, No. 1 MANSE PLACE, the former Monifieth Parish Manse, was built in 1829. Two storeys, with a piended platform roof. Ashlar front of three bays, the parapet higher and with anthemion-finialled corners at the slightly advanced centre from which projects a porch, the entrance through a screen of Doric columns *in antis*. Pediments at the centres of the rubble-built sides. HILL STREET runs across the N end of Church Street. On its W corner with Queen Street, Monifieth South Church (*see* Churches, above). Just to the E, on the W corner of Hill Street and VICTORIA STREET, SEAVIEW, a big and bare late C19 Jacobethan villa with a pyramidal-roofed low tower. Opposite, another sizeable villa, ASHLEA (No. 4 Victoria Street), by *J. Murray Robertson*, 1892. Red sandstone walls, the roofs covered with green slates. Corner turrets, their ogee-profiled roofs repeated in larger but flatter form at the centre. At the N end of Victoria Street, the Ashludie Hospital (*see* Public Buildings, above).

Ferry Road continues Maule Street to the W. GRANGE ROAD leads off to the N. On its W side, the white-harled MILTON INN (formerly GRANGE COTTAGE) which was given its present informal laird's house appearance by *Thoms & Wilkie* in 1912. Crowstepped gables and segmental dormerheads over the first-floor windows.

MONIKIE 5030

Just a handful of houses by the church. Larger development on the far side of the Monikie Reservoirs to the E.

MONIKIE PARISH CHURCH. Rubble-built kirk, by *David Neave*, 1811–12, but altered in the 1880s and again by *James H. Langlands*, 1901–3. The general shape is Neave's, a tall box, the W gable surmounted by a birdcage bellcote with Roman Doric piers and a weathercock; stone acorn finial on the E gable. Also by Neave are the tall hoodmoulded and pointed Y-traceried windows in the centre of the S side and the two round-headed doors* (now built-up) at the ends of that side. But in place of Neave's double tier of Tudor-arched windows in the second

* Although Neave's elevational drawing shows the doors as Tudor-arched.

and fifth bays there are now tall pointed lights, probably of 1901. Certainly of 1901 are the three tall pointed windows of the N wall and the depressed-arched window in the E gable. The broad pointed gallery window in the W gable may be of 1811–12 but the pointed door below is an insertion of 1901. NE vestry added in 1860.

The interior was remodelled by Langlands who changed the position of the pulpit from the centre of the S side to the E end, removed the N and E galleries and provided a new W gallery. Compartmented plaster ceiling of 1812 with small pendants at the intersection of the ribs and large Tudorish ventilators. The PULPIT of 1901 is high and backed by a display of Gothic PANELLING. In front, COMMUNION TABLE of 1913, the front carved with a relief of grapes. – The WEST GALLERY's slender fluted cast-iron columns and panelled front look like reused work of 1812. – Simple PEWS of 1901. On the N end of the E wall, a First World War memorial TABLET, its top displaying the Burning Bush emblem of the Church of Scotland, the bottom carved standards bearing the Royal Arms and Union flag. – At the wall's S end, a mid-C20 bronze Second World War memorial TABLET with a relief of saints and soldiers above the inscription. – STAINED GLASS E window (Our Lord and the Samaritan Woman, flanked by figures of St Peter and a female saint), 1901.

GRAVEYARD. At the NW corner, HEARSE HOUSE of 1795, rubble-built with a stone-slabbed roof. – There are a good number of late C18 and early C19 HEADSTONES with inscriptions in elegantly flowing lower-case lettering. – S and SW of the church is a remarkable collection of carved C18 headstones, all with shaped tops containing angels' heads (souls) and several displaying mantled coats of arms. Among them, to the SW of the church, a headstone erected in 1765 by Edward Gibson to commemorate his children, the carving on the front including the relief of a weaver. – S of this, a stone of 1778 put up by William Webster to his wife, Mathilda Clark, and his children, with a panel displaying weavers' tools. – Several stones stand in a line running S from the centre of the church. They begin with one to Margaret Webster †1744, its top carved with emblems of death, the front with the high relief of a girl under a crown flanked by the heads of chubby-cheeked angels. – Then, an C18 stone to John Morgan, merchant in Dundee and tenant of Ballhill ('revised', presumably re-cut, in 1815), with a small relief of a half-length man with scales on the l. and a plough on the r. – S of this, a stone of 1778 to James Hog, with the figure of a weaver under an angel's head and crown. – Again to the S, Robert Wat †1733, with a strapwork cartouche bearing tailor's scissors and an iron. – Immediately W of this line, a GRAVE-SLAB to James Mude †1656, carved with a long inscription and an hourglass and grave-digger's tools. – A little to its E, another slab (to GA and RA), probably C18, a mantled and helmet-crested shield at the top and reminders of death at the bottom. – Just SE of the church, a

HEADSTONE dated 1775 to Henry Fairlie and his wife, Elizabeth Ramsay. On the front, the relief of a man and woman, each holding the hand of a child (a son and daughter respectively); above, a rather grand shield bearing a coat of arms.

To the E, the harled MANSE of 1794, enlarged to an L in 1827.

MONIKIE MEMORIAL HALL, 1.8 km. SW. By *James H. Langlands*, 1927. Broad and tall single-storey rubble-walled symmetrical edifice, covered by prominent piended slate roofs. Semicircular windows flank the entrance porch.

KIRKTON OF MONIKIE. Big rubble-built steading, probably of the mid C19. On the N side of the road, a single-storey cottage and stable range dated 1778. Built into its front wall, two triangular DORMERHEADS, the lower carved with weathered decoration, the upper bearing the date 1587 and the initials BE and DL (perhaps for David Lindsay of Monikie and his wife); they are fragments of the demolished Monikie Tower which stood 0.23 km. N of the Parish Church.

CAMUS' CROSS, 0.9 km. S. On a path through the woodland of Camustane Hill, a free-standing stone cross of the C10. It has been formed from a rough stone slab, the cross carved with notches at the intersections of the arms and shaft. Weathered carving on the faces and narrow sides. The W face is the more worn. It is divided into three panels. The top panel, occupying the head and arms, displays a relief of Our Lord on the Cross; beneath his outstretched arms, a pair of beasts. On the upper of the shaft's two panels, the depiction of a *sagittarius*. The lowest panel bears scrolls of foliage. On the E face, another three panels in the same positions. The top contains a depiction of a beardless Christ worshipped by rather small angels. Each of the shaft's panels contains the figures of two ecclesiastics holding books, perhaps intended to portray the Evangelists. On the sides, foliage scrolls.

PANMURE TESTIMONIAL, 1.1 km. S. Poking above the trees of a wood covering the top of Downie Hill, the 32 m.-high monument designed by *John Henderson* and erected in 1839 by the tenantry of the Panmure estate in honour of their landlord, William Ramsay Maule, first Lord Panmure of Brechin and Navar, 'to perpetuate the memory of a nobleman who, through a long life, made the interests and comforts of his tenantry his sole and unwearied object'. The stonework is all of red sandstone polished ashlar, channelled at the corniced octagonal base which is covered with a very shallow roof and contained rooms for the reception of visitors. Projecting from the corners of the base are plinths on which stand the tall turret-like ends of flat-topped flying buttresses. Piercing each flying buttress, a huge round-headed arch. These buttresses join to the high octagonal base of a column, its circumference ringed by slender pilasters surmounted by blocky consoles under the column's cornice and parapet. Rising within the parapet, a low lantern ringed by more consoles under its cornice. Topping the lantern, an urn finial. *p. 616*

Panmure Testimonial.
Engraving, 1848

AFFLECK CASTLE AND HOUSE. *See* p. 289.
PANMURE HOUSE. *See* p. 654.

7050

MONTROSE

Sited at the mouth of the River South Esk which provides a natural harbour, Montrose was a royal burgh by the mid C12. Its medieval layout comprised a single main street (Castle Street and

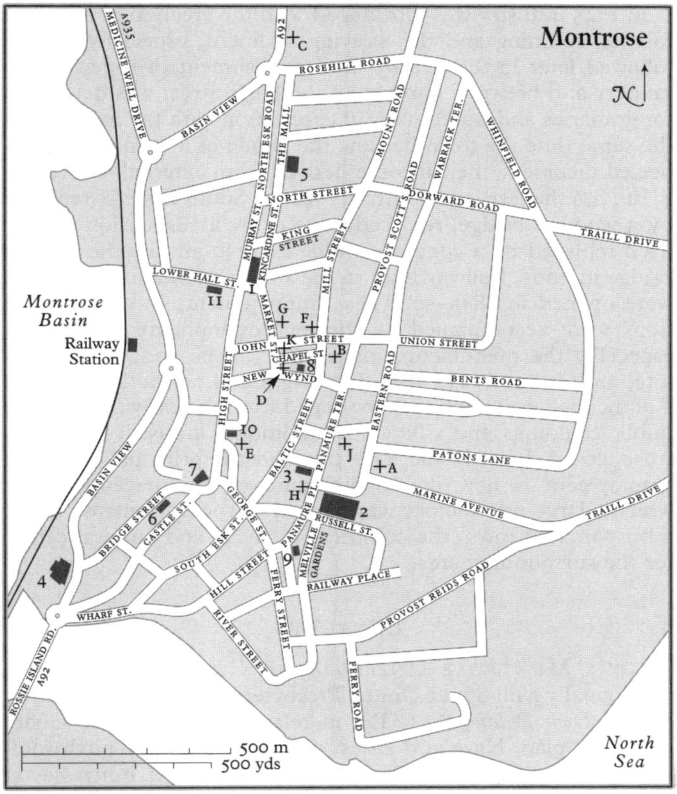

A	Chapel Works	1	Masonic Hall
B	Knox's Montrose United Free Church	2	Montrose Academy
C	Lochside Church	3	Montrose Museum
D	Methodist Church	4	Montrose Royal Infirmary
E	Old Parish Church	5	Montrose Swimming Pool
F	St John	6	Post Office
G	St Margaret (R.C.)	7	Public Library
H	St Mary (Episcopal)	8	Registration Office
J	St Mary and St Peter (Episcopal)	9	Town Hall
K	United Association Church	10	Town House
		11	YMCA

High Street) running N from the shore and with the burgh church about halfway along it. By the the late C17 Montrose was described* as 'a very handsome, well-built toune', the inhabitants including 'mightie fyne burgesses and delicat painfull merchants', its prosperity based on local trade and the export of salmon caught in large quantities in the Rivers South and North Esk.

* By John Ochterlony of the Guynd, quoted in Walter Macfarlane, *Geographical Collections*, ed. Arthur Mitchell, ii (Scottish History Society, 1907), 41–2.

In 1745 industry was introduced with the erection of a factory for flax spinning and the weaving of linens, especially canvas, followed later in the C18 by the establishment of ropeworks, a tannery and brewery. Land SE of the High Street was developed for granaries and warehouses in connection with the harbour. At the same time the town became the abode of a number of well-heeled incomers, their income derived from external sources.

In 1796 the ferry to Montrose over the South Esk was replaced by a wooden bridge, replaced in 1839 by a suspension bridge, itself replaced by a concrete bridge in 1930 and by the present bridge in 2005. Railway lines to the S of Scotland and Aberdeen were opened in 1848–50. These improvements in communications were accompanied by further development of industry, especially the manufacture of textiles (linens and, in the C20, jute) and, from the late C19, distilling. Land on the Links to the E of the medieval town was developed from the early C19 for new public buildings and villas. The traditional industries of Montrose closed down in the later C20 and the principal source of employment is now the manufacture of pharmaceuticals for which a large new factory was opened in 1992. Montrose is still a busy market town, the commercial, social and cultural centre for the surrounding area.

CHURCHES

KNOX'S MONTROSE UNITED FREE CHURCH, Mill Street. Originally Mill Street United Presbyterian Church. Gothic, by *John Dick Peddie*, 1851. Tall in relation to its almost square ground plan. Nave and aisles, each with a double-pitch roof. Two-storey front of buff-coloured ashlar. Angle buttresses at the outer corners. Flanking the nave gable are buttresses topped by octagonal pinnacles. In the front gable of each aisle, a door under a window, both hoodmoulded. At the lower storey of the nave's gable, a pair of round windows under a large window of three lancet lights in a stepped arrangement, the hoodmould's label stops now missing. On the N side of the church, a low HALL added by *John Sim* in 1885.

The interior is a rich Victorian combination of pitch-pine woodwork and colourful stained glass. Dividing the aisles from the nave are wooden columns which sprout brackets under the roof and under the deep-fronted galleries filling the aisles and W end. Boarded flat ceilings over the aisles. Over the nave, a boarded pointed tunnel vault crossed by transverse ribs and decorated with stencilled borders; in the centre of the ceiling, an ornamental ventilator boss. – At the E end, a PULPIT with a tabernacled Gothic back; it is a replacement of *c.* 1890 by *Archibald Macpherson*. – Flanking the pulpit, the two halves of the ORGAN provided by *Eustace Ingram*, 1890. – STAINED GLASS. In the E wall, two pointed lights and a roundel (Parables), probably of 1887. – In the main W window, glass (post-Resurrection appearances of Our Lord) dated 1891. – In the round windows under the W gallery, depictions of flowers and fruit, dated 1889. – The side windows' coloured borders and panels decorated with foliage may be of the 1850s.

LOCHSIDE CHURCH, North Esk Road. Built as a mission hall by *John Sim*, 1888. Cheap Gothic, a gableted 'bellcote' feature on the N gable.

MELVILLE SOUTH PARISH CHURCH, Castle Street. Built in 1859–60 as St Paul's Free Church. Village Gothic, a rose window with foiled lights in the front gable. In the NE inner angle of the nave and transepts, a plain steeple, the spire rising from a splayed base. The hall at the back was added by *Aitkenhead & Mason* in 1876.

Former METHODIST CHURCH, Market Street and Chapel Street. Secularized. Simple rendered rectangle, built in 1814. Pointed windows, their heads still with intersecting wooden tracery.

METHODIST CHURCH, New Wynd. Smallish rectangular church of 1873–4, all the windows acutely pointed lancets. Sturdily buttressed E side facing Mill Street, its masonry of hammer-dressed ashlar. More hammer-dressed ashlar at the front (S) gable, its outer corners with angle buttresses. The gable's centre is marked off by diagonal buttresses to suggest a nave from which projects an angle-buttressed and gabled porch. Pointed entrance, its hoodmould's label stops carved with human heads, one badly weathered. In the main gable behind, a stepped arrangement of three hoodmoulded lancets under a hoodmoulded circular recess containing a trefoiled opening. Narrow gableted 'bellcote'. In the S end of each 'aisle', a hoodmoulded lancet window under a hoodmoulded recess containing a quatrefoil. – Simpler and lower HALL at the N end, again Gothic in manner.

MONTROSE UNITED REFORMED CHURCH, Museum Street. Built in 1841. Two-storey ashlar-faced hall-like building. S front of three bays with the centre slightly advanced. At the ground-floor, a pilastered and parapeted porch flanked by windows with consoled shallow pediments, their round-arched lights and narrow wooden mullions probably a late C19 alteration. Rectangular first-floor windows linked by a sill course. Above the main cornice and parapet, an attic, whose moulded sloping sides over the end bays suggest an overall pediment but this is broken by a central pedimented aedicule whose coupled pilasters lack capitals and have to make do with the metopes of its Doric frieze. On the outer corners of the main parapet and the corners of the attic's centrepiece, heavy domed octagonal finials. Plain side elevation to Baltic Street.

At the N of the church, the Georgian survival MEMORIAL HALL of 1877–8. One tall storey, the windows with lugged architraves. Boldly projecting parapeted porch with corner piers. – N of this, a second and rather Baroque MEMORIAL HALL. It is by *John Sim*, 1895–6. Tall two storeys and three bays, the broad centre recessed and containing a three-light window with pilaster-mullions at each floor. At the outer bays, narrow architraved ground-floor windows; at the first-floor, segmental-pedimented inscription panels. Over the end bays, the sloping stone skews of the main gable decorated with scrolled ends. Their rise towards the apex of the roof is halted by pedimented fluted piers framing the centrepiece's pedimented attic storey.

OLD PARISH CHURCH, High Street. Large but plain Georgian kirk, the height and architectural ambition of its later steeple dominating the town. The church itself was built in 1791 to a design by *David Logan*. Tall rubble-built box of four bays by two. In the end bays of each long side, two tiers of pointed windows, each of two cusped lights under a trefoiled head, the tracery an embellishment of 1855, the upper windows very squat. At the centre of the S side, a broad semi-octagonal apse added by *John Sim* in 1885. In the canted faces, tall two-light windows, their surrounds and tracery reused from the windows formerly in the centre of the S wall. Across the N side of the church, a single-storey outshot added by *Thomson, McCrea & Sanders* in 1954–5, incorporating some work from the porches which used to stand on this side. Rubble walling surmounted by a parapet of polished ashlar. Central entrance, with a blind head to its pointed arch, flanked by piers decorated with Gothic panels. On the outshot's W end, blind arcading and a battlement, a spiky pinnacle on its corner.

The W end of the church was refronted in ashlar in 1832–4 when the medieval W tower was replaced by a new steeple. The architect of both the new W front and the steeple was *James Gillespie Graham*, perhaps assisted by *A. W. N. Pugin* who acted as his occasional draughtsman at this time. At the church's W front, sloped battlements and stepped diagonal buttresses, their faces decorated with Gothic panels, their crocketed pinnacles topped by foliaged finials. Flanking the steeple are very tall windows, each of two cusped lights under a quatrefoil, their hoodmoulds' label stops carved, like all those of the 1830s work, as male and female heads.

19 The design of the steeple itself is clearly derived from the steeple at Louth Parish Church (Lincolnshire). It is of four stages, marked off by string courses. At each corner, an octagonal turret-buttress topped by two tiers of gablets under a crocketed and foliage-finialled pinnacle. In each of the N and S faces of the lowest stage, a hoodmoulded two-light Tudor window. In the W front, a Tudor-arched entrance with four orders of bell-capitalled shafts. Its hoodmould is ogee-arched, crocketed and topped by a large foliaged finial. In each face of the second stage, a hoodmoulded three-light window with quite elaborate Perp tracery. Above, a low clock stage with blind arcading (crossing the buttresses) and a round clock face in each front. At the belfry above, pairs of splay-sided cusped openings, their ogee hoodmoulds with large foliaged finials. The tower's moulded cornice, like the string courses below, is carried round the buttresses. It supports a parapet pierced by Gothic arcading. Inside the parapet, a lavishly crocketed octagonal needle spire with ogee-headed lucarnes. The spire is tied

to the pinnacles of the tower's turret-buttresses by lacy flying buttresses which are pierced by traceried circles and decorated with cusped soffits and flattish crockets.

The church's interior is a huge space covered by a plain plaster ceiling. Around the W, N and E sides and canted across the NE and NW corners, a two-tier gallery supported on superimposed Tuscan columns, the upper columns smaller than those below. On the N side, the lower gallery's front bulges out, the upper gallery's front is recessed and filled with organ pipes (placed here in the alterations of 1954–5). Tudorish arch into the S apse, added in 1885 to house the organ but now containing the PULPIT. This is of double-decker type, with a sounding board. Like the boxy limba wood pews in the area it dates from the alterations made by *Thomson, McCrea & Sanders* in 1954–5. – In front of the pulpit, the Lorimerian Late Gothic COMMUNION TABLE of *c.* 1923. – Hanging above the table, a brass CHANDELIER ('THE HEARSE') of 1624. Two tiers of branches; on top, a figure of St Margaret of Antioch, her foot on the head of a dragon. – ORGAN, now in the gallery, by *Brindley & Foster*, 1886; rebuilt in 1955 by *Willis*.

In the first-floor room (the Coutts Room) of the steeple, DONATION BOARDS recording gifts and bequests made to the burgh and parish from 1646 to 1883. – In the belfry, four BELLS. The oldest is of 1676, made by *Peter Osteus* of Rotterdam. The others are all by *Thomas Mears* of London, two dated 1801 and 1836, the third probably also early C19.

ST ANDREW, George Street and Baltic Street. Built as a Free church in 1843–4; *William Middleton* was the architect. Two aisles, the W shorter than the E, the inner angle containing a porch, the Free Church emblem of the Burning Bush carved over its entrance. The front (S) gable of each aisle has parapets aligned with the pitches of the roof but, at the inner side, the downward slope is halted above the eaves and the parapet becomes horizontal. On the horizontal section of the E aisle, a large and very solid-looking birdcage bellcote, its pyramidal roof covered with stone slabs. In the S gables, round-arched windows. On the church's E side, two porches containing round-headed doors. In 1896–7 *Matthews & Mackenzie* filled the space between them with a hall, its windows mullioned and transomed. Transeptal vestry of the 1840s at the NE, its mullioned window containing two round-headed lights.

ST JOHN, John Street. Secularized and the interior subdivided 20
as offices. Greek Revival, by *William Smith*, 1827–9. Front built of vertically droved ashlar. It is two-storeyed, of five bays with a first-floor sill course and heavy cornice topped by a low parapet. Projecting from the three centre bays, a tetrastyle Ionic pedimented portico. Behind the portico, three architraved doors. On the front of the main roof, a tall octagonal belfry-cupola. In each of its four main faces, a big round-arched opening; attached Doric columns at the much narrower other sides. The cupola is finished with a circular drum under a copper-covered dome. Tall round-arched windows in the side

elevations of the church, their mullions and circled heads probably part of *John Sim*'s alterations of 1892 when the English Baroque HALL was built at the back.

ST MARGARET (R.C.), Market Street. By *Robert Keith*, 1886. Lanceted Gothic with a gableted W 'bellcote'. Small rectangular chancel. The flèche is now missing from the nave. Interior covered by an open wooden roof. – Contemporary CLERGY HOUSE attached to the S side of the church.

ST MARY (Episcopal), Panmure Place. Now a hall. Lancet Gothic, by *John Henderson*, 1844. Cruciform, with a nave, low transepts and a short chancel. Diagonally buttressed E gable faced with broached ashlar and containing a a stepped arrangement of three hoodmoulded lights. Harled sides. SW porch added in 1878 by *Alexander Ross* who extended the nave to the W at the same time.

ST MARY AND ST PETER (Episcopal), Mid Links. Sizeable church (originally St Peter's) built in 1858 to replace an early C18 chapel destroyed by fire the year before. It was remodelled and enlarged in the 1920s and 1930s after a union with St Mary's (Episcopal) Church (for which, *see* above).

The church of 1858, designed by *John Henderson*, consisted of a tall unaisled nave and slightly lower transepts, with a steeple in the SW inner angle and a two-storey porch in the NW angle. Stugged masonry of local pinkish sandstone. The style was Dec and Dec tracery survives in the unaltered five-light W window. On each side of the nave was a three-light window rising into a big gablet. Two-light window to the N porch. Large windows in the transept gables. Steeple consisting of an angle-buttressed tower broached to an octagonal top stage surmounted by the spire rising from a splayed base.

In 1925–7 *H. O. Tarbolton* enlarged the church by the addition of an austere chancel flanked by a low vestry on the N and a taller Lady Chapel on the S. At the same time the N and S windows of the nave and transepts were altered to form paired lancet lights (the traceried heads of the 1850s nave windows surviving above) in which was placed stained glass taken from St Mary's Church. The straightforward Gothic W porch was added in 1938–9.

Inside, the nave and transepts are covered by open wooden roofs, their collar-braces springing from small moulded wooden corbels except at the crossing where the corbels are of stone and the roofs meet in an elaborate display of joinery. Plain pointed stone arch into the chancel of 1925–7. Here, an idiosyncratically simplified hammerbeam roof, the hammerposts supporting the principal rafters but not the collar which is skied above. In the Lady Chapel S of the chancel, a wagon roof, the E panels crossed by intersecting diagonal ribs with carved and gilded emblems on the central bosses.

Behind the high altar, a Caen stone REREDOS made in 1899 for St Mary's Church and moved here in 1927. It was designed by *Ross & Macbeth* and executed by *Alexander Neilson*. Gothic, with seven compartments, the two outer compartments on each side containing high-relief figures of the four Evangelists. In the three centre compartments, mosaics by *James Powell & Sons* depicting the Virgin and Child, flanked by the Magi and the Shepherds. Statues of angels on top. – On the N side of the sanctuary, a recessed three-seat oak SEDILIA of 1927. – Also of 1927 the simple oak CHOIR STALLS. – ORGAN on the N side of the chancel, by *Blackett & Howden*, 1926; rebuilt and enlarged in 1963 by *Degens & Rippin Ltd.* – Simplified Gothic wooden PULPIT of 1958. – Nave PEWS of 1858. – Strongly coloured STAINED GLASS (Saints) in the choir, transepts, and side windows of the nave, all by *Alexander Gibbs*, 1878–87 and formerly in St Mary's Church. – In the vestry, one light (St Joseph), also late C19 and from St Mary's Church.

In the Lady Chapel, an ALTAR of veined Siena marble designed by *H. O. Tarbolton* and executed in 1927. On the retable, shields bearing emblems of the Passion; the central tabernacle door is carved with a chalice. – Above, a contemporary carved and painted wooden TRIPTYCH, also designed by Tarbolton and executed by *John Sime*, of *Thomas Good*. Elaborate coloured and gilded Late Gothic frame. In the centre panel, a high relief of Our Lord on the Cross flanked by Our Lady and St John. – On each wing, depictions of four saints painted by *Morris* and *Alice Meredith Williams*. – Double-sided oak LECTERN of *c.* 1925, its base carved with emblems of the Evangelists.

GRAVEYARD surrounding the church. In its NW corner, several TABLE STONES with panels placed between their baluster legs. They are probably late C18. – Early C19 sarcophagus MONUMENT to Alicia Scott, the wife of George Bell, †1819, with swagged drapery over the oval panels on its long sides and swags at the ends. – Plenty of HEADSTONES of the later C18 and C19.

UNITED ASSOCIATE CHURCH, Market Street and John Street. Secularized. By *William Smith*, 1823–4. Broad pilastered and pedimented W front with two tiers of round-headed windows. Tall windows, round-headed again, in the three-bay side to John Street. The front has been overlaid by a C20 extension, less tactful than intended. Not even trying to be tactful are the rectangular windows inserted in the side.

CEMETERIES

INCHBRAOCH CEMETERY, Braoch Road. The graveyard of a medieval parish church which was demolished in the early C17. Just NE of the entrance, a HEADSTONE to members of the Findlay family, dated 1837, decorated on the front and back with reliefs of sailing ships. – Another relief of a ship on the large HEADSTONE of 1807 commemorating the children of Andrew Wast, seaman in Ferryden. – E of this, a couple of C18 TOMB-CHESTS, the sides of one formed by panels set between balusters, those of the other panelled. The top slabs of both are carved with mantled shields above reminders of death; on one, two angels' heads (souls). – Immediately to the E, the HEADSTONE of Alexander Strachan, blacksmith, dated 1827, with the relief of a hand holding a crowned hammer (the emblem of the smiths) above an anvil. – S of this, the BURIAL ENCLOSURE of the Scotts of Rossie. Set into the nondescript rubble walls are seven pedimented dormerheads, probably of the later C17, with scrolls on their sides and fleur-de-lis finials. They bear heraldic shields, two displaying the impaled arms of Scott. Did they come from the demolished Rossie Castle? – Immediately S of the enclosure, an early C19 TOMB-CHEST with swagged drapery on the sides and ends. At the corners, acanthus-capitalled pilasters, their shafts decorated with rosettes set in a guilloche pattern. More rosettes on the fluted frieze.

ROSEHILL CEMETERY, Rosehill Road. Laid out in 1839–40. Along Rosehill Road, waist-high ashlar-built dwarf walls, their railings now missing. At each end, a single-storey pedimented 'lodge' front with two segmental-arched dummy windows. Behind the E is a shed; the W fronts a much altered house. In the centre of the cemetery's front wall, tall panelled gatepiers with mutuled cornices and shallow pyramidal tops; they are dated 1839. At the cemetery's N side, Jacobean gatepiers of 1861 form the entrance into an extension of the same date. On the E side, gatepiers very similar to those of the main entrance but presumably of 1876, the date of the E extension to which they give access.

SLEEPYHILLOCK CEMETERY, Brechin Road. Laid out in 1893–4 by *McCulloch & Fairley* as a lavishly planted arboretum, yews appropriately prominent. – Poised on the steeply rising ground just inside the entrance, a LODGE of 1894. Vertical Baronial, the entrance in a tower crowned with a witch's-hat spire; a smaller spire on an angle turret.

PUBLIC BUILDINGS

BURGH HALL, Baltic Street and Museum Street. Now in other use. Late C19. Picturesque Gothic on a small scale.

DORWARD HOUSE, Dorward Road. Built in 1838–9 as a house of refuge for paupers and orphans, it was endowed by William Dorward, a Montrose merchant, and designed by *James Brewster*. Gentle Italianate, fronted with ashlar and with bracketed broad eaves. Symmetrical build-up from well set-back two-storey pyramid-roofed pavilions joined by one-bay links to broad gabled blocks which have, paired narrow lights at both floors, those of the first floor round-headed. Then, another couple of one-bay links, their ground-floor windows round-headed. Main block of five bays, the ends rising as four-storey towers with shallow pyramid roofs, the three-bay centrepiece a storey lower. Central door under a piend-roofed canopy supported by pairs of heavy moulded corbels. Round-headed ground-floor windows. Corbelled sloping stone canopies over the first-floor windows, the centre one of three lights. At the second floor, the windows of the centrepiece are smaller and almost square, the centre bay again marked by a tripartite window. Tall narrow windows at this floor of the end bays whose top windows are dummies, each of three round-headed lights.

HARBOUR. Quays and wharfs of the C19 and C20 along the N bank of the River South Esk, the FISH QUAY at the W (by *David Cunningham*, 1884–5) faced with ashlar. At the E end, a LIGHTHOUSE, by *Robert Stevenson*, 1818, a tapering circular rubble-walled tower, a railed walkway around the cupola-lantern on the top.

MASONIC HALL (THE HOLY ROYAL LODGE 'KILWINNING'), Upper Hall Street. A two-storey Late Georgian building dressed up in 1909–10 in enjoyable Artisan Mannerist style.

MELVILLE MISSION HALL, Southesk Street. Now in other use. By *John Sim*, 1888. Built of badly weathered sandstone ashlar, the lower courses bull-nosed. At the S end, a two-storey house, its round-arched entrance in a granite surround and topped by a Venetian window (the sidelights dummies), both entrance and window framed by giant pilasters rising to the eaves to support a segmental pediment which is broken by the triangular-pedimented base of a conical-spired bellcote. To the N, a tall single-storey hall. Frontage of four bays, the broad end windows with French Renaissance lights.

MONTROSE ACADEMY, Academy Square. Greek Revival, by 74
David Logan, 1815–16. Two-storey main block of five broad bays by three, the upper windows almost square. W front with giant Ionic attached columns across the three recessed centre bays in which are a trio of doors under semicircular fanlights.

Montrose Academy.
Front elevation, *c.* 1814

In each end bay, a tall architraved and consoled-pedimented window. Above the boldly projecting cornice, a fluted parapet supporting a central panel flanked and topped by scrolls. Rising behind the parapet, a drum pierced by circular windows (a clock face to the front) and roofed with a gilded copper dome surmounted by a cupola formed by a second domed drum.

In 1841 the Academy was extended by the addition of flanking single-storey pavilions linked to the main block by screens of Ionic columns *in antis*. The front of each pavilion is of three bays, the centre slightly recessed, the windows dignified with architraves and aprons. Over each pavilion, a high parapet with a scroll-sided pedimental feature at its centre.

Behind the C19 buildings, a large courtyard extension by the *Angus County Council Architect's Office*, 1960–1. Flat-roofed ranges, their rubble and drydash walling and traditionally proportioned windows deferential to the earlier buildings but far from matching their elegance. A pair of boldly painted bridges join the 1960s extension to the two-storey PRIMARY DEPARTMENT added by *Tayside Regional Council*, 1987–90. Walls of brown brick enlivened by horizontal bands of yellow brick and brightly coloured metal window frames. Shallow-pitched roofs and a few Postmodern touches.

MONTROSE MUSEUM, Panmure Place and Museum Street. By
79 *John Henderson*, 1837–42. Greek Revival, built of local purplish coloured stone, the E front of channelled polished ashlar, the N side of rougher stugged ashlar, the plain S side of rubble. Front of three bays. At the recessed centre, giant Ionic columns *in antis* and a narrow door whose corniced architrave is given marked entasis. Cornices and entasis again at the outer bays' aproned ground-floor windows. These contain elaborate metal glazing bars and borders decorated with a sort of Vitruvian scroll. Instead of windows at the upper floor, panels, each bearing a variant of a Greek key pattern, a motif used by Sir John Soane for the breakfast-room chimneypiece at his house in Lincoln's Inn Fields, London, which he illustrated in his *Description* of that house published in 1832.

Henderson's N side is of four bays, the ground-floor windows of the same design as those of the front but with larger panels above. At the W end, an addition of 1889 by *John Sim*, its N front a slightly broader and more pompous version of the 1830s E front.

Inside, Henderson's museum room rises the full height of the building under a coffered elliptical tunnel vault. Round all four sides, a gallery on slender cast-iron columns, the iron front with foliaged decoration at the intersection of its latticework.

MONTROSE ROYAL INFIRMARY, Bridge Street. Competent but unexciting Greek Revival, by *James Collie*, 1837–9. Two storeys and nine bays, the two-bay parapeted ends joined by slightly recessed one-bay links, also parapeted, to the boldly advanced three-bay centrepiece. At the centrepiece, fluted Doric columns supporting a pediment. On the frieze below the pediment, empire garlands. Entrance with a cornice skied above the rectangular fanlight. Pediments at the three-bay gables, the S overlaid by a later outshot. At the back, plain additions of 1865–6. The Infirmary was further extended by *William Alexander*, 1892–4, and again in 1924–8.

MONTROSE SWIMMING POOL, The Mall. By *John B. Wingate & Partners*, 1961–2. Shed-like, the walls faced with 'Fyfestone' and drydash.

POST OFFICE, Bridge Street. By *W. T. Oldrieve* of *H.M. Office of Works*, 1905–7. Tall two storeys and an attic, the manner free Wrenaissance except at the attic where Scottish allusions are introduced. This has steeply gabled dormerheads at the ends and, between them, three keel-shaped dormerheads. All these are carved with specifically Scottish emblems (thistles and lions rampant) except the centre one which bears a rose but this is presumably in honour of the burgh.

PUBLIC LIBRARY, Castle Place. By *J. Lindsay Grant* of Manchester, 1903–5. Scots Jacobean Renaissance with only a hint of Baronial, the walls built of red Closeburn (Dumfriesshire) ashlar, the bellcast-eaved roofs covered with green Westmoreland slates, the mullioned-and-transomed windows all containing rectangular leaded panes. *p. 628*

The main block's principal (SE) front is symmetrical, of five bays, the centre slightly advanced under a pediment containing an empty shield. Pendants of fruiting foliage flank the centre first-floor window and the panel below inscribed with the building's name; a cornice over the ground-floor central window. At the ground-floor windows of the outer bays, blocky bold keystones and steep pediments. Lugged architraves at the openings above. At the first floor of the main block's broad NE gable, a shallowly canted bay window recessed in a broad rectangular surround; under the consoles of the window's cornice, cherubs' heads and more pendants of fruiting foliage. On the centre of the main block's roof, a square cupola-ventilator rising from a battered base. At each face, Roman Doric columns carrying an open pediment; on top, a low ogee dome with a stalk-and-ball finial.

The entrance is placed in a recessed and gabled bay on the l. of the main front. Round-arched door with a big console-keystone. It is framed by an aediculed surround with small cherubs' heads peeping out of the capitals of the Ionic pilasters; heraldic achievement of the burgh of Montrose carved by *Earp, Hobbs & Miller* in the steep pediment. Four-light window above. The NW elevation is less formal. Projecting from the side of the entrance bay, an octagon with a low spired roof topped by a large weathervane, the letters of the cardinal points sticking out of an openwork ball. To the l. of this octagon, a trio of gables, the r. with a four-light stair window, the taller and broader centre gable with a balustraded broad and shallow bay window. At the projecting l. gable, a small Venetian first-floor window. In the inner angle of these two last gables, a

Montrose Library.
Engraving, 1905

round turret projected on continuous corbelling, a stalk-and-ball finial on its ogee roof.

The entrance, its fanlight containing stained-glass roses, opens into a square vestibule with green-tiled walls. Beyond, an octagonal hall with doors to the reading rooms. These rooms open into each other through round-arched screens. On the hall's SW side, a Roman Doric-columned screen marks off the stair but continuity is provided by carrying through the hall's high dado of dark crimson tiles. In the stair window, stained glass depicting cherubs holding garlands of roses under the English translation of the burgh motto (THE SEA ENRICHES THE ROSE ADORNS) and mermaid supporters of the burgh of Montrose. On the first floor, a gallery with a plastered elliptical tunnel vault.

RAILWAY STATION, Railway Place. Now Caledonian House. Built for the Aberdeen Railway in 1848 and converted to a community centre in 1987. Symmetrical cottage-picturesque, built of purplish stugged ashlar with creamy sandstone dressings. Round-headed doors and windows; bracketed broad eaves. The glazed platform awning is a replacement of 1987.

RAILWAY STATION, off Western Road. The station building opened by the Dundee & Arbroath Railway in 1881 has been replaced by a late C20 waiting room. There survives a lattice-girder FOOTBRIDGE of 1881.

REGISTRATION OFFICE, John Street. Built as the Parish Council Chambers in 1915–16, incorporating fabric of an Evangelical Union church of 1849, it is by *D. Wishart Galloway*. Authoritarian English Baroque on a tiny scale. Single-storey with a projecting and higher centrepiece where the parapet is carved with swagged drapery and fruit with, at the centre, a man's head above a shield bearing the burgh coat of arms.

Inside, the back part of the church (now MARRIAGE ROOM) survives, a tunnel-vaulted room with an early C20 rectangle of enriched plasterwork and a round-headed N window.

SOUTHESK PRIMARY SCHOOL, Hill Place. Polite but unimaginative Scots Renaissance, by *John Sim*, 1890–1. Two storeys, of polished ashlar. In each of the broad step-gabled ends, a giant overarch framing a three-light ground-floor window and, at first floor, a Venetian window under a bullseye. Three-bay links, each with a segmental-pedimented aediculed doorpiece, the columns without capitals, join the ends to the three-storey centre tower. At its ground floor, rusticated corners surmounted by paired anta-pilasters at the upper storeys. A two-light window at each floor. Slated ogee roof topped by cresting; pilastered and pedimented attic aedicule at the front.

TOWN HALL, Melville Gardens. Built in 1851–2 as Melville Church to a design of *William Middleton* but recast and refronted for its present use in 1962–3. Broad gable front with a large rectangular window and cantilevered canopy over the entrance.

TOWN HOUSE, High Street. Prominently sited but restrained Neo-Palladian expression of civic dignity, the product of two stages of development. The first took place in 1763–4 when *John Hutcheon*, land surveyor in Montrose, designed a two-storey block of five bays by three. In 1819 *William Smith* remodelled the building, raised it to three storeys, and added a full-height jamb at the SW. 73

The main N and W fronts are each of five bays, faced with ashlar, channelled at the ground floor and with rusticated quoins above. At the ground floor, round-headed arches which open at the N front and the two N bays of the W into a piazza. At the W front's three S bays the arches used to form overarches for recessed windows but these were enlarged (one into a door) c. 1900 to fill the full width of each opening. Band course under the first floor whose N windows are architraved and corniced, the cornices of the centre and end windows carried on consoles. The W windows were treated similarly but have lost their cornices. Architraves at the second-floor windows of the N front but now missing on the W. On each elevation, a mutuled cornice and central pediment flanked and topped by urns. In the N pediment, a clock face; in the W, an oval panel carved with the heraldic achievement of the burgh of Montrose. Over the outer bays of the N front, a balustrade with urns at the corners. Parapet on the W front. The other elevations are rubble-built and unpretentious. In the E side of the jamb, an open round-headed arch into a space which contains C18 tombs, this part of the Town House having been built over the W end of the graveyard of the Old Parish Church.

YOUNG MEN'S CHRISTIAN ASSOCIATION, Murray Street. Dated 1908 on the downpipes' hoppers. Tall two storeys of thrifty Free Jacobean, an ogee-roofed octagonal turret corbelled out at the NE corner.

BRIDGE AND VIADUCTS

BRIDGE over the South Esk. By the *Carl Bro Group*, 2005. Three elliptical spans, just missing elegance.

INCHBRAOCH VIADUCT. *See* Ferryden.

RAILWAY VIADUCT over the South Esk. By *W. R. Galbraith*, 1882–3. Sixteen spans, with elliptically topped lattice-girder trusses supported on pairs of riveted-iron columns.

DESCRIPTION

Town centre

NORTH ESK ROAD is the town's principal entry from the N. On
71 its E side, THE TOWER, designed as a water tower by *William Middleton*, 1841. It is Tudor, of three tall stages marked off by string courses. Octagonal, the principal faces with rusticated stonework at the ground floor and stugged ashlar above, all of pinkish local sandstone. Originally the first- and second-floor windows were alternately of two and three lights, the tripartites hoodmoulded, but most of the mullions were removed and metal-framed glazing introduced when the building was converted to a house in 1972–4. Overall parapet rising into pinnacled gablets at alternate faces; at each corner, a ball-finialled stalk. S of The Tower, Lochside Church (*see* Churches, above), a little before the corner of Rosehill Road, for whose eponymous Cemetery *see* Cemeteries, above.

THE MALL, set back at a higher level but parallel to North Esk Road, is prosperous villadom. On its S corner with Graham Street, a cottagey double house (THE GABLES and CRANES MEADOW) of 1900, by *T. Martin Cappon*. Two storeys, of red brick, with harling and half-timbering in the bargeboarded gables and some tile-hanging. Red-tiled roofs. In the apex of each front gable, a carved angel's head. Along the S side of the front garden of Cranes Meadow, a low single-storey brick-built cottage, probably of the late C18 but made English picturesque in 1900 when the windows were given leaded lights and jettied gablets decorated with harling and half-timbering. Also of 1900 is the cottage's low addition towards the street, with a gablet which contains a Dutch tile decorated with a man's face framed by flowers and a surround inscribed JAN.COUPER.DEVENTRE./ TEXEL/1708. FAIRFIELD next door is mid-C19 Georgian survival, with a corniced doorpiece and rosetted skewputts. A little further S and set well back, MALL HOUSE of the earlier C19 with Roman Doric columns at the entrance. Near the S end of The Mall, the Montrose Swimming Pool (*see* Public Buildings, above), a utilitarian jolt to the gentility.

MURRAY STREET continues the line of North Esk Road. On the W side, the cement-rendered Nos. 10–14, dated 1902.

Light-hearted Jacobean Gothick of generally C18 inspiration but with carved bears' heads projecting from two of the crowstepped front gables. Behind, in a close entered through a pend, No. 18 of the later C19. Two tall storeys, with a cement-rendered two-bay pedimented gable front. At the ground floor, angle pilasters carrying an egg-and-dart cornice. Above, panelled Corinthian angle pilasters and windows with pulvinated friezes under consoled pediments. A rosette in the building's overall pediment. For the rest, Murray Street is low-key, mostly C19 vernacular with some C20 intrusions. A little smarter than the average is the ashlar-fronted BLACK HORSE INN of 1890. At the splayed corner to Lower Hall Street, a rectangular oriel window topped by a steep pyramidal spire with a horse weathervane. For the Young Men's Christian Association opposite, *see* Public Buildings, above.

In LOWER HALL STREET, Nos. 2–6, next to the Black Horse Inn, comprise a block of *c.* 1815 which has lost some architectural detail but is still given modest pretension by three-light windows at the centre of the first floor and of the attic whose wall-head gablet is dignified by columns at the sides. Further down the street, on the S side, the late C19 Nos. 29–37, covered with cement render masquerading as bull-nosed ashlar, enjoy a piece of folk art in the form of a large cement roundel bearing the arms of the burgh of Montrose flanked by the heads of Edward VII and Queen Alexandra; it was probably put up for the King's coronation in 1902. For the Masonic Hall in UPPER HALL STREET to the E of Murray Street, *see* Public Buildings, above.

MURRAY STREET'S S stretch is more consistently Late Georgian but with few frills. On the E side, No. 121 with a gable front. On the W, Nos. 122–126, its slightly advanced centre rising to a chimney-gableted attic. At this centre bay, a three-light second-floor window and a Venetian window at the attic, both with dummy sidelights. At the S end and half blocking the streetline, a block of *c.* 1815 (Nos. 128 Murray Street and Nos. 2–4 High Street). It is of three storeys and an attic, ashlar-faced, with rusticated quoins at the NE angle and panelled masonry on its rounded corner at the entry of Murray Street into High Street. Boldly projecting cornice at the NE angle and the S front but not carried across the E gable. The pilastraded shopfronts seem original. At the back, a bowed stair-tower with a segmental-arched entrance containing attached piers supporting an entablature and fanlight. This rear elevation is reached through a pend under the L-plan Nos. 6–10, late C18 but very plain and rather altered.

HIGH STREET continues the S progress of Murray Street but broadens out to the W. The S focus is on the Town House and the steeple of the Old Parish Church behind (*see* Public Buildings and Churches, above). On the E side, the rendered Nos. 1–5 was built in 1816 as the TRADES HALL. Two storeys and an attic, of three bays. Boldly projecting cornice; large first-floor windows, now with C20 metal-framed glazing. Under its

S end, a narrow pend into TRADES CLOSE where a couple of pilastered doorpieces dignify the rather altered and low mid-C19 housing. At the end of the close, St Margaret's (R.C.) Church (*see* Churches, above). High Street continues with Nos. 7–11, a late C19 ashlar-fronted building with some heavy Renaissance detail. The Late Georgian front block at Nos. 13–15 is quite plain and with altered windows but, in the close behind, is a rear wing formed of late C18 three-storey houses, the W's segmental-arched entrance containing an elegantly simple fan-light and sidelights, the entrance to No. 17 round-headed. The next block fronting High Street (Nos. 19–21) is of 1866. The manner is generally Georgian survival but Jacobean touches are provided by the stepped central gablet and a lozenge panel on its crowning chimney. Humble two-storey early C19 Nos. 23–27. The gable-ended No. 29, on the corner of John Street, is probably mid-C18 but clad in cheerless C20 drydash.

JOHN STREET, opened in 1818, is a detour. Of about that date are the unassuming two-storey vernacular buildings which lead off its N side. They are followed by a slightly later ashlar-faced three-storey tenement (Nos. 23–39), its doors grouped in three lots of three, the centre opening of each trio surmounted by a cornice carried on tall consoles. On the S side and stretching down Market Street, a busy Neo-vernacular drydashed development of 1995. On the SE corner with Market Street, the former United Associate Church (*see* Churches, above). The E stretch of John Street is mostly Georgian survival of the earlier C19 but including the Registration Office of 1915 (*see* Public Buildings, above). At the E end, the classical presence of the former St John's Church (*see* Churches, above). Some items of interest among the buildings in the streets off John Street. In MARKET STREET, St Margaret's (R.C.) Church and, on the corner of Chapel Street, the former Methodist Church (*see* Churches, above). Opposite the second of these, the early C19 No. 1 CHAPEL STREET, its windows with moulded architraves and cornices, its doorpiece pilastered and corniced. In MILL STREET further E, Knox's Montrose United Free Church and, on the corner of New Wynd, the Methodist Church (*see* Churches, above). Opposite the Methodist Church, No. 71 Mill Street of *c.* 1800 with a central chimney gablet. The rubble-built two-storey store to its N looks a bit earlier.

HIGH STREET'S E side S of John Street begins with the BANK OF SCOTLAND by *William Burn*, 1839, a big piend-roofed block, its character still Georgian with sill courses under the architraved windows of the two upper floors and a large anta-pilastered doorpiece. Of the same height is the adjoining block (Nos. 35–37) of *c.* 1880 but the architectural inspiration is from 'Greek' Thomson and the stonework badly weathered. Behind this, a mid-C19 Neo-Jacobean rear wing, its boldly projecting lid-like cornice projected on brackets decorated with strap-work. Nos. 39–41 High Street began as a Late Georgian building with moulded architraves to the windows, the openings at the original third floor quite small, but the ground and first floors were united as a single tall shop *c.* 1960. Corniced first-floor windows at the early C19 Nos. 43–45. The cornice over the door of its contemporary back wing is carried on rosetted consoles. At Nos. 47–49, a lower three-storey front block of *c.* 1800, built of rough ashlar, with a band course between the first and second floors; the roof is piended towards the street. The adjoining cement-rendered building (Nos. 51–55), also of *c.* 1800, is crushed under a C20 'mansard' roof.

S of New Wynd, No. 59 High Street, a small late C20 block, makes nothing of the potential of its site. Beside it, the former ROYAL BANK OF SCOTLAND is by *Peddie & Kinnear*, 1864 (the architects' initials and the date carved on the second-floor sill course), a three-storey five-bay palazzo fronted with polished ashlar. At the tall ground floor, a console-corniced door; the flanking windows have been converted to entrances into a loggia in front of the shops which now occupies the space intended for the banking hall. Sill course linking the first-floor windows, the spandrels of their shouldered arches carved with rosettes. More rosettes on the guilloche decoration of the second-floor sill course running under windows which are each of two segmental-arched lights divided by a foliage-capitalled column-mullion. Rosettes again between the consoles under the overall cornice. No. 67 next door is late C20, attempting to replicate some of the character of its C18 gable-ended predecessor but with a flashy modernistic shopfront. This is carried brutally across Nos. 71–77, a big three-storey-and-attic five-bay block of 1885. Up to the consoled main cornice its style is Georgian survival, with corniced first-floor windows, the centre one pedimented, and a sill course under the architraved windows of the second floor. But the attic shows inspiration from an earlier period and displays a Dutch gablet containing a round-arched window in a pilastered and corniced surround. The wall-head height is continued by the adjacent former BRITISH LINEN CO. BANK of 1815. Four bays of polished ashlar, rusticated at the ground floor where the console-corniced doorpieces of the end bays are later embellishments. Cornices at the first-floor windows, plain architraves at the second floor. Above the main cornice, a blocking course, its taller centrepiece a fluted panel. Stretching down the close behind, the bank's rear wing, with a big Roman Doric-columned doorpiece. At the end of this close, IVY HOUSE, a smart early C19 town house. Elegant doorpiece, the cornice carried on tall consoles, the frieze with incised Soanean decoration. High Street continues with No. 83, plain Late Georgian but sadly bereft of its chimneys, followed by Nos. 85–87, the late C20's unfaithful copy of an C18 gable-ender. Genuine mid-C18 gable-ender at Nos. 89–91 but it has been given an unsuitable shopfront and the first-floor windows have been enlarged. Then a plain block (Nos. 93–95) of *c.* 1840 and a lower vernacular building (Nos. 97–99) of about a century earlier. The scale jolts up with the NATIONAL (now Royal) BANK OF SCOTLAND, a characteristic work of *David MacGibbon*, 1864.

Scottish Baronial, without obviously martial features but clad in aggressive hammer-dressed masonry. It is studiously asymmetrical, with one splay-sided oriel jettied out on continuous corbelling and another oriel in the form of a shallow rectangular projection supported by moulded individual corbels. Battlement broken by crowstepped gablets rising above panels carved with the National Bank's emblem of St Andrew, its motto and coat of arms. There follows a large but plain late C18 block (Nos. 105–109). Informal collection of C18 buildings in the close behind. At its end, No. 107, the former SHIP INN, built in the mid C18 but given a porch with an anta-pilastered doorpiece in the early C19. Back in High Street, Nos. 111–115 of *c.* 1840, dignified, with consoled cornices over the first-floor windows, a second-floor sill course, and urns on the pierced parapet. At the S end of this stretch of High Street, the four-storey Nos. 119–121 of *c.* 1790 in its present form but incorporating inside parts of an earlier structure. It is L-plan, the main block running E from the Town House (*see* Public Buildings, above), its N jamb pierced by the pend into a court. The S side of this court is filled by the rendered and white-painted MOORAN HOUSE (No. 117 High Street), its main part (probably incorporating some earlier work) built for James Scott of Brotherton *c.* 1750. This is of two storeys over a basement. The N front to the court is obscured by a C19 lean-to addition but the C18 S elevation overlooking the graveyard of the Old Parish Church originally had five ground-floor windows grouped 3:2 and four regularly spaced windows at the first floor. A further S bay with a three-light ground-floor window seems to be an extension of the early C19, perhaps the date of the short laundry wing which forms a NE jamb. Inside the house, a fragment of mid-C18 panelling (perhaps not *in situ*) at the staircase down to the basement.

High Street's W side starts at the N with a vernacular gable-ended block (Nos. 12–14), probably mid-C18 but now dry-dashed. Down the close at its side, a couple of C18 houses, one of four storeys, the other of three. The ashlar-fronted but severe Nos. 16–18 High Street may be late C18. So too may be the three cement-rendered buildings (Nos. 20–30) to its N, one (Nos. 24–26) enlivened by a Victorian shopfront with Corinthianish capitals to its cast-iron columns. Jolly folk art appears at the ROYAL ARCH bar (Nos. 32–34) of *c.* 1860. It is Georgian survival with a straightforward Victorian pub front but, atop this and between the two first-floor windows is a large panel carved with the high-relief painted figures of Freemasons ministering to a widow, orphan and half-naked man holding a club (a lunatic?) placed in front of a classical backdrop. No. 36 next door consists only of a late C20 shopfront. Beyond this puncture in the streetscape, a block of the earlier C19 (Nos. 40–42). Ashlar front with a pilastraded shopfront, architraved and corniced first-floor windows, and more architraves at the second-floor openings. A taller version of this, also of the earlier C19, next door (Nos. 44–46) but it is of only two bays and has been given Victorian shopfronts. After the slightly later Georgian survival No. 48, the early C19 polished ashlar frontage of Nos. 50–52, plain except for a heavy console which survives from a mid-C19 shopfront (since replaced). This console is at the pend arch to a close to which the building's back wing displays a smart Ionic pilastered and corniced doorpiece, with rosettes on the frieze. The High Street frontages continue with the rendered Late Georgian Nos. 54–56, its austerity relieved only by a second-floor sill course. No. 58 of the earlier C19 is a little more ambitious with architraves and horizontal glazing at the upper floors' windows, those of the first floor with cornices. After the flat-roofed Nos. 60–62 of *c.* 1930, Nos. 66–68 of the earlier C19, the first-floor windows corniced. Probably contemporary but perhaps a remodelled C18 gable-fronted building is the block at Nos. 70–72, with a second-floor sill course and a chimney-topped pediment. A mid-C18 gable-ender with a prominent chimney does survive at Nos. 74–76. Much grander is the ashlar-fronted three-storey former CROWN HOTEL (Nos 78–84) of *c.* 1815. Five bays, the centre three slightly advanced and rising above the main cornice as a pedimented attic. Three-light first- and second-floor windows in the end bays. Shallow vases on the corners of the building and its central pediment. Then straightforward early C19 buildings (Nos. 86–108). On the S side of the long and narrow RAILWAY CLOSE running downhill to the E, a range of C19 stabling. The three-storey former NORTH OF SCOTLAND (now Clydesdale) BANK at Nos. 110–116 High Street is large-scale Italianate by *James Matthews*, *c.* 1866–9. The framework of the façade is provided by channelled pilaster-strips at the outer corners and an overall balustraded cornice projected on moulded corbels. Within this frame, a slightly recessed two-bay centre. The ground floor originally had plain shopfronts (the S still unaltered) flanking the premises of the bank itself whose relative grandeur has been lost by its being given a late C20 front of commercial rather than civic status. The detail above has survived. At each end of the first floor, a tripartite window, its lights' stilted round-headed arches springing from foliage-capitalled pilasters. At the centrepiece, two windows of the same type but without pilasters and with the foliage of the capitals continued across as a decorative band at the arches' springing level. Second-floor windows with elliptical-arched heads and shouldered architraves. On the corner with Hume Street, the former CENTRAL HOTEL, by *John Sim*, 1892. French Renaissance of a sort, its canted corner topped by an octagonal turret under a fish-scale-slated truncated spire surmounted by iron cresting. In the middle of High Street opposite the hotel, a more than life-size stone STATUE of the politician, Joseph Hume, by *Calder Marshall*, 1858–9, who depicted his subject as addressing the House of Commons; battered and corniced plinth. To the S, a much smaller though life-size bronze STATUE ('Bill the Smith') by *William Lamb*, 1937. On the N side of HUME

STREET, the former LA SCALA CINEMA (now The Picture House bar) by *W. M. Patrick & Co.*, 1932, a long rendered front with pedimented ends and immensely broad mutuled eaves at the four-bay centrepiece.

On the S corner with Hume Street, Nos. 138–142 High Street, by *James Parr & Associates*, 1965, its pair of artificial stone gables a weak balance to the former Central Hotel. Then, Nos. 144–148, plain Late Georgian but now dressed in cement render masquerading as bull-nosed rubble. At the end of the close behind, No. 146 was remodelled *c.* 1800 when it was given a console-corniced doorpiece but contains a fireplace dated 1673. In the close behind Nos. 150–152 (a Late Georgian block covered in bull-nosed render), No. 154, a harled L-plan three-storey building of *c.* 1700, a corniced doorpiece at the NE wing. In the next close, again with an unappealingly rendered Late Georgian front block (Nos. 156–158), the early C19 ashlar-fronted COUTTS HOUSE (No. 158), the former town house of the Coutts of Hallgreen and Fullerton. It is L-plan, the main (E) front a single piend-roofed bay. Broad entrance, the cavetto-splayed door and sidelights surmounted by a segmental-arched fanlight. Above, a three-light window with Roman Doric column-mullions. More column-mullions at the two-light windows of the NE wing. Bow-fronted W elevation to the garden behind. After the plain Georgian survival Nos. 162–164, Nos 166–168 of 1870 with tripartite windows, those of the first floor with extravagantly stilted segmental-arched lights. The block at Nos. 170–174 High Street is dated 1888. Free Renaissance, with pilasters marking off the narrow end bays from the centrepiece whose two-light first-floor windows are contained in a large basket overarch. On the N side of the close behind, a harled Late Georgian block. At the close's end, the narrow early C19 gable, partly overlaid by the buildings each side, of HOLLY HOUSE, its rear part of *c.* 1700. High Street continues with Nos. 176–178 and Nos. 180–184, both of the earlier C19, with corniced shopfronts, Nos. 176–178 now with late C19 iron cresting at the eaves, Nos. 180–184 with cornices over the first-floor windows. At the W end of the close, an C18 house (No. 182), its architraved doorpiece now sheltered by an early C19 wooden portico with skinny Doric columns. The rendered front block of Nos. 186–190 High Street, set back from the streetline, is early C18 with irregular five-bay fenestration at the upper floors. Behind is THE RETREAT, the ashlar-fronted early C18 L-plan town house of the Ouchterlonies. Corniced doorpiece with fluted pilasters. The large block fronting the street at Nos. 192–194 was built in the later C18 as a grand town house of three storeys and attic, the two centre bays under a pediment topped by a half-round urn projecting from the crowning chimney. In 1877 the building was remodelled by *William Aitkenhead* as the COMMERCIAL BANK OF SCOTLAND, the two lower floors thrown together to form the banking hall which was given a front of French Renaissance inspiration with panelled pilasters and a round-arched and keystoned central door. Drydashed block of *c.* 1800 at Nos. 198–200 followed by the straightforward early C19 ashlar frontage of Nos. 202–204. Then the former ABERDEEN TOWN AND COUNTY BANK (Nos. 208–212), a big three-storey five-bay block of *c.* 1870. Weird detail in a sort of Venetian manner. Windows placed in recesses with diagonally banded surrounds. More diagonal banding on the attached columns at the ends of the upper floors. Over the entrance, massive corbelling carrying a balustraded balcony in front of a two-light window. Three-light second-floor window. Corbelled cornice and parapet with heavy blocky detail.

Most of the E side of HIGH STREET S of the Town House and Old Parish Church (*see* Public Buildings and Churches, above) is formed by an ashlar-fronted terrace (Nos. 133–145) of *c.* 1870. Three storeys and an attic, the ground-floor shopfronts surmounted by a heavily consoled cornice, the first-floor windows all with cornices and some also with consoles and dentils but the result just missing symmetry. Moulded architraves to the second-floor windows; dentils under the parapet. At the back of the Carlton Hotel (No. 139), a Jacobean villa of *c.* 1840, its main front facing E with hoodmoulds over the first-floor windows and a narrow centrepiece carried up as a curvilinear gablet flanked by a pair of chimneys. The canted bay window at the S end of this front is a late C19 addition. In High Street, S of the terrace, a couple of humble two-storey houses (Nos. 147–149), probably of the C18, their front gardens now filled with late C19 shops, and Nos. 151–157, a mid-C19 Georgian survival block added to the front of an C18 house. More Georgian survival at the bowed corner with GEORGE STREET. In the middle of this stretch of High Street, a stone STATUE (now painted) of Sir Robert Peel, looking determined but priggish, by *A. Handyside Ritchie*, 1852.

CASTLE PLACE continues the town's main thoroughfare to the SW. Its NW side is filled by the Public Library (*see* Public Buildings, above). On the SE and set back, CASTLESTEAD (now Jobcentre Plus). The ashlar-faced and battlemented front block is of *c.* 1815. Single-storey over a basement; three bays, the outer with canted bay windows. At the centre, the entrance in a round-headed overarch, itself framed by a rectangular overarch with small corbels under the lintel. Behind, a taller and rendered C18 block. In front, a bronze STATUE of the armour-clad figure of James Graham, first Marquess of Montrose, by *Michael Snowden*, 2005. Along the SW side of Castlestead's forecourt, a rubble-built range of two and three storeys, probably C18. The NW house was altered in the early C19 when it was given a new roof, piended at the front gable which was itself refronted with ashlar and provided with a parapet and three-light first-floor window. Fronting the street are the Late Georgian Nos. 7–8 and 9–11, plain except for second-floor sill courses, rusticated quoins and blocking courses. A pend at No. 10 leads to the garden of STRATON HOUSE, a brick-fronted merchant's house built for John Straton in 1762. At the Late

Victorian Nos. 12–13 Castle Place, a cast-iron shopfront, its columns with heavily foliaged capitals. Then Lloyds TSB Scotland (former TRUSTEE SAVINGS BANK), by *John Sim*, 1899–1900. Almost frivolous North European Renaissance gable front of two tall storeys and an attic, largely filled by windows. At the first floor, a frieze carved with cornucopiae; griffons at the outer corners.

BRIDGE STREET starts with a short E–W stretch. On its S side, a plain early C19 block (Nos. 1–9) with a recessed bow at its corner to Castle Street; delicate Adamish fanlight at No. 5. Opposite, just W of the Public Library, a small red brick PAVILION, built as a ladies' toilet *c.* 1900. In each face, an elliptically arched mullioned-and-transomed window. Bracketed broad eaves and a red-tiled ridge at the piended roof. Bridge Street then swings l. to run S. On its E side, the Post Office (*see* Public Buildings, above). Opposite, THE ELMS (No. 8) of *c.* 1825. Ashlar front, the ground-floor windows aproned, the door with a consoled cornice; first-floor sill course. Then, on the l., CASTLEGATE of *c.* 1815. Large round-arched windows lighting the basement; skinny Roman Doric columns at the door. Nos. 31–33 are mid-C19 Georgian survival but with heavy banded Roman Doric columns at the ground floor whose shops have been converted to housing; at the first floor, a canted oriel window with column-mullions. The street continues with generally straightforward Late Georgian buildings, some now covered with cement render imitating bull-nosed masonry. Rosetted consoles under the cornice of No. 26's doorpiece. At No. 36, a rusticated ground floor and deep aprons under the first-floor windows. Urns on the ends of the low parapet. Nos. 38A and 38B form a double house of *c.* 1840. Paired doors sharing a consoled cornice at the slightly advanced centre which rises into a pedimented attic. Bridge Street's lower stretch is more ragged and mostly of the later C19 but Nos. 54–56 are of *c.* 1830 with consoled cornices over the openings at the ground floor whose windows are aproned. At the end of the W side, the Montrose Royal Infirmary (*see* Public Buildings, above). To the S, the railway viaduct and bridge over the South Esk (*see* Bridges and Viaducts, above).

Harbour area

WHARF STREET beside the River South Esk is one-sided. At its W corner with Bridge Street, Nos. 1–2, a harled two-storey vernacular block, probably of the later C18. Beside it, the plain ashlar-fronted early C19 No. 4. No. 6, also early C19, is more ambitious. At its ground floor, a narrow door with a semicircular fanlight, flanked by broad segmental-arched shop openings, now partly built up to give privacy to the flats which now lie behind. At the first and second floors, three-light windows in the outer bays, those of the first floor with hoodmoulds. Mutuled cornice. Again of the early C19 but without ambition is No. 8. It is followed by the drydashed front, proably C18, of

Nos. 9–11 (the former SAILORS' HALL) and Nos. 12–13 of *c.* 1840, both buildings reconstructed by the Angus Housing Association in the late C20. More late C20 housing before reaching No. 26 which is perhaps late C18 but covered with charmless render. Much better is the early C19 block at Nos. 28–33, with a pilastrade at the ground floor and a blocking course above the main cornice. On the corner with Shore Wynd, the harled mid-C19 SOUTH ESK INN with a prominent wall-head chimney. On the other side of the street, two bronze STATUES. The W ('Bamse'), a colossal figure of a Norwegian St Bernard dog who served on a minesweeper during the Second World War, is by *Alan Beattie Heriot*, 2006. The E ('The Seafarer') was modelled by *William Lamb*, *c.* 1940 but not cast until *c.* 1977, an accomplished piece of realism.

HILL STREET runs uphill to the NE. On its SE side, overlooking the W end of the Harbour (*see* Public Buildings, p. 625), a plain mid-C19 WAREHOUSE, now drydashed, its roof piended towards the street. For the Southesk Primary School fronting Hill Place and the Melville Mission Hall in Southesk Street to its N, *see* Public Buildings, above.

RIVER STREET to the SE of Hill Street runs parallel to the Harbour from which it is separated by warehouses. On its NE side, more warehouses probably of the earlier C19, the walls generally of rubble with some cherry-cock pointing in stone or brick but one gable is of brick; all now covered with corrugated iron roofs. In AMERICA STREET to the SW, the mid-C19 No. 3 is a Georgian survival mixture of offices, warehousing and housing round a courtyard. Back in River Street, SE of California Street, is TOWER HOUSE (No. 12). The main block is a plain rendered house, probably of *c.* 1800. A three-storey battlemented ashlar-faced tower was added to the centre of the front *c.* 1830. Pointed ground-floor windows containing Y-tracery and horizontal glazing. More horizontal glazing in the tall rectangular windows of the first floor. At the top floor, big dummy keyhole gunloops. Opposite, the early C19 No. 5 River Street, its centre emphasized by a wall-head gable and three-light windows. This house has suffered the addition of a C20 box dormer. So too has the early C19 No. 1 (RIVERDALE HOUSE), now too badly altered for mention were it not that its garden gatepiers are still topped by urns from which springs an anthemion-foliaged iron overthrow lampholder.

On MERIDIAN STREET'S SE side, a long two-storey warehouse of coursed squared rubble, dated 1905 at the segment-headed S gable. Closing the street's NE view are the mid-C19 DOCK BUILDINGS which fill the width between Ferry Street and Erskine Street. Built of ashlar, polished at the ground floor and stugged above; rusticated quoins. Thirteen-bay front, the centre carried up a floor higher than the three storeys of the rest and topped by an open pediment containing a clock face. Elliptical-arched centre door in a corniced surround of vermiculated masonry. At the other front entrances the surrounds are channelled. Behind, facing CALEDONIA STREET, the slightly later and lumpier rubble-built CALEDONIA GRANARY, of four storeys and an attic. Front of six bays, the centre two topped by a large gablet pierced by a round window. At Caledonia Street's W end, a long ashlar-clad tenement development of 1850 (Nos. 1–5 Caledonia Street and Nos. 43–77 Ferry Street), its main front to FERRY STREET. Three-storey ends, their roofs piended at the outer gables. At each of these end blocks, a trio of doors, the centre one under a consoled open pediment, and cornices and aprons at the first-floor windows. Long centre of two storeys and an attic with bowed dormers. Again the doors are tripleted with a cornice over the centre of each threesome. First-floor windows with aprons but no cornices. At Ferry Street's N end, on the corner of Commerce Street, a V-plan Art Deco block of flats by *W. M. Patrick & Co.*, 1937–8, the cream-harled walls originally enlivened by horizontal strips of red brickwork (now also painted cream), the would-be modernity belied by the pitched roofs just visible above the parapet. Cantilevered concrete balconies project into the courtyard behind.

Mid Links and neighbourhood

MID LINKS, formerly a golfing area, was laid out from the 1870s as a string of municipal gardens, bowling greens and tennis courts that run almost the length of the town, a genteel and arboreal contrast to the traffic-choked commercialism of the parallel High Street. On the N side of Erskine Place, at the corner with GIBSON PLACE, a square three-storey pyramid-roofed and ball-finialled pavilion of an early C19 warehouse. Here begins Mid Links' S section, laid out as a garden in 1875–6, the bowling green at its N end formed in 1878 and provided with a cottagey pavilion in 1911. This green space is overlooked from the E by MELVILLE GARDENS which starts with a short two-storey-and-attic terrace (Nos. 8–10), probably of the 1870s, the detail faintly Italianate but heavy-handed, the dormer windows' wrought-iron finials welcome survivors. At the gable of No. 8 what seems at first glance to be a lower extension of that house but actually belongs to Melville Gardens' next development (of 1887) and serves as a hinge covering the obtuse-angled join of the two sections, its idiosyncratic detail not providing a gentle transition from one style to another but unrelated to both. It is bow-fronted, built of ashlar, the main walling bull-nosed but crossed by polished band courses below the windows. The ground-floor window is flanked by dummy arrowslits, all with shouldered arches. Above, dummy windows flank a column-mullioned oriel. On the polished ashlar parapet, the inscription: VICTORIA VILLAS, the name of Nos. 3–7 Melville Gardens. After this roguish introduction the houses form a fairly conventional Neo-Jacobean terrace, the polished ashlar masonry channelled at the ground floor. Each of the three-storey-and-attic houses is of two bays, composed of a two-storey canted bay window and a segmental-arched door under a rectangular oriel projected on heavy moulded corbels and surmounted by a glazed conservatory roof. On the front face of each oriel, oval panels framed by carved foliage; rosettes on the necking of the column-mullion of each oriel's two-light window. Over the end houses, shaped gablets. Just off the centre of the terrace, a very small pediment broken by an open-centred stone oval, a nagging reminder that the terrace is one house too long or too short for symmetry. To the N, the Town Hall (*see* Public Buildings, above). Then, two villas of *c.* 1860, PARK HOUSE, expensive Italianate, and ESK HOUSE, symmetrical Jacobean of a sort, the bay windows' parapets pierced by round-headed arcading.

ACADEMY SQUARE to the N serves as a forecourt to Montrose Academy (*see* Public Buildings, above). Then, a broad formal garden (DEAN'S GREEN) laid out *c.* 1880 with St Mary's and St Peter's Episcopal Church (*see* Churches, above) at its far end. At the S end of Dean's Green, a SUNDIAL on a bulbous baluster stem. It was erected in Melville Gardens in 1876 and moved here in 1965. To its N, the DEAN'S LAMP, a cast-iron lamppost-cum-fountain by *McDowall, Steven & Co.*, of the *Milton Ironworks*, 1881. Elaborate Victorian Renaissance, decorated with the heads of dolphins, lions and cherubs, mistletoe and acorns. Further N again, a stone STATUE of Robert Burns by *W. Birnie Rhind*, commissioned in 1889 but not erected here until 1912. The poet is depicted standing in front of corn sheaves. On each face of the Gothic pedestal, a figure in high relief. On the W side of Academy Square and Dean's Green, the mid-C19 houses of PANMURE PLACE. First, a *cottage orne* (No. 8) with extravagantly large and wavy bargeboards, bay windows and a fish-scale-slated iron-crested truncated spire. Mid or late C19 Georgian survival houses to the N. Beyond the former St Mary's Episcopal Church (*see* Churches, above), No. 1 Panmure Place (DUNGEITH), by *Thoms & Wilkie*, 1925, its squared-up Scottish Arts and Crafts a contrast to the polished classicism of the adjacent Montrose Museum (*see* Public Buildings, above). PANMURE TERRACE, built by *Japp*, *c.* 1850, takes 86
its cue from the Museum. Palace-front of polished ashlar, channelled at the ground floor. At each end, a flatted block of three storeys and an attic, the outer ends of the roofs piended, with an Ionic-columned doorpiece in the centre of the front (the capitals of No. 7's replaced with unmoulded blocks). Aprons under the first-floor windows, a band course below the smaller windows of the second floor. Between these end blocks, four houses grouped as two pairs, each pair sharing an acanthus-decorated cast-iron balcony. Three of the original bowed dormers survive; the fourth has been replaced by a box.

EASTERN ROAD on the E side of Dean's Green contains the front of the Chapel Works (*see* below) whose buildings stretch back along Marine Avenue and Paton Lane. On the N side of Paton Lane, at its W end, YELLOW TUBS, an early C19 ashlar-fronted house with a consoled cornice over the door and an overall parapet.

SCOTT'S PARK, the portion of Mid Links between St Peter's Road and Melville Road, was laid out *c.* 1882, trees forming a border and also a saltire across the grass in the middle. At the centre of the saltire, a MONUMENT to Provost George Scott, by *D. Wishart Galloway*, 1903–4. Square pier with battered sides and a domed top, executed in red Dumfriesshire sandstone ashlar. The ball finial (restored) was added in 1905, together with a wrought-iron finial (later removed). At the SW face, a round-arched granite-columned recess containing a bronze plaque bearing a relief portrait of Scott. On the W side of Scott's Park, CHAPEL PLACE. At its S end, late C20 housing, a busy brick and drydash evocation of traditional burgh architecture of the C16 or C17 including gables to the street and a jettied timber outshot, not entirely appropriate in this genteel C19 context. To the N, the early C19 Nos. 8–10, a round-headed window in the central wall-head gablet. After the shoddy-looking infill of *c.* 1967 at Nos. 6–7, mid-C19 houses, No. 5 with the cornice over the door carried on elegant tall consoles and with a Jacobean chimneyed gablet at the centre of the wall-head, the asymmetrical Nos. 2–3 with gableted dormerheads. The front of No. 1 Chapel Place has been covered in bull-nosed render and its ground-floor windows altered but the small upper windows suggest an C18 date. On the E side of Scott's Park, ST PETER'S PLACE. Nos. 6–10 form a terrace of mid-C19 cottages, the cornices over the doors of Nos. 8–10 carried on ridiculously heavy consoles.

GREEN PARK, formed with a central avenue *c.* 1890, and HOPE PATON GARDENS, laid out with a garden and bowling green by the Montrose Burgh Surveyor, *S. L. Christie*, 1904,* fill Mid Links between Melville Road and Wellington Street. In Hope Paton Gardens, the burgh's WAR MEMORIAL designed by *George Washington Browne*, 1922–4. Bronze figure of Victory (by *H. S. Gamley*) on a tall granite stepped pedestal. Flanking granite blocks topped by bronze laurels (cast by *George Mancini*) were added by *William Lamb* in 1948–9 as a Second World War memorial. To the N, the bowling green with a small PAVILION of 1904. On the S corner of JOHN STREET to the W, LINKS LODGE, an idiosyncratically smart ashlar-clad villa of the earlier C19. Main block of two storeys, a basement and attic, with three-light ground- and first-floor windows at its r. bay. Across this block's N side is stretched a second block of only a single storey. On its E end, an Ionic portico. Canopied windows at its three-bay N front to John Street. On John Street's N corner, a mid-C19 villa (the PARK HOTEL), now much altered and extended. Further up John Street, on the N side, the former St John's Church (*see* Churches, above) followed by a Georgian survival terrace (Nos. 53–57) of *c.* 1845, the Registration Office (*see* Public Buildings, above) and more mid-C19 Georgian survival housing.

* The design based on one by Christie's predecessor, *J. R. Findlay*.

On the E side of Mid Links, UNION PLACE. At its S end, No. 3 of 1892, with canted bay windows corbelled out to the square and topped by bargeboarded gables. They flank the curly-topped door over which a window rises into a a bargeboarded dormerhead. Then two terraces (Nos. 4–7 and 8–11) of *c.* 1840, each containing four houses grouped as pairs marked off by rusticated quoins. At Nos. 4–7, tall consoles under the doors' cornices; at Nos. 8–11, aproned ground-floor windows and round-headed fanlit entrances. Between these two terraces is the entry to UNION STREET which contains more Georgian survival of *c.* 1840. At No. 7, an unusually broad entrance, the recessed door flanked by pilasters. At Nos. 17–19 (its top floor now drydashed), paired doors under a pediment.

JAMIESON PATON PARK, formed in 1904–5, continues the formal layout of Mid Links. In the middle of its saltire-plan planting, a Gothic FOUNTAIN of red and grey granite with a foliage-finialled spired top, erected in 1905. The ground to the N was laid out in 1912 as a lavish municipal garden. In WHITE'S PLACE to the W, Nos. 26–33 form a terrace of paired cottages with bay windows linked by verandas which shelter the twinned entrances. At White's Place's N end, on the corner of Dorward Street, DORWARD COURT, sheltered housing by *Baxter, Clark & Paul*, *c.* 1989. Modern-traditional with canted corners and a tall recessed window. On the E side of Jamieson Paton Park, another terrace, Nos. 1–6 WELLINGTON PLACE of 1868. At its S end, a round corner turret, a fish-scale-slated spire rising within the battlement; steep Jacobean spike-finialled gablet on No. 4.

The N end of Mid Links is occupied by tennis courts and a low PAVILION of 1925 but still Edwardian in spirit; it is by the Burgh Surveyor, *David Maxwell*. In DORWARD PLACE to the W, Nos. 1–4, a pair of Late Victorian single-storey-and-attic double houses. At each pair, advanced Jacobean gabled ends and bay windows at the centre. Baroque consoles to the doors' cornices.

DORWARD ROAD goes E towards the Links of Montrose (the present golf courses). At the road's start, Dorward House (*see* Public Buildings, above) set well back. The E end of the road becomes TRAILL DRIVE. On its N side, overlooking the Links, GREY HARLINGS, a rambling harled and half-timbered villa of *c.* 1900, with a display of oriel windows and jettying. On the S, the ROYAL MONTROSE GOLF CLUB, uninspired early C20 with an equally uninspired late C20 extension. To its S, the MONTROSE MERCANTILE GOLF CLUB of 1902–3. Single-storey Jacobean Renaissance, its Dutch gables decorated with scrawny birds. The l. gable also bears the relief of a golfer. S of this, ROO'S LEAP, a heavy late C19 villa with broad eaves and aggressively hammer-dressed masonry.

CHAPEL WORKS, Eastern Road, Marine Avenue and Paton's Lane. Huge industrial complex developed as a flax-spinning works from 1828 when the Montrose merchants and ship-owners, J. & G. Paton, built a mill and warehouse near the NW corner of the site. Expansion of the works continued through most of the C19. Textile manufacture here ceased in 1967 when the works were taken over as a bottling plant and some of the buildings converted to bonded warehouses. Since 1989, when this use ceased, parts have been demolished and replaced by housing, the rest apparently left to dereliction.

The S RANGE along Marine Avenue was built *c.* 1875 on the site of a ropeworks. Sixty-nine bays of stugged ashlar masonry, all single-storey except for two short two-storey sections (the W a beam-engine house) and quite plain, the sheer length impressive. The severe but dignified front block facing Eastern Road was built *c.* 1875. Tall single-storey. Seventeen bays, the two at each end and the two each side of the central entrance slightly advanced and with rusticated quoins and higher parapets. Above the round-arched entrance, the date 1795 (presumably commemorating the foundation of the firm), the style of the numerals innocent of any attempt to suggest that this is C18 work. Behind, what now forms a central range but until the 1870s the S range of the mill. It dates from the earlier C19, with regular fenestration, the top windows quite small. The E range of *c.* 1855 contained flax warehouses. Two storeys, the seven bays alternately advanced and recessed, with rusticated quoins and parapets at the projecting bays and segmental-arched doors at the others.

3030

MUIRHEAD AND BIRKHILL

Originally two villages but now conjoined, Muirhead (the W) predominantly late C19 and dour, Birkhill a mixture of mid and late C19 cottages and C20 housing.

MUIRHEAD CHURCH, Coupar Angus Road. Built as Liff Free Church in 1843. Rubble-walled box with round-headed windows. Corniced birdcage bellcote on the N gable; ventilator, probably a late C19 addition, on the centre of the roof.

BIRKHILL PRIMARY SCHOOL NURSERY CLASS, Coupar Angus Road. By *William Paterson*, 1846, and originally a Free Church school. Small and quite simple, the walls of rubble, the S front of three bays.

MUIRHEAD SCHOOL, School Wynd. Now housing. By *Thoms & Wilkie*, 1911–12. Squared-up free Wrenaissance. Single-storey, with tall windows rising into piended dormerheads, and ogee-domed and wrought-iron-finialled cupolas on the gambrel-gabled roof.

4030

MURROES

Murroes Church and Murroes House standing almost alone above the Murroes Burn.

MONIFIETH FREE CHURCH, Hillock, 1.3 km. SE. Now housing. Rubble-walled oblong built in 1846–7. Corbelled out from the W gable, a birdcage bellcote whose cast-iron columns support the ogee-profiled and ball-finialled stone-slabbed roof. Ball-finialled porch at the W end, session house at the E. – Mid-C19 piend-roofed MANSE to the E.

MURROES CHURCH. By the Dundee Town's Architect, *William Scott*, 1848. Gothic, built of squared rubble, a T with a N jamb and, in the inner angles, full-height outshots, the W containing the gallery stair, the E the vestry. Low gabled porches at the E and W ends of the main block. Diagonal buttresses at all corners. In the main block's S side, four broad lancet windows, their hoodmoulds with pendant label stops. The outer windows are each of two lights with wooden mullions and tracery, the two centre windows were remodelled in 1892 as single lights with stone tracery. In the E and W gables, large rose windows containing wooden tracery. Corbelled out from the W gable, an octagonal bellcote, its faces gabled; stone spire of bellcast profile. Foliate crosses on the E gable and the N gable of the jamb. In the jamb's gable, a large stone-mullioned window of three lights, its window also with pendant label stops. In this gable are set two early or mid-C17 stones, one carved with the coat of arms and initials of Thomas Fothringham of Powrie, the other with those of his wife, Margaret Gibson. In the jamb's W side, a stone finished with a flat-topped pediment bearing the coats of arms and monogrammed initials of Thomas Fothringham and Margaret Gibson together with the date 1642.

Inside, the PULPIT, covered by an elaborate and heavily detailed Tudor Gothic canopy, stands at the centre of the S side facing the panel-fronted GALLERY in the jamb. – Boxy PEWS. – In the gallery, a CHAMBER ORGAN of the 1830s, originally installed in a private house and later in Balgay Church, Dundee, and moved here in 1924. – Set into the jamb's E wall, an early or mid-C17 STONE carved with eight coats of arms identified as those of Fothringham, Scott, Lyndsay (twice), Gibson, Craigie, Ærthe and Herit representing the progenitors of Thomas Fothringham and Margaret Gibson. – STAINED GLASS. In the Gothic screen erected in 1893 to cut off the end of the jamb, a heraldic light displaying the coat of arms of Robert McGavin of Ballumbie. – In the end windows of the S wall, glass of 1885, the surrounds and central narrative scenes (the Baptism of Our Lord and the Sermon on the Mount; the Crucifixion and Ascension) apparently by different artists. – In the two centre windows flanking the pulpit, glass (Faith; Blessed are the Pure in Heart) by *James Ballantine & Son* and *A. Ballantine & Gardiner*, 1885 and 1892. – In the N wall of the vestry, a single light (St Matthew) of 1885.

GRAVEYARD. Propped against the church's NW outshot, the GRAVE-SLAB of William Couper, hammerman, †1649 and his wife †1646, the top bearing the crowned hammer of the smiths between the initials WC, the bottom incised with a pair of skulls and crossbones. – Against the graveyard's N wall, some C18 HEADSTONES carved variously with angels' heads (souls), reminders of death and shields displaying trade emblems. – Beside the N gateway, a stone fragment, probably of *c.* 1600, carved with the torso of an angel clad in doublet and ruff and bearing a shield with the Fothringham coat of arms. – Against the N end of the graveyard's E wall, a large egg-and-dart-bordered GRAVE-SLAB, perhaps of the mid C18, carved in relief with a pair of angels' heads above a prostrate skeleton. – Between this and the church's E end, the HEADSTONE erected in 1762 by James Nicol, tailor in Buckler-heads, to the memory of his children. The E face is carved with an aedicular frame containing an angel's head above a panel bearing the iron, shears and pressing board of a tailor. – Just S of the church, various TABLE STONES and GRAVE-SLABS with angels' heads at their top and emblems of death at the bottom. – W of the church, the TABLE STONE of Alexander Edward †1655 and his twin grandchildren †1660, the top of the slab with a floating angel blowing a trumpet, the bottom with four naked human figures. – Just S of the graveyard's W gateway, a pair of crisply carved HEADSTONES. One is of 1762 and commemorates Alexander Lindsay, the pilastered and swan-neck-pedimented W face bearing a high relief of a helm-crested and mantled shield under an angel's head. The other, of 1756, is similar but the shield bears a weaver's loom and shuttle and there are emblems of death at the base. – More emblems of death and angels' heads on a couple of TABLE STONES to the SE. – SE again the HEADSTONE erected by John Gibson and Barbara Swan to her father, George. It is a swan-neck-pedimented aedicule. Inside, a central panel bears a shield with George Swan's initials and the date 1765 above a pair of angels' heads.

N of the graveyard, U-plan STABLES AND COACHHOUSE (now CHURCH HALL) of the former manse of 1811 (demolished, *c.* 1970). Single-storey under a loft and rubble-walled.

MURROES HOUSE. A secondary residence of the Fothringhams of Powrie built in the mid or later C16 and extended *c.* 1600. It is a rubble-walled crowstep-gabled oblong of two storeys, the upper windows rising through the eaves to catslide dormerheads, perhaps added in the C19. The earliest part is at the N end, a square house with, at its SW corner, a bowed stair-tower which was given a conical roof (replacing a swept roof) in 1942. In the E side, gunloops beneath ground- and first-floor windows; forestair to a porch, perhaps of the early C19, at the N end which encloses the C16 first-floor roll-moulded entrance. Ball finial on the N gable in which there is another gunloop. More gunloops and shot-holes in this part's W elevation, both at the main block and the stair-tower. The piend-roofed S extension of *c.* 1600 is of the same width and height but longer. Shot-holes in its W side. Single-storey S addition of the 1960s.

Inside, the ground floor of the N part (the original house) is occupied by the kitchen but this may originally have been a hall. The base of the turnpike stair is below ground-floor level and carried on a pair of moulded corbels. On the first floor, the walls of the 'laird's room' at the N are lined with panelling of 1859 from the demolished Fothringham House.

KINGENNIE HOUSE, 1.4km. E. Ensconced on a wooded hillside, a harled three-storey Arts and Crafts villa of markedly vertical emphasis, by *T. Martin Cappon*, *c.* 1905. Main block with a tall and narrow centrepiece, the house's entrance and its sidelights under a broad elliptical-arched fanlight. This is squeezed between a pair of gables, their lower two-thirds covered by boldly advanced and generously sized two-storey bows. Lower two-storey lateral wing set back at the W end, an oriel window at its upper floor.

FORT AND BROCH, Craighill, 3 km. W. The W end of a steep-sided promontory in a bend of the Pithie Burn has been fortified in the first millennium B.C. by the cutting of a ditch and the construction of a rampart behind. In the resulting enclosure, foundations of a broch, probably erected in the first millennium A.D. It is 19.8 m. in diameter, the wall *c.* 4.6 m. thick.

GAGIE HOUSE. *See* p. 491.

NEVAY *see* KIRKINCH

NEWBIGGING

4030

Straggle of C19 houses and cottages.

NEWBIGGING UNITED PRESBYTERIAN CHURCH. Disused. By *James Maclaren*, 1864. Rubble-built box, the side walls with round-headed windows. Diagonally buttressed front (E) gable whose hoodmoulded Gothic two-light windows flank the slightly advanced centrepiece topped by a gableted bellcote. Here, a pointed door under an ogee hoodmould; above, a narrow Gothic light and a round clock face.

DOOCOT, Pitairlie, 0.8 km. N. Rubble-built and crowstep-gabled lectern doocot, probably of the C17. Along the back wall, a couple of projecting rat courses which have returned across the gables and presumably the front. A large entrance for machinery has been inserted in the front wall and the roof covered with corrugated iron.

SOUTERRAIN, Ardestie, 1.8 km. S. On a low hill, an underground passage, now excavated and unroofed, and associated surface structures, all constructed *c.* 100 A.D. The main passage was entered from the SW through a narrow 3 m.-long downward-sloping passage, the walls formed of boulders and flagstones and inclined towards the top; at its entry from the surface, a pair of squared stone pillars. The entrance to the curved main passage is marked by a pair of large flagstones set on edge. This passage, now curtailed but still *c.* 20 m. long, is *c.* 2 m. wide and the inwardly corbelled walls, also of boulders and flagstones, probably rose originally to a height of *c.* 2 m. so its roof must have pushed above ground level. The floor is paved irregularly, again with flagstones and boulders. In it, for two-thirds of its length, has been inserted a drain, an afterthought necessitated by the souterrain having been dug in boulder clay. On the surface and SW of the main passage there survives the base of walling and the paving of four interconnected structures, also built of boulders and flagstones. The NW has had an external entrance, the SE a door into the souterrain.

SOUTERRAIN, Carlungie, 1.3 km. E. In a fenced-off grassy enclosure in the middle of a field, a souterrain constructed *c.* 100 A.D. This is an irregularly curved underground passage, *c.* 39 m. long, the walls built of drystone boulders and flags, the roof now missing. Two S spurs off the main passage and one to the N. On the surface of the ground outside and associated with the souterrain are eight paved areas, probably the remains of dwellings or workshops.

6060

NEWTONMILL HOUSE

2 km. SW of Stracathro

Late C17 harled laird's house, altered in the C18 and C19 and restored by *Robert Hurd & Partners*, 1959, to an approximation of the original appearance. The house is of two storeys and an attic, the present canted dormer windows additions of 1959. Sandstone ashlar strip quoins and surrounds to the door and windows of the S front. This is of five bays, the openings grouped 2:1:2; in the centre, a moulded stone doorpiece of late C17 type and, above, an oval first-floor window, both provided in 1959. Two rear wings, both probably mid-C18, the space between infilled later. Inside, a late C17 stair with moulded stone risers. Some panelling of early C18 appearance but it is of plaster and perhaps of 1959. Extending W from the main block, a rubble-built SCREEN WALL, perhaps of *c.* 1820, its higher centre section with ball finials. Behind, a piend-roofed two-storey COTTAGE (former laundry), rubble-built and probably also early C19.

GARDEN directly S of the house, the walls of rubble and perhaps dating from the late C18. They are high on three sides but low on the N allowing a view into the garden from the house. In the garden's SE corner, a rubble-walled and pyramidal-roofed square DOOCOT, probably of the C18. Inside, stone nesting boxes placed at a high level on the walls. – Just S of the garden, an early C19 rubble-built and piend-roofed single-storey COTTAGE. S front of three bays with Gothic windows and a later wooden porch.

STABLES W of the house, a harled and piend-roofed two-storey mid-C18 block. Rusticated quoins at the outer corners of the E front. This is of five bays with round openings at the first floor of the outer bays. Broad centrepiece, its crowning pediment with a small dummy oculus. Pilastered and basket-arched carriage entrance and, above, a rectangular opening flanked by circular dummy windows. – N of the stables, a two-storey rubble-built late C18 MILL (now housing). – On its W, the harled single-storey-and-attic GARDENER'S HOUSE (former mill house), also late C18 in origin but the prettily carved bargeboards of the dormer window and the gabled porch are mid-C19.

LODGE at the end of the E drive, of *c.* 1800, a small rubble-walled oblong under a broad-eaved piended roof; at the E front, a window in a segmental-headed overarch. Contemporary corniced GATEPIERS of channelled ashlar, now with *Coade* stone swagged urns of 1765.

NEWTYLE

2040

Planned village laid out on a gridiron plan by *George Mathewson* in 1832. The first inhabitants were mainly agricultural labourers, many of whom also worked as weavers. The houses now are predominantly of the C19 and earlier C20, the earlier mostly rubble-walled, the later harled.

NEWTYLE CHURCH, corner of Dundee Road and Kirkton Road. By *Andrew Heiton Jun.*, 1870–2, a Presbyterian-planned kirk clad in carefully detailed Early English dress, the squared masonry of bull-nosed red sandstone. Oblong main block with N and S transepts. In the S transept's E inner angle with the main block, a helm-roofed tower surmounted by a weather-cock and with tall two-light belfry openings under quatrefoil lights; in the E face, the church's principal entrance.

At each gable of the main block, a window of four lights, the openings grouped 2:2 under a plate-traceried head. Shallow N transept flanked by mirror-image low outshots housing the vestry and session house. The triple-gabled S transept is much bolder and broader, its internal gallery lit from plate-traceried rose windows.

The tower door opens into a vestibule containing the stair to the S transept's gallery and, on the r., the entrance to the church. Over the body of the church, an open kingpost-truss roof with collar-braces pierced by quatrefoils and with small hammerbeams. Over the 'crossing' the collar-braces are placed as intersecting diagonals, their S ends supported on corbels carved as human heads; the other supporting corbels are foliate. At the S transept, cast-iron columns with large foliaged capitals support the transverse roofs and laird's loft, its front decorated with quatrefoils. The N transept now contains the ORGAN (by *William Hill & Son and Norman & Beard*, 1937; rebuilt by *David W. Loosley* in 1977), its oak case fronted by the oak PULPIT of 1963 and COMMUNION TABLE of 1939, both in a Lorimerian manner. – PEWS of 1872, their ends pierced by quatrefoils. – E of the pulpit, a bronze MONUMENT to Edward, third Baron and first Earl of Wharncliffe, designed by

R. Rowand Anderson in 1906, a large coat of arms accompanying the inscription. – STAINED GLASS. In the N transept, a strongly coloured narrative window (the Risen Christ flanked by Scenes of Charity) of 1908, formerly in Newtyle United Free Church. – The S transept's three rose windows are filled with depictions of birds and flowers by *A. Carrick Whalen*, 1989–90. – The clearly drawn W window (Scenes from the Life of Our Lord) is of 1924–5. – In the vestibule, one light (St Michael) by *Alexander L. Russell*, 1948.

GRAVEYARD. At the E entrance, Tudorish octagonal GATE-PIERS of *c.* 1840, topped by shallow pyramids. The wrought-iron GATES AND OVERTHROW are of the later C20. – On the graveyard's W side, a range of ashlar-fronted BURIAL ENCLOSURES of the earlier C19, the elliptical-arched entrances set between battered and panelled piers, also with pyramidal tops. – S of the church, an C18 TABLE STONE to members of the Jobson family, its top panel carved in high relief with human figures, an angel's head (the soul) and hourglass, the bottom with emblems of death. – Immediately to the S, the TABLE STONE commemorating James Jobsone †1674, its centre bearing the low relief of a skull and bones. – SE of the church, a couple of C18 HEADSTONES (one dated 1768) which bear weavers' shuttles.

White-harled MANSE set back from the S side of Kirkton Road. The two-storey main block is of 1771, a three-light window at the r. of the front's upper floor. The l. part of the front is overlaid by a full-height addition, probably of 1894.

NEWTYLE FREE CHURCH, Belmont Street. Now LEGION HALL. By *William Paterson*, 1844–5. Church-cum-school, of the humblest sort, now with a corrugated iron roof.

NEWTYLE UNITED FREE CHURCH, Castle Street. Now church hall. By *John Robertson* of Meigle, 1901. Simple Gothic, the walls of stugged brownish masonry with dressings of red Keithock sandstone. T-plan with transepts forming the S cross-bar. On the S side a square tower, the top stage with three-light belfry openings; a red-tiled small spire rises within the battlement.

NEWTYLE UNITED SECESSION CHURCH, Church Street. Now WHARNCLIFFE HALL. By *Peter Scott*, 1835. Rubble-built broad box with Y-traceried pointed windows.

NEWTYLE PRIMARY SCHOOL, Dundee Road. By *James F. Stephen*, 2006–7. Determinedly cheerful with brightly coloured rendered walls and opposed ribbed metal curved roofs.

RAILWAY STATION, corner of Commercial Street and Knox Close. Built in 1831–2 as the terminus of the Dundee & Newtyle Railway. Goods shed of a single tall storey, the walls of rubble with broached ashlar dressings, the roof now of corrugated iron. In the S gable, two segmental-arched entrances of different sizes. At the N end, a single large entrance, also segmental-arched. The W end of this gable is overlaid by a platform on which stands a lower single-storey passenger station, its E front brick-walled, the N gable and back wall of rubble; slated roof.

BANNATYNE HOUSE, Kirkton Road. A much altered and extended white-harled house begun *c.* 1575 for James Bannatyne. The earliest part is at the W, a crowstep-gabled two-storey-and-attic main block, the three-light windows, very tall at the first floor, probably altered in the late C18. At the N corners, conical-roofed turrets on continuous corbelling, the W a late C19 addition, the two-storey E turret probably late C16, its lower part bowed, the upper corbelled to the square. The remainder is of the C19 and early C20, partly by *C. & L. Ower*, 1897 and 1916, but reduced in size and remodelled in 1962. In the E face of the low SE wing, a stone bearing impaled coats of arms and the initials T^{M}B for Mr Thomas Bannatyne, a lawyer who built an addition (later removed) to the original house in 1589. At this wing's S end, a late C20 L-plan turreted screen wall into which are set a couple of large dormerheads of the late C16 or early C17, one carved with thistles, the other with a sunburst.

KINPURNEY TOWER, Kinpurney Hill, 2.6 km. E. Hilltop landmark, a three-stage tower built as a folly by James Stuart-Mackenzie of Belmont and Rosehaugh in 1774. It is a rubble-walled oblong, *c.* 9 m. by 6 m. and 12 m. high. Rising flush with the wall-head, tall merlons making a crude battlement on three sides, the S side originally lower but later heightened although without a battlement.

PRIVY'S PRAP, Keillor Hill, 2.2 km. SW. Ball-finialled 6 m.-high tapering round column constructed of solid rubble. It was erected in 1774 by James Stuart-Mackenzie of Belmont and Rosehaugh to be used in conjunction with a mark on the lawn of Belmont Castle to indicate the meridian passage of the sun.

HATTON CASTLE. *See* p. 519.

KINPURNIE CASTLE. *See* p. 566.

NORANSIDE 4060

1.2 km. SW of Fern

Competent but uninspired two-storey late C18 classical mansion house built for a London merchant, John Mill, and extended for his son and namesake in 1797.

Long and harled S front. Five-bay piend-roofed main block, its slightly advanced centrepiece of three bays marked off by pilasters, their capitals remodelled in simplified form, which carry a pediment containing an oculus. Sidelit entrance under a semicircular fanlight with delicate cast-iron tracery and flanked by corniced ground floor windows. The main block is joined by one-bay recessed links of 1797, their ground-floor windows round-headed, to the broader and taller pedimented contemporary ends on the same plane as the main block. Each of these ends is also of a single bay, its front ground-floor window of three lights with Roman Doric pier-mullions and covered by a semicircular dummy fanlight.

Inside, the entrance hall ceiling enriched with swagged plaster drapery. Further swagged embellishment on the lintel of the N door. This opens onto the stair hall, the stair itself with anthemion-decorated balusters. Doorways with fan decoration in their semicircular heads. The main block's principal rooms face S. The W, probably the drawing room, has a swagged frieze under the simple cornice. Painted pine and gesso chimneypiece with reeded jambs and lintel, the lintel bearing swags and urns. The E room was probably the dining room. Bowed N end and plaster-panelled walls. Another painted pine and gesso chimneypiece, the lintel decorated with a basket of fruit, urns and anthemion; foliaged pendants on the jambs.

Extensive but low and unassertive additions to the N and W, built for the house's late C20 use as an open prison (closed in 2011).

Early C19 STABLES to the SW. At each end of the S front, an ashlar-faced pavilion with a carriage entrance under a semicircular dummy fanlight. Lower two-storey three-bay rubble-built links, their upper windows of horizontal proportion, join to the tall gabled centrepiece. Like the ends, this is ashlar-faced and contains a carriage entrance, its semicircular fanlight with wooden tracery.

4050

OATHLAW

Small village, the houses C19 and late C20.

OATHLAW PARISH CHURCH. Now housing. Tall crowstep-gabled and rubble-walled box, the N side now harled, built in 1815. The windows are tall and pointed except the E gable's which was remodelled with plate tracery by *John Carver*, 1881. On the centre of the S side, a battlemented tower of three stages, the ground floor with Gothic windows in the E and W faces. The tower's S door, its hoodmould with spiral-carved pendant label stops, and upper stages' paired windows are all round-headed.

GRAVEYARD. S of the church, several C18 HEADSTONES crisply and variously carved with angels' heads, shields bearing trade emblems, and reminders of death. One, commemorating Kathleen Watson †1750, also has foliate-capitalled pilasters.

Former MANSE (now Oathlaw House) just to the E. Harled and piend-roofed L of two storeys. The main block was built by *James Winter*, wright in Forfar, in 1812. The slightly taller wing projecting from the r. bay of the front was added in 1833, as may have been the flat-roofed porch in the inner angle.

OATHLAW TANNADICE PARISH CHURCH. *See* Tannadice.

DOOCOT, Milton of Finavon, 1.6 km. ENE. Large harled double-chamber lectern doocot, probably built in the earlier C20 and much restored in the later C20. Crowsteps on the gables and central partition wall. Rat course formed by thin projecting slabs placed just below the eaves along the S front; at the eaves it steps up and returns along the back wall *c.* 1.8 m. below a string course. In the front a pair of doors under the central moulded surround of a missing panel. On the roof a couple of low horizontally proportioned dormers containing the flight entrances. The back wall rises above the roof as a parapet which rises into crowstepped and ball-finialled gablets at the centre and ends; obelisk finials between the gablets.

FINAVON CASTLE. *See* p. 465.

PANBRIDE

5030

Just the Parish Church, its Victorian former MANSE (now Panbride Glebe) and the school.

PANBRIDE FREE CHURCH. *See* Carnoustie: Carnoustie Panbride Church.

PANBRIDE PARISH CHURCH. Plain Gothic T-plan kirk of 1851, built of snecked and stugged grey stone. Doors with shouldered arches. Lancet windows; at the slightly advanced and gabled centre of the S side and the W gable and the gable of the N jamb they are in stepped three-light arrangements. Bellcote on the W gable; fleur-de-lis finials on the other gables.

Attached to the E end of the church is the PANMURE AISLE, the mausoleum of the Earls of Panmure, built or reconstructed in 1681. Lower than the church, it is of two storeys, built of squared rubble, with a moulded cornice along the N and S sides and pinnacles at the outer corners of the E gable. On top of this gable, a bellcote (dated 1681), its panelled pedestal surmounted by four birdcage tiers, their size progresively diminishing; the top tier has battered sides and is finished with a pinnacle. At the ground floor of the Aisle, plain doors in the E gable and S side; in the W end of the N wall, a square window. At the first floor, a two-light E window with chamfered margins; above, a weathered coat of arms in a moulded frame. Windows of the same type in the S side, both rising above the eaves and finished with pinnacled-pedimented dormerheads. In the pediment over the l. window, the initials of George Maule, third Earl of Panmure, and, in the r., those of his wife, Jean Fleming, Countess of Panmure, under the badly weathered carving of a coronet (presumably there was originally also a carved coronet in the l. pediment). Hanging on the S wall, a JOUGS, perhaps of the C18.

Inside the church, a Tudorish plaster ceiling; galleries along the E, W, and N sides. In the centre of the S wall, a PULPIT brought here in 1952 from St Bride's Hall in Carnoustie (q.v.); it is of 1901. – Pictorial STAINED GLASS window (the Risen Lord) of 1897.

GRAVEYARD. Most of the monuments are C19 and C20 but a few earlier ones are worth searching out. Immediately E of the church, a HEADSTONE erected in 1750 by James Stroak, merchant, to his wife, Elizabeth Gibson. The back is carved with a shell flanked by a crossed scythe and arrow and cross-bones. On the front, floral decoration against which stands out a cartouche bearing a merchant's scales with an angel's head (the soul) above. – S of the church, more C18 HEADSTONES, those to David Watt (dated 1797) and William Anderson (dated 1795) with angels' heads with exceptionally large wings in the fashion of the immediate area at that time (cf. the Parish Churchyard at Barry). Another, dated 1755, has Ionic pilasters at the sides and a shield with a mantled helm on the front. Also mid-C18 is the stone commemorating the children of George Anderson and Margaret Webster, its top carved with reminders of death, the sides with torches, the front with the figure of a boy holding a flower and, above, a crown flanked by pudgy angels' heads. – Just to the S of the church's W end, a couple of weathered GRAVE-SLABS (now placed upright) carved with crossed bones. Both look late C17. – Behind them, the HEADSTONE of William Sinclair †1751 aged thirteen, the front showing two angels' heads above the figure of a boy holding a book.

SCHOOL. Harled two-storey three-bay school house, dated 1799 at the lintel of the central first-floor window. Above this window, a chimneyed pedimental gablet containing a blind oculus. C20 porch. Attached to the E gable is the school itself, built in 1816, with round-headed windows and a ball-finialled birdcage bellcote. Its inscription (1886 PANBRIDE PUBLIC SCHOOL) presumably refers to the plain Victorian rear additions.

5030 PANMURE HOUSE

1.9 km. E of Monikie

Panmure House, designed in 1666 by *John Mylne Jun.* for George, second Earl of Panmure, and reconstructed and extended by *David Bryce* in 1852–5, was one of Angus's major mansion houses but was demolished in 1953. The surrounding LANDSCAPE, its present layout mostly mid-C19, and ancillary buildings remain.

EAST GATES AND LODGES by *David Bryce*, 1852. The gateway itself is in the grand late C17 classical manner of the West Gate (*see* below). Large corniced and scroll-sided gatepiers, their stonework of faceted blocks; coroneted ball finials Wrought-iron gates under a monogrammed overthrow. From the gatepiers balustraded low screen walls, their ashlar stugged, join to corniced and strapworked pedestrian entrances. These flank the mirror-image two-storey lodges, also of 1852 but their design reminiscent of early rather than late C17 work.

Each is a crowstep-gabled T, the gable of the E jamb bowed at the ground floor and covered by a rectangular upper storey carried on continuous corbelling. The main block's gable towards the drive is placed between diagonally set full-height projections, the upper storey also on continuous corbelling and surmounted by a broken segmental pediment standing in front an ogee-profiled roof. On each main gable, a carved heraldic achievement and, at the top, barley-sugar chimneys. Pushing out from the lodges are tall stugged ashlar screen walls ending at corniced and ball-finialled piers.

The East Gates open onto the straight avenue which led to the mansion house set back to its N. On the S side of the avenue, opposite the site of the mansion house, the mid-C19 STABLES. Their main part consists of two-storey crowstep-gabled ranges round a rectangular courtyard, the central N entrance a round-arched pend contained in a gable. Single-storey U-plan ranges to the SW, with Scots Jacobean Renaissance ornament and a domed octagonal low tower at the NW corner.

SE of the stables, beside a secondary drive running parallel to the main E avenue, MARGARET'S MOUNT, a terraced mound surmounted by an early C18 monument. This was erected by Lady Margaret Hamilton, wife of James, fourth Earl of Panmure, to celebrate her husband's escape to France after he had taken part in the Jacobite rising of 1715–16. Corniced square pedestal of polished ashlar, one face bearing a swagged oval inscription panel. On the pedestal, a large urn decorated with carved oval rosettes.

At the end of a path running S from the stables is the rubble-walled GARDEN, also of the mid C19. Immediately to its W, the GARDEN HOUSE by Bryce, 1852. Picturesqely gabled and gableted single-storey-and-attic rambling large cottage. – Just SE of the garden, the low remains of PANMURE CASTLE occupying a natural ridge beside the Monikie Burn and the landward N approach cut through by a ditch. It may be of C13 origin.

In Pillar Wood, N of the stables and site of the mansion house, a polished ashlar PILLAR, *c.* 16.8 m. high, erected (according to the inscriptions) by James, fourth Earl of Panmure, and his wife, Margaret Hamilton, to commemorate their marriage in 1694. Above a square pedestal, the corniced pillar itself, each face bearing a full-height pilaster decorated with horizontal panels carved with faceted stone blocks. Between the panels and carried across the faces of the main pillar, pulvinated bands of stonework. The pillar supports a large and richly carved urn. – E of the pillar, a Gothick ARTIFICIAL RUIN of the later C18, a landscape ornament intended to evoke an imaginary monastic past.

W of the stables is the MONTAGU BRIDGE over the Monikie Burn, constructed in 1854, probably to Bryce's design. Three tall round-headed arches, their masonry of rusticated ashlar, carry corbelled string courses under battlements. – To the W, the rubble-built WEST GATE BRIDGE, probably of the late C18 and consisting of a single segmental arch. – In Corriera Den, SE of the bridges and overlooking the Monikie Burn, a pair of stone GARDEN SEATS, probably originally constructed *c.* 1690 as parts of a garden wall but resited here after the wall's demolition and the recasting of Panmure House's setting in the later C18. They are identical, each placed in a shallow rectangular recess flanked by coupled attached Doric columns, the lintel with a Doric entablature.

WEST GATE, W of the Montague and West Gate Bridges, designed by *Sir William Bruce* and built for George, third Earl of Panmure, in 1672. Tall square corniced gatepiers, the ashlar stonework crossed by horizontal bands of masonry. Coroneted ball finials. Wrought-iron gates of elaborate but delicate design incorporating floral and foliage motifs. Flanking the gatepiers are vertical panels, each displaying a heraldic stone. Extending from these, balustraded low screen walls in a late C17 manner but probably dating from the 1850s.

3050

PEARSIE HOUSE

2.9 km. W of Cortachy

Substantial white-harled mansion. The three-storey piend-roofed main block was built in 1805 by Charles Wedderburn some years after his return from India. S front of five bays, the centre three forming a bowed projection containing the entrance set in a framework of skinny Roman Doric columns topped by a cornice. The upper floors are marked off by string courses; first-floor sill course. At the end bays the first-floor windows are Venetians set in round-headed overarches. Lower back (NW) wings, perhaps of C17 or C18 origin but plain and rather altered.

Inside, the entrance opens into an oval hall, its white marble chimneypiece with an allegorical scene on the frieze's central panel. Behind, a flying stair with lyre-shaped cast-iron balustrades.

6060

PERT

Remains of the church in a graveyard beside the A90.

PERT PARISH CHURCH. Now roofless but the gables and substantial parts of the side walls still stand. Rubble-walled oblong, the gables and some of the N wall probably C13, much of the rest probably of the C16 or C17. The E gable contains a pair of lancets with tall rere-arches; between them, an external buttress. In the S wall, remains of rectangular windows and end doors with chamfered surrounds, all probably late C16 or early C17 in their present form. In the W gable, a small lancet window, presumably C13. The birdcage bellcote atop the gable bears the date 1676. Probably C13 is the shouldered arch doorway (blocked) W of the centre of the N side. Inside, near the N wall's E end, the head of a pointed arch, perhaps from an aumbry.

GRAVEYARD. Some HEADSTONES worth note. Just W of the church's W end, a badly worn C18 stone bearing a depiction of Adam and Eve. – In a railed enclosure S of the W door of the church's S side, the large headstone to Elizabeth Fife †1737, its E face carved with a pair of angels' heads (souls) at the top. At the bottom, an angel blowing a trumpet to wake a skeleton who pierces a coffin with a spear; above the coffin, an hour-glass. On the W face, figures of men in C18 dress arranged in the shape of a cross. – To the E, several worn GRAVE-SLABS of the C17 and early C18 bearing angels' heads, shields and emblems of death.

UPPER NORTH WATER BRIDGE, 0.4 km. E. Built in the later C16 but repaired and reconstructed by *John Gibb*, 1841. Masonry of rough ashlar, the parapets late C20 replacements. Three segmental arches with ribbed soffits.

PITSCANDLY HOUSE

4050

0.8 km. E of Lunanhead

Harled two-storey laird's house built, probably in the late C17, for the Lindsays of Pitscandly. Bellcast eaves to the piended roof of the main block, its walling enlivened with ashlar strip quoins at the corners, an eaves course and window surrounds. The S front has an advanced centrepiece, its pediment pierced by a bullseye window. Here are two windows to the first floor and, below, a pair of windows flank the moulded doorpiece surmounted by a pulvinated frieze and steep pediment. Set well back from the front are the piended gables of two-storey NE and NW wings, perhaps early C18 additions, the inner angle of the main block and NE wing filled with a flat-roofed extension added by *Maclaren, Soutar & Salmond* in 1926. The main block's N front is similar to the S. Seven bays, the centre three advanced under a pediment containing a bullseye window. One bay of the centrepiece is overlaid by a small late C20 piend-roofed single-storey addition. The main block and wings enclose three sides of a courtyard, both wings with forestairs to the first floor, small windows and straight N gables.

GARDEN behind the house, three of its walls rubble-built, the N faced internally with brick, all perhaps of the late C18. Over the S entrance, a Victorian stone dragon gargoyle and, above the centre of the N wall, a Celtic cross finial, also late C19, both probably from a demolished church and placed here in the C20. – Lectern DOOCOT, probably of the C17, E of the house. Walls of white-painted rubble crossed by a single rat course; entrance in the S side.

6050

RED CASTLE

0.5 km. S of Lunan

Tall fragments of a castle of enclosure and a tower house built inside its courtyard, all constructed of the local red sandstone from whose colour the castle takes its name.

The site is a promontory at the mouth of the Lunan Water with naturally steep banks on three sides; the rather gentler approach from the S was probably protected by a marsh. The promontory is cut through by a N–S hollow, probably a natural feature rather than an artificial ditch, and the CASTLE OF ENCLOSURE has occupied the E part of the site. This may have been built in the C13. There survives a 32 m. stretch of the W wall, *c.* 1.8 m. thick and over 6 m. high, built of mortared layers of large boulders faced with rubble. Near the top, under the remains of the parapet, are stone spouts, some complete and others fragmentary, which have drained the wall walk. Joist holes and a roof-raggle show that a lean-to structure has been built against the wall's exterior, perhaps in the C17 or C18. The internal side of the wall has been robbed of much of its lower facing but, at a height of *c.* 4.4 m. and a little N of centre, its stonework provides evidence of the first-floor fireplace of a building on this site and a corbel to the N may mark the position of a wooden partition wall. A second wall returns to the E, at a slightly obtuse angle, from the N end of the W wall and runs for *c.* 7.6 m. before turning SE towards the NE corner of the tower house, this last stretch of curtain almost entirely missing. This N wall is slightly thinner than the W and seems to have been built later, perhaps in the C15 at the same time as the tower house; some foundations of an earlier wall further to the N survive. A roof raggle and corbel indicate that there has been a lean-to building in the courtyard's NW, replaced in the early C19 by a coastguard's cottage.

The TOWER HOUSE was built in the late C15 for the Stewarts, Lords Innermeath. It is oblong, *c.* 13.4 m. by 10 m., ashlar-faced and of four storeys and an attic in height. There still stand the N gable, most of the E wall and about half the W. Joist holes for the floors show that these were all wooden and that, unusually for a house of this quality and date, there was no internal vaulting. The ground floor, lit from a slit window in each side wall, seems to have contained storage. Hall on the first floor with a large N fireplace and tall E window, its arched embrasure apparently having contained stone seats. Upper hall at the second floor, one jamb of its canopied W fireplace surviving. E window and, in the N gable, a slit-windowed garderobe. The third floor has contained a N fireplace and W window. The attic storey is set back from the wall-head to allow for a wall-walk. At the main wall-head, individual moulded corbels under a now missing battlement and, at the corners, continuous corbelling below angle-rounds or turrets, also now missing.

RESCOBIE

5050

Church and former Manse on a hillside overlooking Rescobie Loch.

RESCOBIE PARISH CHURCH. Rubble-walled box built in 1820, a birdcage bellcote on the W gable, a stone cross of 1907 on the E. In the S side wall, tall pointed windows with intersecting wooden tracery, their central mullions broadened in 1907. The N windows, also pointed, are smaller and now built up; above them, elliptical-headed openings which originally lit a gallery. Each gable contains a door with a pointed fanlight (the E door blocked in 1907 when the W was widened) under an elliptical-arched window and a circular dummy opening. Placed at the centre of the S wall is the late C17 MONUMENT to members of the family of David Lindsay, Minister of Rescobie. It is an aedicule, the fluted Roman Doric piers supporting an entablature, the frieze carved with angels' heads. Above, a gable suggestive of a pediment containing a coat of arms and surmounted by ball finials incised with the initials D^{M}L (for Mr David Lindsay). The bases of the piers are carved with skulls; below the inscription panel, a depiction of crossbones.

The interior was remodelled in 1907 by *Carver & Symon* who removed the galleries and provided new FURNISHINGS, changing the position of the pulpit and communion table from the centre of the S side to the E end.

GRAVEYARD. W of the church are weathered C17 and C18 GRAVE-SLABS, some bearing coats of arms or trade emblems and symbols of death. – E of the church, the HEADSTONE of Thomas Findly †1750, the W face with a serious-looking angel and a shield displaying a ploughshare; reminders of mortality on a panel at the bottom of the E face.

Former MANSE to the W, built in 1837. Piend-roofed and rubble-walled main block looking like a very superior farmhouse.

RESWALLIE HOUSE, 0.8 km. SW. Two-storey laird's house of 1794, now extracted from sizeable late C19 additions. Panelled pilasters at the ends of the ashlar-faced S front. This is of three bays, the centre with a chimney-topped wall-head gablet and corniced doorpiece. – U-plan GARAGE AND OFFICE COURT of *c.* 1900 to the NW. Broad-eaved piended roofs covered with red Rosemary tiles; cupolas over the central and SW ranges. At the central range, a half-timbered gable above the elliptical-arched vehicle entrance. – Contemporary single-storey LODGE at the W entrance to the drive. Harled with sandstone dressings. At the S front, the entrance is set back between Roman Doric columns which support the broad eaves of the roof; barge-boarded gables to the outer bays.

FORT (KEMP'S CASTLE), Turin Hill, 1.5 km. N. Hilltop fortification, now cut through by a farm wall, showing various stages of development from *c.* 500 B.C. to the early centuries of the first millennium A.D. The first stage saw the construction of a roughly oval 2.7 ha. fort, *c.* 274 m. by 122 m. in extent, enclosed on three sides by a double rampart; on the S is a cliff making no artificial defence necessary. Downhill to the E, a single roughly concentric rampart is probably contemporary with this first stage and enclosed a smaller annex. The second stage of development is probably of the late first millennium B.C. This entailed the erection of a roughly oblong and much smaller fort in the SW corner of the first. This second fort was *c.* 152 m. by 40 m. and defended by a single broad rampart. In the third stage, probably in the early centuries of the first millennium A.D, three circular homesteads or duns were built along the S edge of the side, the W outside the ramparts of the oval fort. The central and best-preserved, its wall up to 4 m. thick, is built on top of the side walls of the oblong fort which must have been abandoned by then. These structures stand in line and are *c.* 120 m. apart from each other. Does this mean that they are contemporary or are the alignment and regular spacing coincidental?

4050

RESTENNETH PRIORY

0.9 km. S of Lunanhead

Remains of a medieval priory surrounded by fields, the site originally the promontory of a loch which was drained in the late C18.

A religious establishment, presumably of *Céli Dé*, had probably been founded here by the later C11. In the early or mid C12 this was replaced by or transmogrified to a priory of Augustinian canons, formally confirmed as a pendicle of Jedburgh Abbey in 1161. The conventual buildings were abandoned after the Reformation and the priory church, formerly serving the surrounding parish, after 1591 when a parish church was established at Forfar. The ruins were transferred to the Office of Works in 1919 and are now maintained by Historic Scotland.

The NAVE, rebuilt in the mid or later C13 and now reduced to the lowest courses of the walls, has been an unaisled rectangle, *c.* 18 m. by 8.5 m, with buttresses at the N side's corners and centre. Walling of ashlar above a splay-topped plinth. Door in the N gable and probably another from the cloister which stood on the S side.

The place of the crossing in larger conventual churches is
8 here occupied by a square TOWER with a passage on its N side, the tower's S wall continuing the line of this side of the nave, the passage's N wall set back from that of the nave but aligned with the choir's. The lowest stage of the tower is constructed of roughly squared masonry mixed with some thin slabs. This survives from an earlier church, perhaps of the C11, which it served apparently as a short nave, only *c.* 3 m. long internally. Towards the W end of its S face, a narrow round-headed door

decorated with a band of moulded stripwork carried up the jambs and round the arch-head which is carved from a massive single stone. In the centre of the E face, a large chancel arch, its semicircular head carried on projecting imposts and set back from the line of the jambs; voussoirs with tails of varying lengths. Similar W arch but it is slightly off-centre, has a rough filling of small stones next to the jambs and the tails of the voussoirs form a uniform outer ring; clearly it is an insertion, probably of the C12 after the church had been taken over by the Augustinians and when a new and longer nave was built to the W. Also probably C12 are the tower's upper stages, their masonry formed from large blocks of close-jointed roughish ashlar cut across by raggles for the roofs of the C13 nave, choir and E cloister range. The lower of these two added stages is tall. Round opening to the W under the roof of the C13 nave, a slit window on the S just above the line of the cloister roof and, in the E face, a narrow rectangular doorway which probably opened onto a loft at this end of the choir. The tower's top stage is marked off by a string course. At each face, a triangular-headed window. Simple wall-head cornice. The tower is finished with an octagonal splay-footed stone spire, added probably *c.* 1500. At the bottom of each of the four faces to the cardinal points, a single gabled lucarne containing a segmental-headed opening.

The CHOIR, rebuilt in the C13 when it was broadened to the N, extends 21.5 m. E of the tower, its walling of rubble above a splay-topped ashlar base. In the N side, relatively tall and narrow hoodmoulded lancet windows with chamfered margins, those in the second and third bays from the E formed *c.* 1870 when a wall was built in the position of the medieval one which had separated the choir from a sacristy to the N. The lower part of a buttress between the windows of the two W bays survives. Minimally projecting clasping buttresses at the corners of the E gable which is pierced by three lancets, their arch-heads now missing. On the choir's S side, E of the cloister, a procession of lancet windows between buttresses (their bases surviving) followed by the E bay which is longer than the others and without a window. Along the two W of these bays, a row of weathered corbels, perhaps not *in situ*. The W bay, formerly covered by the cloister's E range, is a survival from a C12 choir. In it, a blocked tall and round-headed door which gave access from the dormitory to the church.

Inside the choir, the E windows are flanked by narrow image niches. The side windows have hoodmoulds linked by a string course. At the E end of the S wall, a PISCINA, the head of its pointed arch formed of two stones, the l.'s soffit carved with what may have been foliaged bosses. – Immediately W, remains of an elliptically arched SEDILIA and, to its W, a CUPBOARD. W of that the moulded elliptical arch of a TOMB-RECESS. – Another recess is in the W end of the N wall but the head of its moulded arch has been cut into to accommodate a Late Georgian monument, itself now mutilated.

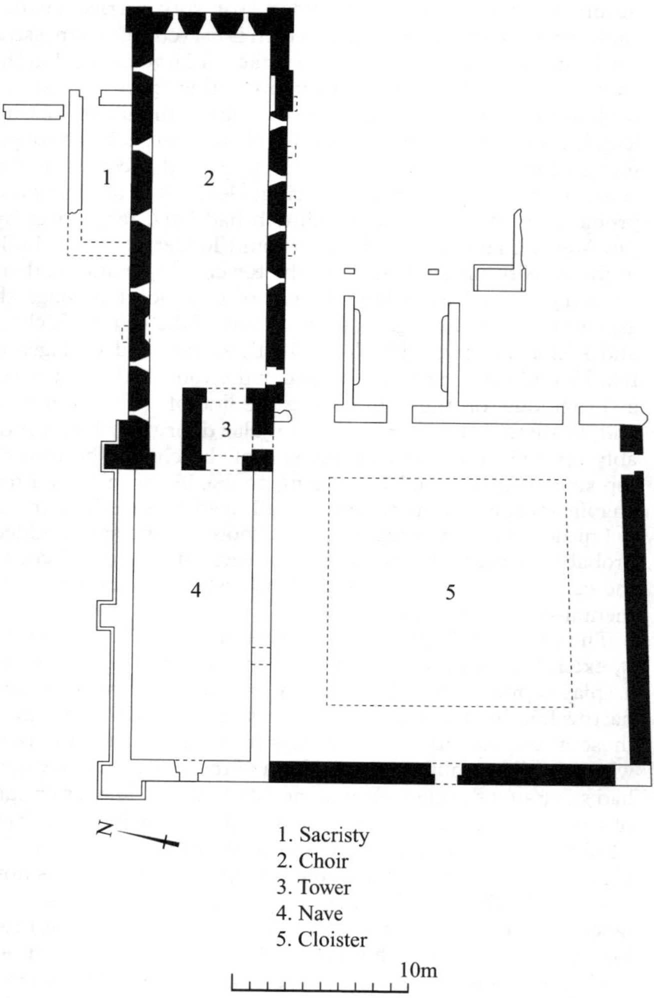

Restenneth Priory.
Plan

Only the wall bases survive of the E range of the CLOISTER BUILDINGS. They perhaps date largely from the C13 but are now almost featureless. Two roof-raggles show that the dormitory abutting the church was originally of a single storey and attic and later raised to two storeys. In the chapter house, vestiges of stone benches along the N and S sides. The inner walls of the two-storey S and W ranges stand, each with an impressive display of putlog holes and a rectangular door incised with a roll-and-hollow moulding. Just below the wall-head, rounded corbels which have supported the cloister's high-set roof.

Inside the tower, various stone FRAGMENTS and, on its N wall, a broken early C16 GRAVE-SLAB incised with a cross above the figure of a woman, her hands clasped in prayer. – Set into the grassy floor of the nave, more GRAVE-SLABS, probably C16, one incised with a cross, another with a very crude skull.

PRIOR HOUSE beside the approach from the NW is a white-painted farmhouse of *c.* 1800. – To its W, HUNTER LIBRARY (ANGUS ARCHIVES) of 1972. Single-storey flat-roofed pavilion, the walls of timber, stone, render and glass.

RUTHVEN

2040

Church of a rural parish and its former manse standing beside the River Isla.

RUTHVEN CHURCH. By *John Carver*, 1858–9. Small buttressed and lancet-windowed rectangle, the walling of stugged red sandstone with some cherry-cock pointing, the roof with bands of fish-scale slating. Tiny 'chancel' at the E end. Gabled porch at the W end of the S side. At this side's E end, a bell-tower of two stages, the lower square and containing the cusped-pointed door, the upper broached to an octagon and pierced by narrow pointed belfry openings, also cusped. Built into the church's W gable, FRAGMENTS of two medieval stones, the l. crudely incised with a cross, the r. with the relief of a ringed cross-head.

The interior, covered by a collar-braced roof, is focused on the Gothic pulpit at the W end. The 'chancel', divided from the body of the church by a stone arch, contains seating for the lairds of Ruthven House.

GRAVEYARD. S of the church, a few Late Georgian HEADSTONES including one erected in 1833 by *John Leslie*, mason, for his daughter, the W face bearing a shield which displays dividers and a setsquare placed among the masons' emblem of three castles. Flanking the shield, a pair of Ionic columns topped by humanoid depictions of the Sun and Moon. – Further S, a stone, probably of the C18, with an angel's head (the soul) above a mantled shield bearing tools; grisly reminders of death at the base.

Plain former MANSE (now Kirkhowe) to the W, also built of stugged red sandstone masonry and designed by *John Carver* but of 1873–4. – Further W and probably contemporary, the MANSE OFFICES, now altered on their conversion to a house. The lintel over the W entrance is a reused medieval GRAVE-SLAB carved with a sword and ringed cross and very similar to a grave-slab at Kingoldrum Church (*see* Kirkton of Kingoldrum).

RUTHVEN HOUSE

2 km. SE

Laird's house of unostentatious dignity (originally known as Islabank House) built for James Ogilvy of Ruthven in 1790. Oblong block of two storeys over a half-sunk basement, faced with creeper-clad red sandstone rough ashlar, cherry-cock-pointed below the ground floor sill course; lintel course linking the basement windows. Five bays by three, the taller ground-floor windows denoting the *piano nobile*. In the centre of the W side, the main entrance placed between paired acanthus-capitalled pilasters and fronted by a corniced portico, its columns also paired and with acanthus capitals. Piended platform roof, its half-sunk gabled dormers mid-C19 additions.

Attached to the main block's rear corners are single-storey and basement straight links of the mid C19. These join to contemporary two-storey-and-basement piend-roofed pavilions. At the one-bay front of each, a basement window in a rock-rusticated surround. Corniced and pilastered ground floor windows of three lights, the outer openings dummies, and three-light windows also at the first floor but here they are low and horizontally proportioned.

Inside, a long entrance hall divided by side pilasters and plastered beams into three compartments, each with pendentives supporting not the expected dome but an oval flat ceiling, its central parasol rose perhaps of 1790 but possibly an embellishment of about a century later. At the hall's E end, a round-headed arch to a lower and shorter compartment, its bowed end covered by a plaster dome enriched with a plasterwork fan. On the S is the dining room, its bracketed and rosetted cornice a mid-C19 replacement. Adamish painted wood and gesso chimneypiece of 1790, its frieze with vine swags flanking an oval containing a figure of Diana. N of the entrance hall the drawing room, its swagged cornice of 1790. So too is the chimneypiece, also Adamish and of painted wood and gesso, the frieze with urns at the ends and anthemion enrichment in the centre. At the back of the room, an archway with paired skinny pilaster strips topped by panels displaying lions' heads and surmounted by tall foliaged consoles. Over the archway, plaster fan decoration under a row of beads below a flat cornice. The archway opens into a smaller back room, its end wall with an archway of the same design opening onto a recess. In this room, another Adamish chimneypiece, its frieze's central panel with thistle enrichment. The mid-C19 N and S pavilions were gutted in the later C20 but the N contained a ground floor library, the S a basement kitchen.

WALLED GARDEN, probably of *c.* 1790, W of the house. Protruding from its NE corner, a rubble-walled and piend-roofed two-storey garden store of Late Georgian appearance, its ground floor a survival of RUTHVEN CASTLE, the house built for the Crichtons of Ruthven in the mid C16. In each of the E and W sides and the bowed E end, a wide-mouthed oval gunloop at the ground floor; slit window to the E. The ground floor contains a single tunnel-vaulted store room.

LODGE at the S end of the drive of *c.* 1900 in an Arts and Crafts manner.

ST VIGEANS

6040

Tiny village which has just managed to avoid absorption into Arbroath.

ST VIGEANS PARISH CHURCH, Kirkstyle. Dominantly placed on a steep-sided natural mound rising in a bend of the Brothock Burn above the cottages of the village. This is the epitome of a prosperous medieval kirk although its present appearance dates very largely from *R. Rowand Anderson*'s reconstruction of 1871–2. 9

Numerous fragments of sculptured crosses and grave-slabs discovered here and now in the St Vigeans Museum show that this was a graveyard of some importance by the C8. Although the earliest documentary record of a church here dates from 1178, the discovery in the 1870s of Romanesque carved stones from the arch of a door or window which were discovered in the 1870s re-used in the walling of the S aisle makes it likely that that church had been built in the first half of the C12. An early C12 date is also consistent with the stonework of the E gable of the present main N aisle and the rubble walling of that aisle's W gable. In plan (as established in the 1870s) this first identifiable church on the site was a simple unaisled rectangle (*c.* 18.3 m. by 8.0 m. externally), with no structural division between the nave and chancel, and covered the site of the present main N aisle and about half of the present nave.

The chronology of the building's subsequent development is clear enough. First, probably in the early C15, came the enlargement of the rectangular single-cell building *c.* 4.6 m to the S and the construction of an arcade marking off the N third of the enlarged church as an aisle. The next phase entailed the construction of a tower covering the S half of the nave's W gable. This may have followed soon after completion of the previous work but is clearly a second stage of development since the tower covers the external intake and splayed base course of the gable. Erection of the tower was, in turn, followed by the addition of a S aisle, slightly narrower than the N, and a heightening and remodelling of the tower. Completion of this work can be closely dated by a new consecration of the church in 1485, an event which was said a few years later to have marked the church's rebuilding. After the Reformation the church was reordered internally and galleries put up in the N aisle and the W end of the nave; an E gallery was erected in 1770. External remodelling took place in the early C19. In 1802 the side walls of the N and S aisles were rebuilt, the new masonry thinner than that of its medieval predecessor. Further work, including enlargement of the windows of the S aisle, was carried out in 1822 and in 1827 a transeptal jamb or 'aisle' was added to the N side of the main N aisle. Probably either in 1822 or 1827 the upper part of the W tower was remodelled in a simple Georgian castellated manner.

R. Rowand Anderson's reconstruction of 1871–2, undertaken at the instigation of the antiquarian William Duke who was then minister of St Vigeans, was a determined attempt to restore medieval character to the church and to rearrange the interior along 'ecclesiological' lines. Much of the work was concerned with repair including rebuilding of the S nave arcade (reusing the original stones) and the clearstorey above, and the restoration of detail (e.g. of the windows) to its possible medieval appearance, but included remodelling the top of the tower, replacement of the N jamb of 1827 by an outer N aisle 'in architectural harmony with the church', and the addition of a semi-octagonal chancel at the E end of the nave.

9 Walling all of local red sandstone, mostly snecked rubble. Anderson's additions are unfussy Gothic. At his apse, heavy buttresses, their tops aggressively stepped; three-light Y-traceried windows. His outer N aisle, shorter than the medieval nave and aisles, is covered by a double-pitch roof. Two-light Y-traceried windows in the gables of this aisle. The aisle's rectangular windows, each containing two segmental-arched lights, are identical to those he provided for the W bay of the medieval N aisle and for the S aisle 'based on ancient examples' and following a supposed 'tradition' that the S aisle's windows had been rectangular before being Gothicized in the 1820s. The clearstorey windows of the nave, substantially medieval in their external form although repaired or replicated by Anderson, consist of rectangular openings to the N and segmental-arched lights to the S. In the W bay of each medieval aisle, a door of 1871–2; over the S door, a sundial dated 1871. Also of 1871–2 is the buttress at the N corner of the W gable of the nave. At the E end of the S aisle's side wall, a consecration cross, and another on the E gable of the N aisle.

The placing of the tower so that it covers the S half of the nave's W gable is curious unless it was intended to serve also as a buttress for the SW corner of the nave. The tower's two lower stages are substantially original, both with a gentle batter, the short second stage intaken. In the W face of the bottom stage, a plain round-arched door. At the second stage, a slit window in each outer face, the W and S restored. Below and to the E of the slit window in the N face, a blocked rectangular opening. Above the second stage, another intake on the N and W faces but not now on the S where the walling was thickened externally *c.* 1480.* In this tall upper part of the tower which again has a slight batter, chamfered rectangular windows to the S and N (two of them built up). The top of the tower was rebuilt and heightened in 1871–2 when Anderson provided a pointed

* The N and W walls were thickened at the same time but with the extra masonry added to their internal faces.

belfry opening in each face. Above, sturdy unmoulded corbels carry an uncrenellated parapet from which project half-round stone spouts. Inside the gable, a crowstep-gabled saddleback-roofed caphouse whose design was, claimed Anderson, in accordance with the recollection of 'an old inhabitant of the Parish who remembers the original structure', the general effect not dissimilar to that of the towers of Dunning and Muthill Parish Churches (Perth and Kinross). In the inner angle of the tower and S aisle Anderson provided a stair-turret which begins as a square before being broached to an octagon finished with a stone-slabbed squat spire.

Inside the tower, a stone tunnel vault (now plastered) over the ground floor. This vault must have been an afterthought, perhaps of *c.* 1480, since it blocks windows in the tower's N face. In the E side of the tower, an off-centre round-arched door into the nave. Inside the church itself, the C15 four-bay nave arcades survive (the S a careful rebuild of the 1870s). Both have segmental arches with broad notched splays but the piers of the N arcade are round and have caps formed of two shaft-rings, the piers of the S arcade octagonal with simple moulded caps. On the soffit of the arch at each end, a consecration cross. Anderson's three-bay arcade into his outer N aisle is low with elliptical arches springing from round piers. The clearstorey windows above the medieval arcades now have stone segmental rere-arches, the S side's replicas of those which existed here before the wall was rebuilt in 1871–2, the N's replacements for oak-lintelled rectangular openings. Simple open roofs of the 1870s described by Anderson as 'characteristic of the fifteenth century period when the church was rebuilt'. Plastered walls except in the apsidal chancel where they are faced with ashlar. Tall pointed chancel arch. At the chancel's E wall Anderson provided a SEDILIA with three ogee arches over the seats. The chancel is floored with routine encaustic TILES which are used also as borders to the stone-paved passages of the nave and aisles.

FURNISHINGS of 1871–2 arranged on High Presbyterian or 'ecclesiological' lines with the communion table in the chancel, and the chancel arch flanked by a small stone font and a pulpit of linenfold panelling on an ashlar base. Simple pews. – In the W gallery, an ORGAN by *Harrison*, 1874–5.

STAINED GLASS. In the chancel's five windows, depictions of the Nativity, Baptism, Crucifixion, Resurrection and Ascension of Our Lord, erected in 1872–80. – In the E bay of the S aisle, a window (the Martyrdom of St Stephen) by *Field & Allan*, 1874. – Also in this aisle a characteristically stylized work (Our Lord and the Centurion) by *Gordon Webster*, 1976. – The laughably bad E window of the outer N aisle (scenes from the life of King David) is signed by *Mayer & Co.*, *c.* 1875. – In this aisle's N wall, a clear and well-coloured window (Our Lord and the Disciples on the road to Emmaus) by *C. E. Kempe & Co.*, 1925.

MONUMENTS in the main N aisle. On the W wall, a white marble monument to John Henderson †1836, with the statue of a kneeling angel writing the inscription. It is signed by *Peter Rouw Yr.* – On the E wall, a small but elaborate Gothic monument of brownish alabaster to the Rev. John Muir †1865, designed by *R. Rowand Anderson*, 1871. – On the N wall of the outer N aisle, a veined white marble MONUMENT to John Dempster of Dunnichen †1753, with scrolls at the bottom of the tablet; at the top a swan-neck pediment broken by an urn. Swagged drapery and a man's head on the frieze.

GRAVEYARD. Immediately S of the church, the mid-C18 HEADSTONE commemorating members of the Kyd family, the front carved with a relief of two children under an angel's head (the soul). – On the steep slope below, the HEADSTONE of the children of John Spink, mariner in Auchmithie, dated 1805, decorated with a fishing boat, anchor and fishes, under a smiling angel's head. – To its E, a HEADSTONE, probably late C18, bearing the initials IB, HS and the head of a sorrowful angel. – W of the church, a HEADSTONE to William Johnston, dated 1751, the front displaying an angel's head above a shield carved with initials and crested with a mantled helm; on top of the stone, the figures of two sleeping children. – S of this, the HEADSTONE to David Crool and Jean Watson, dated 1755 and carved with a shield and a crude version of mantling under an angel's head; grisly reminders of death at the bottom. – At the E end of the graveyard, some C18 STONES carved variously with angels' heads, shields crested with mantled helms, and reminders of death; one bears the relief of a man.

ST VIGEANS MUSEUM, Kirkstyle. A pair of C18 cottages converted to a museum to house the remarkable collection of Early Christian carved stones of the C8–C10 unearthed in the Parish Church and graveyard in the late C19. First housed in the church porch, they were moved here in 1960. Some are mere fragments but many deserve a brief description. The face of one, a Pictish slab, perhaps of the C9, bears a ringed cross carved with interlacing and with a pair of interlaced knots under the arms; below the knots, relief of a pair of ecclesiastics. On the back, depictions of four figures, the upper pair seated and probably representing St Paul the Hermit and St Antony of Egypt, the lower a pair of ecclesiastics (the r. figure almost obliterated) walking towards each other and holding staffs. – The front of another slab is carved with a cross, also decorated with interlacing, the arms notched at their intersection. Panels of interlaced work under the arms, a pair of birds above. On the badly weathered back, reliefs of two saints and more interlacing. – A third and larger slab is carved with a notched cross, its base with interlace decoration, the shaft with spiralling interlace, the arms diaper-patterned; a roundel of interlacing at the intersection. Under the r. arm, the seated figures of St Paul the Hermit and St Antony of Egypt sharing bread in the desert; below, a cow and crouching human. Under the l. arm of the cross, two standing figures. The slab's back, now badly weathered, has also been carved with a cross decorated with interlacing. – Another slab, perhaps of the C8, displays the shaft of a cross (its arms and head missing) decorated with panels of interlaced work. This is flanked by worn Pictish symbols. On the l., a 'mirror-and-comb', on the r., 'snake and Z-rod' above an eagle. – Another Pictish symbol (the 'double-disc and Z-rod', only a little of the 'Z-rod' now visible) on the small fragment of a carved stone, its other face with interlacing. – Perhaps of the C9 is the fragment of a slab, one face bearing the head and l. arm of a ringed cross; the relief of a manticore stands on the arm. On the back, the relief of a recumbent deer. – Fragment of another stone carved with a 'double disc' symbol. – The 'double disc' also appears, together with a staff and the top of a hooded man, on the fragment of another slab whose other face bears part of a ringed cross decorated with interlaced work. Another fragment of this slab displays more of the ringed cross and, on its back, a horse's head. – The 'DROSTEN STONE' is probably of the earlier C9 and the most impressive of these sculptured slabs. This missing part of its top has been restored in unadorned fashion. On the face, a notched cross decorated with interlace. Flanking the shaft are elongated fantastic beasts; perched on the l. arm is an angel. On the top of the back, a hunting scene. In the middle of this side, Pictish symbols ('double-disc and Z-rod', 'crescent' and 'mirror and comb'). Below, a menagerie of wild beasts and birds and, at the bottom, a bowman taking aim at a boar. Vine-scroll decoration on one of the narrow edges. On the other, interlacing above a panel inscribed DROSTEN: IRE UORET [E]TT FORCUS, possibly translatable as 'Drosten, in the reign of Uoret and Forcus'. – The side of a recumbent grave-slab, perhaps of the C9 or C10, is incised with a depiction of dogs or wolves hunting deer; at the r., a manticore looks on balefully. – Another recumbent grave-slab has an interlaced border round the top where one end is pierced by a socket, perhaps for an upright cross. On the side, a relief of Daniel in the Lions' Den. – A third recumbent slab also has an interlaced border at the top and, in its centre, a panel carved with a cross. – Fragments of a slab (now joined together by a replacement panel), one face bearing a cross with interlacing, the other the relief of a mounted warrior.

DESCRIPTION. Curving round the N side of the base of the mound on which sits the Parish Church is a line of single-storey C18 cottages (KIRKSTYLE), their walls of red sandstone rubble, their roofs covered with stone slabs; two now form the St Vigeans Museum (*see* above). The detached No. 1 at the E end was built in the late C18 as a SCHOOL with bowed ends. To its E, a small rubble-built BRIDGE over the Brothock Burn, probably C18 in origin but remodelled in the mid C19. Two segmental arches; triangular cutwaters.

LETHAM HOUSE, 0.7 km. NW. Relaxed classical two-storey mansion house (now flatted) of 1756 built for the Stephens of Letham, its walling of warm red sandstone. Long S front of seven bays, the outer windows each side grouped 2:1; dummy windows at the two r. bays of the ground floor. Slightly advanced ashlar centrepiece with rusticated quoins and a pediment. This contains the entrance, its surround and that of the window above rusticated and corniced. At the E end of a forecourt in front of the house, urn-topped C18 GATEPIERS to a garden. At the forecourt's W end, a pair of rubble-walled two-storey square PAVILIONS with flattened ogee-profiled roofs, probably of 1756 although looking earlier. Between the pavilions, a dwarf wall now surmounted by classical columns.

6040

SEATON HOUSE

2.4 km. NE of Arbroath

Now the centre of a caravan park and holiday village, the barrack-like red sandstone mansion house built by Alexander Strachan of Tarrie *c.* 1800. Three-storey main block of five bays, its ashlar façade with rusticated quoins and tall first-floor windows to delineate the *piano nobile*; wall-head parapet, rising higher over the second and fourth bays and higher again at the centre. Parapeted portico with coupled Roman Doric columns. At each end, a slightly recessed two-storey one-bay link to a lateral wing, also two-storeyed and of three bays, its parapet stepped up over the centre. In the N wing's rubble-built gable, a dummy window of three lights under a segmental fanlight.

STABLES of 1855 N of the house. Tudorish, built of coursed brown masonry. Over the centre, a spire-roofed lantern with louvred sides. – NW of the house, a slender octagonal TOWER, also of *c.* 1800 and built of cherry-cock-pointed rough ashlar. Pointed door in one face of the lowest stage. Off-set tall second stage, alternate faces with pointed dummy windows. Above a string course, the low top stage, its quatrefoil panels placed above the second stage's blind faces. Wall-head cornice and parapet. – S of the house, a rubble-walled GARDEN, probably also of *c.* 1800.

6060

STRACATHRO

Church of a rural parish sitting in isolation, the woodland of Stracathro House a little to the E.

STRACATHRO PARISH CHURCH. Tall but plain Gothic T, the walls of red sandstone rubble. The cross-bar was built in 1799, a pair of Y-traceried two-light windows in the S side and the W gable's birdcage bellcote its principal features. The N jamb, the L-plan W porch and vestry and the small E porch were added in 1883–4.

Inside, a W gallery of 1883–4. – FURNISHINGS mostly of the 1880s with simple oak pews and, at the E end, a Neo-Jacobean communion table with the pulpit to its r. – STAINED GLASS. E window (the Good Shepherd) by *Marjorie Kemp*, 1939, originally in the now disused former Blairgowrie Parish Church (Perth and Kinross) and placed here in 1978.

GRAVEYARD. S of the church a few C17 and C18 HEADSTONES, their fairly vigorous but badly weathered carved decoration including shields, angels' heads (souls) and emblems of death.

AUCHENREOCH HOUSE, 1.7 km. W. Small late C18 piend-roofed and two-storey mansion house of the Turnbulls of Stracathro. The original main front faced W. It is of rendered rubble, the broad centre slightly advanced under a pediment and containing a moulded doorpiece flanked by windows. At the end of the C18 the estate was bought by a Calcutta merchant, Archibald Gibson, who seems to have given the house its present early C19 S front, perhaps in 1828–9. This is faced with cherry-cock-pointed ashlar; strip quoins at the corners and a first-floor sill course under the eaves. Three bays, the minimally advanced centre slightly higher and pedimented; boldly projecting porch.

MILLDEN HOUSE, 0.5 km. NE. Two rubble-walled early C19 buildings, one a mill, the other a house, linked by a harled central section designed in an early C18 manner by *Marcus Dean*, *c.* 1997. The two-storey 1990s block's N front is of six bays, the centre two advanced under a pediment pierced by an oculus. Short bowed quadrants join to the earlier buildings which now appear as two-storey piend-roofed pavilions. The E (former miller's house) faces E, a block-consoled doorpiece at the centre of its front.

STRACATHRO HOUSE

0.8 km. ESE

Greek Revival mansion designed by *Archibald Simpson* in 1827 53
for Alexander Cruikshank who had made a fortune in Jamaica. It stands on the edge of a hospital complex opened as an Emergency Medical Services hospital in 1939 and still has much of the air of a makeshift expedient.

The main block, built of polished buff-coloured sandstone ashlar, faces S. Two-storey front with slightly advanced two-bay ends, their ground-floor windows tall and aproned, their wall-head parapets surmounted by balustrades. Between these stolid book-ends are seven bays delineated by giant Corinthian pilasters, each of the end bays half the width of the others. The exceptionally tall lower windows rise from ground level; consoled cornice over the central door. In front of the outer bays, a screen of giant columns, also Corinthian, carrying a wall-head entablature. At the three-bay centrepiece, the screen breaks boldly forward as a pedimented and Corinthian-columned *porte cochère*. Straightforward end elevations, each of five bays with aprons to the ground-floor windows and balustraded parapets like those at the ends of the S front. At the rear (N), a shorter narrow block runs parallel to the main building.

Originally, this was of the same height but with a fully exposed basement set behind a loggia, the channelled masonry of its front and sides pierced by elliptical-headed arches; at the front's end bays, round-headed niches. The loggia's front wall is surmounted by an urn-finialled balustrade stretched between polished ashlar parapets; behind the balustrade, the loggia's flat roof forms a terrace in front of the house's principal ground-floor rooms. The two main floors are treated very simply, the only flourish a corniced three-light window at the centre of the ground floor. The unhappily detailed mansard roof was added by *Peddie & Forbes Smith* in 1914.

Extending from the ends of this N block are wings added *c.* 1850. These are identical, each of one storey above a basement which is hidden at the front but fully exposed at the ends and rear, its masonry channelled like that of the N loggia and with elliptical-arched windows and round-headed niches. To the S the wings present tall aproned windows and central pedimented openings of three pilastered lights. Pilastered and pedimented E and W gables with anthemion finials. The wings' ground-floor N elevations are simply treated, the end bays pilastered, the windows (mostly dummies) aproned.

INTERIOR. The entrance opens onto a plain and passage-like vestibule, an austere introduction to the INNER HALL at the centre of the house. This is a noble double-height space, the inspiration from Rome rather than Athens, the walls covered with yellow scagliola decoration. Oblong but the E and W ends are divided off by Corinthian-columned screens from the central square. Here the floor is laid with panels of black marble in white marble borders radiating from a central circle. In the corners of the central space, L-plan pilasters, a half-face on each of two walls. The N and S walls are divided by pilasters into three bays. In the centre of the S, the entrance from the vestibule; round-headed recesses in the outer bays. Round-headed recesses also in the N wall, the outer containing doors, the centre placed in a rectangular frame and designed to contain a fireplace. Entablature round the central space, its frieze decorated with painted rosettes. Above the entablature each wall rises as a segmental-arched panel painted with a stylized floral design. Dome on pendentives, each painted with portrait of a female emblematic of the unexciting but estimable virtues of 'Regularity', 'Diligence', 'Hospitality' and 'Provi-
55 dence'. The dome itself is panelled with long coffers which taper towards the centre and are painted with stylized foliage, anthemion the principal motif. The centre of the dome is glazed, the glass painted with stylized patterns. Over the hall's lower E and W arms beyond the screens, coffered ceilings enriched with plaster rosettes.

The two doors in the N wall of the Inner Hall's central square open onto the ANTE-ROOM, the central of the house's enfilade of three principal rooms (Drawing Room, Ante-Room and Dining Room) which extend the full length of the original N block. In all these rooms, coffered and painted ceilings with rosettes at the intersections of the beams and almost identical plasterwork to the coffers; doorcases enriched with anthemion ornament. At the N wall of the Ante-Room, a pair of exceptionally widely spaced Corinthian columns *in antis*, the shafts of scagliola, the capitals gilded. These form a screen in front of the immense window of three equal-sized lights which rise from the floor to the room's entablature. The entablature's frieze is enriched with anthemion, its cornice with anthemion and palmette decoration. The ceiling is an elliptically arched shallow tunnel vault, its painted decoration predominantly in turquoise and red, bordered by a band decorated with rosettes. On the beams, Greek key and star ornament; the panels of the coffers are painted identically with stylized foliage. The plain white marble chimneypiece, with paired consoles under the mantelshelf, was introduced in 1914 by *Peddie & Forbes Smith*, the design copied from the Dining Room chimneypiece. In the DINING ROOM to the E the ceiling's beams are painted in blue and green with a different pattern of stylized floral decoration, the plaster rosettes at the intersections gilded. Each of the coffer's panels is painted with a design of stylized floral decoration on a brown ground. Round the room, a Victorian frieze of richly embossed Tynecastle Tapestry. Veined black marble chimneypiece, the design like that in the Ante-Room. E of the Dining Room, in the addition of *c.* 1850, are a lobby and pantry. Above a door in the lobby, a panel with a Neoclassical plaster relief. In the pantry's W wall, a blocked door, apparently an 1820s external entrance to the Dining Room. On the E of the lobby is the mid-C19 Billiard Room, top-lit and plain.

The DRAWING ROOM, W of the Ante-Room, is the same size as the Dining Room and with a very similar ceiling but the beams are painted with key pattern and stars and the coffer panels' stylized foliage decoration is modelled in shallow-relief plasterwork. All this is also painted, brown and green the dominant colours. Anthemion and palmette cornice round the room. Alabaster chimneypiece, its jambs with decorously clad caryatids wearing volutes as hats. Rosettes on the ends of the frieze and, between them, rinceau enrichment ending in female angels who flank an oval panel depicting a classical scene. The Drawing Room opens at the W into the CONSERVATORY added *c.* 1850. This is entered through a tunnel-vaulted passage between Corinthian pilastered and columned aedicules (one bricked off to form a small room). On the E wall of the S of these, an oval plaque bearing the relief of Hebe, goddess of Youth. The Conservatory's main space is covered with a cast-iron hammerbeam roof with circles piercing the spandrels of its side arches and at the apex of the centre.

Off the W end of the Drawing Room's S side is the BOUDOIR of *c.* 1830, covered with a coffered quadripartite vault, the panels painted with birds and stylized foliage. Extending S from the W end of the Inner Hall and parallel to the Vestibule, the LIBRARY, the frieze of its wide N doorcase with anthemion decoration. In the centre of the E wall, a plain chimneypiece; it is flanked by built-in bookcases set between Corinthian pilasters. On the upper part of the walls are painted garlands. Painted ceiling whose rosetted border encloses square panels depicting fruiting foliage.

Placed between the Library and the Boudoir is the MAIN STAIR, its wrought-iron balustrade decorated with curling foliage. Painted decoration on the stair-hall walls with panels of birds and flowers. Over the top landing, a trabeated ceiling, its side panels painted with stars, its centre rising as a glass-walled rectangular lantern with anthemion finials round its base and a star-painted ceiling. Off the Main Stair a first-floor corridor covered with quadripartite vaulting runs the length of the house from E to W. Near its E end, beside the Inner Hall, is a service stair, its cast-iron balustrade with anthemion decoration.

GATEPIERS of *c.* 1830, 0.8 km. S, at the S end of the drive passing through the hospital. Corniced, with rosetted friezes and swagged urn finials. – Of the same date, at the N end of this drive, on its W side, a cast-iron three-span FOOTBRIDGE. Bundle-shafted columns carry the segmental-headed arches with fretted Gothic soffits and spandrels pierced by quatrefoils, circles and mouchettes. The walkway's balustrades are decorated with stylized foliage of the same design as the mansion's Main Stair. On the approach at each end, lattice-sided balustrades, probably afterthoughts.

STABLES also of *c.* 1830, 0.1 km. W of the mansion house,
68 the main elevations of reddish-coloured polished sandstone ashlar. At each end of the principal (S) range, an anta-pilastered and pedimented pavilion of one tall storey with an elliptical-arched coachhouse doorway. Two-bay links of two storeys, the upper windows very low and horizontally proportioned, join to the centrepiece. This is of only one storey but taller, its large round-headed entrance framed by coupled pilasters carrying a Doric entablature. At the centre of the back (N) range is an octagonal tower with tall round-headed dummy windows to the upper stage. Under the stone brackets supporting the eaves are small round-headed flight-holes for pigeons to enter the doocot inside. Low pavilion roof with a weathervane.

WALLED GARDEN 0.3 km. W of the mansion house, also of *c.* 1830 and roughly D-plan. Walls of red sandstone, the centre of the curved N side rising above the rest to allow height for the main lean-to greenhouse built against it. Against this part's external face, a square pavilion-roofed three-storey tower, the sides of its top floor glazed almost continuously, the three-light windows at each face set between broad pilasters at the outer corners and slender mullion-piers at the centre. Extending laterally from the tower are single-storey lean-to ranges, their gables pierced by circular dummy openings.

NEWTONMILL HOUSE. *See* p. 648.

STRATHMARTINE PARISH CHURCH
see DUNDEE: ARDLER

STRATHMARTINE PARISH CHURCHYARD
see BRIDGEFOOT

TANNADICE

4050

Rather inchoate small village, the houses mostly harled.

OATHLAW TANNADICE PARISH CHURCH. Originally Tannadice Parish Church. By *John Carver*, 1866. Buttressed Gothic box, the walls of stugged ashlar, the eaves of the roof supported on stone corbels. In the side walls, hoodmoulded two-light windows. The placing of the E gable's buttresses hints at a nave and aisles behind, the 'aisle' windows hoodmoulded single lancets, the 'nave' window also hoodmoulded but of two cusped lights, a circular opening in the head. Projecting from the 'nave', an angle-buttressed porch, its door's hoodmould with headstops. SE steeple, the tower's lowest stage square, the second broached to an octagon, the third with Gothic panels, the intermediate faces pierced by windows; octagonal stone spire. At the W end, a low two-storey HALL added by *The Parr Partnership*, 2002–3, its upper floor's main window reused from the 1866 vestry which stood here.

The interior is covered by an elaborate open roof which combines hammerbeams and kingposts. E gallery. PEWS of 1935–6 designed by *Waterston & Graham* and originally in St James's Church, Forfar. At the W end, a simple Gothic communion table by *Steele & Balfour*, 1894, and formerly in Partick Old Parish Church (Glasgow). It stands in front of the 1866 PULPIT, also Gothic, behind which hangs an iron CROSS designed and made by *Tony Fleming* in 1994. – STAINED GLASS. Flanking the pulpit, a pair of windows (St Columba and St Francis) of 1976, brightly coloured and realistic. – In the N wall, the First and Second World War memorial windows (an Angel and Faithful Knight; Abraham and Melchizedek) from Oathlaw Parish Church. They are by *James Ballantine II*, 1923, and *Douglas Hamilton*, 1949. – In the porch, a medieval octagonal stone FONT bowl with rope decoration at the base.

In the GRAVEYARD some C17 and C18 HEADSTONES to the S of the church. Just to the N, the former MANSE (now Kirkside House) by *Samuel Bell*, 1797–8, a harled two-storey house; Victorian porch at the three-bay front.

BRIDGE, Justinhaugh, 1.7 km. SW. Steel bowstring girder bridge, by *Crouch & Hogg*, 1907–8. Wrought-iron scrolls at the ends of the structure abut low battlemented stone turrets.

INSHEWAN HOUSE, 3 km. SW. At the end of a long drive, the piend-roofed small mansion house built in 1827–8 for John

Ogilvy of Inshewan. Two storeys over a basement, the walling of red sandstone ashlar, a band course between the ground and first floors. Front of five bays, the advanced and pedimented centre containing the fanlit entrance under a three-light window. Pair of short single-storey rear wings at basement level. – Rubble-built and piend-roofed quadrangular C18 STEADING on the approach.

MARCUS, 3.5 km. SE. Two-storey *cottage orné*, built for Major (later, Lieutenant-General) Thomas Robert Swinburne in 1834–5, the design provided by *James Ross* who had acted as Archibald Simpson's clerk of works during the construction of Stracathro House (q.v.) a few years before. Harled walling with ashlar dressings; broad eaves and bargeboarded gables. Restrained Jacobean detail, some of the windows, those of the ground floor taller than the first floor's, hoodmoulded, others containing round-headed lights, several surmounted by block-consoled cornices and all probably originally with horizontal-paned glazing. N-facing L-plan entrance front. In the inner angle, a semi-octagonal projection, its gabled N face topped by a chimney, its ground floor with a segmental-arched dorway and fronted by a veranda. At the back, sympathetically detailed late C19 additions; some chimneys have been removed but without evident loss of character.

Inside, an octagonal vestibule, the ribs of its groin-vaulted plaster ceiling meeting at a foliaged boss. Behind, a spacious stair-hall, the stair's balustrades decorated with twining leaves very similar to the slightly earlier work at Stracathro House or Archibald Simpson's contemporary Linton House (Aberdeenshire). The principal rooms all face NE. Drawing room at the N, its ceiling enriched with a parasol centre. The chimneypiece, its frieze's central panel carved with face-to-face griffons, is in a late C18 manner but may be Late Victorian, probably a replacement for a simple white marble chimneypiece like that in the adjacent study. At the NE wing's S end, the 1830s dining room (now sitting room), its ceiling rose with heavily modelled foliage, the black marble chimneypiece original but adorned in 1965 with gilded silhouette sphinxes. Also of 1965 the pedimented bookcases. Bedrooms on the first floor; above the ground-floor vestibule, an octagonal dressing room.

Rubble-walled GARDEN, also of the 1830s, to the W. – To the NE, in line with the drawing room's end window, an early C21 white limestone OBELISK. – Small STABLE block, again of the 1830s, to the N, a round-headed carriage entrance in the front's gabled centre.

TANNADYCE HOUSE, 1.2 km. SE. Stolid mansion house, the product of several building stages, all harled and with red sandstone dressings. The first stage, *c.* 1805, was undertaken by Dr Charles Ogilvy after his return from service with the East India Company. This was a piend-roofed block of two storeys above a basement, the front of three bays. Soon after the estate's purchase by a Dundee lawyer, William Neish, in 1870 the house was remodelled, its front acquiring a Jacobean porch flanked by V-shaped bay windows and its upper windows red sandstone surrounds which break up through the eaves into dormerheads. Neish also added Jacobean strapwork pediments to the sides' ground-floor windows and dormerheads over the first-floor openings. A sizeable rear addition in similar style was added in 1895 after a fire.

At the head of the N drive, a mid-C19 rubble-built U-plan SERVICE COURT, a pavilion-roofed tower at the centre of the N range.

TARFSIDE

4070

Estate hamlet of the mid C19, the single-storey DALHOUSIE COTTAGES with bargeboarded porches.

MAULE MEMORIAL CHURCH, 0.4 km. SE. Originally Lochlee Free Church. Standing on a hillock, a well-sited Early Christian edifice, by *J., W. H. & J. M. Hay*, 1857–8. Oblong, with a pyramidal-roofed tower at the E end of the N side, a small porch in its W inner angle; a second porch near the S side's W end. Rubble walling with a band of herringbone-patterned stonework above the base. Round-headed windows with projecting imposts. In the S porch, stone seats along the sides.

Simple interior covered by a collar-braced roof. The focus is on the COMMUNION TABLE at the E end and the PULPIT behind. These are by *J. Raitt* with carving by *James Bremner*, 1901, and formerly in the now demolished Edzell United Free Church. – Gothic FONT by Bremner and also of 1901 from Edzell United Free Church. – Boxy Victorian PEWS. – STAINED GLASS. Two windows flanking the pulpit, both by *James Ballantine & Son*, 1881, the centre panel of the l. (a memorial to Fox Maule Ramsay, Earl of Dalhousie) heraldic, and of the r. (a memorial to Dr Thomas Guthrie, the Free Church divine and frequent holiday-maker in the parish) floral.

ST DROSTAN (Episcopal). By *Matthews & Mackenzie*, 1879–80. Early English, built of cherry-cock-pointed squared granite rubble. Corner-buttressed nave with a porch at the W end of the N side and a vestry at the E end of the N; apse-ended lower chancel at the E, an organ chamber on its N side. Projecting from below the head of the W gable, a corbelled bellcote covered with a half-domed slated roof. The nave walls' windows are each of two pointed lights with a circular opening in the head. Single lancets to the chancel.

Inside, the porch is paved with red and black ENCAUSTIC TILES which continue along the nave's central aisle and, in more elaborate form, the chancel but are now covered by carpeting. Collar-braced kingpost-truss roof over the nave. Stone chancel arch and another stone arch from the chancel to the former organ chamber. Over the chancel, a ribbed and boarded tunnel vault. – At the W end, a stone FONT by *Thomas Goodwillie*, 1880, from a design by *Matthews & Mackenzie*, the octagonal bowl supported by granite-shafted columns with foliate capitals. – ALTAR by *Jones & Willis*, also of 1880 and of stone. Marble-shafted columns divide the front into five panels, the centre and ends decorated with crosses. – STAINED GLASS. Three lights of 1880 in the chancel (Christ the Good Shepherd flanked by St Andrew and St Peter), examples of strongly coloured Victorian realism.

BRIDGE. Rubble-built gently humpbacked bridge over the Water of Tarf erected in 1830. Segmental arch over the river. Piers at the ends of the parapet.

WAR MEMORIAL. Erected *c.* 1920, a stepped steep pyramid of granite.

CROSS-STONE, 0.9 km. W. Rough boulder, its face incised with a cross, perhaps *c.* 700.

MAULE MONUMENT, Hill of Rowan, 2.1 km. W. By *Jenkins & Marr*, 1866. Hilltop cairn erected by Fox Maule Ramsay, eleventh Earl of Dalhousie, to commemorate dead and still living members of the Maule family. Large rubble-built truncated cone topped by a bullet-shaped finial.

4030

TEALING

Hamlet, the houses mostly C20, the former Parish Church a little to the W.

TEALING PARISH CHURCH, Kirkton of Tealing, 1 km. W. Disused. Rubble-walled and rectangular-windowed oblong of 1806, a spired birdcage bellcote on the W gable. In each of the long N and S sides a double tier of windows at the end bays. Tall windows at the centre of the S wall; at the centre of the N wall, a piend-roofed vestry and classroom added by *Alexander Johnston* in 1895–6. At the gables, gallery windows under circular openings; porches, also additions of 1895–6 by Johnston.

(The INTERIOR was remodelled in 1895–6. – On the N wall, the GRAVE-SLAB of Ingram of Kethenys, Archdeacon of Dunkeld, †1380, the inscription, unusually for the date, in English. – Also on this wall, the grey-painted stone MONUMENT to John Ramsay, Minister of Tealing, †1618. It is an aedicule with paired pilasters and a pedimental head carved with a skull above the monogrammed initials of Mr John Ramsay and Elizabeth Kinloch, his wife. The main panel depicts Ramsay kneeling before a lectern on which rests an open book. – On the W wall, the fragment of a SACRAMENT HOUSE of *c.* 1500. It consists of the lintel, its ends carved with the foliage-finialled pinnacles which topped the missing jambs. On the lintel itself, a badly defaced depiction of the face of Our Lord flanked by angels. – On the S wall, marble MONUMENTS to William Forsyth †1814 and Patrick Scrymsoure †1815 (by *Thomas Campbell*). – In the E porch, the grave-slab erected by Elizabeth Kinloch in memory of her husband, John Ramsay, Minister of

Tealing, †1618. Strapworked border. Above the inscription panel, a skull. Below, a larger panel with a blank central shield flanked by the initials IR and EK and surrounded by more shields, their coats of arms identified on inscribed ribbons as those of Strauchin, Levingstoun, Guthrie and Carnegy.)

GRAVEYARD. At the N entrance, an early C19 HEARSE HOUSE, a basket-arched entrance in the W gable. – A BURIAL ENCLOSURE extends from the centre of the church's S wall. In it, the MONUMENT erected in 1867–8 to commemorate James Scrymsoure Fothringham of Powrie and Tealing, a large polished granite inscription tablet above a heraldic achievement; it was designed by *Edward & Robertson* and executed by *John Rhind*. – Also within the enclosure and propped against the church wall are various GRAVESTONES and FRAGMENTS, probably all of the C17, displaying emblems of death. They include two which bear the coats of arms of the Maxwells of Tealing, one of these with the initials DM (for David Maxwell) and the date 1605. One grave-slab's inscription panel is set between strapworked sides and with a skeleton at the bottom. At the top, an angel's head (the soul) surmounted by four shields, their coats of arms identified by inscriptions as those of Maxwell, Butter, Gordon and Gray in celebration of the marital alliances of the Maxwells of Tealing. Another grave-slab, to Helen Maxwell, lady of Tealing, †1639, is carved with the Maxwell coat of arms and a pair of skulls and bones. – Outside the enclosure but also propped against the church's S wall, the FRAGMENTS of a large stone, perhaps C17, one decorated with the figure of a coffined corpse at the base. – On the ground E and S of the enclosure C17 GRAVE-SLABS with reminders of death and shields bearing trade emblems. – Also the HEADSTONE of 1765 erected by Thomas Kar to commemorate his wife, Margaret Fairweather, its E face carved with the figure of a woman in C18 dress accompanied by a boy and girl. – Just SE of the church, an C18 TABLE STONE, the top of the slab decorated with an angel's head above a helm-crested shield, the bottom with an extensive display of emblems of death.

TEALING HOME FARM. Steading of various dates but now predominantly early C19. U-plan stables and cartshed at the E (now housing), with segmental-arched carriage openings and a pointed window in the S gable of the E wing which is surmounted by onion-like finials.

DOOCOT immediately SW. It is a rubble-built and crowstep-gabled double-pitch-roofed oblong, the SE skewputt carved with the date 1595 and the coat of arms and initials of David Maxwell of Tealing. In the centre of the S side, the entrance in a chamfered surround, its lintel inscribed with the monogrammed initials of Maxwell and Helen Gray, his wife. A boldly projecting rat course runs below the eaves and across the end walls. In each gable, a flight-hole slit above a stone ledge. Inside, stone nesting boxes on all sides.

SOUTERRAIN in a field to the W. Excavated in 1871 and now without its roofing slabs, this is an underground storage chamber of *c.* 100 A.D. It is passage-like, roughly semicircular, sloping down from the NE entrance, and contains two compartments totalling *c.* 28 m. in length. Walls, *c.* 2 m. high, constructed of boulders corbelled inwards towards the top. Just inside the entrance and on the r., a stone bearing cup-and-ring marks, probably dating from Neolithic times and reused here later.

TEALING HOUSE. Harled mansion house which has developed in a makeshift classical manner. It may have been begun in the late C16 as a two-storey laird's house built for the Maxwells of Tealing. In the early C18, perhaps soon after the estate had been acquired by John Scrymsoure, a former Provost of Dundee, the house was remodelled and enlarged. The original building was heightened to three storeys and given a new front of four bays, the centre two advanced under a pediment, an oculus in its tympanum. At the same time the house was made double-pile by the addition of a rear block. Further extension and remodelling was carried out for James Scrymsoure Fothringham in 1827, the designs by *William Burn* executed under the supervision of *James Black*. The principal addition of 1827 was a three-storey W block, its N and S gables pedimented. At the same time a parapeted porch was erected at the l. bay of the early C18 S front. Further alterations, made later in the C19, included the addition of a bay window on the W side of Burn's W wing. About 2000 the house was rescued from dereliction and accretions cleared from the E and N sides, the E side acquiring a garage opening.

7050

USAN HOUSE

1.7 km. S of Ferryden

Classical country house built in 1820 for George Keith who had used a fortune made in the West Indies to purchase the estate.

Two storeys above a fully exposed basement; mutuled cornice at the wall-head. Five-bay entrance (S) front of polished ashlar, V-jointed at the basement and with rusticated quoins at the urn-finialled corners. The centre is advanced under a pediment, also urn-finialled. Here, a flight of steps to the Ionic portico, its columns' necking with acanthus-leaf ornament; first-floor window of three lights.

W elevation also of five bays but harled and with strip quoins at the corners. The centre is again pedimented and topped by swagged urns but only slightly advanced and with a three-light window to each floor, the ground-floor and low basement windows set behind a 'portico' of coupled giant Ionic columns. At the E side's N end, a pedimented billiard room addition by *H. O. Tarbolton*, *c.* 1910.

STABLES of *c.* 1820 to the NE. Rubble-built, a pyramidal-roofed tower with bellcast eaves and a ball finial the principal feature. – At the NE end of the drive, a single-storey LODGE (now drydashed) also of *c.* 1820 with primitivist pedimented Tuscan portico. Contemporary corniced GATEPIERS, their masonry V-jointed, topped by swagged urns. – To the N, a large rubble-walled GARDEN, probably also of *c.* 1820.

VAYNE CASTLE

4050

2 km. SE of Fern

Roofless and partly demolished ruin of the house built for Alexander Lindsay, a younger son of Sir David Lindsay of Edzell, after his acquisition of the lands of Vayne in 1550. This was a rubble-walled three-storey Z, the oblong main block having a square jamb at its NE corner and a round tower at the SW; bowed stair-tower in the jamb's S inner angle with the main block. A round turret on continuous corbelling projects in the main block's inner angle with the tower. Wide-mouthed oval gunloops at the ground floor of the main block, jamb and tower. The original entrance was in the E segment of the tower. A second doorway has been inserted, perhaps in the late C17, in the S side of the main block.

Inside, the SW jamb contained a stair to the first floor. Passage from the foot of this stair into the main block's ground floor which contained two cellars, both covered with semicircular tunnel vaults. In the NW corner of the W was originally a tight turnpike stair to the hall, so this seems to have been the house's wine cellar. Another cellar, also with a semicircular tunnel vault, in the NE jamb. Another turnpike stair but tighter than the SW in the turret in this jamb's inner angle with the main block.

WEST FERRY *see* BROUGHTY FERRY

WEST NEWTON HOUSE

6040

3.2 km. S of Inverkeilor

Small piend-roofed villa-mansion house of *c.* 1800, the walls white-harled and with red sandstone dressings. The main block is of two storeys. W front of three bays with large windows to the ground floor; strip quoins at the corners, first-floor sill course and a wall-head which rises over the slightly advanced centre. This contains the entrance, flanked by recessed Roman Doric columns and topped by a semicircular fanlight. Set back at either end are single-storey piend-roofed wings, probably additions of *c.* 1820. In the front of each, a window under a semicircular fanlight.

Inside, a very smart entrance hall in a late Adam manner, the plaster ceiling embellished with an oval enclosing a sunburst and surrounded by swags; at the ends, rectangular panels containing depictions of wheat sheaves. Acanthus leaf cornice.

At the hall's E end, a trio of round-headed arches springing from Corinthian columns *in antis*, the outer arches framing narrow recesses, the taller and broader central arch containing a door opening onto the flying stair behind. In the head of each arch is a fan ornament; on the wall above the arches, swags containing rosettes. Either side of the entrance hall are the dining and drawing rooms, their doorpieces' outer faces with latticework enrichment; in the top corners, reliefs of lions' heads and, at the centre of each lintel, a foliaceous rosette. Inner surround with guilloche decoration. On each inner face of these doorpieces, reeded jambs under lions' heads in the upper corners. In these rooms, delicately panelled window shutters. In the dining room, perhaps originally the drawing room, a pine and gesso chimneypiece, the jambs with acanthus-capitalled pilasters under anchors; on the lintel, reliefs of shells and a central figure of Hope.

Contemporary rubble-walled GARDEN to the S, its W wall curved; bee-bolls in the N wall. – Behind the garden, a late C19 red sandstone two-storey COACHHOUSE, its W front with a crowstep-gabled slightly advanced centrepiece flanked by a pair of dormer windows, also crowstep-gabled.

Pair of LODGES of *c.* 1800 at the W end of the drive, both single-storey, piend-roofed and harled with red sandstone dressings. Each has a bowed and parapeted front gable containing a Venetian window.

GLOSSARY

Numbers and letters refer to the illustrations (by John Sambrook) on pp. 694-701

ABACUS: flat slab forming the top of a capital (3a).

ACANTHUS: classical formalized leaf ornament (3b).

ACCUMULATOR TOWER: *see* Hydraulic power.

ACHIEVEMENT: a complete display of armorial bearings (i.e. coat of arms, crest, supporters and motto).

ACROTERION: plinth for a statue or ornament on the apex or ends of a pediment; more usually, both the plinth and what stands on it (4a).

ADDORSED: descriptive of two figures placed back to back.

AEDICULE (*lit.* little building): architectural surround, consisting usually of two columns or pilasters supporting a pediment.

AFFRONTED: descriptive of two figures placed face to face.

AGGREGATE: *see* Concrete, Harling.

AISLE: subsidiary space alongside the body of a building, separated from it by columns, piers or posts. Also (Scots) projecting wing of a church, often for special use, e.g. by a guild or by a landed family whose burial place it may contain.

AMBULATORY (*lit.* walkway): aisle around the sanctuary (q.v.).

ANGLE ROLL: roll moulding in the angle between two planes (1a).

ANSE DE PANIER: *see* Arch.

ANTAE: simplified pilasters (4a), usually applied to the ends of the enclosing walls of a portico (q.v.) *in antis*.

ANTEFIXAE: ornaments projecting at regular intervals above a Greek cornice, originally to conceal the ends of roof tiles (4a).

ANTHEMION: classical ornament like a honeysuckle flower (4b).

APRON: panel below a window or wall monument or tablet.

APSE: semicircular or polygonal end of an apartment, especially of a chancel or chapel. In classical architecture sometimes called an *exedra*.

ARABESQUE: non-figurative surface decoration consisting of flowing lines, foliage scrolls etc., based on geometrical patterns. Cf. Grotesque.

ARCADE: series of arches supported by piers or columns. *Blind arcade* or *arcading*: the same applied to the wall surface. *Wall arcade*: in medieval churches, a blind arcade forming a dado below windows. Also a covered shopping street.

ARCH: Shapes *see* 5c. *Basket arch* or *anse de panier* (basket handle) three-centred and depressed, or with a flat centre. *Nodding*: ogee arch curving forward from the wall face. *Parabolic*: shaped like a chain suspended from two level points, but inverted.
Special purposes. *Chancel*: dividing chancel from nave or crossing. *Crossing*: spanning piers at a crossing (q.v.). *Relieving* or *discharging*: incorporated in a wall to relieve superimposed weight (5c). *Skew*: spanning responds not diametrically opposed. *Strainer*: inserted in an opening to resist inward pressure. *Transverse*: spanning a main axis (e.g. of a vaulted space). *See also* Jack arch, Overarch, Triumphal arch.

ARCHITRAVE: formalized lintel, the lowest member of the classical entablature (3a). Also the moulded frame of a door or window (often borrowing the profile of a classical architrave). For *lugged* and *shouldered* architraves *see* 4b.

ARCUATED: dependent structurally on the arch principle. Cf. Trabeated.

ARK: chest or cupboard housing the tables of Jewish law in a synagogue.

ARRIS: sharp edge where two surfaces meet at an angle (3a).

ASHLAR: masonry of large blocks wrought to even faces and square edges (6d). *Broached ashlar* (Scots): scored with parallel lines made by a narrow-pointed chisel (broach). *Droved ashlar*: similar but with lines made by a broad chisel.

ASTRAGAL: classical moulding of semicircular section (3f). Also (Scots) glazing-bar between window panes.

ASTYLAR: with no columns or similar vertical features.

ATLANTES: *see* Caryatids.

ATRIUM (plural: atria): inner court of a Roman or C20 house; in a multi-storey building, a toplit covered court rising through all storeys. Also an open court in front of a church.

ATTACHED COLUMN: *see* Engaged column.

ATTIC: small top storey within a roof. Also the storey above the main entablature of a classical façade.

AUMBRY: recess or cupboard, especially one in a church, to hold sacred vessels used for the Mass.

BAILEY: *see* Motte-and-bailey.

BALANCE BEAM: *see* Canals.

BALDACCHINO: freestanding canopy, originally fabric, over an altar. Cf. Ciborium.

BALLFLOWER: globular flower of three petals enclosing a ball (1a). Typical of the Decorated style.

BALUSTER: pillar or pedestal of bellied form. *Balusters*: vertical supports of this or any other form, for a handrail or coping, the whole being called a *balustrade* (6c). *Blind balustrade*: the same applied to the wall surface.

BARBICAN: outwork defending the entrance to a castle.

BARGEBOARDS (corruption of 'vergeboards'): boards, often carved or fretted, fixed beneath the eaves of a gable to cover and protect the rafters.

BARMKIN (Scots): wall enclosing courtyard attached to a tower house.

BARONY: *see* Burgh.

BAROQUE: style originating in Rome *c.* 1600 and current in England *c.*1680–1720, characterized by dramatic massing and silhouette and the use of the giant order.

BARROW: burial mound.

BARTIZAN: corbelled turret, square or round, frequently at an angle (8a).

BASCULE: hinged part of a lifting (or bascule) bridge.

BASE: moulded foot of a column or pilaster. For *Attic* base *see* 3b. For *Elided* base *see* Elided.

BASEMENT: lowest, subordinate storey; hence the lowest part of a classical elevation, below the piano nobile (q.v.).

BASILICA: a Roman public hall; hence an aisled building with a clerestory.

BASTION: one of a series of defensive semicircular or polygonal projections from the main wall of a fortress or city.

BATTER: intentional inward inclination of a wall face.

BATTLEMENT: defensive parapet, composed of *merlons* (solid) and *crenelles* (embrasures) through which archers could shoot (8a); sometimes called *crenellation*. Also used decoratively.

BAY: division of an elevation or interior space as defined by regular vertical features such as arches, columns, windows etc.

BAY LEAF: classical ornament of overlapping bay leaves (3f).

BAY WINDOW: window of one or more storeys projecting from the face of a building. *Canted*: with a straight front and angled sides. *Bow window*: curved. *Oriel*: rests on corbels or brackets and starts above ground level; also the bay window at the dais end of a medieval great hall.

BEAD-AND-REEL: *see* Enrichments.

BEAKHEAD: Norman ornament with a row of beaked bird or beast heads usually biting into a roll moulding (1a).

BEE-BOLL: wall recess to contain a beehive.

BELFRY: chamber or stage in a tower where bells are hung. Also belltower in a general sense.

BELL CAPITAL: *see* 1b.

BELLCAST: *see* Roof.

BELLCOTE: bell-turret set on a roof or gable. *Birdcage bellcote*: framed structure, usually of stone.

BERM: level area separating a ditch from a bank on a hillfort or barrow.

BILLET: Norman ornament of small half-cylindrical or rectangular blocks (1a).

BIVALLATE: of a hillfort: defended by two concentric banks and ditches.

BLIND: *see* Arcade, Baluster, Portico.

BLOCK CAPITAL: *see* 1a.

BLOCKED: columns etc. interrupted by regular projecting blocks (*blocking*), as on a Gibbs surround (4b).

BLOCKING COURSE: course of stones, or equivalent, on top of a cornice and crowning the wall.

BÖD: *see* Bü.

BOLECTION MOULDING: covering the joint between two different planes (6b).

BOND: the pattern of long sides (*stretchers*) and short ends (*headers*) produced on the face of a wall by laying bricks in a particular way (6e).

BOSS: knob or projection, e.g. at the intersection of ribs in a vault (2c).

BOW WINDOW: *see* Bay window.

BOX FRAME: timber-framed construction in which vertical and horizontal wall members support the roof. Also concrete construction where the loads are taken on cross walls; also called *cross-wall construction*.

BRACE: subsidiary member of a structural frame, curved or straight. *Bracing* is often arranged decoratively, e.g. quatrefoil, herringbone. *See also* Roofs.

BRATTISHING: ornamental crest, usually formed of leaves, Tudor flowers or miniature battlements.

BRESSUMER (*lit.* breast-beam): big horizontal beam supporting the wall above, especially in a jettied building.

BRETASCHE (*lit.* battlement): defensive wooden gallery on a wall.

BRICK: *see* Bond, Cogging, Engineering, Gauged, Tumbling.

BRIDGE: *Bowstring*: with arches rising above the roadway which is suspended from them. *Clapper*: one long stone forms the roadway. *Roving*: *see* Canal. *Suspension*: roadway suspended from cables or chains slung between towers or pylons. *Stay-suspension* or *stay-cantilever*: supported by diagonal stays from towers or pylons. *See also* Bascule.

BRISES-SOLEIL: projecting fins or canopies which deflect direct sunlight from windows.

BROACH: *see* Spire and 1c.

BROCH (Scots): circular tower-like structure, open in the middle, the double wall of dry-stone masonry linked by slabs forming internal galleries at varying levels; found in W and N Scotland and mostly dating from between 100 B.C. and A.D. 100.

BÜ or BÖD (Scots, esp. Shetland; *lit.* booth): combined house and store.

BUCRANIUM: ox skull used decoratively in classical friezes.

BULLSEYE WINDOW: small oval window, set horizontally (cf. Oculus). Also called *oeil de boeuf*.

BURGH: formally constituted town with trading privileges. *Royal Burghs*: monopolized foreign trade till the C17 and paid duty to the Crown. *Burghs of Barony*: founded by secular or ecclesiastical barons to whom they paid duty on their local trade. *Police Burghs*: instituted after 1850 for the administration of new centres of population and abolished in 1975. They controlled planning, building etc.

BUT-AND-BEN (Scots, *lit.* outer and inner rooms): two-room cottage.

BUTTRESS: vertical member projecting from a wall to stabilize it or to resist the lateral thrust of an arch, roof or vault (1c, 2c). A *flying buttress* transmits the thrust to a heavy abutment by means of an arch or half-arch (1c).

CABLE or ROPE MOULDING: originally Norman, like twisted strands of a rope.

CAMES: *see* Quarries.

CAMPANILE: freestanding bell-tower.

CANALS: *Flash lock*: removable weir or similar device through which boats pass on a flush of water. Predecessor of the *pound lock*: chamber with gates at each end allowing boats to float from one level to another. *Tidal gates*: single pair of lock gates allowing vessels to pass when the tide makes a level. *Balance beam*: beam projecting horizontally for opening and closing lock gates. *Roving bridge*: carrying a towing path from one bank to the other.

CANDLE-SNUFFER ROOF: conical roof of a turret (8a).

CANNON SPOUT: *see* 8a.

CANTILEVER: horizontal projection (e.g. step, canopy) supported by a downward force behind the fulcrum.

CAPHOUSE (Scots): small chamber at the head of a turnpike stair, opening onto the parapet walk (8a). Also a chamber rising from within the parapet walk.

CAPITAL: head or crowning feature of a column or pilaster; for classical types *see* 3a; for medieval types *see* 1b.

CARREL: compartment designed for individual work or study, e.g. in a library.

CARTOUCHE: classical tablet with ornate frame (4b).

CARYATIDS: female figures supporting an entablature; their male counterparts are *Atlantes* (*lit.* Atlas figures).

CASEMATE: vaulted chamber, with embrasures for defence, within a castle wall or projecting from it.

CASEMENT: side-hinged window. Also a concave Gothic moulding framing a window.

CASTELLATED: with battlements (q.v.).

CAST IRON: iron containing at least 2.2 per cent of carbon, strong in compression but brittle in tension; cast in a mould to required shape, e.g. for columns or repetitive ornaments. *Wrought iron* is a purer form of iron, with no more than 0.3 per cent of carbon, ductile and strong in tension, forged and rolled into e.g. bars, joists, boiler plates; *mild steel* is its modern equivalent, similar but stronger.

CATSLIDE: *see* 7.

CAVETTO: concave classical moulding of quarter-round section (3f).

CELURE or CEILURE: enriched area of roof above rood or altar.

CEMENT: *see* Concrete.

CENOTAPH (*lit.* empty tomb): funerary monument which is not a burying place.

CENTRING: wooden support for the building of an arch or vault, removed after completion.

CHAMBERED TOMB: Neolithic burial mound with a stone-built chamber and entrance passage covered by an earthen barrow or stone cairn.

CHAMFER (*lit.* corner-break): surface formed by cutting off a square edge or corner. For types of chamfers and *chamfer stops see* 6a. *See also* Double chamfer.

CHANCEL: E end of the church containing the sanctuary; often used to include the choir.

CHANTRY CHAPEL: often attached to or within a church, endowed for the celebration of Masses principally for the soul of the founder.

CHECK (Scots): rebate.

CHERRY-CAULKING or CHERRY-COCKING (Scots): decorative masonry technique using lines of tiny stones (*pins* or *pinning*) in the mortar joints.

CHEVET (*lit.* head): French term for chancel with ambulatory and radiating chapels.

CHEVRON: V-shape used in series or double series (later) on a Norman moulding (1a). Also (especially when on a single plane) called *zigzag*.

CHOIR: the part of a church E of the nave, intended for the stalls of choir monks, choristers and clergy.

CIBORIUM: a fixed canopy over an altar, usually vaulted and supported on four columns; cf. Baldacchino.

CINQUEFOIL: *see* Foil.

CIST: stone-lined or slab-built grave.

CLACHAN (Scots): a hamlet or small village; also, a village inn.

CLADDING: external covering or skin applied to a structure, especially a framed one.

CLEARSTOREY: uppermost storey of the nave of a church, pierced by windows. Also high-level windows in secular buildings.

CLOSE (Scots): courtyard or passage giving access to a number of buildings.

CLOSER: a brick cut to complete a bond (6e).

CLUSTER BLOCK: *see* Multi-storey.

COADE STONE: ceramic artificial stone made in Lambeth 1769–*c.*1840 by Eleanor Coade (†1821) and her associates.

COB: walling material of clay mixed with straw.

COFFERING: arrangement of sunken panels (coffers), square or polygonal, decorating a ceiling, vault or arch.

COGGING: a decorative course of bricks laid diagonally (6e). Cf. Dentilation.

COLLAR: *see* Roofs and 7.

COLLEGIATE CHURCH: endowed for the support of a college of priests, especially for the saying of masses for the soul(s) of the founder(s).

COLONNADE: range of columns supporting an entablature. Cf. Arcade.

COLONNETTE: small column or shaft.

COLOSSAL ORDER: *see* Giant order.

COLUMBARIUM: shelved, niched structure to house multiple burials.

COLUMN: a classical, upright structural member of round section with a shaft, a capital and usually a base (3a, 4a).

COLUMN FIGURE: carved figure attached to a medieval column or shaft, usually flanking a doorway.

COMMENDATOR: receives the revenues of an abbey *in commendam* ('in trust') when the position of abbot is vacant.

COMMUNION TABLE: table used in Protestant churches for the celebration of Holy Communion.

COMPOSITE: *see* Orders.

COMPOUND PIER: grouped shafts (q.v.), or a solid core surrounded by shafts.

CONCRETE: composition of *cement* (calcined lime and clay), *aggregate* (small stones or rock chippings), sand and water. It can be poured into *formwork* or *shuttering* (temporary frame of timber or metal) on site (*in-situ* concrete), or *pre-cast* as components before construction. *Reinforced*: incorporating steel rods to take the tensile force. *Prestressed*: with tensioned steel rods. Finishes include the impression of boards left by formwork (*board-marked* or *shuttered*), and texturing with steel brushes (*brushed*) or hammers (*hammer-dressed*). *See also* Shell.

CONDUCTOR (Scots): down-pipe for rainwater; *see also* Rhone.

CONSOLE: bracket of curved outline (4b).

COPING: protective course of masonry or brickwork capping a wall (6d).

COOMB or COMB CEILING (Scots): with sloping sides corresponding to the roof pitch up to a flat centre.

CORBEL: projecting block supporting something above. *Corbel course:* continuous course of projecting stones or bricks fulfilling the same function. *Corbel table*: series of corbels to carry a parapet or a wall-plate or wall-post (7). *Corbelling*: brick or masonry courses built out beyond one another to support a chimney-stack, window etc. For *continuous* and *chequer-set* corbelling see 8a.

CORINTHIAN: *see* Orders and 3d.

CORNICE: flat-topped ledge with moulded underside, projecting along the top of a building or feature, especially as the highest member of the classical entablature (3a). Also the decorative moulding in the angle between wall and ceiling.

CORPS-DE-LOGIS: the main building(s) as distinct from the wings or pavilions.

COTTAGE ORNÉ: an artfully rustic small house associated with the Picturesque movement.

COUNTERSCARP BANK: low bank on the downhill or outer side of a hillfort ditch.

COUR D'HONNEUR: formal entrance court before a house in the French manner, usually with flanking wings and a screen wall or gates.

COURSE: continuous layer of stones etc. in a wall (6e).

COVE: a broad concave moulding, e.g. to mask the eaves of a roof. *Coved ceiling*: with a pronounced cove joining the walls to a flat central panel smaller than the whole area of the ceiling.

CRADLE ROOF: *see* Wagon roof.

CREDENCE: shelved niche or table, usually beside a piscina (q.v.), for the sacramental elements and vessels.

CRENELLATION: parapet with crenelles (*see* Battlement).

CRINKLE-CRANKLE WALL: garden wall undulating in a series of serpentine curves.

CROCKETS: leafy hooks. *Crocketing* decorates the edges of Gothic features, such as pinnacles, canopies etc. *Crocket capital*: *see* 1b.

CROSSING: central space at the junction of the nave, chancel and transepts. *Crossing tower*: above a crossing.

CROSS-WINDOW: with one mullion and one transom (qq.v.).

CROWN-POST: *see* Roofs and 7.

CROWSTEPS: squared stones set like steps, especially on a crowstepped gable (7, 8a).

CRUCKS (*lit.* crooked): pairs of inclined timbers (*blades*), usually curved, set at bay-lengths; they support the roof timbers and, in timber buildings, also support the walls. *Base*: blades rise from ground level to a tie-or collar-beam which supports the roof timbers. *Full*: blades rise from ground level to the apex of the roof, serving as the main members of a roof truss. *Jointed:* blades formed from more than one timber; the lower member may act as a wall-post; it is usually elbowed at wall-plate level and jointed just above. *Middle*: blades rise from halfway up the walls to a tie-or collar-beam. *Raised*: blades rise from halfway up the walls to the apex. *Upper*: blades supported on a tie-beam and rising to the apex.

CRYPT: underground or half-underground area, usually below the E end of a church. *Ring crypt*: corridor crypt surrounding the apse of an early medieval church, often associated with chambers for relics. Cf. Undercroft.

CUPOLA (*lit.* dome): especially a small dome on a circular or polygonal base crowning a larger dome, roof or turret. Also (Scots) small dome or skylight as an internal feature, especially over a stairwell.

CURSUS: a long avenue defined by two parallel earthen banks with ditches outside.

CURTAIN WALL: a connecting wall between the towers of a castle. Also a non-load-bearing external wall applied to a C20 framed structure.

CUSP: *see* Tracery and 2b.

CYCLOPEAN MASONRY: large irregular polygonal stones, smooth and finely jointed.

CYMA RECTA and CYMA REVERSA: classical mouldings with double curves (3f). Cf. Ogee.

DADO: the finishing (often with panelling) of the lower part of a wall in a classical interior; in origin a formalized continuous pedestal. *Dado rail*: the moulding along the top of the dado.

DAGGER: *see* Tracery and 2b.

DEC (DECORATED): English Gothic architecture *c.* 1290 to *c.* 1350. The name is derived from the type of window tracery (q.v.) used during the period.

DEMI- or HALF-COLUMNS: engaged columns (q.v.) half of whose circumference projects from the wall.

DENTIL: small square block used in series in classical cornices (3c). *Dentilation* is produced by the projection of alternating headers along cornices or string-courses.

DIAPER: repetitive surface decoration of lozenges or squares flat or in relief. Achieved in brickwork with bricks of two colours.

DIOCLETIAN or THERMAL WINDOW: semicircular with two mullions, as used in the Baths of Diocletian, Rome (4b).

DISTYLE: having two columns (4a).

DOGTOOTH: E.E. ornament, consisting of a series of small pyramids formed by four stylized canine teeth meeting at a point (1a).

DOOCOT (Scots): dovecot. When freestanding, usually *Lectern* (rectangular with single-pitch roof) or *Beehive* (circular, diminishing towards the top).

DORIC: *see* Orders and 3a, 3b.

DORMER: window projecting from the slope of a roof (7). *Dormer head*: gable above a dormer, often formed as a pediment (8a).

DOUBLE CHAMFER: a chamfer applied to each of two recessed arches (1a).

DOUBLE PILE: *see* Pile.

DRAGON BEAM: *see* Jetty.

DRESSINGS: the stone or brickwork worked to a finished face about an angle, opening or other feature.

DRIPSTONE: moulded stone projecting from a wall to protect the lower parts from water. Cf. Hoodmould, Weathering.

DRUM: circular or polygonal stage supporting a dome or cupola. Also one of the stones forming the shaft of a column (3a).

DRY-STONE: stone construction without mortar.

DUN (Scots): small stone-walled fort.

DUTCH or FLEMISH GABLE: *see* 7.

EASTER SEPULCHRE: tomb-chest, usually within or against the N wall of a chancel, used in Holy Week ceremonies for reservation (entombment) of the sacrament after the mass of Maundy Thursday.

EAVES: overhanging edge of a roof; hence *eaves cornice* in this position.

ECHINUS: ovolo moulding (q.v.) below the abacus of a Greek Doric capital (3a).

EDGE RAIL: *see* Railways.

EDGE-ROLL: moulding of semicircular section or more at the edge of an opening.

E.E. (EARLY ENGLISH): English Gothic architecture *c.* 1190–1250.

EGG-AND-DART: *see* Enrichments and 3f.

ELEVATION: any face of a building or side of a room. In a drawing, the same or any part of it, represented in two dimensions.

ELIDED: used to describe a compound feature, e.g. an entablature, with some parts omitted. Also, parts of, e.g., a base or capital, combined to form a larger one.

EMBATTLED: with battlements.

EMBRASURE: splayed opening in a wall or battlement (q.v.).

ENCAUSTIC TILES: earthenware tiles fired with a pattern and glaze.

EN DELIT: stone laid against the bed.

ENFILADE: reception rooms in a formal series, usually with all doorways on axis.

ENGAGED or ATTACHED COLUMN: one that partly merges into a wall or pier.

ENGINEERING BRICKS: dense bricks, originally used mostly for railway viaducts etc.

ENRICHMENTS: the carved decoration of certain classical mouldings, e.g. the ovolo with *egg-and-dart*, the cyma reversa with *waterleaf*, the astragal with *bead-and-reel* (3f).

ENTABLATURE: in classical architecture, collective name for the three horizontal members (architrave, frieze and cornice) carried by a wall or a column (3a).

ENTASIS: very slight convex deviation from a straight line, used to prevent an optical illusion of concavity.

ENTRESOL: mezzanine floor subdividing what is constructionally a single storey, e.g. a vault.

EPITAPH: inscription on a tomb or monument.

EXEDRA: *see* Apse.

EXTRADOS: outer curved face of an arch or vault.

EYECATCHER: decorative building terminating a vista.

FASCIA: plain horizontal band, e.g. in an architrave (3c, 3d) or on a shopfront.

FENESTRATION: the arrangement of windows in a façade.

FERETORY: site of the chief shrine of a church, behind the high altar.

FESTOON: ornamental garland, suspended from both ends. Cf. Swag.

FEU (Scots): land granted, e.g. by sale, by the *feudal superior* to the *vassal* or *feuar*, on conditions that usually include the annual payment of a fixed sum of *feu duty*. Any subsequent proprietor of the land becomes the feuar and is subject to the same obligations.

FIBREGLASS (or glass-reinforced polyester (GRP)): synthetic resin reinforced with glass fibre. GRC: glass-reinforced concrete.

FIELD: *see* Panelling and 6b.

FILLET: a narrow flat band running down a medieval shaft or along a roll moulding (1a). It separates larger curved mouldings in classical cornices, fluting or bases (3c).

FLAMBOYANT: the latest phase of French Gothic architecture, with flowing tracery.

FLASH LOCK: *see* Canals.

FLATTED: divided into apartments. Also with a colloquial (Scots) meaning: 'He stays on the first flat' means that he lives on the first floor.

FLÈCHE or SPIRELET (*lit.* arrow): slender spire on the centre of a roof.

FLEURON: medieval carved flower or leaf, often rectilinear (1a).

FLUSHWORK: knapped flint used with dressed stone to form patterns.

FLUTING: series of concave grooves (flutes), their common edges sharp (arris) or blunt (fillet) (3).

FOIL (*lit.* leaf): lobe formed by the cusping of a circular or other shape in tracery (2b). *Trefoil* (three), *quatrefoil* (four), *cinquefoil* (five) and *multifoil* express the number of lobes in a shape.

FOLIATE: decorated with leaves.

FORE-BUILDING: structure protecting an entrance.

FORESTAIR: external stair, usually unenclosed.

FORMWORK: *see* Concrete.

FRAMED BUILDING: where the structure is carried by a framework - e.g. of steel, reinforced concrete, timber - instead of by load-bearing walls.

FREESTONE: stone that is cut, or can be cut, in all directions.

FRESCO: *al fresco*: painting on wet plaster. *Fresco secco*: painting on dry plaster.

FRIEZE: the middle member of the classical entablature, sometimes ornamented (3a). *Pulvinated frieze* (*lit.* cushioned): of bold convex profile (3c). Also a horizontal band of ornament.

FRONTISPIECE: in C16 and C17 buildings the central feature of doorway and windows above linked in one composition.

GABLE: peaked external wall at end of double-pitch roof. For types *see* 7. Also (Scots): whole end wall of whatever shape. *Pedimental gable*: treated like a pediment.

GADROONING: classical ribbed ornament like inverted fluting that flows into a lobed edge.

GAIT or GATE (Scots): street, usually with a prefix indicating use, direction or destination.

GALILEE: chapel or vestibule usually at the W end of a church enclosing the main portal(s).

GALLERY: a long room or passage; an upper storey above the aisle of a church, looking through arches to the nave; a balcony or mezzanine overlooking the main interior space of a building; or an external walkway.

GALLETING: small stones set in a mortar course.

GAMBREL ROOF: *see* 7.

GARDEROBE: medieval privy.

GARGOYLE: projecting water spout, often carved into human or animal shape. For cannon spout *see* 8.

GAUGED or RUBBED BRICKWORK: soft brick sawn roughly, then rubbed to a precise (gauged) surface. Mostly used for door or window openings (5c).

GAZEBO (jocular Latin, 'I shall gaze'): ornamental lookout tower or raised summer house.

GEOMETRIC: English Gothic architecture *c.* 1250–1310. *See also* Tracery. For another meaning, *see* Stairs.

GIANT or COLOSSAL ORDER: classical order (q.v.) whose height is that of two or more storeys of the building to which it is applied.

GIBBS SURROUND: C18 treatment of an opening (4b), seen particularly in the work of James Gibbs (1682–1754).

GIRDER: a large beam. *Box*: of hollow-box section. *Bowed*: with its top rising in a curve. *Plate*: of I-section, made from iron or steel plates. *Lattice*: with braced framework.

GLACIS: artificial slope extending out and downwards from the parapet of a fort.

GLAZING-BARS: wooden or sometimes metal bars separating and supporting window panes.

GLAZING GROOVE: groove in a window surround into which the glass is fitted.

GNOMON: vane or indicator casting a shadow onto a sundial.

GRAFFITI: *see* Sgraffito.

GRANGE: farm owned and run by a religious order.

GRC: *see* Fibreglass.

GRISAILLE: monochrome painting on walls or glass.

GROIN: sharp edge at the meeting of two cells of a cross-vault; *see* Vault and 2b.

GROTESQUE (*lit.* grotto-esque): wall decoration adopted from Roman examples in the Renaissance. Its foliage scrolls incorporate figurative elements. Cf. Arabesque.

GROTTO: artificial cavern.

GRP: *see* Fibreglass.

GUILLOCHE: classical ornament of interlaced bands (4b).

GUNLOOP: opening for a firearm (8a).

GUSHET (Scots): a triangular or wedge-shaped piece of land or the corner building on such a site.

GUTTAE: stylized drops (3b).

HALF-TIMBERING: archaic term for timber-framing (q.v.). Sometimes used for non-structural decorative timberwork.

HALL CHURCH: medieval church with nave and aisles of approximately equal height. Also (Scots C20) building for use as both hall and church, the double function usually intended to be temporary until a separate church is built.

HAMMERBEAM: *see* Roofs and 7.

HARLING (Scots, *lit.* hurling): wet dash, i.e. a form of roughcasting in which the mixture of aggregate and binding material (e.g. lime) is dashed onto a wall.

HEADER: *see* Bond and 6e.

HEADSTOP: stop (q.v.) carved with a head (5b).

HELM ROOF: *see* 1c.

HENGE: ritual earthwork with a surrounding ditch and outer bank.

HERM (*lit.* the god Hermes): male head or bust on a pedestal.

HERRINGBONE WORK: *see* 6e (for brick bond). Cf. Pitched masonry.

HEXASTYLE: *see* Portico.

HILLFORT: Iron Age earthwork enclosed by a ditch and bank system.

HIPPED ROOF: *see* 7.

HOODMOULD: projecting moulding above an arch or lintel to throw off water (2b, 5b). When horizontal often called a *label.* For label stop *see* Stop.

HORIZONTAL GLAZING: with panes of horizontal proportions.

HORSEMILL: circular or polygonal farm building with a central shaft turned by a horse to drive agricultural machinery.

HUNGRY-JOINTED: *see* Pointing.

HUSK GARLAND: festoon of stylized nutshells (4b).

HYDRAULIC POWER: use of water under high pressure to work machinery. *Accumulator tower*: houses a hydraulic accumulator which accommodates fluctuations in the flow through hydraulic mains.

HYPOCAUST (*lit.* underburning): Roman underfloor heating system.

IMPOST: horizontal moulding at the springing of an arch (5c).

IMPOST BLOCK: block between abacus and capital (1b).

IN ANTIS: *see* Antae, Portico and 4a.

INDENT: shape chiselled out of a stone to receive a brass. Also, in restoration, new stone inserted as a patch.

INDUSTRIALIZED or SYSTEM BUILDING: system of manufactured units assembled on site.

INGLENOOK (*lit.* fire-corner): recess for a hearth with provision for seating.

INGO (Scots): the reveal of a door or window opening where the stone is at right angles to the wall.

INTERCOLUMNATION: interval between columns.

INTERLACE: decoration in relief simulating woven or entwined stems or bands.

INTRADOS: *see* Soffit.

IONIC: *see* Orders and 3c.

JACK ARCH: shallow segmental vault springing from beams, used for fireproof floors, bridge decks etc.

JAMB (*lit.* leg): one of the vertical sides of an opening. Also (Scots) wing or extension adjoining one side of a rectangular plan making it into an L-, T- or Z-plan.

JETTY: the projection of an upper storey beyond the storey below. In a stone building this is achieved by corbelling. In a timber-framed building it is made by the beams and joists of the lower storey oversailing the wall; on their outer ends is placed the sill of the walling for the storey above.

JOGGLE: the joining of two stones to prevent them slipping by a notch in one and a projection in the other.

KEEL MOULDING: moulding used from the late C12, in section like the keel of a ship (1a).

KEEP: principal tower of a castle.

KENTISH CUSP: *see* Tracery.

KEY PATTERN: *see* 4b.

KEYSTONE: central stone in an arch or vault (4b, 5c).

KINGPOST: *see* Roofs and 7.

KNEELER: horizontal projecting stone at the base of each side of a gable to support the inclined coping stones (7).

LABEL: *see* Hoodmould and 5b.

LABEL STOP: *see* Stop and 5b.

LACED BRICKWORK: vertical strips of brickwork, often in a contrasting colour, linking openings on different floors.

LACING COURSE: horizontal reinforcement in timber or brick to walls of flint, cobble etc.

LADE (Scots): channel formed to bring water to a mill; mill-race.

LADY CHAPEL: dedicated to the Virgin Mary (Our Lady).

LAIGH or LAICH (Scots): low.

LAIR (Scots): a burial space reserved in a graveyard

LAIRD (Scots): landowner.

LANCET: slender single-light, pointed-arched window (2a).

LANTERN: circular or polygonal windowed turret crowning a roof or a dome. Also the windowed stage of a crossing tower lighting the church interior.

LANTERN CROSS: churchyard cross with lantern-shaped top.

LAVATORIUM: in a religious house, a washing place adjacent to the refectory.

LEAN-TO: *see* Roofs.

LESENE (*lit.* a mean thing): pilaster without base or capital. Also called *pilaster strip*.

LIERNE: *see* Vault and 2c.

LIGHT: compartment of a window defined by the mullions.

LINENFOLD: Tudor panelling carved with simulations of folded linen.

LINTEL: horizontal beam or stone bridging an opening.

LOFT: gallery in a church. *Organ loft*: in which the organ, or sometimes only the console (keyboard), is placed. *Laird's loft*, *Trades loft* etc. (Scots): reserved for an individual or special group. *See also* Rood (loft).

LOGGIA: gallery, usually arcaded or colonnaded along one side; sometimes freestanding.

LONG-AND-SHORT WORK: quoins consisting of stones placed with the long side alternately upright and horizontal, especially in Saxon building.

LOUVRE: roof opening, often protected by a raised timber structure, to allow the smoke from a central hearth to escape. *Louvres*: overlapping boards to allow ventilation but keep the rain out.

LOWSIDE WINDOW: set lower than the others in a chancel side wall, usually towards its W end.

L-PLAN: *see* Tower house and 8b.

LUCARNE (*lit.* dormer): small gabled opening in a roof or spire.

LUCKENBOOTH (Scots): lock-up booth or shop.

LUGGED ARCHITRAVE: *see* 4b.

LUNETTE: semicircular window or blind panel.

LYCHGATE (*lit.* corpse-gate): roofed gateway entrance to a churchyard for the reception of a coffin.

LYNCHET: long terraced strip of soil on the downward side of prehistoric and medieval fields, accumulated because of continual ploughing along the contours.

MACHICOLATIONS (*lit.* mashing devices): series of openings between the corbels that support a projecting parapet through which missiles can be dropped (8a). Used decoratively in post-medieval buildings.

MAINS (Scots): home farm on an estate.

MANOMETER or STANDPIPE TOWER: containing a column of water to regulate pressure in water mains.

MANSARD: *see* 7.

MANSE: house of a minister of religion, especially in Scotland.

MARGINS (Scots): dressed stones at the edges of an opening. 'Back-set margins' (RCAHMS) are actually set forward from a rubble wall to act as a stop for harling (q.v.). Also called *rybats*.

MARRIAGE LINTEL (Scots): door or window lintel carved with the initials of the owner and his wife and the date of building work, only coincidentally of their marriage.

MATHEMATICAL TILES: facing tiles with the appearance of brick, most often applied to timber-framed walls.

MAUSOLEUM: monumental building or chamber usually intended for the burial of members of one family.

MEGALITHIC: the use of large stones, singly or together.

MEGALITHIC TOMB: massive stonebuilt Neolithic burial chamber covered by an earth or stone mound.

MERCAT (Scots): market. The *Mercat Cross* of a Scottish burgh was the focus of market activity and local ceremonial. Most examples are post-Reformation with heraldic or other finials (not crosses).

MERLON: *see* Battlement.

MESOLITHIC: Middle Stone Age, in Britain *c.* 5000 to *c.* 3500 B.C.

METOPES: spaces between the triglyphs in a Doric frieze (3b).

MEZZANINE: low storey between two higher ones or within the height of a high one, not extending over its whole area.

MILD STEEL: *see* Cast iron.

MISERICORD (*lit.* mercy): shelf on a carved bracket placed on the underside of a hinged choir stall seat to support an occupant when standing.

MIXER-COURTS: forecourts to groups of houses shared by vehicles and pedestrians.

MODILLIONS: small consoles (q.v.) along the underside of a Corinthian or Composite cornice (3d). Often used along an eaves cornice.

MODULE: a predetermined standard size for co-ordinating the dimensions of components of a building.

MORT-SAFE (Scots): device to secure corpse(s): either an iron frame over a grave or a building where bodies were kept during decomposition.

MOTTE-AND-BAILEY: C11 and C12 type of castle consisting of an earthen mound (motte) topped by a wooden tower within or adjoining a bailey, an enclosure defended by a ditch and palisade, and also, sometimes, by an inner bank.

MOUCHETTE: *see* Tracery and 2b.

MOULDING: shaped ornamental strip of continuous section; *see* Cavetto, Cyma, Ovolo, Roll.

MULLION: vertical member between window lights (2b).

MULTI-STOREY: five or more storeys. Multi-storey flats may form a *cluster block*, with individual blocks of flats grouped round a service core; a *point block*, with flats fanning out from a service core; or a *slab block*, with flats approached by corridors or galleries from service cores at intervals or towers at the ends (plan also used for offices, hotels etc.). *Tower block* is a generic term for a high multi-storey building.

MULTIVALLATE: of a hillfort: defended by three or more concentric banks and ditches.

MUNTIN: *see* Panelling and 6b.

MUTULE: square block under the corona of a Doric cornice.

NAILHEAD: E.E. ornament consisting of small pyramids regularly repeated (1a).

NARTHEX: enclosed vestibule or covered porch at the main entrance to a church.

NAVE: the body of a church W of the crossing or chancel, often flanked by aisles (q.v.).

NEOLITHIC: New Stone Age in Britain, *c.* 3500 B.C. until the Bronze Age.

NEWEL: central or corner post of a staircase (6c). For Newel stair *see* Stairs.

NIGHT STAIR: stair by which religious entered the transept of their church from their dormitory to celebrate night offices.

NOGGING: *see* Timber-framing.

NOOK-SHAFT: shaft set in the angle of a wall or opening (1a).

NORMAN: *see* Romanesque.

NOSING: projection of the tread of a step (6c). *Bottle nosing*: half round in section.

NUTMEG: medieval ornament with a chain of tiny triangles placed obliquely.

OCULUS: circular opening.

OEIL DE BOEUF: *see* Bullseye window.

OGEE: double curve, bending first one way and then the other, as in an *ogee* or *ogival arch* (5c). Cf. Cyma recta and Cyma reversa.

OPUS SECTILE: decorative mosaic-like facing.

OPUS SIGNINUM: composition flooring of Roman origin.

ORATORY: a private chapel in a church or a house. Also a church of the Oratorian Order.

ORDER: one of a series of recessed arches and jambs forming a splayed medieval opening, e.g. a doorway or arcade arch (1a).

ORDERS: the formalized versions of the post-and-lintel system in classical architecture. The main orders are *Doric*, *Ionic* and *Corinthian*. They are Greek in origin

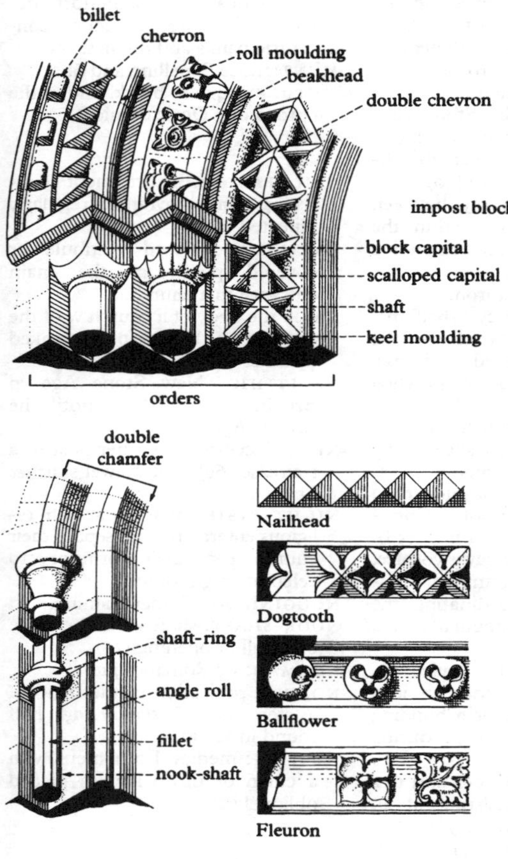

a) MOULDINGS AND ORNAMENT

b) CAPITALS

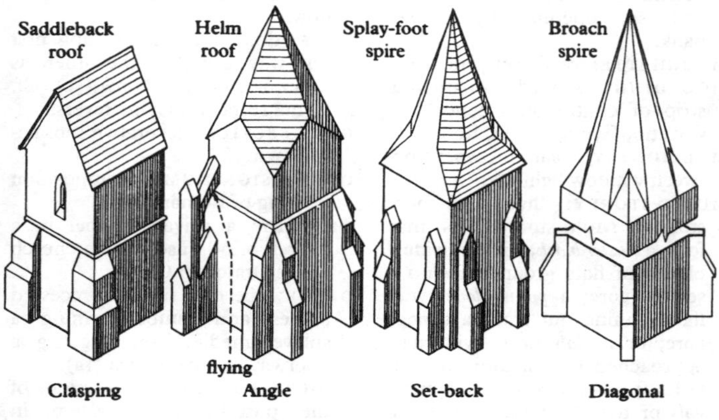

c) BUTTRESSES, ROOFS AND SPIRES

FIGURE 1: MEDIEVAL

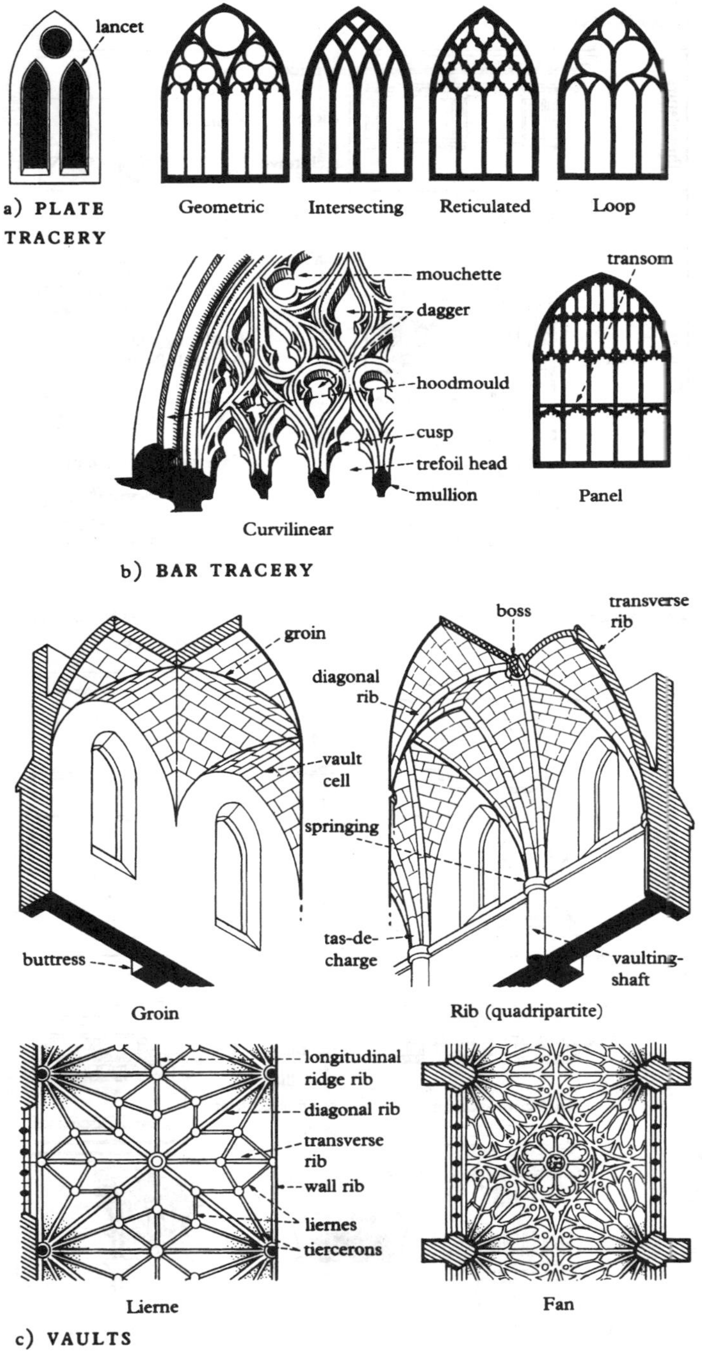

FIGURE 2: MEDIEVAL

ORDERS

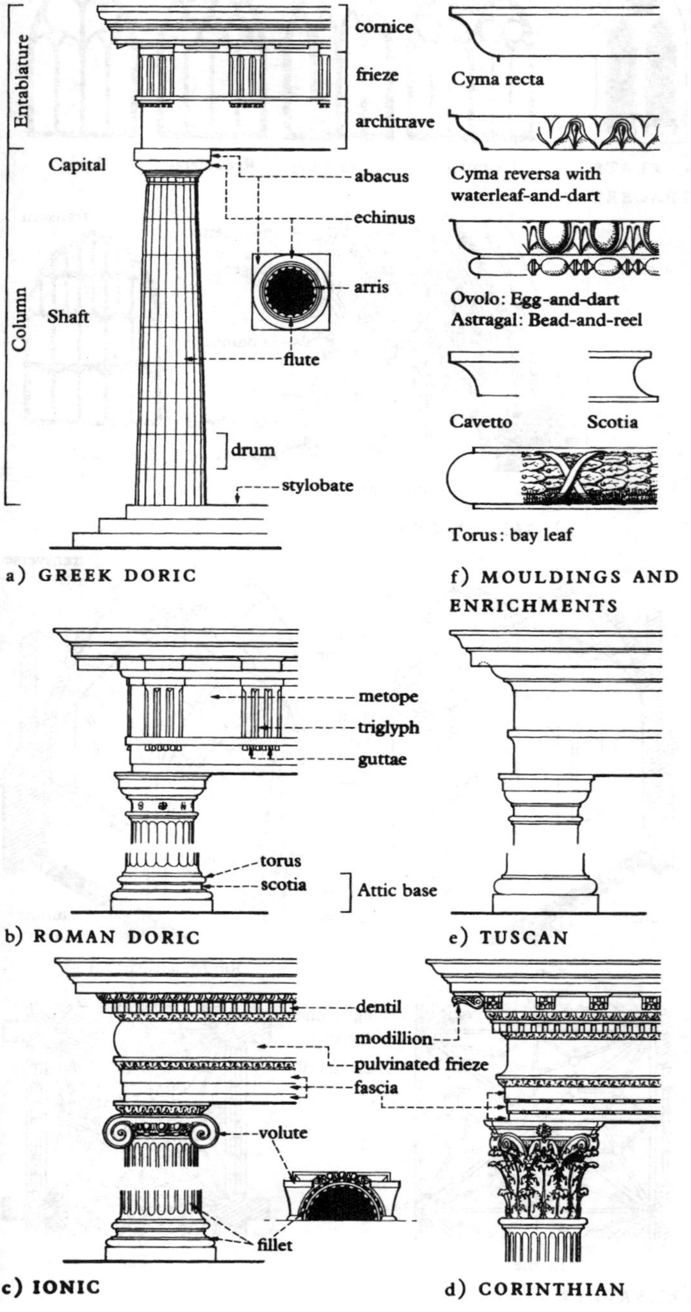

FIGURE 3: CLASSICAL

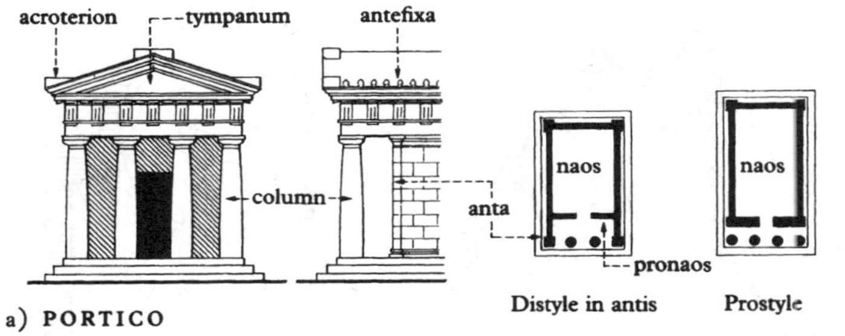

a) PORTICO

b) ORNAMENTS AND FEATURES

FIGURE 4: CLASSICAL

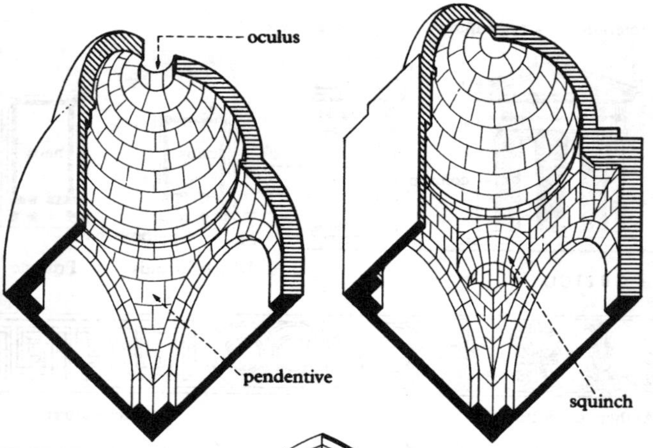

a) DOMES

b) HOODMOULDS

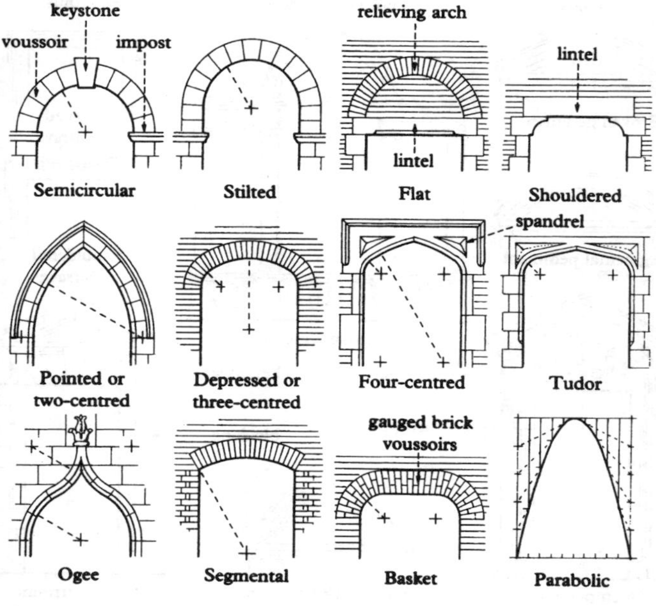

c) ARCHES

FIGURE 5: CONSTRUCTION

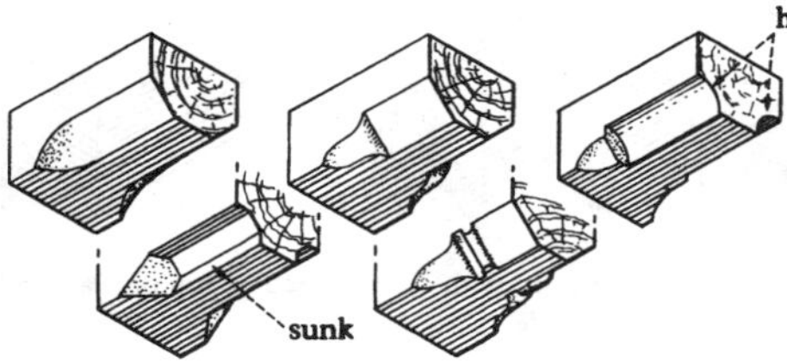

a) CHAMFERS AND CHAMFERSTOPS

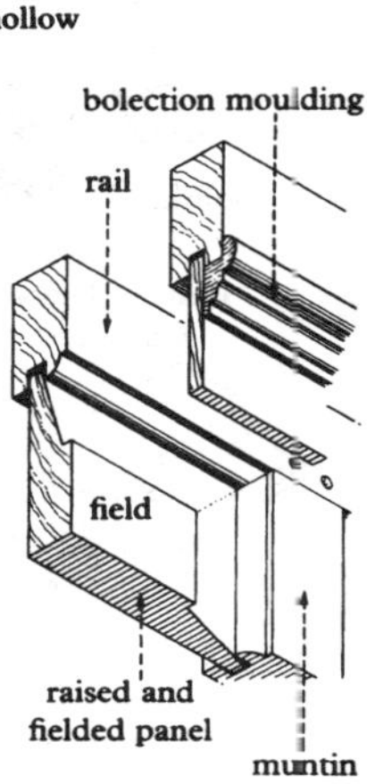

b) PANELLING

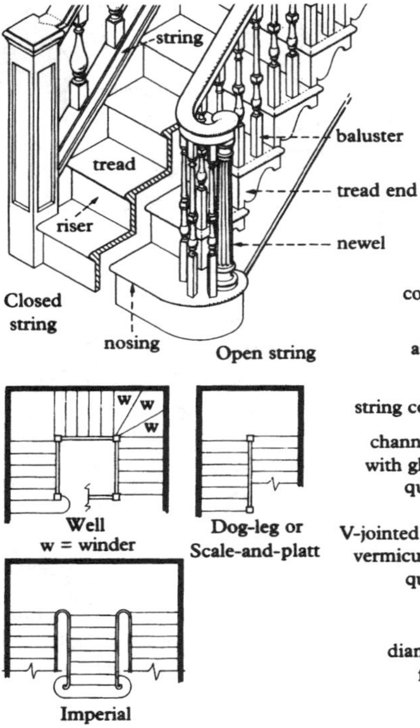

c) STAIRS

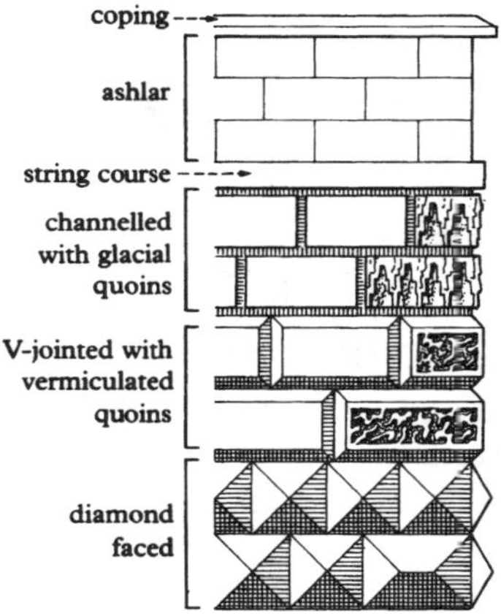

d) RUSTICATION

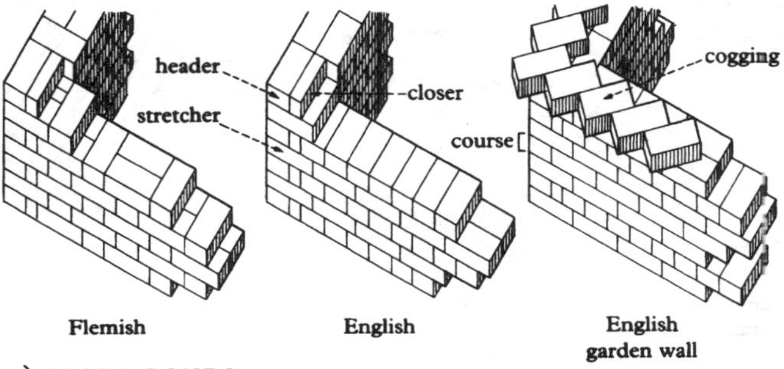

e) BRICK BONDS

FIGURE 6: CONSTRUCTION

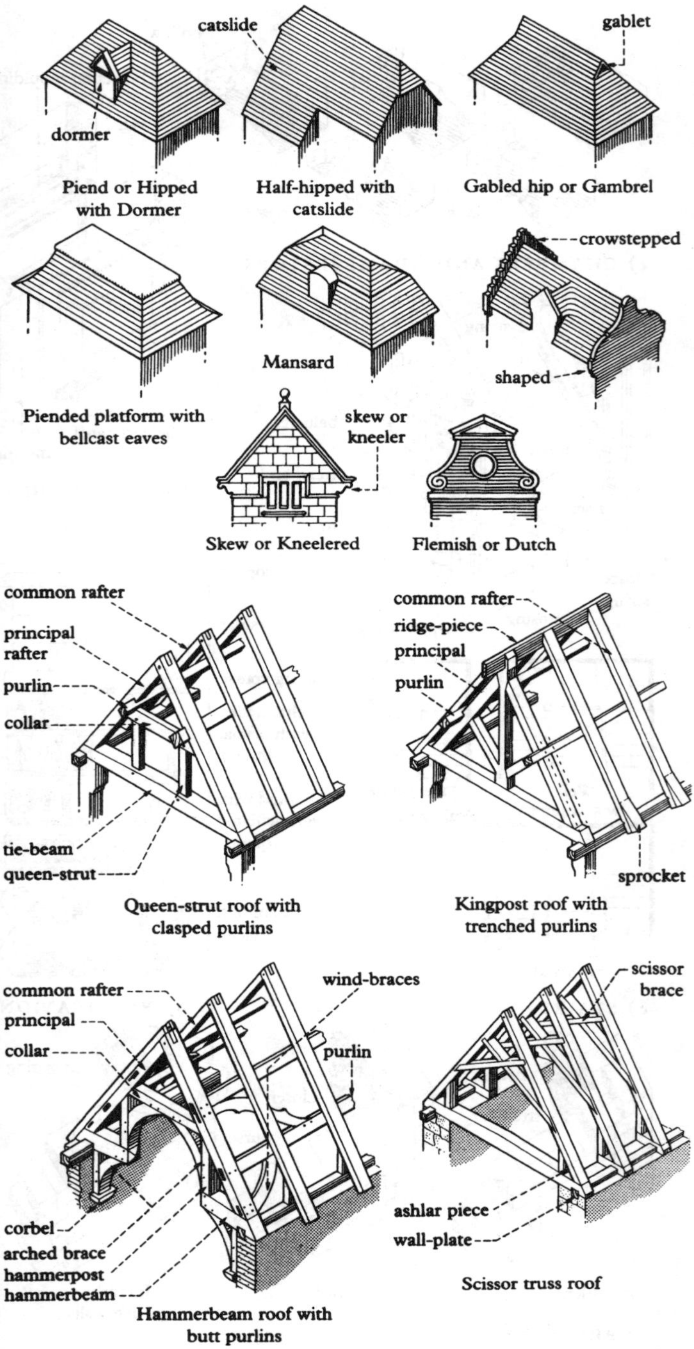

FIGURE 7: ROOFS AND GABLES

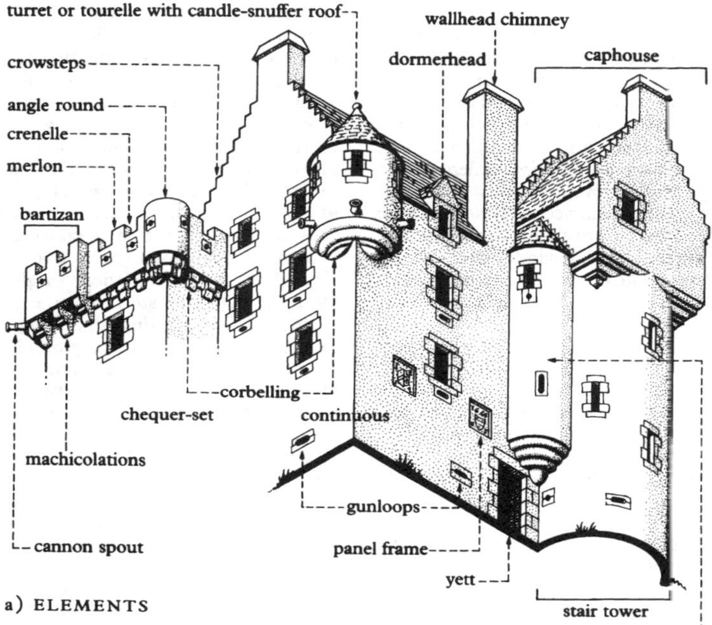

a) ELEMENTS

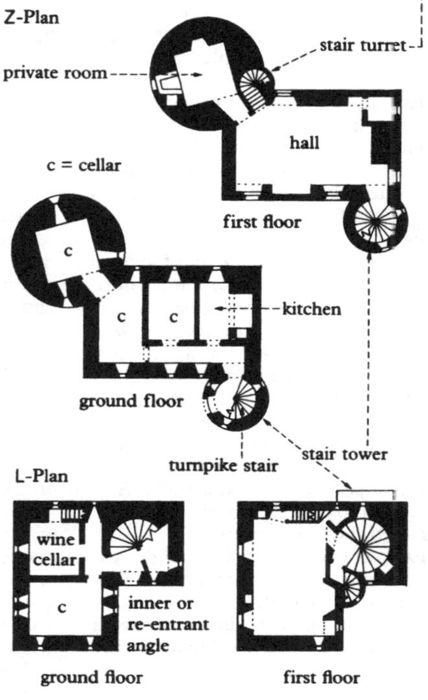

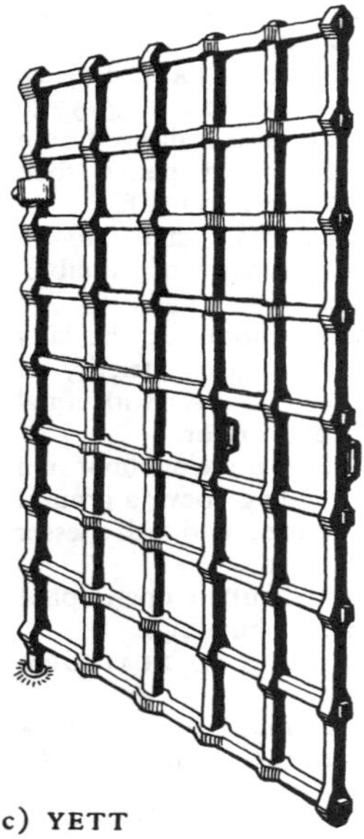

c) YETT

b) FORMS

FIGURE 8: THE TOWER HOUSE

but occur in Roman versions. *Tuscan* is a simple version of Roman Doric. Though each order has its own conventions (3), there are many minor variations. The *Composite* capital combines Ionic volutes with Corinthian foliage. *Superimposed orders*: orders on successive levels, usually in the upward sequence of Tuscan, Doric, Ionic, Corinthian, Composite.

ORIEL: *see* Bay window.

OVERARCH: framing a wall which has an opening, e.g. a window or door.

OVERDOOR: painting or relief above an internal door. Also called a *sopraporta*.

OVERTHROW: decorative fixed arch between two gatepiers or above a wrought-iron gate.

OVOLO: wide convex moulding (3f).

PALIMPSEST: of a brass: where a metal plate has been reused by engraving on the back; of a wall painting: where one overlaps and partly obscures an earlier one.

PALLADIAN: following the examples and principles of Andrea Palladio (1508–80).

PALMETTE: classical ornament like a palm shoot (4b).

PANEL FRAME: moulded stone frame round an armorial panel, often placed over the entrance to a tower house (8a).

PANELLING: wooden lining to interior walls, made up of vertical members (*muntins*) and horizontals (*rails*) framing panels: also called *wainscot*. *Raised-and-fielded*: with the central area of the panel (*field*) raised up (6b).

PANTILE: roof tile of S section.

PARAPET: wall for protection at any sudden drop, e.g. at the wallhead of a castle where it protects the *parapet walk* or wall-walk. Also used to conceal a roof.

PARCLOSE: *see* Screen.

PARGETING (*lit.* plastering): exterior plaster decoration, either in relief or incised.

PARLOUR: in a religious house, a room where the religious could talk to visitors; in a medieval house, the semi-private living room below the solar (q.v.).

PARTERRE: level space in a garden laid out with low, formal beds.

PATERA (*lit.* plate): round or oval ornament in shallow relief.

PAVILION: ornamental building for occasional use; or projecting subdivision of a larger building, often at an angle or terminating a wing.

PEBBLEDASHING: *see* Rendering.

PEDESTAL: a tall block carrying a classical order, statue, vase etc.

PEDIMENT: a formalized gable derived from that of a classical temple; also used over doors, windows etc. For variations *see* 4b.

PEEL (*lit.* palisade): stone tower, e.g. near the Scottish-English border.

PEND (Scots): open-ended ground-level passage through a building.

PENDENTIVE: spandrel between adjacent arches, supporting a drum, dome or vault and consequently formed as part of a hemisphere (5a).

PENTHOUSE: subsidiary structure with a lean-to roof. Also a separately roofed structure on top of a C20 multi-storey block.

PEPPERPOT TURRET: bartizan with conical or pyramidal roof.

PERIPTERAL: *see* Peristyle.

PERISTYLE: a colonnade all round the exterior of a classical building, as in a temple which is then said to be *peripteral*.

PERP (PERPENDICULAR): English Gothic architecture *c.* 1335–50 to *c.* 1530. The name is derived from the upright tracery panels then used (*see* Tracery and 2a).

PERRON: external stair to a doorway, usually of double-curved plan.

PEW: loosely, seating for the laity outside the chancel; strictly, an enclosed seat. *Box pew*: with equal high sides and a door.

PIANO NOBILE: principal floor of a classical building above a ground floor or basement and with a lesser storey overhead.

PIAZZA: formal urban open space surrounded by buildings.

PIEND AND PIENDED PLATFORM ROOF: *see* 7.

PIER: large masonry or brick support, often for an arch. *See also* Compound pier.

PILASTER: flat representation of a classical column in shallow relief. *Pilastrade*: series of pilasters, equivalent to a colonnade.

PILE: row of rooms. *Double pile*: two rows thick.

PILLAR: freestanding upright member of any section, not conforming to one of the orders (q.v.).

PILLAR PISCINA: *see* Piscina.

PILOTIS: C20 French term for pillars or stilts that support a building above an open ground floor.

PINS OR PINNINGS (Scots): *see* Cherry-caulking.

PISCINA: basin for washing Mass vessels, provided with a drain; set in or against wall to S of an altar or freestanding (*pillar piscina*).

PITCHED MASONRY: laid on the diagonal, often alternately with opposing courses (*pitched and counterpitched* or herringbone).

PIT PRISON: sunk chamber with access from above through a hatch.

PLATE RAIL: *see* Railways.

PLATEWAY: *see* Railways.

PLATT (Scots): platform, doorstep or landing. *Scale-and-platt stair*: *see* Stairs and 6c.

PLEASANCE (Scots): close or walled garden.

PLINTH: projecting courses at the foot of a wall or column, generally chamfered or moulded at the top.

PODIUM: a continuous raised platform supporting a building; or a large block of two or three storeys beneath a multi-storey block of smaller area.

POINT BLOCK: *see* Multi-storey.

POINTING: exposed mortar jointing of masonry or brickwork. Types include *flush*, *recessed* and *tuck* (with a narrow channel filled with finer, whiter mortar). *Bag-rubbed*: flush at the edges and gently recessed in the middle. *Ribbon*: joints formed with a trowel so that they stand out. *Hungry-jointed*: either with no pointing or deeply recessed to show the outline of each stone.

POPPYHEAD: carved ornament of leaves and flowers as a finial for a bench end or stall.

PORTAL FRAME: C20 frame comprising two uprights rigidly connected to a beam or pair of rafters.

PORTCULLIS: gate constructed to rise and fall in vertical gooves at the entry to a castle.

PORTE COCHÈRE: porch large enough to admit wheeled vehicles.

PORTICO: a porch with the roof and frequently a pediment supported by a row of columns (4a). A portico *in antis* has columns on the same plane as the front of the building. A *prostyle* porch has columns standing free. Porticoes are described by the number of front columns, e.g. tetrastyle (four), hexastyle (six). The space within the temple is the *naos*, that within the portico the *pronaos*. *Blind portico*: the front features of a portico applied to a wall.

PORTICUS (plural: porticūs): subsidiary cell opening from the main body of a pre-Conquest church.

POST: upright support in a structure.

POSTERN: small gateway at the back of a building or to the side of a larger entrance door or gate.

POTENCE (Scots): rotating ladder for access to doocot nesting boxes.

POUND LOCK: *see* Canals.

PREDELLA: in an altarpiece, the horizontal strip below the main representation, often used for subsidiary representations.

PRESBYTERY: the part of a church lying E of the choir where the main altar is placed. Also a priest's residence.

PRESS (Scots): cupboard.

PRINCIPAL: *see* Roofs and 7.

PRONAOS: *see* Portico and 4a.

PROSTYLE: *see* Portico and 4a.

PULPIT: raised and enclosed platform for the preaching of sermons. *Three-decker*: with reading desk below and clerk's desk below that. *Two-decker*: as above, minus the clerk's desk.

PULPITUM: stone screen in a major church dividing choir from nave.

PULVINATED: *see* Frieze and 3c.

PURLIN: *see* Roofs and 7.

PUTHOLES or PUTLOG HOLES: in wall to receive putlogs, the horizontal timbers which support scaffolding boards; not always filled after construction is complete.

PUTTO (plural: putti): small naked boy.

QUARRIES: square (or diamond) panes of glass supported by lead strips (*cames*); square floor-slabs or tiles.

QUATREFOIL: *see* Foil.

QUEEN-STRUT: *see* Roofs and 7.

QUILLONS: the arms forming the cross-guard of a sword.

QUIRK: sharp groove to one side of a convex medieval moulding.

QUOINS: dressed stones at the angles of a building (6d).

RADBURN SYSTEM: pedestrian and vehicle segregation in residential developments, based on that used at Radburn, New Jersey, U.S.A., by Wright and Stein, 1928–30.

RADIATING CHAPELS: projecting radially from an ambulatory or an apse (*see* Chevet).

RAFTER: *see* Roofs and 7.

RAGGLE: groove cut in masonry, especially to receive the edge of a roof-covering.

RAIL: *see* Panelling and 6b.

RAILWAYS: *Edge rail*: on which flanged wheels can run. *Plate rail*: L-section rail for plain unflanged wheels. *Plateway*: early railway using plate rails.

RAISED AND FIELDED: *see* Panelling and 6b.

RAKE: slope or pitch.

RAMPART: defensive outer wall of stone or earth. *Rampart walk*: path along the inner face.

RATCOURSE: projecting string-course on a doocot to deter rats from climbing to the flight holes.

REBATE: rectangular section cut out of a masonry edge to receive a shutter, door, window etc.

REBUS: a heraldic pun, e.g. a fiery cock for Cockburn.

REEDING: series of convex mouldings, the reverse of fluting (q.v.). Cf. Gadrooning.

RENDERING: the covering of outside walls with a uniform surface or skin for protection from the weather. *Lime-washing*: thin layer of lime plaster. *Pebble-dashing*: where aggregate is thrown at the wet plastered wall for a textured effect. *Roughcast*: plaster mixed with a coarse aggregate such as gravel. *Stucco*: fine lime plaster worked to a smooth surface. *Cement rendering*: a cheaper substitute for stucco, usually with a grainy texture.

REPOUSSÉ: relief designs in metalwork, formed by beating it from the back.

REREDORTER (*lit.* behind the dormitory): latrines in a medieval religious house.

REREDOS: painted and/or sculptured screen behind and above an altar. Cf. Retable.

RESPOND: half-pier or half-column bonded into a wall and carrying one end of an arch. It usually terminates an arcade.

RETABLE: painted or carved panel standing on or at the back of an altar, usually attached to it.

RETROCHOIR: in a major church, the area between the high altar and E chapel.

REVEAL: the plane of a jamb, between the wall and the frame of a door or window.

RHONE (Scots): gutter along the eaves for rainwater: *see also* Conductor.

RIB-VAULT: *see* Vault and 2c.

RIG (Scots): a strip of ploughed land raised in the middle and sloped to a furrow on each side; early cultivation method (runrig) usually surrounded by untilled grazing land.

RINCEAU: classical ornament of leafy scrolls (4b).

RISER: vertical face of a step (6c).

ROCK-FACED: masonry cleft to produce a rugged appearance.

ROCOCO: style current between *c.* 1720 and *c.* 1760, characterized by a serpentine line and playful, scrolled decoration.

ROLL MOULDING: medieval moulding of part-circular section (1a).

ROMANESQUE: style current in the C11 and C12. In England often called Norman. *See also* Saxo-Norman.

ROOD: crucifix flanked by representations of the Virgin and St John, usually over the entry into the chancel, painted on the wall, on a beam (*rood beam*) or on top of a *rood screen* or pulpitum (q.v.) which often had a walkway (*rood loft*) along the top, reached by a *rood stair* in the side wall. *Hanging rood*: cross or crucifix suspended from roof.

ROOFS: For the main external shapes (hipped, gambrel etc.) *see* 7. *Helm* and *Saddleback*: *see* 1c. *Lean-to*: single sloping roof built against a vertical wall; also applied to the part of the building beneath. *Bellcast*: sloping roof slightly swept out over the eaves.
Construction. *See* 7.
Single-framed roof: with no main trusses. The rafters may be fixed

to the wall-plate or ridge, or longitudinal timbers may be absent altogether.

Double-framed roof: with longitudinal members, such as purlins, and usually divided into bays by principals and principal rafters.

Other types are named after their main structural components, e.g. *hammerbeam*, *crown-post* (*see* Elements below and 7).

Elements. *See* 7.

Ashlar piece: a short vertical timber connecting an inner wall-plate or timber pad to a rafter.

Braces: subsidiary timbers set diagonally to strengthen the frame. *Arched braces*: curved pair forming an arch, connecting wall or post below with a tie- or collar-beam above. *Passing braces*: long straight braces passing across other members of the truss. *Scissor braces*: pair crossing diagonally between pairs of rafters or principals. *Wind-braces*: short, usually curved braces connecting side purlins with principals; sometimes decorated with cusping.

Collar or *collar-beam*: horizontal transverse timber connecting a pair of rafter or cruck blades (q.v.), set between apex and the wall-plate.

Crown-post: a vertical timber set centrally on a tie-beam and supporting a collar purlin braced to it longitudinally. In an open truss lateral braces may rise to the collar-beam; in a closed truss they may descend to the tie-beam.

Hammerbeams: horizontal brackets projecting at wall-plate level like an interrupted tie-beam; the inner ends carry *hammerposts*, vertical timbers which support a purlin and are braced to a collar-beam above.

Kingpost: vertical timber set centrally on a tie-or collar-beam, rising to the apex of the roof to support a ridge piece (cf. Strut).

Plate: longitudinal timber set square to the ground. *Wall-plate*: along the top of a wall to receive the ends of rafters; cf. Purlin.

Principals: pair of inclined lateral timbers of a truss. Usually they support side purlins and mark the main bay divisions.

Purlin: horizontal longitudinal timber. *Collar purlin* or *crown plate*: central timber which carries collar-beams and is supported by crown-posts. *Side purlins*: pairs of timbers placed some way up the slope of the roof, which carry common rafters. *Butt* or *tenoned purlins* are tenoned into either side of the principals. *Through purlins* pass through or past the principal; they include *clasped purlins*, which rest on queenposts or are carried in the angle between principals and collar, and *trenched purlins* trenched into the backs of principals.

Queen-strut: paired vertical, or near-vertical, timbers placed symmetrically on a tie-beam to support side purlins.

Rafters: inclined lateral timbers supporting the roof covering. *Common rafters*: regularly spaced uniform rafters placed along the length of a roof or between principals. *Principal rafters*: rafters which also act as principals.

Ridge, ridge piece: horizontal longitudinal timber at the apex supporting the ends of the rafters.

Sprocket: short timber placed on the back and at the foot of a rafter to form projecting eaves.

Strut: vertical or oblique timber between two members of a truss, not directly supporting longitudinal timbers.

Tie-beam: main horizontal transverse timber which carries the feet of the principals at wall level.

Truss: rigid framework of timbers at bay intervals, carrying the longitudinal roof timbers which support the common rafters. *Closed truss*: with the spaces between the timbers filled, to form an internal partition.

See also Cruck, Wagon roof.

ROPE MOULDING: *see* Cable moulding.

ROSE WINDOW: circular window with tracery radiating from the centre. Cf. Wheel window.

ROTUNDA: building or room circular in plan.

ROUGHCAST: *see* Rendering.

ROUND (Scots): bartizan, usually roofless.

ROVING BRIDGE: *see* Canals.

RUBBED BRICKWORK: *see* Gauged brickwork.

RUBBLE: masonry whose stones are wholly or partly in a rough state. *Coursed*: coursed stones with rough faces. *Random*: uncoursed stones in a random pattern. *Snecked*: with courses broken by smaller stones (snecks).

RUSTICATION: *see* 6d. Exaggerated treatment of masonry to give an effect of strength. The joints are usually recessed by V-section chamfering or square-section channelling (*channelled rustication*). *Banded rustication* has only the horizontal joints emphasized. The faces may be flat, but can be *diamond-faced*, like shallow pyramids, *vermiculated*, with a stylized texture like worm-casts, and *glacial* (frost-work), like icicles or stalactites.

RYBATS (Scots): *see* Margins.

SACRAMENT HOUSE: safe cupboard in a side wall of the chancel of a church and not directly associated with an altar, for reservation of the sacrament.

SACRISTY: room in a church for sacred vessels and vestments.

SADDLEBACK ROOF: *see* 1c.

SALTIRE CROSS: with diagonal limbs.

SANCTUARY: part of church at E end containing high altar. Cf. Presbytery.

SANGHA: residence of Buddhist monks or nuns.

SARCOPHAGUS: coffin of stone or other durable material.

SARKING (Scots): boards laid on the rafters to support the roof covering.

SAXO-NORMAN: transitional Romanesque style combining Anglo-Saxon and Norman features, current *c.* 1060–1100.

SCAGLIOLA: composition imitating marble.

SCALE-AND-PLATT (*lit.* stair and landing): *see* Stair and 6c.

SCALLOPED CAPITAL: *see* 1a.

SCARCEMENT: extra thickness of the lower part of a wall, e.g. to carry a floor.

SCARP: artificial cutting away of the ground to form a steep slope.

SCOTIA: a hollow classical moulding, especially between tori (q.v.) on a column base (3b, 3f).

SCREEN: in a medieval church, usually at the entry to the chancel; *see* Rood (screen) and Pulpitum. A *parclose screen* separates a chapel from the rest of the church.

SCREENS or SCREENS PASSAGE: screened-off entrance passage between great hall and service rooms or between the hall of a tower house and the stair.

SCRIBE (Scots): to cut and mark timber against an irregular stone or plaster surface.

SCUNTION (Scots): reveal.

SECTION: two-dimensional representation of a building, moulding etc., revealed by cutting across it.

SEDILIA (singular: sedile): seats for clergy (usually for a priest, deacon and sub-deacon) on the S side of the chancel.

SEPTUM: dwarf wall between the nave and choir.

SESSION HOUSE (Scots): a room or separate building for meetings of the minister and elders who form a kirk session. Also a shelter by the church or churchyard entrance for an elder collecting for poor relief, built at expense of kirk session.

SET-OFF: *see* Weathering.

SGRAFFITO: decoration scratched, often in plaster, to reveal a pattern in another colour beneath. *Graffiti*: scratched drawing or writing.

SHAFT: vertical member of round or polygonal section (1a, 3a). *Shaft-ring*: at the junction of shafts set *en délit* (q.v.) or attached to a pier or wall (1a).

SHEILA-NA-GIG: female fertility figure, usually with legs apart.

SHELL: thin, self-supporting roofing membrane of timber or concrete.

SHEUGH (Scots): a trench or open drain; a street gutter.

SHOULDERED ARCH: *see* 5a.

SHOULDERED ARCHITRAVE: *see* 4b.

SHUTTERING: *see* Concrete.

SILL: horizontal member at the bottom of a window-or door-frame; or at the base of a timber-framed wall into which posts and studs are tenoned.

SKEW (Scots): sloping or shaped stones finishing a gable upstanding from the roof. *Skewputt*: bracket at the bottom end of a skew. *See* 7.

SLAB BLOCK: *see* Multi-storey.

SLATE-HANGING: covering of overlapping slates on a wall. *Tile-hanging* is similar.

SLYPE: covered way or passage leading E from the cloisters between transept and chapter house.

SNECKED: *see* Rubble.

SOFFIT (*lit.* ceiling): underside of an arch (also called *intrados*), lintel etc. *Soffit roll*: medieval roll moulding on a soffit.

SOLAR: private upper chamber in a medieval house, accessible from the high end of the great hall.

SOPRAPORTA: *see* Overdoor.

SOUNDING-BOARD: *see* Tester.

SOUTERRAIN: underground stone-lined passage and chamber.

SPANDRELS: roughly triangular spaces between an arch and its containing rectangle, or between adjacent arches (5c). Also non-structural panels under the windows in a curtain-walled building.

SPERE: a fixed structure screening the lower end of the great hall from the screens passage. *Spere-truss*: roof truss incorporated in the spere.

SPIRE: tall pyramidal or conical feature crowning a tower or turret. *Broach*: starting from a square base, then carried into an octagonal section by means of triangular faces; *splayed-foot*: a variation of the broach form, found principally in the south-east of England, in which the four cardinal faces are splayed out near their base, to cover the corners, while oblique (or intermediate) faces taper away to a point (1c). *Needle spire*: thin spire rising from the centre of a tower roof, well inside the parapet: when of timber and lead often called a *spike*.

SPIRELET: *see* Flèche.

SPLAY: of an opening when it is wider on one face of a wall than the other.

SPRING OR SPRINGING: level at which an arch or vault rises from its supports. *Springers*: the first stones of an arch or vaulting-rib above the spring (2c).

SQUINCH: arch or series of arches thrown across an interior angle of a square or rectangular structure to support a circular or polygonal superstructure, especially a dome or spire (5a).

SQUINT: an aperture in a wall or through a pier, usually to allow a view of an altar.

STAIRS: *see* 6c. *Dog-leg stair* or (Scots) *Scale-and-platt stair*: parallel flights rising alternately in opposite directions, without an open well. *Flying stair*: cantilevered from the walls of a stairwell, without newels; sometimes called a *geometric* stair when the inner edge describes a curve. *Turnpike* or *newel stair*: ascending round a central supporting newel (8b); also called a *spiral stair* or *vice* when in a circular shaft, a *winder* when in a rectangular compartment. (Winder also applies to the steps on the turn.) *Well stair*: with flights round a square open well framed by newel posts. *See also* Perron.

STAIR TOWER: full-height projection from a main block (especially of a tower house) containing the principal stair from the ground floor (8a).

STAIR TURRET: turret corbelled out from above ground level and containing a stair from one of the upper floors of a building, especially a tower house (8a).

STALL: fixed seat in the choir or chancel for the clergy or choir (cf. Pew). Usually with arm rests, and often framed together.

STANCHION: upright structural member, of iron, steel or reinforced concrete.

STANDPIPE TOWER: *see* Manometer.

STEADING (Scots): farm building or buildings; generally used for the principal group of buildings on a farm.

STEAM ENGINES: *Atmospheric*: worked by the vacuum created when low-pressure steam is condensed in the cylinder, as developed by Thomas Newcomen. *Beam engine*: with a large pivoted beam moved in an oscillating fashion by the piston. It may drive a flywheel or be *non-rotative*. *Watt* and *Cornish*: single-cylinder; *compound*: two cylinders; *triple expansion*: three cylinders.

STEEPLE: tower together with a spire, lantern or belfry.

STIFFLEAF: type of E.E. foliage decoration. *Stiffleaf capital*: *see* 1b.

STOP: plain or decorated terminal to mouldings or chamfers, or at the end of hoodmoulds and labels (*label stop*), or stringcourses (5b, 6a); *see also* Headstop.

STOUP: vessel for holy water, usually near a door.

STRAINER: *see* Arch.

STRAPWORK: decoration like interlaced leather straps, late C16 and C17 in origin.

STRETCHER: *see* Bond and 6e.

STRING: *see* 6c. Sloping member holding the ends of the treads and risers of a staircase. *Closed string*: a broad string covering the ends of the treads and risers. *Open string*: cut into the shape of the treads and risers.

STRINGCOURSE: horizontal course or moulding projecting from the surface of a wall (6d).

STUCCO: decorative plasterwork. *See also* Rendering.

STUDS: subsidiary vertical timbers of a timber-framed wall or partition.

STUGGED (Scots): of masonry hacked or picked as a key for rendering; used as a surface finish in the C19.

STUPA: Buddhist shrine, circular in plan.

STYLOBATE: top of the solid platform on which a colonnade stands (3a).

SUSPENSION BRIDGE: *see* Bridge.

SWAG: like a festoon (q.v.), but representing cloth.

SYSTEM BUILDING: *see* Industrialized building.

TABERNACLE: safe cupboard above an altar to contain the reserved sacrament or a relic; or architectural frame for an image or statue.

TABLE STONE or TABLE TOMB: memorial slab raised on freestanding legs.

TAS-DE-CHARGE: the lower courses of a vault or arch which are laid horizontally (2c).

TENEMENT: holding of land, but also applied to a purpose-built flatted block.

TERM: pedestal or pilaster tapering downward, usually with the upper part of a human figure growing out of it.

TERRACOTTA: moulded and fired clay ornament or cladding.

TERREPLEIN: in a fort the level surface of a rampart behind a parapet for mounting guns.

TESSELLATED PAVEMENT: mosaic flooring, particularly Roman, made of *tesserae*, i.e. cubes of glass, stone or brick.

TESTER: flat canopy over a tomb or pulpit, where it is also called a *sounding-board*.

TESTER TOMB: tomb-chest with effigies beneath a tester, either freestanding (tester with four or more columns), or attached to a wall (*half-tester*) with columns on one side only.

TETRASTYLE: *see* Portico.

THERMAL WINDOW: *see* Diocletian window.

THREE-DECKER PULPIT: *see* Pulpit.

TIDAL GATES: *see* Canals.

TIE-BEAM: *see* Roofs and 7.

TIERCERON: *see* Vault and 2c.

TIFTING (Scots): mortar bed for verge slates laid over gable skew.

TILE-HANGING: *see* Slate-hanging.

TIMBER-FRAMING: method of construction where the structural frame is built of interlocking timbers. The spaces are filled with non-structural material, e.g. *infill* of wattle and daub, lath and plaster, brickwork (known as *nogging*) etc., and may be covered by plaster, weatherboarding (q.v.) or tiles.

TOLBOOTH (Scots; *lit.* tax booth): burgh council building containing council chamber and prison.

TOMB-CHEST: chest-shaped tomb, usually of stone. Cf. Table tomb, Tester tomb.

TORUS (plural: tori): large convex moulding, usually used on a column base (3b, 3f).

TOUCH: soft black marble quarried near Tournai.

TOURELLE: turret corbelled out from the wall (8a).

TOWER BLOCK: *see* Multi-storey.

TOWER HOUSE (Scots): for elements and forms *see* 8a, 8b. Compact fortified house with the main hall raised above the ground and at least one more storey above it. A medieval Scots type continuing well into the C17 in its modified forms: *L-plan* with a jamb at one corner; *Z-plan* with a jamb at each diagonally opposite corner.

TRABEATED: dependent structurally on the use of the post and lintel. Cf. Arcuated.

TRACERY: openwork pattern of masonry or timber in the upper part of an opening. *Blind* tracery is tracery applied to a solid wall.

Plate tracery, introduced *c.* 1200, is the earliest form, in which shapes are cut through solid masonry (2a).

Bar tracery was introduced into England *c.* 1250. The pattern is formed by intersecting moulded ribwork continued from the mullions. It was especially elaborate during the Decorated period (q.v.). Tracery shapes can include circles, *daggers* (elongated ogee-ended lozenges), *mouchettes* (like daggers but with curved sides) and upright rectangular *panels*. They often have *cusps*, projecting points defining lobes or *foils* (q.v.) within the main shape: *Kentish* or *split-cusps* are forked.

Types of bar tracery (*see* 2b) include *geometric(al)*: *c.* 1250–1310, chiefly circles, often foiled; *Y-tracery*: *c.* 1300, with mullions branching into a Y-shape; *intersecting*: *c.* 1300, formed by interlocking mullions; *reticulated*: early C14, net-like pattern of ogee-ended lozenges; *curvilinear*: C14, with uninterrupted flowing curves; *loop*: *c.* 1500–45, with large uncusped loop-like forms; *panel*: Perp, with straight-sided panels, often cusped at the top and bottom.

TRANSE (Scots): passage.

TRANSEPT: transverse portion of a cruciform church.

TRANSITIONAL: generally used for the phase between Romanesque and Early English (*c.* 1175–*c.* 1200).

TRANSOM: horizontal member separating window lights (2b).

TREAD: horizontal part of a step. The *tread end* may be carved on a staircase (6c).

TREFOIL: *see* Foil.

TRIFORIUM: middle storey of a church treated as an arcaded wall passage or blind arcade, its height corresponding to that of the aisle roof.

TRIGLYPHS (*lit.* three-grooved tablets): stylized beam-ends in the Doric frieze, with metopes between (3b).

TRIUMPHAL ARCH: influential type of Imperial Roman monument.

TROPHY: sculptured or painted group of arms or armour.

TRUMEAU: central stone mullion supporting the tympanum of a wide doorway. *Trumeau figure*: carved figure attached to it (cf. Column figure).

TRUMPET CAPITAL: *see* 1b.

TRUSS: braced framework, spanning between supports. *See also* Roofs.

TUMBLING or TUMBLING-IN: courses of brickwork laid at right angles to a slope, e.g. of a gable, forming triangles by tapering into horizontal courses.

TURNPIKE: *see* Stairs.

TUSCAN: *see* Orders and 3e.

TUSKING STONES (Scots): projecting end stones for bonding with an adjoining wall.

TWO-DECKER PULPIT: *see* Pulpit.

TYMPANUM: the surface between a lintel and the arch above it or within a pediment (4a).

UNDERCROFT: usually describes the vaulted room(s) beneath the main room(s) of a medieval house. Cf. Crypt.

UNIVALLATE: of a hillfort: defended by a single bank and ditch.

VAULT: arched stone roof (sometimes imitated in timber or plaster). For types *see* 2c.

Tunnel or *barrel vault*: continuous semicircular or pointed arch, often of rubble masonry.

Groin vault: tunnel vaults intersecting at right angles. *Groins* are the curved lines of the intersections.

Rib vault: masonry framework of intersecting arches (ribs) supporting *vault cells*, used in Gothic architecture. *Wall rib* or *wall arch*: between wall and vault cell. *Transverse rib*: spans between two walls to divide a vault into bays. *Quadripartite* rib vault: each bay has two pairs of diagonal ribs dividing the vault into four triangular cells. *Sexpartite* rib vault: most often used over paired bays, has an extra pair of ribs springing from between the bays. More elaborate vaults may include *ridge-ribs* along the crown of a vault or bisecting the bays; *tiercerons*: extra decorative ribs springing from the corners of a bay; and *liernes*: short decorative ribs in the crown of a vault, not linked to any springing point. A *stellar* or *star* vault has liernes in star formation.

Fan vault: form of barrel vault used in the Perp period, made up of halved concave masonry cones decorated with blind tracery.

VAULTING-SHAFT: shaft leading up to the spring or springing (q.v.) of a vault (2c).

VENETIAN or SERLIAN WINDOW: derived from Serlio (4b). The motif is used for other openings.

VERMICULATION: *see* Rustication and 6d.

VESICA: oval with pointed ends.

VICE: *see* Stair.

VILLA: originally a Roman country house or farm. The term was revived in England in the C18 under the influence of Palladio and used especially for smaller, compact country houses. In the later C19 it was debased to describe any suburban house.

VITRIFIED: bricks or tiles fired to a darkened glassy surface. *Vitrified fort*: built of timber-laced masonry, the timber having later been set on fire with consequent vitrification of the stonework.

VITRUVIAN SCROLL: classical running ornament of curly waves (4b).

VOLUTES: spiral scrolls. They occur on Ionic capitals (3c). *Angle* volute: pair of volutes, turned outwards to meet at the corner of a capital.

VOUSSOIRS: wedge-shaped stones forming an arch (5c).

WAGON ROOF: with the appearance of the inside of a wagon tilt; often ceiled. Also called *cradle roof*.

WAINSCOT: *see* Panelling.

WALLED GARDEN: in C18 and C19 Scotland, combined vegetable and flower garden, sometimes well away from the house.

WALLHEAD: straight top of a wall. *Wallhead chimney*: chimney rising from a wallhead (8a). *Wallhead gable*: gable rising from a wallhead.

WALL MONUMENT: attached to the wall and often standing on the floor. *Wall tablets* are smaller with the inscription as the major element.

WALL-PLATE: *see* Roofs and 7.

WALL-WALK: *see* Parapet.

WARMING ROOM: room in a religious house where a fire burned for comfort.

WATERHOLDING BASE: early Gothic base with upper and lower mouldings separated by a deep hollow.

WATERLEAF: *see* Enrichments and 3f.

WATERLEAF CAPITAL: Late Romanesque and Transitional type of capital (1b).

WATER WHEELS: described by the way water is fed on to the wheel. *Breastshot*: mid-height, falling and passing beneath. *Overshot*: over the top. *Pitchback*: on the top but falling backwards. *Undershot*: turned by the momentum of the water passing beneath. In a *water turbine*, water is fed under pressure through a vaned wheel within a casing.

WEALDEN HOUSE: type of medieval timber-framed house with a central open hall flanked by bays of two storeys, roofed in line; the end bays are jettied to the front, but the eaves are continuous.

WEATHERBOARDING: wall cladding of overlapping horizontal boards.

WEATHERING: or SET-OFF: inclined, projecting surface to keep water away from the wall below.

WEEPERS: figures in niches along the sides of some medieval tombs. Also called *mourners*.

WHEEL HOUSE: Late Iron Age circular stone dwelling; inside, partition walls radiating from the central hearth like wheel spokes.

WHEEL WINDOW: circular, with radiating shafts like spokes. Cf. Rose window.

WROUGHT IRON: *see* Cast iron.

WYND (Scots): subsidiary street or lane, often running into a main street or gait (q.v.).

YETT (Scots, *lit.* gate): hinged openwork gate at a main doorway, made of iron bars alternately penetrating and penetrated (8c).

Z-PLAN: *see* Tower house and 8b.

INDEX OF ARCHITECTS AND ARTISTS

INDEX OF PLACES

Principal references are in **bold** type; demolished buildings are shown in *italic*.

Dundee is indexed in two separate entries: 'Dundee City Centre', covering pp. 79–142, and 'Dundee outer areas', which covers the Waterfront and Nethergate sections (pp. 142–83) and the suburbs (pp. 183–286). See maps on pp. 80–81, 151 and 184–5.